Comprehensive COBOL

Andrew S. Philippakis

Leonard J. Kazmier

Arizona State University

Mitchell **McGRAW-HILL**

New York St. Louis San Francisco Auckland Bogotá Caracas Hamburg
Lisbon London Madrid Mexico Milan Montreal New Delhi Paris
San Juan São Paulo Singapore Sydney Tokyo Toronto Watsonville

Mitchell **McGraw-Hill**
55 Penny Lane
Watsonville, CA 95076

Comprehensive COBOL

1 2 3 4 5 6 7 8 9 0   SEM SEM   9 0 9 8 7 6 5 4 3 2 1

ISBN: 0-07-049828-8

The sponsoring editor was Steve Mitchell.
The production supervisor was Betty Drury.
The production manager was Greg Hubit, Bookworks.
The text and cover designer was Gary Palmatier.
The compositor was Ideas to Images.
The printer and binder was Semline, Inc.

Library of Congress Catalog Card Number 90-83377

Contents

Preface

The title of this book, *Comprehensive COBOL*, accurately indicates its contents. Increasingly, courses in COBOL are taken by students who have a *serious* professional interest in business programming, and for this purpose a casual acquaintance with the language is not sufficient. Students interested in a general introduction to programming typically choose to study a language other than COBOL. On the employer side, the need is for graduates who have had a *rigorous* exposure to COBOL concepts and programming techniques.

In this environment, there is a need for a textbook that can support courses intended for professional preparation. This classroom-tested book is unique in its thorough coverage of *both* the COBOL language features and the underlying information processing concepts and methods.

Although the content of the book is comprehensive, we have made special efforts to assure that it is *user friendly*. Every chapter begins with clearly stated **learning objectives.** Included with every main section of every chapter are **interactive reviews,** so that the student can combine review and self-testing throughout the chapter. The **summary** at the end of each chapter then reviews and reinforces all of the concepts and techniques. There are **extensive end-of-chapter** partial and complete **programming exercises,** with **sample data and tested program solutions available on disk to text adopters.**

The organization of the book reflects a spiral-learning approach. By Chapter 4 the student has covered a complete, though limited, set of COBOL instructions. Thus the student's self-confidence develops through the ability to write complete programs for simplified exercises early in the course. Later chapters impart successively broader views and more detailed methods and concepts. Overall, this book emphasizes long-lasting learning by presenting fundamental concepts first, *followed* by programming details, rather than focusing on programming minutia.

One-Semester Course

The book is structured to that it easily accommodates either a one-semester course or a two-course sequence. The first 13 chapters are intended for the first course and present a complete set of topics, including basic commands, structured programming concepts in COBOL, extensive coverage of conditional statements, control break processing, sequential files, file sorting and merging, and single-level table handling. Chapter 13 consists of an expanded "case" example of sequential file processing and serves as a capstone for the one-semester experience.

Enriched courses for those with previous programming experience can include one or more topics from later chapters, such as additional file processing techniques, multilevel table handling, or program design and testing.

Full Year Course

The second semester in a two-semester course typically would cover Chapters 14 through 26. However, complete coverage of all 13 chapters requires an intensive effort. Typically, some chapters would be omitted or covered lightly, with the selection of such chapters depending on instructor preference. File processing, which is the "heart" of business information systems, has five of the 13 chapters devoted to it, including the comprehensive "case" example that constitutes the last chapter in the book. The example involves multiple files, all three file organization methods, and the application of concepts concerned with a "system" of interrelated programs.

Coverage in the last half of the book extends beyond language features, in that file processing is also studied in terms of *information systems* processing concepts and procedures. Interactive processing and subprograms/nested programs are developed well beyond the level that is common in other COBOL books, while the inclusion of a chapter on data structures provides instructors with the opportunity to lay a foundation for a subsequent database course.

Instructor's Guide

An *Instructor's Guide* is available to adopters of the textbook. It comes with the aforementioned data disk as well as the program solutions on disk. Documentation and overhead transparency master information is contained in the *Instructor's Guide*.

ACKNOWLEDGMENTS

We express appreciation to Marian Lamb for her technical editing assistance with the original manuscript and preparation of the book index. We thank Deepa Luthra for her outstanding programming support during the development of this book. The timely publication of this book would not have been possible without the commitment of Greg Hubit and his staff at Bookworks, the editorial planning of Raleigh Wilson, and the coordinating activities of Denise Nickeson at Mitchell Publishing.

COBOL is an industry language and is not the property of any company or group of companies, or of any organization or group of organizations.

No warranty, expressed or implied, is made by any contributor or by the CODASYL Programming Language Committee as to the accuracy and functioning of the programming system and language. Moreover, no responsibility is assumed by the contributor, or by the committee, in connection therewith.

The authors and copyright holders of the copyrighted material used herein

FLOW-MATIC (trademark of Sperry Rand Corporation), Programming for the UNIVAC® I and II, Data Automation Systems, copyrighted 1958, 1959, by Sperry Rand Corporation; IBM Commercial Translator Form No. F28-8013, copyrighted 1959 by IBM; FACT, DSI 27A5260-2760, copyrighted 1960 by Minneapolis-Honeywell

have specifically authorized the use of this material in whole or in part, in the COBOL specifications. Such authorization extends to the reproduction and use of COBOL specifications in programming manuals or similar publications.

COBOL in the '90s and Beyond

YOU ARE ABOUT TO MAKE *a large investment of your time and effort by studying COBOL programming.*

The length of this book tells you something obvious: COBOL is a language for the professional programmer. Whether you spend one semester studying about half this book, or you complete the whole book in two semesters, you will undertake a serious learning task.

It is only natural that you should want to know if the study of COBOL represents a good investment. We try to give you a realistic assessment using a question-answer approach.

Question: *Who uses COBOL today?*

Answer: The main users of COBOL are medium and large organizations, to do their "business" processing. Manufacturing, retailing, insurance, banking, government agencies, hospitals, school districts, colleges, and universities are typical extensive COBOL users. In fact, information processing in medium and large organizations throughout the world is based on COBOL, and this has been true for the last two decades.

Question: *What about the use of other languages for information processing?*

Answer: There are many programming languages in use. Many small companies use the RPG languages rather than COBOL. But as small companies grow, they often join the larger ones in also using COBOL. Other languages, such as BASIC and Pascal, are used by both small and large organizations, but usually on a limited basis and for specialized projects. More recently C, and to a lesser extent Ada, are finding increasing use in developing new computer applications.

Information processing is a multilingual environment, to be sure. And the trend of using more than one language in the same organization is well established. A successful computer professional should be familiar with more than one language. Most programmers tend to develop their main competency in one language, but the successful ones can move to another language when the need arises.

Question: *Why do you think that COBOL will continue to be the language of business information processing?*

Answer: It may be useful to consider an analogy. If you visit an old city and look at the way its streets are laid out, it's not practical to contemplate changing the layout of the streets. You may think of changes and improvements in transportation systems, but the basic infrastructure is already there.

Something analogous has happened with COBOL. Organizations have made heavy commitments over the past two decades in developing COBOL-based computer applications. The cumulative total of these developments represents a major asset. To see this point, consider Table 1, which estimates the total dollar investment for different combinations of number of years and number of programmers in an organization. The numbers in the table are based on a reasonable average of $30,000 per person per year, which is low for today's salaries, but high for the long past.

The cumulative investment in COBOL-based programs in organizations is so large, and the applications are so extensive, that COBOL is here to stay for a long time. Any notion of "clearing the decks" and starting over again with some other language is no more practical than thinking of redesigning the street layout for an established city.

Question: *What is happening in terms of improved use of COBOL?*

Answer: The use of COBOL is not static. New things are happening to increase the productivity of COBOL programmers. Companies are acquiring a variety of "productivity tools" to facilitate the design, coding, and revision of COBOL programs. Some of these tools facilitate writing reports (report generators), others make it easier to write interactive programs (screen formatters), to re-use similar code across several programs (libraries), to re-use data definitions (dictionaries), and to correct errors (on-line debuggers). Such productivity tools increase the programmer's output per hour of work, improve the quality of the programs, and enrich the programmer's job.

TABLE 1
Cumulative Investment in Millions of Dollars

TOTAL NUMBER OF YEARS	NUMBER OF PROGRAMMERS EMPLOYED				
	5	10	25	50	100
10	$1.50	$3.00	$7.50	$15.00	$30.00
15	2.25	4.50	11.25	22.50	45.00
20	3.00	6.00	15.00	30.00	60.00

Many of these productivity tools are available on personal computers, as well as large, shared computers (minicomputers and mainframes). Unfortunately, colleges and universities often do not have such productivity tools available for instruction. This is due both to limited budgets and to the objective of teaching fundamental concepts rather than training the student to become a fluent programmer. A recent survey that we conducted revealed that the vast majority of colleges use large computers to teach COBOL, and this limits the availability of many productivity tools that are less expensive when purchased for use with personal computers.

Question: *What else is happening in the use of COBOL today?*

Answer: Many organizations find that program "maintenance" has become an overwhelming activity. Maintaining a program means that it is changed to adapt to the changing needs of the organization. As programs undergo multiple changes over the years, they become complicated and difficult to keep changing. Therefore organizations are gradually redesigning their old systems. One approach to redesigning programs is to take the old programs and convert them to modern forms of program structure. The practice of *reverse engineering* relies on the use of specialized programs that take existing COBOL programs and help convert them to well-structured programs that are less complex and more understandable.

Another development is the use of *Computer Assisted Software Engineering* (CASE). CASE relies on methods and special programs that automate much of the design and coding of COBOL programs. Use of graphics is common in CASE, since visual tools increase the conceptual power of the programmer. CASE tools are in limited use at colleges, partly because they are new, and partly because the hardware and software required to implement CASE are rather expensive.

Question: *What are the prospects for COBOL over the next 10 years?*

Answer: The most likely occurrence during the next ten years is a high level of activity in organizations aimed at modernizing their program libraries and designing new or redesigning existing major application systems. Increasing the use of power tools will be a high priority as organizations try to manage the costs of these major undertakings. More important for the prospective student is the fact that organizations will need well-educated and open-minded professional programmers. From this standpoint, experience is not as much a factor. In fact, many experienced programmers, who grew up thinking in the old ways, have difficulty adapting to the new features of COBOL. Through this course you will be educated in the current version of the language and the modern ways of conceiving and designing high-quality structured programs. In this respect you can expect to have something of a competitive advantage as you graduate and enter the market as a programmer-analyst.

Of course, computing is a dynamic field that has had a continuing stream of changes in conceptual and physical tools. To compete and succeed as a professional programmer, you need to keep learning new methods and adopting new tools. Learning COBOL now will provide you with a solid foundation for business uses of computers. As time goes on, you will need to keep adding to your store of knowledge, including the ability to use other languages that may interface with COBOL.

In summary, over the next ten years we foresee COBOL remaining the main language for business applications of computers in medium and large organizations. However, it will continuously be supplemented by capabilities and tools that will require frequent updating of your knowledge of how to use COBOL in a particular programming environment.

It is impractical to try to predict the more distant future with a high degree of confidence. But if any major changes do occur, it is almost certain that they will develop over long periods of time. There are too many existing programs, and all of these systems have a huge human component. The bottom line is that the time and effort that you spend in learning COBOL programming is an investment that will yield positive long-run returns to you.

I

Fundamentals of COBOL Programming

1 Introduction

IN THIS CHAPTER *you will first briefly consider the differences between business data analysis and scientific computing. Then you will study some* **general issues** *in computer programming. These include levels of computer languages, the operating systems of computers, characteristics of good computer programs, and steps in a programming project.*

After this general foundation you will be introduced to some **design and testing concepts** *for COBOL programs. Included are the use of program structure charts, use of pseudocode, and procedures of debugging and testing a COBOL program.*

In the last several sections of the chapter you will focus specifically on the COBOL **language.** *Included is an introduction to the overall structure of COBOL programs, the use of data-names and constants, and finally, a complete sample COBOL program.*

BUSINESS DATA PROCESSING VS. SCIENTIFIC COMPUTING

Business data processing has distinct characteristics and requirements. Business operations involve such transactions as sales, payments, shipments, and purchases. *Transaction processing* involves the input of data for transactions, and the output of reports that reflect the consequences of the transactions. For example, when a product is sold, input data about the sale transaction are used to change (update) the customer file, the inventory file, and the accounts receivable file. As a result of transaction processing, various output reports also are generated. For example, the daily sales transactions can be reported according to categories of products and according to different retail store locations.

Business data processing reflects the structure and operations of an organization. Since organizations consist of many interrelated parts (departments, divisions, etc.) that have a large variety of operations, it follows that business data processing involves a great variety of input data, many and varied data files (personnel, materials, sales, financial, and so on), and a complex series of programs to process transaction data in order to update the multiple files. Finally, most organizations have a variety of scheduled activities that involve data processing, such as payroll every two weeks, billing of customers every month, and financial reports every quarter. This time-associated processing is another major distinguishing feature of data processing.

By way of contrast, *scientific computing* has quite different characteristics. Scientific computing tends to focus on individual projects rather than interrelated organizational operations. Such projects tend to involve extensive calculations. If they involve a lot of data, such as do geological and space exploration projects, the data tend to be limited in form, consisting mostly of numeric values. Business data tend to be varied in form, consisting of long records containing large numbers of fields of both numeric and character data.

In general, business data processing is different enough from scientific computing that there are distinct computer programming concepts and methods for each type of computing. Reflecting the specialized needs of business data processing, a special computer language, COBOL (COmmon Business Oriented Language), has been developed.

LEVELS OF COMPUTER LANGUAGES

A *computer program* is a set of instructions that directs a computer to perform a series of operations. A *computer language* is a set of characters, words, and rules that can be used to write a computer program.

Every computer model has its own language, which is determined by its hardware structure. Such "native" computer languages are referred to as *machine languages*. These languages are, of course, machine dependent. They appear highly obscure because they consist of strings of numeric codes. Early computer programming was almost exclusively machine-language programming. Although machine language is natural to the hardware of a computer, it is quite unnatural to people. A step in the direction of making computer programming easier was taken with the development of *symbolic languages*. Symbolic languages use codes that are easier to remember, such as ADD, to represent machine instructions. For instance, a machine instruction such as 21300400, meaning to add (indicated by "21") the value stored in location 300 to the value stored in location 400, could be written as ADD AMOUNT1, AMOUNT2.

Such codes as ADD are not directly understood by a computer. They have to be translated into machine-language form. An *assembler* is a machine-language program that translates symbolic-language instructions into machine-language instructions. Symbolic languages are machine dependent in that a set of such codes is applicable only to a particular computer model; therefore the programmer has to be familiar with the particular instruction set of the machine being programmed. This is a serious disadvantage when programming efforts are extensive and hardware is continually changing.

The next stage in the development of programming language was the advent of *higher-level languages* that are procedure oriented rather than machine oriented. Such languages focus on the data processing procedure to be accomplished rather than on the coding requirements of particular machines. Further, higher-level languages are *not* machine dependent; such programs are not restricted to use with particular computer models.

Even though such instructions are not designed to correspond to the way a particular computer model operates, they must, of course, ultimately be executed on some particular machine. Again the process of translation is used to obtain the required machine-language program. A computer program written in a higher-level language is referred to as a *source program*. A *compiler* is a machine-language program that translates (or compiles) the source program into a machine-language program. This machine-language program is referred to as the *object program*. The object program is then input into the machine to perform the required task. Thus a compiler is a program whose function is to convert source programs into object programs. The main difference between a compiler and an assembler is that compilation is a more complex process than assembly. Assembly typically involves a one-for-one translation from a word code to a machine code; compilation involves a many-for-one translation: one higher-level instruction may be the equivalent of several machine-level instructions.

Figure 1-1 illustrates the compilation and execution process. In the first phase the source program and the compiler serve as input. The output includes the object program, which is stored on disk, and a listing of the source program on

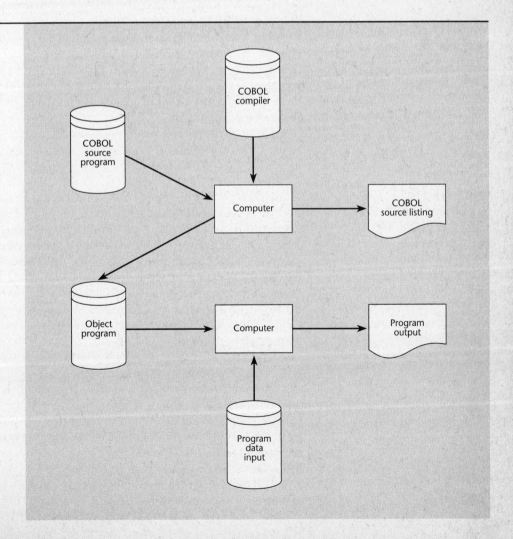

FIGURE 1-1
COBOL Program Compilation-Execution Process

the printer, along with diagnostic error messages, if any. If no serious errors are detected, the object program is entered into the computer. Based on the program instructions, input data are then read and processed, and output data are written onto files or printed reports.

COBOL is a programming language that has been designed expressly for data processing. It is a higher-level language and, as such, is designed to be machine independent.

The idea of developing the language was conceived at a Pentagon meeting in May 1959. At that meeting representatives from the U.S. government, from business users, and from computer manufacturers decided that it was feasible to proceed with the development of a higher-level language that would satisfy the specific needs of administrative data processing, as contrasted to scientific computing. A preliminary version of COBOL appeared in December 1959. This version was followed in 1961 by COBOL '61, which became the cornerstone for the development of later versions of the language. In 1968 a standard version of the language was approved by what now is called the *American National Standards Institute* (ANSI), and revised versions were adopted by ANSI in 1974 and again in 1985. Thus, the three standard versions of the language are COBOL '68, COBOL '74, and COBOL '85. The language is continuously evolving and being enhanced by the addition of new programming capabilities and the deletion of obsolete functions. Proposed changes in the COBOL language are documented annually in the *Journal of Development*. These changes are tentative, however, until ANSI adopts a new standard.

It is estimated there are millions of existing programs written in COBOL '74, so it will take a long time before the features associated with COBOL '85 are fully implemented. Therefore in this text we make a clear distinction between COBOL '74 and the COBOL '85 standard. Overall, the new standard is principally concerned with achieving greater programming flexibility and capability; it does not change the fundamental structure of COBOL programs.

COBOL in either version is *the* language of choice for administrative applications of the computer. The vast majority of large business and governmental organizations have developed extensive libraries of COBOL programs and continue to use COBOL as their principal programming language for data processing.

THE OPERATING SYSTEM AND THE EXECUTION OF COMPUTER PROGRAMS

All modern computer systems are controlled by an *operating system* that consists of a set of programs designed to facilitate the automatic operation of the computer system and to reduce the programming task for system users. In a modern mainframe computer system, operators continuously input the programs to be processed (often simultaneously in different locations), while the operating system maintains control over the program-to-program execution sequence, checks availability of resources (tapes, disk space, printers), and, when needed, transfers control from one program to another in an attempt to maximize throughput.

Operating systems require extensive programming efforts. In fact, programming is differentiated into systems programming (systems software is an associated term) and applications programming. *Systems programming* relates to operating systems and includes various general-purpose machine management and data management functions. *Applications programming,* on the other hand, is oriented toward the use of the computer for some data processing task. Thus a COBOL programmer clearly is an applications programmer. All applications programs require the use of systems programs in their processing, and therefore it is essential to have a basic understanding of the operating system of the computer with which the applications programmer is working.

Each computer manufacturer has an operating system that differs from the others, and often has different operating systems for different computer models. Therefore we cannot explain the specifics of particular operating systems in this text. We will, however, discuss the general concepts that relate COBOL programming to operating systems, and we assume that the reader has access to information about the specific operating system used by his or her computer. Our comments concern large mainframe computers shared by many users. The basic concepts apply to personal computers as well, but many things are simplified for personal computers.

In order for a COBOL program to be run, the programmer needs to communicate certain things to the operating system. Typical areas of information include the following:

- Identify the user as a legitimate user of the machine.

- Indicate the fact that a COBOL program is being used. (In a typical installation, programs are written in several languages and they need to be differentiated.)

- Request compilation of the COBOL source program into object-program form.

- Indicate whether the compilation output (object program) is to be saved on disk, tape, etc.

- Request the use of tapes, disks, printers, and other devices.

- Request execution of the compiled program.

The communication process between the programmer and the operating system is effected by means of system commands known collectively as the *Job Control Language (JCL)*. The JCL, of course, is not standardized. Figure 1-2 portrays a typical COBOL program setup. In the past, the JCL statements were punched onto cards referred to as *program control cards*. Although punched cards as such are

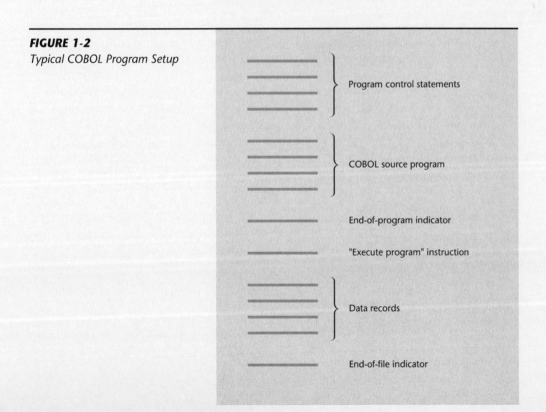

FIGURE 1-2
Typical COBOL Program Setup

Program control statements

COBOL source program

End-of-program indicator

"Execute program" instruction

Data records

End-of-file indicator

not used anymore, it is still not unusual to refer to "cards" in this context. In general, the first card identifies the user by account number or by name and may set parameters on maximum time, maximum number of pages, and the like. Then there are one or more JCL statements to invoke the compiler and to indicate the disposition of the object program. The source program follows, possibly with an end-of-program indicator. Then there are one or more JCL statements to ready the object program for execution. The "execute" type of instruction often is followed by the data and by an end-of-file indicator.

Overall, then, program control statements serve to transmit certain categories of information to the operating system. On the basis of this information, execution of the program is scheduled and monitored.

R E V I E W . . . .

1. A computer program is essentially a set of instructions that directs the operation of a machine. When the set of instructions is written in a language that consists of a series of numeric codes that can be used with a particular computer model only, the language is referred to as a _____ language.

   machine

2. The next stage in the development of computer languages made possible the use of word codes, such as ADD, in place of numeric codes. As is the case for machine languages, such languages are also machine dependent. Because of the type of code system used, such languages are called _____ languages.

   symbolic

3. The third stage in the development of computer languages was the formulation of higher-level, or procedure-oriented, languages that [are also / are not] machine dependent. An example of such a language is _____ .

   are not; COBOL (or BASIC, FORTRAN, Pascal, etc.)

4. Both symbolic languages and procedure-oriented languages have to be translated into machine-language form before they can be used to direct computer operations. The program that translates a symbolic-language program into machine-language form is called a(n) _____ , whereas the program that translates a procedure-oriented language program is called a(n) _____ .

   assembler; compiler

5. In the context of using a procedure-oriented language, the program written in such a language is often referred to as the _____ program, whereas the translated version of the program is referred to as the _____ program.

   source; object

6. The major procedure-oriented language that has been designed specifically to satisfy programming needs associated with administrative data processing is _____ .

   COBOL

7. Development of the COBOL language is a continuing process. New versions of the language are approved periodically by the _____ .

   American National Standards Institute (ANSI)

8. The set of programs designed by the computer manufacturer to facilitate the automatic operation of the computer is called the _____ .

   operating system

9. The types of computer programs that are concerned with such functions as disk-space allocation and copying data from tape to disk are called _____ programs.

systems

10. The types of computer programs concerned with actual data processing tasks are called _____ programs.

applications

11. A programmer who uses COBOL as the programming language is a(n) [systems / applications] programmer.

applications

12. An applications programmer communicates with the operating system of a computer through the use of a set of commands called the _____ .

Job Control Language (JCL)

· ·

CHARACTERISTICS OF GOOD PROGRAMS

The traditional approach to the programming process was to view a computer program as a personal creation by an individual. The distinguishing characteristic of a good programmer was the ability to write clever programs—"clever" often being synonymous with complex and obscure. The trouble with such programs is that it is difficult for persons other than the author of the program to understand them, and even the author may have difficulty when months or years have passed. Therefore particular emphasis is now given to the principles and concepts by which good programs can be written. The following is a list of several characteristics associated with a good computer program:

1. It is correct.

2. It is understandable.

3. It is easy to change.

4. It has been written efficiently.

5. It executes efficiently.

Of course, the identification of these characteristics does not in itself tell us how to write such programs. However, the following sections of this chapter are directed toward describing some of the concepts and techniques by which these objectives can be achieved.

The first, and usually most important, characteristic of a good program is that it is *correct*. The program should carry out the task for which it was designed and do so without error. To achieve this objective, a complete and clear specification of the purpose and functions of the program must be developed. Thus program "errors" can be due to outright mistakes on the part of a programmer or to a lack of a clear description regarding the processing detail and the required output of the program.

The second characteristic of a good program is that it is *understandable*. Although a computer program is a set of instructions for a computer, it also should be comprehensible to people. A person other than the author should be able to read and understand the purpose and functions of the program. Higher-level programming languages such as COBOL are intended for direct comprehension by people, and are intended for machine use only indirectly, through compilation.

Third, a computer program should be *easy to change.* Changes in products, changes in company procedures, new government regulations, and the like, all lead to the necessity of modifying existing computer programs. As a result most established computer installations devote considerable time and effort to changing, or *maintaining,* existing programs. A good program not only fulfills its original purpose but also is adapted easily in response to changing needs.

The fourth characteristic of a good program is that it has been *written efficiently.* This refers to the amount of time spent in writing the program. Of course, this objective is secondary to the program being correct, understandable, and easy to change. In practice, the easiest way to write a program quickly is to write it partly correct, leave it difficult to understand, or allow its obscurity to make it difficult to change, but none of these ways is cost effective. The main cost of a programming project is the programmer's time. Thus the best programming techniques economize this time while still satisfying the objectives that the program be correct, understandable, and easy to change.

The final characteristic of a good program that we consider is that it *executes efficiently.* The program should be written so that it does not use more computer storage nor more computer processing time than is necessary. This objective also is secondary to the primary objectives that a program be correct, understandable, and easy to change. Furthermore, as hardware costs have decreased relative to programmers' salaries, overall cost considerations often justify reducing the concern about a high level of efficiency in program execution. A programmer should be alert, nevertheless, to the techniques by which efficient program execution can be achieved.

STEPS IN A PROGRAMMING PROJECT

A programmer goes through a number of steps in completing a COBOL program. These steps are summarized in Table 1-1.

We begin the project by first designing the *overall program structure.* This is achieved by preparing a structure chart and associated pseudocode for the programming project, as explained and illustrated in the following two sections of this chapter. Then the actual first draft of the program is written on the *COBOL Coding Form.* This coding form is included as Figure 1-9 with the sample COBOL program in the last section of this chapter. After these first two steps in Table 1-1 are completed, the third step begins a process of review and revision of the program that continues with the rest of the steps in the listing.

All of the steps beginning with the third step are collectively called *program debugging and testing.* We shall return to this topic, and to Table 1-1, after the next two sections on structure charts and pseudocode.

TABLE 1-1
Steps Included in a Programming Project

- Design the overall program structure.
- Write the program on a COBOL coding form.
- Review and correct the handwritten program.
- Key-in the program in machine-readable form.
- Obtain a listing of the program for review.
- Compile the program and review any diagnostic error messages.
- Recompile the program until no error diagnostics are issued.
- Execute the program with some limited test data.
- Review the output for the test data and determine the causes of any erroneous output.

PROGRAM STRUCTURE CHARTS

A *structure chart* is a visual representation of the main functions and subfunctions of a program. Figure 1-3 presents a structure chart for a typical COBOL programming task. The single block at the top of the chart stands for the entire programming task. Having identified the overall task, we then ask, what are the main functions that need to be carried out to do the task? The four functions identified at the second level of the structure chart in Figure 1-3 are *Print report heading, Read customer record, Process customer detail,* and *Print report footing.* The completion of these four functions would constitute the complete program.

Next, we consider each of the main functions individually and determine what subfunctions need to be carried out to complete that function. For instance, we could ask, what activities need to be carried out to accomplish the function *Print report heading*? Because this task is a simple one, we conclude that it is not necessary to break it down into subordinate functions in Figure 1-3. However, when the function *Process customer detail* is considered, four subfunctions are identified. In other words, we conclude that to accomplish the function *Process customer detail,* four specific tasks have to be completed: *Compute net sales, Accumulate totals, Print customer detail data,* and *Read customer record.* Because *Read customer record* is a function that is used in more than one place in the structure chart, the upper-right corner of the block is shaded to indicate such repetition.

The programmer continues the process of considering each function and subfunction in turn to determine if it can be broken down into more specific tasks. For example, for the function *Compute net sales* in Figure 1-3 we would ask, what needs to be done to compute net sales? The answer is that the unit price needs to be determined, and the units sold need to be multiplied by the unit price. We could have chosen to show these two tasks as subordinate functions of *Compute net sales* in Figure 1-3. We chose not to do so because showing the additional detail would not add much to the usefulness of the structure chart. At what level of detail should the analysis of functions be stopped? This judgment is based largely on experience with similar programming projects. As a general rule, the structure chart should have sufficient detail to be a useful guide in developing the program but not so much detail that the blocks in the structure chart are direct alternatives to COBOL program statements.

Structure charts provide a comprehensive overview of the functions to be performed. Notice that no consideration is given to the timing or sequence of

FIGURE 1-3
Structure Chart for a Typical COBOL Programming Task

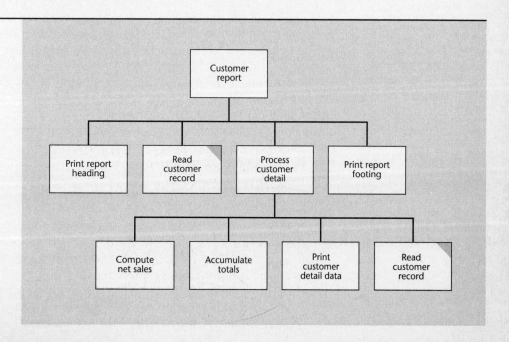

FIGURE 1-4
Pseudocode for the Programming Task Example

CUSTOMER REPORT PROGRAM

PERFORM

    Print the report heading

    Read a record from the customer file

    PERFORM UNTIL the end of customer file

        Determine appropriate price

        Compute net sales

        Accumulate totals

        Print customer detail line

        Read a record from the customer file

    END-PERFORM

    Print the report footing

END-PERFORM

Stop execution of the program

tasks in developing a structure chart. In contrast, such a concern is fundamental in the development of flowcharts, as described in the Sample Program section at the end of this chapter. The matter of the time flow of the specific tasks to be performed is also considered in the use of pseudocode, as described in the following section.

PSEUDOCODE

After development of a structure chart, it may be useful to write the program outline in *pseudocode*. As the name implies, we do *not* write the program code according to the rules of COBOL. Instead we concentrate on the logical flow of the program, using ordinary language to represent the main functions in the program.

Pseudocode is incomplete and limited, but it is very useful because it can communicate the essence of a program without being bogged down in precise detail. Figure 1-4 presents a set of pseudocode statements for the programming task described by the structure chart in Figure 1-3.

Notice that the functions taken from the structure chart are listed *sequentially* in the pseudocode. That is, not only are the functions to be performed listed, but also attention is given to the time flow and the program logic as it relates to time.

Since pseudocode is not standardized, there is not much point in trying to offer exact rules on how to write pseudocode; however, some organizations do have in-house guidelines to follow. A common-sense rule is to write pseudocode in a way that has meaning for its author and can be understood easily by others.

DEBUGGING AND TESTING A PROGRAM

Having described the use of structure charts and pseudocode as aids in designing the overall program structure, we now return to the steps in a programming project as listed in Table 1-1 shown again on the next page. As we indicated when this table was first discussed, the steps beginning with the third step all constitute the process of *debugging and testing* the program initially written.

The programmer begins by reviewing and correcting the handwritten program, followed by entering the program into the computer system by the use

TABLE 1-1 *(Repeated)*
Steps Included in a Programming Project

- Design the overall program structure.
- Write the program on a COBOL coding form.
- Review and correct the handwritten program.
- Key-in the program in machine-readable form.
- Obtain a listing of the program for review.
- Compile the program and review any diagnostic error messages.
- Recompile the program until no error diagnostics are issued.
- Execute the program with some limited test data.
- Review the output for the test data and determine the causes of any erroneous output.

of a terminal, and obtaining a program listing that is again reviewed. Only after such a "double review" should the programmer compile the program. Use of the COBOL compiler results in the source program written in COBOL being translated into the machine-language object program. Given that there are some *diagnostic error messages,* which is typical, the program is recompiled until no error messages are issued.

The absence of diagnostic error messages indicates that the technical requirements of the language have been satisfied. However, the absence of such errors in itself says nothing about whether the data processing objectives of the program have been achieved. Although the test data used for trial execution of the program are described as being "limited" in Table 1-1, they are limited only in the number of data items. The test data should include not only all of the extremes of values for each type of data item, but also combinations of extreme values for different data items. Finally, these extreme values should include "impossible" values, such as an hourly employee having a work week of 140 hours.

If the test run gives erroneous output, the programmer can find the source of the problem by a process called *tracing.* This procedure often is the most difficult part of programming. The programmer "walks through" or "desk checks" the program step by step by applying each program instruction sequentially and checking the results at each step. This includes a listing of program output for every step of processing in the program. If the nature of the output error indicates that the program error probably occurred in a particular routine, we trace and compare program execution in the suspected routine first, rather than starting from the beginning of the program. There may be an early error, however, that does not surface until later in the program. For instance, it may be that a total is incorrect at the end of program execution because we forgot to set an accumulator equal to zero at the beginning of the program.

Experience and insight are very useful in debugging and testing; however, the best way to avoid debugging and testing problems is to be very careful in the initial design and writing of the program. It is a fact that the student who writes a program with little design and review effort is the one who gets involved in seemingly endless attempts to correct a poorly written program. A programmer who spends 10 hours designing, writing, and reviewing a program may spend two hours correcting compiler diagnostics and program testing. On the other hand, a programmer with similar abilities who spends just five hours designing, writing, and reviewing the same program will likely spend 15 hours in debugging the program.

R E V I E W . . . .

1. The most important characteristic of a good computer program is that it is
   _____ .

   correct

2. Probable later reference to the program by individuals other than the original
   programmer dictates that it should be _____ , while
   unavoidable changes in data processing requirements in most organizations
   make it desirable that the program be _____ .

   understandable; easy to change

3. To economize the programmer's time, a program should be _____
   efficiently; to economize the use of computer hardware, the program should
   _____ efficiently.

   written; execute

4. The type of chart used as a programming aid that is a visual representation of the
   main functions and subfunctions of a program is the
   _____ .

   structure chart

5. In a structure chart the entire programming task is represented by the single
   block at the [top / bottom] of the chart.

   top

6. The upper-right corner of a structure-chart block is shaded for functions that are
   _____ in the chart.

   repeated

7. The analysis of functions and associated subfunctions to be carried out in a
   programming project is fundamental to the development of a
   _____ chart.

   structure

8. A program outline written in approximately ordinary language that concentrates
   on the logical flow of the program is described as being outlined in
   _____ .

   pseudocode

9. A program outline using pseudocode generally would be written immediately
   following development of the program _____ chart.

   structure

10. The overall process of checking a program for correctness is called program
    debugging and _____ .

    testing

11. After the keyed-in version of the program is listed and reviewed, the program is
    compiled to obtain a printout of the COBOL source program and a listing of
    diagnostic _____ messages.

    error

12. Corrections and changes to the program are made by reviewing all of the
    diagnostics. When no diagnostic error messages are obtained upon recompiling
    the program, the program is then executed using limited _____ .

    test data

13. When a programmer arranges to list every record or the result of every sequential
    processing step that is associated with an output error, the procedure is called
    program _____ .

    tracing

. . . .

OVERALL STRUCTURE OF COBOL PROGRAMS

Every COBOL program consists of four *divisions* that are included in the following order:

- IDENTIFICATION DIVISION

- ENVIRONMENT DIVISION

- DATA DIVISION

- PROCEDURE DIVISION

The *IDENTIFICATION DIVISION* identifies the COBOL program to the computer by providing a program name.

The *ENVIRONMENT DIVISION* specifies the computer equipment and operating environment that are required to execute the program.

The *DATA DIVISION* includes all of the data format specifications for input, output, and temporary storage. This includes the assignment of data-names and the definition of constants, as will be described in the following sections of this chapter.

The *PROCEDURE DIVISION* is the executable part of the COBOL program. That is, this division contains the specific input, data processing, and output statements that are to be executed to achieve the overall data processing objectives.

The next two sections of this chapter explain the assignment of data-names and the definition of constants in COBOL. Following these explanations the final section of the chapter presents a sample COBOL program that includes, in order, the IDENTIFICATION DIVISION, ENVIRONMENT DIVISION, DATA DIVISION, and PROCEDURE DIVISION. Also included for the program are the program structure chart, pseudocode, COBOL Coding Form, and flowchart.

DATA-NAMES

A *data-name* in COBOL is analogous to a *variable* in algebra. It is a general symbol or name that can have different values. Another way of viewing a data-name is that it is a label for a storage location that may contain various, and different, values at different times. In this sense any computer program consists of a set of instructions to manipulate central storage areas that are referenced by their corresponding data-names. In COBOL, data-names and their formats are specified in the DATA DIVISION.

Data-names are coined at the discretion of the programmer, except that there are certain rules that must be followed:

1. A data-name can be up to 30 characters in length and can include alphabetic characters, numeric characters, and hyphens.

2. At least one character must be alphabetic.

3. The only special symbol permitted is the hyphen. A hyphen must always be *embedded;* that is, it cannot be the first or last character of the data-name.

4. Blanks cannot be included in the data-names.

5. Within the above rules the programmer may use any data-name, with the exception of the approximately 300 COBOL *reserved words* listed in Appendix A. (Manufacturers often add some of their own words to the ANSI list.)

Some examples of legitimate data-names are these:

HOURS	PREMIUM
ENDING-INVENTORY	A527157
SALES-TAX-TOTAL	31576X5

As illustrated above, data-names do not have to be meaningful English words. A programmer can choose to use such data-names as X, Y, Z, X1, X2, and the like. However, even though such data-names are typically shorter than those that are inherently meaningful as names, they increase the likelihood of subsequent confusion. COBOL was designed specifically to allow *self-documentation*, which means that by reading the program one should be able to understand what the program does and what data it uses. The problem with using terse data-names is that their meanings are forgotten by the programmer and are difficult to understand by others even if a list of definitions is supplied.

In addition to data-names, *constants* also are defined in the DATA DIVISION. We defer discussion of the types of constants and their use until Chapter 3, which focuses particularly on writing the DATA DIVISION of a COBOL program.

R E V I E W . . . .

1. Of the four divisions of a COBOL program, the one that identifies the COBOL program to the computer by providing a program name is the
_____ DIVISION.

IDENTIFICATION

2. The division of the COBOL program in which the computer equipment to be used is specified is the _____ DIVISION.

ENVIRONMENT

3. The division that includes the data format specifications for both input and output is the _____ DIVISION.

DATA

4. The division of a COBOL program that includes the executable instructions directly concerned with the overall objectives of the program is the
_____ division.

PROCEDURE

5. The order in which the four divisions of a COBOL program appear is
_____ , _____ , _____ , and
_____ .

IDENTIFICATION; ENVIRONMENT; DATA; PROCEDURE

6. IN COBOL a label for a field of data that can contain different values at different times is called a(n) _____ .

data-name

7. A data-name must not be more than _____ (number) characters in length and can include [alphabetic characters only / alphabetic and numeric characters].

30; alphabetic and numeric characters

8. Every data-name must include at least one [alphabetic / numeric] character, and the only special symbol permitted is the _____ .

alphabetic; hyphen

9. Place a check mark before each of the following that is a legitimate data-name in COBOL.

a. _____ INVENTORY

b. _____ END OF YEAR BALANCE

c. _____ 2735B5

d. _____ 27-35B5

e. _____ BALANCE-DUE-

f. _____ 57

g. _____ END-OF-YEAR-BALANCE-DUE-ON-ACCOUNT

h. _____ DATA

i. _____ BALANCE

a. ✔

b. spaces not allowed

c. ✔

d. ✔

e. hyphens must be embedded

f. at least one alphabetic character must be included

g. must be less than 30 characters in length

h. a reserved COBOL word (a bit of a trick question—see Appendix A)

i. ✔

10. Each field of internal storage has a unique data-name, or label, associated with it. Each data-name [must / need not] be unique and [must / need not) imply something about the meaning of the content.

must; need not

. . . .

SAMPLE COBOL PROGRAM

In this section you will study the sample program from a broad point of view only, not in terms of the meaning and function of each of the specific COBOL statements included in the program. In the next chapter, Basic Commands, you will focus on the specific commands included in another sample program.

Program Function

The function of the sample program is simply to read all the student records in a file and to print each name on the printer.

Input

The student file consists of records that have the following format:

- Columns 1-10:   Contains the first name

- Columns 11-25:   Contains the last name

- Columns 26-80:   Contains other data, not used by this program.

The sample input looks like this:

J	O	S	E	P	H					A	N	D	E	R	S	O	N							
R	O	B	E	R	T	A		J	O	B	R	O	W	N										
D	A	N	I	E	L					C	A	S	T	E	L	L	O	R	I					
L	I	N	D	A						C	H	R	I	S	T	I	A	N	S	O	N			
K	A	T	H	E	R	I	N	E		D	R	I	N	K	W	A	T	E	R					

Output

The output will be a printed listing with the following format:

- Columns 1-10:   Will contain blank spaces
- Columns 11-20:   Will contain the first name
- Columns 21-22:   Will contain blank spaces
- Columns 23-37:   Will contain the last name
- Columns 38-132:   Will contain blank spaces

Based on the sample input on the preceding page, the corresponding output would differ by the fact that there will be at least two blank spaces between the first and the last name. Short first names, of course, will have more than two blank spaces following since the last names will be vertically aligned.

Structure Chart

Figure 1-5 is a structure chart for the sample program. The MAIN-LOGIC module has two immediate subordinate modules: READ-STUDENT and PRINT-STUDENT. The READ-STUDENT module then also is subordinate to PRINT-STUDENT because after each customer record is printed the next input record needs to be read.

The number at the top-right of each module identifies the paragraph number in the corresponding PROCEDURE DIVISION of the COBOL program. Of course, this number can be known only after the program is written. Thus a structure chart evolves through several stages. Initially, which is the point we are at now, it serves as a graphical tool in designing the main functions of the program and their relationships. After the program is completed and the paragraph numbers are inserted, another reviewer of the program can compare the structure chart with the program code to understand more easily the program and the relationships of the main functions (paragraphs). We will refer back to the structure chart in Figure 1-5 after the COBOL program is presented to you.

FIGURE 1-5

Structure Chart for the Sample Program

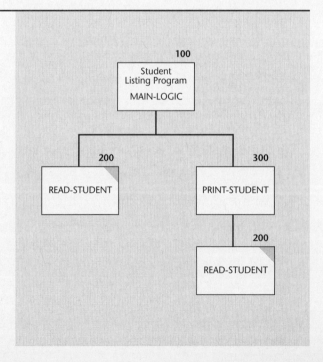

Pseudocode

Figure 1-6 presents pseudocode for the sample program. In part (a) of the figure the pseudocode is written in a general way, while in part (b) the pseudocode is written to correspond rather closely to the COBOL language. As we stated earlier in this chapter, pseudocode is not standardized. Its main function is to help the

FIGURE 1-6

Pseudocode for the Sample Program

Part (a) — Generalized Pseudocode

STUDENT LISTING PROGRAM

PERFORM

    Open the input and output files

    Read student record

    PERFORM UNTIL end of student records

        Clear the output print report record

        Move the name from the input to the output record

        Write the output record on the printer

        Read the next student record

    END-PERFORM

    Close the files

END-PERFORM

Stop program execution

Part (b) — COBOL-Oriented Pseudocode

STUDENT LISTING PROGRAM

100-MAIN-LOGIC.

    Open the input and output files

    PERFORM 200-READ-STUDENT

        to read the first record from the student file

    PERFORM 300-PRINT-STUDENT

        UNTIL the end of the student file

    Close the files

    Stop run

200-READ-STUDENT.

    Read a record from the student file

        and if it is the end of the file, set a flag on

300-PRINT-STUDENT.

    Clear the print report record

    Move the first and last name from the input

        student file record to the report record

    Write the report record (on the printer)

    PERFORM 200-READ-STUDENT

        to read the next record from the student file.

End of Program

programmer develop the program. You can think of part (a) in Figure 1-6 as the first-pass pseudocode; you would develop such a pseudocode when your main focus is on the programming task. Later, as you think about translating the task into COBOL statements, you might develop pseudocode such as in part (b) of Figure 1-6, where we have chosen to use paragraph names that are the same as the function names in the structure chart. Further, we anticipate the syntax required in COBOL programs by assigning unique numbers to the paragraphs. In fact, each of the three numbered paragraph names exactly follows the required COBOL format, including the use of the period at the end of each paragraph name. However, the detail under each paragraph name follows no special format, but does list the subfunctions in logical, sequential order.

The COBOL Program Listing

Figure 1-7 presents the COBOL program to accomplish the desired task. The four divisions that you considered earlier in this chapter are included in the required order: IDENTIFICATION DIVISION, ENVIRONMENT DIVISION, DATA DIVISION, and PROCEDURE DIVISION.

  The IDENTIFICATION DIVISION gives the name of the program in the PROGRAM-ID paragraph as being STUDLIST.

  The ENVIRONMENT DIVISION identifies the SOURCE-COMPUTER and the OBJECT-COMPUTER in their respective paragraphs. The FILE-CONTROL paragraph is concerned with specific hardware assignments.

FIGURE 1-7

Sample COBOL Program

```
    ****************************************************************
    *  This is a sample program that reads a student file     *
    *  and lists its contents (student names) on the printer  *
    ****************************************************************
    *
     IDENTIFICATION DIVISION.
    *
     PROGRAM-ID. STUDLIST.
    *
    *
     ENVIRONMENT DIVISION.
    *
     SOURCE-COMPUTER.  ABC-480.
    *
     OBJECT-COMPUTER.  ABC-480.
    *
     INPUT-OUTPUT SECTION.
    *
     FILE-CONTROL.
    *
         SELECT STUDENT-FILE  ASSIGN TO   STUDFILE.
         SELECT REPORT-FILE   ASSIGN TO   PRINTER.
    *
    *
     DATA DIVISION.
    *
     FD   STUDENT-FILE
```

FIGURE 1-7

Sample COBOL Program
(continued)

```
                      LABEL RECORDS ARE STANDARD.
           *
            01    STUDENT-RECORD.
                  05   FIRST-NAME-IN      PIC X(10).
                  05   LAST-NAME-IN       PIC X(15).
                  05   FILLER             PIC X(55).
           *
            FD    REPORT-FILE
                  LABEL RECORDS ARE OMITTED.
           *
            01    REPORT-RECORD.
                  05   FILLER             PIC X(10).
                  05   FIRST-NAME-OUT     PIC X(10).
                  05   FILLER             PIC X(02).
                  05   LAST-NAME-OUT      PIC X(15).
                  05   FILLER             PIC.X(95).
           *
            WORKING-STORAGE SECTION.
           *
            01    END-OF-FILE             PIC X(03) VALUE 'NO '.
           *
            PROCEDURE DIVISION.
           *
            100-MAIN-LOGIC.
           *
                  OPEN INPUT    STUDENT-FILE
                  OPEN OUTPUT   REPORT-FILE
           *
                  PERFORM 200-READ-STUDENT
           *
                  PERFORM 300-PRINT-STUDENT
                      UNTIL END-OF-FILE = 'YES'
           *
                  CLOSE STUDENT-FILE
                  CLOSE REPORT-FILE
           *
                  STOP RUN.
           *
            200-READ-STUDENT.
           *
                  READ STUDENT-FILE RECORD
                    AT END MOVE 'YES' TO END-OF-FILE.
           *
            300-PRINT-STUDENT.
           *
                  MOVE SPACES        TO REPORT-RECORD
                  MOVE FIRST-NAME-IN TO FIRST-NAME-OUT
                  MOVE LAST-NAME-IN  TO LAST-NAME-OUT
           *
                  WRITE REPORT-RECORD AFTER ADVANCING 1 LINE
           *
                  PERFORM 200-READ-STUDENT.
```

The DATA DIVISION includes the specification of data-names to be used in the PROCEDURE DIVISION, including special FILLER fields that describe fields not referenced by the PROCEDURE DIVISION, but needed for certain data description purposes. An explanation of what the data specifications mean is included with the sample program in the next chapter. For now we continue focusing on an overall, broad understanding of the program. Notice that the DATA DIVISION includes detailed specifications for the input in the STUDENT-RECORD description and detailed specifications for the output in the REPORT-RECORD description.

The PROCEDURE DIVISION includes the statements that are executed to achieve the desired data processing and data output. The 100-MAIN-LOGIC paragraph begins with the required OPEN statement for the INPUT and OUTPUT files. Then the program goes through the sequence of read and print for each record in the input file. The detail associated with the input process, including the necessity to test for the end of the file, is contained in the 200-READ-STUDENT paragraph. Similarly, the detail associated with the output process is contained in the 300-PRINT-STUDENT paragraph. In the 100-MAIN-LOGIC paragraph execution of the first PERFORM statement results in the reading of an input record, and the subsequent execution of the second PERFORM statement results in the printing of an output record. Each execution of the 300-PRINT-STUDENT paragraph includes the next READ operation, because the last statement in that paragraph is PERFORM 200-READ-STUDENT. Notice how this second reference to the 200-READ-STUDENT paragraph corresponds exactly with the relationships shown for the functions in the structure chart in Figure 1-5. Notice also the correspondence between the paragraph numbers in the program and the numbers entered at the top-right of the modules in Figure 1-5.

The sample program in Figure 1-7 complies with the 1974 COBOL standard. Use of the features available in the 1985 standard can result in a PROCEDURE DIVISION that is somewhat different from that in the figure. The PROCEDURE DIVISION for our sample program based on COBOL '85 is presented in Figure 1-8. Using COBOL '85, we could write the entire PROCEDURE DIVISION as one paragraph, and therefore the program in Figure 1-8 does not correspond to the structure chart in Figure 1-5. This need not always be the case; it occurs for this example only because the programming task is such a simple one. In any event a program written using the rules of COBOL '74 can always be compiled by a COBOL '85 compiler. Such a relationship is called *upward compatibility*. Because most existing COBOL programs in organizations have been written using the 1974 version, and given the upward compatibility, it is important that you be familiar with COBOL '74 as well as COBOL '85.

The COBOL Coding Form

The COBOL Coding Form for our sample program is presented in Figure 1-9. Blank copies of this form are included in the back of this book for your use. Historically this form was designed to coincide with the standard 80-column format of the punched card. Of course, nowadays input terminals are used to enter COBOL programs into a computer.

The first six positions of the COBOL Coding Form are reserved for the optional *sequence number*. The programmer may assign a sequence number to each program line so that the lines are numbered in order. A common practice has been to use the first three columns as a page number corresponding to the number of coding form pages used. Then the next three columns can indicate line numbers, such as 010, 020, 030, and so on, leaving gaps in the numbering for possible program changes. Given that this program is quite short, we chose not to assign any sequence numbers in Figure 1-9. In any case the practice of using sequence numbers in a COBOL program is now generally unnecessary. Most programs are

FIGURE 1-8
PROCEDURE DIVISION for the
Sample Program Based on the
1985 ANSI COBOL Standard

```
*
PROCEDURE DIVISION.
*
PRINT-STUDENT-REPORT.
*
    OPEN INPUT    STUDENT-FILE
    OPEN OUTPUT   REPORT-FILE
*
    PERFORM UNTIL FILE-END
*
        READ STUDENT-FILE RECORD
*
            AT END SET FILE-END TO TRUE
*
            NOT AT END
*
                MOVE SPACES TO REPORT-RECORD
                MOVE FIRST-NAME-IN TO FIRST-NAME-OUT
                MOVE LAST-NAME-IN  TO LAST-NAME-OUT
*
                WRITE REPORT-RECORD
                    AFTER ADVANCING 1 LINE
*
        END-READ
*
    END-PERFORM
*
    CLOSE STUDENT-FILE
*
    CLOSE REPORT-FILE
*
    STOP RUN.
*
```

now keyed-in using a text editor or word processing program. Such programs allow for insertion and deletion of individual lines and automatically keep track of line numbers.

Column 7 is used to indicate that a line contains a *comment* entry, shown by entering an *asterisk* (*) in that column. Whatever is written on such a line is listed with the source program but is not compiled. Comments can be used to enter explanations about a portion of the program; however, a well-written program should have a limited need for comments. Back in Figure 1-7, the first four lines were comment lines that gave a brief description of the program. Several lines throughout the coding form in Figure 1-9 have an asterisk in column 7, but with nothing else on the line. The effect is that when the program is listed, these lines will be left blank, thereby enhancing the readability of the program listing.

Finally, readability of a program listing can be enhanced by causing a portion of the program to be listed on a *new page* on the printer. This can be accomplished by entering a *slash* (/) in column 7, as illustrated at the top of the second page of Figure 1-9. Incidentally, it is coincidental that the signal for the page break in the program listing happened to be exactly at the top of the second

FIGURE 1-9

COBOL Coding Form for the Sample Program

COBOL Coding Form

SYSTEM | PROGRAM | PROGRAMMER | DATE 5/25/91 | PUNCHING INSTRUCTIONS | GRAPHIC | PUNCH | PAGE OF | CARD FORM #

SEQUENCE (PAGE) (SERIAL) | CONT. | A | B | COBOL STATEMENT | IDENTIFICATION

```
       IDENTIFICATION DIVISION.
       PROGRAM-ID.    STUDLIST.
      *
       ENVIRONMENT DIVISION.
       CONFIGURATION SECTION.
       SOURCE-COMPUTER.  ABC-480.
       OBJECT-COMPUTER.  ABC-480.
       INPUT-OUTPUT SECTION.
       FILE-CONTROL.
           SELECT STUDENT-FILE ASSIGN TO STUDFILE
           SELECT REPORT-FILE  ASSIGN TO PRINTER.
      *
       DATA DIVISION.
       FILE SECTION.
       FD  STUDENT-FILE LABEL RECORDS ARE STANDARD.
       01  STUDENT-RECORD.
           05 FIRST-NAME-IN        PIC X(10).
           05 LAST-NAME-IN         PIC X(15).
           05 FILLER               PIC X(55).

       WORKING-STORAGE SECTION.
       01  END-OF-FILE             PIC X(3) VALUE 'NO '.
           88 FILE-END             VALUE 'YES'.
```

AMPAD 23-401

COBOL Coding Form

SYSTEM | PROGRAM | PROGRAMMER | DATE 5/25/91 | PUNCHING INSTRUCTIONS | GRAPHIC | PUNCH | PAGE OF | CARD FORM #

SEQUENCE (PAGE) (SERIAL) | CONT. | A | B | COBOL STATEMENT | IDENTIFICATION

```
      /
       PROCEDURE DIVISION.
       100-MAIN-LOGIC.
           OPEN INPUT   STUDENT-FILE
           OPEN OUTPUT  REPORT-FILE
           PERFORM 200-READ-STUDENT
           PERFORM 300-PRINT-STUDENT
               UNTIL END-OF-FILE = 'YES'
           CLOSE STUDENT-FILE
           CLOSE REPORT-FILE
           STOP RUN.
      *
       200-READ-STUDENT.
           READ STUDENT-FILE RECORD
               AT END MOVE 'YES' TO END-OF-FILE.
      *
       300-PRINT-STUDENT.
           MOVE SPACES TO REPORT-RECORD
           MOVE FIRST-NAME-IN TO FIRST-NAME-OUT
           MOVE LAST-NAME-IN TO LAST-NAME-OUT
           WRITE REPORT-RECORD AFTER ADVANCING 1 LINE
           PERFORM 200-READ-STUDENT.
```

AMPAD 23-401

page of Figure 1-9. The point at which we would like a page break in the program listing generally is unrelated to where we happen to begin a new page on the COBOL Coding Form.

Program Flowchart

Figure 1-10 presents the flowchart for the sample program. Flowcharts are useful for *understanding* the overall logic and the sequential relationships of functions in

FIGURE 1-10

Flowchart for the Sample Program

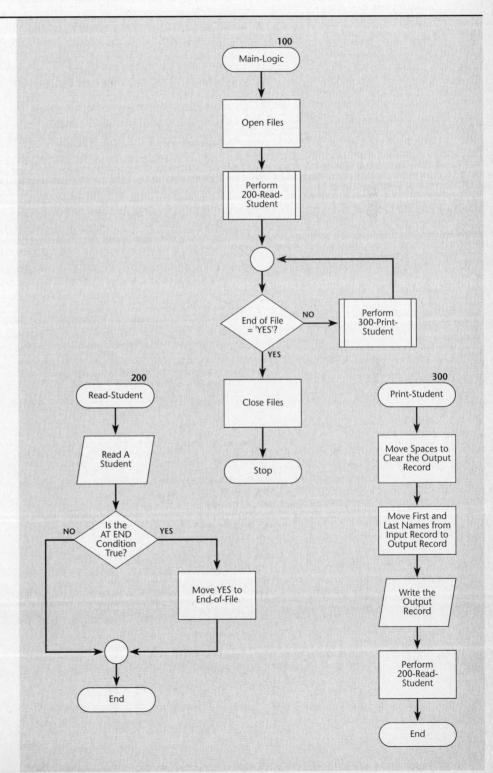

a program, and therefore are important for program documentation. However, flowcharts are not as useful in *designing and writing* a COBOL program as are the combined use of structure charts and pseudocode.

SUMMARY

The contents of this chapter were designed to provide you with a broad but thorough introduction to COBOL programming by focusing on three categories of topics: (1) an overview of some *general issues* in computer programming; (2) program *design and testing* concepts as they apply specifically to COBOL programming; and (3) some specific concepts and rules associated with the COBOL *language,* including the review of the development of a simple, but complete, COBOL program.

The following topics were considered in the category of *general issues:*

- *Business data processing* differs from *scientific computing* in that data processing typically involves a larger volume and variety of data, more complex processing logic, but less mathematical manipulation.

- A computer language can be at the level of being a *machine language, symbolic language,* or *higher-level language.* A program written in a higher-level language such as COBOL is called a *source program.* A *compiler* is a machine-language program that translates a source program into an *object program* that can be processed by the machine.

- COBOL was first developed in 1959. The two standard versions of COBOL that are now in use are COBOL '74 and COBOL '85.

- An *operating system* is a set of programs supplied by a manufacturer to facilitate the automatic operation of a computer system. *Systems programs* are part of the operating system while *applications programs* are end-user programs, such as those written in COBOL. The *Job Control Language* (JCL) for a computer installation provides the means of communication between the user and the operating system.

The following topics were considered with respect to the *design and testing* of a COBOL program:

- A *good computer program* is one that is correct, understandable, and easy to change, has been written efficiently, and executes efficiently.

- Following the identification of the *program function,* a COBOL programming project begins by designing the overall program structure, preferably by constructing a *structure chart* and writing *pseudocode.* Then the first draft of the COBOL program is written, followed by *program debugging and testing.*

- Every COBOL program includes four divisions. The IDENTIFICATION DIVISION provides a program name. The ENVIRONMENT DIVISION specifies the computer equipment that is required. The DATA DIVISION has the data format specifications for both input and output. The PROCEDURE DIVISION has the commands specifically concerned with carrying out the program function.

The following topics were covered in the category of specific concepts and rules associated with the COBOL *language:*

- A *data-name* in COBOL is analogous to a variable in algebra. It is a label for a storage area (field) that can be referenced by the program.

- The last section of the chapter includes a complete COBOL program for reading a set of customer records and printing the name of each customer. Use of a *structure chart* and *pseudocode* are illustrated. Following the program listing, a *COBOL Coding Form* and a *program flowchart* are included.

EXERCISES

1.1 Describe some of the main characteristics of business data processing and contrast those with scientific computing.

1.2 Give examples of some data processing tasks that would be done in one of these types of organizations: a library, a college, a hospital, a retail store, a manufacturing plant. What are some typical files and typical transactions that would take place in the organization of your choice?

1.3 Name and briefly discuss three levels of computer languages.

1.4 Explain these three related concepts: source program, object program, and compiler. Draw a diagram to illustrate how these three entities are related to one another in a typical COBOL program run.

1.5 What does it mean when we say: "COBOL programs should be substantially self-documenting"?

1.6 What is the operating system of a computer? What is the usual name for the type of language that we use to give commands to the operating system?

1.7 Programming is not a single step but is best thought of as a process. Describe the main steps included in the programming process.

1.8 Give the name and the role for each of the divisions that make up a COBOL program.

1.9 Take the sample program in Figure 1-7 and use it as a basis for learning how to compile and execute a COBOL program with your computer.

1.10 Modify the sample program in Figure 1-7 so that the order of the first and the last name is reversed in the output report.

2

Basic Commands

THE **MAIN PURPOSE** of this chapter is to provide you with a working knowledge of a basic set of executable commands in COBOL.

As discussed in Chapter 1, each COBOL program consists of four divisions. The first three— IDENTIFICATION, ENVIRONMENT, and DATA DIVISION—contain specifications about the program rather than executable statements as such. They set the stage for the fourth division, the PROCEDURE DIVISION to contain the commands that will be carried out during program execution.

In this chapter you will focus your attention on the PROCEDURE DIVISION and study a limited number of basic commands: OPEN, READ, WRITE, CLOSE, MOVE, ADD, PERFORM, and STOP RUN. A sample program is first described and then referenced throughout the chapter, so that you can relate the use of these commands to a concrete example.

THE SAMPLE REPORT PROGRAM

Program Function

This is a simple program designed to read records from a customer file and to print a report about those records. The report will consist of a *report heading,* a set of *detail records* corresponding to the records in the customer file, and a *report footing* consisting of a total value. Figure 2-1 is a sample printed report that specifically identifies the three report groups.

Data Definition

There are three main categories of data in any COBOL program: *input data* read from one or more input files, *working storage data* used during program execution, and *output data* written to one or more output files. Although the typical form of output is a printed report, outputting to magnetic disk, to magnetic tape, or to a terminal screen is also common.

For our sample report program, the *input file* is a disk file that contains customer records. Each customer record is described by means of the *record layout chart* in Figure 2-2. Each customer record consists of three fields:

- Columns 1–13:   Customer name
- Columns 14–16:   Number of units sold for a particular product
- Columns 17–80:   Other data not used by this program

Following is a listing of sample input data:

```
SAMPLE INPUT DATA
ADAMS        100
BROWN        075
GROVER       030
MOORE        025
PETERSON     060
WILLIAMS     010
```

FIGURE 2-1

Desired Output for the Report Program

```
CUSTOMER NAME          UNITS SOLD   ⎫ Report Heading

    ADAMS                 100       ⎫
    BROWN                  75       ⎪
    GROVER                 30       ⎪
    MOORE                  25       ⎬ Customer Detail
    PETERSON               60       ⎪
    WILLIAMS               10       ⎭

    TOTAL                 300       ⎫ Report Footing
```

FIGURE 2-2

Record Layout Chart for the Report Program

Field name	Customer name	Units sold	Unused
Field positions	1–13	14–16	17–80

The desired program output is described by means of the *printer spacing chart* shown in Figure 2-3. Blank copies of this chart are included in the back of this book for your use. The printer spacing chart provides an effective means of defining report data. Typically, these charts provide 132 columns because this is the number of print positions on "computer paper" that is 13½ inches wide. As you can see in Figure 2-3, we wish to print the report heading starting with column 11 and extending through column 43. The "H" at the left margin of line 1 on the print chart indicates that the first line of the report is a heading.

Next, the chart shows the layout of the detail (D) lines on line 3, following one blank line below the report heading. Each detail line consists of four *fields*. The first field consists of blank spaces in columns 1–10. The Customer Name is in columns 11–23, followed by a field of 13 blank spaces in columns 24–36, and the numeric field for the Units Sold in columns 37–39. The report detail records repeat for as many lines as there are customers in the input file. Therefore it is not possible to specify the line number for the third type of report group, the report footing. Again referring to Figure 2-3, you can see the spacing designed for the report footing (F), which gives the total units sold to all of the customers listed on the report. There are 10 blank spaces in columns 1–10, the word TOTAL in columns 11–15, 20 blank spaces in columns 16–35, and then the Total Units Sold field in columns 36–39. Note that the Totals field in the report footing consists of four columns instead of the three columns allocated to the Units Sold field in the detail lines. The reason is that a total field is likely to need more positions than the individual values.

The record layout chart for the input data and the printer spacing chart for the output constitute the two main data definitions for this program. There is

FIGURE 2-3

Printer Spacing Chart for the Report Program

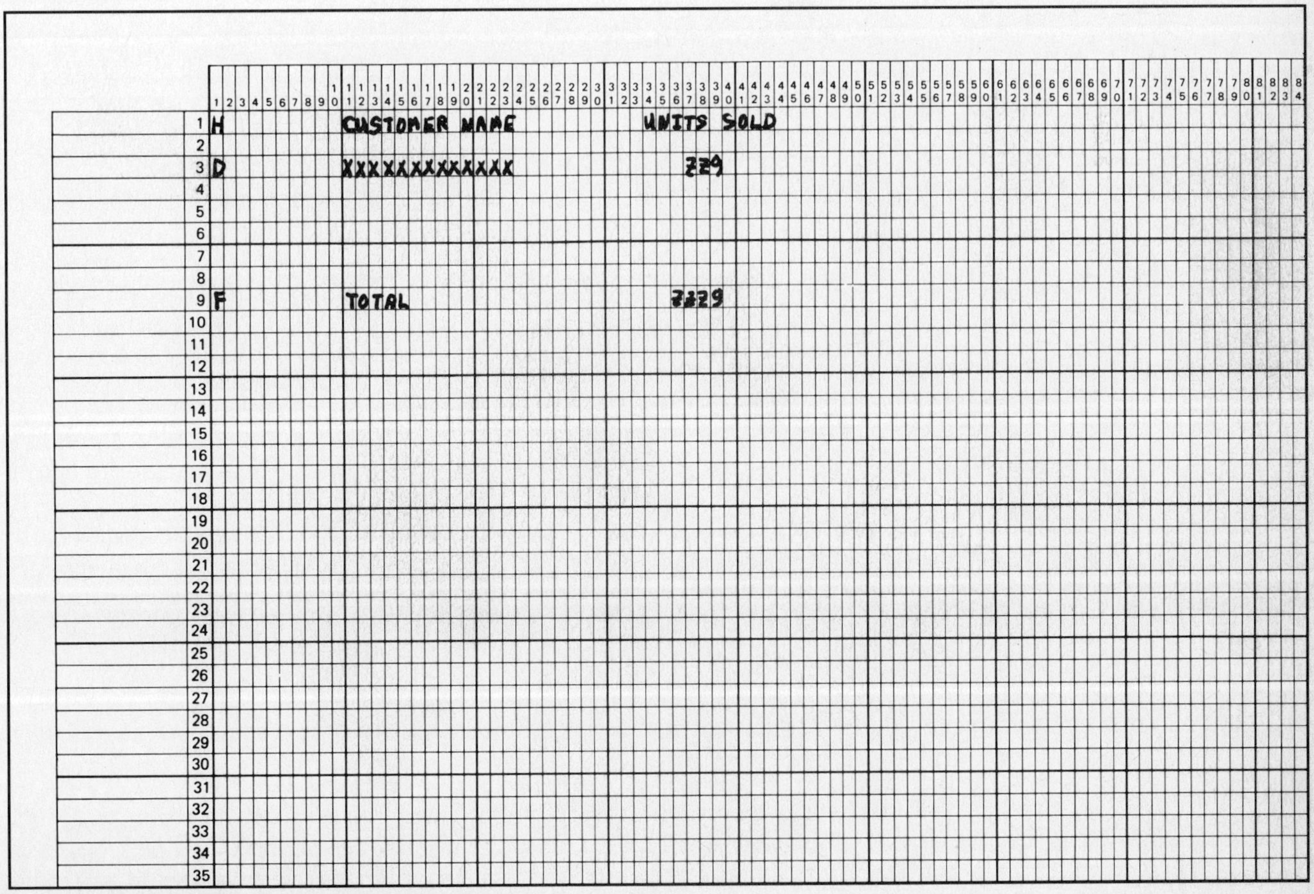

also a need for some other data fields to be used in the program, and these are described in the WORKING-STORAGE of the program. However, we will not discuss them at this point, in order to attend to our main objective, which is to learn some basic PROCEDURE DIVISION commands.

Structure Chart

Figure 2-4 is a structure chart designed for the sample program. It consists of just four modules for the relatively simple program function. The module for the overall programming task, or *root module,* is labeled PROGRAM-SUMMARY. The root module has two immediate subordinates, the READ-CUSTOMER-RECORD and the PROCESS-CUSTOMER-DETAIL modules. Each module has an identification number at its top right for cross-reference with the corresponding paragraph in the COBOL program. As explained with the sample program in Chapter 1, we develop the structure chart *before* writing the COBOL program, and therefore we would not know the paragraph numbers at the time that the structure chart is constructed. However, here we show the structure chart as it would look *after* the program is written. Thus a structure chart initially is used to help us design the program, and then subsequently it can also serve as a reference for a person reading the program. The READ-CUSTOMER-RECORD module is shaded in the upper right corner to mark it as a module that is used in more than one place. In this case it is subordinate to both PROGRAM-SUMMARY and the PROCESS-CUSTOMER-DETAIL modules.

Pseudocode

As introduced in Chapter 1, pseudocode is a method of describing the programming logic without having to follow the syntax rules of any programming language. For a simple program like the one in this case, we could write a rather simple version of pseudocode:

> CUSTOMER REPORT
> PERFORM
> > Open input and output files
> > Print the report heading
> > Read record in customer file
> > > PERFORM UNTIL end of customer file
> > > > Accumulate the units sold into the total
> > > > Move the customer data to the output record
> > > > Write the output record
> > > > Read the next customer record
> > > END-PERFORM
> > Print the report footing
> END-PERFORM
> Stop program

However, it is more typical in the COBOL environment to develop pseudocode that resembles the way of thinking that the language requires. As a positive result of this approach, the actual COBOL program then can be developed in a parallel

FIGURE 2-4

Structure Chart for the Report
Program

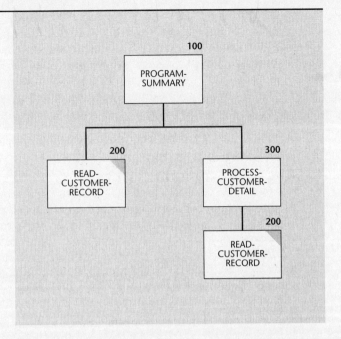

FIGURE 2-5

Pseudocode for the Report
Program

Pseudocode for the Customer Report Program

   Written by Chris Anthony

   Date: 06-10-89

100-PROGRAM-SUMMARY

   Open the input and output files

   Print the report heading

   Perform 200-READ-CUSTOMER-RECORD
      to read the first record from the customer file

   Perform 300-PROCESS-CUSTOMER-DETAIL
      until the end of the customer file

   Print the report footing showing the total units sold

   Close the files

   Stop

200-READ-CUSTOMER-RECORD

   Read a record from the customer file
      and if it is the end of the file, set a flag on

300-PROCESS-CUSTOMER-DETAIL

   Accumulate the total units

   Move the customer name and units sold to the output record

   Print the output record

   Perform 200-READ-CUSTOMER-RECORD to read the next record.

END OF PROGRAM

way with the pseudocode. Figure 2-5 presents a set of pseudocode statements for the sample program. It would be useful, as well as typical, to think of the pseudocode in Figure 2-5 as being the next version of the set of pseudocode statements above. In Figure 2-5 we took the basic concepts in the above sample and developed them into more detailed descriptions that parallel the COBOL syntax. Delineating modules by name, opening and closing the files, and "performing" the modules are all counterparts of what eventually will be written as a COBOL program.

The COBOL Program Listing

Figure 2-6 presents a listing of the COBOL program written for the task. On the right margin of the program a commentary highlights the meaning of each group of statements.

As is true for all COBOL programs, the complete program in Figure 2-6 consists of four divisions: IDENTIFICATION, ENVIRONMENT, DATA, and PROCEDURE. The IDENTIFICATION DIVISION is written first:

```
IDENTIFICATION DIVISION.
PROGRAM-ID.  CUSTRPRT.
```

It consists of one paragraph-name, in this case PROGRAM-ID, which then identifies this program by the name CUSTRPRT.

The ENVIRONMENT DIVISION is written next. The basic function of this division is to make reference to the computer system and the file devices required for this program. We defer any study of this division until Chapter 4.

The DATA DIVISION follows. It is used to identify the data-names that will be used in the program. This division consists of a FILE SECTION and a WORKING-STORAGE SECTION.

The last division is the PROCEDURE DIVISION, which constitutes the executable part of the program. In this division the programmer writes the specific data processing instructions to be carried out by the computer.

The purpose of this chapter is to focus on a basic set of PROCEDURE DIVISION commands. However, a few comments are necessary with respect to the DATA DIVISION, because it defines the data-names that are used in the PROCEDURE DIVISION.

Notice the definition of the input file in Figure 2-6:

```
FD  CUSTOMER-FILE
    LABEL RECORDS ARE OMITTED
    RECORD CONTAINS 80 CHARACTERS
    DATA RECORD IS CUSTOMER-RECORD.
01  CUSTOMER-RECORD.
    05 CUSTOMER-NAME      PIC X(13).
    05 CUSTOMER-UNITS     PIC 999.
    05 FILLER             PIC X(64).
```

The input file is called CUSTOMER-FILE, and each record is referenced by the name CUSTOMER-RECORD. Referring to the input record layout chart presented earlier, it is easy to see the correspondence between the record layout chart and the data description in the program. This correspondence is made explicit in Figure 2-7.

Figure 2-8 presents an analysis of one of the data description entries used. The *level-number* indicates whether a field is part of another field. The highest level-number in the hierarchy is 01. Thus 05 CUSTOMER-NAME indicates that the

FIGURE 2-6
Listing of the COBOL Program

```
    IDENTIFICATION DIVISION.                          The beginning of the program and the
    PROGRAM-ID. CUSTRPRT.                             program name.
*
    ENVIRONMENT DIVISION.
*
*
*
    CONFIGURATION SECTION.                            This section identifies the computer
    SOURCE-COMPUTER. ABC-480.                         system being used.
    OBJECT-COMPUTER. ABC-480.
*
    INPUT-OUTPUT SECTION.
    FILE-CONTROL.
        SELECT CUSTOMER-FILE   ASSIGN TO CUSTFILE.    Designation of the two files and their
        SELECT REPORT-FILE     ASSIGN TO PRINTER.     hardware assignment.

    DATA DIVISION.
*
    FILE SECTION.
*

    FD CUSTOMER-FILE                                  Description of the input
       LABEL RECORDS ARE OMITTED                      customer data file.
       RECORD CONTAINS 80 CHARACTERS
       DATA RECORD IS CUSTOMER-RECORD.
    01 CUSTOMER-RECORD.
       05 CUSTOMER-NAME       PIC X(13).
       05 CUSTOMER-UNITS      PIC 999.
       05 FILLER              PIC X(64).
*
    FD REPORT-FILE                                    Description of the output report file.
       LABEL RECORDS ARE OMITTED
       RECORD CONTAINS 132 CHARACTERS
       DATA RECORD IS REPORT-RECORD.
    01 REPORT-RECORD          PIC X(132).
*
    WORKING-STORAGE SECTION.
*
    01 END-OF-FILE            PIC XXX VALUE 'NO'.      A "flag" field used to signal the end of file.
*
    01 REPORT-HEADING.                                A record containing the report heading.
       05 FILLER              PIC X(10) VALUE SPACES.
       05 REPORT-HEADING-LINE PIC X(31)
       VALUE 'CUSTOMER NAME     UNITS SOLD'.
*
    01 REPORT-FOOTING.
       05 FILLER              PIC X(10) VALUE SPACES.
       05 FILLER              PIC X(5)  VALUE 'TOTAL'.  A record containing the report footing.
       05 FILLER              PIC X(18) VALUE SPACES.
       05 REPORT-TOTAL-UNITS  PIC ZZZ9.
*
```

FIGURE 2-6

Listing of the COBOL Program (continued)

```
 01 REPORT-DETAIL-RECORD.                          A record consisting of the report
    05 FILLER              PIC X(10) VALUE SPACES.  detail data fields.
    05 REPORT-CUST-NAME    PIC X(13).
    05 FILLER              PIC X(10) VALUE SPACES.
    05 REPORT-UNITS        PIC ZZ9.
 01 TOTAL-UNITS            PIC 9999 VALUE ZERO.     A units accumulator.
/
 PROCEDURE DIVISION.
*
 100-PROGRAM-SUMMARY.
*
    OPEN INPUT   CUSTOMER-FILE                      Declare the input/output files and get
         OUTPUT   REPORT-FILE.                      them open.
*
    MOVE REPORT-HEADING TO REPORT-RECORD            Print the report heading on
    WRITE REPORT-RECORD AFTER ADVANCING PAGE.       a new page.
*
    MOVE SPACES TO REPORT-RECORD                    Print a blank line to double space.
    WRITE REPORT-RECORD AFTER ADVANCING 1 LINE
*
    PERFORM 200-READ-CUSTOMER-RECORD.               Read the (first) customer record.
*
    PERFORM 300-PROCESS-CUSTOMER-DETAIL             Keep processing customers until the
         UNTIL END-OF-FILE = 'YES'.                 end of the file.
*
    MOVE TOTAL-UNITS TO REPORT-TOTAL-UNITS          Print the report footing, double
    MOVE REPORT-FOOTING TO REPORT-RECORD            spacing after the last line.
    WRITE REPORT-RECORD AFTER ADVANCING 2 LINES
*
    CLOSE CUSTOMER-FILE                             Close the files.
          REPORT-FILE.
*
    STOP RUN.                                       Terminate the program.
*
 200-READ-CUSTOMER-RECORD.
*
    READ CUSTOMER-FILE RECORD                       Read a record from the customer file. If
         AT END MOVE 'YES' TO END-OF-FILE.          it is the end, set a flag to YES.
*
 300-PROCESS-CUSTOMER-DETAIL.
*
    ADD CUSTOMER-UNITS TO TOTAL-UNITS               Accumulate total units.
*
    MOVE CUSTOMER-NAME TO REPORT-CUST-NAME          Move data from the input record to
    MOVE CUSTOMER-UNITS TO REPORT-UNITS             report detail.
*
    MOVE REPORT-DETAIL-RECORD TO REPORT-RECORD      Print a customer detail line.
    WRITE REPORT-RECORD AFTER ADVANCING 1 LINE.
*
    PERFORM 200-READ-CUSTOMER-RECORD.               Read (another) customer record.
```

FIGURE 2-7

Relationship of the Defined Data-Names to the Record Layout Chart

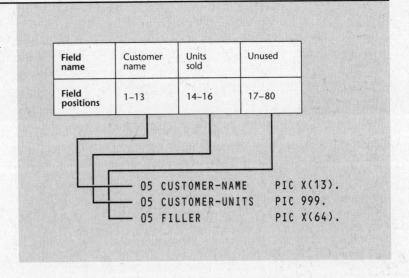

FIGURE 2-8

Analysis of One Data Definition Entry

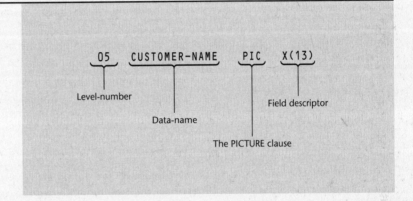

name field is under, and part of, the 01 CUSTOMER-RECORD. Similarly, 05 CUSTOMER-UNITS and 05 FILLER are all fields within 01 CUSTOMER-RECORD. Because these three fields all have the same 05 level-number, none of them is part of the other two fields. Chapter 3 will provide you with a more in-depth explanation of the use of level-numbers.

The *data-name* plays the obvious role of naming the field. In Figure 2-8 the data-name is CUSTOMER-NAME. As discussed in Chapter 1, COBOL specifies a number of rules for forming data-names. One data-name used frequently is FILLER, which is a reserved word and is designed to define fields that are not needed to be referenced in the program. In other words, there will never be a statement such as MOVE FILLER in a program. We use FILLER fields in records to define portions of a record that are not of interest in a specific program. We also use FILLER frequently in the WORKING-STORAGE SECTION, to define fields that contain such constant data as headers:

```
05  FILLER   PIC X(5) VALUE 'TOTAL'
```

In the example the keyword PIC (abbreviation for PICTURE) is used to introduce the field description in terms of a *picture string* that follows. In Figure 2-8 the picture string X(13) specifies that this is an alphanumeric field by using the X code, and that it is 13 bytes long, by the number within the parentheses.

Continuing with the example above, the field of five bytes will contain the characters in quotes. By the way, VALUE, as we will study in Chapter 3, is a *keyword* used in the DATA DIVISION to define the initial contents of fields. For example, in examining Figure 2-6 you will see clauses like VALUE ZERO or VALUE SPACES.

You will study the DATA DIVISION features in greater detail in Chapter 3. For now we can summarize two other main types of PIC clauses, in addition to the PIC X, by the following examples:

```
05 CUSTOMER-UNITS PIC 999
```
This is a numeric field by use of the 9 code, and it is 3 bytes long because there are 3 9's.

```
05 REPORT-TOTAL-UNITS PIC ZZZ9
```
This is a numeric edited field. The Z code specifies suppression of leading zeros, if any, in the first three positions. The total field is four bytes long, one byte for each character in the ZZZ9 picture code.

The other data definitions in the DATA DIVISION of the sample program are not discussed at this point. However, because of their self-documenting names it is easy to get an intuitive understanding of their purpose. We will make reference to all of them as we discuss the PROCEDURE DIVISION statements that make reference to these fields.

Program Flowchart

Figure 2-9 presents a flowchart for the program in Figure 2-6. Study this flowchart to gain an understanding of the sequence of tasks included in the PROCEDURE DIVISION.

AN OUTLINE FOR YOUR COBOL PROGRAMS

As a student learning the COBOL language for the first time, you will probably find it convenient to create a program outline similar to the one presented in Figure 2-10. Using a text editor, you can create such an outline and save it as a text file. Then whenever you are about to key-in a new program, copy the outline and add the appropriate instructions. In Figure 2-10 blank spaces indicate the locations of required data, data-names, and so forth in the program. Using a program outline will save you program entry time as well as help to avoid the inadvertent omission of required keywords or sections.

PROCEDURE DIVISION FOR THE SAMPLE REPORT PROGRAM

Reviewing the function for the report program, we begin with a file of customer records, with each record containing a customer name and number of units sold for a particular product. The program is designed to read each record in the file and to produce the report portrayed in Figure 2-1. The complete program in Figure 2-6 is referenced throughout the remainder of this chapter so that you can relate the various types of language statements to a concrete example.

The IDENTIFICATION, ENVIRONMENT, and DATA DIVISION in a COBOL program perform "housekeeping tasks" in that they provide background information so that the program can be executed after compilation. On the other hand, the instructions that directly result in execution of the program are given in the PROCEDURE DIVISION. Most of these executable instructions operate on storage locations, or fields, that have been defined in the DATA DIVISION. The keywords PROCEDURE DIVISION identify the beginning of this division and

FIGURE 2-9
Flowchart for the Report Program

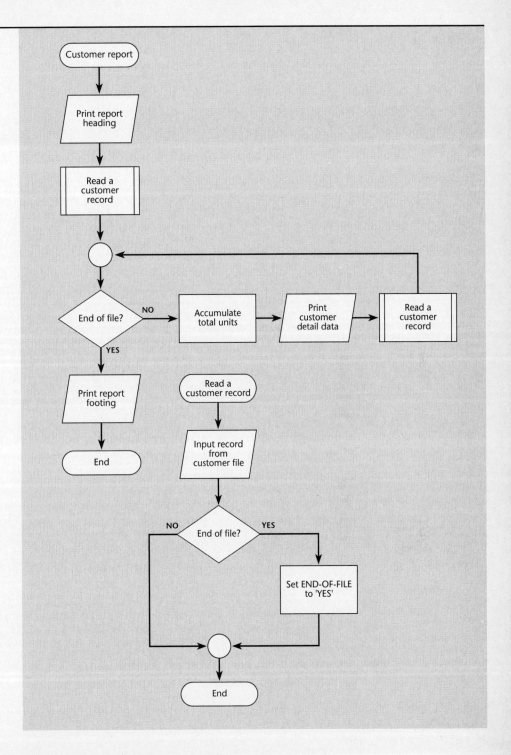

begin at the A margin of the COBOL Coding Form, followed by a period, as illustrated by the following excerpt:

FIGURE 2-10
An Outline for COBOL Programs

```
IDENTIFICATION DIVISION.
PROGRAM-ID. _____.


ENVIRONMENT DIVISION.


CONFIGURATION SECTION.


SOURCE-COMPUTER. _____.
OBJECT-COMPUTER. _____.


INPUT-OUTPUT SECTION.
FILE-CONTROL.
    SELECT _____ ASSIGN TO _____
    SELECT _____ ASSIGN TO _____.


DATA DIVISION.


FILE SECTION.


FD _____

    LABEL RECORDS ARE OMITTED
    RECORD CONTAINS ___ CHARACTERS
    DATA RECORD IS _____.


01 _____

FD _____

    LABEL RECORDS ARE OMITTED
    RECORD CONTAINS ___ CHARACTERS
    DATA RECORD IS _____.


01 _____


WORKING-STORAGE SECTION.


PROCEDURE DIVISION.
```

The PROCEDURE DIVISION consists of paragraphs, each paragraph containing at least one sentence. Each paragraph starts with a paragraph-name beginning in column 8 (A margin) of the COBOL Coding Form and ends with a required period. Paragraph-names are coined by the programmer following the rules of data-name formation, with one additional option: paragraph-names may be all numeric. Sentences and statements are written in the B area of the coding form, which includes columns 12–72.

In the sample report program in Figure 2-6 the PROCEDURE DIVISION consists of three paragraphs:

```
PROCEDURE DIVISION.
100-PROGRAM-SUMMARY.
200-READ-CUSTOMER-RECORD.
300-PROCESS-CUSTOMER-DETAIL.
```

These three paragraphs correspond to the three unique modules in the structure chart in Figure 2-4. Except for the first paragraph, 100-PROGRAM-SUMMARY, the order of the other two paragraphs is not important because they are executed by reference with a PERFORM statement. You can see this by reading the contents of the 100-PROGRAM-SUMMARY paragraph in Figure 2-6. Notice that the last statement in that paragraph is a STOP RUN, which terminates the execution of the program. So the program execution flow is to begin with the first statement in the first paragraph, to branch to and return from PERFORMed paragraphs referenced in that first paragraph, and to stop execution when we reach the last statement in the first paragraph, which normally will be a STOP RUN. Now it is obvious why we used 100-PROGRAM-SUMMARY for the name of the first paragraph. Another common name for such a module is 100-MAIN-LOGIC, although the rules of the language allow us to call any paragraph by any name.

The two most commonly used types of PROCEDURE DIVISION statements are imperative and conditional statements. An *imperative statement* consists of a verb that indicates action, plus appropriate operands involved in the action. In this chapter we will concentrate on imperative statements. The following imperative verbs are described in the following sections of this chapter:

- Input-output verbs: OPEN, READ, WRITE, CLOSE
- Data transfer verb: MOVE
- Arithmetic verb: ADD
- Control verbs: PERFORM, STOP RUN

A *conditional statement* allows the program to test for the existence of a condition, and to execute one or more commands selectively depending on the result of the test. Two basic conditional expressions are covered in this chapter: The AT END and the UNTIL conditional clauses. The AT END is used in READ statements, while the UNTIL is used in PERFORM statements.

R E V I E W . . . .

1. Of the four divisions that make up any COBOL program, the one that always is first in the sequence of presentation is the _____ DIVISION.

    IDENTIFICATION

2. The next division in the program, which makes reference to the computer hardware that is required, is the _____ DIVISION.

    ENVIRONMENT

3. The division of our sample COBOL program that consists of a FILE SECTION and a WORKING-STORAGE SECTION is the _____ DIVISION.

    DATA

4. In the DATA DIVISION the hierarchical relationship of a field with other data fields is indicated by the _____-number that is assigned to the field.

level

5. The name of a field is indicated in the DATA DIVISION by the assignment of a _____-name.

data

6. The field description PIC X(13) in the sample program identifies a field as being [numeric / alphanumeric], and ____ (number) bytes long.

alphanumeric; 13

7. The field description PIC 999 in the sample program identifies a field as being _____ , and ____ bytes long.

numeric; 3

8. The field description PIC ZZZ9 in the sample program identifies a field as being numeric and 4 bytes long, and for which up to 3 _____ _____ , if any, will be suppressed in the printed output.

leading zeros

9. The division of a COBOL program that includes the executable statements directly related to the overall program function is the _____ DIVISION.

PROCEDURE

10. Of the two commonly used types of statements in the PROCEDURE DIVISION, the type that includes a verb that indicates action—such as OPEN, MOVE, ADD, or PERFORM—is the _____ statement.

imperative

11. The type of statement in the PROCEDURE DIVISION that includes use of the AT END or the UNTIL clause is a _____ statement.

conditional

· ·

INPUT-OUTPUT VERBS

In this section we consider four input-output verbs: OPEN, READ, WRITE, and CLOSE.

Before an input or an output file can be used by the program, it must be OPENed. For the report program the following statement can be seen in the first paragraph of the PROCEDURE DIVISION in Figure 2-6:

```
OPEN INPUT    CUSTOMER-FILE
     OUTPUT   REPORT-FILE.
```

The file named CUSTOMER-FILE is opened as input, so that we can READ from it. The file named REPORT-FILE is opened as output; in our example the printer is assigned as the output file, and we will WRITE on it. Thus the OPEN verb declares the input or output function of the file. As in the above, it is common to write each file-name on a *separate* line rather than on the same line, and *not* to repeat the OPEN verb for each file. This practice makes for better readability than is true for the following alternative version of the above commands:

```
OPEN INPUT CUSTOMER-FILE OPEN OUTPUT REPORT-FILE.
```

At this point we should note that the file names appear in two other divisions of the program. In the ENVIRONMENT DIVISION the two files are referenced in the corresponding entries in Figure 2-6:

```
SELECT CUSTOMER-FILE ASSIGN TO  CUSTFILE.
SELECT REPORT-FILE   ASSIGN TO  PRINTER.
```

The statements above designate the hardware assignment for each file. CUSTFILE and PRINTER are assumed to be the names of the two files in the operating system; CUSTOMER-FILE and REPORT-FILE are the chosen file-names within the COBOL program. Then in the DATA DIVISION the FD entries name and describe certain characteristics of each file. For instance, in Figure 2-6 we have the following:

```
FD  REPORT-FILE
    LABEL RECORDS ARE OMITTED
    RECORD CONTAINS 132 CHARACTERS
    DATA RECORD IS REPORT-RECORD.
```

Thus when references to files are made in the PROCEDURE DIVISION, it is understood that the above type of information about the files has already been given in the ENVIRONMENT DIVISION and DATA DIVISION.

The basic format of the READ instruction is

READ file-name RECORD

    AT END imperative-statement.

In Figure 2-6, in the 200-READ-CUSTOMER-RECORD paragraph of the PROCEDURE DIVISION, the input instruction is

```
READ CUSTOMER-FILE RECORD
    AT END MOVE 'YES' TO END-OF-FILE.
```

Each time the command READ CUSTOMER-FILE RECORD is executed, the data contained in the next record of the customer file on disk is copied into central storage in the area referenced by the record-name CUSTOMER-RECORD. For example, whatever data is in columns 1–13 of the disk record is copied into columns 1–13 of CUSTOMER-RECORD (which is designated by the data-name CUSTOMER-NAME).

Each execution of the READ statement causes the previous content of the corresponding record in central storage to be erased. This means that normally one record at a time is processed, and, when a next record is read, there is no longer any use for the content of the preceding record.

As part of the READ instruction, we also need to indicate what the computer should do after all the input records have been read. The AT END clause serves this purpose. When a record is read, it is examined to see if it is an end-of-file record. The specific form of an end-of-file record differs according to the computer used, but in general it contains data codes that designate it as such. Only when such a record is read, is the "imperative-statement" following AT END executed. Thus AT END is a conditional clause: it indicates that the statement following the AT END should be executed if the record just read is an end-of-file record.

In our sample program, the imperative statement following AT END enters a YES in the END-OF-FILE field so that the program will be able to test the content of this "flag" field and determine when all the data have been read. This test is done by the UNTIL clause in the PERFORM verb discussed later.

The output verb WRITE is similar to the input verb READ, except that reference is made to a *record-name* rather than a file-name:

    WRITE record-name AFTER ADVANCING integer LINES

or

    WRITE record-name AFTER ADVANCING PAGE.

Consider the following excerpt from Figure 2-6:

```
MOVE REPORT-HEADING TO REPORT-RECORD
WRITE REPORT-RECORD AFTER ADVANCING PAGE.
```

The contents of the WORKING-STORAGE field called REPORT-HEADING are MOVEd (copied) to REPORT-RECORD, which is the record of the output file (recall the OPEN . . . OUTPUT REPORT-FILE). The AFTER ADVANCING PAGE clause in the excerpt above specifies that the printer should skip to the start of a new page and then write the data. PAGE is another reserved word in COBOL and signals the start of a page. As also illustrated in Figure 2-6, we can control the number of lines between printed output. To single space, we say WRITE . . . AFTER ADVANCING 1 LINE. To double space, we say AFTER ADVANCING 2 LINES, and so on.

As illustrated in Figure 2-6, in COBOL we do not write data directly. First we transfer whatever is to be written to an output file record, and then we issue the command WRITE. The output record is like a gate through which all output passes. For this reason the description of the REPORT-RECORD in the DATA DIVISION of our sample program specifies one long field of 132 bytes:

```
01   REPORT-RECORD   PIC X(132).
```

There is no point in subdividing the above field of 132 bytes into subfields, since a variety of output may be moved to the field. For instance, we will print a report heading, detail lines, and a report footing. Incidentally, as we mentioned earlier, the choice of 132 bytes is in reference to the common width of printers in mainframe computers. If our output device were a video monitor or a typical, 80-column personal computer printer, we would have used another record size, such as PIC X(80).

We conclude this discussion of input-output verbs with the CLOSE verb, which is used after a file is no longer needed and which must be used before the end of the program. At the end of the PROGRAM-SUMMARY paragraph in Figure 2-6, we see

```
CLOSE CUSTOMER-FILE
      REPORT-FILE.
```

The CLOSE verb is particularly meaningful in the context of magnetic tapes and disk files. File-names are written on separate lines simply to enhance readability, and the CLOSE is written only once by style choice. For the second line it would be equally correct to write CLOSE REPORT-FILE.

R E V I E W . . . .

1. Input of data into the central storage of the computer is accomplished by executing a READ statement. Before a READ statement can be executed, a checking procedure must be carried out to determine file availability by executing a(n) _____ statement.

OPEN

2. As each record of a file is read into storage, the previous content of that storage location, which typically represents data from the preceding record that was read, is automatically [moved / erased].

erased

3. The part of the READ statement that indicates what should be done after all the records of the input file have been read is the _____ clause.

AT END

4. Output of data from a designated output file is accomplished by executing a(n) _____ instruction.

WRITE

5. Just as is true for a READ STATEMENT, before a WRITE statement can be executed, availability of the output file must be ascertained by executing an appropriate _____ statement.

OPEN

6. An option available with the WRITE statement allows control of the vertical spacing in the printed output. The clause used to designate spacing instruction is the AFTER _____ clause.

ADVANCING

7. When a data processing operation is completed, the availability of both the input and output files that have been used should be terminated. This is accomplished by an appropriate _____ instruction.

CLOSE

. . . .

THE MOVE INSTRUCTION

The MOVE verb is used to copy data from a sending field to a receiving field. Despite what the word MOVE implies, data items are not moved but, rather, are simply copied. Thus the instruction MOVE A to B designates that B should contain a copy of the content of A which also retains its content. Examples of the MOVE instruction in Figure 2-6 are

```
MOVE      REPORT-HEADING TO REPORT-RECORD
MOVE      SPACES TO REPORT-RECORD
MOVE      CUSTOMER-NAME TO REPORT-CUST-NAME
```

The sending field should not be longer than the receiving field, for otherwise some data would be truncated. When a sending field such as REPORT-HEADING is moved to a larger receiving field such as REPORT-RECORD, the extra spaces to the right are filled with blanks. When moving numeric data, the programmer must observe many rules. The MOVE operation will be described in further detail in Chapter 4.

THE ARITHMETIC VERB: ADD

In this section we consider the ADD arithmetic verb which is used in the first line of the 300-PROCESS-CUSTOMER-DETAIL paragraph in Figure 2-6:

```
ADD CUSTOMER-UNITS TO TOTAL-UNITS.
```

The instruction says to add the value in CUSTOMER-UNITS to the existing value in TOTAL-UNITS. If the first field had a content of 30 and the second a content of 20, the ADD instruction would change the content of TOTAL-UNITS to 50 and would leave the value in CUSTOMER-UNITS unchanged.

TOTAL-UNITS in the above example serves as an accumulator. We keep adding to it the values of CUSTOMER-UNITS being read from the CUSTOMER-FILE records. It is important to start the accumulator with a zero value; otherwise we would be adding to an already existing value. Therefore the DATA DIVISION specifies

```
01  TOTAL-UNITS   PIC 9999   VALUE ZERO.
```

The VALUE ZERO clause assures us that the accumulator will have a zero initial value. If we forgot to include the VALUE ZERO clause, we would generate improper totals, since the initial content of the field is not likely to be zero.

The ADD verb, as well as other arithmetic verbs, has many variations. You will study these verbs in some detail in Chapters 4 and 7.

R   E   V   I   E   W   .   .   .   .

1. The verb that is used for data transfer is the _____ verb.

    MOVE

2. Execution of a MOVE instruction results in the content of a sending field being [moved / copied] into the receiving field.

    copied

3. The sending field should not be [smaller / larger] than the receiving field.

    larger

4. The verb that is used to achieve the accumulation of values that are stored in two different fields is the _____ verb.

    ADD

5. When the statement ADD DAILY-SALES TO SALES-TOTAL is executed, the record field whose content remains unchanged because of its position in the above statement is _____.

    DAILY-SALES

6. When the statement ADD DAILY-SALES TO SALES-TOTAL is executed, the field whose content is changed, given that the other field had a nonzero value, is

    _____.

    SALES-TOTAL

7. The clause in the DATA DIVISION record description that is used to ensure that a field used as an accumulator has an initial value of zero is the _____ clause.

    VALUE ZERO

.   .   .   .

CONTROL VERBS

Program instructions in the PROCEDURE DIVISION are executed in the order in which they are written, from top to bottom, except when control verbs interrupt this normal flow. In this section we describe some basic forms of program control by use of the PERFORM and STOP RUN verbs.

The PERFORM verb provides a powerful mechanism for program control. Referring to the 100-PROGRAM-SUMMARY paragraph of the PROCEDURE DIVISION in Figure 2-6, you can observe the following instruction:

```
PERFORM 200-READ-CUSTOMER-RECORD.
```

The 200-READ-CUSTOMER-RECORD is a paragraph-name. The effect of the above instruction is to branch to the specified paragraph, execute all the instructions in the paragraph, and then resume with the statement immediately following the PERFORM.

When the PERFORM 200-READ-CUSTOMER-RECORD is executed, we read the next record in CUSTOMER-FILE. If that record happens to be the end-of-file record, the field named END-OF-FILE would then contain a YES because of the READ statement that has already been executed:

```
READ CUSTOMER-FILE RECORD
    AT END MOVE 'YES' TO END-OF-FILE.
```

Again a PERFORM statement says "go execute the named paragraph and come back." In the 100-PROGRAM-SUMMARY paragraph in Figure 2-6 we have two PERFORM statements in succession:

```
PERFORM 200-READ-CUSTOMER-RECORD.
PERFORM 300-PROCESS-CUSTOMER-DETAIL
        UNTIL END-OF-FILE = 'YES'.
```

The second PERFORM statement has a different format from that of the first one, as will be explained below. But apart from that consideration, when the program comes to the second PERFORM, a record has already been read from the CUSTOMER-FILE and the AT END test in the READ statement has been executed.

The PERFORM verb also can be used to execute an *iterative procedure,* or *loop,* as in the second PERFORM statement discussed above:

```
PERFORM 300-PROCESS-CUSTOMER-DETAIL
        UNTIL END-OF-FILE = 'YES'.
```

Recall that the END-OF-FILE contains YES only when the end-of-file record has been read in the CUSTOMER-FILE. The above PERFORM operates as follows: the conditional expression END-OF-FILE = 'YES' is tested; if it is true, the program leaves the associated PERFORM statement and continues execution with the next statement, which starts with MOVE TOTAL-UNITS. If the condition is not true, then 300-PROCESS-CUSTOMER-DETAIL is executed again. The entire process is repeated until the condition is true. At this point, it would be a good idea for you to turn to the flowchart in Figure 2-9 to get a visual view of the interrelationships in the program logic.

It is important to recognize that the specialized conditional UNTIL . . . is executed first, and if END-OF-FILE is YES, then the associated PERFORM 300-PROCESS-CUSTOMER-DETAIL is *not* executed. To understand fully the control structure in the sample program, notice that the last statement in the 300-PROCESS-CUSTOMER-DETAIL paragraph in Figure 2-6 is PERFORM 200-READ-CUSTOMER-RECORD. Thus every time we repeat execution of the PERFORM . . . UNTIL, a new record is read and checked for the end-of-file condition. Furthermore, before the PERFORM . . . UNTIL is executed for the very first time, a record has already been read due to the first PERFORM statement in the 100-PROGRAM-SUMMARY paragraph.

Figure 2-11 portrays the control structure of the PERFORM . . . UNTIL in flowchart form. As an additional aid in understanding the control structure involved, we consider a few special cases in the following paragraphs.

Suppose that the customer file contains only two customer records. How many times would the 200-READ-CUSTOMER-RECORD paragraph be executed? The answer is three times. The first time is caused by the first PERFORM in the 100-

FIGURE 2-11

Flowchart Showing the Effect of Executing the Conditional UNTIL

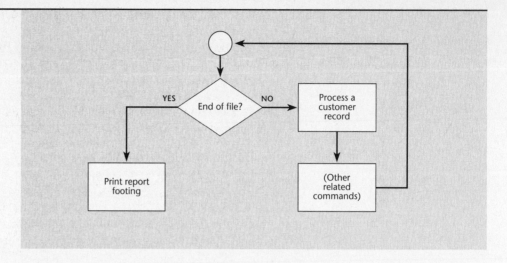

FIGURE 2-12

Sequence of Program Execution Steps Involving PERFORM Statements

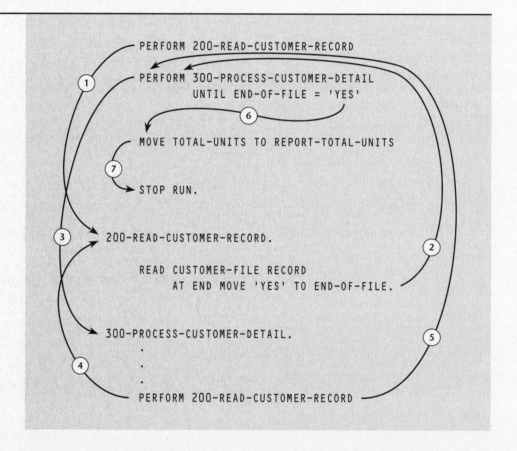

PROGRAM-SUMMARY. The second and third times are caused by the PERFORM in the 300-PROCESS-CUSTOMER-DETAIL paragraph. Of course, the third record would not be a customer record; it would be an end-of-file record that would cause YES to be moved to END-OF-FILE, which in turn would cause the PERFORM . . . UNTIL not to execute 300-PROCESS-CUSTOMER-DETAIL, and would lead to printing of the report footing and the termination of the program via execution of the STOP RUN command.

The flowchart in Figure 2-9 and the examples above may not make it obvious how program control returns to the PERFORM . . . UNTIL statement after each customer record has been read. To illustrate how this occurs, Figure 2-12 portrays the sequence of program execution for the usual data situation in which there is at least one customer record. Study Figure 2-12 as you read the following paragraph.

As a result of executing the PERFORM 200-READ-CUSTOMER-RECORD statement in the 100-PROGRAM-SUMMARY paragraph, the 200-READ-CUSTOMER-RECORD paragraph is executed. The first record is a customer record. As is always the case, program execution now returns to the statement following the PERFORM that was just executed. The next statement is the PERFORM . . . UNTIL. Because the record that was read was *not* the end-of-file record, the 300-PROCESS-CUS-TOMER-DETAIL paragraph is now executed, culminating with the last statement in that paragraph, which is PERFORM 200-READ-CUSTOMER-RECORD. Execution of this statement results in program control returning to the 200-READ-CUSTOMER-RECORD paragraph. If the record that is read is a customer record, the record is then simply available for processing. If the record is the end-of-file record, YES is moved to END-OF-FILE. After executing the 200-READ-CUSTOMER-RECORD command, program execution then would continue with the statement following the PERFORM statement in the 300-PROCESS-CUSTOMER-DETAIL paragraph. But there is no statement following that embedded PERFORM statement, because it is the last statement in that paragraph. Therefore, control returns to the PERFORM . . . UNTIL statement after every record is read.

A LOGIC TEMPLATE FOR INPUT PROCESSING LOOPS

Most COBOL programs are input-driven and involve the following general structure:

> We read a record from an input file, process that record, and then we continue so reading and processing until we reach the end of the input file. At that point, we either terminate the program or we do other tasks, such as print summary totals.

Because this structure is so common, we suggest that you take the time to learn how to code this general logic in a "standard" way so that you don't have to stop and "re-invent the wheel" every time that you wish to do such data processing. Figures 2-13 and 2-14 present two recommended standard templates for handling the logic of iteration for input from a file. Figure 2-13 presents the template based on the 1974 ANSI COBOL standard and follows the procedure used in the sample program. Figure 2-14 presents the template based on the 1985 standard.

The main difference between COBOL '74 and COBOL '85 is that in the 1985 version we have available a number of new features, such as the in-line PERFORM and the NOT AT END clause in the READ statement. The details of these features will be discussed in Chapter 4. For now we will stay with a rough, but simple explanation of some of the COBOL '85 features. The in-line PERFORM does not make reference to another paragraph; instead, it means to say, "perform what follows." Thus in the template in Figure 2-14 you can observe that what follows the in-line PERFORM . . . UNTIL is a READ statement that specifies what to do for both the AT END and the NOT AT END cases. Finally, the END-READ and END-PERFORM are "scope terminators" that define the end of the effect of the corresponding statement. We are proceeding on the assumption that these are intuitive enough features that make sense for now, and we will return to them in Chapter 4.

THE STOP RUN STATEMENT

The STOP RUN statement is the control statement that terminates program execution. When this statement is encountered, program execution terminates immediately. Therefore you should take care to include this command only at the appropriate point or points in terms of the logic of the program.

FIGURE 2-13

A Logic Template for Handling Input-Driven Iteration Using COBOL '74

Set up a Read-Input-File paragraph that reads the input file and, if it is the end of the file, it sets a flag to a value such as "yes".

Set up a Process-Record paragraph that does the necessary processing.

The last statement in this paragraph performs the Read-Input-File paragraph.

    PERFORM the Read-Input-File paragraph
       to read the first record from the file.

    PERFORM the Process-Record paragraph
       UNTIL the end-of-file condition is true.

Example:

    OPEN the input and output files.

    PERFORM 200-READ-CUSTOMER-RECORD.

    PERFORM 300-PROCESS-CUSTOMER-DETAIL

       UNTIL END-OF-FILE = 'YES'.

    Other instructions, such as processing summary totals, etc.

    CLOSE the files.

    STOP RUN.

200-READ-CUSTOMER-RECORD.

    READ CUSTOMER-FILE RECORD

       AT END MOVE 'YES' TO END-OF-FILE.

300-PROCESS-CUSTOMER-DETAIL.

       instructions to process the record

    PERFORM 200-READ-CUSTOMER-RECORD

R E V I E W . . . .

1. The COBOL verbs that interrupt the normal sequential execution of program statements are called _____ verbs.

          control

2. The control verb that makes it possible to branch to a specified paragraph, execute it, and then return to the statement immediately following the statement containing the control verb is the _____ verb.

          PERFORM

3. The control verb that is used to terminate program execution is the _____ verb.

          STOP RUN

4. The STOP RUN statement [is / need not be] the last statement in a program.

          need not be

FIGURE 2-14
A Logic Template for Handling Input-Driven Iteration Using COBOL '85

```
PERFORM UNTIL end-of-file-condition is true
    READ a record from the input file
        AT END SET end-of-file-condition TO TRUE
        NOT AT END
            Process the input record, either by writing the instructions
            right here, or by writing a PERFORM that references a paragraph
            that does the processing
    END-READ
END-PERFORM


Example:
OPEN input and output files
PERFORM UNTIL END-OF-INPUT
    READ CUSTOMER-FILE RECORD
        AT END SET END-OF-INPUT TO TRUE
        NOT AT END
            PERFORM
                instructions to process the record
            END—PERFORM
    END-READ
END-PERFORM
CLOSE the files
STOP RUN.
```

SUMMARY

The overall purpose of this chapter was to introduce you to a basic set of PROCEDURE DIVISION commands. A sample program was referenced throughout the chapter as a concrete example.

The *program function* was to read records from a customer file and to print a report that includes a *report heading,* a set of *detail records,* and a *report footing.* A *printer spacing chart* was used to plan program output. A *structure chart* was prepared, *pseudocode* was written, and a *flowchart* was developed in the process of program design, culminating in a listing of the COBOL program.

As a necessary prerequisite for discussion of the PROCEDURE DIVISION commands, the way that data specifications are written in the DATA DIVISION was briefly described. The elements of such a specification include the *level-number, data-name, PICTURE (PIC) clause,* and the *field descriptor* (such as 999) associated with the PICTURE clause.

After reviewing the overall logic of the sequence of paragraphs in the sample PROCEDURE DIVISION, two types of PROCEDURE DIVISION statements were identified: imperative statements and conditional statements. This chapter focused particularly on imperative statements.

An *imperative statement* consists of a verb that indicates action, plus the appropriate operands involved in the action. The imperative verbs whose uses were described in this chapter are

- Input-output verbs: OPEN, READ, WRITE, CLOSE
- Data transfer verb: MOVE
- Arithmetic verb: ADD
- Control verbs: PERFORM, STOP RUN

A *conditional statement* allows the program to test for the existence of a condition, and to execute one or more commands selectively depending on the result of the test. Two conditional expressions were described in this chapter: the AT END and the UNTIL. The AT END is used in READ statements, while the UNTIL is used in PERFORM statements, and such uses are included in the sample program.

EXERCISES

2.1   Write COBOL statements for the following tasks.

(a) Set the value of a data-name A equal to 150.

(b) Set the value of ACCUMULATOR equal to zero.

(c) Add the value of BONUS to PAY.

2.2   Write COBOL statements to exchange the contents of two fields, A and B. (You may assume any additional data-names that you need.)

2.3   A program contains the statement

```
PERFORM REPORT-PRINTING
        UNTIL END-OF-DATA = 'YES'.
```

Explain how END-OF-DATA is defined in the program, and illustrate how it is used as a control mechanism. Assume that END-OF-DATA refers to an input file called CUSTOMER-FILE.

2.4   The following program segment contains a logical error. Find and correct the error.

```
PROCEDURE DIVISION.
FIRST-PARAGRAPH.
    READ PRODUCT-FILE RECORD
        AT END MOVE 'YES' TO END-OF-FILE.
```

2.5   Write a statement to make an output file called TRANSACTIONS-FILE available for subsequent use.

2.6   Assume that we have the following program excerpt.

```
PROGRAM-SUMMARY.
. . . (other statements of no interest here)
    PERFORM PROCESS-INPUT
        UNTIL END-OF-FILE = 'YES'
```

```
READ-INPUT.
        _____
        _____

PROCESS-INPUT.
        . . . (other statements of no interest here)
        PERFORM READ-INPUT.   (last statement in paragraph)
```

Write statements to determine if an input file called PAYABLES has been read-in completely and, if it has, to terminate the program. Assume that PAYABLES and RECEIVABLES are the input and output files that had been used in the program. Fill in the blank spaces indicated in the program segment.

2.7 Write statements to print two records from a file whose record is called MONTHLY-REPORT, leaving two blank lines between the records. The first record will print the contents of HEADER-1 and the second will print the contents of HEADER-2.

2.8 Consider the following main-logic paragraph of a program.

```
MAIN-LOGIC.
    . . . (other statements of no interest here)
        PERFORM PROCESSING
             UNTIL END-OF-FILE = 'YES'

        _____
        _____

STOP RUN.
```

After the PERFORM PROCESSING instruction, write statements to print the (last) record of a file called FINAL-REPORT. The record-name of FINAL-REPORT is called MONTHLY-REPORT. The record written will be double-spaced from the previous record written and it will contain the data in a field called MONTHLY-SUMMARY.

2.9 Using the PERFORM verb, write PROCEDURE DIVISION instructions to read 10 records from a file called SALES-FILE. Each record contains a field called AMOUNT-SOLD. We want to accumulate the sum of the AMOUNT-SOLD values in a field called TOTAL-AMOUNT. The DATA DIVISION has been written so that TOTAL-AMOUNT has an initial value of zero.

(*Hint:* Set up a field and call it RECORD-COUNTER, to count the records read-in and to test for the value of the counter in the PERFORM . . . UNTIL statement, to determine termination.)

Assume that after the 10 records have been read-in, the program continues with other statements that are not of interest to us.

```
PROCEDURE DIVISION.
PROGRAM-SUMMARY.
        OPEN. . . (etc., not of interest here)
        PERFORM READ-SALES-FILE   (initial read)
        _____
        PERFORM ACCUMULATE-SALES
             UNTIL _____
        (etc., not of interest to us here)
READ-SALES-FILE.
        _____
        _____
```

```
ACCUMULATE-SALES.

    _____
    _____
```

2.10 We have a file on disk that contains employee records. Each record in the input file contains the following fields:

Employee Name in columns	1–15
Hours Worked in columns	16–17
Unused by this program:	18–80

The Employee Name field will not be used directly by the program, so it could be designated as a FILLER field. Nevertheless, we describe the content of this field anyway, to make the exercise more meaningful.

We want to write a program that will read each record in the file, count the number of employee records in the file, and accumulate the total hours worked by all employees. The output of the program consists of one line that gives these totals. The following input and output samples illustrate these points.

SAMPLE INPUT

```
ANDERSON, P.  40
BROWN, S.     32
GARCIA, M .   40
LORENZO, K.   40
NICHOLSON, J. 36
PHILLIPS, P.  44
REEBOCK, A.   40
```

SAMPLE OUTPUT

```
        EMPLOYEE WORK SUMMARY
NUMBER OF EMPLOYEES =   7    TOTAL HOURS =  272
```

Your assignment is to write the required program by completing the missing parts of the program below. After completing the program, compile and execute it on your computer, using the sample input above.

```
        IDENTIFICATION DIVISION.
        PROGRAM-ID.  EMPLRPRT.
*
        ENVIRONMENT DIVISION.
*
        CONFIGURATION SECTION.
        SOURCE-COMPUTER. ABC-480.
        OBJECT-COMPUTER. ABC-480.
*
        INPUT-OUTPUT SECTION.
        FILE-CONTROL.
            SELECT EMPLOYEE-FILE ASSIGN TO _____.
            SELECT REPORT-FILE   ASSIGN TO _____.
*
        DATA DIVISION.
*
        FILE SECTION.
*
```

```
      FD  EMPLOYEE-FILE
          LABEL RECORDS ARE STANDARD
          RECORD CONTAINS 80 CHARACTERS
          DATA RECORD IS EMPLOYEE-RECORD.
      *
       01  EMPLOYEE-RECORD.
           05 EMPLOYEE-NAME         PIC X(15).
           05 EMPLOYEE-HOURS-WORKED PIC 99.
           05 FILLER               PIC X(63).
      *
      FD  REPORT-FILE
          LABEL RECORDS ARE OMITTED
          RECORD CONTAINS 132 CHARACTERS
          DATA RECORD IS PRINT-LINE.
      *
       01  PRINT-LINE              PIC X(132).
      *
      *

          WORKING-STORAGE SECTION.
      *
       01  END-OF-FILE-TEST        PIC XXX VALUE 'NO'.
      *
       01  EMPLOYEE-COUNTER        PIC 999 VALUE ZERO.
      *
       01  TOTAL-HOURS-WORKED      PIC 9999 VALUE ZERO.
      *
       01  REPORT-HEADING.
           05 FILLER               PIC X(12) VALUE SPACES.
           05 FILLER               PIC X(21) VALUE
              'EMPLOYEE WORK SUMMARY'.
      *
       01  REPORT-TOTALS.
           05 FILLER               PIC X(5) VALUE SPACES.
           05 FILLER               PIC X(22)
              VALUE 'NUMBER OF EMPLOYEES = '.
           05 REPORT-EMPL-COUNTER   PIC ZZ9.
           05 FILLER               PIC X(5) VALUE SPACES.
           05 FILLER               PIC X(14)
              VALUE 'TOTAL HOURS = '.
           05 REPORT-TOTAL-HOURS    PIC ZZZ9.


          PROCEDURE DIVISION.
      *
          100-PROGRAM-SUMMARY.
      *
              OPEN INPUT  _____
                   OUTPUT _____
      *
              _____
              _____
              _____
              _____
              PERFORM 200-_____
              PERFORM 300-_____
                      UNTIL END-OF-FILE = 'YES'
```

Write instructions to print the report heading on top of page and print a blank line afterwards. (*Hint:* See Figure 2-6.)

```
            MOVE EMPLOYEE-COUNTER TO REPORT-EMPL-COUNTER
            MOVE _____
            WRITE _____
                        AFTER ADVANCING PAGE
    *
            CLOSE _____
    *
            STOP RUN.
    *
    *
      200-_____.
            READ EMPLOYEE-FILE RECORD
                AT END _____.
    *
    *
      300-_____.
    *
    *
            ADD 1 TO _____
    *
            ADD  EMPLOYEE-HOURS-WORKED TO_____
    *
    *
            PERFORM _____.
    *
```

2.11 Key-in and run the sample program given in Figure 2-6. Use as input the sample data given below. Even though this exercise will not involve programming effort on your part, it will provide you with the opportunity to familiarize yourself with the ENVIRONMENT DIVISION entries pertinent to your computer, and the program-submission procedures of your installation.

SAMPLE INPUT DATA

```
ADAMS        100
BROWN        075
GROVER       030
MOORE        025
PETERSON     060
WILLIAMS     010
```

2.12 Write a COBOL program that will take a set of input records and list these records double-spaced on the printer. Each source record read in should be moved to the output file and be written in the exact form that was input, double-spacing between records.

Following are parts of the program for the first three divisions. Refer to the "standard" outline for COBOL programs that we showed in Figure 2-10.

```
    FD  SOURCE-FILE   LABEL RECORDS ARE OMITTED
                      RECORD CONTAINS 80 CHARACTERS
                      DATA RECORD IS SOURCE-REC.
    01  SOURCE-REC    PIC X(80).
    *
    FD  OUTPUT-FILE   LABEL RECORDS ARE OMITTED
                      RECORD CONTAINS 132 CHARACTERS
```

```
                                   DATA RECORD IS OUTPUT-REC.
             01  OUTPUT-REC    PIC X(132).
             *
             WORKING-STORAGE SECTION.
             01  END-OF-FILE   PIC X(3) VALUE 'NO '.
```

2.13   Figure 2-15 provides the first three divisions of a COBOL program. You are
        asked to write the PROCEDURE DIVISION for this program and then
        compile and execute the entire program.

        The function of this program is to read source records containing the
        three data fields, NAME-IN, STREET-IN, and CITY-IN, as you can see in the

---

FIGURE 2-15

*Partial Program Listing for
Exercise 2.13*

```
IDENTIFICATION DIVISION.
PROGRAM-ID.  LABELS.
*
ENVIRONMENT DIVISION.
*
CONFIGURATION SECTION.
SOURCE-COMPUTER. ABC-480.
OBJECT-COMPUTER. ABC-480.
*
INPUT-OUTPUT SECTION.
FILE-CONTROL.
    SELECT ADDRESS-FILE ASSIGN TO INFILE.
    SELECT PRINT-FILE   ASSIGN TO PRINTER.
*
DATA DIVISION.
*
FILE SECTION.
*
FD  ADDRESS-FILE
    LABEL RECORDS ARE OMITTED
    DATA RECORD IS ADDRESS-RECORD.
*
01  ADDRESS-RECORD.
    02 NAME                   PIC X(25).
    02 STREET                 PIC X(25).
    02 CITY                   PIC X(30).
*
FD  PRINT-FILE
    LABEL RECORDS ARE OMITTED
    DATA RECORD IS PRINT-RECORD.
*
01  PRINT-RECORD.
    02 FILLER                 PIC X(2).
    02 PRINT-LINE             PIC X(30).
    02 FILLER                 PIC X(100).
*
WORKING-STORAGE SECTION.
*
01  END-OF-DATA-INDICATOR     PIC XXX VALUE 'NO '.
```

DATA DIVISION under the FD for ADDRESS-FILE. These three fields are located, respectively, in columns 1–25, 26–50, and 51–80 in the source records. The program should print each of these three fields on a separate line, double-spacing between address records.

Output from two sample records would appear as follows:

```
ALLEN M. JOHNSON
1532 E. WASHINGTON ST.
CHICAGO, ILLINOIS 60186

PATRICIA K. WALTON
2252 PALM BOULEVARD
MIAMI, FLORIDA 33322
```

The program can be used with adhesive labels so that a mailing could be made to a group of individuals whose names and addresses are available in ADDRESS-FILE. The input file, called ADDRESS-FILE, has been ASSIGNed to a device assumed to be called INFILE. Obviously this part of the program may have to be changed to adapt it to your own computer. Similarly, the output file, PRINT-FILE, has been ASSIGNed to a device, PRINTER, which may also need revision. A field in WORKING-STORAGE is called END-OF-DATA-INDICATOR and is initialized to a value of 'NO'. It is assumed that in your PROCEDURE DIVISION you will write

```
READ ADDRESS-FILE RECORD
    AT END MOVE 'YES' TO END-OF-DATA-INDICATOR
```

and you will PERFORM the repeated function of the program UNTIL END-OF-DATA-INDICATOR = 'YES'.

3

Data Definition and Editing

IN THIS CHAPTER *you will develop an understanding of the purpose, structure, and coding details for writing the DATA DIVISION of a COBOL program.*

Specifically, you will learn (1) how to define elementary and group data fields; (2) how to define initial contents in data fields, including the definition of constants; (3) how to use the features in the FILE and WORKING-STORAGE sections; and (4) how to use the PICTURE clause to define and edit data fields.

With respect to PICTURE description, the material in this chapter is more extensive than what you can reasonably apply at this point in your studies. Therefore you should plan to make continued reference to this chapter as you study examples of, or write, PICTURE descriptions in later chapters.

INTRODUCTION

As you learned in the previous chapters, the DATA DIVISION is that part of the COBOL program in which data fields are defined. The executable programming instructions in the PROCEDURE DIVISION make reference to these data fields, as in, for examples, MOVE A TO B and ADD 1 TO TOTAL. In addition to defining the data fields, the DATA DIVISION is also the place in which we specify desired editing. Editing is used to improve the readability of output on a printed report or video monitor by eliminating leading zeros, entering dollar signs, inserting commas in long numbers, and the like.

OVERALL STRUCTURE OF THE DATA DIVISION

The DATA DIVISION commonly includes two sections: the FILE SECTION and the WORKING-STORAGE SECTION. Figure 3-1 outlines the overall structure of the DATA DIVISION. The FILE SECTION is used to define each file used by the program, as will be explained in some detail later in this chapter. The WORKING-STORAGE SECTION is used to define fields that are used in the course of program execution but are not directly related to input or output files. Examples of WORKING-STORAGE fields are report headings, totals accumulators, and "flag" fields used for testing whether or not certain conditions exist.

Although the FILE SECTION and WORKING-STORAGE SECTION commonly are the only sections included in the DATA DIVISION, there may in fact be as many as three more sections: the REPORT SECTION, LINKAGE SECTION, and COMMUNICATION SECTION. However, these latter three sections are rather specialized. The REPORT SECTION and LINKAGE SECTION will be covered in later chapters. The COMMUNICATION SECTION is so specialized and so rarely used that we consider it to be outside the scope of this book.

DATA-NAMES AND CONSTANTS

As introduced in Chapter 1, a data-name in COBOL is analogous to a variable in algebra. It is a general symbol or name that can have different values. The specific rules that must be followed in choosing data-names were presented in Chapter 1, in the section on data-names.

FIGURE 3-1

Outline of a Typical DATA DIVISION

```
DATA DIVISION.

FILE SECTION.

FD   file-name
     other clauses describing the file

01   record-name
     other clauses describing fields
     within the record

FD   file-name... (as many FDs as there are files)

WORKING-STORAGE SECTION.

77   elementary field description

     (as many 77-type descriptions as needed)

01   field description(s)
     with possible subordinate field descriptions

     (as many 01 descriptions as needed)
```

In addition to data-names, COBOL makes use of constants that also need to be defined in the DATA DIVISION. Up to now we have side-stepped this discussion in favor of describing data-names and covering a basic set of PROCEDURE DIVISION commands.

There are three distinct types of constants in COBOL: numeric literals, figurative constants, and nonnumeric literals.

As an example of a *numeric literal,* suppose that the sales tax rate in a particular state is 0.06 of sales. Within the COBOL program we need a way to multiply the amount of sales by 0.06. One way of accomplishing this without using a numeric literal is to define a storage field, assign to it a data-name, such as TAX-RATE, and input the value 0.06 into the field. Conceptually, the internal storage location has the following structure:

TAX-RATE	Data-name
0 0 6	Content

The decimal point is not shown above, but is understood to be located in the appropriate position. With this approach the reference to TAX-RATE will make available the 0.06 value stored in this field. Another approach that is available in COBOL, however, is simply to write the numeric literal 0.06 in the PROCEDURE DIVISION of the program itself and use this value directly. Conceptually, the internal storage location has the following structure in this case:

0 0 6	Data-name
0 0 6	Content

Numeric literals without a decimal point are understood to be integers (whole numbers). If a decimal point is used, it must not be the last character. Thus, 35. is not correct, whereas 35.0 is acceptable. The reason for this rule is that in COBOL programming, the period is always used to signal the end of a sentence, just as in English. Therefore it would be ambiguous as to whether a point following a number is a decimal point or a period.

The second type of constant used in COBOL is the *figurative constant.* The most common figurative constants are ZERO, ZEROS, ZEROES, SPACE, and SPACES, although a few others are available. These refer to zeros or blanks, respectively. Their general use can be illustrated by the following brief examples. Suppose we want to set the data-name AMOUNT equal to zero. We can write MOVE ZERO TO AMOUNT to accomplish this objective. Similarly, if we wish to ensure that blanks are contained in the field called TITLE, we can write MOVE SPACES TO TITLE.

The third type of constant is the *nonnumeric literal.* As contrasted to numeric literals and figurative constants, the nonnumeric literal is any alphanumeric value enclosed in quotation marks. For example, suppose we want to print the title INCOME STATEMENT as the heading of a report. The words INCOME and STATEMENT are not intended to refer to data-names; rather, we simply want these exact words printed. This can be done by enclosing them in quotation marks and making reference to 'INCOME STATEMENT' in the COBOL command. Incidentally, the COBOL language specifications allow use of the single or double quotation marks for nonnumeric literals. Thus for the example above we could have "INCOME STATEMENT". However, some compilers accept only the single quotes or only the double quotes for nonnumeric literals. Therefore you should check as to what your compiler allows.

As an example of how a nonnumeric literal might be used in a decision context, suppose we want to know if a customer's last name is BROWN. We could write the following:

```
IF LAST-NAME EQUAL 'BROWN' (etc.)
```

Unlike a data-name, a nonnumeric literal can include blanks. The nonnumeric literal also can be composed entirely of numeric characters. This may seem like a contradiction, but it is not. The term "nonnumeric" refers to how the characters are handled within the computer, and not to their form as letters or numbers. For a nonnumeric literal, *the numbers are handled as being symbols, as are alphabetic letters, and not as being quantities or values.*

DEFINING AN ELEMENTARY DATA FIELD

The most basic data definition is that of describing an elementary data field. "Elementary" here means a single field that, unlike "group" fields, is not subdivided into subfields. An example is a field designed to store the last name of a customer:

```
05   LAST-NAME   PIC X(15).
```

The definition consists of three parts:

1. The level-number, in this case 05, which is used to describe the relationship of this field to other fields, as will be explained below.

2. The data-name, in this case, LAST-NAME, which can be used to reference the field. For example, MOVE SPACES TO LAST-NAME. Several specific rules for forming data-names were presented in Chapter 1.

3. The PIC (abbreviation of PICTURE) clause, which is used to define the size and the data type of the field. In the above example PIC X(15) defines a field of 15 alphanumeric positions (X indicates the alphanumeric type of field).

The three parts of the definition above enable us to define individual data fields at the elementary level. To do so, we need to know how to assign level-numbers, how to create data-names, and how to define PICTURE clauses. You will study these topics in subsequent sections of this chapter. First, however, let us consider two other topics for elementary fields: the use of the FILLER generic data-name and how to put initial contents into data fields.

R E V I E W . . . .

1. Of the four divisions of a COBOL program, the one concerned with the identification and description of storage fields is the _____ DIVISION.

                                                                    DATA

2. The two sections commonly included in the DATA DIVISION are the _____ and the_____ .

                                            FILE SECTION; WORKING-STORAGE SECTION

3. IN COBOL a label for a field of data that can contain different values at different times is called a(n) _____ .

                                                                    data-name

4. Three classes of constants were described. They are the
_____ , _____ , and
_____ .

   numeric literal; figurative constant; nonnumeric literal

5. In the following listing, place an NL before those expressions that can serve as numeric literals in a COBOL program, an FC for figurative constants, and a NON-L for nonnumeric literals; leave a blank for expressions not exemplifying any of the classes of constants.

   a. _____ 'DEPRECIATION SCHEDULE'   g. _____ 25.32

   b. _____ '12%'   h. _____ SPACES

   c. _____ 237   i. _____ 100.0

   d. _____ INTEREST-DUE   j. _____ "SPACE"

   e. _____ 125.   k. _____ '325'

   f. _____ ZEROS

a. NON-L	g. NL
b. NON-L	h. FC
c. NL	i. NL
d. no quotation marks	j. NON-L
e. cannot end with a decimal point	k. NON-L
f. FC	

· ·

FILLER — A NONSPECIFIC DATA-NAME

The use of data-names is an essential part of programming. There are many instances, however, when we need to define a data field in the DATA DIVISION that will not be referenced in the PROCEDURE DIVISION. In such instances we use the name FILLER, which is a reserved COBOL word.

A common use of FILLER is in describing report-record formats. For example, suppose we want to define a record that will be printed at the end of a report to show certain totals. We desire the following format:

- Columns 1-5   filled with blanks
- Columns 6-10   to contain the word TOTAL
- Columns 11-20   filled with blanks
- Columns 21-24   to contain the total sales in units
- Columns 25-32   filled with blanks
- Columns 33-40   to contain the total sales in dollars

We could write the following record description:

```
01  REPORT-FOOTING.
    02  FILLER              PIC  X(05)      VALUE  SPACES.
    02  FILLER              PIC  X(05)      VALUE  'TOTAL'.
    02  FILLER              PIC  X(10)      VALUE  SPACES.
    02  REPORT-TOT-UNITS    PIC  ZZZ9.
    02  FILLER              PIC  X(08)      VALUE  SPACES.
    02  REPORT-TOT-SALES    PIC  ZZZZ9.99.
```

Although parts of the preceding description will not be fully clear at this point, note the four FILLER fields. Through use of the VALUE clause, three of these FILLER fields contain blank spaces, but one contains the nonnumeric literal TOTAL. This is a good place to emphasize that the use of FILLER does *not* imply anything about the contents of that field; specifically, it does not mean a field containing blanks, as the word "FILLER" might imply.

The choice of FILLER in the above example is not necessary, of course. We could have used data-names of our choice instead of FILLER in each case. It is just simpler not to assign unique data names for fields that will not be referenced in the program.

In the 1985 standard the recognition that there are fields in a program that will not be referenced explicitly has led to the option of omitting entirely the generic data-name FILLER. Thus we can specify "nameless" fields, as follows:

```
01  REPORT-FOOTING.
    02                        PIC   X(05)     VALUE   SPACES.
    02                        PIC   X(05)     VALUE   'TOTAL'.
    02                        PIC   X(14)     VALUE   SPACES.
    02  REPORT-TOT-UNITS      PIC   ZZZ9.
    02                        PIC   X(08)       VALUE   SPACES.
    02  REPORT-TOT-SALES      PIC   ZZZZ9.99.
```

For the above entries that contain no data-names, the record description is treated exactly as if FILLER had been specified.

DEFINING INITIAL CONTENTS WITH THE VALUE CLAUSE

The example included in our discussion of FILLER fields in the preceding section illustrates that we often need to define the contents of fields *before* program execution begins. In addition to defining storage fields with respect to their size and type by using the PICTURE clause, it is often desirable to assign initial values to WORKING-STORAGE fields. Such a value may remain unchanged throughout the program, as in the case of a tax rate, or it may change in the course of program execution, as in the case of a totals accumulator. Such initial values must not be assigned to FILE SECTION items, since such fields receive their data either from an external file via a READ instruction, or from some other storage location as the result of program execution.

An initial value can be assigned by the use of the VALUE clause. The VALUE clause is usually written after the PIC definition of an elementary data field, as in this example:

```
05  TOTAL-UNITS   PIC 999   VALUE ZERO.
05  REPORT-TOTALS PIC X(21) VALUE 'TOTAL SALES FOR MONTH'.
```

Actually, the order of the PIC and VALUE clauses is interchangeable; either one can precede the other.

The assigned value can be one of these three choices:

ASSIGNMENT TYPE	EXAMPLE
A numeric literal	VALUE 125
A figurative constant	VALUE SPACES
A nonnumeric literal	VALUE 'CUSTOMER NAME'

A very common use of the VALUE clause is the definition of report formats, as the example in the preceding section illustrated. Data stored on disk or tape are written so as to save space by omitting the kind of spacing that we like to see when we read a report on paper or on a video monitor. It is very common for the WORKING-STORAGE SECTION of a COBOL program to contain a large number of report-related definitions with suitable VALUE clauses to define the contents of report headings, spacing between columns of data, and so on. Rather than elaborate on the VALUE clause at this point, we will let its use become evident as we progress through the chapter and use the clause in conjunction with PICTURE descriptions.

Use of VALUE in the DATA DIVISION is not the only way of defining the initial contents of data fields. It is also possible to achieve the same result by writing instructions in the PROCEDURE DIVISION to enter appropriate contents into a field. For example, instead of writing

```
05  TOTAL-UNITS  PIC 999  VALUE ZERO
```

we could write

```
MOVE ZERO TO TOTAL-UNITS
```

early in the PROCEDURE DIVISION, before the TOTAL-UNITS field is referenced by another instruction. While this is possible, the preferred way is to define initial contents with the VALUE clause in the DATA DIVISION. It is a safer practice to adopt.

R E V I E W . . . .

1. The data-name often used in the DATA DIVISION to define a field that is not referenced in the PROCEDURE DIVISION is the reserved COBOL word _____ .

   FILLER

2. If a field has been named FILLER, this indicates that the field [is / is not necessarily] filled with blanks.

   is not necessarily

3. As an example of being filled with something other than blanks, a FILLER field could contain a _____ .

   nonnumeric literal

4. Initial values can be assigned to WORKING-STORAGE fields by use of the _____ clause.

   VALUE

5. The VALUE clause [always precedes / always follows / can either precede or follow] the PICTURE clause in a WORKING-STORAGE entry.

   can either precede or follow

. . . .

USING LEVEL-NUMBERS TO DEFINE GROUP STRUCTURES

Data used in business applications of the computer come in a variety of forms and structure. Such data are commonly organized in the form of records. A record typically consists of several fields, sometimes hundreds of fields. For example, the record of a college student will involve fields such as name, campus street address, city and state, zip-code, telephone number, home address, parents' or guardians' name and address, high school(s) attended, test scores, other colleges attended, courses taken, grades and credits earned, and grade-point average. It is easy to see how such a record may consist of a very large number of fields and possibly be a few thousand bytes in length. In such an environment it is very important to be able to define data in a variety of ways and to be able to structure data fields into logical groups. The PICTURE clauses enable us to define the variety of data types, but it is through *level-numbers* that we define the group structures comprising a record.

Let us begin with a common example. We have records that consist of names. In the course of program execution we may need to refer to individual parts of the name record, such as the last name, first name, and middle initial. Alternately, we may need to refer to the entire name as a unit. We can define the record as follows:

```
01  NAME-RECORD.
    05  LAST-NAME        PIC X(15).
    05  FIRST-NAME       PIC X(15).
    05  MIDDLE-INITIAL   PIC X(01).
```

The 01 level-number must be used to define a *record*. It is the highest level-number, and it is used to define a group of fields as a record. The data-name associated with the 01 level-number refers to the collection of all the fields having higher level-numbers until another 01 record is defined (or a new SECTION or DIVISION begins). Level-numbers are allowed in the range 01-49. A level number other than 01 indicates that the field to which it is attached is a subordinate field. In the example above, we chose 05 as the level-number of all three subordinate fields. The choice of 05 is arbitrary. We could have used any number between 02 and 49 inclusive. Many programmers tend to use level numbers that are multiples of 5, but this is not a required practice.

The three fields LAST-NAME, FIRST-NAME, and MIDDLE-INITIAL, are all *elementary* fields, because none of them has any subordinate field. Further, because they all have the same level-number, none of the fields in this group is subordinate to any other field in the group. On the other hand, consider the following example:

```
01  NAME-RECORD.
    03  LAST-NAME        PIC X(15).
    03  NAME-INITIALS.
        05  FIRST-INITIAL   PIC X(01).
        05  MIDDLE-INITIAL  PIC X(01).
```

In this case we have chosen to define a record that is subdivided into the elementary field LAST-NAME, and the group field NAME-INITIALS. A *group field* is defined by the fact that it is followed by two or more fields with a higher level-number, in this case, 05. The main purpose of defining a group field is so that we can reference the whole group by one name. In this example we could write the following type of statements:

```
MOVE NAME-INITIALS TO INITIALS-FIELD
```
or
```
MOVE FIRST-INITIAL TO FIRST-INITIAL-OUT
MOVE MIDDLE-INITIAL TO MIDDLE-INITIAL-OUT.
```

The first MOVE transfers the contents of two fields together as a group, while each of the other two MOVE instructions transfers each field individually. Also by the same reasoning, MOVE NAME-RECORD would transfer the contents of all the subordinate fields of this group field. The subordinate fields in this case are the LAST-NAME elementary field and the MIDDLE-INITIALS group field, for a total of 17 bytes. The length of the NAME-RECORD group can be calculated by adding up the length of all the elementary fields in the group. The length is defined in the PIC descriptions, which in this case are 15 bytes for LAST-NAME and one byte each for the initials fields.

It should be noted that group fields do not have PIC clauses attached to them. PIC descriptions are included only for elementary fields. The group field then is the sum of its parts.

Another important point is that a group field is always treated as an *alphanumeric field,* even if its subordinate elementary fields are defined to be numeric ones, as in the following:

```
05  WEEKLY-SALES.
    10  GROSS-SALES   PIC 999.
    10  NET-SALES     PIC 999.
```

The PIC 999 field descriptions above indicate numeric data. However, writing MOVE WEEKLY-SALES... would transfer both sales quantities as a string of data. Also, writing ADD 1 TO WEEKLY-SALES would be an incorrect instruction (and the compiler would so diagnose the instruction and disallow it). This is consistent with common sense and numeric accuracy. If GROSS-SALES contained 125 and NET-SALES contained 100, the combined field 125100 does not mean a quantity, but rather, consists of two three-digit numbers strung together.

Use of level-numbers to define data records and their appropriate subdivisions is further explained by using the following example. Figure 3-2 represents a 67-byte record designed to contain customer addresses. A glance at the figure shows that there are many fields, they vary in size, and they are organized into groups. For instance, NAME is a data-name that consists of the combination of the two subordinate fields called FIRST-NAME and LAST-NAME. COBOL derives a great deal of its suitability for business applications from the fact that it allows the programmer to construct such hierarchies of data structures.

As we have already discussed, a useful distinction is made between elementary and group items in COBOL. An elementary item has no subordinate parts. With reference to Figure 3-2, FIRST-NAME and ZONE are the first and last of the eight elementary items, from left to right. The data-name NAME, on the other hand, is an example of a group item. A group item can consist of one or more other group items, rather than any elementary items, as is the case with CUSTOMER-ADDRESS in the illustration.

Reference to Figure 3-2 makes the concept of group item rather obvious, but in a programming language we cannot construct figures, and so we need a

FIGURE 3-2

Conceptual Structure of Information in Internal Storage

Data name	CUSTOMER-ADDRESS							
Data name	NAME		STREET		CITY-STATE		ZIP-CODE	
Data name	FIRST-NAME	LAST-NAME	STREET-NUMBER	STREET-NAME	CITY	STATE	PO	ZONE
Content	R O N A L D	J O H N S O N	1 0 5 7	M O N T E R E Y D R I V E	T E M P E	A R I Z O N A	8 5 2	8 2
		10	22	27	42	52	62	65 67

means of communicating the same information in symbolic form. COBOL provides such a symbolic form by means of level-numbers. Here is an example of how level numbers can represent the same hierarchical (grouping) structure as in Figure 3-2:

```
01   CUSTOMER-ADDRESS
     02   NAME
          03 FIRST-NAME
          03 LAST-NAME
     02   STREET
          03 STREET-NUMBER
          03 STREET-NAME
     02   CITY-STATE
          03 CITY
          03 STATE
     02   ZIP-CODE
          03 PO
          03 ZONE
```

The first level number, 01, is associated with CUSTOMER-ADDRESS. A 01 level number indicates the highest level in a data hierarchy. Reference to the data-name at the 01 level is a reference to the *entire data set,* or *record.* There is only one data-name at the 01 level for each record, as it is the all-inclusive data-name. All data-names that follow this one and are part of this record have level numbers that are higher than 01, and are in the allowable range 02-49.

The 02 NAME introduces NAME as a data-name subordinate to the 01 level. Reading from top to bottom corresponds to left to right in Figure 3-2. We observe a total of four data-names at the 02 level: NAME, STREET, CITY-STATE, and ZIP-CODE. Since they are all at the same level, 02, none of them is subordinate to the others in the group (but each is subordinate to the 01 level).

As in Figure 3-2, we are interested in specifying that NAME is a group item and that it consists of two other data-names, FIRST-NAME and LAST-NAME. This relationship is expressed by assigning the 02 level-number to NAME and the 03 level-number to FIRST-NAME and LAST-NAME. Notice that, as we read from top to bottom, STREET is not confused as being subordinate to NAME because both are assigned to the 02 level.

In terms of format or style, the indentations are preferred but not required. In addition, level numbers need not increase by consecutive values. The following example illustrates these two points:

```
01   CUSTOMER-ADDRESS
03   NAME
05   FIRST-NAME
03   STREET
04   STREET-NUMBER
04   STREET-NAME
```

Notice the absence of indentation in this example and observe that it is much harder to read and understand the intended data structure, as compared to the preceding example. Also notice that level numbers do not increase by 1. The 03 NAME specifies that NAME is subordinate to CUSTOMER-ADDRESS, because 03 is greater than 01. Similarly, 05 FIRST-NAME is subordinate to NAME, because 05 is greater than 03. In the case of 04 STREET-NUMBER, it is understood that STREET-NUMBER is subordinate to the data-name just above it, which has a lower level-number. Thus, the 04 level is perfectly proper in the example, and it preserves the intended grouping of Figure 3-2. Also notice that once NAME is assigned to the 03 level, STREET must also be assigned to the same level, since NAME and STREET have the same immediate superior, CUSTOMER-ADDRESS.

As illustrated in the above examples, level-numbers combine with data-names to represent the desired organization of data. Many times, however, there is no need to describe data in detail. For instance, suppose that we wish to write a program for which the input is the customer file containing the data described in Figure 3-2 and the output is an analysis of the ZIP code information. For such an analysis we are not concerned with the first 62 bytes of data in each record, and therefore we may choose to describe the data record as follows:

```
01  CUSTOMER-ADDRESS.
    02 FILLER            PIC  X(62).
    02 ZIP-CODE.
        03 P0            PIC  999.
        03 ZONE          PIC  99.
```

As explained earlier in this chapter, the reserved word FILLER is a generic data-name. It is not unique and therefore cannot be used in the PROCEDURE DIVISION. In the above example its main purpose is to allow us to specify (although indirectly) that ZIP-CODE begins with byte 63 in CUSTOMER-ADDRESS.

RECORD LAYOUT

As much as COBOL allows great flexibility and ease in describing the organization of data, planning the record layout is a time-consuming and detail-oriented task. When designing a new program or referring to an existing program, it is convenient to use certain graphic representation tools, such as record layout charts and printer spacing charts, to simplify the process.

A *record layout chart* is intended to help specify and visualize the organization of data within a record. The illustration in Figure 3-2 is certainly capable of serving as a record layout chart, but it is too elaborate for such use and too time consuming to prepare. Instead, we prefer a simpler chart, such as the two samples illustrated in Figure 3-3. Figure 3-3(a) is a table-like chart that is rather easy to scan

FIGURE 3-3
Sample Record Layout Representations

COLUMNS	CONTENT	DATA-NAME
1–15	Employee's name	NAME-IN
16	Sex code	SEX-CODE
17–23	Salary	SALARY-IN
24–80	Unused	FILLER

(a)

EMPL-RECORD			
NAME-IN	SEX-CODE	SALARY-IN	FILLER
1 – 15	16	17–23	24 – 80

Data name / Columns

(b)

and understand. Figure 3-3(b) is a more visually oriented chart that corresponds to the left-right concept of data representation. These are simply illustrations. Many organizations use special forms for record layouts. The main point of this brief discussion is that the supporting documentation for a program should include easy-to-read record layout charts to help convey the organization of data used in the program. Record layout charts are particularly useful for the type of individual records encountered in using disk and tape files. For report files, however, the focus is on the visualization and description of an entire report rather than single records. Since reports are most often printed, we refer to such charts as *printer spacing charts,* as introduced at the beginning of Chapter 2. Actually, their use is equally valid for planning the display of data on a video monitor.

Figure 3-4 presents a *printer spacing chart* for a simple salary report. The underlying programming task involves reading records from an employee file, as described in Figure 3-3, and producing the report form specified in Figure 3-5. The

---

FIGURE 3-4

Printer Spacing Chart Illustration

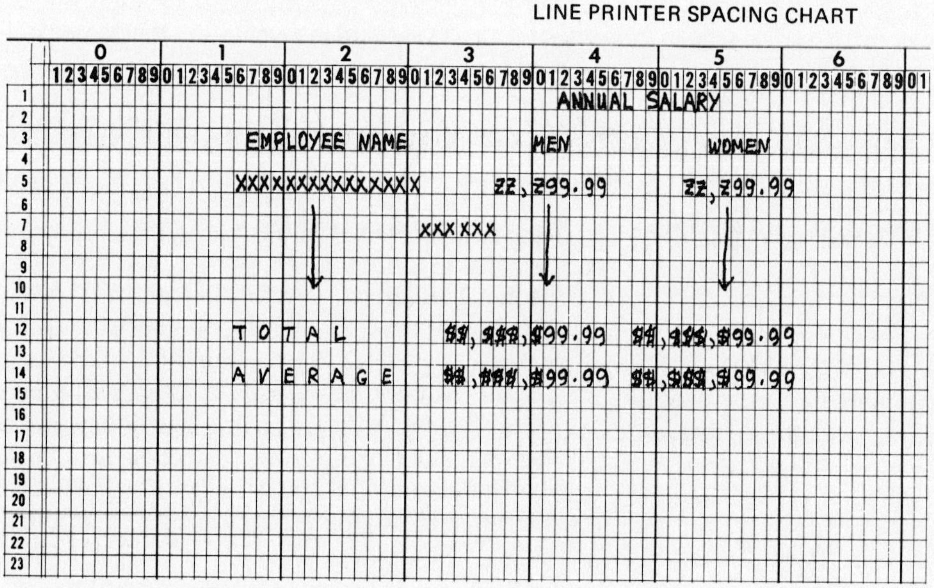

LINE PRINTER SPACING CHART

FIGURE 3-5

Sample Salary Report

```
                        ANNUAL SALARY

        EMPLOYEE NAME        MEN           WOMEN


        JONES, A.        28,200.00
        ANDERSON, P.     22,000.00
        ROBERTS, M.                      25,000.00
        PROUST, K.  ******
        NICHOLSON, J.    29,600.00
        PHILLIPS, P.                     28,500.00
        WORK, A.                         30,000.00


        T O T A L       $79,800.00      $83,500.00


        A V E R A G E   $26,600.00      $27,833.33
```

line with asterisks in Figure 3-5 was chosen to represent cases in which there was an error. Employee Proust in Figure 3-5 could not be classified as either male or female because there was an error in the data.

A printer spacing chart such as the one in Figure 3-4 allows a visual summary of a report, and can be used as a valuable aid in writing the corresponding DATA DIVISION specifications. To help you appreciate the value of a printer spacing chart, we ask two questions:

- How many record formats are required in the DATA DIVISION for this report output?

- How many blank columns will separate the last digit of men's salary from the first digit of women's salary in each report detail line?

In answering the first question, one can observe that five different records are portrayed in Figure 3-4: lines 1, 3 , and 5, and the total and average report lines in the report footing. Finally, in response to the second question, one can observe that there are six blank columns separating the two fields in the printer spacing chart, and therefore an appropriate entry in the DATA DIVISION would be

```
...FILLER PIC X(6) VALUE SPACES.
```

As stated in Chapter 2, blank copies of printer spacing charts are included in the back of this book for your use.

R E V I E W . . . .

1. In COBOL programming, a data-name that has no subordinate items is called a(n) _____ item, while one that does have subordinate items is called a(n) _____ item.

   elementary; group

2 For a given data set, the all-inclusive data-name generally is defined at the _____ level-number.

   01

3. All fields in the record that are directly subordinate to the overall record commonly are assigned the level number _____ (number).

   02 or higher

4. A data item that is directly subordinate to one at the 02 level [must / need not] be assigned to the 03 level.

   need not

5. The chart that is used to specify and visualize the organization of data in a record is called a _____ chart.

   record layout

6. The chart that is used to portray the layout of a report, whether printed or to be presented on a video monitor, is the _____ chart.

   printer spacing

7. The record layout chart and printer spacing chart are particularly useful with respect to writing specifications in the _____ DIVISION of a COBOL program.

   DATA

FILE SECTION

The function of the FILE SECTION is to describe each file used in the program by specifying four things:

1. The name of the file
2. The name assigned to the record in the file
3. The hierarchical structure of the data fields in the record
4. The field size and type of data in each storage field of the record

The general format presented thus far in the illustrations in preceding chapters is as follows:

```
FD  file-name
    LABEL RECORDS ARE OMITTED
    RECORD CONTAINS integer CHARACTERS
    DATA RECORD IS record-name.
01  record-name.
```

The FD is a COBOL reserved word and designates that this is a file description. There is an FD entry for each file involved in a program, and it includes a complete description of the named record. The description begins with the record name, which is always at the 01 level, and includes the data specifications for the data fields in the record. For instance:

```
DATA DIVISION.
*
FILE SECTION.
*
FD  CUSTOMER-FILE
    LABEL RECORDS ARE STANDARD
    RECORD CONTAINS 80 CHARACTERS
    DATA RECORD IS CUSTOMER-RECORD.
*
01  CUSTOMER-RECORD.
    02  CUSTOMER-NAME      PIC X(13).
    02  CUSTOMER-UNITS     PIC 999.
    02  FILLER             PIC X(64).
```

The LABEL clause will be discussed in Chapter 10, "Sequential File Processing." Until then we simply use the LABEL clause to indicate either STANDARD or OMITTED. The RECORD CONTAINS clause is used for documentation. The size of the record is specified indirectly by the sum of the individual PICTURE descriptions, which should correspond to the number of characters identified in the RECORD CONTAINS clause. For the above example the sum of the individual PIC descriptions is 13 + 3 + 64 = 80, which corresponds to the RECORD CONTAINS 80 CHARACTERS. Then the DATA RECORD IS specifies the name of the record, which is described beginning with the 01 level-number.

In COBOL '85, the LABEL, RECORD and DATA clauses in the FD entry are all optional. Therefore we could have written this:

```
FD  CUSTOMER-FILE.
01  CUSTOMER-RECORD.
    02 . . . (etc.)
```

Some reasons for making those clauses optional are as follows: The LABEL aspect of a file generally is dependent on the operating system rather than on

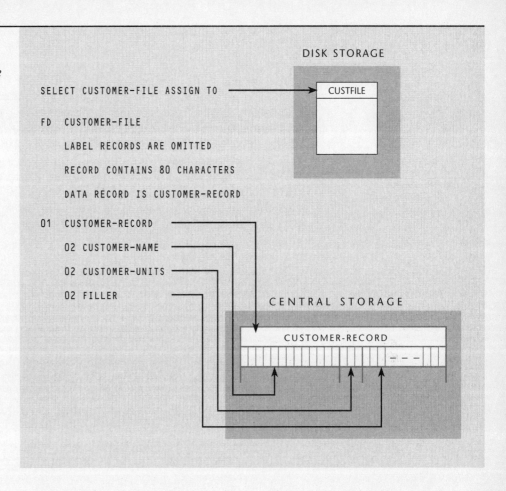

FIGURE 3-6

Relationship of File-Names and Data-Names to Hardware Storage

COBOL specifications, even in the 1974 version of the language. The RECORD CONTAINS has always been optional, and the DATA RECORD is redundant, since the subsequent 01 entry always specifies the record-name in any event.

Figure 3-6 should help explain some fundamental concepts about files, records, and fields in a COBOL program. Within the program we use a file-name such as CUSTOMER-FILE. However, that file-name may be designated by other means in terms of the operating system of the computer. In the example the customer file is a disk file and is called CUSTFILE, as illustrated in Figure 3-6.

The 01 record entry describes the central storage area referenced by the record-name CUSTOMER-RECORD. Similarly, the fields CUSTOMER-NAME, CUSTOMER-UNITS, and FILLER also refer to central storage locations, as illustrated in Figure 3-6.

Assuming CUSTOMER-FILE to be an input file, we can give an instruction to copy a data record from the disk into central storage by use of the READ verb. After a READ operation we can then give instructions to operate on the data in central storage by instructions such as ADD CUSTOMER-UNITS TO . . .

CUSTOMER-NAME and CUSTOMER-UNITS are data-names referencing fields in the record. As illustrated in Figure 3-6, CUSTOMER-NAME refers to the first 13 bytes of the CUSTOMER-REC, while CUSTOMER-UNITS refers to the next 3 bytes. The size and type of each field would be specified by the PIC clause. The third field in CUSTOMER-RECORD is named FILLER.

Storage fields associated with the file records receive data from, or are used to send data to, external input-output devices, such as disks, tapes, printers, and video terminals. In addition to such storage fields, there also is a need for storage of header data and the like. The WORKING-STORAGE SECTION is used to define such fields.

WORKING-STORAGE SECTION

The WORKING-STORAGE SECTION immediately follows the FILE SECTION in the program. It is possible for a program not to have either a FILE SECTION or a WORKING-STORAGE SECTION, as discussed in Chapter 23 in the case of subprograms. Whereas the FILE SECTION describes the files used in the program, the WORKING-STORAGE SECTION provides for the storage of data items that are not part of any file, such as intermediate calculations, report headings for printing, and numeric constants for use in calculations.

The WORKING-STORAGE SECTION consists of group items and elementary items, as is also the case in the FILE SECTION. In older versions of COBOL it was common to use a special level-number, 77, to describe all elementary independent items; that is, elementary items that are not part of a group. These elementary independent items preceded all the group (or record) items which were introduced at the 01 level as in the following example:

```
WORKING-STORAGE SECTION.
77  TOTAL-SALES    PIC 9999 VALUE ZERO.
77  NO-OF-CUST     PIC 99   VALUE ZERO.
01  REPORT-HEADING.
    02  FILLER... etc.
```

However, whether the elementary independent items are designated by the level 77 or 01 makes no difference in program processing, and this is the main reason why the use of level 77 was largely abandoned in the late 1970s.

Consider the following example of a WORKING-STORAGE SECTION:

```
WORKING-STORAGE SECTION.
01  END-OF-FILE            PIC XXX     VALUE 'NO '.
01  REPORT-HEADING         PIC X(40)   VALUE
    'CUSTOMER NAME  UNITS SOLD      NET SALES'.
01  REPORT-FOOTING.
    02  FILLER             PIC X(5)    VALUE 'TOTAL'.
    02  FILLER             PIC X(14)   VALUE SPACES.
    02  REPORT-TOTAL-UNITS PIC ZZZ9.
    02  FILLER             PIC X(9)    VALUE SPACES.
    02  REPORT-TOTAL-SALES PIC ZZZZ9.99.
```

Each 01 entry defines a record in central storage. The first entry defines a field called END-OF-FILE that is 3 bytes long (PIC XXX) and is initialized to the value "NO". As we discussed earlier, the VALUE clause is used to define the contents of a record/field at the start of the program execution. Thus the 40-byte REPORT-HEADING is initialized with the desired report heading. Note that the 40-byte literal does not fit on the same line as the data-name and the PIC description, so we switched to the next line to write the literal for the VALUE clause. A nonnumeric literal can be as long as 120 bytes in the 1974 standard (160 in the 1985 version).

If we have a long literal that does not fit on one line, there is a special way to split it across two lines: column 7 of the COBOL Coding Form can be used to signal continuation of an entry to the following line. Recall that in Chapter 1 we first introduced use of this column to signal a comment entry by an asterisk (∗) and to signal that printer output of the source program listing should begin on a new page by a slash (/). When the literal is too long for one line, a *hyphen* (–) is entered in column 7 of the next line, and the entry is continued starting with column 12

FIGURE 3-7

Example of Continuing a Literal on the Next Line of the COBOL Coding Form

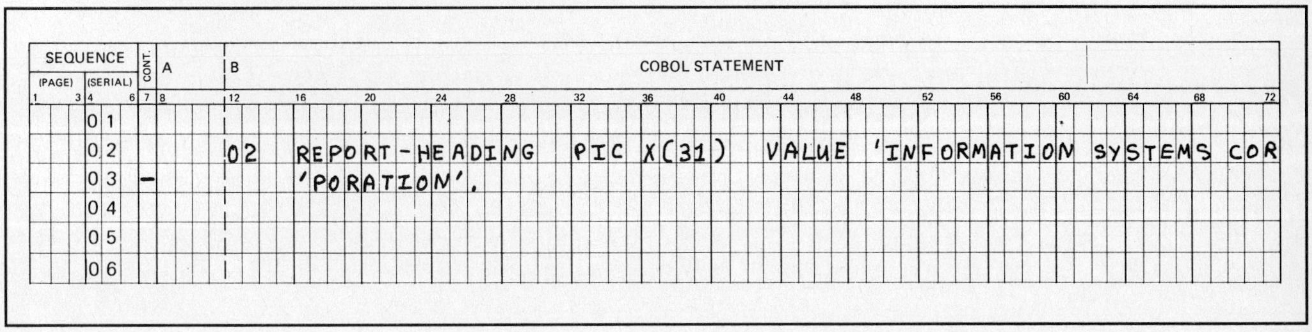

or to the right of column 12. When a nonnumeric literal is being continued, not only do we enter a hyphen in column 7, but we also start the continued line with a quotation mark in column 12 or to the right of it and conclude with a quotation mark. Figure 3-7 includes an example of continuation for a literal that is split between two lines. Notice the hyphen in column 7 and the opening and closing quotation marks on the second line.

Continuing with the example of a WORKING-STORAGE SECTION above, the first two FILLER fields in the REPORT-FOOTING record specify the characters TOTAL followed by 14 blanks. We used two FILLER fields for convenience, because 14 blanks in a literal are difficult to count visually and may lead to errors. Still, it would have been just as correct to write

```
01  REPORT-FOOTING.
    02  FILLER   PIC X(19) VALUE 'TOTAL
    02  REPORT-TOTAL-UNITS . . .
```

In the above program segment the nonnumeric literal value of FILLER contains 14 blanks to the right of TOTAL and inside the quotation marks.

There is little to say about the organization of the WORKING-STORAGE SECTION except that it is a recommended practice to group related items together under a common group to enhance reader awareness of their relationships. For example, consider the following DATA DIVISION entries:

```
01  SALARY-TOTALS.
    02  MEN-TOTAL-SALARY     PIC 9(7)V99 VALUE ZERO.
    02  WOMEN-TOTAL-SALARY   PIC 9(7)V99 VALUE ZERO.
```

Assuming that we never make use of the data-name SALARY-TOTALS in the program, the 01 group item in this program segment is used only for readability. An alternative to this structure would be to write the two elementary independent items as follows:

```
01  MEN-TOTAL-SALARY     PIC 9(7)V99 VALUE ZERO.
01  WOMEN-TOTAL-SALARY   PIC 9(7)V99 VALUE ZERO.
```

In this alternative program segment, the similarity in the data-names and their physical consecutive order implies a relationship between them, but the association is much clearer when a group data-name is used to indicate the relationship between the two data items.

R   E   V   I   E   W . . . .

1. The section of the DATA DIVISION concerned with describing each file used in the program is the _____ SECTION.

    FILE

2. In the FILE SECTION we designate that an entry is a file description by beginning the entry with the COBOL reserved word _____ .

    FD

3. After the name of the file is given, the next item of information given in the FD entry is the name of the _____ included in the file.

    record

4. The section of the DATA DIVISION that provides for the storage of such data items as intermediate calculations and report headings is the _____ SECTION.

    WORKING-STORAGE

5. In lieu of the older practice of using the special level-number 77 for elementary independent data items in WORKING-STORAGE, current practice favors use of the level number _____ for such items.

    01

6. When two or more elementary items are logically related, rather than place them in the program as elementary independent items, documentation is improved by _____ .

    lacing them under a common group (etc.)

7. An initial content can be established in a WORKING-STORAGE field by use of the _____ clause.

    VALUE

8. The VALUE clause can be used in the WORKING-STORAGE SECTION to establish field values that are [numeric only / numeric or nonnumeric].

    numeric or nonnumeric (for example, a nonnumeric
    literal such as 'ANNUAL SALARY' can be assigned)

. . . .

THE PICTURE CLAUSE FOR DATA DESCRIPTION

The general form of the PICTURE clause was introduced in Chapter 2, in the example of a complete program. The purpose of this DATA DIVISION feature is to describe the data included in the data items. We use the word PICTURE, or its abbreviated form PIC, and the optional word IS, followed by a string of characters that describe the data. In the following subsections we consider in turn each of the PICTURE characters that can be used to describe data fields that are defined in the DATA DIVISION.

The X PICTURE Character

The X PICTURE character denotes that data contained in that field are treated as alphanumeric. NAME X(20), for example, signifies a field of 20 alphanumeric positions, which can include alphabetic characters, numeric characters, and special symbols. In the following examples a "b" represents a blank space in the storage location. Notice that when the characters do not fill an X field completely, they are left-justified, with blanks filling the remaining positions on the right.

DESCRIPTION	EXAMPLE	REPRESENTED IN STORAGE AS
02 PART-NAME PICTURE XXXXX	DIODE	DIODE
02 PART-NAME PICTURE X(5)	TUBE	TUBEb
02 NAME PICTURE X(20)	JOHN F. ANDREWS	JOHNbF.bANDREWSbbbbb
02 MESSAGE-CODE PICTURE X(8)	AB13C,$M	AB13C,$M

The A PICTURE Character

The A PICTURE character is similar to the X character, except that it indicates that only alphabetic characters and blanks are intended to be contained in a field. Excluded therefore are numeric characters and special symbols. Since the first two statements in the preceding examples concerned storage locations containing only alphabetic information, the A PICTURE character could have been used instead of the X, as indicated in the following table:

DESCRIPTION	EXAMPLE	REPRESENTED IN STORAGE AS
02 PART-NAME PICTURE AAAAA	DIODE	DIODE
02 PART-NAME PICTURE A(5)	TUBE	TUBEb

The reader is cautioned against using the A character in what seems a natural use: a field containing people's names. Names such as O'Neal do not consist of alphabetic characters alone. The X character is better suited for use in such fields. In fact, use of the A PICTURE is rare, because use of the X field is satisfactory for all cases of nonnumeric data fields.

The 9 PICTURE Character

The numeric 9 indicates that a storage position should contain only any of the numeric digits from 0 to 9. In this context a blank is not considered equivalent to the numeric 0 and thus is not a numeric character. The field size of the item is indicated by the number of successively written 9s in the PICTURE clause; thus PICTURE IS 999 means a field of three numeric positions. An alternative is to write a 9 followed by parentheses enclosing the number of positions in the field. For example, the statement 03 AMT PICTURE IS 9(5) indicates that AMT is a five-position numeric field. Some examples of using the 9 PICTURE character are as follows:

DESCRIPTION	NUMERIC VALUE	REPRESENTED IN STORAGE AS
02 SCHOOL-ENROLLMENT PICTURE IS 9(6)	12,327	012327
02 STOCK-ON-HAND PICTURE 9999	8,956	8956
04 POPULATION-OF-CITY PICTURE 9(10)	1,563,813	0001563813
03 UNION-MEMBERSHIP PICTURE IS 9999	285	0285

Again note that a numeric field can contain only the digits 0-9. Blanks are not numeric characters. When entering data, you should be careful to zero-fill a field with leading zeros; otherwise you may be in for some surprising results. Thus in a field of five positions the numeric value 532 should be entered as follows:

0	0	5	3	2

The V PICTURE Character

The V character indicates the position of an assumed decimal point. "Assumed" means that the decimal point is not written as part of the field and therefore is not included as part of the field size. Instead, the information about decimal point location is stored elsewhere (as part of the instructionns that do arithmetic computations), so that any arithmetic computations can be done correctly. For example, if two items are multiplied and each is assumed to have two positions to the right of the decimal, the product will be understood to have four positions to the right of the decimal point.

If the V character is omitted, it is understood that the decimal point is at the extreme right of the numeric field. It is not necessary, therefore, to place a V as the last character in a PICTURE clause. Of course, no more than one V is permitted in a field. Refer to the following table and note that, if we printed HOURS-WORKED without any editing, the value represented in storage, 385, would be printed without a decimal. The V character establishes the position of the decimal for purposes of arithmetic manipulation but does not make the decimal point as such available for printout. Some examples of using the V character are given in this table. The *caret* (∧) indicates the position of the assumed decimal point.

DESCRIPTION	NUMERIC VALUE	REPRESENTED IN STORAGE AS
03HOURS-WORKED PICTURE 99V9	38.5	38∧5
03NET-PAY PICTURE 9(4)V99	452.39	452∧39
02TON-CAPACITY PICTURE 999	550	550∧
02BALANCE PICTURE IS 99999V99	23561.00	23561∧00

The P PICTURE Character

The P PICTURE character is used in conjunction with the V character to indicate the position of a decimal point in cases in which the decimal point is not within the number. This character is used, for example, when it is understood that a value held in storage represents thousands of units and we wish to indicate the decimal position for this value. The following examples indicate the use of this character. As before, the caret indicates the position of an assumed decimal point.

DESCRIPTION	NUMERIC VALUE	ARITHMETIC EQUIVALENT
02 AMOUNT PICTURE IS 99PPPV	12	12000∧
02 AMOUNT PICTURE VP(3)9(4)	1023	∧0001023

The P character is not used very much in administrative applications. It is suited best to scientific computational needs, which are likely to be better satisfied by the use of languages other than COBOL.

The S PICTURE Character

The S character is used to designate a numeric field that is signed; that is, one that can be negative in value. In COBOL all fields are considered positive unless the S has been used. For instance, for a field containing the checking account balance of a bank customer, when the account is overdrawn, the only way the balance will become negative is to designate the balance field as a signed one by use of the S character. Otherwise, if the dollar balance in the field is 23.50 and a check is written for 50.00, the balance will become 26.50!

Only one S character may be used in a field, and it must be the leftmost character. The S is not counted in the size of the field; therefore S99 is a field of two positions. In the following examples the negative sign (−) in machine representation is shown as a "⁻" above the rightmost digit in order to preserve the concept that it does not take up an extra position.

DESCRIPTION	NUMERIC VALUE	REPRESENTED IN STORAGE AS
02 BALANCE PICTURE S9999V99	−1251.16	1251ₐ1$\bar{6}$
02 BALANCE PICTURE S9(4)V99	− 0.10	0000ₐ1$\bar{0}$
02 BALANCE PICTURE 9(4)V99	− 325.18	0325ₐ1$\bar{8}$

The reason for not needing an extra position is related to how numeric values and their signs are represented by specific bit combinations in internal storage. For example, a value of negative 32 might be written as 3K, the K representing the bit combination of the digit 2 and the negative sign. Further, the specific representation would depend on the system in use (as will be further discussed in Chapter 16, "Special Data-Oriented Division Features"). If this seems a bit alarming, keep in mind that in business data processing, input data are almost never negative. Instead, we define categories of positive data that may then be treated as negative in the program logic. Consider this example: A customer returns an item and receives refund. One could think of this as a negative sale represented by a negative number. But that is not the way it is done. Instead, a "sales" record would have a field that identifies the type of sale, as perhaps purchase or return, by means of a code. When the record is processed, we would specify something like this:

> If it is a purchase
>> add the amount to the customer's balance
>
> else
>> if it is a return
>>> subtract the amount from the customer's balance.

As the above example illustrates, negative values are not used directly in input files. When we want to show negative values in reports, we use the special editing PICTURE character "-" as explained in the next section of this chapter, on the use of the PICTURE clause for data editing.

R E V I E W . . . .

1. We have discussed thus far six PICTURE characters that can be used in a PICTURE clause to describe the contents of a field. These are the X, A, 9, V, P, and S PICTURE characters. The character used to indicate that a field can contain either alphabetic, numeric, or special symbols is the _____ character, whereas the character that indicates alphabetic content only is the _____ character.

X; A

2. The character that indicates numeric content only is the _____ character. If the stored values can be negative as well as positive, the PICTURE clause should include the _____ character as the leftmost character.

9; S

3. The character used to indicate the position of an assumed decimal point is the _____ character. This character is used only with PICTURE clauses that also contain the _____ PICTURE character.

V; 9

4. When we wish to identify the correct decimal position for a field whose numeric value is understood to be in thousands of units, we use the _____ PICTURE character.

P

5. When a value does not fill a numeric 9 field completely, the value is justified to the [right / left], and the extra positions are filled with [blanks / zeros].

right; zeros

6. When an item does not fill an A field or an X field completely, the item is justified to the [right / left], and the extra positions are filled with [blanks / zeros].

left; blanks

· · · · · · · · · · · · · · · · · · · ·

THE PICTURE CLAUSE FOR DATA EDITING

As contrasted to the field definition characters we have described so far, the PICTURE characters that follow are editing symbols. The editing function involves a change in the form of data. For example, we may suppress leading zeros, we may use commas to make long numeric values more legible, we may insert a dollar sign in front of a value, and so forth. *The purpose of editing is to make data more suitable for human reading.* Thus, in its most common use, editing is associated with printing data on the printer. A great many of the applications of COBOL involve the production of reports that are to be read by people, and data editing greatly enhances the visibility of data in such reports.

The $ PICTURE Insertion Character

By use of the $ PICTURE character, the dollar sign is written in the position in which it is to appear in the output. Because the $ sign is counted in the size of the field, the field should be assigned at least one more position than the maximum number of significant digits expected. The $ sign also may be *floated,* by which we mean that it will not necessarily be entered in the leftmost position of a field but, rather, will be entered to the left of the first significant digit in the field and be preceded by blanks. For example, if we have the statement 02 AMT PICTURE $$$99V99, when a data value is to be entered in AMT, a test is performed. The leftmost digit is examined first. If it is zero, the next digit is examined. If this next digit is not zero, then the dollar sign is inserted directly to the left of that digit. For the PICTURE clause above, the $ sign can appear in any one of the first three positions, according to the value stored in the field. The following examples further illustrate the use of the $ PICTURE insertion character. The last example shows that, when the $ sign appears in all positions and the value is zero, the effect is to blank the field.

DESCRIPTION			NUMERIC VALUE	REPRESENTED IN STORAGE AS
02	AMT PICTURE	$999V99	125.13	$125ₐ13
02	AMT PICTURE	$9(5)V99	100.0	$00100ₐ00
02	AMT PICTURE	$$99V99	12.49	b$12ₐ49
02	AMT PICTURE	$$$9V99	150.10	$150ₐ10
02	AMT PICTURE	$$$$V99	0.15	bbb$ₐ15
02	AMT PICTURE	$$$$V$$	0.0	bbbbₐbb

For the example just given let us consider what the result in storage would be if the value to be written in AMT were 0.05. In this case the presence of the V would stop the dollar sign float, and the value would be represented in storage as bbb$ₐ05. If the decimal point did not terminate the float, the result in storage would be bbbbbₐ$5, which is clearly not the desired representation. Therefore the presence of the decimal point stops the float except when the entire field is zero. Further examples involving use of the $ PICTURE character are included in the discussion immediately following. Actually, we would not use a $ and a V in the same field, since the V does not result in a visible decimal point. The above examples make more sense if we use the decimal point editing character, discussed next.

The Decimal and the Comma PICTURE Insertion Characters

Each of these insertion characters is used to indicate the position of the indicated character in the storage location. Because the . (decimal) PICTURE character indicates the position of the decimal point and serves to align the actual decimal values in the field, only one such character may appear in a field. Further, a field cannot contain both a V and a . PICTURE character. On the other hand, a field may include more than one , (comma) PICTURE character if the size of the field warrants it.

The following examples illustrate the use of the . and the , PICTURE insertion characters in conjunction with the $ insertion characters. Notice some of these points. The $ float stops when either the first nonzero digit or the . or V is encountered. The only exception is when the $ is written in all positions and the value is zero, in which case the entire field (including any . and ,) is blanked. If a comma happens to precede the first nonzero item, the comma is replaced by the dollar sign, which is the format generally desired for purposes of output.

DESCRIPTION			NUMERIC VALUE	REPRESENTED IN STORAGE AS
02	AMT PICTURE	$9,999.99	2,350.22	$2,350.22
02	AMT PICTURE	$9,999.99	150.31	$0,150.31
02	AMT PICTURE	$$999.99	150.31	b$150.31
02	AMT PICTURE	$$,$$$.99	25.40	bbb$25.40
02	AMT PICTURE	$$,$$$.999	0.019	bbbbb$.019
02	AMT PICTURE	$$,$$$.$$$	0.009	bbbbb$.009
02	AMT PICTURE	$$,$$$.$$$	0.0	bbbbbbbbbb
02	AMT PICTURE	$$,$$9.999	2,210.2	$2,210.200
02	AMT PICTURE	$$,999.9	2,210.2	$2,210.2
02	AMT PICTURE	$$,999.9	2,210.256	$2,210.2
02	AMT PICTURE	$9,999.9999	23	$0,023.0000
02	AMT PICTURE	$$,$$$.$$9	0.002	bbbbb$.002

The Z PICTURE Character

The Z PICTURE character is used to replace leading zeros by blanks and thus performs a function identical to that of the floating $ character, except for insertion of the $ itself. As for the floating $, zero suppression terminates when the first nonzero digit or the . character is encountered, whichever occurs first. As with the $ PICTURE character, the only exception occurs when Zs have been designated for all positions in a field and the value to be inserted in that field is zero, in which case the entire field is blanked. The following examples illustrate the use of the Z PICTURE character:

DESCRIPTION		NUMERIC VALUE	REPRESENTED IN STORAGE AS
02 AMT PICTURE	Z99	25	b25
02 AMT PICTURE	ZZZ.99	25	b25.00
02 AMT PICTURE	ZZZ.99	0.10	bbb.10
02 AMT PICTURE	ZZZ.ZZZ	0.052	bbb.052
02 AMT PICTURE	ZZZ.ZZZ	0.0	bbbbbbb
02 AMT PICTURE	$ZZZ.9	13.2	$b13.2
02 AMT PICTURE	$ZZZZ.Z	13.2	$bb13.2
02 AMT PICTURE	$Z,ZZZ,ZZZ.ZZ	156,320.18	$bb156,320.18
02 AMT PICTURE	$Z,ZZZ,ZZZ.ZZ	3,156,320.18	$3,156,320.18
02 AMT PICTURE	$$,$$Z.ZZZ	0.001	bbbb$b.001

The + and − PICTURE Insertion Characters

Each of these editing characters can be inserted into the leftmost or rightmost position in a PICTURE. When the + character is used, positive values receive a + sign and negative values receive a − sign. On the other hand, when the − PICTURE character is used, positive values are represented in storage without a sign, while negative values receive a − sign. In either case a negative sign associated with a value always is represented in storage.

The − PICTURE insertion character differs from the S character in that the use of the S character identifies a field as a signed one for computational purposes, but the sign does not occupy a position as such. An edited field that contains such editing characters as the negative sign (as well as $, ., etc.) is *not* a numeric field and cannot be used in computations. Thus the compiler will issue a diagnostic error if we try to ADD 1 TO A, and the PIC string for A contains editing characters. Use of the − PICTURE character leads to a field in which the sign occupies a character position.

The + character and the − character also can be floated; in this respect they are similar to the $ PICTURE character. However, the +, −, and $ are mutually exclusive as floating characters. If we want to have both $ float and + or − sign representation, we write the + or − to the right of the field, as illustrated in the last two of the following examples:

DESCRIPTION		NUMERIC VALUE	REPRESENTED IN STORAGE AS
02 BALANCE PICTURE	+ 999.9	35.2	+035.2
02 BALANCE PICTURE	999.9 +	35.2	035.2+
02 BALANCE PICTURE	999.9 +	− 35.2	035.2−
02 BALANCE PICTURE	+ + 9.9	− 001.3	b−1.3
02 BALANCE PICTURE	+ + + 9.99	.05	bb+0.05
02 BALANCE PICTURE	+ + + 9.99	− .05	bb−0.05

DESCRIPTION			NUMERIC VALUE	REPRESENTED IN STORAGE AS
02	BALANCE PICTURE	+ + + +.+ +	.01	bbb+.01
02	BALANCE PICTURE	– – – –.– –	0.0	bbbbbbb
02	BALANCE PICTURE	– 99.99	– 10.25	b–10.25
02	BALANCE PICTURE	– 999.99	100.25	b100.25
02	BALANCE PICTURE	999.99–	– 10.2	010.2–
02	BALANCE PICTURE	$$$$.99–	20.35	b$20.35b
02	BALANCE PICTURE	$$$$.99+	20.35	b$20.35+

R E V I E W . . . .

1. Several $ signs included in a PICTURE clause signify that [several dollar signs should appear in the output / the output should contain the dollar sign in one of several possible positions].

    the output should contain the dollar sign in one of several possible positions

2. Both the V PICTURE character and the . PICTURE character indicate _____ positions.

    decimal point

3. The difference in the use of the V and the . PICTURE characters is that the V signifies an _____ decimal point, whereas the . signifies an _____ decimal point.

    assumed; actual

4. Arithmetic computations can be performed with fields whose decimal point designation is [V only / "." only / V or "."].

    V only

5. In general, the $ float stops when the first nonzero digit is encountered or when the _____ PICTURE character is encountered. The only exception occurs when the value in the field is zero and the $ is written in all positions, in which case the field is filled with _____ .

    V or . (decimal); blanks

6. The PICTURE insertion character that is similar to the . PICTURE character but can appear more than once in a field is the _____ PICTURE character.

    , (comma)

7. The character in a PICTURE clause which is used to replace with blanks the leading zeros in a value is the _____ PICTURE character.

    Z

8. Representation of the algebraic sign of a numeric value is accomplished by the use of the _____ or _____ PICTURE character.

    +; –

9. If the – PICTURE insertion character is used, a value held in storage will have associated with it either a – sign or [+ / no] sign. If the + PICTURE character is used, a value held in storage will have associated with it either a + sign or [– / no] sign.

    no; –

10. Fields that contain editing characters, such as $, +, or –, [can / cannot] be used in computations.

    cannot

. . . .

The DB and CR PICTURE Characters

In accounting applications there is often need to identify values that represent debits or credits. The COBOL language facilitates such differentiation by means of the DB (debit) and CR (credit) editing characters. As indicated in the following examples, the DB or CR symbol is written only to the right of a field in the PICTURE clause, and in both cases it is represented in storage for the purpose of subsequent output only when the value is negative.

DESCRIPTION	NUMERIC VALUE	REPRESENTED IN STORAGE AS
02 RECEIPT PICTURE $999.99DB	135.26	$135.26bb
02 RECEIPT PICTURE $999.99DB	–135.26	$135.26DB
02 RECEIPT PICTURE $,$$9.99CR	–10.50	bb$10.50CR

Notice that the edited field does not provide for negative values as such. A value such as –10.50 would have been stored previously in a signed numeric field and then sent to the edited field. For example, if the original field is described by 03 PAY PICTURE S9(4)V99, then executing the instruction MOVE PAY TO RECEIPT will generate the stored content represented on the last line of the preceding table.

The following table summarizes the effects of the storage location associated with the use of the +, –, CR, and DB PICTURE editing symbols. Note that for positive values the + is included in the edited field only when the + PICTURE character appears in the PICTURE clause. Note also that for negative values the – sign is included in the edited field if either the + or – PICTURE character has been used, and that the CR or DB appears only if the numeric value is negative.

PICTURE CHARACTER USED	STORAGE REPRESENTATION WHEN VALUE IS POSITIVE	STORAGE REPRESENTATION WHEN VALUE IS NEGATIVE
+	+	–
–	Blank	–
DB	Blank	DB
CR	Blank	CR

The B PICTURE Character

This is an insertion editing character resulting in blanks being entered in the designated positions. For example, suppose the first two characters in the storage location NAME always represent the initials of a person's first name and middle name, as follows: RBSMITH. If we wish to print the name with spaces included between the two initials and between the initials and the last name, we can set up the editing field 02 EDNAME PICTURE ABABA(1O). If we then execute the instruction MOVE NAME TO EDNAME and subsequently print the contents of EDNAME, the output will be R B SMITH.

The 0 (Zero) PICTURE Character

The zero insertion character causes zeros to be inserted in the positions in which it appears. For example, we can use this option if the value represented in the storage is understood to be in thousands and we want to edit it to show the full value. Thus if we had 1365 as the value of AMT and we set up EDSUM PICTURE 9(4)000, we could execute MOVE AMT TO EDSUM, giving the following result in EDSUM: 1365000.

The * PICTURE Character

The * character is referred to as a check-protect character and normally is used to protect dollar amounts written on checks or other negotiable documents. As indicated by the following examples, it works very much like the floating $ or the Z PICTURE character. In this case, however, instead of the $ sign being floated or positions being filled with blanks, the * character is entered in each zero-suppressed position as designated in the PICTURE clause.

DESCRIPTION	NUMERIC VALUE	REPRESENTED IN STORAGE AS
02 CHECK-VALUE PICTURE $***.99	256.18	$256.18
02 CHECK-VALUE PICTURE $***.99	10.13	$*10.13
02 CHECK-VALUE PICTURE $***.99	0.15	$***.15

The / (Stroke) PICTURE Character

Each / (stroke) in the PICTURE character string represents a character position into which the stroke character will be inserted. For example, suppose we have

```
02 NUMERIC-DATE      PIC 9(6) VALUE 040792.
02 EDITED-DATE       PIC 99/99/99.
```

The instruction MOVE NUMERIC-DATE TO EDITED-DATE will cause EDITED-DATE to contain 04/07/92.

R E V I E W . . . .

1.   The editing characters that can be used in a PICTURE clause to identify debits and credits, respectively, are the _____ and the _____ characters.

DB; CR

2.   In order for a DB or CR to be included in an editing field, the value entered in that field must be [positive / negative / positive for DB but negative for CR].

negative

3.   The insertion editing character that results in blanks being entered in the designated positions is the _____ PICTURE character, whereas the insertion editing character that results in zeros being entered in designated positions is the _____ PICTURE character.

B; 0

4.   The insertion editing character that is referred to as the check-protect character is the _____ PICTURE character.

*

5.   Use of the / (stroke) insertion character results in the stroke character being inserted in designated character positions [only when those positions are blank / to achieve visual separation of values].

to achieve visual separation of values

. . . .

TABLE 3-1

Types of Characters Available for Use in Picture Clauses

TYPE OF CHARACTER	SYMBOL	USE
Field definition characters	9	Numeric field
	A	Alphabetic field
	X	Alphanumeric field
Numeric field special character	V	Assumed decimal point
	P	Decimal scaling
	S	Operational (arithmetic) sign included
Editing characters	$	Dollar sign
	Z	Zero suppression
	*	Check protection
	.	Decimal point
	,	Comma
	+	Plus sign
	–	Minus sign
	DB	Debit
	CR	Credit
	B	Blank insertion
	0	Zero insertion
	/	Stroke insertion

Summary of PICTURE Clause Options

Table 3-1 lists all the PICTURE characters. As indicated, the characters that identify the type of content in a storage field are the 9, A, and X characters. Special-purpose characters associated with numeric fields only are the V, P, and S characters. All the other characters listed in Table 3-1 are used for editing purposes.

Instead of listing the characters that can be used in PICTURE clauses, another way of summarizing the material presented in this section is to consider the categories of data that can be contained in a storage location and the PICTURE characters that can be used with each category. Accordingly, Table 3-2 identifies five categories of data: numeric, alphabetic, alphanumeric, numeric edited, and alphanumeric edited. Notice that the PICTURE clause for alphanumeric items cannot contain all 9s or all A's; all 9s would be indicative of a numeric field, and all A's would indicate an alphabetic field. Note also that numeric edited items can include appropriate combinations of all 12 editing characters included in Table 3-1. On the other hand, alphanumeric edited items can include the B and 0 (zero insertion) and / (stroke) editing characters only.

R E V I E W . . . .

1. Three of the PICTURE characters discussed are used for the purpose of defining the type of content in a storage field, namely, the _____ , _____ , and _____ characters. On the other hand, the three special characters used

TABLE 3-2
The Five Catagories of Data

Numeric items	The PICTURE may contain suitable combinations of the following characters: 9 V P and S.
Alphabetic items	The PICTURE clause contains only the A character.
Alphanumeric items	The PICTURE clause consists of A 9 and X characters. It cannot contain all A or all 9 characters, but it may contain a mixture of A and 9 characters.
Numeric edited items	The PICTURE clause can contain suitable combinations of the following characters: B P V Z O 9 , . + – CR DB $ and /.
Alphanumeric edited items	The PICTURE clause can contain combinations of the following characters: Z X 9 B O and /.

in conjunction with computational numeric fields are the ____ , ____ , and ____ PICTURE characters. (Refer to Table 3-1 if you wish.)

9, A, X; V, P, S

2. The only editing PICTURE character used in conjunction with an alphabetic field is the ____ character, whereas the three editing characters that can be used in conjunction with an alphanumeric field are the ____ , ____ , and ____ PICTURE characters.

B; B, 0, /

. . . .

THE BLANK WHEN ZERO CLAUSE

Use of this clause achieves the same result as Z PICTURE, but it is more general. Consider the statement 02 AMOUNT PIC ZZ9.99 BLANK WHEN ZERO. If AMOUNT contains a zero value, the field will be blanked (six blanks); otherwise the PICTURE string will provide the editing.

THE CURRENCY AND DECIMAL-POINT CLAUSES

These two clauses actually refer to the ENVIRONMENT DIVISION. However, they are directly applicable to the subject of this chapter because they define aspects of the operating environment that have a direct impact on DATA DIVISION features associated with PICTURE strings for editing.

COBOL includes provisions for international usage with respect to monetary currencies and numeric values. Changing the dollar sign and using a comma in lieu of a decimal point can be accommodated by the use of two special clauses, as explained below.

By use of the following format specification in the SPECIAL-NAMES paragraph of the CONFIGURATION SECTION of the ENVIRONMENT DIVISION, one can thereafter use a sign other than $ in PICTURE clauses that are included in the program.

<u>CURRENCY</u> SIGN IS <u>literal</u>

For example, suppose that 'F' is the appropriate currency sign. We could write:

```
ENVIRONMENT DIVISION.
CONFIGURATION SECTION.
SOURCE-COMPUTER. . . .
OBJECT-COMPUTER. . . .
SPECIAL-NAMES.
    CURRENCY SIGN IS 'F'.
```

Then in PICTURE clauses we would use 'F' in place of $ as in the following two contrasting but equivalent examples:

```
02  AMOUNT  PIC FF,FFF,FFF.99.

02  AMOUNT  PIC $$,$$$,$$$.99.
```

The currency sign cannot be chosen from the following:

1. The digits 0 through 9

2. The alphabetic characters consisting of the uppercase letters A, B, C, D, P, R, S, V, X, Z; the lowercase letters a through z; or the space

3. The special characters * + − , . : ( ) " = /

In many countries outside of the United States the functions of the decimal point and comma are reversed. Thus the values 1,35 and 2.534,99 would be equivalent to the U.S. 1.35 and 2,534.99, respectively. The format of the clause in the SPECIAL-NAMES paragraph to accommodate the difference in these conventions is

<u>DECIMAL-POINT</u> IS <u>COMMA</u>

Once this clause has been used, the function of the comma and period are interchanged in the character string of the PICTURE clause and in numeric literals. Suppose we use the following specification in the ENVIRONMENT DIVISION:

```
SPECIAL-NAMES.
    CURRENCY SIGN IS 'F'
    DECIMAL-POINT IS COMMA.
```

Given the above specification, the following PICTURE definition is valid in the DATA DIVISION:

```
02 AMOUNT-1 PIC FF.FFF.FF9,99.
```

The floating currency sign in the PICTURE definition above is the character 'F' and the roles of the decimal point and comma have been reversed. Thus in the statement MOVE 1000,56 TO AMOUNT, the value is one thousand units and fifty-six hundredths of the F-currency units.

Keep in mind that given the CURRENCY and DECIMAL-POINT specifications above, a PICTURE definition cannot include the floating $ sign nor the "usual" use of the comma and decimal point in a PICTURE definition.

R E V I E W . . . .

1. Changing the dollar sign to a symbol associated with another currency can be achieved by use of the _____ clause.

CURRENCY

2. The clause that makes it possible to interchange the meaning and function of the comma and decimal-point symbols in PICTURE strings is the _____ clause.

DECIMAL-POINT

3. The specification of the CURRENCY and DECIMAL-POINT clauses is written in the _____ paragraph of the _____ SECTION of the ENVIRONMENT DIVISION.

SPECIAL-NAMES; CONFIGURATION

. . . .

SAMPLE DATA DIVISION

We conclude our discussion with a sample DATA DIVISION that includes many of the features described in this chapter. The sample is based on a salary-report programming task. The task consists of reading records in an employee file and producing a report such as that previously illustrated in Figure 3-5. The input record layout chart was presented in Figure 3-3, while the printer spacing chart was presented in Figure 3-4. Finally, Figure 3-8 presents the DATA DIVISION written for the programming task. The PROCEDURE DIVISION for the task is presented and discussed at the end of the following chapter.

FIGURE 3-8
DATA DIVISION for the Salary Report Program

```
DATA DIVISION.
*
FILE SECTION.
*
FD  EMPLOYEE-FILE
    LABEL RECORDS ARE OMITTED
    RECORD CONTAINS 80 CHARACTERS
    DATA RECORD IS EMPLOYEE-RECORD.
01  EMPLOYEE-RECORD.
    02 EMPLOYEE-NAME          PIC X(15).
    02 EMPLOYEE-SEX-CODE      PIC 9.
       88 MALE                VALUE 1.
       88 FEMALE              VALUE 2.
       88 ERROR-SEX-CODE      VALUE ZERO 3 THRU 9.
    02 EMPLOYEE-SALARY        PIC 9(5)V99.
    02 FILLER                 PIC X(57).
*
FD  REPORT-FILE
    LABEL RECORDS ARE OMITTED
    RECORD CONTAINS 132 CHARACTERS
    DATA RECORD IS PRINT-LINE.
01  PRINT-LINE                PIC X(132).
*
WORKING-STORAGE SECTION.
*
```

FIGURE 3-8

DATA DIVISION for the Salary
Report Program (continued)

```
 01  END-OF-FILE-TEST            PIC XXX VALUE 'NO'.
     88  END-OF-EMPLOYEE-FILE    VALUE 'YES'.
 *
 01  EMPLOYEE-COUNTERS.
     02  NO-OF-MEN               PIC 99 VALUE ZERO.
     02  NO-OF-WOMEN             PIC 99 VALUE ZERO.
 *
 01  SALARY-TOTALS.
     02  MEN-TOTAL-SALARY        PIC 9(7)V99 VALUE ZERO.
     02  WOMEN-TOTAL-SALARY      PIC 9(7)V99 VALUE ZERO.
 *
 01  REPORT-HEADINGS.
     02  HEADING-L.
         03  FILLER              PIC X(36) VALUE SPACES.
         03  FILLER              PIC X(13) VALUE
                 'ANNUAL SALARY'.
 *
     02  HEADING-2.
         03  FILLER              PIC X(16) VALUE SPACES.
         03  FILLER              PIC X(13) VALUE
                 'EMPLOYEE NAME'.
         03  FILLER              PIC X(10) VALUE SPACES.
         03  FILLER              PIC X(3) VALUE 'MEN'.
         03  FILLER              PIC X(13) VALUE SPACES.
         03  FILLER              PIC X(5) VALUE 'WOMEN'.
 *
 01  REPORT-DETAIL-LINE.
     02  FILLER                  PIC X(15) VALUE SPACES.
     02  REPORT-EMPL-NAME        PIC X(15).
     02  REPORT-ERROR-CODE       PIC X(6) VALUE SPACES.
     02  REPORT-MEN-SALARY       PIC ZZ,Z99.99
                                     BLANK WHEN ZERO.
     02  FILLER                  PIC X(8) VALUE SPACES.
     02  REPORT-WOMEN-SALARY     PIC ZZ,Z99.99
                                     BLANK WHEN ZERO.
 *
 01  REPORT-TOTALS-LINE.
     02  FILLER                  PIC X(15) VALUE SPACES.
     02  FILLER                  PIC X(9) VALUE 'T O T A L'.
     02  FILLER                  PIC X(8) VALUE SPACES.
     02  REPORT-TOT-MEN-SALARY   PIC $$,$$$,$99.99.
     02  FILLER                  PIC X(4)  VALUE SPACES.
     02  REPORT-TOT-WOMEN-SALARY PIC $$,$$$,$99.99.
 *
 01  REPORT-AVERAGES-LINE.
     02  FILLER                  PIC X(15) VALUE SPACES.
     02  FILLER                  PIC X(13) VALUE
             'A V E R A G E'.
     02  FILLER                  PIC X(4) VALUE SPACES.
     02  REPORT-AVG-MEN-SALARY   PIC $$,$$$,$99.99.
     02  FILLER                  PIC X(4)    VALUE SPACES.
     02  REPORT-AVG-WOMEN-SALARY PIC $$,$$$,$99.99.
```

The only DATA DIVISION feature in Figure 3-8 that has not been previously discussed is the special level number, 88, which is used to define the condition of a field having a specified value. For example, in the figure we have

```
02 EMPLOYEE-SEX-CODE          PIC 9.
   88 MALE                     VALUE 1.
```

MALE is a *condition-name* that defines a condition that corresponds to the value of "1." Henceforth in the program IF MALE can be used in lieu of IF EMPLOYEE-SEX-CODE = "1." The subject of condition-names is covered more fully in Chapter 5.

For convenience we selectively outline the DATA DIVISION in Figure 3-9, discussing some of the highlights.

FIGURE 3-9

Explanation of Selected DATA DIVISION Entries in Figure 3-8

FD EMPLOYEE-FILE	The input file-name.
01 EMPLOYEE-RECORD.	The name of the input file record.

02 EMPLOYEE-SEX-CODE
    88 MALE
    88 FEMALE
	In the data field identifying the sex category of the employee. Notice use of the 88 level-numbers to specify the condition-names MALE and FEMALE.

88 ERROR-SEX-CODE	Another condition-name, which identifies the condition of EMPLOYEE-SEX-CODE having any of the values of zero or 3 through 9.
01 END-OF-FILE TEST. 88 END-OF-EMPLOYEE-FILE	A data-name used for purposes of testing whether the end-of-file record has been read. Again, a condition-name is used for convenience in testing whether or not the end-of-file condition is true.

01 EMPLOYEE-COUNTERS.
    02 NO-OF-MEN
    02 NO-OF-WOMEN
	The EMPLOYEE-COUNTERS group item is used for documentation purposes. There will be no reference to EMPLOYEE-COUNTERS as such in the PROCEDURE DIVISION. The references will be to either NO-OF-MEN or NO-OF-WOMEN, as appropriate in each case. These counter fields were created in recognition of the need to report the average salary, the computation of which requires a count of the number of men and women, respectively.

01 SALARY-TOTALS.
    02 MEN-TOTAL-SALARY
    02 WOMEN-TOTAL-SALARY
	These data-names were defined in recognition of the fact that the required report presents the total salary for each of the two categories of employees.

01 REPORT-HEADINGS.
    02 HEADING-l
        .
        .
        .
    02 HEADING-2
	The report heading consists of two title lines. For better documentation we coined a group item REPORT-HEADINGS to refer to both of them, and then delineated each heading under HEADING-1 and HEADING-2. Blank lines between these headings can be specified by PROCEDURE DIVISION instructions (. . . ADVANCING . . . LINES), so we do not bother to specify blank line headings in the DATA DIVISION.

01 REPORT-DETAIL-LINE.	This item represents the format for producing each of the detail lines in the report.
02 REPORT-ERROR-CODE	This field is normally blank. However, as illustrated in the sample report in Figure 3-5, we want to print six asterisks in any field for which the employee is not classified as being either male or female. *(continued on next page)*

FIGURE 3-9

Explanation of Selected DATA DIVISION Entries in Figure 3-8 (continued)

---

02 REPORT-MEN-SALARY	Notice the PIC clause illustrating the use of zero suppression, comma and decimal point insertion, and use of BLANK WHEN ZERO. The thinking is that if an employee record is for a woman, then we want spaces to be in the REPORT-MEN-SALARY, and vice versa for men. Therefore we plan to move zeros to the field, which then are converted to spaces by the BLANK WHEN ZERO clause. (MOVE SPACES TO REPORT-MEN-SALARY would be improper because COBOL does not allow moving inconsistent categories of data. In this example the alphanumeric data, SPACES, cannot be moved to the numeric edited field, REPORT-MEN-SALARY.)
01 REPORT-TOTALS-LINE. . . .	These are specifications for the last two lines in the report, which constitute the footing, and include the total and average salary for each category.
01 REPORT-AVERAGES-LINE. . . .	Notice the use of floating dollar signs and the larger field size. Since this is a sum, it should be larger than the field from which we add the data being accumulated. The BLANK WHEN ZERO clause (or the equivalent of $$,$$$,$$$.$$) is not used because we wish to print the zero rather than have a space if the total is in fact zero dollars.
02 REPORT-AVG-MEN-SALARY	

SUMMARY

The purpose of this chapter was to present and explain quite a few of the coding details for writing the DATA DIVISION of a COBOL program. The two sections commonly included in a DATA DIVISION are the FILE SECTION and the WORKING-STORAGE SECTION.

Data fields are defined in both the FILE SECTION and the WORKING-STORAGE SECTION. Therefore the first several sections of this chapter were concerned with defining data fields. In these sections you learned how elementary data fields are defined, the use of FILLER as a nonspecific data-name, the use of the VALUE clause to define initial contents, the use of level-numbers to define group structures, and methodology associated with record layout.

Particular attention was given to *constants* as contrasted to data-names. COBOL has three types of *constants*. A *numeric literal* is a stored numeric value that is analogous to a constant in algebra. A *figurative constant* includes such verbalized constants as ZEROS and BLANKS; these are often used to "fill" a field, such as filling a data field to serve as an accumulator with zeros before it is used. A *nonnumeric literal* is enclosed in quotation marks and typically is used for such functions as a printed heading in a report.

The function of the FILE SECTION is to describe each file used in the program. Each FD entry is followed by a file-name. Then the name assigned to the record in the file is given. The hierarchical structure of the data fields included in the records is defined by use of level-numbers, with the whole record being at the 01 level.

The WORKING-STORAGE SECTION provides descriptions of data items that are not part of any file, such as intermediate calculation values and report headings. Special attention was given to the use of the VALUE clause in defining the initial contents of WORKING-STORAGE fields.

97

PICTURE clauses are used in both the FILE SECTION and the WORKING-STORAGE SECTION to describe the type of content in elementary data fields. We considered separately the use of PICTURE clauses for data description as contrasted to data editing. These parts of the chapter are quite detailed and include the types of definitions that you will continue to reference in later chapters.

The chapter concluded with a sample DATA DIVISION that illustrates many of the features presented in this chapter.

EXERCISES

3.1 Consider the following record description outline:

```
01  A
      03  B-0
            05  B-1
            05  B-2
      03  C-0
            05  C-1
                  07  C-1-1
                  07  C-1-2
            05  C-2
```

Answer the following questions with respect to the above:

a. How many group fields are described? List them.

b. Which field descriptions should have a PIC clause?

c. Which data-names should be followed by a period?

d. If every elementary field has a PIC of X(5), how long is the entire record in terms of bytes?

3.2 A data field contains social security identification numbers (SSN) and has been defined as follows:

```
01  SOC-SEC-NO-IN  PIC 9(9).
```

We want to MOVE the contents of that field into an edited field that would contain hyphens before the fourth and the sixth digits in SOC-SEC-NO-IN. For example, if the SSN is 233154389, we want to have it available in the form 233-15-4389. Write the data definition for that edited field, name it SOC-SEC-NO-OUT, and explain how you would use the MOVE instruction to accomplish the task.

3.3 Indicate the size of each of the following fields in terms of the number of bytes:

PICTURE	SIZE
99V99	_____
9(3).9	_____
S999V9	_____
ZZ,ZZZ	_____
+(3).99	_____
$***,**9.99	_____
VPP99	_____
ZZZ000	_____

3.4   Complete the DATA DIVISION description for the following WORKING-STORAGE record so that it corresponds to the record layout that follows. Use your own choice of data-names.

```
01  TOTALS-LINE.

    02  _____  PIC _____  VALUE _____

    02  _____  PIC _____  VALUE _____

    02  _____  PIC _____  VALUE _____

    02  _____  PIC _____

    02  _____  PIC _____  VALUE _____

    02  _____  PIC _____
```

1–16	17–25	26–35	36–45	46–50	51–60
Blank	TOTAL	Blank	Men's total salary, showing decimal point and 2 decimal places	Blank	Women's total salary, showing decimal point and 2 decimal places

3.5   Referring to the following schematic representation, write a DATA DIVISION record description using the information:

DEPT	2 letters
NAME	15 characters
RATE	4 digits, 2 decimal places, used for arithmetic
SKILL	1 letter
REGULAR	7 digits, 2 decimal places, used for arithmetic
OVERTIME	6 digits, 2 decimal places, used for arithmetic
SS-TAX	5 digits, 2 decimal places, used for arithmetic

PAY-RECORD						
EMPLOYEE		RATE	SKILL	YEAR-TO-DATE		
DEPT	NAME			GROSS		SS-TAX
				REGULAR	OVERTIME	

3.6   Write DATA DIVISION entries for the WORKING-STORAGE record named SALES-DATA whose description is given in the following table. Data are moved from the items whose PICTURE description is shown.

SOURCE ITEM PICTURE	RECEIVING ITEM-NAME	PRINT POSITIONS	EDITING REQUIRED
99999	SALE-NUMBER	1-5	Suppress all leading zeros.
		6-7	Blank
(X)25	NAME	8-32	None
		33–34	Blank

SOURCE ITEM PICTURE	RECEIVING ITEM-NAME	PRINT POSITIONS	EDITING REQUIRED
S9999V99	DOLLARS	35–?	Insert comma, decimal point. Dollar sign immediately to the left of leftmost nonzero digit. Show negative sign if negative.
		2 positions	Blank
S9(3)V9(4)	PROFIT		Show decimal point. Suppress leading zeros. Show negative sign to left of leftmost nonzero digit.

3.7 Following the format below are DATA DIVISION entries for fields that contain the data to be printed as the CHECK-REGISTER record. The output resulting from printing of the CHECK-REGISTER record should have approximately the following format (header titles are shown for clarity only):

VENDOR NAME	VENDOR NUMBER	CHECK NUMBER	DATE	DEBIT	DISCOUNT	CASH
ACME CORP.	1234	12345	01/03/86	$1,030.57	$20.13	$1,010.44

```
01  CHECK-NUMBER    PICTURE 9(5).
01  DEBIT           PICTURE 9(6)V99.
01  DISCOUNT        PICTURE 9(4)V99.
01 CASH             PICTURE 9(6)V99.
01  VENDOR-DATA.
    02  V-NAME      PICTURE X(15).
    02  V-NUMBER    PICTURE X(4).
01  DATE.
    02  MONTH       PICTURE 99.
    02  DAY         PICTURE 99.
    02  YEAR        PICTURE 99.
```

Write DATA DIVISION entries to form the CHECK-REGISTER record so that the output is printed approximately in the desired format. Make sure that the date is in the form MM/DD/YY. Use a printer spacing chart from the supply at the end of the text to assist your output report effort.

3.8 It is required that two lines having the following general format be printed:

```
SUMMARY STATISTICS
AVERAGE BAL.$XXX,XXX.XX  MAX$XXX,XXX.XX  MIN$XXX,XXX.XX
```

Assume the following DATA DIVISION entries:

```
FD  PRINT-FILE LABEL RECORDS OMITTED DATA RECORD IS
        PRINT-LINE.
01  PRINT-LINE   PICTURE X(132).
WORKING-STORAGE SECTION.
01  MAX-BAL      PICTURE 9(6)V99.
01  MIN-BAL      PICTURE 9(6)V99.
01  AVER-BAL     PICTURE 9(6)V99.
```

Write WORKING-STORAGE SECTION entries to set up the required fields to print these two lines.

3.9   Suppose that it has become necessary to change an existing COBOL program. The original version of the relevant DATA DIVISION entries is as follows:

```
02  FIELD-A
    03  FIELD-B
    03  FIELD-C
    03  FIELD-D
02  FIELD-E
```

In the revised version it is required that the fields be restructured so that (a) reference can be made to all the fields as one unit; (b) reference can be made to fields B and C as a unit; and (c) reference can be made to fields D and E as a unit. Show how this can be done.

3.10   Assume that in all cases the following two instructions apply:

```
MOVE A TO B
MOVE B TO C
```

Field C has been defined as follows:

```
01  C  PIC X(11).
```

Show the resulting contents of C in each of the cases included in the following table, assuming that each cell stands for one character position.

CONTENT OF A	PICTURE OF B	RESULTING CONTENT IN C										
10.125	999V99											
10000.00	Z,ZZZ.ZZ											
900.15	$$,$$Z.99											
0.08	$$,$ZZ.ZZ											
50.50	$***.99DB											
−25.25	+,+++.99											
25.25	$$$$.99−											
WELCOME	XXXBXXX											

4

Writing Complete Programs

THE MAIN OBJECTIVE *of this chapter is to develop your knowledge of COBOL to the point that you will be able to write complete programs.*

You will begin by first considering the coding conventions by which COBOL programming options are presented, and then you will review the features of the IDENTIFICATION DIVISION, ENVIRONMENT DIVISION, and DATA DIVISION. Recall that the DATA DIVISION was covered in some detail in the preceding chapter. Your study in this chapter will focus on the PROCEDURE DIVISION, and you will learn how to use a complete set of PROCEDURE DIVISION statements.

The chapter concludes with coverage of the PROCEDURE DIVISION for the employee salary-report programming task for which the DATA DIVISION was written in the preceding chapter.

COBOL LANGUAGE FORMATS

Before turning our attention to PROCEDURE DIVISION statements, we need to describe the method by which programming options are presented in this book. COBOL is characterized by great flexibility in the form of options available to the programmer. To communicate these options, we use a *metalanguage*, a language about a language. The form of presentation used here is not unique to this book but generally is followed in all books concerned with COBOL program statements. The method is used to describe how each type of statement should be structured, and to identify the options available to the programmer for each type of statement. In other words, the style of presentation is necessary because we wish to talk about types of statements in general, rather than about specific and particular program instructions. For this purpose, then, the following set of conventions is followed:

1. Words presented entirely in uppercase letters are always COBOL reserved words.

2. Uppercase words that are underlined are words that are required in the type of program statement being described. Uppercase words that are not underlined are optional and are used only to improve the readability of the program.

3. Lowercase words are used to indicate the points at which data-names or constants are to be supplied by the programmer. In addition to the words "data-name" and "literal," the term "identifier" is used to indicate a data-name, but it has a slightly broader meaning. It refers to either of the following cases: data-names that are unique in themselves, or data-names that are not unique in themselves but are made unique through qualification. Qualification is discussed in Chapter 16. For now, you may safely assume the words "data-name" and "identifier" to be equivalent. Other lowercase words used to indicate items to be inserted by the programmer are

file-name	condition
record-name	statement
integer	any imperative statement
formula	any sentence

4. Items enclosed in braces { } indicate that one of the enclosed items must be used.

5. Items enclosed in brackets [ ] indicate that the items are optional, and one of them may be used at the option of the programmer.

6. An ellipsis (. . .) indicates that further information may be included in the program instruction, usually in the form of repeating the immediately preceding element any desired number of times.

As an example of the use of these conventions, consider the ADD statement. With the COBOL language format a basic form of ADD is

$$\underline{ADD} \begin{Bmatrix} \text{identifier -1} \\ \text{literal -1} \end{Bmatrix} \begin{bmatrix} \text{, identifier -2} \\ \text{, literal -2} \end{bmatrix} \ldots \underline{TO} \text{ identifier-m}$$

If we apply the rules just presented, the word ADD is a reserved COBOL word because it is in uppercase, and it is required because it is underscored. The word TO is governed by the same rules. The braces following ADD indicate that one of the two alternatives enclosed must be used. Thus the required word ADD must be followed by either an identifier or a literal. Incidentally, it also is understood that, for this specific instruction, the identifier must be an elementary numeric (nonedited) field and the literal must be a numeric literal. The square brackets indicate that identifier-2 and literal-2 are both optional. In other words, the identifier or literal that immediately follows ADD may or may not be followed by a second identifier or literal. The commas also are optional; they may be included to improve readability, or they may be omitted. The ellipsis indicates that the preceding element (in square brackets) may be repeated as many times as desired. Finally, the identifier-m indicates that an identifier must follow the word TO. Note that it is not enclosed in braces because it is the only option; braces are used when we may choose among alternatives. Utilizing this general format, we see that the following examples are legitimate ADD statements:

```
ADD AMOUNT TO TOTAL
ADD 100 TO TOTAL
ADD REGULAR OVERTIME TO GROSS
ADD 10 BONUS 100.25 TO GROSS
```

R E V I E W . . . .

1. In presenting COBOL statement instructions, words that are entirely in uppercase letters designate _____ words.

   COBOL reserved

2. When a reserved COBOL word is underlined in the format presentation, this indicates that the word [may / must] be used as part of a program instruction.

   must

3. Items to be inserted in the program instruction, such as data-names, identifiers, constants, and expressions, are indicated by [lowercase / uppercase] words.

   lowercase

4. When two or more items are enclosed within brackets [ ], this indicates that one of them [may / must] be included in the program instruction. When two or more items are enclosed within braces { } this indicates that one of them [may / must] be included.

   may; must

5. To indicate that further information, such as additional data-names, can be included in an instruction, a(n) _____ is used.

   ellipsis (. . .)

. . . .

IDENTIFICATION DIVISION

The function of the IDENTIFICATION DIVISION is to supply information about the program to others who may read or use the program. On the COBOL Coding Form we start in column 8 with the words IDENTIFICATION DIVISION. The first and only required paragraph is the PROGRAM-ID, which is followed by the program-name chosen by the programmer. For example, we may have

```
IDENTIFICATION DIVISION.
PROGRAM-ID. CUSTRPRT.
```

In this case the word CUSTRPRT is the name the programmer has chosen to identify the program. This name must start with an alphabetic character and may consist of up to 30 alphabetic or numeric characters unless the specific compiler limits the number to fewer characters. The two lines shown in the example are sufficient content for the IDENTIFICATION DIVISION. All other paragraphs are optional but, if they are used, they must be written in the order shown. The following example includes optional paragraphs. The underlined words are COBOL reserved words, which are required; the other words are a matter of the programmer's choice.

IDENTIFICATION DIVISION.

PROGRAM-ID. SALARY.

AUTHOR. LEE WALTERS.

INSTALLATION. XYZ CORPORATION.

DATE-WRITTEN. JANUARY 14, 1990.

DATE-COMPILED.

SECURITY.   THIS PROGRAM RESTRICTED TO ALL
            PERSONNEL EXCEPT THOSE AUTHORIZED
            BY THE OFFICE OF THE CONTROLLER.

All paragraph-names start in column 8 and, as stated earlier, all paragraphs are optional with the exception of PROGRAM-ID. The compiler does not process what follows the COBOL words but only prints that content. Thus after DATE-WRITTEN we could have written DURING THE SPRING OF 1990. The compiler derives no more meaning from JANUARY or from SPRING than from a nonsense word; therefore the programmer should be concerned simply with choosing verbal descriptions that will be meaningful to the potential readers of the program.

Note that the DATE-COMPILED paragraph is left blank. The compiler will insert the actual date, and the source listing will include that date.

An entry in the IDENTIFICATION DIVISION may extend to more than one line, as illustrated in the case of the SECURITY paragraph. In such a case the lines subsequent to the first line must all start in column 12 or to the right of column 12. The PROGRAM-ID paragraph, however, is restricted to one word, which must not exceed 30 characters in length. (Some exceptions to these rules are discussed in Chapter 23, in connection with subprograms.)

R   E   V   I   E   W   .   .   .   .

1. The order in which the four divisions of a COBOL program appear is:
    _____ , _____ , _____ , and
    _____ .

                            IDENTIFICATION; ENVIRONMENT; DATA; PROCEDURE

2. Other than the division name itself, the only paragraph required in the
    IDENTIFICATION DIVISION is the one named _____ .

                                                            PROGRAM-ID

3. Although other entries in the IDENTIFICATION DIVISION may extend to more
    than one line, the PROGRAM-ID paragraph is restricted to one word which must
    not exceed _____ (number) characters in length.

                                                                        30

4. Overall, the purpose of the IDENTIFICATION DIVISION of a COBOL program is
    to _____ .

                                    describe the program to potential users (etc.)

.   .   .   .

ENVIRONMENT DIVISION

This division is designed to describe the computer system "environment" in which the program is compiled and executed. With a few important exceptions, this division provides documentation type of information. In the 1985 standard this is an optional division. Still, for the vast majority of programs, and in both the '74 and the '85 versions, there are parts of the ENVIRONMENT DIVISION that define very necessary and important information. This importance will become much more evident in the chapters that deal with file processing (chapters 10, 20, and 21).

The following illustration of an ENVIRONMENT DIVISION is a typical one. Again, as for the IDENTIFICATION DIVISION, the underlined words are COBOL reserved words.

ENVIRONMENT DIVISION.

CONFIGURATION SECTION.

SOURCE-COMPUTER. ABC-480.
OBJECT-COMPUTER. ABC-480.

INPUT-OUTPUT SECTION.

FILE-CONTROL.

    SELECT CUSTOMER-FILE   ASSIGN TO CUSTFILE.

    SELECT REPORT-FILE   ASSIGN TO PRINTER.

There are two sections included in the ENVIRONMENT DIVISION in this example: the CONFIGURATION SECTION and the INPUT-OUTPUT SECTION. The SOURCE-COMPUTER and OBJECT-COMPUTER paragraphs serve documentation purposes. They are intended to provide information about the computer system used for compilation (SOURCE-COMPUTER) and the system used for execution (OBJECT-COMPUTER). The name ABC-480 is fictitious in the example and would be replaced by a manufacturer's name and model number, such as IBM-3081, OR DEC-VAX-8650.

This example has one paragraph in the INPUT-OUTPUT SECTION, the FILE-CONTROL paragraph. The SELECT statement identifies the name of a file, in this case CUSTOMER-FILE. This file-name is the programmer's choice and is formed in compliance with COBOL name formation rules (although some compilers place further restrictions, such as that the first 12 characters must be unique). The ASSIGN statement declares that this file will be associated with the file identification that follows, in this case CUSTFILE. Similarly, REPORT-FILE identifies another file-name, and the hardware device with which this file will be associated is PRINTER (thus this file will include the output information). Device names are neither COBOL words nor programmer supplied; they are *implementor-names,* which means they are specific to the compiler and operating system used. Sometimes the implementor-names can be rather cryptic, as in

```
SELECT CUSTOMER-FILE ASSIGN TO SYS005-UR-2540R-S.
```

We illustrate the common practice in IBM mainframe environments because they are so widely used for business applications in the large corporations that often hire the students who have learned COBOL in college. Figure 4-1 presents an outline of a complete JOB Control Language (JCL) stream for an IBM mainframe system. Included in the figure is an illustration of how file-names in the COBOL program are associated with the operating system file-names. In Figure 4-1 the names in the ASSIGN TO clauses are highlighted, as are the corresponding "DD-names" in the JCL (Job Control Language) stream.

FIGURE 4-1

Sample JCL Stream for an IBM Mainframe Computer

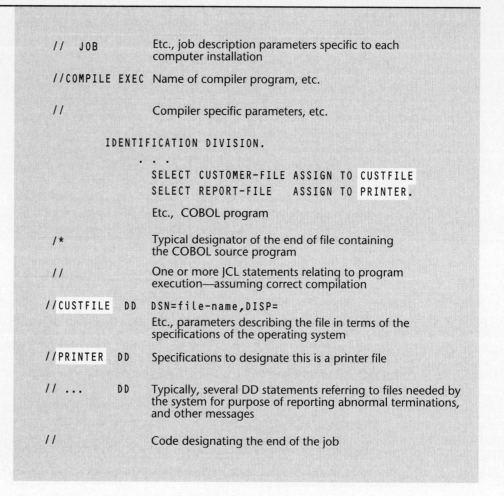

```
// JOB                Etc., job description parameters specific to each
                      computer installation

//COMPILE EXEC        Name of compiler program, etc.

//                    Compiler specific parameters, etc.

         IDENTIFICATION DIVISION.
            . . .
         SELECT CUSTOMER-FILE ASSIGN TO CUSTFILE
         SELECT REPORT-FILE   ASSIGN TO PRINTER.

         Etc.,  COBOL program

/*                    Typical designator of the end of file containing
                      the COBOL source program

//                    One or more JCL statements relating to program
                      execution—assuming correct compilation

//CUSTFILE  DD  DSN=file-name,DISP=
                      Etc., parameters describing the file in terms of the
                      specifications of the operating system

//PRINTER  DD         Specifications to designate this is a printer file

// ...     DD         Typically, several DD statements referring to files needed by
                      the system for purpose of reporting abnormal terminations,
                      and other messages

//                    Code designating the end of the job
```

Each computer system has its own way of designating computer files. Therefore in this book such entries usually are presented in a general conceptual form rather than in a computer-specific form.

R E V I E W . . . .

1. Of the four divisions of a COBOL program, the one written with an orientation to a particular computer system and its equipment is the _____ DIVISION.

   ENVIRONMENT

2. The ENVIRONMENT DIVISION is optional in the [1974 / 1985] standard version of COBOL.

   1985

3. Two sections of the ENVIRONMENT DIVISION are the CONFIGURATION SECTION and the INPUT-OUTPUT SECTION. Of these, the one that serves to identify the equipment to be used and is the only section specifically required is the _____ SECTION.

   CONFIGURATION

4. The section of the ENVIRONMENT DIVISION concerned with the assignment of specified files to particular devices is the _____ SECTION.

INPUT-OUTPUT

5. The division of a COBOL program that supplies general information about the program is the _____ DIVISION; the division that specifies the equipment to be used is the _____ DIVISION.

IDENTIFICATION; ENVIRONMENT

. . . .

DATA DIVISION

The DATA DIVISION was the main subject of Chapter 3. As a brief review, it serves to define file and working-storage fields and their names. Commonly, it consists of two sections: the FILE SECTION and the WORKING-STORAGE SECTION.

An example FILE SECTION is

```
FILE SECTION.
FD  CUSTOMER-FILE
    LABEL RECORDS ARE STANDARD
    RECORD CONTAINS 80 CHARACTERS
    DATA RECORD IS CUSTOMER-RECORD.
01  CUSTOMER-RECORD.
    05  CUSTOMER-NAME  PIC X(13).
    05  CUSTOMER-UNITS PIC 999.
    05  FILLER         PIC X(64).
```

The FD designation is needed at the beginning of each file description. It is always followed by a file-name—in the case above, by CUSTOMER-FILE.

The clause LABEL RECORDS ARE STANDARD or LABEL RECORDS ARE OMITTED will be discussed in Chapter 10, on sequential file processing. For now we will use it in either the STANDARD or OMITTED versions and will understand that it states whether the file has standard or omitted identifying labels.

The optional statement RECORD CONTAINS . . . CHARACTERS is used to declare the size of the record. In the CUSTOMER-FILE each record is 80 characters in length, and we refer to such a record by means of the name CUSTOMER-RECORD, which is designated in the clause DATA RECORD IS CUSTOMER-RECORD.

Following the FD entry we see the record description. The 01 level-number introduces the record-name CUSTOMER-RECORD, referring to the entire record. Then there are three entries, each starting with the appropriate level-number.

Assuming CUSTOMER-FILE to be an input file, we can give an instruction to copy a data record from the disk into central storage (by use of the READ verb). Subsequent to a READ operation we can then give instructions to operate on the data in central storage—for example, by instructions such as ADD CUSTOMER-UNITS TO . . .

CUSTOMER-NAME and CUSTOMER-UNITS are data-names referencing fields in the record. CUSTOMER-NAME refers to the first 13 bytes of CUSTOMER-RECORD while CUSTOMER-UNITS refers to the next 3 bytes. The third field in CUSTOMER-RECORD is named FILLER.

Storage fields associated with the file records receive data from, or are used to send data to, external input-output devices, such as disks, tapes, printers, and video terminals. In addition to such storage fields, there also is a need for storage of header data, intermediate arithmetic results, and the like. The WORKING-STORAGE SECTION is used to define such fields, as discussed in Chapter 3.

R E V I E W . . . .

1. Of the four divisions of a COBOL program, the one concerned with the identification and description of storage fields is the _____ division.

   DATA

2. In the FILE SECTION of the DATA DIVISION, we designate that an entry is a file description by beginning the entry with the COBOL reserved word _____ .

   FD

3. After the name of the file, the next item of information given in the FD entry is the name of the _____ contained in the file.

   record

4. The level-number assigned to the whole record is always _____ (number).

   01

5. All fields in the record that are directly subordinate to the overall record commonly are assigned the level-number _____ (number).

   02 or higher

. . . .

FILE INPUT AND OUTPUT

The general functions performed by an input statement and an output statement are, respectively, to transfer data from an external storage medium to central storage, and to transfer data from central storage to an external storage medium. The file storage medium involved in each case is specified in the ENVIRONMENT DIVISION by the corresponding SELECT file-name and ASSIGN TO . . . statements.

The OPEN and CLOSE Verbs

Before a file can be used, we must OPEN that file and designate whether it is an input file or an output file. The format is

$$\text{OPEN} \begin{Bmatrix} [\underline{\text{INPUT}} \text{ file-name-1} & [\text{file-name-2} \dots]] \\ [\underline{\text{OUTPUT}} \text{ file-name-3} & [\text{file-name-4} \dots]] \end{Bmatrix}$$

The full meaning and purpose of the OPEN verb is explained in Chapter 10; for now, we simply will say that it must be used prior to writing into or reading from a file.

We can use an OPEN statement for each file, or we can use one OPEN statement for several files as a group:

```
OPEN INPUT   EMPL-FILE
OPEN OUTPUT  REPORT-FILE


OPEN INPUT   FILE-A
             FILE-B
     OUTPUT  FILE-C
             FILE-D
             FILE-E.
```

The practice of writing only one file-name per line simply enhances documentation. We could also have written all file-names on one line.

Before a program terminates execution with a STOP RUN statement, we must use a CLOSE statement for each file that was opened. The meaning and purpose of this statement will be explained further in Chapter 10.

The following is the format for the CLOSE verb; just as for the OPEN verb, we can use one CLOSE statement for each file or we can reference several files from one CLOSE.

CLOSE file-name-1   [file-name-2] . . .

The READ Verb

One format of the READ verb is

READ file-name RECORD [INTO identifier]

[AT END imperative-statement]

Each execution of the READ transfers the data contained in the subsequent physical record of the file to the internal record described in the 01 entry that follows the FD specification. In effect, the READ is a "copy" command; it copies data from file storage to central storage.

The INTO option is a short form for moving the data from the file-record field to another field so that the data can be copied without a separate MOVE statement. Here are examples of two equivalent versions:

```
READ INPUT-FILE RECORD INTO OUTPUT-RECORD
    AT END MOVE 'YES' TO END-OF-FILE.
IF  END-OF-FILE = 'NO'
    WRITE OUTPUT-RECORD . . .
```

The INTO OUTPUT-RECORD function could be replaced by the equivalent use of MOVE:

```
READ INPUT-FILE RECORD
    AT END MOVE 'YES' TO END-OF-FILE.
IF  END-OF-FILE = 'NO'
    MOVE INPUT-RECORD TO OUTPUT-RECORD
    WRITE OUTPUT-RECORD . . .
```

Thus the INTO OUTPUT-RECORD is simply a "shorthand" substitute for MOVE INPUT-RECORD TO OUTPUT-RECORD. The AT END is indicated as being optional; however, until we discuss alternatives in Chapter 10, we will treat it as being required. Each computer system has one or more special characters for indicating the end of the file. When a record that contains such a character is read, the AT END condition is true and the imperative-statement is executed.

In the 1985 standard the format has been expanded as follows:

READ file-name RECORD [INTO identifier]

[AT END imperative-statement-1]

[NOT AT END imperative-statement-2]

[END READ]

As indicated above, in COBOL '85 the NOT AT END and the END-READ enhancements provide for an IF . . . ELSE . . . type of program structure, as

FIGURE 4-2
Examples of READ Statements

COBOL '74	COBOL '85
| ```
MOVE 'NO' TO END-OF-FILE
READ EMPLOYEE-FILE RECORD
    AT END MOVE 'YES' TO END-OF-FILE.
IF END-OF-FILE = 'YES'
    PERFORM PRINT-SUMMARY
ELSE
    PERFORM PRINT-DETAIL.
PERFORM XYZ.
``` | ```
READ EMPLOYEE-FILE RECORD
    AT END
        PERFORM PRINT-SUMMARY
    NOT AT END
        PERFORM PRINT-DETAIL
END-READ
PERFORM XYZ.
``` |

illustrated in the two contrasting examples in Figure 4-2. In this figure notice that there is no need to use a field such as END-OF-FILE in the revised version since the AT END and NOT AT END allow for the dual alternatives to be expressed in the one READ statement.

The END-READ marks the termination of the READ statement. It could be omitted in the revised language provided that a period is placed after PERFORM PRINT-DETAIL. Such a period terminates the AT END conditional, and there is no ambiguity that PERFORM XYZ is to be executed regardless of whether AT END is true or false.

The WRITE Verb

The WRITE statement, as used with the printer, has the following format:

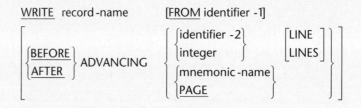

The FROM option is the counterpart of the INTO option for the READ verb. For example, we could write

```
MOVE HEADER TO OUTPUT-RECORD
WRITE OUTPUT-RECORD . . .
```

or we could use the FROM:

```
WRITE OUTPUT-RECORD FROM HEADER . . .
```

The ADVANCING clause is used only with files assigned to a printer, and it is used to control the vertical spacing on the printer. We can write WRITE . . . AFTER ADVANCING 2 LINES to achieve double spacing, for instance. We also can have variable spacing, as the sample in the following paragraph illustrates.

Suppose that a sales invoice form has space for 10 items on each invoice, and we always wish to print the total billing on the last line of the invoice. We can use a storage field (NO-OF-ITEMS) as a counter to keep track of the number of items on each invoice. If an invoice contains four items, the value stored in NO-OF-ITEMS will be 4; if an invoice contains six items, the value will be 6, and so on.

To print the total billing on the last line of the invoice, the number of lines to be skipped (let's call it LINE-COUNT) will always be 10 spaces minus NO-OF-ITEMS. For this example we are assuming that there will never be more than 10 items; therefore the following statements provide the basis for skipping the appropriate number of lines:

```
SUBTRACT NO-OF-ITEMS FROM 10 GIVING LINE-COUNT
WRITE REP-LINE AFTER ADVANCING LINE-COUNT LINES.
```

Use of the AFTER ADVANCING in the above example indicates the "skipping" of as many printer lines as the value of LINE-COUNT.

When a mnemonic-name is used, (see the presence of "mnemonic-name" in the general format for the WRITE verb, at the beginning of this subsection), it is specified in a special paragraph, the SPECIAL-NAMES paragraph of the ENVIRON-MENT DIVISION. Such mnemonic-names are specified differently for each operating system. As an example, consider a system where C12 is defined to mean channel 12 on the printer carriage control tape, where channel 12 defines the bottom of a printer page. We could have the following:

```
ENVIRONMENT DIVISION.
    CONFIGURATION SECTION.
    SOURCE-COMPUTER.
    OBJECT-COMPUTER.
    SPECIAL-NAMES.
        C12 IS BOTTOM-OF-PAGE.
INPUT-OUTPUT SECTION.
(etc.)
```

In the PROCEDURE DIVISION the statement

```
WRITE PRINT-RECORD AFTER ADVANCING BOTTOM-OF-PAGE
```

is understood to mean to skip to the bottom of the page. The SPECIAL-NAMES paragraph in the CONFIGURATION SECTION is used to designate such special names as printer spacing codes and "alphabet" designations, as will be discussed in Chapter 16.

R E V I E W . . . .

1. Prior to inputting data from a file, a(n) _____ statement must be executed.

   OPEN INPUT

2. Prior to writing data onto a file, a(n) _____ statement must be executed.

   OPEN OUTPUT

3. Before a program terminates execution with STOP RUN, a _____ statement must be executed for every file that was opened.

   CLOSE

4. Data are entered into central storage by use of the _____ verb.

   READ

5. The option that results in the same data being available in two different places after a READ statement has been executed (often in one input record and one output record) is the _____ option.

INTO

6. Similar to the AT END option available with the READ statement, COBOL '85 also makes available the _____ option.

NOT AT END

7. The verb that is used to output data from central storage onto an external file is the _____ verb.

WRITE

8. In conjunction with a WRITE statement, data are moved from an identifier to the output record being written by use of the _____ option.

FROM

9. Variable vertical spacing of output on the printer can be accomplished by using the _____ clause in conjunction with a WRITE statement.

ADVANCING

· ·

THE MOVE STATEMENT

The word "MOVE" in COBOL is, in fact, a misnomer because the function performed is duplicating, not moving. When we write MOVE A to B, the contents of A are duplicated in B, with the contents of A remaining unchanged.

The format for the MOVE instruction is

$$\underline{\text{MOVE}} \begin{Bmatrix} \text{identifier -1} \\ \text{literal -1} \end{Bmatrix} \underline{\text{TO}} \text{ identifier-2 [, identifier-3] } \ldots$$

In any use of the MOVE instruction caution should be exercised so that the receiving field is not smaller than the sending field. If the receiving field is too small, truncation will result in the loss of part of the value or information being transferred. The rules for moving data are many and relate to the form of data moved. One important point to remember is the following: numeric data are aligned according to the decimal point. If the receiving field is larger than the sending, the extra positions are filled with zeros. If the receiving field is smaller, then truncation takes place as needed, to the right, left, or both right and left of the decimal point. In the following illustrations the caret (∧) implies a decimal point:

SENDING FIELD	RESULT IN RECEIVING FIELD
0 1 3 5 2∧	0 0 1 3 5∧2 0
2 5 2 3∧5	2 5 2 3∧5
2 5 2 3∧5	5 2 3∧5
2 5 2 3∧5	5 2 3∧

A second important point is that alphabetic or alphanumeric data are left-justified in the receiving field (unless the programmer uses the JUSTIFIED RIGHT clause described in Chapter 16). If the receiving field is larger than the sending field, the additional positions are filled with blanks. If the receiving field is smaller, then truncation takes place from the right. The following examples illustrate some typical cases:

SENDING FIELD	RECEIVING FIELD
B O N A N Z A	B O N A N Z A
B O N A N Z A	B O N A N Z A
B O N A N Z A	B O N A N

Table 4-1 indicates the types of data transfer that are and are not permitted in COBOL. You may want to review Table 3-2 in the preceding chapter, which defines the various categories of data to which reference is made in Table 4-1. Most compilers incorporate the rules presented in this table, so the programmer will be warned of illegal MOVE statements. Still, it is not difficult to internalize most of these rules.

Refer to the last line of Table 4-1. In the 1985 standard it is permissible to move a numeric edited field to a numeric unedited field. This new option allows for *de-editing* of data, something not permitted in the 1974 version. As examples, consider these statements:

```
02   COMP-AMOUNT          PIC 9(5)V99.
02   EDIT-AMOUNT          PIC $$,$$9.99.
.
.
.
MOVE 1234.56 TO EDIT-AMOUNT
MOVE EDIT-AMOUNT TO COMP-AMOUNT.
```

When these statements have been executed, EDIT-AMOUNT would contain $1,234.56 while COMP-AMOUNT would correctly contain 01234ᴀ56. The last

TABLE 4-1

Legal and Illegal MOVE Commands

CATEGORY OF SENDING DATA; DATA ITEM	CATEGORY OF RECEIVING DATA ITEM		
	ALPHABETIC	ALPHANUMERIC; ALPHANUMERIC EDITED	NUMERIC INTEGER; NUMERIC NONINTEGER; NUMERIC EDITED
Alphabetic	Yes	Yes	No
Alphanumeric	Yes	Yes	No
Alphanumeric edited	Yes	Yes	No
Numeric integer	No	Yes	Yes
Numeric noninteger	No	No	Yes
Numeric edited	No	Yes	No (Yes in revised language)

statement, MOVE EDIT-AMOUNT to COMP-AMOUNT, strips the data of such editing characters as the dollar sign, the comma, and the decimal point, and moves the numeric data to the numeric unedited field. Such a move is not valid in the 1974 version of COBOL.

It is often assumed that the DATA DIVISION description of a field as being numeric somehow guards against the moving of nonnumeric data into that field. We present the following example to dispel such a notion:

```
01  SAMPLE-FIELD.
    02  A   PIC XX.
    02  B   PIC 99V99.
    .
    .
    .
    MOVE 'ROBERT' TO SAMPLE-FIELD.
```

After the MOVE is executed, B contains the letters "BERT"! How can that be? It is very simple. SAMPLE-FIELD is a group-item that is six bytes long; two of these constitute A and four make up B. Therefore when we move 'ROBERT' into SAMPLE-FIELD, the last four bytes of the field contain the last four characters in the literal.

The above example constitutes a valid action in COBOL and shows the flexibility that the language provides. On the other hand, it would not be correct to do arithmetic involving the B field after the above MOVE. For example,

```
MOVE 'ROBERT' TO SAMPLE-FIELD
ADD 1 TO B
```

would be an incorrect program as far as logic is concerned. However, from the standpoint of COBOL the ADD is a valid statement, because it is phrased independently of the content of B. Fortunately, many compilers add program code to check whether a numeric field does indeed contain numeric data before doing arithmetic with that field. You may wish to test the above illustration on the available compiler to see what happens.

To guard against such possible errors, COBOL provides for class condition tests, discussed in Chapter 8. The following illustrates such a class condition test:

```
IF  B  IS  NUMERIC
    ADD 1 TO B
ELSE
    PERFORM ERROR-ROUTINE.
```

R E V I E W . . . .

1. When data are transferred by use of the MOVE instruction, one might say more correctly that the data have been _____ rather than moved.

                                          duplicated

2. When numeric data are moved from a sending field to a receiving field, alignment takes place with respect to the _____ .

                                        decimal point

3. When nonnumeric data are moved from a sending field to a receiving field, alignment takes place at the [left / right] margin.

                                        left

4. Movement of numeric data into a numeric edited field is valid [in both COBOL '74 and '85 / only in COBOL '85].

in both COBOL '74 and '85

5. De-editing involves movement of numeric edited data into a numeric field and is valid [in both COBOL '74 and '85 / only in COBOL '85].

only in COBOL '85

6. Nonnumeric data can be moved inadvertently into a numeric field when the field is part of a _____-item that is alphanumeric, for example.

group

. . . .

THE PERFORM VERB

The PERFORM verb is generally used to specify the sequence of execution of a modular program, represented by paragraphs or sections, or to specify the repeated execution of such modules to achieve program looping. We already have seen the use of the PERFORM verb in the program examples in the preceding chapters. In this section we review and expand our description of the uses of this verb by presenting basic formats associated with the PERFORM verb. This is a highly flexible verb, and additional formats for its use will be presented in later chapters.

The simplest format of the PERFORM is

PERFORM procedure-name

The procedure-name referenced in this format is either a paragraph-name or a section-name (sections are discussed in Chapter 11). Simply stated, the PERFORM directs program execution to the named procedure, at which point the procedure is executed and program execution returns to the next statement following the PERFORM. In this respect it follows that the named procedure must allow the program to return; that is, the procedure must not contain a GO TO (see Chapter 7) or a STOP RUN statement. However, the paragraph that is performed may itself contain another PERFORM instruction.

The PERFORM . . . UNTIL

Another format of PERFORM is shown here:

COBOL '74	COBOL '85
PERFORM procedure-name UNTIL condition	PERFORM procedure-name $\left[\text{WITH } \underline{\text{TEST}} \left\{ \begin{array}{l} \underline{\text{BEFORE}} \\ \underline{\text{AFTER}} \end{array} \right\} \underline{\text{UNTIL}} \text{ condition} \right]$ [END-PERFORM]

The simplest form of the 1985 version omits the WITH TEST clause and the END-PERFORM terminator, and thereby is the same as the 1974 version. An example is

```
PERFORM PROCESS-DETAIL
        UNTIL END-OF-FILE = 'YES'.
```

In this program segment the UNTIL condition is tested before the procedure is executed. The END-OF-FILE first is tested for 'YES'. If END-OF-FILE is equal

FIGURE 4-3
PERFORM . . . UNTIL with Use of
TEST Option

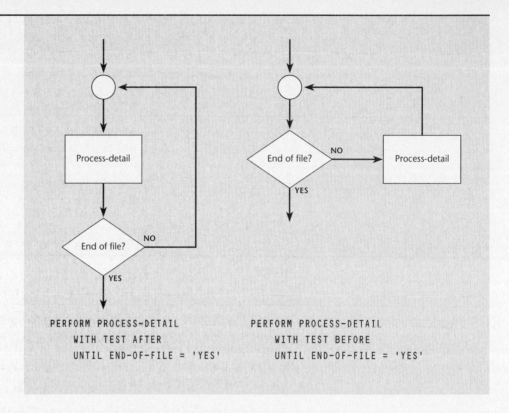

```
PERFORM PROCESS-DETAIL              PERFORM PROCESS-DETAIL
    WITH TEST AFTER                     WITH TEST BEFORE
    UNTIL END-OF-FILE = 'YES'           UNTIL END-OF-FILE = 'YES'
```

to YES, the program continues with the next statement. If it is not equal to YES, then PROCESS-DETAIL is executed, and the process is repeated until END-OF-FILE = 'YES'.

COBOL '85 allows for greater control over the repeated execution of a procedure. If we want to do a procedure and then determine if it should be done again, we use the WITH TEST AFTER option. If we want to determine if a procedure should be done beforehand, then we can either use the TEST BEFORE option or leave the TEST option out altogether. Figure 4-3 presents a flowchart and an example of each of the two TEST options in the PERFORM . . . UNTIL statement.

The In-Line PERFORM in COBOL '85

In the 1985 standard it is also possible to use an *in-line* PERFORM, which does not make reference to a procedure-name. As an example, consider the case in accounting in which we need to form the "sum of the digits" for depreciating an asset over N years, where N has an integer value. We need to form the sum of $1 + 2 + 3 + \ldots + (N - 1) + N$. Thus if N is 5, we have $1 + 2 + 3 + 4 + 5$. Here is a routine for doing this task:

```
MOVE ZERO TO SUM-OF-DIGITS
MOVE 1 TO YEAR-COUNTER
PERFORM UNTIL YEAR-COUNTER > N
    ADD YEAR-COUNTER TO SUM-OF-DIGITS
    ADD 1 TO YEAR-COUNTER
END-PERFORM.
```

Notice the absence of a procedure-name between the words PERFORM and UNTIL. This signifies that the command(s) to be performed follows the basic PERFORM UNTIL statement and is marked by the END-PERFORM terminator.

Thus the two ADD statements constitute the procedure to be executed in the example above. This format of the PERFORM allows for an immediately following "nameless" procedure, in essence. Contrast the above example with the following equivalent one:

```
MOVE ZERO TO SUM-OF-DIGITS
MOVE 1 TO YEAR-COUNTER
PERFORM FORM-SUM UNTIL YEAR-COUNTER > N
       .
       .
       .
FORM-SUM.
   ADD YEAR-COUNTER TO SUM-OF-DIGITS
   ADD 1 TO YEAR-COUNTER.
```

We can see that the in-line PERFORM is more convenient when, as in this example, the procedure is so simple that it does not warrant setting up a separate paragraph.

R   E   V   I   E   W . . . .

1. The COBOL verb used to execute a paragraph and return to the instruction immediately following that command is the _____ verb.

    PERFORM

2. The format of the PERFORM statement that permits conditional execution of the procedure-name depending on the result of a test is the PERFORM . . . _____ .

    UNTIL

3. In COBOL '74 when the PERFORM . . . UNTIL format is used, the condition is tested [before / after / either before or after] the object of PERFORM is executed.

    before

4. In COBOL '85 when the PERFORM . . . UNTIL format is used, the condition is tested [before / after / either before or after] the object of PERFORM is executed.

    either before or after

5. The version of the PERFORM command that does not make reference to a procedure-name, but rather has the commands to be executed immediately follow the PERFORM UNTIL conditional statement, is the _____ PERFORM.

    in-line

. . . .

ARITHMETIC VERBS

COBOL has five arithmetic verbs: ADD, SUBTRACT, MULTIPLY, DIVIDE, and COMPUTE. The first four verbs are used to execute the arithmetic operations corresponding to their respective names. COMPUTE is a general-purpose verb and can be used in lieu of any of the other four, as well as to write more complex operations that combine several arithmetic steps. A rich variety of statement formats will be studied in detail in Chapter 7, "Additional PROCEDURE DIVISION Statements." In this section we present an overview of arithmetic statements and limit our scope to the very basic options.

We begin with the ADD verb and show three formats:

1. <u>ADD</u> literal <u>TO</u> identifier
2. <u>ADD</u> identifier <u>TO</u> identifier
3. <u>ADD</u> two or more literals or identifiers <u>GIVING</u> identifier

The following examples illustrate each of the three formats:

1. `ADD 123 TO TOTAL`
2. `ADD STATE-TAX TO TOTAL-TAX`
3a. `ADD 123 AMOUNT GIVING TOTAL`
3b. `ADD STATE-TAX FED-TAX GIVING TOTAL-TAX`
3c. `ADD 0.05 RATE-1 RATE-2 GIVING RATE`

The result of the additions must always be an identifier. Thus in the first example it would be wrong to attempt to write ADD TOTAL TO 123. The identifier following the TO is incremented. If TOTAL contained a value of 100 before the first ADD, then as a result of the ADD, TOTAL would contain 223.

The GIVING option differs from the TO option because the identifier following the GIVING is not incremented. Instead, its former content is replaced by the result of the addition. Considering example 3a above, if TOTAL contained the value 1000 before the ADD and AMOUNT contained 456, TOTAL will contain 579 after the addition. That is, TOTAL would contain 579 after the addition regardless of what it contained before. Thus the GIVING implies a *replace* operation. In essence, it says, "do the addition and then store the result in the identifier that follows the GIVING."

Having discussed the ADD verb in some detail, we now present simplified formats for the other three verbs by means of examples. Detailed coverage of arithmetic verbs will be found in Chapter 7.

Figure 4-4 presents a number of examples. In each example it should be obvious that the generalized format involves arithmetic literals or identifiers in all cases except where the result field is involved. The result must be an identifier, not a numeric literal. For instance, in the case of the SUBTRACT consider these two examples:

```
SUBTRACT TAX 100 FROM GROSS-PAY
SUBTRACT TAX 100 FROM 1000 GIVING NET-PAY
```

In the first case GROSS-PAY is reduced by the sum of TAX and 100, so the item following FROM must be an identifier. In the second case, because of the presence of GIVING, it is permissible to write FROM 1000 because it is NET-PAY that receives the result. As in the case of the GIVING in the ADD statement, the value of the identifier following the GIVING is replaced, not just "changed."

Referring now to Figure 4-4, note that we have labeled a number of columns with simplified data-names, their respective PICTURE definition, and their initial contents. Thus it is possible to follow the change in the contents of the data fields involved in the illustrated arithmetic statements in detail.

The negative sign is shown as a horizontal bar above the last digit in each signed negative field. For example, the initial value of W is negative 10. Also, the assumed decimal point (V PIC character), is shown as a caret (∧) in each case.

Note a few special cases:

• Example 5 illustrates that a negative result is stored as an absolute value (without sign) if the numeric field does not include the S PICTURE character.

FIGURE 4-4
Examples of the Use of Arithmetic Verbs

	W	X	Y	Z
PICTURE:	S999V99	999V99	999V99	999
INITIAL VALUE:	010,0̄0	090,00	030,00	040
1. ADD X TO Y			120,00	
2. ADD X Y TO Z				160
3. ADD 5 Y GIVING W	035,00			
4. SUBTRACT Y FROM X		060,00		
5. SUBTRACT X FROM Y			060,00	
6. SUBTRACT X Y FROM W	130,0̄0			
7. SUBTRACT W FROM X GIVING Y			100,00	
8. MOVE 10 TO X		010,00		
MULTIPLY X BY Y			300,00	
9. MULTIPLY X BY Y			700,00	
10. DIVIDE Y INTO X		003,00		
11. DIVIDE X INTO Y			000,33	
12. DIVIDE Z INTO 100 GIVING Y			002,50	
13. DIVIDE 12.2 INTO Y GIVING Z				002

- Example 6 illustrates the application of the rule of arithmetic that subtracting from a negative value is equivalent to adding the number to be subtracted to that negative value.

- Example 9 illustrates that truncation will occur if the number is larger than the defined field.

R E V I E W . . . .

1. Complete the following table by entering the numeric result of each arithmetic operation:

	W	X	Y	Z
PICTURE:	99V9	99	99V9	S999V9
INITIAL VALUE:	15,0	10	12,8	100,0
1. ADD W, Y TO X				
2. ADD W, Y GIVING X				
3. SUBTRACT W FROM Y				
4. SUBTRACT W FROM Y GIVING Z				
5. MULTIPLY W BY Y				
6. MULTIPLY X BY Y GIVING Z				
7. DIVIDE X INTO Y				
8. DIVIDE X INTO Y GIVING Z				

1. X = 37   5. Y = $92_\wedge 0$
2. X = 27   6. Z = $128_\wedge 0$
3. Y = $02_\wedge 2$ 7. Y = $1_\wedge 2$
4. Z = $002_\wedge \overline{2}$ 8. Z = $1_\wedge 28$

. . . .

CONDITIONAL STATEMENTS

Conditional statements allow the program to test for a condition and to execute one or more commands selectively, depending on the result. Chapter 5 is dedicated to this subject. Therefore here we provide only a brief introduction to conditional statements.

In the following program segment we determine the appropriate price as follows:

```
IF CUSTOMER-UNITS > 20
    MOVE DISCOUNT-PRICE TO PRICE
ELSE
    MOVE FULL-PRICE TO PRICE.
```

The conditional statement begins with the IF followed by a *conditional expression*. In the example above, the conditional expression is CUSTOMER-UNITS > 20. A conditional expression is either true or false. If it is true, the command that follows the IF statement is executed (MOVE DISCOUNT-PRICE TO PRICE); if it is false, the command that follows the ELSE is executed (MOVE FULL-PRICE TO PRICE).

Although the conditional IF statement often includes the ELSE option, it is not necessary to include the option in the command. In the absence of the ELSE option, when the condition tested by the IF statement is true, the command that follows the IF is executed. When it is false, that command is not executed and program execution continues with the next sentence in the program. For example:

```
MOVE FULL-PRICE TO PRICE.
IF  CUSTOMER-UNITS > 20
    MOVE DISCOUNT-PRICE TO PRICE.
MULTIPLY CUSTOMER-UNITS BY PRICE . . .
```

We conclude this introductory presentation by considering the AT END conditional statement, as in

```
READ CUSTOMER-FILE RECORD
    AT END MOVE 'YES' TO END-OF-FILE.
```

The AT END is a specialized conditional expression that really means "IF END" and refers to the condition of reading the end-of-file record. The specialized AT END conditional statement is used only with the READ verb and specifies what is to be done when our end-of-file type of record is read. In the sample program we MOVE 'YES' TO END-OF-FILE. Just as in any other conditional statement, the period is important, although in this particular example it happens that the AT END statement is also the last statement in the paragraph.

R E V I E W . . . .

1. Whereas the AT END clause is an example of a specialized conditional expression, more general conditional expressions make use of the _____ verb.

IF

2. If the condition specified in the IF clause is met, then program execution continues with [the statement that directly follows the IF / the next sentence / the next paragraph].

the statement that directly follows the IF

3. If the condition specified in the IF clause is not met, then program execution continues with [the statement that directly follows the IF / the next sentence / the next paragraph].

the next sentence

4. The option used in conjunction with the IF clause that makes it possible to execute one of two alternative statements is the _____ option.

ELSE

•   •

SAMPLE PROCEDURE DIVISION

The sample program task involves reading records from an employee file and producing a report such as the one illustrated in Figure 4-5. This is the same report for which the DATA DIVISION was prepared in the preceding chapter, and presented in Figure 3-8. Each record in the employee file contains the individual's name (columns 1–15), a code classifying the person as a man or woman (column 16), and the annual salary (columns 17–23), as previously presented in the record layout in Figure 3-3. Should there be an error and a record does not include a valid sex code, then asterisks are printed in the report to highlight the error. The occurrence of such an error is illustrated in Figure 4-5 for the case of the employee named PROUST, K., where a group of asterisks appears in the report line.

A structure chart for the program is presented in Figure 4-6, and a more detailed view of the program logic is presented in the pseudocode in Figure 4-7. As usual, the structure chart portrays the overall processing logic for the programming task, whereas the pseudocode goes into detailed program-oriented descriptions and anticipates the eventual program structure.

The PROCEDURE DIVISION is listed in Figure 4-8. Reviewing the sample output in Figure 4-5, we notice that there is need for a report heading at the beginning of the task, and a report footing, showing the total and average values,

FIGURE 4-5
Sample Salary Report

		ANNUAL SALARY	
EMPLOYEE NAME	MEN		WOMEN
JONES, A.	28,200.00		
ANDERSON, P.	22,000.00		
ROBERTS, M.			25,000.00
PROUST, K.	******		
NICHOLSON, J.	29,600.00		
PHILLIPS, P.			28,500.00
WORK, A.			30,000.00
TOTAL	$79,800.00		$83,500.00
AVERAGE	$26,600.00		$27,833.33

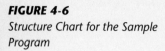

FIGURE 4-6
Structure Chart for the Sample Program

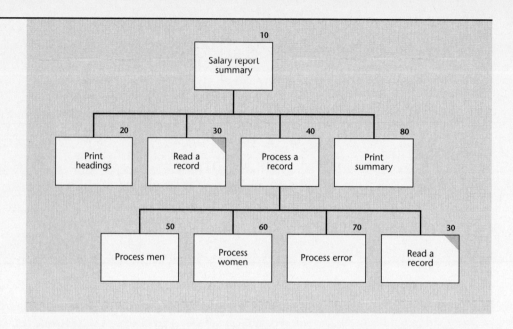

at the end of the task. Corresponding to these two needs, we see the two paragraphs, 20-PRINT-REPORT-HEADINGS and 80-PRINT-REPORT-FOOTINGS. Between these two paragraphs the program logic involves reading employee records, identifying them as pertaining to one of three categories, and processing each category in a separate paragraph. Specifically, employee records are identified as referring to a record whose EMPLOYEE-SEX-CODE meets the MALE, FEMALE, and ERROR-SEX-CODE conditions defined by the respective 88-level condition names. (You may want to refer to Figure 3-9 for a brief explanation of 88-level condition-names in the DATA DIVISION.) Each category is processed in a separate paragraph: 50-PROCESS-MEN, 60-PROCESS-FEMALE, and 70-PROCESS-ERROR-CODE. The content of each of these three paragraphs is simple enough that we could have incorporated their statements into the 40-PROCESS-EMPLOYEE-RECORD paragraph, as in this example:

```
40-PROCESS-EMPLOYEE-RECORD.
    IF  MALE
        MOVE EMPLOYEE-SALARY TO REPORT-MEN-SALARY
        MOVE ZERO TO REPORT-WOMEN-SALARY
        ADD 1 TO NO-OF-MEN
        ADD EMPLOYEE-SALARY TO MEN-TOTAL-SALARY.
    IF  FEMALE...
        etc.
```

However, each employee category represents a distinct logical function in the program and therefore it is a good idea to separate such functions into distinct modules (paragraphs). By this approach it is much easier to change the program if different processing logic is needed for different employee categories in the future. Such a provision is associated with good program design and structure, and will be discussed in Chapters 6 and 14.

The program illustrates use of one more figurative constant, ALL. In 70-PROCESS-ERROR-CODE notice the statement MOVE ALL '*' TO REPORT-ERROR-CODE. The ALL figurative constant signifies that the receiving field should be filled with the nonnumeric literal '*'. This is a convenient way of specifying the move of as many repetitions of the literal as the size of the receiving field in the MOVE statement will allow. Recall that a statement such as MOVE SPACES TO A is

FIGURE 4-7

Pseudocode for the Salary Report Program

PROGRAM-SUMMARY

    Open Files

    Perform Print-Headings

    Perform Read-Record

    Perform Process-Record until no more records

    Perform Print Summary

    Close Files

    Stop

PRINT-HEADINGS

    Write two lines on top of new page and double space after the second line

READ-RECORD

    Read a Record

    If it is the end of the file set an indicator on

PROCESS-RECORD

    If the record represents a man

        Perform Process-Man

    If the record represents a woman

        Perform Process-Woman

    If the record represents neither man nor woman

        Perform Process-Error

    Print a report line

    Perform Read-Record

PROCESS-MAN

    Add 1 to number of men

    Add the salary to the total salary for men

    Move the salary data to the men's column

PROCESS-WOMAN

    Add 1 to number of women

    Add the salary to the total salary for women

    Move the salary data to the women's column

PROCESS-ERROR

    Move asterisks to the salary fields

PRINT-SUMMARY

    Print the accumulated total salaries

    Compute the averages (e.g., divide number of men into total salary of men)

    Print the averages

FIGURE 4-8

PROCEDURE DIVISION for the
Salary Report Program

```
    PROCEDURE DIVISION.
*
  10-PROGRAM-SUMMARY.
        OPEN INPUT   EMPLOYEE-FILE
             OUTPUT REPORT-FILE
*
        PERFORM 20-PRINT-REPORT-HEADINGS
*
        PERFORM 30-READ-EMPLOYEE-RECORD
*
        PERFORM 40-PROCESS-EMPLOYEE-RECORD
                  UNTIL END-OF-EMPLOYEE-FILE
*
        PERFORM 80-PRINT-REPORT-FOOTINGS
*
        CLOSE EMPLOYEE-FILE
              REPORT-FILE
*
        STOP RUN.
*
  20-PRINT-REPORT-HEADINGS.
        WRITE PRINT-LINE FROM HEADING-1
              AFTER ADVANCING PAGE
        WRITE PRINT-LINE FROM HEADING-2
              AFTER ADVANCING 2 LINES
        MOVE SPACES TO PRINT-LINE
        WRITE PRINT-LINE AFTER ADVANCING 2 LINES.
*
  30-READ-EMPLOYEE-RECORD.
        READ EMPLOYEE-FILE RECORD
            AT END MOVE 'YES' TO END-OF-FILE-TEST.
*
  40-PROCESS-EMPLOYEE-RECORD.
        IF MALE    PERFORM 50-PROCESS-MEN.
*
        IF FEMALE PERFORM 60-PROCESS-FEMALE.
*
        IF ERROR-SEX-CODE PERFORM 70-PROCESS-ERROR-CODE.
*
        MOVE EMPLOYEE-NAME TO REPORT-EMPL-NAME
        WRITE PRINT-LINE FROM REPORT-DETAIL-LINE
              AFTER ADVANCING 1 LINE
*
        MOVE SPACES TO REPORT-DETAIL-LINE
*
        PERFORM 30-READ-EMPLOYEE-RECORD.
*
  50-PROCESS-MEN.
        MOVE EMPLOYEE-SALARY TO REPORT-MEN-SALARY
        MOVE ZERO TO REPORT-WOMEN-SALARY
*
```

FIGURE 4-8
PROCEDURE DIVISION for the
Salary Report Program (continued)

```
        ADD 1 TO NO-OF-MEN
        ADD EMPLOYEE-SALARY TO MEN-TOTAL-SALARY.
    *
     60-PROCESS-FEMALE.
        MOVE EMPLOYEE-SALARY TO REPORT-WOMEN-SALARY
        MOVE ZERO TO REPORT-MEN-SALARY
    *
        ADD 1 TO NO-OF-WOMEN
        ADD EMPLOYEE-SALARY TO WOMEN-TOTAL-SALARY.
    *
     70-PROCESS-ERROR-CODE.
        MOVE ALL '*' TO REPORT-ERROR-CODE.
    *

     80-PRINT-REPORT-FOOTINGS.
        MOVE MEN-TOTAL-SALARY TO REPORT-TOT-MEN-SALARY
        MOVE WOMEN-TOTAL-SALARY TO REPORT-TOT-WOMEN-SALARY

        WRITE PRINT-LINE FROM REPORT-TOTALS-LINE
                AFTER ADVANCING 3 LINES
     *
        DIVIDE NO-OF-MEN INTO MEN-TOTAL-SALARY
                GIVING REPORT-AVG-MEN-SALARY
        DIVIDE NO-OF-WOMEN INTO WOMEN-TOTAL-SALARY
                GIVING REPORT-AVG-WOMEN-SALARY
     *
        WRITE PRINT-LINE FROM REPORT-AVERAGES-LINE
                AFTER ADVANCING 2 LINES.
```

a specialized version of this case, and is equivalent to saying MOVE ALL ' ' TO A, where there is a blank space between the quotes. Thus the ALL can do with any literal what we can do with other figurative constants (such as ZERO and SPACE).

We complete our description of the sample program by presenting a detailed flowchart in Figure 4-9. Normally, a structure chart and a pseudocode are sufficient tools for developing the program. In this case we also show a flowchart as a more detailed aid for the beginning COBOL programmer. Learning to read flowcharts is a useful skill because detailed flowcharts were a strong tradition in the past, and many "old" programs are documented by accompanying flowcharts rather than by structure charts or pseudocode.

SUMMARY

In this chapter we first presented and discussed the set of conventions by which COBOL programming options are presented. This involved such matters as the use of uppercase words, lowercase words, underlining, braces, brackets, and the ellipsis. We then reviewed the functions of the IDENTIFICATION DIVISION, ENVIRONMENT DIVISION, and DATA DIVISION in a COBOL program.

The function of the IDENTIFICATION DIVISION is to supply information about the program. The first and only required paragraph is the PROGRAM-ID, which includes the program-name.

FIGURE 4-9

Complete Flowchart for the Salary Report Program (The numbers in the upper right-hand corner of some entries serve as cross-references between modules and their respective blocks.)

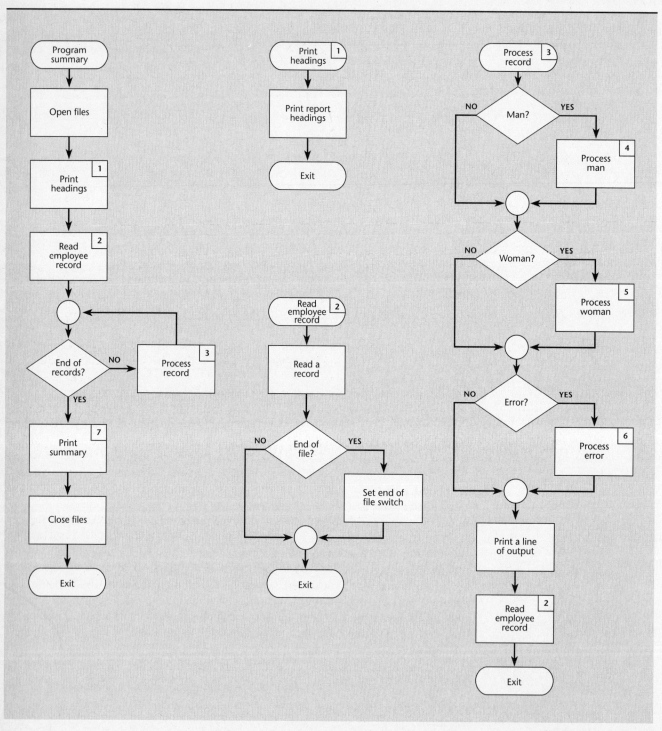

(continued on next page)

The function of the ENVIRONMENT DIVISION is to describe the computer system on which the program has been compiled and executed. Although this division is optional in COBOL '85, the information that is supplied is very important and necessary for most programs. Two sections were included in the

FIGURE 4-9

Complete Flowchart for the Salary Report Program (continued)

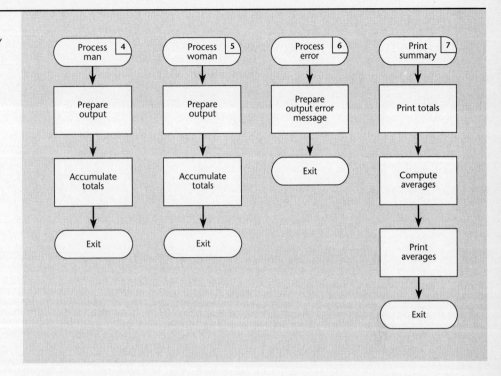

brief chapter example of an ENVIRONMENT DIVISION: the CONFIGURATION SECTION and the INPUT-OUTPUT SECTION. The CONFIGURATION SECTION contains the SOURCE-COMPUTER and OBJECT-COMPUTER paragraphs. The INPUT-OUTPUT SECTION includes the FILE-CONTROL paragraph.

The DATA DIVISION was covered in some detail in the preceding chapter, in addition to being reviewed in this chapter. It serves to define files and their records, and working-storage fields. The FD designation is required at the beginning of each file description. Each file description then includes the name of the file and the name of the record in the file. The level-number assigned to each record as a whole is 01, with other numbers then assigned to the fields in the record according to the data structure.

Following the reviews of the first three divisions of any COBOL program, the chapter focused on the study of the PROCEDURE DIVISION, and specifically, on the use of various verbs. In the category of file input and output, we studied the OPEN and CLOSE verbs, the READ verb, and the WRITE verb. Uses of the MOVE statement were then described, followed by study of the PERFORM and the associated PERFORM . . . UNTIL option.

The use of arithmetic verbs in COBOL then was described briefly. Examples of using the ADD, SUBTRACT, MULTIPLY, and DIVIDE verbs in arithmetic operations were studied.

Next, we included a section on the use of conditional statements in the PROCEDURE DIVISION. The key verb is the IF, followed by a conditional expression. The ELSE option is often included, but it is not required. In the absence of the ELSE option, if the conditional expression is false, then program execution continues with the next sentence in the program. The next chapter is devoted to further study of conditions and conditional statements.

The final section of this chapter presented and discussed the PROCEDURE DIVISION for the employee salary-report programming task for which the DATA DIVISION was written in the preceding chapter. Taken together, we have a complete programming example for the task.

EXERCISES

4.1 This exercise involves a somewhat expanded version of the sample program in Chapter 2. As before, the data are a file of customer records, with each record containing a customer name and number of units sold of a particular product:

COLUMNS	FIELD
1–13	Customer name
14–16	Units sold — an integer field
17–80	Unused by this program

Sample input is as follows:

```
ADAMS        100
BROWN        075
GROVER       030
MOORE        025
PETERSON     060
WILLIAMS     010
```

The program will read the records in this file and produce as output a report as shown in the following example:

```
CUSTOMER NAME      UNITS SOLD    NET SALES

ADAMS                 100         950.00
BROWN                  75         712.50
GROVER                 30         285.00
MOORE                  25         237.50
PETERSON               60         570.00
WILLIAMS               10         100.00


TOTAL                 300        2855.00
```

The NET SALES column in the output results from the following computational basis: If the number of units sold is 20 or fewer, the unit price is $10.00. If the number of units sold is greater than 20, the unit price is discounted to $9.50. The net sales value then is computed by multiplying the number of units sold by the appropriate unit price.

a. Construct a structure chart for the programming task.

b. Write pseudocode.

c. Write, compile, and execute a complete program.

4.2 A file contains data on the number of vehicles passing a certain point on the highway. Each record contains a whole number in columns 1–4 that corresponds to one day's traffic. We are interested in reading the data file and producing a report such as that shown below. For each week we list the daily data and a statistical summary for the week. The last week of data may be a partial week—that is, fewer than seven days. The output format is illustrated by the following, with the report for each week being printed on a new page:

```
DAILY TRAFFIC REPORT
   WEEK 03
   2,345
   1,000
     500
   2,000
   1,400
   1,331
     809
MINIMUM =    500  MAXIMUM = 2,345 WEEKLY TOTAL =  9,385
```

Note that the program should be able to compute the minimum and maximum value for each week.

4.3 Write a COBOL program to read a file of records containing data about accounts-receivable and to print a summary of the overdue and forthcoming receivables. An extended description follows, including variable names and a partial DATA DIVISION.

The input consists of a set of records having the following content:

COLUMNS	COBOL NAME
1–6	ACCOUNT-NO
7–8	FILLER (blank)
9–11	DAY-DUE
12–13	YEAR-DUE
14–21	AMOUNT-DUE
22–80	FILLER

The records are sorted in ascending sequence on ACCOUNT-NO, and there should be only one record per account. The program checks for correct sequencing. Records out of sequence are to be printed as shown on the sample output below. Note that the data on such records are excluded from the total.

DATA DIVISION entries are provided below, except that you are asked to write WORKING-STORAGE entries to provide the header with the words STATUS, NUMBER OF ACCOUNTS, and DOLLAR VALUE, as shown in the sample output at the end of the description of this assignment.

```
DATA DIVISION.
FILE SECTION.
FD  REC-FILE LABEL RECORDS OMITTED
            DATA RECORD RECEIV-RECORD.
01  RECEIV-RECORD.
    02   ACCOUNT-NO          PIC X(6).
    02   FILLER              PIC XX.
    02   DAY-DUE             PIC 999.
    02   YEAR-DUE            PIC 99.
    02   AMOUNT-DUE          PIC 9(6)V99.
    02   FILLER              PIC X(59).
FD  REPORT-FILE LABEL RECORD OMITTED
            DATA RECORD REPORT-RECORD.
01  REPORT-RECORD            PIC X(132).
```

```
WORKING-STORAGE SECTION.
01  END-OF-DATA-FLAG              PIC X VALUE 'NO'.
    88  END-OF-DATA                     VALUE 'YES'.
01  TODAYS-DATE.
    02  THIS-YEAR                 PIC 99.
    02  TODAY                     PIC 999.
*
01  PREVIOUS-ACCT-NO             PIC X(6).
01  NO-OVERDUE                   PIC 9(4).
01  TOTAL-OVERDUE                PIC 9(7)V99.
01  NO-RECEIVABLE                PIC 9(4).
01  TOTAL-RECEIVABLE             PIC 9(7)V99.
01  ERROR-MESSAGE.
    02  FILLER                   PIC X(23)
        VALUE 'ACCOUNT OUT OF SEQUENCE'.
    02  FILLER                   PIC X(3) VALUE SPACES.
    02  ERROR-NUMBER             PIC X(6).
01  REPORT-LINE.
    02  STATUS-TYPE              PIC X(13).
    02  FILLER                   PIC X(10) VALUE SPACES.
    02  HOW-MANY                 PIC Z(3)99.
    02  FILLER                   PIC X(15) VALUE SPACES.
    02  DOLLAR-VALUE             PIC $$$,$$$,$$9.99.
```

The day on which the account is due is expressed as a 3-digit number (Julian calendar). Thus January 10 is 010 and February 28 is 059.

Use the ACCEPT verb (to be discussed in Chapter 7) to access today's date by writing the following at the beginning of the PROCEDURE DIVISION:

```
ACCEPT TODAYS-DATE FROM DAY
```

The statement above will fill the field TODAYS-DATE with the last two digits of the year in THIS-YEAR and the 3-digit day value in TODAY. Notice that in the WORKING-STORAGE SECTION we have defined the following fields:

```
01  TODAYS-DATE.
    02  THIS-YEAR   PIC 99.
    02  TODAY       PIC 999.
```

Thus if you ran your program on February 18, 1992, as a result of the above ACCEPT statement, THIS-YEAR would contain 92, and TODAY would contain 049.

A few other data-names merit explanation:

PREVIOUS-ACCT-NO stores the previously read account number so that each record can be compared with the preceding one to see that the records are in ascending sequence. Initially, PREVIOUS-ACCT-NO is set equal to zero. NO-OVERDUE stores the number of overdue accounts, TOTAL-OVERDUE stores the total dollar value of overdue accounts, NO-RECEIVABLE stores the number of accounts that are not overdue, and TOTAL-RECEIVABLE stores the total value of accounts that are not overdue.

SAMPLE INPUT FOR DAY 101 OF 1991

```
012345  0909200010000
023467  1509100020020
001234  1409100030030
123456  1309200040040
```

SAMPLE OUTPUT

```
ACCOUNT OUT OF SEQUENCE 001234
```

STATUS	NUMBER OF ACCOUNTS	DOLLAR VALUE
OVERDUE	02	$300.20
RECEIVABLE	01	$400.40
TOTALS	03	$700.60

5

Conditions and Conditional Statements

COMPUTER PROCESSORS *derive their logic capability from their ability to test for the truth or falsity of conditions. You can appreciate the fundamental nature of this ability by considering what computer programs would be like without conditional logic. It would be impossible to write most computer programs without the use of conditional instructions.*

The COBOL language recognizes the importance of this need and provides a rich set of conditions and conditional statements.

In general, a **condition** *is an expression that is either true or false in a particular circumstance; that is, the condition either holds or it does not hold. You have already studied some conditional statements in preceding chapters.*

In this chapter you will expand your knowledge of conditions and conditional statements. You will begin with a study of the general rules associated with use of the IF statement. Then you will study four specific types of conditional statements that involve use of the IF: (1) relation conditions; (2) condition-name conditions; (3) nested conditions; and (4) compound conditions.

THE IF STATEMENT

In general, the IF statement is used by the programmer to arrange for the conditional execution of one or more statements. A test is made to determine whether or not a condition is true. Depending on the result of that test, one or more statements may or may not be executed. The IF statement is very common, and it is used in a variety of program statements. In this section we will discuss simple IF statements, while in subsequent sections we discuss more complex IF statements. Still, use of even the simple IF comes in a variety of forms.

SIMPLE IF STATEMENT

IF condition-is-true

      executable statement(s).

An example of a simple IF statement is

```
IF  EXAM-SCORE  =  100
        ADD 1 TO PERFECT-SCORES.
ADD EXAM-SCORE TO EXAM-SCORE-TOTAL
```

In the above the condition-is-true test is EXAM-SCORE = 100. This is one of several types of conditions that can be tested with the IF and will be discussed later in this chapter. Specifically, it is a relational condition. Execution of the statement ADD 1 TO PERFECT-SCORES, is conditional on the condition being true, as indicated in the following flowchart:

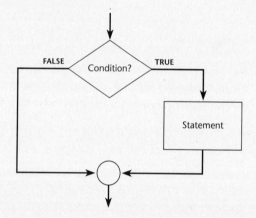

If the condition is not true (false), then the ADD 1 ... statement is not executed; it is bypassed. *The period at the end of the ADD 1 ... statement is significant.* It terminates the scope of the IF statement. Thus, because the statement ADD EXAM-SCORE ... follows the period, it is outside the scope of the IF and it will be executed unconditionally (regardless of what happened within the IF). To see the significance of the period at the end of the IF statement, consider the following example.

```
IF  HOURS-WORKED  >  40
        SUBTRACT 40 FROM HOURS-WORKED GIVING OVER-HOURS
        ADD OVER-HOURS TO TOTAL-OVER-HOURS
        PERFORM COMPUTE-OVERTIME-PAY.
PERFORM COMPUTE-PAY
```

This example illustrates that the scope of a simple IF statement may encompass several statements. Thus, if the condition HOURS-WORKED > 40 is true, three statements will be executed: SUBTRACT ..., ADD ..., and PERFORM. The period at the end of COMPUTE-OVERTIME-PAY terminates the scope of the IF statement, and as a result PERFORM COMPUTE-PAY is executed unconditionally.

A slightly more advanced version of the IF allows us to write *IF-ELSE* types of statements:

SIMPLE IF ... ELSE STATEMENT

IF condition-is-true

     executable statement(s)

ELSE

     executable statement(s).

An IF statement may be written to specify that if a condition is true, one or more statements should be executed, but if it is false, then one or more *other* statements should be executed.

The following flowchart portrays the execution of an IF ... ELSE statement:

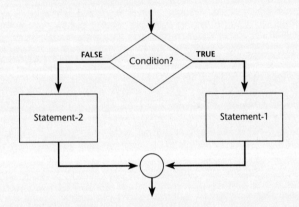

If the condition being tested is true, then we execute one set of statements; if the condition is false, we execute another set of statements. Consider the following example:

```
IF  EXAM-SCORE  =  100
    ADD 1 TO PERFECT-SCORES
ELSE
    ADD 1 TO NORMAL-SCORES.
ADD EXAM-SCORE TO EXAM-SCORE-TOTAL
```

In this example we will ADD 1 either to PERFECT-SCORES or NORMAL-SCORES. Again, the period is significant in defining the *scope* (termination) of the IF statement. Thus, the last statement, ADD EXAM-SCORE ..., will be executed regardless of the truth or falsity of the condition because it is written after the period. A common programming error is to omit the period that terminates the IF statement. In the above example omitting the period would cause the last statement to be executed only when the condition was false!

There can be one or more statements executed in either or both of the "legs" of the IF ... ELSE statement, as in this example:

```
IF  HOURS-WORKED  >  40
    SUBTRACT 40 FROM HOURS-WORKED GIVING OVER-HOURS
    ADD OVER-HOURS TO TOTAL-OVER-HOURS
    PERFORM COMPUTE-OVERTIME-PAY.
ELSE
    PERFORM COMPUTE-REGULAR-PAY.
```

The condition being tested in an IF statement may be of a variety of types. In the following section we discuss one of the most common forms, relation conditions.

R E V I E W . . . .

1. When the condition specified in the IF clause is met, then program execution continues with [the statement that directly follows the IF / the next sentence / the next paragraph].

the statement that directly follows the IF

2. The option used in conjunction with an IF clause that makes it possible to execute one of two alternative statements without having to use two separate IF conditionals is the _____ option.

ELSE

3. In the absence of the ELSE option, when the condition specified in the IF clause is not met, then program execution continues with [the statement that directly follows the IF / the next sentence / the next paragraph].

the next sentence

. . . .

RELATION CONDITIONS

Relation conditions are concerned with comparisons between two items. The items being compared (the *comparands*) may be one of three things: identifier, literal, and arithmetic expression. The type of comparison is indicated by the *relational operator*, which may be in the form of words or symbols. The general format for forming relational conditions is

$$
\underline{IF}
\begin{Bmatrix}
\text{identifier -1} \\
\text{literal -1} \\
\text{arithmetic -expression -1}
\end{Bmatrix}
\begin{Bmatrix}
\text{IS [\underline{NOT}] \underline{LESS} THAN} \\
\text{IS [\underline{NOT}] <} \\
\text{IS [\underline{NOT}] \underline{EQUAL} TO} \\
\text{IS [\underline{NOT}] =} \\
\text{IS [\underline{NOT}] \underline{GREATER} THAN} \\
\text{IS [\underline{NOT}] >} \\
\text{IS \underline{GREATER} THAN \underline{OR EQUAL} TO} \\
\text{IS > =} \\
\text{IS \underline{LESS} THAN \underline{OR EQUAL} TO} \\
\text{IS < =}
\end{Bmatrix}
\begin{Bmatrix}
\text{identifier -2} \\
\text{literal -2} \\
\text{arithmetic -expression -2}
\end{Bmatrix}
$$

The last four operators above (greater than or equal, and less than or equal) were added in the 1985 standard, so they cannot be used with earlier compilers.

Studying the format, we see that we can compare one identifier to another, and one arithmetic expression to another. Comparing one literal to another does not make sense since we would already know the "answer." Thus, writing IF 22 > 25, or IF 'MARY' = 'ANN' violates common sense and the rules of the language. The following examples illustrate use of the above general format:

```
IF AMOUNT IS LESS THAN 100
IF AMOUNT < 100
```

```
IF BALANCE IS NOT EQUAL TO CREDIT-LIMIT
IF BALANCE IS NOT = CREDIT-LIMIT
IF HOURS - 40 > ZERO
IF QUANTITY GREATER OR EQUAL MAX-SIZE
IF QUANTITY > = MAX-SIZE
```

As these examples illustrate, one can use either the symbolic (<, =, >) or the verbal (LESS, EQUAL, GREATER) operators; they are equivalent forms, and it is a matter of personal preference as to which is used.

The fifth example above illustrates use of an arithmetic expression (HOURS-40). Rules for forming and evaluating such arithmetic expressions will be discussed in Chapter 7, in connection with the COMPUTE arithmetic verb.

The meaning of relational tests involving numeric values is obvious. If RATE-1 and RATE-2 are numeric fields, the conditional statement IF RATE-1 > RATE-2 PERFORM PAR-A leads to PAR-A whenever the numeric (algebraic) value of RATE-1 is greater than the numeric value of RATE-2, regardless of the field size. In nonnumeric comparisons, however, certain things are not so obvious. A comparison involving two alphabetic items proceeds from left to right in pairs of characters until the first unequal pair occurs. Thus, in comparing

| T | H | O | R | P | to | T | H | A | L | E | S |

the first pair of characters to be compared involves two T characters, the second pair involves two H's, but then the first field is determined to be greater than the second when the O-A pair is compared. The size of the fields in this case is irrelevant. But suppose we are comparing the following two fields:

| S | A | N | D | E | R | S | | S | A | N | D | E | R | S | O | N |

In this case the first field is considered to be smaller in value. The shorter field is treated as if it had enough trailing blanks to make it equal in size to the longer field. Then, when a blank is compared to the letter "O" in the eighth field position, the first field is determined to be smaller in value.

As a third case of alphabetic comparison, consider this:

| S | M | I | T | H | | S | M | I | T | H | | |

These two items are considered equal, even though their field size is unequal. In this case the first field is treated as if it had enough trailing blanks to be equal in size to the second field.

Now consider the following two alphanumeric fields:

| X | A | - | 1 | 2 | 3 | | X | . | B | - | 3 |

In this case determining the "larger" of the two fields is not as obvious. Still, these are characters and can be compared in pairs as before. For this purpose, we rely on the *collating sequence* of a computer system. The collating sequence is simply a defined sequence that states the relative "size" of each possible character in a computer's storage. For example, in the widely used IBM large mainframe computers, the EBCDIC collating sequence for some selected characters is as indicated by the following ascending order of listing:

> blank
> . (period or decimal point)
> (
> + (plus sign)
>)
> – (hyphen or minus)
> / (stroke)
> , (comma)
> ' (single quote)
> " (double quote)
> letters A–Z
> numbers 0–9

Thus, when comparing 3-A/ and Z/9K, the 3-A/ is the greater. In any collating sequence there is a smallest and a largest character. COBOL recognizes that constant fact about collating sequences and provides two special figurative constants as a means of referencing them:

> LOW-VALUE
>
> LOW-VALUES
>
> HIGH-VALUE
>
> HIGH-VALUES

In the above the singular and the plural versions have identical meanings. Thus, LOW-VALUE and LOW-VALUES reference the smallest character. Consider an example:

```
02  PREVIOUS-ACCOUNT-NO  PIC  X(5).
        .
        .
        .
    MOVE LOW-VALUES TO PREVIOUS-ACCOUNT-NO.
```

The MOVE statement will fill PREVIOUS-ACCOUNT-NO with as many LOW-VALUE characters as the field size (5, due to the PIC string). It should be noted that LOW-VALUE does not refer to the blank space. Typically, the smallest character is some other character formed by a particular configuration of binary bits, as will be explained in Chapter 16. In fact, in the ASCII collating sequence, the blank space is the 32nd character; there are 31 others that are "smaller" in value than the blank space.

The HIGH-VALUE figurative constant defines the other end of the collating sequence. For example, if we write

```
MOVE HIGH-VALUES TO PREVIOUS-ACCOUNT-NO
```

then any comparison such as

```
IF CURRENT-ACCOUNT-NO < PREVIOUS-ACCOUNT-NO
```

will be true, unless CURRENT-ACCOUNT-NO also contains the HIGH-VALUE character.

There are several collating sequences in use, and one should be aware of the possible differences in program results arising from differences in collating sequences. The standard one is the American Standard Code for Information Interchange (ASCII). The subject of collating sequences and character representation is treated in some detail in Chapter 16.

R E V I E W . . . .

1. Relation conditions are concerned with comparisons between two items. The words or symbols that serve to indicate the type of comparison to be made are called relational _____ .

   > operators

2. As indicated above, relational operators can be in the form of either words or symbols. In the following spaces, enter the symbols that are equivalent to the listed relational operators:

   ```
   _____   LESS THAN
   _____   EQUAL TO
   _____   GREATER THAN
   _____   LESS THAN OR EQUAL TO
   _____   GREATER THAN OR EQUAL TO
   ```

   > <   =   >   <=   >=

3. Of the following three relation conditions, the one that is invalid as a COBOL expression is the one identified by the letter [a / b / c].

   a. IF GROSS-PAY IS GREATER THAN 99 . . .

   b. IF 100 < ORDER-AMT . . .

   c. IF 500 > 400 . . .

   > c

4. An ordering that defines the relative rank of all the valid characters in a computer system is referred to as the _____ for the system.

   > collating sequence

5. The smallest-valued character in the collating sequence is referenced by the reserved COBOL word LOW-VALUE or LOW-VALUES, which is a figurative constant. Similarly, the largest-valued character is referenced by the figurative constant _____ or _____ .

   > HIGH-VALUE; HIGH-VALUES

. . . .

CONDITION-NAME CONDITIONS

As discussed in Chapter 1, figurative constants such as ZERO and SPACE are words that signify constant values. For example, the figurative constants ZERO and SPACES mean values of zero and blanks, respectively. In effect, the use of *condition-names* enables the programmer to define additional specialized figurative constants to be used in condition tests in the COBOL program. We begin by considering an example:

```
01  END-OF-FILE-FLAG   PIC  XXX.
    88  END-OF-FILE    VALUE 'YES'.
```

In this case END-OF-FILE is a condition-name. It signifies the condition of END-OF-FILE-FLAG containing the value 'YES'. The condition is true if that field contains YES; it is false otherwise. The statement IF END-OF-FILE is equivalent to the statement IF END-OF-FILE-FLAG = 'YES'. We define a condition-name representing a specified value in a data field and then we can test if the condition is true. That is, we test as to whether the data field associated with the condition-name contains the value defined by the condition-name.

The use of the condition-name option always is indicated by the special level 88 entry, whose format is

$$88 \text{ data-name} \begin{Bmatrix} \underline{VALUE} \text{ IS} \\ \underline{VALUES} \text{ ARE} \end{Bmatrix} \text{literal-1 } [\underline{THRU} \text{ literal-2}]$$

$$[\text{literal-3 } [\underline{THRU} \text{ literal-4}]] \ldots$$

For example, we can define condition-names for testing whether an employee is male or female based on data in a record:

```
02  EMPLOYEE-SEX-CODE   PIC  X.
    88  MALE              VALUE 'M'.
    88  FEMALE            VALUE 'F'.
```

Based on this data definition, we could write

```
IF  MALE
    PERFORM  PROCESS-MALE-STATISTICS
ELSE
    PERFORM PROCESS-FEMALE-STATISTICS.
```

The above is equivalent to the following, alternate code:

```
IF  EMPLOYEE-SEX-CODE  =  'M'
    PERFORM  PROCESS-MALE-STATISTICS
ELSE
    PERFORM  PROCESS-FEMALE-STATISTICS.
```

Use of condition-names makes the program more self-documenting. It is much easier to understand the meaning of a condition-name such as "MALE" than a code such as "M". The following example provides a more extended illustration of the documentation feature as well as the general use of condition-names.

Suppose that the personnel record used in a company contains the number of years of education, among other things. The information is contained in a field called EDUCATION and is so coded that the number indicates the last school grade completed. Thus a code number less than 12 indicates that the person did not complete high school, 12 indicates a high school graduate, 13-15 indicate some college education, 16 indicates a college graduate, and a number greater than 16 indicates some graduate or postgraduate work. If we wish to process for educational level using these categories, we could write such PROCEDURE DIVISION statements as

```
IF EDUCATION IS LESS THAN 12 . . .
```
or
```
IF EDUCATION IS EQUAL TO 12 . . . etc.
```

However, an alternative is to define condition-names in the DATA DIVISION that will then stand for the indicated values. Thus we can write

```
01   PERSONNEL-DATA.
     02  ID-NUMBER . . .
     02  NAME . . .
     02  ADDRESS . . .
     02  EDUCATION PICTURE IS 99.
         88  LESS-THAN-H-S-GRAD  VALUES ARE 0 THRU 11.
         88  H-S-GRAD           VALUE IS 12.
         88  SOME-COLLEGE       VALUES ARE 13 THRU 15.
         88  COLLEGE-GRAD       VALUE IS 16.
         88  POST-GRAD          VALUES ARE 17 THRU 20.
         88  ERROR-CODE         VALUES ARE 21 THRU 99.
```

Note the use of the THRU option. It allows us to define a condition-name for a range of values. Thus SOME-COLLEGE is true if EDUCATION contains either 13 or 14 or 15. Thus one advantage of using condition-names is that they allow the programmer to write complex tests in simple form in the PROCEDURE DIVISION.

The use of condition-names improves the readability of a computer program and also makes it easier to change programs. Statements such as IF EDUCATION < 12 and IF SEX-CODE = 'M' require that we remember the arbitrary meaning of the symbolic codes. Their equivalent condition-names, however, are self-documenting when reference is made to LESS-THAN-H-S-GRAD or MALE. In terms of program changes, suppose that we decide to change a code from 1 to 2. In the absence of having used a condition-name, we would have to search the entire PROCEDURE DIVISION to make sure that every instance of the use of this code is changed. If, however, a condition-name has been used, all we have to do is to change the definition of the condition-name from VALUE IS 1 to VALUE IS 2 in the DATA DIVISION.

Next, we discuss another important factor in using condition-names that has to do with the choice of the PIC definition. Let us consider an example:

```
02   EMPLOYEE-CODE      PIC  9.
     88   MALE          VALUE  1.
     88   FEMALE        VALUE  2.
     88   ERROR-SEX-CODE  VALUES ARE ZERO, 3 THRU 9.
```

This example illustrates a potential programming error. One would reason that since EMPLOYEE-CODE is a one-digit numeric field and since MALE and FEMALE account for the 1 and 2 values, ERROR-SEX-CODE correctly covers all other possibilities. However, this is not necessarily true. The PIC 9 specification does not mean that the field must contain numeric data. As we explained in Chapter 4 in conjunction with discussion of the MOVE statement, a PIC 9 field may contain nonnumeric data. So let us write a broader condition-name that covers all possibilities of an error code. Here is a rewritten specification:

```
02   EMPLOYEE-CODE      PIC  X.
     88   MALE          VALUE  '1'.
     88   FEMALE        VALUE  '2'.
     88   ERROR-SEX-CODE  VALUES ARE LOW-VALUES THRU ZERO,
                          '3' THRU HIGH-VALUES.
```

In the above program segment we allow for the possibility that EMPLOYEE-CODE is not a numeric field in the quantitative sense. The code values are simply characters that identify each employee; they are not measures of quantity. Thus a code of 2 is not a larger value than a code of 1; they are simply different values. Recognizing the nominal nature of the code, it makes more sense to use PIC X rather than PIC 9, and then the 88-level condition-name can be used to capture all error cases. Specifically, we used the LOW-VALUES figurative constant, which refers to the smallest character in the collating sequence, and the HIGH-VALUES, which refers to the highest value. This approach would "sense" any incorrect value in the field. For a review on the LOW-VALUES and HIGH-VALUES figurative constants refer to the preceding section of this chapter, on relation conditions.

As a last point related to the example above, we should notice the use of nonnumeric literals such as '1', '2', and '3'. For example, the MALE condition-name refers to EMPLOYEE-CODE having the character 1 as its content. The PIC X specification defines the field as alphanumeric and we should stay consistent with that definition when using literals. It would not be correct to define VALUE 1 (without quotes) in conjunction with the PIC X specification.

Despite the preceding discussion, it is common practice to use numeric definitions for fields containing such codes as EMPLOYEE-CODE in the above example. The reason that this practice works is that it is typical to test data for correctness when the data are added to a file. For example, we could assume that a "class" test has been performed (as will be discussed in Chapter 8) such as IF EMPLOYEE-CODE IS NOT NUMERIC.... Such class tests can ascertain that the data are indeed numeric, and therefore condition-names that apply to the range 0–9 are a valid programming practice.

R E V I E W . . . .

1. An entry in which a condition-name is defined is always assigned the level-number _____ (number).

                                                                                                88

2. Suppose that for the data-name MARITAL-STATUS the possible values are 1 = married, 2 = divorced, 3 = widowed, 4 = single, and all other values are errors. Assuming numeric data, write suitable 88-level entries to define condition-names for

   a. condition of being or having been married

   b. condition of being single

   c. condition of error code.

   ```
   03  MARITAL-STATUS PICTURE 9.
       88 _____ .
       88 _____ .
       88 _____ .
   ```

                                        a. IS-OR-WAS-MARRIED VALUES ARE 1 THRU 3.
                                                         b. SINGLE VALUE IS 4.
                                           c. ERROR-CODE VALUES ARE ZERO 5 THRU 9.

3. Given that a numeric code is used to identify categories rather than quantities in condition-name descriptions, then the preferred PICTURE for such a one-digit code is [PIC 9 / PIC X].

                                                                                              PIC X

4. When PIC X specification is used for a data item used for condition-names, then a condition represented by the numeric code 3 correctly has the defined value [VALUE 3 / VALUE '3'].

                                                                                          VALUE '3'

5. Suppose that for a PIC X field, a value other than 1, 2, or 3 is invalid. Complete the following statement to write a condition-name that defines the condition of invalid.

```
88  INVALID-DATA VALUES ARE _____

    _____ .
```

LOW-VALUE THRU ZERO
4 THRU HIGH-VALUE

. . . .

THE SET VERB FOR CONDITION-NAMES

COBOL '85 provides for a convenient way to move data into fields for which condition-names have been defined. The 88-level condition-name feature of COBOL is very meaningful for conducting tests as to whether a condition is true. But in COBOL '74 there is something lacking with respect to moving values that correspond to defined condition-names. Consider this example:

```
01  TOTAL-CREDIT-HOURS    PIC 999.
01  STUDENT-CLASS-CODE     PIC X.
    88  FRESHMAN           VALUE   '1'
    88  SOPHOMORE          VALUE   '2'.
    .
    .
    .
    IF  TOTAL-CREDIT-HOURS < 33
        MOVE '1' TO STUDENT-CLASS-CODE
    ELSE
        MOVE '2' TO STUDENT-CLASS-CODE.
```

In the above IF example a statement like MOVE '1' TO STUDENT-CLASS-CODE does not take advantage of the 88 FRESHMAN condition-name specification. But consider the following program revision that uses the specialized SET verb:

```
IF  TOTAL-CREDITS < 33
    SET FRESHMAN TO TRUE
```

The SET verb above has been used to take advantage of the convenient condition-names provided by the 88-level items.

The general format of the SET verb for this purpose is given below. Other uses of the SET verb are presented in Chapter 19, on table-searching features.

```
SET {condition-name-1} . . . TO TRUE
```

In this format the SET verb specifies that the value defined in the condition-name VALUE clause is to be moved to the field associated with the condition-name definition. If a range of values is specified, then the first value is moved, as in the following example.

```
01  STUDENT-CLASS-CODE     PIC X.
    88 UNDERGRADUATE        VALUES ARE '1' '2' '3' '4'.
    88 GRADUATE             VALUES ARE '5' THRU '8'.
```

Use of SET UNDERGRADUATE TO TRUE then is equivalent to saying MOVE '1' TO STUDENT-CLASS-CODE. As the example above illustrates, a range can be specified in detail, as in the first case, or by use of the THRU, as in the second case.

If multiple condition-names are specified in the same SET statement, the effect is the same as using multiple SET statements. This is illustrated in the following example.

```
01  CREDIT-RATING        PIC XX.
    88 DOUBLE-A           VALUE 'AA'.
    88 GOOD               VALUES ARE 'A' THRU 'BB'.
01  ACCOUNT-CLASS         PIC X.
    88 INSTITUTIONAL      VALUE 'I'.
    88 PERSONAL           VALUE 'P'.
    .
    .
    .

    SET DOUBLE-A PERSONAL TO TRUE.
```

The above SET statement is equivalent to

```
    SET DOUBLE-A TO TRUE
    SET PERSONAL TO TRUE.
```

or

```
    SET DOUBLE-A
        PERSONAL TO TRUE.
```

The last two versions are preferred because they make it clear that two condition-names are set to true.

Of course, in either form it would not be logical to use two condition-names from the same field, such as

```
    SET DOUBLE-A TO TRUE
    SET GOOD     TO TRUE.
```

The 88 condition-names included in a given field are mutually exclusive categories, and only one of them can apply. The corresponding data-name cannot contain more than one value at any one time!

R E V I E W . . . .

1. The verb that can be used to move values that correspond to defined condition-names by reference to the condition-name itself is the _____ verb.

   SET

2. The SET verb is available in [COBOL '74 AND '85 / COBOL '85 only].

   COBOL '85 only

3. Given that the DATA DIVISION specification is 88 MALE VALUE '1', then the SET verb statement for an individual that is a male is: SET MALE TO _____ .

   TRUE

. . . .

NESTED CONDITIONS

Before discussing nested conditions, let us consider the general format for the IF statement.

$$\underline{\text{IF}} \text{ condition THEN } \begin{Bmatrix} \text{statement -1} \\ \underline{\text{NEXT SENTENCE}} \end{Bmatrix} \begin{Bmatrix} \underline{\text{ELSE}} \text{ \{statement -2\} } \dots \underline{[\text{END-IF}]} \\ \underline{\text{ELSE NEXT SENTENCE}} \\ \underline{\text{END-IF}} \end{Bmatrix}$$

The possible unique structures are many, and, since the IF statement is so very common and so very useful an instruction, we will do well to spend some time studying it. Here are some of the forms we can have:

IF condition statement-1.

IF condition statement-1 ELSE NEXT SENTENCE.

IF condition statement-1 ELSE statement-2.

IF condition NEXT SENTENCE ELSE statement-2.

The first case shows that we can omit the ELSE portion as, for example, IF TAX < 5000 MOVE ZERO TO DEDUCTIONS. The statement that follows will be the NEXT SENTENCE, and so it would be redundant to write ELSE NEXT SENTENCE, although it would not be wrong.

As a further review of the IF statements, study the following example.

```
IF  AMOUNT IS GREATER THAN CREDIT LIMIT
    WRITE PRINT-LINE FROM CREDIT-OVERDRAW
ELSE
    MOVE AMOUNT TO BILLING-FIELD
    WRITE PRINT-LINE FROM BILL-AREA.
ADD AMOUNT TO TOTAL-VALUE.
```

The flowchart for this program segment appears in Figure 5-1. The program statements that correspond to the flowchart descriptions are as follows:

FLOWCHART DESCRIPTION	CORRESPONDING PROGRAM STATEMENT
Condition	`IF AMOUNT IS GREATER THAN CREDIT-LIMIT`
Statement-1	`WRITE PRINT LINE FROM CREDIT-OVERDRAW`
Statement-2	`MOVE AMOUNT TO BILLING-FIELD WRITE PRINT-LINE FROM BILL-AREA`
Next sentence	`ADD AMOUNT TO TOTAL-VALUE`

Notice that statement-1 and statement-2 need not be single statements. Statement-2 illustrates the case in which two statements are included.

The NEXT SENTENCE option is one way of expressing the null leg of a condition, as in this example:

```
IF  DEBITS = CREDITS
    NEXT SENTENCE
ELSE
    PERFORM OUT-OF-BALANCE.
```

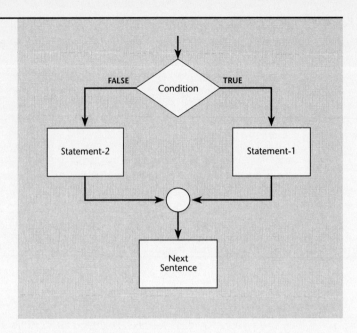

The NEXT SENTENCE in the preceding code provides a clear way of expressing the fact that no action is taken if the condition is true. Contrast the example just given to the equivalent:

```
IF  DEBITS NOT = CREDITS
     PERFORM OUT-OF-BALANCE.
```

The first version is preferred for its clarity.

In the general format for the IF statement, statement-1 and statement-2 are not restricted to being imperative statements; rather, they themselves may be conditional expressions, giving rise to nested IF statements. A relatively simple example of a nested IF statement, or a *nested conditional,* is the following:

```
IF  AMOUNT  <  100
     IF  AMOUNT  >  50
          MOVE 0.3 TO RATE
     ELSE
          MOVE 0.4 TO RATE
ELSE
     MOVE 0.2 TO RATE.
```

This COBOL statement corresponds to the following rule:

AMOUNT	RATE
Less than or equal to 50	0.4
Greater than 50 but less than 100	0.3
Equal to or greater than 100	0.2

A flowchart corresponding to this example is shown in Figure 5-2.

You will find it useful in interpreting nested conditionals to look for the first ELSE; it always pertains to the immediately preceding IF. The second ELSE pertains to the IF just preceding the inner IF, and so on. Schematically, the relationships can be portrayed as follows:

```
IF . . . IF . . . IF . . . ELSE . . . ELSE . . . ELSE . . .
```

FIGURE 5-2
Nested Conditional Structure to
Determine Rate

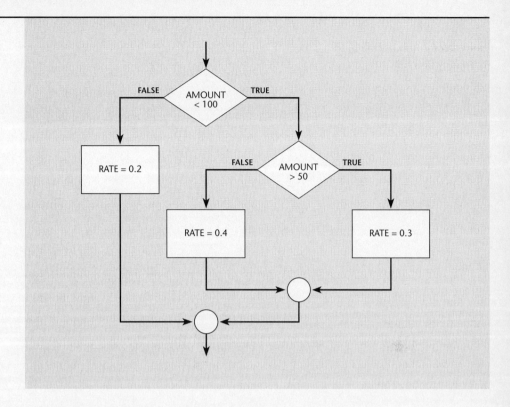

Nested conditions can be very useful in writing program statements, but they also can be misused. This is done by nesting conditions so deeply that program logic is difficult to follow. Because nested conditions are important, we present an additional example.

Consider a code that can have legitimate values in the range 1–5. Figure 5-3 depicts a nested conditional structure that tests for the value of the code and executes a suitable procedure (the strange spelling of KODE is because the more natural CODE is a reserved COBOL word). The corresponding nested IF could be written as

```
IF KODE = 1
    PERFORM ADDITION
ELSE
    IF KODE = 2
        PERFORM DELETION
    ELSE
        IF KODE = 3
            PERFORM CHANGE-ADDRESS
        ELSE
            IF KODE = 4
                PERFORM CHANGE-NAME
            ELSE
                IF KODE = 5
                    PERFORM CHANGE-CREDIT
                ELSE
                    PERFORM ERROR-CODE.
PERFORM NEXT-P.
```

We have nested to five levels, which tests the limits of our ability to understand the program logic inherent in the nesting. In general, many programming managers

FIGURE 5-3
*Sample Nested Conditional
Structure that Includes Five Levels*

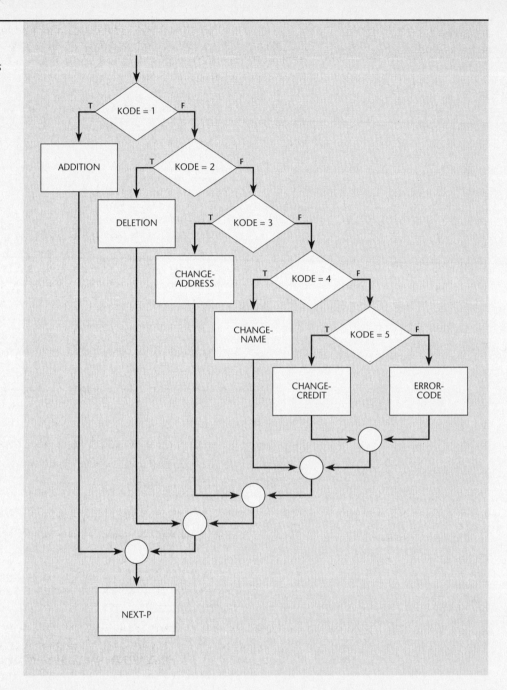

advise against nesting more than three levels. In this particular example the structure is rather easy, however, because of the null alternatives involved. In this sense we can say that, even though we have nested to five levels, it is a "clean" program structure.

The above example represents a "case structure," a subject that will be discussed in the following chapter, on structured programming. One way of implementing the case structure is by means of nested IF statements as in this illustration. Other ways of implementing the case structure will be discussed in Chapter 8 in connection with the GO TO ... DEPENDING ON and EVALUATE statements.

THE END-IF SCOPE TERMINATOR

Nested structures are sometimes a bit awkward to code in the 1974 version of COBOL. Consider the flowchart in Figure 5-4(a). When the GOOD-RISK condition is true, we want to PERFORM GROSS and PERFORM NET regardless of the value of QUANT. Figure 5-4(b) presents the programming statements based on the 1974 standard. The statements PERFORM GROSS and PERFORM NET are written twice to achieve the desired logic. In contrast, Figure 5-4(c) presents the program statements that include use of the END-IF scope terminator. This terminator marks the end of the preceding IF statement, and therefore the PERFORM GROSS and PERFORM NET are executed conditionally on GOOD-RISK being true and unconditionally on the value of QUANT. A second END-IF is used just before the PERFORM INVOICE statement in Figure 5-4(c). A period would play the same role as the second END-IF because a period would also terminate the scope of the main IF GOOD-RISK statement.

While the END-IF plays a useful role, you should not conclude that the 1974 standard is always deficient in ease and clarity of program structure. To make that point, suppose that instead of just the two PERFORM GROSS and PERFORM NET statements we had, say, 20 statements. Duplicating all such statements as was done in Figure 5-4(b) is unappealing, but the following program segment illustrates an improved way of achieving the desired result:

```
IF GOOD-RISK
    IF QUANT > 1000
        MOVE HIGH-RATE TO DISCOUNT
        PERFORM COMPUTATIONS
    ELSE
        MOVE LOW-RATE TO DISCOUNT
        PERFORM COMPUTATIONS
ELSE
    PERFORM BAD-RISK.
PERFORM INVOICE.
COMPUTATIONS.
    PERFORM GROSS
    PERFORM NET.
```

In the above segment we created a new paragraph, COMPUTATIONS, which contains all of the statements whose execution is conditional on GOOD-RISK and unconditional on QUANT. Thus the duplicated code consists of only one statement, PERFORM COMPUTATIONS.

R E V I E W . . . .

1. For the following program instructions, identify the program statement that corresponds to each IF statement element. Refer to the general format for the IF statement if you wish.

```
IF  QUANTITY < 100
    NEXT SENTENCE
ELSE
    MULTIPLY DISCOUNT BY PRICE.
MULTIPLY PRICE BY QUANTITY GIVING NET.
```

FIGURE 5-4

Illustration of Nested IF Without and With END-IF

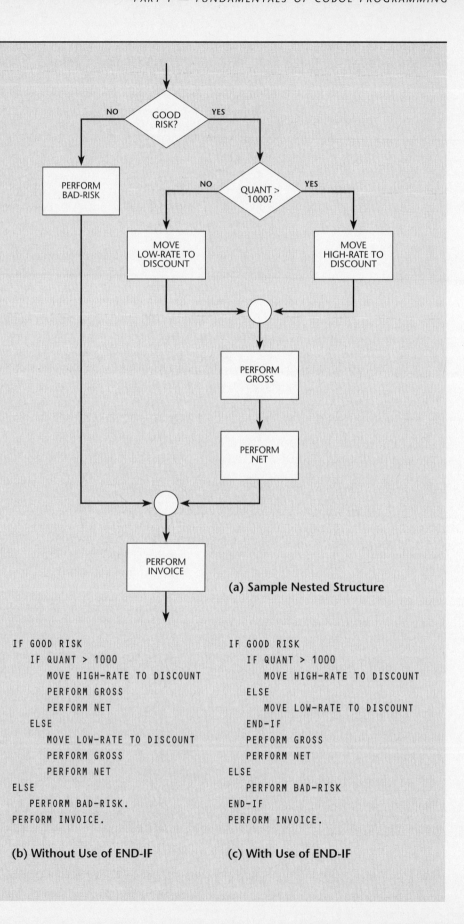

(a) Sample Nested Structure

```
IF GOOD RISK
    IF QUANT > 1000
        MOVE HIGH-RATE TO DISCOUNT
        PERFORM GROSS
        PERFORM NET
    ELSE
        MOVE LOW-RATE TO DISCOUNT
        PERFORM GROSS
        PERFORM NET
ELSE
    PERFORM BAD-RISK.
PERFORM INVOICE.
```

```
IF GOOD RISK
    IF QUANT > 1000
        MOVE HIGH-RATE TO DISCOUNT
    ELSE
        MOVE LOW-RATE TO DISCOUNT
    END-IF
    PERFORM GROSS
    PERFORM NET
ELSE
    PERFORM BAD-RISK
END-IF
PERFORM INVOICE.
```

(b) Without Use of END-IF   **(c) With Use of END-IF**

IF STATEMENT ELEMENT	CORRESPONDING PROGRAM STATEMENT
a. Condition	_____
b. Statement-1	_____
c. Statement-2	_____
d. Next sentence	_____

a. QUANTITY < 100

b. Not used as such (NEXT SENTENCE was used instead)

c. MULTIPLY DISCOUNT BY PRICE

d. MULTIPLY PRICE BY QUANTITY GIVING NET

2. Construct a flowchart corresponding to this program segment:

```
IF  QUANTITY < 100
    NEXT SENTENCE
ELSE
    MULTIPLY DISCOUNT BY PRICE.
MULTIPLY PRICE BY QUANTITY GIVING NET.
```

3. Using the following COBOL statement, complete the table below.

```
IF  GRSPAY < 1000.00
    IF  GRSPAY > 500.00
        MOVE 0.05 TO RETRMNT-DEDUC
    ELSE
        MOVE 0.03 TO RETRMNT-DEDUC
ELSE
    MOVE 0.07 TO RETRMNT-DEDUC.
```

AMOUNT OF GROSS PAY	RETIREMENT DEDUCTION RATE
Equal to or greater than 1,000	_____
Greater than 500 but less than 1,000	_____
Less than or equal to 500	_____

0.07; 0.05; 0.03

•   •

COMPOUND CONDITIONS

It is possible to combine the simple (individual) conditionals we have described into *compound conditionals* by the use of the logical operators OR, AND, and NOT. OR means *either or both,* and AND means *both.* Consider the following statement:

```
IF  BALANCE < ZERO AND DAYS-OVERDUE > 10
    PERFORM PAR-A.
```

The instruction indicates that the program should execute PAR-A when both the balance is negative and the number of overdue days exceeds 10.

On the other hand, consider the following statement:

```
IF  INPUT-DATA IS NONNUMERIC OR NAME-IS-MISSING
    MOVE 'CANT PROCESS, INCORRECT DATA' TO ERR-MESSAGE.
```

The program will move the indicated message to ERR-MESSAGE if either the condition-name NONNUMERIC condition is true or the condition-name condition defined as NAME-IS-MISSING is true.

There is a rather complex set of rules associated with the writing and evaluation of compound conditionals. In this chapter we shall limit our attention to the use of parentheses to clarify the meaning, whereas in Chapter 8 we shall expand on the subject. For example, we can write

```
IF  (AGE IS GREATER THAN 28) OR ((EXPERIENCE = 4)
    AND (EDUCATION IS GREATER THAN HS)) . . .
```

This condition holds either if age is greater than 28 or if both experience = 4 and education is greater than high school.

As another example, consider the following:

```
IF  ((CUST-CODE = 2) OR (CUST-CODE = 5)) AND (BALANCE = 0)
    PERFORM DISCOUNT-COMP
ELSE
    PERFORM FULL-PRICE-COMP.
```

In this example the first condition is true if BALANCE is equal to zero and CUST-CODE is either equal to 2 or equal to 5.

Using nested IF statements, we might write

```
IF  CUST-CODE = 2
    IF  BALANCE = 0
        PERFORM DISCOUNT-COMP
    END-IF
ELSE
    IF  CUST-CODE = 5
        IF  BALANCE = 0
            PERFORM DISCOUNT-COMP
        END-IF
    ELSE
        PERFORM FULL-PRICE-COMP.
```

Looking at the nested IF above, we see clearly that by the use of compound conditionals we can write conditional tests that otherwise would require very long expressions consisting of several nested IF statements.

R E V I E W . . . .

1. In contrast to the use of simple conditionals, a combination of tests can be included in one statement by the use of _____ conditionals.

                                                                        compound

2. The use of a compound conditional requires the use of one of the logical operators: _____ , _____ , or _____ .

OR; NOT; AND

3. When the logical operator OR is used in a compound conditional test, the presence of [either / both / either or both] of the conditional states constitutes a true condition.

either or both

4. When the logical operator AND is used in a compound conditional test, the presence of [either / both / either or both] of the conditional states constitutes a true condition.

both

. . . .

SUMMARY

We began this chapter with a discussion of the general rules associated with the use of the IF statement, and then we covered four specific types of conditional statements: (1) relation conditions; (2) condition-name conditions; (3) nested conditions; and (4) compound conditions.

When the condition specified in the IF statement is met, program execution continues with the statement or statements that directly follow that statement. Otherwise, program execution continues with the next sentence. The ELSE option makes it possible to execute one of two alternative statements (or sets of statements) through the use of one IF before continuing to the next sentence.

Relation conditions are always concerned with comparisons. The words or symbols that indicate the type of comparison to be made are called *relational operators*. We can compare one identifier to another identifier, one arithmetic expression to another arithmetic expression, literals to identifiers or expressions, and identifiers to expressions. For nonnumeric comparisons, it is necessary to know the *collating sequence* of the computer system. The EBDIC collating sequence is used by many IBM mainframe computers, while ASCII is the standard collating sequence.

The use of *condition-names* enables the programmer to define specialized figurative constants for use in condition tests. Instead of testing for a particular value for a data field, one can test for a condition-name instead, such as, IF MALE. Such use of condition-names enhances the readability of programs. The SET verb, available in COBOL '85, can be used to move values that correspond to defined condition-names.

A *nested conditional statement* involves the use of a sequence of IF clauses followed by a sequence of ELSE clauses. The first ELSE pertains to the immediately preceding IF; the second ELSE pertains to the IF just preceding the inner IF; and so on. In using nested designs, care must be taken to ensure that program logic is easy to follow. Use of the END-IF scope terminator available in COBOL '85 can help keep program logic clear.

Compound conditions are formed by joining several simple conditional statements into one statement by use of the logical operators OR, AND, and NOT. Such conditionals make it possible to write conditional tests that otherwise would require very long expressions consisting of several nested IF statements.

EXERCISES

5.1   Write PROCEDURE DIVISION statements to implement the logic included in the following flowchart.

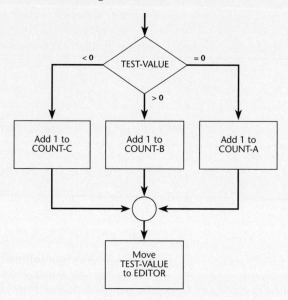

5.2   Using the 88-level-number indicator in the DATA DIVISION and suitable condition-name clauses, the following obvious identifiers have been defined:

MALE	WIDOWED-M
FEMALE	SINGLE-F
SINGLE-M	MARRIED-F
MARRIED-M	DIVORCED-F
DIVORCED-M	WIDOWED-F

Assume we want to tabulate the number of individuals falling into the last eight classes, as, for example, the number of single males (SINGLE-M). We thus want to test the field containing the identifying code and ADD 1 TO the corresponding counter. Assume the following fields are to be used as counters: SM, MM, DM, WM, SF, MF, DF, WF (where SM stands for single males, etc.).

a.   Draw a flowchart corresponding to your program logic.

b.   Write one nested conditional expression to accomplish the required testing and tabulating.

5.3   Consider the following DATA DIVISION entries relating to a personnel record:

```
02  EDUCATION              PIC 99.
    88  H-S GRAD               VALUE 12.
    88  COLLEGE-GRAD           VALUE 16.
    88  MASTERS-GRAD           VALUE 17.
    88  DOCTORATE-GRAD         VALUE 20.
02  YEARS-OF-EXPERIENCE    PIC 99.
```

```
02  SEX-CODE                PIC 9.
    88  MALE                    VALUE 1.
    88  FEMALE                  VALUE 2.
02  GEOGRAPHIC-PREFERENCE   PIC 9.
    88  EAST                    VALUE 1.
    88  MIDWEST                 VALUE 2.
    88  WEST                    VALUE 3.
    88  SOUTH                   VALUE 4.
    88  WILLING-TO-TRAVEL       VALUE 5.
```

Suppose that we want to find individuals who fulfill one of these three sets of requirements:

a. Five years of experience, male, high school graduate, willing to travel

b. Male, one year of experience, master's degree, preferring the West or South

c. Three years of experience, female, doctorate, preferring the East

Write one compound conditional sentence by which we can check whether a record in question fulfills the first, second, or third of these requirements. If one of these sets of requirements is met, we PERFORM PAR-A. If no set of requirements is met, we execute PAR-B.

5.4 Consider the following table of conditions:

QUANTITY	PRICE	RATING	DISCOUNT
>100	>10	<2	0.05
–100	>10	≥2	0.10
–100	≤10	<2	0.15
>100	≤10	≥2	0.20
≤100	$\begin{cases} < \\ =10 \\ > \end{cases}$	$\begin{cases} < \\ = 2 \\ > \end{cases}$	0.25

a. Write instructions using nested IF to MOVE to DISCOUNT the value shown depending on the conditions. Do not use END-IF.

b. Use the END-IF scope terminator to do the task.

c. Draw a flowchart corresponding to the specifications in the above table.

5.5 Draw a flowchart representing the following nested conditional statements. C1, C2, ... stand for condition names.

```
IF  C1 AND (C2 OR C3)
    PERFORM F1
    PERFORM F2
ELSE
    IF  C2 OR (C6 AND C7)
        PERFORM F3
    ELSE NEXT SENTENCE.
```

5.6 Write a program corresponding to the flowchart in Figure 5-5. Assume that the input file is defined as follows:

```
FD  EMPLOYEE-FILE  LABEL RECORDS STANDARD
                        DATA RECORD EMPL-REC.
01  EMPL-REC.
    02  FILLER          PIC X(5)
    02  HOURLY-OR-SAL   PIC X.
        88  HOURLY          VALUE '1'.
        88  SALARIED        VALUE '2'.
    02  UNION-CODE      PIC X.
        88  UNION           VALUE '1'.
        88  NONUNION        VALUE '2'.
    02  SEX-CODE        PIC X.
        88  MALE            VALUE '1'.
        88  FEMALE          VALUE '2'.
    02  FILLER          PIC X(72).
```

The following sample input and output data serve the purpose of describing the required logic. In summary, we want to count the number of employees who belong to the labor union and to show separately the number of men from the number of women union members.

SAMPLE INPUT

```
111
121
222
211
122
111
121
212
111
112
112
```

SAMPLE OUTPUT

```
        UNION MEMBERSHIP
MEN          3
WOMEN        2
TOTAL        5
```

FIGURE 5-5

Flowchart for Exercise 5.6

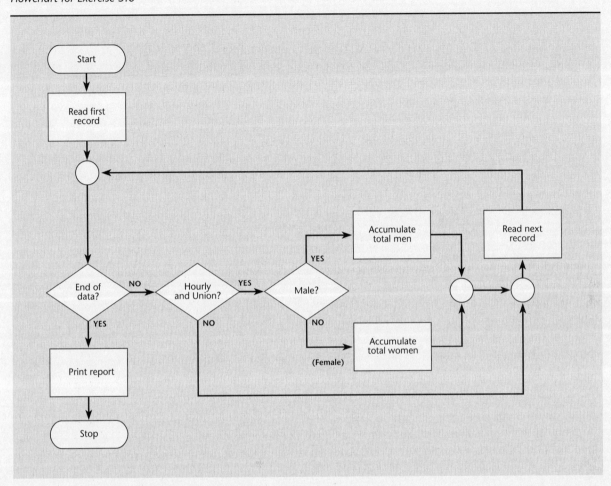

6 Structured Programming in COBOL

IN EARLY PROGRAMMING *practice, most programs were characterized by "spaghetti bowl logic." This involved the repeated transfer of program execution and control from one part of the program to another, particularly by the use of GO TO types of statements. Programmers had no clear concepts or guidelines on which to rely for writing good programs in a systematic way. Programs differed in their structure depending on the intuition and experience level of individual programmers. By the mid-1970s concepts and methods were developed that could be used to write good programs that have common structural elements.* **Structured programming** *is the label that was given to this development.*

Programs developed under the structured programming approach are less error-prone and can be understood and modified more easily than programs not so developed.

In this chapter you will study the key concepts and techniques associated with structured programming in COBOL. You will begin by considering the several basic types of program structures that you can use. You will then study the application of partitioning to good program design and the use of structure charts in establishing good modular design. You will conclude this chapter by studying a set of rules for formatting COBOL programs.

FIGURE 6-1
Standard Program Structures

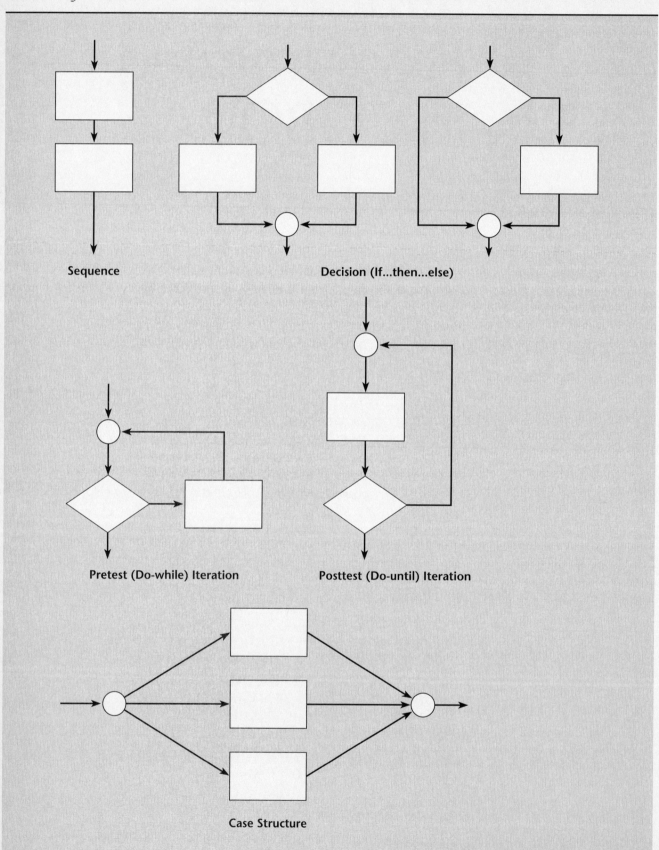

Sequence

Decision (If...then...else)

Pretest (Do-while) Iteration

Posttest (Do-until) Iteration

Case Structure

BASIC PROGRAM STRUCTURES

Briefly stated, structured programming is based on the use of the five standard structures presented in Figure 6-1: Sequence, Decision, Pretest Iteration, Posttest Iteration, and the Case Structure. For a program to be considered structured, one should be able to portray the program by the use of any combination of these five standard structures, and only these structures.

COBOL now provides for convenient implementation of all five basic program structures. In some cases COBOL '74 is incapable of straightforward implementation of all of these structures, but COBOL '85 has removed such deficiencies. A series of examples are presented in this section to demonstrate how COBOL language statements can be used to implement each of the basic structures.

Sequence Structure

Figure 6-2 presents the implementation of the *sequence structure* in COBOL. This is the most basic form of structure, and simply represents the *successive* execution of statements or modules in a program. As exemplified by the set of statements for the second module in that figure, a conditional statement that is properly marked by an END-IF scope terminator in COBOL '85 may be viewed as one step (block) in the sequence. In fact, as we shall see in a later section in this chapter, on levels of abstraction, program can be portrayed as a sequence structure. This is so because all the forms in Figure 6-1 are characterized by one entry and one exit, and can therefore be viewed, in the abstract, as being blocks in a sequence.

The Decision Structure

The implementation of the *decision structure* (also called the *selection* or *if-then-else* structure) is illustrated in Figure 6-3.

There are two forms of the decision structure. The first form is used when we have an IF ... ELSE case. One or more actions are taken given that the condition is true, and another action is taken given that the condition is false.

In the second form one of the "legs" is null, and no action is taken in that case. Either the "true" or the "false" case may be null. An IF without the ELSE, and

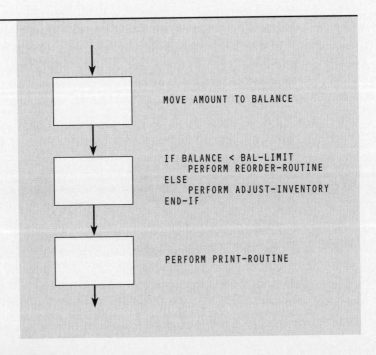

FIGURE 6-2
COBOL Implementation of Sequence Structure

```
MOVE AMOUNT TO BALANCE



IF BALANCE < BAL-LIMIT
    PERFORM REORDER-ROUTINE
ELSE
    PERFORM ADJUST-INVENTORY
END-IF



PERFORM PRINT-ROUTINE
```

FIGURE 6-3
COBOL Implementation of
Decision Structure

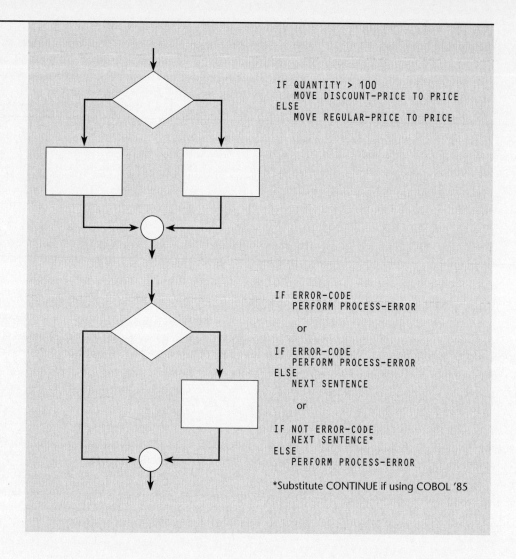

```
IF QUANTITY > 100
    MOVE DISCOUNT-PRICE TO PRICE
ELSE
    MOVE REGULAR-PRICE TO PRICE
```

```
IF ERROR-CODE
    PERFORM PROCESS-ERROR
```

        or

```
IF ERROR-CODE
    PERFORM PROCESS-ERROR
ELSE
    NEXT SENTENCE
```

        or

```
IF NOT ERROR-CODE
    NEXT SENTENCE*
ELSE
    PERFORM PROCESS-ERROR
```

*Substitute CONTINUE if using COBOL '85

terminating with a period or END-IF, is one way of writing the corresponding COBOL implementation. An alternate way, as shown in the last two examples of Figure 6-3, is use of the NEXT SENTENCE option to indicate the null leg.

Iteration Structures

As presented in Figure 6-4, there are two *iteration structures:* the *pretest* (or *do-while*) and the *posttest* (or *do-until*). In the pretest iteration, a test is performed before any execution of a module, whereas in the posttest iteration, the module is executed once, and then may be executed more times according to the result of the test that follows. The pretest iteration can be implemented with a PERFORM . . . UNTIL command in both COBOL '74 and COBOL '85. The WITH TEST AFTER clause in the 1985 version is optional, and its omission implies exactly what PERFORM ... UNTIL does in COBOL '74.

There is no direct way of implementing the posttest iteration structure in COBOL '74. As shown in the last example in Figure 6-4, we need to write two PERFORM statements to implement the posttest iteration in COBOL '74. The first PERFORM is unconditional execution of the target procedure, while the second PERFORM is a pretest PERFORM ... UNTIL. However, this deficiency has been removed in COBOL '85 with the addition of the PERFORM ... WITH TEST AFTER option.

FIGURE 6-4
COBOL Implementation of
Iteration Structures

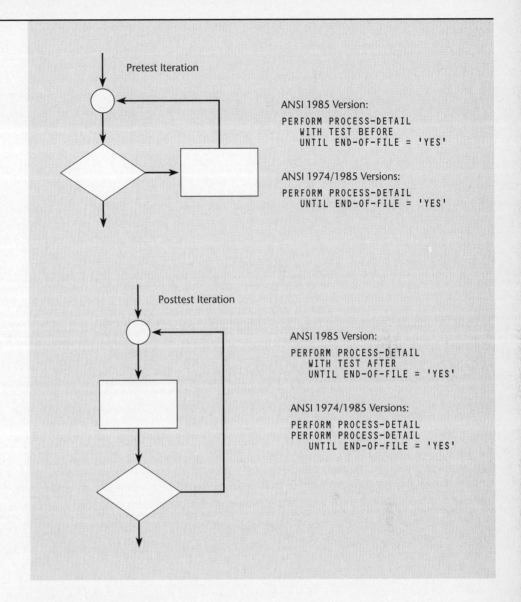

The Case Structure

The *case structure* is useful when we need to select one from among several alternatives. Rather than having one true-false type of condition, we have a number of possibilities, one of which is true, as for example the processing of one of many possible types of transactions in a file update program. Figure 6-5 illustrates case implementation using nested IF statements. Such an approach can be used with both COBOL '74 and COBOL '85.

However, the case structure can be implemented in other ways, as well. A better approach is to use the EVALUATE verb, which will be discussed in Chapter 8. Another possibility is use of the specialized verb GO TO ... DEPENDING ON, also described in Chapter 8. In general, the nested IF illustrated in Figure 6-5 is a good approach when the number of alternatives is relatively small. When the number of alternatives is large, the EVALUATE statement is preferred because it avoids the use of a deeply nested IF structure. The implementation using GO TO ... DEPENDING ON, is suitable only if we have a numeric code that assumes consecutive numeric values ranging as 1, 2, ... , *n*. For instance, if the numeric code represents the last school grade completed from the first grade through the fourth

FIGURE 6-5
Sample Nested Conditional Structure that Includes Five Levels

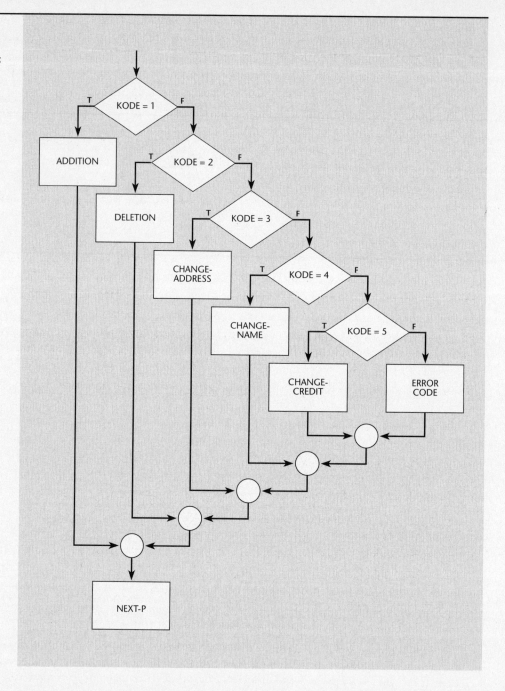

year of college, and we process each of the 16 possibilities separately, then GO TO ... DEPENDING ON implementation would be convenient as well as compatible with both COBOL '74 and COBOL '85.

R E V I E W . . . .

1. Structured programming is based on the use of [any one / any combination] of the standard structures presented in Figure 6-1.

    any combination

2. The program structure that simply indicates that processing is to continue with the next statement or module is the _____ structure.

sequence

3. The type of structure that involves a selection of one of two alternative actions, or of one action versus no action, is the _____ structure.

decision (or selection, or if-then-else)

4. The two forms of program structure that represent a repeating process, or program loop, are the _____ structures.

iteration

5. The form of the iteration structure in which a test is done before the execution of a program module is the _____ iteration.

pretest (or do while)

6. The form of the iteration structure in which the program module is executed once, and then may be executed more times according to the result of a test, is the _____ iteration.

posttest (or do until)

7. The type of program structure in which selection of program modules is made from more than two alternatives is the _____ structure.

case

8. When the number of alternative modules is small, the preferred COBOL code to implement the case structure is to use [GO TO ... DEPENDING / nested IF] statements.

nested IF

.   .   .   .

PARTITIONING PROGRAM MODULES

A fundamental concept of program design is that of *partitioning,* which refers to the process of subdividing a large programming task into smaller parts or functions.

The use of partitioning is common in many fields. One form of partitioning in organizations is based on the division of labor, or functional specialization. For example, an automobile manufacturing plant includes departmental units that may be further subdivided according to specific functions. A Painting Department, for instance, could include such separate functions as cleaning, spraying, baking, inspecting, and the like. Similarly, an Information Systems Department could include such separate functions as programming, systems analysis, data entry, and input-output control. In general, we find it not only beneficial, but also necessary, to partition large and complex tasks into smaller and more specialized tasks.

A computer programming task generally is complex enough to make partitioning desirable. In the context of computer programming, a widely used term associated with partitioning is *modularity.* A *program module* is a well-defined program segment. Modular programming has been recognized as a desirable practice for many years. In practice, all programs include some degree of modularity by necessity; no programmer can write a monolithic program that is not partitioned into some kinds of parts, or modules. Thus, it is not just the presence of modularity that is important. Rather, we need to develop an understanding of how to design programs whose modules are so constructed as to lead to good programs.

To be useful, a module should not only be a program segment, but also a *well-defined* program segment. More specifically, a module should be a *named* program segment that carries out a *specific program function*. In the context of COBOL programming, a module eventually is represented in one of four forms in the program:

1. As a single paragraph

2. As a series of two or more consecutive paragraphs that are the object of a PERFORM PAR-A THRU PAR-Z, where PAR-A and PAR-Z stand for the first and last paragraphs in a series (as will be discussed in the next chapter)

3. As a single SECTION (as will be discussed in Chapter 11)

4. As a subprogram (as will be discussed in Chapter 23)

R E V I E W . . . .

1. The process of subdividing a large programming task into smaller, more specific tasks is called _____ .

                                                                                                    partitioning

2. In terms of its general application, partitioning is a [long-standing / recently developed] concept.

                                                                                                    long-standing

3. "A named program segment that carries out a specific program function" is a definition of a program _____ .

                                                                                                    module

4. Program modularity can be described as being effective when it leads to the development of _____ programs.

                                                                                                    good

. . . .

LEVELS OF ABSTRACTION AND STRUCTURE CHARTS

As we stated in the preceding section, a good program should be partitioned into modules that perform a specific function. For purposes of designing a good program, a module can be viewed as a *black box*. A black box is a means of representing a program task, or procedure, in an abstract way. When we concentrate on the *what* rather than the *how* aspect of a task, we thereby introduce the idea of abstraction, which is concerned with a summary representation, free of detail.

An important consideration in program design is the partitioning of a whole task into smaller, interrelated modules. To achieve effective partitioning of a task, we must be able to look at the parts in abstract form rather than in detail. If a program consists of one hundred modules and each module averages 10 lines of code, it is impossible to comprehend the whole program at once. This is where the black box concept comes in handy. We describe each module as a black box, thus abstracting from its detail. So, for the above example, we would need to consider the one hundred modules rather than the 1,000 lines of code as such. While this is an improvement, we would still find it hard to comprehend the 100 modules viewed all at one time.

The way we manage the large number of modules in program design is to organize them in a systematic fashion. Just as a large college is organized into departments, fields of specialization, and individual faculty, so we organize program modules into a hierarchical structure. *Structure charts* are the best way of depicting

FIGURE 6-6
Rectangular and Angular Structure Charts

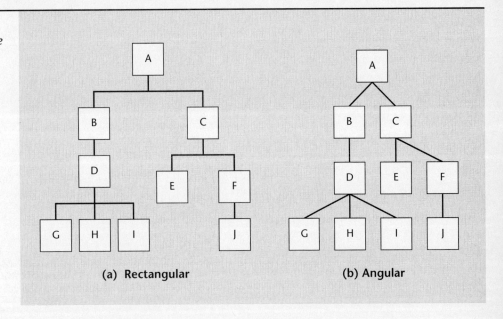

(a) **Rectangular**   (b) **Angular**

the hierarchical structure of programs. Figure 6-6 presents two sample hierarchical structure charts, one showing rectangular connecting lines, the second one showing angular connections. The type of connecting lines that are used is simply a matter of preference and has nothing to do with the meaning of a structure chart.

The critical characteristics of a hierarchical structure are

1. There is only one top module (the *root* module), and it represents the entire program. This module is superior to all other modules.

2. Any given module may have subordinate modules. These are shown below their immediate superior and are connected with lines to show this superior-subordinate relationship. In Figure 6-6, for example, D is a module that is subordinate to B and superior to modules G, H, and I.

3. Any given module, except the top one, should have one, and only one, superior in the structure chart. Yet there are situations in which the same module may need to be subordinate to more than one superior. In such cases we draw the subordinate module as if it were a unique subordinate to each respective superior in the structure chart, but we shade the upper-right corner to indicate the fact that it is a duplicate representation. Module Q is such a module in Figure 6-7. Notice that we have included the Q block four times in the structure chart, rather than the alternative of presenting it once and showing four connecting lines leading to the module. By this method of duplicate representation, the requirement that a module should have only one superior shown in the structure chart is satisfied.

In all cases a superior module is superior by the fact that it issues a PERFORM to execute the given subordinate. So in operational terms, a module A is superior to another module B when A contains a "PERFORM B" statement. The PERFORM itself is a means of using abstract references. When a PERFORM is written, it specifies a black box approach; it says what to do, without including the specific procedure of how to do the task. Therefore a structure chart is an abstract representation of a program because it represents a summary of the functions performed by the program.

FIGURE 6-7

Structure Chart Illustrating a Common Function (Q)

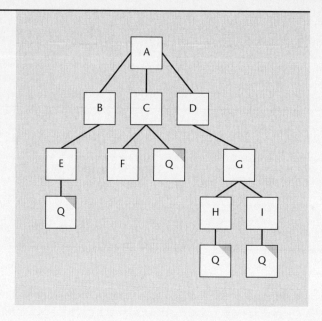

Furthermore, a given module is a summary representation of all of its subordinates. Module C in Figure 6-7 is superior to F and Q, which means it contains "PERFORM F" and "PERFORM Q" statements in it. So when execution of C has been completed, F and Q have also been executed. Similarly, when module A in Figure 6-7 has been executed, the entire program has been executed. Thus a given module provides a high-level, or abstract, representation of its subordinates.

The use of *abstraction* and the *omission of detail* is our best weapon against overwhelming complexity. A structure chart representing a program of 100 modules need not be overwhelming. The hierarchical structure allows us to focus on parts of the total without losing sight of the whole. When we view one module to find out "how it fits in the whole picture," we simply look up to its superior and, if need be, to the superior of its superior, and so on.

In addition to describing the hierarchical relationships, a structure chart can also be enhanced to include

- *Loops* (repetitive execution of subordinate modules)

- *Decision points* (conditional execution of subordinate modules)

- *Data* (input to and output from modules)

Figure 6-8 is a structure chart that includes these additional features. Module A passes X as input data to module B, which returns output data Y to module A. Then modules C and D are executed repetitively, as indicated by the curved arrows below B; the inner loop involves module C while the outer loop involves both C and D. Finally, module F executes modules G and H conditionally, as indicated by the diamond symbol at F.

It may be useful at this point to contrast a structure chart with a *flowchart*. A structure chart is based on hierarchical program structure, whereas a flowchart is based on sequential procedure. To design a good program, first a good structure chart should be developed. After the structure chart has been completed, a flowchart may then be developed as an additional aid for coding the program logic into program procedures; however, a *pseudocode* version of the program is a preferred approach.

We conclude this section with a brief discussion of how the concept of levels of abstraction is also relevant for flowcharts as well as structure charts. As we

FIGURE 6-8

Structure Chart Showing Data,
Loops, and Decision Point

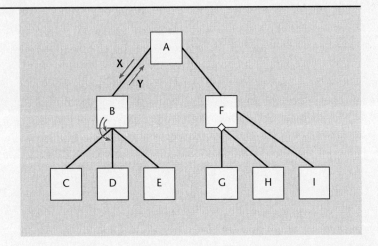

recall from the discussion in the beginning of this chapter on the basic flowchart forms of program structure, a fundamental property of the five basic structures is that each has *one entry* and *one exit*. Based on that property, we may represent a structure either in detail or in summary form. A given block structure may represent a series of interrelated blocks with the same entry and exit point. Figure 6-9 illustrates the property. The rectangular borders in Figure 6-9(a) illustrate how we can use different levels of abstraction depending on our needs. In part (b) one block has been substituted for the entire diagram in part (a). This is the highest level of abstraction. Then in part (c) we represent the entire part (a) structure as a simple selection. Finally, part (d) presents more detail by demonstrating the nested selection structure of part (a).

The one-entry, one-exit property can be used as a powerful tool both when developing a new program and when trying to review or comprehend a program already written. We can deal with the details of the code or we can focus on higher levels of abstraction, as needed.

R E V I E W . . . .

1. The process by which the overall programming task is subdivided into several more specific tasks is called _____ .

    partitioning

2. The type of chart that represents the hierarchical organization of program modules is the _____ .

    structure chart

3. In terms of structure chart representation, the entire program is represented by the [top / bottom] module.

    top

4. Any given module in the structure chart can have [only one / any number of] subordinate module(s).

    any number of

5. Except for the top module, which has no superior module, any module in the structure chart representation has [only one / any number of] superior module(s).

    only one

FIGURE 6-9
Illustration of Levels of Abstraction Based on the One-Entry One-Exit Property

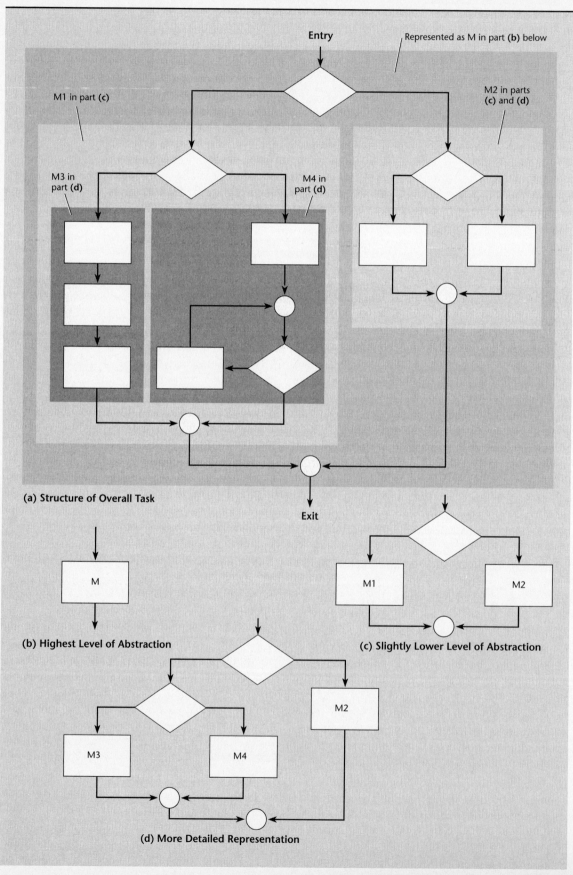

6. When a given module is in fact subordinate to more than one superior in terms of program logic, that module is _____ in the structure chart.

repeated (and shaded)

7. If module C is the superior of module D in a structure chart, this indicates that module C includes in it the PROCEDURE DIVISION command, _____ , in some form.

PERFORM D

8. As contrasted to the structure chart, which is based on hierarchical program structure, the type of chart that is based on sequential procedure is the _____ .

flowchart

9. A fundamental property of the basic structures is the existence of [only one / several] entry point(s) and [only one / several] exit point(s).

only one; only one

·   ·   ·   ·   ·   ·   ·   ·   ·   ·   ·   ·   ·   ·   ·   ·   ·   ·   ·

ALTERNATIVE FORMS OF STRUCTURE CHARTS

The preceding section presented some basic conventions for representing program structure in the form of charts. However, there is no one universal format for drawing such charts; rather, there are several somewhat competing alternative formats. Each alternative encompasses a design methodology that provides a standard set of conventions for representing program structure, data structure, and program code. In a given organization it makes good sense to use one of the alternative formats consistently, so that efficient and clear communication among programming professionals in that organization is achieved. In a general context, such as in this book, it is impractical to attempt the simultaneous use of different diagramming conventions. For this reason a simplified set of formats is used in the text examples, leaving the choice of a specific convention to your preference.

Of the several available diagrammatic conventions for representing program structure, we present a brief overview of two of them: HIPO charts and Warnier-Orr charts.

Hierarchical Input-Process-Output (HIPO) is the set of diagramming conventions developed by IBM that focuses on the inputs, processes, and outputs of programs. Figure 6-10 includes a sample HIPO chart. Figure 6-10(a) is a *Visual Table of Contents (VTOC,* pronounced "vee-tok") diagram that essentially is a hierarchical structure chart very similar to the type used throughout this book. At the lower right corner of each block in the VTOC diagram, a number is included as a reference to an associated HIPO chart. The HIPO chart included in Figure 6-10(b) is for block 1.0, which is the root module representing the entire program. As illustrated in Figure 6-10(b), a HIPO chart consists of three portions, labeled INPUT, PROCESS, and OUTPUT, respectively. As part of the HIPO methodology, a similar chart would be prepared for each of the 12 blocks in the VTOC chart in Figure 6-10(a). Thus HIPO charts provide documented detail for the input, process, and output for each module or function in the program, and therefore can be used as the basis for writing the program code.

Warnier-Orr charts are named after Jean-Dominique Warnier and Ken Orr, who were the principal developers of this approach to representing program structure. Figure 6-11 presents a Warnier-Orr chart corresponding to the structure chart in Figure 6-10(a). The notable characteristic of such charts is that they use *horizontally arranged brackets* rather than vertically placed blocks to represent the

FIGURE 6-10

A Hierarchical Structure Chart and One Associated HIPO Chart

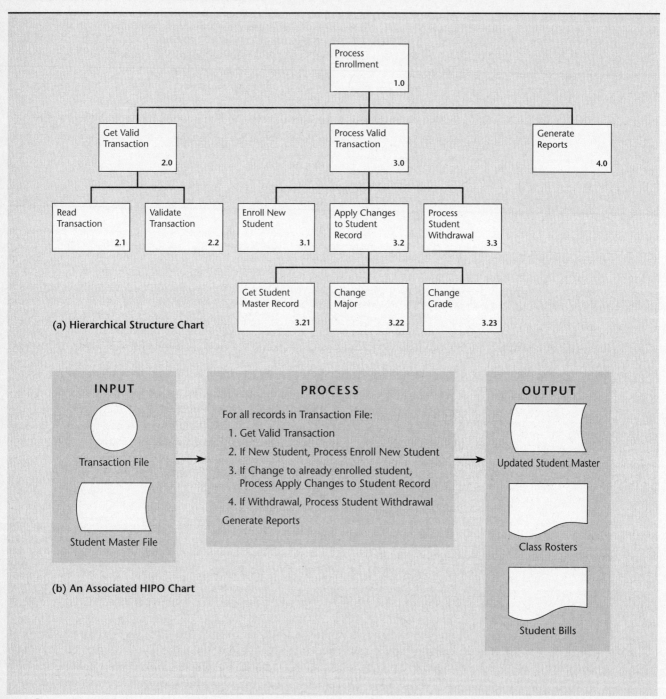

(a) **Hierarchical Structure Chart**

(b) **An Associated HIPO Chart**

hierarchical structure of a program. Warnier-Orr charts focus on the hierarchical relationships of the functions to be performed, and, as is the case for HIPO charts, they can be used as the basis for developing the program code. Warnier-Orr charts are generally more compact than corresponding HIPO charts because they incorporate the functions of both the VTOC and HIPO charts into one diagram. However, combining the two types of functions into one chart results in a somewhat more complex diagram.

FIGURE 6-11

Sample Warnier-Orr Chart

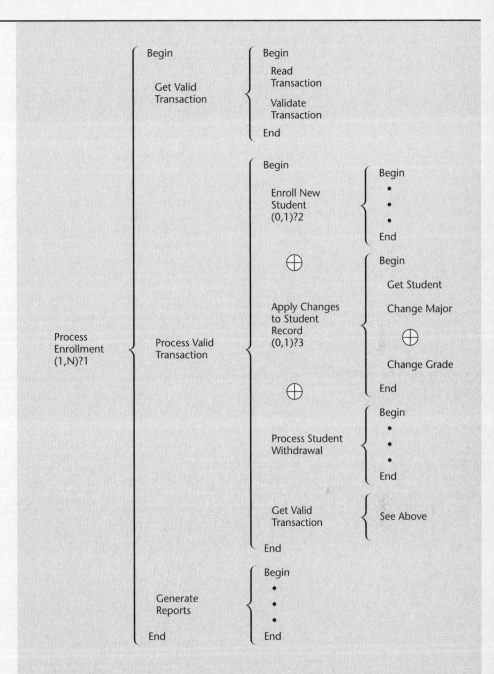

(1,N) means that this process is repeated N times and ?1 is an indication that there is a footnote and it is labeled 1. Warnier-Orr diagrams use footnotes to explain control logic; for this example, footnote 1 might state that the N repetitions are terminated when the end-of-file condition is true. ⊕ is a symbol to indicate the exclusive *or*; for example, either Enroll New Student *or* Apply Changes to Student Record will be executed.

R E V I E W . . . .

1. The type of chart developed by IBM that focuses on the inputs, processes, and outputs of programs is the _____ chart.

HIPO

2. Reflecting the focus of such a chart, the term HIPO stands for
   _____ .

Hierarchical Input-Process-Output

3. The type of chart that utilizes horizontally arranged brackets rather than vertically placed blocks to represent the hierarchical structure of a program is the
   _____ chart.

Warnier-Orr

4. Of the two additional approaches to diagrammatic representation that were described, the one that requires that two types of associated charts be prepared is the _____ chart.

HIPO

5. Of the two approaches to diagrammatic representation that were discussed, the one that incorporates all information in one rather than two types of charts, with greater complexity generally resulting in the one chart, is the
   _____ chart.

Warnier-Orr

. . . .

FORMATTING RULES FOR PROGRAMS

Form and substance often are highly interrelated. A number of the benefits associated with structured programming derive from use of certain forms. Proper substance must be there as a prerequisite to good programming, but proper substance cast in obscure form is hardly worthwhile. In this section we provide some basic guidelines for writing structured programs in readable form. These guidelines are neither exhaustive nor required, but they represent collectively the consensus of good formatting rules practiced in the field.

1. In the source program use physical spacing to enhance visibility and to denote logical groupings.

   - Use asterisks in column 7 of the COBOL coding form to separate major items. For instance, precede each new 01 item in the WORKING-STORAGE with a blank line containing an asterisk in column 7 on the COBOL Coding Form. Similarly, in the PROCEDURE DIVISION, separate logical groups by a comment line, as in the following:

     ```
     *
     *THE FOLLOWING TWO RECORDS DESCRIBE THE REPORT FORMAT
     *
      01  SALES-REP-HEADING.
          05 . . .
     *
      01  SALES-REP-DETAIL
          05 . . .
     ```

   - If there is a series of MOVE statements and then a WRITE, put a blank comment line before the WRITE to block together the MOVEs that perform a common function, as in the following:

     ```
     *
     *THE FOLLOWING STATEMENTS MOVE AND WRITE THE DATA FOR THE
     *SALES REPORT SUMMARY
     ```

```
*
        MOVE . . .
        MOVE . . .
        MOVE . . .
*
        WRITE . . .
```

- Use the stroke (/) in column 7 of the COBOL coding form to start a new page. For instance, always begin the DATA DIVISION on a new page and the PROCEDURE DIVISION on a new page. Then within each of these divisions, start a new page when a major logical unit begins. If you have, for example, three 01 heading descriptions and they require about 20 lines of codes, it is much better to start a new page and to precede the program code with a comment such as

```
*THE FOLLOWING THREE ITEMS DESCRIBE THE PAGE HEADERS OF THE
*SALES REPORT.
```

  Then the reader can quickly grasp the common element in the items on the page, and can choose either to give attention to the page or to bypass it.

- In the PROCEDURE DIVISION it is a good practice to list a PROGRAM SUMMARY type of module on the first page and, if there is enough space, also to list all its immediate subordinates. If there is not enough space for all the immediate subordinates, then start a new page for each first-level module and, similarly, place all its immediate subordinates on one page.

2. Use vertical alignment of similar items to convey similarity of function.

- Align all PICTURE and VALUE clauses on the same column when possible, especially with respect to each 01-level item. For example:

```
01  A.
        02 B      PIC  9(6).
        02 C      PIC  X(2)     VALUE  'ABC'.
        02 D      PIC  99V9.
        02 E      PIC  99V9.
        02 F      PIC  X(3)     VALUE  'XYZ'.
        02 G      PIC  X(29)    VALUE
                  'LONG LITERAL ON SEPARATE LINE'.
```

- Align similar verbs and their operands in the PROCEDURE DIVISION, as in the following:

```
OPEN INPUT  FILE-A
            FILE-B
     OUTPUT FILE-C
     .
     .
     .
MOVE AMOUNT       TO ED-AMOUNT
MOVE RATE         TO FACTOR
MOVE PREVIOUS-BAL TO TEST-VALUE.
```

- Indent subordinate clauses under the main clause. In the DATA DIVISION, for instance, 88 items should be indented as follows:

```
02   TRANS-CODE          PIC   X.
     88  CHANGE-RATE              VALUE '1'.
     88  CHANGE-BAL               VALUE '2'.
     88  ERROR-CODE               VALUE LOW-VALUES THRU ZERO
                                        3 THRU HIGH-VALUES.
```

In the PROCEDURE DIVISION we can use indentation, as in the following examples:

```
READ SOURCE-FILE RECORD
     AT END . . .
WRITE DISK-FILE RECORD
PERFORM PROCESS-RATE-CHANGE
        UNTIL AMOUNT-OWED > MAX-LIMIT
             OR ERROR-CODE
MOVE LAST-NAME OF TRANSACTION-FILE-REC
     TO LAST-NAME OF REPORT-REC
```

The above illustrations should serve to suggest the various possibilities. There is no reason why one should commit to memory any detailed rules of indentation. Instead, one should develop a general practice and a state of mind to indent to advantage. Within a given organization there may be "standard" indentation rules developed, but petty adherence to any strict set of rules may defeat the main purpose of indentation, which is to facilitate writing readable programs.

3. Use group labels to convey common functions.

- In the DATA DIVISION it is desirable to group similar items under the same group item. For instance, if four totals are accumulated in a report-generating program, it is preferable to write them under one group name:

```
01   REPORT-TOTALS.
     02  PRODUCT-TOTAL
     02  SALESPERSON-TOTAL
     02  DEPARTMENT-TOTAL
     02  GRAND-TOTAL
```

- In the PROCEDURE DIVISION, group labels can be written in many ways. As one approach a comment line preceding a group of statements may, in effect, be a group label that explains the common function:

```
*TEST WHETHER GROSS-PAY FALLS WITHIN REASONABLE LIMITS
*
 IF  SALARIED-EMPL
     IF  GROSS-PAY-THIS-WEEK > MIN-SAL-LEVEL
         AND GROSS-PAY-THIS-WEEK < MAX-SAL-LEVEL
         PERFORM COMPUTE-NET
     ELSE
         PERFORM UNREASONABLE-SALARY
 ELSE . . .
```

Another way of creating a group label is, of course, by the paragraph-name. It should be chosen to convey the function of the paragraph.

- Whenever a series of paragraphs constitute a logical unit, then the SECTION name should be used to give a name to the function of the whole group. (SECTIONs are discussed in Chapter 11, but we mention them here for completeness.) Remember, though, that the end of a section is signaled when another section begins. Thus if there is one section, there must be at least one additional section unless the single section is in the last physical position in the program. In general, instead of using PERFORM A THRU B (see Chapter 7) it is better to give a section name to the paragraphs A through B and then say "PERFORM section-name" instead.

4. Use similar names for similar items.

   - In most programs we encounter fields such as Name or Employee-Number that are present in an input file record, an output file record, and a report record. All three records contain similar items, and we should use a naming convention that facilitates recognition of this similarity. One way to approach the nomenclature is to use qualification, which is explained in Chapter 7, as follows:

     ```
     MOVE NAME OF EMPL-SOURCE-FILE
       TO NAME OF PAY-REG-REPORT
     MOVE ADDRESS OF EMPL-SOURCE-REC
       TO ADDRESS OF EMPL-NEW-MAST-REC.
     ```

     But qualification requires more extensive writing; therefore programmers avoid qualification in their hurry to complete the program. Actually, the typing effort associated with a programming task is a very small portion of the total programming effort, but programmers tend to place undue weight on the amount of typing involved. Therefore qualification should be considered a good approach to naming similar items and achieving good program documentation.

   - Another way of naming similar items is to use a mnemonic prefix or suffix to differentiate the items. For example:

     ```
     NAME-IN     [IN is understood to mean the input file]
     NAME-WS     [WS = WORKING-STORAGE]
     ```

5. Use a numerical prefix to indicate the physical order of paragraphs.

   - Structure charts allow for a two-dimensional representation of the program modules and their relationships. However, programs are written in one dimension—top to bottom, or beginning to end. In large programs such a statement as PERFORM GROSS-CALC provides no clue as to where the paragraph GROSS-CALC is located. We may need to scan many pages of listing to find the paragraph. To make it easy to "navigate" through the program, a numerical prefix is assigned as part of a section or paragraph name and serves as the indicator of the physical location of the section or paragraph. For example, inclusion of the numerical prefix in PERFORM 260-GROSS-CALC makes it much easier to find the paragraph-name.

R E V I E W . . . .

1. The purpose of this section has been to present the consensus of rules relating to the _____ of structured COBOL programs.

                                                                format

2. Many of the rules are concerned with spacing and indentation, with the objective particularly being to make the programs easier to [read / write].

    read

3. The use of group labels in the program and the use of similar data-names for similar items particularly [minimize writing time / enhance readability] for the program.

    enhance readability

4. The physical location of paragraphs in a program can be made explicit by assigning a numerical _____ to each paragraph name.

    prefix

5. The rules presented in this section [should be followed strictly / are general guidelines] for establishing the format for a COBOL program.

    are general guidelines

. . . .

SUMMARY

This chapter was concerned with the concepts and techniques of structured programming, which is now accepted as being the appropriate method for writing COBOL programs.

We began the chapter with a study of five standard structures that are used in structured programs. Included were the COBOL commands that can be used to implement them. (1) The *sequence structure* represents the successive execution of program statements or modules. (2) The *decision structure* has two forms. The first form is the IF ... ELSE, while in the second form one of the "legs" is null, and no action is taken in that case. (3) In *pretest iteration* (or *do while*) a test is performed *before* any execution of a module. (4) In *posttest iteration* the module is executed first, and then may be executed more times according to the result of each subsequent test. (5) The *case structure* is concerned with the selection of an alternative from among several possible alternative statements or modules.

Partitioning refers to the process of subdividing a large programming task into smaller parts or functions. To achieve partitioning in a programming project, we first establish *program modules,* each of which is a *named* and *well-defined* program segment.

For purposes of designing a good program, a module can be viewed as being a *black box.* That is, we take an abstract point of view and focus on *what* the task is for each module, rather than on *how* the task is carried out. Such modules then can be organized systematically in a hierarchical structure in which there is only one top module. Each module in the resulting *structure chart* can have only one superior, but may have many subordinates.

Whereas a structure chart is based on hierarchical structure, a *flowchart* is based on sequential procedure. Because each of the five basic structures described above has *one entry* and *one exit,* their use in flowcharts permits one to focus on the detail or the summary of individual processes.

Two of the several available diagrammatic conventions for representing program structure were overviewed in this chapter. *Hierarchical Input-Process-Output (HIPO)* was developed by IBM and focuses on the *inputs, processes,* and *outputs* of programs, as the name of the approach indicates. The *Visual Table of Contents (VTOC)* diagram is the hierarchical structure chart used with this approach. In contrast, *Warnier-Orr charts* use horizontally arranged brackets rather than vertically placed blocks to represent the hierarchical structure of a program. Since these two methods are not the only ones available and no method has been accepted as the standard, in this book we use hierarchical structure charts as a simplified diagrammatic representation of programs.

Formatting rules and guidelines used with structured COBOL programs were described and illustrated in the final section of this chapter. Major consideration was given to (1) use of physical spacing in the source program; (2) use of vertical alignment of similar items to convey similarity of function; (3) use of group labels to convey common functions; (4) use of similar names for similar items; and (5) use of numerical prefixes to indicate the physical order of the paragraphs in the program.

EXERCISES

6.1 Demonstrate each of the five fundamental structures for programming in flowchart form and also through COBOL programming examples.

6.2 Figure 6-12 presents a detailed flowchart segment of a program.

FIGURE 6-12

Flowchart for Exercise 6.2

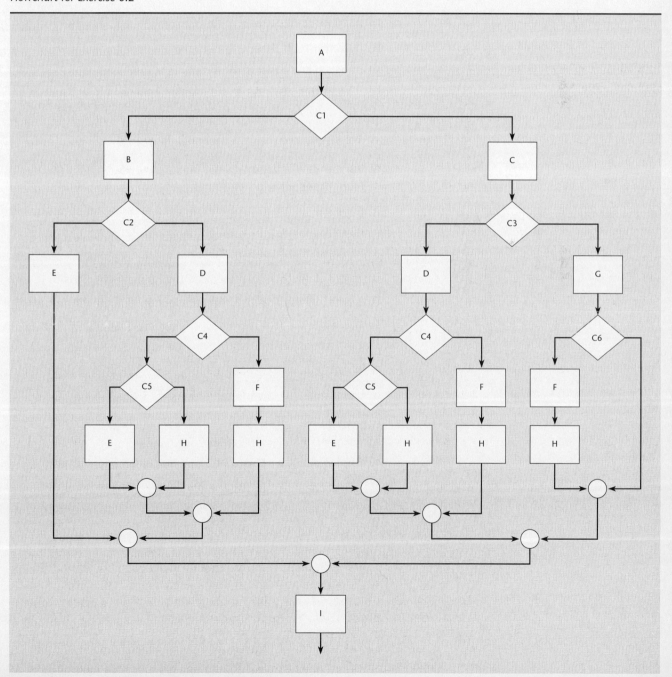

a. Demonstrate your understanding of the concept of levels of abstraction by drawing two revised versions of the flowchart—one at a high and one at an intermediate level of abstraction.

b. Draw a structure chart of the functions included in Figure 6-12. Each rectangular block in the flowchart is assumed to stand for a PERFORMed procedure. For example, the B block in the upper left of the flowchart should be visualized to be the name of a paragraph which is executed if condition C1 is false.

6.3 A program is to be developed to represent the basic logic and function of a vending machine that accepts nickels, dimes, and quarters, dispenses a 30-cent snack, and provides the correct change, if any. Coins other than nickels, dimes, and quarters are rejected. We assume that we want to develop a program that reads data records, with each data record representing one coin. The program reads the data, processes it, and either "delivers" a product and the change or reads another record representing another coin. The last record in the input file contains a special code that indicates the end of the data. After processing such a record, the program stops.

a. Draw a structure chart of the program. Remember that the purpose of a structure chart is to list the functions to be done as black boxes. For example Compute-Change would be one of the functions.

b. Write the program outline in pseudocode.

c. Draw a flowchart of the program logic.

6.4 A sales file consists of records having the following format:

Salesperson Name	Date	Amount of Sale	Other Data

For a given salesperson there may be many records. The records are sorted so that the records for each salesperson are together, in sequence.

A program is to be written to produce a report similar to the following format:

```
SALESPERSON NAME              DATE          AMOUNT OF SALE

JOHNSON, A. J.              03/11/90            132.29

                           03/20/90            150.15

TOTAL                                          282.44
```

(new page)

```
SALESPERSON NAME              DATE          AMOUNT OF SALE

NOWAK, C. J.               04/01/90            300.00
```

(etc. for each salesperson)

Note that when a new salesperson begins, we print the total for the previous one, we skip to a new page, we print the heading, the name of the new salesperson, the date, and amount of sale. This report will be repeated for as many salespeople as there are in the file, with sales for each salesperson reported starting with a new page. Assume that no salesperson will need more than one page for his/her report.

a. Design a structure chart for such a program.

b. Write a pseudocode outline for such a program.

Additional
COBOL
Instructions

7

Additional Procedure Division Statements

IN THIS CHAPTER *you will do what the title directly indicates: you will study a variety of PROCEDURE DIVISION statements. The purpose of this chapter is to complete the description of the main verbs that are available in the PROCEDURE DIVISION, as a follow-up to the introduction in Chapter 2.*

An obvious characteristic of COBOL is the rich set of available commands. Unlike many other languages, COBOL consists of many specialized statements, and features within statements.

In this chapter you will study a relatively large number of verbs and the options associated with them. However, you should not expect to master all of the verbs at this point. This chapter is intended to serve as a useful reference as you continue to develop your COBOL programming skills.

THE FOUR ARITHMETIC VERBS

Chapter 4 introduced the *four basic arithmetic verbs:* ADD, SUBTRACT, MULTIPLY, and DIVIDE. Now we complete the discussion of these verbs in greater detail. Figure 7-1 presents the standard formats for the four principal arithmetic verbs. As can be seen in this figure, a variety of statement formats can be written. Rather than discuss every format, we present a number of selected and representative examples to illustrate the format and effect of executing different arithmetic statements. However, before considering the examples, we first discuss two specialized clauses that can be used with arithmetic statements in the following two subsections: the ROUNDED and ON SIZE ERROR clauses.

The ROUNDED Clause

A need frequently exists for *rounding* numeric values. For example, even though prices or rates of interest may be quoted to three or four decimal places, any billing must be rounded to two decimal places, since the smallest monetary unit is the cent. COBOL provides automatic rounding by use of the ROUNDED clause, which can be used with all arithmetic verbs.

Execution of the statement ADD A TO B ROUNDED will result in a rounded number in B. If B were specified as containing two decimal places in a PIC 999V99 description, for example, rounding would be accomplished by adding 0.005 to the result of the addition and truncating the third place. Thus if A had the value 1.286 and B had the value 2.00, ADD A TO B ROUNDED would result in the value 3.29 being stored in B. Therefore, when the remainder that is to be dropped begins with a 5 or higher value, the number is rounded up; otherwise, it is rounded down. If B were specified to contain one place to the right of the decimal (say PIC 999V9), 0.05 is added to the result of the addition, and the second place is truncated.

The ON SIZE ERROR Clause

The case may arise in which an arithmetic result is larger than anticipated, in terms of the number of digit positions available. For example, a person earning $10.00 per hour should have a weekly gross pay well under $999.99. But suppose that by some mistake in the input the computed weekly pay is over $1,000.00. Rather than allow truncation of this figure to occur, such "overflows" can be detected by use of the ON SIZE ERROR clause. For example, assume GROSS has PICTURE 999V99. We can write

```
MULTIPLY RATE BY HOURS GIVING GROSS
    ON SIZE ERROR
        MOVE "GROSS PAY EXCEEDS $999.99" TO ERR-MESSAGE.
```

The ON SIZE ERROR clause is simply a conditional statement that says, if the size of a value does not fit in the field, do whatever is indicated in the statement that follows in that sentence. The statement that follows must be imperative; that is, it cannot be conditional. When ON SIZE ERROR is used and the condition is met, the arithmetic operand intended to receive the result is not altered from its previous value. In other words, it is as if the arithmetic operations had not happened.

In addition to "large" results, the ON SIZE ERROR condition also is met when there is a division by zero. As you may recall from algebra, division by zero is an undefined operation yielding an "infinitely" large quotient.

In COBOL '85 two enhancements have been made that are included as the last two lines in each of the formats presented in Figure 7-1. These are the NOT

FIGURE 7-1

Standard COBOL Formats for the
Four Arithmetic Verbs

ADD $\left\{ \begin{array}{l} \text{identifier -1} \\ \text{literal -1} \end{array} \right\}$ $\left[\begin{array}{l} \text{identifier -2} \\ \text{literal -2} \end{array} \right]$ . . . TO identifier-m [ROUNDED]

[identifier-n [ROUNDED]] . . . [ON SIZE ERROR imperative-statement-1]

[NOT ON SIZE ERROR imperative-statement-2]

[END-ADD]

ADD $\left\{ \begin{array}{l} \text{identifier -1} \\ \text{literal -1} \end{array} \right\}$ $\left[\begin{array}{l} \text{identifier -2} \\ \text{literal -2} \end{array} \right]$ $\left[\begin{array}{l} \text{identifier -3} \\ \text{literal -3} \end{array} \right]$ . . .

GIVING identifier-m [ROUNDED] [identifier-n [ROUNDED]] . . .

[ON SIZE ERROR imperative-statement-1]

[NOT ON SIZE ERROR imperative-statement-2]

[END-ADD]

SUBTRACT $\left\{ \begin{array}{l} \text{identifier -1} \\ \text{literal -1} \end{array} \right\}$ $\left[\begin{array}{l} \text{identifier -2} \\ \text{literal -2} \end{array} \right]$ . . . FROM identifier-m [ROUNDED]

[identifier-n [ROUNDED]] . . . [ON SIZE ERROR imperative-statement-1]

[NOT ON SIZE ERROR] imperative-statement-2]

[END-SUBTRACT]

SUBTRACT $\left\{ \begin{array}{l} \text{identifier -1} \\ \text{literal -1} \end{array} \right\}$ $\left[\begin{array}{l} \text{identifier -2} \\ \text{literal -2} \end{array} \right]$ . . . FROM $\left\{ \begin{array}{l} \text{identifier -m} \\ \text{literal -m} \end{array} \right\}$

GIVING identifier-n [ROUNDED] [identifier-o [ROUNDED]] . . .

[ON SIZE ERROR imperative-statement-1]

[NOT ON SIZE ERROR imperative-statement-2]

[END-SUBTRACT]

MULTIPLY $\left\{ \begin{array}{l} \text{identifier -1} \\ \text{literal -1} \end{array} \right\}$ BY identifier-2 [ROUNDED]

[identifier-3 [ROUNDED]] . . . [ON SIZE ERROR imperative-statement-1]

[NOT ON SIZE ERROR imperative-statement-2]

[END-MULTIPLY]

MULTIPLY $\left\{ \begin{array}{l} \text{identifier -1} \\ \text{literal -1} \end{array} \right\}$ BY $\left\{ \begin{array}{l} \text{identifier -2} \\ \text{literal -2} \end{array} \right\}$ GIVING identifier-3 [ROUNDED]

[identifier-4 [ROUNDED]] . . . [ON SIZE ERROR imperative-statement-1]

[NOT ON SIZE ERROR imperative-statement-2]

[END-MULTIPLY]

DIVIDE $\left\{ \begin{array}{l} \text{identifier -1} \\ \text{literal -1} \end{array} \right\}$ INTO identifier-2 [ROUNDED]

[identifier-3 [ROUNDED]] . . . [ON SIZE ERROR imperative-statement-1]

[NOT ON SIZE ERROR imperative-statement-2]

[END-DIVIDE]

DIVIDE $\left\{ \begin{array}{l} \text{identifier -1} \\ \text{literal -1} \end{array} \right\}$ INTO $\left\{ \begin{array}{l} \text{identifier -2} \\ \text{literal -2} \end{array} \right\}$ GIVING identifier-3 [ROUNDED]

[identifier-4 [ROUNDED]] . . . [ON SIZE ERROR imperative-statement-1]

[NOT ON SIZE ERROR imperative-statement-2]

[END-DIVIDE]

FIGURE 7-1
Standard COBOL Formats for the
Four Arithmetic Verbs (continued)

$$\underline{DIVIDE} \begin{Bmatrix} \text{identifier -1} \\ \text{literal -1} \end{Bmatrix} \underline{BY} \begin{Bmatrix} \text{identifier -2} \\ \text{literal -2} \end{Bmatrix} \underline{GIVING} \text{ identifier-3 } [\underline{ROUNDED}]$$

$\underline{REMAINDER}$ identifier-4 [ON $\underline{SIZE ERROR}$ imperative-statement-1]

[$\underline{NOT}$ ON $\underline{SIZE ERROR}$ imperative-statement-2]

[$\underline{END-DIVIDE}$]

$$\underline{DIVIDE} \begin{Bmatrix} \text{identifier -1} \\ \text{literal -1} \end{Bmatrix} \underline{INTO} \begin{Bmatrix} \text{identifier -2} \\ \text{literal -2} \end{Bmatrix} \underline{GIVING} \text{ identifier-3 } [\underline{ROUNDED}]$$

[identifier-4 [ROUNDED]] . . . [ON $\underline{SIZE ERROR}$ imperative-statement-1]

[$\underline{NOT}$ ON $\underline{SIZE ERROR}$ imperative-statement-2]

[$\underline{END-DIVIDE}$]

$$\underline{DIVIDE} \begin{Bmatrix} \text{identifier -1} \\ \text{literal -1} \end{Bmatrix} \underline{BY} \begin{Bmatrix} \text{identifier -2} \\ \text{literal -2} \end{Bmatrix} \underline{GIVING} \text{ identifier-3 } [\underline{ROUNDED}]$$

$\underline{REMAINDER}$ identifier-4 [ON $\underline{SIZE ERROR}$ imperative-statement-1]

[$\underline{NOT}$ ON $\underline{SIZE ERROR}$ imperative-statement-2]

[$\underline{END-DIVIDE}$]

ON SIZE ERROR clause and the END-verb terminators. Figure 7-2 presents code and corresponding flowcharts for purposes of illustrating and contrasting COBOL '74 and COBOL '85. The flowcharts are intended to show the actual meaning of the program statements. As can be seen in the figure, because the 1974 version does not have the NOT ON SIZE ERROR and END-ADD features, a test flag field (SIZE-ERR-TEST) was used to code the required logic. In contrast, the program code for the 1985 version is much more straightforward.

The ON SIZE ERROR and other conditionals such as the AT END are actually specialized IF statements; in this vein, they apply until a period is encountered. In COBOL '74 the ON SIZE ERROR provides for a course of action when the condition is true, but it does not provide for a course of action when it is false. The 1985 version allows for a symmetrical specification with the ON SIZE ERROR and NOT ON SIZE ERROR dual alternatives, as illustrated in the flowchart in the second column of Figure 7-2.

The END-verb clause provides for termination of the SIZE ERROR conditional statement. Notice that in the example in Figure 7-2, there is no period after the END-ADD, and none is required. As the flowchart illustrates, the MOVE Z TO A is executed regardless of the truth or falsity of the SIZE ERROR condition.

As a final point, let us test our understanding of the difference in the two sample program codes in Figure 7-2. Suppose that in each case the following program statement preceded the code:

```
    .
    .
    .
W    PIC  9.
    .
    .
    .
MOVE 3  TO W
MOVE 10 TO X
MOVE 20 TO Y
```

Deliberately, W has been defined with PIC 9 in the DATA DIVISION, which then invariably will result in the SIZE ERROR condition being true in the example

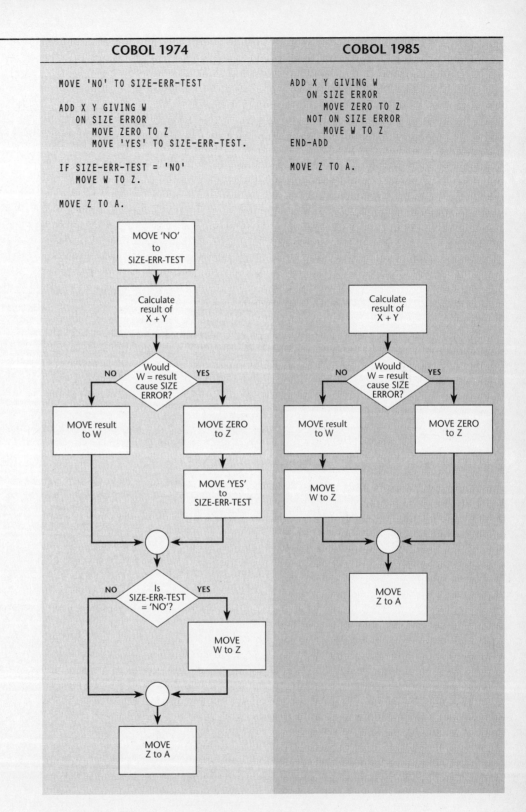

FIGURE 7-2
ON SIZE ERROR Illustration

COBOL 1974	COBOL 1985

```
MOVE 'NO' TO SIZE-ERR-TEST

ADD X Y GIVING W
   ON SIZE ERROR
      MOVE ZERO TO Z
      MOVE 'YES' TO SIZE-ERR-TEST.

IF SIZE-ERR-TEST = 'NO'
   MOVE W TO Z.

MOVE Z TO A.
```

```
ADD X Y GIVING W
   ON SIZE ERROR
      MOVE ZERO TO Z
   NOT ON SIZE ERROR
      MOVE W TO Z
END-ADD

MOVE Z TO A.
```

above. What is the value stored in A at the completion of each program version in Figure 7-2? The answer is, A is equal to zero.

Use of the Arithmetic Verbs

Figure 7-3 presents a set of examples involving the use of the arithmetic verbs. Review these examples and note the effects of the various forms of the instructions

FIGURE 7-3
Examples of the Use of Arithmetic Verbs

	W	X	Y	Z
PICTURE:	S999V99	999V99	999V99	999
INITIAL VALUE:	010.00	090.00	030.00	040
1. ADD X TO Y			120.00	
2. ADD X, Y TO Z				160
3. ADD 5 Y GIVING W	035.00			
4. ADD X, 12.456 TO Y ROUNDED			132.46	

5. ADD 1000.25 TO Y ROUNDED
    ON SIZE ERROR
       MOVE ZERO TO Z
				000

6. SUBTRACT Y FROM X		060.00		
7. SUBTRACT X FROM Y			060.00	
8. SUBTRACT X Y FROM W	130.00			
9. SUBTRACT W FROM X GIVING Y			100.00	

10. SUBTRACT 1260.256 FROM Y
     ROUNDED
     ON SIZE ERROR
        MOVE ZERO TO Z
				000

11. MOVE 10 TO X MULTIPLY X BY Y		010.00	300.00	
12. MULTIPLY X BY Y			700.00	

13. MULTIPLY X BY Y
     ON SIZE ERROR
        MOVE ZERO TO Z
				000

14. MULTIPLY Y BY 0.2453 GIVING X ROUNDED		077.36		
15. DIVIDE Y INTO X		003.00		
16. DIVIDE X INTO Y			000.33	
17. DIVIDE Z INTO 100 GIVING Y			002.50	
18. DIVIDE 12.2 INTO X Y ROUNDED		007.37	002.46	
19. DIVIDE 12.2 INTO Y GIVING Z REMAINDER X		005.60		002
20. DIVIDE Z BY 12.2 GIVING Y ROUNDED REMAINDER X		000.10	003.28	

on the data fields. Negative values are indicated by a negative sign above the rightmost digit of a number, while decimal points are indicated by a caret ($\wedge$). In addition, the following paragraphs direct your attention to some particular results.

Example 4 illustrates the effect of the ROUNDED clause. The result of 132.456 has been rounded to 132.46 because Y has two decimal positions.

Example 5 shows the effect of the ON SIZE ERROR clause. Since Y has three positions to the left of the decimal point, the result 1030.25 is too large. Incidentally, if the ON SIZE ERROR had not been used, the result in Y would have been stored as 030.25 due to truncation of the first significant digit.

Example 7 illustrates that a negative result is stored as an absolute value (without sign) if the numeric field does not include the S PICTURE character.

Example 8 illustrates the application of the rule of arithmetic that subtracting from a negative value is equivalent to adding the number to be subtracted to that negative value.

Example 12 illustrates that truncation will occur if the number is larger than the defined field.

Example 18 shows the effects of the absence of ROUNDED in the result in X and the presence of ROUNDED in the result in Y. Incidentally, it is permissible to write DIVIDE 12.2 INTO X ROUNDED Y ROUNDED.

Example 19 illustrates the storage of the integer result in Z (since the PICTURE of Z is integer) and storage of the remainder in X. The remainder is determined as follows. Because the integer quotient is 30.00 / 12.2 = 2, the remainder is 30.00 – (2 x 12.2) = 5.6.

Example 20 shows that the value is stored in the REMAINDER field before the rounding takes place. Thus the unrounded quotient is 3.278, which, if stored in Y, would have been stored unrounded as 3.27. The remainder is, then, 40 – (3.27 x 12.2) = 0.106, which is stored (right-truncated) in X as 0.10.

R E V I E W . . . .

1. If the result of an arithmetic operation is 45.4545, rounding to three decimal places will result in the value _____ being placed in a storage location, whereas rounding to two places will result in the value _____ being placed in the storage location.

    45.455; 45.45

2. If the ROUNDED option is not used, 45.4545 reported to three places would result in the value _____ , whereas the value reported to two places would be _____ .

    45.454; 45.45

3. When the number of digits of an arithmetic result is greater than the number defined in the PIC specifications, such an overflow can be signaled by use of the _____ clause.

    ON SIZE ERROR

4. In addition to the availability of the ON SIZE ERROR clause, COBOL '85 provides for a course of action when there is no such error by the _____ clause.

    NOT ON SIZE ERROR

5. In COBOL '85 termination of the SIZE ERROR statement, or processing associated with any verb, is signalled clearly by the _____-verb clause.

    END

6. Complete the following table by entering the numeric result of each arithmetic operation:

	W	X	Y	Z
PICTURE:	99V9	99	99V9	S999.9
INITIAL VALUE:	15$_\wedge$0	10	12$_\wedge$8	100$_\wedge$0

1. ADD W, Y TO X

2. ADD W, Y GIVING X ROUNDED

3. SUBTRACT W FROM Y

4. SUBTRACT W FROM Y GIVING Z

5. MULTIPLY W BY Y

6. MULTIPLY X BY Y GIVING Z ROUNDED

7. DIVIDE X INTO Y ON SIZE ERROR MOVE ZERO TO X

8. DIVIDE X INTO Y ROUNDED REMAINDER Z

1.	X = 37	5.	Y = 92$_\wedge$0
2.	X = 28	6.	Z = 128$_\wedge$8
3.	Y = 02$_\wedge$2	7.	Y = 1$_\wedge$2
4.	Z = 002$_\wedge\bar{2}$	8.	Y = 1$_\wedge$3; Z = 008$_\wedge$8
			[= 12.8 – (1.2 x 10)]

• •

THE COMPUTE VERB

Use of the four arithmetic verbs we have studied thus far is well suited for single arithmetic operations, but suppose it is required that an answer be obtained by use of such a formula as $a = 3b - c + b(d - 2)$. If we were to use the four arithmetic verbs to evaluate this expression, a large number of statements would be required. However, use of the COMPUTE verb along with symbolic arithmetic operators makes it possible to write compact arithmetic statements for mathematical expressions.

Table 7-1 lists the symbols used for the arithmetic operations of addition, subtraction, multiplication, division, and exponentiation. Only the symbols for multiplication and exponentiation are different from the symbols commonly used in mathematics. In addition to the symbols, parentheses can be used to designate the *order of operations;* however, unlike their use in algebra, parentheses never are used to designate multiplication.

TABLE 7-1

The Five Arithmetic Operations in COBOL

+	Addition
–	Subtraction
*	Multiplication
/	Division
**	Exponentiation (raising to a power)

An *arithmetic expression* is formed by the use of arithmetic operators and data-names or literals. At least one space must separate each operator symbol from the preceding and following data-names, with parentheses used to designate or clarify the order of operations. Some examples of arithmetic expressions are shown here.

ALGEBRAIC EXPRESSION	COBOL ARITHMETIC EXPRESSION
$a + b$	A + B
$a - b + (a - 5)c$	A − B + (A − 5) * C
$a^2 - \dfrac{b + c}{2}$	A ** 2 − (B + C) / 2

When parentheses are used, the operations within the parentheses are completed first, with order of priority given to the innermost sets, working from left to right in the arithmetic expression. In the absence of parentheses, the arithmetic operations are performed according to the following order of priority:

1. Exponentiation
2. Multiplication and division from left to right in the order written
3. Addition and subtraction from left to right in the order written

Consider the following COBOL examples:

COBOL ARITHMETIC EXPRESSION	ALGEBRAIC EXPRESSION
A + B / C	$a + \dfrac{b}{c}$
(A + B) / C	$\dfrac{a + b}{c}$
A + (B / C)	$a + \dfrac{b}{c}$

The first and third COBOL expressions represent the same algebraic expression. This is so because in the first example the rule that division takes priority over addition applies. Nevertheless, it is good programming practice to include the parentheses in such cases, since it improves documentation.

In addition to the five arithmetic operations, COBOL defines a " + " and a " − " *unary* operator. The operator is simply an instruction to multiply a variable by +1 or −1, respectively. Thus, if we want to multiply variable B times the negative value of variable A, we could use the unary operator as follows:

```
B * (- A)
```

The "−" in the above expression is the unary operator. In this example parentheses are used to avoid having two consecutive arithmetic operators.

Returning to the COMPUTE verb, we note that the general format associated with the use of this verb is

COMPUTE {identifier-1 [ROUNDED]} . . . = arithmetic-expression-1

    [ON SIZE ERROR imperative-statement-1]

    [NOT ON SIZE ERROR imperative-statement-2]

    [END-COMPUTE]

A simple example of using the COMPUTE verb is

```
COMPUTE GROSS = (REGULAR * WAGE) + 1.5 * (OVERTIME * WAGE).
```

An example that includes use of the ROUNDED and ON SIZE ERROR options is

```
COMPUTE GROSS ROUNDED =
    (REGULAR * WAGE) + 1.5 * (OVERTIME * WAGE)
    ON SIZE ERROR
        PERFORM GROSS-TOO-BIG.
```

The NOT ON SIZE ERROR clause and the END-COMPUTE terminator are available only in the 1985 standard. These additional features are used for the same purposes as for the arithmetic verbs, as described in the preceding section of this chapter.

The identifier-1 in the COMPUTE format is the storage field that receives the results. It should be noted that it can be a numeric or numeric edited item. It really corresponds to the GIVING identifier clause in the other arithmetic verbs. All identifiers on the right-hand side, however, must be elementary numeric (nonedited) items.

The arithmetic operators +, –, *, and / correspond to the verbs ADD, SUBTRACT, MULTIPLY, and DIVIDE, respectively. The arithmetic operator ** has no corresponding verb and can be used only with the COMPUTE. Since exponentiation is a general mathematical process, it can be used to extract square roots as well as to raise numbers to various powers. Thus A**2 means a^2, but A**0.5 means $\sqrt{A}$. This facility to extract roots increases the usefulness of the exponentiation operator. In general, however, COBOL has limited computational capabilities. COBOL is used for data processing tasks rather than for computational tasks. Thus logarithmic and trigonometric functions are not available in COBOL, although they commonly are available in languages developed for scientific work.

R E V I E W . . . .

1. As an alternative to the arithmetic verbs, arithmetic operators can be used in conjunction with the _____ verb.

   COMPUTE

2. The arithmetic symbols used with the COMPUTE verb—which indicate the operations addition, subtraction, multiplication, division, and exponentiation—are _____ , _____ , _____ , _____ , and _____ , respectively.

   +, –, *, /, and **

3. The COBOL arithmetic expression corresponding to the algebraic expression $a^2 - 2ac + c^2$ is _____ .

   (A**2) – (2 * A * C) + (C**2) (See further comment in the next review item.)

4. Suppose that all the parentheses included in the above answer were omitted. The algebraic expression that corresponds to the resulting COBOL expression would be _____ .

   $a^2 - 2ac + c^2$ (Discussion continued in the next review item.)

5. Therefore, because of the order in which the arithmetic operations always are performed, no parentheses are required in the COBOL expression just given. However, such parentheses usually are included to improve readability of the program. In the absence of parentheses, the order of priority for the arithmetic operations is such that _____ always is performed first, followed by _____ and _____ , and culminating with _____ and _____ .

   exponentiation; multiplication; division; addition; subtraction

6. Typically, however, the use or nonuse of parentheses *does* make a difference in the way a COBOL arithmetic expression is evaluated. For each of the following COBOL expressions, indicate the equivalent algebraic expression:

COBOL ARITHMETIC EXPRESSION	ALGEBRAIC EXPRESSION
((A + (B * C)) / D)**2	_____
(A + (B * C)) / D**2	_____
A + (B * C) / D**2	_____
A + B * C / D**2	_____

$$\left(\frac{a+bc}{c}\right)^2; \quad \frac{a+bc}{d^2}; \quad a+\frac{bc}{d^2}; \quad a+\frac{bc}{d^2}$$

7. An example of the use of the unary operator in a simple COBOL expression involving multiplication is _____ .

A * (−B) (or other similar example)

8. In the general format associated with the COMPUTE verb, the results of the arithmetic operation are stored in [identifier-1 / arithmetic-expression-1].

identifier-1

. . . .

ADDITIONAL PERFORM OPTIONS

The PERFORM ... TIMES

There are tasks in which a procedure needs to be executed a definite number of times, and in such cases the TIMES option is useful. The format is

PERFORM [procedure -name] $\begin{Bmatrix} \text{integer} \\ \text{identifier} \end{Bmatrix}$ TIMES

[imperative -statement]

[END-PERFORM]

As an example, in accounting applications we sometimes need to form the "sum of the digits" for depreciating an asset over N years, where N is always an integer (whole number). In general, the required sum is 1 + 2 + 3 + ... + (N−1) + N. Thus, if N = 5, we have 1 + 2 + 3 + 4 + 5 = 15. In a COBOL program, we can form the sum-of-digits for N, by using the TIMES option, as follows:

```
MOVE ZERO TO SUM-OF-DIGITS
MOVE 1 TO YEAR-COUNTER
PERFORM FORM-SUM N TIMES
    .
    .
    .
FORM-SUM.
    ADD YEAR-COUNTER TO SUM-OF-DIGITS
    ADD 1 TO YEAR-COUNTER.
```

Alternatively, using the in-line PERFORM of COBOL '85, we could write

```
MOVE ZERO TO SUM-OF-DIGITS
MOVE 1 TO YEAR-COUNTER
PERFORM N TIMES
    ADD YEAR-COUNTER TO SUM-OF-DIGITS
    ADD 1 TO YEAR-COUNTER
END-PERFORM.
```

The PERFORM ... THRU

Instead of PERFORMing one procedure, it is possible to reference a series of procedures that are all written in sequence by referencing the first and the last procedure. In general, whenever we have "procedure-name" in a PERFORM format, we can substitute

$$\underline{\text{PERFORM}} \quad \text{procedure-name-1} \begin{Bmatrix} \underline{\text{THROUGH}} \\ \underline{\text{THRU}} \end{Bmatrix} \text{procedure-name-2}$$

Consider the following example:

```
PERFORM PROCESS-DETAIL-START THRU PROCESS DETAIL-EXIT
    UNTIL END-OF-FILE = 'YES'.
    .
    .
    .
PROCESS-DETAIL-START.
    ADD . . . .
COMPUTE-SPECIAL-PRICE.
    IF . . .
READ-RECORD.
    READ CUSTOMER-FILE
        AT END MOVE 'YES' TO END-OF-FILE.
PROCESS-DETAIL-EXIT.
    EXIT.
```

The example, in effect, states that the group of paragraphs that begin with the one named PROCESS-DETAIL-START through the one named PROCESS-DETAIL-EXIT are to be executed in sequence, one after another. When the last statement in the last-named paragraph is executed, then program execution returns to the original PERFORM statement. In everyday language the PERFORM ... THRU states

> Perform the group of consecutive paragraphs that begins with the first-named paragraph and ends with the second-named paragraph.

With use of the PERFORM ... THRU option, it is common practice to use the specialized EXIT verb to mark the last paragraph in the THRU range. The last paragraph consists of only one statement, the EXIT statement. In effect, the EXIT is a do-nothing, or "no-op" (no-operation) statement. It allows the programmer to identify a place in the program but it does not require any processing. In the above example the only purpose for the EXIT is program documentation: it simply makes it easier for the reader of the program to see that PROCESS-DETAIL-EXIT is the last paragraph in a PERFORM ... THRU range of paragraphs. At other times the EXIT statement is used in conjunction with the GO TO verb, discussed later in this chapter. Briefly, if we want to bypass execution of some paragraph(s) in a range of paragraphs referenced by a PERFORM ... THRU, we could include a statement such as

```
IF some condition is true
    GO TO PROCESS-DETAIL-EXIT.
```

The effect of this code would be to reach the end of the range and return to the original PERFORM ... THRU without executing anything else (recall that EXIT is a no-op type of statement).

Although the THRU option is available, we do not recommend its use except for very special circumstances. The reason is that it relies heavily on the physical position of paragraphs. For instance, in the above example, if the COMPUTE-SPECIAL-PRICE paragraph were moved elsewhere in the program, a most serious error would result.

Instead of using the THRU option, we recommend using one paragraph that, in turn, includes PERFORM commands that make reference to each of the other paragraphs. Using such an approach for the above example, we have

```
PERFORM PROCESS-CUSTOMER
    UNTIL END-OF-FILE = 'YES'.
        .
        .
        .
PROCESS-CUSTOMER.
    PERFORM PROCESS-DETAIL
    PERFORM COMPUTE-SPECIAL-PRICE
    PERFORM READ-RECORD.
PROCESS-DETAIL.
    ADD . . .
COMPUTE-SPECIAL-PRICE.
    IF . . .
READ-RECORD.
    READ CUSTOMER-FILE . . .
```

In this revised structure the physical position of paragraphs is irrelevant, and the relationship among the paragraphs is clear.

Alternatively, in COBOL '85 we can use an in-line PERFORM, as follows:

```
PERFORM UNTIL END-OF-FILE = 'YES'
    PERFORM PROCESS-DETAIL
    PERFORM COMPUTE-SPECIAL-PRICE
    PERFORM READ-RECORD
END-PERFORM.
```

Nested PERFORM statements

We have already seen examples of *nested PERFORM statements:* one paragraph performs another paragraph, which, in turn, performs another paragraph, and so on. Such nesting is common and useful. In a structure chart it corresponds to blocks at systematically lower levels. However, one important rule is that we cannot have *cyclical (recursive) nesting.* Consider this example:

```
PAR-A.
    PERFORM PAR-B.
PAR-B.
    PERFORM PAR-C.
PAR-C.
    PERFORM PAR-A
    PERFORM PAR-B.
```

Both PERFORM statements in PAR-C are in error; it is not valid to issue a PERFORM backwards. What will happen if we do? In general, the results are unpredictable, and often are very strange, depending on the particular compiler used. In fact, if a program compiles without errors and then during execution does "strange" things, it may be well worth the effort to check for the possibility of cyclical PERFORM statements.

When the THRU option is exercised, it is possible to have one or more PERFORM statements included in the range of procedure-1 to procedure-2. These are nested PERFORM statements. It is also possible to have PERFORM statements whose range is totally outside the range of the first PERFORM. The following two examples illustrate the two permitted structures:

CORRECT STRUCTURE

```
A.      . . . PERFORM B THRU F.
B.                                              ⌐─── B
C.      . . . PERFORM D THRU E.
D.                                              │   ⌐─ D
E.                                              │   └─ E
F.                                              └───── F
```

CORRECT STRUCTURE

```
A.      . . . PERFORM B THRU D.
B.                                              ⌐─ B
C.      . . . PERFORM M THRU Q.                 │      . . . PERFORM M THRU Q.
D.                                              └─ D
G.
M.                                              ⌐─ M
I.
Q.                                              └─ Q
```

Finally, the following example illustrates an incorrect structure:

INCORRECT STRUCTURE

```
A.      . . . PERFORM B THRU E.                 ⌐──── B
B.                                              │ ⌐── D
C.      . . . PERFORM D THRU F.                 │ │
D.                                              │ │
E.                                              └─┼─ E
F.                                                └─ F
```

R E V I E W . . . .

1. The format of the PERFORM statement that specifies execution of a procedure a definite number of times is the PERFORM ... _____ .

TIMES

2. The PERFORM ... THRU format permits the execution of [two / two or more] procedures.

two or more

3. Suppose that four consecutive paragraphs are to be executed by use of the PERFORM ... THRU command. The PERFORM statement specifically would include reference to [two / four] procedure-names.

two

4. Because a change in the physical position of paragraphs generally would disrupt the intent of a PERFORM ... THRU command, the use of this format has to be considered as being _____-prone.

error

5. When a PERFORM statement results in execution of a paragraph that itself contains another PERFORM statement (and so forth), the program structure is described as having a _____ PERFORM structure.

nested

6. The type of nesting of PERFORM statements that is not allowed, and may have unpredictable results upon program execution, is _____ nesting.

cyclical (recursive)

7. The "no-op" type of verb discussed in this section that is always used alone in a paragraph is the _____ verb.

EXIT

8. A common use of the EXIT verb is to indicate the _____ of a PERFORM ... THRU range of paragraphs for documentation purposes.

end (or last paragraph)

. . . .

THE GO TO VERB

For a long time the GO TO was one of the most frequently used verbs in all programming languages. However, it has been found that its unrestricted use is likely to create difficulty in reading a program and may contribute to the development of error-prone programs. With some minor exceptions in this book we refrain from the use of GO TO. Still, programs written in the first quarter-century of programming history are full of GO TO statements, and the reader should be familiar with this control verb.

GO TO is an unconditional branch to a paragraph or section name (sections are discussed in chapter 11). Consider the following example, which incorporates use of the GO TO:

```
READING-DATA.
    READ EMPLOYEE-FILE
        AT END GO TO WRAP-UP.
    PERFORM PROCESS-EMPLOYEE
    GO TO READING-DATA.
PROCESS-EMPLOYEE.
    .
    .
    .
WRAP-UP.
    PERFORM. . . .
    CLOSE. . .
    STOP RUN.
```

Notice that AT END the program specifies GO TO WRAP-UP, which terminates the program, among other things. If the AT END is not true, PERFORM PROCESS-EMPLOYEE is executed and then execution continues with GO TO READING-DATA. This last GO TO implements an iterative procedure, and it does so by referring to its own paragraph name.

Use of the GO TO in simple programs, such as the above example, seems straightforward and even, perhaps, appealing. However, in programs of typical size and complexity, use of GO TO is likely to cause unnecessary complications in logic. Of course, it should be made very clear that the use of the GO TO in the above example is unstructured code!

R E V I E W . . . .

1. The COBOL verb that provides the programmer with the capability of achieving unconditional branching in a program without returning to the point of original branching is the _____ .

GO TO

2. The GO TO verb has been used in both COBOL and other programming languages. The use of this verb steadily has been [increasing / decreasing] in recent years.

decreasing

. . . .

THE ACCEPT AND DISPLAY VERBS

Up to this point we always have discussed input and output in connection with files. Such is the normal use of input and output verbs, but it also is possible to execute input and output in conjunction with storage fields that are not part of any files. This typically is done to permit the input and/or output of short data items to or from devices such as video terminals, the system console, and printers. The verbs that allow such input and output are ACCEPT and DISPLAY.

The ACCEPT Verb

There are two general formats associated with use of the ACCEPT verb. The first format is

FORMAT 1

ACCEPT identifier [FROM mnemonic-name]

This format can be used as in this example:

```
ACCEPT STARTING-CHECK-NO FROM OPERATOR-CONSOLE.
```

As a result of executing this instruction, the computer will input data into the STARTING-CHECK-NO storage field from the device previously defined as OPERA-TOR-CONSOLE in the SPECIAL-NAMES paragraph of the ENVIRONMENT DIVI-SION, as in, for instance:

```
ENVIRONMENT DIVISION.
CONFIGURATION SECTION.
SOURCE-COMPUTER.  . . .
OBJECT-COMPUTER.  . . .
SPECIAL-NAMES.
    CONSOLE IS  OPERATOR-CONSOLE.
```

If this device is a keyboard, further program execution is delayed until the operator enters the appropriate input. If the device referenced in the ACCEPT is a file, the next record will be read, and data will be input into STARTING-CHECK-NO.

Data input via ACCEPT is treated as if it were alphanumeric with respect to positioning. Suppose that STARTING-CHECK-NO has been defined with a PICTURE 99999. If ACCEPT is executed with reference to the operator's control terminal and the operator types in 12345, the receiving field will contain 12345. On the other hand, if the operator types 12, the 12 will be stored left-justified in

STARTING-CHECK-NO, followed by three blanks. In general, an entire record is moved from the input device to the identifier specified in ACCEPT. Thus, when we typed 12 above, we were, in effect, transmitting a whole line from the terminal with blanks trailing the 12.

The second general format of ACCEPT is

FORMAT 2

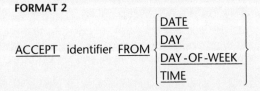

This format of ACCEPT can be used to move the contents of the COBOL pre-defined fields DATE, DAY, DAY-OF-WEEK, or TIME to a specified identifier. These latter fields are not defined by the programmer but are made available by the compiler. Their implicit definition is

1. DATE	PIC 999999
2. DAY	PIC 99999
3. DAY-OF-WEEK	PIC 9
4. TIME	PIC 99999999

1. The DATE field contains the year, month, and day. Assume that TODAY was defined as follows:

    ```
    02  TODAY.
        03  T-YEAR     PIC 99.
        03  T-MONTH    PIC 99.
        03  T-DAY      PIC 99.
    ```

    The instruction ACCEPT TODAY FROM DATE issued on February 1, 1990, will cause the content of DATE, 900201, to be moved to TODAY.

2. The DAY field contains the year and the day of the year, counting from January 1 as 001 to December 31 as 365 (assuming a nonleap year). Thus, February 1, 1990, would be stored as 90032.

3. The DAY-OF-WEEK yields a one-digit code that corresponds to the days of the week as follows: 1 = Monday, 2 = Tuesday, ..., 7 = Sunday. For example, if we define

    ```
    02  DAY-NAME-CODE  PIC 9.
        88  MONDAY      VALUE 1.
        88  TUESDAY     VALUE 2.
          .
          .
          .
        88  SUNDAY      VALUE 7.
    ```

Then we can use program statements like the following:

```
ACCEPT DAY-NAME-CODE FROM DAY-OF-WEEK
IF MONDAY PERFORM MONDAY-ROUTINE.
IF TUESDAY PERFORM TUESDAY-ROUTINE.
    .
    .
    .
```

4. TIME contains hours, minutes, seconds, and hundredths of a second, based on elapsed time after midnight on a 24-hour-clock. Thus, 8:30 p.m. is stored as 20300000. The smallest value of TIME is 00000000, and the largest is 23595999.

The DISPLAY Verb

The general format associated with use of the DISPLAY verb is

$$\underline{\text{DISPLAY}} \left\{ \begin{array}{l} \text{identifier -1} \\ \text{literal -1} \end{array} \right\} \left[\begin{array}{l} \text{, identifier -2} \\ \text{, literal -2} \end{array} \right] \ldots [\underline{\text{UPON}} \text{ mnemonic-name}]$$

$$[\text{WITH } \underline{\text{NO ADVANCING}}]$$

Notice that DISPLAY can reference a series of identifiers or literals. Thus, we can write

```
DISPLAY
    AMOUNT-A, 'IS A VALUE OUT OF RANGE' UPON OPERATOR-CONSOLE.
```

Execution of this statement will result in the contents of the storage field AMOUNT-A followed by the literal message in the quotation marks being output on the device named OPERATOR-CONSOLE.

In some computer installations ACCEPT and DISPLAY can be used only with devices predefined by the installation itself; thus the device will not be named in the statement. For example, writing ACCEPT CODE-A may be valid and would refer to some specific device in the particular installation, such as the operator's console. Similarly, DISPLAY ERR-MESSAGE-1 may be valid in installations in which the DISPLAY verb is associated automatically with a particular device, such as the operator's console or a specific printer.

A common use of DISPLAY is for program debugging purposes. For instance, if we encounter an error in results associated with a field MEN-TOTAL-SALARY, we may want to DISPLAY the contents of this field each time a value is added to it, as in the following example:

```
DISPLAY
  'MEN-TOTAL-SALARY BEFORE ADDING = '  MEN-TOTAL-SALARY
ADD EMPLOYEE-SALARY TO MEN-TOTAL-SALARY
DISPLAY
  '                AFTER  ADDING = '  MEN-TOTAL-SALARY
```

As an illustration, the output resulting from execution of the above statements might be:

```
MEN-TOTAL-SALARY BEFORE ADDING = 0125000
                AFTER  ADDING = 0149250
```

These statements allow the programmer to trace the accumulation of values in the target field and, perhaps, provide a clue as to the cause of the error. We could, of course, use the WRITE verb to do the same thing, but it would require additional specifications and commands. For instance, a WORKING-STORAGE group item consisting of two elementary fields would have to be defined: one field for the explanatory header in the above examples and one for the content of MEN-TOTAL-SALARY. Then we would MOVE and WRITE the appropriate data.

In the 1985 standard a new enhancement of DISPLAY has been introduced that includes the WITH NO ADVANCING option. This option is useful when writing on a video monitor because it prevents the cursor from moving to the next line, which is the normal action after a DISPLAY command.

The ACCEPT and DISPLAY verbs are also used to handle input and output on a video monitor. Cursor positioning, and special print effects such as a message in bold or in blinking mode, are features that we want to be able to program for interactive processing. Unfortunately, there is no standard set of commands in COBOL for programming such features. Still, the subject is discussed in Chapter 22. (The high chapter number does not imply that the topic is advanced. Rather, it is placed toward the end of this book because video monitor programming is different for each compiler or computer system).

R E V I E W . . . .

1. The verb used to input data items not usually part of any file as such is the _____ verb, whereas the verb similarly used for output, often on a CRT terminal or video monitor, is the _____ verb.

    ACCEPT; DISPLAY

2. DATA input by use of the ACCEPT verb is always treated as being [alphabetic / numeric / alphanumeric].

    alphanumeric

3. Because the DISPLAY verb can reference literals as well as identifiers, it can be used to convey certain _____ , as well as data items.

    messages

4. Although the DISPLAY verb has limited use in computer programs for regular data processing applications, it is used frequently in conjunction with the _____ of computer programs.

    debugging

. . . .

QUALIFICATION AND THE MOVE CORRESPONDING

This section covers two related subjects. First, we discuss *qualification,* which allows us the flexibility of defining nonunique data-names in the DATA DIVISION but then using qualifiers as a means of clarifying which data-name we are actually referencing. Second, we discuss the MOVE verb with the CORRESPONDING option, which is also related to the subject of nonunique data-names.

Qualification

Up to this point in the book, we always have indicated that every data-name must be unique in a given program. This requirement will be modified now by introducing the use of qualifiers. A *qualifier* is a data-name of higher hierarchical level than the name it qualifies. The use of qualifiers results in having unique data-names for names that otherwise would not be unique, thus providing more flexibility in the assignment of data-names in the program. The following DATA

DIVISION segment is an example of a case in which qualification would be necessary in the PROCEDURE DIVISION:

```
02  WEEKLY-TOTALS.
    03 TOTAL-HOURS        PIC 99V9.
    03 WAGE-RATE          PIC 99V99.
    03 ...
02  MONTHLY-TOTALS.
    03 TOTAL-HOURS        PIC 999V9.
    03 (etc.)
```

Notice that TOTAL-HOURS seems to be used twice, but with respect to two different items, namely, the total hours for the week and the total hours for the month. If reference were made simply to TOTAL-HOURS, it would not be clear which storage field should be used. However, the use of qualifiers results in unique data-names and could be accomplished as follows in the PROCEDURE DIVISION instructions:

```
MOVE TOTAL-HOURS OF WEEKLY-TOTALS TO ...
MOVE TOTAL-HOURS IN MONTHLY-TOTALS TO ...
```

The OF and IN are equivalent, and use of either word after a data-name serves to signal the use of a qualifier. Since a data-name that is not unique in the program must always be qualified, the use of nonunique names always results in longer statements in the PROCEDURE DIVISION. Despite this disadvantage, qualifiers are often used because they improve documentation. For instance, the statements in the above example make it quite clear that we are working with weekly and monthly hours, respectively.

A common use of qualifiers is with files whose record descriptions have corresponding fields. If an employee has an assigned identification number that is included in the record of each of two files, the following type of instruction can be included in the PROCEDURE DIVISION:

```
IF EMPLOY-NUMBER IN MASTER-RECORD
    IS EQUAL TO EMPLOY-NUMBER IN TRANSACTION-RECORD ...
```

The documentation aspect of the program is enhanced in this example in that it is quite clear what is being compared.

At times qualification requires several qualifiers. Consider the following example:

```
01  OLD-RECORD.              01  NEW-RECORD.
    02  TODAYS-DATE...            02  TODAYS-DATE ...
        03 MONTH...                   03 MONTH....
        03 YEAR ...                   03 YEAR ...
    02  LAST-PERIODS-DATE ...    02  LAST-PERIODS-DATE ...
        03 MONTH ...                  03 MONTH ...
        03 YEAR. ...                  03 YEAR. ...
        03 TOTAL ...                  03 TOTAL ...
```

In this example the OLD-RECORD and NEW-RECORD are assumed to be in the same program. Notice that there are four fields named MONTH. Thus a qualifier such as MONTH OF LAST-PERIODS-DATE does not provide a unique reference because there are two such fields, one in the OLD-RECORD and one in the NEW-RECORD. Therefore two qualifiers are needed to reference a unique field, such as

$$\text{MONTH} \begin{Bmatrix} \text{OF} \\ \text{IN} \end{Bmatrix} \text{LAST-PERIODS-DATE} \begin{Bmatrix} \text{OF} \\ \text{IN} \end{Bmatrix} \text{OLD-RECORD}$$

Since the TOTAL field in the preceding program example occurs only once in each record, only a single qualifier is required; therefore TOTAL IN OLD-RECORD is an adequate reference in this case. The use of two qualifiers, such as TOTAL OF LAST-PERIODS-DATE IN OLD-RECORD is acceptable but unnecessary for the purpose of unique identification.

The CORRESPONDING option

The CORRESPONDING option, available for use with MOVE and with the ADD and SUBTRACT arithmetic verbs, simplifies programming in cases in which the same operation is to be performed on one or several identically named pairs of elementary data-names. In this section we discuss the MOVE verb. Use of the CORRESPONDING feature with the ADD and SUBTRACT is rare, so we simply direct you to Appendix B, which presents the complete formats of these verbs.

Let us consider an example. Suppose we have the following two records:

```
01  PAY-RECORD.
    02   GROSS      PIC 9999V99.
    02   NET        PIC 9999V99.
    02   TAXES      PIC 999V99.
01  EDITED-RECORD.
    02   GROSS      PIC ZZZ9.99.
    02   TAXES      PIC ZZ9.99.
    02   NET        PIC ZZZ9.99.
```

If we want to move PAY-RECORD to EDITED-RECORD, we cannot do it in one statement. Writing MOVE PAY-RECORD to EDITED-RECORD would be incorrect, because the order of the fields NET and TAXES is not the same in the two records and because there are edited fields in the receiving record (editing works only when we move an individual elementary field to another elementary edited field). Of course, the move could be accomplished by a separate MOVE statement for each of the three fields; however, the same result can be accomplished more easily by use of the CORRESPONDING option:

```
MOVE CORRESPONDING PAY-RECORD TO EDITED-RECORD.
```

The general format associated with the use of the CORRESPONDING option is

$$\underline{\text{MOVE}} \begin{Bmatrix} \underline{\text{CORRESPONDING}} \\ \underline{\text{CORR}} \end{Bmatrix} \text{identifier-1} \ \underline{\text{TO}} \ \text{identifier-2}$$

CORR is the abbreviated form of the option. Unlike the situation in the previous example, the two data-names may contain only some items that correspond, as in the following example:

```
      02  INSPECTION.
          03  TOTAL-QUANTITY . . .
          03  REJECTED . . .
          03  ACCEPTED . . .
          03  QUALITY-RATIO . . .
  01  QUALITY-REPORT.
      02  TOTAL-QUANTITY . . .
      02  QUALITY-RATIO . . .
```

With respect to the above, executing the statement

```
MOVE CORR INSPECTION TO QUALITY-REPORT
```

will result in the two corresponding fields, TOTAL-QUANTITY and QUALITY-RATIO, being moved.

In order for the CORRESPONDING option to be used, there must be pairs of data items having the same name in two group items, and at least one of the items in each pair must be at the elementary level. (We also now mention some other details for future reference, even though the related subjects are covered in later chapters.) Another rule is that any items that are subordinate to identifier-1 and identifier-2 and have RENAMES, REDEFINES, or OCCURS clauses are ignored in the move. Therefore we cannot use the MOVE CORRESPONDING option to move a table of values, for example. However, the identifier-1 and identifier-2 items themselves may have REDEFINES or OCCURS clauses or may be subordinate to data items with such clauses.

In general, the CORRESPONDING option should be avoided or used sparingly with respect to the MOVE as well as the ADD or SUBTRACT arithmetic verbs. Use of the CORRESPONDING option may result in errors when programs are modified subsequently, as in the case of changing a data-name and not being aware that its other "name-sake" was involved in a CORRESPONDING reference.

R E V I E W . . . .

1. The use of qualifiers makes it possible to use the same data-name for variables that otherwise would have different data-names assigned to them. The main advantage of using qualifiers is that _____ thereby is improved.

    documentation (or interpretation of the program, etc.)

2. When a qualifier is used, it always [precedes / follows] the referenced data-name, and its use is signaled by one of two words: _____ or _____ .

    follows OF; IN

3. Assume that the record-name for one file is MASTER-RECORD and the record-name of another file is TRANSACTION-RECORD. Both records contain a field called CUSTOMER-NUMBER. To determine that we are dealing with two records of the same customer, we say:

    ```
    IF CUSTOMER-NUMBER OF _____ IS EQUAL TO
    CUSTOMER-NUMBER OF _____
    ```

    MASTER-RECORD; TRANSACTION-RECORD (either order)

4. A sufficient number of qualifiers must be used to differentiate a particular data field from all other data fields in the program that are identified by the same data-name. Suppose that a qualifier is used with a data-name that is unique and thus requires no qualifier. From the standpoint of programming requirements,

the qualifier is unnecessary [and the program will terminate / but will not affect program execution].

> but will not affect program execution
>
> (again, such a qualifier might be used to improve documentation)

5. The abbreviated form of the CORRESPONDING option is _____ . Use of this option in conjunction with the MOVE instruction results in transfer of only the _____ items contained in two records.

> CORR; common (or corresponding)

6. When the MOVE CORRESPONDING option is used, an item will be moved if at least one of the items in each pair is at the _____ level and only if the receiving group item has an item with the same [storage capacity / name].

> elementary; name

. . . .

CHARACTER PROCESSING VERBS

COBOL includes a number of verbs intended to execute tasks that involve data as *characters* rather than as numeric values. These verbs are specialized and very powerful. We will discuss five such verbs: INITIALIZE, COPY, STRING, UNSTRING, and INSPECT. Then we will present a sample program that illustrates use of these verbs in the following section of this chapter.

The INITIALIZE Verb

This verb is available only in COBOL '85. The INITIALIZE statement provides for a convenient way to move data to selected fields. The most common use of this verb is for setting numeric fields to zero and nonnumeric fields to spaces.

Figure 7-4 presents the general format and some examples of using the INITIALIZE verb. When used without the REPLACING option, spaces are moved to alphabetic, alphanumeric, and alphanumeric edited data items, while zeros are moved to numeric and numeric edited items. When identifier-1 is a group item, as in the first INITIALIZE A example, it is as if we wrote a series of elementary MOVE statements to move either spaces or zeros, depending on the receiving data item category.

When the REPLACING option is used, only items matching the specified category are initialized. Thus the third example in Figure 7-4b illustrates that only D is affected by the INITIALIZE statement.

Overall, we can observe that the INITIALIZE serves as a convenient alternative to the VALUE clause in the DATA DIVISION and the use of MOVE in the PROCEDURE DIVISION.

The COPY Verb

COBOL provides for a library facility. By *library* we mean a collection of COBOL source program elements recorded on tape or disk and accessible by reference to text-names. A text-name is similar to a file name, and it serves as the identifier for one or more preprogrammed COBOL items.

For example, suppose that we have stored the following record description in a source library under the text-name CUST-REC.

```
05  CUST-NO     PIC 9(5).
05  CUST-NAME   PIC X(20).
```

FIGURE 7-4
Format and Sample Uses of
INITIALIZE

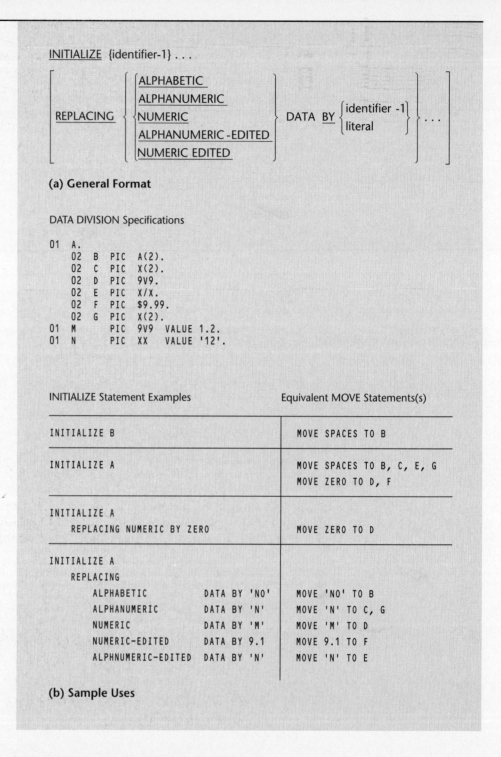

```
INITIALIZE {identifier-1} ...
```

(a) **General Format**

DATA DIVISION Specifications

```
01  A.
    02  B  PIC  A(2).
    02  C  PIC  X(2).
    02  D  PIC  9V9.
    02  E  PIC  X/X.
    02  F  PIC  $9.99.
    02  G  PIC  X(2).
01  M      PIC  9V9   VALUE 1.2.
01  N      PIC  XX    VALUE '12'.
```

INITIALIZE Statement Examples	Equivalent MOVE Statements(s)
`INITIALIZE B`	`MOVE SPACES TO B`
`INITIALIZE A`	`MOVE SPACES TO B, C, E, G` `MOVE ZERO TO D, F`
`INITIALIZE A` `   REPLACING NUMERIC BY ZERO`	`MOVE ZERO TO D`

`INITIALIZE A`
`   REPLACING`
`      ALPHABETIC          DATA BY 'NO'`
`      ALPHANUMERIC        DATA BY 'N'`
`      NUMERIC             DATA BY 'M'`
`      NUMERIC-EDITED      DATA BY 9.1`
`      ALPHNUMERIC-EDITED  DATA BY 'N'`
	`MOVE 'NO' TO B`
	`MOVE 'N' TO C, G`
	`MOVE 'M' TO D`
	`MOVE 9.1 TO F`
	`MOVE 'N' TO E`

(b) **Sample Uses**

Then in a program we could write as follows:

```
01  CUSTOMER-RECORD  COPY  CUST-REC.
```

As a result, the program would be compiled as if we had written

```
01  CUSTOMER-RECORD.
    05  CUST-NO     PIC 9(5).
    05  CUST-NAME   PIC X(20).
```

The COPY facility not only saves time for the programmer, but even more importantly, it serves to reduce errors from inconsistent descriptions of the same file data. Commonly, the same file will be used by several programs. In such a case it is very productive to have the description of the file stored in a text library, so that all the programs using that file will copy exactly the same descriptions.

The COPY can be used throughout the COBOL program. For instance, assuming that TEXT-1 refers to specific program elements, we could write

```
SOURCE-COMPUTER.  COPY TEXT-1.
        .
        .
        .

SELECT PRODUCT-FILE COPY TEXT-15.
        .
        .
        .

FD  PRODUCT-FILE COPY TEXT-3.
        .
        .
        .

BILLING-PARAGRAPH.  COPY TEXT-14.
        .
        .
        .
```

In this fashion we need not rewrite those portions of the program that have already been written and stored in the library.

Building the library commonly is done outside the COBOL language by means of JCL (Job Control Language) statements. Use of a library is a very local practice, and we direct the readers to their own computer system for details.

R E V I E W . . . .

1. In effect, the INITIALIZE verb available in the 1985 standard represents a more efficient alternative to the use of the _____ verb.

    MOVE

2. The most common use of this verb is for setting numeric fields to _____ and nonnumeric fields to _____ .

    zero; spaces

3. The verb that makes it possible to reference a precoded program segment from a library of such program segments is the _____ verb.

    COPY

4. When the COPY verb is used to obtain a record description from a library, the record-name used in the program and in the library [must / need not] be the same.

    need not

The STRING Verb

The STRING verb is designed to facilitate transfer of data from *several sources into one destination,* while the UNSTRING verb is designed to facilitate transfer of data *from one source to many destinations.* In effect, use of these verbs allows one statement to be used in lieu of multiple uses of the MOVE verb and, possibly, in lieu of some DATA DIVISION entries.

We begin with two examples that illustrate uses of the STRING verb.

Suppose that EDIT-SOC-SEC contains a social security number, including hyphens after the third and fifth digits, as, for instance, '123-45-6789'. We wish to move the social security number to SOC-SEC while also removing the hyphens. The following data description entries are given:

```
01  SOC-SEC            PIC X(9).
01  EDIT-SOC-SEC.
    02  PART-1          PIC 999.
    02  FILLER          PIC X VALUE '-'.
    02  PART-2          PIC 99.
    02  FILLER          PIC X VALUE '-'.
    02  PART-3          PIC 9999.
```

We now use the STRING statement:

```
STRING   PART-1 DELIMITED BY SIZE
         PART-2 DELIMITED BY SIZE
         PART-3 DELIMITED BY SIZE
   INTO   SOC-SEC.
```

The STRING specifies moving the three fields, PART-1, PART-2, and PART-3, and positioning them adjacent to each other. The transfer of data can be thought of as taking place character by character. Thus the data in PART-1 would be transferred into the first three positions of SOC-SEC, the data in PART-2 would be transferred into the next two positions of SOC-SEC, and so on. The DELIMITED BY SIZE clause specifies that the transfer of data from the associated field will stop at (be delimited by) the point when as many characters have been transferred as the size of the source field.

The next example illustrates the availability of other alternatives.

Assume that we want to print a report that lists a company name in columns 5–19, a city name starting with column 26, 1 blank space, and then the ZIP code. The source of data is VENDOR-RECORD:

```
01  VENDOR-RECORD.
    02  COMPANY-NAME       PIC X(15).
    02  STREET             PIC X(40).
    02  CITY-STATE         PIC X(20).
    02  ZIP                PIC 9(5).
```

The data in CITY-STATE are recorded so that the city-name is followed by a comma, a space, and then the state code, as in LOS ANGELES, CA.

The output record is described as

```
01  OUTPUT-REC PIC X(132).
```

We use the STRING verb as follows:

```
MOVE SPACES TO OUTPUT-REC
MOVE 5 TO STARTING-PLACE.
STRING COMPANY-NAME DELIMITED BY SIZE
       '      '  DELIMITED BY SIZE
       CITY-STATE   DELIMITED BY ','
       SPACE, ZIP   DELIMITED BY SIZE
  INTO OUTPUT-REC
  WITH POINTER STARTING-PLACE.
```

The first MOVE statement clears the output record of any previous contents. The second MOVE sets STARTING-PLACE to a value of 5 so that the beginning of data transfer into OUTPUT-REC will begin in column 5 (WITH POINTER STARTING-PLACE). Of course, STARTING-PLACE is an arbitrary name chosen by the programmer; but it must be an integer field for obvious reasons.

The STRING statement specifies that, in effect, five fields will be transferred: COMPANY-NAME, the 6-byte nonnumeric literal '   ', CITY-STATE, the figurative constant SPACE, and ZIP. Thus, starting with column 5 of OUTPUT-REC, the entire (DELIMITED BY SIZE) COMPANY-NAME is transferred and it is followed by the 6-blank nonnumeric constant to account for columns 20-25. The next data item to be transferred comes from CITY-STATE; this data item is transferred character by character until a comma is encountered (DELIMITED BY ','). We deliberately omitted the state code. Thus if CITY-STATE contained LOS ANGELES, CA, the DELIMITED BY ',' stops the transfer when the comma is encountered. Then we string one blank (SPACE) and then the contents of the ZIP code field. It should be pointed out that use of figurative constants, such as SPACE, ZEROS, or the like, always means one occurrence of the implied character. Thus, we would obtain one blank even if we had used SPACES instead of SPACE.

The general format for the STRING verb is presented in Figure 7-5.

Our two examples have illustrated all but the OVERFLOW option. If the data specified to be transferred are greater than the size of the receiving item (identifier-7) during execution of a STRING statement, then the imperative statement of the OVERFLOW clause is executed. If the optional OVERFLOW is not used and the overflow condition arises, then the STRING operation is discontinued and

FIGURE 7-5
General Format for the STRING Verb

$$\underline{\text{STRING}} \begin{Bmatrix} \text{identifier-1} \\ \text{literal-1} \end{Bmatrix} \begin{bmatrix} \text{, identifier-2} \\ \text{, literal-2} \end{bmatrix} \ldots \underline{\text{DELIMITED}} \text{ BY} \begin{Bmatrix} \text{identifier-3} \\ \text{literal-3} \\ \underline{\text{SIZE}} \end{Bmatrix}$$

$$\left\{ \begin{Bmatrix} \text{identifier-4} \\ \text{literal-4} \end{Bmatrix} \begin{bmatrix} \text{, identifier-5} \\ \text{, literal-5} \end{bmatrix} \ldots \underline{\text{DELIMITED}} \text{ BY} \begin{Bmatrix} \text{identifier-6} \\ \text{literal-6} \\ \underline{\text{SIZE}} \end{Bmatrix} \right\} \ldots$$

<u>INTO</u> identifier-7 [WITH <u>POINTER</u> identifer-8]

[<u>ON OVERFLOW</u> imperative-statement-1]

[<u>NOT</u> ON <u>OVERFLOW</u> imperative-statement-2]

[<u>END-STRING</u>]

the next program statement is executed. During execution, identifier-8, if used, is incremented by 1 as each character is transferred. It is the value of this identifier that is checked in determining an overflow condition. If the identifier-8 option is not used, an implied counter is used to fulfill the same function. When the STRING operation has been completed, the value of identifier-8 is one higher than the number of characters transferred. This feature is used in the sample program at the end of the chapter. The NOT ON OVERFLOW and the END-STRING options apply only to the 1985 standard.

The UNSTRING Verb

The UNSTRING verb, as its name implies, acts in the reverse direction of the STRING verb. The UNSTRING verb facilitates transfer of data from *one source* to *many destinations*. We present two examples to illustrate use of this verb.

Suppose that data are recorded in free form (without predefined fields) as follows:

```
TED S BROWN,4,15,3.52
TINA LORI CHRISTIANSON,1,12,2.50
```

As we can see, name fields are separated by one or more blank spaces; then commas separate the remaining three fields. We would like to move these data fields to a fixed-format record:

```
01  STUDENT-RECORD.
    02   FIRST-NAME              PIC X(15).
    02   MIDDLE-NAME             PIC X(15).
    02   LAST-NAME               PIC X(20).
    02   CLASSIFICATION          PIC 9.
    02   CREDIT-LOAD             PIC 99.
    02   GPA                     PIC XXXX.
```

Assuming that the source data are in

```
01  FREE-FORM-RECORD PIC X(57).
```

we can write

```
UNSTRING FREE-FORM-RECORD
    DELIMITED BY ALL SPACES OR ','
        INTO      FIRST-NAME
                  MIDDLE-NAME
                  LAST-NAME
                  CLASSIFICATION
                  CREDIT-LOAD
                  GPA.
```

The DELIMITED clause above specifies that fields in the source record are separated by one or more blank spaces (ALL SPACES), or single commas (OR ','). In essence, the source record is scanned character by character from left to right. When a blank or a comma appears in FREE-FORM-RECORD, it is assumed that a new field begins. The delimiters in this case are blanks or commas, and they are not included in the data transfer, although the UNSTRING statement does include an option allowing the transfer of delimiters themselves.

FIGURE 7-7
General Format for the UNSTRING Verb

UNSTRING identifier -1 $\left\{\text{\underline{DELIMITED} BY [\underline{ALL}]}\begin{Bmatrix}\text{identifier -2}\\\text{literal -1}\end{Bmatrix}\right.$

$\left\{\text{\underline{OR} [\underline{ALL}]}\begin{Bmatrix}\text{identifier -3}\\\text{literal -2}\end{Bmatrix}\right\}\ldots$ \underline{INTO} identifier -4 [, \underline{DELIMITER} IN identifier -5]

[, \underline{COUNT} IN identifier-6] [, identifier-7 [, \underline{DELIMITER} IN identifier-8]]

[, \underline{COUNT} IN identifier-9] . . . [WITH \underline{POINTER} identifier-10]

[\underline{TALLYING} IN identifier-11] [ON \underline{OVERFLOW} imperative-statement-1]

[\underline{NOT} ON \underline{OVERFLOW} imperative-statement-2]

[END-UNSTRING]

R   E   V   I   E   W   .   .   .   .

1. The verb that is used to transfer data from several sources to one destination is the _____ verb.

    STRING

2. The verb that is used to transfer data from one source to many destinations is the _____ verb.

    UNSTRING

3. When the DELIMITED BY SIZE clause is used in conjunction with the STRING verb, transfer of data from the sending field stops when the number of characters that have been transferred equals the size of the [sending / receiving] field.]

    sending (unless the receiving field is shorter than the sending field)

4. If an OVERFLOW clause is not used in conjunction with a STRING verb and an overflow condition occurs, then [the STRING operation / program execution] is terminated.

    the STRING operation

5. Used in conjunction with the UNSTRING verb, the DELIMITED BY clause specifies the basis used to signal the beginning of a new [sending / receiving] field.

    sending

6. The clause that is used if delimiters themselves, such as commas or spaces, are to be transferred to receiving fields during the UNSTRING operation is the _____ clause.

    DELIMITER IN

. . . .

The INSPECT Verb

At times we need to access and manipulate individual characters in a field. One very common use is to edit input data, such as replacing leading blanks by zeros. COBOL provides the INSPECT verb to accomplish such character manipulations.

The INSPECT verb is powerful but a bit complicated. Three formats are available, and these are presented in the format specifications in Appendix B.

Discussion of the complete set of options would exceed the intended scope of this text. We present some examples to illustrate the basic options.

EXAMPLE 1   Suppose we want to replace all leading blanks by leading zeros in a field called TEST. We could write

```
INSPECT TEST REPLACING LEADING ' ' BY '0'.
```

EXAMPLE 2   Suppose we want to replace all blanks (not just leading ones) by zeros in a field called TEST. We could write

```
INSPECT TEST REPLACING ALL ' ' BY '0'.
```

EXAMPLE 3   If we want to replace the first zero by a + , we write

```
INSPECT TEST REPLACING FIRST '0' BY '+'.
```

EXAMPLE 4   Suppose we want to ask the question: How many dollar signs are in TEST? We write

```
INSPECT TEST TALLYING DOLLAR-COUNT FOR ALL '$'.
```

After this instruction is executed, the numeric field DOLLAR-COUNT will contain a value equal to the number of $ in TEST. (DOLLAR-COUNT would have been defined in the DATA DIVISION.)

EXAMPLE 5   Suppose we want to ask the question: How many zero characters are there to the left of the decimal point and how many zeros are there to the right of the decimal point? We write

```
INSPECT TEST TALLYING COUNT-B FOR ALL '0' BEFORE INITIAL '.'
                      COUNT-A FOR ALL '0' AFTER '.'.
```

This instruction would result in COUNT-B containing the number of zeros before the decimal point and COUNT-A containing the number of zeros after the decimal point.

EXAMPLE 6   We want to count the number of dollar signs in TEST and replace all dollar signs after the first one by asterisks. We write

```
INSPECT TEST TALLYING COUNT-A FOR ALL '$'
             REPLACING ALL '$' BY '*' AFTER INITIAL '$'.
```

EXAMPLE 7   We want to ask the question: Assuming that TEST contains a name left-justified, how long is the name? (Unused positions are blank.) We write

```
INSPECT TEST TALLYING COUNT-A FOR CHARACTERS BEFORE INITIAL ' '.
```

EXAMPLE 8   We want to convert all uppercase letters to lowercase. We could write

```
INSPECT TEST REPLACING ALL 'A' BY 'a'
                           'B' BY 'b'
                            .
                            .
                            .
                           'Z' BY 'z'.
```

In some instances the compiler may limit the number of literal pairs used in one INSPECT statement, so that for the example we may need to write two INSPECT statements, say, one for replacing the letters A through M and another one for the letters N through Z.

In COBOL '85 there is an easier way to do the above tests by using the CONVERTING option:

```
INSPECT TEST CONVERTING 'ABCDEFGHIJKLMNOPQRSTUVWXYZ'
                     TO 'abcdefghijklmnopqrstuvwxyz'
```

The above statement specifies to change any "A" to "a", and so on, exactly as the REPLACING ALL statement does at the beginning of this example.

EXAMPLE 9　An integer field, ABC, of six positions may have leading blanks and a sign. We want to move the correct numeric value represented in ABC to S-ABC whose PIC is S9(6). We could write

```
MOVE ZERO TO PLUS-SIGN, MINUS-SIGN
INSPECT ABC
    TALLYING  PLUS-SIGN FOR ALL '+'
              MINUS-SIGN FOR ALL '-'
    REPLACING
              LEADING SPACES BY ZERO
              FIRST '+' BY ZERO
              FIRST '-' BY ZERO.
IF  ABC IS NOT NUMERIC
    PERFORM INCORRECT-DATA
ELSE
    MOVE ABC TO S-ABC
    IF MINUS-SIGN NOT = ZERO
    MULTIPLY -1 BY S-ABC.
```

We initialize two counters, PLUS-SIGN and MINUS-SIGN, to zero and we use them for TALLYING the occurrence of + and –, respectively. Notice, however, that we use REPLACING ... FIRST. In the unlikely event that more than one like sign is present, the statement IF ABC IS NOT NUMERIC would sense the presence of the unconverted extra sign(s). If the field is unsigned or positive, MOVE ABC to S-ABC is sufficient. If the field is negative, however, then MINUS-SIGN would have a nonzero value and we multiply S-ABC by –1 to attain the proper sign. We could also test PLUS-SIGN and MINUS-SIGN to determine how many signs were present, if any.

R E V I E W . . . .

1. Individual characters in a field can be accessed and possibly changed by use of the _____ verb.

   INSPECT

2. Use of the TALLYING option in conjunction with the INSPECT verb makes it possible to _____ designated characters.

   count

3. Use of the REPLACING option in conjunction with the INSPECT verb makes it possible to _____ designated characters.

   change

4. In the 1985 STANDARD, a more efficient way than use of the REPLACING
    option by which a series of designated characters can be changed is use of the
    option, _____ .

                                                                            CONVERTING

·   ·   ·   ·   ·   ·   ·   ·   ·   ·   ·   ·   ·   ·   ·   ·   ·   ·   ·

SAMPLE PROGRAM

We wish to create a file that contains records consisting of persons' names
compressed so as to leave the trailing blanks out of each name. We might want to
do something like this to save storage space, or to save transmission costs if we are
sending the data via telecommunications.

It will be easiest to begin with an example of some input and the desired
corresponding output, as presented in Figure 7-8. Observing the sample *output*, we
can see that names are written without trailing spaces, with a # serving as a
delimiter to separate each name from the next one. If a first name or a middle
name is missing, there are two consecutive # symbols. For example, at the end of
the first output record, SOTELO THOMAS has no middle name, and WILSON in
the third output record has no first name.

The output records are fixed length, in this case 80 characters long. If a
complete name does not fit at the end of such a record, we "pad" the end of the
output record with * symbols, as shown in the first, third, and fourth sample
output records.

FIGURE 7-8
Input and Output for the Sample Program

INPUT FILE

DOAKS	MARY	BETH
LURVEY	ALEXANDER	RALPH
NEWMAN	ANNETTE	MARIE
SOTELO	THOMAS	
ELLIOTT	C	W
RICHARDSON	NICKOLAUS	ANDREW
THOMPSON	PAMELA	ANN
SPENCER	GARY	MARTIN
LIN	CHIN	CHI
RIBBENTROP	RONALD	GENE
WILSON		D
TRAN	TONY	H
WOELFEL	KATHRYN	P
JANES	BEVERLY	EDWARD
MURPHEY	DAN	E

PROGRAM OUTPUT

```
DOAKS#MARY#BETH#LURVEY#ALEXANDER#RALPH#NEWMAN#ANNETTE#MARIE#SOTELO#THOMAS##*****

ELLIOTT#C#W#RICHARDSON#NICKOLAUS#ANDREW#THOMPSON#PAMELA#ANN#SPENCER#GARY#MARTIN#

LIN#CHIN#CHI#RIBBENTROP#RONALD#GENE#WILSON##D#TRAN#TONY#H#WOELFEL#KATHRYN#P#****

JANES#BEVERLY#EDWARD#MURPHEY#DAN#E#**********************************************
```

Figure 7-9 presents a complete program for the task. Notice that the input file (STRING-FILE), contains fields for LAST-NAME, FIRST-NAME, and MIDDLE-NAME, each 15 bytes long. Thus, the longest compressed name could be 48 bytes long when we consider insertion of the delimiting # symbols (two within the name and one at the end of the name). The shortest compressed name could be, conceivably, a person with a single-letter last name and no first and no middle name, in which case the compressed version of the name would be four bytes long.

The logic used in the 200-COMPRESS-DATA paragraph of the sample program STRINGs the full name into a WORKING-STORAGE field named NAME-BUFFER, which has been defined to be 49 bytes in length. We use the WITH

FIGURE 7-9

COBOL Program for the STRING Example

```
*
  IDENTIFICATION DIVISION.
  PROGRAM-ID. STRINGIT.
*
  ENVIRONMENT DIVISION.
*
  CONFIGURATION SECTION.
  SOURCE-COMPUTER. ABC-480.
  OBJECT-COMPUTER. ABC-480.
*
  INPUT-OUTPUT SECTION.
*
  FILE-CONTROL.
      SELECT STRING-FILE ASSIGN TO STRING-DAT.
      SELECT STRING-OUT   ASSIGN TO STRING-RPT.
*
  DATA DIVISION.
*
  FILE SECTION.
*
  FD   STRING-FILE LABEL RECORDS ARE OMITTED
                   RECORD CONTAINS 80 CHARACTERS
                   DATA RECORD IS STRING-RECORD.
  01   STRING-RECORD.
       05 FILLER                              PIC X(4).
       05 LAST-NAME                           PIC X(15).
       05 FIRST-NAME                          PIC X(15).
       05 MIDDLE-NAME                         PIC X(15).
       05 FILLER                              PIC X(31).
*
  FD   STRING-OUT   LABEL RECORDS ARE OMITTED
                    RECORD CONTAINS 80 CHARACTERS
                    DATA RECORD IS STRING-LINE.
  01   STRING-LINE                            PIC X(80).
*
  WORKING-STORAGE SECTION.
*
  01 END-OF-FILE-TEST                         PIC X(3) VALUE "NO".
     88  END-OF-FILE                          VALUE "YES".
*
```

FIGURE 7-9
COBOL Program for the STRING
Example (continued)

```
01  NAME-LENGTH                              PIC 9(2).
01  STARTING-PT                              PIC 9(2).
01  SPACE-LEFT                               PIC 9(2).
01  NAME-BUFFER                              PIC X(49).
01  STRING-LENGTH                            PIC 9(2) VALUE 80.
*
PROCEDURE DIVISION.
*
000-MAIN-ROUTINE.
    OPEN INPUT  STRING-FILE
         OUTPUT STRING-OUT

    PERFORM 100-READ-EXPANDED-REC
    MOVE ALL "*" TO STRING-LINE
    MOVE 1 TO STARTING-PT
    PERFORM 200-COMPRESS-DATA
       UNTIL END-OF-FILE

    WRITE STRING-LINE

    CLOSE STRING-FILE
          STRING-OUT
    STOP RUN.
*
100-READ-EXPANDED-REC.
    READ STRING-FILE RECORD
       AT END SET END-OF-FILE TO TRUE
*
200-COMPRESS-DATA.
    MOVE SPACES TO NAME-BUFFER
    MOVE 1 TO NAME-LENGTH
    STRING LAST-NAME DELIMITED BY SPACE
           "#" DELIMITED BY SIZE
           FIRST-NAME DELIMITED BY SPACE
           "#" DELIMITED BY SIZE
           MIDDLE-NAME DELIMITED BY SPACE
           "#" DELIMITED BY SIZE
             INTO NAME-BUFFER
             WITH POINTER NAME-LENGTH
    END-STRING
*
    SUBTRACT 1 FROM NAME-LENGTH
    COMPUTE SPACE-LEFT = STRING-LENGTH - STARTING-PT + 1
    IF SPACE-LEFT < NAME-LENGTH
        WRITE STRING-LINE
        MOVE ALL "*" TO STRING-LINE
        MOVE 1 TO STARTING-PT
    END-IF
*
    STRING NAME-BUFFER DELIMITED BY SPACE
           INTO STRING-LINE
           WITH POINTER STARTING-PT
    END-STRING
*
    PERFORM 100-READ-EXPANDED-REC.
```

POINTER option in the string operation as a way of determining the length of a compressed name. If a name should happen to be 45 bytes long, the pointer (NAME-LENGTH) will have a value 49. The value 49 is desired based on the following analysis. There will be three # delimiters incorporated in the 45-byte name, which accounts for a value of 48. Then we add 1 to account for the fact that the value of the POINTER field at the end of the STRING operation is one higher than the number of characters transferred, as explained in the earlier section of this chapter on the STRING statement. Thus, the pointer will have a value 1 greater than the length of the compressed name in NAME-BUFFER. For this reason we insert SUBTRACT 1 FROM NAME-LENGTH after the STRING statement.

The COMPUTE SPACE-LEFT statement calculates whether there is room in the current output record for storing the just-compressed name in NAME-BUFFER. Notice that the size of the output record (80 bytes) has been stored in the data-name STRING-LENGTH which was defined in working storage. Thus, if we wanted to change the size of the output records to, say, 132 bytes, all we would have to do is change the VALUE clause for STRING-LENGTH.

If the name in NAME-BUFFER does not fit in the output record, we WRITE STRING-LINE to output the record and then MOVE ALL " * " TO STRING-LINE to prepare it for the next record. By filling the entire record with asterisks initially, we know that the remaining positions at the end of a partially name-filled record will contain asterisks.

The task is completed by a STRING statement that strings the data in NAME-BUFFER into STRING-LINE WITH POINTER STARTING-PT. The pointer value is equal to 1 plus the ending point of the previous string operation; thus the pointer automatically keeps track of where to begin stringing. Finally, the DELIMITED BY SPACE in the last STRING statement is used because at the beginning of the 200-COMPRESS-DATA we have written MOVE SPACES TO NAME-BUFFER, and therefore when a blank space is encountered we have reached the end of the name data in NAME-BUFFER.

One of the exercises at the end of this chapter asks you to do the reverse of the operation in this sample program: to take compressed data and to reformat it into typical, fixed-length fields.

SUMMARY

As indicated in the chapter objectives, the coverage in this chapter was intended to complete the presentation of the main verbs available in COBOL, as a follow-up to the introduction to PROCEDURE DIVISION commands in Chapter 2.

The four basic *arithmetic verbs* that were reviewed and discussed further were the ADD, SUBTRACT, MULTIPLY, and DIVIDE. A variety of examples, including use of the ROUNDED and ON SIZE ERROR clauses, were considered. The use of the END-verb, available in COBOL '85, also was explained.

The COMPUTE verb makes it possible to write compact arithmetic statements for mathematical expressions. The arithmetic operators +, −, *, and / correspond to the verbs ADD, SUBTRACT, MULTIPLY, and DIVIDE, respectively. The ** operation provides for exponentiation.

Features associated with the PERFORM verb that were covered in this chapter are the PERFORM ... TIMES and PERFORM ... THRU options, and the use of nested PERFORM statements. The format of the PERFORM statement that specifies execution of a procedure a definite number of times is the PERFORM ... TIMES. Associated with the PERFORM ... THRU, we can use the EXIT statement to mark the end of the THRU range of procedures referenced by such a PERFORM. Because a change in the physical position of paragraphs in the PROCEDURE DIVISION can disrupt the intent of a PERFORM ... THRU command, use of this option is discouraged. A *nested* PERFORM structure is exemplified when a PERFORM statement results in execution of a paragraph that itself contains another PERFORM statement.

The GO TO verb is an *unconditional branch* to a paragraph or section name. Because extensive use of this verb makes a program difficult both to read and to modify, the GO TO verb should be used very sparingly.

The ACCEPT verb is used for input and the DISPLAY verb is used for output for storage fields that are *not* part of any files, usually in conjunction with using such hardware devices as video monitors. Use of the DISPLAY verb is particularly useful for the debugging of COBOL programs.

Two general approaches for handling *nonunique data-items* in the PROCE-DURE DIVISION are by use of *qualification* and use of the CORRESPONDING option with the MOVE verb. The use of qualifiers results in having unique data-names for names that otherwise would not be unique. The presence of a qualifier is signalled by use of either OF or IN after a data-name, such as in MOVE TOTAL-HOURS OF WEEKLY-TOTALS TO … . To use the CORRESPONDING option with the MOVE verb, there must be pairs of data items having the same name in each of two group items, and at least one of the items must be at the elementary level.

The last major section of the chapter, before the sample program, was concerned with *character processing verbs.* These are verbs that process data as *characters,* rather than as numeric values. The five verbs described were the INITIALIZE, COPY, STRING, UNSTRING, and INSPECT.

The INITIALIZE verb, available only in COBOL '85, is used to set numeric fields to zero and nonnumeric fields to spaces. For such applications, it is a more efficient alternative to the use of the MOVE verb.

The COPY verb makes it possible to reference a program segment from a library of such precoded segments and to copy it into the source program.

The STRING verb facilitates the transfer of data from *several sources* into *one destination.* For example, by use of a STRING command we can specify that three separate data-names and/or nonnumeric literals be moved and positioned adjacent to one another.

The UNSTRING verb facilitates the transfer of data from *one source* to *many destinations.* For example, by use of an UNSTRING command one field can be "split up" and transferred to three different fields.

As indicated by its name, the general purpose of the INSPECT verb is to access, and possibly change, individual characters in a data field. A number of options make the INSPECT verb useful for data editing.

The sample program in the final section of this chapter focuses particularly on the use of the STRING verb and some of its options.

EXERCISES

7.1 Assume the following DATA DIVISION entries:

```
01  A.
    02  X.
        03  Y.
    02  W.
        03  Y.
01  B.
    02  X.
        03  Y.
    02  W.
        03  Y.
```

Write PROCEDURE DIVISION statement(s) to move the last elementary item in A to the first elementary item in B.

7.2 Write a COBOL program to compute depreciation schedules, using the sum-of-the-digits method of depreciation. The sum-of-the-digits method works as follows: Suppose that you have an asset of original value $1,000.00 to be depreciated over 3 years. The following table shows the nature of the calculations involved:

YEAR	DEPRECIATION RATE	DEPRECIATION
1	$\dfrac{3}{1+2+3} = \dfrac{3}{6}$	$1,000 \times \dfrac{3}{6} = 500.00$
2	$\dfrac{2}{1+2+3} = \dfrac{2}{6}$	$1,000 \times \dfrac{2}{6} = 333.33$
3	$\dfrac{1}{1+2+3} = \dfrac{1}{6}$	$1,000 \times \dfrac{1}{6} = 166.67$

Notice that the depreciation rate varies from year to year, but that the rate is applied to the same (original) asset dollar value. The rate consists of a denominator that is the sum of the digits from 1 up to the number of years over which the asset is to be depreciated. To test your understanding of the concept, compute the denominator value for five years. The answer is 15. The numerator of the depreciation rate varies from the number of years over which depreciation is to be taken down to 1, in steps of 1. Thus, for a five-year depreciation schedule the numerator values are 5, 4, 3, 2, 1.

Input: This is in the form of a set of records with the following data format:

COLUMNS	CONTENT
1-5	Asset number
6-14	Original asset value in dollars and cents
15-16	Blank
17-18	Number of years over which the asset is to be depreciated
19-80	Blank

Output: This should be on a new page for each asset and should have approximately the following format:

ASSET 12345   ORIGINAL VALUE: $1,000.00

YEAR	DEPRECIATION	ACCUMULATED DEPRECIATION	BOOK VALUE
1	$ 500.00	$ 500.00	$ 500.00
2	333.33	833.33	166.67
3	166.67	1,000.00	0.00

Note: In order always to show a final accumulated depreciation equal to the original value, as well as a final book value equal to zero, the depreciation of the last year is to be computed as follows:

Last year depreciation = original value − accumulated depreciation

Write and run a COBOL program to produce the desired output. Use as test data those shown in the preceding description.

7.3   The data processing objective of this program is to compute and print the monthly schedule of payments resulting from a credit purchase. Given the amount of the credit purchase and the number of monthly payments planned, the amount of the monthly payment is computed as follows:

$$\text{Payment due} \ = \ \frac{\text{amount of credit purchase}}{\text{number of payments}} + 0.015 \text{ of unpaid balance}$$

Of course, this formula presumes an interest charge of 0.015 per month on the unpaid balance in the account. For example, suppose that a customer has purchased an item valued at $1,200.00 and is going to pay for it over a 12-month period. The payment due at the end of the first month is

$$\text{Payment due} \ = \ \frac{\$1,200.00}{12} + 0.015 \ (\$1,200.00)$$

$$= \$100.00 + 0.015 \ (\$1,200.00) = \$100.00 + \$18.00 = \$118.00$$

Similarly, for the second month the payment is

$$\text{Payment due} \ = \ \frac{\$1,200.00}{12} + 0.015 \ (\$1,100.00)$$

$$= \$100.00 + 0.015 \ (\$1,100.00) = \$100.00 + \$16.50 = \$116.50$$

The monthly payment consists of a constant element, which is the original amount of the credit purchase divided by the number of monthly payments, and a variable element, which is the monthly interest charge on the unpaid balance. With each monthly payment, the unpaid balance is decreased by the amount of the constant element.

The desired output for this program is illustrated in Figure 7-10. This case involves a credit transaction of $4,291.50. It is assumed that the letterhead is preprinted, but that the name and address, all column headings, and the numeric values will be printed as the result of program execution. Since the column headings are always the same, in practice these headings also would be preprinted on the form. However, in our example we will print the headings to illustrate how this can be accomplished through the use of COBOL. For each monthly payment, the numeric information provided is the amount of the monthly interest charge, the total payment due that month, and the unpaid balance remaining after that month. Note also that the spacing of the computer printout is designed for use with a window envelope, thereby eliminating the need for separate addressing of envelopes.

Program input: This will consist of a file, with one record per customer. The record format and the layout of these data is as follows:

COLUMNS	CONTENT
1–20	Customer's name
21–45	Number and street
46–70	City, state, and ZIP code
71–78	Amount of credit purchase
79–80	Number of monthly payments

Write a COBOL program to accomplish the task we have described. Use the input for Figure 7-10 as test data for your program, and compare your output with the output in this figure.

FIGURE 7-10

Desired Form of Output for Exercise 7.3

ABC COMPANY
5000 East Camelback Road
Phoenix, Arizona 85033

ALBERT ROBINSON
3150 NORTH ST.
TEMPE, AZ 85282

Fold here

SCHEDULE OF PAYMENTS
ORIGINAL AMOUNT $4,291.50

MONTH	INTEREST	TOTAL PAYMENT	UNPAID BALANCE
1	64.37	422.00	3,933.87
2	59.00	416.63	3,576.25
3	53.46	411.27	3,218.62
4	48.27	405.90	2,861.00
5	42.91	400.54	2,503.37
6	37.55	395.18	2,145.75
7	32.18	389.81	1,788.12
8	26.82	384.45	1,430.50
9	21.45	379.08	1,072.87
10	16.09	373.72	714.25
11	10.72	368.35	357.62
12	5.36	362.99	.00

Envelope

ABC COMPANY
5000 East Camelback Road
Phoenix, Arizona 85033

Window

ALBERT ROBINSON
3150 NORTH ST.
TEMPE, AZ 85282

7.4 A file contains data about the inventory of a company. Each inventory item is identified by a unique item number. The file is sorted on item number. There are three types of records in the file. A balance record contains the amount in inventory as of the last time the data were processed. A receipt record contains the amount of a shipment received. An issue record contains the amount sold. For each shipment received and each sale made, a separate record is created. We wish to read the records, process the data, produce an inventory report on the printer, and produce a set of new balance records.

Input is as follows:

COLUMN	CONTENT
1–5	Item number
6–20	Part name (on balance records only)
21	Type code 1 = balance 2 = receipt 3 = issue
22–25	Quantity

(*Note:* The records in the input file have been sorted on item number. For each item the balance record precedes the receipt and issue records.)

Sample input is as follows:

```
01212TRANSFORMER    12350
01212               26000
01212               30150
01212               33050
01212               31600
01515GEAR TRAIN     11000
01515               30600
02010METAL PLATE    14000
```

Sample output: The printer output resulting from the previously given sample input is

```
ITEM NUMBER   PART NAME      PREVIOUS BALANCE   NEW BALANCE
01212         TRANSFORMER         2350             3550
01515         GEAR TRAIN          1000              400
02010         METAL PLATE         4000             4000
```

The balance records resulting from the sample input are

```
01212TRANSFORMER    103550
01515GEAR TRAIN     100400
02010METAL PLATE    104000
```

These balance records serve as input to the next program run, along with the receipt and issue records created between processing runs.

Write and run a COBOL program to accomplish the desired result. Assume all data are correct.

7.5 A file contains customer names in free form. Each record in that file consists of a field of 45 bytes containing the name, and a FILLER field of 35 bytes.

The last name is written first, followed by a comma, followed by the first name or initial, followed by a comma, and finally followed by the middle name or initial. Write a program to read data from that file and print the data in the following fixed format:

- Columns 11–30   Last name
- Columns 32–45   First name
- Columns 47–60   Middle name

Print the data under suitable headings and use the following test data:

```
BROWN,AL,GEORGE
GARCIA,P.,K.
LONGNAME,VALERIE,GEORGIA
```

7.6 Write a program to reverse the action of the sample program in this chapter. The input file will consist of compressed records, each record 80 bytes long and containing names separated by # symbols, as described in the explanation of the sample program.

The output will be a file containing names in fixed-length fields:

- Columns 1–15   Last name
- Columns 16–30   First name
- Columns 31–45   Middle name

If a name (middle or first) is missing, the corresponding field in the output file will contain blanks.

8 More About Conditional Statements

AS YOU MAY RECALL, *a number of features relating to conditional expressions and conditional statements were described in Chapter 5. In the present chapter you will review some of the points covered in that earlier chapter, and expand your study of conditional statements.*

You will begin with a review of the concept of nested conditional statements and extend its applications to more complex cases. Then you will study some types of conditions that expand on your knowledge of relational conditions and condition-name conditions from Chapter 5. These additional conditions are class conditions, sign conditions, and switch-status conditions. You will also review and expand on the subject of compound conditions that was introduced in Chapter 5. The CONTINUE verb, which can help to handle compound conditionals in some instances, will be included in your study.

Following the coverage of conditional statements, you will continue with the EVALUATE statement, available only in COBOL '85. This verb empowers you to write well-structured and easily understood case structures. Then you will study the GO TO ... DEPENDING statement, which provides yet another alternative for programming case structures.

A final sample program illustrates some of the COBOL '85 features and their impact on conditional statements within a complete program.

THE IF STATEMENT AND NESTED CONDITIONS

We begin with a review of the general format of the IF statement presented in Figure 8-1. As you may recall, in this format condition-1 is either a simple or compound conditional expression. Statement-1 and statement-2 represent either an imperative or a conditional statement optionally preceded by an imperative statement. The ELSE NEXT SENTENCE phrase may be omitted if it immediately precedes the terminal period of the sentence. The END-IF is the scope terminator. If the END-IF, available only in COBOL '85, is specified, then the ELSE NEXT SENTENCE must not be specified. Also, COBOL '85 provides the CONTINUE statement (discussed in the next section of this chapter), which can be used in lieu of NEXT SENTENCE for the null side of an IF statement.

When statement-1 and/or statement-2 in the IF statement format are conditional statements, then a nested conditional exists. Nested conditions can be quite extensive. Figure 8-2(a) illustrates an extensively nested condition in flowchart form. At first glance it appears that the flowchart is rather easily comprehensible. However, a flowchart is a good learning tool, but not a good programming tool, because flowcharts are difficult to modify. Figure 8-2(b) presents the corresponding program in both COBOL '74 and COBOL '85. The 1974 version does not include the END-IF scope terminator. As a result, we used duplicate code for the PERFORM G and PERFORM B statements. That is, we had to repeat PERFORM G three times because procedure G is to be executed unconditionally on C3, and the END-IF is not available.

Use of the END-IF scope terminator in the 1985 version helps to block off and identify related units of code in Figure 8-2(b). Still, as the levels of nesting are increased, it becomes difficult to follow the logic of the program. Figure 8-3 illustrates a deeply nested structure that would be very difficult to comprehend without a pictorial aid such as a flowchart. But rather than creating diagrammatic aids to cope with such complexity, our objective should be to reduce the complexity and thereby make the program logic more understandable and easier to code. One effective way of reducing program complexity is to decompose a complex structure into simpler but interrelated modules. Figure 8-4 illustrates one possible decomposition of the nested structure in Figure 8-3. At the top of the figure, we have summarized the entire logic into an abbreviated structure consisting of one IF statement and two modules, M1 and M2. (You may want to review the concept of levels of abstraction, covered in Chapter 6.) Each of the two M modules can be referenced by a PERFORM statement, as follows:

```
IF  C1

    PERFORM M1

ELSE

    PERFORM M2.
```

FIGURE 8-1
General Format for the IF Statement

$$\underline{IF} \ condition\text{-}1 \ \ THEN \left\{ \begin{array}{l} \{statement\text{-}1\} \dots \\ \underline{NEXT \ SENTENCE} \end{array} \right\} \left\{ \begin{array}{l} \underline{ELSE} \ \{statement\text{-}2\} \dots \ [\underline{END\text{-}IF}] \\ \underline{ELSE \ NEXT \ SENTENCE} \\ \underline{END\text{-}IF} \end{array} \right\}$$

FIGURE 8-2
Illustration of Deeply Nested Program Structure

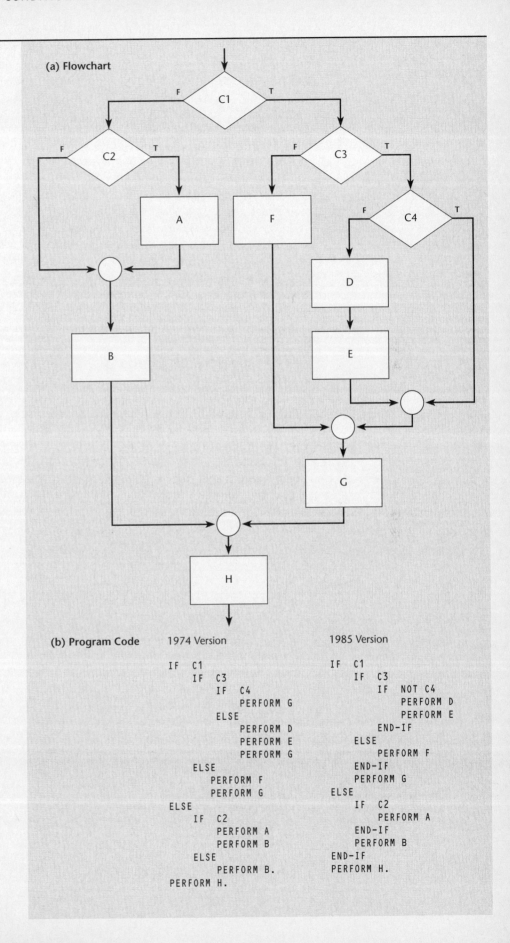

(a) Flowchart

(b) Program Code

1974 Version

```
IF  C1
    IF  C3
        IF  C4
            PERFORM G
        ELSE
            PERFORM D
            PERFORM E
            PERFORM G
    ELSE
        PERFORM F
        PERFORM G
ELSE
    IF  C2
        PERFORM A
        PERFORM B
    ELSE
        PERFORM B.
PERFORM H.
```

1985 Version

```
IF  C1
    IF  C3
        IF  NOT C4
            PERFORM D
            PERFORM E
        END-IF
    ELSE
        PERFORM F
    END-IF
    PERFORM G
ELSE
    IF  C2
        PERFORM A
    END-IF
    PERFORM B
END-IF
PERFORM H.
```

FIGURE 8-3
Sample Deeply Nested Conditional Structure

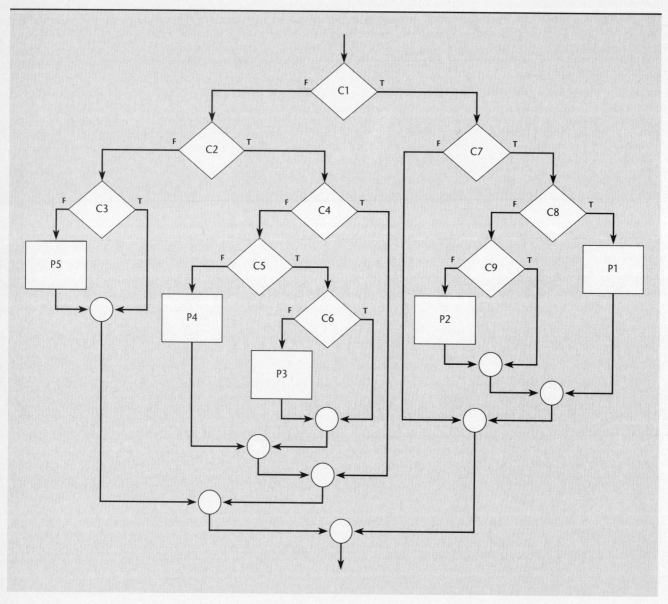

The flowchart for module M1 includes a reference to module M3, which is detailed in the lower left flowchart segment in Figure 8-4. Thus the corresponding code for M1 would be

```
M1.
    IF  C2
        PERFORM M3
    ELSE
        IF  C3
            NEXT SENTENCE
        ELSE
            PERFORM P5.
```

FIGURE 8-4
Decomposition of a Deeply Nested Conditional Structure

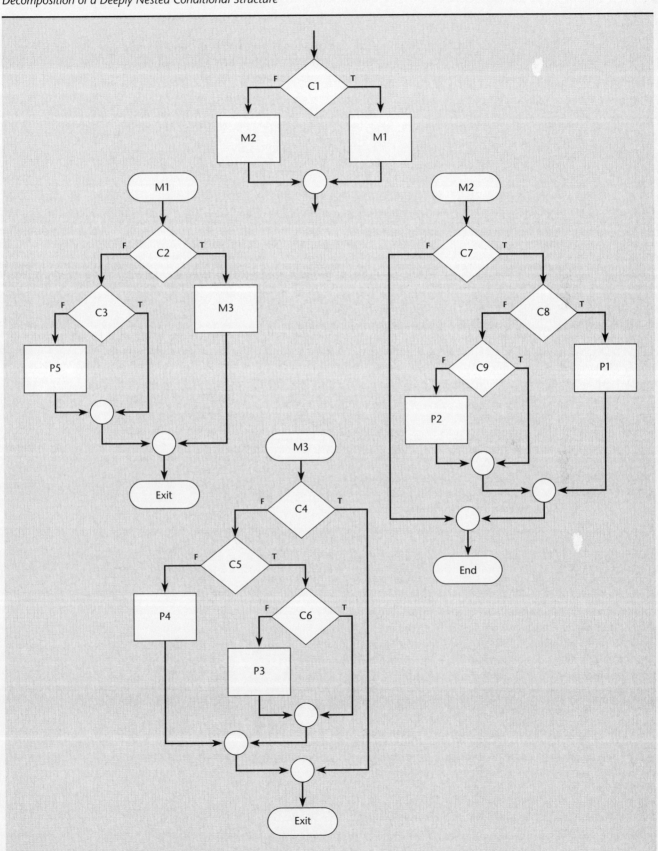

In this particular example we have used simplified and brief references, such as PERFORM P5, which may cause us to wonder if decomposition is worth the bother. We should keep in mind that in a typical program there are multiple lines of code in place of the abbreviated references in the example. In such more complex settings, it is much easier to partition the task into modules such as M1, M2, etc. By this approach we can focus our attention on a single module, rather than trying to relate to all aspects of the complex program module simultaneously.

In summary, nested conditionals should be constructed only up to the level of depth that the program author or a future reader can easily understand.

R E V I E W . . . .

1. A nested conditional is said to exist when statement-1 and/or statement-2 in the IF statement format are themselves _____ .

    conditional

2. Related units of code that are associated with an IF statement can be blocked and readily identified with the statement by use of the _____ scope terminator.

    END-IF

3. One way of eliminating deeply nested structures, and thereby reducing program complexity, is to decompose a complex structure into simpler but interrelated _____ .

    modules

. . . .

THE CONTINUE STATEMENT

The CONTINUE verb is available only in the 1985 standard, and is used to indicate that no executable statement is present. It may be used anywhere that a conditional statement or an imperative statement may be used. Its most likely use is in the null branch of a conditional statement. Consider the following example:

```
IF  C1
    IF  C2
        PERFORM P-1
    ELSE
        CONTINUE
    END-IF
ELSE
    IF  C3
        CONTINUE
    ELSE
        PERFORM P-2
    END-IF
END-IF.
```

As the example illustrates, use of the CONTINUE option allows the programmer to preserve the symmetry of the If-Then-Else structure. The NEXT SENTENCE resembles the CONTINUE, except that in a nested statement it takes us out of the range of the entire IF statement. Thus, instead of using the CONTINUE in the above example, suppose we had written the following program segment:

```
IF C1
    IF  C2
        PERFORM P-1
    ELSE
        NEXT SENTENCE
    END-IF
END-IF
    .
    .
    .
```

In this case, when C2 is false, program execution will continue with the statement following the second END-IF. Thus the CONTINUE can play a very useful role in nested conditional statements.

In terms of function, CONTINUE is a "no-op" type of instruction, just like the EXIT discussed in Chapter 7. However, the EXIT has more specialized requirements: it must be used as the only statement in a paragraph, and therefore, is not an alternative to the CONTINUE in conditional statements.

Another convenient use of CONTINUE is to form "do-nothing" paragraphs, marking the end of a section or the last paragraph in a PERFORM procedure-1 THRU procedure-n series of paragraphs. In such cases the CONTINUE serves as an alternative to using the EXIT command.

R E V I E W . . . .

1. The verb that can be used to indicate that no executable statement is present is the _____ verb.

   CONTINUE

2. The CONTINUE statement [is / is not] a "no-op" type of statement and [must / need not] be the only statement in a paragraph.

   is; need not

3. When the CONTINUE statement is the only statement in a paragraph, a "do-nothing" paragraph has been formed. The usual function for such a paragraph is to mark the _____ of a section or series of paragraphs.

   end

. . . .

CLASS CONDITIONS

The use of a class condition test makes it possible to determine whether contents of a data field are *numeric, alphabetic, alphabetic lowercase,* or *alphabetic uppercase.* Further, by use of a combination of such conditionals, we also can determine if the field contains *alphanumeric data.* The general format for the class condition test is

$$\text{identifier -1 is } [\underline{\text{NOT}}] \left\{ \begin{array}{l} \underline{\text{NUMERIC}} \\ \underline{\text{ALPHABETIC}} \\ \underline{\text{ALPHABETIC - LOWER}} \\ \underline{\text{ALPHABETIC - UPPER}} \\ \text{class -name} \end{array} \right\}$$

The two options dealing with the lowercase and uppercase aspect of alphabetic data are available only in the 1985 standard.

As an example, we can write statements like

```
IF  SALARY IS NUMERIC
    PERFORM PROCESS-PAY
ELSE
    PERFORM NON-NUMERIC-DATA-ERROR.
```

In general, the class condition test is useful as a check to determine if data fields contain the types of data as defined in the DATA DIVISION: numeric, alphabetic, or alphanumeric. The tests for NUMERIC and ALPHABETIC are straightforward, such as these:

```
IF AMOUNT IS NUMERIC ...
IF NAME IS NOT ALPHABETIC ...
```

In effect, the first statement directly tests the appropriateness of the content in the numeric field called AMOUNT, whereas the second statement tests for inappropriateness of the content in the alphabetic field called NAME.

The identifier being tested can be described as *numeric* (with the 9, V, and possibly S PIC characters), *alphanumeric* (with X characters in the PIC description), or *alphabetic* (with A characters in the PIC string). A data field is considered to be numeric if it contains only the digits 0–9, with or without an operational sign. Alphabetic items, on the other hand, consist of the letters A–Z and/or blanks. It is not valid to perform a NUMERIC class test on an alphabetic field or an ALPHABETIC class test on a numeric field. Thus, suppose we have the following DATA DIVISION specifications:

```
AMOUNT      PIC   9(4)V99.
NAME        PIC   A(15).
```

It would be improper to write

```
IF AMOUNT IS ALPHABETIC ...
```
```
        or
```
```
IF NAME IS NUMERIC ...
```

Instead, the AMOUNT field in the above example can be tested to determine if the content is, in fact, NUMERIC or if it is NOT NUMERIC. Similarly, the NAME field

TABLE 8-1

Valid Uses of the Class Condition Test for Different Kinds of Fields

FIELD CLASS	VALID TEST
Numeric	NUMERIC, NOT NUMERIC
Alphabetic	ALPHABETIC, NOT ALPHABETIC
Alphanumeric	NUMERIC, NOT NUMERIC, ALPHABETIC, NOT ALPHABETIC

can be tested only to determine if the content is ALPHABETIC or NOT ALPHABETIC.

A common case of a numeric field not containing numeric data involves reading a field from a record that contains one or more blanks. Specifying the PICTURE with 9s does not guarantee that the field will contain numeric digits. Table 8-1 summarizes the valid uses of the class condition test for different kinds of fields. Note that any of the condition tests may be used with an alphanumeric field.

Since an alphanumeric field can have both alphabetic and numeric content, the alphanumeric content can be ascertained indirectly by determining that the content is not entirely numeric and that it is not entirely alphabetic, as follows:

```
IF  FIELD-A IS NOT NUMERIC
    IF  FIELD-A IS NOT ALPHABETIC
        PERFORM ALPHA-NUM-PAR ...
```

For later reference we mention here that the class condition test cannot be used with numeric items whose USAGE has been declared COMPUTATIONAL. Thus the usage must be explicitly or implicitly DISPLAY. The COMPUTATIONAL and DISPLAY clauses are discussed in Chapter 16.

The ALPHABETIC-LOWER and ALPHABETIC-UPPER are new with the 1985 standard and provide a way of testing the content of a nonnumeric field for the presence of lowercase and uppercase alphabetic characters, respectively. Although data fields may contain lowercase letters, programs written in COBOL '74 themselves must be written in uppercase, except for the nonnumeric literals. For example, the following statements are valid:

```
02 NAME-FIELD PIC X(8) VALUE 'John Doe.'
MOVE 'incompatible codes' TO ERR-MESSAGE.
```

In COBOL '85 we can also use lowercase letters in the COBOL program itself to specify nonreserved words, as in the following:

```
MOVE last-name-in TO last-name-out
PERFORM 250-Report-Detail
    UNTIL  salesperson-no NOT = previous-salesperson-no.
```

Also, many compilers allow reserved COBOL words to be in lowercase.

Because of the multitude of existing programs written in uppercase code, in this book we have chosen *not* to use the 1985 option of using lowercase letters in the program samples.

The fifth class condition in the general format for class conditions at the beginning of this section, *class-name,* can be used for a user-defined class. Such a class can be defined in the SPECIAL-NAMES paragraph of the ENVIRONMENT DIVISION. The user defines a set of characters, assigns them a class-name, and then can refer to that class-name to test whether it is true or false that a data item consists exclusively of the characters identified in the definition of the class-name. Here is an example:

```
ENVIRONMENT DIVISION.
CONFIGURATION SECTION.
SOURCE-COMPUTER.  ABC-480.
OBJECT-COMPUTER.  ABC-480.
```

```
SPECIAL-NAMES.
     CLASS  SPOKEN-NUMERIC
          IS  '0' THRU '9'
                    'o', 'O'.  (These are the lowercase and uppercase letter "o")
```

In the above example SPOKEN-NUMERIC is defined as the set of 10 numeric digits and the letter "o", to allow for the use of "o" as an alternate to zero, such as in "the course number is three-o-two" (perhaps as heard and interpreted by a speech-recognition data-input device). In the PROCEDURE DIVISION we now write

```
IF STREET-NUMBER IS SPOKEN-NUMERIC ...
```

The condition is true if STREET-NUMBER contains only the characters in the defined set SPOKEN-NUMERIC, which consists of the 10 digits and the letter "o", as defined above.

R E V I E W . . . .

1. The purpose of a class condition test is to determine if the actual content of a storage field is _____ , _____ , or
_____ .

   numeric; alphabetic; alphanumeric

2. Suppose that a field named VENDOR has been defined as an alphabetic field in the DATA DIVISION, with PICTURE A(12). If we wish to check for the possibility that numeric data have been entered into this field, we could do so by the following statement:

   IF VENDOR IS _____

   NOT ALPHABETIC

3. Suppose that a field named ADDRESS has been defined as an alphanumeric field in the DATA DIVISION. If we wish to PERFORM PAR-A when the content of the field is, in fact, alphanumeric, we can do so by the following statement:

   _____
   _____
   _____

   IF ADDRESS IS NOT NUMERIC
   IF ADDRESS IS NOT ALPHABETIC
   PERFORM PAR-A

4. In the 1985 standard the content of a nonnumeric field can be tested for the presence of lowercase and uppercase alphabetic characters by the respective keywords _____ and
_____ .

   ALPHABETIC-LOWER; ALPHABETIC-UPPER

5. In COBOL '85 we can use lowercase letters in the program itself to specify _____ words.

   nonreserved

6. The clause in the SPECIAL-NAMES paragraph that can be used to define a set of characters and to assign a class-name to them is the _____ clause.

   CLASS

. . . .

THE SIGN CONDITION

The sign condition determines whether or not the algebraic value of an identifier or arithmetic expression is greater than, less than, or equal to zero. The general format for the sign condition is

$$\text{IF} \begin{Bmatrix} \text{identifer} \\ \text{arithmetic -expression} \end{Bmatrix} \text{IS [NOT]} \begin{Bmatrix} \underline{\text{POSITIVE}} \\ \underline{\text{NEGATIVE}} \\ \underline{\text{ZERO}} \end{Bmatrix} \dots$$

The subject of the condition must be a numeric field or an arithmetic expression. If the value contained in the field is greater than zero, it is POSITIVE; if the value is equal to zero, it is ZERO; and if it is less than zero, it is NEGATIVE.

As was true for the class condition test, the sign condition is used frequently to check on the appropriateness of data. For example, if an inventory value cannot be negative by definition, the presence of a negative value can be detected using the sign condition test, such as in IF INV-QUANTITY IS NEGATIVE. This is a bit more convenient than the equivalent relational test, IF INV-QUANTITY < ZERO. As can be seen by the above two examples, the sign test provides a minor improvement in documentation. By the way, this is a good point to recall that, in order for a field to contain a negative value, it must have been defined with an S character in its PIC string. Also, note that the + and – editing characters do *not* signify algebraic values, since they are not operational signs.

SWITCH-STATUS CONDITIONS

The implementor of a compiler may define certain "switches" and give them associated names. Then such switches can be set as being "on" or "off" at program execution time through the operating system, and the executing program can include a test to determine the status of the switch.

The implementor-name and the ON and OFF values associated with each switch are specified in the SPECIAL-NAMES paragraph of the ENVIRONMENT DIVISION. The following example serves to illustrate such a specification:

```
ENVIRONMENT DIVISION.
CONFIGURATION SECTION.
SOURCE-COMPUTER.  ABC-480.
OBJECT-COMPUTER.  ABC-480.
SPECIAL-NAMES.
    UPSI-0 ON  STATUS IS END-OF-MONTH
           OFF STATUS IS NOT-END-OF-MONTH.
```

The example above defines an external switch by the implementor-name UPSI-0. It is to be referenced by the condition-names END-OF-MONTH and NOT-END-OF-MONTH as corresponding to the ON and OFF status, respectively. The switch is set by an action external to the COBOL program, usually through the operating system. The definition could be applied in the following PROCEDURE DIVISION segment:

```
IF  END-OF-MONTH
    PERFORM CLOSE-THE-BOOKS
ELSE
    PERFORM DAILY-PROCESSING.
```

In essence, the above program segment says: If the external switch called UPSI-0 is ON at the time of program execution, do one thing; if it is OFF, do another thing. The program can then "sense" the operating environment at the time of program execution and take the appropriate action. It is clear that this is not a feature used in a student environment, but in keeping with the "comprehensive" nature of this book, we present the feature for your future reference.

R   E   V   I   E   W . . . .

1. The sign condition can be used to test for three specific types of conditions in regard to the content held in a particular field: whether it is positive, _____ , or _____ .

   negative; zero

2. The subject of the sign condition must be a _____ field or expression.

   numeric

3. As indicated by its name, the purpose of a switch-status conditional is to determine if a switch is in an _____ or _____ condition.

   ON; OFF

4. The implementor-names and the ON and OFF values associated with each such switch are specified in the _____ paragraph of the ENVIRONMENT DIVISION.

   SPECIAL-NAMES

. . . .

COMPOUND CONDITIONS

The subject of compound conditions was introduced in Chapter 5. Here we review and expand on the subject. A *compound condition* is formed by combining two or more simple and/or compound conditions with the logical connectors AND, OR, or NOT. The word *OR* means *either or both,* while *AND* means *both.* Consider the following statement:

```
IF  AMT-DUE IS POSITIVE AND DAYS-OVERDUE > 30
    PERFORM PAR-A.
```

The instruction indicates that the program should execute PAR-A when *both* AMT-DUE is positive and DAYS-OVERDUE exceeds 30.

On the other hand, consider the following statement:

```
IF  AMT-DUE IS POSITIVE OR DAYS-OVERDUE > 30
    PERFORM PAR-A.
```

In this case PAR-A will be executed when *either* AMT-DUE is positive or DAYS-OVERDUE exceeds 30.

Parentheses can be and are used to clarify the meaning of a compound condition. For example, consider the following:

```
IF  ((KODE = 2) OR (KODE = 3)) AND (BALANCE-CODE = 1)
    MOVE SPACES TO ERROR-MESSAGE
    PERFORM OLD-ITEM-2.
```

In this example the condition is true if KODE is equal to 2 or 3 *and* BALANCE-CODE is equal to 1.

In the absence of parentheses the order of precedence (priority) in execution is NOT, AND, and OR. Thus

```
IF  A > B OR NOT C = 10 AND D < K
```

is equivalent to

```
IF  A > B OR ((NOT C = 10) AND D < K)
```

With reference to the examples above, it is obvious that omission of parentheses may result in unnecessarily greater difficulty in understanding a compound conditional expression.

A compound condition can also be abbreviated by omitting the subject of the relation condition or by omitting both the subject and the relational operator in any relational condition except the first. The format for the abbreviated combined relation condition is

$$\text{relation -condition} \left\{ \left\{ \begin{array}{c} \text{AND} \\ \hline \text{OR} \end{array} \right\} \underline{[\text{NOT}]} \text{ [relational operator] object} \right\} \dots$$

Presented below are some relational examples in both expanded and abbreviated form:

- Expanded

  ```
  (A NOT = B) OR (A NOT = C)
  ```

- Abbreviated

  ```
  A NOT = B OR C
  ```

- Expanded

  ```
  ((A > B) and (A NOT < C)) OR (A NOT < D)
  ```

- Abbreviated

  ```
  A > B AND NOT < C OR D
  ```

- Expanded

  ```
  (NOT (A = B)) OR (A = C)
  ```

- Abbreviated

  ```
  NOT A = B OR C
  ```

- Expanded

  ```
  NOT ((((A NOT > B) AND (A NOT > C)) AND (NOT (A NOT > D))))
  ```

- Abbreviated

  ```
  NOT (A NOT > B AND C AND NOT D)
  ```

Brevity of expression may or may not be desirable, depending on the conditional expression. For instance, in the last example above, the multiple parentheses in the expanded version are somewhat confusing, and the abbreviated version is easier to understand. In the immediately preceding example, however, the expanded version is less likely to be misinterpreted than is the abbreviated version.

The above examples use abstract data-names to provide a concise presentation of the subject. Using more conventional data-names, the very last example above could be

```
IF  NOT (INCOME NOT > MEDIAN-INCOME
                 AND COLLEGE-LIMIT
                 AND NOT SCHOLARSHIP-LEVEL)
```

In ordinary language we would say: the condition is true if all three of the following are false:

> income is greater than the value in median-income
>
> income is greater than the value in college-limit
>
> income is not greater than the value in scholarship-level

If you feel that these examples seem confusing, you are justified in your reaction. In many cases, however, it is the nature of the task that requires complex logical tests. Also, previously written programs often use "clever" conditional tests that are unnecessarily complex, and you will need to understand their meaning even if you personally would not have chosen to write such expressions. Programmers can improve documentation by not using unnecessarily complicated expressions. For instance compare the following equivalent pairs:

```
IF  A  NOT >  B              IF  A  <=  B
                         or IF  A  < B  OR  A = B

IF  NOT (A NOT  >  B)        IF  A  >  B
```

The equivalent statements on the right are easier to understand.

R E V I E W . . . .

1. In contrast to the use of simple conditionals, a combination of tests can be included in one statement by the use of _____ conditionals.

    compound

2. The use of a compound conditional requires the use of one of the logical operators: _____ , _____ , or _____ .

    OR; NOT; AND

3. When the logical operator OR is used in a compound conditional test, the presence of [either/ both / either or both] of the conditional states constitutes a true condition.

    either or both

4. When the logical operator AND is used in a compound conditional test, the presence of [either / both / either or both] of the conditional states constitutes a true condition.

    both

5. Generally, the abbreviated form of a compound conditional requires [more / fewer] parentheses and is [easier / more difficult] to interpret in terms of meaning.

    fewer; easier

. . . .

THE EVALUATE STATEMENT

The EVALUATE verb, available only in COBOL '85, provides a powerful and convenient way of implementing the "case" structure in structured programming. Use of the EVALUATE statement eliminates the need to use complicated nested IF statements and allows the programmer to express conditional logic in a well-documented manner. The general format of the statement is presented in Figure 8-5.

As the general format indicates, there are many options available in using the EVALUATE statement, hence its power and flexibility. Let us begin by considering the following simple example:

```
EVALUATE TRANSACTION-CODE
    WHEN 1      PERFORM P-A
    WHEN 2      PERFORM P-B
    WHEN 3      PERFORM P-C
    WHEN OTHER PERFORM P-D.
```

The above statement says to "evaluate" TRANSACTION-CODE and if it is equal to 1, to PERFORM P-A; if it is equal to 2, to PERFORM P-B, and so on. If TRANSACTION-CODE is not 1, 2, or 3, then it is to PERFORM P-D. TRANSACTION-CODE is the

FIGURE 8-5
Format of the EVALUATE Statement

```
           {identifier-1 }  [       {identifier-2 } ]
           {literal-1    }  [       {literal-2    } ]
EVALUATE   {expression-1 }  [ ALSO  {expression-2 } ] ...
           {TRUE         }  [       {TRUE         } ]
           {FALSE        }  [       {FALSE        } ]

{{WHEN
 {ANY                                                                                    }
 {condition-1                                                                            }
 {TRUE                                                                                   }
 {FALSE                                                                                  }
 {      {identifier-3              } [ {THROUGH} {identifier-4              } ]          }
 {[NOT] {literal-3                 } [ {THRU   } {literal-4                 } ]          }
 {      {arithmetic-expression-1   } [           {arithmetic-expression-2   } ]          }

[       {ANY                                                                          }      ]
[       {condition-2                                                                  }      ]
[       {TRUE                                                                         }      ]
[ ALSO  {FALSE                                                                        } ... ] ...
[       {      {identifier-5            } [ {THROUGH} {identifier-6            } ]    }      ]
[       {[NOT] {literal-5               } [ {THRU   } {literal-6               } ]    }      ]
[       {      {arithmetic-expression-3 } [           {arithmetic-expression-4 } ]    }      ]

imperative-statement-1} ...
[WHEN OTHER imperative-statement-2]
[END-EVALUATE]
```

evaluation subject, and as we shall explain below, multiple evaluation subjects may be included in an EVALUATE statement.

The literals 1, 2, and 3 and the keyword OTHER that follow each WHEN in the above example are the evaluation *objects.* Again, as explained below, there may be a single object or multiple objects associated with each WHEN. Execution of an EVALUATE statement involves evaluating each subject with respect to each corresponding object for each of the WHEN statements. Evaluation means substituting each subject and each object with one of the following:

TRUE or FALSE	a. if these very keywords are written as a subject or object
	b. if the subject/object is a condition
A value (numeric or alphanumeric)	a. if the subject/object is a literal or an identifier
	b. if the subject/object is an arithmetic expression
A range of values (numeric or alphanumeric)	if the object is written with the THROUGH or THRU option

The evaluation subject(s) and the corresponding object(s) are compared for each WHEN statement. If they match, then the imperative statement that follows the WHEN is executed. If no such statement immediately follows the WHEN, then the next encountered imperative statement associated with a subsequent WHEN is the one executed, as will be illustrated later in this section in Figure 8-10.

We now illustrate the uses of the EVALUATE command by a series of sample applications.

Figure 8-6 presents a sample case structure that is implemented in Figure 8-7 by use of an EVALUATE statement. Figure 8-8 represents the EVALUATE

FIGURE 8-6
Sample Case Structure

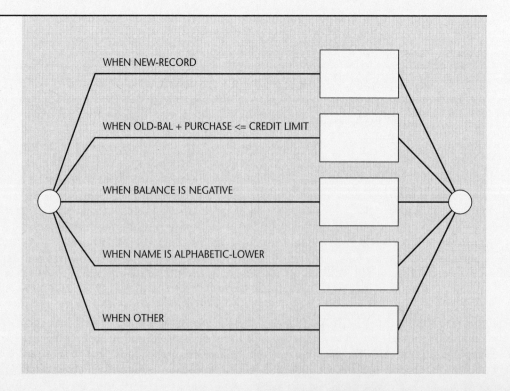

FIGURE 8-7
Sample EVALUATE Statement

```
EVALUATE TRUE                                           }  The evaluation subject is "TRUE".

    WHEN NEW-RECORD                                     }  NEW-RECORD is a condition-name and is the first
                                                           evaluation object. If the condition NEW-RECORD is true
        PERFORM P-1                                        then P-1 is executed and A is MOVED to B and
                                                           program control continues with execution of P-6.
        MOVE A TO B

    WHEN OLD-BAL + PURCHASE <= CREDIT LIMIT             }  The second evaluation object is a relational condition.
                                                           If it is true, then P-2 is executed and program control
        PERFORM P-2                                        continues with execution of P-6.

    WHEN BALANCE IS NEGATIVE

        PERFORM P-3

        IF  X > Y

            THEN                                        }  The third evaluation object is a sign condition. If it is
                                                           true, P-3 is executed, followed by the conditional
                MOVE P TO Q                                statement and then program control continues with
                                                           execution of P-6.
            ELSE

                MOVE R TO Q

        END-IF

    WHEN NAME IS ALPHABETIC-LOWER                       }  The fourth evaluation object is a class condition. If it is
                                                           true then P-4 is executed and program control
        PERFORM P-4                                        continues with P-6.

    WHEN OTHER                                          }  If none of the above four evaluation objects were
                                                           TRUE, then P-5 is executed and program control
        PERFORM P-5                                        continues with P-6.

    END-EVALUATE

    PERFORM P-6
```

statement in flowchart form in order to focus on the chronological order of execution of the commands. Finally, Figure 8-9 presents an equivalent nested IF coding of the same logic, so that this approach can be contrasted with the EVALUATE code in Figure 8-7.

Figure 8-10 illustrates use of the EVALUATE statement with multiple subjects and objects. There are three evaluation subjects: TRUE, TRUE, and FALSE; therefore, each WHEN (except a WHEN OTHER) must have three evaluation

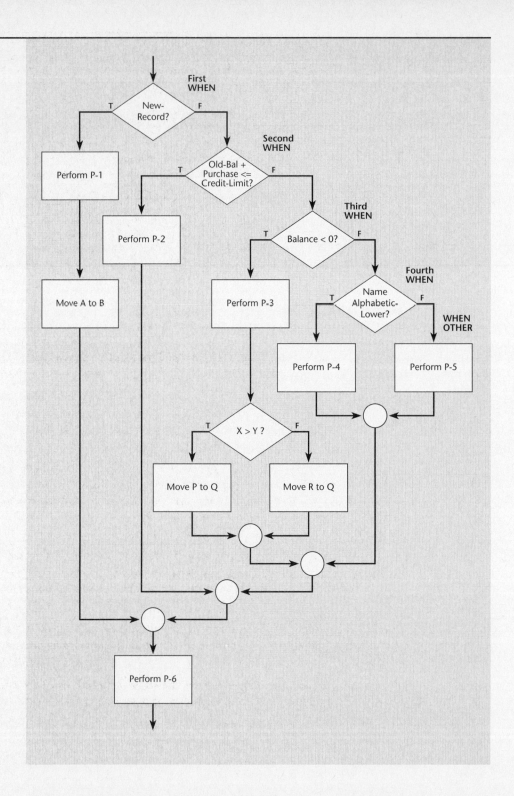

FIGURE 8-8
Flowchart Representation of Sample EVALUATE Statement

objects, although some may include the null ANY, which satisfies any comparison. Notice that the third and fourth WHEN "share" the PERFORM P-C imperative statement. If either of these two WHEN statements is satisfied, P-C is executed.

Figure 8-11 illustrates the incorporation of the EVALUATE verb in a conditional statement and omission of the optional WHEN OTHER clause. Notice the third evaluation subject, which is an arithmetic expression: BALANCE + (PRICE * QUANTITY) < CREDIT-LIMIT.

FIGURE 8-9
Nested IF Alternative to Sample
EVALUATE Statement

```
IF  NEW-RECORD
    THEN
        PERFORM P-1
        MOVE A TO B
    ELSE
        IF  OLD-BAL + PURCHASE <= CREDIT-LIMIT
            THEN
                PERFORM P-2
            ELSE
                IF  BALANCE IS NEGATIVE
                    THEN
                        PERFORM P-3
                        IF  X > Y
                            THEN
                                MOVE P TO Q
                            ELSE
                                MOVE R TO Q
                        END-IF
                    ELSE
                        IF  NAME IS ALPHABETIC-LOWER
                            THEN
                                PERFORM P-4
                            ELSE
                                PERFORM P-5
                        END-IF
                END-IF
        END-IF
END-IF
PERFORM P-6.
```

FIGURE 8-10
Additional Sample EVALUATE Illustration

EVALUATE	TRUE	ALSO	TRUE	ALSO	FALSE
WHEN	ACCOUNTANT **PERFORM P-A**	ALSO	EXPERIENCED	ALSO	WILLING-TO-TRAVEL
WHEN	ACCOUNTANT **PERFORM P-B**	ALSO	INEXPERIENCED	ALSO	WANTS-TO-STAY-PUT
WHEN	COMPUTER-SCIENTIST	ALSO	ANY	ALSO	UNDERPAID
WHEN	SYSTEM-ANALYST **PERFORM P-C**	ALSO	EXPERIENCED	ALSO	ANY
WHEN	EXPERIENCED **PERFORM P-D**	ALSO	ANY	ALSO	ANY

FIGURE 8-11

Sample EVALUATE as Part of a Conditional Statement

```
IF  A = B
    THEN
        EVALUATE TRUE   ALSO    BALANCE  ALSO  BALANCE + (PRICE * QUANTITY) < CREDIT-LIMIT
            WHEN EXCELLENT       ALSO                ANY                ALSO            ANY
                PERFORM P-1
            WHEN AVERAGE         ALSO  LOW-BAL  THRU MEDIUM-BAL         ALSO            ANY
                PERFORM P-2
            WHEN MARGINAL        ALSO  LOW-BAL  THRU HIGH-BAL           ALSO            TRUE
                PERFORM P-3
            WHEN DAYS-SINCE-LAST-PMT < LATE-LIMIT  ALSO  ANY           ALSO            TRUE
                PERFORM P-4
        END-EVALUATE
    ELSE
        PERFORM P-A
END-IF
```

As the final example of using the EVALUATE statement, Figure 8-12 presents a decision table that shows two fields, YEAR-CODE and LETTER-GRADE. There are four alternative actions specified, depending on the joint values of the two fields. For instance, when YEAR-CODE has a value of 4, then the procedure called PROC-3 is executed regardless of the value of LETTER-GRADE. Figure 8-12 also includes an EVALUATE statement to implement the decision table. For example, the first WHEN clause is interpreted as follows:

> If the value of YEAR-CODE is 1 thru 2 and the value of LETTER-GRADE is A thru C, then PERFORM PROC-1.

The ANY option in the third WHEN in Figure 8-12 specifies that any value of LETTER-GRADE fulfills the evaluation criterion for this WHEN conditional. Finally, the WHEN OTHER refers to both the YEAR-CODE and LETTER-CODE; it is equivalent to saying

> Any combination of values of YEAR-CODE and LETTER-GRADE other than the ones specified in the previous WHEN statements.

THE GO TO ... DEPENDING ON STATEMENT

This is a specialized version of the GO TO verb introduced in Chapter 7. It is a conditional statement designed to implement a case structure. However, it is limited to only certain situations. The general format is

> <u>GO</u> TO {procedure-name-1} . . . <u>DEPENDING</u> ON identifier-1

An example of using this format is

```
GO TO WEEKLY-REPORT
      MONTHLY-REPORT
      QUARTERLY-REPORT
   DEPENDING ON PERIOD-FLAG.
```

FIGURE 8-12

Sample Use of the EVALUATE Verb

CONDITION		ACTION
YEAR-CODE	LETTER-GRADE	
1 or 2	A, B, or C	Execute PROC-1
3	A or B	Execute PROC-2
4	any	Execute PROC-3
any other	any	Execute PROC-4

```
EVALUATE YEAR-CODE  ALSO  LETTER-GRADE

    WHEN 1 THRU 2   ALSO  'A' THRU 'C'  PERFORM PROC-1

    WHEN 3          ALSO  'A' THRU 'B'  PERFORM PROC-2

    WHEN 4          ALSO  ANY           PERFORM PROC-3

    WHEN OTHER PERFORM PROC-4

END-EVALUATE
```

This example says to check the value of PERIOD-FLAG (identifier-1 in the format) and if the value is equal to 1, to GO TO the paragraph named WEEKLY-REPORT; if the value of PERIOD-FLAG is equal to 2, to GO TO MONTHLY-REPORT; and if it is equal to 3, to GO TO QUARTERLY-REPORT. Thus the statement is the equivalent of a series of mutually exclusive branching instructions.

A special feature, and a limitation, is that the identifier used in the statement must have values of 1, or 2, or 3, and so on. Then we can specify an implied GO TO statement corresponding to each of these consecutive values. Thus there must be as many procedure-names written as the possible values of identifier-1. If, however, the identifier has a value outside the implied range of values, then the program bypasses this GO TO, and execution continues with the next statement in the program. For example, if PERIOD-FLAG, above, had a value other than 1, 2, or 3, then the whole GO TO ... DEPENDING would be bypassed.

Although it may seem that the statement includes some very restrictive requirements, it is not unusual to have situations where these restrictions apply. For instance, suppose that student records in a college contain a field that serves as a code for the year of studies, such that 1 = freshman, 2 = sophomore, 3 = junior, and 4 = senior. This is typical of many situations where a code is used and the range of values assigned to the code is 1, 2, etc.

We now illustrate use of the application of the GO TO ... DEPENDING statement as a means of implementing case structures. We also take the opportunity to use the example to put together four alternative ways that a case structure can be implemented. Figure 8-13 consists of four parts and illustrates the implementation of the required case structure by use of the (a) EVALUATE statement; (b) nested IF; (c) GO TO ... DEPENDING; and (d) simple conditionals with GO TOs. In the example we assume that we have a field, YEAR-OF-STUDIES, which contains values in the range 1–4, indicating freshman through senior. In each of the four cases we want to execute a specialized procedure, such as FROSH-PAR. If the value in YEAR-OF-STUDIES is not within the valid range, we want to execute ERROR-PAR.

The sample code in parts (a) and (b) of Figure 8-13 is routine. Part (c) shows the use of the GO TO ... DEPENDING. Notice that we have made the effort

FIGURE 8-13

Alternative COBOL
Implementations of Case Structure

```
EVALUATE TRUE
    WHEN     FRESHMAN        PERFORM      FROSH-PAR
    WHEN     SOPHOMORE       PERFORM      SOPH-PAR
    WHEN     JUNIOR          PERFORM      JUNIOR-PAR
    WHEN     SENIOR          PERFORM      SENIOR-PAR
    WHEN     OTHER           PERFORM      ERROR-PAR
END-EVALUATE
```

(a) Case Implementation using the EVALUATE Statement (ANSI 1985)

```
IF   FRESHMAN
     PERFORM FROSH-PAR
ELSE
    IF   SOPHOMORE
         PERFORM SOPH-PAR
    ELSE
        IF   JUNIOR
             PERFORM JUNIOR-PAR
        ELSE
            IF   SENIOR
                 PERFORM SENIOR-PAR
            ELSE
                 PERFORM ERROR-PAR
```

(b) Case Implementation using Nested IF Statements

to preserve the one-entry, one-exit concept of structured programming even while using GO TO statements. The initial GO TO ... DEPENDING branches to one of four paragraphs implementing the case structure. However, at the end of each of those four paragraphs, we have included a GO TO EXIT-PAR statement which brings program flow to one converging point so that there is a common exit.

In the ENTRY-PAR paragraph, notice the very last line following the DEPENDING ON YEAR-OF-STUDIES. It consists of the statement GO TO ERROR-PAR. If YEAR-OF-STUDIES does not contain a value in the range 1–4, the program will not have branched to any of the four named procedures. Instead, execution will bypass the GO TO ... DEPENDING statement and will "fall through" to the unconditional GO TO statement. Thus the counterpart of the OTHER option in the EVALUATE statement is the statement following the GO TO ... DEPENDING.

For completeness Figure 8-13 also illustrates use of simple conditionals with the GO TO statement in part (d) of the figure. Again, we have used GO TO EXIT-PAR for all cases to force convergence of program control flow to one exit point. As a final remark about the example in Figure 8-13(d), we should mention that we could have used nested IF with GO TOs just as well, but we chose to use simple IF statements. This choice would have been even more appropriate if the number of alternatives was large and we did not want to write a very deeply nested IF.

FIGURE 8-13
Alternative COBOL
Implementations of Case Structure
(continued)

```
02   YEAR-OF-STUDIES   PIC 9.          (Notice that values start with 1 and
       88  FRESHMAN      VALUE 1.      are consecutive—a requirement for
       88  SOPHOMORE     VALUE 2.      correct use of the GO TO . . .
       88  JUNIOR        VALUE 3.      DEPENDING ON statement.)
       88  SENIOR        VALUE 4.
  ENTRY-PAR.
       GO TO FROSH-PAR
             SOPH-PAR
             JUNIOR-PAR
             SENIOR-PAR
       DEPENDING ON YEAR-OPF-STUDIES.
       GO TO ERROR-PAR.


  FROSH-PAR.
       -------------------
       -------------------
       GO TO EXIT-PAR.


  SOPH-PAR.
       -------------------
       -------------------
       GO TO EXIT-PAR.


  JUNIOR-PAR.
       -------------------
       -------------------
       GO TO EXIT-PAR.


  SENIOR-PAR.
       -------------------
       -------------------
       GO TO EXIT-PAR.


  ERROR-PAR
       -------------------
       -------------------
       GO TO EXIT-PAR.          (In case EXIT-PAR is not physically contiguous.)


  EXIT-PAR.          (This is the converging point for all cases, so that the one-entry,
                     one-exit structure is preserved and GO TOs are in control.)
```

(c) Case Implementation using GO TO . . . DEPENDING ON . . . .

FIGURE 8-13

Alternative COBOL Implementations of Case Structure (continued)

```
        IF   FRESHMAN
             PERFORM FROSH-PAR
             GO TO EXIT-PAR.


        IF   SOPHOMORE
             PERFORM SOPH-PAR
             GO TO EXIT-PAR.


        IF   JUNIOR
             PERFORM JUNIOR-PAR
             GO TO EXIT-PAR.


        IF   SENIOR
             PERFORM SENIOR-PAR
             GO TO EXIT-PAR.


        PERFORM ERROR-PAR
        GO TO EXIT-PAR.           (In case EXIT-Par is not physically contiguous.)


    EXIT-PAR.        (This is the converging point for all cases, so that the one-entry,
                      one-exit structure is preserved and GO TOs are in control.)
```

(d) Case Implementation using Simple Conditionals and GO TO

VERB-RELATED CONDITIONS

Several verbs in COBOL contain "built-in" conditionals. These are summarized in Table 8-2 along with the verb or verbs with which each of these conditionals is associated. Many of the verbs shown in Table 8-2 will be discussed in subsequent chapters. However, we have included them in this chapter for future reference since the subject falls naturally under the topic of conditional statements. COBOL uses such specialized conditionals to serve as special-purpose "if" statements, in contrast with the general-purpose IF.

R E V I E W . . . .

1. A powerful and convenient way of implementing the "case" type of program structure in COBOL '85 is provided by use of the _____ statement.

   EVALUATE

2. For each of the WHEN statements, execution of an EVALUATE verb involves evaluating each _____ with respect to its corresponding _____ .

   subject; object

3. The conditional GO TO verb that can be used in either COBOL '74 or COBOL '85 to implement the "case" type of program structure is the GO TO ... _____ verb.

   DEPENDING (or DEPENDING ON)

TABLE 8-2
Specialized Conditionals Related to Control Verbs

CONDITIONAL	RELATED VERB
AT END	READ, SEARCH
[NOT] AT END	READ
[NOT] AT $\left\{ \begin{array}{l} \text{END-OF-PAGE} \\ \text{EOP} \end{array} \right\}$	WRITE
[NOT] INVALID KEY	DELETE, READ, REWRITE, START, WRITE
[NOT] ON EXCEPTION	CALL
[NOT] ON OVERFLOW	STRING, UNSTRING
[NOT] ON SIZE ERROR	ADD, COMPUTE, DIVIDE, MULTIPLY, SUBTRACT
UNTIL	PERFORM
WHEN	EVALUATE, SEARCH

4. The [NOT] ON OVERFLOW and [NOT] ON SIZE ERROR conditionals are
   examples of _____-related conditionals.

                                                                                verb

5. In its effect, a verb-related conditional serves as a special "_____" statement.

                                                                                if

·   ·   ·   ·   ·   ·   ·   ·   ·   ·   ·   ·   ·   ·   ·   ·   ·   ·   ·   ·

SAMPLE PROGRAM USING COBOL '85

We conclude the chapter by presenting a revised version of the sample program in
Figure 4-8 in Chapter 4. The revised program is presented in Figure 8-14.
It includes use of selected COBOL '85 features, such as the in-line PERFORM,
SET condition-name, and NOT AT END, and the scope terminators END-IF,
END-READ, and END-PERFORM. The cumulative effect of these features is to
allow us to write the entire PROCEDURE DIVISION as one paragraph. This particular
occurrence is incidental to this case. Still, the general effect of using scope
terminators is to enable COBOL '85 programs to reduce the number of paragraphs
without impacting the self-documentation and clarity of the programs.

SUMMARY

The purpose of this chapter was to review and expand your knowledge of the use
of conditional statements in COBOL.

     The IF command is the fundamental type of conditional statement. A
nested conditional is said to exist when statement-1 or statement-2 in the general
format are themselves conditional statements. Use of the END-IF scope terminator
in COBOL '85 helps to block off and identify units of code in a nested design. The
CONTINUE verb, also available only in COBOL '85, is used to indicate that no

FIGURE 8-14

Sample Program Using COBOL '85

```
    PROCEDURE DIVISION.
*
    000-MAIN-ROUTINE.
        OPEN INPUT  EMPLOYEE-FILE
             OUTPUT REPORT-FILE.
*
*   PRINT REPORT HEADINGS
        WRITE PRINT-LINE FROM HEADING-1 AFTER ADVANCING PAGE
        WRITE PRINT-LINE FROM HEADING-2 AFTER 2 LINES
        MOVE SPACES TO PRINT-LINE
        WRITE PRINT-LINE AFTER 2 LINES
*
*   PROCESS AND PRINT EACH RECORD
        PERFORM UNTIL END-OF-EMPLOYEE-FILE
            READ EMPLOYEE-FILE
                AT  END
                    MOVE "YES" TO END-OF-FILE-TEST
                NOT AT  END
                    IF  MALE
                        MOVE EMPLOYEE-SALARY TO REPORT-MEN-SALARY
                        MOVE ZERO TO REPORT-WOMEN-SALARY
                        ADD 1 TO NO-OF-MEN
                        ADD EMPLOYEE-SALARY TO MEN-TOTAL-SALARY
                    ELSE
                        IF  FEMALE
                            MOVE EMPLOYEE-SALARY TO REPORT-WOMEN-SALARY
                            MOVE ZERO TO REPORT-MEN-SALARY
                            ADD 1 TO NO-OF-WOMEN
                            ADD EMPLOYEE-SALARY TO WOMEN-TOTAL-SALARY
                        ELSE
                            MOVE ALL "*" TO REPORT-ERROR-CODE
                        END-IF
                    END-IF
                    MOVE EMPLOYEE-NAME TO REPORT-EMPL-NAME
                    WRITE PRINT-LINE FROM REPORT-DETAIL-LINE BEFORE
                        ADVANCING 1 LINE
                    MOVE SPACES TO REPORT-DETAIL-LINE
            END-READ
        END-PERFORM
*
*   PRINT REPORT FOOTINGS
        MOVE MEN-TOTAL-SALARY TO REPORT-TOT-MEN-SALARY
        MOVE WOMEN-TOTAL-SALARY TO REPORT-TOT-WOMEN-SALARY
        WRITE PRINT-LINE FROM REPORT-TOTAL-LINE AFTER 3 LINES
*
        DIVIDE NO-OF-MEN INTO MEN-TOTAL-SALARY
                GIVING REPORT-AVG-MEN-SALARY
        DIVIDE NO-OF-WOMEN INTO WOMEN-TOTAL-SALARY
                GIVING REPORT-AVG-WOMEN-SALARY
*
        WRITE PRINT-LINE FROM REPORT-AVERAGES-LINE AFTER 2 LINES
*
        CLOSE EMPLOYEE-FILE
              REPORT-FILE
*
        STOP RUN.
```

executable statement is present, and thereby also helps to block off and identify units of code.

The use of a *class condition test* makes it possible to determine whether the contents of a data field are *numeric, alphabetic, alphabetic lowercase, alphabetic uppercase, alphanumeric,* or belong to a user-defined class. The main purpose for such tests is to ascertain that the designated data classes in fact contain the types of data as defined in the DATA DIVISION or the SPECIAL-NAMES paragraph of the ENVIRONMENT DIVISION. On the other hand, the *sign condition test* is used to determine whether the content in a numeric data field or the value of an arithmetic expression is *positive, negative,* or *zero.* The purpose of a *switch-status conditional* is to test for the status of an "on" or "off" switch. The implementor-names and the ON and OFF values associated with each such switch are specified in the SPECIAL-NAMES paragraph of the ENVIRONMENT DIVISION.

A *compound condition* is formed by combining two or more simple and/or compound conditionals with the logical connectors AND, OR, or NOT. Parentheses are often used to clarify the meaning of compound conditions. A compound condition can be abbreviated by omitting the subject, or both the subject and relational operator, in any relational condition except the first one in the expression. As illustrated by a number of examples, the abbreviated version generally requires fewer parentheses.

The EVALUATE verb, available only in COBOL '85, is particularly useful for implementation of the *case* type of program structure. This is the type of structure that provides for the execution of one of *several* alternatives. The GO TO ... DEPENDING statement, available in both COBOL versions, also can be used to implement the "case" structure. However, it is more limited in its applications than is the EVALUATE verb. Examples of implementing the "case" structure by several different approaches were given in the chapter.

Finally, *verb-related conditionals* were briefly overviewed. These are verbs that contain "built-in" conditionals, such as the AT END and [NOT] ON SIZE ERROR verbs.

EXERCISES

8.1 An input field has been defined as

    03 IN-FIELD PICTURE X(10).

Two other fields in WORKING-STORAGE have been defined as

    01 AMOUNT PICTURE 9(10).

    01 NAME   PICTURE A(10).

We wish to test the content of IN-FIELD and, if it contains a number, to store it in AMOUNT; if it contains a name, to store it in NAME; and if a mixture of characters, to execute a paragraph called ERRORS.

a. Write PROCEDURE DIVISION statements to accomplish this task.

b. Suppose that if the IN-FIELD contains a number, it is actually in dollars and cents. What would you do to make the number available in dollars and cents instead of as an integer?

8.2. We want to write a program to "edit" input data. In this context, editing means to check the data for accuracy and compliance with certain rules.

The data are in the following file:

```
FD  EMPLOYEE-FILE    LABEL RECORDS STANDARD
                     RECORD CONTAINS 80 CHARACTERS
                     DATA RECORD IS EMPLOYEE-RECORD.
01  EMPLOYEE-RECORD.
    02  EMPL-NAME          PIC X(15).
    02  EMPL-NO            PIC 9(4).
    02  PAY-CODE           PIC X.
        88  SALARIED       VALUE 'S'.
        88  HOURLY         VALUE 'H'.
        88  VALID-PAY-CODE VALUE 'H', 'S'.
        88  ERROR-PAY-CODE VALUE ... (You insert the value.)
    02  PAY-RATE           PIC 9(4)V99.
    02  FILLER             PIC X(54)
    .
    .
    .

WORKING-STORAGE SECTION.
01  PAY-LIMITS.
    02  MINIMUM-SALARY  PIC 9(4)V99 VALUE 940.00.
    02  MAXIMUM-SALARY  PIC 9(4)V99 VALUE 6800.00.
    02  MINIMUM-WAGE    PIC 9(2)V99 VALUE 5.50.
    02  MAXIMUM-WAGE    PIC 9(2)V99 VALUE 18.99.
```

We want to read the data and screen them for the kinds of errors implied by the above data definitions and by the sample output in Figure 8-15. As you can see in the sample output, if a record contains one or more errors, the record itself is printed, followed by the appropriate error messages.

Write a program to do this data editing task, and use the sample input in Figure 8-15 as test data.

FIGURE 8-15
*Sample Input and Output for
Exercise 8.2*

INPUT FILE

```
BROWN,R.K.           1234S156035
DAVIS,M.O.           5246H250603
GARCIA,L.A.          3345H000676
HARRISON,P.N         21005000700
MARTIN,A.C.          5123S12000
MARTINEZ,P.M.        4433S800000
PETERSON,R.A.        6161H0001256
                     8990H000600
```

PROGRAM OUTPUT

```
                        INPUT DATA ERROR LISTING
                   (RECORD PRECEDES ITS ERROR MESSAGES)

BROWN,R.K.       1234S156035
                 UNREASONABLE PAY RATE FOR HOURLY EMPLOYEE


DAVIS,M.O.       5246H250603
                 UNREASONABLE PAY RATE FOR HOURLY EMPLOYEE


HARRISON,P.N     21005000700
                 PAY CODE IS NEITHER S NOR H


MARTIN,A.C.      5123S12000
                 PAY RATE CONTAINS NON-NUMERIC CHARACTERS
                 UNREASONABLE PAY RATE FOR HOURLY EMPLOYEE


MARTINEZ,P.M.    4433S800000
                 UNREASONABLE PAY RATE FOR SALARIED EMPLOYEE


PETERSON,R.A.    6161H0001256
                 UNREASONABLE PAY RATE FOR HOURLY EMPLOYEE


                 8990H000600
                 EMPLOYEE NAME IS MISSING
```

9 Control Break Processing for Reports

IN THIS CHAPTER *you will develop a basic level of expertise for producing reports. A report may consist of a* **report heading**, *the* **report body**, *and a* **report footing.** *The report body then is made up of pages, and you will learn what distinct types of parts can be included on each page from the standpoint of required programming. Then you will consider the topic of* **control breaks** *in programming for reports, and the general logical structure that applies to most such programs.*

Following this overall study of the topic, you will then be "walked through" two examples of preparing reports with control breaks: one relatively simple and the other more advanced. Your study will conclude with some specialized options in the WRITE verb that facilitate report generation.

THE GENERAL STRUCTURE OF REPORTS

Report output is a common and important purpose associated with the use of computers in business. People use computer data through reports. A *report* is a formatted collection of data recorded either as printed output or on a display screen.

Figure 9-1 presents the general structure of a report. There may be a *report heading* at the beginning of the report, which may contain such information as the report title, the date, the name of the person who prepared the report, intended recipients of the report, and the like. Then the *report body* consists of one or more pages. A page is a formatted collection of lines. Usually, pages are defined on the basis of some physical characteristics of the output medium. For instance, printed reports are usually printed on paper that is 11 inches in vertical length, while display-screen reports tend to be equal in vertical length to the size of the screen (about 24 lines). A page is subdivided into five parts, or types of report groups: a *page heading, control heading(s), report detail lines, control footing(s),* and a *page footing.*

A *page heading* is included to enhance the readability of long reports by including such information as page numbers and column headings. The report data are included in *detail lines* of one or more formats. A *control heading* is used to introduce a new category of data, such as a new department or a new salesperson. A *control footing* typically is used to summarize the data presented in the preceding group of detail lines, such as the total sales for the salesperson whose detail sales were just reported. Finally, the end of each page may include a *page footing* that contains summary data for the page or simply serves as an alternate page-numbering position (unless page numbers were included in the page heading).

After all pages have been presented, a *report footing* may be included to designate the end of the report and to provide summary data about the report as a whole.

FIGURE 9-1
General Report Structure

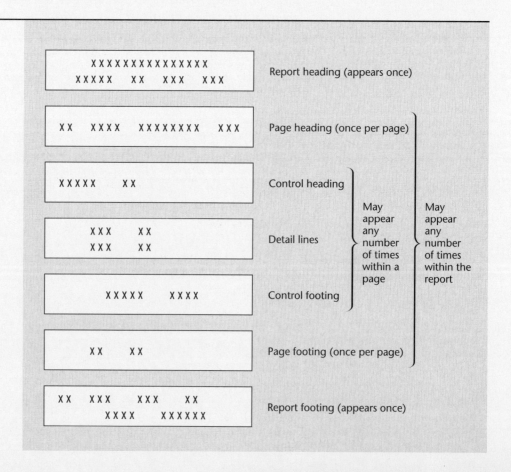

Figure 9-2 illustrates most of these report group types by means of a brief example. In the output the report heading consists of the first two lines. It is assumed that it appears only once at the beginning of the report. The indicated line serving as page heading consists of column headings to help the reader interpret the meaning of the report data. The control heading in this example is very simple, but nevertheless, distinct. When the report shows sales data for a new product number, the product number is listed; it is not repeated on every line, thus making the report easy to read. The fact that we do something distinctive when a new group of data is reported constitutes the control heading in this case.

The detail lines show the amount of individual sales transactions for each product. In the example we have two transactions for the first product and three for the second one. Notice that the control heading in this example (the line with the product number) happens to include the detail data (sales amount) for the first detail line. This need not be the case, but often it is so.

The control footing consists of the total sales for each product. In a less simple report, the control footing would typically include additional data. Finally, Figure 9-2 illustrates the idea of a report footing by means of the last line showing the grand total of sales figures for the report.

Report generation is characterized by common logical program procedures. Because of the common characteristics and the frequent need for report programs, a large number of report writer program products have been developed. These proprietary report writers are of two types. One type uses a specialized language that the programmer can use to compose a report-generating program. Such specialized languages are, of course, nonstandard and are unique to each program product. Many are "user-friendly" languages that can be used by "layman" users with just a few hours of training. A second type of report writer is the parameter-driven report writer. The program requires specifications about headings, totals, etc., as parameters, and then uses these to generate the desired report.

In the context of COBOL programming many report-generating programs are coded in the usual fashion. However, a special *report writer feature,* which facilitates report programming and also has the property of being standardized, is available. This COBOL feature is a language type of report writer. In essence, the report writer feature is a specialized language embedded in the

FIGURE 9-2
Sample Report Groups

ACME CORPORATION			Report Heading
SALES REPORT FOR JULY, 1990			
PRODUCT NO.	SALES AMOUNT	TOTAL SALES	Page heading
123	125.27		Control heading
	100.00		Detail line
		$225.27	Control footing
345	50.00		
	110.25		
	10.09		
		$170.34	
GRAND TOTAL		$395.61	Report footing

COBOL framework for use in report-generating programs. The report writer is described in Chapter 24.

R E V I E W . . . .

1. In general, a report may consist of a report heading, a report body, and a report _____.

                                                                                          footing

2. The report body is normally subdivided into _____.

                                                                                          pages

3. Of the subdivisions in a page of a report, the type of heading that introduces a new category of data is the _____ heading.

                                                                                          control

4. Data that have been presented in the preceding group of data lines are summarized in the control _____.

                                                                                          footing

5. With respect to commercially available report writer programs, one type is based on the use of specialized _____ while the second type requires specification of _____ for the desired report.

                                                                                          languages; parameters

6. The COBOL feature that facilitates the programming of report-generating programs, is called the _____ feature.

                                                                                          report writer

. . . .

CONTROL BREAKS IN REPORT WRITING

Most reports pertain to data that are associated with categories that bear a hierarchical relation to each other. Very often the categories correspond to organizational departments or groupings. For instance, suppose that we are producing a report listing student enrollment for a college. We have students enrolled in a course section, sections belonging to a course, courses belonging to a department, and departments belonging to a college. Suppose that we are interested in having the enrollment reported in a way that makes these relationships meaningful. To achieve this objective, we designate that each course section begin on a new page with a heading, that there be a heading for each course, and that there be a heading for each department. Further, we designate that total enrollment be reported for each section, for each course, for each department, and for the entire college.

In the above example we would say that we have three control breaks: *course section, course,* and *department.* We speak of department as the *major* control, course as the *intermediate* control, and section as the *minor* control. Of course, we may have more than three control levels. Regardless of the number of control levels, each level is subordinate to its superior and all are subordinates to one control level—the major control. In other words, control levels are nested in a hierarchical structure so that the report groups are clearly related.

As the report is being produced, we want to break the report routine whenever a new course section, a new course, or a new department begins. The control is based on the content of the fields that designate the course section, course, and department. We would expect that the report program logic would check the course section, for instance; and, if it changed value, we would want to print the total enrollment for the course section just listed. But it may be that the section did not change (say, section 1 of a one-section course), but the course changed from CIS-302 to CIS-402. The report program then also must be checking the course designation to capture the change. A similar checking procedure is required for department designation. In simple terms, as the report is being produced, the program has to be checking for a new department, a new course, and a new course section.

The highest level of control break is called the *final control,* which is, of course, nonrecurring. In essence, it is a means of controlling the report action when all the detail data have been processed. In the above student registration example, a final control break would occur when the last course section in the last course of the last department in the college had been processed. At that point the final control might involve reporting the enrollment for the entire college.

A point that relates to the control breaks is the fact that they are used to present control headings and control footings. As we explained at the beginning of the chapter, a *control heading* is a report group (one or more lines of output) that is presented when a control break occurs. For example, a control heading specified for the department field could be used to print the department name and start a new page. As the name implies, a *control footing* is a report group that is presented at the end of a group and before the next category begins. In our example, at the end of each course we might desire a control footing to write the accumulated total enrollment of all the sections in that course. Typically, control footings are used for accumulating and reporting totals, while control headings are used for printing headers.

It should be noted that the control fields and the sort order of the input file are related. In our example we would expect that the data have been sorted by student within section, by section within course, by course within department, and by department within the college. This sorting would be appropriate to establishing control breaks that treat department as a more inclusive control than course, course as more inclusive than section, and so forth.

R E V I E W . . . .

1. When control breaks are used in conjunction with a report program, the category that is at the highest hierarchical level compared with the other categories is termed the _____ control.

    major

2. In addition to the major control breaks, other levels of such breaks are the _____ and _____ controls.

    intermediate; minor

3. When all the report detail data have been processed, the last break is associated with the output of grand totals for all of the categories and is called the _____ control break.

    final

4. A heading (or footing) that is printed just before (or just after) a data group that is associated with a control break is called a _____ heading (or footing).

    control

FIGURE 9-3
Sample Report Logic Flowchart for Three Control Breaks

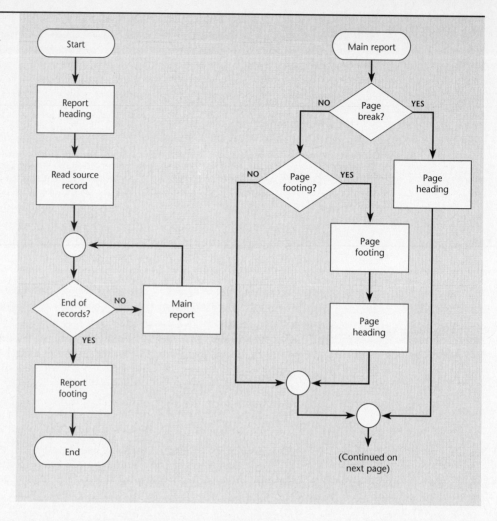

LOGIC OF REPORT PROGRAMS

The logical structure of report-generating programs tends to be similar regardless of the specific characteristics of the individual report. Figure 9-3 outlines this general logic in flowchart form. The figure is based on a report with three control breaks that are associated with the three fields: Dept., Month, and Part. Although the flowchart references these three control breaks, it is easy to see that it applies in concept to any report program with three levels of control breaks. Also, if we have a different number of control breaks, the flowchart can be easily adapted to that need.

In the flowchart of Figure 9-3, notice that a test for page break is made first. A condition of needing to start a new page is similar to the condition of a control heading or control footing: we need to pause the report routine and do something special. In the logic of a report program the page break case is hierarchically superior to the other control groups. If it is time to start a new page, we need to take care of that situation regardless of whether we do or do not have a new department, or a new month, etc.

Further studying the flowchart in Figure 9-3, notice that we test for Dept. break first, for Month next, and for Part last. We can assume that these represent the major, intermediate, and minor control levels, respectively. Thus if the program logic is "looking" at data for a new Dept., there is no need to know if it is a new Month or new Part; it is time to process a control footing for Dept., regardless.

FIGURE 9-3

Sample Report Logic Flowchart for Three Control Breaks (continued)

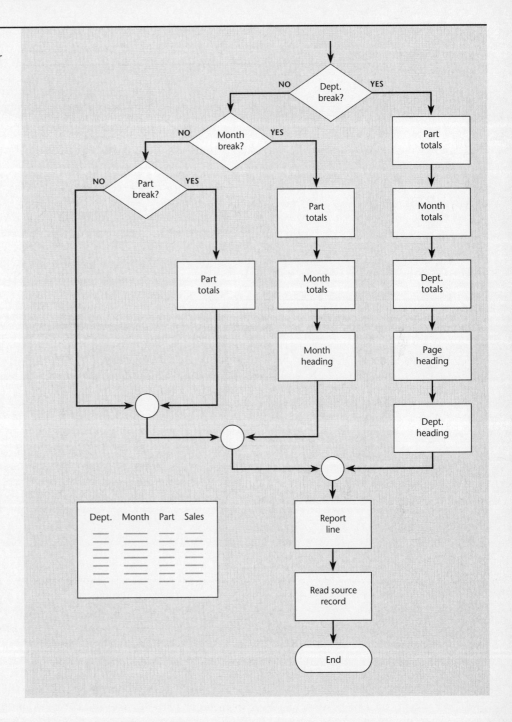

A SIMPLE REPORT PROGRAM

We present first a simple report program that illustrates many of the general concepts about report writing without being overwhelming in detail. Then we present a more advanced example in the next section of this chapter.

The objective of this program is to read records in a file and produce a report such as that shown in Figure 9-4. The input records are sorted so that all records pertaining to a given product are grouped together. The input records have the format and sample input presented in Figure 9-5.

Figure 9-6 presents a structure chart for the program, while Figure 9-7 is the corresponding COBOL program itself.

FIGURE 9-4

Output of the Report Program

PRODUCT NO.	SALES AMOUNT	TOTAL SALES
123	125.27	
	100.00	
		$225.27
345	50.50	
	110.25	
	10.09	$170.84

FIGURE 9-5

Input Record Format and Sample Records

RECORD FORMAT

FILLER	PRODUCT-NO	SALES-AMOUNT	FILLER
PIC X(15)	PIC 999	PIC 9(4)V99	PIC X(56)

SAMPLE INPUT

```
123012527
123010000
345005050
345011025
345001009
```

We can observe several key points that are typical of such report-generating programs. First, the initial record that is input is treated separately. Whereas we have to check all subsequent records to determine whether the current record is for the same product as the previous record, this is not the case for the first record, for which there is no previous record. The 010-PROCESS-FIRST-SALES-RECORD in the PROCEDURE DIVISION of the program, and the corresponding block in the structure chart, are designed to handle this special case.

After the first record has been processed, the remaining records are handled by the logic in 050-PROCESS-RECORD, which tests for a control break first by the statement IF PRODUCT-NUMBER = PREVIOUS-PRODUCT-NUMBER. The typical detail line is handled in 060-PROCESS-REPORT-LINE, while the case of a control break is handled in the 070-PROCESS-NEW-RECORD. The latter paragraph presents a control footing that, in this case, is simply the MOVE PRODUCT-TOTAL TO TOTAL-SALES-OUT statement followed by printing the control footing through execution of 040-PRINT-LINE. Then the control heading for the new product is handled by executing the 030-PRINT-NEW-PRODUCT-LINE.

Notice that all the actual printing is handled through the 040-PRINT-LINE procedure. Having one single printing point gives us easy control over the printing

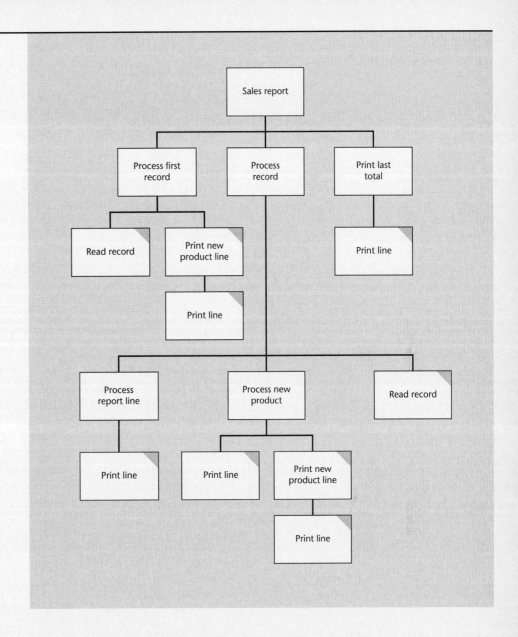

FIGURE 9-6
Structure Chart for the Report Program

of a page heading at the top of each page. As we are about to print a report line, we check to see if we should be starting a new report page, in which case we should print a page heading. In the structure chart for the program, in Figure 9-6, Print Line is a module that is subordinate to five different modules. The reason for the repeated use of this module is that the page-heading logic is included in this module; therefore, it involves more than just printing a line. In a report-oriented program it is always best to do the printing in one module, rather than dispersing this function throughout the program. Report formats often need to be changed, and it is much easier to change one cohesive module than to attempt changing scattered statements throughout the program. In the program we assume that each page will consist of 25 lines, and we have defined a constant, PAGE-SIZE, in the WORKING-STORAGE SECTION for this value. Should we want to generate the report with a different number of lines per page, all we would have to do is change the VALUE clause of PAGE-SIZE.

As a final point in discussing the sample program, notice that the last input record is handled as another special case. After the AT END is true, we

FIGURE 9-7

*Example Program with One
Control Break*

```
      IDENTIFICATION DIVISION.
      PROGRAM-ID. SALEREP1.
      *

      ENVIRONMENT DIVISION.
      *

      CONFIGURATION SECTION.
      SOURCE-COMPUTER. IBM-3081.
      OBJECT-COMPUTER. IBM-3081.
      *

      INPUT-OUTPUT SECTION.
      *

      FILE-CONTROL.
          SELECT SALES-FILE  ASSIGN TO S-CARDS.
          SELECT REPORT-FILE ASSIGN TO S-PRINTER.
      *

      DATA DIVISION.
      *

      FILE SECTION.
      *

      FD  SALES-FILE     LABEL RECORDS ARE OMITTED
                         RECORD CONTAINS 80 CHARACTERS
                         DATA RECORD IS SALES-RECORD.
      01  SALES-RECORD.
          02  FILLER               PIC X(15).
          02  PRODUCT-NUMBER       PIC 9(3).
          02  SALES-AMOUNT         PIC 9(4)V99.
          02  FILLER               PIC X(56).
      *
      FD  REPORT-FILE    LABEL RECORDS ARE OMITTED
                         DATA RECORD IS REPORT-RECORD.
      01  REPORT-RECORD            PIC X(132).
      *


      WORKING-STORAGE SECTION.
      *

      01  PREVIOUS-VALUES.
          02  PREVIOUS-PRODUCT-NUMBER PIC 9(3).
      *

      01  END-OF-FILE-INDICATOR    PIC XXX    VALUE 'NO'.
          88 END-OF-FILE                      VALUE 'YES'.
          88 NOT-END-OF-FILE                  VALUE 'NO'.
      *

      01  PAGE-SIZE                PIC 99     VALUE 25.
      *

      01  PAGE-LINE-COUNTER        PIC 99     VALUE 25.
      *

      01  PRODUCT-TOTAL            PIC 9(5)V99 VALUE ZERO.
      *
```

FIGURE 9-7

Example Program with One
Control Break (continued)

```
01  REPORT-HEADING.
    02 FILLER                    PIC X(10) VALUE SPACES.
    02 FILLER                    PIC X(11) VALUE 'PRODUCT NO.'.
    02 FILLER                    PIC X(3)  VALUE SPACES.
    02 FILLER                    PIC X(12) VALUE 'SALES AMOUNT'.
    02 FILLER                    PIC X(4)  VALUE SPACES.
    02 FILLER                    PIC X(11) VALUE 'TOTAL SALES'.
*
01  REPORT-LINE.
    02 FILLER                    PIC X(14) VALUE SPACES.
    02 PRODUCT-NUMBER-OUT        PIC 999.
    02 FILLER                    PIC X(9)  VALUE SPACES.
    02 SALES-AMOUNT-OUT          PIC Z,ZZ9.99.
    02 FILLER                    PIC X(7)  VALUE SPACES.
    02 TOTAL-SALES-OUT           PIC $$$,$$9.99.
*

PROCEDURE DIVISION.
*
000-PROGRAM-SUMMARY.
    OPEN INPUT SALES-FILE
         OUTPUT REPORT-FILE.
*
    PERFORM 010-PROCESS-FIRST-SALES-RECORD.
*
    PERFORM 050-PROCESS-RECORD
       UNTIL END-OF-FILE.
*
    PERFORM 080-PRINT-LAST-TOTAL.
*
    CLOSE SALES-FILE
          REPORT-FILE.
*
    STOP RUN.
*
010-PROCESS-FIRST-SALES-RECORD.
    PERFORM 020-READ-SALES-RECORD.
*
    IF NOT-END-OF-FILE
       MOVE PRODUCT-NUMBER TO PREVIOUS-PRODUCT-NUMBER
       MOVE SALES-AMOUNT TO PRODUCT-TOTAL
       PERFORM 030-PRINT-NEW-PRODUCT-LINE
       PERFORM 020-READ-SALES-RECORD
    END-IF.
*
020-READ-SALES-RECORD.
    READ SALES-FILE RECORD
       AT END SET END-OF-FILE TO TRUE.
*
```

```
030-PRINT-NEW-PRODUCT-LINE.
    MOVE SPACES TO REPORT-LINE
    MOVE PRODUCT-NUMBER TO PRODUCT-NUMBER-OUT
    MOVE SALES-AMOUNT TO SALES-AMOUNT-OUT
*
    PERFORM 040-PRINT-LINE.
*
040-PRINT-LINE.
    IF PAGE-LINE-COUNTER = PAGE-SIZE
        WRITE REPORT-RECORD FROM REPORT-HEADING
                AFTER ADVANCING PAGE
        MOVE SPACES TO REPORT-RECORD
        WRITE REPORT-RECORD AFTER ADVANCING 1 LINE
        MOVE 2 TO PAGE-LINE-COUNTER
    END-IF
*
    WRITE REPORT-RECORD FROM REPORT-LINE
        AFTER ADVANCING 1 LINE
*
    ADD 1 TO PAGE-LINE-COUNTER.
*
050-PROCESS-RECORD.
    IF PRODUCT-NUMBER = PREVIOUS-PRODUCT-NUMBER
        PERFORM 060-PROCESS-REPORT-LINE
    ELSE
        PERFORM 070-PROCESS-NEW-RECORD
    END-IF
*
    ADD SALES-AMOUNT TO PRODUCT-TOTAL
*
    PERFORM 020-READ-SALES-RECORD.
*
060-PROCESS-REPORT-LINE.
    MOVE SPACES TO REPORT-LINE
    MOVE SALES-AMOUNT TO SALES-AMOUNT-OUT
*
    PERFORM 040-PRINT-LINE.
*
070-PROCESS-NEW-RECORD.
    MOVE SPACES TO REPORT-LINE
    MOVE PRODUCT-TOTAL TO TOTAL-SALES-OUT
    PERFORM 040-PRINT-LINE
*
    MOVE ZERO TO PRODUCT-TOTAL
*
    PERFORM 030-PRINT-NEW-PRODUCT-LINE
*
    MOVE PRODUCT-NUMBER TO PREVIOUS-PRODUCT-NUMBER.
*
080-PRINT-LAST-TOTAL.
    MOVE SPACES TO REPORT-LINE
    MOVE PRODUCT-TOTAL TO TOTAL-SALES-OUT
    PERFORM 040-PRINT-LINE.
*
```

PERFORM 080-PRINT-LAST-TOTAL. This is another case of having a control break, but it is different from having a new product number. When the last record has been read in, we want to execute the control footing logic to show the total for the previous product, as usual. But there is no need to show the control heading for the next product, because there is no next product. Thus, the logic in 070-PROCESS-NEW-RECORD would not be correct, and we have developed, instead, the 080-PRINT-LAST-TOTAL procedure to handle this special case.

In a report program it is natural to distinguish three cases: the first record, the last record, and the ones between. Each of these types requires special processing. In our case we developed three distinct paragraphs to handle these three cases. An alternate approach would be to combine the processing of more than one of these cases in the same physical paragraph. For instance, we could have written this:

```
070-PROCESS-NEW-RECORD.
    MOVE SPACES TO REPORT-LINE
    MOVE PRODUCT-TOTAL TO TOTAL-SALES-OUT
    PERFORM 040-PRINT-LINE
    IF  END-OF-FILE
        NEXT SENTENCE
    ELSE
        MOVE ZERO TO PRODUCT-TOTAL
        PERFORM 030-PRINT-NEW-PRODUCT-LINE
        MOVE PRODUCT-NUMBER TO PREVIOUS-PRODUCT-NUMBER.
```

In this alternative code we have used the end-of-file condition to differentiate the processing of the last versus the "middle" records. It is easy to see that we could take a similar approach with the special case of the first record. We could set a flag at the beginning of the program:

```
01  FIRST-TIME-FLAG PIC X VALUE 'Y'.
    88  FIRST-RECORD  VALUE 'Y'.
```

Then we could modify the 050-PROCESS-RECORD paragraph as follows:

```
050-PROCESS-RECORD.
    IF  NOT FIRST-RECORD
        IF  PRODUCT-NUMBER = PREVIOUS-PRODUCT-NUMBER
            PERFORM 060-PROCESS-REPORT-LINE
        ELSE
            PERFORM 070-PROCESS-NEW-RECORD
        END-IF
        ADD SALES-AMOUNT TO PRODUCT-TOTAL
        PERFORM 020-READ-SALES-RECORD
    ELSE
    following is the case of the first record
        MOVE 'N' TO FIRST-TIME-FLAG
        MOVE PRODUCT-NUMBER TO PREVIOUS-PRODUCT-NUMBER
        MOVE SALES-AMOUNT TO PRODUCT-TOTAL
        PERFORM 030-PRINT-NEW-PRODUCT-LINE
        PERFORM 020-READ-SALES-RECORD.
```

In the above illustration we have used the 1985 version END-IF scope terminator to delimit the second nested IF. In the 1974 version either we would have to repeat the two lines now following the END-IF and place them in front of the first ELSE, or we would set up a separate paragraph (which defeats the very point of the illustration about using one paragraph for multiple functions).

Although programmers differ in their preferences, we certainly advocate using distinct physical procedures/paragraphs for distinct functions. Use of flags, etc., complicates the logic for both the original program writer and the subsequent reader.

A MORE ADVANCED EXAMPLE

We now consider a revised version of the previous task that involves a report with *two* control breaks: Salesman Name and Product No. We have modified the source data file for the simple example in the previous section by including a SALESMAN-NAME instead of the FILLER in the first 15 bytes:

```
01  SALES-RECORD.
    SALESMAN-NAME        PIC X(15).
    PRODUCT-NUMBER       PIC 9(3).
    SALES-AMOUNT         PIC 9(4)V99.
    FILLER               PIC X(56).
```

We want to report sales by salesman as well as by product number. Figure 9-8 presents the output resulting from the following input:

```
ADAMSON, JOHN  123012527
ADAMSON, JOHN  123010000
ADAMSON, JOHN  345005000
ADAMSON, JOHN  345011025
ADAMSON, JOHN  345001029
ROSELLE, LINDA 123400000
WILLIAMS, MARY 123020000
WILLIAMS, MARY 123050000
WILLIAMS, MARY 123030000
WILLIAMS, MARY 123112500
```

Notice in Figure 9-8 that we have two control footings, one for the product and one for the salesman. Additionally, each footing includes an explanatory message and repeats the Product Number or Salesman Number for easier reading. There is a report heading and also a report footing that shows the total sales for the report.

Before considering the details of this program, we first consider a simplified structure chart for such a two-level control break program in Figure 9-9. The first sales record is handled as a special case, as discussed in the previous example. Then, in the main repeating module that processes sales records, we determine the control break level and we identify three possibilities: no control break, a control break due to a new product, or a control break due to a new salesman. Separate modules have been designed for product footing, product heading, salesman footing, and salesman heading. Finally, a "print line" module and its subordinates are common to many modules. Figure 9-10 presents simplified pseudocode for the two-level program. It is easy to extrapolate this approach to programs with additional control levels. We would simply have more control heading and footing groups.

Figure 9-11 presents the structure chart for the specific example program. The sample program that corresponds to the structure chart in Figure 9-11 is presented in Figure 9-12.

FIGURE 9-8

Sample Output for a Program with Two Control Breaks

```
                  SALES REPORT FOR ACME CORPORATION

     SALESMAN NAME      PRODUCT NO.    SALES AMOUNT      TOTAL SALES

     ADAMSON, JOHN      123               125.27
                                          100.00

        * TOTAL FOR PRODUCT   123                          $225.27

     ADAMSON, JOHN      345                50.00
                                          110.25
                                           10.29

        * TOTAL FOR PRODUCT   345                          $170.54

      ** TOTAL FOR SALESMAN   ADAMSON, JOHN                $395.81

     ROSELLE, LINDA     123             4,000.00

        * TOTAL FOR PRODUCT   123                        $4,000.00

      ** TOTAL FOR SALESMAN   ROSELLE, LINDA             $4,000.00

     WILLIAMS, MARY     123               200.00
                                          500.00


     ---------- (page break here) -----------


     SALESMAN NAME      PRODUCT NO.    SALES AMOUNT      TOTAL SALES

     WILLIAMS, MARY     123               300.00
                                        1,125.00

        * TOTAL FOR PRODUCT   123                        $2,125.00

      ** TOTAL FOR SALESMAN   WILLIAMS, MARY             $2,125.00

       *** TOTAL SALES FOR REPORT                        $6,520.81
```

Reviewing Figure 9-11, notice the module labeled 030-DETERMINE-CNTRL-BRK-LEVEL. What was the basis for including this module in the chart? We asked the question: "What is needed in order to select execution of particular control headings and footings?" We then realized that their execution is dependent on the particular control break. So we concluded that a module is needed to do the task of "sorting out" the control break situation.

FIGURE 9-9
Structure Chart for Two-Level Control Break Logic

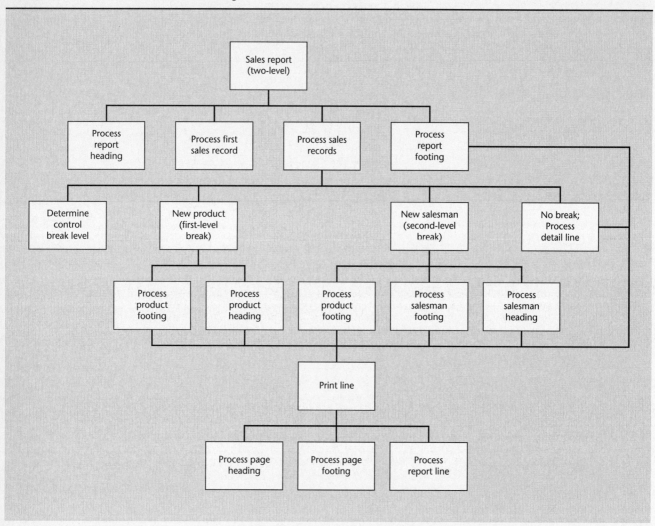

The 100-PRINT-LINE module(s) in Figure 9-11 do not show subordinates, unlike the counterpart in the more abstract case in Figure 9-9. Since no page footing is needed in this case, and since the page heading is a minor task, we chose to combine these functions in one module. However, should we later need to add more elaborate page heading and/or page footing functions, it would be easy to make such additions both to the chart and to the program.

As in the case of the simple program in the preceding section of this chapter, we have designed specialized modules for the first, the in-between, and the last records: 010-PRINT-REPORT-HEADING, 015-PROCESS-FIRST-SALES-RECORD, 020-PROCESS-SALES-RECORDS, and 110-END-OF-REPORT-FOOTING. The last of these three paragraphs combines the processing of the last record and the report footing. Because these are simple and related functions, we combined them in the same paragraph. If the report footing were more extensive, we would want to create a distinct module for processing the last record and another one for the report footing.

Let's discuss some points in the 020-PROCESS-SALES-RECORDS procedure of the program in Figure 9-12. First, we PERFORM 030-DETERMINE-CNTRL-BRK-

FIGURE 9-10

Pseudocode for Two-Level Report Program

```
Two-Level Report Program with Control Breaks

PERFORM
    Open Input and Output Files
    Print Report Headings
    Process First Input Record
    PERFORM  UNTIL End of Input File
        If No Control Break
            Then Process Detail Line
        Else
            If Second-Level (Product) Control Break
                Then    Process Second-Level (Product) Footing
                        Process Second-Level (Product) Heading
            Else
                Process Second-Level (Product) Footing
                Process First-Level (Salesman) Footing
                Process First-Level (Salesman) Heading
            End-If
        End-If
    END-PERFORM
    Process Report Footing
END-PERFORM
```

LEVEL, which is designed to "decide" what type of control break there is, if any. In this program there are two control fields, SALESMAN-NAME and PRODUCT-NUMBER. By having a distinct module, it is easy to see that we can expand the logic to accommodate any number of control break levels. Then the 020 paragraph of the program continues with

```
EVALUATE TRUE
    WHEN NO-BREAK         PERFORM 080-PRINT-DETAIL-LINE
    WHEN PRODUCT-BREAK    PERFORM 022-NEW-PRODUCT
    WHEN SALESMAN-BREAK   PERFORM 025-NEW-SALESMAN
END-EVALUATE
```

In both the 022-NEW-PRODUCT and 025-NEW SALESMAN, we first perform 070-PRINT-PRODUCT-FOOTING. Since PRODUCT-NUMBER is the minor level, if we do have any control break, we need to process the product control footing regardless of the specific control break. In other words, we want to show the sales total for the previous product if there is either a new salesman or a new product.

To see this point better, suppose that we have *three* levels: Department, Salesman, and Product, with Department being the highest level. We could write

FIGURE 9-11
Structure Chart for Sample Report Program

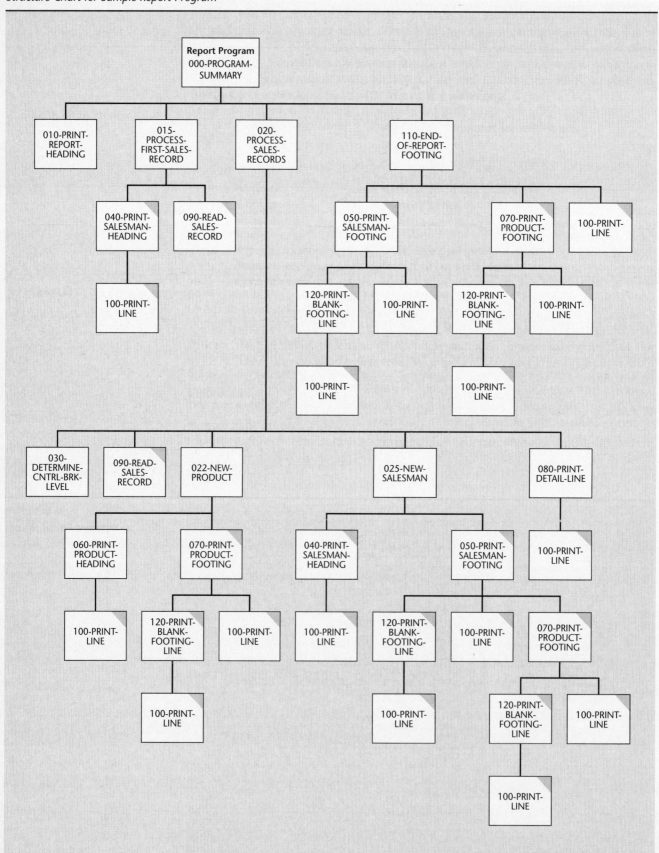

FIGURE 9-12

Example Program with Two
Control Breaks

```
        IDENTIFICATION DIVISION.
        PROGRAM-ID. CTRLBRK.
*
        ENVIRONMENT DIVISION.
*
        CONFIGURATION SECTION.
        SOURCE-COMPUTER. ABC-490.
        OBJECT-COMPUTER. ABC-490.
*
        INPUT-OUTPUT SECTION.
*
        FILE-CONTROL.
            SELECT SALES-FILE   ASSIGN TO CTRLBRK.IN.
            SELECT REPORT-FILE  ASSIGN TO CTRLBRK.OUT.
*
        DATA DIVISION.
*
        FILE SECTION.
*
        FD  SALES-FILE    LABEL RECORDS ARE OMITTED
                          RECORD CONTAINS 80 CHARACTERS
                          DATA RECORD IS SALES-RECORD.
        01 SALES-RECORD.
            02 SALESMAN-NAME          PIC X(15).
            02 PRODUCT-NUMBER         PIC 9(3).
            02 SALES-AMOUNT           PIC 9(4)V99.
            02 FILLER                 PIC X(56).
*
        FD  REPORT-FILE   LABEL RECORDS ARE OMITTED
                          DATA RECORD IS REPORT-RECORD.
        01  REPORT-RECORD            PIC X(132).
*
        WORKING-STORAGE SECTION.
*
        01 PREVIOUS-VALUES.
            02  PREVIOUS-SALESMAN-NAME  PIC X(15).
            02  PREVIOUS-PRODUCT-NUMBER PIC 9(3).
*
        01 PROGRAM-FLAGS.
            02  END-OF-FILE-INDICATOR  PIC XXX     VALUE 'NO'.
                88 END-OF-FILE                     VALUE IS 'YES'.
*
            02  CONTROL-BREAK-LEVEL    PIC 9.
                88 NO-BREAK                         VALUE ZERO.
                88 PRODUCT-BREAK                    VALUE 1.
                88 SALESMAN-BREAK                   VALUE 2.
*
            02  FOOTING-INDICATOR      PIC XXX     VALUE 'NO'.
                88  NO-FOOTING                      VALUE 'NO'.
                88  YES-FOOTING                     VALUE 'YES'.
*
        01  PAGE-SIZE                  PIC 99      VALUE 25.
        01  PAGE-LINE-COUNTER          PIC 99      VALUE 25.
```

FIGURE 9-12

*Example Program with Two
Control Breaks (continued)*

```
*
01  PAGE-HEADING.
    02  FILLER                  PIC X(10)    VALUE SPACE.
    02  FILLER                  PIC X(13)
            VALUE 'SALESMAN NAME'.
    02  FILLER                  PIC X(4)     VALUE SPACES.
    02  FILLER                  PIC X(11)
            VALUE 'PRODUCT NO.'.
    02  FILLER                  PIC X(3)     VALUE SPACES.
    02  FILLER                  PIC X(12)
            VALUE 'SALES AMOUNT'.
    02  FILLER                  PIC X(4)     VALUE SPACES.
    02  FILLER                  PIC X(11)
            VALUE 'TOTAL SALES'.
*
01  REPORT-HEADING.
    02  FILLER                  PIC X(20)    VALUE SPACES.
    02  FILLER                  PIC X(33)    VALUE
            "SALES REPORT FOR ACME CORPORATION".
*
01  REPORT-LINE.
    02  FILLER                  PIC X(10)    VALUE SPACES.
    02  SALESMAN-NAME-OUT       PIC X(15).
    02  FILLER                  PIC X(2)     VALUE SPACES.
    02  PRODUCT-NUMBER-OUT      PIC 999.
    02  FILLER                  PIC X(11)    VALUE SPACES.
    02  SALES-AMOUNT-OUT        PIC Z,ZZ9.99.
    02  FILLER                  PIC X(8)     VALUE SPACES.
    02  TOTAL-SALES-OUT         PIC $$$,$$9.99.
*
01  SALESMAN-FOOTING.
    02  FILLER                  PIC X(12)    VALUE SPACES.
    02  FILLER                  PIC X(24)
            VALUE '** TOTAL FOR SALESMAN '.
    02  SALESMAN-NAME-FOOTING   PIC X(15).
    02  FILLER                  PIC X(3)     VALUE SPACES.
    02  TOTAL-SALESMAN-FOOTING  PIC $$,$$$,$$9.99.
*
01  PRODUCT-FOOTING.
    02  FILLER                  PIC X(14)    VALUE SPACES.
    02  FILLER                  PIC X(21)
            VALUE '*TOTAL FOR PRODUCT '.
    02  PRODUCT-NUMBER-FOOTING  PIC 999.
    02  FILLER                  PIC X(16)    VALUE SPACES.
    02  TOTAL-PRODUCT-FOOTING   PIC $$,$$$,$$9.99.
*
01  REPORT-FOOTING.
    02  FILLER                  PIC X(18)    VALUE SPACES.
    02  FILLER                  PIC X(26)
            VALUE '*** TOTAL SALES FOR REPORT'.
    02  FILLER                  PIC X(10)    VALUE SPACES.
    02  TOTAL-REPORT-FOOTING    PIC $$,$$$,$$9.99.
```

FIGURE 9-12

*Example Program with Two
Control Breaks (continued)*

```
*
  01   SALES-TOTALS.
       02   PRODUCT-TOTAL-SALES      PIC 9(6)V99 VALUE ZERO.
       02   SALESMAN-TOTAL-SALES     PIC 9(6)V99 VALUE ZERO.
       02   REPORT-TOTAL-SALES       PIC 9(7)V99 VALUE ZERO.
*
  PROCEDURE DIVISION.
*
  000-PROGRAM-SUMMARY.
       OPEN  INPUT   SALES-FILE
       OPEN  OUTPUT  REPORT-FILE
*
       PERFORM 010-PRINT-REPORT-HEADING
*
       PERFORM 015-PROCESS-FIRST-SALES-RECORD
*
       PERFORM 020-PROCESS-SALES-RECORDS
                UNTIL END-OF-FILE
*
       PERFORM 110-END-OF-REPORT-FOOTING
*
       CLOSE SALES-FILE
              REPORT-FILE
*
       STOP RUN.
*
  010-PRINT-REPORT-HEADING.
       MOVE REPORT-HEADING TO REPORT-RECORD
       WRITE REPORT-RECORD AFTER ADVANCING PAGE
       MOVE PAGE-HEADING TO REPORT-RECORD
       WRITE REPORT-RECORD AFTER ADVANCING 2 LINES
       MOVE SPACES TO REPORT-RECORD
       WRITE REPORT-RECORD AFTER ADVANCING 1 LINE
       MOVE 4 TO PAGE-LINE-COUNTER.
*
  015-PROCESS-FIRST-SALES-RECORD.
       PERFORM 090-READ-SALES-RECORD
       IF NOT END-OF-FILE
           MOVE SALESMAN-NAME TO PREVIOUS-SALESMAN-NAME
           MOVE PRODUCT-NUMBER TO PREVIOUS-PRODUCT-NUMBER
           PERFORM 040-PRINT-SALESMAN-HEADING
           PERFORM 090-READ-SALES-RECORD.
*
  020-PROCESS-SALES-RECORDS.
*
       PERFORM 030-DETERMINE-CNTRL-BRK-LEVEL
*
       EVALUATE TRUE
           WHEN NO-BREAK        PERFORM 080-PRINT-DETAIL-LINE
           WHEN PRODUCT-BREAK   PERFORM 022-NEW-PRODUCT
           WHEN SALESMAN-BREAK  PERFORM 025-NEW-SALESMAN
       END-EVALUATE
```

```
     *
         PERFORM 090-READ-SALES-RECORD.
     *
      022-NEW-PRODUCT.
          PERFORM 070-PRINT-PRODUCT-FOOTING
          PERFORM 060-PRINT-PRODUCT-HEADING.
     *
      025-NEW-SALESMAN.
          PERFORM 070-PRINT-PRODUCT-FOOTING
          PERFORM 050-PRINT-SALESMAN-FOOTING
          PERFORM 040-PRINT-SALESMAN-HEADING.
     *
      030-DETERMINE-CNTRL-BRK-LEVEL.
          IF  SALESMAN-NAME NOT = PREVIOUS-SALESMAN-NAME
              SET SALESMAN-BREAK TO TRUE
          ELSE
              IF  PRODUCT-NUMBER NOT = PREVIOUS-PRODUCT-NUMBER
                  SET PRODUCT-BREAK TO TRUE
              ELSE
                  SET NO-BREAK TO TRUE.
     *
      040-PRINT-SALESMAN-HEADING.
          MOVE SPACES TO REPORT-LINE
          MOVE SALESMAN-NAME TO SALESMAN-NAME-OUT
          MOVE PRODUCT-NUMBER TO PRODUCT-NUMBER-OUT
          MOVE SALES-AMOUNT TO SALES-AMOUNT-OUT
          PERFORM 100-PRINT-LINE
          ADD SALES-AMOUNT TO PRODUCT-TOTAL-SALES.
     *
      050-PRINT-SALESMAN-FOOTING.
          MOVE PREVIOUS-SALESMAN-NAME TO SALESMAN-NAME-FOOTING
          MOVE SALESMAN-TOTAL-SALES TO TOTAL-SALESMAN-FOOTING
          MOVE SALESMAN-FOOTING TO REPORT-LINE
          MOVE 'YES' TO FOOTING-INDICATOR
          PERFORM 100-PRINT-LINE
          MOVE 'NO' TO FOOTING-INDICATOR
          PERFORM 120-PRINT-BLANK-FOOTING-LINE
          ADD SALESMAN-TOTAL-SALES TO REPORT-TOTAL-SALES
          MOVE ZERO TO SALESMAN-TOTAL-SALES
     *
          MOVE SALESMAN-NAME TO PREVIOUS-SALESMAN-NAME
          MOVE PRODUCT-NUMBER TO PREVIOUS-PRODUCT-NUMBER.
     *
      060-PRINT-PRODUCT-HEADING.
          MOVE SPACES TO REPORT-LINE
          MOVE SALESMAN-NAME TO SALESMAN-NAME-OUT
          MOVE PRODUCT-NUMBER TO PRODUCT-NUMBER-OUT
          MOVE SALES-AMOUNT TO SALES-AMOUNT-OUT
          PERFORM 100-PRINT-LINE
          ADD SALES-AMOUNT TO PRODUCT-TOTAL-SALES.
     *
```

FIGURE 9-12

Example Program with Two Control Breaks (continued)

```
070-PRINT-PRODUCT-FOOTING.
    PERFORM 120-PRINT-BLANK-FOOTING-LINE
    MOVE PREVIOUS-PRODUCT-NUMBER TO PRODUCT-NUMBER-FOOTING
    MOVE PRODUCT-TOTAL-SALES TO TOTAL-PRODUCT-FOOTING
    MOVE PRODUCT-FOOTING TO REPORT-LINE
    MOVE 'YES' TO FOOTING-INDICATOR
    PERFORM 100-PRINT-LINE
    MOVE 'NO' TO FOOTING-INDICATOR
    PERFORM 120-PRINT-BLANK-FOOTING-LINE
    ADD PRODUCT-TOTAL-SALES TO SALESMAN-TOTAL-SALES
    MOVE ZERO TO PRODUCT-TOTAL-SALES
*
  MOVE PRODUCT-NUMBER TO PREVIOUS-PRODUCT-NUMBER.
*
 080-PRINT-DETAIL-LINE.
    MOVE SPACES TO REPORT-LINE
    MOVE SALES-AMOUNT TO SALES-AMOUNT-OUT
    PERFORM 100-PRINT-LINE
    ADD SALES-AMOUNT TO PRODUCT-TOTAL-SALES.
*
 090-READ-SALES-RECORD.
    READ SALES-FILE RECORD
        AT END SET END-OF-FILE TO TRUE.
*
 100-PRINT-LINE.
    IF  PAGE-LINE-COUNTER > PAGE-SIZE OR
        PAGE-LINE-COUNTER = PAGE-SIZE
        WRITE REPORT-RECORD FROM PAGE-HEADING
            AFTER ADVANCING PAGE
        MOVE SPACES TO REPORT-RECORD
        WRITE REPORT-RECORD AFTER ADVANCING 1
        MOVE 2 TO PAGE-LINE-COUNTER
*
        IF  NO-FOOTING
            MOVE SALESMAN-NAME TO SALESMAN-NAME-OUT
            MOVE PRODUCT-NUMBER TO PRODUCT-NUMBER-OUT.
*
    WRITE REPORT-RECORD FROM REPORT-LINE
        AFTER ADVANCING 1
    ADD 1 TO PAGE-LINE-COUNTER.
*
 110-END-OF-REPORT-FOOTING.
    PERFORM 070-PRINT-PRODUCT-FOOTING
    PERFORM 050-PRINT-SALESMAN-FOOTING
    MOVE REPORT-TOTAL-SALES TO TOTAL-REPORT-FOOTING
    MOVE REPORT-FOOTING TO REPORT-LINE
    MOVE 'YES' TO FOOTING-INDICATOR
    PERFORM 100-PRINT-LINE.
*
 120-PRINT-BLANK-FOOTING-LINE.
    IF  PAGE-LINE-COUNTER < PAGE-SIZE
        MOVE SPACES TO REPORT-LINE
        PERFORM 100-PRINT-LINE.
```

the following type of logic (using nested IF, instead of EVALUATE, just to show that either approach can be used):

```
IF Department-break
        perform Product control footing
        perform Salesman control footing
        perform Department control footing
        perform Department control heading
ELSE
    IF Salesman-break
            perform Product control footing
            perform Salesman control footing
            perform Salesman control heading
    ELSE
        IF Product-break
                perform Product control footing
                perform Product control heading
```

Continuing with the 020-PROCESS-SALES-RECORDS paragraph in Figure 9-12, notice the use of the EVALUATE statement to select the appropriate case to execute: detail, product heading, or salesman heading. Of course, if we were using the 1974 standard, we would have used simple or nested IF statements in lieu of the EVALUATE. Also, we could use GO TO ... DEPENDING ON CONTROL-BREAK-LEVEL. However, either we would need to have defined the values of CONTROL-BREAK-LEVEL to be 1, 2, and 3 instead of 0, 1, and 2, or, alternatively, we could increment the value of that field by 1 just before the GO TO ... was executed.

Another feature in the sample program in Figure 9-12 is the handling of page breaks. The 100-PRINT-LINE paragraph uses a field called PAGE-LINE-COUNTER to keep track of the number of lines printed so far, and compares it to PAGE-SIZE, which contains the number of desired lines per page. After printing a control footing, we want to double-space. However, when the footing is the last line on the page we do not want to print a blank line, because it would be printed on the next page. The 120-PRINT-BLANK-FOOTING-LINE paragraph serves the purpose of controlling for such a case.

When we have a page break, we want to repeat the SALESMAN-NAME and the PRODUCT-NUMBER values at the top of the new page. For this reason, in the two footing paragraphs (050 and 070) we use a FOOTING-INDICATOR field as a flag to tell 100-PRINT-LINE that we are printing a control footing and it must not print the salesman name and the product number when there is a page break. Thus, 100-PRINT-LINE contains the following statement:

```
IF  NO-FOOTING
    MOVE SALESMAN-NAME TO SALESMAN-NAME-OUT
    MOVE PRODUCT-NUMBER TO PRODUCT-NUMBER-OUT.
```

As you review some of these detailed points in the sample program, it is likely that you wonder whether there could have been a simpler way to code these printer-spacing details. In particular, one might wonder if having a single point for printing all output (100-PRINT-LINE) does not make things more complex than they have to be. Our answer to such questions is that for a relatively simple program such as the current example, it might be easier to distribute the printing function throughout the program. However, the program structure that we have used is robust. It can be used with more complex program tasks without major modifications to the basic logical structure of the sample program. Thus, we suggest that you use this sample program as a generalized prototype for writing report programs with control breaks.

THE WRITE VERB WITH THE LINAGE CLAUSE

We conclude the chapter with discussion of some specialized options in the WRITE statement that facilitate report generation. Figure 9-13 presents the expanded format for the WRITE verb. We observe the AT END-OF-PAGE conditional statement. When specified, a check is made to determine if the END-OF-PAGE (abbreviated EOP) condition is met. If it is, then the imperative statement is executed.

The END-OF-PAGE condition is defined by means of the LINAGE clause in the DATA DIVISION, which has the format presented in Figure 9-14. Let us consider an example. We want to produce a report with the following format:

LINE NUMBER	CONTENTS
1–5	Not used
6	The page heading
7–56	The body of the report
57–59	The page totals
60–66	Not used

We could proceed as follows:

```
DATA DIVISION.
   .
   .
   .
FD   PRINT-FILE LABEL RECORD OMITTED
               DATA RECORD IS PRINT-REC
               LINAGE IS 54 LINES
                  WITH FOOTING AT 51
                  LINES AT TOP 5
                  LINES AT BOTTOM 7.
```

The page will consist of 66 lines, which is the sum of the values referenced in each phrase except for the FOOTING phrase (54 + 5 + 7 = 66). Five lines are unused at the top (lines 1–5), and 7 at the bottom (lines 60–66).

FIGURE 9-13
General Format for the WRITE Verb

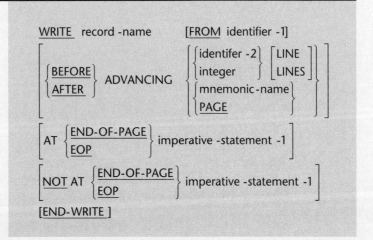

FIGURE 9-14
General Format for the LINAGE Clause

$$\underline{LINAGE} \text{ IS } \begin{Bmatrix} data\text{-}name\text{-}1 \\ integer\text{-}1 \end{Bmatrix} LINES \left[\text{WITH } \underline{FOOTING} \text{ AT } \begin{Bmatrix} data\text{-}name\text{-}2 \\ integer\text{-}2 \end{Bmatrix} \right]$$

$$\left[LINES \text{ AT } \underline{TOP} \begin{Bmatrix} data\text{-}name\text{-}3 \\ integer\text{-}3 \end{Bmatrix} \right] \left[LINES \text{ AT } \underline{BOTTOM} \begin{Bmatrix} data\text{-}name\text{-}4 \\ integer\text{-}4 \end{Bmatrix} \right]$$

In the PROCEDURE DIVISION the statement

```
WRITE PRINT-REC FROM TOP-HEADER
      AFTER ADVANCING PAGE
```

will cause printing of the content of TOP-HEADER on line 6 because now PAGE is associated with line 6, since LINES AT TOP 5 means that 5 lines will be left blank at the top of the page. (TOP-HEADER in this example is assumed to contain the desired header.)

Now consider the following commands, assumed to be executed iteratively under control of a PERFORM . . . UNTIL or other such statement:

```
        WRITE PRINT-REC FROM BODY-OF-REPORT-LINE
              AFTER ADVANCING 1 LINE
          AT END-OF-PAGE PERFORM TOTALS.
          .
          .
          .
TOTALS.
        WRITE PRINT-REC FROM TOTALS-LINE
              AFTER ADVANCING 3 LINES
        WRITE PRINT-REC FROM TOP-HEADER
              AFTER ADVANCING PAGE.
```

With reference to the above, we will keep printing data from BODY-OF-REPORT-LINE until we have reached line 56 (51 + 5), which is defined as the footing: WITH FOOTING AT 51. At that point the END-OF-PAGE condition will hold, and we will PERFORM TOTALS, in which we print data on line 59 (triple-spacing) and then skip to the next page (line 6 of the next page) to print the page header TOP-HEADER.

A special counter is used whenever LINAGE is specified. It is called LINAGE-COUNTER, a COBOL reserved word. It is set to 1 when a print file is opened or when an ADVANCING PAGE is encountered. Afterward, the counter is automatically incremented the appropriate number of lines implied in each WRITE statement. When LINAGE-COUNTER is equal to the value of the FOOTING phrase, then an END-OF-PAGE condition occurs. The LINAGE-COUNTER may not be modified by the program, but it may be accessed. Thus, it is legitimate to write IF LINAGE-COUNTER = 25 PERFORM MID-PAGE ROUTINE, for example.

It can be seen that this version of the WRITE statement can be used to automate the process of counting lines in a report program and testing for the end of the page. In the two sample programs in this chapter we defined a field to which we added a number equal to the number of lines printed in each case. Then we kept comparing the value of that line-counter field to the page length, to determine if it was the end of the page.

The LINAGE clause, the reserved field LINAGE-COUNTER, and the AT END-OF-PAGE test of the WRITE statement can be used for similar purposes. There are, in fact, some advantages to using these options. For instance, if instead of defining the LINAGE values, we define data-names containing the same values and then use them accordingly, we may need to write some additional statements. For example, if we want to begin the page heading on line 6, as in the above example, we could have defined TOP-LINES with a VALUE of 5 and then have written

```
MOVE SPACES TO PRINT-LINE
WRITE PRINT-LINE AFTER ADVANCING PAGE
```

```
WRITE PRINT-LINE FROM PAGE-HEADER
    AFTER ADVANCING TOP-LINES.
```

As the above example illustrates, we cannot write in one statement to advance to the top of a new page *and* to skip a given number of lines. We must use two WRITE commands, one to position the printer to the top of a new page by printing a blank line there, and another WRITE to print the desired data after skipping a number of lines. We conclude by observing that although there are some advantages to the WRITE and LINAGE options, they are relatively minor.

R E V I E W . . . .

1. When an END-OF-PAGE (EOP) condition is specified in conjunction with a WRITE statement, then the description of the number of lines and their use has to be defined in a(n) _____ clause in the DATA DIVISION.

   LINAGE

2. The special counter that is a reserved word and is used implicitly whenever the LINAGE option is specified is the _____.

   LINAGE-COUNTER

3. Assume the following page specifications:

   ```
   LINAGE IS 25 LINES
       WITH FOOTING AT 21
           LINES AT TOP 2
           LINES AT BOTTOM 3
   ```

   Fill in the missing numbers in the following page mock-up:

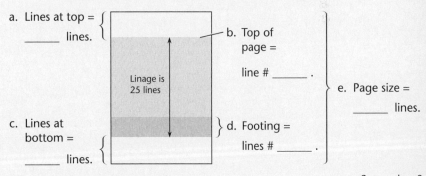

a. Lines at top = _____ lines.

b. Top of page = line # _____ .

Linage is 25 lines

c. Lines at bottom = _____ lines.

d. Footing = lines # _____ .

e. Page size = _____ lines.

a. 2   b. 3
c. 3   d. 23 to 27
e. 24 + 2 + 3 = 30

. . . .

SUMMARY

This chapter was concerned with the knowledge that you need to write COBOL programs for producing reports.

In terms of overall structure, a report may contain a *report heading*, *report body*, and *report footing*. The report body consists of one or more pages, each of which is a formatted collection of lines. A page contains five types of report groups: *page heading*, *control heading(s)*, *report detail lines*, *control footing(s)*, and *page footing*.

Control breaks in report writing are associated with the hierarchical categories of data in a report. For example, a report of vehicle registrations by city, county, and state would involve three control breaks. State would be the *major* control, county would be the *intermediate* control, and city would be the *minor* control, which follows the hierarchical structure of the data.

A general logical structure in flowchart form was presented in Figure 9-3 for the case of three control breaks. This flowchart can be easily adapted for use with any other number of control breaks as well.

Two example programs for producing reports were described in detail in this chapter. The "simple" program involves one control break, while the "more advanced" program involves two control breaks.

The last section of this chapter described specialized options in the WRITE statement when the LINAGE clause has been used in a data description. This included the END-OF-PAGE option and use of the LINAGE-COUNTER.

EXERCISES

9.1   Student registration records have the following format:

```
01  STUD-REC.
    05  DEPT-NO      PIC XXX.
    05  COURSE-NO    PIC X(7).
    05  SECTION-NO   PIC X.
    05  STUD-NAME    PIC X(20).
```

We want to read the records in the file and produce a report such as the following example:

```
DEPARTMENT NUMBER: ACC   COURSE NUMBER: MIS-101   SECTION: 1
------------------------------------------------------------
        STUDENT NAME
ANDERSON, ROSE ANN
BROWN, LORI BETH
CRAWFORD, CHRIS L.
DONALD, DON DANIEL

    TOTAL STUDENTS IN SECTION:  4

                        Section page  2
                        Report  page  9
```

Each course section must begin on a new page. For the assignment, assume that each page has room for up to six students. The total enrollment for each section is shown on the last page only. Notice that at the bottom of each page we print the section page number as well as the report page number.

Write a program to produce such a report.

9.2   Revise the sample program in Figure 9-12 so that a third control break is included. Each record includes a department name in columns 25–34, as well as the salesperson name in columns 1–15, the product number in columns 16–18, and the sales amount in columns 19–24.

Assume that department is the major control break. In other words, salespersons are grouped within departments, and products are grouped under salespersons. Include a page number at the bottom of each page.

Figure 9-15 shows sample input and the corresponding 3-page output. Draw a structure chart and write a complete program.

FIGURE 9-15
Sample Input and Output for Exercise 9.2

INPUT FILE

```
ADAMSON, JOHN  123012527DEPRTMENT1
ADAMSON, JOHN  123010000DEPRTMENT1
ADAMSON, JOHN  345005000DEPRTMENT1
ADAMSON, JOHN  345011025DEPRTMENT1
ADAMSON, JOHN  345001029DEPRTMENT1
ROSELLE, LINDA 123400000DEPRTMENT1
WILLIAMS, MARY 123020000DEPRTMENT1
WILLIAMS, MARY 123050000DEPRTMENT1
WILLIAMS, MARY 123030000DEPRTMENT1
WILLIAMS, MARY 123112500DEPRTMENT1
ADAMSON, JOHN  123012527DEPRTMENT2
ADAMSON, JOHN  123010000DEPRTMENT2
ADAMSON, JOHN  345005000DEPRTMENT3
ADAMSON, JOHN  345011025DEPRTMENT3
ADAMSON, JOHN  345001029DEPRTMENT3
ROSELLE, LINDA 123400000DEPRTMENT3
WILLIAMS, MARY 123020000DEPRTMENT3
WILLIAMS, MARY 123050000DEPRTMENT3
WILLIAMS, MARY 123030000DEPRTMENT3
WILLIAMS, MARY 123112500DEPRTMENT3
```

PROGRAM OUTPUT

```
DEPT. NAME   SALESMAN NAME    PRODUCT NO.   SALES AMOUNT   TOTAL SALES

DEPRTMENT1   ADAMSON, JOHN    123               125.27
                                                100.00

             * TOTAL FOR PRODUCT  123                          $225.27

             ADAMSON, JOHN    345                50.00
                                                110.25
                                                 10.29

             * TOTAL FOR PRODUCT  345                          $170.54

           ** TOTAL FOR SALESMAN   ADAMSON, JOHN               $395.81

             ROSELLE, LINDA   123             4,000.00

             * TOTAL FOR PRODUCT  123                        $4,000.00

           ** TOTAL FOR SALESMAN   ROSELLE, LINDA            $4,000.00

             WILLIAMS, MARY   123               200.00
                                                500.00
                                                300.00
                                              1,125.00
```

────────── (page break here) ──────────

FIGURE 9-15

Sample Input and Output for Exercise 9.2 (continued)

```
DEPT. NAME    SALESMAN NAME    PRODUCT NO.    SALES AMOUNT    TOTAL SALES

              * TOTAL FOR PRODUCT  123                         $2,125.00

              ** TOTAL FOR SALESMAN   WILLIAMS, MARY           $2,125.00

            *** TOTAL FOR DEPARTMENT DEPRTMENT1                $6,520.81


DEPRTMENT2    ADAMSON, JOHN         123           125.27
                                                  100.00

              * TOTAL FOR PRODUCT  123                          $225.27

              ** TOTAL FOR SALESMAN   ADAMSON, JOHN            $225.27

            *** TOTAL FOR DEPARTMENT DEPRTMENT2                 $225.27


DEPRTMENT3    ADAMSON, JOHN         345            50.00
                                                  110.25
                                                   10.29

              * TOTAL FOR PRODUCT  345                          $170.54

              ** TOTAL FOR SALESMAN   ADAMSON, JOHN            $170.54

            ---------- (page break here) -----------

DEPT. NAME    SALESMAN NAME    PRODUCT NO.    SALES AMOUNT    TOTAL SALES

DEPRTMENT3    ROSELLE, LINDA   123             4,000.00

              * TOTAL FOR PRODUCT  123                        $4,000.00

              ** TOTAL FOR SALESMAN   ROSELLE, LINDA          $4,000.00

              WILLIAMS, MARY   123               200.00
                                                 500.00
                                                 300.00
                                               1,125.00
            *** TOTAL FOR DEPARTMENT DEPRTMENT3               $4,170.54


              * TOTAL FOR PRODUCT  123                        $2,125.00

              ** TOTAL FOR SALESMAN   WILLIAMS, MARY          $2,125.00

              *** TOTAL SALES FOR REPORT                     $10,916.62
```

9.3 A file contains data pertaining to student grades. Each record consists of the following:

```
01  STUDENT-RECORD.
    05  NAME       PIC X(15).
    05  COURSE     PIC X(7).
    05  CREDITS    PIC 9.
    05  GRADE      PIC X.
```

For each student we want to produce a semester grade report illustrated in the following example:

```
                      SEMESTER GRADE REPORT
NAME               COURSE-NO    CREDITS      GRADE      G.P.A
ANDERSON, A. J.     CIS-200        3           A
                    ACC-101        4           B
                    CSC-200        3           B
                    ART-111        2           C
                                                         3.08
```

The grade point average (G.P.A.) is computed by assigning the following point values to letter grades: A = 4, B = 3, C = 2, D = 1, E = 0. We multiply credits times the numeric grade, sum the total products, and divide by the total number of credits.

The report for each student begins on a new page.

Write a program to produce such a report.

10 Sequential File Processing

I N THIS CHAPTER *you will learn how to create and update sequential files. For such files the records are written and accessed in a serial order.*

Often, the storage device that is used dictates the method of file storage. For example, sequential file storage must be used for data stored on magnetic tape. Therefore a discussion of such devices and their storage characteristics is included early in this chapter.

You will then study the COBOL instructions that are associated with sequential files. This will include the FILE-CONTROL specification in the ENVIRONMENT DIVISION, the file description entry in the DATA DIVISION, and use of specialized verbs in the PROCEDURE DIVISION.

Finally, you will study a sample program to create a sequential file, and another sample program to update a sequential file.

FILE ORGANIZATION The concept of *file organization* refers to the manner in which data records are arranged on a file-storage medium. There are three principal methods of file organization in COBOL: sequential, indexed, and relative.

In a *sequential file* the records are written in a serial order and are accessed (read) in the same order as written. The serial order is chronological and need not be in any particular logical sequence, such as according to account number. Files assigned to printers and magnetic tape drives are always organized as sequential files. On the other hand, files stored on magnetic disk and other direct access storage devices may be sequential, indexed, or relative files.

Although the language does not require it, sequential files on tape or disk most commonly are sorted so that the records are in some logical sequential order. For instance, if we have a customer file, we might choose to sort the records on the basis of customer number. Then, if customer numbers are unique, each successive record read from the file should have a higher customer number than the one before. This practice of sorting the records is convenient when processing "batch" jobs, such as payroll. In such jobs, we sort the "transaction" data, such as time cards, in the same order as the employee payroll file. Then we process the time cards by reading the two files from beginning to end without the need to go back and forth looking for employee records in random order.

Indexed file organization means that an index has been created so that records can be located directly without accessing them in sequence. We describe this file organization method in Chapter 20. *Relative* file organization means that the file is stored in such a way that each record can be accessed directly by means of its relative position in the file. Such positions are the first, second, third, etc., record in the file. This method is covered in Chapter 21.

R E V I E W . . . .

1. The manner in which data records are arranged on a file-storage medium is referred to as file _____ .

    organization

2. The type of file for which the records are written in a serial order and for which the records must be accessed in the same order as written is the _____ file organization.

    sequential

3. The type of file for which the records have been read and stored in a serial order, but for which access can be direct, is the _____ file organization.

    indexed

4. The type of file for which records are both stored and accessed directly according to the relative position of the record is the _____ file organization.

    relative

5. If a file is assigned to a printer or magnetic tape drive, it must be organized as a(n) _____ file.

    sequential

6. A file that can be organized by any of the three methods described in this section is one for which the records are stored on magnetic _____ .

    disk

. . . .

FILE STORAGE DEVICES

While the characteristics of the data processing task dictate which method of file organization is preferred, the storage device that is used determines which methods are possible. As related to file organization, it is useful to distinguish two main categories of storage devices: *magnetic tape* and *direct access storage devices* (DASD, pronounced das-dee). The latter category refers mainly to magnetic disk, but it also includes other direct access storage devices, such as cartridge systems. As indicated in the preceding section, only the sequential file organization can be used for files stored on magnetic tape, whereas any method of file organization can be used for files stored on direct access storage devices.

The *magnetic tape unit* is the specialized input-output device used for reading and writing magnetic tapes. As illustrated in Figure 10-1, it includes two

FIGURE 10-1
IBM 3420 Magnetic Tape Drive
(IBM Corporation)

FIGURE 10-2

Magnetic Disk Storage Device and Schematic Representation of Tracks on a Disk Surface (IBM Corporation)

 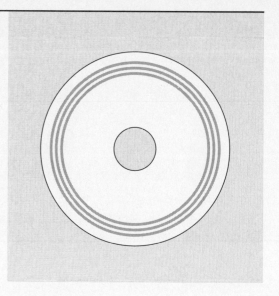

reels. The *file reel* contains the tape to be read or to be written on, and the *machine reel* contains the tape that has already been processed. The tape is threaded through a *read-write head* capable of performing the functions of reading and writing; thus, the tape transport unit works very much like a home tape recorder. Use of magnetic tape in cartridges is becoming common. These cartridges resemble VCR or audio cassette tapes, and the two reels are less evident in the enclosed structure of the cartridge.

A *magnetic disk* is a magnetically sensitive circular surface resembling a phonograph record. Data are recorded on this disk surface in designated circular bands called *tracks*. Figure 10-2 portrays a magnetic disk storage device and includes a diagram of tracks on the surface of a disk. There may be up to several hundred usable tracks on the surface of a magnetic disk, depending on the size of the unit. Each track can contain a few thousand characters around its circular length. Each track is separate from the others, and all tracks have the same capacity, even though the circles become smaller as we move away from the periphery. Tracks are referenced in numeric order from 0 up to the last track. Thus, if we have 200 tracks, the first is designated as track 000 and last as track 199.

A *disk pack* refers to a group of disks stacked on a vertical spindle. The disks are parallel to each other but physically separated from one another. Such packs may be removable as a unit, so that we can change disk packs for the same reasons that we change reels of magnetic tape.

Typically, for each disk surface in a disk pack there is a *read-write head*—a device that can read data from or write data on the surface. These heads are fixed to a vertical column and can move as a unit toward or away from the center of the disk pack. Figure 10-3 illustrates the read-write head mechanism.

Data are recorded on any magnetic storage device in the form of *blocks*. Each block consists of a grouping of data written (or read) in one continuous operation. Several formats are possible for the data included in the block, as illustrated in Figures 10-4 and 10-5, which illustrate blocks on magnetic tape. The *gap* is an unused space that serves as a separator between blocks. Disk files do not need the same gap between blocks due to the more precise nature of the hardware device.

Data records handled in a program are called *logical records,* as distinguished from the *physical records* written on a file device such as a tape or disk. A physical record is defined as a group of bytes written or read in one I/O (input-output)

FIGURE 10-3

Disk Access Mechanism (IBM Corporation)

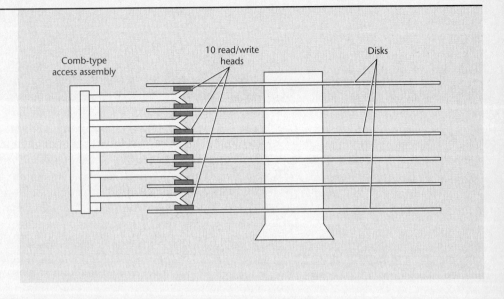

FIGURE 10-4

Tape Recording Format Containing One Record Per Block

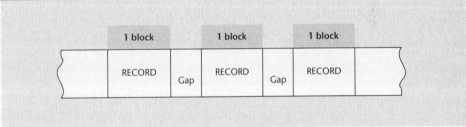

FIGURE 10-5

Tape Recording Format Containing Four Records Per Block

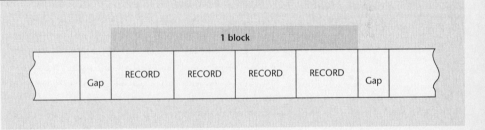

operation. The physical and logical records are related to each other in various ways:

- They may be identical.

- A physical record may consist of several complete logical records.

- A physical record may consist of a portion of one logical record or may consist of a mixture of several complete and partial logical records. (These possibilities are uncommon in practice, however.)

The term *block* often is used as being synonymous with physical record, while the term *blocking factor* denotes the number of logical records per block. When the blocking factor is 1, the physical and logical records are equivalent, and we often refer to them as *unblocked records*. When the blocking factor is greater than 1, then a block contains several logical records, and we refer to them as *blocked records.* Finally, if the blocking factor is less than 1, we have *spanned records,* in which case a logical record is written in two or more physical records.

Logical records may be *fixed-length* or *variable-length.* For example, an employee record that contains the names of dependents would be a candidate for variable-length format, since some employees may have no dependents while others may have a number of dependents. If we used fixed-length records in such a case, all records would have the length required for the record with the maximum number of dependents, thus wasting a lot of file storage.

When records vary in length, blocks normally would contain *padding.* For instance, suppose block length is fixed at 1,000 bytes and we have records of 300, 450, and 280 bytes. The first block could contain the first two records and 250 bytes of padding (special characters recognized as not being data).

Record blocking is done to compact data in file storage media and to improve processing time. For magnetic tape files, blocking results in data compaction because of the fact that a "dead space" interblock gap is necessary between physical blocks. With typical-length records of a few hundred bytes, unblocked records on magnetic tape can have as much as 80 to 90 percent of the tape devoted to interblock gaps. For both tape and disk, blocking also improves processing time because the number of physical read and write operations is reduced by the blocking factor. I/O operations are very slow compared to central processing, and blocking helps reduce the incidence of a program being "I/O-bound," that is, waiting for the reading or writing of data before processing can continue. To further improve I/O, operating systems use double-buffering, as described below.

A *buffer* is a storage space. Data read from a file medium are always stored in an I/O buffer; similarly, data are always sent to the file device from an I/O buffer. This I/O buffer must be at least equal to the block size, so that a complete block is read from or written into a file. *Double-buffering* refers to the nearly universal practice of allocating twice the buffer size needed to store a block of data from a given file. If the file is an input file, anticipatory double-buffering is practiced. When an OPEN command is encountered, the system proceeds to read the first block and store it in the first buffer and then continues reading the second block into the second buffer. When the program has read and processed all the records from the first buffer, processing continues with the records in the second buffer while the first buffer is being refilled with the third block of data. In a similar fashion, when a block has been completed in one buffer for an output file, formation of the second block begins in the second buffer while the first buffer is being emptied. Thus double-buffering cuts down on the waiting period between read-write operations. Of course, one can see that the advantage of double-buffering is enhanced as the blocking factor is increased. However, as the block size increases, so does the amount of central storage needed for the program.

In addition to the number of records contained in each block, the *size* of each record is also of importance. In using magnetic storage, the record size is not restricted to any particular limit. The records can be as long as is suitable for the applications involved. In the case of disk files, the track size is a natural upper limit on the block size. Furthermore, the records can be either fixed or variable in length. Just as record size can be variable, so can the number of records per block. Overall, then, we can have fixed-length or variable-length records and fixed-length or variable-length blocks. Variable-length records and blocks are discussed in Chapter 17.

R E V I E W . . . .

1. The magnetic tape unit requires the use of two reels when it is used: the machine reel and the file reel. The reel that contains the tape to be written on or read is

the _____ reel. The reel that contains the tape that already has been processed is the _____ reel.

file; machine

2. A group of magnetic disks stacked on a vertical shaft in a parallel fashion is called a(n) _____ .

disk pack

3. A grouping of data that is written on a magnetic storage device in one continuous operation, and that may include one or more records, is called a _____ .

block

4. In addition to the number of records contained in each block, block size also is determined by the length of each record. Whereas both the record size and the block size can be fixed, variable size is possible [only for records / only for blocks / also for both records and blocks].

also for both records and blocks

5. The type of record that is defined as a group of bytes written or read in one I/O operation is the _____ record.

physical

6. In contrast to physical records, the data records handled in a program are called _____ records.

logical

7. The term "block" is another name for a [logical / physical] record.

physical

8. The blocking factor represents the number of _____ per block.

logical records

9. When the records are described as being "unblocked," then by definition the blocking factor has the value _____ .

1

10. The logical records in a program may be fixed-length or variable-length. If fixed-length blocks are used with variable-length records, then each block can be restricted to an integer number of records by filling in the unused portion of the block with _____ .

padding

11. In terms of actual practice, records are most often [fixed / variable] in length and [blocked / unblocked].

fixed; blocked

12. Principal advantages of record blocking are that it results in data compaction and a reduction in the physical read and write operations, thereby also reducing processing _____ .

time

13. In addition to using blocking, the practice associated with defining the buffer size that further reduces the time devoted to I/O operations is called _____ .

double-buffering

14. Given a particular number of records all of the same length and given that blocking is used, the larger the block size, the [smaller / larger] is the total physical file size for magnetic tape files.

smaller

· · · ·

FILE LABELS

Each magnetic file, such as a reel of tape or a disk pack, is identified by two means. Externally, an adhesive label is attached so that the human operator can identify the contents of the file by reading this label. In addition, magnetic labels are included with the file itself. In general, two types of magnetic labels are used: the header label and the trailer label.

As implied by the name, a *header label* is located at the beginning of the file. This label contains such information as

- File identification: in terms of a file name or a file number

- Retention period: the date prior to which the file cannot be overwritten

- Creation date: the date the file was established

- Sequence number: the sequence number for a multivolume file that consists of several volumes (reels or disk packs).

The header label not only serves as a means of verifying the correct identity of an input file but also is used as a means of preventing inadvertent overwriting as explained below.

The *trailer label* is a record written as the last record on the file. Typically, it contains the same information as the header label, but in addition it contains a block count, which is a count of the number of data blocks written on the file.

The trailer label differs depending on whether a file is a single-volume or a multivolume file. If it is a single-volume file, the trailer is as described above. If it is a multivolume file, the trailer label of each volume indicates the volume (reel or disk pack) number as well.

As far as label processing is concerned, we can differentiate the processing on the basis of whether a file is opened for *output* or *input*.

When a file is used in the output mode, the three main actions are OPEN, WRITE, and CLOSE. The following general operations take place with respect to label processing:

- When the file is OPENed for OUTPUT, the beginning label is checked for the field that contains the expiration date of the previously written file. If the expiration date has not yet been reached, then the label processing results in some appropriate diagnostic message and prevention of the output function. Thus, a file is protected from inadvertent overwriting. If the expiration date indicates that the previous file can be overwritten, then the header label of the new file is written.

- WRITE operations proceed normally until the physical end of the file is reached. If the file is on magnetic tape and it is to be continued on another reel, a trailer label is written indicating that this is the end of the reel and not the end of the file. Then the operator is notified to make the next reel available by replacing the present reel with a "fresh" reel on the same tape drive or by providing for continuation on another drive. A beginning-volume label and a header label are then inserted before the next record block is written on the new reel. Thus three label records are written between the last data record on the first reel and the first data record on the new reel: the trailer label on the previous volume, a beginning-volume label, and a header label on the next volume.

- If the file is stored on magnetic disk and it is to continue on another disk, the actions parallel those of tape. However, in the case of a disk file, the physical end of the file may be reached without it being the end of the volume. For example, we may have allocated cylinders 21 to 80 to the file, but the file now requires more than 60 cylinders. In such a case the operating system will issue a diagnostic message to the operator and the job will be abnormally terminated (although some operating systems may expand file size automatically).

- When a CLOSE file command is carried out, the resulting operation is the writing of a trailer label at the end of the file. As records are written into the file, their number typically is accumulated by the label-processing routine, and this "block count" is written as a field in the trailer label. When the file is used as input on future occasions, the counting is repeated, and the new count is compared to the count in the trailer label to ascertain that all the records in the file have been read by the time the trailer label is processed. In a sequential input file we must have read all of the records in the file if we are at the end of the file.

When a file is used in the INPUT mode, the three main actions are OPEN, READ, and CLOSE. The following general operations take place with respect to label processing:

- When the file is OPENed for INPUT, the beginning labels are read to ascertain that the file identification provided in the job control statements agrees with the information in the label record.

- The READ operation proceeds normally until the trailer label is reached. If the label signifies the end of the file, then the operating system communicates this information to the program (recall READ ... AT END ...) and aborts the program if a further attempt is made to read from the file. If the file is a multivolume file, the end-of-volume label will signify such a condition and will result in reading and processing the volume and file header labels on the next volume. Of course, the label-processing routine will check to see that the correct sequence of volumes is presented.

- When an INPUT file is CLOSEd, the trailer label is processed to verify that all records have been read. If the file is on tape, the reel is normally rewound as a result of closing the file. In rare instances it is desirable to read a file in reverse order, in which case an "open reverse" command may be issued after a suitable "close with no rewind" command. The trailer label then acts as a header label.

In general, label processing involves a number of specialized functions having to do with proper identification of data files and ensuring the data integrity in such files. As stated earlier, it is a function governed by localized conventions and procedures, and the programmer has to obtain specific instructions from the particular installation.

R E V I E W . . . .

1. Magnetic files are identified by two general types of labels: _____ labels for human use and _____ labels for machine use.

   external, magnetic

2. Magnetic labels used with files are of two types. The label included at the beginning of a file is called the _____ label, while the label at the end of the file is called the _____ label.

   header; trailer

3. For a multivolume file, both the header and trailer labels include a
    _____ number.

    sequence

4. For a file used in the output mode, the three main actions (COBOL verbs) are
    _____ , _____ , and _____ .

    OPEN; WRITE; CLOSE

5. For a file used in the input mode, the three main actions (COBOL verbs) are
    _____ , _____ , and _____ .

    OPEN; READ; CLOSE

6. The specific procedures associated with label processing [have generally been
    standardized / are governed by localized conventions].

    are governed by localized conventions

.   .   .   .

COBOL INSTRUCTIONS FOR SEQUENTIAL FILES

A number of COBOL instructions have been designed for use with sequential file processing. In the following sections we present most of the common options. Additional features are discussed in Chapter 17. We then conclude the chapter with two sample programs that illustrate the application of such instructions in some typical tasks.

THE FILE-CONTROL SPECIFICATION

For sequential files the FILE-CONTROL specification in the ENVIRONMENT DIVISION has the format presented in Figure 10-6.

The OPTIONAL specification is used for files that may or may not be present. For example, we could have a file on which we output end-of-month reports only when it is the end of the month. In a program using such a file we would specify the file as OPTIONAL and we include some test in the PROCEDURE DIVISION to determine whether the file is used.

OPTIONAL files must be OPENed in the INPUT, I-O, or EXTEND modes (the latter two modes are discussed later in this chapter).

In the ASSIGN statement, *implementor-name-1* refers to the way each particular operating system designates files. Such designation varies. For example, for IBM mainframes the designation consists of a so-called data-set definition name, which is associated with a corresponding job control language statement, as in this example:

```
        SELECT STUDENT-FILE ASSIGN TO STUFILE
        .
        .
        .
//STUFILE DD DSN=  ...  etc.        (This is a JCL statement,
                                    not a COBOL statement.)
```

In the 1985 standard a file can be ASSIGNed to literal-1 in Figure 10-6, which may be a file name. For example, for a diskette file on the "B:" drive of a personal computer we could have

```
SELECT STUDENT-FILE ASSIGN TO "B:STUDENT.DAT".
```

The ORGANIZATION clause is optional for sequential files. When it is omitted, as has been done in this book up to now, the specification defaults to

FIGURE 10-6
FILE-CONTROL Format for Sequential Files

```
FILE -CONTROL.

    SELECT [OPTIONAL] file-name

        ASSIGN TO  { implementor -name-1 }  . . .
                   { literal -1           }

        [ [ORGANIZATION  IS]  SEQUENTIAL ]

        [ PADDING CHARACTER IS  { data -name-1 } ]
        [                       { literal -2    } ]

        [ RECORD DELIMITER  IS  { STANDARD -1          } ]
        [                       { implementor -name -2 } ]

    [ACCESS MODE IS SEQUENTIAL ]

    [FILE STATUS IS data -name -2]
```

ORGANIZATION IS SEQUENTIAL. As one might guess, with indexed and relative files their organization is declared to be INDEXED and RELATIVE, respectively, as will be illustrated in later chapters.

The PADDING CHARACTER option available in COBOL '85 allows the programmer to specify the character to be used to fill the remainder of a partially filled block. If a block is 6000 bytes long and the records require 200 bytes each, there could be 30 records per block. If the total number of records in the file is 125, the last block would contain 5 data records, and the remaining (30 – 5) x 200 = 5000 bytes would be "padded" with the specified characters.

Both data-name-1 and literal-2 must be one character long. When a PADDING option is not specified, then the padding character is the default character used by that particular operating system.

The RECORD DELIMITER is a 1985 feature that allows the programmer to specify either the standard or a specific alternative method for delimiting variable-length records. Such a method is used to determine the length of each record when records are variable. Variable-length records are discussed in Chapter 17.

The optional ACCESS MODE clause serves mainly a documentation role in the case of sequential files, since SEQUENTIAL is the default case even if the clause is not used. However, for indexed and relative files the clause has a more important role.

The final optional clause, FILE STATUS IS, has to do with exception processing during input or output operations. When executing an I/O operation, there may be exceptions. For example, we may have attempted to close an unopened file, and the like.

As a case in point, consider the AT END clause associated with the READ statement. Its purpose is to provide for specific processing when a particular exception occurs during input, namely, when an end-of-file condition occurs. Other I/O verbs, such as OPEN, WRITE, and CLOSE, do not have clauses paralleling the AT END feature of READ. Yet it is important for the programmer to be able to test for exceptions and treat them under control of program logic. For example, if we attempt to open a file and for some reason the command is not successfully completed, we should be able to recognize the exceptional condition and be able to continue with appropriate processing.

The FILE STATUS clause designates a field into which a code is placed after each I/O statement execution (such as OPEN, CLOSE, READ, WRITE, REWRITE). Let us consider an example:

```
SELECT CUSTOMER-FILE ASSIGN TO file-name
        ORGANIZATION IS SEQUENTIAL
        ACCESS MODE IS SEQUENTIAL
        FILE STATUS IS CUST-FILE-IO-STATUS.
        .
        .
        .
WORKING-STORAGE SECTION.
        .
        .
        .
01 CUST-FILE-IO-STATUS PIC X(2).
```

Notice that we chose CUST-FILE-IO-STATUS as the data-name for a two-byte field in WORKING-STORAGE. As each input/output command involving CUSTOMER-FILE is executed, the operating system places a two-byte code in the designated field. Figure 10-7 presents these codes and their meaning.

The FILE STATUS field can then be tested to ascertain the outcome of an I/O operation. For example, we may have

```
OPEN INPUT CUSTOMER-FILE
IF  CUST-FILE-IO-STATUS = "00"
    PERFORM READ-CUSTOMER
ELSE
    IF  CUST-FILE-IO-STATUS = "10"
        PERFORM NO-MORE-CUSTOMERS
    ELSE
        PERFORM ERROR-ROUTINE.
```

The first IF statement checks to determine if the OPEN command was executed successfully (see Figure 10-7 for the meaning of the codes), while the second IF statement checks for the end-of-file condition.

This approach of using the FILE STATUS feature enables the programmer to have better control over exception processing. The program can test for specific exception conditions and take the appropriate action.

R E V I E W . . . .

1. In the FILE-CONTROL statement the specification that is included for files that may or may not be present is the _____ specification.

    OPTIONAL

2. The implementor-name-1 in the ASSIGN statement designates a file according to the method of the particular _____ system being used.

    operating

3. When the ORGANIZATION clause is omitted in the FILE-CONTROL statement, program execution defaults to ORGANIZATION IS _____ .

    SEQUENTIAL

FIGURE 10-7
File Status Codes and Their Meanings

I-O STATUS CODE	EXPLANATION
00	Successful execution.
04	A record whose length is inconsistent with the record description for the file that has been read.
05	Attempt to OPEN a file that is not available.
07	The file storage device is not magnetic tape, yet a CLOSE or OPEN involved a corresponding NO REWIND, REEL, FOR REMOVAL phrase.
10	End-of-file condition.
15	Attempt to read an optional file which is not present.
16	A READ statement was executed while the at end condition is true (attempt to read past the end of the file).
30	A permanent error exists; no further information is available.
34	An attempt is made to write beyond the boundaries of the file.
35	Attempt to OPEN as INPUT, I-O, or EXTEND a nonoptional file.
37	Attempt to OPEN a file that should be on mass storage but is not.
38	Attempt to OPEN a file that has been CLOSED with LOCK.
39	Error during OPEN execution, due to inconsistency between the file description and the actual file.
41	Attempt to OPEN a file that is already opened.
42	Attempt to CLOSE a file that is not open.
43	A successful READ did not precede execution of the current REWRITE command.
44	A boundary violation due to attempt to WRITE or REWRITE a record of improper length.
46	Attempt to READ the next nonexistent record.
47	Attempt to READ from a file not open in INPUT or I-O mode.
48	Attempt to WRITE on a file not open in OUTPUT or EXTEND mode.
49	Attempt to REWRITE on a file not open in I-O mode.
9X	An error condition defined by the particular system in use.

4. The clause available in the 1985 version by which the character that is to be used to fill the remainder of a partially filled block can be specified is the
    _____ clause.

    PADDING CHARACTER

5. If the optional ACCESS MODE clause is used, the only mode available in the clause is SEQUENTIAL. If the clause is not used, the default mode is the
    _____ mode.

    SEQUENTIAL

6. The optional clause that makes it possible to test for exceptional conditions during program execution and thereby achieve better program control and the processing of exceptional conditions is the _____ IS clause.

    FILE STATUS

• • • • • • • • • • • • • • • • • • • •

THE FILE DESCRIPTION ENTRY

Figure 10-8 presents the general format of the file description entry used for sequential files in the DATA DIVISION.

FD marks the beginning of a file description entry and is followed immediately by the name of the file. The name of the file already has been declared in the SELECT statement of the ENVIRONMENT DIVISION, where it was assigned to a hardware device.

If records are grouped together, the BLOCK CONTAINS clause is used. If each record constitutes one block, the clause may be omitted or the equivalent BLOCK CONTAINS 1 RECORD can be used. When a block contains several records, then the clause must be used. Typically, this clause is used with the RECORDS option. In such a case it references the number of records per block. For example, if we have

```
FD PAYROLL-FILE BLOCK CONTAINS 10 RECORDS
```

each block will contain 10 records.

Because of the widespread use of IBM systems, we now mention the common convention in such environments, which is to use

```
BLOCK CONTAINS 0 RECORDS
```

Zero records per block is not a logical statement. However, it is a special convention that states that the blocking factor for this file will be specified in the accompanying JCL statements. Thus the same program can be executed with files of different blocking factors, thereby introducing flexibility at the time of program execution.

The VARYING clause is used to specify variable-length records, as will be discussed in Chapter 17.

The LABEL RECORDS clause is required for all files in the 1974 version but is optional in the 1985 standard. The OMITTED option indicates that the file either has no beginning or ending label (as is the case with printer files), or they are ignored if they exist. If the STANDARD option is used, it is understood to be the standard label for the particular computer installation. As we mentioned earlier, the label record contains data that identify the file, and obviously each file is identified uniquely. There are two basic ways of saying what the label contents should be. By the first approach this information is communicated through

FIGURE 10-8
Format for a FILE DESCRIPTION Entry

```
FD file-name
  [ BLOCK CONTAINS [ integer-1 TO] integer-2 { RECORDS    } ]
  [                                          { CHARACTERS } ]

  [         { CONTAINS integer -3 CHARACTERS                                       } ]
  [ RECORD  { IS VARYING IN SIZE [ [FROM integer -4] [TO integer -5] CHARACTERS ]   } ]
  [         {      [DEPENDING on data-name-1]                                       } ]
  [         { CONTAINS integer -6 TO integer -7 CHARACTERS                          } ]

  [ LABEL { RECORD IS    } { STANDARD } ]
  [       { RECORDS ARE  } { OMITTED  } ]

  [ VALUE OF { implementor-name-1 IS { data-name-2 } } . . . ]
  [                                  { literal-1   }         ]

  [ DATA { RECORD IS   } {data-name-3} . . . ]
  [      { RECORDS ARE }                     ]
```

program control statements submitted with the COBOL program. In other words, this information is not communicated, strictly speaking, in the COBOL program language. Another way of communicating the contents of label records is by use of the VALUE OF clause in Figure 10-8. For example, we could have this for a particular case:

```
FD  PAYROLL-FILE BLOCK CONTAINS 10 RECORDS
                 LABEL RECORDS ARE STANDARD
                 VALUE OF IDENTIFICATION IS "A2359"
                 RETENTION-PERIOD IS 090
                 DATA RECORD IS PAY-REC.
```

The words IDENTIFICATION and RETENTION-PERIOD above are meaningful in a particular installation, and indicate that the STANDARD label contains a field called IDENTIFICATION, whose content should be A2359. When the file is opened, the field is checked to ascertain that A2359 is there (to check that the correct file is mounted). The RETENTION-PERIOD field implies that this file cannot be written on until 90 days have elapsed. Of course, other similar fields are used in the VALUE clause for more complete label specification, depending on the conventions at each computer system.

The VALUE clause has been marked as being obsolete in the 1985 version. This means that it should not be used in new programs and that it will he deleted in a future version of COBOL. The "obsolete" category allows for a transitional period so that "old" features can be phased out of the language. The VALUE clause is not in common use. Most implementors provide means external to COBOL for specifying file label contents.

The DATA RECORD clause is optional and identifies the name of the record(s) in the file. A file may contain more than one type of record as will be discussed in Chapter 16. For example:

```
DATA RECORDS ARE CHARGE-REC
                PAY-REC.
```

In the above example, there are two records in the file.

The DATA RECORD clause mainly serves a documentation role, since it is followed immediately by the data record names and the 01 level-number.

As a way of summarizing the discussion in this section, the following are examples of file descriptions in the DATA DIVISION:

```
FD PAYROLL-FILE BLOCK CONTAINS 10 RECORDS
                RECORD CONTAINS 80 CHARACTERS
                LABEL RECORDS ARE OMITTED
                DATA RECORD IS SAMPLE-REC.

FD FILE-A       BLOCK CONTAINS 600 CHARACTERS
                LABEL RECORD IS STANDARD
                VALUE OF IDENTIFICATION IS "A1-2B"
                DATA RECORD IS REC.

FD FILE-B       LABEL RECORDS OMITTED
                DATA RECORD IS SIMPLE-REC.

FD FILE-85      (this is a minimum specification for COBOL '85)
```

R E V I E W . . . .

1. With reference to the sample file descriptions just given, the names of the four files are _____ , _____ , _____ , and _____ , respectively.

    PAYROLL-FILE; FILE-A; FILE-B; FILE-85

2. The file description just given in which each block contains one record is the [first / second / third] description. The file description in which the record size may be variable is the [first / second / third] description.

    third; second

3. The file description that includes a label record is the [first / second / third] description. The file description that includes the optional VALUE OF clause is the [first / second / third] description.

    second; second

. . . .

THE OPEN AND CLOSE VERBS

The OPEN verb initiates processing of a file and performs appropriate label processing. If the file is to be used as output, when the file is opened, the existing label is checked to ascertain that the previous file can be overwritten by the new one. If so, the new header label is written on the file. Similarly, if the file is opened for input, its label is read and checked for proper identification.

If an error condition arises as a result of such label processing, either it is reported by the operating system, which normally terminates the program, or it is handled by the program itself through use of the FILE STATUS feature discussed earlier in this chapter.

The OPEN verb has the following format:

$$
\underline{\text{OPEN}} \left\{
\begin{array}{ll}
\underline{\text{INPUT}} & \text{file-name [with } \underline{\text{NO REWIND}} \text{]} \\
\underline{\text{OUTPUT}} & \text{file-name [with } \underline{\text{NO REWIND}} \text{]} \\
\underline{\text{I-O}} & \text{file-name} \\
\underline{\text{EXTEND}} & \text{file-name}
\end{array}
\right\}
$$

In the general format the INPUT and OUTPUT modes contain the NO REWIND option that can be used with magnetic tape files. Absence of the NO REWIND implies that the reel should be rewound, if necessary, so that it is at its beginning. If the NO REWIND is used, it is assumed that a previous CLOSE ... WITH NO REWIND has resulted in the multifile tape being positioned at the beginning of the next desired file (by being at the end of the previous file that was just closed).

The I-O option can be used only for disk or other DASD (direct access storage device) files. It allows the program to both input from and output on the file. It is used if we want to change a record that we have just read. With tape files, however, we cannot rewrite a record that we have just read in.

The EXTEND option positions the file after its last record. It can be used to add new records at the end of the file and is really a special case of the OUTPUT mode option.

Correct use of input-output verbs depends on the option, or mode, used in the OPEN statement. Table 10-1 summarizes this relationship, with an X designating each permissible combination. For instance, if the INPUT mode option is used, then the READ verb can be used, but the WRITE and REWRITE verbs cannot be used.

The CLOSE verb has the following expanded format:

$$
\underline{\text{CLOSE}} \text{ file-name} \left[
\left\{
\begin{array}{l}
\underline{\text{REEL}} \\
\underline{\text{UNIT}}
\end{array}
\right\}
\left[
\begin{array}{l}
\text{WITH } \underline{\text{NO REWIND}} \\
\text{FOR } \underline{\text{REMOVAL}}
\end{array}
\right]
\text{ WITH }
\left\{
\begin{array}{l}
\underline{\text{NO REWIND}} \\
\underline{\text{LOCK}}
\end{array}
\right\}
\right] \ldots
$$

Prior to closing, a file must have been opened. "CLOSE file-name" results in end-of-file procedures. If label records have not been omitted, a trailer label is written; and if a tape file, the tape is rewound automatically.

TABLE 1

Permissible Combinations of OPEN Mode Options and Input-Output Verbs

	OPEN MODE			
STATEMENT:	INPUT	OUTPUT	I/O	EXTEND
READ	X		X	
WRITE		X		X
REWRITE			X	

With tape files, if the option CLOSE file-name REEL is used, this results in closing that reel but not the file as such. The file itself still will be in an open status. The common circumstance under which the REEL option is used is in the case of multireel files, when the processing of a particular reel for a file may have been completed but other reels for the file still might remain to be processed. If we are using disk files, then the term UNIT is used instead of REEL. The NO REWIND option prevents the rewinding that otherwise is caused automatically by the CLOSE verb. As also explained in connection with the OPEN statement above, one circumstance in which the user would not want to rewind the tape is when a second file subsequently is to be read from or written on the same tape reel. When the LOCK option is used instead of the NO REWIND, the file is locked and can be reopened only by restarting the program. The LOCK option serves as protection against accidentally opening and misusing a file whose data have already been processed. The FOR REMOVAL option is used to allow the operator to intervene, remove the reel or disk unit (at least logically), and replace it with another reel. The specific procedure that should take place in conjunction with using the FOR REMOVAL option is not defined by COBOL; rather, it is determined by the implementor.

R E V I E W . . . .

1. Processing of a file is initiated by the use of the _____ verb.

                                                                              OPEN

2. If the READ verb is to be used subsequent to a file being opened, then the INPUT mode option should be included in the OPEN statement. Similarly, if the WRITE verb is to be used then the _____ mode option should be included in the OPEN statement.

                                                                    OUTPUT (or EXTEND)

3. End-of-file procedures are specified by use of the _____ verb.

                                                                              CLOSE

4. The option of the OPEN verb that enables us to rewrite a disk record that has been read is the _____ option.

                                                                                I-O

5. The option in the closing routine that serves to protect the file from use (and misuse) is the [NO REWIND / LOCK] option, whereas the option that permits further use of the reel is the [NO REWIND / LOCK] option.

                                                                    LOCK; NO REWIND

. . . .

THE READ, WRITE, AND REWRITE VERBS

The format for the READ verb is

> <u>READ</u> file-name-1 [<u>NEXT</u>] [<u>INTO</u> identifier-1]
>
>   [AT <u>END</u> imperative-statement-1]
>
>   [<u>NOT</u> AT <u>END</u> imperative-statement-1]
>
> [<u>END-READ</u>]

This is the same format as we have encountered before, with one small exception: the NEXT option. This option is available only in COBOL '85. The NEXT option serves mainly a documentary role for sequential files, but it has a much more important role in indexed and relative files, as explained in later chapters.

The AT END clause is optional. In its place we can use the FILE STATUS feature to check whether an end-of-file (as well as any other) condition has occurred while reading. However, some compilers require the AT END specification for all sequential files.

If a file was designated as OPTIONAL in the SELECT statement and the file is not present, the AT END condition occurs when the first READ is executed. As Table 10-1 indicates, a READ is valid when a file has been opened as INPUT or I-O.

The NOT AT END and the END-READ options apply to the 1985 standard only.

The relevant WRITE format for a sequential file is

WRITE record -name [FROM identifier]

[NOT] AT $\begin{Bmatrix} \text{END-OF-PAGE} \\ \text{EOP} \end{Bmatrix}$ imperative -statement

[END-WRITE]

As discussed in Chapter 9, the END-OF-PAGE option is meaningful only for files assigned to a printer device. Also, the END-WRITE is a 1985-only feature.

As Table 10-1 indicates, the file must be opened as either OUTPUT or EXTEND if the WRITE verb is to be used.

If a BLOCK CONTAINS clause was used in the file description, the system will control automatically the operations needed to form an appropriate block prior to a physical write of the block itself. The programmer need not be concerned about the blocking operation.

The REWRITE statement is a specialized instruction for direct access storage files. Its format is

REWRITE record-name [FROM identifier]

To update a sequential file on disk, we may use "OPEN I-O file-name." Then, after issuing a READ command that accesses the record to be updated, we use the REWRITE verb to replace the updated record in the same file instead of WRITE on a different file. With magnetic tape files, we must read a record from one file and MOVE and write the updated record on a new file.

It should be noted that REWRITE can be used only to update an existing file. If we are creating a new file, we must use the WRITE verb.

R E V I E W . . . .

1. If the OPEN verb is to be used, the file must be opened in the _____ or _____ mode.

   INPUT; I-O

2. If the WRITE verb is to be used, the file must be opened in the _____ or _____ mode.

   OUTPUT; EXTEND

3. The verb that is used to update an existing file is the _____ verb. To use this verb, the file must be opened in the _____ mode.

   REWRITE; I-O

SAMPLE PROGRAM TO CREATE A SEQUENTIAL FILE

Figure 10-9 illustrates the process of creating a sequential file on magnetic tape or disk. The source records are assumed to be in CUST-SOURCE-FILE. The new file will be CUST-MAST-FILE and is defined so that BLOCK CONTAINS 5 RECORDS.

The PROCEDURE DIVISION illustrates use of the file status feature after the OPEN OUTPUT CUST-MAST-FILE statement. CUST-FILE-STATUS was declared to be the FILE STATUS for this file in the SELECT statement of the ENVIRONMENT DIVISION. Recall from the earlier discussion of file status that a "00" value means that the I/O operation (OPEN in this case) was successful. If after the OPEN statement CUST-FILE-STATUS does not contain a "00" value, then we PERFORM 400-I-O-EXCEPTION, which prints an explanatory error message containing the file status value and sets the ABEND (abnormal end) condition-name condition to true, so that the program will terminate.

If the OPEN command is successfully executed, then we execute the 100-CREATE-MASTER which controls the execution of 200-READ-SOURCE. In the latter paragraph we check the file status after the READ statement. A value of "10" indicates an end-of-file condition, as you can verify by reviewing Figure 10-7, which lists the file status values and their meanings. If the file status is not "10" and it is not "00", then, again, we execute 400-I-O-EXCEPTION.

Each record read in is checked in 300-CHECK-WRITE-READ for sequence on a field called CUST-NO in columns 1–5. If a record is not in ascending sequence, it is listed on the printer for visual review. In this manner we know that after the new file has been created, the records are in sequence in ascending order of the CUST-NO field.

Figure 10-10 shows sample input and output from execution of the sample program in Figure 10-9. Notice that the sample input contained one sequence error, which was reported in the error file.

Figure 10-11 presents the same program using features from the 1985 standard. We have used two paragraphs, 000-CREATE-MASTER and 100-I-O-EXCEPTION. The capability of using the in-line PERFORM and END-IF scope terminators allows us to consolidate the logic into fewer paragraphs. This is

FIGURE 10-9

Program to Create a Sequential File

```
      IDENTIFICATION DIVISION.
      PROGRAM-ID. CREATE-FILE.
      *
      ENVIRONMENT DIVISION.
      *
      CONFIGURATION SECTION.
      SOURCE-COMPUTER. ABC-490.
      OBJECT-COMPUTER. ABC-490.
      *
      INPUT-OUTPUT SECTION.
      FILE-CONTROL.
          SELECT CUST-MAST-FILE ASSIGN TO MASTOUT.
      *
          SELECT CUST-SOURCE-FILE    ASSIGN TO SOURCE
              FILE STATUS IS CUST-FILE-STATUS.
      *
          SELECT ERROR-FILE          ASSIGN TO PRINTER.
      *
```

FIGURE 10-9

Program to Create a Sequential File (continued)

```
DATA DIVISION.
*
FILE SECTION.
*
FD  CUST-MAST-FILE
    LABEL RECORDS ARE STANDARD
    BLOCK CONTAINS 5 RECORDS
    DATA RECORD IS CUST-MAST-REC.
01  CUST-MAST-REC            PIC X(75).
*
FD  CUST-SOURCE-FILE
    LABEL RECORDS OMITTED
    DATA RECORD IS CUST-SOURCE-REC.
01  CUST-SOURCE-REC.
    02  CUST-NO              PIC 9(5).
    02  CUST-NAME            PIC X(20).
    02  CUST-ADDRESS         PIC X(50).
    02  FILLER               PIC X(5).
*
FD  ERROR-FILE
    LABEL RECORDS ARE OMITTED
    DATA RECORD IS ERROR-REC.
01  ERROR-REC                PIC X(132).
*
WORKING-STORAGE SECTION.
*
01  END-OF-FILE-INDICATOR    PIC XXX    VALUE 'NO'.
    88  END-OF-FILE                     VALUE 'YES'.
*
01  CUST-FILE-STATUS         PIC XX.
*
01  PREVIOUS-CUST-NO         PIC 9(5)  VALUE ZERO.
*
01  SEQ-ERROR-MESSAGE.
    02  FILLER               PIC X     VALUE SPACE.
    02  FILLER               PIC X(13) VALUE
                'ERROR RECORD:'.
    02  RECORD-OUT           PIC X(75).
*
01  I-O-ERROR-MESSAGE.
    02  FILLER               PIC X(25) VALUE
                    'CUST-MASTER I/O EXCEPTION'.
    02  FILLER               PIC X(16) VALUE
                    ' FILE STATUS = '.
    02  ERR-MESS-FILE-STATUS PIC XX.
*
01  JOB-TERMINATOR           PIC XXX    VALUE 'NO'.
    88  ABEND                           VALUE 'YES'.
*
*
```

FIGURE 10-9

Program to Create a Sequential
File (continued)

```
/
      PROCEDURE DIVISION.
*
  000-MAIN-ROUTINE.
      OPEN INPUT CUST-SOURCE-FILE
           OUTPUT ERROR-FILE.
*
      OPEN OUTPUT CUST-MAST-FILE.
*
      IF  CUST-FILE-STATUS = '00'
          PERFORM 100-CREATE-MASTER
      ELSE
          PERFORM 400-I-O-EXCEPTION.
*
      CLOSE CUST-SOURCE-FILE
      ERROR-FILE
      CUST-MAST-FILE.
*
      STOP RUN.
*
  100-CREATE-MASTER.
*
      PERFORM 200-READ-SOURCE
*
      PERFORM 300-CHECK-WRITE-READ
          UNTIL END-OF-FILE
              OR ABEND.
*
  200-READ-SOURCE.
      READ CUST-SOURCE-FILE RECORD
      IF  CUST-FILE-STATUS = '10'
          MOVE 'YES' TO END-OF-FILE-INDICATOR
      ELSE
          IF CUST-FILE-STATUS NOT = '00'
          PERFORM 400-I-O-EXCEPTION.
*
  300-CHECK-WRITE-READ.
      IF  CUST-NO NOT > PREVIOUS-CUST-NO
          MOVE CUST-SOURCE-REC TO RECORD-OUT
          WRITE ERROR-REC FROM SEQ-ERROR-MESSAGE AFTER 2
      ELSE
          WRITE CUST-MAST-REC FROM CUST-SOURCE-REC
          MOVE CUST-NO TO PREVIOUS-CUST-NO.
*
      PERFORM 200-READ-SOURCE.
*
  400-I-O-EXCEPTION.
      MOVE CUST-FILE-STATUS TO ERR-MESS-FILE-STATUS
      WRITE ERROR-REC FROM I-O-ERROR-MESSAGE AFTER 1
      MOVE 'YES' TO JOB-TERMINATOR.
```

FIGURE 10-10
Sample Input and Output for the
Program in Figure 10-9

```
CUSTOMER SOURCE FILE

11111NAME-1              ADDRESS-1
22222NAME-2              ADDRESS-2
33333NAME-3              ADDRESS-3
44444NAME-4              ADDRESS-4
10000SEQUENCE ERROR
55555NAME-5              ADDRESS-5
60000NAME-6              ADDRESS-6


CUSTOMER MASTER FILE

11111NAME-1              ADDRESS-1
22222NAME-2              ADDRESS-2
33333NAME-3              ADDRESS-3
44444NAME-4              ADDRESS-4
55555NAME-5              ADDRESS-5
60000NAME-6              ADDRESS-6


ERROR FILE

ERROR RECORD:10000SEQUENCE ERROR
```

FIGURE 10-11
Program to Create a Sequential
File Using COBOL '85

```
IDENTIFICATION DIVISION.
PROGRAM-ID. CREATE-FILE-85.
*
ENVIRONMENT DIVISION.
INPUT-OUTPUT SECTION.
FILE-CONTROL.
    SELECT CUST-MAST-FILE     ASSIGN TO MASTOUT.
*
    SELECT CUST-SOURCE-FILE   ASSIGN TO SOURCE-FILE
           FILE STATUS IS CUST-FILE-STATUS.
*
    SELECT ERROR-FILE         ASSIGN TO PRINTER.
*
DATA DIVISION.
*
FILE SECTION.
FD  CUST-MAST-FILE    LABEL RECORDS ARE STANDARD
                      BLOCK CONTAINS 5 RECORDS.
01  CUST-MAST-REC             PIC X(75).
*
```

```
     FD   CUST-SOURCE-FILE LABEL RECORDS OMITTED.
     01   CUST-SOURCE-REC.
          02   CUST-NO               PIC 9(5).
          02   CUST-NAME             PIC X(20).
          02   CUST-ADDRESS          PIC X(50).
          02   FILLER                PIC X(5).
     *
     FD   ERROR-FILE      LABEL RECORDS ARE OMITTED.
     01   ERROR-REC                  PIC X(132).
     *
     WORKING-STORAGE SECTION.
     *
     01   END-OF-FILE-INDICATOR      PIC XXX    VALUE 'NO'.
          88   END-OF-FILE                      VALUE 'YES'.
     *
     01   CUST-FILE-STATUS           PIC XX.
     *
     01   PREVIOUS-CUST-NO           PIC 9(5)   VALUE ZERO.
     *
     01   SEQ-ERROR-MESSAGE.
          02   FILLER                PIC X      VALUE SPACE.
          02   FILLER                PIC X(13) VALUE
                    'ERROR RECORD:'.
          02   RECORD-OUT            PIC X(75).
     *
     01   I-O-ERROR-MESSAGE.
          02   FILLER                PIC X(25) VALUE
                    'CUST-MASTER I/O EXCEPTION'.
          02   FILLER                PIC X(16) VALUE
                    ' FILE STATUS = '.
          02   ERR-MESS-FILE-STATUS    PIC XX.
     *
     01   JOB-TERMINATOR             PIC XXX    VALUE 'NO'.
          88   ABEND                            VALUE 'YES'.
     *
     /
     PROCEDURE DIVISION.
     *
     000-CREATE-MASTER.
     *
          OPEN INPUT  CUST-SOURCE-FILE
               OUTPUT ERROR-FILE
                      CUST-MAST-FILE
     *
          IF  CUST-FILE-STATUS NOT = '00'
              PERFORM 100-I-O-EXCEPTION
              SET ABEND TO TRUE
          END-IF
     *
          PERFORM UNTIL END-OF-FILE  OR ABEND
     *
```

FIGURE 10-11

Program to Create a Sequential File Using COBOL '85 (continued)

```
        READ CUST-SOURCE-FILE RECORD
        IF  CUST-FILE-STATUS = '10'
            SET END-OF-FILE TO TRUE
        ELSE
            IF  CUST-FILE-STATUS NOT = '00'
                PERFORM 100-I-O-EXCEPTION
            ELSE
                IF  CUST-NO NOT > PREVIOUS-CUST-NO
                    MOVE CUST-SOURCE-REC TO RECORD-OUT
                    WRITE ERROR-REC FROM SEQ-ERROR-MESSAGE
                        AFTER ADVANCING 2 LINES
                ELSE
                    WRITE CUST-MAST-REC FROM CUST-SOURCE-REC
                    MOVE CUST-NO TO PREVIOUS-CUST-NO
                END-IF
            END-IF
        END-IF
*
    END-PERFORM
*
    CLOSE CUST-SOURCE-FILE
          ERROR-FILE
          CUST-MAST-FILE
*
    STOP RUN.
*
 100-I-O-EXCEPTION.
    MOVE CUST-FILE-STATUS TO ERR-MESS-FILE-STATUS
    WRITE ERROR-REC FROM I-O-ERROR-MESSAGE AFTER 1
    SET ABEND TO TRUE.
```

especially appealing when the logic of a module, or a whole PROCEDURE DIVISION in this case, can fit on one page; we can easily scan the logic up-and-down, without needing to jump from one paragraph to another. Of course, the exceptionally small size of this program is not representative.

SEQUENTIAL FILE UPDATING

Files on magnetic tape or disk are maintained or updated to reflect changes that take place. We speak of *master* and *transaction* files as being involved in the updating process.

A *master* file contains reference data that reflect the cumulative status as of a point in time. For example, a payroll master file would contain data on each employee, such as name, address, pay rate, year-to-date earnings, and so forth.

A *transaction* file contains records that either reflect events or indicate changes to the master file. For example, a transaction record at a bank might be a deposit made or a check written. Other examples of transactions would be the addition of a new customer to the master file, deletion of a former customer's record, or a change of the customer's address.

File *updating* involves processing the transaction file against the master file. Figure 10-12 illustrates the general procedure involved in updating magnetic tape and disk files. Beginning with the top of the figure, we assume that the

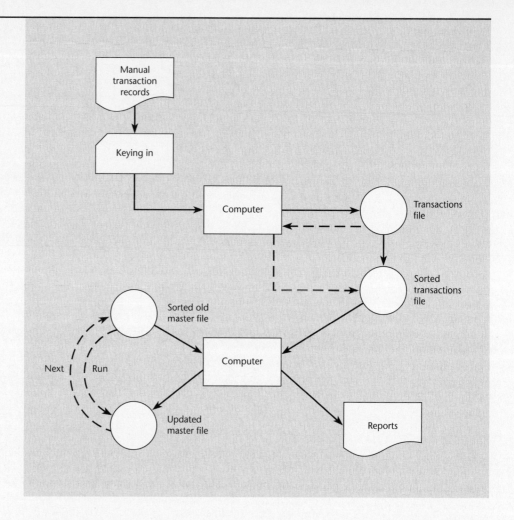

transactions originally were recorded manually and then were keyed in and transferred onto a magnetic tape or disk file. The old master file then is processed against the sorted transactions file to produce the updated master file. In addition, related reports might be produced on the printer.

As indicated by the dashed lines in Figure 10-12, what is now the updated master file becomes the old master file in the next update run, and the old master file from the first run will be used for entry of the updated master file on the next update run. This is known as a parent/child file relationship. However, the procedure we have described results in each case in destruction of the file for the period preceding the one being updated. If we want to have more historical backup, we could use a third file in this procedure, giving rise to a grandparent/parent/child relationship.

To update a master file, both the master file and the transaction file must be sorted on the same basis. Typically, they are sorted according to part number, account number, employee number, or the like.

In the case of a master file stored on disk, it is not necessary to create a new file. We could REWRITE each updated record in its original location. However, we should realize that doing so eliminates our backup capability. If something went wrong in the previous update run, we would not find it easy to reconstruct the file and rerun the update program. Thus, even with disk storage it often is preferable to create a new master file. Also, we cannot add new records to a sequential file unless we create a new, updated file. New records cannot be "squeezed in" between existing records.

R E V I E W . . . .

1. The file that contains cumulative data as of a point in time is called the
    _____ file.

    master

2. The file that contains records that reflect required changes to the master file is
    the _____ file.

    transaction

3. In the process of updating, the updated master file becomes the _____
    master file in the next update run.

    old

4. An existing master file can be updated directly, rather than by creating a new
    master file, when the existing file is stored on [tape / disk].

    disk

. . . .

SAMPLE SEQUENTIAL FILE UPDATE PROGRAM

We illustrate the general logic involved in a sequential file update by means of a simple example.

Master records consist of a customer number, a customer name, and an address. Transaction records consist of a customer number, a transaction code, a name field, and an address field. The transactions are of three general types: changing the content of a specified customer's master record, adding a new customer record, and deleting a customer record. The "change" transactions are of two types: change name and change address. In more complex tasks, there may be a large number of types of transactions. However, whether we have two types or ten, the programming logic is similar. Another point is that we may have several transaction records corresponding to one master record. In our simple example we could have both a change of name and a change of address for a given customer.

A structure chart for the program is presented in Figure 10-13, a complete program listing is included in Figure 10-14, and sample input and output are shown in Figure 10-15.

The main function involved is to process a transaction record against a master record. The 000-MAIN-LOGIC paragraph in Figure 10-14 begins with an OPEN command for the four files involved. Then we execute what is called a "primal read" to read the first record from each file:

```
PERFORM 010-READ-TRANS
PERFORM 020-READ-MASTER
```

At any point in the program logic we are in a position of having a record read from the master and transaction files. We repeatedly execute the 030-COMPARE-M-TO-T procedure to find out which of the three cases we have: the master record customer number is equal to, less than, or greater than the transaction record. We need to discuss each of these cases individually. However, first let us consider the 010 and 020 paragraphs that read the two input files.

To make sure that both files are in sequence, the 010-READ-TRANS and 020-READ-MASTER paragraphs perform appropriate sequence checking. In each case we save the value of the respective previous record and store it in PREVIOUS-TRANS-NO and PREVIOUS-MAST-NO, both of which were initialized with a VALUE ZERO. In the case of the transaction file a sequence error is indicated when a new

FIGURE 10-13

Structure Chart for the Update Program

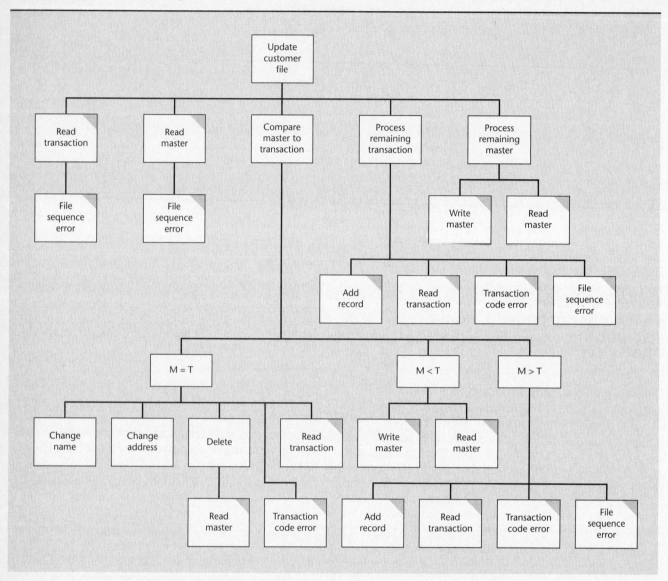

transaction record is smaller than the previous record. If it is equal, it simply means that we have a second, third, and so forth, transaction for the same customer. For the master file an out-of-sequence condition exists if the new record read does not have a customer number value greater than the one before it, since we cannot have two master records with the same customer number.

In the 020-READ-MASTER, notice that we READ OLD-CUST-MASTER RECORD INTO NEW-MAST-REC, thereby storing a copy of the record read into the record area of the new master. The purpose of this action will become clear as we continue with our explanation.

In 040-M-EQUALS-T when a master record is equal to a transaction record, we execute one of four possible cases: 070-NAME-CHANGE, 080-ADDRESS-CHANGE, 090-DELETION, or 130-TRANS-CODE-ERROR. Use of the EVALUATE statement from the 1985 standard is appropriate here, but we stay with the nested IF because there are so many existing programs before the 1985 standard, and if anything, the EVALUATE is easier to understand.

FIGURE 10-14

Program to Update a Sequential File

```
IDENTIFICATION DIVISION.
PROGRAM-ID.  SIMPLUPD.
*
ENVIRONMENT DIVISION.
*
CONFIGURATION SECTION.
SOURCE-COMPUTER. ABC-480.
OBJECT-COMPUTER. ABC-480.
*
INPUT-OUTPUT SECTION.
*
FILE-CONTROL.
    SELECT OLD-CUST-MASTER ASSIGN TO A
           ORGANIZATION IS SEQUENTIAL
           ACCESS MODE IS SEQUENTIAL.
    SELECT NEW-CUST-MASTER ASSIGN TO B
           ORGANIZATION IS SEQUENTIAL
           ACCESS MODE IS SEQUENTIAL.
    SELECT TRANS-FILE ASSIGN TO CARDS.
    SELECT REPORT-FILE ASSIGN TO PRINTER.
/
DATA DIVISION.
*
FILE SECTION.
*
FD  OLD-CUST-MASTER
    LABEL RECORDS ARE STANDARD
    BLOCK CONTAINS 5 RECORDS
    DATA RECORD IS OLD-MAST-REC.
*
01  OLD-MAST-REC.
    02  CUST-NO            PIC X(5).
    02  CUST-NAME          PIC X(20).
    02  CUST-ADDRESS       PIC X(50).
*
FD  NEW-CUST-MASTER
    LABEL RECORDS ARE STANDARD
    BLOCK CONTAINS 5 RECORDS
    DATA RECORD IS NEW-MAST-REC.
*
01  NEW-MAST-REC.
    02  CUST-NO            PIC X(5).
    02  CUST-NAME          PIC X(20).
    02  CUST-ADDRESS       PIC X(50).
*
FD  TRANS-FILE
    LABEL RECORDS OMITTED
    DATA RECORD IS TRANS-REC.
*
```

FIGURE 10-14

Program to Update a Sequential File (continued)

```
01  TRANS-REC.
    02  CUST-NO               PIC X(5).
    02  TRANS-CODE            PIC 9.
        88  NEW-NAME          VALUE 1.
        88  NEW-ADDRESS       VALUE 2.
        88  NEW-RECORD        VALUE 3.
        88  DELETE-RECORD     VALUE 4.
        88  ERROR-TRANSACTION VALUES ZERO, 5 THRU 9.
    02  CUST-NAME             PIC X(20).
    02  CUST-ADDRESS          PIC X(50).
    02  FILLER                PIC X(4).
*
 FD REPORT-FILE
    LABEL RECORDS OMITTED
    DATA RECORD REPORT-REC.
*
 01 REPORT-REC               PIC X(132).
*
/
 WORKING-STORAGE SECTION.
*
 01 END-OF-FILE-SWITCHES.
    02  END-OF-TRANS-SWITCH  PIC XXX VALUE 'NO'.
        88  TRANS-ENDED      VALUE 'YES'.
    02  END-OF-MASTER-SWITCH PIC XXX VALUE 'NO'.
        88  MASTER-ENDED     VALUE 'YES'.
*
 01 TERMINATION-SWITCH       PIC XXX VALUE 'NO'.
        88  TERMINAL-ERROR   VALUE 'YES'.
*
 01 PREVIOUS-REC-VALUES.
    02  PREVIOUS-TRANS-NO    PIC 9(5) VALUE ZEROS.
    02  PREVIOUS-MAST-NO     PIC 9(5) VALUE ZEROS.
*
 01 ERROR-MESSAGE-RECORD.
    02  FILLER               PIC X VALUE SPACE.
    02  MESSAGE-FIELD        PIC X(75).
*
 01 PREVIOUS-VALUES-OUT.
    02  FILLER               PIC X VALUE SPACE.
    02  FILLER               PIC X(18)
                             VALUE 'PREVIOUS TRANS NO'.
    02  TRANS-NO-OUT         PIC 9(5).
    02  FILLER               PIC X(3) VALUE SPACES.
    02  FILLER               PIC X(17) VALUE
                             'PREVIOUS MAST NO'.
    02  MAST-NO-OUT          PIC 9(5).
/
```

FIGURE 10-14

Program to Update a Sequential File (continued)

```
*
  PROCEDURE DIVISION.
*
  000-MAIN-LOGIC.
      OPEN INPUT  OLD-CUST-MASTER
                  TRANS-FILE
           OUTPUT NEW-CUST-MASTER
                  REPORT-FILE.
*
      PERFORM 010-READ-TRANS
      PERFORM 020-READ-MASTER
*
      PERFORM 030-COMPARE-M-TO-T UNTIL TRANS-ENDED
                                    OR MASTER-ENDED
                                    OR TERMINAL-ERROR.
*
      CLOSE OLD-CUST-MASTER
            NEW-CUST-MASTER
            TRANS-FILE
            REPORT-FILE
*
      STOP RUN.
*
  010-READ-TRANS.
      READ TRANS-FILE RECORD
           AT END MOVE 'YES' TO END-OF-TRANS-SWITCH
              MOVE HIGH-VALUES TO CUST-NO OF TRANS-REC.
*
      IF  TRANS-ENDED
          NEXT SENTENCE
      ELSE
          IF  CUST-NO OF TRANS-REC < PREVIOUS-TRANS-NO
              MOVE 'TRANSACTION FILE OUT OF SEQUENCE'
                            TO MESSAGE-FIELD
              PERFORM 120-FILE-SEQUENCE-ERROR
          ELSE
              MOVE CUST-NO OF TRANS-REC TO PREVIOUS-TRANS-NO.
*
  020-READ-MASTER.
      READ OLD-CUST-MASTER RECORD INTO NEW-MAST-REC
          AT END MOVE 'YES' TO END-OF-MASTER-SWITCH
                 MOVE HIGH-VALUES TO CUST-NO OF OLD-MAST-REC.
*
      IF  MASTER-ENDED
          NEXT SENTENCE
      ELSE
          IF CUST-NO OF OLD-MAST-REC NOT > PREVIOUS-MAST-NO
              MOVE 'MASTER FILE OUT OF SEQUENCE' TO MESSAGE-FIELD
              PERFORM 120-FILE-SEQUENCE-ERROR
          ELSE
              MOVE CUST-NO OF OLD-MAST-REC TO PREVIOUS-MAST-NO.
*
```

FIGURE 10-14

*Program to Update a Sequential
File (continued)*

```
    030-COMPARE-M-TO-T.
        IF  CUST-NO OF TRANS-REC = CUST-NO OF OLD-MAST-REC
            PERFORM 040-M-EQUALS-T
        ELSE
            IF  CUST-NO OF TRANS-REC > CUST-NO OF OLD-MAST-REC
                PERFORM 050-M-LESS-THAN-T
            ELSE
                PERFORM 060-M-GREATER-THAN-T.
*
    040-M-EQUALS-T.
        IF  NEW-NAME
            PERFORM 070-NAME-CHANGE
        ELSE
            IF  NEW-ADDRESS
                PERFORM 080-ADDRESS-CHANGE
            ELSE
                IF  DELETE-RECORD
                    PERFORM 090-DELETION
                ELSE
                    PERFORM 130-TRANS-CODE-ERROR.
*
        PERFORM 010-READ-TRANS.
*
    050-M-LESS-THAN-T.
        PERFORM 110-WRITE-MASTER
        PERFORM 020-READ-MASTER.
*
    060-M-GREATER-THAN-T.
        IF  NEW-RECORD
            PERFORM 100-ADD-RECORD
            PERFORM 010-READ-TRANS
        ELSE
            IF  ERROR-TRANSACTION
                PERFORM 130-TRANS-CODE-ERROR
                PERFORM 101-READ-TRANS
            ELSE
                MOVE 'FILES OUT OF SEQUENCE' TO MESSAGE-FIELD
                PERFORM 120-FILE-SEQUENCE-ERROR.
*
    070-NAME-CHANGE.
        MOVE CUST-NAME OF TRANS-REC TO CUST-NAME OF NEW-MAST-REC.
*
    080-ADDRESS-CHANGE.
        MOVE CUST-ADDRESS OF TRANS-REC
            TO CUST-ADDRESS OF NEW-MAST-REC.
*
    090-DELETION.
        PERFORM 020-READ-MASTER.
*
    100-ADD-RECORD.
        MOVE CUST-NO OF TRANS-REC TO CUST-NO OF NEW-MAST-REC
        MOVE CUST-NAME OF TRANS-REC TO CUST-NAME OF NEW-MAST-REC
        MOVE CUST-ADDRESS OF TRANS-REC
                TO CUST-ADDRESS OF NEW-MAST-REC.
*
```

FIGURE 10-14
Program to Update a Sequential File (continued)

```
          PERFORM 110-WRITE-MASTER
*
      IF  NOT MASTER-ENDED
          MOVE OLD-MAST-REC TO NEW-MAST-REC.
*
* THE ABOVE MOVE RESTORES THE CONTENTS OF NEW-MAST-REC
* WHICH WERE DESTROYED BY THE NEW RECORD JUST ADDED.
* RECALL THAT IN READ-MASTER PARAGRAPH AS EACH OLD-MAST-REC
* IS READ IN IT IS MOVED INTO NEW-MAST-REC.
*
  110-WRITE-MASTER.
      WRITE REPORT-REC FROM NEW-MAST-REC
                  AFTER ADVANCING 1 LINE
*
      WRITE NEW-MAST-REC.
*
  120-FILE-SEQUENCE-ERROR.
      WRITE REPORT-REC FROM ERROR-MESSAGE-RECORD
                  AFTER ADVANCING PAGE.
*
      MOVE 'TRANSACTION RECORD AT TIME OF ERROR'
                  TO MESSAGE-FIELD
      WRITE REPORT-REC FROM ERROR-MESSAGE-RECORD
                  AFTER ADVANCING 2 LINES
      MOVE TRANS-REC TO MESSAGE-FIELD
      WRITE REPORT-REC FROM ERROR-MESSAGE-RECORD
                  AFTER ADVANCING 2 LINES
*
      MOVE 'MASTER RECORD AT TIME OF ERROR'
                  TO MESSAGE-FIELD
      WRITE REPORT-REC FROM ERROR-MESSAGE-RECORD
                  AFTER ADVANCING 2 LINES
      MOVE OLD-MAST-REC TO MESSAGE-FIELD
      WRITE REPORT-REC FROM ERROR-MESSAGE-RECORD
                  AFTER ADVANCING 2 LINES
*
      MOVE PREVIOUS-TRANS-NO TO TRANS-NO-OUT
      MOVE PREVIOUS-MAST-NO TO MAST-NO-OUT
      WRITE REPORT-REC FROM PREVIOUS-VALUES-OUT
*
      MOVE 'YES' TO TERMINATION-SWITCH.
*
  130-TRANS-CODE-ERROR.
      MOVE SPACES TO REPORT-REC
      WRITE REPORT-REC
                  AFTER ADVANCING 1 LINE
      MOVE 'THE FOLLOWING RECORD CONTAINS A CODE ERROR'
                  TO MESSAGE-FIELD
      WRITE REPORT-REC
                  AFTER ADVANCING 1 LINE
      WRITE REPORT-REC FROM TRANS-REC
                  AFTER ADVANCING 1 LINE
      MOVE SPACES TO REPORT-REC
      WRITE REPORT-REC
                  AFTER ADVANCING 1 LINE.
```

FIGURE 10-15

Sample Input and Output for the Update Program in Figure 10-14

INPUT TRANSACTION FILE

```
222221NEW-NAME
234563NEW-CUSTOMER          ADDRESS OF NEW
4000032ND-NEW-CUSTOMER      ADDRESS OF 2ND NEW
444444 DELETE EXAMPLE
555555WRONG CODE EXAMPLE
555554                      NEW ADDRESS
543211 SEQ ERROR
666663 3RD NEW
```

OLD CUSTOMER MASTER FILE

```
11111NAME-1                 ADDRESS-1
22222NAME-2                 ADDRESS-2
33333NAME-3                 ADDRESS-3
44444NAME-4                 ADDRESS-4
55555NAME-5                 ADDRESS-5
60000NAME-6
```

NEW CUSTOMER MASTER

```
11111NAME-1                 ADDRESS-1
22222NEW-NAME               ADDRESS-2
23456NEW-CUSTOMER           ADDRESS OF NEW
33333NAME-3                 ADDRESS-3
400002ND-NEW-CUSTOMER       ADDRESS OF 2ND NEW
```

ERROR REPORT OUTPUT

```
555555WRONG CODE EXAMPLE

 TRANSACTION FILE OUT OF SEQUENCE
 TRANSACTION RECORD AT TIME OF ERROR
 543211 SEQ ERROR
 MASTER RECORD AT TIME OF ERROR
 60000NAME-6
 PREVIOUS TRANS NO 55555   PREVIOUS MAST NO 60000
```

If the master record is less than the transaction record, then we execute 050-M-LESS-THAN-T in which we first PERFORM 110-WRITE-MASTER. The latter paragraph writes the new master record on the printer first and then writes it onto the new master file. At this point we should emphasize that a WRITE instruction is destructive. After the WRITE NEW-MAST-REC command, for instance, the data in NEW-MAST-REC are unavailable. The basic reason is that while an output record is being "sent" to the file, the operating system defines a new space in memory to refer to the record, and the contents of that space are "garbage," that is they are dependent on what happened to be in that place in memory at that moment in time. Thus, if in 110-WRITE-MASTER we were to reverse the order of the two WRITE statements, the data in REPORT-REC would come as a surprise, since they would be unpredictable.

Returning to the content of the 050-M-LESS-THAN-T paragraph in Figure 10-14, we can better understand its purpose by considering the following simple example:

TRANSACTION	MASTER
10 change name	10
10 change address	15
20 change address	20

Customer 10 has two transactions. When we compare the first transaction to the master we find them to be equal. We process the first transaction, which changes the name in the copy of the 10 master record in the new master record (recall that when we read a master record, we also make a copy of it in the new master record). We read the second transaction, which changes the address of the 10 new master record. When we read the third transaction, we have the case of the master record (10) being less than the transaction record (20). As indicated in 050-M-LESS-THAN-T, at that point we write the already updated 10 master record into the new master file and PERFORM 020-READ-MASTER, which results in customer 15 being read in. In this case when we compare the two records, the master (15) is less than the transaction (20). Again we write the new master record to its file, but in this case it is simply a copy of the original record, since there have been no updates to the record of customer 15. Thus, the logic in 050-M-LESS-THAN-T is based on the premise that NEW-MAST-REC already holds the appropriate content.

If the master record is higher than the transaction record, then it must be an "add" transaction to be valid. The 100-ADD-RECORD paragraph handles the addition of new records. Consider an example set of data:

TRANSACTION	MASTER
10 change	10
12 add new	15
20 change	20

When transaction 12 is read in, the program takes the path to 050-M-LESS-THAN-T, where we write the updated record for customer 10 and we read the next master, record 15. Now the program executes 060-M-GREATER-THAN-T since 15 is greater that 12. Since transaction 12 is an add transaction, we execute 100-ADD-RECORD, in which the data in the transaction record are MOVEd to the NEW-MAST-REC and written onto the new master file. However, when the master record for customer 15 was read in, it was also copied (READ ... INTO) in NEW-MAST-REC, and the process for creating the new record for customer 12 erased the data for customer 15 in NEW-MAST-REC. Thus the statement

```
IF NOT MASTER-ENDED
    MOVE OLD-MAST-REC TO NEW-MAST-REC
```

in 100-ADD-RECORD will restore the data for customer 15 in NEW-MAST-REC.

Observing the main iteration instruction in 000-MAIN-LOGIC, we see

```
PERFORM 030-COMPARE-M-TO-T
    UNTIL TRANS-ENDED AND MASTER-ENDED
        OR TERMINAL-ERROR.
```

Then, in the 010 and 020 paragraphs, when either the transaction or old master file is at the end, we make the TRANS-ENDED and MASTER-ENDED conditions true, and we MOVE HIGH-VALUES TO the respective CUST-NO. Consider these two cases:

TRANS.	MASTER	TRANS.	MASTER
10	10	10	10
20	eof	eof	20
30			30
eof			eof
(a)		(b)	

The "eof" represents the last (end of file) record. In case (a) the old master file's last record is for customer 10. The transactions for customers 20 and 30 would be add types, unless they were errors. In case (b) the transaction file ends before the old master, and the records for customers 20 and 30 will need to be copied unchanged onto the updated new master file. When transaction 20 is read in case (a), the 050-M-LESS-THAN-T is executed, which writes the updated record for customer 10; and through PERFORM 020-READ-MASTER the end-of-file record is read, and we MOVE HIGH-VALUES TO CUST-NO OF OLD-MAST-REC. From that point on, 060-M-GREATER-THAN-T will be executed, since HIGH-VALUES is always greater than any customer-number value in the transaction record. However, when the eof record is read from the transaction file, then the compound TRANS-ENDED AND MASTER-ENDED condition is true, and the PERFORM in 000-MAIN-LOGIC will terminate the iteration. Before the eof record is read from the transaction file in case (a), however, the comparison of 30 to the HIGH-VALUES contained in the customer-number field of the old master record will have caused 060-M-GREATER-THAN-T to execute, and record 30 will have been added to the new file. You are asked to trace processing of the records in case (b) on your own.

Two kinds of error messages are produced in the sample program in Figure 10-14. The first one is generated in 120-FILE-SEQUENCE-ERROR when the files are found to be out of sequence. We then terminate the program, printing first the records involved and then the immediately preceding records, for reference. It is not always necessary to terminate the program, but in this case it seems the reasonable thing to do. The second type of error has to do with incorrect transaction codes, and it is processed in 130-TRANS-CODE-ERROR. When such errors occur, we write an error message on a separate file, which we assume also is ASSIGNed to the printer device.

The printed output for this program is a simple listing of the updated file. Generally, there would be a list of updated, new, and deleted records printed, rather than the complete file. Exercise 10.2 at the end of this chapter asks for such a modification to the program.

The sample program in Figure 10-14 hopefully is sufficiently self-documenting that you should be able to follow it. This program can be used as the basis for most sequential updating programs, because the basic logic of all such programs is very similar. Chapter 17 presents an expanded discussion and further examples of processing sequential files.

SUMMARY

The three principal methods of file organization in COBOL are the *sequential, indexed,* and *relative.* In this chapter we focused on sequential file processing, in which records are written and accessed in a serial order.

The storage device that is used often determines which methods of file organization are possible. If the storage device is *magnetic tape,* then sequential file organization must be used. In the chapter, characteristics of magnetic tape and *magnetic disk* were considered.

Data are recorded on any magnetic storage device in the form of *blocks.* The *blocking factor* denotes the number of *logical* (as contrasted to *physical*) records included in each block. Some of the factors that need to be considered in enhancing storage efficiency, and therefore reducing processing time, are *padding, buffering, double-buffering,* and the use of *fixed-length* or *variable-length* records.

In the FILE-CONTROL paragraph of the ENVIRONMENT DIVISION, a sequential file organization is designated either by ORGANIZATION IS SEQUENTIAL, or by omitting this option, in which case the default is the SEQUENTIAL choice. The use of other options in the FILE-CONTROL paragraph as they relate to sequential files also was described.

In the DATA DIVISION the FD entry is followed immediately by the file name that was declared in the ENVIRONMENT DIVISION, where it was assigned to a hardware device. Again, the various options in the file description entry as they relate to sequential files were described.

Processing of a file is initiated by use of the OPEN verb in the PROCEDURE DIVISION, while end-of-file procedures are specified by use of the CLOSE verb. The READ, with its available options, is used with respect to *file input.* The WRITE, with its available options, is used with respect to *file output.* The REWRITE can be used with respect to *updating* an existing disk file. Exceptions or errors can be identified by use of the FILE STATUS feature, which results in a two-digit code that identifies the status of each input or output operation. The programmer can test the contents of that field and decide on the next program sequence.

In general, updating a sequential file involves processing a *transaction file* against a *master file* and generating a *new master file* as backup.

The chapter concluded with detailed discussion of two sample COBOL programs: one for *creating* a sequential file, and the other for *updating* an established sequential file.

EXERCISES

10.1 Modify the sample update program in Figure 10-14 so that transaction error records are saved on a tape or disk file and are printed after the update process has been completed. In a process chart form, we should have this:

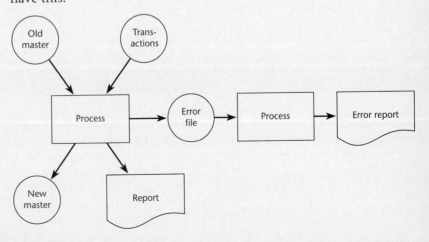

10.2 Modify the sample update program in Figure 10-14 so that during the update process only those master records that were in some way altered are output on the printer. Where appropriate, show both the old and the new record for visual reference and comparison. If a record is added or deleted, however, only one master record is relevant. The report should have the following format:

```
                    Changes to Customer Master
                            MM/DD/YR


       RECORD                                  ACTION


       OLD: xxxxxxxxxxxxxx                      CHANGED ADDRESS
       NEW: xxxxxxxxxxxxxx
       NEW: xxxxxxxxxxxxxx                      NEW RECORD ADDED
       OLD: xxxxxxxxxxxxxx                      DELETED RECORD
       OLD: xxxxxxxxxxxxxx                      CHANGED NAME
       NEW: xxxxxxxxxxxxxx
```

10.3 A company maintains inventory data on a master file sorted on part number. Each record contains the following types of data for each item held in inventory:

FIELD	SIZE
Part number	5 numeric positions
Part name	15 alphanumeric positions
Quantity	5 numeric positions

For the sake of simplicity, there are two types of transactions: receipts and issues. Each transaction has the following format:

FIELD	SIZE
Part number	5 numeric positions
Transaction code 1 = receipt 2 = issue	1 numeric position
Quantity	5 numeric positions

Batches of transaction records are accumulated and then processed to update the master file and to print a report that lists each part number, name, previous quantity balance, and new balance. When the transaction code is 1, the quantity is added; if the code is 2, the quantity is subtracted.

a. Write a program to create the master file. Sample input for the master tape is as follows:

```
035611/2 HP EL MOTOR02000
10513TRANSFORMER    08000
30561GEAR TRAIN-A   07890
30562GEAR TRAIN-B   10250
30564GEAR TRAIN-C   04650
30579GEAR TRAIN-G   08529
40100STEEL PLATE-1A 06099
```

```
40110STEEL PLATE-2A 00852
40120STEEL PLATE-3A 00996
40130STEEL PLATE-4A 01250
40140STEEL PLATE-5B 02899
40150STEEL PLATE-3C 08192
51000BRASS FTNGS-A  12695
51020BRASS FTNGS-B  08569
51030BRASS FTNGS-C  09992
60256BALL BEARING-A201695
60257BALL BEARING-A302561
60258BALL BEARING-A410883
60259BALL BEARING-A513429
60260BALL BEARING-A608866
60261BALL BEARING-A706219
```

b. Write a program to update the master file, given a set of transaction records. The program should perform a sequence check to ascertain that the transaction input records are in the same sequence as the master records. It is possible that some items may have no corresponding transactions, but no transactions are present for items not on the master file. Sample input for transactions is as follows (the master file input is the same as shown in part (a):

```
10513200200
10513110000
30562200500
30562200800
30562200900
30564108000
40100112000
40100204000
40100203000
40140110000
51030200200
51030200965
60261200600
60261200500
60261200900
60261104000
```

Sample output is presented in Figure 10-16 on the following page.

FIGURE 10-16

Sample Output for Exercise 10.3

```
   ITEM NUMBER        PART NAME        PREVIOUS BALANCE     NEW BALANCE

      03561        1/2 HP EL MOTOR          2000               2000
      10513        TRANSFORMER              8000              17800
      30561        GEAR TRAIN-A             7890               7890
      30562        GEAR TRAIN-B            10250               8050
      30564        GEAR TRAIN-C             4650              12650
      30579        GEAR TRAIN-G             8529               8529
      40100        STEEL PLATE-1A           6099              11099
      40110        STEEL PLATE-2A           0852               0852
      40120        STEEL PLATE-3A           0996               0996
      40130        STEEL PLATE-4A           1250               1250
      40140        STEEL PLATE-5B           2899              12899
      40150        STEEL PLATE-3C           8192               8192
      51000        BRASS FTNGS-A           12695              12685
      51020        BRASS FTNGS-B            8569               8569
      51030        BRASS FTNGS-C            9992               8827
      60256        BALL BEARING-A2          1695               1695
      60257        BALL BEARING-A3          2561               2561
      60258        BALL BEARING-A4         10883              10883
      60259        BALL BEARING-A5         13429              13429
      60260        BALL BEARING-A6          8866               8866
      60261        BALL BEARING-A7          6219               8219
```

11 Sorting and Merging Sequential Files

THE PURPOSE OF THIS CHAPTER *is to learn how to use the COBOL sort feature to sort data in a sequential file according to a desired sequence. In addition, you will study the related operation of merging two or more presorted files to form one combined file.*

You will begin by studying some general concepts about file sorting. You will then observe the use of the specialized COBOL statements that are used for sorting by means of two example programs. This will be followed by detailed consideration of the formats in the DATA DIVISION and the PROCEDURE DIVISION for the specialized statements.

The chapter concludes with a general discussion of file merging, and the COBOL specialized instructions for file merging.

INTRODUCTION

In our description of sequential file processing in the preceding chapter, it was evident that sequential files must be sorted in sequence. In file updating, the master file and the transaction file must both have been sorted in the same order. The basis for the sequence is dependent on the situation. For example, in the processing of sales transactions, we may sort the data in the order of customer number. Then we may want to use the same transaction data to update the inventory master file. So next we sort the transaction file in the order of product number to match the sequence of the product inventory master. In addition, we may need reports organized by salesperson, by date, and by geographic area. It should be rather evident that sorting is a very common activity.

Sorting files is so common and so important in business applications of the computer that people have devoted special efforts to devise efficient ways of sorting. When a company acquires a computer, invariably it will acquire indispensable software, such as the operating system, one or more programming language compilers, and a number of "utility" programs. *Utilities* are programs designed to do general-purpose tasks that are not specific to a single application. Typical utilities include programs to create files (catalog their given name in the system table of files, allocate disk space, etc.); to copy a file from, say, magnetic tape to disk; and to sort or merge files. Sorting and merging are so interrelated that the name "sort-merge" is the common way of referring to such a utility program.

Usually the computer hardware vendor will supply a basic set of utilities, including sort-merge, along with the operating system. However, many companies have devised more efficient ways of sorting, and they sell their programs as software products. There are a number of such "proprietary" sorting programs on the market, and their exact method of sorting is the very value of their product. So file sorting can be done in a variety of ways, and the details of each proprietary method are trade secrets. Still, there are many sorting algorithms in the public domain, and it can be presumed that all sort programs use the same basic principles. Where they differ is in critical details.

Basically, all sort routines proceed along these general lines:

- Read a group of records into the central memory of the computer and sort the records in that group using the high speed of the central memory. However, the file is much larger than the central memory, so we can read and sort internally only a relatively small set of records.

- Write the sorted group of records out to a file (disk or tape).

- Read another group of records, sort them internally, and write them out to another file. Keep repeating this process, writing sorted groups of records to two or several files, until all the initial records have been so processed.

- Next, there will be a phase of repeated merging of the sorted groups. The reasons for needing possibly several merging operations require more detailed explanation than is warranted by our intended scope of coverage at this time. Suffice it to say that merging is used to eventually combine the sorted groups into one sorted file. Thus, merging and sorting are related operations in practice.

Sorting is frequently done as a separate program step. A file containing the data is input into a sort utility program, and a sorted file is created that can then be used as input to a COBOL program for further processing. Another approach is to do the sorting or merging operation as part of a COBOL program, not as a separate program. In this chapter we concentrate on the latter approach, that of using COBOL itself for sorting and merging files.

THE COBOL SORT FEATURE

Since file sorting is such a common need, the COBOL language incorporates a sort feature that makes it possible to accomplish this operation with minimal programming. The programmer need not be concerned with the details of any sort algorithm in using this feature, but may simply specify the files to be sorted, the sort key (or keys) to be used, and any special procedures for the handling of files before or after the sort. We illustrate here the COBOL sort feature by means of two examples.

Example 1

Assume that we have a sequential file with the following record description in the DATA DIVISION:

```
01  INPUT-RECORD.
    02  ACCOUNT-NUMBER        PICTURE 9(8).
    02  NAME                  PICTURE X(20).
    02  TRANSACTION-DATE.
        03  DAY-OF-YEAR       PICTURE 999.
        03  YEAR              PICTURE 99.
    02  OTHER-DATA            PICTURE X(47).
```

Suppose we wish to sort the file in *ascending sequence* according to AC-COUNT-NUMBER and in *descending sequence* according to YEAR. That is, for each account, all records are to be arranged from the most recent to the least recent YEAR. Also assume that the sorted file is to be called SORTED-FILE. The sorting process can be portrayed as involving three files, INPUT-FILE, SORT-FILE, and SORTED-FILE, as follows:

Because the sorting procedure is preprogrammed, you need not be concerned about the detail of the SORT-FILE. In concept, SORT-FILE represents a preprogrammed file whose description has been embedded in the sorting routine. As the above diagram illustrates, data from the INPUT-FILE are transferred to the SORT-FILE where they are sorted, and the sorted data are then output onto the SORTED-FILE (these specific file names are, of course, arbitrary choices).

The SORT-FILE is a conceptual file that may involve several physical files. Typically, the sort routine uses several sequential files to execute the sort. Since the sort routine is automated, however, the COBOL programmer describes the file as if it were one physical file, and it is through JCL statements that we describe the physical structure of the file.

Figure 11-1 presents the COBOL program that can be used to sort the file described in this example problem, including sample input and output. In the ENVIRONMENT DIVISION three files are identified in the SELECT statements. Notice that SORT-FILE has been ASSIGNed as if it were one physical file.

In the DATA DIVISION the INPUT-FILE is described in the usual fashion. However, the SORT-FILE is introduced with the special SD level indicator (which stands for Sort Descriptor). The SD level indicator specifies that this is a file to be used in conjunction with the sort routine. Notice that there is no LABEL clause given for such a file.

As far as the record description for the SORT-FILE is concerned, it is just like any other such description. We used the same description as we used for the

FIGURE 11-1

*SORT Program for Example 1,
Including Sample Input and
Output*

```
      IDENTIFICATION DIVISION.
      PROGRAM-ID. SORT1.
*
* THIS PROGRAM ILLUSTRATES SORTING A SEQUENTIAL
* FILE CALLED INPUT-FILE AND MAKING THE SORTED FILE
* AVAILABLE IN SORTED-FILE.
*
      ENVIRONMENT DIVISION.
*
      CONFIGURATION SECTION.
      SOURCE-COMPUTER. ABC-480.
      OBJECT-COMPUTER. ABC-480.
*
      INPUT-OUTPUT SECTION.
      FILE-CONTROL.
          SELECT INPUT-FILE  ASSIGN TO CARD.
          SELECT SORT-FILE   ASSIGN TO SORTWK.
          SELECT SORTED-FILE ASSIGN TO PRINTER.
*
      DATA DIVISION.
*
      FILE SECTION.
      FD  INPUT-FILE LABEL RECORD OMITTED
                   DATA RECORD IS INPUT-RECORD.
*
      01  INPUT-RECORD.
          02  ACCOUNT-NUMBER    PIC 9(8).
          02  NAME              PIC X(20).
          02  TRANSACTION-DATE.
              03  DAY-OF-YEAR   PIC 999.
              03  YEAR          PIC 99.
          02  OTHER-DATA        PIC X(47).
*
      SD  SORT-FILE DATA RECORD IS SORT-RECORD.
*
      01  SORT-RECORD.
          02  ACCOUNT-NUMBER    PIC 9(8).
          02  NAME              PIC X(20).
          02  TRANSACTION-DATE.
              03  DAY-OF-YEAR   PIC 999.
              03  YEAR          PIC 99.
          02  OTHER-DATA        PIC X(47).
*
      FD  SORTED-FILE LABEL RECORD OMITTED
              DATA RECORD IS SORTED-RECORD.
*
      01  SORTED-RECORD         PIC X(80).
*
```

FIGURE 11-1
SORT Program for Example 1,
Including Sample Input and
Output (continued)

```
       PROCEDURE DIVISION.
     *
       000-SORTING-PARAGRAPH.
           SORT SORT-FILE
     *
               ON ASCENDING KEY ACCOUNT-NUMBER OF SORT-RECORD
                  DESCENDING KEY YEAR OF SORT-RECORD
     *
               USING INPUT-FILE
     *
               GIVING SORTED-FILE.
     *
           STOP RUN.

     INPUT FILE

     99881111NAME1        10080
     88772222NAME2        20076
     99873333NAME3        14580
     99874444NAME4        00380
     99985555NAME5        01076
     66789666NAME6        30076
     99887777NAME7        02284
     88888888NAME8        32284
     99999999NAME9        11180
     10000000NAME0        23380

     PROGRAM OUTPUT

     10000000NAME0        23380
     66789666NAME6        30076
     88772222NAME2        20076
     88888888NAME8        32284
     99873333NAME3        14580
     99874444NAME4        00380
     99881111NAME1        10080
     99887777NAME7        02284
     99985555NAME5        01076
     99999999NAME9        11180
```

INPUT-FILE, and qualification is used to differentiate between the two records in the SORT statement (ACCOUNT-NUMBER OF SORT-RECORD).

Finally, the SORTED-FILE record has been described as one field of 80 characters to illustrate one possible variation. Since the program is concerned only with the sorting of the file, there is no need to describe the specific fields in the records that constitute this file.

The relevant PROCEDURE DIVISION is simple and consists of just one paragraph. The SORT verb is very powerful in that the programmer need only specify the sort keys and the source and destination of the file records. The statement SORT SORT-FILE identifies the name of the file to be sorted—which should be the same file introduced by an SD entry in the DATA DIVISION. The ASCENDING KEY ACCOUNT-NUMBER OF SORT-RECORD clause specifies that the file is to be sorted in ascending ACCOUNT-NUMBER OF SORT-RECORD sequence. The DESCENDING KEY YEAR OF SORT-RECORD clause specifies that, within each ACCOUNT-NUMBER OF SORT-RECORD, we wish to sort in descending sequence with respect to the values contained in the YEAR OF SORT-RECORD field. Thus the following would be examples of an unsorted and a sorted file, respectively:

UNSORTED			SORTED	
ACCOUNT	YEAR		ACCOUNT	YEAR
237	1990		134	1992
134	1992		134	1991
345	1991		237	1990
134	1991		345	1991
345	1990		345	1990

The key written first in the SORT statement is the principal basis for the sort. Other keys are of decreasing sorting significance as we proceed from one to the next. Consider the following KEY clauses:

```
SORT ... ON
     ASCENDING KEY STATE-NAME
     ASCENDING KEY COUNTY-NAME
     ASCENDING KEY CITY-NAME
```

The order of listing of these clauses indicates that STATE-NAME is the principal basis for the sort. Put another way, CITY-NAME will be sorted within COUNTY-NAME, and COUNTY-NAME will be sorted within STATE-NAME. The fields used for the sort order are often referred to as *sort keys,* and the terms "major," "intermediate," and "minor" sort keys are used to describe multiple sort keys. Thus in the above example STATE-NAME is the major sort key, COUNTY-NAME is the intermediate sort key, and CITY-NAME is the minor sort key. Of course, if we have more than three sort keys, then this three-level terminology is not directly applicable.

Note that the sort keys are written according to the desired order of the sort, and not according to the order in which the keys appear in the record. For this example, it could very well be that the three fields used as sort keys are in the following physical order in the record: CITY-NAME, STATE-NAME, COUNTY-NAME, and there could even be other field definitions intervening between them.

The USING INPUT-FILE clause in Figure 11-1 specifies the file that is the source of the records, while the GIVING SORTED-FILE clause simply specifies the file on which the sort output is to be recorded. Finally, note that in the present example the programmer does not OPEN or CLOSE any of the three files involved. The use of the SORT verb automatically takes care of such procedures.

In the above example the whole function of the PROCEDURE DIVISION is to sort a file. This need not be the case. The SORT is simply one of the COBOL verbs and, as such, it comprises only one statement in the program. The following example illustrates the point:

```
IF  TIME-TO-SORT
    PERFORM ROUTINE-A
    SORT CUST-SORT-FILE
       ON ASCENDING KEY NAME
       USING CUSTOMER-SOURCE-FILE
```

```
          GIVING CUSTOMER-SORTED-FILE
       PERFORM ROUTINE-B
   ELSE
       PERFORM ROUTINE-C.
```

Example 2

We now illustrate use of the COBOL sort feature with a more complex data processing task. Suppose we want to read a set of records, add a field to each record to indicate its original sequential order, sort the file, store the sorted file, and print the sorted file. Figure 11-2 presents the COBOL program designed to accomplish this task, including sample input and output. Notice that there are four files, called INPUT-FILE, SORT-FILE, SORTED-FILE, and PRINT-FILE. DATA DIVISION entries follow the usual format, except for the use of SD to identify SORT-FILE as the sort file, as was the case in the preceding example. In the present example the WORKING-STORAGE SECTION is used to form the SEQUENCE-NUMBER.

Figure 11-3 presents the program logic in flowchart form. Comparing the SORT statement in the PROCEDURE DIVISION in Figure 11-2 with the flowchart, notice that even though the SORT statement is one statement in form, it consists of three executable steps in function. These three steps are

1. Execute the section identified by INPUT PROCEDURE IS.

2. Execute the SORT itself.

3. Execute the section identified by OUTPUT PROCEDURE IS.

In the PROCEDURE DIVISION we first specify that we wish to sort the SORT-FILE on ASCENDING KEY NAME OF SORT-RECORD. Thus the NAME field is the sort key. INPUT PROCEDURE IS 100-READING-SEQUENCING indicates that records will become available to the SORT-FILE according to instructions contained in a section called 100-READING-SEQUENCING. A *section* is a group of paragraphs that can be referenced as a group. To declare the beginning of a section, we give it a name followed by the keyword SECTION and a period. In the example in Figure 11-2 we can see 100-READING-SEQUENCING SECTION.

The first paragraph in the 100-READING-SEQUENCING SECTION, called 110-INPUT-SET-UP, serves to open the INPUT-FILE as input. Then we enter a loop involving the 130-SEQ-RELEASE paragraph. Each record is read, and in each case a four-digit sequence number is assigned to the field called DATA-TO-BE-INSERTED:

```
ADD 1 TO SEQUENCE-NUMBER
MOVE SEQUENCE-NUMBER TO DATA-TO-BE-INSERTED.
```

Then we use the RELEASE SORT-RECORD FROM INPUT-RECORD statement. This simply says to move the contents of INPUT-RECORD to SORT-RECORD and then to write the SORT-RECORD on its file. The RELEASE command can be thought of as a specialized form of the WRITE instruction. If we are writing a record into a file that has been declared with SD rather than the usual FD descriptor, we use the specialized RELEASE verb to do the "write" function. Of course, we use RELEASE only in a section referenced with the INPUT PROCEDURE of the SORT statement. So the analogy between RELEASE and WRITE exists, but they cannot be used interchangeably.

The loop terminates when the last record is read, at which point the program branches to 140-END-OF-INPUT-SECTION, after INPUT-FILE is closed. The 140-END-OF-INPUT-SECTION paragraph is the last paragraph of the 100-READING-SEQUENCING SECTION, and is indicated by the EXIT verb. Recall that

FIGURE 11-2

Sort Program for Example 2, Including Sample Input and Output

```
*
 IDENTIFICATION DIVISION.
 PROGRAM-ID. SORT2.
*
 ENVIRONMENT DIVISION.
*
 CONFIGURATION SECTION.
 SOURCE-COMPUTER. ABC-480.
 OBJECT-COMPUTER. ABC-980.
*
 INPUT-OUTPUT SECTION.
*
 FILE-CONTROL.
     SELECT INPUT-FILE ASSIGN TO CARDS.
*
     SELECT SORT-FILE ASSIGN TO SORTWK.
*
     SELECT SORTED-FILE ASSIGN TO SORTOUT.
*
     SELECT PRINT-FILE ASSIGN TO PRINTER.
*
 DATA DIVISION.
 FILE SECTION.
*
 FD  INPUT-FILE LABEL RECORD OMITTED
     DATA RECORD IS INPUT-RECORD.
 01  INPUT-RECORD.
     02  FILLER                 PIC X(10).
     02  NAME                   PIC X(15).
     02  FILLER                 PIC X(51).
     02  DATA-TO-BE-INSERTED    PIC 9999.
*
 SD  SORT-FILE DATA RECORD IS SORT-RECORD.
 01  SORT-RECORD.
     02  FILLER                 PIC X(10).
     02  NAME                   PIC X(15).
     02  FILLER                 PIC X(55).
*
 FD  SORTED-FILE LABEL RECORD STANDARD
     BLOCK CONTAINS 77 RECORDS
     DATA RECORD IS SORTED-RECORD.
*
 01  SORTED-RECORD             PIC X(80).
*
 FD  PRINT-FILE LABEL RECORD OMITTED
     DATA RECORD IS PRINT-LINE.
*
 01  PRINT-LINE               PIC X(132).
*
 WORKING-STORAGE SECTION.
*
 01  END-OF-DATA              PIC XXX.
*
```

FIGURE 11-2

Sort Program for Example 2, Including Sample Input and Output (continued)

```
 01  SEQUENCE-NUMBER              PIC 9(4) VALUE ZEROS.
*
 PROCEDURE DIVISION.
*
 000-MAIN-SORT-ROUTINE.
     MOVE ZERO TO SEQUENCE-NUMBER.
*
     SORT SORT-FILE ASCENDING KEY NAME OF SORT-RECORD
*
         INPUT  PROCEDURE IS 100-READING-SEQUENCING
*
         OUTPUT PROCEDURE IS 200-RETURNING-PRINTING.
 STOP RUN.
*
 100-READING-SEQUENCING SECTION.
 110-INPUT-SET-UP.
     OPEN INPUT INPUT-FILE.
     MOVE 'NO' TO END-OF-DATA.
*
     PERFORM 120-READ-DATA
*
     PERFORM 130-SEQ-RELEASE
         UNTIL END-OF-DATA = 'YES'
     CLOSE INPUT-FILE
     GO TO 140-END-OF-INPUT-SECTION.
*
 120-READ-DATA.
     READ INPUT-FILE RECORD
        AT END MOVE 'YES' TO END-OF-DATA.
*
 130-SEQ-RELEASE.
     ADD 1 TO SEQUENCE-NUMBER.
     MOVE SEQUENCE-NUMBER TO DATA-TO-BE-INSERTED.
*
     RELEASE SORT-RECORD FROM INPUT-RECORD.
*
     PERFORM 120-READ-DATA.
*
 140-END-OF-INPUT-SECTION.
     EXIT.
*
 200-RETURNING-PRINTING SECTION.
 210-OUTPUT-SET-UP.
     OPEN OUTPUT SORTED-FILE
                 PRINT-FILE
     MOVE 'NO' TO END-OF-DATA
*
     PERFORM 220-RETURN-DATA
*
     PERFORM 230-WRITE-DATA
         UNTIL END-OF-DATA ='YES'.
     CLOSE SORTED-FILE PRINT-FILE
     GO TO 240-END-OF-OUTPUT-SECTION.
```

FIGURE 11-2

Sort Program for Example 2,
Including Sample Input and
Output (continued)

```
*
   220-RETURN-DATA.
       RETURN SORT-FILE RECORD INTO SORTED-RECORD
             AT END MOVE 'YES' TO END-OF-DATA.
*
   230-WRITE-DATA.
       WRITE PRINT-LINE FROM SORTED-RECORD
       WRITE SORTED-RECORD.
*
       PERFORM 220-RETURN-DATA.
*
   240-END-OF-OUTPUT-SECTION.
       EXIT.
```

INPUT FILE

```
NAME-1
NAME-2
NAME-3
ANDERSON
JOHNSON
SMITH
ADAMS
LILAC
BROWN
```

PROGRAM OUTPUT

```
ADAMS                 0007
ANDERSON              0004
BROWN                 0009
JOHNSON               0005
LILAC                 0008
NAME-1                0001
NAME-2                0002
NAME-3                0003
SMITH                 0006
```

the execution of the 100-READING-SEQUENCING SECTION was initiated by execution of the INPUT PROCEDURE statement in the SORT statement. In fact, the INPUT PROCEDURE statement has the same effect as if we had written PERFORM 100-READING-SEQUENCING. Program execution branches to that section, and, when it is completed, the next statement is executed. The next statement in the present example is the sorting operation itself, as illustrated in the flowchart of Figure 11-3, which depicts the chronological order of execution.

After the sorting has been completed, the statement executed next is OUTPUT PROCEDURE IS 200-RETURNING-PRINTING. Thus program execution proceeds to the 200-RETURNING-PRINTING SECTION.

The first paragraph of the 200-RETURNING-PRINTING SECTION is the 210-OUTPUT-SET-UP, which opens two output files. Then we PERFORM

FIGURE 11-3

Flowchart Representation of
Sample SORT Program

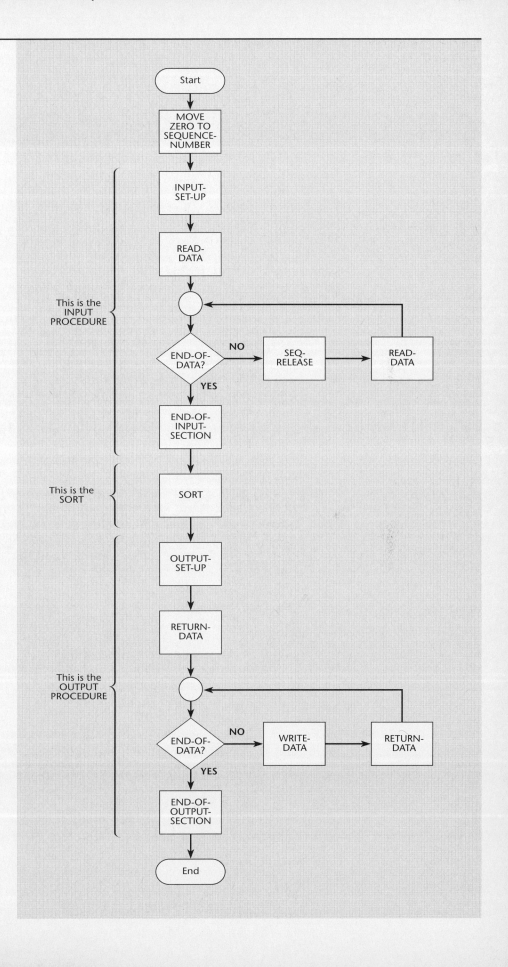

220-RETURN-DATA and enter a loop involving 230-WRITE-DATA. The RETURN SORT-FILE RECORD INTO SORTED-RECORD statement is simply a special form of saying, "Read a record from the SORT-FILE and move it to the SORTED-RECORD." Notice the use of AT END, which parallels the same clause in the READ verb. After each record is RETURNed, we employ an implicit move (FROM SORTED-RECORD) and we WRITE PRINT-LINE. It should be emphasized that use of the RETURN ... INTO option is not required. The RETURN, just like the READ, allows for use of the INTO option as a shorthand way of saying MOVE SORT-RECORD TO SORTED-RECORD. In the sample program we happened to choose to so move each record read from the file containing the sorted records to the record of a file that we called SORTED-FILE. If we had not used the INTO option, the 230-WRITE-DATA paragraph would have been:

```
230-WRITE-DATA.
    WRITE PRINT-LINE FROM SORT-RECORD
    WRITE SORTED-RECORD FROM SORT-RECORD.
```

The RETURN, exactly like the READ, transfers a record from the file to the record area. In this case SORT-RECORD is the record area for the file involved in the SORT.

Notice in the 230-WRITE-DATA paragraph that we WRITE twice. This is so because we wanted to write the sorted records onto two files. The first time we write to the printer (WRITE PRINT-LINE FROM SORTED-RECORD), and the second time we write onto the SORTED-FILE, which will be the sorted file.

The process of reading a record and writing it on the printer and the sorted file is repeated until the END-OF-DATA = 'YES' condition holds. Then we close the files and GO TO 240-END-OF-OUTPUT-SECTION, which is the end of the section, and we execute the no-op instruction EXIT.

When the EXIT has been executed, we have finished the 200-RETURNING-PRINTING SECTION, and program control then returns to the statement that follows the statement, OUTPUT PROCEDURE IS 200-RETURNING-PRINTING. The statement in question is STOP RUN and signifies the logical end of the program.

Thus, in this example we have demonstrated that, by using the INPUT PROCEDURE and the OUTPUT PROCEDURE options of the SORT verb, we can specify the procedure to be executed both before the sort takes place and after the sort takes place. Within these procedures we can execute any COBOL statements, but in addition we must use two specialized I/O verbs:

1. When data are ready to be written onto the sort file (the one with the SD level indicator), we use the RELEASE instead of the WRITE verb.

2. When data are ready to be read from the sort file, we use the RETURN instead of the READ verb.

You may question why the SORT statement was written with this second format. We could reason that if we want to execute some procedure before and/or after the data are sorted, we could do something like the following:

```
PERFORM INPUT-PROC
SORT file-name-1 ASCENDING KEY key-name
    USING file-name-2
    GIVING file-name-3
PERFORM OUTPUT-PROC.
```

In the above example we assume that INPUT-PROC executes some procedure that generates the presorted data in file-name-2. We SORT ... USING file-name-2 and obtain the sorted output in file-name-3 (GIVING file-name-3). Then the OUTPUT-PROC can execute whatever procedure we want to do with the sorted output.

The above approach is correct, but it has the disadvantage that it will consume more I/O processing time than the use of the INPUT PROCEDURE and OUTPUT PROCEDURE options included in Figure 11-2. In the above approach we read the input file once in INPUT-PROC and then read it a second time during the USING file-name-2 routine. Also, the sorted data are read and possibly written twice, once during the GIVING phase, and a second time during the OUTPUT-PROC. In summary, the example in Figure 11-2 has the advantage that the INPUT PROCEDURE is executed while the data are being transferred from the source file to the sort file. Similarly, the OUTPUT PROCEDURE is executed while the data are transferred from the sort file.

We should also point out that we can mix these options, as in

```
SORT ...
    USING file-name
    OUTPUT PROCEDURE IS procedure-name.
```

In this example we combined USING and OUTPUT PROCEDURE. The fourth, and last, alternative would be to use INPUT PROCEDURE and GIVING.

R E V I E W . . . .

1. The COBOL language feature by which a file can be sorted without having to write a sorting algorithm as such is called the COBOL _____ feature.

   sort

2. In order to use the sort feature, the programmer must specify the _____ to be sorted and the _____ to be used as the basis for the sort.

   file; key (or keys)

3. If a file is to be sorted on the basis of more than one key, the key that is written [first / last] is the principal basis for the sort.

   first

4. In the second example problem in this section two options of the SORT verb were used to branch to other parts of the program to perform required processing tasks. These were the _____ and _____ options of the SORT verb.

   INPUT PROCEDURE; OUTPUT PROCEDURE

. . . .

DATA DIVISION FORMAT SPECIFICATIONS

In the DATA DIVISION the relevant format associated with use of the sort feature is presented in Figure 11-4.

The level indicator SD identifies the beginning of a sort file sort description. Notice that, other than the SD, the file description has the usual format, except that there is no LABEL RECORD nor BLOCK CONTAINS option. Whether or not any blocking is possible or desirable is determined automatically by the preprogrammed sort routine.

The first two options of the RECORD clause are applicable only in the 1985 version of COBOL. The RECORD CONTAINS integer-1 CHARACTERS specifies fixed-length records, while the RECORD IS VARYING IN SIZE ... specifies

FIGURE 11-4
SORT File Description Entry

SD file-name-1

$$\left[\text{RECORD} \left\{ \begin{array}{l} \text{CONTAINS integer -1 CHARACTERS} \\ \text{IS } \underline{\text{VARYING}} \text{ IN SIZE} \\ \quad [\ [\text{FROM integer -2}] \ [\underline{\text{TO}} \text{ integer -3}] \text{ CHARACTERS }] \\ \quad [\ [\underline{\text{DEPENDING}} \text{ on data-name-1}] \\ \text{CONTAINS } [\text{ integer -4 } \underline{\text{TO}}] \text{ integer -5 CHARACTERS} \end{array} \right\} \right]$$

$$\left[\underline{\text{DATA}} \left\{ \begin{array}{l} \underline{\text{RECORD}} \text{ IS} \\ \underline{\text{RECORDS}} \text{ ARE} \end{array} \right\} \{\text{data-name-2}\} \ldots \right]$$

variable-length records. In the 1974 version of the language, variable-length records are specified by RECORD CONTAINS integer-4 to integer-5 CHARACTERS.

Note that in Figure 11-4 both the RECORD and the DATA clauses are optional. Usually the function of the RECORD clause is embedded in the sort routine itself, while the DATA clause is always optional.

PROCEDURE DIVISION FORMAT SPECIFICATIONS

The SORT verb is the basic verb in the COBOL sort feature. The format is presented in Figure 11-5.

The verb SORT always is required. File-name-1 is the file designated in an SD entry in the DATA DIVISION. At least one KEY must be specified. If more than one sort key is used and several are ascending (or descending), they can be written in the following form:

```
SORT file-name ON ASCENDING KEY ACCOUNT, NAME, YEAR
                DESCENDING KEY AMOUNT, REGION.
```

Here we have specified an ascending sort by ACCOUNT, by NAME within AC-COUNT, and by YEAR within NAME. Or, we could have used the word ASCEND-ING (or DESCENDING) in conjunction with each KEY, as follows:

```
SORT file-name ON ASCENDING KEY ACCOUNT
                ON ASCENDING KEY NAME (etc.)
```

The COLLATING SEQUENCE clause is a seldom used one that allows the programmer to specify whether the data in the file to be sorted are to be ordered according to a special "alphabet" or collating sequence. Chapter 16 provides some additional discussion on the subject of alphabet-names.

The WITH DUPLICATES IN ORDER clause can be used to specify that if there are records with duplicate sort-keys, they should be kept in their original order with respect to each other. Thus, if the source file contains ten records whose name-field contains SMITH, these ten records will be in their original order relative to each other.

The INPUT PROCEDURE and the OUTPUT PROCEDURE options refer to a *section-name* in the 1974 standard. In the 1985 standard they can be paragraph-names *or* section-names, thus allowing for greater flexibility. In the example in Figure 11-2 we used the section choice, and as a result we had to use the GO TO verb to reach the end-paragraph in the section. The 1985 version allows us to eliminate the END-OF-INPUT-SECTION and the END-OF-OUTPUT-SECTION types

FIGURE 11-5
The SORT Statement

SORT file-name-1

$$\left\{ ON \left\{ \begin{array}{l} \underline{ASCENDING} \\ \underline{DESCENDING} \end{array} \right\} KEY \{data\text{-}name\text{-}1\} \ldots \right\} \ldots$$

[COLLATING SEQUENCE IS alphabet-name-1]

[WITH DUPLICATES IN ORDER]

$$\left\{ \begin{array}{l} \underline{INPUT\ PROCEDURE}\ IS \left\{ \begin{array}{l} section\text{-}name\text{-}1 \\ procedure\text{-}name\text{-}1 \end{array} \right\} \left[\left\{ \begin{array}{l} \underline{THROUGH} \\ \underline{THRU} \end{array} \right\} \left\{ \begin{array}{l} section\text{-}name\text{-}2 \\ procedure\text{-}name\text{-}2 \end{array} \right\} \right] \\ \underline{USING}\ [file\text{-}name\text{-}2] \ldots \end{array} \right\}$$

$$\left\{ \begin{array}{l} \underline{OUTPUT\ PROCEDURE}\ IS \left\{ \begin{array}{l} section\text{-}name\text{-}3 \\ procedure\text{-}name\text{-}3 \end{array} \right\} \left[\left\{ \begin{array}{l} \underline{THROUGH} \\ \underline{THRU} \end{array} \right\} \left\{ \begin{array}{l} section\text{-}name\text{-}4 \\ procedure\text{-}name\text{-}4 \end{array} \right\} \right] \\ \underline{GIVING}\ [file\text{-}name\text{-}3] \ldots \end{array} \right\}$$

of paragraphs as well as the two GO TO statements in Figure 11-2. In the 1974 version the only way to avoid use of GO TO is to make all paragraphs as sections.

The THRU option is used to specify a *range* of paragraphs.

The section or paragraph referenced by the INPUT PROCEDURE specifies the processing tasks to be performed prior to the sort, while OUTPUT PROCEDURE specifies the processing to be done after the sorting has been completed and the sorted data are in the file referenced in the SORT statement.

If the INPUT PROCEDURE is used, the verb RELEASE must be used somewhere in that procedure. If the OUTPUT PROCEDURE is used, the verb RETURN must be used somewhere in that procedure. The USING file-name-2 option in Figure 11-5 is used when records are made available to the sort from file-name-2 without any processing. The GIVING file-name-3 option specifies that the sorted file is to be recorded on file-name-3.

The RELEASE Verb

The general format of the RELEASE IS

RELEASE record-name [FROM identifier]

The RELEASE verb can be used only in a procedure referenced by the INPUT PROCEDURE. The record-name in this format refers to a record in the sort file. If the FROM option is used, it resembles the WRITE ... FROM. The effect is to move the contents of identifier to the record-name and then to RELEASE. In effect, RELEASE is a specialized form of the WRITE verb.

The RETURN Verb

The RETURN verb, which is used in conjunction with the OUTPUT PROCEDURE of the SORT verb, has the format presented in Figure 11-6.

The RETURN verb has the effect of a READ verb. The file-name is the name of the sort file. When the INTO option is used, the effect is the same as execution

FIGURE 11-6
The RETURN Statement

RETURN file-name-1 RECORD [INTO identifier]

    AT END imperative -statement -1

    [NOT AT END imperative -statement -2]

    [END-RETURN]

of the two statements RETURN file-name and MOVE record-name TO identifier. The AT END clause is required.

Note that the NOT AT END and the END-RETURN options in the RETURN statement are available only in the 1985 standard. These options can be used for handling conditionals more easily. For example, we could modify the 200-RETURNING-PRINTING SECTION of Figure 11-2 as follows (including omission of the SECTION requirement):

```
          .
          .
          .
       OUTPUT PROCEDURE IS 200-RETURNING-PRINTING
          .
          .
          .
     200-RETURNING-PRINTING.
         OPEN OUTPUT SORTED-FILE
                     PRINT-FILE
         MOVE 'NO' TO END-OF-DATA
         PERFORM 220-RETURN-DATA
             UNTIL END OF DATA = 'YES'.
         CLOSE SORTED-FILE
               PRINT-FILE.
     220-RETURN-DATA.
         RETURN SORT-FILE RECORD INTO SORTED-RECORD
             AT END
                 MOVE 'YES' TO END-OF-DATA
             NOT AT END
                 WRITE PRINT-LINE FROM SORTED-RECORD
                 WRITE SORTED-RECORD
         END-RETURN.
```

Notice that OUTPUT PROCEDURE makes reference to a paragraph, thus avoiding the need to use a GO TO statement to reach the end of the section, as in Figure 11-2. Also, the END-RETURN is not necessary. However, if we wanted to execute a statement regardless of the outcome of the AT END condition test, we would need to use the END-RETURN scope terminator so that the statement(s) that follow the END-RETURN are executed unconditionally.

R E V I E W . . . .

1. In the DATA DIVISION the file to be sorted is identified by the level indicator
    _____.

2. The option of specifying a variable-length record depending on a data-name in the sort description is available only in the [1974 version / 1985 version] of COBOL.

1985 version

3. If the INPUT PROCEDURE option is used in conjunction with the SORT verb, designated processing is performed [before / after] the sort, and the verb _____ must be used somewhere in the procedure.

before; RELEASE

4. If the OUTPUT PROCEDURE option is used in conjunction with the SORT verb, designated processing is performed [before / after] the sort, and the verb _____ must be used somewhere in the procedure.

after; RETURN

5. In COBOL '74 the subject of INPUT PROCEDURE and OUTPUT PROCEDURE must be a section-name. In COBOL '85 it can be either a section-name or a _____.

paragraph-name

6. The RELEASE verb can be considered a specialized form of the _____ verb, while the RETURN verb can be considered a form of the _____ verb.

WRITE; READ

7. In order to handle conditionals more easily, the NOT AT END and the END-RETURN options can be used in a RETURN statement that utilizes the [1974 version / 1985 version] of COBOL.

1985 version

• •

FILE MERGING

Essentially, *merging* refers to the process by which two or more sorted files are combined to form one file. Merging is often a required step in the process of sorting. Merging is also often used simply to combine two or more presorted files. For example, the sales transactions in a department store might be processed on a daily basis, thus creating a daily sales tape sorted by item number. Then, at the end of each week it may be desirable to merge the several daily tapes to form a weekly sales tape for batch processing use. The procedure of combining the several daily tapes to form one weekly tape exemplifies the merging process.

The simplest case of merging is the one in which there are two sorted files A and B, and they are merged to form one file. The process consists of reading a record from each input file, comparing the two records, and writing the "smaller" of the two onto the output file, based on a reference, or "sort key," field. Then another record is read from the file that supplied the last smaller record, and the comparison is repeated. To illustrate the procedure, consider these two input files:

```
File A:  12   15   22
File B:  13   14   20   30
```

Merging these two files involves initially reading records 12 and 13, one from each file. The smaller record, 12, is written onto the output file C, and another record is read from file A. Next, records 15 and 13 are being compared. The 13 record is written onto C and the 14 record is read in from B. The 14 record goes to C and

20 record is read. The process continues until all records have been read in from both files, forming the merged file C:

File C: 12   13   14   15   20   22   30.

Suppose, however, that *five* daily transaction files are to be merged to form one weekly file. In such a case the process of merging requires a more complex logic. In each comparison five records are involved, one from each respective daily file, and the smallest of the five is to be written on the output file. The flowchart in Figure 11-7 indicates the essential logic of the comparisons that are required to find the smallest record. In this figure, A, B, C, D, and E are the five records from the five input files. File F is the output file. Notice that the process described in Figure 11-7 ignores end-of-file conditions to keep the illustration simple.

When merging multiple files on magnetic tape, the number of tape drives available is an important factor. In general, we prefer to use all available drives, since merging is more efficient with a greater number of tape drives. Still, when the number of files is larger than the number of tape drives, we may have to choose the right merging sequence to avoid unnecessary processing. For example, suppose that we have 12 files to be merged. These files are identified by the letters A through L in Figure 11-8. If four tape drive units are available, three units would be used for input and one would be used for output. As illustrated in Figure 11-8, in such a case we could merge A, B, and C to form file 1, D, E, and F to form file 2, and G, H, and I to form file 3. Next we could merge files J and K to form file 4. Then files 3, 4, and L can be merged to form file 5, and finally, files 1, 2, and 5 can be merged to form file 6.

An alternative way of merging the 12 files, which is not as efficient, would be to merge files J, K, and L to form one file, as illustrated in Figure 11-9. Notice, however, that this alternative merging procedure would take longer to accomplish. To see this, let us count the number of file passes that are required by each approach. By *file pass* we mean the process of inputting and merging the contents of a file with the contents of one or more other files. Thus, by the procedure portrayed in Figure 11-9, the formation of files 1, 2, 3, and 4 requires 3 file passes each. The formation of file 5 requires 9 file passes because the contents of 9 original input files are involved. Similarly, the formation of file 6 requires 12 file passes. Thus, in total 33 file passes are required to merge the files by the procedure portrayed in Figure 11-9.

However, by the procedure portrayed in Figure 11-8 only 29 file passes are required. As it happens, given the 12 input files and four tape units, the 29 file passes associated with the procedure in Figure 11-8 is the optimum result. A computational procedure, or algorithm, is available to determine the optimum merge configuration, given the number of files to be merged and the tape units available. The algorithm is included in most merge program packages, so that its application is automatic without the user having to determine the optimum merging routine for each situation.

Frequently, the files to be merged are not stored on magnetic tape. Rather, it may be that designated disk areas constitute files. In such a case the limitation of the number of available input-output units does not apply and the need to merge, say, 20 files could conceivably be accomplished by one merge operation.

R E V I E W . . . .

1. When two or more sequential files are combined to form one sequential file, the process is called _____.

merging

FIGURE 11-7

Flowchart for the Process of Merging Five Files

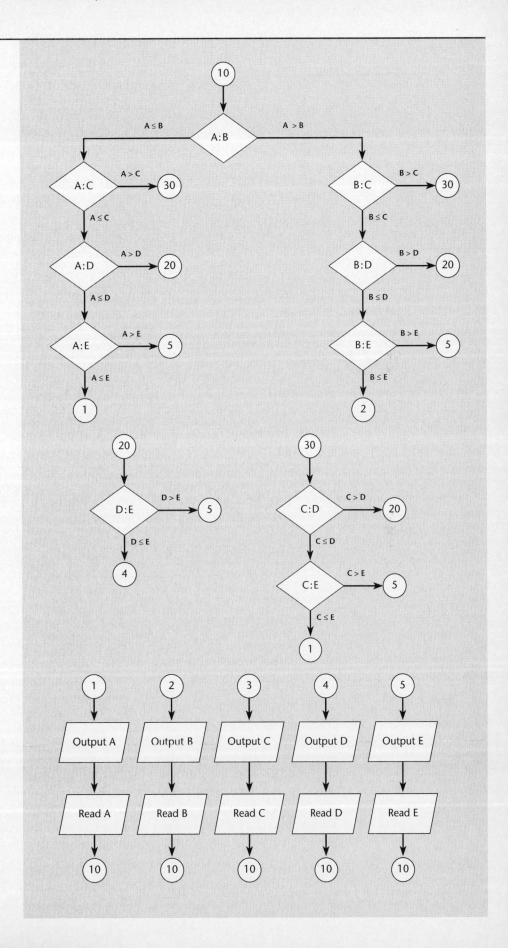

FIGURE 11-8

Schematic Diagram for the Process of Merging 12 Tape Files by the Use of Four Tape Transport Units

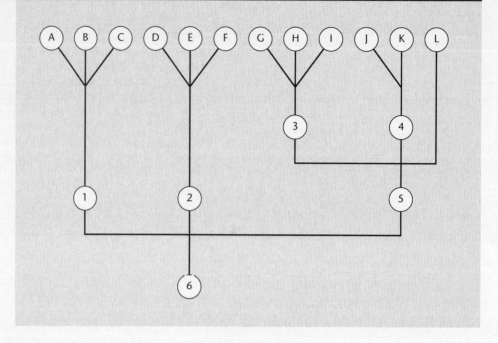

FIGURE 11-9

Schematic Diagram for an Alternative Way of Merging 12 Tape Files by the Use of Four Tape Transport Units

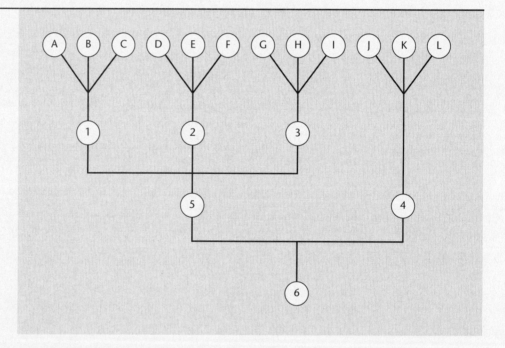

2. The simplest case of merging is the one in which _____ (number) files are merged.

    two

3. The optimum merge configuration to be used in merging several tape files generally is determined [by each user / by the merge program package].

    by the merge program package

FILE MERGING IN COBOL

Merging is implemented in COBOL as a very-high-level language feature, in the form of the MERGE statement.

Let us consider an example. A business firm generates a sales history file at the end of the quarter. Each record in the file contains a department number and a product number, as well as many other fields. This quarterly file is sorted, with department number being the major sort key and product number being the minor sort key. At the end of the year we are interested in merging the four quarterly sales history files into one. Figure 11-10 presents an outline of the

---

FIGURE 11-10

Outline for a MERGE Program

```
FD   FIRST-QUARTER LABEL RECORDS STANDARD
                      DATA RECORD   SALES-HISTORY.
01   SALES-HISTORY.
     02 DEPT-NO             PIC 999.
     02 PROD-NO             PIC 99999.
     .
     .
     .
FD   SECOND-QUARTER...
     .
     .
     .
FD   THIRD-QUARTER...
     .
     .
     .
FD   FOURTH-QUARTER...
     .
     .
     .
FD   YEARLY LABEL RECORDS STANDARD
          DATA RECORD   CUMULATIVE-SALES.
01   CUMULATIVE-SALES.
     02  DEPT-NO           PIC 999.
     02  PROD-NO           PIC 99999.
     .
     .
SD   MERGE-FILE DATA RECORD   MERGE-RECORD.
01   MERGE-RECORD.
     02  DEPARTMENT         PIC 999.
     02  PRODUCT            PIC 99999.
     .
     .

PROCEDURE DIVISION.
     .
     .
     .
     MERGE MERGE-FILE    ON ASCENDING KEY DEPARTMENT
                         ON ASCENDING KEY PRODUCT
          USING FIRST-QUARTER, SECOND-QUARTER,
                THIRD-QUARTER, FOURTH-QUARTER
          GIVING YEARLY.
```

relevant parts of the program. Four files are introduced with an FD entry, one for each quarter. The fifth FD entry is for the output file. Then the SD introduces the file to be used for the merge, which in this example is called MERGE-FILE. Notice that the data record description for this file corresponds to the record description of the four quarterly files. The MERGE statement in the PROCEDURE DIVISION references the SD file and specifies that the merge will proceed on the basis of DEPARTMENT being the major key and PRODUCT being the minor key. As is the case with the SORT verb, the keys decrease in significance in the order written. The ASCENDING option specifies that the next record of each of the four quarterly files will be examined; and the record sent to the output file next is the one that has the highest department number, or the highest product number if the department numbers are equal. If all four records have identical department and product values, then the records will be sent to the output file in the order in which the file names are written in the merge statement.

The USING clause specifies the files to be merged, which are the input files. These files must be closed at the time of merging. Opening is carried out by the MERGE statement implicitly.

The GIVING clause specifies the output file. This file will contain the combined set of the four quarterly files. This new file will be in the same sort order as the quarterly files. Note that in order for the merge process to take place correctly, the input files must be in the sort order indicated by the KEY specifications.

The general format of the MERGE statement is presented in Figure 11-11.

The OUTPUT PROCEDURE option parallels the one available with the SORT verb. A RETURN statement is used within the output procedure to make merged records available for processing, just as is the case with SORT. Unlike SORT, MERGE does not include any INPUT PROCEDURE options; thus the input files must be in proper form for merging before a MERGE instruction is executed.

R E V I E W . . . .

1. The COBOL language feature by which monthly summaries of transactions can be combined to create an annual summary is the _____ statement.

                                                                                                    MERGE

FIGURE 11-11
The MERGE Statement

<u>MERGE</u> file-name-1

$\left\{ \text{ON} \left\{ \begin{array}{l} \underline{\text{ASCENDING}} \\ \underline{\text{DESCENDING}} \end{array} \right\} \text{KEY } \{\text{data-name-1}\} \ldots \right\} \ldots$

[COLLATING <u>SEQUENCE</u> IS alphabet-name-1]

<u>USING</u> file-name-2 {file-name-3} . . .

$\left\{ \underline{\text{OUTPUT PROCEDURE}} \text{ IS} \left\{ \begin{array}{l} \text{section-name-1} \\ \text{procedure-name-1} \end{array} \right\} \left[\left\{ \begin{array}{l} \underline{\text{THROUGH}} \\ \underline{\text{THRU}} \end{array} \right\} \left\{ \begin{array}{l} \text{section-name-2} \\ \text{procedure-name-2} \end{array} \right\} \right] \right\}$

<u>GIVING</u> {file-name-4} . . .

2. If 12 monthly summaries are to be combined to form an annual summary, then in addition to the one SD entry, the number of FD entries required in the associated MERGE program is _____ (number).

13

3. In order for the merge process to take place correctly, it [is / is not] necessary that each input file be in the exact sort order indicated by the KEY specifications.

is

. . . .

SUMMARY

This chapter covered the general concepts and specialized COBOL statements for sorting and merging sequential files. The requirement that sequential files be sorted is pervasive. For example, it is the basis by which different types of reports, such as "by product" as contrasted to "by region" can be produced.

In the COBOL *sort feature,* the sorting procedure is preprogrammed. In the ENVIRONMENT DIVISION the source file, the file used for the sort, and the output file are assigned to hardware devices in the FILE-CONTROL paragraph of the INPUT-OUTPUT SECTION. In the DATA DIVISION the source and output files are described in the usual fashion, while the sort file is introduced with the special SD level indicator. In the PROCEDURE DIVISION the SORT verb incorporates the sort keys and the source and destination of the file records. The sort key written first is the principal basis for the sort (*major* key). Other keys are referred to as being *intermediate* and *minor* sort keys.

Two complete examples of sorting sequential files were presented. In the first a file was sorted in ascending sequence according to ACCOUNT-NUMBER and in descending order according to YEAR. In the second example the INPUT PROCEDURE and OUTPUT PROCEDURE options of the SORT verb were used to branch to other parts of the program to perform required processing tasks.

Following the above examples, detailed attention was given to the specific format specifications of the COBOL sort-associated statements. In the DATA DIVISION this included consideration of the options associated with the RECORD clause. In the PROCEDURE DIVISION this included consideration of the SORT statement and its options, and then of the RELEASE and RETURN verbs.

File merging is the process by which two or more sorted files are combined to form one file. Of course, the greater the number of files, the more complex is the merging operation. The MERGE verb is the specialized COBOL verb that is used for merging presorted sequential files. The example in the chapter showed how this verb can be used to merge four quarterly sales history files for the purpose of producing one cumulative sales file for the entire year.

EXERCISES

11.1 A sort file has been defined as SORT-FILE, and, in part, its DATA DIVISION entries include

```
02   DEPT-CODE          PIC X(3).
02   COURSE-NUMBER      PIC 99.
02   STUDENT-NAME       PIC X(6).
```

Using the following data, write a SORT statement that could cause the sorted data shown. The original data come from SOURCE-FILE, and we want to have the sorted data in SORTED-FILE. Be sure to specify which are the major, intermediate, and minor sort keys.

ORIGINAL DATA	SORTED DATA
CIS20BILL	MGT10BRENDA
CIS30LINDA	QBA10JILL
QBA10BRENDA	CIS20MARY
CIS30XAVIER	CIS20JOHN
MGT10JILL	CIS20BILL
CIS20JOHN	CIS30XAVIER
CIS20MARY	CIS30LINDA

11.2   A file contains data about students and has the following record format:

```
FIRST-NAME    PIC   X(10).
LAST-NAME     PIC   X(15).
YEAR          PIC   X(2).
MAJOR         PIC   X(3).
GPA           PIC   9V99.
```

Write a program to sort the file so that student records are in order by year of studies (YEAR) within major field of study (MAJOR) and in descending order of GPA. In addition, the sorted file must have a different format from the original file: the FIRST-NAME and LAST-NAME fields must be reversed:

```
LAST-NAME     PIC   X(15).
FIRST-NAME    PIC   X(10).
YEAR          PIC   X(2).
MAJOR         PIC   X(3).
GPA           PIC   9V99.
```

The sorted file is to be saved as a separate file as shown below:

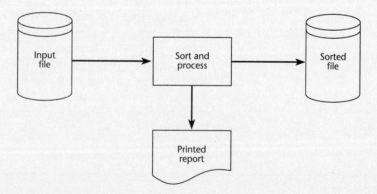

It is also desired to produce a report from the newly sorted file as presented in Figure 11-12. Use the sample data given in Figure 11-13 on page 354 as input for your program.

11.3   Using any data file available, write a program incorporating the COBOL sort feature to sort a file. For example, you could modify any of the exercises at the end of Chapter 10 to sort the master file or the transaction file in the required order.

FIGURE 11-12
Report Format for Exercise 11.2

```
MAJOR FIELD: XXX      (New page for each new field)

STUDENT NAME        YEAR      GPA       AVG. GPA

    L1      F1       FR       3.40
    L2      F2       FR       2.00
    L3      F3       FR       1.90
                                          2.43

    L4      F4       SO
                      .
                      .
                      .
                     JR
                      .
                      .
                      .
                     SR
                      .
                      .
                      .

AVG. GPA FOR XXX MAJOR FIELD = 9.99
```

11.4 Consider the following to be the contents of the four quarterly files discussed in the merging example in this chapter. Show the content of the output file.

FIRST QUARTER	SECOND QUARTER	THIRD QUARTER	FOURTH QUARTER
345 12345	123 00112	345 56111	931 00001
345 25936	987 56111		999 99999
619 01110			

11.5 Using any two sorted data files, write a program incorporating the MERGE feature to combine the two files into one file.

FIGURE 11-13

Sample Input Data for
Exercise 11.2

MAURICE	HOLLMAN	03CIS273
ADAM	LENHARDT	01ACC205
ROBERT	HAYWOOD	04MKT312
ALLAN	TEEGARDEN	05MGT400
JAMES	NORVELL	02F1N302
ROGER	WHITTIER	02F1N395
MARGARET	AKIN	05ACC295
CHRIS	NORTON	01ACC271
JIM	BEECHER	01CIS240
TOD	FORBES	03MGT362
FLOYD	MCNEELY	04ACC314
MICHAEL	DERKS	04MGT268
DEAN	WERNER	01MKT250
CORDELIA	MONTGOMERY	04MKT400
MAGGIE	WILSON	03F1N254
JACK	HOLT	02ACC267
LEONARD	LESMEISTER	02MGT332
DONALD	FAUBERT	04ACC348
WILLARD	FICKER	01F1N257
EDWARD	EASTON	03MKT260
MICHAEL	VOLRICH	02C1S378
RITA	SOLANO	02ACC400
BRYON	ELLIS	01F1N285
FRANCIS	QUIGLEY	04C1S395
CORNELIUS	CLAXTON	03F1N215
HERBERT	SCHAEFER	03MGT400
ROSELLA	MCGOWEN	04MKT390
LAURA	HOFSTATTER	03CIS268
GORDON	PETRIE	01FIN240
TRACY	ZIMMERMAN	03ACC272
EVELYN	RAGSDALE	02FIN278
SIDNEY	KRAMER	01MKT179
GIBSON	GORMAN	02MKT349
LINDSEY	YOUNGBLOOD	03MGT311
STANLEY	FORRESTER	04CIS329
ROBERT	UPDIKE	04FIN268
LESTER	CROWLEY	03ACC287
ELWOOD	ISAAC	01F1N305
MORRIS	JACOBY	02CIS298
JESSIE	LANGFORD	04MGT205
MERRILL	ORMSBEE	03CIS400

12

Single-Level Table Handling

IN THIS CHAPTER *you will learn the basic concepts and methods for processing tables of data. First you will study the specialized COBOL instructions that are used for defining tables and for manipulating data in such tables. Then two sample programs will be presented to provide illustrations of table handling.*

The function of the first program is to output a monthly sales forecast for the next several months. The function of the second program is to present graphic output in the form of a bar chart, using table-processing techniques.

INTRODUCTION

A table, like a file, is a collection of logically related entries. Examples are tax rates for different municipalities in a metropolitan area, commission rates for different product classes, and income tax rates for different levels of income and numbers of dependents. Such data are normally short enough to be placed in central storage and thus constitute a table. Table handling is fundamental to data processing. COBOL recognizes this fact and includes specialized instructions for table definition and manipulation.

**SUBSCRIPTING AND
THE OCCURS CLAUSE**

A great deal of the documentation in COBOL derives from the use of appropriate data-names, that is, names that provide a direct clue to the type of data contained in the named storage location. There are situations, however, when practicality dictates that we dispense with the use of such names. For example, suppose we are processing data on the average income per household in each of the 50 states in the United States. If we chose to name the average income for each state uniquely, we could have such data names as ALABAMA-INCOME, ALASKA-INCOME, and so on, for a total of 50 names. It is easy to imagine the problems that this practice would cause. For example, 50 MOVE statements would be required before the results could be printed.

The use of tables and subscripts is a programming feature that is particularly useful in such situations. A *table* is simply a set of values stored in consecutive storage locations and assigned one data-name. Reference to specific entries in the table is made by the use of the one name along with a subscript that identifies the location of the particular entry. Entries in a *single-level,* or *one-dimensional,* table are numbered sequentially 1, 2, 3, ... , on to the last. Thus, in our example of the average household income for the 50 states, imagine that we have a table of 50 entries. If the entries are arranged alphabetically and we wish to reference the average income for the third state, Arizona, the subscript will have a value of 3. Similarly, the subscripts for the last two states, Wisconsin and Wyoming, will be 49 and 50, respectively. Use of the OCCURS clause in conjunction with the PICTURE clause enables the programmer to set up tables so that reference can be made to entire tables or individual values in tables by means of subscripts. A DATA DIVISION entry involving an OCCURS clause includes the data-name assigned to the table, the number of levels or dimensions, the number of entries in each level, and the field characteristics of the entries.

A *level* or *dimension* (the terms are synonymous) in a table refers to a category of data. For instance, if a table contains sales data for each of five departments as one dimension and for the 12 months of the year as the other dimension, we have a two-dimensional table: the first level being department, and the second level being month. In this chapter we consider single-level tables only, such as the one for the average household income in the 50 states; in Chapter 18 we discuss two-level and higher-level tables.

Assume that the data for average income is contained in a WORKING-STORAGE table, although it could be a FILE SECTION table just as well. Thus we have

```
WORKING-STORAGE SECTION.
  .
  .
  .
01  STATE-INCOME-TABLE.
    02 AVERAGE-INCOME OCCURS 50 TIMES
                 PICTURE 9(6)V99.
```

The OCCURS 50 TIMES clause sets up a table in storage that has the conceptual structure portrayed in Figure 12-1. The 01 group-name STATE-INCOME-TABLE

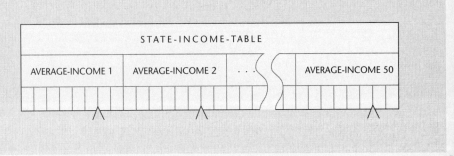

FIGURE 12-1
Conceptual Structure of a Table of Average Income by State

includes the entire set of 50 elementary data items that are defined at the 02 level. Execution of the statement

```
MOVE STATE-INCOME-TABLE TO FIELD-X
```

will result in the entire table of 50 fields being moved.

To reference a single field or entry in the table, a subscript is included in parentheses. For instance, the 12th occurrence of the average income value is referenced as follows:

```
MOVE AVERAGE-INCOME (12) TO ....
```

The subscript may be a variable instead of a constant, but it always must be a positive integer (whole number) with a value greater than zero. To illustrate the need for a subscript that is a variable, consider the following example. Suppose that source records have the following layout:

```
01   STATE-REC.
     02   STATE-NUMBER     PIC 99.
     02   INCOME           PIC 9(6)V99.
```

The value in columns 1–2 is a number assigned to each state signifying its alphabetical order. The value in columns 3–10 is the average household income for that state. The following statement can be used to insert the income value in the appropriate place in the table after the record has been read:

```
MOVE INCOME TO AVERAGE-INCOME (STATE-NUMBER).
```

As a result of this statement, if the state number were 49, the income value would be inserted in the forty-ninth entry of the average-income table.

The OCCURS clause can be written with any level-number item, except the 01 level. In other words, we cannot have a table of records. Of course, that is not a significant restriction, since we can use any level-number in the range 02 to 49, but it is a rule of the language that must be obeyed. Thus the minimum table definition will consist of two lines, as in

```
01   TABLE-GROUP-ITEM.
     02   TABLE OCCURS 10 TIMES PIC XXX.
```

The OCCURS clause need not be used alone in a record definition; other reference entries may be included as well. For example, the record might have been structured as follows:

```
01   STATE-INCOME-TABLE.
     02   AVERAGE-INCOME OCCURS 50 TIMES      PIC 9(6)V99.
     02   NATIONAL-AVERAGE                    PIC 9(6)V99.
```

Notice, however, that the all-encompassing group name STATE-INCOME-TABLE now refers to more than the table of 50 entries. If we want to make specific reference to the entire table of 50 entries, we will have to write something like this:

```
01   STATE-INCOME-TABLE.
     02   AV-TABLE.
          03 AVERAGE-INCOME OCCURS 50 TIMES
                          PIC 9(6)V99.
     02   NATIONAL-AVERAGE  PIC 9(6)V99.
```

As a further illustration of a single-level table, assume that we want to include the names of the states along with their corresponding average-income values:

```
01   STATE-INCOME-TABLE.
     02   NAME-INCOME OCCURS 50 TIMES.
          03 NAME         PIC X(12).
          03 INCOME       PIC 9(6)V99.
```

The OCCURS 50 TIMES clause sets up a table in storage that has the structure portrayed in Figure 12-2. Each NAME-INCOME is a group item consisting of the two elementary items NAME and INCOME. STATE-INCOME-TABLE refers to the entire table of 100 fields.

If we write NAME (1), we are referring to a storage field of 12 positions, whereas INCOME (1) refers to an 8-position field. If we write NAME-INCOME (1), we are referring to a storage field of 20 positions. Thus, when an OCCURS clause defines a table at the group level, either the group item or each of its subordinates may be subscripted. In the above example NAME-INCOME is the group item with the OCCURS clause, specifying that we want to define a table of 50 STATE-INCOME items. Since each STATE-INCOME is subdivided into two fields (NAME and INCOME), we must use a subscript to reference one of the 50 name values or one of the 50 income values.

A point to be made clear is that in the above example we have a *single-level table*. Each entry in the table happens to consist of two fields, but this is still a table of one level or category, the STATE-INCOME category. To have a two-level table, we need multiple occurrences nested within multiple occurrences. For example, if

FIGURE 12-2

Structure of a Table of Average Income that Includes State Names

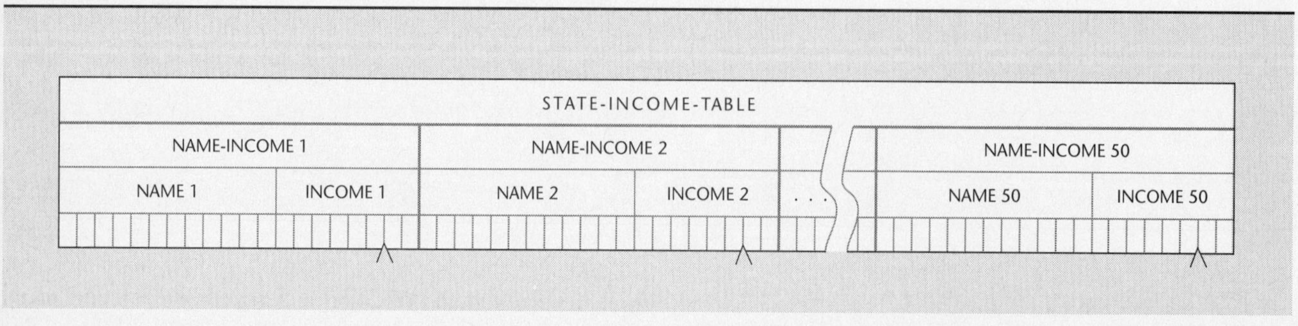

we had a table of 50 names and for each name we had, say, 12 monthly income values, then we would have a two-level table. Again, tables involving more than one level are the subject of Chapter 18.

R E V I E W . . . .

1. The programmer can set up tables by using the _____ clause in the DATA DIVISION.

    OCCURS

2. The OCCURS clause indicates the maximum number of _____ in the table.

    entries

3. Suppose a STATE-POPULATION-TABLE is to include the population figures for 50 states in alphabetical order. Complete the description below by writing the appropriate OCCURS clause. Assume that the PICTURE for POPULATION is 9(8).

    ```
    01 STATE-POPULATION-TABLE.
    _____
    ```

    ```
    02 POPULATION OCCURS 50 TIMES
                       PIC 9(8).
    ```

4. Suppose that both the state names and the population figures are read in and we wish to set up a STATE-POPULATION record such that the 50 state names are located first as a table, followed by the 50 population figures. Complete the following description, assuming that the PICTURE for NAME is X(12).

    ```
    01 STATE-POPULATION.
    _____
    _____
    ```

    ```
    02 NAME OCCURS 50 TIMES PIC X(12).
    02 POPULATION OCCURS 50 TIMES PIC 9(8).
    ```

5. The STATE-POPULATION record set up in the preceding question will have a total of _____ (number) fields.

    100

6. For the table in #4, above, suppose we wish to obtain data about Wyoming, which is the 50th state alphabetically. If we make reference to POPULATION (50), the storage field includes the [state name / state population / both state name and population].

    state population

7. For the record in #4, suppose we make reference to NAME-POPULATION (50). The storage field referenced is [the state name and population for Wyoming / one that has not been defined].

    one that has not been defined

8. The STATE-POPULATION description in #4 is an example of a [single-level / two-level] table.

    single-level

. . . .

READING VALUES INTO A TABLE

Let us suppose that we have defined a tax table to contain 10 deduction rates, thus:

```
01  TAX-TABLE.
    02 TAX-RATE OCCURS 10 TIMES    PIC V999.
```

We want to read in 10 values from a source file and store them in the above table. Assume that the source file is called RATE-FILE, and that the specific field containing the rate is called RATE. We will use a data-name, N, to specify the subscript value. Initially, we want to read the first record and store the value of RATE in the first cell of the TAX-TABLE. Then we want to increase the value of N and repeat the process, storing each newly read value in the Nth place of TAX-TABLE. The following PROCEDURE DIVISION entries can accomplish the rate-reading objective.

```
        MOVE 'NO' TO DATA-END
        MOVE 1 TO N
        PERFORM TABLE-READ UNTIL N > 10 OR DATA-END = 'YES'.
            .
            .
            .
    TABLE-READ.
        READ RATE-FILE RECORD AT END MOVE 'YES' TO DATA-END.
        IF DATA-END = 'YES'
           PERFORM NOT-ENOUGH-DATA
        ELSE
           MOVE RATE TO TAX-RATE (N)
           ADD 1 TO N.
    NOT-ENOUGH-DATA.
                (etc.)
```

Notice that we account for the possibility of fewer than 10 records in the input file, in which case we execute an error routine called NOT-ENOUGH-DATA.

ENTERING CONSTANT VALUES INTO A TABLE

It is often desirable to build tables that contain specified constant values. One way to accomplish this objective was illustrated in the example we just reviewed. We define the table by using the OCCURS clause in the DATA DIVISION and then read in the desired values through suitable PROCEDURE DIVISION instructions. This approach generally is used when there are a large number of constant values to be entered into the table or the values could change from time to time and we do not want to recompile the program every time the data changes. For small tables of constant values other approaches, as described in the following subsections, are commonly used.

Use of the REDEFINES Clause

Suppose that we want to have a table that contains the names of the 12 months of the year, so that we can reference these names by use of the table name and a subscript. For instance, we may want to reference the fifth month or the twelfth month, and so on. Using numeric values to reference the months is desirable, because arithmetic can be performed with numeric values. For instance, if we are on the sixth month and we want to reference the next month, we can simply add

1 to 6 and then make reference to the resulting month. The following example illustrates the common way of accomplishing this task:

```
01  MONTH-TABLE.
    02    FILLER    PICTURE X(9)  VALUE 'JANUARY  '.
    02    FILLER    PICTURE X(9)  VALUE 'FEBRUARY '.
    02    FILLER    PICTURE X(9)  VALUE 'MARCH    '.
    02    FILLER    PICTURE X(9)  VALUE 'APRIL    '.
    02    FILLER    PICTURE X(9)  VALUE 'MAY      '.
    02    FILLER    PICTURE X(9)  VALUE 'JUNE     '.
    02    FILLER    PICTURE X(9)  VALUE 'JULY     '.
    02    FILLER    PICTURE X(9)  VALUE 'AUGUST   '.
    02    FILLER    PICTURE X(9)  VALUE 'SEPTEMBER'.
    02    FILLER    PICTURE X(9)  VALUE 'OCTOBER  '.
    02    FILLER    PICTURE X(9)  VALUE 'NOVEMBER '.
    02    FILLER    PICTURE X(9)  VALUE 'DECEMBER '.
01  MONTHS REDEFINES MONTH-TABLE.
    02    MONTH PICTURE X(9) OCCURS 12 TIMES.
```

Notice that the record MONTH-TABLE consists of 12 equal-sized fields, with each field containing the name of a month. The VALUE clause is used to assign the constant (nonnumeric literal) values. The record called MONTHS is described by the use of the REDEFINES clause. MONTHS simply is an alternate definition of MONTH-TABLE. Thus both MONTHS and MONTH-TABLE are synonyms for the same storage area. The subject of REDEFINES is further discussed in Chapter 16. Here we use it for a limited, specific purpose. The data-name MONTH-TABLE is a field of 108 (12 x 9 = 108) bytes. Instead of the 12 FILLER definitions, we could have defined one long FILLER 108 bytes in size and given it a long literal value, as in

```
... VALUE 'JANUARY  FEBRUARY MARCH    APRIL ...'
```

Instead of such a long literal, we chose to divide the record into 12 fields corresponding to the twelve months.

MONTHS is also a field of the same 108 bytes because it is simply another name redefining the same field. But MONTHS has been subdivided into the table called MONTH, which OCCURS 12 TIMES and has a PIC of X(9). Therefore each of the PIC X(9) FILLER fields corresponds to one of the 12 table entries. Each entry can be referenced by the use of MONTH and a subscript. Thus, executing the instruction MOVE MONTH (3) TO PRINT-AREA WRITE PRINT-AREA results in the word MARCH being printed. A practical example is given later in this chapter, using the table of months.

Use of the VALUE Clause

Another approach that is available in both the 1974 and the 1985 versions of COBOL permits the entry of different constants into the different table positions. The technique involves use of the VALUE clause at a level superior to the OCCURS clause, as illustrated in the following example:

```
01  ALPHABET-TABLE  VALUE 'ABCDEFGHIJKLMNOPQRSTUVWXYZ'.
    02  LETTER OCCURS 26 TIMES PIC X.
```

By using the VALUE clause at the 01 level in the example above, we built a table of 26 cells, each cell containing a different letter of the alphabet.

If we want to fill a table with the same constant in all positions, there is a difference between the 1974 and 1985 standards. In the 1974 version of COBOL we *cannot* use the OCCURS and VALUE clauses to enter the same constant into all of the positions. However, in the 1985 version we can write

```
01   SAMPLE-TABLE.
     02  TABLE-CELL OCCURS 100 TIMES
                PIC 9(5)V99
                VALUE ZERO.
```

When the above program segment is compiled, each of the 100 fields in the table is set to zero. In the 1974 version, typically we would utilize the approach below, using the MOVE verb.

Use of the MOVE Verb

Another way of entering either the same or different constants into the various positions of a table is to reference the superior level of the OCCURS clause in an appropriate MOVE statement. For example, we could write

```
01   SAMPLE-TABLE.
     02  TABLE-CELL OCCURS 100 TIMES
                PIC 9(5)V99.
                .
                .
                .
     MOVE ZEROS TO SAMPLE-TABLE.
```

The MOVE statement fills the 700-byte SAMPLE-TABLE field with zeros. As a result, each of the 7-byte TABLE-CELL fields will also contain zero values.

Also, we can use the COBOL '85 INITIALIZE option:

```
INITIALIZE SAMPLE-TABLE.
```

The INITIALIZE would insert zeros into all numeric fields comprising the table.

As a final example of moving data to the group level, we could rewrite the alphabet example as

```
01   ALPHABET-TABLE.
     02  LETTER OCCURS 26 TIMES PIC X.
         .
         .
         .
     MOVE 'ABCDEFGHIJKLMNOPQRSTUVWXYZ' TO ALPHABET-TABLE.
```

As a result of executing the program segment above, each LETTER will contain one of the letters of the alphabet.

R E V I E W . . . .

1. One way of establishing a table of constant values without reading them in through PROCEDURE DIVISION statements is through use of the
    _____ clause in conjunction with the OCCURS option.

                                                                        REDEFINES

2. Another approach, by which only the same constant can be entered into all positions of the table, concerns use of the combination of the OCCURS and VALUE clauses. This approach is available only with the [1974 version / 1985 version] of COBOL.

    1985 version

3. A table may be filled with zeros or blanks, depending on its PIC description, using the COBOL '85 feature _____ .

    INITIALIZE

4. With both versions of COBOL, another way that the VALUE clause can be used, and which permits entry of different constants into different table positions, is to use the VALUE clause at a level [superior / subordinate] to the OCCURS clause.

    superior

5. The third approach for entering constants into a table, and by which either the same or different constants can be entered, is by use of the _____ verb.

    MOVE

. . . .

THE PERFORM VERB AND TABLE HANDLING

The PERFORM verb has already been discussed in several chapters. We now continue our study of the PERFORM verb by introducing additional formats and emphasizing the use of this verb for table-handling applications.

Beginning with an example, suppose that we have monthly sales data for the 12 months of the year, and we wish to compute the average monthly sales. The data have been stored in SALES-TABLE as follows:

```
01  SALES-TABLE.
    02  MONTHLY-SALES   PIC 9(6)V99 OCCURS 12 TIMES.
```

To compute the average monthly sales, we can write
```
        MOVE ZERO TO TOTAL-SALES
        MOVE ZERO TO N
        PERFORM SUMMATION 12 TIMES
        DIVIDE TOTAL-SALES BY 12 GIVING AVERAGE-SALES.
                .
                .
                .
    SUMMATION.
        ADD 1 TO N
        ADD MONTHLY-SALES (N) TO TOTAL-SALES.
```

Instead of an explicit reference, such as PERFORM ... 12 TIMES, we can use an identifier whose value is subject to change. For instance, the previous example could be modified by using K as the identifier that contains the number of months for which we want to compute a sales average:

```
        MOVE ZERO TO TOTAL-SALES
        MOVE ZERO TO N
        PERFORM SUMMATION K TIMES
        DIVIDE TOTAL-SALES BY K GIVING AVERAGE-SALES.
                .
                .
                .
```

```
SUMMATION.
    ADD 1 TO N
    ADD MONTHLY-SALES (N) TO TOTAL-SALES.
```

However, there is a format of the PERFORM verb that provides a more convenient way of processing data in tables. This format is presented in Figure 12-3.

It will be easier to understand the components of this version of PERFORM if we first consider an example. Let us take the example that we have been describing and rewrite those instructions, applying the PERFORM format:

```
MOVE ZERO TO TOTAL-SALES
PERFORM SUMMATION VARYING N FROM 1 BY 1
    UNTIL N > 12
    DIVIDE TOTAL-SALES BY 12 GIVING AVERAGE-SALES.
    .
    .
    .
SUMMATION.
    ADD MONTHLY-SALES (N) TO TOTAL-SALES.
```

The use of PERFORM ... VARYING allows us to execute an object paragraph or paragraphs while systematically varying an identifier. Of course, this identifier (in the above example, N) must have been defined in the DATA DIVISION. Most often, the identifier varied also is used as a subscript, as in this example; however, it could be used simply as a counter to control the number of executions of the object of the PERFORM verb. The flowchart in Figure 12-4 portrays the control logic involved in the execution of PERFORM with the VARYING option.

The WITH TEST BEFORE and WITH TEST AFTER options are available only in the 1985 standard. Omitting use of the WITH TEST ... clause defaults to the 1974 standard, which tests the UNTIL condition prior to each iteration. Use of WITH TEST AFTER tests the condition at the end of each iteration.

FIGURE 12-3
Format of the PERFORM ...
VARYING Statement

PERFORM [procedure -name -1 $\left[\begin{matrix} \text{THROUGH} \\ \text{THRU} \end{matrix} \right\}$ procedure -name -2]

$\left[\text{WITH} \underline{\text{TEST}} \left\{ \begin{matrix} \underline{\text{BEFORE}} \\ \underline{\text{AFTER}} \end{matrix} \right\} \right]$

$\underline{\text{VARYING}}$ identifier -1 $\underline{\text{FROM}} \left\{ \begin{matrix} \text{identifier -2} \\ \text{literal -1} \end{matrix} \right\}$

$\underline{\text{BY}} \left\{ \begin{matrix} \text{identifier -3} \\ \text{literal -2} \end{matrix} \right\} \underline{\text{UNTIL}}$ condition -1

[imperative -statement -1 $\underline{\text{END-PERFORM}}$]

Also, if no procedure-name is given, we have a 1985 version in-line PERFORM, as in the following:

```
MOVE ZERO TO TOTAL-SALES
PERFORM VARYING MONTH-NUMBER
                FROM 1  BY 1
                UNTIL MONTH-NUMBER > 12
     ADD MONTHLY-SALES (MONTH-NUMBER) TO TOTAL-SALES
END-PERFORM
DIVIDE TOTAL-SALES BY 12 GIVING AVERAGE-SALES.
```

It is worthwhile to consider some further examples to illustrate the potential of PERFORM ... VARYING. Let us say a home mortgage company issues a set of payment coupons at the beginning of each year. There are 12 coupons, numbered 1 to 12, each containing the name of the month in which the payment is due and the amount. What is required to prepare the coupons, then, is a repetitive execution (12 times) of a task with two variable factors: the coupon number (01 to 12) and the month-name. The amount of payment due will be the same for each of the months, and our present example is not concerned with the determination of this amount.

FIGURE 12-4

Flowchart Illustrating the Control Logic Associated with Using the VARYING Option with the PERFORM Verb

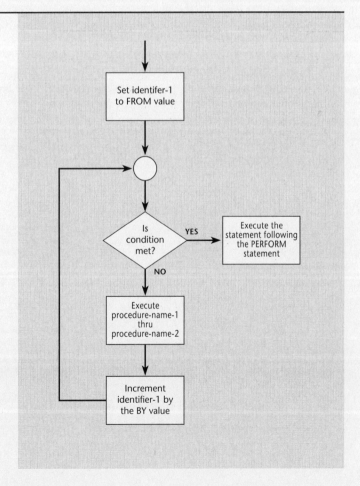

First, let us set up partial DATA DIVISION entries:

```
01  MONTH-NUMBER          PICTURE 99.
01  MONTHS-TABLE.
    02 MONTH              PICTURE X(9) OCCURS 12 TIMES.
01  COUPON-LINE.   (fillers omitted for simplicity)
    02 COUPON-NUMBER      PICTURE 99.
    02 MONTH-NAME         PICTURE X(9).
    02 EDITED-AMOUNT      PICTURE $$,$$9.99.
```

The MONTHS-TABLE will be filled with the names of the 12 months. Assume that the names are to be read from a file, the first record containing the name JANUARY and the twelfth record containing the name DECEMBER, in a field called IN-MONTH. The following PROCEDURE DIVISION program segment can be used to accomplish this task:

```
PERFORM MONTH-READING
    VARYING MONTH-NUMBER FROM 1 BY 1
    UNTIL MONTH-NUMBER > 12.
    .
    .
    .

MONTH-READING.
    READ MONTH-FILE RECORD
        AT END MOVE 'YES' TO END-OF-DATA.
    IF END-OF-DATA = 'YES'
        NEXT SENTENCE
    ELSE
        MOVE IN-MONTH TO MONTH (MONTH-NUMBER).
```

Once the 12 month-names have been entered in the MONTHS-TABLE by execution of the above program segment, the set of statements required to print the 12 coupons, each with a coupon number, month-name, and edited amount, can be written as

```
PERFORM COUPON-PRINTING
    VARYING COUPON-NUMBER FROM 1 BY 1
    UNTIL COUPON-NUMBER > 12.
    .
    .
    .

COUPON-PRINTING.
    MOVE MONTH (COUPON-NUMBER) TO MONTH-NAME.
    MOVE AMOUNT TO EDITED-AMOUNT.
    WRITE PRINT-LINE FROM COUPON-LINE.
```

Note that COUPON-NUMBER, which is varied by PERFORM, is used in three ways:

1. To control the number of executions

2. As the coupon number

3. As the subscript to retrieve the corresponding month-name from MONTHS-TABLE

It now is appropriate to review the overall procedure by which the VARYING option is carried out, as already outlined in the flowchart in Figure 12-4. The procedure is as follows:

1. The identifier to be varied is set at its initial value, the value indicated by the following clause:

$$\underline{FROM} \begin{Bmatrix} \text{identifier -2} \\ \text{literal} \end{Bmatrix}$$

2. If the 1974 standard is used, or the 1985 option WITH TEST BEFORE applies, a test is made to determine if the condition specified by UNTIL is met. If it is met, PERFORM is skipped and control passes to the next statement. If the condition is not met, then the paragraph(s) specified is(are) executed once.

3. The value of the varied identifier is incremented by the amount shown in the following clause:

$$\underline{BY} \begin{Bmatrix} \text{identifier -3} \\ \text{literal} \end{Bmatrix}$$

4. If the 1985 option WITH TEST AFTER is used, then a test is made to determine if the condition specified by UNTIL is met. If it is met, PERFORM is skipped and control passes to the next statement. If the condition is not met, then the paragraph(s) specified is(are) executed once and step 3 is repeated.

5. If the 1974 standard or the 1985 WITH TEST BEFORE is used, then the procedure in steps 2 and 3 is repeated.

The condition need not refer to the value of the identifier-1, which is varied, even though the examples given illustrate only such cases. The condition can refer to other identifiers, but in all cases it must refer to identifiers that have their values altered by the paragraphs under PERFORM control. Otherwise the loop will repeat indefinitely, as in the following example:

```
        MOVE 10 TO AMOUNT
        PERFORM ABC VARYING L FROM 1 BY 1
            UNTIL AMOUNT > 20.
    ABC.
        MOVE AMOUNT TO REPORT-LINE
        WRITE REPORT-LINE.
```

The problem with this segment is that, whereas the value of L is being incremented, the value of AMOUNT is being tested. Since AMOUNT never is altered by the ABC paragraph, there will be no end to the loop!

Now consider one more example that further illustrates use of the VARYING option and utilizes the STRING verb described in Chapter 7. Suppose that a header is to be centered with respect to column 40 of a printed page. The size of the header is variable, but it is always 20 or fewer characters long. The header is stored in the field called HEADER, and we wish to move it and print it from the output record called OUTPUT-RECORD.

Consider the following DATA and PROCEDURE DIVISION entries:

```
01  CHECK-FIELD          PIC X.
01  I                    PIC 99.
01  HEADER.
    02 INDIV-CHAR         PIC X OCCURS 20 TIMES.
    .
    .
    .
    MOVE SPACE TO CHECK-FIELD
    PERFORM DETERMINE-SIZE VARYING I FROM 20 BY -1
            UNTIL CHECK-FIELD NOT = SPACE
                OR I = ZERO.
    ADD 1 TO I
    COMPUTE I = 40 - (I/2)
    MOVE SPACES TO OUTPUT-RECORD
    STRING HEADER DELIMITED BY SIZE
        INTO OUTPUT-RECORD
        WITH POINTER I.
    WRITE OUTPUT-RECORD ...
    .
    .
    .
DETERMINE-SIZE.
    IF INDIV-CHAR (I) NOT = SPACE
        MOVE 'X' TO CHECK-FIELD.
```

The PERFORM DETERMINE-SIZE statement results in searching the HEADER field, character by character, from the right end of the field. The negative increment value in the PERFORM ... VARYING I FROM 20 BY -1 causes I to assume the values 20, 19, 18, etc. Thus we can vary a variable by either adding a value to it or subtracting a value from it. When a nonblank character is encountered or the entire field has been searched, the search is terminated. A value of 1 is then added to I to restore it to the value that identifies the proper length. For example, if the data in HEADER consisted of ACME COMPANY, the Y character would cause an "X" to be moved to CHECK-FIELD. Then, by nature of the PERFORM VARYING, I would be incremented by -1 and would become 11 before the UNTIL test was executed. Thus the ADD 1 to I would restore I to the true length value of 12. Next, the procedure shows that we divide I by 2 and subtract this integer quotient from 40, which is the centering column. In this example the data in HEADER is 12 characters long and I would be I = 40 - (12/2) = 34. Then use of the WITH POINTER I clause in the STRING verb would move the HEADER data into OUTPUT-RECORD, beginning with column 34.

R E V I E W . . . .

1. In general, use of the PERFORM ... VARYING verb allows
    _____ execution of program modules.

    repetitive

2. When using PERFORM ... VARYING, control of PERFORM is associated with
    systematically incrementing the value of a(n) _____ .

    identifier

3. The key programming word that indicates that an identifier is to be systematically incremented in value is the COBOL reserved word _____ .

VARYING

4. The test made to determine if the condition specified for terminating PERFORM control has been met is indicated by the COBOL reserved word _____ .

UNTIL

5. In the 1985 standard two more options are available with the PERFORM ... VARYING that are not part of the 1974 version. One of these options allows omission of a reference to procedure-name, thereby forming a(n) _____ PERFORM structure.

in-line

6. Continuing from #5, above, the other option has to do with the point in time that the UNTIL condition is evaluated during each iteration; it is expressed with one of the two options WITH TEST _____ or WITH TEST _____ .

BEFORE; AFTER

• • • • • • • • • • • • • • • • • • •

SAMPLE PROGRAM I — FORECASTING

The example we present in this section illustrates an application of tables and subscripts. The function of the program is to output a sales forecast for the next several months, as specified, by month. The input values are

- NEXT-MONTH: A numeric value that designates the first month to be included in the forecast

- HOW-MANY-MONTHS: A 2-digit number that designates the number of months to be included in the forecast

- BASE: A dollar value used as the base for the forecast formula

- COEFFICIENT: A numeric coefficient used in the forecast formula

The forecasting formula used is

$$F_i = B + cN$$

The forecast for month i (F_i) is equal to the base (B) plus a coefficient (c) times the number of months (N) from the starting point. If the first month is 2 (February), then the forecast for May will be

$$F_{May} = B + c(3)$$

Thus N = 3 in this case, since May is 3 months after February, which is the starting month.

If the following input were used, the resulting output would be as shown in Figure 12-5.

```
NEXT-MONTH          05
HOW-MANY-MONTHS     09
BASE                0010000000
COEFFICIENT         0000025.000
```

FIGURE 12-5
Illustrative Computer Output

	PROJECTED SALES
MAY	100250.00
JUNE	100500.00
JULY	100750.00
AUGUST	101000.00
SEPTEMBER	101250.00
OCTOBER	101500.00
NOVEMBER	101750.00
DECEMBER	102000.00
JANUARY	102250.00

A sample program listing for the forecasting task is given in Figure 12-6. Notice that the setting up of the MONTH-TABLE in the WORKING-STORAGE SECTION is the same as presented in the earlier section of this chapter.

In the PROCEDURE DIVISION, the paragraph called 010-CALCULATION-ROUTINE is performed HOW-MANY-MONTHS times. In this case the input field, HOW-MANY-MONTHS, contains the number of desired executions of the forecasting computation.

The MONTH-FROM-NOW field corresponds to the N in the forecasting formula $F_i = B + cN$. Finally, the subscript WHICH-ONE is used to reference the name of the month relating to each successive line of output. Since we have only 12 months, we may need to "wraparound" the MONTH-TABLE entries. For instance, if NEXT-MONTH = 5 and HOW-MANY-MONTHS = 9, the last month is not the thirteenth (4 + 9); rather, it is the first month of the next year. Thus, when the month subscript called WHICH-ONE exceeds 12, we subtract 12 from it to "bend" it down around the table.

SAMPLE PROGRAM II — PRINTER GRAPHIC OUTPUT

This section of the chapter presents a sample program that utilizes table-handling concepts to produce graphic printer output in the form of a bar chart. The output format is illustrated in Figure 12-7. For each common stock issue, we print a bar whose length corresponds to the percent yield of the stock.

The yield is computed as the percent ratio of the dividend-per-share to the price-per-share. It is assumed that no yield can exceed 50 percent, but if the computed yield does exceed this percentage, a special message is printed.

The input consists of records containing the stock name, the stock price, and the dividend. Figure 12-8 presents the program listing. The graphic output is prepared in the two paragraphs named 030-FILL-BAR and 040-MOVE-X-TO-BAR.

```
030-FILL-BAR.
    MOVE SPACES TO BAR-CHART
    PERFORM 040-MOVE-X-TO-BAR VARYING I FROM 1 BY 1
                    UNTIL I > PERCENT-YIELD.
*
040-MOVE-X-TO-BAR.
    MOVE 'X' TO BAR-CELL (I).
```

We first clear the group field BAR-CHART by filling it with spaces. Since it is the group-name that includes the entire BAR-CELL table, the 50 entries in the table will be filled with blank spaces. Then the PERFORM ... VARYING varies the

FIGURE 12-6

Sample Forecast Program

```
*
    IDENTIFICATION DIVISION.
    PROGRAM-ID. FORECAST.
*
    ENVIRONMENT DIVISION.
    CONFIGURATION SECTION.
    SOURCE-COMPUTER. ABC-480.
    OBJECT-COMPUTER. ABC-480.
*
    INPUT-OUTPUT SECTION.
    FILE-CONTROL.
        SELECT INPUT-DATA  ASSIGN TO CARD.
        SELECT OUTPUT-FILE ASSIGN TO PRINTER.
*
    DATA DIVISION.
*
    FILE SECTION.
*
    FD  INPUT-DATA     LABEL RECORDS ARE OMITTED
                       DATA RECORD IS INCARD.
    01  INCARD.
        02  NEXT-MONTH          PIC 99.
        02  HOW-MANY-MONTHS      PIC 99.
        02  BASE                PIC S9(8)V99.
        02  COEFFICIENT         PIC S9(8)V99.
        02  FILLER              PIC X(56).
*
    FD  OUTPUT-FILE    LABEL RECORDS OMITTED
                       DATA RECORD IS OUT-LINE.
    01  OUT-LINE               PIC X(132).
*
    WORKING-STORAGE SECTION.
*
    01  WHICH-ONE              PIC 99.
    01  MONTHS-FROM-NOW        PIC 99.
    01  SALES                 PIC S9(9)V99.
    01  DATA-END              PIC X(3).
*
    01  HEADER.
        02  FILLER              PIC X(15) VALUE SPACES.
        02  FILLER              PIC X(15) VALUE 'PROJECTED SALES'.
*
    01 PRINT-RECORD.
        02  FILLER              PIC X VALUE SPACES.
        02  MONTH-NAME          PIC X(12).
        02  FILLER              PIC X(5) VALUE SPACES.
        02  EDIT-SALES          PIC ------99.99.
*
```

FIGURE 12-6
Sample Forecast Program
(continued)

```
01 MONTH-TABLE.
    02  JANUARY              PIC X(9) VALUE 'JANUARY  '.
    02  FEBRUARY             PIC X(9) VALUE 'FEBRUARY '.
    02  MARCH                PIC X(9) VALUE 'MARCH    '.
    02  APRIL                PIC X(9) VALUE 'APRIL    '.
    02  MAY                  PIC X(9) VALUE 'MAY      '.
    02  JUNE                 PIC X(9) VALUE 'JUNE     '.
    02  JULY                 PIC X(9) VALUE 'JULY     '.
    02  AUGUST               PIC X(9) VALUE 'AUGUST   '.
    02  SEPTEMBER            PIC X(9) VALUE 'SEPTEMBER'.
    02  OCTOBER              PIC X(9) VALUE 'OCTOBER  '.
    02  NOVEMBER             PIC X(9) VALUE 'NOVEMBER '.
    02  DECEMBER             PIC X(9) VALUE 'DECEMBER '.
*
01 MONTHS REDEFINES MONTH-TABLE.
    02  MONTH                PIC X(9) OCCURS 12 TIMES.
*
PROCEDURE DIVISION.
*
000-MAIN-ROUTINE.
    OPEN INPUT INPUT-DATA
         OUTPUT OUTPUT-FILE
    MOVE 'NO' TO DATA-END
*
    READ INPUT-DATA RECORD
        AT END MOVE 'YES' TO DATA-END.
*
    IF  DATA-END = 'NO'
        WRITE OUT-LINE FROM HEADER AFTER PAGE
        MOVE SPACES TO OUT-LINE
        WRITE OUT-LINE AFTER 1 LINE
        MOVE ZERO TO MONTHS-FROM-NOW
        MOVE NEXT-MONTH TO WHICH-ONE
*
        PERFORM 010-CALCULATION-ROUTINE
            HOW-MANY-MONTHS TIMES
    ELSE
        MOVE 'NO DATA AVAILABLE' TO OUT-LINE
        WRITE OUT-LINE AFTER 1 LINE
    END-IF
*
    CLOSE INPUT-DATA, OUTPUT-FILE
    STOP RUN.
*
010-CALCULATION-ROUTINE.
    ADD 1 TO MONTHS-FROM-NOW
    IF  WHICH-ONE IS GREATER THAN 12
        SUBTRACT 12 FROM WHICH-ONE
    END-IF
    COMPUTE SALES = MONTHS-FROM-NOW * COEFFICIENT
    ADD BASE TO SALES
    MOVE MONTH (WHICH-ONE) TO MONTH-NAME
    MOVE SALES TO EDIT-SALES
    WRITE OUT-LINE FROM PRINT-RECORD AFTER 1 LINE
    ADD 1 TO WHICH-ONE.
```

FIGURE 12-7

Sample Graphic Output for The Stock-Yield Program

```
                            PERCENT YIELD
                   0    5   10   15   20   25   30   35   40   45   50
        STOCK NAME I    I    I    I    I    I    I    I    I    I    I
                   I
FORD MOTOR CO.     IXXXXXXXXXX
                   I
GENERAL MOTORS CORP. IXXXXXXXXXXXXXXXXXXX
                   I
CONTROL DATA CORP. IXXXXXXXX
                   I
IBM CORP.          IXXXXXXXXXXX
                   I
SPERRY RAND CORP.  IXXXXXXXXXXXXXXXXXXXXXXXXXXXXXXXXXXXXXXXX
                   I
HONEYWELL CORP.    IXXXXXXXXXXX
                   I
DIGITAL EQUIPMENT CO IXXXXXXXXXXXX
                   I
EXAMPLE ERROR-1    IINVALID INPUT DATA
                   I
EXAMPLE ERROR-2    IINVALID INPUT DATA
                   I
JACK-POT CORP.     IYIELD HIGHER THAN 50%
```

FIGURE 12-8

Listing of the Program for Graphic Output

```
IDENTIFICATION DIVISION.
PROGRAM-ID. GRAPH.
*
ENVIRONMENT DIVISION.
*
CONFIGURATION SECTION.
SOURCE-COMPUTER. ABC-480.
OBJECT-COMPUTER. ABC-480.
*
INPUT-OUTPUT SECTION.
FILE-CONTROL.
*
    SELECT STOCK-FILE ASSIGN TO CARD.
    SELECT REPORT-FILE ASSIGN TO PRINTER.
*
DATA DIVISION.
*
FILE SECTION.
*
```

FIGURE 12-8
*Listing of the Program for Graphic
Output (continued)*

```
       FD  STOCK-FILE     LABEL RECORDS OMITTED
                          DATA RECORD IS STOCK-REC.
       01  STOCK-REC.
           02  STOCK-NAME          PIC X(20).
           02  STOCK-PRICE         PIC 9(3)V99.
           02  STOCK-DIVIDEND      PIC 9(2)V99.
           02  FILLER              PIC X(51).
       *
       FD  REPORT-FILE    LABEL RECORDS OMITTED
                          DATA RECORD IS REPORT-REC.
       01  REPORT-REC             PIC X(132).
       *
       WORKING-STORAGE SECTION.
       *
       01  END-OF-FILE-SWITCH     PIC XXX    VALUE 'NO'.
           88  END-OF-FILE                   VALUE 'YES'.
       *
       01  PERCENT-YIELD          PIC 99.
       *
       01  I                      PIC 99.
       *
       01  GRAPH-LINE.
           02  FILLER              PIC X(5) VALUE SPACES.
           02  STOCK-NAME          PIC X(20).
           02  FILLER              PIC X(2 ) VALUE SPACES.
           02  FILLER              PIC X     VALUE 'I'.
           02  BAR-CHART.
               03  BAR-CELL OCCURS 50 TIMES PIC X.
       *
       01  HEADING-1.
           02  FILLER              PIC X(40) VALUE SPACES.
           02  FILLER              PIC X(13) VALUE 'PERCENT YIELD'.
       *
       01  HEADING-2.
           02  FILLER              PIC X(27) VALUE SPACES.
           02  FILLER              PIC X(51) VALUE
               '0   5   10  15  20  25  30  35  40  45   50'.
       *
       01  HEADING-3.
           02  FILLER              PIC X(10) VALUE SPACES.
           02  FILLER              PIC X(10) VALUE 'STOCK NAME'.
           02  FILLER              PIC X(7)  VALUE SPACES.
           02  FILLER              PIC X     VALUE 'I'.
           02  FILLER              PIC X(50) VALUE ALL '....I'.
       *
       01  EMPTY-LINE.
           02  FILLER              PIC X(27) VALUE SPACES.
           02  FILLER              PIC X     VALUE 'I'.
       *
       PROCEDURE DIVISION.
       *
```

FIGURE 12-8

*Listing of the Program for Graphic
Output (continued)*

```
000-MAIN-ROUTINE.
    OPEN INPUT STOCK-FILE
        OUTPUT REPORT-FILE
*
    PERFORM 010-READ-STOCK-REC.
*
    WRITE REPORT-REC FROM HEADING-1 AFTER PAGE
    WRITE REPORT-REC FROM HEADING-2 AFTER 2
    WRITE REPORT-REC FROM HEADING-3 AFTER 2
*
    PERFORM 020-PRINT-GRAPH
        UNTIL END-OF-FILE
*
    CLOSE STOCK-FILE
        REPORT-FILE.
*
    STOP RUN.
*
010-READ-STOCK-REC.
    READ STOCK-FILE RECORD
        AT END MOVE 'YES' TO END-OF-FILE-SWITCH.
*
020-PRINT-GRAPH.
    WRITE REPORT-REC FROM EMPTY-LINE
*
    IF  STOCK-PRICE NOT NUMERIC
        OR STOCK-DIVIDEND NOT NUMERIC
        OR STOCK-PRICE NOT > ZERO
        MOVE 'INVALID INPUT DATA' TO BAR-CHART
    ELSE
        COMPUTE PERCENT-YIELD ROUNDED =
            STOCK-DIVIDEND * 100.0 / STOCK-PRICE
*
        IF  PERCENT-YIELD > 50
            MOVE 'YIELD HIGHER THAN 50%' TO BAR-CHART
        ELSE
            PERFORM 030-FILL-BAR
        END-IF
    END-IF
    MOVE STOCK-NAME OF STOCK-REC
        TO STOCK-NAME OF GRAPH-LINE
*
    WRITE REPORT-REC FROM GRAPH-LINE
    WRITE REPORT-REC FROM EMPTY-LINE
*
    PERFORM 010-READ-STOCK-REC.
*
030-FILL-BAR.
    MOVE SPACES TO BAR-CHART
    PERFORM 040-MOVE-X-TO-BAR VARYING I FROM 1 BY 1
                                UNTIL I > PERCENT-YIELD.
*
040-MOVE-X-TO-BAR.
    MOVE 'X' TO BAR-CELL (I).
```

variable I, which is used as the subscript for BAR-CELL. A stock for which the percent yield is 4%, for example, will thus result in four X characters being moved to the first four locations of the BAR-CELL table.

SUMMARY

This chapter was concerned with the basic concepts and methods used in defining tables and manipulating the associated table data. Only *single-level* table handling was considered. That is, our focus was on *one-dimensional tables*. Chapter 18 presents more advanced methods and language features for table handling, including higher-level tables.

The OCCURS clause in the data description indicates the number of entries in the table for that data item. Consider the following data description:

```
01   REGION-OUTLETS-TABLE.
     02 REGION-OUTLETS OCCURS 6 TIMES.
        03 REGION   PIC X(8).
        03 OUTLETS  PIC 9(3).
```

The table above has six entries. However, each of the entries is subdivided into two elementary fields: one with the REGION name, and the other with the number of OUTLETS in that region. Reference to REGION-OUTLETS-TABLE is a reference to the entire table of data. Reference to REGION-OUTLETS (4) is to the name of the fourth REGION *and* the number of OUTLETS in that region. Reference to REGION (4) is to the name of the fourth REGION, but *not* to the number of outlets. Even though the data item with the OCCURS clause is subdivided into two elementary fields, the table in this example, nevertheless, is a single-level table.

Variable data or constants can be entered into a table by use of the READ command. However, there are three other ways by which constants can be entered into a table. One way of establishing a table of constant values without reading them in through PROCEDURE DIVISION statements is by use of the REDEFINES clause in conjunction with the OCCURS option. Another approach concerns using the OCCURS and VALUE clauses in combination; depending on how these are used, either the same constant will be entered into all positions of the table, or different constants will be entered into different positions. The 1985 verb INITIALIZE can be used to fill a table with zeros or blank spaces. A final approach for entering constants into a table is with the MOVE verb.

Use of the VARYING option with the PERFORM verb makes possible the repetitive execution of program modules. The VARYING option permits us to systematically increment the value of an identifier (subscript) for a data item that is part of a table. The UNTIL option can be used to determine if the condition specified for terminating the PERFORM has been met.

The chapter concluded with two sample programs. The function of the first program was to output a monthly sales forecast for the next several months. The function of the second program was to perform graphic output for table data in the form of a bar chart.

EXERCISES

12.1   Write DATA DIVISION entries to set up a table that is to contain annual dollar sales for 12 years. Use the data-name ANNUAL-SALES at the 01 level and then use a name of your choice for the table. No value will exceed $100,000,000.00.

12.2   Write DATA DIVISION entries to set up a table to contain dollar and unit sales for the years 1980–1992. We want to be able to reference the dollar sales or the unit sales individually for each year, as well as to reference as a group the dollar sales and unit sales pertaining to a given year. The general format of the table is as follows:

YEAR	DOLLAR SALES	UNIT SALES
1980		
1981		
.	.	.
.	.	.
.	.	.
1992		

Do not insert the YEAR values through the DATA DIVISION definition. Instead, write a paragraph called STORE-YEARS that will store the year values in the appropriate place in the table.

12.3 Use DATA DIVISION entries to form a table containing the names of the days of the week so that the names are referenced by a subscript; thus Monday would be referenced by a subscript for which the value is 1, and Sunday would be referenced by a subscript value of 7.

12.4 Assume that TAX-TABLE contains 30 values (V999). Write the PROCE-DURE and DATA DIVISION statements required to print the contents of the table. Write appropriate DATA DIVISION descriptions needed for the tasks below:

a. Print the 30 values in one column of 30 lines.

b. Print the 30 values at the rate of seven per line for as many lines as are needed.

12.5 For the following table write the necessary program instructions to find the smallest value and to place it in SMALLEST. Disregard the possibility of ties.

```
02 TABLE OCCURS 50 TIMES    PICTURE X(12).
```

Write DATA DIVISION descriptions for any additional data-names necessary for the task.

12.6 A sales file contains the following types of data:

COLUMNS	FIELD DESCRIPTION
1	Quarter during which sales occurred; PIC 9, values are in range of 1–4.
2–6	Sales amount; PIC 999V99.

Write a program to read such a sales file and produce the following type of report:

QUARTER	TOTAL SALES	% OF YEAR TOTAL
1	100.00	20%
2	50.00	10%
3	300.00	60%
4	50.00	10%
YEAR TOTAL	$500.00	100%

Use a table to store the quarterly sales; do *not* use four individual data-names. Each value in the TOTAL SALES column may represent the sum of several sales values. In other words, there may be several records that have the same quarter, as, for instance:

QUARTER	SALES
1	20.00
2	35.00
1	10.00
4	100.00

In this example the total sales for the first quarter would be 30.00. As the example demonstrates, the data are not in any order.

12.7   A customer file contains customer names, among other data. We are interested in conducting a frequency analysis of the first letter of customer names. In other words, a table such as the following is to be produced:

BEGINNING LETTER	NUMBER OF NAMES
A	10
B	15
.	.
.	.
.	.
Z	1

Input records have the following format:

COLUMNS	FIELD DESCRIPTION
1–12	Customer name
13–80	Other data

Write a program to do the above task.

13

An Expanded Example of Sequential File Processing

IN THIS CHAPTER *you will study an expanded file-processing example to accomplish two main objectives. First, such an example provides you with the opportunity to review and apply a large number of the statements that you studied in previous chapters. Second, and more important, the example demonstrates what is often missing in a student environment: a system of* **interrelated programs.**

When initially learning COBOL, it is only natural to be involved in studying and writing individual, fairly short programs. However in the "real world" of programming practice, data processing tasks are complex enough to be developed as **systems** *consisting of several programs.*

INTRODUCTION

In this chapter we define and illustrate a system of three interrelated programs. Nevertheless, this is still a limited, if not trivial, example in terms of the size and complexity of real-world computer programming. However, if we attempted to tackle a system of realistic size and complexity, it would require a large and wasted amount of time on your part. For instance, in the sample program we define a limited number of data fields, and we screen input data for a few error conditions. In a realistic program we might have, say, 30 data fields and over 100 error-condition possibilities. Our viewpoint is that if we understand programming logic with respect to three data fields and four error conditions, there is no special benefit to a larger example. Thus, given the limited time available to a student, we try to strike a balance between realism and practical simplicity.

OVERVIEW OF THE TASK

The example deals with a business environment in which we have customers who are involved in such transactions as purchases and payments. We could think of a retail store as the assumed environment. The example is structured as three programs.

The first program illustrates the *creation of a master file* for customer records. We input records from a source file, we screen them for a number of possible errors, and we write the correct records onto a new master file. We then sort the master file in order of the account number in each customer record.

The second program demonstrates a *daily process*. Each day we have sales transactions involving the customers. For purposes of the daily processing, we have an abbreviated version of the customer master file. In this file we store the account number used for identification, the authorized credit limit, and the current balance. The thinking is that because the daily processing is frequent and therefore extensive, we need not do unnecessary processing. Thus the abbreviated daily customer file does *not* contain the customer address. In a realistic setting, the difference in record size would be much greater than simply omitting the address, but the basic point is the same.

As part of the daily processing, we read the daily transactions file and we update the daily master. In the course of the program execution we produce a daily transaction register on paper for managerial review, we generate a report on any error transactions, and, of course, we update the daily master file with the new customer balance. Customers whose current balance exceeds their authorized credit limit are reported for managerial review. Finally, today's daily transactions are merged with the ones from the days before. As is typical in this kind of environment, we have a monthly billing cycle. During each business day of the month we accumulate transactions that are then processed at the end of the month to update the full customer file and to generate monthly billing statements.

The *monthly processing* is the subject of the third programming task in the example. The accumulated monthly transactions are processed against the full (not the abbreviated daily) master file. In the process the full master file is updated, any errors are reported, and monthly billing statements are produced. Actually, this last programming task is illustrated only in part, saving its full detail as an exercise at the end of the chapter.

THE PROGRAM TO CREATE THE MASTER FILE

The first program illustrates creation of the customer master file. Figure 13-1 outlines the main processing steps. The original data are in a source file. Figure 13-2 shows sample input and output, while Figure 13-3 presents the complete program.

The 300-CREATE-MASTER paragraph in the PROCEDURE DIVISION in Figure 13-3 is rather routine. We read the records in the source file and we check

FIGURE 13-1

Overview of File Create Task

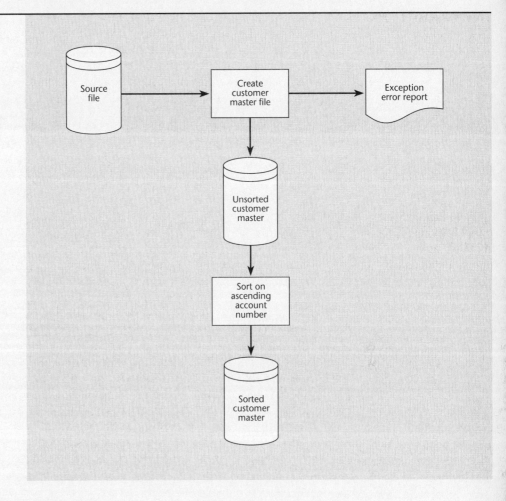

FIGURE 13-2

Sample Input and Output for the File Create Task

INPUT FILE

```
12345JOHN L. ANDERSON    080000000150251020 N. 10TH STREET   MESA    AZ 85280
13345                    0003450000000505 S. ROOSEVELT RD. TEMPE     AZ 85280
33456LINDA M. BREWSTER   100000000500001929 NORTHERN AVE.  TUCSON    AZ 85701
23465LESLIE J. CROWN     050000          400 WASHINGTON BLVD.  MESA  AZ 85202
32222PAT N. THOMPSON     0004000400000010 EAST PLAZA RD.  ANYTOWN    AZ 85281
41231ELMER J. GUSTON     09000000450002350 SOUTHERN AVE.   CHANDLER  AZ 85501
18234JAMES J. JONES      11000000045050
19876JEAN L. PENDLETON   400000002300002888 W. PLAZA RD.  ANYTOWN    AZ 85702
```

UNSORTED MASTER

```
12345JOHN L. ANDERSON    080000000150251020 N. 10TH STREET   MESA   AZ 85280
33456LINDA M. BREWSTER   100000000500001929 NORTHERN AVE   TUCSON   AZ 85701
41231ELMER J. GUSTON     09000000450002350 SOUTHERN AVE.   CHANDLER AZ 85501
19876JEAN L. PENDLETON   400000002300002888 W. PLAZA RD.  ANYTOWN   AZ 85702
```

FIGURE 13-2

Sample Input and Output for the File Create Task (continued)

NEW (SORTED) MASTER

```
12345JOHN L. ANDERSON      080000000150251020 N. 10TH STREET   MESA    AZ 85280
19876JEAN L. PENDLETON     400000002300002888 W. PLAZA RD.   ANYTOWN  AZ 85702
33456LINDA M. BREWSTER     100000000500001929 NORTHERN AVE.   TUCSON  AZ 85701
41231ELMER J. GUSTON       090000000450002350 SOUTHERN AVE.    CHANDLER  AZ 85501
```

ERROR REPORT

```
                EXCEPTION REPORT
   ERROR MESSAGE                    INVALID RECORD
-------------------------------------------------------------------------------------------------------------

   CUSTOMER NAME IS MISSING         13345              0003450000000505 S. ROOSEVELT RD. TEMPE   AZ 85280
   BALANCE AMOUNT NOT VALID         23465LESLIE J. CROWN   050000        400 WASHINGTON BLVD.   MESA    AZ 85202
   CUSTOMER'S BALANCE EXCEEDS LIMIT 32222PAT N. THOMPSON   0004000400000010 EAST PLAZA RD.   ANYTOWN  AZ 85281
   CUSTOMER ADDRESS IS MISSING      18234JAMES J. JONES    11000000045050
```

FIGURE 13-3

COBOL Program to Create the
Master File

```
        IDENTIFICATION DIVISION.
        PROGRAM-ID.  CREATMAS.
       *
        ENVIRONMENT DIVISION.
        CONFIGURATION SECTION.
        SOURCE-COMPUTER. ABC-480.
        OBJECT-COMPUTER. ABC-480.
       *
        INPUT-OUTPUT SECTION.
       *
        FILE-CONTROL.
       *
            SELECT CUST-SOURCE-FILE   ASSIGN TO SOURCE-FIL.
            SELECT CUST-MAST-FILE     ASSIGN TO CUST-MAS.
            SELECT ERROR-FILE         ASSIGN TO PRINT-ERR.
            SELECT NEW-MASTER-FILE    ASSIGN TO NEW-MAS.
            SELECT SORT-FILE          ASSIGN TO SORT-WORK.
       *
        DATA DIVISION.
       *
        FILE SECTION.
       *
        FD  CUST-SOURCE-FILE
            LABEL RECORDS ARE OMITTED
            DATA RECORD IS CUST-SOURCE-RECORD.
       *
```

FIGURE 13-3
COBOL Program to Create the
Master File (continued)

```
01  CUST-SOURCE-RECORD.
    02  CUST-ACCOUNT-NO         PIC 9(05).
    02  CUST-NAME               PIC X(20).
    02  CUST-CR-LIMIT           PIC 9(04)V99.
    02  CUST-BALANCE            PIC S9(06)V99.
    02  CUST-ADDRESS            PIC X(40).
    02  FILLER                  PIC X(01).
*
FD  CUST-MAST-FILE
        LABEL RECORDS STANDARD
        DATA RECORD IS CUST-MAST-RECORD.
*
01  CUST-MAST-RECORD           PIC X(80).
*
FD  ERROR-FILE
        LABEL RECORDS OMITTED
        DATA RECORD IS ERROR-RECORD.
*
01  ERROR-RECORD.
    02  FILLER                 PIC X(132).
*
SD  SORT-FILE
        DATA RECORD IS SORT-RECORD.
*
01  SORT-RECORD.
    02  S-ACCOUNT-NO           PIC 9(05).
    02  FILLER                 PIC X(75).
*
FD  NEW-MASTER-FILE
        LABEL RECORDS STANDARD
        DATA RECORD IS NEW-MASTER-RECORD.
*
01  NEW-MASTER-RECORD          PIC X(80).
*
WORKING-STORAGE SECTION.
*
01  END-OF-FILE-INDICATOR      PIC X(03)  VALUE 'NO'.
    88  END-OF-FILE                       VALUE 'YES'.
*
01  ERROR-FLAG                 PIC X(03)  VALUE 'NO'.
    88  NO-ERROR-FOUND                    VALUE 'NO'.
    88  ERROR-FOUND                       VALUE 'YES'.
*
01  EXCEPTION-RECORD-FORMAT.
*
    02  ERROR-HEAD1.
        03  FILLER             PIC X(20)  VALUE SPACES.
        03  FILLER             PIC X(16)  VALUE
            'EXCEPTION REPORT'.
*
```

FIGURE 13-3

COBOL Program to Create the
Master File (continued)

```
        02  ERROR-HEAD2.
            03 FILLER                PIC X(05)  VALUE SPACES.
            03 FILLER                PIC X(13)  VALUE
                'ERROR MESSAGE'.
            03 FILLER                PIC X(22)  VALUE SPACES.
            03 FILLER                PIC X(14)  VALUE
                'INVALID RECORD'.
    *
        02  ERROR-HEAD3.
            03 FILLER                PIC X(04)  VALUE SPACES.
            03 FILLER                PIC X(115) VALUE ALL '-'.
    *
        02  ERROR-BLANK.
            03  FILLER               PIC X(132) VALUE SPACES.
    *
        02  ERROR-DETAIL-LN.
            03  FILLER               PIC X(05)  VALUE SPACES.
            03  ERROR-MESSAGE        PIC X(35).
            03  FILLER               PIC X(01)  VALUE SPACES.
            03  ERROR-SOURCE-RECORD  PIC X(80).
    *
     PROCEDURE DIVISION.
    *
     100-PROGRAM-SUMMARY.
         PERFORM 200-START-UP
         PERFORM 300-CREATE-MASTER
    *
         CLOSE CUST-SOURCE-FILE
               ERROR-FILE
               CUST-MAST-FILE.
    *
         SORT SORT-FILE ON ASCENDING KEY S-ACCOUNT-NO
               USING CUST-MAST-FILE
               GIVING NEW-MASTER-FILE.
    *
         STOP RUN.
    *
     200-START-UP.
         OPEN INPUT  CUST-SOURCE-FILE
              OUTPUT ERROR-FILE
              OUTPUT CUST-MAST-FILE.
    *
         WRITE ERROR-RECORD FROM ERROR-HEAD1 AFTER PAGE
         WRITE ERROR-RECORD FROM ERROR-HEAD2 AFTER 2 LINES
         WRITE ERROR-RECORD FROM ERROR-HEAD3 AFTER 1 LINE
         WRITE ERROR-RECORD FROM ERROR-BLANK AFTER 1 LINE.
    *
     300-CREATE-MASTER.
         PERFORM 400-READ-SOURCE
    *
```

FIGURE 13-3

COBOL Program to Create the
Master File (continued)

```
            PERFORM 500-CHECK-WRITE-READ
                UNTIL END-OF-FILE.
*
    400-READ-SOURCE.
        READ CUST-SOURCE-FILE RECORD
             AT END SET END-OF-FILE TO TRUE
        END-READ.
*
    500-CHECK-WRITE-READ.
        PERFORM 600-VALIDATE-FIELDS
*
        IF  NO-ERROR-FOUND
            WRITE CUST-MAST-RECORD FROM CUST-SOURCE-RECORD
        ELSE
            MOVE CUST-SOURCE-RECORD TO ERROR-SOURCE-RECORD
            WRITE ERROR-RECORD FROM ERROR-DETAIL-LN AFTER 2
        END-IF
*
        PERFORM 400-READ-SOURCE.
*
    600-VALIDATE-FIELDS.
        SET NO-ERROR-FOUND TO TRUE
*
        EVALUATE TRUE
            WHEN CUST-ACCOUNT-NO IS NOT NUMERIC
                 SET ERROR-FOUND TO TRUE
                 MOVE 'ACCOUNT NUMBER NOT NUMERIC' TO ERROR-MESSAGE
*
            WHEN CUST-NAME IS EQUAL TO SPACES
                 SET ERROR-FOUND TO TRUE
                 MOVE 'CUSTOMER NAME IS MISSING' TO ERROR-MESSAGE
*
            WHEN CUST-CR-LIMIT IS NOT NUMERIC
                 SET ERROR-FOUND TO TRUE
                 MOVE 'CREDIT LIMIT NOT VALID' TO ERROR-MESSAGE
*
            WHEN CUST-BALANCE IS NOT NUMERIC
                 SET ERROR-FOUND TO TRUE
                 MOVE 'BALANCE AMOUNT NOT VALID' TO ERROR-MESSAGE
*
            WHEN CUST-ADDRESS IS EQUAL TO SPACES
                 SET ERROR-FOUND TO TRUE
                 MOVE 'CUSTOMER ADDRESS IS MISSING' TO ERROR-MESSAGE
*
            WHEN NO-ERROR-FOUND
                 IF  CUST-CR-LIMIT < CUST-BALANCE
                     SET ERROR-FOUND TO TRUE
                     MOVE 'CUSTOMER'S BALANCE EXCEEDS LIMIT'
                          TO ERROR-MESSAGE
                 END-IF
*
        END-EVALUATE.
*
```

for five types of errors in the EVALUATE statement of 600-VALIDATE-FIELDS. The first four types of errors pertain to the individual contents of fields. The fifth type of error compares CUST-CR-LIMIT to CUST-BALANCE to ascertain that when we create a new customer record the credit limit is consistent with the balance owed, if any, by the customer. Notice that if we find an error, we do *not* continue with that record to determine if there are any other errors in the same record. Changing the program to check for *all* five error types in each input record is asked as the first exercise at the end of the chapter.

In 100-PROGRAM-SUMMARY we see that after the CREATE-MASTER process has been completed, we close the three files that were involved (CUST-SOURCE-FILE, ERROR-FILE, and CUST-MAST-FILE) and we proceed with

```
SORT SORT-FILE ON ASCENDING KEY S-ACCOUNT-NO
     USING CUST-MAST-FILE
     GIVING NEW-MASTER-FILE.
```

Thus the customer master file is sorted in ascending order of the account number fields in its records.

DAILY MASTER PROCESSING

Figure 13-4 presents an overview of the daily master update program. The old daily customer master file and the transactions for the day serve as the initial input. There are two printed reports, the Daily Transaction Register and the Transaction Error Report, both of which are illustrated in Figure 13-5. As you can see in the sample transaction register, there are four types of transactions: Purchase, Payment, Return, and Adjustment. The asterisks on the fourth line of the transaction register example signify that the authorized credit limit has been exceeded by that customer.

Sample related input and output data for the daily master processing are shown in Figure 13-6.

Continuing with Figure 13-4, the update process results in a new version of the daily master file. After the update process has been completed, a file merging operation is done conditional on there being an optional transaction file from previous days. On the first day of each month, for instance, the "today's transaction" file would be the only such file, and so a merge operation would not be required.

Figure 13-7 presents the complete program for the daily processing task. The 070-UPDATE-MAST paragraph in the PROCEDURE DIVISION is executed until the transactions and old daily master files have been completely read in. In this paragraph we use the EVALUATE statement to select which of the three conditions is true. If OLD-ACCOUNT-NO = TRANS-ACCOUNT-NO, we enter a loop of PERFORMing 080-APPLY-TRANSACTION UNTIL either we have a transaction for a new customer or it is the end of the transaction file. Thus, on the expectation that we may have several transactions for the same account number, we keep the program logic control for reading and processing possibly *several* transactions at this level, rather than returning to the main PERFORM 070-UPDATE-MAST in the 000-PROGRAM-SUMMARY paragraph. This is a typical way to design the program logic for handling multiple transactions for the same master record.

Because there may be error conditions encountered in processing the transactions, in the 070-UPDATE-MAST procedure we check the following:

```
IF WRITE-REC
   WRITE DAILY-MAS-REC FROM WORK-MAS-REC
```

FIGURE 13-4

*Overview of Daily Master Update
Program*

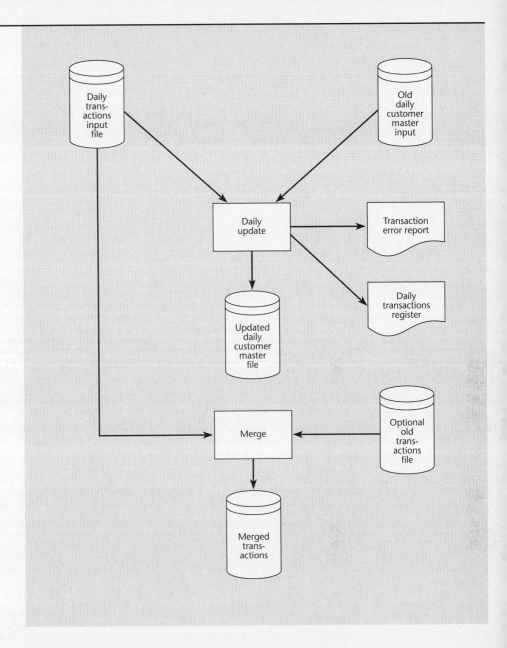

The WRITE-REC condition-name is set to false (SET NOT-WRITE-REC TO TRUE) in the WHEN OTHER alternative of the EVALUATE statement in the 070-UPDATE-MAST procedure. The WORK-MAS-REC is the WORKING STORAGE area in which we prepare the new master record. Alternatively, we could have used the record area in the updated master file (DAILY-MAS-REC in DAILY-MASTER).

The processing logic for the transaction register and the error transaction report have been combined in 100-WRITE-TRANS-REC. Provision for a page heading has been made for the transaction register but not for the error report (being optimists about the number of errors!).

As a last comment on the sample program in Figure 13-7, the paragraph 110-WRITE-TOTALS illustrates limited use of table-processing relating to the last two lines of the transaction register output. In the DATA DIVISION we set up two tables under the headings DAY-TOTAL1 and DAY-TOTAL2. These tables are to contain the total number of transactions and the dollar value for each type of transaction: Purchase, Payment, Return, and Adjustment. The 110-WRITE-TOTALS

FIGURE 13-5
Daily Transaction Register and Error Report

TRANSACTIONS REPORT

```
                          DAILY TRANSACTION REGISTER
                                  06/13/89


    ACCOUNT    DATE    PRODUCT NO    QUANTITY    PRICE    PURCHASE    PAYMENT    RETURN    ADJUSTMENT
--------------------------------------------------------------------------------------------------------


     19876   05/28/89   0608            1       $100.00    $100.00
     19876   05/28/89                                                 $2,400.00
     19876   05/29/89   0011           10       $100.00                                  $1,000.00
**** 33456   06/01/89   8333            1      $8,000.00   $8,000.00
     33456   06/10/89                                                                                 $900.00
     41231   06/19/89                                                  $400.00


                          TRANSACTIONS PROCESSED                 2          2          1           1
                          TOTAL DOLLAR AMOUNTS          $8,100.00  $8,100.00  $1,000.00   $8,000.00
```

ERROR REPORT

```
                      ERROR TRANSACTION REPORT
              ERROR MESSAGE                        TRANSACTION RECORD
--------------------------------------------------------------------------------


          NO MATCH IN MASTER              12341104218801000001005000
          INVALID TRANSACTION CODE        12345504218800000001000000
          NO MATCH IN MASTER              20000305298955891111555555500240000
          NO MATCH IN MASTER              50000107108999980001010000000040000
```

FIGURE 13-6
Sample Input and Output for Daily Master Processing

OLD TRANSACTION — INPUT FILE

```
198761061089023200100002350
19876X06108902300100000235
334561061389677701000003000
334562061489          00500000
412311061789004500020000300
412314062089          00011000
```

DAILY TRANSACTION — INPUT FILE

```
1234110421880100000100500
1234550421880000000010000
1987610528890608000101000
198762052889          00240000
1987630529890011001001000
20000305298955891111555555
334561060189833300018000
334564061089          00090000
412312061989          00040000
500001071089999800010100
```

FIGURE 13-6

Sample Input and Output for Daily Master Processing (continued)

OLD MASTER — INPUT FILE

```
12345JOHN L. ANDERSON    0800000000150251020 N. 10TH STREET   MESA
AZ 85280
19876JEAN L. PENDLETON   4000000002300002888 W. PLAZA RD.
ANYTOWN  AZ 85702
33456LINDA M. BREWSTER   1000000005000001929 NORTHERN AVE.
TUCSON  AZ 85701
41231ELMER J. GUSTON     0900000004500002350 SOUTHERN AVE.
CHANDLER  AZ 85501
```

DAILY MASTER — OUTPUT FILE

```
12345JOHN L. ANDERSON    08000000015025
19876JEAN L. PENDLETON   40000000100000
33456LINDA M. BREWSTER   10000000760000
41231ELMER J. GUSTON     09000000005000
```

COMBINED TRANSACTION — OUTPUT FILE

```
12341104218801000001005000
12345504218800000001000000
19876106108902320010002350
19876105288906080001010000
198762052889              00240000
19876305298900110010010000
19876X06108902300100000235
20000305298955891111555555
33456106138967770100003000
33456106018983330001800000
334562061489              00500000
334564061089              00090000
41231106178900450020000300
412312061989              00040000
412314062089              00011000
50000107108999980001010000
```

paragraph is used to do the appropriate processing for outputting the results. First, we fill the DAY-NO-TRANSACTIONS and DAY-TRANS-AMOUNTS tables with spaces. Then we use the INITIALIZE statement to move zeros to the numeric fields in the two tables. Actually, since we MOVE data to the subscripted numeric fields DAY-TOTAL-NO and DAY-AMOUNTS in the second and third PERFORM VARYING statements of 110-WRITE-TOTALS, there is no need to INITIALIZE them with zero values. But we do so anyhow to illustrate use of the statement.

FIGURE 13-7
COBOL Program for the Daily
Processing

```
              IDENTIFICATION DIVISION.
              PROGRAM-ID. UPDMAS.
          *
              ENVIRONMENT DIVISION.
              CONFIGURATION SECTION.
              SOURCE-COMPUTER. ABC-480.
              OBJECT-COMPUTER. ABC-480.
          *
              INPUT-OUTPUT SECTION.
          *
              FILE-CONTROL.
          *
                  SELECT OPTIONAL OLD-TRANS-FILE  ASSIGN TO OLD-TRANS.
                  SELECT DAILY-TRANS-FILE         ASSIGN TO DAY-TRANS.
                  SELECT MERGE-FILE               ASSIGN TO MERGE-FILE.
                  SELECT OLD-MASTER               ASSIGN TO OLD-MAS.
                  SELECT DAILY-MASTER             ASSIGN TO DAY-MAS.
                  SELECT NEW-TRANS-FILE           ASSIGN TO COMBINED-TRANS.
                  SELECT ERROR-FILE               ASSIGN TO PRINT-ERR.
                  SELECT REPORT-FILE              ASSIGN TO REPORT-FIL.
          *
              DATA DIVISION.
          *
              FILE SECTION.
          *
              FD  OLD-TRANS-FILE
                  BLOCK CONTAINS 50 RECORDS
                  LABEL RECORDS ARE OMITTED
                  DATA RECORD IS OLD-TRANS-RECORD.
          *
               01  OLD-TRANS-RECORD            PIC X(34).
          *
              FD  DAILY-TRANS-FILE
                  BLOCK CONTAINS 50 RECORDS
                  LABEL RECORDS ARE OMITTED
                  DATA RECORD IS DAY-TRANS-RECORD.
          *
               01  DAY-TRANS-RECORD.
                  02  TRANS-ACCOUNT-NO        PIC X(5).
                  02  TRANS-CODE              PIC 9.
                  02  TRANS-DATE              PIC X(6).
                  02  TRANS-PRODUCT-NO        PIC 9(4).
                  02  TRANS-QUANTITY          PIC 9(4).
                  02  TRANS-PRICE             PIC 9(4)V99.
                  02  TRANS-PMT-ADJ-AMT       PIC 9(6)V99.
          *
              FD  OLD-MASTER
                  BLOCK CONTAINS 50 RECORDS
                  LABEL RECORDS OMITTED
                  DATA RECORD IS OLD-MASTER-RECORD.
          *
```

FIGURE 13-7
COBOL Program for the Daily
Processing (continued)

```
01   OLD-MASTER-RECORD.
     02   OLD-ACCOUNT-NO           PIC X(5).
     02   FILLER                   PIC X(20).
     02   OLD-CREDIT-LIMIT         PIC 9(4)V99.
     02   OLD-BALANCE              PIC S9(6)V99.
*
 FD  DAILY-MASTER
     BLOCK CONTAINS 50 RECORDS
     LABEL RECORDS STANDARD
     DATA RECORD IS DAILY-MAS-REC.
*
 01  DAILY-MAS-REC                 PIC X(39).
*
 FD  NEW-TRANS-FILE
     BLOCK CONTAINS 50 RECORDS
     LABEL RECORDS ARE OMITTED
     DATA RECORD IS COMBINED-TRANS-REC.
*
 01  COMBINED-TRANS-REC            PIC X(34).
*
 FD  ERROR-FILE
     LABEL RECORDS OMITTED
     DATA RECORD IS ERROR-RECORD.
*
 01  ERROR-RECORD                  PIC X(132).
*
 FD  REPORT-FILE
     LABEL RECORDS OMITTED
     DATA RECORD IS REPORT-RECORD.
*
 01  REPORT-RECORD                 PIC X(132).
*
 SD  MERGE-FILE
     DATA RECORD IS MERGE-TRANS-RECORD.
*
 01  MERGE-TRANS-RECORD.
     02   MERGE-ACCOUNT-NO         PIC X(5).
     02   MERGE-TRANS-CODE         PIC X(1).
     02   FILLER                   PIC X(28).
*
 WORKING-STORAGE SECTION.
*
 01  END-OF-TRANS                  PIC X(3) VALUE "NO".
     88   TRANS-ENDED              VALUE "YES".
*
 01  END-OF-MASTER                 PIC X(3) VALUE "NO".
     88   MASTER-ENDED             VALUE "YES".
*
 01  WRITE-TRANS-SWITCH            PIC X(3) VALUE "YES".
     88   WRITE-TRANS              VALUE "YES".
     88   NOT-WRITE-TRANS          VALUE "NO".
*
```

FIGURE 13-7

COBOL Program for the Daily
Processing (continued)

```
01  WRITE-FLAG                     PIC X(3) VALUE "YES".
    88  WRITE-REC                  VALUE "YES".
    88  NOT-WRITE-REC              VALUE "NO".
*
 01  WORK-MAS-REC.
    02  WORK-ACCOUNT-NO            PIC X(5).
    02  FILLER                     PIC X(20).
    02  WORK-CREDIT-LIMIT          PIC 9(4)V99.
    02  WORK-BALANCE               PIC S9(6)V99.
    02  FILLER                     PIC X(41).
*
 01  WS-DATE-ITEMS.
    02  WS-DATE.
        03  WS-YR                  PIC 9(2).
        03  WS-MO                  PIC 9(2).
        03  WS-DA                  PIC 9(2).
*
 01  END-OLD-TRANS-FLAG            PIC X(3) VALUE "NO".
    88  END-OF-OLD-TRANS           VALUE "YES".
    88  NOT-END-OF-OLD-TRANS       VALUE "NO".
*
 01  WS-SUBSCRIPTS.
    02  SUB                        PIC 9(2) VALUE ZERO.
*
 01  SUMMARIZE-TRANS-TABLE.
    02  TRANS-TYPE                 OCCURS 4 TIMES.
        03  TRANS-TOTAL-AMOUNT     PIC 9(6)V99.
        03  TRANS-TOTAL-NUMBER     PIC 9(3).
*
 01  WS-NUMERIC-ITEMS.
    02  LN-COUNTER                 PIC 9(2) VALUE ZERO.
    02  PAGE-SIZE                  PIC 9(2) VALUE 35.
    02  WS-TRANS-AMOUNT            PIC 9(6)V99.
*
OUTPUT REPORT RECORD DESCRIPTION:
*
 01  DAILY-REPORT-FORMAT.
*
    02  DAY-HEAD1.
        03  FILLER                 PIC X(44) VALUE SPACES.
        03  FILLER                 PIC X(27) VALUE
            "DAILY TRANSACTION REGISTER".
*
    02  DAY-HEAD2.
        03  FILLER                 PIC X(55) VALUE SPACES.
        03  D-MONTH                PIC 9(2).
        03  FILLER                 PIC X(1) VALUE "/".
        03  D-DAY                  PIC 9(2).
        03  FILLER                 PIC X(1) VALUE "/".
        03  D-YEAR                 PIC 9(2).
*
```

FIGURE 13-7

COBOL Program for the Daily
Processing (continued)

```
02  DAY-HEAD3.
    03  FILLER              PIC X(5) VALUE SPACES.
    03  FILLER              PIC X(7) VALUE "ACCOUNT".
    03  FILLER              PIC X(5) VALUE SPACES.
    03  FILLER              PIC X(4) VALUE "DATE".
    03  FILLER              PIC X(5) VALUE SPACES.
    03  FILLER              PIC X(10) VALUE "PRODUCT NO".
    03  FILLER              PIC X(8) VALUE SPACES.
    03  FILLER              PIC X(8) VALUE "QUANTITY".
    03  FILLER              PIC X(6) VALUE SPACES.
    03  FILLER              PIC X(5) VALUE "PRICE".
    03  FILLER              PIC X(7) VALUE SPACES.
    03  FILLER              PIC X(8) VALUE "PURCHASE".
    03  FILLER              PIC X(6) VALUE SPACES.
    03  FILLER              PIC X(7) VALUE "PAYMENT".
    03  FILLER              PIC X(7) VALUE SPACES.
    03  FILLER              PIC X(6) VALUE "RETURN".
    03  FILLER              PIC X(7) VALUE SPACES.
    03  FILLER              PIC X(10) VALUE "ADJUSTMENT".
*
02  DAY-HEAD4.
    03  FILLER              PIC X(132) VALUE ALL "-".
*
02  DAY-BLANK.
    03  FILLER              PIC X(132) VALUE SPACES.
*
02  DAY-DETAIL.
    03  FILLER              PIC X(1) VALUE SPACES.
    03  FILLER1             PIC X(4) VALUE SPACES.
    03  FILLER              PIC X(1) VALUE SPACES.
    03  D-ACCOUNT           PIC X(5).
    03  FILLER              PIC X(4) VALUE SPACES.
    03  D-DATE              PIC XX/XX/XX.
    03  FILLER              PIC X(6) VALUE SPACES.
    03  D-PRODUCT-NO        PIC X(4).
    03  FILLER              PIC X(13) VALUE SPACES.
    03  D-QUANTITY          PIC X(4).
    03  FILLER              PIC X(6) VALUE SPACES.
    03  D-PRICE             PIC $$,$$9.99 BLANK WHEN ZERO.
    03  FILLER              PIC X(4) VALUE SPACES.
    03  D-PURCHASE          PIC $$$,$$9.99 BLANK WHEN ZERO.
    03  FILLER              PIC X(4) VALUE SPACES.
    03  D-PAYMENT           PIC $$$,$$9.99 BLANK WHEN ZERO.
    03  FILLER              PIC X(4) VALUE SPACES.
    03  D-RETURN            PIC $$$,$$9.99 BLANK WHEN ZERO.
    03  FILLER              PIC X(4) VALUE SPACES.
    03  D-ADJUSTS           PIC $$$,$$9.99 BLANK WHEN ZERO.
*
```

```
        02  DAY-TOTAL1.
            03  FILLER              PIC X(36) VALUE SPACES.
            03  FILLER              PIC X(25) VALUE
                "TRANSACTIONS PROCESSED   ".
            03  DAY-NO-TRANSACTIONS OCCURS 4 TIMES.
                04  FILLER          PIC X(11).
                04  DAY-TOTAL-NO    PIC ZZ9.

        02  DAY-TOTAL2.
            03  FILLER              PIC X(38) VALUE SPACES.
            03  FILLER              PIC X(21) VALUE
                "TOTAL DOLLAR AMOUNTS".
            03  DAY-TRANS-AMOUNTS   OCCURS 4 TIMES.
                04  FILLER          PIC X(5).
                04  DAY-AMOUNTS     PIC $,$$$,$$9.99.
   *
   **ERROR FILE RECORD DESCRIPTION:
   *
    01  ERROR-RECORDS.
        02  ERROR-HEAD1.
            03  FILLER              PIC X(26) VALUE SPACES.
            03  FILLER              PIC X(24) VALUE
                "ERROR TRANSACTION REPORT".
   *
        02  ERROR-HEAD2.
            03  FILLER              PIC X(10) VALUE SPACES.
            03  FILLER              PIC X(13) VALUE
                "ERROR MESSAGE".
            03  FILLER              PIC X(27) VALUE SPACES.
            03  FILLER              PIC X(18) VALUE
                "TRANSACTION RECORD".
   *
        02  ERROR-HEAD3.
            03  FILLER              PIC X(80) VALUE ALL "-".
   *
        02  ERROR-BLANK.
            03  FILLER              PIC X(132) VALUE SPACES.
   *
        02  ERROR-DETAIL.
            03  FILLER              PIC X(10) VALUE SPACES.
            03  ERROR-MESSAGE       PIC X(40).
            03  ERROR-TRANS         PIC X(82).
   *
    PROCEDURE DIVISION.
   *
    000-PROGRAM-SUMMARY.
        PERFORM 010-STARTUP
        PERFORM 040-READ-FIRST-PAIR
        PERFORM 070-UPDATE-MAST UNTIL
            TRANS-ENDED AND MASTER-ENDED
        PERFORM 110-WRITE-TOTALS
        CLOSE DAILY-TRANS-FILE,
              OLD-MASTER,
              DAILY-MASTER,
              ERROR-FILE,
              REPORT-FILE.
```

FIGURE 13-7

COBOL Program for the Daily
Processing (continued)

```
*
        OPEN INPUT OLD-TRANS-FILE.
        READ OLD-TRANS-FILE RECORD
            AT END SET END-OF-OLD-TRANS TO TRUE
        END-READ
*
        CLOSE OLD-TRANS-FILE.
*
        IF  NOT-END-OF-OLD-TRANS
            MERGE MERGE-FILE ON ASCENDING KEY MERGE-ACCOUNT-NO
                            ON ASCENDING KEY MERGE-TRANS-CODE
                USING OLD-TRANS-FILE, DAILY-TRANS-FILE
                GIVING NEW-TRANS-FILE
        END-IF.
*
        STOP RUN.
*
    010-STARTUP.
        OPEN INPUT  OLD-MASTER
                    DAILY-TRANS-FILE
             OUTPUT DAILY-MASTER
                    ERROR-FILE
                    REPORT-FILE.
*
        MOVE ZEROS TO SUMMARIZE-TRANS-TABLE
        MOVE ZEROS TO D-PURCHASE, D-PAYMENT, D-RETURN, D-ADJUSTS
*
        ACCEPT WS-DATE FROM DATE
        MOVE WS-YR TO D-YEAR
        MOVE WS-MO TO D-MONTH
        MOVE WS-DA TO D-DAY
*
        PERFORM 020-WRITE-TRANS-HEADINGS
        PERFORM 030-WRITE-ERROR-HEADINGS.
*
    020-WRITE-TRANS-HEADINGS.
        WRITE REPORT-RECORD FROM DAY-HEAD1 AFTER PAGE
        WRITE REPORT-RECORD FROM DAY-HEAD2 AFTER 1
        WRITE REPORT-RECORD FROM DAY-HEAD3 AFTER 2
        WRITE REPORT-RECORD FROM DAY-HEAD4 AFTER 1
        WRITE REPORT-RECORD FROM DAY-BLANK AFTER 1
        MOVE 6 TO LN-COUNTER.
*
    030-WRITE-ERROR-HEADINGS.
        WRITE ERROR-RECORD FROM ERROR-HEAD1 AFTER PAGE
        WRITE ERROR-RECORD FROM ERROR-HEAD2 AFTER 2
        WRITE ERROR-RECORD FROM ERROR-HEAD3 AFTER 1
        WRITE ERROR-RECORD FROM ERROR-BLANK AFTER 1.
*
    040-READ-FIRST-PAIR.
        PERFORM 050-READ-TRANS
        PERFORM 060-READ-MASTER.
```

```
*
  050-READ-TRANS.
      READ DAILY-TRANS-FILE
          AT END MOVE HIGH-VALUES TO TRANS-ACCOUNT-NO
          SET TRANS-ENDED TO TRUE
      END-READ.
*
  060-READ-MASTER.
      READ OLD-MASTER
          AT END MOVE HIGH-VALUES TO OLD-ACCOUNT-NO
          SET MASTER-ENDED TO TRUE
      END-READ.
*
  070-UPDATE-MAST.
      EVALUATE TRUE
          WHEN OLD-ACCOUNT-NO = TRANS-ACCOUNT-NO
              MOVE OLD-MASTER-RECORD TO WORK-MAS-REC
              PERFORM 080-APPLY-TRANSACTION
                  UNTIL (OLD-ACCOUNT-NO NOT EQUAL TRANS-ACCOUNT-NO)
                      OR TRANS-ENDED
              PERFORM 060-READ-MASTER
          WHEN OLD-ACCOUNT-NO < TRANS-ACCOUNT-NO
              MOVE OLD-MASTER-RECORD TO WORK-MAS-REC
              PERFORM 060-READ-MASTER
          WHEN OTHER
              MOVE OLD-MASTER-RECORD TO WORK-MAS-REC
              SET NOT-WRITE-REC TO TRUE
              PERFORM 090-TRANS-ERROR
                  UNTIL (OLD-ACCOUNT-NO NOT > TRANS-ACCOUNT-NO)
                      OR TRANS-ENDED
      END-EVALUATE.
*
      IF  WRITE-REC
          WRITE DAILY-MAS-REC FROM WORK-MAS-REC
      ELSE
          SET WRITE-REC TO TRUE
      END-IF.
*
  080-APPLY-TRANSACTION.
      IF  TRANS-CODE IS NUMERIC AND
          (TRANS-CODE > 0 AND TRANS-CODE < 5)
          IF  TRANS-CODE = 1 OR TRANS-CODE = 3
              MULTIPLY TRANS-QUANTITY BY TRANS-PRICE
                  GIVING WS-TRANS-AMOUNT
          END-IF
          ADD WS-TRANS-AMOUNT TO TRANS-TOTAL-AMOUNT(TRANS-CODE)
          ADD 1 TO TRANS-TOTAL-NUMBER(TRANS-CODE)
          SET WRITE-TRANS TO TRUE
      END-IF
*
```

FIGURE 13-7

COBOL Program for the Daily
Processing (continued)

```
                    EVALUATE TRUE
                        WHEN TRANS-CODE = 1
                            MOVE WS-TRANS-AMOUNT TO D-PURCHASE
                            ADD WS-TRANS-AMOUNT TO WORK-BALANCE
                            IF  WORK-BALANCE > WORK-CREDIT-LIMIT
                                MOVE "****" TO FILLER1
                            END-IF
                        WHEN TRANS-CODE = 2
                            MOVE TRANS-PMT-ADJ-AMT TO D-PAYMENT
                            SUBTRACT TRANS-PMT-ADJ-AMT FROM WORK-BALANCE
                        WHEN TRANS-CODE = 3
                            MOVE WS-TRANS-AMOUNT TO D-RETURN
                            SUBTRACT WS-TRANS-AMOUNT FROM WORK-BALANCE
                        WHEN TRANS-CODE = 4
                            MOVE TRANS-PMT-ADJ-AMT TO D-ADJUSTS
                            SUBTRACT TRANS-PMT-ADJ-AMT FROM WORK-BALANCE
                        WHEN OTHER
                            SET NOT-WRITE-TRANS TO TRUE
                    END-EVALUATE
             *
                    PERFORM 100-WRITE-TRANS-REC
                    PERFORM 050-READ-TRANS.
             *
              090-TRANS-ERROR.
                    MOVE "NO MATCH IN MASTER" TO ERROR-MESSAGE
                    MOVE DAY-TRANS-RECORD TO ERROR-TRANS
                    WRITE ERROR-RECORD FROM ERROR-DETAIL AFTER 1
                    PERFORM 050-READ-TRANS.
             *
              100-WRITE-TRANS-REC.
                    IF  WRITE-TRANS
                        MOVE TRANS-ACCOUNT-NO TO D-ACCOUNT
                        MOVE TRANS-DATE TO D-DATE
                        IF  TRANS-CODE = 1 OR TRANS-CODE = 3
                            MOVE TRANS-PRODUCT-NO TO D-PRODUCT-NO
                            MOVE TRANS-QUANTITY TO D-QUANTITY
                            MOVE TRANS-PRICE TO D-PRICE
                        ELSE
                            MOVE ZEROS TO D-PRODUCT-NO, D-QUANTITY, D-PRICE
                        END-IF
                        IF  PAGE-SIZE < LN-COUNTER
                            PERFORM 020-WRITE-TRANS-HEADINGS
                        END-IF
                        WRITE REPORT-RECORD FROM DAY-DETAIL AFTER 1
                        ADD 1 TO LN-COUNTER
                        MOVE ZERO TO D-PAYMENT,
                                     D-PURCHASE,
                                     D-ADJUSTS,
                                     D-RETURN
                        MOVE SPACES TO FILLER1
                    ELSE
                        MOVE "INVALID TRANSACTION CODE" TO ERROR-MESSAGE
                        MOVE DAY-TRANS-RECORD TO ERROR-TRANS
                        WRITE ERROR-RECORD FROM ERROR-DETAIL AFTER 1
                        SET WRITE-TRANS TO TRUE
                    END-IF.
```

FIGURE 13-7
COBOL Program for the Daily
Processing (continued)

```
     *
        110-WRITE-TOTALS.
            PERFORM VARYING SUB FROM 1 BY 1
                UNTIL SUB > 4
                MOVE SPACES TO DAY-NO-TRANSACTIONS( SUB ),
                              DAY-TRANS-AMOUNTS( SUB )
                INITIALIZE DAY-NO-TRANSACTIONS( SUB ),
                           DAY-TRANS-AMOUNTS( SUB )
            END-PERFORM
     *
            PERFORM VARYING SUB FROM 1 BY 1
                UNTIL SUB > 4
                MOVE TRANS-TOTAL-NUMBER ( SUB ) TO DAY-TOTAL-NO( SUB )
            END-PERFORM
     *
            WRITE REPORT-RECORD FROM DAY-TOTAL1 AFTER 2
     *
            PERFORM VARYING SUB FROM 1 BY 1
                UNTIL SUB > 4
                MOVE TRANS-TOTAL-AMOUNT( SUB ) TO DAY-AMOUNTS( SUB )
            END-PERFORM
     *
            WRITE REPORT-RECORD FROM DAY-TOTAL2 AFTER 1.
     *
```

MONTHLY PROCESSING

Figure 13-8 outlines the monthly processing. The daily transactions have been merged as part of the daily processing during the month. The combined transactions file for the month is used as input along with the full-version customer master file. Recall that we distinguished between the abbreviated master used on a daily basis and the full master file used once during the monthly processing. In a more realistic example, we would include transactions to update the full master file with respect to the addition of new customers, name and address changes, and deletion of customer records. However, for the sake of simplicity, we limit the type of transactions to those processed during the daily runs: purchases, payments, returns, and adjustments. As a result of the processing, the customer balance field in the master file is updated, a billing statement is produced, and error transactions are reported.

Figure 13-9 shows sample input and output for the monthly processing. The sample output includes billing statements and an error transaction report. Since the daily processing program checked transactions for error codes, we should not have any at the end of the month. However, it is not unusual to have redundant checking, as illustrated in this case. It may be that the monthly transaction file contains error transactions due to inadvertent merging of error transactions, mislabeling of files, and other hard-to-predict error possibilities. Because processing financial data is a critical operation, it is usually wise to include testing logic to screen out error data if there is any possibility that such data could have slipped through the system.

Figure 13-10 presents the first three divisions of the COBOL program for the monthly processing task. Writing the PROCEDURE DIVISION is left as an exercise.

FIGURE 13-8
Overview of Monthly Processing

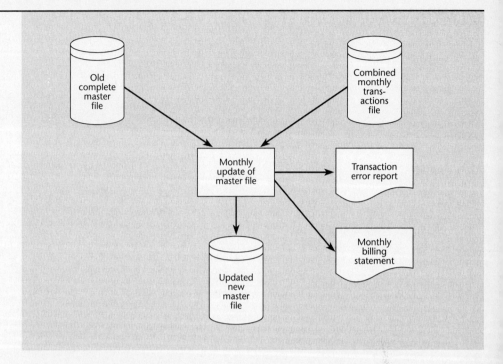

FIGURE 13-9
Sample Input and Output for
Monthly Processing

OLD MASTER — INPUT FILE

```
12345JOHN L. ANDERSON    080000000150251020 N. 10TH STREET  MESA
 AZ 85280
19876JEAN L. PENDLETON   400000002300002888 W. PLAZA RD.   ANYTOWN
AZ 85702
33456LINDA M. BREWSTER   100000000500001929 NORTHERN AVE.   TUCSON
AZ 85701
41231ELMER J. GUSTON     090000000450002350 SOUTHERN AVE.
CHANDLER AZ 85501
```

COMBINED TRANSACTION — INPUT FILE

```
123411042188010000001005000
123455042188000000001000000
198761061089023200010002350
198761052889060800001010000
198762052889           00240000
198763052989001100100010000
19876X0610890230010000235
200003052989558911111555555
334561061389677701000003000
334561060189833300018000000
334562061489           00500000
334564061089           00090000
412311061789004500200000300
412312061989           00040000
412314062089           00011000
500001071089999980001010000
```

FIGURE 13-9
Sample Input and Output for Monthly Processing (continued)

NEW MASTER—OUTPUT FILE

```
12345JOHN L. ANDERSON    080000000150251020 N. 10TH STREET  MESA    AZ 85280
19876JEAN L. PENDLETON   400000000765002888 W. PLAZA RD. ANYTOWN    AZ 85702
33456LINDA M. BREWSTER   100000005600001929 NORTHERN AVE.  TUCSON   AZ 85701
41231ELMER J. GUSTON     090000000000002350 SOUTHERN AVE.   CHANDLER  AZ 85501
```

```
06/13/89                                                    PAGE  1
                          ACME ANYTHING CORP.
                          STATEMENT OF ACCOUNT


12345
JOHN L. ANDERSON


SALE DATE      PRODUCT NO        PURCHASE       PAYMENT      RETURN     ADJUSTMENT
----------------------------------------------------------------------------------

                      **** NO ACTIVITY IN THIS PERIOD ****

                          NEW BALANCE       $150.25
                    AVAILABLE CREDIT LINE    $649.75




06/13/89                                                    PAGE  1
                          ACME ANYTHING CORP.
                          STATEMENT OF ACCOUNT


19876
JEAN L. PENDLETON


SALE DATE      PRODUCT NO        PURCHASE       PAYMENT      RETURN     ADJUSTMENT
----------------------------------------------------------------------------------


 06/10/89        0232             $235.00
 05/28/89        0608             $100.00
 05/28/89                                       $2,400.00
 05/29/89        0011                                      $1,000.00


                          NEW BALANCE       $765.00CR
                    AVAILABLE CREDIT LINE   $4,000.00
```

FIGURE 13-9

Sample Input and Output for Monthly Processing (continued)

```
06/13/89                                                   PAGE  1
                         ACME ANYTHING CORP.
                         STATEMENT OF ACCOUNT


33456
LINDA M. BREWSTER

 SALE DATE     PRODUCT NO       PURCHASE      PAYMENT     RETURN      ADJUSTMENT
------------------------------------------------------------------------------


 06/13/89        6777         $3,000.00
 06/01/89        8333         $8,000.00
 06/14/89                                   $5,000.00
 06/10/89                                                            $900.00


                              NEW BALANCE   $5,600.00
                     AVAILABLE CREDIT LINE      $0.00



06/13/89                                                   PAGE  1
                         ACME ANYTHING CORP.
                         STATEMENT OF ACCOUNT


41231
ELMER J. GUSTON

 SALE DATE     PRODUCT NO       PURCHASE      PAYMENT     RETURN      ADJUSTMENT
------------------------------------------------------------------------------


 06/17/89        0045           $60.00
 06/19/89                                    $400.00                 $110.00
 06/20/89


                              NEW BALANCE       $0.00
                     AVAILABLE CREDIT LINE    $900.00
```

ERROR REPORT

```
                      ERROR TRANSACTION REPORT
          ERROR MESSAGE                     TRANSACTION RECORD
-------------------------------------------------------------------------


     NO MATCH IN MASTER             123411042188010000001005000
     INVALID TRANSACTION CODE       123455042188000000001000000
     INVALID TRANSACTION CODE       19876X061089023001000000235
     NO MATCH IN MASTER             200003052989558911111555555
     NO MATCH IN MASTER             500001071089999980001010000
```

FIGURE 13-10

First Three Divisions of the COBOL
Program for Monthly Processing

```
       IDENTIFICATION DIVISION.
       PROGRAM-ID. MONTHUPD.
      *
       ENVIRONMENT DIVISION.
       CONFIGURATION SECTION.
       SOURCE-COMPUTER. ABC-480.
       OBJECT-COMPUTER. ABC-480.
      *
       INPUT-OUTPUT SECTION.
      *
       FILE-CONTROL.
      *
           SELECT OLD-MASTER              ASSIGN TO OLD-MAS.
           SELECT COMB-TRANS-FILE         ASSIGN TO COMBINED-TRANS.
           SELECT NEW-MASTER              ASSIGN TO NEW-MAS.
           SELECT ERROR-FILE              ASSIGN TO PRINT-ERR.
           SELECT REPORT-FILE             ASSIGN TO REPORT-FIL.
      *
       DATA DIVISION.
      *
       FILE SECTION.
      *
       FD  COMB-TRANS-FILE
           BLOCK CONTAINS 50 RECORDS
           LABEL RECORDS ARE OMITTED
           DATA RECORD IS COMB-TRANS-RECORD.
      *
       01  COMB-TRANS-RECORD.
           05  TRANS-ACCOUNT-NO           PIC X(5).
           05  TRANS-CODE                 PIC 9.
           05  TRANS-DATE                 PIC X(6).
           05  TRANS-PRODUCT-NO           PIC 9(4).
           05  TRANS-QUANTITY             PIC 9(4).
           05  TRANS-PRICE                PIC 9(4)V99.
           05  TRANS-PMT-ADJ-AMT          PIC 9(6)V99.
      *
       FD  OLD-MASTER
           LABEL RECORDS OMITTED
           DATA RECORD IS OLD-MASTER-RECORD.
      *
       01  OLD-MASTER-RECORD.
           02  OLD-ACCOUNT-NO             PIC X(5).
           02  OLD-NAME                   PIC X(20).
           02  OLD-CREDIT-LIMIT           PIC 9(4)V99.
           02  OLD-BALANCE                PIC S9(6)V99.
           02  OLD-ADDRESS                PIC X(40).
           02  FILLER                     PIC X(1).
      *
       FD  NEW-MASTER
           LABEL RECORDS STANDARD
           DATA RECORD IS NEW-MAS-REC.
      *
       01  NEW-MAS-REC                    PIC X(80).
```

FIGURE 13-10

First Three Divisions of the COBOL
Program for Monthly Processing
(continued)

```
 *
   FD  ERROR-FILE
       LABEL RECORDS OMITTED
       DATA RECORD IS ERROR-RECORD.
 *
   01  ERROR-RECORD              PIC X(132).
 *
   FD  REPORT-FILE
       LABEL RECORDS OMITTED
       DATA RECORD IS REPORT-RECORD.
 *
   01  REPORT-RECORD            PIC X(132).
 *
   WORKING-STORAGE SECTION.
 *
   01  END-OF-TRANS             PIC X(3) VALUE "NO".
       88  TRANS-ENDED          VALUE "YES".
 *
   01  END-OF-MASTER            PIC X(3) VALUE "NO".
       88  MASTER-ENDED         VALUE "YES".
 *
   01  ACTIVITY-FLAG            PIC X(3) VALUE "NO".
       88  ACTIVITY-ON          VALUE "YES".
       88  NO-ACTIVITY          VALUE "NO".
 *
   01  WRITE-TRANS-SWITCH       PIC X(3) VALUE "YES" .
       88  WRITE-TRANS          VALUE "YES".
       88  NOT-WRITE-TRANS      VALUE "NO".
 *
   01  WRITE-FLAG               PIC X(3) VALUE "YES".
       88  WRITE-REC            VALUE "YES".
       88  NOT-WRITE-REC        VALUE "NO".
 *
   01  WORK-MAS-REC.
       02  WORK-ACCOUNT-NO      PIC X(5).
       02  FILLER               PIC X(20).
       02  WORK-CREDIT-LIMIT    PIC 9(4)V99.
       02  WORK-BALANCE         PIC S9(6)V99.
       02  FILLER               PIC X(41).
 *
   01  WS-DATE-ITEMS.
       02  WS-DATE.
           03  WS-YR            PIC 9(02).
           03  WS-MO            PIC 9(02).
           03  WS-DA            PIC 9(02).
 *
   01  WS-NUMERIC-ITEMS.
       02  LN-COUNTER           PIC 9(2) VALUE ZERO.
       02  PAGE-SIZE            PIC 9(2) VALUE 35.
       02  WS-TRANS-AMOUNT      PIC 9(6)V99.
       02  PG-COUNTER           PIC 99 VALUE ZERO.
       02  WORK-AVAILABLE-LIMIT PIC 9(6)V99.
 *
```

FIGURE 13-10

*First Three Divisions of the COBOL
Program for Monthly Processing
(continued)*

```
   OUTPUT REPORT RECORD DESCRIPTION:
*
   01  STATEMENT-REPORT-FORMAT.
       02  STATE-HEAD1.
           03  FILLER            PIC X(02) VALUE SPACES.
           03  S-MONTH           PIC 9(02).
           03  FILLER            PIC X(01) VALUE "/".
           03  S-DAY             PIC 9(02).
           03  FILLER            PIC X(01) VALUE "/".
           03  S-YEAR            PIC 9(02).
           03  FILLER            PIC X(62) VALUE SPACES.
           03  FILLER            PIC X(5) VALUE "PAGE ".
           03  S-PAGE            PIC Z9.
*
       02  STATE-HEAD2.
           03  FILLER            PIC X(30) VALUE SPACES.
           03  FILLER            PIC X(19) VALUE
               "ACME ANYTHING CORP.".
*
       02  STATE-HEAD3.
           03  FILLER            PIC X(29) VALUE SPACES.
           03  FILLER            PIC X(20) VALUE
               "STATEMENT OF ACCOUNT".
*
       02  STATE-HEAD4.
           03  FILLER            PIC X(2) VALUE SPACES.
           03  S-ACCOUNT-NO      PIC X(5).
*
       02  STATE-HEAD5.
           03  FILLER            PIC X(2) VALUE SPACES.
           03  S-NAME            PIC X(20).
*
       02  STATE-HEAD6.
           03  FILLER            PIC X(2) VALUE SPACES.
           03  FILLER            PIC X(9) VALUE "SALE DATE".
           03  FILLER            PIC X(6) VALUE SPACES.
           03  FILLER            PIC X(10) VALUE "PRODUCT NO".
           03  FILLER            PIC X(9) VALUE SPACES.
           03  FILLER            PIC X(8) VALUE "PURCHASE".
           03  FILLER            PIC X(7) VALUE SPACES.
           03  FILLER            PIC X(7) VALUE "PAYMENT".
           03  FILLER            PIC X(7) VALUE SPACES.
           03  FILLER            PIC X(6) VALUE "RETURN".
           03  FILLER            PIC X(5) VALUE SPACES.
           03  FILLER            PIC X(10) VALUE "ADJUSTMENT".
*
       02  STATE-HEAD7.
           03  FILLER            PIC X(90) VALUE ALL "-".
*
       02  STATE-BLANK.
           03  FILLER            PIC X(132) VALUE SPACES.
*
```

FIGURE 13-10
First Three Divisions of the COBOL
Program for Monthly Processing
(continued)

```
        02  STATE-DETAIL.
            03  FILLER              PIC X(4) VALUE SPACES.
            03  S-DATE              PIC XX/XX/XX.
            03  FILLER              PIC X(09) VALUE SPACES.
            03  S-PRODUCT-NO        PIC X(4).
            03  FILLER              PIC X(10) VALUE SPACES.
            03  S-PURCHASE          PIC $$$,$$9.99 BLANK WHEN ZERO.
            03  FILLER              PIC X(4) VALUE SPACES.
            03  S-PAYMENT           PIC $$$,$$9.99 BLANK WHEN ZERO.
            03  FILLER              PIC X(4) VALUE SPACES.
            03  S-RETURN            PIC $$$,$$9.99 BLANK WHEN ZERO.
            03  FILLER              PIC X(04) VALUE SPACES.
            03  S-ADJUSTS           PIC $$$,$$9.99 BLANK WHEN ZERO.
            03  FILLER              PIC X(4) VALUE SPACES.
       *
        02  STATE-DETAIL2.
            03  FILLER              PIC X(28) VALUE SPACES.
            03  FILLER              PIC X(36) VALUE
                "**** NO ACTIVITY IN THIS PERIOD ****".
       *
        02  STATE-TOTAL1.
            03  FILLER              PIC X(31) VALUE SPACES.
            03  FILLER              PIC X(12) VALUE "NEW BALANCE ".
            03  STATE-BALANCE-NOW   PIC $,$$$,$$9.99CR.
       *
        02  STATE-TOTAL2.
            03  FILLER              PIC X(22) VALUE SPACES.
            03  FILLER              PIC X(21) VALUE
                "AVAILABLE CREDIT LINE".
            03  STATE-CR-AMT        PIC $,$$$,$$9.99.
       *
       **ERROR FILE RECORD DESCRIPTION:
       *
        01  ERROR-RECORDS.
            02  ERROR-HEAD1.
                03  FILLER          PIC X(26) VALUE SPACES.
                03  FILLER          PIC X(24) VALUE
                    "ERROR TRANSACTION REPORT".
       *
            02  ERROR-HEAD2.
                03  FILLER          PIC X(10) VALUE SPACES.
                03  FILLER          PIC X(13) VALUE "ERROR MESSAGE".
                03  FILLER          PIC X(27) VALUE SPACES.
                03  FILLER          PIC X(18) VALUE
                    "TRANSACTION RECORD".
       *
            02  ERROR-HEAD3.
                03  FILLER          PIC X(80) VALUE ALL "-".
       *
            02  ERROR-BLANK.
                03  FILLER          PIC X(132) VALUE SPACES.
       *
            02  ERROR-DETAIL.
                03  FILLER          PIC X(10) VALUE SPACES.
                03  ERROR-MESSAGE   PIC X(40).
                03  ERROR-TRANS     PIC X(82).
```

SUMMARY

In this chapter we presented and discussed a system of three interrelated COBOL programs concerned with sequential file processing.

The first program illustrated the creation of a master file for customer records. The second program demonstrated the processing of daily transactions and updating of the daily master. The third program was concerned with monthly activities, and processed the transactions for the month against the full master file.

The expanded example was intended to provide you with a programming illustration that goes beyond the usual, more-limited text examples. Although the system of programs in this chapter are not at the level of complexity to be "real-world" examples, they serve to illustrate some of the practical issues that guide program development in organizations.

EXERCISES

13.1 Modify the sample program in Figure 13-3 so that each input record is checked for *all* five possible errors. Each error encountered should be included in the error report.

13.2 Write the PROCEDURE DIVISION for the monthly processing program, using the first three divisions in Figure 13-10 as well as the task description in the last section of the chapter.

Advanced
COBOL
Programming

14 Program Design

THIS CHAPTER *and the following one cover a number of conceptual issues about designing and testing COBOL programs. At about the midpoint in the book you pause, as it were, to consider the process of designing and testing good programs. In this chapter you deal with the process of program design, which is concerned with how individual modules are synthesized into a complete program.*

As stated in Chapter 1, the ultimate objective of program design is to produce good programs. In the first three sections of this chapter you will study **program cohesion,** *which has to do with the properties associated with good modules. The emphasis in this topic is on the* **individual module.** *In contrast, in the remaining sections of this chapter you will consider overall program design, which has to do with* **intermodule relationships** *and overall structure-chart considerations.*

COHESION IN PROGRAMS

As we discussed in Chapter 6, to achieve good program design, a program module should have the property of being a *black box*. The black box concept means that a module should be capable of being described in terms of the *function* that it performs, rather than the *procedure* by which it performs the function. In addition to each module representing a black box, a well-designed program should consist of modules that have as much cohesion as possible. A module is *cohesive* if it performs only *one function* and all program statements in the module are directly related to that function only. A well-designed program ideally should be so partitioned that it consists of specific functions, each of which is represented by a cohesive module in the program.

From the practical standpoint this question arises: What is a cohesive function? Unfortunately, there is no specific and comprehensive definition of a cohesive function. Nevertheless, a working knowledge of this concept can be developed by understanding some of its characteristics. Generally speaking, a cohesive function refers to a *single task* that can be described in just a few words of language. An example is "Compute this week's F.I.C.A. tax for the employee." But what about the function "Process the payroll for this week"? The latter function is too broad and should be partitioned into several more specific tasks or functions. At the other extreme, however, the printing of one line of information or the addition of two numbers are tasks that are too specific to be represented as distinct program modules. Thus both experience and judgment serve as the basis for defining cohesive program modules. Still, the following two guidelines can be useful:

- A cohesive module, when coded in COBOL, should not exceed a page of program statements (about 50 lines). However, the module may be represented by only 1 or 2 lines of program code if they constitute a distinct, cohesive function.

- The module should be capable of being described in ordinary language without the use of multiple verbs, the conjunction "and," or use of a series of words such as "first," "then," and the like.

The above guidelines rely on indirect indicators that can alert the programmer to the existence of noncohesive functions. To further assist us in designing and recognizing cohesive modules, the next section of this chapter describes several types of cohesion that can characterize a module.

R E V I E W . . . .

1. A module that performs only one function, and whose program statements are all directed toward that function, is described as being _____ .

   cohesive

2. Generally speaking, when a cohesive module is coded in COBOL, the program statements should not exceed about _____ (number) lines.

   50

3. Generally speaking, the description of a cohesive module [may / should not] include a series of words such as "first," "then," and "next."

   should not

TYPES OF COHESION

Functional Cohesion

Functional cohesion represents the highest form of cohesion and is the only type to which reference specifically was made in the preceding section of this chapter. Such a module's design is based on the definition of the function involved, and all the processing in the module is directly related to the defined function. For instance, a module described as Process-Transactions as contrasted to the module Process-Payment-Transactions illustrates the difference between a *composite* as contrasted to a *cohesive* function. Consider now the following widely used type of paragraph in COBOL programs:

```
READ-RECORD.
    READ CUST-FILE RECORD
        AT END MOVE 'YES' TO FILE-END-FLAG.
```

It must be admitted that technically this is not a cohesive function. Its description would include two statements, such as "Read the next record, and if it is an end-of-file record, set a flag." The use of the conjunction "and" reveals the absence of functional cohesion. But the simplicity of the module, plus the fact that the language syntax requires the AT END to be associated with a READ statement, make it desirable to create such a module. Thus functional cohesion is a programming objective that may not be strictly attainable in all situations because of practical considerations.

Coincidental Cohesion

Essentially, *coincidental cohesion* represents the other extreme from functional cohesion. A module has coincidental cohesion if it consists of a more-or-less random collection of statements or procedures. In reviewing programs one can often find a "catchall" paragraph that includes a series of relatively unrelated statements, such as

```
PAR-X.
    MOVE SPACES TO PRINTLINE
    MOVE CUST-NO TO SAVE-CUST-NO
    ADD TOT-1 TO TOT-ALL
    MOVE ZERO TO OLD-AMOUNT.
```

A practical way to recognize a module based on coincidental cohesion is to try to describe it with a simple statement. Module PAR-X above defies such description. Another practical test is to ask if it would make any difference if the single module were partitioned into two or more modules. For example, we could partition PAR-X above into PAR-X1 and PAR-X2 without impacting the cohesion of the new modules in any way:

```
PAR-X1.
    MOVE SPACES TO PRINTLINE
    MOVE CUST-NO TO SAVE-CUST-NO.
PAR-X2.
    ADD TOT-1 TO TOT-ALL
    MOVE ZERO TO OLD-AMOUNT.
```

Programs that are designed to try to balance the size of modules instead of concentrating on the functional cohesion would tend to have program procedures split across two or more modules, and the program would be difficult to understand and difficult to modify.

Class-Oriented Cohesion

Modules characterized by *class-oriented cohesion* are formed by inclusion of elements that refer to the same broad class of logical processes or functions. A common example of class-oriented cohesion is the type of module that is often labeled "Validate Data." Data validation is a general class of functions, and it would be better to construct a module for each specific type of data validation. For instance, we could have modules such as Validate Financial Data and Validate Customer Account Number.

Another common example of the use of class-oriented cohesion is a module that might be labeled Process-Transactions. Such a module often includes multiple functions, as indicated in the following program outline:

```
PROCESS-TRANSACTIONS.
    IF PAYMENT-TRANSACTION
                statements to process payment ...
    ELSE
        IF CHARGE-TRANSACTION
                statements to process charge ...
        ELSE
            IF NEW-RECORD-TRANSACTION
                statements to process new record ...
```

From the standpoint of good design logic, PROCESS-TRANSACTIONS is a composite-functions module because it includes the logic for several distinct transaction types. Consideration should be given to partitioning the one composite into several modules, each with strong functional cohesion, such as by defining separate modules for processing payment transactions and for processing charge transactions.

The above example is so common in programming practice that it warrants further consideration. Is it really wrong to design a module such as Process-Transactions? Not necessarily. In general, modules characterized by class-oriented cohesion are not as good as modules based on functional cohesion. As a practical matter, however, if the Process-Transactions module is fairly simple, it has to be admitted that such a composite-functions module does no real harm. But what do we mean by "simple"? If there are just a few types of transactions included in the module, perhaps not more than five, and their processing logic is not extensive or difficult, then we would be hard-pressed to argue against the composite module. Such a class-oriented module could be relatively easily comprehended, developed, and modified in the future. In particular, grouping several transaction-types in the same module does no harm if the processing logic of each transaction-type is distinct. The harm occurs if transaction-types share common procedures and the module is so designed that processing logic from several transaction-types is interwoven. In such a case an understanding of the processing of one transaction-type depends on an understanding of how it relates to the processing of one or more other transaction-types, thereby violating the concept of cohesiveness and resulting in poor partitioning of the program.

At this point it is appropriate to differentiate the appropriate orientation of a programmer during the design stage of a programming project as contrasted to the program-writing stage. At the *design stage* we should not be concerned about the eventual implementation into program code. At the *program-writing* stage we may choose to implement a composite module because of the limited extent of code and the simplicity of logic in such cases as the use of nested IF or EVALUATE statements. Nevertheless, in the long run we will write better programs if we design them apart from coding considerations. Such an approach would lead us to recognize, for instance, the processing of Payments, Charges, and New Records as distinct functions. As a likely result, we would probably end up with a coding structure that is improved in the long run. For example, instead of the program outline with one class-oriented module developed earlier in this section, we might have the following outline, which includes one class-oriented module and then several modules with functional cohesion:

Using Nested If
    Process-Transactions.
       If payment-transaction
          Perform Apply-Payment
       Else
          If charge-transaction
             Perform Apply-Charge
          Else
             If new-record-transaction
                Perform Add-New-Record
.
.
.

    Apply-Payment.
.
.
.

    Apply-Charge.
.
.
.

    Add-New-Record.

Using EVALUATE
    Process-Transactions.
       Evaluate true
          When payment-transaction
             Perform Apply-Payment
          When charge-transaction
             Perform Apply-Charge
          When new-record-transaction
             Perform Add-New-Record.
.
.
.

Now the modules Apply-Payment, Apply-Charge, and Add-New-Record have functional cohesion. If the credit department of the company should institute a new procedure for processing charges, for example, we need focus only on that module without being concerned about the other modules.

Time-Related Cohesion

In *time-related cohesion* the only reason for combining the elements of a module into one unit is that they occur together in time. A common example of time-related cohesion is a module often named "Initialize," in which files are opened, counters and flags are set, headers are printed, and the like. Most programs contain such a module, even though such a module lacks functional cohesion.

Improved program design suggests that the use of time-related modules should be *minimized*. If an accumulator is to be set equal to zero, for example, it would be best to do so within a module for which this process is necessary to carry out a specific function. As we have acknowledged with respect to class-oriented cohesion, in many instances it is convenient to utilize time-oriented cohesion and to group steps that occur together in time. But it is better not to think in the time-oriented context of beginning, middle, and end when designing a program. Rather, the program designer should give principal attention to the functions to be carried out.

Procedural Cohesion

Procedural cohesion involves a grouping of items that are associated with a particular type of procedure. The two most common procedures that serve as the basis for such a module are a program loop and a decision element. The program designer may identify the repeated performance of a series of steps and therefore choose to develop a module corresponding to the loop. For example, a program could include repeated analysis of company sales for each of the last 12 months. As much as possible, the repetition aspect of processing should *not* serve as the basis for module design. Instead, the focus should be on the functions to be performed.

As an example of a decision step serving as the basis for a program module, suppose that product prices are determined to be either "standard" or "exception." In such a case the program designer may choose to design a module that encompasses the processing for such prices. Again, the decision step is not the appropriate basis for module design, but rather the focus should be on function. Using function as the basis, we would disregard the decision aspect and proceed to design two (or more) modules to correspond to the functions involved in standard-price and exception-price processing. At the *programming stage* we may indeed end up writing a paragraph based on the decision aspect of the code. But at the *design stage* we should focus only on the *what,* not the *how*. Program designers who rely on flowcharts as the basis for design tend to develop modules that are heavily procedure-oriented.

Data-Related Cohesion

As the name implies, *data-related cohesion* is based on data categories. Such modules are most likely to be developed when a program is viewed in terms of data flow. For example, a module called Transactions Register might be developed based on transactions data being input and listed. The reason for the module is recognition of the data flow. Many program processes have the characteristic that data output with respect to one step is data input with respect to another step, and there is a tendency to combine the two steps into one module when data-related cohesion is applied. Again, this approach is less than ideal because the cohesion is not based on function and may result in multiple functions being combined into one module or one function being split into several modules.

Sequential Cohesion

Modules exemplifying *sequential cohesion* are designed on the basis of processing steps that occur in sequence. Therefore the two or more steps that are combined may form a module with weak cohesion, because the module may include either a partial function or multiple functions. As an example, suppose that there are three processing steps, A, B, and C, in sequence.

A ...
B ...
C ...

Further, suppose that in terms of logical cohesion steps A and B, in fact, constitute one function, while C is another, distinct function. If sequence alone were the basis for modular design, any of the following four modular groupings would be possible:

(A,B,C)	A and (B,C)
(A,B) and C	A and B and C

Of the possible groupings above, the only one that is functionally cohesive is the one consisting of the two modules, (A,B) and C.

Again, anticipation of program coding should *not* be considered in designing program modules. Suppose a program segment consists of 15 statements occurring in sequence. On a superficial basis (and before actual program coding) one might apply sequential cohesion and create a module (paragraph) containing all 15 lines. However, suppose the first 10 lines represent one function and the last 5 lines represent another function. Should a new module (paragraph) be defined beginning at line 11 even though the 15 lines will always be executed in the same sequential order in any event? We maintain that such partitioning of the module should be done. The separation leads to better documentation and makes future modification of the program easier.

R E V I E W . . . .

1. In terms of general priority in program design, the highest form of cohesion for a module is _____ cohesion.

   functional

2. Modules that are not functionally cohesive [should never / may sometimes] be included in a well-designed COBOL program.

   may sometimes

3. Modules that are formed by inclusion of elements that belong in the same broad class of logical processes or functions are said to exhibit_____ cohesion.

   class-oriented

4. For the programmer to anticipate program coding considerations during the program design stage, and to define modules accordingly, is [desirable / undesirable].

   undesirable

5. The type of modular cohesion based on grouping items that occur together in time is _____ cohesion.

   time-related

6. Although establishing a program module on the basis of time-oriented considerations is sometimes useful, the program designer should give principal attention to the _____ to be carried out by the module.

   function

7. When items in a module are grouped because they are associated with a particular programming procedure, the basis for cohesion is described as _____ cohesion.

                                                                        procedural

8. The two most common procedures that serve as a basis for procedural cohesion are the existence of a program _____ and a _____ element, or step.

                                                                        loop; decision

9. The program designer who is likely to develop modules that are heavily procedure-oriented is one who relies on _____ as the basis for design.

                                                                        flowcharts

10. The type of module that is defined on the basis of the commonality of data exhibits is _____ cohesion.

                                                                        data-related

11. Data-related cohesion is most likely to be used by a program designer who views the program in terms of _____ .

                                                                        data flow

12. The type of cohesion that reflects a more-or-less random collection of the statements or procedures included in a module is _____ cohesion.

                                                                        coincidental

13. In general, a well-designed program is one that [minimizes / maximizes] the use of coincidental cohesion in the formation of program modules.

                                                                        minimizes

14. Modules that are based on including the processing steps that occur sequentially are said to exemplify _____ cohesion.

                                                                        sequential

15. Generally, a module that is based on sequential cohesion [would also / would not] incorporate functional cohesion.

                                                                        would not

* * * * * * * * * * * * * * * * * *

LEVELS OF COHESION

As indicated earlier, functional cohesion is the most desirable basis for modular design, while coincidental cohesion is the least desirable basis. Where do the other forms of cohesion fall with respect to these two extremes? It has been suggested that the order from most desirable to least desirable forms of cohesion is as listed in Table 14-1.

Of course, the general rule is that functional cohesion should be achieved when possible. If functional cohesion is not attainable, the higher forms of cohesion in Table 14-1 should be preferred to the lower ones listed. But in actual programs it is difficult to justify any particular priority of types of cohesion other than functional cohesion. That is, for a given program and particular circumstance a class-oriented basis for module cohesion may be preferred to a data-related basis. Given the overall design of the program, there may be, in fact, little choice regarding the basis for a particular module of the program.

The most useful viewpoint to develop in studying the different forms of cohesion is to develop an awareness of the variety of approaches possible, but to follow a functional approach as the basic foundation for program design. As you

TABLE 14-1
Preferred Order of Cohesion

Functional

Sequential

Data-Related

Procedural

Time-Related

Class-Oriented

Coincidental

design a program, you might ask yourself: "Am I inadvertently relying on sequence to develop the program modules?" Such a questioning attitude leads to improved program design from the very start. Once a program has been designed and found to be wanting, it is very difficult then to redesign the program. *It is fundamentally easier to design a program correctly in the first place.* Still, it must be acknowledged that program design is an iterative process. We have to sketch a design, erase and resketch, and occasionally scrap the whole design and start all over.

R E V I E W . . . .

1. While the preferred order for the various forms of cohesion may vary to some extent from program to program, the most desirable is _____ cohesion while the least desirable is _____ cohesion.

   functional; coincidental

2. If the concepts of good modular design are followed, iterative procedures involving revisions of early design attempts [are nevertheless / are not] required.

   are nevertheless

. . . .

PROGRAM DESIGN

The first part of this chapter was concerned with issues about good design of individual modules. In the remainder of the chapter we discuss principles of program design that are aimed at *relationships between modules*. A good program should consist of well-designed cohesive modules. Additionally, these well-designed modules must be placed in a total program structure that leads to good program design.

Content Coupling

One of the issues regarding between-module relationships is *content coupling*. Two program modules are content-coupled when one module references the contents of the other module. A general rule of good program design is that such coupling should be minimized. Content coupling is common in unstructured programs with abusive use of GO TO statements. For example, consider the program modules in Figure 14-1. Modules A, B, C, and D are highly content-coupled because in essence each module contains part of one or more other modules. The GO TO indicates continuation of the module's logic; so in order to follow the logic of the entire module we have to read the module referenced by the GO TO as well.

But the GO TO command is not the only culprit. Programs without this command can also include content coupling. Refer to Figure 14-2, which employs a PERFORM ... THROUGH structure. The A and B paragraphs constitute a logical module because they are referenced jointly by the PERFORM A THROUGH B statement. However, since module C PERFORMs B, part of the first module is also the content of C. Notice that the problem is caused by the PERFORM ... THROUGH, which implies that A and B constitute a cohesive module. If, indeed, B is a separate function, we should set up a separate function B which is PERFORMed by A and C. However, B must be defined as a distinct module with functional strength. If B by itself is a series of statements with little functional meaning, we should repeat the B program code within C rather than confusing the structure by avoiding the repetition of the code through the use of the PERFORM B statement.

Many times, as we write program code, we may find that a number of consecutive lines are repeated in two or more places in the program. We may then conclude that such lines of code should not have to be repeated, and so we put those statements under a paragraph name and PERFORM them from the several different places in the program. But such a paragraph does not have an *independent* functional purpose of its own, and results in content coupling among several paragraphs.

FIGURE 14-1
Content-Coupled Modules
Using GO TO

FIGURE 14-2
Illustration of Content Coupling
Without the GO TO

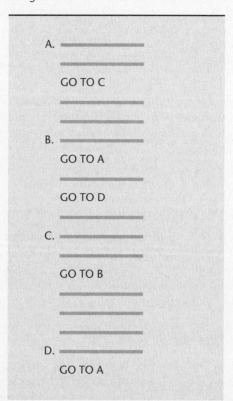

1. When one program module references the contents of another module, the two modules are described as being _____ .

    content-coupled

2. Frequent use of the GO TO command leads to [many / few] modules being content-coupled.

    many

3. A principal problem associated with content coupling is that the functional _____ of modules is destroyed.

    cohesiveness

. . . .

Module Size

In the first part of this chapter we indicated that the size of a module is governed by the concept of functional cohesion. Thus it might seem that module size as such is not relevant as an indicator of good program design. However, in practice, well-designed programs tend to have modules that are not systematically too small or too large. At the preferred limits, any given module cannot be smaller than 1 line and should not be much larger than a page (about 50 lines). But even within these limits a program may become too complex because of a large number of modules that are very small or a small number of modules that are very large.

As illustrated in Figures 14-3 and 14-4, the basic solution for modules that are too large is to partition them into smaller modules. In Figure 14-3(a) the large

FIGURE 14-3

Reducing Module Size by Hierarchical Partitioning

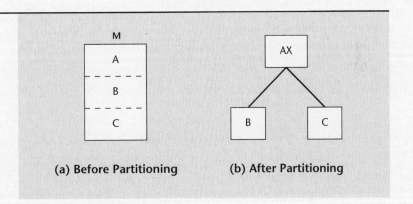

(a) Before Partitioning (b) After Partitioning

FIGURE 14-4

Reducing Module Size by Partitioning at the Same Hierarchical Level

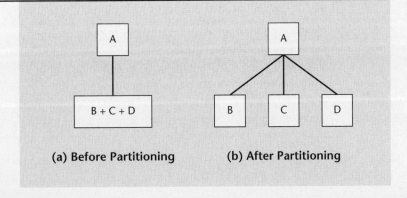

(a) Before Partitioning (b) After Partitioning

module M consists of elements A, B, and C. We create a new hierarchical level in Figure 14-3(b) with AX as the superior module and modules B and C as the subordinates. AX includes the original element A plus the coordinative elements to control B and C. In the case of Figure 14-4 the one module subordinate to A is partitioned into three modules, but at the same hierarchical level as before partitioning.

Similarly, modules that are too small can be combined to form larger modules, as illustrated in Figures 14-5 and 14-6. In Figure 14-5 modules B and C are combined into one module at the same hierarchical level. In the case of Figure 14-6 the two subordinates are incorporated into their superior to form a larger module. For instance, suppose the small module B is

```
B.
    MOVE SPACES TO XYZ.
```

Instead of the statement PERFORM B in module A, that module could include the statement

```
MOVE SPACES TO XYZ.
```

Sometimes it is desirable to have small modules because they provide programming flexibility and facilitate future modifications of the program. Refer to Figure 14-7. In Figure 14-7(a), before any combining of modules, X is a data item given to B as input from module A. On the basis of X, B invokes either

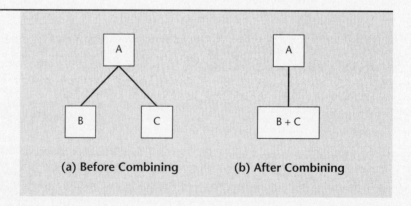

FIGURE 14-5

Increasing Module Size by Combining at the Same Hierarchical Level

(a) Before Combining   (b) After Combining

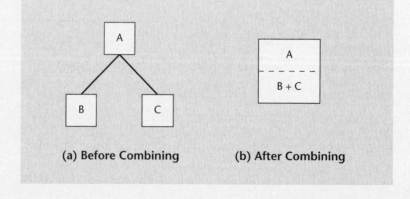

FIGURE 14-6

Increasing Module Size by Combining Subordinates into a Superior

(a) Before Combining   (b) After Combining

module C or module D, and that is the extent of the function of module B in the program. For example, the following program code could constitute B:

```
B.
    IF  X = 'DO-C'
        PERFORM C
    ELSE
        IF X = 'DO-D'
            PERFORM D.
```

The logical question arises: Why not incorporate module B into module A, as in Figure 14-7(b)? But suppose that a future modification would require that the C vs. D selection be invoked by the new modules P and Q, as shown in Figure 14-7(c). It is now clear that although module B is small and simple, it can play a useful role as a functional subordinate to several superior modules.

Of course, in all cases the primary consideration is the functional cohesion of each module. Our discussion above does not mean that we strive for "proper" module size as a main objective. Instead, module size is often an indirect indicator of functional cohesion, and we consider size changes only as an objective that is secondary to functional cohesion.

R E V I E W . . . .

1. The usual limits on module size are from _____ line(s) to approximately _____ lines of program code.

    1; 50

2. When modules are too large, the basic solution is to _____ them into smaller (but cohesive) modules.

    partition

3. Partitioning of modules [cannot / may] lead to more hierarchical levels in the structure chart.

    may

FIGURE 14-7

Should the Small Module B Be Eliminated?

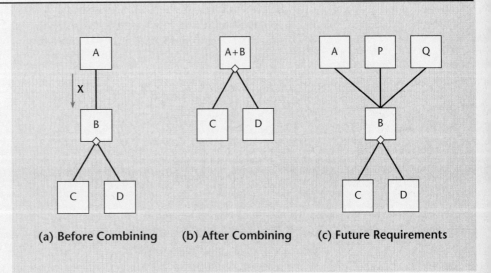

(a) Before Combining   (b) After Combining   (c) Future Requirements

4. Program modules that are too small often can be _____ to form larger modules without impacting the cohesion of each module.

combined

5. Combining small modules to form larger modules [cannot / may] lead to fewer hierarchical levels in the structure chart.

may

6. When a small program module is subordinate to several superior modules, it is generally [desirable / undesirable] to combine the module with one of the superior modules.

undesirable

.   .   .   .

Fan-out: The Span of Control

The *span of control* is defined by the number of subordinates for a given superior module. In organization and management there is a counterpart concept that refers to the number of people that report directly to an organizational superior. In program design it is generally true that well-designed programs tend to have balanced spans of control in the range of 2 to about 7. A span of control of 1 suggests the possibility of composite functions that should be partitioned, while a span exceeding about 7 suggests that the modules may be too small and perhaps should be combined. Visual inspection of a structure chart often is sufficient to determine if the spans generally are too small or too large. For example, the unbalanced spans of control are readily observed in the two structure charts in Figure 14-8.

The term *fan-out* is also used to express the span of control. The fan-out of a given module is the number of its subordinates, and the term is derived from the structure-chart representation of the superior with respect to its subordinates. Another descriptive term is *pancaking,* which refers to a very wide span of control such as portrayed in Figure 14-8(a).

A span of control that is too narrow can be increased either by incorporating subordinates into their superiors or by partitioning and increasing the number of modules at a given level. Which approach is followed is, of course, reflective of the reason for the span being too narrow in the first place. Refer to Figure 14-9. The span of control has been increased for this structure by incorporating subordinates into their superiors and thereby also reducing the number of levels in the hierarchy. On the other hand, in Figure 14-10 the span of control has been increased by partitioning module B into Bl, B2, and B3. Of course, in all cases span of control is an objective that is subordinate to the main objective of having functionally cohesive modules.

R E V I E W .   .   .   .

1. The number of subordinates for a given superior module defines the concept of

_____ .

span of control

2. Generally, the span of control should be within the range of _____ to about _____ subordinate modules.

2;7

FIGURE 14-8
Unbalanced Spans of Control

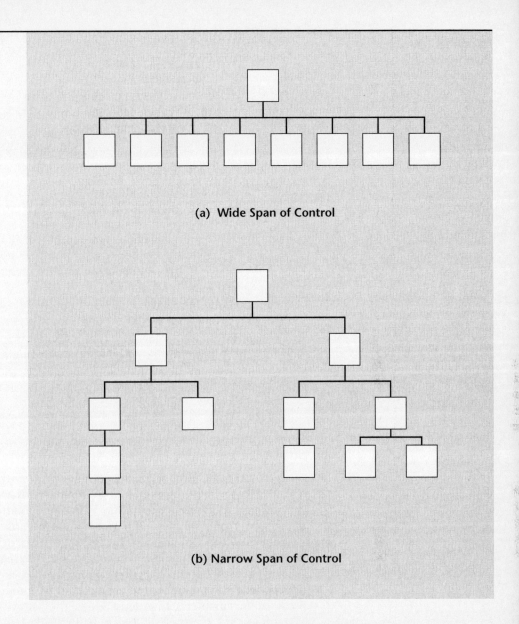

(a) Wide Span of Control

(b) Narrow Span of Control

FIGURE 14-9
Increasing Span of Control by Incorporating Subordinates into Superiors

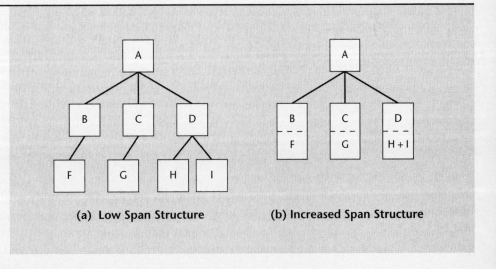

(a) Low Span Structure

(b) Increased Span Structure

FIGURE 14-10

Increasing Span of Control by Partitioning Modules

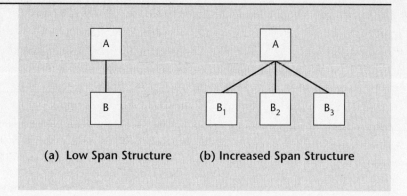

(a) Low Span Structure   (b) Increased Span Structure

3. If a span of control that is too wide is reduced through combining modules at the same level, then the number of levels in the structure chart is [reduced / unaffected].

                                                                        unaffected

4. If a span of control that is too narrow is increased by combining modules at different levels (i.e., by incorporating subordinates into their superiors), then the number of levels in the structure chart is [reduced / unaffected].

                                                                        reduced

· ·

Fan-In

The term *fan-in* refers to the number of superiors with respect to a given module. Refer to Figure 14-11. Figure 14-11(a) illustrates that module E has a fan-in of 4. Even though a strict hierarchy should not have modules with multiple superiors, in practice a high fan-in often is desirable because it reduces the amount of program code and provides the opportunity to develop well-tested common functions. From a program-coding standpoint we may well ask how high fan-in modules should be implemented. One approach is to set up such modules as independent subprograms that are CALLed by their superiors (subprograms are discussed in Chapter 23). Alternatively, they may be set up within the main program as paragraphs or sections to be PERFORMed.

Occasionally, there may be objection to frequent use of the PERFORM (and CALL) commands because of the processing time required. If these commands are to be avoided, an alternative is to develop and test the high-fan-in module separately and then duplicate it into each of its superiors, as illustrated in Figure 14-11(b). However, the avoidance of the CALL or PERFORM commands is generally not warranted except, perhaps, for a program with high data volume that is processed in a computer facility with minimum capacity.

A few words of caution are necessary regarding fan-in. Modules with multiple superiors (high fan-in) introduce a new form of relationship that may undermine the concept of hierarchical independence described in Chapter 6. In Figure 14-12, for example, modules B and C are hierarchical peers and therefore should be independent in their processing. Yet their sharing of module G as a subordinate introduces a form of relationship that may make them content-dependent on one another. For instance, suppose that a modification in C requires that G be modified. The modification in G may then lead to the requirement that B also be modified. Thus, the modules B and C have become dependent on one another because of the fan-in with respect to module G. Note that the fan-in

FIGURE 14-11
High-Fan-in Modules

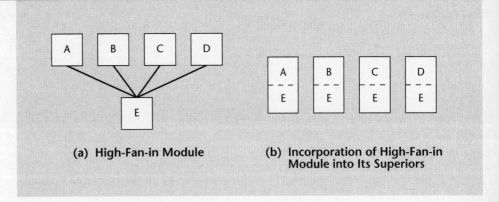

(a) High-Fan-in Module

(b) Incorporation of High-Fan-in Module into Its Superiors

FIGURE 14-12
Structure Chart with Fan-in at Module G

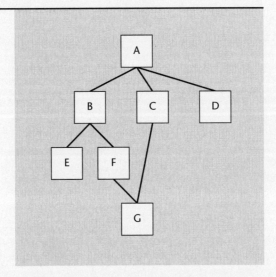

need not be direct. In this example B is not the direct superior of G, but is one level removed in the hierarchy.

The possible adverse effects associated with sharing modules as subordinates makes it necessary that such sharing be clearly documented. In Figure 14-12 the sharing is documented by the multiple lines branching into module G. However, in structure charts with several high-fan-in modules, the result may be many crossing lines, as illustrated in Figure 14-13(a). To avoid such a potentially confusing chart, the shared modules may be repeated in the chart with respect to each subordinate, and the repeated modules are then shaded in the upper right corner, as illustrated in Figure 14-13(b). But structure charts are only one form of documentation. Most compilers can produce a cross-reference listing that shows all of the PERFORM and CALL references to a given module, thereby providing a complete list of the superiors for that module. With such documentation being available, the programmer can maintain proper control over modification of shared modules. Whenever a change is required in such a module, one should review all instances of its use to ascertain whether the change applies in all cases. For example, suppose that a change in module H in Figure 14-13 results in module F having to be changed, but that F should not be changed with respect to its also being a subordinate to modules B and C. A new module, say Fl, should be created as the subordinate of H, leaving the original module F unchanged as a subordinate of B and C.

FIGURE 14-13
*Documentation of High Fan-in
Structure Charts*

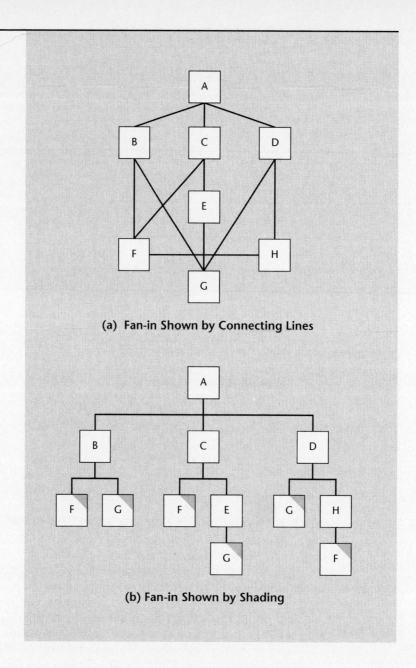

(a) **Fan-in Shown by Connecting Lines**

(b) **Fan-in Shown by Shading**

Sometimes programmers change the procedure of a shared module so that it "knows" whether it is being executed under the control of one or another of its superior modules, and does one function or another, accordingly. For example, we can have the following:

```
PAR-A.
   .
   .
   .
   MOVE 'A' TO WHO-PERFORMS-ME-FLAG
   PERFORM PAR-X
   .
   .
   .
```

```
PAR-B.
    .
    .
    .
    MOVE 'B' TO WHO-PERFORMS-ME-FLAG
    PERFORM PAR-X
    .
    .
    .
PAR-X.
    IF WHO-PERFORMS-ME-FLAG = 'A'
    .
    .
    .
    ELSE
        IF WHO-PERFORMS-ME-FLAG = 'B'
    .
    .
    .
```

Such a practice is error-prone and leads to noncohesive modules. It is preferable to create two separate modules instead of the one PAR-X, each module corresponding to the distinct logic relating to PAR-A or PAR-B, respectively.

R E V I E W . . . .

1. The term that designates the number of superiors with respect to a given module is _____ .

   fan-in

2. From the standpoint of reducing the amount of program code, high fan-in generally is considered [desirable / undesirable].

   desirable

3. An adverse effect associated with high-fan-in modules is that the common superiors of such modules may become content-dependent on one another, thereby undermining the concept of hierarchical _____ .

   independence

4. When modules with multiple superiors are repeated in a structure chart, such shared modules are coded, or tagged, by

   _____ .

   shading the upper right corner of such modules

5. When a shared subordinate module has to be changed, it [is / is not] important to determine if the change is appropriate for its use with respect to all other superiors.

   is

. . . .

Control Based On Physical Contiguity

In a strict program hierarchy, a program should be so designed as to have *one single superior* for the entire structure. The superior controls the execution of its subordinates which, in turn, do the same with respect to their subordinates.

Subordinate control should be *explicit,* and as indicated earlier in this chapter, should be exercised by use of PERFORM or CALL statements. However, many programs include a third form of control structure that is implicit and tends to be error-prone. This kind of control is based on *physical contiguity* of modules in the program.

Figure 14-14(a) illustrates an example of a program outline with control based on physical contiguity. Module A is assumed to contain no end-of-program or GO TO statements. Thus, when module A finishes executing, then B starts to execute. B is, in effect, a subordinate of A by virtue of its physical position in the program. If a programmer later inserts a new module between A and B, the implied control structure between these two modules may be overlooked, resulting in programming errors. Similarly, modules D and E have the same control relationship because of their physical contiguity.

A related point is illustrated in Figure 14-14(b). Notice that PERFORM I THRU L in module A establishes the I through L sequence of paragraphs as one module. One would therefore expect that I THRU L constitutes a cohesive function. But then notice that later in the program module N contains PERFORM J THRU K, which is part of the I THRU L sequence. One of two reasons most likely led to this program structure. One possible reason is that I THRU L is really a composite function that includes the J THRU K function. If such is the case, the J through K sequence should be set up as a separate module. The other possibility is that I THRU L is, in fact, one cohesive function and the J THRU K sequence is a module with coincidental cohesion; the programmer noticed a sequence of code that was also needed in module N, and so made reference to J THRU K instead of writing the code again at N.

The two illustrations of programs that include control by physical contiguity in Figure 14-14 represent weak structures from the standpoint of program design. They are particularly likely to lead to errors when programs are altered or revised, and therefore control based on physical contiguity should be minimized.

FIGURE 14-14
Illustrations of Improper Structures Involving Control by Physical Contiguity

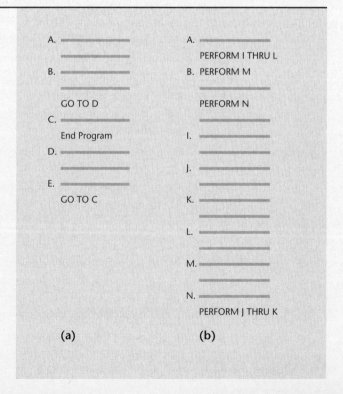

R E V I E W . . . .

1. In a well-designed program, program control of a given module always originates from its _____ .

superior

2. Explicit execution of a subordinate module is achieved by use of the verb _____ in the superior module.

PERFORM

3. When a particular module H is executed because it happens to follow module G in the program, module H, in effect, is a [superior / subordinate] of module G.

subordinate

4. The type of control of the execution of module H described in #3 illustrates control based on _____ .

physical contiguity

5. A general rule in program design is that control based on physical contiguity should be [maximized / avoided].

avoided

. . . .

TOP-DOWN DESIGN

In the preceding sections of this chapter we have described operational guidelines and characteristics of well-designed programs. We now describe the process by which well-partitioned modular programs can be structured into *hierarchies*. The process is known as *top-down design*.

In top-down design we begin by identifying one module that describes the overall function of the program. Then we proceed to partition this overall function into its main components. For example, suppose that the overall function is Process Payroll. We ask ourselves: What has to be done to process the payroll? In response to this question we might initially identify four main functions, as shown in Figure 14-15: Edit Input Data, Process Transactions Against Master, Produce Paychecks, and Produce Reports. We then review these functions and determine whether the breakdown is complete and whether it contains redundancies. For instance, we might question whether or not the two modules Produce

FIGURE 14-15

Initial Design Structure for the Payroll Program

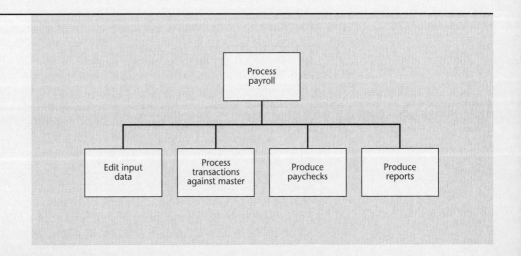

FIGURE 14-16

*First Revision and Expansion of the
Structure Chart in Figure 14-15*

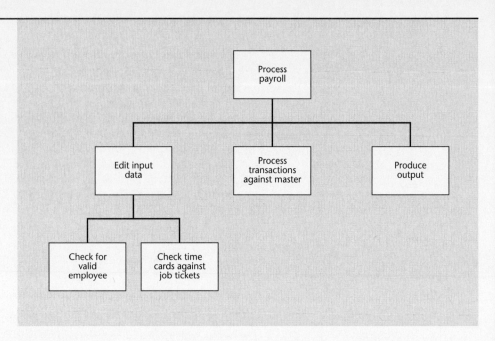

Paychecks and Produce Reports are really different functions, and if not, whether they could be replaced by a single module that could be called Produce Output. Or we might come up with a new module such as Sort Transactions.

When we are satisfied with the modules comprising the second level in the structure chart, we repeat the process, considering each of these modules in turn as if it were the top module. That is, for each main subfunction of the overall task we identify specific subfunctions that comprise that function. For example, we first ask: What are the main subfunctions that can be developed for Edit Input Data? As presented in Figure 14-16, two subfunctions are identified: Check For Valid Employee and Check Time Cards Against Job Tickets. Although we do not continue with the analysis in Figure 14-16, the next step would be to determine subfunctions for the remaining second-level functions of Process Transactions Against Master and Produce Output.

The general process of identifying subfunctions continues with each lower level in turn. We stop when no function at any level can be partitioned any further, given that each function is a cohesive task that ultimately can be expressed in one cohesive module.

The top-down design by which modules are developed within a hierarchical structure permits the designer to concentrate on a *single module* at a time and to consider the relationship of that module to its subordinates only. By this approach a large, complex programming task, in essence, can be reduced to a set of subtasks, each of which is substantially smaller and easier than the total task. The property of independence in a structure chart is the one that allows us to proceed in this simplifying manner. Recall that each module should be independent in function from its peers. Thus, when we consider the Edit Input Data module in Figure 14-15, we need not focus on any of the other three modules that are its peers.

Top-down design is a well-tested and effective method for developing good program designs. Although the programmer should aspire to follow this approach closely, there are often reasons why top-down design cannot be followed strictly. For instance, one rule associated with top-down design is that all modules at a given level be reviewed and partitioned before proceeding to the next level. In practice, it may be necessary to violate this rule, as in a case in which there is a pressing need to implement a main function quickly. A function such as Edit Input Data may represent a priority function for operating reasons.

Further, try as we may to achieve perfect partitioning of modules, continued work at lower levels of the structure chart almost invariably brings to light the need for additional functions at a higher level or the desirability of consolidating certain higher-level functions. Thus *some* bottom-up design is inevitable in most cases. Nevertheless, top-down design is the best general approach, and it is clearly superior to the bottom-up approach that was prevalent among programmers for many years. Attempts to structure a hierarchy by defining bottom-level functions and then assembling them into hierarchies leads to higher-level modules with low cohesion and to improper hierarchical dependencies.

R E V I E W . . . .

1. The approach to program design that begins by describing the one module for the overall function of the program and then proceeds to partition this function into its main components is called _____ design.

    top-down

2. In terms of top-down design the programmer directs primary attention at partitioning [a single module / all modules at a single hierarchical level] at any one time.

    a single module

3. A general rule associated with top-down design is that all modules at a given level [should / need not] be partitioned before proceeding to the next level.

    should

4. An approach to program design that begins by defining bottom-level functions first and that leads to modules with low cohesion and to improper hierarchical dependencies is the _____ approach.

    bottom-up

. . . .

SUMMARY

In the first part of this chapter you studied *program cohesion,* which has to do with the properties associated with good modules. In contrast, the second part of the chapter was concerned with *intermodule relationships* and overall structure-chart considerations.

To achieve good program design, each module should be viewed as a *black box,* with emphasis being on *function,* rather than procedure. Generally, a *cohesive function* is one that can be described in just a few words and without the use of multiple verbs.

Several types of cohesion can characterize program modules. *Functional cohesion* is the preferred type, and is based on the defined function of the module. *Coincidental cohesion* is exhibited by a module with a "catchall" set of unrelated statements. Modules that focus on the same broad class of logical processes or functions exhibit *class-oriented cohesion.* When the only reason for combining the program statements as a module is because they occur together in time, then *time-related cohesion* is involved. *Procedural cohesion* concerns the grouping together into one module of statements that are all associated with a particular type of procedure. *Data-related cohesion* is based on data flow. Finally, when a module is formed on the basis of including the processing steps that occur in sequence, then *sequential cohesion* is involved. The order of desirability of the various types of cohesion is summarized in Table 14-1.

In our coverage of program design we next focused on *relationships between modules,* and we covered several topics concerned with overall program structure, as follows.

Content coupling is exemplified when one module references the contents of another module. A general rule of good program design is that such coupling should be minimized. In terms of *module size,* well-designed programs should have modules that are not systematically too small *or* too large. At issue is the possibility that a program may be too complex *either* because of having a large number of very small modules *or* because of having a small number of very large modules.

Span of control refers to the number of subordinate modules for a given superior module. Well-designed programs tend to have balanced spans of control in the range of about 2 to 7. The *fan-out* of a given module refers to the number of its subordinates. In contrast, *fan-in* refers to the number of superiors for a given module. Even though a strict hierarchical approach would result in every module having only one superior, high fan-in can reduce the amount of program code and result in well-tested common functions.

The control of subordinate modules should be *explicit,* with the superior module being the source of control. An implicit type of control structure is based on *physical contiguity,* in which a module is executed at a given point in program processing because it follows another module in the listed program. Such programs are error-prone, particularly if they are modified and the physical contiguity is changed.

Overall, well-partitioned modular programs can be structured into hierarchies by the process of *top-down design.* By this process, the programmer begins with the one module that describes the overall program function and partitions that function into its second-level subordinates. Then each of the second-level subordinates is similarly partitioned, and so on down the hierarchy. The attempt to design programs by defining bottom-level functions first is called *bottom-up design,* and leads to the development of programs with low cohesion and improper hierarchical dependencies.

EXERCISES

14.1 Is cohesion an attribute of programs or of modules within programs?

14.2 Explain what is meant by "cohesion" in the context of program design.

14.3 Discuss several measures of cohesion and identify the highest and the lowest levels of cohesion.

14.4 Suppose that sales transactions are processed in a programming task. When a sales transaction is processed, all of the following steps are required:

- Check the credit of the customer.

- Change the amount on hand in the inventory file.

- Update the accounts receivable file.

Should these steps be included in one module, or should they be partitioned into more than one module? Explain.

14.5 Why is content coupling via GO TO statements undesirable?

14.6 Suppose that a module has a size of 120 program lines. Is this necessarily a poorly designed module? Explain.

14.7 Consider the diagrams. If the (a) version represents an original design and (b) and (c) two alternative modifications, what reasons would lead to choosing (b) or (c)? In other words, should we increase span by partitioning at the same level or by hierarchical partitioning?

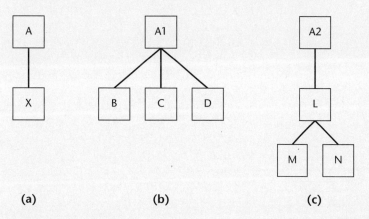

(a)   (b)   (c)

14.8 Consider the diagrams. If version (a) represents an original design and (b) and (c) two alternative modifications, what reasons would lead to choosing (b) or (c)? In other words, should we combine at the same hierarchical level, or should we combine subordinates into a superior?

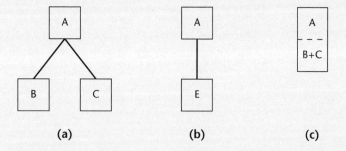

(a)   (b)   (c)

14.9 Explain the term "fan-in" of a module and discuss both why it is desirable to have a high fan-in as well as the need to be cautious about high fan-ins.

14.10 Why is control based on physical contiguity undesirable?

14.11 Describe the top-down design approach to programs in your own words. Why is this approach preferred to the bottom-up approach?

15 Program Testing

IN THIS CHAPTER *you will study the concepts and techniques of program testing. Your learning objective will be to establish a frame of mind, as well as a familiarity with particular ideas and techniques. The frame of mind that you should develop is that of following an* **organized** *and* **disciplined** *approach to program testing. Such an approach is required in all three areas of designing, coding, and testing COBOL programs in professional practice.*

You will begin by studying two common approaches to developing and testing programs at some length: the top-down approach and the bottom-up approach. Each of these two orientations to program testing has its good points as well as its weaknesses, but top-down testing is generally preferred. You will next study several techniques used in program testing, such as the use of test data sets, two types of walkthroughs, traces, and core dumps.

You will then overview a number of common COBOL programming errors and learn how they can be avoided. Because a program to be tested may be a revised version of an earlier program that was written (by someone else) in unstructured form, you will conclude the chapter by learning how to convert existing unstructured programs to structured form.

INTRODUCTION

Program testing refers to the steps and procedures undertaken to ascertain that the program is correct—that is, that the program does what it was intended to do. The programmer goes through a number of steps in completing a programming project. These steps are summarized in Figure 15-1. As indicated in this outline, the actual program coding is just one of a large number of steps, and it constitutes only a relatively small part in the overall process. Program testing is involved in a multitude of single attempts, each not as time-consuming as initial coding, but in total usually summing up to a large multiple of the coding time requirement.

Casual, sketchy, or haphazard approaches to program development results in a heavy penalty in error-correcting efforts. Well-managed installations have long recognized the importance of thoughtful, organized approaches to program development and demand that special emphasis and extensive effort be devoted to good program design. It is a fact that the greater the effort devoted to the first five steps in Figure 15-1, the less effort needed for the steps after coding. Good design is actually a high-yielding investment. A person who spends 5 days in design efforts may spend 3 days in program testing. In contrast, a person of comparable skills who spends 2 days in design efforts for the same task may spend 15 days in testing. Further, the second person will be working in the frustrating effort of endless error-correcting attempts, and will develop a program that is much more likely to be found in error in the future when untested conditions are encountered.

Ideally, we would like to produce programs with zero defects. In reality, we have no practical way to ascertain that a program is indeed correct. Well-designed and properly tested programs have a high probability of being error-free, but we have no logical way of ascertaining their absolute correctness. Inexperienced programmers and "laymen" often believe that exhaustive testing can remove all errors. They think that test data can be created to test the program under all possible conditions. Unfortunately, this is far from the truth. It has been shown that even for relatively small programs, testing of all possible paths under all possible data combinations would require hundreds or even thousands of years of continuous computer running!

There have been some efforts to develop a theoretical foundation for constructing unambiguous proofs of program correctness, comparable to the mathematical logic that guarantees the correctness of mathematical theorems. However, these developments are presently at an embryonic stage. Program development will remain an art for the foreseeable future. Like any other art, it can be practiced well, or it can be practiced poorly. The current professional consensus is that programs can be developed so that errors are minimized and occasionally totally absent. Further, programs should be so constructed that errors, when discovered, can easily be traced to their causes and be corrected. Thus, as a philosophy, we can say that we should strive for minimal errors and easily correctable programs.

R E V I E W . . . .

1. With respect to an overall programming project, program design generally requires [less / more] time than program coding.

    more

2. The more time devoted to establishing the functions of a program, designing the program structure, and defining test data, the [less / more] time generally is required for program testing.

    less

FIGURE 15-1

Steps Included in a Programming Project

- Define the function of the program.

- Define required data and record layouts.

- Design the program structure.

- Define test data and expected test results.

- Transform the program structure into a pseudocode program outline.

- Write the program in COBOL.

- Review and correct obvious syntactical or logical errors in this original version.

- If initial version was handwritten, key-in the program in machine-readable form; obtain a listing of the keyed-in version, correct typing errors, and obtain revised listing.

- Compile the program and review syntactical and logical errors diagnosed by the compiler.

- Recompile the program until all compiler-detectable errors have been corrected.

- Execute the program using test data.

- Compare program results to established test results and revise the program. Repeat this step until satisfied that the program is correct.

- Execute the program with selected "real" data and verify correctness of processing. If errors are discovered, further revise the program until correct processing is achieved.

- Store program on library and release it for operation.

3. As a general philosophy, the objective in programming projects is to develop programs that have [zero / minimal] errors.

minimal

. . . .

TOP-DOWN PROGRAM DEVELOPMENT AND TESTING

One approach to program development and testing places emphasis on the system, where the system is the total program that consists of a collection of interrelated modules. This *top-down* testing approach requires that testing be implemented in stages, each stage corresponding to one hierarchical level in the program structure.

In a typical program structure, such as is illustrated in Figure 15-2, top-down testing would proceed as follows. First, we test module 1 to see that it performs its function correctly. Next, we test module 1 together with modules 2, 3, and 10 to ascertain their correctness. The third test incorporates modules 4, 5, 6, and 7 along with 1, 2, 3, and 10, while the final test would also involve modules 8 and 9 in addition to the other modules.

FIGURE 15-2

Sample Hierarchical Program Structure

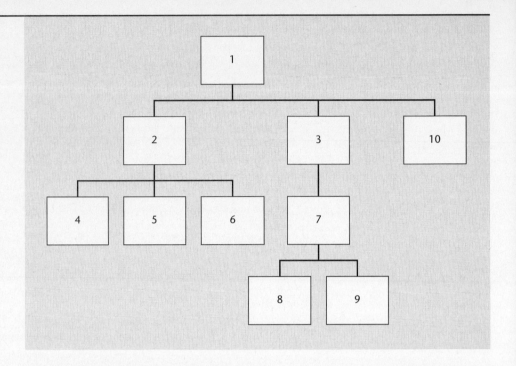

In general, the top-down testing approach is associated with a top-down approach to program development. The advantage of following a top-down approach is that we make sure that the total program works properly before we refine any of its parts. It may be useful to relate this approach to the construction of a new building, where the total outside structure is created and tested before individual rooms are built inside. The top-down approach avoids "surprises" at the end of a programming project, such as incompatibility among the parts of the program. It is especially useful in large projects involving several programmers, where the need for integration of the parts is very important. But it is also useful in smaller, single-person programs. In either case the approach can be implemented through the development of *stub modules,* as explained in the following paragraph.

To implement the top-down testing approach, we design the entire program module structure first, and then we code in detail at progressively lower-level modules. For example, for the program structure in Figure 15-2 we would first code only module 1 in detail, simply identifying all other modules by module names and by some identification-producing statements. In the next step we would code modules 1, 2, 3, and 10 in detail, while all other modules would be stubs, as illustrated in Figure 15-3. In our example we chose to DISPLAY a message in each stub module, identifying its execution. When we test this partial program, all modules would be executed, albeit the lower-level ones would perform trivial functions.

In this progressive testing approach, when modules 1, 2, 3, and 10 are tested and found to function correctly, we then develop the full detail of modules 4, 5, 6, and 7 and test this expanded program. Finally, modules 8 and 9 are developed, and the whole system of modules is tested to ascertain its correctness.

A variant of the top-down approach is to subdivide the progressive module development and testing into stages that represent vertical rather than horizontal module order. For the example in Figure 15-2 we would first develop and test modules 1, 2, 4, 5, and 6, keeping 3, 7, 8, 9, and 10 as stub modules. In the next step we would expand the module development and testing to include module 3 and its subordinates, and finally we would add module 10.

FIGURE 15-3
Program with Module Stubs

```
MODULE-1.
    .
    .
    .

    PERFORM MODULE-2
    .
    .
    .
    PERFORM MODULE-3
    .
    .
    .
    PERFORM MODULE-10
    .
    .
    .
MODULE-2.
    PERFORM MODULE-4
    PERFORM MODULE-5
    PERFORM MODULE-6
    .
    .
    .
MODULE-3.
    PERFORM MODULE-7
    .
    .
    .
MODULE-10.
    .
    .
    .
MODULE-4.
    DISPLAY 'THIS IS MODULE-4 EXECUTING'.
MODULE-5.
    DISPLAY 'THIS IS MODULE-5 EXECUTING'.
MODULE-6.
    DISPLAY 'THIS IS MODULE-6 EXECUTING'.
MODULEñ7.
    DISPLAY 'THIS IS MODULE-7 EXECUTING'.
MODULE-8.
    DISPLAY 'THIS IS MODULE-8 EXECUTING'.
MODULE-9.
    DISPLAY 'THIS IS MODULE-9 EXECUTING'.
```

The top-down approach has great merit in providing a systematic approach to program development and testing. However, it is often difficult to implement in pure form. Consider, for instance, module 2 in Figure 15-2. It is likely that some of its processing is conditional on the outcome of functions performed in its subordinate modules. The stub approach cannot simulate the required results in a satisfactory way. As a practical matter, then, we may consider two options. One option is to "fake" the results of a given module's assumed function. For instance, if module 2 is to receive an edited record from module 5, we might "hand-code" data in module 5, such as MOVE '123ABCD35982XYZ' TO RECORD-A, where RECORD-A is the one used by module 2 in its further processing. Or, if there is need for multiple records, we might include a READ instruction in module 5 to input manually tested correct records, but without doing the editing functions that will eventually be incorporated into module 5.

COBOL '85 offers another alternative for structuring stub modules. In this version it is permissible to create a program that consists simply of an IDENTIFICATION DIVISION. Such programs require certain other features, as explained in Chapter 23, in which we discuss "nested" or "contained" programs. For now, we illustrate the approach by the following simple example:

```
IDENTIFICATION DIVISION.
PROGRAM-ID.  MAINPROG.
    (etc. as in a usual program)
        CALL STUB1
    (etc., other usual program statements)
IDENTIFICATION DIVISION.
PROGRAM-ID.  STUB1.
END PROGRAM STUB1
END PROGRAM MAINPROG.
```

In the above example MAINPROG is the overall, main program. Then, instead of PERFORMing a module stub that is a paragraph, we CALL a module stub that is actually a program. Reviewing this program, whose name in the example is STUB1, we see that it has no content, no procedures. Alternatively, we could have included a PROCEDURE DIVISION in STUB1 that could contain a suitable DISPLAY message. Finally, notice the last two lines containing the END PROGRAM program-name statements in the above example, which mark the end of each respective program. One can see that STUB1 is a "contained" program because it is fully contained by the outer program, MAINPROG.

A second option is to temper the strict top-down method by fully developing the subordinate modules whose output is required by the superior module to be tested. For example, with respect to Figure 15-2, we might fully code modules 1, 2, 3, 10, and 5 in one stage, rather than keeping module 5 a stub.

R E V I E W . . . .

1. The approach to program testing that places primary emphasis on the total program, and by which program testing begins at the highest hierarchical level of the program structure is the_____ approach.

                                                                    top-down

2. When a module is represented only by an identification statement during program testing, and is not, in fact, involved in data execution, such a module is often referred to as being a _____ module.

                                                                    stub

3. Whereas the basic top-down approach described in this section gives attention to modules according to hierarchical level, an alternative is to subdivide the

progressive development and testing of modules according to [horizontal / vertical] order.

vertical

4. When the output of a subordinate module is required in order to test its superior, two options are available. One option is to enter the required output either by hand-coding the data or by READING the data from a special file. The other is to _____ .

fully develop the subordinate module

. . . .

BOTTOM-UP PROGRAM DEVELOPMENT AND TESTING

The *bottom-up* approach emphasizes complete development and testing of the individual component modules before proceeding to their integration. It is the opposite of the top-down approach in that it proceeds from the lowest-level modules to the higher modules. The bottom-up approach is analogous to the approach taken in manufacturing, where parts are made and tested individually before they are assembled into units that are then tested as subassemblies or final products.

Refer to Figure 15-2. Application of the bottom-up approach would begin by developing and testing modules 8 and 9 individually before developing module 7 and testing all three modules together. In the next phase modules 4, 5, and 6 would be completed, followed by 2, 3, and 10. Finally module 1 would be added and tested in conjunction with all the other modules.

The bottom-up approach is characteristic of programmers driven by a need to "keep working." They prefer to start early into the project by actually coding the most detailed and specific functions. Common candidates for such coding are input- and output-oriented modules. The programmer thinks, "I am going to need a 'read' module for each input file, so I might as well start coding them now." Similarly, printed reports are natural targets for early development, since the report formats and data transfer functions are clear and can be tested independently of the rest of the program.

The preceding paragraph implies some degree of arbitrary selection as to which modules to develop first. This need not be the case. The approach can be organized and systematic, and may dictate a precise order of module development and testing. In the strictest case, we proceed from the lowest level in the hierarchy chart to the top, main module.

To implement bottom-up testing it must be possible to "drive" lower-level modules. If a module is going to be eventually executed under control of a PERFORM, that control must be provided in some way so that the module can actually be executed for the purpose of testing. This is accomplished in one of two ways. One method is to write *test-driver modules* that invoke execution of the modules undergoing testing. The test-driver can be a program that contains a PERFORM for each module to be tested. If modules to be tested are subprograms (see Chapter 23), then a main program that issues the appropriate CALLs is written so that the subprograms can be tested as such.

A second method of arranging for the execution of a lower-level module is to write the module to be tested so that it is an executable program. Instead of being under the control of a PERFORM or CALL, the procedures comprising the module are written as a complete program. For example, in the case of a subprogram the LINKAGE SECTION header (as discussed in Chapter 23) can be written, but with an asterisk placed in column 7 of the COBOL Coding Form. Thus the header is treated as a comment. Similarly, the PROCEDURE DIVISION header would contain no USING clause, although it is recommended that such a clause be included in a comment statement. Finally, STOP RUN would be used rather than EXIT PROGRAM, and thus instead of a subprogram we have an executable (main) program that can be tested by itself. When testing is completed, the module is revised so that it can be used as a subordinate module that is executed under the control of a PERFORM or CALL in the next stage of program development and testing.

As is the case with the top-down approach, availability of necessary data becomes an issue with the bottom-up approach as well. A superior module often provides data upon which a subordinate module performs its function. If the superior module has not been developed as yet, the data output of the superior module needs somehow to be made available. As with the top-down approach, we may hand-code data into the program, or we may include a READ statement preceding the PERFORM or CALL. The READ statement is used to input the needed data from a special test file that is used to simulate the required data.

R   E   V   I   E   W . . . .

1. Modules that are particular candidates for early development in the bottom-up approach are those whose functions are oriented toward either _____ or

    _____ .

                                                                   input; output

2. Modules with PERFORM or CALL statements that are written specifically to invoke execution of the modules undergoing testing are called _____ modules.

                                                                   test-driver

3. Instead of using test-driver modules, the procedure comprising the module to be tested can be written [so that it is under the control of a PERFORM or CALL / as a complete program].

                                                                   as a complete program

4. In testing a module, the required data that would normally be obtained from a superior module can be hand-coded into the program or can be obtained from a special test file of such simulated data by use of the _____ statement.

                                                                   READ

. . . .

TOP-DOWN VS. BOTTOM-UP APPROACHES TO TESTING

Having described each of the two basic approaches to program development and testing, we may now raise the question as to which approach is better. In practice, most organizations are not purists with respect to either method and tend to use a combination of both approaches in the same project. Of course, they are fundamentally opposite approaches, and one must choose one or the other as the main approach.

The trend today favors the top-down approach for most environments. It has been concluded that it provides a better opportunity for continuous coordination and integration of all parts of a program project. But the top-down approach cannot always be successfully applied. Its success is tied to the prior development of a complete and correct program design. Such design is often an aspiration more than a reality because, simply, we are not perfect and we tend to overlook program requirements or make incorrect judgments. Often, it is not until we get into the details that we see some parts that were left out of the design or some misunderstandings and misconceptions upon which the design was based.

As much as possible, we want to proceed on the basis of the top-down approach. On the other hand, we have to accept the reality that design and implementation are iterative processes. We design, we implement, we redesign, and so on. Thus we often use a bottom-up approach to some extent by necessity. We may also incorporate the bottom-up approach by design. If we have difficulty understanding the impact of a module's detailed code on the total program structure, we may choose to develop that module first, even if it is at a lower level. In either case some of the bottom-up approach will thereby be incorporated together with the top-down approach.

From a historical perspective the bottom-up approach has often been associated with "sloppy" programming practices. Very often a team of programmers would work separately on different parts of a system. Then when the time came to integrate the whole, it would be an endless chain of errors and incompatibilities in the parts. Just when the users were told "the system is almost ready; it is all coded and we only need to test it all together," the integration test would require months of effort. Also, on an individual basis, programmers who were not disciplined in their profession would tend to do a lot of coding but little designing, and then would spend endless hours testing the "almost-finished" program.

The top-down approach forces the design phase more explicitly, and for that reason it is the preferred choice. However, either method can be made to work successfully. If we do have a good, complete design, and if we do define clearly the data interfaces between modules, the bottom-up approach can be very effective. Under such circumstances each module is developed and tested within a clearly defined design framework, and incompatibilities and integration problems can be minimized.

The important point to keep in mind is that strict adherence to either the top-down or bottom-up approach is often indicative of narrow-minded management. No approach is the best in all cases. The effective programmer is one who understands all available methods and tools and is wise in selecting the right one for the appropriate occasion.

R E V I E W . . . .

1. The approach to program development and testing that generally is favored for use as the main approach is the _____ approach.

    top-down

2. The approach to program development and testing that historically has been associated with a lack of attention given to program design is the _____ approach.

    bottom-up

3. With reference to program development and testing, it is good organizational policy to use [one or the other approach explicitly / a combination of approaches].

    a combination of approaches

TESTING PROCEDURES

In this section we describe a number of specific procedures used in program testing.

Creation of Test Data

To test a single module or a whole program, we need input test data. Using a sample of real data is not the best approach because the sample is not likely to include all the special conditions to be tested.

The creation of test data requires considerable effort and thought. Inclusion of insufficient cases will allow hidden program deficiencies, or "bugs," to surface gradually over time as the overlooked cases are encountered in actual use of the program. Attempts to include all possible cases are futile, since the combinations of cases are literally overwhelming. We want to choose important cases, such as data in the extremes of the range as well as in the middle of the range of possible values. For instance, if a field can contain signed numeric data, include one positive, one negative, one zero, and one nonnumeric error value, as a minimum.

However, we cannot rely too much on test data to "prove" that the program is correct. If there are 10 numeric fields in the input data, and we want to test for most possibilities, we should include the following for each field: a large negative value, a small negative value, a zero value, a small positive value, a large positive value, and a nonnumeric (error) value. Given these six types of input for each field and considering that there are 10 fields, we would need to provide $6^{10} =$ 60,466,176 sets of test data to include all the possible input combinations! Worse yet, we need to check that many test results to see how the program processed each combination. Thus we cannot rely on test data alone. Our main weapon against errors is the logical construction of the program and then the additional strength provided by well-chosen test data. There are some proprietary commercial software packages that generate test data based on PICTURE descriptions of fields. These are extremely useful aids and can be a great advantage for most routine testing. Having such automatic test data generation allows the programmer to concentrate on constructing special test data combinations.

Walkthroughs—Individual Review

After a program is written, it is important to review the procedure logic of the program by *walking through* it on an individual basis. We take test data and apply the program instructions to it manually, thereby *desk-checking* the program execution. If erroneous results have been obtained from actual processing of the program, such desk-checking can also be used to search for the source of the error.

In the desk-checking review it is useful to maintain a map of storage to keep track of the values stored in the various fields. A useful approach is to write field names as column headings and to enter the values stored in a given field under that column heading. When a value changes as a result of a READ, a MOVE, or an arithmetic instruction, then cross out the old value and write a new value underneath. Do not erase old values, so that you can refer back to a previous step in the program execution.

Walkthroughs—Peer Review

Most programmers have experienced the following situation. The programmer encounters a program error. Many frustrating hours or even days are spent trying to resolve the error, to no avail. Then the program is shown to a colleague and the nature of the error is explained. The colleague glances at the program and diagnoses the error or makes a suggestion as to how to resolve it in just a few minutes. This kind of experience has been actually formalized into an organizational procedure at many computer sites.

The term *structured walkthrough* has been used widely and originated with IBM, which formalized the concept and developed a set of rules and guidelines for such walkthroughs. In general terms, such a walkthrough is a *peer review* of a program. The program (module) author gives a copy of the code along with some documentation to a group of peers who will undertake the review. The group size is normally two to four persons, and may include all members of the team working on the same project. Each person studies the program individually, and then they all meet at an appointed time. During this meeting they "react" to the program by bringing out ambiguities, possible errors, and visible errors. No suggestions are made on how to correct them—that is left to the author. Such a walkthrough lasts one-half to one hour and serves a very beneficial function. The programmer learns to program in understandable ways, tends to design better programs, and avoids "tricky," obscure code. Further, the programmer group as a whole adapts to common company standards.

Many organizations have ritualized the process and are religious in the little details associated with such a review. We cannot, of course, comment on such individual practices. The important point is that it is very helpful to have your program reviewed by a small group of peers. Other people see quickly things that our own myopic view may prevent us from seeing. The author of a program often is so tied to the present structure that he or she cannot look at the program with the fresh viewpoint necessary to identify errors.

Traces

Most computer sites have available a software package that can *trace,* or monitor, program execution at the paragraph or even the data-name level. A printed trace captures the actual sequence of program execution and can be an invaluable aid in program testing and program error correction. Desk-checking a program often suffers from incorrect assumptions about the sequence of instructions to be executed, but a trace provides a record of the actual sequence.

In its simplest form a trace prints the names of each paragraph executed in the order of execution. The programmer can check this sequence against the test data and ascertain that the program does indeed follow the expected paths with the test data. We recommend routine use of such a trace feature during program testing, since it requires a minimum amount of additional printout (a page or two), and it provides an invaluable aid. However, one word of caution is necessary. If the program contains a logical error that results in an interminable loop, you may generate an inordinately long printed trace! To prevent this problem, put an appropriate page limit in your job control statements so that the printing is checked.

If a software package trace is not available, the programmer can develop one rather easily by following each paragraph-name by a DISPLAY or WRITE statement that prints a literal, which is the paragraph-name. When program testing is completed, an asterisk can be placed in column 7 to convert these trace statements into comments. Then, should the program need to be retested in the future, all we need to do is convert these asterisks to spaces and the "home-made" trace is reinstated.

Printing a trace of paragraph-names is a minimum trace. Most trace packages will allow selective control over tracing of individual records or data-names. For instance, if we have specified the tracing of data-name ABC, then when MOVE XYZ TO ABC is executed, the trace will show the name of the field, ABC, its content before the move, and its content after the move. It is also possible to trace "all," in which case every paragraph and every instruction is traced, resulting in voluminous trace printouts. Occasionally such indiscriminate tracing is necessary, but it is usually a waste of time. It is much better to first localize the portion of the program that is likely to contain the suspected error and then, through controls in the trace package, monitor that portion of the program only. There are some trace type packages, mostly available on personal computers, that allow the programmer to step through the program online.

Although it will always be important to make effective use of any testing aid, good program design should be used to minimize errors and testing efforts. No testing aid should be allowed to provide implicit encouragement of "sloppy" programming because of the belief that the testing package will uncover the errors.

Core Dumps

A core dump is a printing of central memory contents at an instant in time. It is a snapshot of central memory. The programmer can use reference data provided during compilation to locate any desired field and view its contents as they were at the moment that the core dump was executed. Normally the programmer uses the required job control statements to specify that a core dump be performed when the program abends. In this way the contents of memory can be viewed as they were at the time of the fatal error, and the programmer can see which record had been read from a given file, what the values of accumulator fields were at that time, and the like.

In many installations core dumps are a routine procedure, and some experienced programmers cannot imagine that anybody can develop and test programs without core dumps being used in the process. The practice can be very beneficial to those who are accustomed to it and know how to use if efficiently and effectively. On the other hand, core dumping has its roots in an era when other diagnostic and testing aids, such as traces, were not available, when compilers were much more prone to erroneous compilation, and when COBOL programmers were, at heart, assembler programmers and wanted to see the "real thing." In today's environment core dumps should have a very small place.

Most core dumps are produced in hexadecimal or other non-people-oriented output, and they take considerable time to read and interpret, even for experienced users. Just like any puzzle, they do generate interest on the part of the user, and many such users actually thrive on the ritual of getting the multipage dump and going through the process of deciphering it. But the practice can be wasteful in programmer time.

A trace can be both more efficient and more effective than a core dump because it is a picture of the dynamics of the program, rather than a static snapshot, and because trace packages are easier to use. There are occasions, however, when core dumps are indispensable, and that is when there is an error caused by the system software. Compiler and operating system software do contain errors, and occasionally they cause a COBOL program to execute in a strange way. When normal procedures cannot resolve an error, then core dump diagnosis is perhaps the only way to proceed. Thus we advocate highly selective use of core dumps and recommend strongly against routine use of this testing procedure for every little program error.

R E V I E W . . . .

1. One appropriate procedure associated with program testing is to apply the program to a set of [actual sample data / specially constructed test data].

specially constructed test data

2. Test data for a numeric field [should / should not] include nonnumeric data.

should

3. The type of walkthrough in which program instructions are applied manually to test data is called _____ .

desk-checking

4. The type of walkthrough in which a programmer other than the original program writer studies a program and its associated output is called _____ .

peer review (or structured walkthrough)

5. A printed output that captures the actual sequence of program execution by including such information as the paragraph-names in the order of their execution is called a _____ .

trace

6. Testing aids, such as trace packages, are becoming increasingly available. Programmers [can therefore / nevertheless should not] be less concerned about program efforts oriented toward minimizing initial programming errors.

nevertheless should not

7. The printing of central memory contents at an instant in time is called a _____ .

core dump

8. In general, a core dump is most appropriate for the diagnosis of apparent errors in [applications programs / system software].

system software

· ·

COMMON ERRORS

The purpose of this section is to describe a few common programming errors. There also are certain errors that are common to each specific computer site rather than being a general source of errors. These errors can be related to the type of applications programmed at that site, the standards adopted, or the systems software in use. Programmers have an extensive and highly efficient "grapevine" for passing along the appropriate warnings to one another. This is so even in the rather fluid college environment, in which any given student may be involved in the programming process for only a few months. In any case, avoiding errors that others have previously encountered makes good sense, and should be supported by documentation as well as informal communication.

Forgetting to Initialize or Reset

Forgetting to initialize or reset is a common error, and it can be avoided only by systematic review of every flag-type field and every accumulator. Fields may be initialized in the DATA DIVISION by using a VALUE clause, or they can be initialized in the PROCEDURE DIVISION by using a MOVE-literal, a SET ... TRUE, or an INITIALIZE instruction. A good practice to follow is to initialize fields in the DATA DIVISION only when the values are to remain constant throughout the program. Fields that are used as "flags" or "switches," and therefore are set and reset during program execution, are best initialized in the PROCEDURE DIVISION, since the latter approach is more self-documenting.

In addition to forgetting to initialize a field, a common error is to forget to reset a value. For instance, in a nested PERFORM structure with iterative processing we may use a flag to control execution. We enter the procedure with the flag set to one value and then we change that value as an indicator that a condition has developed. However, we may forget to reset the flag back to the original value before it is again used in conjunction with the procedure.

Nonnumeric Data in Numeric Fields

Numeric data must consist of the digits 0–9, an operational sign (PIC S), and an implied decimal point (PIC V). Presence of other characters in a numeric field is an error. Some compilers abend the job when attempting to perform arithmetic or comparison (IF) with a numeric field that contains nonnumeric data; worse yet, other compilers process the nonnumeric data, yielding incorrect results. Abending is a nuisance, but incorrect arithmetic is a serious problem. In the latter case the error is hidden and may go undetected for a long time unless proper check-totals are used to detect such errors.

To avoid this kind of error, it is important to review the program to ascertain that all fields used as operands in arithmetic statements have proper data. Data are entered into a field by a MOVE, a VALUE, or an input statement. Most often, it is through input statement execution that nonnumeric data originate. To prevent the error, all such data should be checked by a class-condition test, such as IF NOT NUMERIC ... .

Improper Use of Period

In any IF or other conditional statement the presence of a period is very important, since it terminates the domain of that statement. A common error is to have a period too early in the statement, and as a result to get subtle errors. For instance, if we have

```
IF  QUANT > LIMIT
    MOVE A TO B
    ADD 1 TO LARGE.
```

it makes an important difference as to whether the period is at the end of the second line or the third line. Such a programming error is difficult to detect because the consequences of the error might never be encountered with the test data (recall that it is impossible to test all possible combinations of values). The best way to prevent such errors is to review each conditional statement individually for the proper placement of the period.

Another error associated with a misplaced period is the situation in which the period is in column 73 of the COBOL Coding Form. As the program is scanned, it looks normal, yet it produces incorrect results (if we are fortunate to detect the error during testing). Anything written in columns 73–80 appears as part of the program in the listing, but it is treated as a comment by the compiler.

A related but relatively rare error is the situation in which an operand is written past column 72, such as COMPUTE X = Y + 1 and the "+ 1" is in columns 73–75.

Subscript Out of Range

Tables are defined using OCCURS clauses, which specify their size. If a two-dimensional table consists of 10 x 20 entries, the subscripts should be in the ranges 1–10 and 1–20, respectively. Yet for a variety of causes a subscript may lie outside that range, causing unpredictable results. Almost every programmer has been bitten by this bug. It often results in hidden errors, which are the worst kind. If we are aware of the type of error being committed, then we can try to correct it; but if we do not know what is happening operationally, then we have a serious problem.

Compilers do not generally provide automatic checking for out-of-range subscripts. The programmer can prevent such errors by preceding subscript uses by IF statements to check for invalid subscript values, or by checking input data and program logic to ascertain that the problem cannot occur undetected.

Improper Nesting of PERFORM Statements

Improper nesting of PERFORMs is another common error that results in unpredictable or strange results. Consider these statements:

```
A.
    PERFORM B
    .
    .
    .
B.
    PERFORM C
    .
    .
    .
    PERFORM B.
C.
    PERFORM A.
```

The B paragraph should not PERFORM itself, and the C paragraph should not PERFORM its hierarchical superior. Such errors may lead to strange complications. Desk-checking will not work because the compiled program is, in fact, different from the source program. As you try to follow the source program against a trace of some kind, it makes no sense. Rather than blaming the compiler, we should first check our program logic. If no answer for the difficulty can be found, then have peers review the program. The chances are that there are improper PERFORM statements or subscripts out of range, rather than errors in the compiler.

Processing the Last Input Record Twice

A common error is associated with use of the following type of structure:

```
PERFORM A UNTIL X = 'YES'.
    .
    .
    .
A. READ IN-FILE AT END MOVE 'YES' TO X.
   (Process input record ...)
```

The programmer is thinking that moving 'YES' to X in the READ statement provides proper control. Yet the PERFORM ... UNTIL will not catch the end-of-file condition until after the processing of the input record has taken place. As a result, the last record is still in the buffer, and it is processed twice.

Improper Data Format

Some of the most difficult errors are ones that result from interaction between data and logic. When the program logic appears correct but the program is not performing correctly, good candidates for review are the data definitions and the actual data used as input. Suppose that we have

```
02  PART-NO    PIC 9(4).
02  T-CODE     PIC 9.
02  QUANT      PIC 9(3).
```

If part numbers are, in fact, 5 digits long, the fifth digit of the part number will be treated as a value for T-CODE. By coincidence, in limited testing the fifth digit of part number may have valid values as a T-CODE, and the error may go undetected.

Length of records and length of fields must be checked thoroughly. Additionally, we must accept the premise that input data may be recorded in error and may therefore cause problems, even if the data definitions in the programs are correct. To avoid source-data-related errors, the program should include checks to test the input data. Regardless of verification and checking, input data may still be incorrect. We cannot possibly eliminate all errors. A more realistic objective is to minimize errors and to provide for easy correction when errors do slip through.

Environment-Related Errors

Occasionally there are errors that can be attributed to the environment. That is, they have their causes outside the program itself. For example, the operating system may have undergone a revision that is not compatible with the assumptions of the program about file handling. The human operator may be the cause of error; there may be a hardware malfunction; or a system software error can occur. There are many cases of programmers spending days puzzling over a bug, only to find out its removal was not within their control.

Environment-related errors often are temporary. Now and then a program does not run correctly on a given execution and yet, if resubmitted without any change in program or data, it runs just fine. It could be operator action, system error, or a rare combination of factors that was the cause. Our curiosity may be unsatisfied, but occasionally we have to accept the fact that trying to identify the cause of a temporary error may be futile. Fortunately, such error situations are rare.

R E V I E W . . . .

1. The content of a flag-type field can be initialized in the DATA DIVISION by using a VALUE clause, or it can be initialized in the PROCEDURE DIVISION by using a(n) _____ instruction or a(n) _____ instruction.

    MOVE-literal; INITIALIZE

2. Because, by their very nature, flag-type fields are changed and then reset in value during program execution, it is best to initialize such fields in the [DATA DIVISION / PROCEDURE DIVISION].

    PROCEDURE DIVISION

3. To avoid the inadvertent input of nonnumeric data into a numeric field, such a test procedure as IF NOT NUMERIC... , which is a(n) _____ test, should be employed.

    class-condition

4. A common programming error is that of misplacing the period with respect to
   _____ statements.

   conditional

5. Anything written in columns 73–80 of the COBOL Coding Form, including a
   period in column 73, is treated as a(n) _____ by the compiler.

   comment

6. The possibility of a subscript being out of range of a defined table can be
   detected by checking for invalid subscript values through the use of conditional
   _____ statements.

   IF

7. Improper nesting of PERFORM statements is associated with faulty program
   [coding / logic].

   logic

8. The error of processing the last input record twice typically is associated with the
   use of the PERFORM ... _____ command.

   UNTIL

9. When the program logic has been thoroughly reviewed and appears correct and
   environment-related errors are not a factor, likely sources of errors are the format
   specifications for the _____ and the actual _____ itself.

   data; input data

10. Examples of environment-related errors are those associated with the computer
    operator, _____ malfunction, or system _____ error.

    hardware; software

.   .   .   .

CONVERTING UNSTRUCTURED PROGRAMS TO STRUCTURED FORM

We conclude this chapter with a subject related to program testing, in particular, related to modifying and testing "old" programs. As mentioned in Chapter 6, programs written during the first quarter-century of programming practice do not conform to the recent techniques of structured programming. Still, these programs are in use and may continue to be used for a long time to come. Thus it is a common occurrence for a programmer to be asked to modify an existing program. If the required modification is extensive enough, it may be worth redesigning and rewriting the program "from scratch." In the more typical case, an organization cannot afford to rewrite whole programs, and we have to work with "local" modifications to the program. In such instances it may be helpful to revise the appropriate part of the program into structured form. Again, form and substance are not equivalent. If the program was poorly designed in the first place, the benefit of converting the form without converting the substance is questionable. Still, it is often useful to convert an old program into structured form so that modifications can then be incorporated with minimal risk of error. In this section we describe some conversion approaches that may be useful for unstructured programs.

Use of Duplicate Code to Achieve Structured Form

It is often possible to achieve proper structured form by duplicating the same instructions in several places in the program. First, consider a case such as portrayed in Figure 15-4(a). While the form is, in fact, structured, ANS 1974 COBOL

FIGURE 15-4

Duplication of Code to Implement a Nested Structure in the Absence of the END-IF Scope Terminator

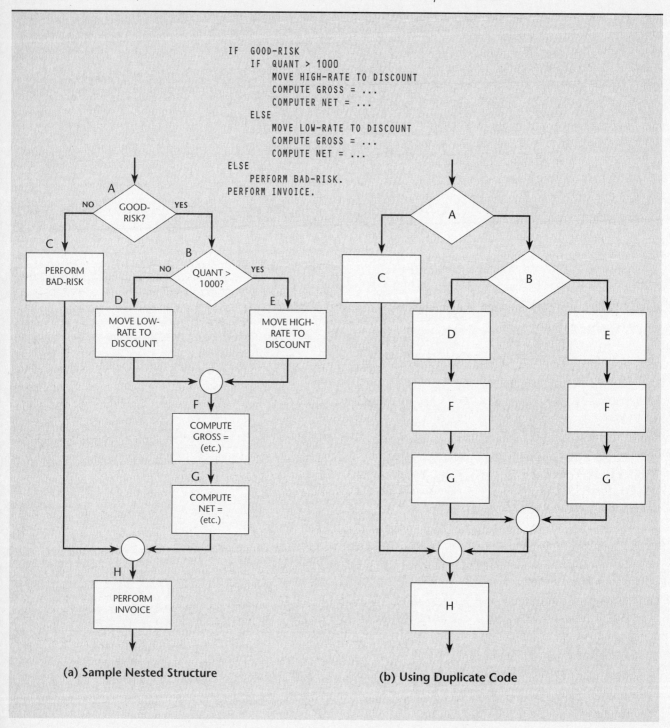

```
IF  GOOD-RISK
    IF  QUANT > 1000
        MOVE HIGH-RATE TO DISCOUNT
        COMPUTE GROSS = ...
        COMPUTER NET = ...
    ELSE
        MOVE LOW-RATE TO DISCOUNT
        COMPUTE GROSS = ...
        COMPUTE NET = ...
ELSE
    PERFORM BAD-RISK.
PERFORM INVOICE.
```

(a) Sample Nested Structure   (b) Using Duplicate Code

cannot represent the form directly without the duplication of code, as illustrated in Figure 15-4(b). We could, of course, create a separate paragraph out of the entire "yes" branch of the first decision, thus avoiding duplicate code. But proliferating paragraphs is not a desirable way of creating structured programs. However, in the

1985 standard the availability of the END-IF makes it possible to code the structured form directly, without the use of duplicate code, as follows:

```
IF  GOOD RISK
    IF  QUANT > 1000
        MOVE HIGH-RATE TO DISCOUNT
    ELSE
        MOVE LOW-RATE TO DISCOUNT
    END-IF
    COMPUTE GROSS = ...
    COMPUTE NET   = ...
ELSE
    PERFORM BAD-RISK
END-IF
PERFORM INVOICE.
```

Lacking the END-IF capability for programs written before the 1985 standard was available, duplicate code has been the most straightforward approach for converting such types of unstructured code segments into structured form.

Now let us apply duplication of code in a more complex and more realistic example. Consider the program outline in Figure 15-5(a) and its associated flow diagram in Figure 15-5(b). Using the concept of duplication of code, we revise the program structure as presented in Figure 15-6. Notice that we have achieved the one-entry, one-exit property at all levels, and we can now make our program modifications much more easily than before. For instance, if we wanted to make a change to the program under condition C4 when the path was from C to C3 to D to C4, we could make the change and leave the rest of the program unaffected.

Duplication of coding appears to be against "efficiency" in program coding. Yet writing a few additional instructions may be a small investment with a high payoff. Further, the duplication is often only conceptual, as illustrated in Figure 15-6(b), where the use of PERFORMs has reduced the actual duplicate code.

Use of a Binary Switch to Control Loop Execution

Unstructured programs often contain intermeshed multiple loops that are difficult to unravel without rewriting the entire program segment involved. To convert an unstructured loop into structured form, we employ the approach illustrated in Figure 15-7. The original form in Figure 15-7(a) is, in fact, structured. We start with an already structured form to better understand the approach. The method relies on setting a switch (S) to an initial value, S = 1 in the example, and forming a revised pretest loop structure based on using this switch as the selection variable.

Now let us illustrate application of this method in a rather difficult but common case of overlapping loops. In Figure 15-8(a) we have a program segment that is diagrammed in part (b). Notice that there are two overlapping loops, and to make matters worse, the selection step of the first loop is the first step of the second loop.

Figure 15-9 represents a conversion of Figure 15-8 into structured form using two binary switches, S1 and S2, to control execution of the two loops. Notice the inset in the upper right corner, which employs the concept of levels of abstraction to highlight the structured form of the converted figure.

An alternative solution is given in Figure 15-10. In this case we first employ duplication of coding to set off the first loop by itself, at the top of the flow diagram. Then we use two switches in the lower half to control iterative execution of the two loops after we have exited from the first loop.

FIGURE 15-5
Sample Unstructured Program

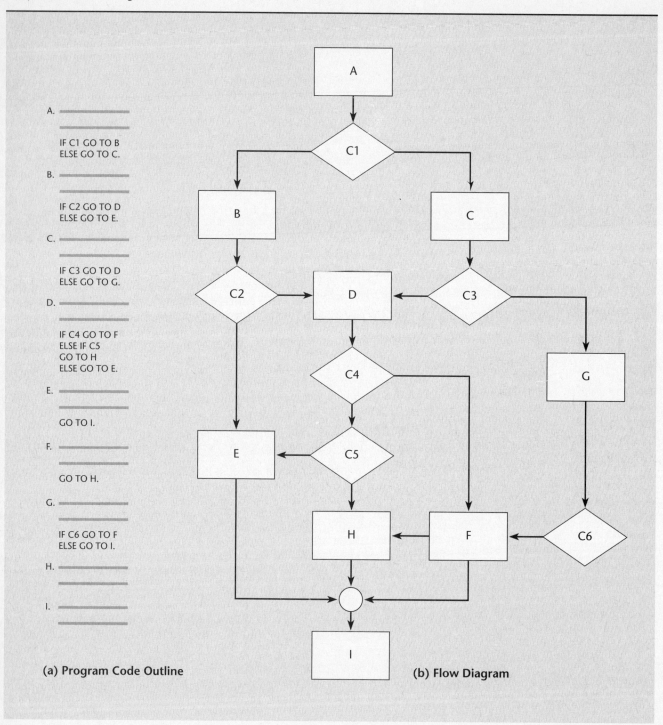

A. ────────
   ────────
   IF C1 GO TO B
   ELSE GO TO C.

B. ────────
   ────────
   IF C2 GO TO D
   ELSE GO TO E.

C. ────────
   ────────
   IF C3 GO TO D
   ELSE GO TO G.

D. ────────
   ────────
   IF C4 GO TO F
   ELSE IF C5
   GO TO H
   ELSE GO TO E.

E. ────────
   ────────
   GO TO I.

F. ────────
   ────────
   GO TO H.

G. ────────
   ────────
   IF C6 GO TO F
   ELSE GO TO I.

H. ────────
   ────────

I. ────────
   ────────

(a) Program Code Outline

(b) Flow Diagram

FIGURE 15-6   *(facing page)*
Structured Version of the Program in Figure 15-5

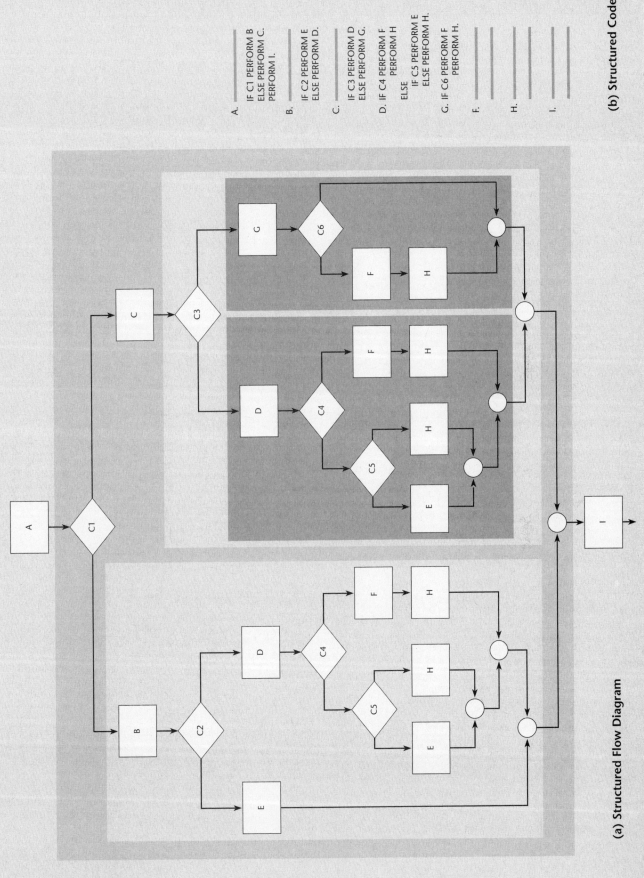

(a) Structured Flow Diagram

(b) Structured Code

A. IF C1 PERFORM B
ELSE PERFORM C.
PERFORM I.

B. IF C2 PERFORM E
ELSE PERFORM D.

C. IF C3 PERFORM D
ELSE PERFORM G.

D. IF C4 PERFORM F
PERFORM H
ELSE
IF C5 PERFORM E
ELSE PERFORM H.

G. IF C6 PERFORM F
PERFORM H.

F.

H.

I.

FIGURE 15-7
*Using a Binary Switch to Control
Loop Execution in Structured Form*

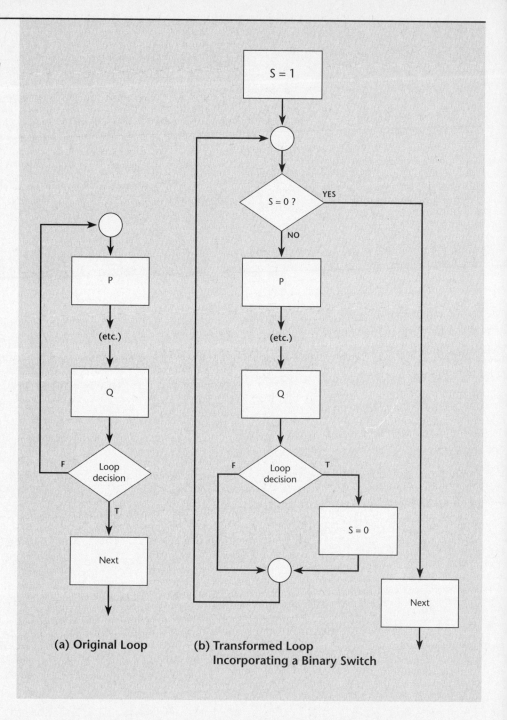

(a) Original Loop

**(b) Transformed Loop
Incorporating a Binary Switch**

The two alternatives in Figures 15-9 and 15-10 serve to demonstrate that the conversion to structured form is not a fixed procedure, but can be done in different ways.

R E V I E W . . . .

1. The need to convert unstructured programs to structured form typically is associated with [the objective that all programs be structured / the need to modify an existing older program].

                    the need to modify an existing older program

FIGURE 15-8

Sample Unstructured Program
Involving Overlapping Loops

```
A.
   WRITE PRINT-REC
   MOVE AMOUNT TO SUBTOTAL.
B.
   MOVE TEMP-SUM TO PREV-TEMP-SUM.


C.
   IF  PROD-CLASS-1
       GO TO B
   ELSE
       MOVE DISC-CODE TO SAVE-CODE
       WRITE PRINT-REC FROM MESSAGE-3.
   IF  CUST-CLASS-B
       GO TO C
   ELSE
       WRITE PRINT-REC FROM MESSAGE-5.
```

(a) Sample Unstructured Code Involving Loops

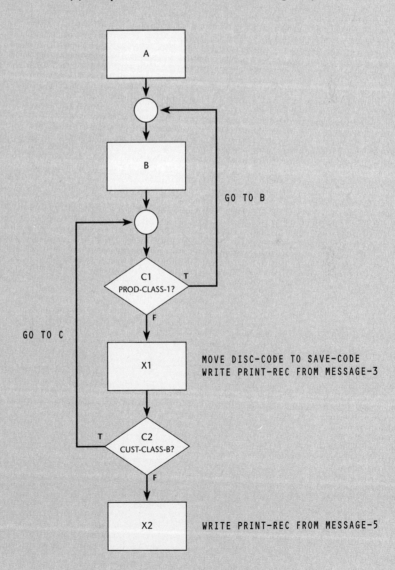

(b) Flow Diagram for Unstructured Code

FIGURE 15-9
Using Two Binary Switches
to Convert the Program in
Figure 15-8 to Structured Form

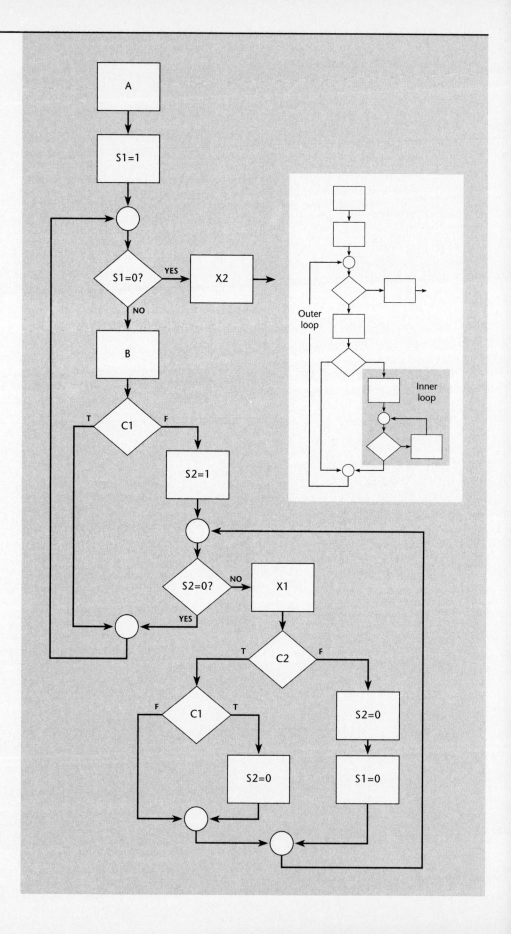

FIGURE 15-10

Using Duplication of Coding and Binary Switches to Convert the Program in Figure 15-8 to Structured Form

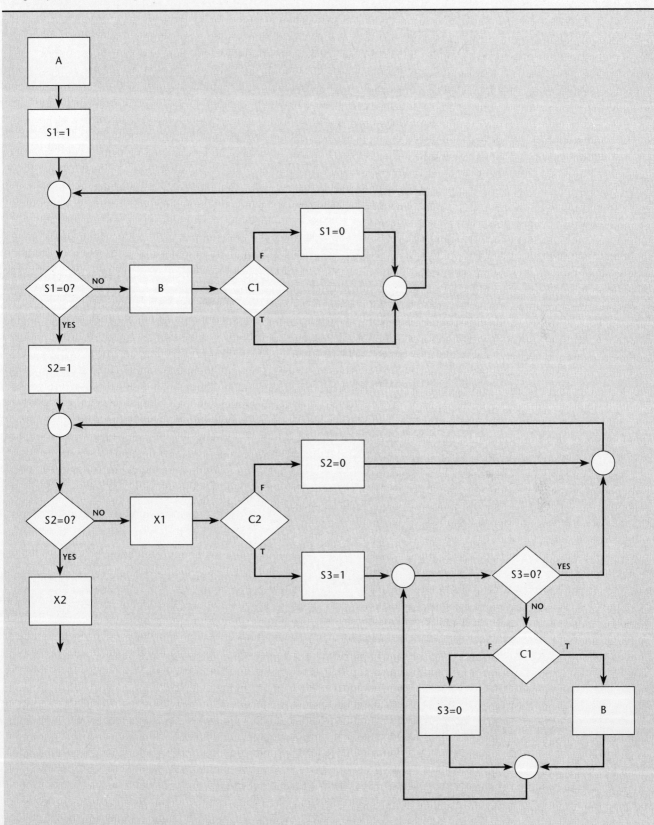

2. Duplication of modules in a structure chart done to achieve structured form [does / does not] thereby result in the program code also being duplicated the same number of times.

does not

3. In the 1985 standard, duplication of code to achieve a structured form can often be avoided by the use of the command _____ .

END-IF

(and other END ... scope terminators)

4. The principal method used to convert overlapping program loops into structured form involves the introduction of binary _____ into the program.

switches

.   .   .   .

SUMMARY

A number of concepts and techniques associated with program testing were covered in this chapter.

Program testing refers to the steps and procedures undertaken to ascertain that the program does what it was intended to do. *Top-down* testing refers to the procedure by which testing begins at the highest hierarchical level of the program structure chart, and then proceeds in stages to each lower level that follows. Thus the initial focus is on execution of the total program, and then to its parts. In the process of such development and testing, lower-level modules that are not yet developed can be represented by module name only, and are called *stub modules*.

The *bottom-up* approach to program development and testing focuses on the complete development and testing of the individual modules *before* proceeding to their integration. Thus initial programming efforts are concerned with the coding of detailed and specific functions, rather than on overall program design considerations. Candidate modules for the earliest programming and testing activities are those concerned with input or output.

In practice, some combination of the top-down and bottom-up approaches is followed in organizations. However, the top-down approach generally is favored because of its emphasis on the development of a complete and correct program design.

Of the procedures in program testing, a common one is the creation of *input test data* that is specially constructed to contain a wider diversity of data conditions, and data errors, than would exist in any limited sample of real data. The walkthrough procedure of applying program instructions manually to the test data is called *desk-checking*, whereas the type in which another programmer studies a program and its associated output is called *peer review*. A program *trace* is printed output of the actual sequence of program execution, including identification of the paragraph-names that are involved in each step. In contrast to such a sequential analysis, a *core dump* is a printing of central memory at some one point in time of program execution.

The common programming errors that were described in this chapter are *forgetting to initialize or reset* flag types of fields and accumulators; the presence of *nonnumeric data in numeric fields; improper use of the period,* thereby affecting the domain of statement execution; inclusion of a *subscript that is outside of the range* of a defined table structure; *improper nesting* of PERFORM statements; *processing the last* input record twice; improper data format; and such *environment-related errors* as hardware malfunction or temporary system errors.

The final section of this chapter was concerned with converting unstructured programs to structured form. The revision and subsequent testing of COBOL programs written some time ago often involves having to deal with unstructured programs. Some of the conversion approaches that were described are the use of *duplicate code,* the use of END-IF commands in the converted program, and use of *binary switches* to convert overlapping program loops into structured form.

EXERCISES

15.1 Describe the top-down and bottom-up approaches to program testing.

15.2 In your own words explain why extensive testing is not a sufficient substitute for good program design.

15.3 Apply the top-down testing approach, using paragraph stubs, with respect to a COBOL program that you have already written.

15.4 Consider the following unstructured program segment:

```
PAR-A.
    IF COND-A GO TO PAR-C.
    PERFORM PAR-M.
PAR-B.
     IF COND-B GO TO PAR-X.
PAR-C.
    PERFORM PAR-N
    GO TO PAR-B.
PAR-M.
    .
    .
    .
PAR-N.
    .
    .
    .
PAR-X.
    .
    .
    .
```

a. Draw the corresponding logic in flowchart form.

b. Apply use of duplicate code to achieve structured form. Show the structured form both by means of flowcharting and by means of program statements.

c. Apply use of binary switches to achieve structured form. Show the structured form both by means of flowcharting and by means of program statements.

15.5   Revise the following chart to structured form using both flowcharting and program statements. Enhance the program logic so that, when either file ends, we exit from this procedure.

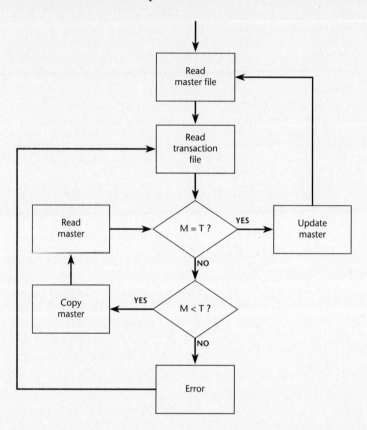

15.6   Consider the following program excerpt, which is not in proper structured form.

```
PAR-1.
    MOVE AMOUNT TO BALANCE
    IF BALANCE IS NEGATIVE GO TO PAR-4.
    PERFORM READ-INVENTORY
    IF END-INV GO TO PAR-3
    ELSE MOVE PART-LOC TO WHSE-CODE
            MULTIPLY QUANT BY PRICE GIVING TOTAL
            MOVE INV-LIMIT TO LIMIT-FIELD.
PAR-2.
    PERFORM CHECK-INVENTORY
    IF TOTAL > MAX-QUANT GO TO PAR-1
    ELSE PERFORM PROCESS-SHIPPING-PREP.
    IF FULL-LOAD PERFORM TRUCK-LOAD
    ELSE PERFORM COMBINE-SHIPMENT.
    IF SHIPPING ERROR GO TO PAR-2.
PAR-3.
    MOVE CUST-ADDRESS TO REPORT-ADDRESS
    PERFORM PRINT-LABEL.
PAR-4.
(etc.)
```

a. Draw a flowchart to highlight the essential control logic of the program.

b. Revise the flowchart constructed in part (a) so that it is in structured form by using binary switch(es) and/or duplicate code.

c. Demonstrate application of the concept of levels of abstraction in your structured flowchart in part (b).

d. Rewrite the program excerpt in proper structured form.

16

Special Data-Oriented Features

YOU WILL STUDY *a number of topics relating to data features that go beyond the elementary level in this chapter. The first four sections describe features that give you flexibility in naming and referring to storage positions. First, you will learn how to handle record definitions for files that contain more than one format of data. For example, a set of bytes in one type of record may represent the name of the high school attended, while the same set of bytes may represent the home address in a different record-type in the same file.*

*Then you will learn how the REDEFINES and RENAMES clauses allow you to use different names to refer to desired positions in storage. The feature of **reference modification** in COBOL '85 makes it possible to refer to a **portion** of a field in storage without having to define that portion as a data-name in the DATA DIVISION.*

*The subject of **data representation** concerns some fundamental notions about how data are represented in storage via a variety of binary bit combinations. You will learn how these fundamental concepts are related to the COBOL features of SIGN, USAGE, SYNCHRONIZED, and JUSTIFIED. These options enable you to exercise some control over the definition and internal representation of data, particularly numeric data.*

*In the concluding section of the chapter you will consider the concept of **collating sequence**. By your definition of an **alphabet** (character set) you can, as a programmer, choose from among several character sets, and even define unique orderings of characters.*

MULTIPLE DATA RECORDS IN THE FILE SECTION

There are many instances in which a file consists of more than one type of record. For example, a file containing sales transactions may also include transactions about a customer change of address. Sales records relating to customers will have a different format from records relating to customer change of address. The following option is available in the file description to indicate the existence of more than one type of data record in a file:

FD file-name LABEL clause . . .

DATA $\left\{ \begin{array}{l} \underline{\text{RECORD}} \text{ IS} \\ \underline{\text{RECORDS}} \text{ ARE} \end{array} \right\}$ record-name-1 [record-name-2] . . .

Consider an example. Suppose that a bank's customers may make three kinds of transactions: deposits, withdrawals, and change of address. A record containing information about a deposit or withdrawal has a different format from one pertaining to a change of address. We assume that all records identify the account by a 5-digit number in the first 5 columns and the type of transaction by a transaction code in column 6. Then, if it is a deposit or withdrawal record, the amount is recorded in columns 7–12, while if it is a change of address, the new address is recorded in columns 7–50. We can write the following data entries:

```
FD   TRANSACTION-FILE
     LABEL RECORDS OMITTED
     DATA RECORDS ARE FINANCIAL-REC
                      ADDRESS-REC.
01   FINANCIAL-REC.
     02   ACCOUNT      PIC 9(5).
     02   TRANS-CODE   PIC 9.
     02   AMOUNT       PIC 9(4)V99.
     02   FILLER       PIC X(38).
01   ADDRESS-REC.
     02   ACCOUNT      PIC 9(5).
     02   TRANS-CODE   PIC 9.
     02   NEW-ADDRESS  PIC X(44).
```

In this example the FD entry has specified two types of data records, named FINANCIAL-REC and ADDRESS-REC. It is important to emphasize that, physically, a record in this file will consist of 50 characters of data (the sum of all PIC clauses in either record description). Use of two record descriptions simply allows us to reference that data by different names and in different ways.

As defined above, both record names reference the entire 50 columns of data. Thus MOVE FINANCIAL-REC or MOVE ADDRESS-REC do exactly the same thing: they MOVE these 50 columns of data. Similarly, ACCOUNT OF FINANCIAL-REC and ACCOUNT OF ADDRESS-REC refer to the same first 5 columns of data, as do the TRANS-CODE names (properly qualified). However, AMOUNT refers to the data in columns 7–12 and, according to the PIC clause, it is assumed that the data are numeric. It should be recalled that a PICTURE clause simply specifies the storage allocation to data, and not the actual contents. The actual contents come about through input or MOVE type operations. Thus, if we were dealing with a change-of-address transaction and columns 7–12 contained the first 6 characters of the new address, a statement such as ADD 1 TO AMOUNT would produce unpredictable results, since we would be performing arithmetic with nonnumeric data. More appropriately, we first should test to see what type of record we actually had before referencing the data in question. For this purpose assume that we use a code of 1 for a deposit, 2 for withdrawal, and 3 for change of address. We could write

```
IF  TRANS-CODE OF FINANCIAL-REC = 1
    PERFORM PROCESS-DEPOSIT,
    (etc.)
```

This statement checks to see if column 6 contains the value 1. Notice that, if we had used IF TRANS-CODE OF ADDRESS-REC = 1, it would be exactly the same thing, since both refer to column 6. To further clarify this point, we could have used this data description for ADDRESS-REC:

```
01  FINANCIAL-REC.
    02  ACCOUNT       PIC 9(5).
    02  TRANS-CODE    PIC 9.
    02  AMOUNT        PIC 9(4)V99.
    02  FILLER        PIC X(38).

01  ADDRESS-REC.
    02  FILLER        PIC X(6).
    02  NEW-ADDRESS   PIC X(44).
```

ACCOUNT and TRANS-CODE need no qualification now, since they are unique names in FINANCIAL-REC. Use of TRANS-CODE still refers to column 6 of the data. In this example the FILLER in ADDRESS-REC refers to the first 6 columns, which we know will contain data—the account number and the transaction code.

Although our example shows both record descriptions as having the same length, this is not necessary. We could have omitted the FILLER PIC X(38) in FINANCIAL-REC.

In general, a file may consist of more than one type of data record. As a rule, there should be a field that designates the type of record involved. In our example we used TRANS-CODE as a field that was in a fixed location no matter what the record type. Then we tested the value of that field to ascertain the type of record. In general, this identifying field should be common to all record types so that, no matter what the data are in other fields, this field can be tested.

R E V I E W . . . .

1. When there is more than one type of data record in a file, the file description in the FILE SECTION of the DATA DIVISION should identify [only one / more than one] file-name.

    only one

2. When there is more than one type of data record in a file, each record description is introduced at the _____ level-number.

    01

3. A coded entry in a specified field serves to differentiate the different records when there is more than one data record. Particularly when the records are of unequal length, the differentiating field should be located in the [left / right] part of the record field.

    left

4. In the case of multiple-type record files, at any given time the internal storage
    can contain [only one / more than one] type of record.

only one

.   .   .   .

THE REDEFINES CLAUSE

The REDEFINES clause can be used to allow the same storage location to be
referenced by different data-names or to allow a regrouping or different description of the data in a particular storage location. The general format associated with
the use of this option is

level-number data-name-1 <u>REDEFINES</u> data-name-2

We first encountered use of the REDEFINES clause in Chapter 12, in
conjunction with entering constants into a table.
The following example illustrates the use of this option:

```
01  SAMPLE.
    02  RECEIVABLE.
        03  CUSTOMER-NUMBER    PIC 9(8).
        03  CUSTOMER-NAME      PIC X(11).
        03  AMOUNT             PIC 9(4)V99.
    02  PAYABLE REDEFINES RECEIVABLE.
        03  VENDOR-NUMBER      PIC 9(6).
        03  VENDOR-NAME        PIC X(12).
        03  VENDOR-OWED-AMOUNT PIC 9(5)V99.
```

In this example, use of the REDEFINES option allows the data-names RECEIVABLE
and PAYABLE to refer to the same 25 positions in internal storage. The format of
these two data items in internal storage can be portrayed as follows:

RECEIVABLE

CUSTOMER-NUMBER	CUSTOMER-NAME	AMOUNT

PAYABLE

VENDOR-NUMBER	VENDOR-NAME	VENDOR-OWED-AMOUNT

In this example notice that the format of the data items was also changed by the
use of the REDEFINES option, but that the overall size of the item was not
changed. However, a redefinition may apply to a shorter field as well.
It should be made clear that the redefinition applies to the storage area
involved and not to the data that may be stored in that area at any point in time.
The programmer is responsible for providing the necessary program logic so that
correct reference is made to the actual data stored. In the previous example, if we
write ADD VENDOR-OWED-AMOUNT TO ..., the result will be to add the contents of the last 7 storage positions, whatever these contents might be.

Under certain conditions the REDEFINES clause cannot be used. Consider the following conditions:

1. The REDEFINES clause cannot be used at the 01 level in the FILE SECTION. The use of multiple data records in the FD entry, as discussed in the preceding section, has the same effect as use of the REDEFINES option, in that it permits use of the same storage location for different records.

2. The REDEFINES clause cannot be used when the levels of data-name-1 and data-name-2 are different. Further, the level-number must not be at the 66- or 88-level. The level 66 designation is discussed in the next section in connection with the RENAMES clause.

3. There can be as many redefinitions of an item as desired. However, all of the redefinitions refer to the first item description. Thus, if item A is the first description, and we needed two redefinitions, we would have

```
... B REDEFINES A ...
... C REDEFINES A ...
```

R E V I E W . . . .

1. The same storage location can be used in conjunction with two different data-names by use of the _____ clause.

                                                                        REDEFINES

2. When the REDEFINES option is used, the format description of the data item [can / can not] be changed as well.

                                                                              can

3. Generally, the REDEFINES clause can be used when the two data items have the same level number. The exceptions are when the special-purpose 66- or 88-level numbers are used and when the level number is at 01 in the _____ SECTION, in which case the REDEFINES clause cannot be used.

                                                                             FILE

. . . .

THE RENAMES CLAUSE

The RENAMES clause provides the programmer with the capability of regrouping elementary data items. In a sense it resembles the REDEFINES clause, except that it can form a new grouping of data items that combines several contiguous items. Use of the RENAMES clause always is signaled by the special 66-level number. The general format is

66   data-name-1 <u>RENAMES</u> data-name-2 [<u>THRU</u> data-name-3]

Consider the following example, which includes use of the RENAMES clause.

```
01  TAX-RECORD.
    02  SOC-SEC-NUMBER      PIC X(9).
    02  NAME.
        03  FIRST-NAME      PIC X(10).
        03  MIDDLE-INITIAL  PIC XX.
        03  LAST-NAME       PIC X(15).
```

```
02  TOTALS-YEAR-TO-DATE.
    03  GROSS-PAY      PIC 9(8)V99.
    03  NET-PAY        PIC 9(8)V99.
    03  FED-TAX        PIC 9(6)V99.
    03  STATE-TAX      PIC 9(4)V99.
66  LAST-GROSS RENAMES LAST-NAME THRU NET-PAY.
```

Schematically, the regrouping of data fields by use of the RENAMES clause in the last statement can be portrayed as follows:

NAME				TOTALS-YEAR-TO-DATE			
SOC-SEC-NUMBER	FIRST-NAME	MIDDLE-INITIAL	LAST-NAME	GROSS-PAY	NET-PAY	FED-TAX	STATE-TAX
			LAST-GROSS				

In the example LAST-GROSS is a storage field that consists of the LAST-NAME, GROSS-PAY, and NET-PAY fields. In this way we can make reference to those three fields as one group, which would be difficult without use of the RENAMES clause, since we are "cutting across" two data-names at the same level.

As an example of another application of the RENAMES clause, suppose that an interactive program asks the user: "DO YOU WANT TO ADD, VIEW, OR DELETE A RECORD?" We may have defined the field in which the user response is entered as follows:

```
01  RESPONSE.
    02  CHARS-1-TO-3  PIC XXX.
    02  CHAR-4        PIC X.
    02  CHARS-5-TO-6  PIC XX.
    66  ADD-RESPONSE
        RENAMES  CHARS-1-TO-3.
    66  VIEW-RESPONSE
        RENAMES  CHARS-1-TO-3 THRU CHAR-4.
    66  DELETE-RESPONSE
        RENAMES  CHARS-1-TO-3 THRU CHARS-5-TO-6.
```

We recognize that the response may be in the first 3, the first 4, or all 6 characters of RESPONSE, according to whether the viewer responded with "ADD," "VIEW," or "DELETE." We could check to see which response was given by statements such as

```
IF  ADD-RESPONSE = 'ADD' ...
IF  VIEW-RESPONSE = 'VIEW' ...
```

Such a structure is particularly useful in subprograms, when passing values of literals as arguments. This point will be elaborated upon in Chapter 23.

R E V I E W . . . .

1. Elementary data items that are part of different storage fields can be regrouped and formed into a new field by use of the _____ clause.

RENAMES

2. The DATA DIVISION statement in which the RENAMES clause is used is always assigned the level-number _____ (number).

66

. . . .

REFERENCE MODIFICATION

In COBOL '85 it is possible to reference a portion of a data field without using REDEFINES or group items in the data description. The general format for such reference is

data-name-1 (leftmost-character-position: [length])

Note the colon (:) character in the above format.

Suppose that we have a field A, containing a 9-digit social security number, and we want to access the last four digits of that number and store them in a field called B. The fields are defined as

```
01  A PIC 9(9).
01  B PIC 9(4).
```

We can use the reference modification feature and write

```
MOVE A (6:4) TO B.
```

The '6' inside the parentheses specifies the starting byte for the MOVE. The colon is the required separator, and the '4' specifies the number of bytes being referenced.

In the general format above note that the "length" item is optional. Its absence implies a reference to the remainder of the field. Thus MOVE A (6:) TO B means to move to B the data stored in A beginning with the sixth byte up to and including the end of the field.

In essence, the reference modification concept is an indirect definition of a field. As such, it reduces the effort that is required to write DATA DIVISION entries. On the other hand, it allows the programmer to define fields "on the fly," so to speak, and thereby runs counter to the documentation spirit of COBOL. Still, let us consider an example that illustrates the time-saving effect of using the reference modification feature. Assume the following field definitions:

```
01  REPORT-LINE.
    02  FILLER             PIC X(10) VALUE SPACES.
    02  SALESMAN-NAME-OUT  PIC X(15).
    02  FILLER             PIC X(5) VALUE SPACES.
    02  PRODUCT-NUMBER-OUT PIC 999.
    02  FILLER             PIC X(11) VALUE SPACES.
    02  SALES-AMOUNT-OUT   PIC Z,ZZ9.99.
    02  FILLER             PIC X(8) VALUE SPACES.
    02  TOTAL-SALES-OUT    PIC $$$,$$9.99.
```

The above field definitions are sufficient for a report containing a salesman heading, product heading, and detail lines. For purposes of footings, however, we need not create separate data definitions. Instead, we can make use of reference modification. For a salesman footing condition, for example, we could write the following:

```
MOVE SPACES TO REPORT-LINE
MOVE '**TOTAL FOR SALESMAN ' TO REPORT-LINE (13:24)
MOVE PREVIOUS-SALESMAN-NAME TO REPORT-LINE (37:15)
MOVE SALESMAN-TOTAL-SALES TO TOTAL-SALES-OUT.
```

The two middle MOVE statements above, which contain the reference modification feature, eliminate the need to define new items. To see the effect of the reference modification feature in the above example, we now present an alternative version *without* the use of reference modification. First, we redefine REPORT-LINE so that we have the two new fields that correspond to the two references above: (13:24), and (37:15). In the example below, SALESMAN-TOT-TITLE-OUT begins at byte 13 and is 24 bytes long, while PREV-SALESMAN-OUT begins at byte 37 and is 15 bytes long.

```
01  SALESMAN-FOOTING REDEFINES REPORT-LINE.
    02  FILLER              PIC X(12).
    02  SALESMAN-TOT-TITLE-OUT  PIC X(24).
    02  PREV-SALESMAN-OUT   PIC X(15).
    02  FILLER              PIC X(9).
    02  TOTAL-SALES-OUT     PIC $$$,$$9.99.
```

We could then write this revised set of statements:

```
MOVE SPACES TO REPORT-LINE
MOVE '**TOTAL FOR SALESMAN ' TO SALESMAN-TOT-TITLE-OUT
MOVE PREVIOUS-SALESMAN-NAME TO PREV-SALESMAN-OUT
MOVE SALESMAN-TOTAL-SALES TO TOTAL-SALES-OUT.
```

As another example of the use of reference modification, Figure 16-1 is a revised version of the sample program in Figure 7-9 in Chapter 7. In the original program we were interested in compressing names so that each name and its parts were separated from each other by the delimiter #, as in the following example:

```
DOAKS$MARY#BETH#LURVEY#ALEXANDER# ...
```

Figure 16-1 shows how reference modification can be used in a case where we cannot use data redefinitions because of the varying conditions. In Figure 16-1 notice the use of STARTING-PT, and ENDING-PT. Respectively, they define the beginning byte for the next compressed name and the ending byte of the previously compressed name. On those occasions when the STRING ... INTO STRING-LINE encounters an OVERFLOW condition, we are in a situation in which part of a name may have been strung and we ran out of room in the receiving record. In such a case we want to "back up" to the ending point of the previously compressed name and fill-in the rest of STRING-LINE with asterisks, thus erasing the partially strung name, and padding the remainder of STRING-LINE as required in the task.

Notice the following statement in both the 000-MAIN-ROUTINE and 200-COMPRESS-DATA paragraphs:

```
MOVE ALL "*" TO STRING-LINE
      (ENDING-PT:STRING-LENGTH - ENDING-PT + 1)
```

As the above example illustrates, we are given considerable power and flexibility in handling reference modification. For instance, we can use a mathematical expression, such as the one above, to define the desired length in the second

FIGURE 16-1

Revised COBOL Program of the Program in Figure 7-9, Using Reference Modification

```
PROCEDURE DIVISION.
*
000-MAIN-ROUTINE.
    OPEN INPUT  STRING-FILE
         OUTPUT STRING-OUT
*
    PERFORM 100-READ-EXPANDED-REC
*
    MOVE 1 TO STARTING-PT
*
    PERFORM 200-COMPRESS-DATA
        UNTIL END-OF-FILE
*
    MOVE ALL "*" TO STRING-LINE
                    (ENDING-PT:STRING-LENGTH - ENDING-PT + 1)
    WRITE STRING-LINE
*
    CLOSE STRING-FILE
          STRING-OUT
    STOP RUN.
*
100-READ-EXPANDED-REC.
    READ STRING-FILE RECORD
        AT END SET END-OF-FILE TO TRUE
    END-READ.
*
200-COMPRESS-DATA.
    STRING LAST-NAME DELIMITED BY SPACE
           "#" DELIMITED BY SIZE
           FIRST-NAME DELIMITED BY SPACE
           "#" DELIMITED BY SIZE
           MIDDLE-NAME DELIMITED BY SPACE
           "#" DELIMITED BY SIZE
               INTO STRING-LINE
               WITH POINTER STARTING-PT
               ON OVERFLOW
                   MOVE ALL "*" TO STRING-LINE
                       (ENDING-PT:STRING-LENGTH - ENDING-PT + 1)
                   WRITE STRING-LINE
                   MOVE 1 TO STARTING-PT
               NOT ON OVERFLOW
                   MOVE STARTING-PT TO ENDING-PT
                   PERFORM 100-READ-EXPANDED-REC
    END-STRING.
```

parameter of the general format of the reference modification shown at the beginning of this section.

The 1974 standard does not include the feature of reference modification. Still, we can handle any task with or without that feature. Lacking reference modification and wanting a flexible reference for variable bytes in a field, the common approach would be to define or redefine such a field as a table of single bytes. Then we can use subscripts and suitable PERFORM ... VARYING statements to access any portion of the field. For example:

```
05   SAMPLE-FIELD    PIC X(50).
05   BYTE-BY-BYTE   REDEFINES SAMPLE-FIELD.
     10 SAMPLE-FIELD-BYTE OCCURS 50 TIMES   PIC X.
```

Now we can access any byte within SAMPLE-FIELD by referencing through subscripts SAMPLE-FIELD-BYTE (...) and processing a set of bytes through iterational instructions.

R E V I E W . . . .

1. The COBOL feature by which a portion of a data field can be referenced in a PROCEDURE DIVISION statement is the

    _____ feature.

    reference modification

2. Suppose we wish to MOVE the 4th through 8th bytes of a 10-byte data field A to field B. The appropriate command is _____ .

    MOVE A (4:5) TO B

3. Suppose we wish to MOVE the 9th and 10th bytes of a 10-byte data field A to field C. The two alternative forms of the command that can be used are MOVE A _____ TO C, or MOVE A _____ TO C.

    (9:2); (9:)

. . . .

DATA REPRESENTATION

We digress now from the COBOL-language orientation of these topics to establish a common foundation for understanding the two special COBOL definitional clauses that are described after the following subsections on character data and numeric data.

Computers utilize the binary characters (bits) of zero and one to represent data because the physical basis of electromagnetic circuitry is binary. However, there is a great variety of ways that these binary bits are used to represent data in computer systems.

Table 16-1 lists the most common ways of representing data. As indicated in the table, we need to make a distinction between *character data,* which are used to represent nonquantitative data, and *numeric data,* which are used to represent quantitative measures. Only a brief explanation of the categories included in Table 16-1 is presented in this section of the chapter. More detailed coverage can be found in introductory texts on computer science and data processing.

Character Data

A *character* may be an alphabetic letter, a numeric digit (but not amenable to arithmetic operations), or any special symbol. Characters are represented by grouping a number of bits together and associating a specific bit pattern with a specific character. Following is a description of each category of character data listed in Table 16-1.

TABLE 16-1
Data Representation

DATA REPRESENTATION	
CHARACTER DATA	**NUMERIC DATA**
6-bit BCD	Binary: *quarterword, halfword, fullword, doubleword*
8-bit ASCII	Scientific Notation: *single-precision, double-precision*
8-bit EBCDIC	Hexadecimal
Other vendor-based codes	Packed Decimal
	Zoned Decimal
	Character Representation: *BCD, ASCII, EBCDIC, other*

BCD. The 6-bit binary-coded decimal code uses 6 binary bits per character. For instance, the letter A is represented as 110001, while the digit 9 is represented as 001001. This coding method is not as widely used today as it was earlier. Its use is natural for 36-bit word-oriented computers, because a 36-bit word can hold an even number of six BCD-type 6-bit characters. The 6-bit BCD can provide $2^6 = 64$ unique bit patterns, so it cannot be used to represent both lowercase and uppercase alphabetic characters as well as other required characters.

ASCII. The American Standard Code for Information Interchange, or ASCII (pronounced "as-kee") uses 8 bits per character and can therefore be used to represent $2^8 = 256$ unique bit patterns. Since there are fewer than 100 characters available in all Western languages, the majority of bit patterns are unused. As the name implies, this is a standard code that can be used to transmit data to all systems that accept this standard.

Figure 16-2 presents the complete ASCII code. As examples, the representations for the characters A,), and 9 are 01000001, 00101001, and 00111001, respectively. For instance, in the ASCII code "null" is the smallest character, with a collating sequence of zero, and the tilde (~) is the largest character, with a value of 126. Note that the bit configurations for the collating sequence 1 through 31 and above 126 are undefined. The collating sequence in a computer is used in alphanumeric comparisons. For instance, in the ASCII system a field whose content is 9A is smaller than a field whose content is aA.

EBCDIC. The Extended Binary Coded Decimal Interchange Code, or EBCDIC (pronounced "eb-se-dik"), is also an 8-bit code developed and favored by IBM. The EBCDIC code is shown in Figure 16-3. As examples, the character representations for A,), and 9 are 11000001 , 01011101, and 11111001, respectively. Notice that in contrast to ASCII, 9A is larger than the value aA.

Numeric Data

A *number* is a collection of digits representing a quantity. Numbers may be signed as positive or negative and may represent integer values or decimal values.

FIGURE 16-2

ASCII Alphabet and Coding Sequence

COLLATING SEQUENCE	BIT CONFIGURATION	SYMBOL	MEANING	COLLATING SEQUENCE	BIT CONFIGURATION	SYMBOL	MEANING
0	00000000		Null	79	01001111	O	
32	00100000	SP	Space	80	01010000	P	
33	00100001	I	Logical OR	81	01010001	Q	
34	00100010	"	Quotation mark	82	01010010	R	
35	00100011	#	Number sign	83	01010011	S	
36	00100100	$	Dollar sign	84	01010100	T	
37	00100101	%	Percent	85	01010101	U	
38	00100110	&	Ampersand	86	01010110	V	
39	00100111	'	Apostrophe, prime	87	01010111	W	
40	00101000	(	Opening parenthesis	88	01011000	X	
41	00101001	)	Closing parenthesis	89	01011001	Y	
42	00101010	*	Asterisk	90	01011010	Z	
43	00101011	+	Plus	91	01011011	[	Opening bracket
44	00101100	,	Comma	92	01011100	\	Reverse slant
45	00101101	–	Hyphen, minus	93	01011101	]	Closing bracket
46	00101110	.	Period, decimal point	94	01011110	^	Circumflex, Logical NOT
47	00101111	/	Slant	95	01011111	_	Underscore
48	00110000	0		96	01100000	'	Grave Accent
49	00110001	1		97	01100001	a	
50	00110010	2		98	01100010	b	
51	00110011	3		99	01100011	c	
52	00110100	4		100	01100100	d	
53	00110101	5		101	01100101	e	
54	00110110	6		102	01100110	f	
55	00110111	7		103	01100111	g	
56	00111000	8		104	01101000	h	
57	00111001	9		105	01101001	i	
58	00111010	:	Colon	106	01101010	j	
59	00111011	;	Semi-colon	107	01101011	k	
60	00111100	<	Less than	108	01101100	l	
61	00111101	=	Equals	109	01101101	m	
62	00111110	>	Greater than	110	01101110	n	
63	00111111	?	Question mark	111	01101111	o	
64	01000000	@	Commercial At	112	01110000	p	
65	01000001	A		113	01110001	q	
66	01000010	B		114	01110010	r	
67	01000011	C		115	01110011	s	
68	01000100	D		116	01110100	t	
69	01000101	E		117	01110101	u	
70	01000110	F		118	01110110	v	
71	01000111	G		119	01110111	w	
72	01001000	H		120	01111000	x	
73	01001001	I		121	01111001	y	
74	01001010	J		122	01111010	z	
75	01001011	K		123	01111011	{	Opening Brace
76	01001100	L		124	01111100	I	Vertical Line
77	01001101	M		125	01111101	}	Closing Brace
78	01001110	N		126	01111110	~	Tilde

FIGURE 16-3

EBCDIC Alphabet and Coding Sequence

COLLATING SEQUENCE	BIT CONFIGURATION	SYMBOL	MEANING	COLLATING SEQUENCE	BIT CONFIGURATION	SYMBOL	MEANING
0	00000000			153	10011001	r	
:				:			
74	01001010	¢	Cent sign	162	10100010	s	
75	01001011	.	Period, decimal point	163	10100011	t	
76	01001100	<	Less than sign	164	10100100	u	
77	01001101	(	Left parenthesis	165	10100101	v	
78	01001110	+	Plus sign	166	10100110	w	
79	01001111	I	Vertical bar, Logical OR	167	10100111	x	
80	01010000	&	Ampersand	168	10101000	y	
:				169	10101001	z	
90	01011010	!	Exclamation point	:			
91	01011011	$	Dollar sign	193	11000001	A	
92	01011100	*	Asterisk	194	11000010	B	
93	01011101	)	Right parenthesis	195	11000011	C	
94	01011110	;	Semi-colon	196	11000100	D	
95	01011111	^	Logical not	197	11000101	E	
96	01100000	–	Minus, hyphen	198	11000110	F	
97	01100001	/	Slash	199	11000111	G	
:				200	11001000	H	
107	01101011	,	Comma	201	11001001	I	
108	01101100	%	Percent sign	:			
109	01101101	_	Underscore	209	11010001	J	
110	01101110	>	Greater than sign	210	11010010	K	
111	01101111	?	Question mark	211	11010011	L	
:				212	11010100	M	
122	01111010	:	Colon	213	11010101	N	
123	01111011	#	Number sign	214	11010110	O	
124	01111100	@	At sign	215	11010111	P	
125	01111101	'	Apostrophe, prime	216	11011000	Q	
126	01111110	=	Equals sign	217	11011001	R	
127	01111111	"	Quotation marks	:			
:				226	11100010	S	
129	10000001	a		227	11100011	T	
130	10000010	b		228	11100100	U	
131	10000011	c		229	11100101	V	
132	10000100	d		230	11100110	W	
133	10000101	e		231	11100111	X	
134	10000110	f		232	11101000	Y	
135	10000111	g		233	11101001	Z	
136	10001000	h		:			
137	10001001	i		240	11110000	0	
:				241	11110001	1	
145	10010001	j		242	11110010	2	
146	10010010	k		243	11110011	3	
147	10010011	l		244	11110100	4	
148	10010100	m		245	11110101	5	
149	10010101	n		246	11110110	6	
150	10010110	o		247	11110111	7	
151	10010111	p		248	11111000	8	
152	10011000	q		249	11111001	9	

Following is a description of each category of numeric data listed in Table 16-1, presented earlier.

Binary. Numeric data in binary representation consist of zeros and ones having position values represented as powers of the (binary) base 2. As an illustration Figure 16-4 presents a 12-bit binary field. The leftmost bit is used for the sign, 0 = positive, 1 = negative. The remaining 11 bits can be used to represent any number ranging from 0 to $2^{11} - 1$. In the illustration the positive decimal quantity +1234 is represented as 010011010010. The number can be converted to its decimal equivalent by multiplying each digit by its position value and forming the sum, as illustrated in the figure. Positions to the right of the "decimal" point have position values of 1/2, 1/4, 1/8, and so forth, and therefore fractional quantities may also be represented. However, note that for a specified number of binary positions to the right of the decimal point some decimal values cannot be represented exactly. For instance, with 2 binary positions to the right of the decimal point we could not represent 1/5, but we could come "close" to it by using 6 positions and writing 0.001101, which is equivalent to 1/8 + 1/16 + 1/64 = 13/64. In administrative uses of the computer, "close" to a value is usually not good enough, and we may choose not to use binary representation for fractional values or to use it only after making appropriate adjustments. For instance, for dollar and cents values we could convert to integer form by multiplying by 100, do the arithmetic in binary form, and then adjust the final result by dividing by 100 in decimal representation.

The number of bits used in a binary field is dependent on the machine used and the size of the values. For IBM mainframe systems, binary fields are either 16 bits (= 2 bytes, or 1 halfword), 32 bits (= 4 bytes, or 1 fullword), or 64 bits (= 8 bytes, or 2 fullwords). For personal computers, binary fields may be either 16 (for instance, the Intel 286 processor) or 32 bits (Intel 386 and 486 processors).

Scientific Notation. Numbers may be represented by a sign bit, a value (mantissa) of fixed length, and an exponent as a power of 10. Thus +12,345,600 and +12,345,666 might both be represented as +1.23456E7, thereby losing the

FIGURE 16-4

Representation of +1234 as a 12-Bit Signed Binary Number

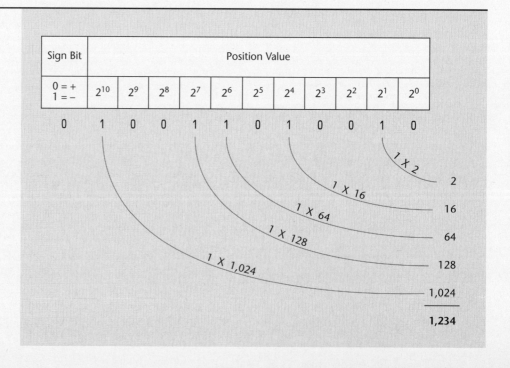

precision of the last two digit positions. This notation is useful in scientific applications but is hardly ever needed in administrative uses, in which precision is as important as the magnitude of quantities.

Hexadecimal. This representation is widely used by large systems and it is externally shown on such printed outputs as "core dumps," which display the contents of memory. Figure 16-5 presents the 16 hexadecimal digits and their binary bit configurations. A hexadecimal digit can have a value from 0 to 15 and can be represented by a group of 4 bits, since 4 bits provide $2^4 = 16$ unique bit patterns. Since many systems use the 8-bit byte as an addressable unit of storage, 2 hexadecimal digits can be stored in 1 byte. Similarly, since a halfword is 2 bytes, a word is 4 bytes, and a doubleword is 8 bytes, there can be 4, 8, and 16 hexadecimal digits stored, respectively, in such units of central storage.

As an illustration, suppose that we have a 2-byte field containing the binary equivalent of the decimal value 1234. As shown in Figure 16-4 and adding 4 leading zeroes to have 2 full bytes, the binary value would be 0000010011010010. In hexadecimal form the content could be represented as 04D2, which can be ascertained by referring to Figure 16-5 and substituting the hexadecimal equivalent for each group of 4 binary bits.

It may be useful to transform 04D2 from hexadecimal to decimal form. The first digit, 0, has zero value. The 4D2 part can be converted, keeping in mind that the position values in the hexadecimal system are, from left to right, ... 16^2, 16^1, 16^0. Thus we have

$$
\begin{aligned}
2 \quad \times \quad 16^0 &= 2 \quad \times \quad 1 \quad = \quad 2 \\
D \quad \times \quad 16^1 &= 13 \quad \times \quad 16 \quad = \quad 208 \\
4 \quad \times \quad 16^2 &= 4 \quad \times \quad 256 \quad = \quad \underline{1{,}024} \\
& \qquad\qquad\qquad\qquad\qquad\quad 1{,}234
\end{aligned}
$$

Packed Decimal. This representation is widely used for numeric computational data by COBOL programs in IBM systems. A packed-decimal field consists of an integer number of bytes and stores 2 digits per byte, except that the last half of the last byte is used to store the sign. For example, +1234 would be stored on 3 bytes even though $2\frac{1}{2}$ bytes would appear to be enough. The hexadecimal representation is 01234C, where the first zero represents 4 leading binary zeroes to make it an even 3-byte field, and the C is the hexadecimal representation of the + sign. The number –1234 is represented in hexadecimal form as 01234D, where D is the negative sign in the rightmost half-byte. Using hexadecimal C for the + sign and D for the negative sign are simply the conventions that have been adopted; there is no special "logic" to these particular choices.

FIGURE 16-5
Hexadecimal Digit Bit Configurations

HEXADECIMAL DIGIT	BIT CONFIGURATION	HEXADECIMAL DIGIT	BIT CONFIGURATION
0	0000	8	1000
1	0001	9	1001
2	0010	A	1010
3	0011	B	1011
4	0100	C	1100
5	0101	D	1101
6	0110	E	1110
7	0111	F	1111

Zoned Decimal. This representation uses a whole byte per decimal digit, but the sign of the field is stored in the last byte along with the last digit. In each byte the first half is the "zone bits" that are essentially unused, while the decimal digit is stored in the second half of the byte. Then, in the last byte the first 4 bits represent the sign, while the last 4 bits represent the last digit.

As an illustration, +1234 would require 4 bytes, 1 for each decimal digit. The hexadecimal representation is FlF2F3C4, where F is represented by the zone bits 1111, as can be observed in Figure 16-5. The C represents the positive sign in the upper half of the last byte. As another example, –1234 has the hexadecimal representation FlF2F3D4, where now D is the negative sign.

Character Representation. Numeric data can be represented as characters. In the 8-bit ASCII code the decimal 19 is represented as 0011000100111001, where the first 8 bits represent 1 and the last 8 bits represent 9. Notice that if we treated this code as a single 16-bit binary number, it would instead represent the quantity 12,345!

Computer systems convert numeric character data into an appropriate computational form before performing arithmetic operations, and then reconvert the data for storage in character form.

The foregoing overview on data representation will be applied to COBOL-related issues in the following sections of this chapter.

R E V I E W . . . .

1. Of the two basic forms of representation, the one that is used to represent nonquantitative data is _____ data.

   character

2. Of the two basic forms of data representation, the one that is used to represent quantitative measures is _____ data.

   numeric

3. The 6-bit BCD, 8-bit ASCII, and 8-bit EBCDIC are all ways of representing _____ data.

   character

4. Binary, scientific notation, hexadecimal, packed decimal, and zoned decimal are all ways of representing _____ data.

   numeric

5. Numeric data can also be represented as characters, and such representation [is / is not] directly amenable to arithmetic operations.

   is not (conversion to a computational form is done)

. . . .

THE USAGE CLAUSE

In COBOL, data in character mode are described as being in DISPLAY mode, while data in numeric mode are described as being in COMPUTATIONAL mode. DISPLAY is the default condition: All data items are assumed to be in DISPLAY mode unless they are declared to be COMPUTATIONAL. The declaration is done in the DATA DIVISION with the USAGE clause. Figure 16-6 presents the general format of this clause. In terms of the character description in the PICTURE clause, numeric data in the DISPLAY mode can be designated PIC 9 or PIC X (numeric or alphanumeric);

FIGURE 16-6
General Format of the USAGE Clause

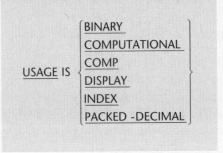

$$\text{USAGE IS} \left\{ \begin{array}{l} \underline{\text{BINARY}} \\ \underline{\text{COMPUTATIONAL}} \\ \underline{\text{COMP}} \\ \underline{\text{DISPLAY}} \\ \underline{\text{INDEX}} \\ \underline{\text{PACKED}}\text{ -DECIMAL} \end{array} \right\}$$

however, data in the COMPUTATIONAL mode can only be PIC 9. Of course, whether data are designated PIC 9 or PIC X, it is understood that any fields involved in arithmetic computations will include only numeric data, and not any letters, spaces, decimal points, or other special symbols. Consider the following examples:

```
02  AMOUNT-1   PIC 99.
02  AMOUNT-2   PIC 99 USAGE DISPLAY.
02  AMOUNT-3   PIC XX USAGE DISPLAY.
02  AMOUNT-4   PIC 99 USAGE COMPUTATIONAL.
02  AMOUNT-5   PIC 99 USAGE COMP.
02  AMOUNT-6   USAGE COMP
               PIC 99 VALUE ZERO.
```

The first example above omits the USAGE clause, and the item will be in DISPLAY mode by default. The second and third examples make the declaration explicit. The fourth and fifth examples illustrate the COMPUTATIONAL declaration in full and abbreviated form, respectively. The last example illustrates the point that the order of USAGE, PIC, and VALUE is immaterial.

The USAGE of a numeric item determines its size in terms of bits, but the size also depends on the coding scheme used. For instance, if we declare USAGE DISPLAY and use an 8-bit code, then there are 8 bits for each 9 or X character in the PICTURE.

For signed numeric DISPLAY items the sign is represented in combination with the last digit in ways similar to the description under the zoned-decimal heading in the preceding section of this chapter. When data are entered on a terminal, we must be careful to cause the correct bit representation by entering an alphabetic character for the last digit.

As will be explained further in the next section of this chapter, the SIGN clause can be used in conjunction with the USAGE clause, and it affects the way that DISPLAY numeric data are treated. For example, suppose that we have

```
... PIC S9999 USAGE IS DISPLAY
          SIGN  IS LEADING.
```

and we have the value –1234. In hexadecimal form (consult Figure 16-5 again) the representation is D1F2F3F4, where D is the leading negative sign in this case. It may be instructive to pause for a moment to further "decode" the hexadecimal form. D1 translates to 11010001, which is the EBCDIC representation of the uppercase letter J, while F2, F3, and F4 are the EBCDIC representations of 2, 3, and 4, respectively. Thus, for the item in this example, J234 is the equivalent of –1234. Had the number been +1234, we would have A234, since a +1 is a C1 in hexadecimal, or A in EBCDIC.

As a further example, suppose that we have

```
... PIC S9999 USAGE IS DISPLAY
        SIGN  IS TRAILING SEPARATE.
```

and we consider the value –1234. Now we need to represent the sign as a separate, trailing character. In hexadecimal form it is FlF2F3F460, where 60 is the hexadecimal negative sign, which is also the EBCDIC (01100000) negative sign. To represent +1234, the hexadecimal form would be FlF2F3F44E, where 4E is the positive sign (01001110).

It is clear from the preceding examples that the COBOL programmer has to have knowledge of the specific coding system that the compiler is using to be able to decode core dumps, or to be able to enter data correctly in DISPLAY usage fields with signed data. Such machine dependence is contrary to the spirit of standardized COBOL, but it is at times necessary to accept the realities of the imperfect world of "standard" languages.

The COMPUTATIONAL option of the USAGE clause specifies that the data are in the form in which the respective machine does its computations. Typically, the form is binary and the size of the field in terms of bits is determined by the compiler. For instance, for some IBM compilers the following rule is used:

DIGITS IN PICTURE CLAUSE	STORAGE OCCUPIED
1–4	2 bytes
5–9	4 bytes
10–18	8 bytes

Care must be taken in handling group fields or records containing USAGE COMP fields. For instance, if we have

```
01  A.
    02  B  PIC X(6).
    02  C  PIC 9(6) USAGE COMP.
```

and we write MOVE A TO ... , we should realize that we are moving 10 bytes, since C now requires just 4 bytes as presented in the preceding table. Without the USAGE COMP we would, of course, be moving 12 bytes!

In addition to the COMP option most compilers will implement additional variants, such as COMP-1, COMP-2, COMP-3, etc. In the case of some compilers, for instance, COMP-1 (or COMPUTATIONAL-1) and COMP-2 mean, respectively, single- and double-precision floating-point scientific notation representation (both of which are rarely used in COBOL programs). Further, COMP-3 for IBM 1974 standard compilers is the packed-decimal representation, which was described in the preceding section, while DISPLAY is the zoned-decimal representation. As discussed below, COBOL '85 eliminates the need for some nonstandard options by introducing the BINARY and PACKED-DECIMAL options.

These options, which include some standard (COMP) and some non-standard (COMP-1, COMP-2, COMP-3) options, provide the programmer with a dubious tool for improving computational efficiency. The case is often made that USAGE COMP in one form or another increases speed of execution because data need not be converted from character mode to computational mode and back. We feel that in terms of today's economics of machine instructions per dollar we should have good reasons before we consider machine efficiency as an important factor in deciding how to write a program. Most COBOL programs do relatively so little arithmetic that it is not worth the trouble to write machine-dependent programs. Particularly, we should not include COMP fields in file descriptions that may need to be portable to other systems.

In a related context it should be noted that moving zeros to a group item whose elementary items contain USAGE COMPUTATIONAL clauses may result in nonzero data. Consider this group item:

```
01 GROUP-ITEM.
    02  AMOUNT-1 PIC 99V99   USAGE COMPUTATIONAL.
    02  AMOUNT-2 PIC 9999V99 USAGE COMPUTATIONAL.
```

With reference to the description above, a statement such as MOVE ZERO TO GROUP-ITEM will move "character" zeros into GROUP-ITEM. A zero in character (DISPLAY) mode is different from a zero in numeric (COMPUTATIONAL) mode. Therefore, if we subsequently write ADD TOTAL TO AMOUNT-1, erroneous results will be obtained from the arithmetic operation, since AMOUNT-1 does not contain a numeric-mode zero value. To avoid such problems, we should move zeros to each individual numeric field that has been defined as USAGE COMPUTATIONAL. Thus MOVE ZERO TO AMOUNT-1, AMOUNT-2 would be the appropriate instruction for setting these two fields equal to zero. Of course, in the absence of the USAGE COMPUTATIONAL clauses, MOVE ZERO TO GROUP-ITEM would have resulted in proper DISPLAY mode zeros in the elementary fields. Another alternative would have been to have declared the GROUP-ITEM USAGE COMPUTATIONAL, in which case a MOVE ZEROS to GROUP-ITEM would have resulted in numeric zeros being stored in the subordinate fields.

Figure 16-6 also includes the BINARY, INDEX, and PACKED-DECIMAL representations as options in the USAGE clause. All three options are COBOL '85 enhancements. The BINARY option specifies that data will be represented in base 2 notation; however, the precise implementation is dependent on the specific implementor. Thus you would have to consult the language manual of your computer to determine the exact form of binary representation. For example, in a 32-bit machine, binary integers may utilize the leading bit as a sign bit (such as 0 = negative and 1 = positive), and the remaining bits may be used for the actual binary values. The number of binary bits that are available must be sufficient to accommodate the maximum range of values specified by the associated decimal PICTURE character string. Consider the following example:

```
02  AMOUNT PIC S9(3) USAGE BINARY.
```

The maximum decimal value is +999, which requires 10 binary bits plus the sign bit (since $2^{10} = 1024$). Whether a particular compiler uses 11 bits or some other, larger number with respect to the above example cannot be known except by reference to the appropriate manual.

The INDEX option of the USAGE clause is described in Chapter 19. Briefly, an *index value* is a value that corresponds to an occurrence number in a table. The specific form of an INDEX item depends on the implementor, so, again, you would need to consult a local source for details.

When the USAGE IS PACKED-DECIMAL option is used, the data are stored in the packed-decimal form described in the preceding subsection of this chapter, "Data Representation." Many computers are designed for efficient execution of computations with respect to data in the packed-decimal form. Therefore for such computers it is advantageous to use such a definition for computational fields.

R   E   V   I   E   W .   .   .   .

1. In COBOL the two modes in which numeric data can be represented are DISPLAY
    and COMPUTATIONAL. The appropriate form of the data can be indicated by
    use of the _____ clause in the DATA DIVISION.

                                                                              USAGE

2. When the USAGE clause is not used, the field is automatically defined as being
    [DISPLAY / COMPUTATIONAL] in form.

                                                                            DISPLAY

3. The option of the USAGE clause that specifies that the data are in the form in
    which the computer does its calculations is the _____
    option.

                                                                     COMPUTATIONAL

4. In addition to the COMP option, most compilers will implement nonstandard
    options designated by such an option name as _____ .

                                                              COMP-1 (or COMP-2, etc.)

5. In general, the use of the COMP options improves [machine / programmer]
    efficiency but as a trade-off against [machine / programmer] time.

                                                                machine; programmer

6. If zeros are moved into a group item that includes elementary items that are
    designated COMP, such zeros will be in the [character / numeric] mode.

                                     character (Unless the USAGE COMP applies to the group item.)

7. If the BINARY option is used in the USAGE clause, the number of binary bits
    available must be sufficient to accommodate the maximum range of values
    specified by the associated decimal _____ character string.

                                                                            PICTURE

8. The option of the USAGE clause that corresponds to an occurrence number in a
    table is the _____ option.

                                                                              INDEX

9. In addition to BINARY, COMPUTATIONAL, DISPLAY, and INDEX USAGE, the
    1985 standard defines the _____ USAGE option.

                                                                     PACKED-DECIMAL

.   .   .   .

THE SIGN CLAUSE

The S PICTURE character specifies that the field is signed. The SIGN clause is used
to specify the position and the mode of representation of the operational sign
when it is necessary to describe these properties explicitly. The general format for
the SIGN clause is

$$[\underline{SIGN} \ IS] \ \left\{ \begin{array}{l} \underline{LEADING} \\ \underline{TRAILING} \end{array} \right\} \ [\underline{SEPARATE} \ CHARACTER]$$

Suppose we write the following:

```
02  AMOUNT-A PICTURE S999
              USAGE DISPLAY
              SIGN IS LEADING.
02  AMOUNT-B PICTURE S999
              USAGE DISPLAY
              SIGN IS TRAILING.
```

By the above descriptions we have specified that these two signed fields contain
the operational sign in the first and in the last digit position, respectively. Thus, if

they both contained the numeric value –243 and the character K happened to represent –2 while L happened to represent –3, the contents of these fields could be shown as follows:

In AMOUNT-A the negative sign is stored in the first byte. Referring back to the discussion about packed-decimal representation, you will recall that a negative sign is a hexadecimal D (1101). Combining the negative sign and the value 2, we have 11010010, which is the letter K in the EBCDIC code in Figure 16-3. In AMOUNT-B, however, the declaration is that the SIGN IS TRAILING, so the combination of the negative sign and the value 3 form the letter L (11010011).

The convention is to store the sign in the rightmost digit position; therefore the absence of the SIGN clause defaults to that case. The choice of LEADING rather than TRAILING is difficult to justify, but the option is available.

When the SEPARATE CHARACTER option is used, then the operational sign is actually represented as a separate leading or trailing character and requires a separate storage position. Consider these examples:

```
02  AMOUNT-A PIC S999
        SIGN IS LEADING SEPARATE CHARACTER.
02  AMOUNT-B PIC S999
        SIGN IS TRAILING SEPARATE CHARACTER.
        .
        .
        .
MOVE 15 TO AMOUNT-A
MOVE -156 TO AMOUNT-B
```

After these MOVE instructions are executed, the contents of these two fields will be

Notice that each field consists of four positions. In AMOUNT-A the + sign is inserted as the first character. A field containing S always contains a sign, whether positive or negative. The leading zero, of course, was inserted by the MOVE so that all the characters in the field are numeric digits. In the case of AMOUNT-B the sign is negative and it is trailing.

Fields containing the SIGN clause must include the S character and are considered numeric. The system treats the sign as part of the field in MOVE and arithmetic operations. A MOVE from an S99 field without a SIGN clause, to S99 SIGN IS ... SEPARATE, will be suitably converted by the system to change the sign representation. Similarly, reversing the sending and receiving fields in the above example will also produce conversion to the appropriate sign representation.

When the SIGN ... SEPARATE clause is used, then the sign is a separate character, and source data may be entered via a terminal with a sign. However, care must be taken to put the sign in the correct place and to use numeric values only, as always. For the field

```
AMOUNT-A PIC S9999 SIGN LEADING SEPARATE
```

all of the following data would be correct: +0010, +1234, –1000, –0001, +0000. Notice that a sign must always be present, even to represent a (positive) zero.

R E V I E W . . . .

1. When it is necessary to describe the position of the operational sign for a field explicitly, the _____ clause is included with the data description.

SIGN

2. Fields containing the sign clause [must / need not] include the S character and [must / need not] be described by 9 PICTURE characters.

must; must

3. The operational sign is represented as a separate character and requires a separate storage position when the _____ option is used in the SIGN clause.

SEPARATE CHARACTER

. . . .

THE SYNCHRONIZED CLAUSE

The SYNCHRONIZED (abbreviated SYNC) clause can be used to improve arithmetic execution speed. It is a machine-dependent instruction, and for that reason unless the need for it is imperative, its use should be avoided. To use the instruction effectively, the programmer has to study the rules that apply to the specific computer system. Even then, it is an error-prone instruction due to the complexity of the rules and the indirect ways by which the instruction works.

By DATA DIVISION descriptions the programmer can specify data items to be stored adjacent to one another in storage. However, execution of arithmetic operations is affected by the extent to which computational items have been "properly" aligned for a given computer system. In other words, there are some naturally good boundaries for computational data, and the SYNCHRONIZED clause provides a means for controlling the alignment to desired advantage. In the course of doing so, however, we typically introduce *slack bytes,* or unused storage interspersed among the useful data. Future oversight of such slack bytes is a main reason for recommending avoidance of the SYNCHRONIZED clause.

Let us consider an example:

```
01  A.
    02  B PIC X(5).
    02  C PIC X(2).
    02  D PIC S9(8)
        USAGE COMPUTATIONAL
        SYNCHRONIZED.
```

For an IBM mainframe system, synchronization would mean the addition of 1 slack byte between items C and D in storage, so that the synchronized item is aligned to start on a fullword boundary (multiple of 4). To be more specific, if a COMP SYNC field has a PICTURE in the range S9 to S9(4), alignment takes place on a halfword. On the other hand, if the item is in the range S9(5) to S9(18), alignment is on a fullword. Rules such as these are machine-dependent, and the reader should be aware that these rules are different for each system.

The programmer should be aware of the availability of the clause. If a program is encountered in which extensive arithmetic computation takes place, the technical manual for the computer system should be consulted for its evaluation of the SYNCHRONIZED clause as a tool for improving program execution.

R   E   V   I   E   W . . . .

1. The option that can be used in elementary field descriptions in the DATA DIVISION to improve efficiency of arithmetic execution by the assignment of aligned storage boundaries is the _____ clause.

   SYNCHRONIZED (or SYNC)

2. Use of the SYNC clause typically introduces some unused storage, or so-called _____ bytes, interspersed among the useful data.

   slack

3. A problem associated with the SYNCHRONIZED option is that its use may make the program incompatible for different [input data / computers].

   computers

. . . .

THE JUSTIFIED RIGHT CLAUSE

The JUSTIFIED RIGHT clause is used with elementary alphabetic or alphanumeric items only, and its effect is to override the convention of left-justifying nonnumeric data. Suppose we have the record description 02 TITLE PIC X(8). If we write MOVE 'JONES' TO TITLE, the effect in TITLE will be

| J | O | N | E | S | | | |

with the name left-justified. However, if in the DATA DIVISION we had written

```
02 TITLE PICTURE X(8) JUSTIFIED RIGHT
```

execution of the above MOVE instruction would result in

| | | | J | O | N | E | S |

As indicated by the above example the JUSTIFIED RIGHT clause is always used in conjunction with the PICTURE clause for elementary items. However, it cannot be used with level-66 or level-88 items, which are concerned with use of the RENAMES and condition-names, respectively. In addition to causing right justification, the JUSTIFIED RIGHT clause also affects truncation. Without the JUSTIFIED RIGHT clause, truncation takes place from the right for alphabetic and alphanumeric data. When the JUSTIFIED RIGHT clause is used, truncation takes place from the left, as is the case for numeric data.

R E V I E W . . . .

1. Elementary alphabetic or alphanumeric items can be positioned in the rightmost portion of the field by the use of the _____ clause in the DATA DIVISION.

JUSTIFIED RIGHT

2. For alphabetic and alphanumeric data, truncation normally occurs from the [left / right]. However, when the JUSTIFIED RIGHT clause is used, truncation occurs from the [left / right].

right; left

. . . .

COLLATING SEQUENCES AND ALPHABETS

Every computer system has a native set of characters, or *alphabet*. The term here has a broader meaning than usually implied, and includes all the characters in use, such as the letters of the alphabet, special symbols, and the numeric digits.

A standard alphabet discussed earlier is the ASCII code, which defines a set of characters and their ordering (collating sequence). COBOL allows the programmer to exercise some control over the alphabet in use. The specification of the chosen alphabet is done in the ENVIRONMENT DIVISION.

To round-out the data-associated coverage of this chapter, we also describe two other options that can be used in the CONFIGURATION SECTION of the ENVIRONMENT DIVISION: the SYMBOLIC CHARACTER clause and the CLASS clause.

Defining Alphabets

Figure 16-7 presents a more complete format for the CONFIGURATION SECTION of the ENVIRONMENT DIVISION than presented earlier in this book. The ALPHABET clause allows the user to name one of the three choices shown in Figure 16-7. STANDARD-1 refers to the American National Standard Code X3.4-1977 for Information Interchange. STANDARD-2 refers to the International Standard 646 Code for Information Processing Interchange. Finally, NATIVE refers to the code that is native to that computer, such as the EBCDIC code used in most IBM mainframe systems. Such codes specify the collating sequence of characters.

We now give some examples to illustrate use of these language facilities.

```
OBJECT-COMPUTER.
    ABC-480
    PROGRAM COLLATING SEQUENCE IS ASCII-CODE.
SPECIAL-NAMES.
    ALPHABET ASCII-CODE IS STANDARD-1.
```

In the above example we have specified that the name ASCII-CODE will refer to the STANDARD-1 alphabet. Since STANDARD-1 is the ASCII code, we would need to write the above specifications only if we were using a computer whose native code was not ASCII. Perhaps we have a file created at another computer site with the ASCII code, and now we want to sort that file. You may have not noticed that in the general format of the SORT verb in Figure 11-5 in Chapter 11, there is this option:

COLLATING SEQUENCE IS alphabet-name-1.

FIGURE 16-7
General Format for the CONFIGURATION SECTION of the ENVIRONMENT DIVISION

```
ENVIRONMENT DIVISION .

CONFIGURATION SECTION .

SOURCE-COMPUTER. [Computer -name [WITH DEBUGGING MODE].]

OBJECT -COMPUTER. [Computer -name

              [PROGRAM COLLATING  SEQUENCE IS alphabet -name].]

SPECIAL -NAMES.

   [implementor -name-1

      ┌ IS mnemonic -name-1
      │     [ON STATUS IS condition -name-1 [OFF STATUS IS condition -name-2]]
      │ IS mnemonic -name-2
      │     [OFF STATUS IS condition -name-1 [ON STATUS IS condition -name-2]]  ...
      │ ON STATUS IS  condition-name-1 [OFF STATUS IS condition -name-2]]
      └ OFF STATUS IS  condition-name-2 [ON STATUS IS condition -name-1]]

   [ALPHABET  alphabet -name-1 IS]                                    ...

      ┌ STANDARD -1
      │ STANDARD -2
      │ NATIVE
      │ implementor -name-2
      │          ┌          ┌ THROUGH ┐            ┐
      │ { literal -1 │ THRU   │ literal -2 ... │ ... }
      └          └          └ ALSO literal -3 ... ┘            ┘

   [ SYMBOLIC CHARACTERS {{symbolic-character -1} ... {IS/ARE} {integer -1} ...} ... [IN alphabet -name -2] ] ...

   ┌ CLASS  class-name IS { literal -4 ┌ THROUGH ┐ literal -5 } ...
   │                              └ THRU   ┘                    ...
   │ [CURRENCY  SIGN IS literal -6]
   └ [DECIMAL -POINT IS COMMA].
```

For our previous example we would write

```
SORT ...
    COLLATING SEQUENCE IS ASCII-CODE ... .
```

Thus we have a means of defining an alphabet-name in the SPECIAL-NAMES paragraph and then using it in the SORT and MERGE statements.

As another example, suppose we want to define a collating sequence that starts with space as the smallest character, followed by the 10 digits, followed by the remaining native sequence. We could write

```
OBJECT-COMPUTER.
    ABC-480
    PROGRAM COLLATING SEQUENCE IS NEW-CODE.
SPECIAL-NAMES.
    ALPHABET NEW-CODE IS
    ' ', '0', '1', '2', '3', '4', '5', '6', '7', '8', '9'.
```

Now in the alphabet named NEW-CODE the figurative constant LOW-VALUE will be the space, since it is listed as the first character in the NEW-CODE alphabet. The characters not explicitly defined remain in their native order and immediately follow the explicitly defined characters.

If we wanted to define the % sign as the largest character (HIGH-VALUE), and if we assume an IBM system whose native code is EBCDIC, we could write

```
NEW-CODE IS 0 THROUGH 107, 109 THRU 249, '%'.
```

When we use numeric literals such as 0, 107, 109, and 249, above, they stand for the characters in the native collating sequence. In other words, we consulted Figure 16-3 and observed that % is 108 in the EBCDIC sequence. In the above example we write 0 THRU 107 to leave the first part of the native sequence intact, and 109 THRU 249 to continue with the remaining native sequence except for character 108 (the % sign), which we wrote last and thereby made it the highest character. We used 249 as the last reference before the % because it is the highest value in the EBCDIC code.

We may also specify equality of characters. For example, if we write

```
ALPHABET CODE-XYZ IS ' ' ALSO '0',
                     'A' THRU 'X', 'Y' ALSO 'Z'
```

the space and the zero, and the Y and the Z, would be equal to one another, respectively. Use of ALSO equates characters in the collating sequence. If CODE-XYZ is used, a nonnumeric field containing zeros would be compared as being equal to another field containing spaces.

As another option, the sequence may be reversed by writing, for example:

```
ALPHABET REVERSE-CODE IS 'Z' THRU 'A', '9' THRU '0'.
```

Now the Z is the smallest letter, followed by Y, and so on, while 9 is the smallest digit for purposes of comparison (but not for purposes of arithmetic). If we were performing a sort on S-FILE and we wrote SORT ... COLLATING SEQUENCE IS REVERSE-CODE (as defined above), the sort would operate in descending order for alphabetic and numeric characters.

Overall, the COLLATING SEQUENCE option is particularly helpful in handling data created under a different alphabet or using a program whose logic is directly dependent on a certain collating sequence that is different from the native sequence. In such cases we can define a new alphabet to simulate the required collating sequence.

R   E   V   I   E   W . . . .

1. The optional clause in the OBJECT-COMPUTER paragraph that identifies the collating sequence to be used during program execution is the _____ clause.

   COLLATING SEQUENCE

2. The native set of characters associated with a computer system, which includes the alphabetic characters, special symbols, and numeric digits, is referred to as the _____ of the system.

   alphabet

3. Associated with every alphabet is a system by which an ordinal value is assigned to each character, which is called the _____ sequence.

   collating

4. STANDARD-1 and STANDARD-2 refer to standard alphabets defined by COBOL. The alphabet that is specific to a given computer is called _____ .

   NATIVE

. . . .

Defining Symbolic Characters

Referring again to the general format of the CONFIGURATION SECTION in Figure 16-7, the SYMBOLIC CHARACTER clause allows the programmer to give a mnemonic-name to a character that may not be in the principal set of characters. For example, consider the following:

```
SPECIAL-NAMES.
    ALPHABET ASCII IS STANDARD-1
    SYMBOLIC CHARACTER BEEP IS 7 IN ASCII.
```

The SYMBOLIC CHARACTER specification uses the alphabet-name ASCII, as defined by ALPHABET ASCII IS STANDARD-1. If the character value 7 in the collating sequence of STANDARD-1 causes the terminal bell to ring, then the following program statements would cause the bell to ring:

```
01  DISPLAY-FIELD PIC X.
    .
    .
    .
    MOVE BEEP TO DISPLAY-FIELD,
    DISPLAY DISPLAY-FIELD ...
```

Defining a Data Class

For purposes of complete presentation, we review the definition of data classes discussed in Chapter 8. The CLASS clause in the SPECIAL-NAMES paragraph of the CONFIGURATION SECTION (see Figure 16-7) can be used to define a set of characters and to assign a class-name to them. The program can then refer to this class-name to test whether it is true or false that a data item consists exclusively of the characters identified in the definition of the class-name. Consider the following example, also discussed in Chapter 8:

```
SPECIAL-NAMES.
    CLASS SPOKEN-NUMERIC
    IS '0' THRU '9'
    'o', 'O'. (these are the lowercase and uppercase letter 'o')
```

In the above example SPOKEN-NUMERIC is defined as the 10 numeric digits and the letter "o", to allow for the use of "o" as an alternate to zero.

R E V I E W . . . .

1. The paragraph in the CONFIGURATION SECTION that provides for a variety of definitions for special features to be used in a COBOL program is the _____ paragraph.

    SPECIAL-NAMES

2. The specification of mnemonic-names in the SPECIAL-NAMES paragraph allows the programmer to use meaningful names in place of _____ -names that may not be meaningful.

    implementor

3. The clause that is used to specify the collating sequence of characters during program processing is the _____ clause.

    ALPHABET

4. The clause that is used to give a name to a character that may not be in the printable set of characters, such as may be useful in causing a bell to ring, is the _____ clause.

    SYMBOLIC CHARACTER

5. The clause in the SPECIAL-NAMES paragraph that can be used to define a set of characters and to assign a class-name to them is the _____ clause.

    CLASS

. . . .

SUMMARY

This chapter was concerned principally with some of the advanced programming features associated with data definition and representation. The first several topics covered features that give the programmer flexibility in naming and referencing storage locations. These topics were multiple data records in the FILE SECTION, the REDEFINES clause, the RENAMES clause, and reference modification.

When there are multiple data records in the same file, there is only one file-name but there are multiple record-names, each corresponding to the separate type of record. Only one type of record can be processed at any one time. The REDEFINES clause is used to allow the same storage location to be referenced by different data-names, or to allow a regrouping of data in a *particular* storage location. The RENAMES clause can be used to regroup elementary data items from *several* contiguous storage locations. Reference modification makes it possible for a PROCEDURE DIVISION statement to reference just a *portion* of a data field.

Following the first four topics in the chapter, *data representation* was then covered to provide a foundation for the subsequent chapter coverage of the USAGE clause and the SIGN clause.

In terms of data representation, *character data* are used to represent nonquantitative data, while *numeric data* are used to represent quantitative measures. Character data can be made up of numeric digits, but such digits *cannot* be used in arithmetic operations. The categories of character data that were described are the BCD, ASCII, and EBCDIC. The categories of numeric data that were described are the binary, scientific notation, hexadecimal, packed decimal, and zoned decimal. The USAGE clause serves to designate whether data are DISPLAY or COMPUTATIONAL. Its use makes for greater machine efficiency. The SIGN clause is used to describe explicitly the position of the operational sign for a field.

The next two topics in the chapter were concerned with the SYNCHRONIZED clause and the JUSTIFIED RIGHT clause. The SYNCHRONIZED clause can be used in elementary field descriptions to improve efficiency of arithmetic execution by the assignment of aligned storage boundaries. Because it is a machine-dependent instruction, its use generally should be avoided. The JUSTIFIED RIGHT clause is used to override the convention of left-justifying nonnumeric data.

The COLLATING SEQUENCE clause in the CONFIGURATION SECTION of the ENVIRONMENT DIVISION identifies the collating sequence being used, while the ALPHABET clause identifies the assigned name for the alphabet that is used as the basis for the collating sequence. Other topics covered in the final section to round-out chapter coverage were use of the SYMBOLIC CHARACTER clause and the CLASS clause.

EXERCISES

16.1 A file contains name and address data for college students and their parents or guardians. The file is arranged so that for each student there are two records. The first record contains the name and address of the student, and the second record contains the name and address of parent or guardian. The record formats are as follows:

STUDENT RECORD		PARENT RECORD	
FIELD	COLUMNS	FIELD	COLUMNS
Student number	1–9	Student number	1–9
Student name	10–30	Parent name	10–30
Street	31–60	Street	31–60
City	61–79	City	61–79
Record code = 1	80	Record code = 2	80

a. Write ENVIRONMENT and DATA DIVISION file and record entries to describe this file.

b. Write PROCEDURE DIVISION statements to read two consecutive records, testing to ascertain that they are student and parent records, respectively. When the first record is read, if it is a student record, it is stored in REC-WORK-AREA. If the first record is not a student record or if the second record is not a parent record for the same student, the program executes a paragraph called ERROR-ROUTINE. If the records are in correct sequence, the program executes a paragraph called PROCESS.

16.2 Suppose it is claimed that the following is equivalent to the example at the end of "The RENAMES Clause" section in this chapter. Explain how this equivalent form can be used instead of the original one. Which form is better? Why?

```
01  RESPONSE.
    02  ADD-RESPONSE    PIC XXX.
    02  CHAR-4          PIC X.
    02  FILLER          PIC XX.
    66  VIEW-RESPONSE RENAMES ADD-RESPONSE THRU CHAR-4.
```

16.3 The following diagram has a record called BIGFIELD. The numbers running from 1 to 13 indicate respective character positions. Thus the record consists of 13 character positions. We want to be able to reference the following positions while also preserving the current structure of the record. Indicate how to accomplish this objective.

BIGFIELD												
GROUP-A							GROUP-B					
AA		AB			AC		BA		BB		BC	
1	2	3	4	5	6	7	8	9	10	11	12	13

a. Reference 1, 2, 3, 4 by one name

b. Reference 5, 6, 7 by one name

c. Reference 8, 9, 10 by one name

d. Reference 11, 12, 13 by one name

e. Reference 1, 2, 3, 4, 5, 6, 7 by one name

f. Reference 8, 9, 10, 11, 12, 13 by one name

g. Reference 3, 4, 5, 6, 7, 8, 9, 10 by one name

16.4 Incorporate the reference modification feature in a program that you have previously written. Evaluate its impact on program documentation.

16.5 Consider the following program segments:

```
01  LAST-NAME PIC X(15).
    .
    .
    .
    PERFORM VARYING I FROM 13 BY -1
        UNTIL I < 1
            OR LAST-NAME (I:3) = 'VEZ'
        CONTINUE
    END-PERFORM
    IF  I < 1
        PERFORM NOT-FOUND
    ELSE
        MOVE LAST-NAME TO ...
    END-IF.
```

a. Describe the function of the program segment above.

b. What would be an alternative way of doing the same task without the use of reference modification?

c. Is reference modification a useful feature for such an application?

16.6 Given that all data in a computer are represented by binary (0,1) bits, in what way are character data different from numeric data?

16.7 How many unique characters can be represented by a 4-bit code? a 6-bit code? a 7-bit code? Generalize to an n-bit code.

16.8 If numeric data is in binary form, how is the sign represented?

16.9 What would be the minimum number of bits required to store a field whose PIC is S999? Explain.

16.10 The discussion in this chapter mentioned that some COBOL systems allocate 2 bytes to COMP fields whose PICTURE clauses include 1 to 4 digits. Suppose that for such a system we have

```
01  A.
    02  B  PIC X(3).
    02  C  PIC S9(3) COMP.
    02  D  PIC 9(5).
    02  E  PIC S9(2) COMP.
```

What is the size of A in terms of bytes? Explain.

16.11 Explain how the SIGN clause can be used with USAGE DISPLAY numeric items.

16.12 Suppose that we have a 36-bit word-oriented computer system and that its COBOL compiler allocates a full word to each SYNC item. Further, assume that we use the ASCII code and have the following DATA DIVISION items:

```
01  X.
    02  A  PIC XX.
    02  B  PIC 99.
    02  C  PIC XXX.
```

a. Draw a storage layout for the above X record, using the diagram below. Be sure to designate the exact starting and ending storage bits for each item.

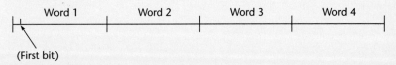

(First bit)

b. Now suppose that everything was the same except that we have 02 B PIC 99 SYNC. Redraw the storage layout and explain the effect of SYNC.

16.13 Are the SYNCHRONIZED and JUSTIFIED clauses related? Explain.

16.14 Give some reasons why a programmer may want to specify an alphabet that is different from the code that is native to a given system.

17

More about Sequential File Processing

THE PURPOSE OF THIS CHAPTER *is to provide additional depth in your understanding of sequential files and the methods for handling such files. Sequential files are the foundation of most business transaction processing systems, such as payroll, billing, general ledger, and other accounting procedures. Therefore it is important that you have a more thorough knowledge of the processing of sequential files than was provided by the introduction in Chapter 10.*

First, you will study a generalized model of sequential file updating logic, so that you can use it as a basic template for writing future sequential updating programs. The generalized logic is then illustrated by means of a sample program that implements the general logic in specific form.

Next, you will learn how to handle variable-length records. These are records whose length depends on some condition, such as the number of items purchased, or the number of checks written during the month.

Another topic in this chapter will teach you a new method for handling input/output processing exceptions in the DECLARATIVES portion of the program by means of the specialized USE statement.

Your study will conclude with a series of sections that impart a deeper conceptual understanding of techniques for editing and validating data, and specialized processing for certain conditions.

A GENERAL PROGRAMMING MODEL FOR UPDATING SEQUENTIAL FILES

Because the updating of sequential files is such a common occurrence, we present a general programming model that can be used as the basis for writing the specific logic for most such programs. Figure 17-1 presents a structure chart for this general program model, while Figure 17-2 presents a program statement outline. The logic is designed to handle the following main types of processing:

- There can be one or many types of transactions.

- There can be one or many transactions pertaining to a given master file record.

- New records may be added to the master file by submitting a suitable transaction record. Such records may be added in the front, in the "middle," or at the end of the master file.

- A new master file record may also be updated by one or more transaction records. The only requirement is that the sort procedure must ensure that the "add-new" transaction precedes the "update"-type transactions.

The meanings of some important data-names used in Figure 17-2 are described below:

- M-I-D: The record key or identifier of a master file record, such as customer number or employee name.

- T-I-D: The record key or identifier of a transaction file record.

- PREV-M-I-D: A WORKING-STORAGE field containing the M-I-D of the previously read master file record. It is used to ascertain that the master file records are in proper sequence.

- PREV-T-I-D: A WORKING-STORAGE field containing the T-I-D of the previously read transaction file record. It is used to ascertain that the transaction records are in proper sequence.

- TRANS-ENDED: A condition-name signifying the end of the transaction file. The condition is true when T-I-D is equal to HIGH-VALUES.

- MASTER-ENDED: A condition-name signifying the end of the old master file. The condition is true when M-I-D is equal to HIGH-VALUES.

- TERMINAL-ERROR: A condition-name signifying the occurrence of a type of error that should result in program termination.

- WORK-NEW-MAST-REC: A WORKING-STORAGE field that is used to build a new master file record or update an existing master file record. When a record is ready to be written into the new master file, it is moved from WORK-NEW-MAST-REC to NEW-MAST-REC.

- PREV-NEW-REC-I-D: A WORKING-STORAGE field containing the T-I-D of an add-new transaction. When such a transaction is read in, its T-I-D is stored in PREV-NEW-REC-I-D. Then the T-I-D of subsequent transactions is compared against the saved value. When T-I-D is not equal to PREV-NEW-REC-I-D, then the new master record is ready to be written into the updated master file. In this way it is possible to add a new master record and update it by a series of transactions that immediately follow the add-new transaction.

Reviewing the program outline in Figure 17-2, we see that paragraphs that are subordinate to more than one module are prefixed with an X and are positioned at the end of the program.

FIGURE 17-1

Structure Chart for General
Sequential File Update Program
Logic

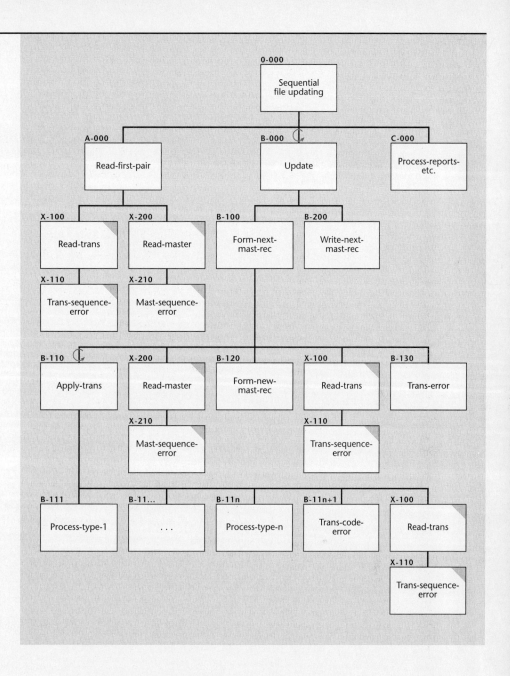

The program outline is substantially self-documenting even though it is context-free. It can be adapted to any specific situation with minimum logic modification.

R E V I E W . . . .

1. This section includes a general model that can be followed for writing program statements to update a _____ file.

sequential

2. In the general procedure for updating sequential files that is presented in this section there can be [only one / many] types of transactions and [only one / many] transactions pertaining to a given master file record.

many; many

FIGURE 17-2

Program Outline for General Sequential File Update Program Logic

```
PROCEDURE DIVISION.
*
0-000-PROGRAM-SUMMARY.
     OPEN INPUT   OLD-MASTER-FILE
                  TRANS-FILE
           OUTPUT  NEW-MASTER-FILE
                   REPORT-FILE
                   ERR-MESS-FILE
     Write any report headings

     PERFORM A-000-READ-FIRST-PAIR
     PERFORM B-000-UPDATE
            UNTIL (TRANS-ENDED AND MASTER-ENDED)
                OR TERMINAL-ERROR
     PERFORM C-000-PRINT-TOTALS-ETC
     CLOSE OLD-MASTER-FILE
           TRANS-FILE
           NEW-MASTER-FILE
           REPORT-FILE
           ERR-MESS-FILE
     STOP RUN.
 A-000-READ-FIRST-PAIR.
     MOVE LOW-VALUES TO PREV-TRANS-ID.
                        PREV-MASTER-ID.
     PERFORM X-100-READ-TRANS.
     PERFORM X-200-READ-MASTER.
*
 B-000-UPDATE.
    PERFORM B-100-FORM-NEXT-MAST-REC.
    PERFORM B-200-WRITE-NEXT-MAST-REC.
*
 B-100-FORM-NEXT-MAST-REC.
*
     EVALUATE TRUE
*
         WHEN M-I-D = T-I-D
             MOVE OLD-MASTER-REC TO WORK-NEW-MAST-REC
             PERFORM B-110-APPLY-TRANS
                 UNTIL (M-I-D NOT = T-I-D)
                     OR TRANS-ENDED
                     OR TERMINAL-ERROR
             PERFORM X-200-READ-MASTER
*
         WHEN M-I-D < T-I-D
             MOVE OLD-MASTER-REC TO WORK-NEW-MAST-REC
             PERFORM X-200-READ-MASTER
*
```

FIGURE 17-2

Program Outline for General
Sequential File Update Program
Logic (continued)

```
                        WHEN ADDITION
                            PERFORM B-120-FORM-NEW-MAST-REC
                            PERFORM X-100-READ-TRANS
                            PERFORM B-110-APPLY-TRANS
                                UNTIL (PREV-NEW-REC-I-D NOT EQUAL T-I-D)
                                    OR TRANS-ENDED
                                    OR TERMINAL-ERROR
        *
                        WHEN OTHER
                            MOVE T-I-D TO PREV-NEW-REC-I-D
                            PERFORM B-130-TRANS-ERROR WITH TEST AFTER
                                UNTIL (PREV-NEW-REC-I-D NOT = T-I-D)
                                    OR TRANS-ENDED
                                    OR TERMINAL-ERROR
                    END-EVALUATE.
        *
            B-110-APPLY-TRANS.
                EVALUATE TRUE
                    WHEN TRANS-TYPE-1
                        PERFORM B-111 PROCESS-TYPE-1
                    WHEN TRANS-TYPE-2
                        PERFORM B-112-PROCESS-TYPE-2
                    WHEN TRANS-TYPE-3
                        PERFORM B-113-PROCESS-TYPE-3

                            .
                            .
                            .

                    WHEN OTHER
                        PERFORM B-114-TRANS-CODE-ERROR
                END-EVALUATE
                PERFORM X-100-READ-TRANS.
        *
            B-111 PROCESS-TYPE-1.
                Process transaction type 1.

            B-112-PROCESS-TYPE-2.
                Process transaction type 2.

            B-113-PROCESS-TYPE-3.
                Process transaction type 3.

                    .
                    .
                    .

            B-114-TRANS-CODE-ERROR.
                Process a transaction whose code does not match any of the defined
                transaction types.
```

FIGURE 17-2
Program Outline for General
Sequential File Update Program
Logic (continued)

```
B-120-FORM-NEW-MAST-REC.
    Transfer data from the source record to WORK-NEW-MAST-REC and do
    the necessary processing.

B-130-TRANS-ERROR.
    Issue appropriate error message to indicate that this is a record with a new
    identifier (T-I-D is less than M-I-D), yet it does not contain an "add-new"
    type transaction code.

B-200-WRITE-NEXT-MAST-REC.
    Do any processing needed before writing the updated record.
    Then, if not a deleted record,

    WRITE NEW-MASTER-REC FROM WORK-NEW-MAST-REC


C-000-PRINT-TOTALS-ETC.
    Do any post-update processing such as calculating totals etc.
*
X-100-READ-TRANS.
    READ TRANS-FILE RECORD
        AT END
            MOVE HIGH-VALUES TO T-I-D
            SET TRANS-ENDED TO TRUE
    END-READ
    IF  NOT TRANS-ENDED
        IF  T-I-D LESS THAN PREV-T-I-D
            PERFORM X-110-TRANS-SEQUENCE-ERROR
            SET TERMINAL-ERROR TO TRUE
        ELSE
            MOVE T-I-D TO PREV-T-I-D
        END-IF
    END-IF.
*
X-110-TRANS-SEQUENCE-ERROR.
    Issue suitable error message indicating that the transaction file is not
    properly sorted, etc.

X-200-READ-MASTER.
    READ OLD-MASTER-FILE RECORD
        AT END
            SET MASTER-ENDED TO TRUE
            MOVE HIGH-VALUES TO M-I-D
    END-READ
    IF  NOT MASTER-ENDED
        IF  M-I-D NOT GREATER THAN PREV-M-I-D
            PERFORM X-210-MAST-SEQUENCE-ERROR
            MOVE 'YES' TO TERMINAL-ERROR-SWITCH
        ELSE
            MOVE M-I-D TO PREV-M-I-D
        END-IF
    END-IF.
X-210-MAST-SEQUENCE-ERROR.
    Issue suitable error message indicating that the master file is not properly
    sorted, etc.
```

3. When a new master record is to be updated, the sort procedure must ensure that update-type transactions [precede / follow] the add-new transactions.

follow

. . . .

SEQUENTIAL UPDATE SAMPLE PROGRAM

Task Description

We wish to write a program to update a simplified payroll master file. The master is sequenced on employee number, and records have the following layout:

Employee number	PIC 9(5)
Employee name	PIC X(20)
Pay rate	PIC 9(2)V99
Withholding rate	PIC V99
Year-to-date gross pay	PIC 9(5)V99
Year-to-date net pay	PIC 9(5)V99

The transaction records are of two types. The first type contains changes to the master file and has the following layout:

Employee number	PIC 9(5)
Employee name	PIC X(20)
Transaction code	PIC X
1 = Create new record	
2 = Delete record	
3 = Change pay rate	
Pay rate	PIC 9(2)V99
Withholding rate	PIC V99

The second type of transaction record is daily time cards that have the following layout:

Employee number	PIC 9(5)
Employee name	PIC X(20)
Transaction code	PIC 9
4 = Time card	
Hours worked	PIC 9(2)V99

In addition to the updated master file, the program should produce a printed report such as illustrated in Figure 17-3.

For each employee a week's gross pay is computed by multiplying pay rate times hours worked for the whole week (remember that time cards are daily records). If the hours worked exceed 40, time-and-a-half is paid for the hours over 40; however, no employee should work more than 10 hours in a given day nor more than 48 hours in a given week. Either condition is an error, and the employee would not be paid; instead, an error message would be printed.

Net pay is computed by multiplying gross pay by the withholding rate and subtracting this amount from the gross pay. The year-to-date gross and net

FIGURE 17-3
Sample Report for the Payroll Program

		THIS WEEK		YEAR TO DATE	
EMPLOYEE NO.	EMPLOYEE NAME	GROSS	NET	GROSS	NET
09000	BROOKS, SHAWN P.	210.00	180.60	210.00	180.60
10000	WELLS, SANIA M.	.00	.00	8,000.00	7,200.00
15000	DOWNEY, ROBERT S.	.00	.00	24,000.00	20,040.00
30003	SAWYER, CATHY H.	.00	.00	10,000.00	9,000.00
50050	SHAFFER, DAVID R.	445.00	400.50	20,445.00	18,400.50
60050	ADD-NEW-ONE	120.00	105.60	120.00	105.60
	T O T A L	775.00	686.70	62,775.00	54,926.70

given in the report include the addition of latest week's gross and the net pay to the previously accumulated amounts.

Structure Chart

Figure 17-4 presents a structure chart developed for the payroll task described above. It should be noticed that the B-200-WRITE-NEXT-MAST-REC module in the generalized structure chart of Figure 17-1 has now been expanded to consist of three subordinate modules, since the writing function is not simple because of the required payroll computations. Such an example demonstrates the relative ease with which the general updating model in Figure 17-1 can be adapted to varying situational needs.

Another point worth mentioning is the development of two "error-handling" modules, B-114-TRANS-CODE-ERROR and B-130-TRANS-ERROR, and their placement under different superior modules. In the course of being ready to apply a transaction, it may be discovered that the transaction code is not a valid one. In such a case B-110-APPLY-TRANS invokes the execution of B-114-TRANS-CODE-ERROR.

A different type of transaction error may also occur, which needs to be handled by a higher-level module than B-110-APPLY-TRANS. Specifically, one of the types of transactions allowed is the addition of new records to the master file, and this is handled by B-120-FORM-NEW-MAST-REC. It is logically necessary that a new record that is to be added must be lower in sequence than the last-read master record. Further, our task description allows transactions (time cards, etc.) to be applied to a new record. There then may be a number of transaction records pertaining to the same employee, and the employee may be a new individual being added to the file. However, it is assumed that in such a case the first of these transactions is the add-new transaction; if it is not, then we have an error condition arising from the presence of transactions pertaining to a nonexisting master record. This type of error condition is handled by B-130-TRANS-ERROR under control of B-100-FORM-NEXT-MAST-REC.

Sample Program

Figure 17-5 presents a program written for the payroll programming tasks. A few comments follow.

FIGURE 17-4

Structure Chart for Payroll Program

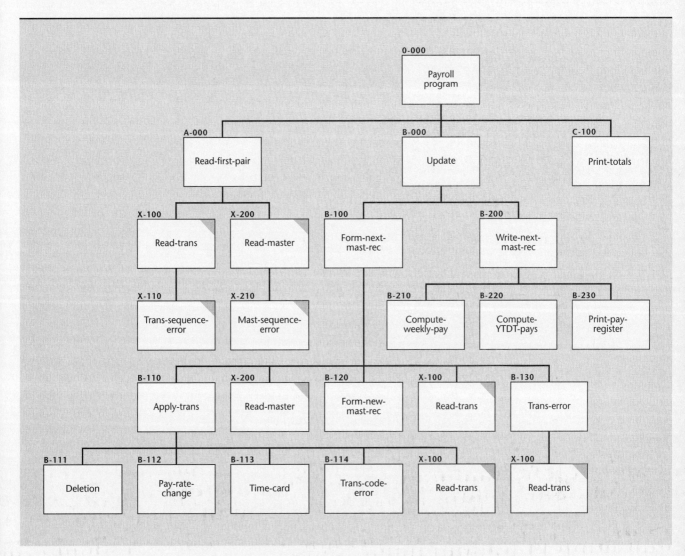

In this sample program the input data are not extensively validated. If we needed to add such a feature, we could easily modify the structure by adding a validation function subordinate to the input module (X-100-READ-TRANS).

Both input files are sequence-checked, and if a record is found to be out of sequence, the program terminates by use of the TERMINAL-ERROR-SWITCH. Such a termination may or may not be appropriate in a given case. However, because the whole logic of sequential file updating is based on the assumption of correctly sequenced files, it is important always to do sequence checking in such programs.

Module B-111-DELETION consists of only one line. One can question the need for creating one-line paragraphs. However, deleting a record is a distinct, cohesive function, and it has clear logical identity. Further, in most cases deleting a record involves a whole procedure, rather than simply omitting the record from the updated file as was done in the abbreviated example. In principle, a separate paragraph is better, especially if the program is modified in the future with respect to the way that deleted records are processed. However, in a specific case like this it would be futile to try to argue either for or against a separate module for the deletion function.

FIGURE 17-5

Listing of the Payroll Program

```
IDENTIFICATION DIVISION.
PROGRAM-ID. PAYROLL.
*
ENVIRONMENT DIVISION.
CONFIGURATION SECTION.
SOURCE-COMPUTER. ABC-480.
OBJECT-COMPUTER. ABC-480.
*
INPUT-OUTPUT SECTION.
*
FILE-CONTROL.
    SELECT OLD-PAY-MASTER  ASSIGN TO OLDMASTR.
    SELECT NEW-PAY-MASTER  ASSIGN TO NEWMASTR.
    SELECT TRANS-FILE      ASSIGN TO TRANS.
    SELECT ERR-MESS-FILE   ASSIGN TO ERRORRPT.
    SELECT REPORT-FILE     ASSIGN TO TRANSRPT.
*
DATA DIVISION.
*
FILE SECTION.
*
FD  OLD-PAY-MASTER LABEL RECORDS OMITTED
            BLOCK CONTAINS 10 RECORDS
            DATA RECORD IS OLD-PAY-MASTER-REC.
01  OLD-PAY-MASTER-REC.
    02  OLD-PAY-MASTER-DATA.
        04  OLD-EMPLOYEE-NO          PIC X(5).
        04  OLD-EMPLOYEE-NAME        PIC X(20).
        04  OLD-PAY-RATE             PIC 99V99.
        04  OLD-WITHHOLDING-RATE     PIC V99.
        04  OLD-YTDT-GROSS           PIC 9(5)V99.
        04  OLD-YTDT-NET             PIC 9(5)V99.
*
FD  NEW-PAY-MASTER LABEL RECORDS STANDARD
            BLOCK CONTAINS 10 RECORDS
            DATA RECORD IS NEW-PAY-MASTER-REC.
01  NEW-PAY-MASTER-REC         PIC X(80).
*
FD  TRANS-FILE LABEL RECORDS OMITTED
            DATA RECORD IS TRANS-REC.
01  TRANS-REC.
    02  TRANS-REC-DATA.
        04  TRANS-EMPLOYEE-NO        PIC X(5).
        04  TRANS-EMPLOYEE-NAME      PIC X(20).
        04  TRANS-CODE               PIC X.
            88  ADDITION             VALUE '1'.
            88  DELETION             VALUE '2'.
            88  PAY-RATE-CHANGE      VALUE '3'.
            88  TIME-CARD            VALUE '4'.
            88  ERROR-CODE           VALUE LOW-VALUE THRU '0'
                                           '5' THRU HIGH-VALUE.
        04  TRANS-PAY-RATE           PIC 99V99.
        04  TRANS-HOURS-WORKED REDEFINES TRANS-PAY-RATE PIC 99V99.
        04  TRANS-WITHHOLDING-RATE   PIC V99.
```

FIGURE 17-5

Listing of the Payroll Program
(continued)

```
*
  FD  REPORT-FILE LABEL RECORDS OMITTED
                    DATA RECORD IS REPORT-REC.
*
  01  REPORT-REC                    PIC X(132).
*
  FD  ERR-MESS-FILE
      LABEL RECORDS ARE OMITTED
      DATA RECORD IS ERROR-REC.
  01  ERROR-REC                     PIC X(132).
*
  WORKING-STORAGE SECTION.
*
  01  WORK-NEW-MAST-REC.
      02  NEW-EMPLOYEE-NO           PIC X(5).
      02  NEW-EMPLOYEE-NAME         PIC X(20).
      02  NEW-PAY-RATE              PIC 99V99.
      02  NEW-WITHHOLDING-RATE      PIC V99.
      02  NEW-YTDT-GROSS            PIC 9(5)V99.
      02  NEW-YTDT-NET              PIC 9(5)V99.
      02  FILLER                    PIC X(35).
*
  01  END-OF-TRANS-SWITCH           PIC XXX     VALUE 'NO'.
      88  TRANS-ENDED                           VALUE 'YES'.
*
  01  END-OF-MASTER-SWITCH          PIC XXX     VALUE 'NO'.
      88  MASTER-ENDED                          VALUE 'YES'.
*
  01  TERMINAL-ERROR-SWITCH         PIC XXX     VALUE 'NO'.
      88  TERMINAL-ERROR                        VALUE 'YES'
*
  01  WRITE-FLAG                    PIC XXX     VALUE 'YES'.
      88  WRITE-REC                             VALUE 'YES'.
      88  NOT-WRITE-REC                         VALUE 'NO'.
*
  01  ACCUMULATORS.
      02  WEEKLY-HOURS              PIC 99V99   VALUE ZEROS.
      02  TEMP-GROSS               PIC 9(6)V99 VALUE ZEROS.
      02  TEMP-NET                 PIC 9(6)V99 VALUE ZEROS.
      02  TOT-GROSS                PIC 9(7)V99 VALUE ZEROS.
      02  TOT-NET                  PIC 9(7)V99 VALUE ZEROS.
      02  TOT-GROSS-YTDT           PIC 9(7)V99 VALUE ZEROS.
      02  TOT-NET-YTDT             PIC 9(7)V99 VALUE ZEROS.
*
  01  HEADER-1.
      02  FILLER                    PIC X(39)   VALUE SPACES.
      02  FILLER                    PIC X(9)    VALUE
          'THIS WEEK'.
      02  FILLER                    PIC X(13)   VALUE SPACES.
      02  FILLER                    PIC X(12)   VALUE
          'YEAR TO DATE'.
*
```

FIGURE 17-5

Listing of the Payroll Program
(continued)

```
01   HEADER-2.
     02  FILLER                         PIC X        VALUE SPACE.
     02  FILLER                         PIC X(28)    VALUE
         'EMPLOYEE NO.   EMPLOYEE NAME'.
     02  FILLER                         PIC X(8)     VALUE SPACES.
     02  FILLER                         PIC X(5)     VALUE 'GROSS'.
     02  FILLER                         PIC X(6)     VALUE SPACES.
     02  FILLER                         PIC X(3)     VALUE 'NET'.
     02  FILLER                         PIC X(7)     VALUE SPACES.
     02  FILLER                         PIC X(5)     VALUE 'GROSS'.
     02  FILLER                         PIC X(7)     VALUE SPACES.
     02  FILLER                         PIC X(3)     VALUE 'NET'.
*
01   HEADER-3.
     02  FILLER                         PIC X(18)    VALUE SPACES.
     02  FILLER                         PIC X(24)    VALUE
         'TRANSACTION ERROR REPORT'.
     02  FILLER                         PIC X(90)    VALUE SPACES.
*
01 REPORT-LINE.
     02  FILLER                         PIC X(4)     VALUE SPACE.
     02  EMPLOYEE-NO                    PIC 9(5).
     02  FILLER                         PIC X(5)     VALUE SPACE.
     02  EMPLOYEE-NAME                  PIC X(20).
     02  WEEK-GROSS                     PIC Z(4),Z(3).99.
     02  WEEK-NET                       PIC ZZZZ,ZZZ.99.
     02  YTDT-GROSS                     PIC ZZZZ,ZZZ.99.
     02  YTDT-NET                       PIC ZZZZ,ZZZ.99.
*
01   PREV-TRANS-ID                      PIC X(5).
*
01   PREV-MASTER-ID                     PIC X(5).
/
PROCEDURE DIVISION.
*
0-000-PROGRAM-SUMMARY.
    OPEN INPUT  OLD-PAY-MASTER
                TRANS-FILE
         OUTPUT NEW-PAY-MASTER
                REPORT-FILE
                ERR-MESS-FILE
    WRITE REPORT-REC FROM HEADER-1.
    WRITE REPORT-REC FROM HEADER-2 AFTER ADVANCING 2 LINES
    WRITE ERROR-REC FROM HEADER-3 BEFORE 3 LINES
    PERFORM A-000-READ-FIRST-PAIR
    PERFORM B-000-UPDATE UNTIL (TRANS-ENDED AND MASTER-ENDED)
                         OR TERMINAL-ERROR
    PERFORM C-000-PRINT-TOTALS
    CLOSE OLD-PAY-MASTER
          TRANS-FILE
          NEW-PAY-MASTER
          REPORT-FILE
          ERR-MESS-FILE
    STOP RUN.
*
```

FIGURE 17-5
Listing of the Payroll Program
(continued)

```
     A-000-READ-FIRST-PAIR.
         MOVE LOW-VALUES TO PREV-TRANS-ID,
                            PREV-MASTER-ID.
         PERFORM X-100-READ-TRANS.
         PERFORM X-200-READ-MASTER.
 *
     B-000-UPDATE.
         PERFORM B-100-FORM-NEXT-MAST-REC.
         PERFORM B-200-WRITE-NEXT-MAST-REC.
 *
     B-100-FORM-NEXT-MAST-REC.
 *
         EVALUATE TRUE
 *
             WHEN OLD-EMPLOYEE-NO = TRANS-EMPLOYEE-NO
                 MOVE OLD-PAY-MASTER-REC TO WORK-NEW-MAST-REC
                 PERFORM B-110-APPLY-TRANS
                     UNTIL (OLD-EMPLOYEE-NO NOT EQUAL TRANS-EMPLOYEE-NO)
                         OR TRANS-ENDED
                         OR TERMINAL-ERROR
                 PERFORM X-200-READ-MASTER
 *
             WHEN OLD-EMPLOYEE-NO < TRANS-EMPLOYEE-NO
                 MOVE OLD-PAY-MASTER-REC TO WORK-NEW-MAST-REC
                 PERFORM X-200-READ-MASTER
 *
             WHEN ADDITION
                 PERFORM B-120-FORM-NEW-MAST-REC
                 PERFORM X-100-READ-TRANS
                 PERFORM B-110-APPLY-TRANS
                     UNTIL (NEW-EMPLOYEE-NO NOT EQUAL TRANS-EMPLOYEE-NO)
                         OR TRANS-ENDED
                         OR TERMINAL-ERROR
 *
             WHEN OTHER
                 MOVE TRANS-EMPLOYEE-NO TO MEW-EMPLOYEE-NO
                 PERFORM B-130-TRANS-ERROR WITH TEST AFTER
                     UNTIL (NEW-EMPLOYEE-NO NOT = TRANS-EMPLOYEE-NO)
                         OR TRANS-ENDED
                         OR TERMINAL-ERROR
                 SET NOT-WRITE-REC TO TRUE
         END-EVALUATE.
 *
     B-110-APPLY-TRANS.
 *
         EVALUATE TRUE
 *
             WHEN DELETION
                 PERFORM B-111-DELETION
 *
             WHEN PAY-RATE-CHANGE
                 PERFORM B-112-PAY-RATE-CHANGE
             WHEN TIME-CARD
                 PERFORM B-113-TIME-CARD
 *
```

FIGURE 17-5

*Listing of the Payroll Program
(continued)*

```
            WHEN OTHER
                  PERFORM B-114-TRANS-CODE-ERROR
        END-EVALUATE
*
        PERFORM X-100-READ-TRANS.
*
    B-111-DELETION.
        SET NOT-WRITE-REC TO TRUE.
*
    B-112-PAY-RATE-CHANGE.
        MOVE TRANS-PAY-RATE TO NEW-PAY-RATE.
*


    B-113-TIME-CARD.
        IF  TRANS-HOURS-WORKED GREATER THAN 10
            MOVE SPACES TO ERROR-REC
            STRING
                    TRANS-REC-DATA,
                  ' TRANSACTION HOURS > 10 HOURS'
                        DELIMITED BY SIZE
                INTO ERROR-REC
            WRITE ERROR-REC
        ELSE
            ADD TRANS-HOURS-WORKED TO WEEKLY-HOURS.
*
    B-114-TRANS-CODE-ERROR.
        MOVE SPACES TO ERROR-REC.
        STRING
                TRANS-REC,
              ' INVALID TRANSACTION CODE'
                    DELIMITED BY SIZE
            INTO ERROR-REC.
        WRITE ERROR-REC.
*
    B-120-FORM-NEW-MAST-REC.
        MOVE SPACES TO WORK-NEW-MAST-REC.
        MOVE TRANS-EMPLOYEE-NO TO NEW-EMPLOYEE-NO.
        MOVE TRANS-EMPLOYEE-NAME TO NEW-EMPLOYEE-NAME.
        MOVE TRANS-PAY-RATE TO NEW-PAY-RATE.
        MOVE TRANS-WITHHOLDING-RATE TO NEW-WITHHOLDING-RATE.
        MOVE ZERO TO NEW-YTDT-GROSS,
                    NEW-YTDT-NET.
*
    B-130-TRANS-ERROR.
        MOVE SPACES TO ERROR-REC.
        STRING
                TRANS-REC-DATA
              ' TRANSACTION SEQUENCE ERROR'
                    DELIMITED BY SIZE
            INTO ERROR-REC
        WRITE ERROR-REC.
        PERFORM X-100-READ-TRANS.
*
```

FIGURE 17-5
Listing of the Payroll Program
(continued)

```
B-200-WRITE-NEXT-MAST-REC.
    IF  WRITE-REC
        IF  WEEKLY-HOURS GREATER THAN 48
            MOVE SPACES TO ERROR-REC
            STRING
                    WORK-NEW-MAST-REC,
                    ' WEEKLY HOURS > 48 HOURS'
                        DELIMITED BY SIZE
                INTO ERROR-REC
            WRITE ERROR-REC
            WRITE ERROR-REC FROM WORK-NEW-MAST-REC
        ELSE
            PERFORM B-210-COMPUTE-WEEKLY-PAY
            PERFORM B-220-COMPUTE-YTDT-PAYS
            PERFORM B-230-PRINT-PAY-REGISTER
            WRITE NEW-PAY-MASTER-REC FROM WORK-NEW-MAST-REC
        END-IF
    END-IF
*
    MOVE ZERO TO WEEKLY-HOURS TEMP-GROSS TEMP-NET
    SET WRITE-REC TO TRUE.
*
B-210-COMPUTE-WEEKLY-PAY.
*
    IF  WEEKLY-HOURS GREATER THAN 40
        COMPUTE TEMP-GROSS = 40.0 * NEW-PAY-RATE
                + (WEEKLY-HOURS - 40.0) * 1.5 * NEW-PAY-RATE
    ELSE
        COMPUTE TEMP-GROSS = WEEKLY-HOURS * NEW-PAY-RATE
    END-IF
    COMPUTE TEMP-NET = TEMP-GROSS -
            (TEMP-GROSS * NEW-WITHHOLDING-RATE).
*
B-220-COMPUTE-YTDT-PAYS.
*
    ADD TEMP-GROSS TO TOT-GROSS
    ADD TEMP-NET TO TOT-NET
    ADD TEMP-GROSS, NEW-YTDT-GROSS TO TOT-GROSS-YTDT
    ADD TEMP-NET, NEW-YTDT-NET TO TOT-NET-YTDT
    ADD TEMP-GROSS TO NEW-YTDT-GROSS
    ADD TEMP-NET TO NEW-YTDT-NET.
*
B-230-PRINT-PAY-REGISTER.
*
    MOVE NEW-EMPLOYEE-NO TO EMPLOYEE-NO
    MOVE NEW-EMPLOYEE-NAME TO EMPLOYEE-NAME
    MOVE TEMP-GROSS TO WEEK-GROSS
    MOVE NEW-YTDT-GROSS TO YTDT-GROSS
    MOVE NEW-YTDT-NET TO YTDT-NET
    MOVE TEMP-NET TO WEEK-NET
    WRITE REPORT-REC FROM REPORT-LIME AFTER 2.
*
```

FIGURE 17-5
Listing of the Payroll Program
(continued)

```
C-000-PRINT-TOTALS.
    MOVE SPACES TO REPORT-LINE.
    MOVE 'T O T A L' TO EMPLOYEE-NAME.
    MOVE TOT-GROSS TO WEEK-GROSS.
    MOVE TOT-NET TO WEEK-NET.
    MOVE TOT-GROSS-YTDT TO YTDT-GROSS.
    MOVE TOT-NET-YTDT TO YTDT-NET.
    WRITE REPORT-REC FROM REPORT-LINE.
*
X-100-READ-TRANS.
    READ TRANS-FILE
        AT END
            MOVE HIGH-VALUES TO TRANS-EMPLOYEE-NO
            SET TRANS-ENDED TO TRUE
        END-READ
        IF NOT TRANS-ENDED
            IF TRANS-EMPLOYEE-NO LESS THAN PREV-TRANS-ID
                PERFORM X-110-TRANS-SEQUENCE-ERROR
                SET TERMINAL-ERROR TO TRUE
            ELSE
                MOVE TRANS-EMPLOYEE-NO TO PREV-TRANS-ID
            END-IF
        END-IF.
*
X-110-TRANS-SEQUENCE-ERROR.
    MOVE SPACES TO ERROR-REC
    STRING
        TRANS-REC-DATA,
        ' TRANSACTION RECORD OUT OF SEQUENCE'
        DELIMITED BY SIZE
        INTO ERROR-REC
    WRITE ERROR-REC.
*
X-200-READ-MASTER.
    READ OLD-PAY-MASTER
        AT END
            SET MASTER-ENDED TO TRUE
            MOVE HIGH-VALUES TO OLD-EMPLOYEE-NO
        END-READ
        IF NOT MASTER-ENDED
            IF OLD-EMPLOYEE-NO NOT GREATER THAN PREV-MASTER-ID
                PERFORM X-210-MAST-SEQUENCE-ERROR
                MOVE 'YES' TO TERMINAL-ERROR-SWITCH
            ELSE
                MOVE OLD-EMPLOYEE-NQ TO PREV-MASTER-ID
            END-IF
        END-IF.
*
X-210-MAST-SEQUENCE-ERROR.
    MOVE SPACES TO ERROR-REC.
    STRING
        OLD-PAY-MASTER-REC,
        ' OLD MASTER RECORD OUT OF SEQUENCE'
        DELIMITED BY SIZE
        INTO ERROR-REC.
    WRITE ERROR-REC.
```

As a final point we consider how the program handles the error condition of there being one or more transactions for a nonexistent master record. As was stated earlier in the comments regarding the structure chart, the assumption is made that the data are sequenced so that an add-new transaction record must precede any other transactions (if any) pertaining to that new record. In the B-100-FORM-NEXT-MAST-REC the following statements implement an appropriate procedure.

```
...WHEN ADDITION
      PERFORM B-120-FORM-NEXT-MAST-REC
      PERFORM X-100-READ-TRANS
      PERFORM B-110-APPLY-TRANS UNTIL
          (NEW-EMPLOYEE-NO NOT EQUAL TRANS-EMPLOYEE-NO)
          OR TRANS-ENDED
          OR TERMINAL-ERROR
   WHEN OTHER
      MOVE TRANS-EMPLOYEE-NO TO NEW-EMPLOYEE-NO
      PERFORM B-130-TRANS-ERROR WITH TEST AFTER UNTIL
          (NEW-EMPLOYEE-NO NOT = TRANS-EMPLOYEE-NO)
          OR TRANS-ENDED
          OR TERMINAL-ERROR
   SET NOT-WRITE-REC TO TRUE
```

Notice that B-130-TRANS-ERROR is executed (possibly) many times, so that if the condition of ADDITION is not signified by the first transaction, all transactions having the same employee number are bypassed. For this purpose the program states

```
... PERFORM B-130-TRANS-ERROR WITH TEST AFTER UNTIL ...
```

to form a do-until type of iterative structure.

PROCESSING VARIABLE-LENGTH RECORDS

There are many occasions when it is advantageous to define and process variable-length records. A classic example is the case of a file containing the monthly transactions for customers in a bank. Some customers may write just a few checks during the month, while others may write a very large number. If we defined fixed-length records, we would have to make all records as long as the longest anticipated record. Variable lengths, on the other hand, would allow records to be as long as needed in each case. Having variable-length records saves file storage and improves the speed of input/output operations on files because we are reading and writing smaller amounts of data.

There are two basic methods for handling variable-length records. The one we will discuss first involves the use of variable-length tables and the specialized OCCURS ... DEPENDING ON clause. The second method defines the variable-length record in the FD entry and is applicable to COBOL '85 only.

The OCCURS ... DEPENDING ON Option

A table may be defined to have a variable number of entries. This is done by use of a special option in the OCCURS clause. This option designates a numeric field as the way of defining the current length of a table. Thus instead of "casting in concrete" the table size in the OCCURS clause, we can define a table of variable length. Consider the following two examples.

FIXED-LENGTH TABLE	VARIABLE-LENGTH TABLE
| ```
05 FAMILY-NAMES.
   10 NAMES
      OCCURS 12 TIMES
      PIC X(12).
``` | ```
05 FAMILY-NAMES.
   10 NO-OF-NAMES PIC 99.
   10 NAMES
      OCCURS 1 TO 12 TIMES
      DEPENDING ON NO-OF-NAMES
      PIC X(12).
``` |

In the variable-length table above notice the OCCURS 1 TO 12 TIMES DEPENDING ON NO-OF-NAMES as the way of defining the minimum and maximum size of a table and the designation of NO-OF-NAMES as the field that defines the current table-length. In the above example the table-length field NO-OF-NAMES happens to be in the same data record definition. This need not be the case. The DEPENDING ON field can be defined anywhere in the DATA DIVISION, but, of course, it must be a numeric unsigned integer field.

To understand the use of variable-length tables in the use of variable-length records, let us consider an example. A bank has a file containing transactions of checking account customers. Some customers have a greater number of transactions than others; that is, they write more checks or make more deposits. Let us assume the following record layout:

FIELD	NUMBER OF POSITIONS
Customer number	6
Number of transactions	3
Transaction code	1
Date	5
Amount	7
Transaction code	1
Date	5
Amount	7

(etc., for up to 100 transactions)

This is a case where a record may contain from 0 to 100 transactions. Notice that the minimum number of character positions is 9: 6 for the customer number and 3 for the number of transactions. The maximum size is 9 + (100 transactions x 13 characters per transaction) = 1,309. We then can have the following file description, assuming blocks of three records each:

```
FD  TRANS-FILE LABEL RECORD STANDARD
        BLOCK CONTAINS 3 RECORDS
        RECORD CONTAINS 9 TO 1309 CHARACTERS
        DATA RECORD IS CHECKING-ACCOUNT-RECORD.
01  CHECKING-ACCOUNT-RECORD.
    02  CUSTOMER-NUMBER            PIC 9(6).
    02  NUMBER-OF-TRANSACTIONS     PIC 999.
    02  TRANSACTION OCCURS 0 TO 100 TIMES
            DEPENDING ON NUMBER-OF-TRANSACTIONS.
        03  TRANSACTION-CODE       PIC 9.
        03  TRANSACTION-DATE       PIC 9(5).
        03  TRANSACTION-AMOUNT     PIC 9(5)V99.
```

Note that NUMBER-OF-TRANSACTIONS, above, does not automatically contain the number of transactions. It is the responsibility of the program logic to store the proper data in the data-name of the DEPENDING ON clause. For example, the following code could be used to add another set of transaction data to the record. Assume that POS-OF-NEW points to the record location where we want to add the new transaction record. For instance, we may have determined through earlier program logic that the new transaction is to be the fifth one.

```
IF  NUMBER-OF-TRANSACTIONS = 100
    MOVE 'RECORD IS FILLED -- CANNOT ADD'
     TO  ERROR-MESSAGE
    WRITE ERROR-REC ... etc.
ELSE
    ADD 1 TO NUMBER-OF-TRANSACTIONS
    PERFORM MOVE-RIGHT
            VARYING J
            FROM NUMBER-OF-TRANSACTIONS BY -1
      UNTIL J = POS-OF-NEW
    MOVE NEW-TRANS TO TRANSACTION (J).
MOVE-RIGHT.
    COMPUTE K = J - 1
    MOVE TRANSACTION (K) TO TRANSACTION (J).
```

The IF statement above checks to see that there is room to add one more transaction. If the table is not full, then we want to execute MOVE-RIGHT iteratively to move the existing transactions to the "right" to make room for the new one. First, we increment the NUMBER-OF-TRANSACTIONS by 1 so that we correctly reference the end of the table. For instance, if the number of transactions was 5 and POS-OF-NEW was 3, we want to lengthen the table to hold 6 transactions, we want to move the fifth transaction to the (new) sixth location, the fourth to the fifth, and the third to the fourth location. Finally, we move the new transaction to location 3.

The general form of the OCCURS ... DEPENDING ON option is

... OCCURS integer-1 TO integer-2 TIMES DEPENDING ON data-name.

The programmer must take care that the DEPENDING ON field is updated before a reference is made to a subscripted entry in a record such as the above. For example, if NUMBER-OF-TRANSACTIONS has a value of 20 and we write MOVE ZERO TO TRANSACTION-AMOUNT (I), where I has a value greater than 20, the results will be erroneous. When the NUMBER-OF-TRANSACTIONS is 20, the operating system allocates only enough space to the record to store 20 occurrences. To avoid such errors, something like the following should be written:

```
MOVE I TO NUMBER-OF-TRANSACTIONS
MOVE ZERO TO TRANSACTION-AMOUNT (I).
```

In other words, we must first update the DEPENDING ON field to a higher value and then make a subscripted reference that is not greater than the value of that field.

As another illustration, suppose that NUMBER-OF-TRANSACTIONS is equal to 20 and we write

```
MOVE CHECKING-ACCOUNT-RECORD TO WORKING-STORAGE-RECORD.
```

Referring back to the earlier definition of CHECKING-ACCOUNT-RECORD, the effective move is for 9 + (13 x 20) = 269 bytes. In other words, at execution time the system checks the value of the DEPENDING ON field to determine the effective size of the record at that time.

COBOL '85 Alternative for Variable-Length Records

The second method of using variable-length records utilizes the IS VARYING IN SIZE clause included in the general format for the FD entry shown in Figure 10-8 in Chapter 10. The following program segment serves to illustrate use of that clause.

```
FD  CUSTOMER-FILE
    BLOCK CONTAINS 1000 CHARACTERS
    RECORD IS VARYING IN SIZE
      FROM 20 TO 100 CHARACTERS
      DEPENDING ON CUST-REC-SIZE
    LABEL RECORDS ARE STANDARD.
01  CUSTOMER-REC.
    05  CUSTOMER-NAME           PIC X(20).
    05  CUSTOMER-ADDRESS        PIC X(80).
WORKING-STORAGE SECTION.
        .
        .
        .
01  CUST-REC-SIZE              PIC 999.
```

In the above example each customer record consists of a 20-byte fixed-length field containing the customer name. A second field in the record, CUSTOMER-ADDRESS, is assumed to be variable in terms of length of content. A customer whose address is not available would be so designated by placing a value of 20 in CUST-REC-SIZE, the field identified in the DEPENDING clause. Similarly, for a customer whose address is 65 bytes long, CUST-REC-SIZE would be set to 85. Then, when outputting of data takes place in CUSTOMER-FILE by use of the WRITE verb, the system strings as many such variable-length records as will fit into each of the 1,000-character blocks. When there is insufficient space for one more whole record in the block, then that block is written onto the file, including end-of-block padding characters.

When a READ is executed successfully, the DEPENDING ON field contains the record size of the record that was just read. Similarly, if the READ ... INTO option is used, the receiving field will also be sent as many bytes as the value in the DEPENDING ON field. With respect to the FD entry above, assume that we also have WORK-REC as follows:

```
WORKING-STORAGE SECTION.
        .
        .
        .
01  WORK-REC.
    05  WORK-NAME        PIC X(20).
    05  WORK-ADDRESS     PIC X(80).
```

If we write READ CUSTOMER-FILE INTO WORK-REC and the specific record that was just read is 60 bytes long, after execution of the READ statement, CUST-REC-

SIZE will contain the value 60, while WORK-REC will contain the appropriate content based on execution of a MOVE statement that sent 60 bytes. Thus WORK-NAME will contain the same 20 bytes as were in the first 20 bytes of CUSTOMER-REC, while WORK-ADDRESS will contain the next 40 bytes of CUSTOMER-REC followed by 40 spaces resulting from the implied move of a shorter sending field (40 bytes) to a longer receiving field (80 bytes). Of course, a MOVE CUSTOMER-REC to WORK-REC would be an identical substitute for the READ ... INTO.

To further explain the process, consider the following example:

```
READ CUSTOMER-FILE ...
SUBTRACT 5 FROM CUST-REC-SIZE
MOVE CUSTOMER-NAME TO WORK-NAME
```

Assuming, as above, that the record read was 60 bytes long, the SUBTRACT 5 would have the effect of shortening the record by 5 bytes. Thus WORK-ADDRESS would receive 35 bytes followed by 45 spaces. Thus the programmer can control the effective length of a record defined by the VARYING clause in the general format of the FD entry back in Figure 10-8 by manipulating the content of the DEPENDING ON field. Of course, care must be taken to avoid incorrect or illogical manipulation. For example, MOVE 120 TO CUST-REC-SIZE would be incorrect. Similarly, ADD 5 TO CUST-REC-SIZE after the file record was read would be illogical, since there are no such additional data. The results of such incorrect operations would depend on the particular compiler and operating system. The most likely effect of lengthening a variable-length record by increasing the DEPENDING ON field is to access "garbage" data that happen to be in storage at the time.

The DEPENDING ON data-name-1 clause in the general format back in Figure 10-8 is optional. If the clause is not used and thus data-name-1 is not specified, then the length of the variable-length record is determined by the record description. Consider the following:

```
FD  CUSTOMER-FILE
    BLOCK CONTAINS 1000 CHARACTERS
    RECORD IS VARYING IN SIZE
        FROM 20 TO 100 CHARACTERS
    LABEL RECORDS STANDARD.
01  CUSTOMER-ADDRESS-REC.
    05  NAME            PIC X(20).
    05  ADDRESS         PIC X(80).
01  CUSTOMER-PURCHASE-DATA.
    05  FILLER          PIC X(20).
    05  NO-OF-PURS      PIC 99.
    05  PURCHASE-DATA OCCURS 0 TO 10 TIMES
                DEPENDING ON NO-OF-PURS.
        10  PUR-NO      PIC 9(5).
        10  PUR-AMT     PIC 999V99.
```

In the above example there are two record definitions for CUSTOMER-FILE. The first record, CUSTOMER-ADDRESS-REC, is now fixed-length consisting of 100 bytes. If we WRITE CUSTOMER-ADDRESS-REC, we will be writing a 100-byte record. The second record, CUSTOMER-PURCHASE-REC, describes a variable-length record employing the OCCURS ... DEPENDING ON clause. Using WRITE CUSTOMER-PURCHASE-REC would write a variable-length record whose fixed length is 21 bytes and whose maximum would be 121 bytes (21 + 10 x 10). To be able to read and process records in the above file, we would need some additional information to be able to tell whether a READ brought in a CUSTOMER-ADDRESS-REC or a CUSTOMER-PURCHASE-REC. Such information could be provided by an "external" source, such as knowing, for example, that every address record is followed by a purchase record. Alternately, we could define the records so as to be able to determine the type of record by such programming logic as this:

```
01   CUSTOMER-ADDRESS-REC.
     05   REC-TYPE        PIC 9.
          88  ADDR-TYPE   VALUE 0.
          88  PURCH-TYPE  VALUE 1.
     05   NAME            PIC X(20).
     05   ADDRESS         PIC X(80).
01   CUSTOMER-PURCHASE-REC.
     05   FILLER          PIC X(21).
     05   NO-OF-PURS      PIC 99.
     05   PURCHASE-DATA   OCCURS 0 TO 10 TIMES
                          DEPENDING ON NO-OF-PURS.
          10  PUR-NO      PIC 9(5).
          10  PUR-AMT     PIC 999V99.
```

The addition of the REC-TYPE field allows us to define the record type by inserting a 0 or 1 value in REC-TYPE before we WRITE; and then when we READ, we can employ tests such as IF ADDR-TYPE ... , and so on.

Thus, when the DEPENDING ON is omitted in conjunction with the RECORD IS VARYING IN SIZE, the record length is determined in one of several ways. If we have multiple record definitions, a WRITE command will reference one of those records. If that record is of fixed length, then that is the record length. If the record is of varying length, it will contain an OCCURS ... DEPENDING ON clause that will serve as the basis for determining the record length. When reading a file with multiple record definitions, then either we know the order of the types of records, or we include a "record-type" field in the original description of the record so that we can determine the type. Finally, if a file consists of only one type of record and we use RECORD IS VARYING IN SIZE *without* a DEPENDING ON clause in the FD, then the record description must include an OCCURS ... DEPENDING ON clause, or else we are attempting an incorrect description.

R E V I E W . . . .

1. The OCCURS ... DEPENDING ON option can be used when the number of entries to be included in a table is [predetermined / variable].

    variable

2. When the DEPENDING ON option is used, the word OCCURS in the program statement always is followed by a specified [value / range of values], and the phrase DEPENDING ON always is followed by a [data-name / specified value].

    range of values; data-name

3. The RECORD IS VARYING IN SIZE clause in the FD entry is available [in both the 1974 and 1985 versions/only in the 1985 version] of standard COBOL.

    only in the 1985 version

4. The DEPENDING ON clause, when used in conjunction with the RECORD IS VARYING IN SIZE, makes reference to a record-length field in [the record description / working storage].

    working storage

5. In the absence of a DEPENDING ON clause in the FD entry, in conjunction with a RECORD IS VARYING IN SIZE, the record length in a WRITE operation is determined by _____.

    the length of the record in the WRITE command

.   .   .   .

USE OF DECLARATIVES FOR I/O EXCEPTION PROCESSING

In Chapter 10 we discussed use of the FILE STATUS feature for handling exceptions during input and output processing. Now we are about to study an alternative way of "trapping" and handling exceptional situations during input and output operations. At the start of a PROCEDURE DIVISION the programmer may include a set of DECLARATIVES, as outlined in Figure 17-6. Notice that we begin immediately after the PROCEDURE DIVISION heading and signify the end by END DECLARATIVES. Within this portion of the program there may be one or more sections. The procedures within each section are conditionally executed on encountering an exception in conjunction with one of the five available choices: INPUT, OUTPUT, I-O, EXTEND, and file-name. The USE AFTER EXCEPTION is really a conditional statement. It can be paraphrased to say: "If an exception is

---

FIGURE 17-6
Outline of Using DECLARATIVES Within a COBOL Program

```
PROCEDURE DIVISION.
DECLARATIVES.
section-name SECTION.

                    ⎰ EXCEPTION ⎱                    ⎰ INPUT     ⎱
    USE AFTER       ⎱ ERROR     ⎰  PROCEDURE ON      ⎱ OUTPUT    ⎰
                                                       I-O
                                                       EXTEND
                                                       file-name

paragraph-1.
    .
    .
    .
paragraph-n.
section-name SECTION.
    USE AFTER . . .
paragraph-1.
    .
    .
    .
paragraph-m.
    .
    .
    .
END DECLARATIVES.
PROGRAM-SUMMARY. (First nondeclarative paragraph)
    .
    .
    .
    (etc.)
```

encountered during INPUT (for instance), execute the instructions in this section." Incidentally, the words ERROR and EXCEPTION are synonyms. Consider an example:

```
PROCEDURE DIVISION.
DECLARATIVES.
CUST-FILE-EXCEPTION SECTION.
    USE AFTER EXCEPTION PROCEDURE ON CUSTOMER-FILE.
WRITE-EXCEPTIONS.
    IF  FILE-STATUS-1 = '34'
        MOVE 'FILE-BOUNDARY VIOLATION' TO ERR-MESSAGE
        WRITE ERROR-RECORD
    ELSE
        MOVE 'UNSPECIFIED ERROR CONDITION' TO ERR-MESSAGE
        WRITE ERROR-RECORD.
PRODUCT-FILE SECTION.
    USE AFTER EXCEPTION PROCEDURE ON PROD-FILE.
OPEN-EXC.
    IF  FILE-CODE-1 = '90'
        MOVE 'FILE CANNOT BE OPENED' TO ERR-MESSAGE
        WRITE ERROR-RECORD
    ELSE
        IF  FILE-CODE-1 = '05'
            MOVE 'LABEL ERROR DURING OPEN' TO ERR-MESSAGE
            WRITE ERROR-RECORD
        ELSE
            MOVE 'UNSPECIFIED ERROR DURING OPEN'
                TO ERR-MESSAGE
            WRITE ERROR-RECORD.
```

In the above example the action resulting from detection of a specific exception is to MOVE and WRITE some message. Obviously, this is only one illustration, and any processing could be done. For instance, we might proceed to the printing of reports accumulated thus far or to providing additional information about the status of the program at the time that the exception occurred.

The first section in the example would work as follows. Every time that WRITE is executed for CUSTOMER-FILE, the system places the corresponding values in the FILE STATUS fields. If unsuccessful completion is indicated, the program executes the WRITE-EXCEPTIONS paragraph as if it were under a PERFORM verb, and finally returns to the statement after the original WRITE (in the non-DECLARATIVES part of the program).

In the OPEN-EXC paragraph of the example, we illustrate the possibility that an implementor has chosen a code of 90 to signify an OPEN exception and a code of 05 to signify a label error. Again this is a hypothetical meaning, not a standardized convention.

The use of DECLARATIVES need not involve use of the FILE STATUS feature. For instance, we could specify a procedure within the DECLARATIVES portion of the program that makes no reference to the file status key. Had we written USE AFTER EXCEPTION PROCEDURE ON I-O, we would know that execution of the associated procedure has to do with I/O (or, alternatively, OUTPUT, EXTEND, or file-name) and we could execute statements without testing the FILE STATUS values.

Overall, through the FILE STATUS feature and/or the DECLARATIVES portion of the PROCEDURE DIVISION we can intervene after I/O operations to treat exceptions. The AT END with READ and the INVALID KEY with the WRITE (see Chapters 20 and 21) already provide for exception processing. With the FILE STATUS and the USE verb in the DECLARATIVES portion, we extend these capabilities to all I/O verbs and also have the choice of implementing AT END (and INVALID KEY) in an alternate way. For example, we can write READ without AT END and use the FILE STATUS or the DECLARATIVES approach to process the AT END exception.

R E V I E W . . . .

1. Both the FILE STATUS feature and DECLARATIVES can be used in conjunction with the processing of _____ for I/O verbs.

   exceptions

2. When DECLARATIVES are used, they are entered into the program immediately after the _____ heading.

   PROCEDURE DIVISION

3. The procedures included within each section of DECLARATIVES portion of the program are executed [conditionally / unconditionally] upon encountering a(n) _____.

   conditionally; exception

4. Overall, the FILE STATUS feature and/or DECLARATIVES can be used to detect and treat exceptions in conjunction with _____ operations.

   I/O (or input-output)

. . . .

MASTER FILE MAINTENANCE

Files on magnetic tape or disk are maintained or updated to reflect changes that take place. We speak of master and transaction files as being involved in the updating process.

A *master file* contains reference data that reflect the cumulative status as of a point in time. For example, a payroll master file would contain data on each employee, such as name, address, pay rate, year-to-date earnings, and so forth.

A *transaction file* contains records that either reflect events or indicate changes to the master file. For example, a transaction record at a bank might be a deposit made or a check written. Other examples of transactions would be the addition of a new customer to the master file, deletion of a former customer's name, or a change of the customer's address.

Updating involves processing the transaction file against the master file. The process of updating varies a little, depending on whether we use magnetic tape or disk for storing the master file.

File maintenance is a primary activity in the batch processing of sequential files. Although it is true that reports are the important result of data processing, it is necessary to maintain the master files to produce the reports. Once the file is in the right state (updated and suitably ordered), report production is simply a matter of extracting the desired information. File maintenance and report production are frequently consolidated in the same run, but this need not be the case.

Since it is the transactions that affect the state of the master file, which in turn reflects the state of the business activity system, it is imperative that the transactions be screened for possible errors prior to being used to update the master file. In this respect, it is useful to distinguish between data verification and data validation.

Verification is concerned with establishing that original data (usually manually produced) have been correctly transcribed into machine processable form. Verification is typically accomplished by duplicating the transcription effort. Since verification that is achieved by duplicating the transcription effort is relatively costly, we should examine whether the value of such verification justifies the cost. For example, verification of hours worked is desirable in a payroll situation but may be questionable when data are to be used in summary form or for statistical analysis in which a small margin of error would not affect the usefulness of the report. Figure 17-7 presents an overview of the file updating process including data verification and validation.

In addition to duplicating the data transcription, the accuracy of certain types of input can be verified by the use of self-checking numbers. A *self-checking number* is one that has a precalculated check digit appended to the basic number to detect input or transmission errors. Normally, the check digit is used in conjunction with such identification codes as employee numbers, customer numbers, and part numbers. A self-checking number that includes the check digit will, of course, contain one more digit than the basic number. For example, a 6-digit customer number would become a 7-digit number.

Although several techniques exist for calculating the check digit, the so-called modulus 10 method is illustrated. The procedure is as follows:

1. The units (rightmost) position and every alternate position thereafter in the basic code number are multiplied by 2.

2. The individual digits in the product and the individual digits in the basic code number that were not multiplied by 2 are summed.

3. The sum is subtracted from the next higher number ending in zero.

4. The difference is the check digit, which is to be appended to the basic code number to form the self-checking number.

An example of calculating a self-checking number is given here:

Basic code number:	345798
Units and every alternate position:	4 7 8
Multiply by 2:	x 2
Product:	956
Digits not multiplied by 2:	359
Sum of individual digits:	9 + 5 + 6 + 3 + 5 + 9 = 37
Next-higher number ending in zero:	40
Subtract sum of individual digits:	− 37
Check digit:	3
Self-checking number:	3457983

When self-checking numbers are used, an error can be detected by the fact that the check digit is not appropriate for the basic number to which it is appended. It is possible that an incorrect basic number will have the same check digit as the original (correct) number. However, this can occur only if there is more than one transcription error in the basic number, and it is therefore a rare occurrence.

FIGURE 17-7
Master File Update Run With Data
Verification and Validation

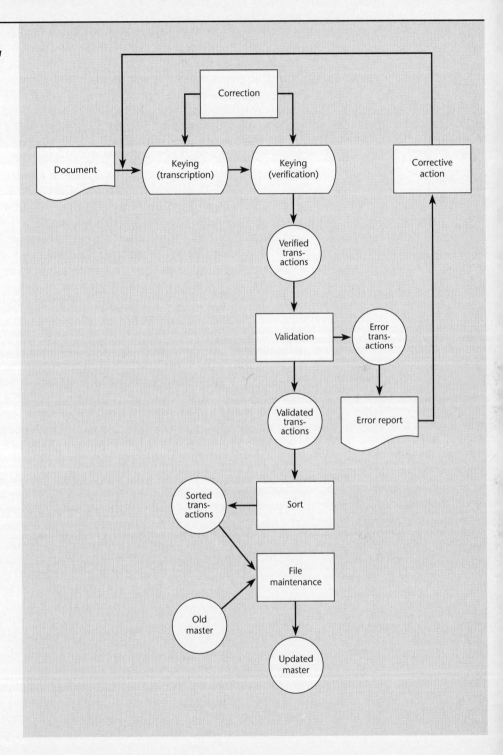

As contrasted to verification, which is concerned with correct individual transactions, *validation* is concerned with the completeness and internal consistency of the set of data. The use of *control totals* is a very common approach to validation, and a *batch total* is one such control total. For example, a bank teller may produce the sum of the amounts deposited for batches of 50 deposits. These batch totals are identified with their corresponding batches and become part of the input for subsequent computer processing. The computer program duplicates the batch total accumulation process and compares these computer-generated totals with the totals determined manually. If they are not equal, an error has been made. In this example the most likely source of error is the transcription process from the manual deposit slip to the magnetically encoded document. Once an error has been detected, we need only search the particular batch to pinpoint the error entry or entries. As can be seen, there is some advantage to keeping batch sizes small. If a batch contains 1,000 entries instead of the 50 described above, we might have to examine as many as 1,000 to locate the error.

A second type of control total is called a *hash total.* When a payroll file is formed, the hash total could be the sum of the identification numbers of all the employees. In subsequent processing of this file the total could be formed again and compared with the previous total. If the two totals are not the same, this may indicate that one or more records were missing. The word "hash" indicates that the total has no meaning of its own and is used only for comparison purposes.

A third type of control total is often referred to as *crossfooting.* For example, the following relationship may apply to each item in an inventory file:

Opening balance + receipts − issues = on hand

Utilizing this known relationship, it must be true that the totals for each of the four fields above for all items processed must also conform to the above formula.

As contrasted to the use of the control totals, another form of validation relies on the use of *range checks.* This approach is based on the fact that classes of transactions must occur within certain numerical limits. For example, a transaction showing the amount charged for a pair of shoes in a discount department store should not exceed $99. Similarly, the Internal Revenue Service can check to determine if deductions exceed a certain percent of income. In a particular form of the range check, we may check as to whether the amount sold is blank—thus performing a check to determine if the amount was left out. Such a determination is referred to as a *completeness check.*

A third form of validation is referred to as a *consistency check.* Such checks are directed toward determining if the input data are consistent with known constraints of reality. For example, hourly rates of pay may always be expressed in dollars and cents rather than whole numbers, and the quantity of a particular item may always be in terms of pounds rather than some other unit of measurement.

The term *data editing* is often used in the context of data validation procedures, even though detection of errors as such may not be involved. Data editing is concerned mainly with accomplishing desired changes in the form of data. For example, blanks might be changed to leading zeros in a numeric field, and a date in the form of XX-XX-XX might be changed to the form XXXXXX, thereby eliminating the hyphens.

When an error is detected through the process of data validation, some corrective action must be taken. Ideally, the computer program should provide the necessary corrective action, and occasionally this is possible. But in most cases there is no way to correct the error based on the input data alone. Therefore, the fact that a certain type of error has been detected is reported for eventual manual correction. Figure 17-7 is a flowchart for a master file update run that includes data verification and validation. In this typical case, manual documents contain the original data, which are keyed and verified, then transferred to magnetic tape, validated, sorted, and finally processed to update the master file. Depending on the extent of data validation, such procedures may be a subpart of a total update job, or they may require a separate computer run. More often than not, validation procedures are a separate run, followed by a sort run, which is in turn followed by the main update run. Thus computer programs concerned with updating master files are not simple programs but rather are concerned with a series of tasks.

R E V I E W . . . .

1. The procedures that are directed toward ascertaining that original data have been correctly transcribed are concerned with the general process called data

    _____.

    verification

2. Data verification is typically accomplished by duplicating the transcription process. However, as an alternate to this approach, certain types of numeric input, such as part numbers, can be verified as to accuracy by the use of _____ numbers.

    self-checking

3. As contrasted to verification, data _____ is concerned with the completeness and internal consistency of a set of data, rather than the accuracy of individual transcriptions taken singly.

    validation

4. Data validation is generally accomplished by making use of various types of _____ totals.

    control

5. When the totals for groups of 100 sales transactions are included with the individual transaction values as the computer input, the type of control total being used for the purpose of validation is the _____ total.

    batch

6. When the sum of all the customer numbers for the account that have had a sales transaction is used for data validation purposes, the control total would be described as being a _____ total. On the other hand, the type of control total that is based on known numerical relationships among such totals as the total amount of payments and total account balances is referred to as

    _____.

    hash; crossfooting

7. As contrasted to the use of control totals, the method of validation based on the fact that certain transactions can occur only within prescribed numerical limits involves the use of _____ checks. A third form of validation is based on the fact that transactions must conform to certain constraints of reality, such as being expressed in certain types of units, and this type of validation is therefore called a _____ check.

    range; consistency

8. The procedure that is sometimes associated with validation procedures and that is concerned with changing the form of the input data, such as replacing $ signs with zeros and eliminating commas included in numeric input, is called

    _____.

    data editing

. . . .

TRANSACTION RECORDS AND FILE MAINTENANCE

There are two basic types of transactions in master file updating: transactions that change the values in the fields in the master records and transactions that result in whole records being added to or deleted from the file. For instance, in the updating of an inventory file the following types of transactions would result in changes in the values of the fields in the master records:

- *Receipt transactions,* indicating a shipment of items received from the vendor

- *Issue transactions,* indicating items taken out of inventory for the purpose of sale to customers or for release to the production floor

- *Adjustment transactions,* indicating corrections of errors, reconciliation of discrepancies between recorded data and physical inventory count, and the like

- *On-order transactions,* indicating items ordered but not yet received

- *Committed-item transactions,* indicating quantities encumbered or reserved for specified future issue

The program used in a file update process will examine the input transaction records, determine the transaction codes, and apply the appropriate adjustments to the records in the master file. For example, for a receipt record corresponding amounts would be added to the "on hand" and "available" fields of the master record for the item in question. Regardless of the specific processing required for such transactions, the final result is the master record updated and written onto the new master file.

The second type of transaction results in the addition or deletion of master records. For example, in a payroll-processing run we will typically have occasion to add new employees to the master file or to delete some employee records from the file. To add a record to the master file, we simply encode the transaction record to indicate the addition of a record, and we include it in the appropriate sequence in the transaction file. Normally, "add-type" transactions are longer than other types. In the payroll example most of the usual transactions will involve only one transaction record containing such input as employee number and hours worked. However, the formation of a master record will probably require several records for such information as full name and address, social security number, rate of pay, tax exemptions, and insurance and other deductions.

Once an add-type of transaction is read, we may simply insert it in the updated file, or we may process any transactions that follow and that pertain to the new record. For example, it could be that we have a new employee and that he or she worked during the pay period of concern. In addition to adding the record to the master file, we must also read the input regarding the amount of time worked and compute the gross pay, taxes, and so on. Note that the inclusion of add-type transactions complicates the processing logic to some extent. In practice, it is not unusual to have one processing run in which the master file is updated with respect to additions and deletions and to have a separate processing run that updates the file with respect to data modifications. This becomes desirable if the number of added or deleted records is large, as it might be for a magazine subscriber list or in a company that has substantial employee turnover.

Deletions from the file are also handled by submitting an encoded transaction record. At first it might seem a simple matter to delete a record from the file: simply do not write the old master record in the updated master file. Practical considerations dictate that a series of steps be followed in the case of deletions, however. For one thing, we will want to print full information regarding the deleted records so that the fact of deletion can be communicated to and reviewed by those who have managerial responsibility over the deleted items. Further, the deletion procedure itself has to take into consideration the continued need to work with the records in certain aspects. For example, in a payroll situation we may owe the employee some back pay and make appropriate adjustments for his or her deductions. We may still want to maintain the record (perhaps on a separate file) for such reasons as end-of-year tax reports.

In addition to transactions that change data on the records and those that alter the composition of the records in a file, a third type of transaction logically could fall into the second category but is usually considered to be a separate type of transaction. It often happens that we need to change the order of records in the master file. One simple example would be the need to change the order of listing in an alphabetical file for individuals who change their last names. If "Zacher" becomes "Brown", the record must be repositioned in the file. Another example would be the situation in which the employee identification number includes a department number, and some employees are transferred between departments. With such examples in mind, let us consider two ways for processing such changes.

One approach is to introduce two transactions in the same run. One involves the addition of a new record, and the other involves the deletion of an old one. In the example of the person who had a change of last name name from Zacher to Brown, we would provide an add-type transaction for Brown and a delete-type transaction for Zacher. If the volume of such changes is low, this is probably a satisfactory approach. However, if the volume of such transactions is high, this approach has the disadvantage that it requires whole new master entries, which may involve considerable work. For instance, in a university each student may have a record approximately 2,000 characters in length, containing his or her name, parents' names, local address, home address, transcript data, and so forth. The prospect of manually recreating a new master record is undesirable, and even the prospect of automatic creation of the data may require reading and searching an entire file.

An alternative approach by which the order of records in a master file can be changed is to alter the record to be relocated, for example, by changing the last name and then writing this altered record on a special "transfer" file, eliminating the record from the currently updated master. This transfer file is then sorted, and in the next run it is merged with the old master file onto the updated master. The chart in Figure 17-8 presents the file processing in this case. By this approach we would read and merge the old master file and the transfers-from-previous-run file as the current transactions are being processed. As the process is portrayed in Figure 17-8, five files are required for the update run: one each for the input old master file, current transactions file, and the transfers from previous run, and one each for output to the updated master file and (new) transfers.

The disadvantages associated with the method portrayed in Figure 17-8 is that the master file is split into two parts. If we wanted to generate a report based on the master file at any other time than during the update procedure, there would be some problems. Figure 17-9 portrays an alternate method that requires an extra merging operation, but that concludes with a complete, updated, and sorted master file.

R E V I E W . . . .

1. Of the two basic types of transactions in the master file updating, one is concerned with transactions that change the values of _____ contained in the master records, while the second is concerned with transactions that result in addition or deletion of whole _____ as such.

   fields; master records

2. Suppose an inventory file is updated and there have been no changes in the items held in the inventory (although particular inventory levels have changed). Such an updating run would be entirely concerned with changing [values of fields in master records / the records composition of the master file].

   values of fields in master records

FIGURE 17-8
File Updating Involving Transfer
Records

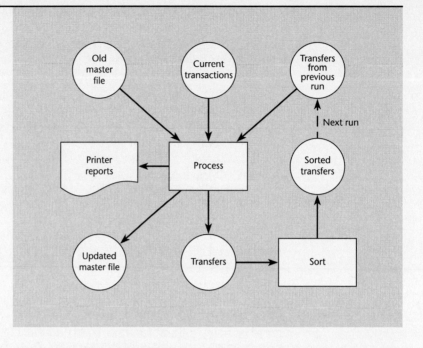

FIGURE 17-9
Alternate Method of File Updating
with Transfer Records

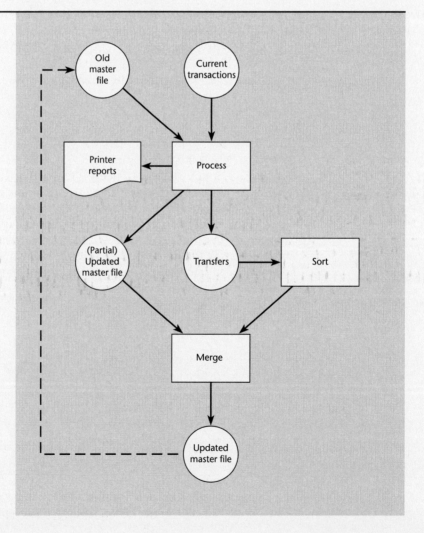

3. Given that employees have been added to and deleted from the payroll since the last payroll processing run, the type of transaction that is required is the type that is concerned with changing [values of fields in master records / the record composition of the master file].

the record composition of the master file

4. A third type of transaction is concerned with changing the order of records held in a master file. One way by which such a change can be accomplished is to alter the record to be relocated, write the record on a special _____ file, and eliminate the record from the currently updated master. On the next processing run the (then) old master file is merged with the _____ file from the previous run to form an updated _____.

transfer; transfer; master file

. . . .

ACTIVITY RATIOS AND FILE MAINTENANCE

The amount of activity over time is different for the various entries, or items, that constitute a master file. For example, suppose we have a warehouse that stocks 20,000 parts. Some of them will experience daily activity, some may average one transaction a week, while others may have transactions just a few times a year. Let us say that we experience an average of 900 transactions a day and that these transactions are concerned with an average of 400 parts in the inventory system—that is, some parts have more than one transaction. Now suppose we update the master file on a daily basis. Since 400 of the 20,000 parts were involved in the transactions, we say that the activity ratio is

$$\frac{400}{20,000} = \frac{1}{50} = 0.02$$

Thus for every 50 records there will be one record for which some processing is done, and 49 records will simply be copied from the old to the updated file. Obviously, the part of the processing concerned with copying is unproductive. As an alternative to updating the file on a daily basis, we might consider processing the file once a week. On the average, there will now be more than 400 active parts per week. However, assuming that there are 5 working days per week, do not be misled into concluding that the number of active parts will be 400 per day x 5 days. Of the 400 average per day, there will be some parts that will be active every day or at least more than once a week. So we may have, say, 1,200 active parts per week, resulting in the activity ratio

$$\frac{1,200}{20,000} = \frac{3}{50} = 0.06$$

The increase in the activity ratio from 0.02 to 0.06 in the above example represents an increase of 300 percent in the value of the ratio, but still represents a small portion of the total. In an extreme case we may wish to process a batch of records only after a very high percentage—say, 98 percent—have had some activity. But this requirement would generally conflict with the need for timely information, since it might well be months before 98 percent of the records experience activity. In a batch processing system we frequently have to balance information needs against data processing efficiency.

In some files the activity ratio is always high. For example, the payroll file for a manufacturing plant with 5,000 employees will include only a small percentage of "inactive" records on any given day (for those who were absent, on vacation, terminated, etc.). Yet payroll records are not processed daily just because the activity ratio is high. Rather, other factors determine the frequency of updating in this case.

When a file is large and activity variations are great, such a file may be subdivided into two master files, one for "active" items and one for relatively "inactive" items. As a practical matter, it is not easy to specify the difference between these two groups of items. One possible way of making the distinction is to set some parameters on the activity. For example, active items might be defined as those that are involved in at least X transactions per designated period—say, 10 transactions per month. All other items would then be considered inactive by definition. Another approach to distinguishing between active and inactive items is based on the nature of the items themselves. For example, we may know from experience that parts for automobiles that are 8 years old or older are inactive, as are parts for the current model year. Parts for the other model years (1 to 7 years old) would then be considered active.

When two master files are used, some procedure is usually required for exit from one class of items and entry to the other class. The process chart in Figure 17-10 illustrates the basic procedure that is used. There are two types of processing runs, one for the active file and one for the inactive file. Typically, there will be several processing runs for the active file to each run of the inactive file. The input for the updating of the active master file includes the old active master, the transactions, and inactive records that have become active. The output consists of the updated active master, those transactions that do not pertain to active records, and those records that have become inactive.

In the maintenance of the inactive file, as portrayed in Figure 17-10, the input consists of the old inactive master, transactions of records not in the active file, and the (formerly) active records that are now inactive. For each of the latter two inputs several files are typically merged because of there being several processing runs for the active master file for each processing run for the inactive master file. Two types of output are generated in addition to the updated inactive master file. One is concerned with error transactions—that is, transactions not applicable to either file. The other type includes the records that were inactive but now have had increased activity and therefore have been reclassified as being active. These reclassified records will be processed in the next maintenance run for the active master file.

R E V I E W . . . .

1. If 300 of 1,000 items are involved in transactions during each week, on the average, the weekly activity ratio has the value _____.

    300/1,000 = 0.30

2. For the example above if the activity ratio is calculated for a typical 2-week period, the value of the ratio is likely to be [less than / equal to / greater than] the value 0.60.

    less than

3. When activity variations among the records of a file are great, such a file is frequently subdivided into two master files—one called the _____ master file and the other called the _____ master file.

    active; inactive

FIGURE 17-10

File Maintenance with Active and
Inactive Master Files

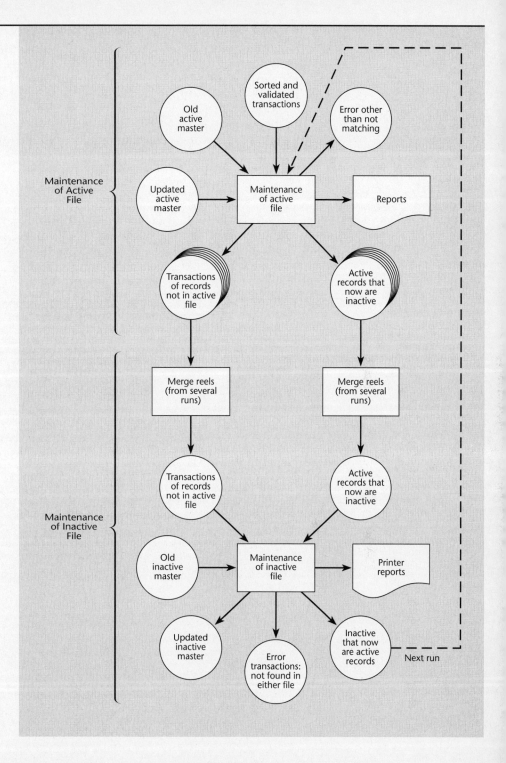

SUMMARY

In this chapter you have studied more advanced concepts about the definition and processing of sequential files. The first two sections of the chapter provided you with a generalized model of sequential update logic. The generalized structure chart and the program outline can be adapted to the vast majority of sequential file updating tasks. This point was demonstrated by the sample program, which used the generalized model as a logic template and then applied it to the specific (payroll) task.

The second major topic discussed in this chapter had to do with the definition and processing of variable-length records. One approach, valid for both COBOL '74 and '85, involves use of the OCCURS ... DEPENDING ON clause to define the variable portion of a record. This approach can be used when we have a series of repeating items, such as the number of checks written by a customer. Another approach involves use of the COBOL '85 feature of specifying that the RECORD IS VARYING IN SIZE in the FD entry of the file. This last approach involves optional use of another version of the DEPENDING ON clause.

Handling of exceptions during input and output was discussed in conjunction with the DECLARATIVES portion of a program and the USE verb to define under what conditions we want the exception processing to take place. This is an alternative approach to using the FILE STATUS feature discussed in Chapter 10, and it has the characteristic that exception-processing instructions are grouped in a separate part of the program, delimited by the DECLARATIVES and END DECLARATIVES keywords at the very beginning of the PROCEDURE DIVISION.

The chapter concludes with a series of conceptual topics about sequential file processing. The activities of *data verification* and *data validation* were discussed as well as a number of controls, such as self-checking numbers, hash totals, and crossfooting procedures. Then we studied alternative ways of handling transactions that change the physical position of records in the master file, such as for a person whose last name changes from Adams to Peterson. Finally, we considered how we can balance currency of information with efficiency in processing, when files are large and many records in a master file are not involved each time we update a file.

EXERCISES

17.1 The county assessor's office maintains a master file of property owners, in the following (simplified) format:

Lot number	9-digit code
Owner name	26 alphanumeric characters
Assessed valuation	8-digit field, including 2 decimal places

An update run involves reading transaction records and creating an updated master file. The input records have the following format:

Lot number	9-digit code
Transaction code	1-digit code

  1 = change owner name

  2 = change assessed valuation

  3 = change both owner and valuation

  4 = add to tax rolls

  9 = remove from tax rolls

Owner name	26 characters
Assessed valuation	8 digits in dollars and cents

If a transaction code of 1 is used, the valuation field is blank. If a code of 2 is used, the owner field is blank. A code of 9 implies that the record is blank from column 11 on.

The printer report should have the approximate layout shown in Figure 17-11.

FIGURE 17-11

Printer Report Layout, Master File, Transaction Records, and Sample Output for Exercise 17.1

LAYOUT FOR PRINTER REPORT

LOT NUMBER	OWNER	ASSESSED VALUE	NEW OWNER	NEW ASSESSMENT	OFF ROLLS
XXXXXXXX	XXXXXXXXXX	$XXXXXX.XX	XXXXXXXXXXX	$XXXXXX.XX	
XXXXXXXX	XXXXXXXXXX	XXXX.XX			***

SAMPLE MASTER FILE

LOT NUMBER	OWNER NAME	ASSESSED VALUATION
000150000	JENKING, ANTHONY	10,872.00
000180000	ANDREWS, JULIA	256,237.00
000290000	THOMAS, THEODORE	162,116.00
000350000	MCDONALD, DONNA	769,276.00
000720000	MARTIN, JANE	99,998.00
001050000	RICHARDSON, PETER	820,600.00
001120000	SILVA, ROBIN	959,999.00

SAMPLE TRANSACTION RECORDS

LOT NUMBER	CODE	OWNER NAME	ASSESSED VALUATION
000180000	1	ANDREWS, THOMAS	
000290000	2		300,000.00
000720000	3	STEINMAN, WILLA	100,000.00
001050000	9		

SAMPLE OUTPUT

LOT NUMBER	OWNER	ASSESSED VALUE	NEW OWNER	NEW ASSESSMENT	OFF ROLLS
00015000	JENKING, ANTHONY	$ 10,872.00			
000180000	ANDREWS, IULIA	$256,237.00	ANDREWS, THOMAS		
000290000	THOMAS, THEODORE	$162,116.00		$300,000.00	
000350000	MCDONALD, DONNA	$769,276.00			
000720000	MARTIN, JANE	$ 99,998.00	STEINMAN, WILLA	$100,000.00	
001050000	RICHARDSON, PETER	$820,600.00			***
001120000	SILVA, ROBIN	$959,999.00			

Whenever an item is eliminated, it is signaled by three asterisks in the OFF ROLLS column.

Write a program to update such a file. The program should check for correct sequence in the transaction and master records and for possibly erroneous codes in the transactions.

A sample master file, sample transaction records, and sample corresponding output are shown in Figure 17-11.

17.2 Perform file maintenance on a sequential customer purchase order master file consisting of variable length records. Master file records have the following format:

```
CUSTOMER ID NUMBER        PIC X(05)
CUSTOMER NAME             PIC X(15)
CUSTOMER PHONE NUMBER     PIC X(08)
NUMBER OF PURCHASE ORDERS PIC 9(02)

DATE OF PURCHASE ORDER    PIC X(06)    These three fields repeat,
PURCHASE ORDER NUMBER     PIC 9(06)    depending on the
PURCHASE ORDER AMOUNT     PIC 9(05)V99 number of transactions.
                                       Maximum = 15.
```

Each record consists of a fixed and a variable part. The variable part consists of data about purchase orders, including the date, number, and dollar amount of each purchase order. A given customer record may have none, one, or up to 15 occurrences of the purchase data. Therefore a field is included in the fixed part of the record to contain the number of occurrences of the variable data. The following is an example of a variable-length record, similar to the one that you will be using:

```
FD  XYZ-FILE
        LABEL RECORDS ARE STANDARD
        RECORD CONTAINS 30 TO 315 CHARACTERS
        BLOCK CONTAINS 1 TO 15 RECORDS
        DATA RECORD IS ABC-REC.
01  ABC-REC.
    05  ID-KEY                        PIC X(05).
    05  FIXED-DATA                    PIC X(23).
    05  NO-OF-VAR-ITEMS               PIC 9(02).
    05  VAR-ITEMS OCCURS 0 TO 15 TIMES
            DEPENDING ON NO-OF-VAR-ITEMS PIC X(19).
```

The RECORD CONTAINS 30 TO 315 CHARACTERS is based on the fact that the fixed portion of the record consists of 30 bytes (5 + 15 + 8 + 2 = 30), the size of each occurrence of the variable portion is 19 (6 + 6 + 7 = 19), and the maximum number of occurrences is 15. Thus the maximum number of characters in the record is 30 + (19 * 15) = 30 + 285 = 315. The specific parameter of 15 in the BLOCK CONTAINS clause is, of course, an arbitrary choice, and it could be some other value as well.

The master file records are in correct sequence by customer ID number. The purchase orders within each record are in sequence by date of purchase order—the most current is the last (e.g., 09/21/90, 09/23/90, 09/27/90).

The format of the transaction file records is as shown here:

TRANSACTION TYPE	TRANS. CODE (COL. 1)	TRANSACTION DATA	COLUMNS
ADD A NEW CUSTOMER	1	CUSTOMER ID NUMBER	2–6
		CUSTOMER NAME	7–21
		CUSTOMER PHONE NUMBER	22–29
CHANGE CUSTOMER NAME	2	CUSTOMER ID NUMBER	2–6
		CUSTOMER NAME	7–21
ADD A NEW PURCHASE ORDER	3	CUSTOMER ID NUMBER	2–6
		DATE OF PURCHASE ORDER	7–12
		PURCHASE ORDER NUMBER	13–18
		PURCHASE ORDER AMOUNT	19–25
DELETE CUSTOMER RECORD	4	CUSTOMER ID NUMBER	2–6
DELETE A PURCHASE ORDER	5	CUSTOMER ID NUMBER	2–6
		DATE OF PURCHASE ORDER	7–12
		PURCHASE ORDER NUMBER	13–18
		PURCHASE ORDER AMOUNT	19–25
ADJUST PURCHASE ORDER AMOUNT	6	CUSTOMER ID NUMBER	2–6
		DATE OF PURCHASE ORDER	7–12
		PURCHASE ORDER NUMBER	13–18
		PURCHASE ORDER AMOUNT	19–25

The remaining columns (up to 80) are unused.

The transaction file records have already been edited and have been sorted in sequence (transaction code within customer ID number.)

There can be more than one purchase order for each date. You must search the record to find the appropriate date, then search further to find the purchase order to be updated.

Purchase order dates must remain in sequence after processing a code 3 transaction. Transaction codes 3 and 5 will change the length of the master record. Transaction codes 2 through 6 require that a master record already exists.

A monthly customer purchase order report is to be printed according to the format shown in Figure 17-12 on the following page.

Start each customer summary on a new page. You are also to print an error report for errors that might occur during an update. The following errors may occur:

a. Deletion or update of a nonexistent customer or purchase order

b. Addition of an already existing customer

c. More than 15 purchase orders for a given customer purchase order record.

17.3 Modify Exercise 17.2 to incorporate use of the COBOL '85 feature RECORD IS VARYING IN SIZE to define the variable-length records.

FIGURE 17-12

Monthly Customer Purchase Order Report for Exercise 17.2

```
                                                            PAGE XX
                                      COMPUMART, INC.
                              CUSTOMER PURCHASE ORDER SUMMARY
                                         09/18/90


                   CUSTOMER ID NUMBER:  XXXXX
                               NAME:  XXXXXXXXXXXXXX
                       PHONE NUMBER:  XXX-XXXX
                   NUMBER OF        DATE OF        PURCHASE       AMOUNT OF
                    P.O.'S      PURCHASE ORDER   ORDER NO.    PURCHASE ORDER
                   -------------------------------------------------------
                      XX         XX/XX/XX         XXXXX        $ XX,XXX.XX
                                 XX/XX/XX         XXXXX          XX,XXX.XX
                                    .               .              .
                                    .               .              .
                                    .               .              .
                   TOTAL DOLLAR AMOUNT OF
                   PURCHASE ORDERS FOR CUSTOMER:  XXXXX      $ XXX,XXX.XX
```

18 Multilevel Table Handling

THIS CHAPTER *is a continuation of the material in Chapter 12, in which you studied single-level table handling. Your focus here is on the definition and processing of tables of data that pertain to* **two or more** *nested categories. You will begin the chapter by considering the concept of higher-level tables and how you can use nested OCCURS clauses to define such tables, and how you can use multiple subscripts to make references to different levels.*

In the second section you will study the mapping of subscripted references to storage locations. You will learn about the physical storage of data in the computer. When you use the COBOL features that allow you to define and process multidimensional tables, you need to understand how such data tables are actually stored in the one-dimensional storage scheme of computer memories.

The next section of the chapter has to do with the use of the PERFORM verb for processing two-level and higher-level tables. Actually, several special features built into the PERFORM facilitate multilevel table processing. As usual, you will distinguish between the features applying to the 1985 as contrasted to the 1974 standard version of COBOL.

Your studies in this chapter will conclude with two sample programs. The first one illustrates the definition and processing of two-dimensional tables, while the second program illustrates the same general concepts for three-dimensional tables. In COBOL '85 we can have up to seven levels; still, if you understand the processing of two-level and three-level tables, the logic is essentially the same for any greater number of levels.

TWO-LEVEL AND HIGHER-LEVEL TABLES

The concept of *levels,* or *dimensions,* refers to the number of levels of categories by which data are organized within tables. As an example, suppose that we have student enrollment data organized as follows:

> By college
>> By department within colleges
>>> By field of specialization within departments
>>>> By year of studies (freshman through senior) within field of specialization

Data so organized in a table would be in four levels or dimensions: college, department, field of specialization, and year of studies. Thus, when data are organized in nested categories, we refer to such categories as levels or dimensions (both terms are used interchangeably).

In the 1974 standard version of COBOL the maximum number of dimensions permitted is three. In the 1985 version the programmer can use up to seven dimensions. In practice, the need for more than three dimensions is rare. Therefore either version of the language is powerful enough for handling most higher-dimensioned tables.

Two-level tables require two subscripts to locate an individual entry, or field. As an example of a two-level table, assume that a particular state has three state universities and we desire to set up a table that will contain the enrollment figures for each university according to class standing: freshman, sophomore, junior, senior, and graduate. Figure 18-1 portrays the required table.

To set up the required storage locations, the following DATA DIVISION entries can be written:

```
01   ENROLLMENT-TABLE.
     02   UNIVERSITY-ENROLLMENT      OCCURS 3 TIMES.
          03   YEAR-ENROLLMENT       OCCURS 5 TIMES.
               04   ENROLLMENT       PIC 9(5).
```

Two levels are specified in the statements above. YEAR-ENROLLMENT, which is at the 03-level and includes an OCCURS clause, is under UNIVERSITY-ENROLLMENT, which is at the 02-level and also includes an OCCURS clause. Thus a data definition

FIGURE 18-1
Required Format of the Enrollment Table

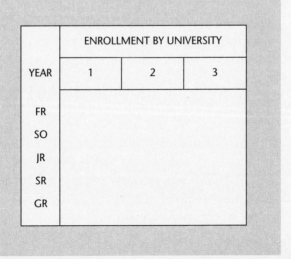

YEAR	ENROLLMENT BY UNIVERSITY		
	1	2	3
FR			
SO			
JR			
SR			
GR			

statement that involves an OCCURS that is subordinate to another OCCURS constitutes a (nested) higher dimension.

Notice the naming conventions illustrated in the above example. The entire collection of data is called ENROLLMENT-TABLE, which seems an appropriate data-name. The first dimension is named UNIVERSITY-ENROLLMENT, a name corresponding to the type of data, while the second dimension is given the data-name YEAR-ENROLLMENT. The 04 ENROLLMENT data-name is at a lower level (04), but since it is the only item at that level, it is really the same as YEAR-ENROLLMENT. However, we use the additional data-name for documentation purposes. The elementary data items in this table refer to enrollment data, and so we wish to use such a name for the data item that has the PIC clause. The 02-level and 03-level items are simply ways of organizing the data. Of course, the 02- and 03-level choices are arbitrary; we could have used 05 and 10 as the level numbers, just as well.

It is instructive to consider the storage layout for the above table. Figure 18-2 illustrates such a table containing hypothetical enrollment data. For instance, we can observe that the junior-year enrollment for the first of the three universities is 1000 students. As the figure illustrates, enrollment data for each of the five enrollment years is stored separately for each of the universities. Thus it is critical as to which OCCURS clause is written first. In our example UNIVERSITY-ENROLLMENT is at the 02-level, followed by YEAR-ENROLLMENT at the 03-level. Accordingly, the data for each university are physically grouped together.

To illustrate use of the table, consider the following examples.

- UNIVERSITY-ENROLLMENT (1) refers to all five fields associated with the first university. Keep in mind that this is a reference to a group-item, and in COBOL all group-items are considered alphanumeric for MOVE purposes. There would be nothing wrong saying MOVE SPACES TO UNIVERSITY-ENROLLMENT (1) since the subscripted data-name refers to a 25-byte (5 x 5) alphanumeric field, not to a numeric field. Even though each of the five individual enrollment figures for each university is a number, the five numbers together do not have any numeric (quantitative) meaning. Thus the collection of these five numbers is simply a string of 25 alphanumeric bytes.

- ENROLLMENT (1, 3) refers to the junior-year (3) enrollment at the first (1) university. ENROLLMENT must always be used with double subscripts. The first subscript refers to the superior dimension defined by the first OCCURS clause, which in this case is UNIVERSITY-ENROLLMENT. The second subscript refers to the subordinate dimension defined by the second OCCURS clause, YEAR-ENROLLMENT.

FIGURE 18-2

Storage Layout of the Two-Dimensional Table

ENROLLMENT TABLE						
UNIVERSITY 1					UNIVERSITY 2	
YEAR 1	YEAR 2	YEAR 3	YEAR 4	YEAR 5	· · ·	
0 0 0 1	0 0 0 5 0	0 1 0 0 0	0 0 2 0 0	0 0 0 3 0 0	· · ·	

- ENROLLMENT (UNIVERSITY, YEAR) refers to the enrollment of the university specified by the value of the UNIVERSITY field and the year defined by the value of YEAR. In order to be correct, UNIVERSITY must have a value in the range 1–3 and YEAR a value in the range 1–5. These ranges correspond to the OCCURS clauses written in the definition of the table.

- ENROLLMENT (1, 3) and YEAR-ENROLLMENT (1, 3) are equivalent. However, we recommend using YEAR-ENROLLMENT for documentation purposes and using ENROLLMENT as the more appropriate data-name for the elementary item.

- Three-dimensional tables involve the use of three subscripts. We can illustrate the statements required to set up a three-dimensional table by adding a further breakdown by male and female to our two-dimensional example, as follows:

```
01  ENROLLMENT-TABLE.
    02  UNIVERSITY-ENROLLMENT      OCCURS    3  TIMES.
        03  YEAR-ENROLLMENT        OCCURS    5  TIMES.
            04  ENROLLMENT-BY-SEX  OCCURS    2  TIMES.
                05  ENROLLMENT     PIC 9(5).
```

Thus ENROLLMENT (2, 3, 1) refers to the enrollment of males (1) in the junior year (3) in the second university (2).

In the 1974 standard, tables of up to only three dimensions are allowed. In contrast, in the 1985 standard up to seven dimensions are allowed. As an example of defining a table with more than three dimensions, the following statements define a table with four dimensions, or levels:

```
01  FOUR-LEVEL-TABLE-EXAMPLE.
    02  STATE-DATA OCCURS 50 TIMES.
        03  YEAR-DATA OCCURS 10 TIMES.
            04  MAJOR-DATA OCCURS 100 TIMES.
                05  GRADE-DATA OCCURS 10 TIMES.
                    06  COURSE-GRADE PICTURE X.
```

Assuming this table contains grade data for a sample of students in each of the 50 states for the last 10 years for each of 100 major field classifications, for each of 10 courses, the reference COURSE-GRADE (49, 10, 28, 8) makes reference to the 8th course grade for the 28th major field for the 10th year in the 49th state.

The following rules serve to summarize the requirements associated with the use of subscripted tables.

1. The OCCURS clause cannot apply to the 01-level. In other words, there cannot be a table of "records." However, this is a language rule and in no way prevents us from assigning a "record" to the 02-level and defining a 01-level name above it, as shown in the following example:

```
01  STATE-INCOME-TABLE.
    02  AVERAGE-INCOME  OCCURS 50 TIMES
                        PIC 9(6)V99.
```

2. The OCCURS clause cannot be used with level 77 items.

3. Subscripted tables may have one, two, or three dimensions in the 1974 standard, or up to seven dimensions in the 1985 version of COBOL.

4. The PICTURE clause applies to the elementary items only. Notice, for instance, the example of the three-dimensional table given previously.

5. Only one PICTURE description can be given for all like entries in a table, but there may be several entries that are not alike. The latter is exemplified by the example given in Chapter 12 and reproduced here:

```
01  STATE-INCOME-TABLE.
    02  NAME-INCOME          OCCURS 50 TIMES.
        03  NAME             PICTURE X(12).
        03  INCOME           PICTURE 9(6)V99.
```

   The same PICTURE clause applies to all 50 Name fields and the 50 Income fields above. Thus OCCURS is used for one or more homogeneous sets of data.

6. The subscripts may be integer constants, or they may be integer variables. Their values must be positive; they must not be zero or negative.

7. The subscript or subscripts are enclosed in one set of parentheses and are separated from the table-name by a space. Multiple subscripts are separated from each other by commas and spaces. Examples are

```
A-TABLE (1)
A-TABLE (IDEN)
B-TABLE (3, COUNT)
C-TABLE (GRADE, CLASS, YEAR)
C-TABLE (GRADE, 3, YEAR)
D-TABLE (GRADE, CLASS, YEAR, STATE)
```

8. Subscripts are enclosed in parentheses, and there must be as many subscripts as there are dimensions corresponding to the subscripted item. Subscripts must be integer literals or integer variables. In the 1985 standard it is also permissible to perform arithmetic operations within the subscript references, as in the following examples:

```
MOVE A (I) TO A (I + 1)
ADD AMOUNT TO B (1, J + 1)
IF C (1, J - K) = C (I + 1, J - K)
```

   In the examples above notice that the plus or minus symbol can be used to increase or decrease the value of a given subscript.

R E V I E W . . . .

1. In the two-dimensional ENROLLMENT-TABLE example, suppose we want the university to be at the lowest hierarchical level, instead of the year. Write the appropriate statements in the following blanks, using a PICTURE of 9(5) for the elementary field.

```
01 ENROLLMENT-TABLE.
    02 _____
        03 _____
            04 _____
                        YEAR-ENROLLMENT OCCURS 5 TIMES.
                          UNIVERSITY-ENROLLMENT OCCURS 3 TIMES.
                            ENROLLMENT PICTURE 9(5).
```

2. For the example in the preceding question, the table location of juniors in the first university is referenced by the subscripted variable
_____ , while the corresponding reference for the original definition of the two-level table is
_____ .

> UNIVERSITY-ENROLLMENT (3, 1), or ENROLLMENT (3, 1)
>
> YEAR-ENROLLMENT (1, 3), or ENROLLMENT (1, 3)

3. The PICTURE clause is used only at the [highest / lowest] hierarchical level of a table.

> lowest

4. The integer subscripts used in conjunction with subscripted variables [may / may not] be constant and [may / may not] be variables.

> may; may

5. A subscript used in conjunction with subscripted variables [may / may not] have a negative value.

> may not

6. In the 1974 standard the maximum number of levels, or dimensions, in a table is _____ , while in the 1985 standard the maximum is _____ .

> 3; 7

7. In the 1985 standard we can reference the *next* and *previous* subscripted references for, say, ABC (I) by the references _____ , and _____ , respectively.

> ABC (I + 1); ABC (I − 1)

∴ ∴ ∴ ∴ ∴ ∴ ∴ ∴ ∴ ∴ ∴ ∴ ∴ ∴ ∴ ∴ ∴ ∴ ∴

MAPPING SUBSCRIPTED REFERENCES TO STORAGE LOCATIONS

Computer storage is one-dimensional. Storage locations are addressable from the lowest to the highest in serial fashion, such as 0000, 0001, 0002, ..., 9999, assuming a 10,000-byte storage. Higher-level tables, in contrast, allow us the convenience of thinking in terms of a multidimensional reference scheme. It is worthwhile to consider the process by which the compiler transforms a multisubscript reference scheme into the one-dimensional reference scheme utilized in central storage. Let us consider a two-dimensional table. Let r (for *row*) and c (for *column*) represent the maximum number of entries in a two-dimensional table of the following definition:

```
02 A    OCCURS r TIMES
    03 B  OCCURS c TIMES ...
        04 T  PIC X(p).
```

We have used generic references for the OCCURS ... TIMES to generalize the description. Also, note that T is p bytes long in this example. Thus the table consists of r x c fields of T, and since each T is p bytes long, the total table consists of r x c x p bytes.

First, let us consider how we can resolve which of the T fields is involved in a two-subscript reference. A two-subscript reference such as B (I, J) can be transformed into a one-dimensional reference by the formula

$$B\ (I, J) = [(I - 1) \times c] + J$$

This formula computes the displacement of a field from the beginning of the table. Thus, if r = 4 and c = 5, T(3, 4) = [(3 – 1) x 5] + 4 = 14, meaning that T(3, 4) is the fourteenth element in the table. We can understand the rationale underlying this formula by thinking of the table as consisting of four groups (r = 4) of five values (c = 5) each. Since T(3, 4) refers to the fourth value in the third group, and each of the first two groups has five values each, we are referring to the fourteenth value (5 + 5 + 4).

If the PICTURE of T in the above example had been X(6), then a reference such as T(3, 4) refers to the field that starts at byte 79 from the beginning of the table. Since each of the 5 T fields at the B level consists of 6 bytes, it follows that each of the A fields (each row of the table) is 5 x 6 = 30 bytes long. Therefore the first two occurrences of A take up 2 x 5 x 6 = 60 bytes, and the first three occurrences of B take up 3 x 6 = 18 bytes, leaving us with the conclusion that T(3, 4) is a 6-byte field that starts at the 60 + 18 + 1 = 79th byte of the table storage. In general terms, the beginning byte of T(I, J) is computed as

$$[(I - 1) \times c \times p] + [(J - 1) \times p] + 1$$

In this formula p = the field size of the elementary item, as defined by the PICTURE clause; c is the number in the OCCURS c TIMES; and I and J are the subscript references. Notice that r, the TIMES value for the major OCCURS, is not involved in the above calculation.

The compilation process stores the beginning address of a table and the c and p values; then during execution of the program, a double-subscript reference is transformed into a storage address by a formula such as the one given above.

The foregoing discussion has two important implications. First, we can observe what happens when we use improper subscripts. If we used OCCURS clauses that defined a 3 x 4 table and then used subscripts (4, 3), then application of the position formula would reference a place in storage that is *past* the table content. In such a case we might get unpredictable results, depending on what happened to be stored at that address and what operation we were executing. Because COBOL compilers (unlike many BASIC compilers, for instance) generally do *not* check for out-of-bounds subscript references, it is particularly important that such errors be avoided. When debugging a table-handling program, it is a good idea to display the subscript value(s) first and then the subscripted reference. For instance, suppose a program abends (abnormally ends) on the following statement:

```
COMPUTE TOTAL = PRICE (I, J) * QUANT (I)
```

We could trace the subscript values as follows:

```
DISPLAY 'VALUES OF I AND J SUBSCRIPTS ' I J
DISPLAY PRICE (I, J)  QUANT (I)
COMPUTE TOTAL = PRICE (I, J) * QUANT (I).
```

By this trace we could readily observe any improper values for I or J.

The inadvertent use of illegal subscript values often is subtle and not immediately obvious, as in the following illustration. In this example we want to scan a table field, A, until we either find the first zero or have scanned the entire table.

```
02  A OCCURS 20 TIMES PIC 9.
    .
    .
    .

PERFORM XYZ VARYING I FROM 1 BY 1
        UNTIL A (I) = ZERO
            OR I > 20.
    .
    .
    .

XYZ.
    CONTINUE.
```

The XYZ paragraph is a "dummy" paragraph containing the do-nothing instruction CONTINUE. All the necessary logic is in the PERFORM instruction. In the 1974 version we lack the in-line PERFORM; however, even in the 1985 version we still need to PERFORM something:

```
PERFORM VARYING I FROM 1 BY 1
        UNTIL A (I) = ZERO
            OR I > 20
    CONTINUE
END-PERFORM.
```

In either version suppose there is no zero value in any of the 20 occurrences of A. Then when I = 21, the A (I) = ZERO test makes reference to an illegal address, namely, to A (21). To avoid such an error, the test should have been written in this order:

```
... UNTIL I > 20
        OR A (I) = ZERO
```

By the above order the I > 20 condition would apply first.

A second implication of the concept that subscripts are transformed into storage addresses is the fact that the decoding of subscripts requires computations. Of course, the number of computations that is required increases substantially with each additional table dimension. While the computations may not be highly time-consuming, in programs involving extensive computations it is advisable to use several tables with a small number of dimensions, for example, rather than one table with a large number of dimensions.

R E V I E W . . . .

1. Suppose we have data for a two-dimensional table that are to be entered into computer storage. For this example the physical storage of the data will have a [one-dimensional / two-dimensional] layout.

                                                          one-dimensional

2. For a two-level table the number of OCCURS clauses that would be included in the data description is [one / two].

two

3. Suppose we have a two-level 3 x 4 table, A, for a set of values, V. Without necessarily using a formula as such, we can conclude that the entry V (2, 3) would be the ______th V in the table.

7

4. For the example in #3 suppose that the PICTURE for V is X(4). Reference to V (2, 3) refers to the portion of the storage field that starts at byte ______ .

25

THE PERFORM VERB AND TABLE HANDLING

In Chapter 12 we described the use of the PERFORM verb for single-level table handling. We now continue the description by presenting a format of the PERFORM verb that is particularly useful for processing two-dimensional and higher-dimensional tables. The extended format of PERFORM is presented in Figure 18-3.

Consider the following example, which illustrates the use of two subscripts. Assume that we have 20 source records, defined as follows:

```
FD  SOURCE-FILE LABEL RECORD OMITTED
            DATA RECORD IS SOURCE-REC.
01  SOURCE-REC.
    02  SALES-VALUE         PIC 9(5)V99.
    02  FILLER              PIC X(73).
```

The data are sales values in each of five sales territories for each of the last four quarters. The records are ordered so that the first record contains the sales value for territory 1, quarter 1; the second record the value for territory 1, quarter 2, and

FIGURE 18-3
Extended Format of the PERFORM ... VARYING Statement

```
PERFORM [procedure-name-1 [{THROUGH} procedure-name-2]]
                           {THRU   }

[with TEST {BEFORE}]
           {AFTER }

VARYING identifier-1 FROM {identifier-2}
                          {literal-1   }

     BY {identifier-3} UNTIL condition-1
        {literal-2   }

[AFTER identifier-4 FROM {identifier-5}         ]
[                        {literal-3   }         ] ...
[                                               ]
[    BY {identifier-6} UNTIL condition-2        ]
[       {literal-4   }                          ]

[imperative-statement-1 END-PERFORM]
```

FIGURE 18-4

Required Format of the Sales Table

QUARTER	SALES TERRITORY				
	1	2	3	4	5
1					
2					
3					
4					

so on. Therefore the twentieth record contains the value for territory 5, quarter 4. We want to read the records and store the sales values in a two-dimensional table as presented in Figure 18-4. The values in records 1–4 are to be stored in column 1, rows 1–4 (according to record sequence). Record values 5–8 are to be stored in column 2, rows 1–4, and so on. Let us first define the table:

```
01   SALES-DATA-TABLE.
     02   SALES-TERRITORY        OCCURS 5 TIMES.
          03   QUARTER-SALES     OCCURS 4 TIMES
                                 PIC 9(5)V99.
```

Since the table is two-dimensional, we will use two subscripts. Let these be defined as

```
01   TERRITORY        PICTURE 9.
01   QUARTER          PICTURE 9.
```

Now we can write PROCEDURE DIVISION statements to accomplish the desired input-storing task, as follows:

```
PERFORM READER
        VARYING TERRITORY FROM 1 BY 1
            UNTIL TERRITORY > 5
        AFTER QUARTER FROM 1 BY 1
            UNTIL QUARTER > 4.
            .
            .
            .
READER.
    READ SOURCE-FILE
        AT END MOVE 'YES' TO END-OF-FILE-SWITCH.
    IF  NOT END-OF-FILE
    MOVE SALES-VALUE
        TO QUARTER-SALES (TERRITORY, QUARTER).
```

Notice that TERRITORY is varied *after* varying QUARTER. Therefore the sequence of values contained in these two fields is as presented in Figure 18-5.

FIGURE 18-5	SALES TERRITORY	QUARTER
Sequence of Values in Sales-Data-Table	1	1
	1	2
	1	3
	1	4
	2	1
	2	2
	2	3
	2	4
	.	.
	.	.
	.	.
	5	1
	5	2
	5	3
	5	4

The paragraph called READER will be executed 20 times, as QUARTER and TERRITORY are varied through their specified ranges. Each time the READER paragraph is executed, the pair of values of the subscripts is unique, so that each value is stored in a new QUARTER-SALES cell of the table.

Now consider the following four-level table that was presented earlier:

```
01  FOUR-LEVEL-TABLE-EXAMPLE.
    02  STATE-DATA  OCCURS 50 TIMES.
        03  YEAR-DATA  OCCURS 10 TIMES.
            04  MAJOR-DATA  OCCURS 100 TIMES.
                05  GRADE-DATA  OCCURS 10 TIMES.
                    06  COURSE-GRADE  PIC X.
```

We wish to tabulate five categories of grades (A, B, C, D, E) into the following one-level table:

```
01  GRADE-SUMMARY-TABLE.
    02  SUMMARY-GRADE OCCURS 5 TIMES  PIC 9(5).
```

The following program code will achieve the above objective:

```
MOVE ZEROS TO GRADE-SUMMARY-TABLE
PERFORM TABULATE-GRADES
        VARYING STATE FROM 1 BY 1
            UNTIL STATE > 50
        AFTER YEAR FROM 1 BY 1
            UNTIL YEAR > 10
        AFTER MAJOR FROM 1 BY 1
            UNTIL MAJOR > 100
        AFTER COURSE FROM 1 BY 1
            UNTIL COURSE > 10.
```

```
TABULATE-GRADES.
    EVALUATE STUD-GRADE (STATE, YEAR, MAJOR, COURSE)
        WHEN 'A' ADD 1 TO SUMMARY-GRADE (1)
        WHEN 'B' ADD 1 TO SUMMARY-GRADE (2)
        WHEN 'C' ADD 1 TO SUMMARY-GRADE (3)
        WHEN 'D' ADD 1 TO SUMMARY-GRADE (4)
        WHEN 'E' ADD 1 TO SUMMARY-GRADE (5).
```

The above example illustrates application of the PERFORM ... VARYING ... AFTER routine when there are four levels involved, and it can be expanded to formulate a similar statement for any number of levels.

As a side point we want to comment on the EVALUATE statement above. Notice that we have used five WHEN statements to decide which of the five grades applies and that we use explicit subscripts (1, 2, 3, 4, 5) to accumulate the total incidence of each grade in SUMMARY-GRADE. If instead of five types of grades we had many more types, say, 20, it is clear that writing 20 WHEN statements would not do. In such a case we could define a table to contain all the possible grade types. Then we would search the table until we found the grade being considered, and we would use a variable subscript corresponding to the location in the table where the match occurred. The subject of searching tables is presented in Chapter 19.

Another important point also relates to the above example of processing a four-level table. You may have noticed that since we used the EVALUATE statement, we were using the 1985 standard, which allows for in-line PERFORMs, and you could have wondered why we bothered to define the TABULATE-GRADES paragraph. The reason for our illustration is that if procedure-name-1 is omitted with respect to the general format presented in Figure 18-3, thus constituting an in-line PERFORM, then the AFTER phrase following the VARYING must not be used. (The AFTER here is not to be confused with the WITH TEST AFTER option, also in the general format of PERFORM.) To use the AFTER phrase with the VARYING option, either procedure-1 must be specified, thereby utilizing an out-of-line PERFORM, or nested multiple in-line PERFORM statements can be used to achieve the same effect. An example of using nested multiple PERFORM statements follows:

```
PERFORM VARYING I FROM 1 BY 1
        UNTIL I > 12
    PERFORM VARYING J FROM 1 BY 1
            UNTIL J > 31
        ADD SALES (I, J) TO TOTAL-SALES
    END-PERFORM
END-PERFORM.
```

The equivalent out-of-line formulation is

```
PERFORM ADD-SALES
        VARYING I FROM 1 BY 1 UNTIL I > 12
        AFTER J FROM I BY I UNTIL J > 31.
ADD-SALES.
    ADD SALES (I, J) TO TOTAL-SALES.
```

Using the WITH TEST Option in PERFORM

Figures 18-6 and 18-7 show the effects of using the COBOL '85 WITH TEST BEFORE and WITH TEST AFTER, respectively, in flowchart form. As can be seen, the difference is that with TEST BEFORE, the specified statements may not be executed even once if the conditions are true. On the other hand, the TEST AFTER

FIGURE 18-6
The PERFORM . . . VARYING
Option with TEST BEFORE

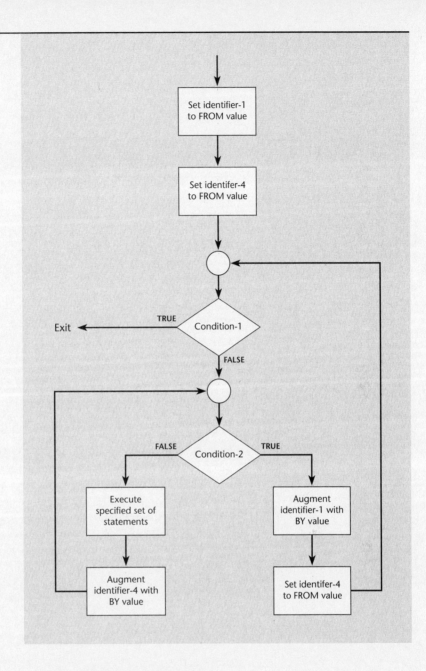

option executes the specified statements at least once before testing whether or not execution should be repeated.

Omission of both the BEFORE and AFTER options is understood to imply the BEFORE option.

Figure 18-8 illustrates the effect of the BEFORE and AFTER options by means of an example. In the TEST AFTER case the conditions are tested after each execution of the iteration; therefore the number of executions is different from the number in the TEST BEFORE case.

R E V I E W . . . .

1. The option of the PERFORM that is particularly useful for iterative references to subscripted entries is the PERFORM ... _____ option.

VARYING

FIGURE 18-7
The PERFORM . . . VARYING
Option with TEST AFTER

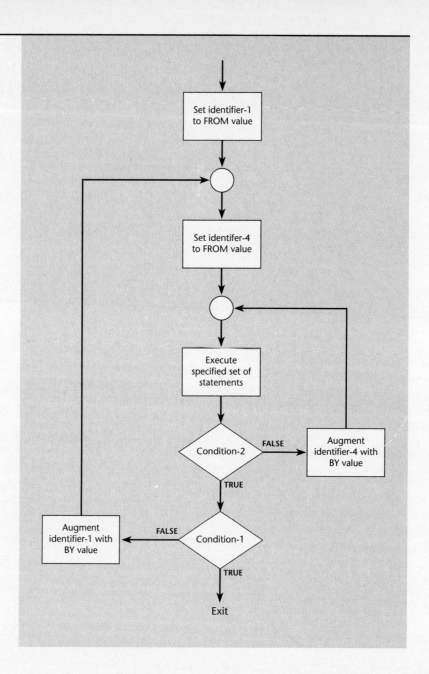

2. If there are two categories in the first dimension of a table, three in the second, and two in the third, addition of all values in the table involves the summation of _____ (number) values.

$$2 \times 3 \times 2 = 12$$

3. The option of the PERFORM by which specified statements are executed at least once before testing whether or not execution should be repeated is the [WITH TEST BEFORE / WITH TEST AFTER] option.

WITH TEST AFTER

4. If neither the BEFORE nor AFTER option is specified in conjunction with a test contained in a PERFORM statement, the default is the [BEFORE / AFTER] option.

BEFORE

FIGURE 18-8
Illustration of TEST BEFORE and TEST AFTER Options

```
Use of TEST BEFORE                    Use of TEST AFTER

    PERFORM LISTING                       PERFORM LISTING
        WITH TEST BEFORE                      WITH TEST AFTER
        VARYING I FROM 1 BY 1                 VARYING I FROM 1 BY 1
            UNTIL I > 2                           UNTIL I > 2
            AFTER J FROM 1 BY 1                   AFTER J FROM 1 BY 1
                UNTIL J > 3.                          UNTIL J > 3.
    LISTING.                              LISTING.
        DISPLAY I J.                          DISPLAY I J.


Resulting Output                      Resulting Output

    I    J                                I    J
    --------                              --------
    1    1                                1    1
    1    2                                1    2
    1    3                                1    3
    2    1                                1    4
    2    2                                2    1
    2    3                                2    2
                                          2    3
                                          2    4
                                          3    1
                                          3    2
                                          3    3
                                          3    4
```

5. If procedure-name-1 is omitted in a PERFORM ... VARYING statement, thus constituting an in-line PERFORM, then the AFTER phrase following the VARYING [must / cannot] be used.

cannot

·   ·   ·   ·   ·   ·   ·   ·   ·   ·   ·   ·   ·   ·   ·   ·   ·   ·   ·

SAMPLE PROGRAM WITH A TWO-LEVEL TABLE

Suppose that data records contain a quarter value in column 1, a region value in column 2, and a sales amount in columns 3-5. We want to read such a file and produce a report that presents sales by quarter and region, as illustrated below.

```
                              REGION
    QUARTER    EAST      SOUTH     MIDWEST    WEST
       1      ZZ,ZZZ    ZZ,ZZZ    ZZ,ZZZ    ZZ,ZZZ
       2        .         .         .         .
       3        .         .         .         .
       4        .         .         .         .
```

Figure 18-9 presents a program to accomplish the task. Notice the definition of the output HEADER-2. Four FILLER fields were used to define the report heading. In the case of the first and fourth FILLER we chose to combine two words in the

VALUE. We could just as well have used six FILLERs, one for each of the five words in the heading and one for the 6-column blank field, or we could have used one long FILLER whose VALUE could have been the entire heading.

The sales data are accumulated in a two-dimensional table, as indicated by the following description included in the WORKING-STORAGE SECTION:

```
01  SALES-TABLE.
    02  QUARTER-DATA OCCURS 4 TIMES
        03  SALES    OCCURS 4 TIMES PIC 9(5).
```

The 020-READ-ACCUMULATE procedure accumulates the total sales data by use of the instruction

```
ADD AMOUNT TO SALES (QUARTER, REGION)
```

which uses the values stored in the input record fields QUARTER and REGION to add the value in AMOUNT to the appropriate cell in the table. Since we are adding to existing values, in the 000-MAIN-ROUTINE we made sure to MOVE ZERO TO SALES-TABLE to zero-fill the entire table before we start adding to it.

Outputting the totals requires two nested PERFORM ... VARYING statements:

```
000-MAIN-ROUTINE.
    .
    .
    .
    PERFORM 040-PRINT-TABLE VARYING QUARTER FROM 1 BY 1
            UNTIL QUARTER IS GREATER THAN 4
    .
    .
    .
040-PRINT-TABLE.
    MOVE SPACES TO OUTPUT-LINE
    PERFORM 050-MOVE-DATA VARYING REGION FROM 1 BY 1
            UNTIL REGION IS GREATER THAN 4
    .
    .
    .
050-MOVE-DATA.
    MOVE SALES (QUARTER, REGION) TO REGION-OUT (REGION).
```

The outer PERFORM varies QUARTER, while the inner one varies REGION. Thus, while QUARTER has a value of 1, REGION varies through 1, 2, 3, 4, and the accumulated sales for the first quarter in SALES-TABLE are transferred to the four REGION-OUT fields in OUTPUT-LINE. In the 040-PRINT-TABLE in Figure 18-9, notice that the statement MOVE QUARTER TO QUARTER-OUT is executed after the inner loop has been executed 4 times; we need to move the quarter number only once for each four region sales values. Similarly, the WRITE statement in 040-PRINT-TABLE is executed once for each quarter.

Instead of writing as many nested PERFORMs as we have levels in the table, we could write one PERFORM that includes the AFTER clause, as illustrated below. However, note that this alternative requires some conditional logic in the 040-PRINT-TABLE procedure to test whether we have completed moving the data for the quarter and we are ready to print a line of output.

FIGURE 18-9
Program for a Quarterly Report

```
IDENTIFICATION DIVISION.
PROGRAM-ID. TABLES.
*
ENVIRONMENT DIVISION.
*
CONFIGURATION SECTION.
SOURCE-COMPUTER.  ABC-480.
OBJECT-COMPUTER.  ABC-480.
*
INPUT-OUTPUT SECTION.
FILE-CONTROL.
*
    SELECT INPUT-FILE  ASSIGN TO CARD.
    SELECT OUTPUT-FILE ASSIGN TO PRINTER.
*
DATA DIVISION.
*
FILE SECTION.
*
FD  INPUT-FILE  LABEL RECORDS OMITTED
                DATA RECORD IS INPUT-RECORD.
01  INPUT-RECORD.
    02  QUARTER            PIC 9.
    02  REGION             PIC 9.
    02  AMOUNT             PIC 999.
    02  FILLER             PIC X(75).
*
FD  OUTPUT-FILE LABEL RECORD IS OMITTED
                DATA RECORD IS OUTPUT-RECORD.
01  OUTPUT-RECORD          PIC X(132).
*
WORKING-STORAGE SECTION.
*
01  END-OF-DATA           PIC XXX.
*
01  SALES-TABLE.
    02  QUARTER-DATA       OCCURS 4 TIMES.
        03  SALES          OCCURS 4 TIMES  PIC 9(5).
*
01  HEADER-1.
    02  FILLER            PIC X(27) VALUE SPACES.
    02  FILLER            PIC X(6)  VALUE 'REGION'.
*
01  HEADER-2.
    02  FILLER            PIC X(17) VALUE
        ' QUARTER     EAST'.
    02  FILLER            PIC X(6)  VALUE SPACES.
    02  FILLER            PIC X(9)  VALUE 'SOUTH    '.
    02  FILLER            PIC X(15) VALUE 'MIDWEST    WEST'.
*
```

FIGURE 18-9

Program for a Quarterly Report
(continued)

```
01   OUTPUT-LINE.
     02   FILLER              PIC X(5).
     02   QUARTER-OUT         PIC 9.
     02   FILLER              PIC X(4).
     02   DATA-OUT            OCCURS 4 TIMES.
          03   FILLER         PIC XX.
          03   REGION-OUT     PIC ZZ,ZZZ.
          03   FILLER         PIC XX.
*
 PROCEDURE DIVISION.
*
 000-MAIN-ROUTINE.
     OPEN INPUT INPUT-FILE
          OUTPUT OUTPUT-FILE
     MOVE 'NO' TO END-OF-DATA
     MOVE ZERO TO SALES-TABLE.
*
     PERFORM 010-READ-DATA.
*
     PERFORM 020-READ-ACCUMULATE
         UNTIL END-OF-DATA = 'YES'
*
     PERFORM 030-HEADERS
*
     PERFORM 040-PRINT-TABLE VARYING QUARTER FROM 1 BY 1
                             UNTIL QUARTER IS GREATER THAN 4
*
     CLOSE INPUT-FILE, OUTPUT-FILE.
*
     STOP RUN.
*
 010-READ-DATA.
     READ INPUT-FILE
         AT END MOVE 'YES' TO END-OF-DATA.
*
 020-READ-ACCUMULATE.
     ADD AMOUNT TO SALES (QUARTER, REGION)
     PERFORM 010-READ-DATA.
*
 030-HEADERS.
     WRITE OUTPUT-RECORD FROM HEADER-1 AFTER PAGE
     WRITE OUTPUT-RECORD FROM HEADER-2 AFTER 3 LINES.
*
 040-PRINT-TABLE.
     MOVE SPACES TO OUTPUT-LINE
     PERFORM 050-MOVE-DATA VARYING REGION FROM 1 BY 1
                           UNTIL REGION IS GREATER THAN 4
*
     MOVE QUARTER TO QUARTER-OUT
     WRITE OUTPUT-RECORD FROM OUTPUT-LINE
         AFTER ADVANCING 2 LINES.
*
 050-MOVE-DATA.
     MOVE SALES (QUARTER, REGION) TO REGION-OUT (REGION).
```

```
                    MOVE SPACES TO OUTPUT-LINE
                    PERFORM 040-PRINT-TABLE VARYING QUARTER FROM 1 BY 1
                                    UNTIL QUARTER > 4
                                AFTER REGION FROM 1 BY 1
                                    UNTIL REGION > 4
                    .
                    .
                    .
            040-PRINT-TABLE.
                MOVE SALES (QUARTER, REGION) TO REGION-OUT (REGION)
                IF  REGION = 4
                    MOVE QUARTER TO QUARTER-OUT
                    WRITE OUTPUT-RECORD FROM OUTPUT-LINE
                        AFTER ADVANCING 2 LINES
                    MOVE SPACES TO OUTPUT-LINE.
```

The test IF REGION = 4 determines whether we have completed moving the sales data for the fourth region, at which point we are ready to print a report line and clear the OUTPUT-LINE to get it ready for the data of the next quarter. Of course, you should have noticed that we placed a MOVE SPACES TO OUTPUT-LINE prior to the PERFORM statement to make sure that we started with a cleared output field.

By the above alternate code we have eliminated the need for the separate 050-MOVE-DATA paragraph, and we have written one compound PERFORM ... VARYING ... AFTER statement instead of two simpler nested ones. On the other hand, we had to introduce some additional logic in the 040-PRINT-TABLE procedure. It is difficult to generalize about when to choose one approach versus the other. The main point is to understand both and be at ease using either approach, depending on specific circumstances.

SAMPLE PROGRAM WITH A THREE-LEVEL TABLE

Figure 18-10 presents the listing of a program that illustrates the processing of a three-dimensional table. The program task is to read source data representing enrollment statistics and to accumulate the enrollment in a three-dimensional ENROLLMENT-TABLE. As can be seen in the definition of the table, the data is organized by semester, within department, within college.

```
            01  ENROLLMENT-TABLE.
                02  COLLEGE-DATA OCCURS 3 TIMES.
                    03  DEPARTMENT-DATA OCCURS 4 TIMES
                        04  SEMESTER-DATA OCCURS 2 TIMES.
                            05  ENROLLMENT PIC 9(4).
```

Each input record in SOURCE-FILE contains data for NUMBER-ENROLLED relating to the categories of college, department, and semester designated by the data-names COLLEGE-IN, DEPT-IN, and SEMESTER-IN. The 030-LOAD-DATA routine contains the characteristic instruction

```
            ADD NUMBER-ENROLLED TO
                ENROLLMENT (COLLEGE-IN, DEPT-IN, SEMESTER-IN).
```

which accumulates the input data in the three-level table in working storage.

As always when dealing with accumulators, we must make certain that their initial values are zero. Paragraph 010-ZERO-ENROLLMENT-TABLES was written

FIGURE 18-10

Sample Program with a Three-Level Table

```
      IDENTIFICATION DIVISION.
      PROGRAM-ID. TBL3D.
     *
      ENVIRONMENT DIVISION.
     *
      CONFIGURATION SECTION.
      SOURCE-COMPUTER.  ABC-480.
      OBJECT-COMPUTER.  ABC-480.
     *
      INPUT-OUTPUT SECTION.
      FILE-CONTROL.
     *
          SELECT SOURCE-FILE   ASSIGN TO CARD.
     *
      DATA DIVISION.
     *
      FILE SECTION.
     *
      FD  SOURCE-FILE
          LABEL RECORDS OMITTED
          DATA RECORD IS SOURCE-RECORD.
      01  SOURCE-RECORD.
          02  COLLEGE-IN                  PIC 9.
          02  DEPT-IN                     PIC 9.
          02  SEMESTER-IN                 PIC 9.
          02  NUMBER-ENROLLED             PIC 99.
          02  FILLER                      PIC X(75).
     *
      WORKING-STORAGE SECTION.
     *
      01  ENROLLMENT-TABLE.
     *
          02  COLLEGE-DATA                OCCURS 3 TIMES.
     *
              03  DEPARTMENT-DATA         OCCURS 4 TIMES.
     *
                  04  SEMESTER-DATA       OCCURS 2 TIMES.
     *
                      05  ENROLLMENT      PIC 9(4).
     *
      01  END-OF-FILE                     PIC XXX VALUE 'NO'.
     *
      01  SUBSCRIPTS.
          02  COLLEGE                     PIC 9.
          02  DEPT                        PIC 9.
          02  SEMESTER                    PIC 9.
     *
      01  TOTALS-TABLES.
          02  COLLEGE-TOTALS-TABLE.
              03  COLLEGE-TOTALS-DATA     OCCURS 3 TIMES.
                  04  FILLER              PIC XXX.
                  04  COLLEGE-TOTALS      PIC 9(4).
     *
```

FIGURE 18-10
Sample Program with a Three-Level Table (continued)

```
          02  DEPT-TOTALS-TABLE.
              03  DEPT-TOTALS-DATA        OCCURS 4 TIMES.
                  04  FILLER              PIC XXX.
                  04  DEPT-TOTALS         PIC 9(4).
      *
          02  SEMESTER-TOTALS-TABLE.
              03  SEMESTER-TOTALS-DATA    OCCURS 2 TIMES.
                  04  FILLER              PIC XXX.
                  04  SEMESTER-TOTALS     PIC 9(4).
      *
          02  ENROLLMENT-TOTAL            PIC 9(4).
      *
      /
       PROCEDURE DIVISION.
      *
       000-MAIN-ROUTINE.
           OPEN INPUT SOURCE-FILE
           PERFORM 010-ZERO-ENROLLMENT-TABLES
           PERFORM 020-READ-DATA
           PERFORM 030-LOAD-DATA UNTIL END-OF-FILE = 'YES'
      *
           PERFORM 040-COLLEGE-SUM
           PERFORM 060-DEPARTMENT-SUM
           PERFORM 080-SEMESTER-SUM
           PERFORM 100-TOTAL-ENROLLMENT-SUM
      *
           CLOSE SOURCE-FILE
           STOP RUN.
      *
       010-ZERO-ENROLLMENT-TABLES.
           MOVE SPACES TO COLLEGE-TOTALS-TABLE
                          DEPT-TOTALS-TABLE
                          SEMESTER-TOTALS-TABLE
           INITIALIZE  ENROLLMENT-TOTAL
                          ENROLLMENT-TABLE
                          COLLEGE-TOTALS-TABLE
                          DEPT-TOTALS-TABLE
                          SEMESTER-TOTALS-TABLE.
      *
       020-READ-DATA.
           READ SOURCE-FILE RECORD
                AT END MOVE 'YES' TO END-OF-FILE.
      *
       030-LOAD-DATA.
           ADD NUMBER-ENROLLED TO
                ENROLLMENT (COLLEGE-IN, DEPT-IN, SEMESTER-IN).
           PERFORM 020-READ-DATA.
      *
       040-COLLEGE-SUM.
           PERFORM 050-ACCUMULATE-COLLEGE-TOTALS
                VARYING COLLEGE FROM 1 BY 1
                        UNTIL COLLEGE > 3
      *
```

FIGURE 18-10

Sample Program with a Three-Level Table (continued)

```
                    AFTER DEPT FROM 1 BY 1
                        UNTIL DEPT > 4
*
                    AFTER SEMESTER FROM 1 BY 1
                        UNTIL SEMESTER > 2.
*
        DISPLAY 'COLLEGE TOTALS   ', COLLEGE-TOTALS-TABLE.
*
    050-ACCUMULATE-COLLEGE-TOTALS.
        ADD ENROLLMENT (COLLEGE, DEPT, SEMESTER)
            TO COLLEGE-TOTALS (COLLEGE).
*
    060-DEPARTMENT-SUM.
        PERFORM 070-ACCUMULATE-DEPT-TOTALS
            VARYING DEPT FROM 1 BY 1
                    UNTIL DEPT > 4
*
                AFTER COLLEGE FROM 1 BY 1
                    UNTIL COLLEGE > 3
*
                AFTER SEMESTER FROM 1 BY 1
                    UNTIL SEMESTER > 2.
*
        DISPLAY 'DEPARTMENT TOTALS', DEPT-TOTALS-TABLE.
*
    070-ACCUMULATE-DEPT-TOTALS.
        ADD ENROLLMENT (COLLEGE, DEPT, SEMESTER)
            TO DEPT-TOTALS (DEPT).
*
    080-SEMESTER-SUM.
        PERFORM 090-ACCUMULATE-SEM-TOTALS
            VARYING SEMESTER FROM 1 BY 1
                    UNTIL SEMESTER > 2
*
                    AFTER COLLEGE FROM 1 BY 1
                        UNTIL COLLEGE > 3
*
                        AFTER DEPT FROM 1 BY 1
                            UNTIL DEPT > 4.
*
        DISPLAY 'SEMESTER TOTALS  ', SEMESTER-TOTALS-TABLE.
*
    090-ACCUMULATE-SEM-TOTALS.
        ADD ENROLLMENT (COLLEGE, DEPT, SEMESTER)
                TO SEMESTER-TOTALS (SEMESTER).
*
    100-TOTAL-ENROLLMENT-SUM.
        PERFORM 110-CALCULATE-ENROLLMENT-TOTAL
            VARYING COLLEGE FROM 1 BY 1
                    UNTIL COLLEGE > 3
                AFTER DEPT FROM 1 BY 1
                        UNTIL DEPT > 4
*
```

FIGURE 18-10
Sample Program with a Three-Level Table (continued)

```
                              AFTER SEMESTER FROM 1 BY 1
                                       UNTIL SEMESTER > 2.
   *
        DISPLAY 'TOTAL ENROLLMENT     ', ENROLLMENT-TOTAL.
   *
     110-CALCULATE-ENROLLMENT-TOTAL.
        ADD ENROLLMENT (COLLEGE, DEPT, SEMESTER)
                    TO ENROLLMENT-TOTAL.
```

to so initialize the tables into which we accumulate the sums. Additionally, we want to blank-fill the FILLER fields in COLLEGE-TOTALS-TABLE, DEPT-TOTALS-TABLE, and SEMESTER-TOTAL-TABLE. Thus we first moved spaces to these three tables, filling their entirety. Then we used the INITIALIZE statement to move zeros to ENROLLMENT-TOTAL, ENROLLMENT-TABLE, and the three tables referenced above. The INITIALIZE does not initialize FILLER fields. Therefore the MOVE SPACES statement in the 010-paragraph filled the three tables with spaces. The INITIALIZE that follows moved zeros *selectively* to the numeric fields. In the absence of the INITIALIZE statement, as in COBOL '74, we would need to write a loop to MOVE ZERO TO each of the three COLLEGE-TOTALS (I, J, K), for instance.

After all the input data have been accumulated through iterative execution of 030-LOAD-DATA, then there are four illustrative modules: 040-COLLEGE-SUM, 060-DEPARTMENT-SUM, 080-SEMESTER-SUM, 100-TOTAL-ENROLLMENT-SUM. The first one, 040-COLLEGE-SUM, forms the enrollment total for each of the three colleges in a WORKING-STORAGE table called COLLEGE-TOTALS-TABLE. Notice use of the VARYING ... AFTER ... AFTER construct. When the accumulation has been completed, we simply DISPLAY the contents of COLLEGE-TOTALS-TABLE to simplify the program, since our objective is to illustrate the table-processing logic rather than the output format.

The second module, 060-DEPARTMENT-SUM, specifies ... VARYING DEPT ... AFTER COLLEGE ... AFTER SEMESTER. Contrast this to the PERFORM statement in 040-COLLEGE-SUM and notice that since we are accessing all the data in the table, the order in which we vary the subscripts does not matter.

The other two modules, 080-SEMESTER-SUM and 100-TOTAL-ENROLL-MENT-SUM, are similar in structure to the first two modules. It should be commented that there is known repetition in the program. Actually, one PERFORM ... VARYING statement would be sufficient to accumulate all four totals by a paragraph such as the following:

```
ACCUMULATE-TOTALS.
    ADD ENROLLMENT (COLLEGE, DEPT, SEMESTER)
        TO COLLEGE-TOTALS (COLLEGE)
            DEPT-TOTALS (DEPT)
            SEMESTER-TOTALS (SEMESTER)
            ENROLLMENT-TOTAL.
```

The program in Figure 18-10 treats each accumulation task independently of the others to provide an illustration of how we could access all the data by each respective category, or dimension. Although the illustration has to do with accumulation of totals, the processing logic would remain essentially the same regardless of the specific task.

SUMMARY

Whereas Chapter 12 covered single-level table handling, this chapter covered multilevel table handling.

The number of levels, or dimensions, refers to the number of groups of categories by which the data are organized. Two-level tables, for example, require two subscripts to locate a particular entry in the table. The PICTURE clause applies only to the lowest hierarchical level of a multilevel table, which is the level of the individual entry. The maximum number of levels for table data is 3 levels in COBOL '74 and 7 levels in COBOL '85.

The number of data categories at each level, or dimension, of a table is indicated in the OCCURS clause for that hierarchical level. Data for multi-dimensional tables are stored in the *one-dimensional* computer storage. By a matter of logic or use of the appropriate mathematical formula, we can determine the position of a table entry in the one-dimensional storage. Similarly, we can also determine the byte positions of a given table entry relative to the beginning of the table.

Use of the VARYING option with the PERFORM verb makes it possible to have iterative references to the subscripted table entries, with associated repetitive execution of program modules for each entry. The option of the PERFORM by which specified program statements are executed at least once before testing for whether or not program execution should be repeated is the WITH TEST AFTER. The option by which the referenced statements may not be executed at all is the WITH TEST BEFORE. The default option is the WITH TEST BEFORE.

The chapter concluded with two sample programs. The first program was concerned with a two-level table, for sales classified by quarter and region. The second sample program was concerned with a three-dimensional table, for student enrollment by college, department, and semester.

EXERCISES

18.1   Consider the following table definition:

```
01  TABLE.
    02  A OCCURS h TIMES.
        03  B OCCURS i TIMES.
            04  C OCCURS j TIMES.
                05  D OCCURS k TIMES.
                    06  T PIC p.   (where p = field length)
```

For a reference such as T (H, I, J, K), develop a formula to compute the displacement value from the start of the table to determine the first byte of the T (H, I, J, K) field.

As a test case, check to determine that your formula agrees with the following: If h = 50, i = 10, j = 100, k = 5, and p = 1, then T (3, 2, 20, 4) begins at byte 10599, counting the first byte in the table as 1.

18.2   A marketing survey conducted by a company involved administering a questionnaire of 25 questions. The responses to each question have been coded by a 1-digit code, ranging from 0 to 9. We want to accumulate a table of the responses to each of the 25 questions, as shown in Figure 18-11.

Write DATA DIVISION entries to form such a table. It should be possible to make reference to each individual cell in the table, as well as each row (question).

FIGURE 18-11
Required Table for Exercise 18.2

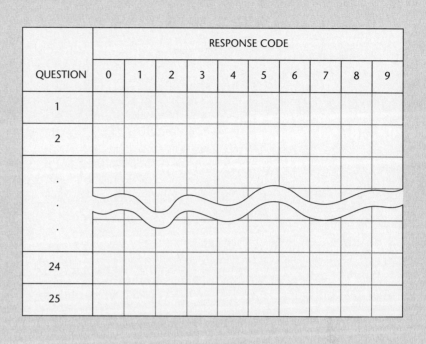

18.3 Suppose that the table described in the following contains 20 values:

```
01  SALES-DATA-TABLE.
    02  SALES-TERRITORY    OCCURS 5 TIMES.
        03  QUARTER-SALES  OCCURS 4 TIMES
                           PIC 9(6)V99.
```

We wish to print the table values with the rows representing quarters and the columns representing sales territories. Write the necessary program instructions.

18.4 Sales records contain data as follows:

COLUMNS	DATA
1–5	Amount (whole dollar)
6	Region code: 1 = West, 2 = Midwest
	3 = South, 4 = East
7–8	Month code (numeric)

We want to read in the data and produce the sales analysis report illustrated in Figure 18-12. Input records that contain error region codes, error month codes, or nonnumeric amounts should be excluded from the tabulation and are to be printed separately with a suitable error message, as shown in Figure 18-13.

Write a program to produce such a sales analysis and error report.

FIGURE 18-12
Sales Analysis Report

```
ACME CORPORATION
SALES ANALYSIS REPORT


                                                           MONTHLY      PERCENT OF
    MONTH       WEST      MIDWEST     SOUTH        EAST      TOTAL      YEAR TOTAL


JANUARY         332          85        157          20        594          1.79
FEBRUARY        356         504        470         300      1,630          4.90
MARCH           170         200        435         201      1,006          3.03
APRIL             0         200        142           0        342          1.03
MAY               0       1,240          0         195      1,435          4.32
JUNE            110         500          0         190        800          2.41
JULY              0         150      1,371         967      2,488          7.48
AUGUST          160         375        417         118      1,070          3.22
SEPTEMBER       692           0      1,050         227      1,969          5.92
OCTOBER         256           0          0      20,296     20,552         61.81
NOVEMBER          0         440        163          30        633          1.90
DECEMBER        115         150        272         193        730          2.20


TOTAL         2,191       3,844      4,477      22,737     33,249        100.00


PERCENT
OF TOTAL       6.58       11.56      13.46       68.38     100.00
```

FIGURE 18-13
Error Report for the Sales Analysis Program of Exercise 18.4

```
                            SOURCE DATA ERRORS

RECORD NO.     RECORD     REGION ERROR   MONTH ERROR   AMOUNT ERROR

    3         00152220                        X
   14         00202100                        X
   15         0015412                         X
   36         00040004         X
   41         00030704         X
   49         /560507          X                             X
   54         70082 01         X


NO. OF ERROR RECORDS =      7
```

18.5   A source file contains data of the following form:

COLUMNS	FIELD
1	Store i.d. (M = Metro, F = Fiesta)
2	Day of the week (1 = Sunday, 2 = Monday, etc.)
3–4	Month (1 = January, etc.)
5–7	Amount of sale (no decimal places)

Assume that the data have been edited so there is no need to check for errors. Write your program with the assumption that all the data are correct.

The program will output a report such as the one illustrated in Figure 18-14.

Notice in the output sample in Figure 18-14 that monthly sales are grouped together into quarters of the year. The program should read each source record, determine its classification, and add the amount of the sale to the corresponding location in the table. For example, if the month value in the input record is 5, we would translate that to a subscript value of 2 since sales data for the 5th month are included in the second grouping (APR-JUN).

The source records are not in any particular order, and there could be more than one record for a given store, day of the week, and month. For example, there could be two records for the Metro store on Sundays in January. In the sample output in Figure 18-14 the value of 50 in the top left corner could be the result of having read in one record with the amount value of 50, or it could be the summation of any number of amounts.

FIGURE 18-14
Required Output for Exercise 18.5

	JAN–MAR		APR–JUN		JUL–SEP		OCT–DEC		DAILY TOTAL		TOTAL	% OF YR. TOTAL	
	American Sales Corporation — Annual Sales by Quarter and Day of the Week												
DAY	METRO	FIESTA	METRO	FIESTA	METRO	FIESTA	METRO	FIESTA	METRO	FIESTA		METRO	FIESTA
SUNDAY	50	30	20	0	30	10	40	20	140	60	200	5%	2%
MONDAY													
.													
.													
.													
SATURDAY													
TOTAL	120	80							1000	2000	3000		
% OF QUARTER TOTAL	60%	40%							33%	66%	100%		

Some data are included in the table to clarify the meaning of the totals and percentages required. For example, the 2% at the extreme right of the SUNDAY row is computed by dividing the total Sunday sales at the Fiesta store (60) by the total sales of the year (3000) and converting to a percentage.

Because this is an extensive assignment, we provide a precoded program in Figure 18-15, excluding the PROCEDURE DIVISION. In particular, you will find the DATA DIVISION to merit some study. We want to print lines consisting of asterisks in lieu of the solid lines used in the table in Figure 18-14. For example, notice HEADING-3, HEADING-6, and OUTPUT-LINE, among many others, involving * characters in the defined formats.

For the most part the data-names used are self-documenting. However, there is one table that needs some explanation:

```
02  STORE-QUART-TOTALS   OCCURS 5 TIMES.
    03  STORE-QUART-TOT  OCCURS 2 TIMES PIC 9(4)V99.
```

Although the report refers to four quarters, we also note that the DAILY TOTAL grouping is logically equivalent to a fifth quarter. Thus in the above definition we say STORE-QUART-TOTALS OCCURS 5 TIMES. Similarly, in OUTPUT-LINE and several other instances, we have defined tables with five entries to simplify the programming. An alternative would be to define two tables in each case, one for the data in the four quarters, and the other for the totals for the four quarters.

Finally, as a way of demonstrating use of some of the data definitions provided, we include an excerpt from our program that does the required task:

```
        PERFORM 230-COMPUTE-STORE-PERCENTS
                VARYING DAY-NO FROM 1 BY 1
                    UNTIL DAY-NO > 7
                AFTER STORE-NO FROM 1 BY 1
                    UNTIL STORE-NO > 2
  *
    230-COMPUTE-STORE-PERCENTS.
        COMPUTE STORE-PERCENT (DAY-NO, STORE-NO) ROUNDED =
            100.0 * ( STORE-DAY-TOTAL (DAY-NO, STORE-NO)
                    / SALES-GRAND-TOTAL).
```

The above code computes the percent values that will be printed in the last two columns of the report.

18.6 We want to write a program to read in numeric data and to output a bar chart depicting the frequency as percent values. Input consists of records of three types: The first record contains a free-form report header. The second record contains three parameter values:

1. The number of classes in the bar chart.

2. The limiting value of the first class: All values equal to or less than this limiting value will be grouped in the first class.

3. The class size: This parameter defines the range of values that constitute a class, or group.

FIGURE 18-15
First Three Divisions of the COBOL Program for Exercise 18.5

```
        IDENTIFICATION DIVISION.
        PROGRAM-ID. STORE-SALES.
*
        ENVIRONMENT DIVISION.
        CONFIGURATION SECTION.
        SOURCE-COMPUTER.  ABC-480.
        OBJECT-COMPUTER.  ABC-480.
*
        INPUT-OUTPUT SECTION.
        FILE-CONTROL.
            SELECT SOURCE-FILE ASSIGN TO Input File
            SELECT REPORT-FILE ASSIGN TO Printer.
*
        DATA DIVISION.
*
        FILE SECTION.
*
        FD  SOURCE-FILE    LABEL RECORDS STANDARD
                           RECORD CONTAINS 7 CHARACTERS
                           DATA RECORD IS SOURCE-RECORD.
        01  SOURCE-RECORD.
            02  STORE-NAME-IN     PIC X.
            02  DAY-NO-IN         PIC 9.
            02  MONTH-NO-IN       PIC 99.
            02  AMOUNT            PIC 9(3).
*
        FD  REPORT-FILE    LABEL RECORDS OMITTED.
*
        01  REPORT-REC            PIC X(102).
*
        WORKING-STORAGE SECTION.
*
        01  END-OF-DATA-TEST      PIC X(3) VALUE 'NO '.
            88  END-OF-FILE   VALUE 'YES'.
*
        01  SUBSCRIPTS.
            02  QUARTER-NO         PIC 9.
            02  DAY-NO             PIC 9.
            02  STORE-NO           PIC 9.
*
        01  DAY-NAMES-1.
            02  FILLER             PIC X(9) VALUE 'SUNDAY   '.
            02  FILLER             PIC X(9) VALUE 'MONDAY   '.
            02  FILLER             PIC X(9) VALUE 'TUESDAY  '.
            02  FILLER             PIC X(9) VALUE 'WEDNESDAY'.
            02  FILLER             PIC X(9) VALUE 'THURSDAY '.
            02  FILLER             PIC X(9) VALUE 'FRIDAY   '.
            02  FILLER             PIC X(9) VALUE 'SATURDAY '.
*
        01  DAY-NAMES-2 REDEFINES DAY-NAMES-1.
            02  DAY-NAME OCCURS 7 TIMES PIC X(9).
*
```

FIGURE 18-15
*First Three Divisions of the COBOL
Program for Exercise 18.5
(continued)*

```
   01   SALES-DATA-TABLES.
*
      02   SALES-TABLE.
         03   QUARTERLY-DATA      OCCURS 4 TIMES.
            04   DAILY-DATA       OCCURS 7 TIMES.
               05   STORE-DATA OCCURS 2 TIMES.
                  06   STORE-SALES PIC 9(4).
*
      02   DAY-TOTAL-DATA         OCCURS 7 TIMES.
         03   STORE-DAY-TOTAL     OCCURS 2 TIMES PIC 9(4).
      02   DAY-GRAND-TOTAL        OCCURS 7 TIMES PIC 9(4).
      02   YEAR-PERCENTS          OCCURS 7 TIMES.
         03 STORE-PERCENT         OCCURS 2 TIMES PIC 999.
*
      02   STORE-QUART-TOTALS     OCCURS 5 TIMES.
         03   STORE-QUART-TOT     OCCURS 2 TIMES PIC 9(4)V99.
      02   SALES-GRAND-TOTAL                  PIC 9(4)V99.
      02   STORE-QUART-PERCNTS    OCCURS 5 TIMES.
         03   STORE-QUART-PRCNT   OCCURS 2 TIMES PIC 999.
*
   01   REPORT-HEADINGS.
*
      02   HEADING-1.
         03   FILLER PIC X(37) VALUE SPACES.
         03   FILLER PIC X(26) VALUE
               'AMERICAN SALES CORPORATION'.
*
      02   HEADING-2.
         03   FILLER PIC X(29) VALUE SPACES.
         03   FILLER PIC X(43) VALUE
               'ANNUAL SALES BY QUARTER AND DAY OF THE WEEK'.
*
      02   HEADING-3.
         03   FILLER PIC X(9)  VALUE SPACES.
         03   FILLER PIC X(78) VALUE ALL '*'.
         03   HD-3-L PIC X(14) VALUE ALL '*'.
*
      02   HEADING-4.
         03   FILLER PIC X(9)  VALUE SPACE.
         03   FILLER PIC X(14) VALUE '*  JAN - MAR  '.
         03   FILLER PIC X(14) VALUE '*  APR - JUN  '.
         03   FILLER PIC X(14) VALUE '*  JUL - SEP  '.
         03   FILLER PIC X(14) VALUE '*  OCT - DEC  '.
         03   FILLER PIC X(21) VALUE '*    DAILY TOTAL    '.
         03   FILLER PIC X(15) VALUE '* % OF YR-TOT *'.
*
      02   HEADING-5.
         03   FILLER PIC X(9)  VALUE SPACES.
         03   FILLER PIC X(70) VALUE ALL '* METRO*FIESTA'.
         03   FILLER PIC X(22) VALUE
               '* TOTAL* METRO*FIESTA*'.
*
```

FIGURE 18-15

First Three Divisions of the COBOL
Program for Exercise 18.5
(continued)

```
        02  HEADING-6.
            03  HD-6-NAME PIC X(9) VALUE SPACES.
            03  FILLER PIC X(79) VALUE ALL '*      *      '.
            03  HD-6-L PIC X(13) VALUE '     *      *'.
    *
    01  OUTPUT-LINE.
        02  DAY-NAME-OUT    PIC X(9).
        02  OUT-1 PIC X(70) VALUE ALL '*      '.
        02  OUT-2 REDEFINES OUT-1.
            03  QUART-DATA-OUT  OCCURS 5 TIMES.
                04  STORE-DATA-OUT OCCURS 2 TIMES.
                    05  FILLER PIC X.
                    05  SALES-OUT PIC Z,ZZZ.
                    05  FILLER PIC X.
        02  FILLER    PIC X VALUE '*'.
        02  DAY-TOT-OUT   PIC ZZ,ZZZ.
        02  FILLER  PIC XX VALUE '* '.
        02  YR-PCNT-OUT-1 PIC X(14) VALUE ALL ' % * '.
        02  YR-PRCNT-OUT-DATA REDEFINES YR-PCNT-OUT-1.
            03  STORE-YR-PRCNT-OUT-DATA OCCURS 2 TIMES.
            04  STORE-YR-PRCNT-OUT  PIC ZZ9.
            04  FILLER              PIC X(4).
    *
    01  QUART-TOT-OUT-DATA.
        02  TOT-NAME-OUT   PIC X(9).
        02  Q-TOT-OUT-1 PIC X(78) VALUE ALL '*    '.
        02  Q-TOT-OUT-2 REDEFINES Q-TOT-OUT-1.
            03  QUART-TOT-OUT  OCCURS 5 TIMES.
                04  STORE-TOT-OUT OCCURS 2 TIMES.
                    05 FILLER PIC X.
                    05 TOT-OUT PIC Z,ZZZ.
                    05 FILLER PIC X.
            03  FILLER PIC X.
            03  GRAND-TOT-OUT  PIC Z,ZZZ.
    *
    01  QUART-PRCNT-OUT-REC.
        02  QUART-NAME-OUT PIC X(9).
        02  Q-PCNT-OUT-1 PIC X(70) VALUE ALL '*    % '.
        02  QUART-PRCNT-OUT-DATA REDEFINES Q-PCNT-OUT-1.
            03  QUART-PRCNT-OUT OCCURS 5 TIMES.
                04  STORE-PRCNT-OUT OCCURS 2 TIMES.
                    05  FILLER PIC XX.
                    05  PRCNT-OUT  PIC ZZ9.
                    05  FILLER PIC XX.
    *
        02  FILLER              PIC XXX VALUE '* '.
        02  COL-100-PRCNT-OUT  PIC ZZZ.
        02  FILLER              PIC XX VALUE '%*'.
```

These three values are sufficient to define the bar chart. For instance, in the sample output of Figure 18-16 the number of classes was 5 (assume the maximum number of classes is 25). The limiting value of the lowest class was 1,000, while the class size is 2,000. Also notice that all values at or above 7,000 in the example are grouped in the highest class.

Write a program that reads in the header and the three parameter values discussed above as well as the data, and prints a bar chart such as shown in Figure 18-16.

The input data should have a PICTURE of S9(7) with 8 values per record. The program should check for nonnumeric data and print out those records that contain such data. However, spaces are not considered errors; they simply indicate the end of data. For instance, if we had 19 data values, there would be 8 values in the first record, 8 values in the second, and 3 values in the third record, followed by blanks. Your program should scan each record and sense the end of data when blanks are encountered. Figure 18-17 presents sample error message output for some records that happened to contain nonnumeric data.

Finally, your program should be capable of printing a statistical summary such as illustrated in Figure 18-18, showing the number of correct data values, the mean of these values, the minimum, and the maximum. The mean is the arithmetic average of the sum of all correct data values divided by the number of correct data values. Use the sample data in Figure 18-19 to check your program. It should give the output shown in Figures 18-16, 18-17, and 18-18.

FIGURE 18-16
Sample Bar Chart for Exercise 18.6

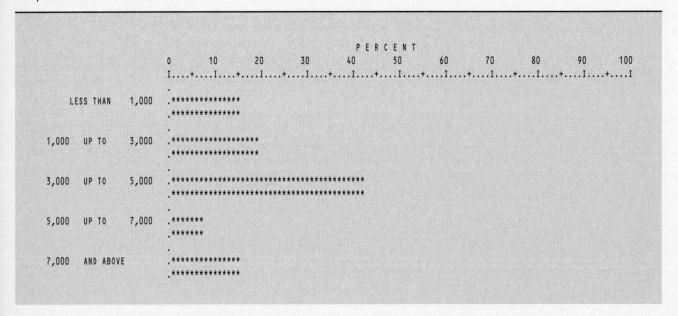

FIGURE 18-17

Sample Output Error Messages for Exercise 18.6

```
SAMPLE BAR CHART
INCORRECT DATA IN THIS CARD
ERROR       0007000    0008000    0002500    0001000    0002000
0007000    0004500
INCORRECT DATA IN THIS CARD
0004500    0003000    A003000    0004400
```

FIGURE 18-18

Sample Output Statistics for Exercise 18.6

```
S U M M A R Y   S T A T I S T I C S

NO. OF VALUES     =    26

MEAN              =     3,611

MINIMUM           =       400

MAXIMUM           =     8,000
```

FIGURE 18-19

Sample Input Data for Exercise 18.6

```
SAMPLE BAR CHART
0500010000002000
0000500    0000400    0003000    0004000    0002000    0001500
0006000    0008000
0000500    0000600    0004000    0003000    0003000    0006000
0004000    0003500
ERROR       0007000    0008000    0002500    0001000    0002000
0007000    0004500
0004500    0003000    A003000    0004400
```

19

Searching and Sorting Tables

I N **CHAPTERS 12 AND 18** *you studied the techniques for defining and processing one-level and higher-level tables. In this chapter you will be concerned with the process of searching tables for particular entries, and sorting such tables according to designated keys.*

*Two common methods that are used to search a table are **linear search** and **binary search.** You will begin by considering the rationale underlying each of these methods. Then you will study the COBOL language options that facilitate table searching, including examples of their use with both one-level and two-level tables. These major sections of the chapter conclude with a sample program that includes indexing and searching.*

*In the final section of this chapter you will study table sorting, which is called **internal sorting,** because the process of sorting is always applied to tables of data that have been entered into the central storage, as is the case for table searching. You will learn three approaches that are used to achieve the internal sorting of tables in this section.*

TABLE SEARCHING

The use of a dictionary to look up the meanings of words is perhaps the most common example of the need to search a table or file for particular entries. Other examples are a sales tax table used by a cashier, an income tax table used by a taxpayer, a rate table used by an electric utility to compute a customer's bill, a listing of rooms available in a hotel, and a list of tickets available for a theatre performance. A table is essentially a file of records. However, tables are short enough to be maintained in their entirety in central storage during program execution, whereas files require an external medium, such as disk or tape, for their storage. Where we *search* a file, it is often said that we *look up* a table.

A table, like a file, is a collection of related records. A record that is sought is always identified by a *key,* such as a part number, first and last name, and the like. A *table* is made up of a group of records, and each record has a field as the key, or identifier. Usually there are other data in the record in addition to the key, but sometimes the key field constitutes the entire record. In any event, the key is the relevant item of information from the standpoint of searching a table. To find a record in a table means to find a key that matches the key of the record being sought.

LINEAR SEARCH

Two common table searching methods are the linear search and the binary search.

In a linear search we employ the access method common to sequential files: beginning with the first record, we access all records in sequential order until the desired record is found or we encounter the end of the table. Application of linear search differs depending on whether the table being searched is known to be sorted in order. If the table is not in order, we search the table until we find the record being sought or we reach the end of the table. For example, assume that the key of the record we want is in REC-SOUGHT and that the table has been defined as follows:

```
02  UNSORTED-TABLE OCCURS 50 TIMES.
    05  RATE-CLASS    PIC X(6).
    05  RATE          PIC 9V99.
```

If we find a matching record in the table, we want to store the corresponding RATE to RATE-FOUND. We can write

```
MOVE 'NO' TO RECORD-FOUND-FLAG
PERFORM SEARCHING VARYING I FROM 1 BY 1
            UNTIL I > 50
                OR RECORD-FOUND.
SEARCHING.
    IF REC-SOUGHT = RATE-CLASS (I)
        MOVE RATE (I) TO RATE-FOUND
        MOVE 'YES' TO RECORD-FOUND-FLAG.
```

Alternately, using COBOL '85 features, we could write

```
SET RECORD-NOT-FOUND TO TRUE
PERFORM VARYING I FROM 1 BY 1
        UNTIL I > 50
            OR RECORD-FOUND
    IF REC-SOUGHT = RATE-CLASS (I)
        MOVE RATE (I) TO RATE-FOUND
        SET RECORD-FOUND TO TRUE
    END-IF
END-PERFORM.
```

If a table is known to be sorted in order, then there is no need to continue the search after we have reached a point in the table that the remaining records have a key value higher than the one being sought. Figure 19-1 presents the logic of linear search for a sorted table.

Assume that we want to search a table to find the entry that matches the content of a field named X. T is the name of the table and therefore $T(I)$ is a subscripted reference to the Ith entry of the table. The subscript I is initialized to a value of 1. We compare X, the key of the record we are seeking, to $T(I)$, the key of the Ith record in the table. If X is less than $T(I)$, this indicates that the point at which the record being sought would have been stored has been passed, and

FIGURE 19-1

Flowchart for the Linear Search of a Sorted (Sequentially Organized) Table

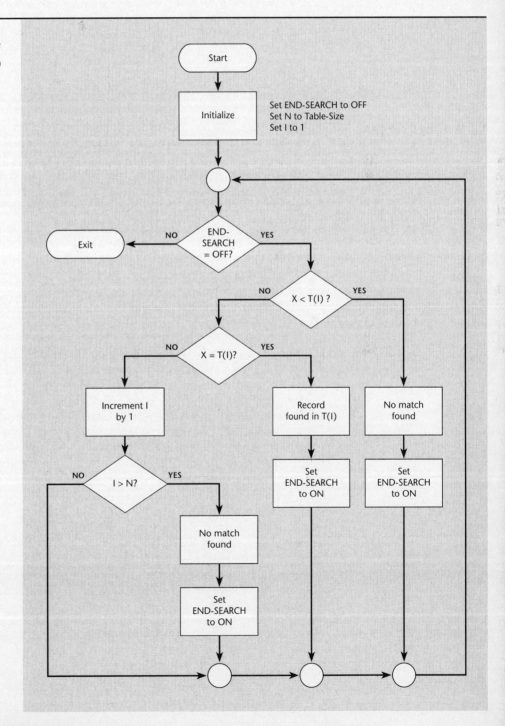

therefore the record is not contained in the table. For instance, if we are seeking employee number 123 and the current (Ith) record being compared has a value of 152, there is no point to continuing the search. All records subsequent to 152 will have key numbers larger than 152. On the other hand, as long as X is greater than T(I), we continue to increment the value of I, but with the provision that I should not exceed N, which is the number of records in the table. We repeat the process until either the record is found or it can be established that the record is not in the table.

The linear search method is generally the simplest procedure to use. It is particularly well suited for unsorted tables, since the method does not require that the table be in any particular order. In practice, many tables are unsorted. If the membership of a table is dynamic, that is, changing often, it may be very costly in terms of overall efficiency to sort the table every time an entry is added to, or deleted from, the table. Furthermore, it may be that other uses of the data require an order that is based on a different key from the one under consideration. The task of sorting the table in one order and then re-sorting back to the original order may not be worth the effort. For example, suppose we are processing daily credit purchases that have been sorted by customer number. For credit-screening purposes we may want to identify the customers who made purchases of $10,000 or more. If we have a block of 20 customers as a table in central storage, it is much simpler to employ a linear search rather than to sort the records by amount of purchase and then re-sort back in customer number order. Of course, for an unsorted table the search should continue until a match occurs, or all entries have been checked, since the record that is sought can be in any location in the table.

BINARY SEARCH

The method of *binary search* is also referred to as *dichotomous search*. It has the feature that each comparison eliminates from further consideration half the entries that could contain the record being sought. The method requires that the table be sorted.

We begin by checking the record at the midpoint of the table. If that record is not the one being sought, it can be determined whether that record is smaller or larger than the one being sought, thereby eliminating half the records from further consideration. For example, if the midpoint record is larger than the one being sought, the record being sought must be in the first half of the table, if it is included in the table at all. Conversely, if the midpoint record is smaller than the record being sought, the first half of the table can be eliminated from further consideration. After half the table is eliminated from consideration, we proceed to the midpoint of the remaining half and again compare the record with the record being sought. The procedure is repeated until the record being sought is found or until it can be concluded that the record is not included in the table. The flowchart in Figure 19-2 presents the logic associated with the binary search method.

Referring to Figure 19-2, we begin by setting two data-names, LO and HI, equal to zero and to the table size plus 1, respectively. The midpoint of the table, MID, is determined by adding LO to HI, dividing by 2, and rounding any fraction upward. Thus, if LO = 0 and HI = 9 for a table with eight entries, MID = $(0 + 9)/2$ = 4.5, which is rounded to 5. MID is then used as the subscript of T, and the value of the record sought, X, is compared with the MIDth record in the table. If X is less than T(MID), the record being sought could only be located before the MID position, and therefore we set HI = MID. Similar reasoning leads to setting LO = MID when X is greater than or equal to T(MID). Then the difference between HI and LO is checked. If it is less than 2, and since any fractional value would have been rounded upward, this indicates that the last record was the last possible location at which the record being sought might have been located, and that the

FIGURE 19-2

Flowchart for the Binary Search of a Sorted Table

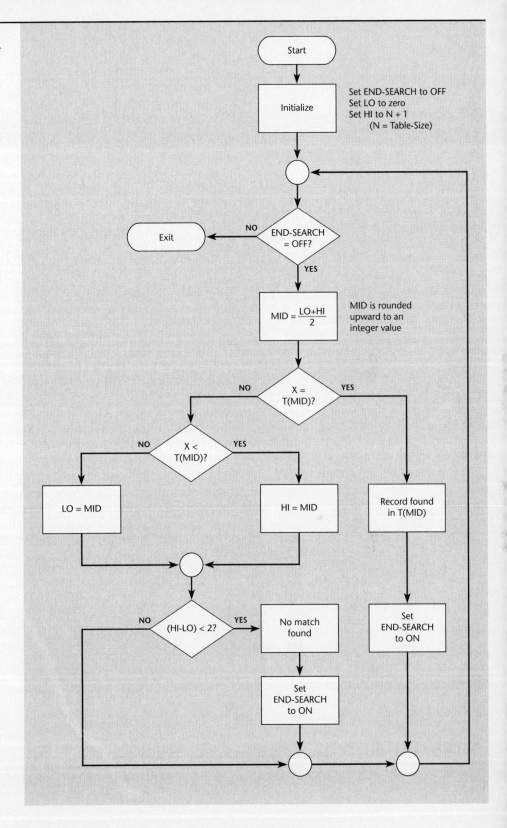

record being sought is not in the table. For example, for a table with eight entries the first MID = 5, as above. Suppose X > T(MID). Then LO = MID = 5 and HI – LO = 9 – 5 = 4, which is not less than 2. The value of MID in the next iteration is (5 + 9)/ 2 = 7. Again, suppose X > T(MID). Then LO = 7 and HI – LO = 9 – 7 = 2. The next

MID = (7 + 9)/2 = 8. If X is unequal to T(MID), the HI – LO comparison will yield one of these two results: If X < T(MID), then HI – LO = 8 – 8 = 0. If X > T(MID), then HI – LO = 9 – 8 = 1. In either case the expression HI – LO will be less than 2, and the search will be terminated with no match found.

Figure 19-3 illustrates the procedure by which the name "Myrtle" would be found in an alphabetically ordered list by means of the binary search method. Notice that a match occurred on the third item considered. If we had been looking for "Mark," one more time through the loop would have been required, for a total of four look-ups. With a table size of 11, four look-ups is, in fact, the maximum number that can be required, as explained below. Figure 19-4 presents the sample code for implementing the binary search logic of Figure 19-2.

Binary search is an efficient method. Its relative efficiency becomes more pronounced as the table size is increased. This is so because the maximum number of comparisons required by this method increases only linearly when the table size increases exponentially. Table 19-1 presents the mathematical relationship involved. Thus, for example, whereas a table with 15 entries requires a maximum of four comparisons, a table with 255 entries requires a maximum of just eight comparisons.

For the reason described above, the binary search method also becomes increasingly more efficient than the linear search method as table size is increased. The general comparison is presented in Table 19-2. The table sizes listed in the first column of Table 19-2 increase exponentially. Note that the maximum number of comparisons for the linear search method also increases exponentially, whereas the maximum number of comparisons for the binary search method increases approximately on a linear basis. The "average" figures reported in Table 19-2 are based on the assumption that the records being sought are randomly and uniformly distributed in the tables. That is, they have not been ordered according to frequency of use. As can be seen in the table, the binary search method outperforms the linear search method by a wide margin, especially when the table size is relatively large. Remember, though, that the binary method specifically requires that the table be sorted, whereas linear search can be used with either a sorted or unsorted table. The time required to sort a table may then have to be balanced against the search time by the linear method. If the membership of a table is stable and the table is used frequently, binary search is likely to be the better choice. Otherwise, linear search may be preferred.

FIGURE 19-3

Illustration of a Binary Search with an Alphabetical List, Where the Record Sought = Myrtle

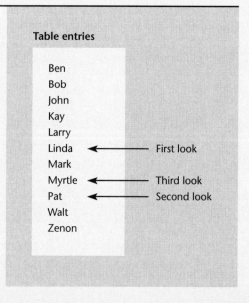

FIGURE 19-4

Sample Binary Search Procedure

```
*
*      We are looking for value X in table T.
*      N is the table size.
*      WHERE-FOUND will contain the subscript value of where X
*          was found in T, or it will contain a zero to signify
*          that X was not found in T.
*      END-SEARCH and NOT-END-SEARCH are logical flags to
*          control the iterative procedure.
*
BINARY-SEARCH
    MOVE ZERO TO LO
    COMPUTE HI = N + 1
    SET NOT-END-SEARCH TO TRUE
    PERFORM UNTIL END-SEARCH
        COMPUTE MID ROUNDED = (LO + HI) / 2
        IF  X = T (MID)
            THEN MOVE MID TO WHERE-FOUND
                SET END-SEARCH TO TRUE
            ELSE
                IF  X < T (MID)
                    THEN MOVE MID TO HI
                    ELSE MOVE MID TO LO
                END-IF
                IF (HI - LO) < 2
                    THEN MOVE ZERO TO WHERE-FOUND
                        SET END-SEARCH TO TRUE
                    ELSE CONTINUE
                END-IF
        END-IF
    END-PERFORM.
```

TABLE 19-1

Maximum Number of Comparisons Required by the Binary Search Method for Tables of Various Sizes

TABLE SIZE		MAXIMUM NUMBER OF COMPARISONS
RANGE	AS A POWER OF 2	
1	2^0	1
2	2^1	2
3–4	2^2	3
5–7	less than 2^3	3
8–15	less than 2^4	4
16–31	less than 2^5	5
32–63	less than 2^6	6
64–127	less than 2^7	7
128–255	less than 2^8	8
256–511	less than 2^9	9

TABLE 19-2
Linear and Binary Search Compared

TABLE SIZE	NUMBER OF COMPARISONS			
	LINEAR		BINARY	
	MAXIMUM	AVERAGE	MAXIMUM	AVERAGE
5	5	3	3	2
10	10	5	4	3
50	50	25	6	5
100	100	50	7	6
1,000	1,000	500	10	9
10,000	10,000	5,000	14	13
100,000	100,000	50,000	17	16

R E V I E W . . . .

1. The two methods of table searching described in this section are _____
    search and _____ search.

                                                                    linear; binary

2. The method of table searching that generally is the simplest to use is
    _____ search.

                                                                              linear

3. The method of table searching that requires that the table data be in sorted
    order is _____ search.

                                                                              binary

4. The table search procedure by which each comparison eliminates from
    consideration half the entries that could contain the record being sought is
    called _____ .

                                                                        binary search

5. Suppose that a sorted table contains 30 entries. By the logic of the binary search
    method the initial value of LO is set equal to _____ and the initial value of HI is
    set equal to _____ .

                                                                              0; 31

6. For Question 5 the value of MID in the first loop through the program would
    be _____ (value).

                                                                                 16

. . . .

COBOL LANGUAGE OPTIONS IN TABLE SEARCHING

Because of the frequency with which table searching is used in computer programs, the COBOL language includes a specialized set of instructions to facilitate programming.

The OCCURS Clause

First, let us consider the format associated with the OCCURS clause:

```
OCCURS integer TIMES

    ⎡⎧ASCENDING ⎫⎤
    ⎢⎨          ⎬⎥ KEY IS  data-name-1 [data-name-2 ... ]
    ⎣⎩DESCENDING⎭⎦

        [INDEXED BY  index-name-1 [index-name-1] ... ]
```

The ASCENDING and DESCENDING KEY options provide a way for the programmer to specify that the data in a table are sorted. For example:

```
02   SAMPLE OCCURS 100 TIMES
            ASCENDING KEY IS   YEAR
                               MONTH.
     03    OTHER-DATA        PICTURE X(20).
     03    MONTH             PICTURE 99.
     03    YEAR              PICTURE 99.
     03    REST-OF-IT        PICTURE X(40).
```

In this example there are two keys, YEAR and MONTH. Keys are listed in decreasing order of significance. Thus the months are sorted in ascending sequence within the years, which are also in ascending sequence. As the example illustrates, the order in which the keys appear in the KEY clause is not related to their physical order in the record (YEAR follows MONTH in physical location within the record).

The sort order for the data in a table is information used by the specialized SEARCH statement (discussed below). In one of the options of the SEARCH we specify using binary search. As we discussed earlier, for the binary search method to work, the data must be sorted, and the OCCURS ... KEY options provide us with a way to tell the compiler how the data are sorted.

Note that use of the KEY clause with the OCCURS simply specifies how the data are *presumed* to be sorted. It is the responsibility of the programmer to make sure that the data are indeed in the order specified by the OCCURS ... KEY ... . The actual data in the table are *not* tested to see if they match the KEY specification. If the data in a table do not match the KEY description and we execute a SEARCH that employs a binary search method, the result of the search generally will be in error—the most likely case being that the record that was sought will not be found, even if it exists in the table.

The last line in the general format of OCCURS includes the INDEXED BY clause. This clause allows us to declare a special variable, an *index*, that is used in lieu of a subscript in reference to the table so INDEXED. We discuss this option in reference to an example.

```
02 SAMPLE  OCCURS 100 TIMES  PIC 9(8)
            INDEXED BY N.
```

In this case we specify an index called N. One of the uses of this index would be in a SEARCH statement as explained in the following subsection of this chapter.

When a table is declared to be INDEXED BY an index item, the index item is expressed in terms of displacement values from the beginning of the table.

Following are the corresponding subscript and index item values for a table defined as TABLE OCCURS 4 TIMES PIC X(3):

SUBSCRIPT VALUE	INDEX ITEM VALUE
1	0
2	3
3	6
4	9

The index item value indicates the position at which the item begins with respect to the beginning of the table; thus, for the above example with PIC X(3), the index value is 6 for a subscript of 3, because the third item in the table begins at the sixth byte from the beginning of the table.

Indexing makes for more efficient table operations. On the other hand, it is not reasonable to require a programmer to think explicitly of the value of index items. For this reason the programmer can think of index items as if they were subscripts. However, when a subscript value is moved to an index, or vice versa, then the special verb SET is used. The SET verb is described later in this chapter. The SET is used to both transform and move values from index variables to "normal" variables, and vice versa. For the example above suppose S is a subscript and I is an index; then if S contains 3, SET I TO S will result in I being set to a value of 6. Conversely, if I = 6, SET S TO I will result in S being set to 3.

Generally, use of index items is required only in SEARCH operations (discussion of SEARCH follows). However, use of index items is encouraged in all table-handling operations because indexes are processed more efficiently than subscripts. An index can be stored in a register during a table operation, whereas a subscript is stored in main memory and has to be brought to a register each time the subscript is used. Also, in serial operations an index is increased by a fixed displacement value. In contrast, a subscript has to be decoded each time by means of multiplication, which is more time-consuming than addition (or subtraction).

The USAGE IS INDEX Clause

Consider now the USAGE IS INDEX clause. We can specify the USAGE of a data item is INDEX, so that the item can be used in conjunction with SET, SEARCH, or PERFORM statements. You may recall from Chapter 16 options such as the USAGE IS DISPLAY and COMPUTATIONAL as shown in the following format:

$$
\underline{\text{USAGE}} \text{ IS} \left\{ \begin{array}{l} \text{BINARY} \\ \text{COMPUTATIONAL} \\ \text{COMP} \\ \text{DISPLAY} \\ \text{INDEX} \\ \text{PACKED -DECIMAL} \end{array} \right\}
$$

As an example of implementing the USAGE IS INDEX clause, consider the following program segment:

```
01 K USAGE IS INDEX.
```

The item called K is an INDEX item; therefore no PICTURE clause is given. All index items are handled according to the rules associated with each particular computer system. Normally, index items are in binary form.

The SEARCH Verb

Consider now the SEARCH verb, which is the cornerstone of a search instruction. Two principal formats are available, as presented in Figure 19-5.

In Format 1 identifier-1 is an item whose description in the DATA DIVISION contains an OCCURS and an INDEXED BY clause. The VARYING option is seldom used, and it must not be confused with the PERFORM VARYING. Because of the similarity to the PERFORM and the naturalness of the expression, it is common to have the inclination to write SEARCH ... VARYING when one should not. The VARYING option is designed for the special cases in which we want to vary a second index, as will be explained in one of the examples later in the chapter.

The AT END clause is optional. If it is omitted, program control will pass to the next sentence when the table has been searched and no match has been found. If AT END is included and imperative-statement-l does not terminate with GO TO, a branch to the next sentence will be made (in effect, bypassing the WHEN clauses). WHEN is a conditional expression.

Format 2 is used with sorted tables, that is, tables for which the OCCURS clause contains a KEY in addition to the INDEXED BY option. The search may be a

FIGURE 19-5

SEARCH Verb Formats

FORMAT 1

SEARCH identifier-1 [VARYING { index-name-1 / identifier-2 }]

[AT END imperative-statement-1]

WHEN condition-1 { imperative-statement-2 / NEXT SENTENCE }

[WHEN condition-2 { imperative-statement-2 / NEXT-SENTENCE }] . . .

[END-SEARCH]

FORMAT 2

SEARCH ALL identifier-1 [AT END imperative-statement-1]

WHEN { data-name-1 { IS EQUAL TO / IS = } { identifier-2 / literal-1 / arithmetic-expression-1 } / condition-name-1 }

[AND { data-name-2 { IS EQUAL TO / IS = } { identifier-3 / literal-2 / arithmetic-expression-2 } / condition-name-2 }] . . .

{ imperative-statement-2 / NEXT SENTENCE }

[END-SEARCH]

binary search, or any other method included in a particular compiler; however, as far as the programmer is concerned, the actual search method is a black box. Only the instructions included in Format 2 are required.

The reserved word that distinguishes between format 1 and format 2 is the ALL. In format 1 we do not use the ALL, whereas we must use it in format 2. So if you have a sorted table and you want to execute a binary search, you write SEARCH ALL ... . This is almost contrary to the natural expectation that the ALL option would be part of the linear search that searches all entries from the first entry to the matching entry, or the end of the table.

Notice that in Format 2 only one WHEN option is available, but multiple AND conditions are allowed. Thus *all* of the conditions must be true for the search to be satisfied. In contrast, whenever multiple WHEN statements are used in Format 1, *any one* of these conditions being true constitutes a sufficient reason for search termination.

Also notice that the conditions tested in the WHEN clauses of Format 1 and Format 2 are different. In Format 1, condition-1 is any condition. For example, we could search a table to find an entry whose squared value plus 100 is greater than some constant. The point is that in a linear search, we can test for any condition, not just the direct content of the table. On the other hand, in the binary search as specified by Format 2, the condition tests for equality of data-name-1 to a specified comparand, or for the truth of a condition-name, which is another form of testing for equality. Since a binary search "jumps around" the table based on the values of the sort keys, it follows that the value of the sort key must be tested at each step of the search. Put another way, in a binary search it would not make any sense to test a WHEN condition that did not involve the sort key(s) (indicated in Format 2 as data-name-1, data-name-2, etc.).

The SET Verb

The SET verb, when used in reference to index items, plays several roles. Two formats are available, as presented in Figure 19-6.

In Format 1 we can use the SET to transform and move data from one index item to another, or from a subscript to a corresponding index. For example, suppose that we have

```
02  ITEM-NO   PIC 99.
     .
     .
     .
03  TABLE OCCURS 10 TIMES
          INDEXED BY I.
     05  TABLE-ITEM-NO   PIC 99.
          .
          .
          .
SEARCH ALL TABLE
     WHEN TABLE-ITEM-NO (I) = ZERO
          SET ITEM-NO TO I
          .
          .
          .
```

As part of the SEARCH operation we want to store in ITEM-NO the subscript value of the item in the table that was equal to zero. Recall that since I is an index item (INDEXED BY I), and since the PIC description in the table is 99, values of I

FIGURE 19-6

SET Verb Formats

FORMAT 1

$$\underline{SET} \begin{Bmatrix} \text{index-name-1 [index-name-2]} \dots \\ \text{identifier-1 [identifier-2]} \dots \end{Bmatrix} \underline{TO} \begin{Bmatrix} \text{index-name-3} \\ \text{identifier-3} \\ \text{integer-1} \end{Bmatrix}$$

FORMAT 2

$$\underline{SET} \text{ index-name-1 [index-name-2]} \dots \begin{Bmatrix} \underline{UP\ BY} \\ \underline{DOWN\ BY} \end{Bmatrix} \begin{Bmatrix} \text{identifier-1} \\ \text{integer-1} \end{Bmatrix}$$

referencing entries in the table will have values such as 0, 2, 4, etc. Thus, if the search operation was successful for the third item in the table, I will have a value of 4. Because ITEM-NO is *not* an index item, we use the SET statement to transfer the data from I to ITEM-NO after converting it to the proper value, which, for our example, should be 3. In a similar manner, suppose that we wanted to begin searching a table from the fifth entry on. We would write

```
SET I TO 5
SEARCH TABLE ...
```

The SET instruction converts the integer 5 to the corresponding value of the index I (for the above example, 8) and then moves the result to I.

As another example, suppose we have two tables, one INDEXED BY A and the other INDEXED BY B. After performing a search and finding a match on the first table, we may want to reference the corresponding entry in the second table. We then SET B TO A so that B can be used as a subscript, or index, in the second table.

In Format 1 of the SET verb, if we use index-name-1, we can set it equal to index-name-3, identifier-3, or integer-1. If identifier-3 is used, it must be defined as an elementary integer item; if integer-1 is used, it must be a positive integer. If we SET identifier-1 and it has not been defined by a USAGE IS INDEX clause, it can be SET only to index-name-3.

In Format 2 in Figure 19-6 we can increase or decrease the value of index-name-1 either by a positive integer (integer-1) or by the value of identifier-1, which must be a field that has not been defined as USAGE IS INDEX. The effect of UP BY is to increase the value of index-name-1, while the effect of DOWN BY is to change index-name-1 by the indicated decrement.

R E V I E W . . . .

1. The COBOL language option used to indicate the total number of table entries and to identify the key or keys associated with the records is the _____ clause.

                                                                    OCCURS

2. The *order* and *name* of each key in an OCCURS clause is indicated by the reserved words ASCENDING KEY or _____ .

                                                            DESCENDING KEY

3. The COBOL options used to identify a particular data item as being an index are the _____ clause and the _____ associated with the OCCURS description.

USAGE; INDEXED BY

4. The COBOL verb that identifies the table to be searched and also includes options to indicate what should be done when a match is found as well as when it is not found is the _____ verb.

SEARCH

5. The COBOL verb that is a variation of the MOVE verb and provides the basis for designating the value to be assigned to an INDEX is the _____ verb.

SET

. . . .

EXAMPLES OF TABLE SEARCHING

We now illustrate application of these language features using some examples. Suppose we have the following table:

```
01  DATA-TABLE.
    02  NAME-NUMBER OCCURS 400 TIMES
        INDEXED BY WHICH-ONE.
        03  NAME        PICTURE X(16).
        03  EMPL-NO     PICTURE 9999.
```

We want to conduct a linear search to find the first zero value, if any, in the EMPL-NO field. We do not want to use the SEARCH verb. However, we *do* want to use the WHICH-ONE index item in a PERFORM ... VARYING loop to take advantage of the efficiency of using index items rather than subscripts. We can carry out such a search as follows:

```
MOVE 'NO' TO EMPL-FOUND-FLAG
PERFORM  SEARCHING
         VARYING WHICH-ONE FROM 1 BY 1
         UNTIL WHICH-ONE > 400
             OR EMPLOYEE-FOUND
    .
    .
    .

SEARCHING.
    IF EMPL-NO (WHICH-ONE) = ZERO
        MOVE 'YES' TO EMPL-FOUND-FLAG.
```

Using the SEARCH verb, the above procedure can be revised as follows:

```
SEARCH  NAME-NUMBER
    AT END MOVE 'NO' TO EMPL-FOUND-FLAG
    WHEN EMPL-NO (WHICH-ONE) = ZERO
        MOVE 'YES' TO EMPL-FOUND-FLAG.
```

Next, suppose that employee data are contained in a sorted table sequenced by employee NAME:

```
01  DATA-TABLE.
    02  NAME-NUMBER OCCURS 400 TIMES
        ASCENDING KEY IS NAME
        INDEXED BY WHICH-ONE.
        03  NAME        PICTURE X(16).
        03  EMPL-NO     PICTURE 9999.
```

Assume that EMPL-NAME is a field that contains a name for which we want to determine the associated employee number (EMPL-NO) and store it in EDIT-NUMBER. To accomplish this task, we can execute the following statements:

```
SEARCH ALL NAME-NUMBER
    AT END PERFORM CANT-FIND
    WHEN NAME (WHICH-ONE) = EMPL-NAME
        MOVE EMPL-NO (WHICH-ONE) TO EDIT-NUMBER.
```

The instruction SEARCH ALL NAME-NUMBER is an application of the second format of the SEARCH verb. Since the table was defined with ASCENDING KEY IS NAME, the SEARCH ALL will result in a binary search on the NAME field. When a match is found, program execution is transferred to the instruction MOVE EMPL-NO (WHICH-ONE) TO EDIT-NUMBER following the WHEN. Notice that WHICH-ONE has the reference value of the record for which the match occurred; thus, it is used as a subscript, or index, to reference the corresponding EMPL-NO.

Next consider an example of a sorted table with *two* sort keys:

```
01  FIND-FLAG   PIC X.
    88  FOUND       VALUE 'Y'.
    88  NOT-FOUND   VALUE 'N'.
01  TABLE.
    02  SALES-DATA OCCURS 100 TIMES
        ASCENDING KEY IS YEAR
        ASCENDING KEY IS MONTH
        INDEXED BY N.
        03  SALES-AMOUNT    PIC 9(4)V99.
        03  YEAR            PIC 99.
        03  MONTH           PIC 99.
          .
          .
          .
```

We want to search the table and add the SALES-AMOUNT to SALES-TOTAL for the entry whose YEAR and MONTH values match YEAR-IN and MONTH-IN. To do this, we can write

```
SEARCH ALL SALES-DATA
    AT END SET NOT-FOUND TO TRUE
    WHEN  YEAR (N) = YEAR-IN
          AND MONTH (N) = MONTH-IN
        SET FOUND TO TRUE
        ADD SALES-AMOUNT (N) TO SALES-TOTAL.
```

In the example above, in the WHEN we test both YEAR (N) and MONTH (N) because the table is sorted on both of these fields.

Searching a table with two or more levels requires some special considerations. The SEARCH verb does not operate across more than one dimension at a time. As a result, we typically write a PERFORM loop to vary an index value over the outer level while the SEARCH controls the index value for the inner level. Let us consider the following example, which involves a two-dimensional table:

```
01  FIND-FLAG   PIC X.
    88  FOUND       VALUE 'Y'.
    88  NOT-FOUND  VALUE 'N'.
01  SALES-TABLE.
    02  QUARTER-SALES OCCURS 4 TIMES
                    INDEXED BY Q.
        03  REGION-SALES OCCURS 10 TIMES
                    ASCENDING KEY SALES
                    INDEXED BY R.
            04  SALES   PIC 9(5).
```

Suppose that we want to find how many regions have a sales value equal to 12345. We are interested in searching for such a value in each region. If there is more than one such value in a given region, we do not care to find that out. Thus we can use binary search (SEARCH ALL) since we are looking for an equality match:

```
PERFORM BINARY-SEARCH VARYING Q FROM 1 BY 1
                    UNTIL Q > 4
                        OR FOUND.
    .
    .
    .
BINARY-SEARCH.
    SET NOT-FOUND TO TRUE
    SEARCH ALL REGION-SALES
        AT END   PERFORM NO-MATCH
        WHEN SALES (Q, R) = 12345
            SET FOUND TO TRUE
            PERFORM YES-MATCH.
```

The PERFORM ... VARYING statement controls the value of Q so that we will execute the SEARCH ALL statement once for each of the four quarters.

Now, suppose we want to count in NO-UNDER-100 the number of sales values that are less than 100. Even though the sales data in the table are sorted within each region, we cannot use binary search; we must use linear search because we want to test for a condition *not* involving equality and we want to find possibly *multiple* occurrences of a match. Recall that in the SEARCH ALL format, the WHEN clause requires a test for equality; searching for a condition of a sales value *less than 100* is *not* a test for equality. Given these considerations, we could code the search in several ways.

First, we will search without use of the SEARCH verb:

```
PERFORM SEARCHING VARYING Q FROM 1 BY 1
                UNTIL Q > 4
                AFTER R FROM 1 BY 1
                UNTIL R > 10
                    OR SALES (Q, R) >= 100.
    .
    .
    .
```

```
SEARCHING.
    IF SALES (Q, R) < 100
        ADD 1 TO NO-UNDER-100.
```

The logic is straightforward. For each quarter and for each region in each quarter we test each sales value to determine if it is less than 100. Also, knowing that the data are sorted within each region, we terminate searching within a region if we encounter a sales value equal to or greater than 100.

As an alternative, we could use the SEARCH verb, and incidentally, the in-line PERFORM:

```
SET Q TO 1
PERFORM UNTIL Q > 4
    SET R TO 1
    PERFORM  UNTIL R > 4
            OR SALES (Q, R) >= 100
        SEARCH REGION-SALES
            WHEN SALES (Q, R) < 100
                ADD 1 TO NO-UNDER-100
                SET R UP BY 1
        END-SEARCH
    END-PERFORM
    SET Q UP BY 1
END-PERFORM
```

The inner PERFORM controls repetitive execution of the SEARCH. We did not use the AT END option with the SEARCH because we needed a "keep performing" command anyway, so it seemed natural to test for the end-of-table condition at the PERFORM rather than at the SEARCH statement. The SET operation in the inner PERFORM serves the purpose of advancing the R index to the next position in the table after a successful SEARCH. For instance, if the sales value in the 5th region was less than 100, we want to repeat the SEARCH starting with the 6th region, and so we SET R UP BY 1. Finally, we chose to vary Q via SET instructions. We could just as well have used

```
PERFORM  VARYING Q FROM 1 BY 1 UNTIL Q > 4.
```

A comparison of the program instructions with and without the SEARCH leads to the conclusion that the first sample code, doing a linear search without use of the SEARCH, is a clear winner in terms of simplicity. The SEARCH was not designed for repetitive searching; use of PERFORM and suitable IF statements may be the preferred approach in such situations.

As another example of searching when there are two sort keys, suppose the following table definitions were written:

```
01  DATA-TABLE.
    02  NAME OCCURS 400 TIMES       PICTURE X(16)
            INDEXED BY NAME-INDEX.
    02  EMPL-NO OCCURS 400 TIMES    PICTURE 9999
            INDEXED BY NO-INDEX.
```

In effect, two tables are defined, one called NAME and the other called EMPL-NO. The NAME table is indexed by NAME-INDEX, while the EMPL-NO table is indexed by NO-INDEX. In relation to these table descriptions, the following statements then can be written:

```
SET NAME-INDEX TO 1.
SET NO-INDEX TO 1.
SEARCH NAME VARYING NO-INDEX
    AT END PERFORM NO-MATCH
    WHEN EMPL-NAME = NAME (NAME-INDEX)
        MOVE EMPL-NO (NO-INDEX) TO EMPL-NO-OUT.
```

The SEARCH statement contains the VARYING option, which, in effect, indicates that NO-INDEX is to be varied in the same way as the index of the table being searched (in this case NAME-INDEX). Thus, for example, when NAME-INDEX refers to the 10th entry, NO-INDEX also refers to the 10th entry. As a result, the EMPL-NO (NO-INDEX) in the MOVE statement corresponds to the NAME for which a match was found. If a match occurred in the 34th position of the NAME table, for example, NAME-INDEX and NO-INDEX both would have a value corresponding to their respective displacement values for the 34th occurrence. Since NAME has PICTURE X(16), NAME-INDEX would have a displacement value of $(34-1) \times 16 = 528$, while NO-INDEX would have a value of $(34-1) \times 4 = 132$. Thus the employee number that is accessed corresponds to the name of the employee for which a match was found. Since the ALL option was not used with the SEARCH verb, the linear search procedure was used, which involves accessing every entry in the table in sequence until a match is found or the entire table is searched.

Note that the VARYING item is incremented from its *initial* value. In the above example we initialized it with SET NO-INDEX TO 1. If NO-INDEX was not so initialized but happened to contain the value 6 from previous operations, it then would be varied to values that correspond to entries 6, 7, 8, ... as NAME-INDEX was varied to values that correspond to entries 1, 2, 3, ...

As a general example of program code that can be applied to the latter situation, the program segment below is concerned with a table of last names for which we are interested in finding the average length of the names:

```
02  NAME-TABLE OCCURS 100 TIMES
            INDEXED BY I.
    03  NAME-LETTERS OCCURS 20 TIMES
            INDEXED BY N.
        04  LETTER          PIC X.
01  K USAGE INDEX.
01  TOTAL-LETTER-COUNT      PIC 9(5).
01  AVG-NAME-LENGTH         PIC 9(2)V9.
    .
    .
    .
    SET K TO 1
    PERFORM VARYING I FROM 1 BY 1
        UNTIL I > 100
        SET N TO 1
        SEARCH NAME-LETTERS VARYING K
            WHEN LETTER (I, N) = SPACE
                NEXT SENTENCE
        END-SEARCH
        SET K DOWN BY 1
    END-PERFORM
    SET TOTAL-LETTER COUNT TO K
    DIVIDE TOTAL-LETTER-COUNT BY 100 GIVING AVG-NAME-LENGTH.
```

In the above program segment, K is a USAGE INDEX item that is not associated with a specific table. It is used as an accumulator of all of the name lengths, because its value is *not* reSET in the program code. Thus, if the first name encountered is 5 characters long, K would be equal to 5. If the second name encountered is 6 characters long, then K would become 11; during the second execution of the SEARCH, K is incremented in the order 6, 7, ... , while N is incremented in the order 1, 2, ... Incidentally, N would be incremented by 1 in the above example because the PIC clause of LETTER was X. If the PIC had been X(4), for instance, N would be incremented by 4 each time. But in the latter case, K would still be incremented by 1 because K is not associated with a table. If the VARYING item (K in this case) were associated with a table (INDEXED BY K), then it would be varied by the amount that is appropriate for its respective table.

SAMPLE PROGRAM WITH INDEXING AND SEARCHING

An input file consists of records containing a student name and the numeric score for each of eight parts of a standardized test. Our objective is to store the data in a table and then to illustrate use of SEARCH to identify those students who either scored 100.0 on any part of the test or scored less than 50.0 on any part of the test.

    The program is presented in Figure 19-7. Notice in the 01 EXAM-TABLE description that S is designated in INDEXED BY S, and then it is used in the PERFORM 020-STORE-RECORD VARYING of the 000-PROGRAM-SUMMARY paragraph. Then observe that, after the PERFORM statement, we write SET S DOWN BY 1. After S is so adjusted, it represents the number of student records that were read in. We then save the value of S in M (SET M TO S) to be used to control the printing task. Notice that M is a WORKING-STORAGE USAGE INDEX item.

FIGURE 19-7

Sample Program with Indexing and Searching

```
IDENTIFICATION DIVISION.
PROGRAM-ID. GRADES.
*
ENVIRONMENT DIVISION.
CONFIGURATION SECTION.
SOURCE-COMPUTER.  ABC-480.
OBJECT-COMPUTER.  ABC-480.
*
INPUT-OUTPUT SECTION.
FILE-CONTROL.
    SELECT EXAM-FILE ASSIGN TO READER.
    SELECT REPORT-FILE ASSIGN TO PRINTER.
*
DATA DIVISION.
*
FILE SECTION.
*
FD  EXAM-FILE      LABEL RECORDS OMITTED
                     DATA RECORD IS EXAM-REC.
01  EXAM-REC.
    02  STUDENT-NAME            PIC X(20).
    02  EXAM-SCORES.
        03 SCORES-IN  OCCURS 8 TIMES  PIC 9(3)V9.
    02  FILLER                  PIC X(28).
*
```

```
FD  REPORT-FILE    LABEL RECORDS OMITTED
                   DATA RECORD IS REPORT-REC.
01  REPORT-REC                PIC X(132).
*
WORKING-STORAGE SECTION.
*
01  END-OF-FILE-SWITCH        PIC XXX VALUE 'NO '.
    88  END-OF-FILE           VALUE 'YES'.
*
01  M    USAGE INDEX.
*
01  EXAM-TABLE.
*
    02  STUDENT-DATA          OCCURS 50 TIMES
                              INDEXED BY  S.
*
        03  STUDENT-NAME      PIC X(20).
*
        03  EXAM-SCORES.
*
            04  SCORE         OCCURS 8 TIMES
                              INDEXED BY Q
                              PIC 9(3)V9.
*
01  HEADING-1.
    02  FILLER                PIC X(50) VALUE SPACES.
    02  FILLER                PIC X(9)  VALUE 'EXAM PART'.
*
01  HEADING-2.
    02  FILLER        PIC X(8)  VALUE SPACES.
    02  FILLER        PIC X(12) VALUE 'STUDENT NAME'.
    02  FILLER        PIC X(12) VALUE SPACES.
    02  FILLER        PIC X(50) VALUE
          '1     2     3     4     5     6     7     8'.
*
01  REPORT-LINE.
    02  FILLER        PIC X(5)  VALUE SPACES.
    02  STUDENT-NAME  PIC X(20).
    02  FILLER        PIC X(2)  VALUE SPACES.
*
    02 SCORE-OUT OCCURS 8 TIMES INDEXED BY R
                      PIC ZZZ99.9.
*
/
PROCEDURE DIVISION.
*
000-PROGRAM-SUMMARY.
    OPEN  INPUT   EXAM-FILE
          OUTPUT  REPORT-FILE.
*
    PERFORM 010-READ-EXAM-REC
*
```

FIGURE 19-7

Sample Program with Indexing and Searching (continued)

```
        PERFORM 020-STORE-RECORD
                VARYING  S  FROM  1  BY  1
                        UNTIL  S > 50
                        OR END-OF-FILE.
    *

        SET  S  DOWN  BY  1
        SET  M  TO  S.
    *

        WRITE REPORT-REC FROM HEADING-1 AFTER PAGE
        WRITE REPORT-REC FROM HEADING-2 AFTER 2
    *

        PERFORM 030-CHECK-SCORES-AND-PRINT
                VARYING  S  FROM  1  BY  1
                        UNTIL  S > M.
    *

        CLOSE EXAM-FILE  REPORT-FILE
    *

        STOP RUN.
    *

     010-READ-EXAM-REC.
        READ EXAM-FILE RECORD
             AT END MOVE 'YES' TO END-OF-FILE-SWITCH.
    *

     020-STORE-RECORD.
        MOVE STUDENT-NAME OF EXAM-REC
             TO STUDENT-NAME OF EXAM-TABLE (S)
    *

        MOVE EXAM-SCORES OF EXAM-REC
             TO EXAM-SCORES OF EXAM-TABLE (S).
    *

        PERFORM 010-READ-EXAM-REC.
    *

     030-CHECK-SCORES-AND-PRINT.
        SET Q TO 1
    *

        SEARCH SCORE
                WHEN   SCORE (S, Q) = 100.0
                     PERFORM 040-PRINT-SCORES;
                WHEN   SCORE (S, Q) < 50.0
                     PERFORM 040-PRINT-SCORES.
    *

     040-PRINT-SCORES.
        PERFORM 050-MOVE-SCORES
                VARYING  Q  FROM  1  BY  1
                         UNTIL  Q > 8.
    *

        MOVE STUDENT-NAME OF EXAM-TABLE (S)
             TO STUDENT-NAME OF REPORT-LINE
        WRITE REPORT-REC FROM REPORT-LINE AFTER 2 LINES.
    *

     050-MOVE-SCORES.
        SET R TO Q
        MOVE SCORE (S, Q) TO SCORE-OUT (R).
```

After the table has been stored, we search it in the 030-CHECK-SCORES-AND-PRINT paragraph. Notice that we did not include the AT END option in this use of Format 1 of the SEARCH, since it was not needed. If neither a score of 100 nor a score of less than 50 is found for a given student, we simply want to continue with the next student without doing anything AT END. When either one of the two search conditions is true, we PERFORM 040-PRINT-SCORES, and the search for that student record terminates. Then, because of the PERFORM 030-CHECK-SCORES-AND-PRINT in the 000-PROGRAM-SUMMARY, we repeat the search for the next student.

The 050-MOVE-SCORES paragraph illustrates again the use of SET. Since SCORE-OUT in 01 REPORT-LINE was indexed by R, we SET R TO Q so that in the MOVE statement we reference the corresponding scores.

Figure 19-8 illustrates sample input and output for the program. The data provide a somewhat contrived set of cases to illustrate the options. Exercise 19.4 at the end of the chapter asks the student to modify the example to incorporate other features of searching.

INTERNAL SORTING

Internal sorting is concerned with sorting procedures (algorithms) used with tables of data held in central storage. Sorting an internal table is a different task from sorting data on external files, such as disk or tape. There are many internal sort algorithms, and new ones continue to be developed for special cases. In this section we present three *interchange sort algorithms*.

There are several versions of the interchange sort approach. Fundamental to all versions is the interchange of two elements in the table. To interchange data

FIGURE 19-8

Input and Output for the Program with Indexing and Searching

INPUT FILE

```
STUDENT-1          09051000082306000900089909770777
STUDENT-2          02000732066605920812085503000600
STUDENT-3          09000820100008320777075306890920
STUDENT-4          07450789082306950765074806780802
STUDENT-5          04500720073010000235024506250213
```

PROGRAM OUTPUT

				EXAM	PART			
STUDENT NAME	1	2	3	4	5	6	7	8
STUDENT-1	90.5	100.0	82.3	60.0	90.0	89.9	97.7	77.7
STUDENT-2	20.0	73.2	66.6	59.2	81.2	85.5	30.0	60.0
STUDENT-3	90.0	82.0	100.0	83.2	77.7	75.3	68.9	92.0
STUDENT-5	45.0	72.0	73.0	100.0	23.5	24.5	62.5	21.3

in two fields, we need a third field for temporary storage. For instance, if we want to interchange the data in T(X) and T(Y), we could write

```
MOVE T(X) TO TEMP
MOVE T(Y) TO T(X)
MOVE TEMP TO T(Y).
```

Any interchange algorithm involves paired comparisons of table elements. The *adjacent comparison-interchange* approach involves comparison of adjacent table values and may require multiple "passes" through the table. In each pass we interchange adjacent elements that are out of order relative to each other. Specifically, in the first pass the first record is compared with the second, the second with the third, and so on until the (N – 1)th record is compared with the Nth record in the table. The two records being compared each time are interchanged whenever the second record is smaller than the first record, assuming that the table is being sorted into ascending order. If no interchange was necessary during an entire pass, this means that the table is already in order. Otherwise, at least one more pass is required.

By the adjacent comparison approach, at the end of the first pass the largest record is driven to the bottom of the table. Thus, in the second pass through the table N – 1 table entries are considered, in the third pass N – 2 are considered, and so forth. Thus the table is sorted from the last entry up, and every pass through the table involves a smaller table for comparisons and interchanges. Eventually only two elements remain to be considered—the first and the second.

Typically, however, the table will come to be sorted correctly before all possible passes through the table are made by the adjacent comparison approach. As indicated above, the fact that no interchange is necessary during a pass through the table serves to indicate that the table is already correctly sorted. To avoid unnecessary passes through the table, it is useful to incorporate a procedure by which such a situation can be detected. One way of doing this is to initialize a data-name with a value such as zero and to change the value to 1 on the occurrence of any interchange. At the end of each pass the value of the data-name is tested. If the value is zero, the table is sorted. If the value is 1, at least one more pass is required.

The procedure associated with the adjacent comparison-interchange method will now be illustrated by means of a COBOL program, which is presented in Figure 19-9. The input consists of records, each of which consists of two fields, NAME-IN and FILLER. The NAME-IN will be used as the sort key, while FILLER is assumed to contain other data. Data are read in by execution of the 100-READ-DATA-IN SECTION, which stores the records in a table called ENTIRE-TABLE. Notice that N is a counter that represents the number of records read (maximum of 50).

The sorting operation takes place in the 200-SORT-DATA SECTION. The PERFORM 220-OUTER-LOOP is executed as long as TEST is not equal to SORTED and as long as I is not equal to N. In essence, this instruction says to keep going through the table as long as it is not sorted after each pass through, but in any case not to go through the table more than N – 1 times. In the 220-OUTER-LOOP paragraph, TEST is set to the value "SORTED" so that if no interchange takes place, that value will stay as such and will terminate execution of the 220-OUTER-LOOP paragraph. Each time through, M is decreased by 1, since the table is effectively shortened as the largest value floats to the bottom. The PERFORM 230-PAIRED-COMPARISONS instruction allows us to compare M-1 pairs and interchange their values as needed.

Finally, the 300-PRINT-DATA SECTION simply lists the data on the printer for visual review. Incidentally, use of SECTIONs in this program was simply

FIGURE 19-9

*COBOL Internal Sort Program
Using the Adjacent Comparison-
Interchange Method*

```
        IDENTIFICATION DIVISION.
        PROGRAM-ID. INSORT.
        ENVIRONMENT DIVISION.
        *
        CONFIGURATION SECTION.
        SOURCE-COMPUTER.  ABC-480.
        OBJECT-COMPUTER.  ABC-480.
        *
        INPUT-OUTPUT SECTION.
        FILE-CONTROL.
            SELECT INPUT-FILE ASSIGN TO CARD.
            SELECT OUTPUT-FILE ASSIGN TO PRINTER.
        *
        DATA DIVISION.
        *
        FILE SECTION.
        FD  INPUT-FILE LABEL RECORD OMITTED
                     DATA RECORD IS INPUT-RECORD.
        *
        01  INPUT-RECORD.
            02  NAME-IN         PIC X(15).
            02  FILLER          PIC X(65).
        *
        FD  OUTPUT-FILE LABEL RECORD OMITTED
                     DATA RECORD IS PRINT-RECORD.
        *
        01  PRINT-RECORD        PIC X(132).
        *
        WORKING-STORAGE SECTION.
        *
        01  ENTIRE-TABLE.
            02  TABLE-REC OCCURS 50 TIMES.
                03  NAME        PIC X(15).
                03  FILLER      PIC X(65).
        *
        01  DATA-END            PIC X(3) VALUE 'NO'.
            88  DATA-ENDED               VALUE 'YES'.
        *
        01  TESTIT              PIC X(8).
        01  N                   PIC 99.
        01  I                   PIC 99.
        01  J                   PIC 99.
        01  K                   PIC 99.
        01  M                   PIC 99.
        01  TEMP-STORE          PIC X(80).
        *
        PROCEDURE DIVISION.
        *
        000-MAIN-ROUTINE.
            OPEN INPUT INPUT-FILE
                 OUTPUT OUTPUT-FILE
```

FIGURE 19-9

COBOL Internal Sort Program
Using the Adjacent Comparison-
Interchange Method (continued)

```
*
        PERFORM 100-READ-DATA-IN
*
        PERFORM 200-SORT-DATA
*
        PERFORM 300-PRINT-DATA
*
        CLOSE INPUT-FILE, OUTPUT-FILE
        STOP RUN.
*
 100-READ-DATA-IN SECTION.
*
 110-SET-UP-TO-READ.
        MOVE 'NO' TO DATA-END
        MOVE ZERO TO N
        PERFORM 120-READ-DATA
*
        PERFORM 130-STORE-READ
            UNTIL DATA-ENDED
                    OR N = 50.
*
        GO TO 140-EXIT-READ.
*
 120-READ-DATA.
        READ INPUT-FILE
            AT END SET DATA-ENDED TO TRUE.
*
 130-STORE-READ.
        ADD 1 TO N
        MOVE INPUT-RECORD TO TABLE-REC (N)
        PERFORM 120-READ-DATA.
*
 140-EXIT-READ.
        EXIT.
*
 200-SORT-DATA SECTION.
*
 210-SET-UP-TO-SORT.
        MOVE 'UNSORTED' TO TESTIT
        MOVE N TO M
*
        PERFORM 220-OUTER-LOOP VARYING I FROM 1 BY 1
                        UNTIL TESTIT = 'SORTED'
                            OR I = N.
        GO TO 240-SORT-ENDED.
*
 220-OUTER-LOOP.
        MOVE 'SORTED' TO TESTIT
        COMPUTE M = M - 1
        PERFORM 230-PAIRED-COMPARISONS VARYING J FROM 1 BY 1
                    UNTIL J > M.
```

FIGURE 19-9

COBOL Internal Sort Program
Using the Adjacent Comparison-
Interchange Method (continued)

```
*
  230-PAIRED-COMPARISONS.
      COMPUTE K = 1 + J
*
      IF NAME (J) IS GREATER THAN NAME (K)
         MOVE TABLE-REC (J) TO TEMP-STORE
         MOVE TABLE-REC (K) TO TABLE-REC (J)
         MOVE TEMP-STORE TO TABLE-REC (K)
         MOVE 'UNSORTED' TO TESTIT
      END-IF.
*
  240-SORT-ENDED.
      EXIT.
*
  300-PRINT-DATA SECTION.
*
  310-PRINT-ROUTINE.
      PERFORM VARYING I FROM 1 BY 1
             UNTIL I > N
         MOVE TABLE-REC (I) TO PRINT-RECORD
         WRITE PRINT-RECORD AFTER ADVANCING 1 LINE
      END-PERFORM.
*
  320-PRINT-END.
      EXIT.
```

programmer preference, and has no relationship to the sort procedure being illustrated.

Another version of the interchange sort algorithm is the *bubble sort-interchange method*. Use of this approach results in the first part of the table being sorted first. By the bubble sort-interchange method the first step is that the second record is compared with the first and, if necessary, they are interchanged. Then the third record is compared with the second. If these two records are interchanged, the (new) second record is compared with the first, interchanging if necessary. Next, the fourth and third records are compared for possible interchange. Again, if an interchange occurs, we go "upward" and compare the third with the second record and then possibly the second with the first record. Thus, at each stage a record rises like a bubble to find its proper place, and hence the name "bubble sort," which is applied to this method.

As an example of using the bubble sort-interchange approach, consider the following set of six records with sort keys as indicated:

```
5
8
10
11
9
15
```

Comparison of the second and first records results in no interchange. Similarly, comparison of the third and second and of the fourth and third records results in no interchange. However, when the fifth and fourth records are compared (9 and 11), an interchange results. Following this, comparison of the fourth and third records (9 and 10) results in another interchange, but then the comparison of the third and second records (9 and 8) results in no further interchange. Finally, the sixth and fifth records are compared (15 and 11). Since this is the last pair of records and no interchange is required, the sort routine is completed.

Another internal sort procedure is one devised by D. L. Shell in 1959 and that bears his name. The main improvement associated with the *Shell sort* is that it has the property of moving records that are far removed from their proper position in fewer steps than either the adjacent comparisons-interchange algorithm or the bubble sort-interchange algorithm. To achieve this result, the procedure uses a distance parameter. Initially, the distance parameter is set to half the table length, thereby comparing the first element with the "middle" element in the table and exchanging the elements if appropriate. The procedure involves multiple passes, as all sorts do; and on each pass, the distance factor is reduced by half until the distance is 1, which is then the last pass. When an exchange occurs, the procedure followed is to examine whether or not additional exchanges should occur by "backing up" in distance-factor increments. A brief illustration will help to explain the procedure. Suppose that we have the following list of values in a table:

$$6 \quad 2 \quad 15 \quad 1 \quad 3 \quad 8 \quad 18 \quad 10 \quad 7 \quad 20$$

Initially, the distance factor is set to 5, resulting in comparison of 6 and 8, 2 and 18, 15 and 10, and so on. When the 15 and 10 are compared, they are interchanged, resulting in the following revised list after the first pass:

$$6 \quad 2 \quad 10 \quad 1 \quad 3 \quad 8 \quad 18 \quad 15 \quad 7 \quad 20$$

On the second pass the distance factor is reduced by half, from 5 to 2 (truncating the fractional quotient), resulting in comparison of 6 and 10, 2 and 1 (and interchange), 10 and 3 (and interchange). At this point in the second pass, the listed order is

$$6 \quad 1 \quad 3 \quad 2 \quad 10 \quad 8 \quad 18 \quad 15 \quad 7 \quad 20$$

Now we back up and compare 3 to 6, since the procedure backs up by the distance factor after an exchange has occurred, when possible. Thus, 6 and 3 would be interchanged and the procedure then would resume with a comparison of 2 and 8, which is where it left off before the backing up. The reason that we did not consider the "backing up" concept earlier in this example is there was no previous occasion in which there was an interchange for which the distance factor allowed us to back up and still be within the limits of the table.

Figure 19-10 presents PROCEDURE DIVISION code to implement the Shell sort. The example includes an algorithm for computing an odd-numbered value as the initial distance factor, DIST, since it has been found that use of an odd-numbered value as the initial distance factor generally results in a faster sort than use of an even-numbered value.

R E V I E W . . . .

1. By "internal sorting" we mean the sorting of a table held in the _____ of the computer.

                                                                internal (or central) storage

FIGURE 19-10
PROCEDURE DIVISION Code for a
Shell Sort Routine

```
*   This is an illustration of the Shell Sort procedure.
*   Also, it demonstrates the options of writing COBOL
*   programs in lower case, omitting the environment
*   division, and no files defined for the program --
*   its output is done using the display verb.
*
*   The data to be sorted are in data-table. For
*   simplicity we insert the data with one move statement.
*
*   Selected data-name definitions:
*     k (...)    is the subscripted reference to the key field
*                   for each record in the table.
*     r (...)    is the whole record (for simplicity it is
*                   only 3 bytes long)
*     ts         is the table size in terms of number of
*                   records
*     dist       is the "distance" parameter
*     i, j, 1, m are used for subscript references
*     temp       is temporary storage for the exchange process
*
  identification division.
  program-id.  shell-sort.
*
  data division.
*
  working-storage section.
*
  01   data-table.
       02 r      occurs 10 times.
          03 k   pic xx.
          03     pic x.
  01   ts        pic 99 value 10.
  01   dist      pic 99.
  01   1         pic 99.
  01   i         pic 99.
  01   j         pic 99.
  01   m         pic 99.
*
  01   flags     pic xxx.
       88 keep-comparing value "aaa".
       88 stop-comparing value "zzz".
*
  01   temp      pic x(3).
*
  procedure division.
*
  shell-sort-routine.
*
       move "06 02 15 01 03 08 18 10 07 20 "
            to data-table
*
```

FIGURE 19-10

PROCEDURE DIVISION Code for a
Shell Sort Routine (continued)

```
*   The following procedure computed an initial odd value
*   for the distance factor
*
    move 1 to dist
    if ts > 3
       perform until dist > ts
         compute dist = dist * 2
       end-perform
       compute dist = (dist / 2) - 1
    end-if.
*
    perform until dist < 1
       compute 1 = ts - dist
       move 1 to j
       perform until j > 1
          compute m = j + dist
          if k(j) > k(m)
             move j to i
             perform exchanger
          end-if
          add 1 to j
       end-perform
       compute dist = dist / 2
    end-perform.
*
    perform varying i from 1 by 1 until i > 10
       display i "   " r(i)
    end-perform.
*
    stop run.
*
  exchanger.
*
    set keep-comparing to true
    perform until stop-comparing
       move r(i) to temp
       compute m = i + dist
       move r(m) to r(i)
       move temp to r(m)
       compute i = i - dist
       if i >= 1
          compute m = i + dist
          if k (i) <= k (m)
             set stop-comparing to true
          else
             continue
          end-if
       else
          set stop-comparing to true
       end-if
    end-perform.
```

2. Several versions of the interchange sort algorithm exist. The feature that is common to all these versions is that in each approach _____ (number) records are compared each time for possible interchange.

2

3. By the adjacent comparison-interchange method, all adjacent records are compared and interchanged, when necessary, during each pass through the table. The fact that the table is correctly sorted is indicated when _____ (number) interchanges are required during a particular pass through the table.

0

4. Another version of the interchange sort algorithm is the bubble sort-interchange. By this approach each record is properly placed before subsequent records are considered, resulting in the [first / last] part of the table being sorted first.

first

5. In the Shell sort procedure the distance parameter used to determine which pairs of items will be compared initially is set at _____ the table length.

one-half

6. In the Shell sort procedure the distance parameter for the last pass through the table is equal to _____ (value).

1

. . . .

SUMMARY

Two methods that are commonly used for searching tables of data held in internal storage are *linear search* and *binary search*. Linear search is similar to the access method used with sequential files, in that the records are accessed in sequential order. Whereas linear search can be used with either sorted or unsorted tables, the method of binary search requires that the table data be in sorted order. The basic idea underlying binary search is that each comparison eliminates from consideration half of the entries remaining at that point in the search.

Several COBOL language features for table searching were described, including examples of their use. The OCCURS clause is included in a data description to indicate the number of entries for a data level, and to identify the sort key that is involved. The INDEXED BY or the USAGE IS INDEX clauses are included in data descriptions to identify a particular data item as being an index. The SEARCH is the verb that includes identification of the table to be searched, and includes options regarding subsequent processing when a match is found vs. when a match is not found. Finally, the SET verb provides a way of designating the value to be assigned to an INDEX.

Examples of table searching were presented for both one-level and two-level tables. These examples were followed by a sample program that incorporates indexing and searching.

The final section of this chapter described *internal sorting*, which is concerned with the sorting of data held in central storage, rather than on external files. Three versions of the *interchange sort algorithm* were described. By the *adjacent comparison-interchange* method all adjacent records are compared and interchanged, when necessary, during each pass through the table. By the *bubble sort-interchange* method each record is properly placed in the file before subsequent records are considered. In the *Shell sort* procedure, a so-called distance parameter is used to determine which pairs of entries will be compared, with the distance factor being reduced with each pass until the sort has been completed.

EXERCISES

19.1 How does COBOL differentiate between searching sorted and unsorted tables?

19.2 What is the difference between an index and a subscript in COBOL?

19.3 Review the meaning of the following search-related COBOL features, explaining the use of each feature:

a. OCCURS accompanied by the ASCENDING (DESCENDING) KEY options

b. INDEXED BY

c. USAGE IS INDEX

d. SEARCH and its several optional forms

e. SET TO and SET UP BY or SET DOWN BY

19.4 Modify the sample program for table searching presented in Figure 19-7 as follows. Assume that the student names are sorted in ascending sequence. After the table is read in, read file records, each of which contains a student name. Search the table and print the test score data for that student. If the name of the student cannot be found, print a suitable error message.

19.5 Consider the following definitions:

```
01  TABLE-OF-NAMES.
    02  NAMES OCCURS 100 TIMES
            INDEXED BY I.
        03  NAME-LETTERS OCCURS 20 TIMES
                INDEXED BY C V.
            04  LETTER     PIC X.
01  VOWEL-FLAG             PIC XXX.
    88  VOWEL-FOUND        VALUE 'YES'.
    88  VOWEL-NOT-FOUND    VALUE 'NO'.
01  CONSONANT-FLAG         PIC XXX.
    88  CONSONANT-FOUND    VALUE 'YES'.
    88  CONSONANT-NOT-FOUND VALUE 'NO'.
```

Write instructions to find the first vowel after the first consonant for a given name, say, the 10th one. If there is a first vowel after the first consonant, then V should contain the location of that vowel and C should contain the location of the first consonant within the name.

Use VOWEL-FLAG and CONSONANT-FLAG as defined above.

(*Note:* When a table is indexed by two index items, as in INDEXED BY C V, if VARYING is used and specifies C or V, then the index specified is the one used in the search. If VARYING is omitted, then the first item, in this case C, is the one used in the search.)

19.6 Suppose that we have a table that contains the following data:

    10   12   04   08   03

If we were using the adjacent comparison-interchange method and if a pair comparison takes 1 microsecond and a pair interchange takes 5 microseconds, what would be the total comparison time and what would be the total interchange time? Be sure to justify your answer.

19.7   Modify the sample program presented in Figure 19-9 to employ the bubble sort method instead of the adjacent comparison method for sorting records.

19.8   *Note: This exercise involves table handling, searching, and report generating. As such, it can be considered as a capstone exercise for both this chapter as well as Chapter 18.*

We want to process salary data and produce three reports that can help management review and control salary expenses. Figures 19-11, 19-12, and 19-13 illustrate the three reports required.

The first output report, in Figure 19-11, summarizes the salary values for each employee, in each department, for each of the six working days of the week.

The second report, shown as Figure 19-12, summarizes the salary data by department and day. The three-level table in Figure 19-11 has been collapsed into a two-level table in Figure 19-12.

FIGURE 19-11
First Required Salary Report for Exercise 19.8

```
                                    ACME ANYTHING CORP.
                                    EMPLOYEE SALARY TABLE

                                     SEPTEMBER 18, 1992

**********************************************************************************************
*             *                     *                     *           *           *           *
* DEPARTMENT*          1            *          2          *     3     *     4     *     5     *
*             *                     *                     *           *           *           *
* * * * * * * * * * * * * * * * * * * * * * * * * * * * * * * * * * * * * * * * * * * * * * * *
*             *                     *                     *           *           *           *
* EMPLOYEE  *  102    106    113  * 103    109    115  *           *           *           *
*             *                     *                     *           *           *           *
**********************************************************************************************
*             *                     *                     *           *           *           *
* MONDAY    *  45.00  35.45  32.00*  0.00 101.00  79.00*           *           *           *
*             *                     *                     *           *           *           *
* * * * * * * * * * * * * * * * * * * * * * * * * * * * * * * * * * * * * * * * * * * * * * * *
*             *                     *                     *           *           *           *
* TUESDAY   *  37.60  43.24  38.07* 22.35   0.00  12.00*           *           *           *
*             *                     *                     *           *           *           *
* * * * * * * * * * * * * * * * * * * * * * * * * * * * * * * * * * * * * * * * * * * * * * * *
*             *                     *                     *           *           *           *
* WEDNESDAY * 11.00 101.00  22.00* 15.00  23.00  18.00*           *           *           *
*             *                     *                     *           *           *           *
* * * * * * * * * * * * * * * * * * * * * * * * * * * * * * * * * * * * * * * * * * * * * * * *
*             *                     *                     *           *           *           *
* THURSDAY  * 45.35  26.00  32.24*100.00  20.00 100.00*           *           *           *
*             *                     *                     *           *           *           *
* * * * * * * * * * * * * * * * * * * * * * * * * * * * * * * * * * * * * * * * * * * * * * * *
*             *                     *                     *           *           *           *
* FRIDAY    * 50.00  30.00  40.00* 21.00  17.75  25.50*           *           *           *
*             *                     *                     *           *           *           *
* * * * * * * * * * * * * * * * * * * * * * * * * * * * * * * * * * * * * * * * * * * * * * * *
*             *                     *                     *           *           *           *
* SATURDAY  *120.00  66.00   0.00*  0.00  24.00   0.00*           *           *           *
*             *                     *                     *           *           *           *
**********************************************************************************************
*             *                     *                     *           *           *           *
* EMP TOTAL *308.95 300.69 165.11*158.35 185.75 234.50*           *           *           *
*             *                     *                     *           *           *           *
**********************************************************************************************

   NOTE: THE FIGURES IN THE ABOVE TABLE ARE FOR THE PURPOSES OF
         DEMONSTRATING THE FORMAT ONLY; OTHER THAN THAT, THEY
         HAVE NO MEANING WHATSOEVER.
```

FIGURE 19-12

Second Required Salary Report for Exercise 19.8

```
                         ACME ANYTHING CORP.
                       DEPARTMENT SALARY EXPENSE

                          SEPTEMBER 18, 1992

   ***************************************************************
   *            *       *       *       *       *       *        *
   *DEPARTMENT*    1    *   2   *   3   *   4   *   5   *  DAILY  *
   *            *       *       *       *       *       *  TOTAL  *
   ***************************************************************
   *            *       *       *       *       *       *        *
   * MONDAY     * 112.45* 180.00*       *       *       * 9999.99 *
   *            *       *       *       *       *       *        *
   * TUESDAY    * 118.91*  34.35*       *       *       *        *
   *            *       *       *       *       *       *        *
   * WEDNESDAY* 134.00 *  56.00*       *       *       *        *
   *            *       *       *       *       *       *        *
   * THURSDAY * 103.59 * 220.00*       *       *       *        *
   *            *       *       *       *       *       *        *
   * FRIDAY     * 120.00*  64.25*       *       *       *        *
   *            *       *       *       *       *       *        *
   * SATURDAY * 186.00 *  24.00*       *       *       *        *
   *            *       *       *       *       *       *        *
   ***************************************************************
   * WEEKLY     *       *       *       *       *       *        *
   * TOTAL      * 774.95* 578.60*       *       *       *99999.99 *
   *            *       *       *       *       *       *        *
   ***************************************************************
```

FIGURE 19-13

Third Required Salary Report for Exercise 19.8

```
                                                      PAGE 1
                         ACME ANYTHING CORP.
                        WEEKLY SALARY REPORT
                   WEEK ENDING: SEPTEMBER 18, 1992

   DEPT#      DAY      EMP#     HRS     PAY RATE      GROSS PAY
                                WORKED

   =============================================================

     1      MONDAY     XXX       X       X.XX          XX.XX
                       XXX       X       X.XX          XX.XX
                       XXX       X       X.XX          XX.XX
                                                     ----------
                                                       XXX.XX

            TUESDAY    XXX       X       X.XX          XX.XX
              :
            WEDNESDAY  ...
              :
            THURSDAY   ...
              :
            FRIDAY     ...
              :
            SATURDAY   XXX       X       X.XX          XX.XX
                       XXX       X       X.XX          XX.XX

         ---------- (page break here) -----------
```

FIGURE 19-13
Third Required Salary Report for
Exercise 19.8 (continued)

```
                                                            PAGE 2
                          ACME ANYTHING CORP.
                          WEEKLY SALARY REPORT
                     WEEK ENDING: SEPTEMBER 18, 1992


        DEPT#   DAY        EMP#      HOURS      PAY RATE      GROSS PAY
                                     WORKED
        ============================================================

          1                XXX        X          X.XX          XX.XX
                                                              --------
                                                              XXX.XX

                                                              --------

                DEPARTMENT 1 WEEKLY TOTAL:                   XXXX.XX
                                                           =============

          2     MONDAY     XXX   .......
                :
          3     MONDAY     XXX   ........
                :
          4     MONDAY     XXX   .........
                :
          5     MONDAY     XXX   .........
                :
                DEPARTMENT 5 WEEKLY TOTAL :                   XXXX.XX
                                                           =============

                COMPANY WEEKLY TOTAL:                    $   XXXXX.XX
                                                           =============
```

The third report, in Figure 19-13, presents a detailed listing of salary data by department, day of the week, and employee. The figure shows sample formats for two pages of output to illustrate continuation of a department report onto a following page. Notice that the totals for department 1 are on page 2.

The source data are in the following file:

COLUMN	FIELD	TYPE
1–3	EMPLOYEE #	ALPHANUMERIC
5	DAY	NUMERIC (1=MON,..,6=SAT)
7	HOURS WORKED	NUMERIC (RANGE 4-8)

It is assumed that the data have already been checked by another program and that there are no data errors.

The input values will be stored in a 3-dimensional table allowing for salary data for 6 days, 5 departments, and 3 employees per department. Each employee's daily salary must be calculated before it is stored in the table.

The rate of pay for each employee and his/her department number can be obtained by searching a WORKING-STORAGE table. The table is to be loaded at the beginning of the program from the following input file:

COLUMN	FIELD	TYPE
1–3	EMPLOYEE #	ALPHANUMERIC
4	DEPARTMENT #	NUMERIC
5–7	PAY RATE	NUMERIC (9V99)

There are three employees in each department. Each employee is identified by an employee number such as 102 or 106, as illustrated in the sample output in Figure 19-11. However, for table-processing purposes, each employee within each department should be referenced by a subscript (or index) item, referencing the employee as 1, 2, or 3. Thus you will need to determine a subscript reference value for each employee after reading in each 3-byte employee number. A natural way will be to search the pay-rate table to find the corresponding employee-department number and use that information to form the subscript/index reference number. For example, by reference to the sample output in Figure 19-11 we can see that the employee whose number is 109 is employee 2 in department 2.

It would also be natural to use table searching to find the pay rate for each employee. Remember that the input data contain only the hours worked. For purposes of reporting the required data we have to calculate the employee earnings, using both the hours worked and the pay rate per hour.

The date for all report headings is to be generated by the program at execution time. Note that the month is to be printed in letters as a name.

With respect to the third report illustrated in Figure 19-13, follow these rules:

- Detail lines within each department are single spaced. Double-space after department daily totals and before department totals. Triple-space between departments and before company total.

- The department number is to be printed only once for each department unless the content related to a department is to be split across several pages; then, print the department number again on the first detail line of each new page.

- Each page will consist of 40 lines. Print page numbers for the third report (Figure 19-13), and include all headings on each page of that report.

Figure 19-14 provides several sections of the required program, allowing you to concentrate your effort on developing the program logic rather than on the definition of variable names, tables, and report formats. You will need to add several additional tables—for instance, one containing the names of the days of the week, and so forth—as well as the table format for producing the report shown in Figure 19-12.

A secondary benefit of the requirement to use a given DATA DIVISION is that it gives you experience in working with data-name definitions created by someone else. Beginning professional programmers, for the most part, are given assignments involving the modification of existing programs. This assignment will give you a sense of that forthcoming experience.

FIGURE 19-14
Partial COBOL Program for
Exercise 19.8

```
        IDENTIFICATION DIVISION.
        PROGRAM-ID. SALREP.
*
        ENVIRONMENT DIVISION.
        CONFIGURATION SECTION.
        SOURCE-COMPUTER.
        OBJECT-COMPUTER.
*
        INPUT-OUTPUT SECTION.
*
        FILE-CONTROL.
*
            SELECT IN-FILE          ASSIGN TO INFILE.
            SELECT EMP-REP-FILE     ASSIGN TO PRINTER1.
            SELECT DEPT-REP-FILE    ASSIGN TO PRINTER2.
            SELECT SUMMARY-REP-FILE ASSIGN TO PRINTER3.
*
        DATA DIVISION.
*
        FILE SECTION.
*
        FD  IN-FILE
                RECORDING MODE IS F   (if you are using an IBM system)
                LABEL RECORDS ARE OMITTED
                BLOCK CONTAINS 10 RECORDS
                DATA RECORD IS IN-REC.
*
        01  IN-REC.
            02  IN-EMP-NUM              PIC X(03).
            02  FILLER                 PIC X(01).
            02  IN-DAY                 PIC 9(01).
            02  FILLER                 PIC X(01).
            02  IN-HOURS               PIC 9(01).
            02  FILLER                 PIC X(73).
*
        FD  EMP-REP-FILE
                LABEL RECORDS OMITTED.
*
        01  EMP-REP                    PIC X(132).
*
        FD  DEPT-REP-FILE
                LABEL RECORDS OMITTED.
*
        01  DEPT-REP                   PIC X(132).
*
        FD  SUMMARY-REP-FILE
*
                LABEL RECORDS OMITTED.
*
        01  SUMMARY-REP                PIC X(132).
/
```

FIGURE 19-14
Partial COBOL Program for
Exercise 19.8 (continued)

```
     WORKING-STORAGE SECTION.
*
*   WORKING-ITEMS:
*
 01  WS-DATE-ITEMS.
     02  WS-DATE.
         03  WS-YR                    PIC 9(02).
         03  WS-MO                    PIC 9(02).
         03  WS-DA                    PIC 9(02).
     02  WS-YEAR                      PIC 9(04).
*
 01  WS-NUMERIC-ITEMS.
     02  WS-LINE                      PIC 9(01).
     02  WS-PAGE                      PIC 9(01)    VALUE 0.
*
     02  WS-SALARY                    PIC 99V99.
     02  WS-PAYRATE                   PIC 9V99.
     02  C-WEEKLY-TOTAL               PIC 9(05)V99 VALUE 0.
*
 01  WS-SUBSCRIPTS.
     02  WS-DAY                       PIC 9(01).
     02  WS-DEPT                      PIC 9(01).
     02  WS-EMP                       PIC 9(01).
*
 01  WS-FLAGS.
     02  INFILE-EOF-FLAG              PIC X(01)  VALUE 'N'.
*
         88  END-OF-INFILE            VALUE 'Y'.
     02  SUBSCRIPT-FOUND-FLAG         PIC X(01)  VALUE 'N'.
*
         88  SUBSCRIPT-FOUND          VALUE 'Y'.
/
*   TABLE DESCRIPTIONS:
*
*
 01  PAY-RATE-TABLE.
     02  T-DEPT                       OCCURS 5 TIMES
                                      INDEXED BY DEPT-IDX.
         03  T-EMP                    OCCURS 3 TIMES
                                      INDEXED BY EMP-IDX.
             04  T-EMPNUM             PIC X(03).
             04  T-DEPTNUM            PIC 9(01).
             04  T-PAYRATE            PIC 9V99.
*
*   TABLE FOR STORING EMPLOYEE SALARIES:
*
 01  SALARY-TABLE.
     02  S-DAY                        OCCURS 6 TIMES.
         03  S-DEPT                   OCCURS 5 TIMES.
             04  S-EMP                OCCURS 3 TIMES.
                 05  SALARY           PIC 99V99.
                 05  HOURS            PIC 9(01).
```

FIGURE 19-14

Partial COBOL Program for
Exercise 19.8 (continued)

```
*
*   TABLES FOR TOTALS:
*
 01   EMPLOYEE-WEEKLY-TABLE.
      02   E-WEEKLY-DEPT              OCCURS 5 TIMES.
           03   E-WEEKLY-EMP          OCCURS 3 TIMES.
                04   E-WEEKLY-TOTAL   PIC 999V99.
*
 01   DEPT-WEEKLY-TABLE.
      02   D-WEEKLY-TOTAL             OCCURS 5 TIMES
                                      PIC 9999V99.
*
 01   DEPT-DAILY-TABLE.
      02   D-DAILY-DEPT               OCCURS 5 TIMES.
           03   D-DAILY-DAY           OCCURS 6 TIMES.
                04   D-DAILY-TOTAL    PIC 999V99.
*
 01   COMP-DAILY-TABLE.
      02   C-DAILY-TOTAL              OCCURS 6 TIMES
                                      PIC 9999V99.
/
*   DESCRIPTION FOR OUTPUT REPORTS:
*
 01   EMPLOYEE-REPORT.
      02   ER-HEAD1.
           03   FILLER                PIC X(53)  VALUE SPACES.
           03   FILLER                PIC X(19)  VALUE
                'ACME ANYTHING CORP.'.
*
      02   ER-HEAD2.
           03   FILLER                PIC X(51)  VALUE SPACES.
           03   FILLER                PIC X(21)  VALUE
                'EMPLOYEE SALARY TABLE'.
*
      02   ER-HEAD3.
           03   FILLER                PIC X(52)  VALUE SPACES.
           03   ER-MONTH              PIC X(09).
           03   FILLER                PIC X(01)  VALUE SPACES.
           03   ER-DA                 PIC Z9.
           03   FILLER                PIC X(02)  VALUE ', '.
           03   ER-YEAR               PIC 9(04).
*
      02   ER-LINE1.
           03   FILLER                PIC X(05)  VALUE SPACES.
           03   FILLER                PIC X(118) VALUE ALL '*'.
*
      02   ER-LINE2.
           03   FILLER                PIC X(05)  VALUE SPACES.
           03   FILLER                PIC X(118) VALUE ALL
                '* '.
```

FIGURE 19-14
Partial COBOL Program for
Exercise 19.8 (continued)

```
*
        02  ER-LINE3.
            03  FILLER                      PIC X(05)  VALUE SPACES.
            03  FILLER                      PIC X(12)  VALUE
                '*          '.
            03  FILLER                      PIC X(105) VALUE ALL
                '*              '.
*
        02  ER-LINE3A.
            03  FILLER                      PIC X(05)  VALUE SPACES.
            03  FILLER                      PIC X(12)  VALUE
                '*          '.
            03  FILLER                      PIC X(105) VALUE ALL
                '*              '.
*
        02  ER-HEAD4 REDEFINES ER-LINE3A.
            03  FILLER                      PIC X(07).
            03  FILLER1                     PIC X(10).
            03  ER-HEAD4-DEPT               OCCURS 5 TIMES.
                04  FILLER                  PIC X(11).
                04  ER-DEPT                 PIC 9(01).
                04  FILLER                  PIC X(09).
*
        02  ER-LINE3B.
            03  FILLER                      PIC X(05)  VALUE SPACES.
            03  FILLER                      PIC X(12)  VALUE
                '*          '.
            03  FILLER                      PIC X(105) VALUE ALL
                '*              '.
*
        02  ER-HEAD5 REDEFINES ER-LINE3B.
            03  FILLER                      PIC X(07).
            03  FILLER2                     PIC X(10).
            03  ER-HEAD5-DEPT               OCCURS 5 TIMES.
                04  ER-HEAD5-EMP            OCCURS 3 TIMES.
                    05  FILLER             PIC X(03).
                    05  ER-EMPNUM          PIC X(03).
                    05  FILLER             PIC X(01).
*
        02  ER-LINE3C.
            03  FILLER                      PIC X(05)  VALUE SPACES.
*
            03  FILLER                      PIC X(12)  VALUE
                '*          '.
            03  FILLER                      PIC X(105) VALUE ALL
                '*              '.
```

FIGURE 19-14

Partial COBOL Program for
Exercise 19.8 (continued)

```
        *
                02   ER-DETAIL REDEFINES ER-LINE3C.
                     03   FILLER                 PIC X(07).
                     03   ER-DAY                 PIC X(09).
                     03   FILLER                 PIC X(01).
                     03   ER-DETAIL-DEPT         OCCURS 5 TIMES.
                          04   ER-DETAIL-EMP     OCCURS 3 TIMES.
                               05   ER-AMT       PIC ZZ9.99.
                               05   FILLER       PIC X(01).
        *
                02   ER-LINE3D.
                     03   FILLER                 PIC X(05)  VALUE SPACES.
                     03   FILLER                 PIC X(12)  VALUE
                          '*           '.
                     03   FILLER                 PIC X(105) VALUE ALL
                          '*                '.
        *
                02   ER-TOTAL-LN REDEFINES ER-LINE3D.
                     03   FILLER                 PIC X(07).
                     03   FILLER3                PIC X(10).
                     03   ER-TOTAL-DEPT          OCCURS 5 TIMES.
                          04   ER-TOTAL-EMP      OCCURS 3 TIMES.
                               05   ER-TOTAL     PIC ZZ9.99.
                               05   FILLER       PIC X(01).
        *
         01   SUMMARY-REP-FORMAT.
                02   SR-HEAD1.
                     03   FILLER                 PIC X(82)  VALUE SPACES.
                     03   FILLER                 PIC X(04)  VALUE 'PAGE'.
                     03   SR-PAGE                PIC ZZ9.
        *
                02   SR-HEAD2.
                     03   FILLER                 PIC X(50)  VALUE SPACES.
                     03   FILLER                 PIC X(19)  VALUE
                          'ACME ANYTHING CORP.'.
        *
                02   SR-HEAD3.
                     03   FILLER                 PIC X(45)  VALUE SPACES.
                     03   FILLER                 PIC X(28)  VALUE
                          'WEEKLY SALARY EXPENSE REPORT'.
        *
                02   SR-HEAD4.
                     03   FILLER                 PIC X(43)  VALUE SPACES.
                     03   FILLER                 PIC X(14)  VALUE
                          'WEEK ENDING: '.
                     03   SR-MONTH               PIC X(09).
                     03   FILLER                 PIC X(01)  VALUE SPACE.
                     03   SR-DA                  PIC Z9.
                     03   FILLER                 PIC X(02)  VALUE ', '.
                     03   SR-YEAR                PIC 9(04).
```

FIGURE 19-14
*Partial COBOL Program for
Exercise 19.8 (continued)*

```
                 *
                         02  SR-HEAD5.
                             03  FILLER                    PIC X(30)  VALUE SPACES.
                             03  FILLER                    PIC X(10)  VALUE
                                 'DEPT#     '.
                             03  FILLER                    PIC X(10)  VALUE
                                 ' DAY      '.
                             03  FILLER                    PIC X(10)  VALUE
                                 'EMP#     H'.
                             03  FILLER                    PIC X(10)  VALUE
                                 'RS   PAY '.
                             03  FILLER                    PIC X(10)  VALUE
                                 'RATE      '.
                             03  FILLER                    PIC X(10)  VALUE
                                 'GROSS PAY '.
                 *
                         02  SR-HEAD6.
                             03  FILLER                    PIC X(58)  VALUE SPACES.
                             03  FILLER                    PIC X(06)  VALUE 'WORKED'.
                 *
                         02  SR-HEAD7.
                             03  FILLER                    PIC X(30)  VALUE SPACES.
                             03  FILLER                    PIC X(60)  VALUE ALL '='.
                 *
                         02  SR-BLANK.
                             03  FILLER                    PIC X(132) VALUE SPACES.
                 *
                         02  SR-LINE1.
                             03  FILLER                    PIC X(80)  VALUE SPACES.
                             03  FILLER                    PIC X(10)  VALUE ALL '-'.
                 *
                         02  SR-LINE2.
                             03  FILLER                    PIC X(77)  VALUE SPACES.
                             03  FILLER                    PIC X(13)  VALUE ALL '='.
                 *
                         02  SR-DETAIL-LN.
                             03  FILLER                    PIC X(32)  VALUE SPACES.
                             03  SR-DEPT1                  PIC Z(01).
                             03  FILLER                    PIC X(07)  VALUE SPACES.
                             03  SR-DAY                    PIC X(09).
                             03  FILLER                    PIC X(01)  VALUE SPACE.
                             03  SR-EMPNUM                 PIC X(03).
                             03  FILLER                    PIC X(07)  VALUE SPACE.
                             03  SR-HRS                    PIC 9(01).
                             03  FILLER                    PIC X(07)  VALUE SPACES.
                             03  SR-PAYRATE                PIC 9.99.
                             03  FILLER                    PIC X(10)  VALUE SPACES.
                             03  SR-SALARY                 PIC ZZ9.99.
                 *
```

FIGURE 19-14
Partial COBOL Program for
Exercise 19.8 (continued)

```
            02  SR-DEPT-DAY-LN.
                03  FILLER                  PIC X(81)  VALUE SPACES.
                03  SR-DEPT-DAY-TOTAL       PIC ZZZ9.99.
        *
            02  SR-DEPT-WEEK-LN.
                03  FILLER                  PIC X(39)  VALUE SPACES.
                03  FILLER                  PIC X(11)  VALUE
                    'DEPARTMENT'.
                03  SR-DEPT2                PIC 9(01).
                03  FILLER                  PIC X(14)  VALUE
                    'WEEKLY TOTAL:'.
                03  FILLER                  PIC X(16)  VALUE SPACES.
                03  SR-DEPT-WEEK-TOTAL      PIC ZZZ9.99.
        *
            02  SR-COMP-WEEK-LN.
                03  FILLER                  PIC X(39)  VALUE SPACES.
                03  FILLER                  PIC X(21)  VALUE
                    'COMPANY WEEKLY TOTAL:'.
                03  FILLER                  PIC X(17)  VALUE SPACES.
                03  FILLER                  PIC X(03)  VALUE '$ '.
                03  SR-COMP-WEEK-TOTAL      PIC Z(04)9.99.
```

20 Indexed Files

I **N CHAPTER 10** *you were introduced to the three methods of file organization:* **sequential,** **indexed,** *and* **relative.** *Then, in Chapter 17 you studied sequential file organization in greater detail. This chapter is devoted to indexed file processing.*

In indexed file organization an index is created so that records can be located directly, without having to access them in sequence, even though they were entered into the file sequentially.

You will first be introduced to two common methods that are used for indexing files, followed by an example of creating such a file. Then you will study the special COBOL instructions for indexed files, which involve the ENVIRONMENT DIVISION and the PROCEDURE DIVISION. Finally, you will consider an example of processing the indexed file that was created earlier in the chapter.

INTRODUCTION

Indexed files represent something of a balance between sequential and relative files, because they allow for sequential storage as well as random access and random processing. The essential feature of an indexed file is that it consists of two parts: the *data file* and the *index(es)*. As the name implies, the data file contains the data records. Each record in the data file is identified uniquely on the basis of one or more keys within the record. When such a file is first created, the data records are written in ascending order of the unique identifying key(s). On the other hand, the index is some kind of "table" structure that facilitates random access. When looking for a particular record, as identified by its key, the index is used to find the (general) location of the record in the file so that the record can be accessed directly.

Indexed files can have multiple indexes. For example, one index could be based on a unique employee-number key in each employee record, while another index could be based on a possibly nonunique employee-name. In such a case we could achieve random access to the file as exemplified by the cases: "Get the record of Employee 1057" or "Get the record of Dorothy Gonzales."

Indexed files are also sequential files with respect to the unique identifier field in each record. For example, we can designate employee-number as the unique identifier field in employee records, create an indexed file, and then use that file as if it were a sequential file. In other words, records can be accessed in ascending order of employee-number just as they would be accessed with a sequential file. However, there are also added flexibilities for indexed files. For one thing, unlike a sequential file, we can do a random access to a particular record, say to employee-number 1057, and then do a sequential access to the following records, thus being able to bypass the records preceding the record for employee 1057.

Another significant difference between indexed and sequential files is that for indexed files both selective and exhaustive updating can be done. Such an option is very useful in applications in which there is natural batch processing as well as a need for occasional selective access to individual records. Payroll, for example, is a natural batch application. All the records in the file need to be processed for each pay period. Yet individual records often need to be accessed between pay periods for such purposes as changing a pay rate, changing a tax deduction, or adding a new employee. Indexed files are an ideal form of file organization to fulfill such needs; however, indexed files can be slower to process than files that are strictly sequential. Therefore indexed files should be used only when their versatility justifies the potentially slower processing time and the more complex environment that is required for the operating system to support such files.

R E V I E W . . . .

1. The type of file organization that allows sequential storage but also facilitates random accessing or processing is called _____ file organization.

   indexed

2. Every indexed file consists of two parts: a _____ file and at least one _____ file.

   data; index

3. Comparing the two, for batch processing applications faster processing time is associated with [indexed / sequential] files.

   sequential

INDEXING METHODS

There is no standard indexing method. Language implementors are responsible for providing their own methods. As far as COBOL is concerned, the language defines the functional aspects of indexing, or the "what." The "how" part of indexing is not part of COBOL. Still, it is useful for the applications programmer to have a basic understanding of common indexing methods. The details of indexing are too complex to be covered in this book. However, in the following two sections of this chapter we present the main concepts associated with two common methods: the *Indexed Sequential Access Method (ISAM),* and the *Virtual Storage Access Method (VSAM).* Both the names and the basic ideas represent specific IBM products. However, they are generic descriptors as well, and therefore their applicability is quite wide.

THE INDEXED SEQUENTIAL ACCESS METHOD (ISAM)

The essential features of ISAM are illustrated in Figure 20-1. The illustration includes use of the same physical file for both the data records and the index records. This example does not imply that this is the way an ISAM file must be constructed, but it does serve to illustrate one possible implementation. At the top of Figure 20-1 is the *cylinder index* for the file. Each record in the index consists of two fields. The *key field* contains the largest key value in the respective cylinder, while the *address field* contains the *address* of the track index for that cylinder. In the figure 68 is the highest key value in cylinder 0, while 01 (cylinder 0 track 1) is the address of the track index for the first cylinder. Notice that the convention generally used is to number both the cylinders and the tracks consecutively with 0,1, 2, and so forth.

The track index for cylinder 0 is in track 1 because track 0 of that cylinder is taken up by the cylinder index. Directing our attention to the track index for

FIGURE 20-1
Sample Indexed File (ISAM Method)

KEY	ADDRESS	KEY	ADDRESS	...		
68	01	460	10		Cylinder Index for Entire File	Track 0 (Cylinder 0)

PRIME INDEX		OVERFLOW INDEX		PRIME INDEX		OVERFLOW INDEX			
KEY	ADDRESS	KEY	ADDRESS	KEY	ADDRESS	KEY	ADDRESS		
68	02	*	*	*	*	*	*	Track Index for Cylinder 0	Track 1 (Cylinder 0)

40	50	54	55	68	Data Records	Track 2 (Cylinder 0)

125	11	200	901	369	12	460	913	Track Index for Cylinder 1	Track 0 (Cylinder 1)

100	101	119	120	125	Data Records	Track 1 (Cylinder 1)
210	250	260	271	369	Data Records	Track 2 (Cylinder 1)

Record 1		Record 2		Record 3		Record 4		Record 5			
132	903	190	912	189	902	380	905	385	911	Track 0	Cylinder 9 (Overflow) Data Records
390	914	200	0	375	904	460	0			Track 1	
										Track 2	

cylinder 0, we see that there are two index entries: the *prime index* and the *overflow index*. Asterisks are used in the example to signify unused entries. Thus there are no overflow data for the first track index entry. The first track index entry consists only of the prime index record, which signifies that the highest key in track 2 of cylinder 0 (address = 02) is 68, with the overflow index being unused in this case. The second pair of prime-overflow index records in track 1 is unused because it would be in reference to the next track of the cylinder (track 03), which does not exist. In this simplified example it is assumed that there are only three tracks per cylinder and, in the case of the first cylinder (0), that the first two tracks are taken up by the cylinder index and the track index, respectively, thereby leaving only one track available for data records.

The second cylinder is a somewhat more typical case. First, referring to the top of Figure 20-1, note that the second record in the cylinder index indicates that the highest record key in the second cylinder has the value 460 and that the address of the track index for that cylinder is cylinder 1, track 0 (10).

Next, consider the data in track 0 of cylinder 1, which is the track index for that cylinder. There are no headings shown for this track in Figure 20-1, but the same headings apply as for track 1 of cylinder 0. The first entry, 125, indicates that the highest prime key is 125 for cylinder 1, track 1 (address 11 in the following entry). The next entry, 200, indicates that the highest overflow key is 200; while the address, 901, indicates that the first record in overflow for this track is located in cylinder 9, track 0, at record 1.

Overflow records are records that have been added to a file after the file was first created. Consider the record at address 901, which is an overflow record for cylinder 1, track 1. Notice that its value, 132, is larger than the last record already included in cylinder 1, track 1 (125), but smaller than the first record in cylinder 1, track 2 (210). A record with a key value such as 132 must precede the first entry in track 2 and, therefore, is placed in overflow for track 1.

Now consider the overflow cylinder, cylinder 9. Each record includes the record value followed by a *pointer field,* which contains the address of the next logical record. For example, the pointer for the first record in cylinder 9, track 0 is 903, meaning that the next logical record is at cylinder 9, track 0, record 3. Following the chain of pointers, we can observe that the last record in overflow for cylinder 1, track 1 is the record with a key value of 200, located at cylinder 9, track 1, record 2. Its pointer value of 0 indicates the end of the chain.

If the file included in Figure 20-1 were accessed sequentially by key value, the records would be retrieved in the following order:

    40, 50, 54, 55, 68, 100, 101, 119, 120, 125, 132, 189, 190,
    200, 210, 250, 260, 271, 369, 375, 380, 382, 390, 460

Figure 20-2 presents a flowchart that indicates the accessing logic associated with sequential processing. Briefly, we begin with the cylinder index, which directs us to the first track index. From the track index we process all the records, both prime and overflow, for the cylinder. These processing steps are repeated for all the cylinders contained in the file. When the last record in the last cylinder and track is processed, the overall processing of the file is completed.

The main appeal of an indexed file, however, is the capability of processing such a file randomly. Figure 20-3 presents a flowchart that indicates the accessing logic associated with random access. Given the key associated with a record, the cylinder index is searched. The search may be sequential or binary. We then access the corresponding track index, which indicates whether the record is located in the prime or overflow area. The appropriate area is searched for a key-equal condition, and the record is accessed.

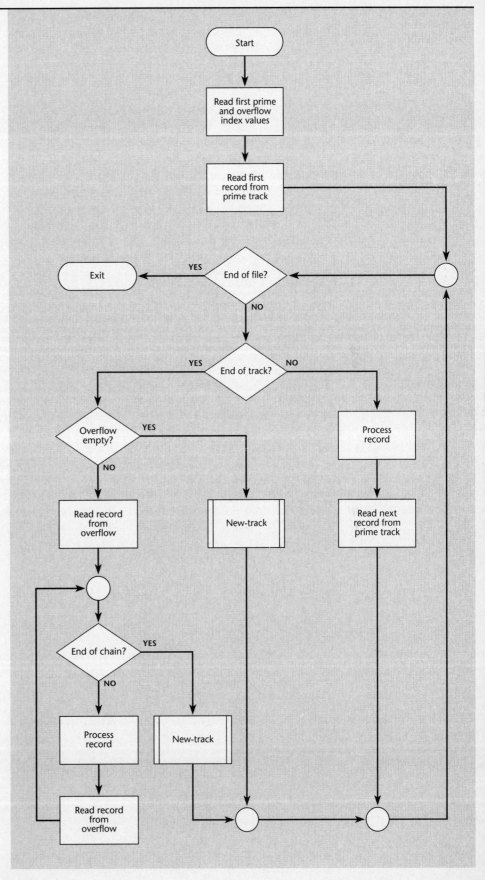

FIGURE 20-2
*Sequential Access with an
Indexed File*

(continued on next page)

FIGURE 20-2

Sequential Access with an Indexed File (continued)

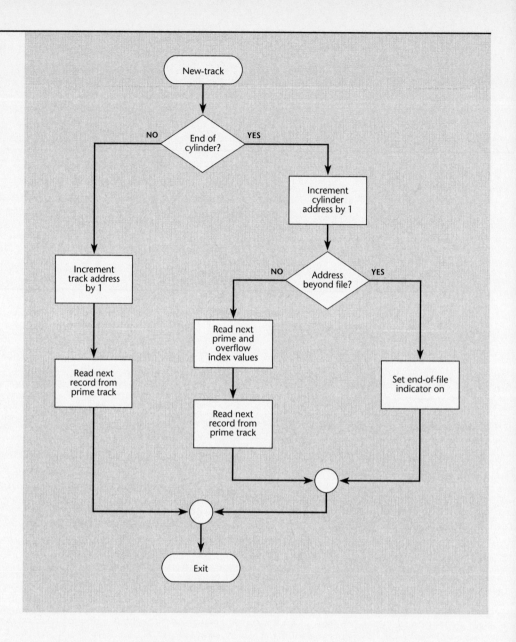

R E V I E W . . . .

1. In the Indexed Sequential Access Method (ISAM), the two types of indexes are the _____ index and the _____ index.

     cylinder; track

2. Each record in a track index consists of four fields: the prime key, the prime address, the _____ , and the

    _____

     overflow key; overflow address

3. When a record that is to be added to an indexed file should logically be located within a prime track, [the record is placed in that track and the last record is "bumped" into overflow / the record in question is entered directly into overflow].

     the record is placed in that track
     and the last record is "bumped" into overflow

FIGURE 20-3
Random Access with an
Indexed File

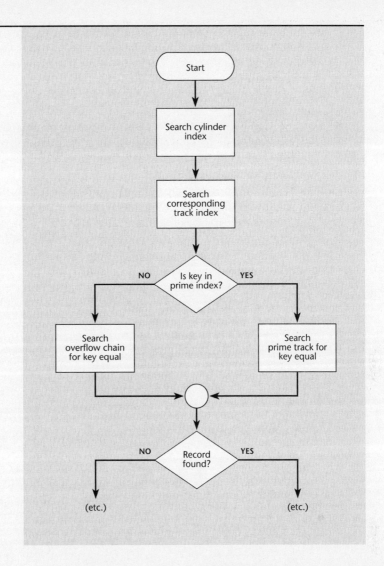

4. When a record that is to be added to an indexed file should logically be located within a particular track in overflow, [it is located in the appropriate position and other records are "bumped" / it is located in the next available position in overflow].

it is located in the next available position in overflow

5. To achieve logical contiguity of the records in overflow for records that may be physically separated, a(n) _____ field is included with each record to identify the location of the next sequential record, if it is located in overflow.

pointer

6. The concept of record chaining is particularly concerned with identifying the appropriate sequencing of records in the [prime / overflow] area of the data file.

overflow

. . . .

THE VIRTUAL STORAGE ACCESS METHOD (VSAM)

The indexed file structure described in the preceding section represents a widely used approach. However, it has one major shortcoming: as the number of records added to the file increases, the average access time grows rather quickly. As you will recall, additions to the file go into overflow space and are no longer in physical sequential order. Other indexing methods have been developed that are more efficient in accommodating additions. One of these methods is IBM's VSAM— Virtual Storage Access Method—which, among other features, incorporates an alternate index structure and can be used with COBOL indexed files. We describe some basic concepts in VSAM so that you have a sufficient background in this widely used index structure.

One of the options in VSAM is to build a *key-sequenced* indexed file that corresponds to COBOL indexed sequential files. In such a file the records are written in storage areas called *control intervals*. A control interval is similar to the concept of a block of records and may be a track in disk storage. A group of control intervals comprise a *control area*. We could think of the control interval as a track and the control area as a cylinder. However, VSAM is a logical method of file structure that is not dependent directly on the physical storage medium in use. For instance, one could have several control intervals per track or two cylinders per control area. Further, VSAM would be, in concept, applicable to nondisk-storage devices, such as solid state memories.

Figure 20-4 illustrates the conceptual structure of a VSAM key-sequenced file. Two control areas are shown, each control area having three control intervals, and each control interval having space for five data records. It should be noted that control intervals A3, B1, and B2 contain some vacant record spaces, while B3 is wholly vacant. VSAM deliberately leaves vacant spaces to facilitate the addition of new records, as will be explained below.

FIGURE 20-4

Sample Conceptual VSAM Structure

Index Set

Highest key in sequence set	115	170
Address of sequence set	I 1	I 2

Sequence Set

		I 1					I 2		
Highest key in control interval	61	100	115	Next sequence set	146	170	Null	Next sequence set
Address of control interval	A1	A2	A3	I2	B1	B2	Null	I . . .

. . .

Data Records

Control Intervals

A1	A2	A3		B1	B2	B3
10	68	105		140	151	V
35	70	110		142	154	A
42	75	112		146	160	C
50	79	115		Vacant	170	A
61	100	Vacant		Vacant	Vacant	N
						T

. . .

Control area 1   Control area 2

Two index levels are used. The higher level is called the *index set,* while the lower level is called the *sequence set.* These two index levels parallel the ISAM cylinder and track indexes discussed earlier in the chapter, but they are more flexible constructs since they are device-independent. Each record in the sequence set contains the value of the highest key in a control interval and the address of that control interval. For instance, the highest key in the A1 interval is the record key 61. In addition to these index values, each sequence set contains the address of the next sequence set. Thus, if we were processing such a VSAM file sequentially, after all records in control area 1 were accessed, we would move to sequence set I2 next, which indexes the control intervals in control area 2.

As an illustration of using the VSAM structure in Figure 20-4, suppose that we wanted to access record 154. The first record in the index set would be accessed and would indicate that record 154 is not in the first control area since the highest key there is 115. The next record in the index set would then be accessed and it would indicate that record 154, if it exists, is in the control area indexed by this record (control area 2). The address of the corresponding sequence set is I2, and the first record in sequence I2 would be accessed next. Since the highest key in the first record of I2 is 146, it would be known that record 154 is not in the first control interval indexed by I2. The next record in I2 has a key value of 170, and therefore record 154 should be in the control interval whose address is B2. Sequential access of the records in control interval B2 would result in retrieval of record 154, which happens to be the second record in the interval. Thus, random access to records can be achieved by using the VSAM index structure.

When records are added to a VSAM file, the resultant action depends on the availability of vacant space. For instance, if record 114 were to be added, record 115 would be moved down one place to the vacant space in control interval A3 and the new record 114 would be written in the space where 115 was; no change in the index structure takes place.

Suppose now that records 162 and 163 are to be added. Logically, they both belong in control interval B2. However, when it would be time to add record 163, there would be no room left in that control interval. VSAM would now cause a *control interval split,* as illustrated in Figure 20-5. The formerly vacant interval B3 is now partially occupied, and the records have been split across intervals B2 and B3, both of which now have some vacant spaces in them. Notice that a third record was added to sequence set I2 but the index set was not affected since 170 remains the highest record in that control area.

Addition of record 80 causes a *control area split,* as illustrated also in Figure 20-5. Record 80 belongs in control interval A2 which happened to have no vacant space in Figure 20-4. Further, no interval in this control area is vacant after the earlier addition of record 114, and therefore an interval split cannot take place as when we added record 163 in the preceding example. VSAM causes an area split by adding another control area, control area 3, and splitting the records across control areas 1 and 3. Notice that intervals A3 and C3 are left vacant so that there will be some time before another split is caused by addition of records in the intervals A1–A3 and C1–C3. As a result of the control area split a new sequence set, I3, has been created, and a new record has been added to the index set to index the new sequence set. Also, notice that if the records were processed sequentially, the next sequence set after I1 is I3, as designated by the last field in I1. Of course, identifiers such as I3 and C1 are used arbitrarily in these illustrations to emphasize the fact that these are new sequence sets and control intervals.

Overall, VSAM avoids creation of overflow record chains by leaving vacant spaces within control intervals and areas and by the use of "splits" as discussed above. These techniques make VSAM a flexible, highly efficient index structure.

FIGURE 20-5

Modification of the Figure 10-4
VSAM Structure to Reflect Addition
of Records 162, 163, and 80.

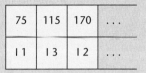

75	115	170	...
I 1	I 3	I 2	...

I 1

50	75	Null	Next sequence set
A1	A2	Null	I 3

I 3

105	115	Null	Next sequence set
C1	C2	Null	I 2

I 2

146	160	170	Next sequence set
B1	B2	B3	I . . .

A1	A2	A3	C1	C2	C3	B1	B2	B3
10	61	V	79	110	V	140	151	162
35	68	A	80	112	A	142	154	163
42	70	C	100	115	C	146	160	170
50	75	A	105	Vacant	A	Vacant	Vacant	Vacant
Vacant	Vacant	N	Vacant	Vacant	N	Vacant	Vacant	Vacant
		T			T			

Control area split   Control interval split

The name "VSAM" is used by IBM, but the general method represented by VSAM is in use by many vendors.

Both ISAM and VSAM types of index structures are more or less transparent to the COBOL programmer. The software needed to create, maintain, and use the indexed file structure is provided as part of the COBOL language processor. Still, it is useful for the COBOL programmer to be familiar with the basic concepts of these methods.

R E V I E W . . . .

1. In the Virtual Storage Access Method (VSAM) data records are written in physical groups called control intervals. Then control intervals are grouped into units called _____ .

   control areas

2. There are two index levels in VSAM. The higher-level index references the highest records in the control areas, and it is called the _____ set; the other index references records in each control interval, and it is called the _____ set.

   index; sequence

3. When a VSAM key-sequenced file is created, disk storage space is [packed / deliberately left vacant].

deliberately left vacant

4. When records are added to a VSAM file, a control interval split takes place when

_____.

no vacancy remains in the appropriate control
interval and no vacant interval remains in the area

. . . .

AN EXAMPLE OF CREATING AN INDEXED FILE

An indexed file can be created with minimal effort on the part of the programmer. The source records first must have been sorted in ascending sequence on a data field that will serve as the primary key for the file. Because an indexed file is a sequential file, the records are positioned in ascending order. We now consider an example to illustrate the process.

Suppose that we have source records that contain data about vendors. Columns 1–8 contain an identifier that is unique for each vendor, and columns 9–80 contain other data. We want to copy these records on disk, forming an indexed file sorted on the basis of the data in columns 1–8. Each disk record will consist of 68 characters, and the source records must have been sorted on columns 1–8.

Figure 20-6 presents a COBOL program written to create an indexed file. Notice the SELECT statement. ORGANIZATION IS INDEXED specifies that this is an indexed file, while ACCESS IS SEQUENTIAL specifies that the access mode for this file is sequential. RECORD KEY IS VENDOR-NUMBER specifies that there is a field called VENDOR-NUMBER, which is a field in the file record and serves as the primary key for the file. In other words, the file will be in ascending order of VENDOR-NUMBER values.

In the DATA DIVISION included in Figure 20-6 observe that VENDOR-NUMBER is a field in the record description of the indexed file (VENDOR-FILE). The RECORD KEY must be a field in the file record, and it must be an alphanumeric field.

In the PROCEDURE DIVISION of Figure 20-6, in the FILE-CREATE paragraph, we move VENDOR-IDENT, a field in the source record, to VENDOR-NUMBER, which was declared to be the RECORD KEY in the SELECT statement. The move of VENDOR-DATA simply transfers 60 bytes from the source record to the output record; notice that the receiving field was defined with PIC X(60). The WRITE statement now includes the INVALID KEY condition. This condition will be true whenever the record key of the record about to be written is not greater than the key of the preceding record in the file. If the INVALID KEY condition is true, the imperative statements that follow are executed. In the example we print an error message and the source record associated with the error condition.

The INVALID KEY test is nonspecific. It could be true because the records are out of order with respect to the values of the RECORD KEY field (including records with duplicate key values), or it could be true because the file is full. As an alternative to the INVALID KEY test, we can use the FILE STATUS or the DECLARATIVES feature, as explained in Chapters 10 and 17 in connection with sequential file processing.

Creation of an indexed file is a complex task, yet the language is very high level with respect to this task. The programmer need write very few instructions to invoke the procedure necessary for the task. In review, these instructions involve a few clauses in the SELECT statement, provision for a record key in the record description of the file, and moving data to the output record in the PROCEDURE

FIGURE 20-6

Sample Program to Create an
Indexed File

```
IDENTIFICATION DIVISION.
PROGRAM-ID. INDEX-CREATE.
*
ENVIRONMENT DIVISION.
CONFIGURATION SECTION.
SOURCE-COMPUTER. ABC-480.
OBJECT-COMPUTER. ABC-480.
INPUT-OUTPUT SECTION.
*
FILE-CONTROL.
    SELECT VENDOR-FILE ASSIGN TO OLDMSTR
                    ORGANIZATION IS INDEXED
                    ACCESS IS SEQUENTIAL
                    RECORD KEY IS VENDOR-NUMBER.
*
    SELECT SOURCE-FILE ASSIGN TO READER.
*
    SELECT PRINT-FILE ASSIGN TO PRINTER.
*
DATA DIVISION.
FILE SECTION.
FD   VENDOR-FILE LABEL RECORDS ARE STANDARD
                    DATA RECORD IS VENDOR-RECORD.
*
01   VENDOR-RECORD.
     02  VENDOR-NUMBER          PIC X(8).
     02  VENDOR-DATA            PIC X(60).
*
FD   SOURCE-FILE LABEL RECORDS ARE STANDARD
                    DATA RECORD IS SOURCE-RECORD.
*
01  SOURCE-RECORD.
    02  VENDOR-IDENT            PIC 9(8).
    02  VENDOR-DATA             PIC X(72).
*
FD   PRINT-FILE LABEL RECORDS OMITTED
                    DATA RECORD IS PRINT-RECORD.
01   PRINT-RECORD             PIC X(132).
*
WORKING-STORAGE SECTION.
*
01  END-OF-DATA-INDICATOR    PIC 9 VALUE ZERO.
    88  INPUT-ENDED               VALUE 1.
*
PROCEDURE DIVISION.
*
MAIN-ROUTINE.
    OPEN INPUT    SOURCE-FILE
         OUTPUT   VENDOR-FILE
                  PRINT-FILE
    READ SOURCE-FILE RECORD
         AT END SET INPUT-ENDED TO TRUE
    END-READ
*
```

FIGURE 20-6

Sample Program to Create an
Indexed File (continued)

```
        PERFORM FILE-CREATE
            UNTIL INPUT-ENDED.
*
    CLOSE SOURCE-FILE
        VENDOR-FILE
        PRINT-FILE
    STOP RUN.
*
  FILE-CREATE.
*
    MOVE VENDOR-IDENT TO VENDOR-NUMBER
*
    MOVE VENDOR-DATA OF SOURCE-RECORD
        TO VENDOR-DATA OF VENDOR-RECORD
*
    WRITE VENDOR-RECORD
      INVALID KEY
        MOVE ' INVALID KEY CONDITION FOR THIS RECORD'
            TO PRINT-RECORD
        WRITE PRINT-RECORD
            AFTER ADVANCING 1 LINE
        WRITE PRINT-RECORD FROM SOURCE-RECORD
            AFTER ADVANCING 1 LINE
    END-WRITE
*
    READ SOURCE-FILE RECORD
        AT END SET INPUT-ENDED TO TRUE
    END-READ.
```

DIVISION. In the following section we study these specialized instructions in a more thorough and comprehensive framework.

R E V I E W . . . .

1. An indexed file must be created in the _____ access mode.

    SEQUENTIAL

2. In the ENVIRONMENT DIVISION, after the file is described as ORGANIZATION IS INDEXED, the basis on which the file is sorted is identified by the COBOL reserved words _____ .

    RECORD KEY

3. The RECORD KEY field must be [alphabetic / alphanumeric] and it [must / need not] be a field in the file record.

    alphanumeric; must

4. The fact that one or more records to be written in an indexed file are not in the appropriate sequence can be detected and identified by using the _____ option in conjunction with the WRITE statement.

    INVALID KEY

ENVIRONMENT DIVISION INSTRUCTIONS FOR INDEXED FILES

Figure 20-7 presents the general format for the SELECT statement. Note that in the ASSIGN portion of the statement the 1985 version of COBOL provides for a literal option as a means for referencing the physical file, just as is true for the sequential file format, as explained in Chapter 10.

The ORGANIZATION statement specifies that this is an indexed file.

The ACCESS MODE clause specifies the way records in the file will be accessed. ACCESS MODE IS SEQUENTIAL specifies that records will be accessed in ascending order of the record key. Omission of the ACCESS clause defaults to the SEQUENTIAL option. The RANDOM option specifies that the order in which records are accessed will be controlled by the programmer. This control is accomplished by moving the value of the key of the desired record into the RECORD KEY field and then issuing an input/output command (READ, WRITE, REWRITE, DELETE).

The DYNAMIC option allows the programmer to change at will from sequential access to random access, using appropriate forms of input/output statements. In its absence the file for a given program must be declared to be either in SEQUENTIAL or in RANDOM access mode, but not in both modes in the same program.

We repeat here a point made in the previous section on creating an indexed file. When the file is first being created, it must be in SEQUENTIAL access mode. In subsequent uses, it may be in any of the three options, SEQUENTIAL, RANDOM, or DYNAMIC.

RECORD KEY references a data-name that must be a field within the record description of the file. If the file description includes multiple records (review the subject of multiple records in Chapter 16), a field from any record description may be given. RECORD KEY specifies the primary key field, on the basis of which the file is sorted.

The ALTERNATE RECORD option specifies a secondary key that is an alternate record key for the file. When alternate keys are used, we can access records either on the basis of the primary key specified in the RECORD KEY clause or on the basis of another ALTERNATE RECORD KEY. When the file is first created, however, the records must have been sorted on the basis of the primary record

---

FIGURE 20-7
General Format for the SELECT Statement for Indexed Files

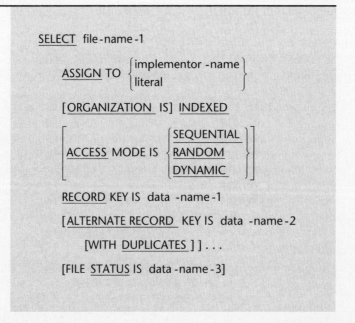

```
SELECT  file-name-1

    ASSIGN TO  {implementor-name}
               {literal         }

    [ORGANIZATION IS] INDEXED

    [                 {SEQUENTIAL} ]
    [ ACCESS MODE IS  {RANDOM    } ]
    [                 {DYNAMIC   } ]

    RECORD KEY IS  data-name-1

    [ALTERNATE RECORD KEY IS  data-name-2

        [WITH DUPLICATES ] ] . . .

    [FILE STATUS IS  data-name-3]
```

key, which is the key declared with the RECORD KEY IS clause. As an example, we could write

```
SELECT STUDENT-FILE ASSIGN TO file-device
            ORGANIZATION IS INDEXED
            ACCESS MODE IS RANDOM
            RECORD KEY IS STUDENT-NO
            ALTERNATE RECORD KEY IS STUDENT-NAME
                            WITH DUPLICATES.
```

This file is indexed on the basis of two keys: STUDENT-NO and STUDENT-NAME. The RECORD KEY is the primary key. This key is used as the basis for the physical position of records in the file. Note that records can be stored in only *one* order in the file. If they are sequentially arranged within disk tracks on the basis of STUDENT-NO, they will be randomly arranged with respect to STUDENT-NAME. Presumably, then the file is sequentially accessed on the basis of STUDENT-NO. If we want to access the records in sequential order of a secondary key such as STUDENT-NAME, processing will take longer because the read/write access arm of the disk will be "jumping" all over the disk cylinders as it follows a random path over the random positions of the records.

The DUPLICATES phrase in the general format in Figure 20-7 specifies that the value of the associated alternate record key may be duplicated within any of the records in the file. Another common example of alternate key values that are duplicates may be the postal code in an address record, where the postal code was specified as an alternate record key. In the absence of the DUPLICATES phrase, the presence of duplicate key values is an error condition. In our example above, we expect the possibility that there may be student records having the same STUDENT-NAME values. Notice that duplicate key values are permitted for alternate keys only. Each record must have a unique primary key.

If the indexed file contains variable-length records, the primary RECORD KEY field must be in the fixed portion of the record. For example, consider the following record description:

```
FD    INDEXED-FILE ...
      RECORD IS VARYING IN SIZE
          FROM 20 TO 200 CHARACTERS ...
```

With respect to the record description above, the RECORD KEY field must be a field within the first 20 bytes in the record.

The FILE STATUS option operates just as explained for sequential files in Chapter 10. Figure 20-8 presents some selected status codes and their explanation. For a complete set of codes it is advisable to refer to your own operating system, since many codes are specific to the implementor.

As an illustration, the sample program in Figure 20-6 can be modified with the following addition of the FILE STATUS clause:

```
SELECT VENDOR-FILE ASSIGN TO OLDMSTR
        ORGANIZATION IS INDEXED
        ACCESS IS SEQUENTIAL
        RECORD-KEY IS VENDOR-NUMBER
        FILE STATUS IS VENDOR-FILE-STATUS.
```

Consistent with the above, the WRITE statement in the FILE-CREATE paragraph of Figure 20-6 can be modified to make use of the FILE STATUS as follows:

```
WRITE VENDOR-RECORD
IF VENDOR-FILE-STATUS NOT = '00' ...
```

In the above program segment the IF statement is used in lieu of the INVALID KEY test.

R E V I E W . . . .

1. In the SELECT statement in the ENVIRONMENT DIVISION, the fact that a file is to be set up as an indexed file is specified by the _____ statement.

   ORGANIZATION

2. A file organized as an indexed file [can / cannot] be accessed in a sequential manner.

   can

3. Omission of the ACCESS clause in the SELECT statement for an indexed file results in the file having to be accessed by the [sequential / random] mode.

   sequential

4. The ACCESS MODE option that allows the programmer to change at will from sequential access to random access is called the _____ mode.

   DYNAMIC

FIGURE 20-8
Selected File Status Codes

SELECTED FILE STATUS CODES	EXPLANATION
00	Successful completion.
02	Successful completion but a duplicate key is detected.
04	A READ statement was executed but the length of the record is inconsistent with the record description.
21	Sequence error exists. The program changed the primary key between a READ and a REWRITE statement.
23	Attempt to read a nonexistent record.
24	An attempt is made to write beyond the boundaries of the file, such as when the file is full.
41	Attempt to OPEN file that is already open.
42	Attempt to CLOSE a file that has not been opened.
43	Attempt to DELETE or REWRITE without the prior execution of a corresponding successful READ.
47	Attempt to READ or START on a file not open in the INPUT or I/O mode.
49	Attempt to DELETE or REWRITE on a file not open in the I/O mode.

5. Even when the ALTERNATE RECORD KEY is used to access a record in a file, when first entered, the file has to be sorted on the basis of the [primary / alternate] key.

primary

6. The ALTERNATE KEY associated with a record [must / need not] be a unique key value in the file.

need not

. . . .

PROCEDURE DIVISION INSTRUCTIONS FOR INDEXED FILES

An indexed file can be opened as INPUT, OUTPUT, or I-O (input-output). Figure 20-9 summarizes the permissible input-output statements for each of these options, depending on the access mode specified.

The READ Statement

Reading records from an indexed file is done by using one of the two READ formats presented in Figure 20-10. The first format must be used if the SEQUENTIAL access mode has been specified either explicitly or implicitly (by default). The NEXT phrase must be specified when a file is declared to be in the DYNAMIC access mode and records are to be retrieved sequentially. Execution of READ ... NEXT RECORD retrieves from the file the next record whose record key is higher

FIGURE 20-9
Permissible INPUT-OUTPUT Statements

FILE ACCESS MODE	STATEMENT	OPEN MODE		
		INPUT	OUTPUT	I-O
Sequential	READ	X		X
	WRITE		X	
	REWRITE			X
	START	X		X
	DELETE			X
Random	READ	X		X
	WRITE		X	X
	REWRITE			X
	START			
	DELETE			X
Dynamic	READ	X		X
	WRITE		X	X
	REWRITE			X
	START	X		X
	DELETE			X

than the one accessed previously. From a logical standpoint, READ ... NEXT operates identically to READ in a sequential file. We use the qualification "from a logical standpoint" because in an indexed file the physical and logical order may not be in direct correspondence, as explained in the descriptions of the ISAM and VSAM methods earlier in this chapter. This happens when an indexed file has new records added to it. Instead of being "squeezed" in between existing records, they are put in a physically separate location (overflow) and connected by address pointers to the records that logically precede and follow them.

Format 2 is used for files in RANDOM access mode; it also is used when records are to be retrieved randomly from a file in DYNAMIC access mode. The KEY clause references the data-name specified as a key either in the RECORD KEY or the ALTERNATE RECORD KEY clause. If the KEY clause is omitted in the Format 2 READ statement, the primary key (RECORD KEY) of the file is assumed by default.

The INVALID KEY condition holds when no record can be located whose record key matches the value of the data-name specified or implied by the KEY IS clause. The NOT INVALID KEY option is not available in the 1974 standard. As an example, we may have

```
MOVE '123456789' TO STUD-NO.
MOVE 'YES' TO VALID-KEY-FLAG
READ STUDENT-MASTER RECORD
    KEY IS STUD-NO
    INVALID KEY
        MOVE 'NO' TO VALID-KEY-FLAG.
IF VALID-KEY-FLAG = 'NO'
   PERFORM READ-ERROR
ELSE
   PERFORM ROUTINE-A
   PERFORM ROUTINE-B.
PERFORM ROUTINE-C.
```

FIGURE 20-10
General Formats for the READ Statement for Indexed Files

FORMAT 1

READ file-name-1 [NEXT] RECORD [INTO identifier-1]

    [AT END imperative-statement-1]

    [NOT AT END imperative-statement-2]

[END-READ]

FORMAT 2

READ file-name-1 RECORD [INTO identifer-1]

    [KEY IS data-name-1]

    [INVALID KEY imperative-statement-3]

    [NOT INVALID KEY imperative-statement-4]

[END-READ]

In this 1974-based example, not having the INVALID ... NOT INVALID option, we set a flag to allow us to test for which of the two conditions is true after the READ. Using COBOL '85, we have

```
MOVE '123456789' TO STUD-NO.
READ STUDENT-MASTER RECORD
     KEY IS STUD-NO
     INVALID KEY
            PERFORM READ-ERROR
     NOT INVALID KEY
            PERFORM ROUTINE-A
            PERFORM ROUTINE-B
END-READ
PERFORM ROUTINE-C.
```

In the above program segment, READ-ERROR will be executed if no record in the file has a STUD-NO key equal to 123456789. If such a record does exist, then ROUTINE-A and ROUTINE-B are executed. ROUTINE-C is executed regardless of the outcome of the READ because of the END-READ scope terminator. Also, STUD-NO is, of course, a key field. Therefore one of the following two clauses is assumed to have been written in the SELECT statement:

```
RECORD KEY IS STUD-NO
```

or

```
ALTERNATE RECORD KEY IS STUD-NO
```

It is instructive also to consider rewriting the above example using the FILE STATUS construct. Assume that in the SELECT statement we had written the clause

```
FILE STATUS IS STUD-MAST-STATUS.
```

Then the example could be rewritten as follows:

```
MOVE '123456789' TO STUD-NO
READ STUDENT-MASTER RECORD
     KEY IS STUD-NO
          INVALID KEY
                  PERFORM CHECK-STATUS-CODE
          NOT INVALID KEY
                  PERFORM ROUTINE-A
                  PERFORM ROUTINE-B
END-READ
PERFORM ROUTINE-C.
CHECK-STATUS-CODE.
IF  STUD-MAST-STATUS = '23'
    PERFORM READ-ERROR
ELSE
    IF STUD-MAST-STATUS = ... .
```

When a FILE STATUS clause has been specified, and prior to the execution of the INVALID ... and NOT INVALID ... tests, the system places the appropriate status code in the FILE STATUS field. Making reference to the codes in Figure 20-8, we see that a code of 00 signifies successful completion. When a read instruction has been successful in the example above, STUD-MAST-STATUS would contain 00 and the NOT INVALID KEY branch would be executed. Within that branch we could look at the contents of STUD-MAST-STATUS, but since it is known to be 00, there is no point in doing so. When the read operation is not successful, the INVALID KEY clause applies, and we execute CHECK-STATUS-CODE, in which we proceed to test for the specific error condition. A code of 23 signifies attempt to read a nonexistent record, as shown in Figure 20-8. Other status codes could also be tested to ascertain the specific cause of the INVALID KEY condition.

In summary, the INVALID KEY condition is generic, whereas the FILE STATUS construct allows us to identify the specific invalid condition.

We take the opportunity here to suggest a more documentative presentation of the file-status specification. Assuming, as above, that we had written FILE STATUS IS STUD-MAST-STATUS, we could write

```
01  STUD-MAST-STATUS       PIC   XX.
    88 VALID-READ              VALUE '00'.
    88 NONEXISTENT-RECORD VALUE '23'.
    88 (etc.)
     .
     .
     .
```

Such a specification would allow replacing statements like IF STUD-MAST-STATUS = '23' by IF NONEXISTENT-RECORD and would remove the hard-to-remember numeric codes from the PROCEDURE DIVISION.

The INVALID KEY and the AT END clauses in the READ statement are shown to be optional in the general format in Figure 20-10. If the INVALID KEY and the AT END are omitted, then there must be a USE AFTER STANDARD EXCEPTION PROCEDURE specified for the corresponding file-name in the DECLARATIVES portion of the program. (You may want to review the discussion on DECLARATIVES in Chapter 17 in connection with sequential file processing.) This rule applies to all of the input/output verbs WRITE, REWRITE and DELETE,

FIGURE 20-11

General Formats for WRITE, REWRITE, and DELETE Statements for Indexed Files

```
WRITE   record-name-1 [FROM identifier-1]
    [INVALID KEY imperative-statement-1]
    [NOT INVALID KEY imperative-statement-2]
[END-WRITE]


REWRITE   record-name-1  [FROM identifier-1]
    [INVALID KEY imperative-statement-1]
    [NOT INVALID KEY imperative-statement-2]
[END-REWRITE]


DELETE  file-name-1  RECORD
    [INVALID KEY imperative-statement-1]
    [NOT INVALID KEY imperative-statement-2]
[END-DELETE]
```

for which the general formats are presented in Figure 20-11. As an example, consider the following PROCEDURE DIVISION statements:

```
PROCEDURE DIVISION.
DECLARATIVES.
I-O-TEST SECTION.
    USE AFTER STANDARD EXCEPTION PROCEDURE
                ON STUDENT-MASTER.
READ-TEST.
  IF VALID-READ
    CONTINUE
  ELSE
    IF NONEXISTENT-RECORD
       MOVE 'CODE 23 ERROR WHILE READING STUDENT-MASTER'
            TO ERROR-MESSAGE
    ELSE
       MOVE 'UNSPECIFIED ERROR WHILE READING STUDENT-MASTER'
            TO ERROR-MESSAGE
    END-IF
    WRITE PRINT-LINE FROM ERROR-MESSAGE
  END-IF.
END-DECLARATIVES.
```

Because of the EXCEPTION PROCEDURE ON STUDENT-MASTER included in the above code, the READ statement does not require the INVALID KEY:

```
MOVE '123456789' TO STUD-NO
READ STUDENT-MASTER RECORD
PERFORM ROUTINE-C.
```

If an exception occurs during execution of the above READ statement, program control will transfer to the READ-TEST paragraph in the DECLARATIVES portion of the program before resuming with execution of the PERFORM ROUTINE-C statement that follows the READ. (Some COBOL compilers require an AT END or INVALID KEY clause after every READ, so the above example may not work in such cases.)

The choice of using INVALID KEY and AT END clauses versus the USE AFTER EXCEPTION construct in the DECLARATIVES portion of the program should depend on the intended focus of program logic with respect to input/ output exceptions. If such exceptions or errors can be viewed as unusual or parenthetical to the task at hand, use of DECLARATIVES is the recommended approach, because it removes these unusual cases from the mainline code. On the other hand, if treatment of errors or exceptions is an integral part of the task logic, then use of the INVALID KEY and the AT END clauses is the recommended approach, because up-front visibility is then given to the logic of handling such exceptions.

The WRITE, REWRITE, and DELETE Statements

New records are written in the file by use of the WRITE statement presented in the first portion of Figure 20-11. When a file is being created, WRITE is used as illustrated in the earlier example in this chapter.

After a file has been created, WRITE is used to add new records to the file. As always, the proper value is moved to the primary record key and to the remaining fields of the record, and the execution of WRITE causes the new record to be inserted in the correct logical position within the file. The INVALID KEY condition is true under the following circumstances:

1. When the file has been opened as OUTPUT, and the value of the primary record key is not greater than the value of the primary record key of the previous record

2. When the file has been OPENed as I-0, and the value of the primary record key is equal to the value of the primary record key of a record already existing in the file

3. When an attempt is being made to write more records than can be accommodated by the available disk storage

4. When there is an equipment failure or other unspecified cause

As with the READ verb, in COBOL '85 the WRITE allows for NOT INVALID ... and END-WRITE options. Further, both the INVALID ... and NOT INVALID clauses are optional and can be replaced by corresponding FILE STATUS-related statements in the DECLARATIVES portion, as illustrated in the preceding program segment for the READ statement.

In updating tasks REWRITE is used to replace a record that exists in the file. The general format is included in the middle portion of Figure 20-11.

At the time of execution of REWRITE, the file must be open in the I-O mode. The record being replaced is the one whose key matches the value of the primary record key. The INVALID KEY holds when the value of the record key in the record to be replaced does not match the value of the record key of the last record read, or the value of the record key does not equal the record key of any record existing in the file.

The DELETE statement logically removes a record from an indexed file. The general format is shown in the last portion of Figure 20-11. A DELETE command can be executed only if the file has been opened in the I-O mode. Notice the explanations associated with codes 43 and 49 in Figure 20-8, which are file-status codes for invalid DELETE (and REWRITE) operations. If the file has been declared to be in RANDOM or DYNAMIC access mode, INVALID KEY is true when the file does not contain a record whose primary record key value matches the value of the record key. Thus the programmer is responsible for moving the key value of the record to be deleted to RECORD KEY.

If the file is in the SEQUENTIAL access mode, then a successful READ must precede the execution of a DELETE. In such a case it is understood that we are deleting the record previously read. If the access mode is RANDOM, then the value placed in the RECORD KEY determines the record to be deleted.

The START Statement

The START verb is used to position the file either at a specific record or at a record whose key meets a particular condition. The START is not an input verb; it must be followed by a READ for a record to be read. A common use of the START is sequential retrieval of records from a point other than the beginning of the file. Thus it is possible to retrieve records sequentially starting with some record in the "middle" of the file, as shown in the general format for the START statement in Figure 20-12.

The file must be in SEQUENTIAL or DYNAMIC access mode and must be open in the INPUT or I-O mode at the time START is executed. The KEY phrase may be omitted, in which case EQUAL is implied. In essence, the START statement

FIGURE 20-12
General Format for the START Statement for Indexed Files

$$
\underline{\text{START}}\ \ \text{file-name-1}\ \ \left[\underline{\text{KEY}}\ \left\{\begin{array}{l} \text{IS}\ \underline{\text{EQUAL}}\ \text{TO} \\ \text{IS}\ = \\ \text{IS}\ \underline{\text{GREATER}}\ \text{THAN} \\ \text{IS}\ > \\ \text{IS}\ \underline{\text{NOT LESS}}\ \text{THAN} \\ \text{IS}\ \underline{\text{NOT}}\ < \\ \text{IS}\ \underline{\text{GREATER}}\ \text{THAN}\ \underline{\text{OR EQUAL}}\ \text{TO} \\ \text{IS}\ >\ = \end{array}\right\}\ \text{data-name-1}\right]
$$

[INVALID KEY imperative-statement-1]

[NOT INVALID KEY imperative-statement-2]

[END-START]

means to position the file to that record whose record key satisfies the explicit or implicit KEY condition. If we simply write

```
START CUSTOMER FILE
    INVALID KEY PERFORM CANT-START
```

we specify that the file is to be positioned at the record whose primary key has a value equal to the current content of the RECORD KEY field. Thus it would be important to have ascertained that the RECORD KEY has an appropriate value. For instance, if the RECORD KEY field contained the value of a deleted record, we would execute CANT-START, since the INVALID KEY condition would be true.

A more typical example would involve use of the KEY clause to specify the key-name (data-name-1) and the condition for determining the "match." For example, if CUSTOMER-NAME is a record key and we want to retrieve the records of customers whose names begin with M or higher, we can write

```
MOVE 'M' TO CUSTOMER-NAME
START CUSTOMER-FILE
    KEY IS NOT LESS THAN CUSTOMER-NAME
    INVALID KEY PERFORM START-ERROR.
PERFORM WITH TEST AFTER
        UNTIL FIRST-LETTER-OF-NAME NOT = 'M'
    READ CUSTOMER-FILE NEXT RECORD
    INVALID KEY
        .
        .
        .
        NOT INVALID KEY
        .
        .
        .
        END-READ
    END-PERFORM
```

In this program segment, MOVE is an alphanumeric move resulting in CUSTOMER-NAME containing the letter M and blanks to the right of M. The KEY IS NOT LESS condition specifies that we want to position the file at the first record whose key is not less than the letter M; in other words, it will be the first name that begins with the letter M, assuming that there is such a record. The first execution of the READ statement then retrieves that record, and additional executions of READ retrieve the following records sequentially. In the above example we wrote the PERFORM loop WITH TEST AFTER to allow execution of at least one READ. The FIRST-LETTER-OF-NAME field is assumed to have been defined as the first byte in the key field so that we terminate the loop when we read a record whose name does not start with the letter M. Of course, if there was a possibility that there is no record beginning with M, we would need to test for that condition after the READ.

The data-name in the KEY phrase can be either a record key (specified as RECORD KEY, or ALTERNATE RECORD KEY) or a data item subordinate to a record key, provided that the data item is the first (leftmost) field in the record key. In other words, we can specify the "first part" of a record key. For the above example we could have the following:

```
... RECORD KEY IS CUSTOMER-NAME ...
           .
           .
           .

02  CUSTOMER-NAME.
    03  FIRST-LETTER-OF-NAME PIC X.
    03  REST-OF-NAME         PIC X(19).
           .
           .
           .

MOVE 'M' TO STARTING-LETTER-OF-NAME
START CUSTOMER-FILE
    KEY IS >= FIRST-LETTER-OF-NAME
    INVALID KEY PERFORM START-ERROR.
```

The INVALID condition is true if the KEY condition cannot be met. For example, consider the following program segment:

```
MOVE 'MICHENER' TO CUSTOMER-NAME.
START CUSTOMER-FILE
    KEY IS EQUAL TO CUSTOMER-NAME
    INVALID KEY PERFORM ERROR-START.
```

ERROR-START will be executed if there is no customer in the file whose record key is equal to 'MICHENER'.

As with all I/O verbs (OPEN, CLOSE, READ, WRITE, REWRITE, DELETE, and START), the FILE STATUS may be used as a more discriminating alternative to the generic INVALID KEY ... , NOT INVALID KEY ... , and the USE AFTER STANDARD EXCEPTION PROCEDURE may be used in lieu of the INVALID KEY approach.

R E V I E W . . . .

1. In the PROCEDURE DIVISION, reading records from an indexed file is accomplished by using the _____ verb.

   READ

2. Whenever records in an indexed file are to be retrieved randomly, the _____ clause indicates (explicitly or implicitly) the data-name to be used to identify each record.

   KEY

3. If the KEY clause is omitted in conjunction with random retrieval of records, the basis for identifying each record is the [RECORD KEY / ALTERNATE RECORD KEY].

RECORD KEY

4. There must be a USE AFTER STANDARD EXCEPTION PROCEDURE specified for the corresponding file-name if the READ statement omits use of both the _____ and the _____ clauses.

INVALID KEY; AT END

5. Records are added to an indexed file by using the _____ verb.

WRITE

6. Execution of a WRITE statement to add a record to an indexed file results in the record being added [at the end of the file / in the correct logical position within the file].

in the correct logical position within the file

7. The verb that is used to modify a record held in an indexed file is the _____ verb.

REWRITE

8. In order for a REWRITE instruction to be executed, the file must be open in the _____ mode.

I-O

9. The verb used to remove a record from an indexed file is the _____ verb.

DELETE

10. A DELETE command can be executed only if the file has been opened in the _____ mode.

I-O

11. The verb that makes it possible to position a file at a record that meets a specified condition is the _____ verb.

START

12. In conjunction with executing a START statement, the data-name used as the key [must / need not] have been specified previously as RECORD KEY or ALTERNATE RECORD KEY.

need not

. . . .

AN EXAMPLE OF PROCESSING AN INDEXED FILE

We present an example here that illustrates the use of most of the language statements and options described in the preceding section. The example involves processing the vendor file created by the example program in Figure 20-6. We now give the following record description to the file.

```
FD  VENDOR-FILE LABEL RECORDS ARE STANDARD
                DATA RECORD IS VENDOR-RECORD.
01  VENDOR-RECORD.
    02  VENDOR-NUMBER       PIC X(8).
    02  VENDOR-NAME         PIC X(15).
    02  VENDOR-ADDRESS      PIC X(45).
```

Transaction records are submitted through a TRANS-FILE and have the record description that follows:

```
01 TRANS-RECORD.
    02  TRANS-CODE PIC 9.
        88   CHANGE-ADDRESS VALUE 1.
        88   ADD-VENDOR     VALUE 2.
        88   DELETE-VENDOR  VALUE 3.
        88   ERROR-CODE VALUES ARE ZERO, 4 THRU 9.
    02  VENDOR-IDENT   PIC 9(8).
    02  VENDOR-NAME    PIC X(15).
    02  VENDOR-ADDRESS PIC X(45).
    02  FILLER         PIC X(11).
```

It is apparent from the self-documenting nature of this record description that we are interested in changing the address of a vendor and in adding or deleting vendors. Figure 20-13 presents a structure chart for the file update task. The simplicity of the structure is its most notable characteristic. You may want to contrast this structure chart with the ones in Figures 17-1 and 17-4, which related to sequential files. The random access feature of indexed files results in a much simpler program structure. In fact, Figure 20-13 could be further simplified by incorporating the function of the 020-UPDATE module into the 010-MAIN-ROUTINE.

In the sample program the 010 module contains a number of functions for purposes of instructional illustration. Such functions would normally be absent in a working environment, and the 020-UPDATE module could be incorporated into the top-level module. Finally, we should point out that the function and name of the 070-SEQUENTIAL-LISTING module is also specific to the sample program. In general, we can think of such a module as being about "post-update" processing; after the file updating has been completed, we want to carry out such tasks as generating reports, or other processes relating to the now updated master file.

Figure 20-14 presents the complete program. Notice in the ENVIRONMENT DIVISION that VENDOR-FILE is in DYNAMIC access mode and that VENDOR-NUMBER is the record key. The PROCEDURE DIVISION is self-documenting and consists of three control portions that illustrate random updating, sequential

FIGURE 20-13

Structure Chart for Sample Indexed File Update Program

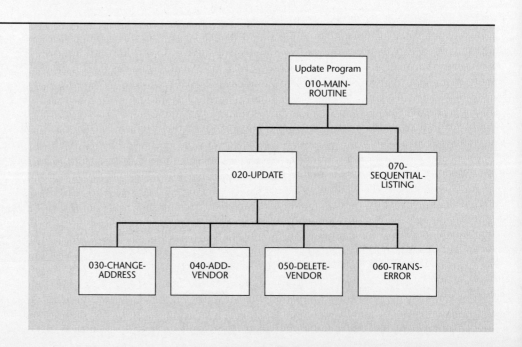

FIGURE 20-14

Sample Program to Update an Indexed File

```
IDENTIFICATION DIVISION.
PROGRAM-ID. UPDATE-INDEX.
*
ENVIRONMENT DIVISION.
CONFIGURATION SECTION.
SOURCE-COMPUTER. ABC-480.
OBJECT-COMPUTER. ABC-480.
*
INPUT-OUTPUT SECTION.
FILE-CONTROL.
    SELECT VENDOR-FILE ASSIGN TO OLDMSTR
                        ORGANIZATION IS INDEXED
                        ACCESS MODE IS DYNAMIC
                        RECORD KEY IS VENDOR-NUMBER.
*
    SELECT TRANS-FILE ASSIGN TO TRANS.
*
    SELECT PRINT-FILE ASSIGN TO PRINTER.
*
DATA DIVISION.
FILE SECTION.
*
FD   VENDOR-FILE LABEL RECORDS ARE STANDARD
                    DATA RECORD IS VENDOR-RECORD.
01   VENDOR-RECORD.
     02 VENDOR-NUMBER      PIC X(8).
     02 VENDOR-NAME        PIC X(15).
     02 VENDOR-ADDRESS     PIC X(45).
*
FD   TRANS-FILE LABEL RECORDS ARE STANDARD
                    DATA RECORD IS TRANS-RECORD.
01   TRANS-RECORD.
     02 TRANS-CODE         PIC 9.
        88 CHANGE-ADDRESS  VALUE 1.
        88 ADD-VENDOR      VALUE 2.
        88 DELETE-VENDOR   VALUE 3.
        88 ERROR-CODE      VALUES ARE ZERO, 4 THRU 9.
     02 VENDOR-IDENT       PIC 9(8).
     02 VENDOR-NAME        PIC X(15).
     02 VENDOR-ADDRESS     PIC X(45).
     02 FILLER             PIC X(11).
*
FD   PRINT-FILE LABEL RECORD OMITTED
                    DATA RECORD PRINTLINE.
01   PRINTLINE            PIC X(132).
*
WORKING-STORAGE SECTION.
01   END-OF-DATA-INDICATOR  PIC 9 VALUE ZERO.
     88 INPUT-ENDED        VALUE 1.
     88 INPUT-NOT-ENDED     VALUE 0.
*
```

FIGURE 20-14

Sample Program to Update an
Indexed File (continued)

```
      PROCEDURE DIVISION.
 *
      010-MAIN-ROUTINE.
 *
 * THIS PORTION ILLUSTRATES RANDOM UPDATING OF INDEXED FILE
 *
           OPEN INPUT    TRANS-FILE
                OUTPUT   PRINT-FILE
                I-O      VENDOR-FILE
           MOVE ' LISTING FROM UPDATE PORTION' TO PRINTLINE
           WRITE PRINTLINE AFTER ADVANCING PAGE
 *
           READ TRANS-FILE RECORD
              AT END SET INPUT-ENDED TO TRUE
           END-READ
 *
           PERFORM 020-UPDATE
                   UNTIL INPUT-ENDED
           CLOSE VENDOR-FILE
 *
 * THIS PORTION ILLUSTRATES SEQUENTIAL RETRIEVAL.
 *
           SET INPUT-NOT-ENDED TO TRUE
           MOVE ' LISTING FROM SEQUENTIAL RETRIEVAL' TO PRINTLINE
           WRITE PRINTLINE AFTER ADVANCING PAGE
           OPEN INPUT VENDOR-FILE
 *
           PERFORM 070-SEQUENTIAL-LISTING
                   UNTIL INPUT-ENDED
           CLOSE VENDOR-FILE
 *
 * THIS PORTION ILLUSTRATES USE OF THE START VERB.
 *
           SET INPUT-NOT-ENDED TO TRUE
           OPEN INPUT VENDOR-FILE
           MOVE '35290001' TO VENDOR-NUMBER
 *
           START VENDOR-FILE
                   KEY IS GREATER THAN VENDOR-NUMBER
                   INVALID KEY
                       SET INPUT-ENDED TO TRUE
           END-START
           MOVE ' LISTING FROM USE OF START VERB' TO PRINTLINE
           WRITE PRINTLINE AFTER ADVANCING PAGE
           PERFORM 070-SEQUENTIAL-LISTING
                   UNTIL INPUT-ENDED
           CLOSE VENDOR-FILE
                 TRANS-FILE
 *
           STOP RUN.
 *
```

```
020-UPDATE.
    MOVE VENDOR-IDENT TO VENDOR-NUMBER
*
    EVALUATE TRUE
       WHEN CHANGE-ADDRESS
            PERFORM 030-CHANGE-ADDRESS
       WHEN ADD-VENDOR
            PERFORM 040-ADD-VENDOR
       WHEN DELETE-VENDOR
            PERFORM 050-DELETE-VENDOR
       WHEN OTHER
            PERFORM 060-TRANS-ERROR
    END-EVALUATE
*
    READ TRANS-FILE RECORD
        AT END SET INPUT-ENDED TO TRUE
    END-READ.
*
030-CHANGE-ADDRESS.
    READ VENDOR-FILE RECORD
       INVALID KEY
          MOVE ' CANNOT FIND VENDOR FOR THIS TRANS '
               TO PRINTLINE
          WRITE PRINTLINE AFTER 1
          WRITE PRINTLINE FROM TRANS-RECORD AFTER 1
       NOT INVALID KEY
          MOVE VENDOR-ADDRESS OF TRANS-RECORD
               TO VENDOR-ADDRESS OF VENDOR-RECORD
          REWRITE VENDOR-RECORD
             INVALID KEY
                MOVE ' CANNOT REWRITE THIS RECORD'
                     TO PRINTLINE
                WRITE PRINTLINE AFTER 1
                WRITE PRINTLINE FROM VENDOR-RECORD AFTER 1
    END-READ.
*
040-ADD-VENDOR.
    MOVE VENDOR-NAME OF TRANS-RECORD
         TO VENDOR-NAME OF VENDOR-RECORD
    MOVE VENDOR-ADDRESS OF TRANS-RECORD
         TO VENDOR-ADDRESS OF VENDOR-RECORD.
    WRITE VENDOR-RECORD
       INVALID KEY
          MOVE ' CANNOT CREATE A RECORD FROM THIS TRANS'
               TO PRINTLINE
          WRITE PRINTLINE AFTER 1
          WRITE PRINTLINE FROM TRANS-RECORD AFTER 1
    END-WRITE.
*
```

FIGURE 20-14

*Sample Program to Update an
Indexed File (continued)*

```
     050-DELETE-VENDOR.
   *
         DELETE VENDOR-FILE RECORD
            INVALID KEY
               MOVE
                 ' CANNOT DELETE RECORD SPECIFIED BY THIS TRANS'
                 TO PRINTLINE
               WRITE PRINTLINE AFTER 1
               WRITE PRINTLINE FROM TRANS-RECORD AFTER 1
         END-DELETE.
   *
     060-TRANS-ERROR.
   *
         MOVE 'WRONG TRANSACTION CODE IN ' TO PRINTLINE
         WRITE PRINTLINE AFTER 1
         WRITE PRINTLINE FROM TRANS-RECORD AFTER 1.
   *
     070-SEQUENTIAL-LISTING.
   *
         READ VENDOR-FILE NEXT RECORD
            AT END
               SET INPUT-ENDED TO TRUE
            NOT AT END
               WRITE PRINTLINE FROM VENDOR-RECORD AFTER 1
         END-READ.
```

retrieval, and use of the START verb, respectively. The first portion illustrates random access and updating.

The first portion of the 010-MAIN-ROUTINE paragraph in the PROCE-DURE DIVISION illustrates random updating of an indexed file. By studying Figure 20-14 we can observe that the 020-UPDATE paragraph analyzes the transaction code. Then we execute the 030-CHANGE-ADDRESS, 040-ADD-VENDOR, 050-DELETE-VENDOR, or 060-TRANS-ERROR paragraph. Each of these paragraphs illustrates, respectively, the replacing of a record (REWRITE), the addition of a record (WRITE), the deletion of a record (DELETE), and the handling of INVALID KEY conditions.

The second portion of the 010-MAIN-ROUTINE procedure illustrates sequential retrieval. When OPEN INPUT VENDOR-FILE is executed, the open instruction causes the file to be positioned at its beginning, so that when the first READ VENDOR-FILE NEXT RECORD is executed, the first record is retrieved.

The third portion of the 010-MAIN-ROUTINE illustrates use of the START verb:

```
MOVE '35290001' TO VENDOR-NUMBER
  .
  .
  .

START VENDOR-FILE KEY IS GREATER THAN VENDOR-NUMBER
   INVALID KEY SET INPUT-ENDED TO TRUE.
```

In this illustration we want to retrieve sequentially all records whose key is greater than 35290001. Since the GREATER THAN option is used, the record whose key equals 35290001 will not be retrieved.

SUMMARY

The three methods of file organization are sequential, indexed, and relative. This chapter covered the creation and processing of indexed files. Techniques for sequential files were described in Chapters 10 and 17, while relative file processing is the subject of Chapter 21.

An indexed file consists of two parts: the data file and the index file(s). Whereas an indexed file allows the data to be stored sequentially, the existence of an index makes possible the random access of specified records.

The two common indexing methods that were described in this chapter are the Indexed Sequential Access Method (ISAM) and the Virtual Storage Access Method (VSAM). The basic concepts associated with each of these techniques were described in the respective sections of this chapter. Even though the software needed to create, maintain, and use an indexed file is provided as part of the COBOL language processor, it is useful for applications programmers to be aware of the basic structure of such software.

Following a sample program (in Figure 20-6) for creating an indexed file, the COBOL language instructions for indexed files were described. In the ENVIRONMENT DIVISION the SELECT statement includes the relevant options. Whereas the ORGANIZATION clause specifies that the file is INDEXED, the ACCESS MODE clause specifies (or defaults to) SEQUENTIAL when an indexed file is being created. In subsequent uses of the file the ACCESS MODE can be SEQUENTIAL, RANDOM, or DYNAMIC. The RECORD KEY clause must reference a data-name that is a field within the record description. The ALTERNATE RECORD option can be used to specify one or more secondary keys.

In the PROCEDURE DIVISION an indexed file can be opened as INPUT, OUTPUT, or I-O. For random access the KEY clause of the READ statement identifies the data-name specified as the key in the RECORD KEY or ALTERNATE RECORD KEY clause. The INVALID KEY clause of the WRITE statement can be used to determine whether a record to be entered in an indexed file is not in the appropriate sequence. Execution of a WRITE statement to add a record to an indexed file results in the record being added in the correct position within the file. Other verbs whose use for indexed files was described are the REWRITE, DELETE, and START.

The chapter concluded with a sample program (in Figure 20-14) that illustrates the processing of the indexed file created by the program in Figure 20-6.

EXERCISES

20.1 Outline a program to re-create an indexed sequential file. Assume that the original file has too many overflow records and that we therefore want to create a new version of the file to eliminate all overflow. Include in your outline the FILE-CONTROL paragraph of the ENVIRONMENT DIVISION and the complete PROCEDURE DIVISION. Assume that OLD-FILE, OLD-REC, NEW-FILE, and NEW-REC are the corresponding file- and record-names.

20.2 Refer to Exercise 10.3 for the program description.

a. Create the master file as an indexed file, using the part number as the RECORD KEY.

b. Update the master file on a random basis, using the part number as the RECORD KEY.

20.3   Refer to Exercise 17.1 for the program description.

    a.   Create the master file as an indexed file, using the lot number as the RECORD KEY.

    b.   Update the master file on a random basis, using the lot number as the RECORD KEY.

20.4   This exercise requires random order file maintenance and sequential processing for an indexed file.

The master file is an indexed file and contains records about products. The format of the product master file record is as follows:

```
PRODUCT ID NUMBER            PIC X(05)
PRODUCT DESCRIPTION          PIC X(25)
QUANTITY ON HAND             PIC S9(03)
REORDER POINT                PIC 9(03)
VENDOR NUMBER                PIC 9(06)
```

The transaction file is defined as follows:

COLUMNS	FIELD DESCRIPTION
1–4	SALESMAN ID NUMBER
5–10	DATE OF PURCHASE ORDER (MMDDYY)

11	TYPE OF PURCHASE ORDER
	   C = PRIVATE CUSTOMER
	   B = BUSINESS

12–17	PURCHASE ORDER NUMBER
18	UNUSED
19–23	PRODUCT ID NUMBER
24–26	QUANTITY ORDERED (INTEGER)
27–32	PRODUCT PRICE (DOLLARS AND CENTS)
33–80	UNUSED

You are required to write two programs:

    a.   The first program will apply sales transactions against the product file and check the inventory to verify that the product specified in the sale transaction is an item that is carried in inventory.

The quantity should be subtracted from the quantity on hand.

An error report is needed to print any transaction errors. The transaction file may contain such errors as

      • A product number that is not in the product master file

      • A quantity ordered that is not numeric

At the end of the update procedure use a utility program at your installation to "dump" the contents of the master file on the printer (dump = print as is, without formatting, column headings, etc.).

    b.   In the second program generate a report of the product file listing in ascending product order.

A sample format of the report for the second program is:

```
                          COMPUMART, INC.
                        PRODUCT FILE LISTING
                            09/18/92
PRODUCT                               QUANTITY    REORDER    VENDOR
ID NO.    PRODUCT DESCRIPTION         ON HAND     POINT      NUMBER
-------------------------------------------------------------------
XXXXX     XXXXXXXXXXXXXXXXXXXXXXXXX   XXX (*****)  XXX        XXXXXX
XXXXX     XXXXXXXXXXXXXXXXXXXXXXXXX   XXX          XXX        XXXXXX
  .                 .                  .            .           .
  .                 .                  .            .           .
  .                 .                  .            .           .
```

Notes:

- If the product quantity on hand is below or equal to the reorder point, place a row of five asterisks next to the product as shown above.

- The quantity on hand may be negative. Do not treat this as an error. It is presumed to represent planned sales against anticipated shipments.

21

Relative File Processing

A S INTRODUCED TO YOU in Chapter 10, the three methods of file organization are the *sequential, indexed,* and **relative.** *You studied sequential file organization in Chapter 10 and 17 and indexed file organization in Chapter 20. You now will study the creation and processing of relative files.*

*In relative file organization the file is stored in such a way that each record can be accessed directly by reference to its relative position in the file. Frequently, such access is based on the record key for the record being transformed into a location address relative to the other records in the file. You will study several such **key-to-address transformation methods** in the early sections of this chapter.*

*Next you will consider the COBOL language options that are applicable for relative files, followed by example programs for creating and updating a relative file. In the final section of this chapter you will study the use of the concept of a **bucket,** or block of records, to reduce the access time in the processing of relative files.*

RELATIVE FILE ORGANIZATION

A *relative file* is one in which records are accessed by reference to their relative position in the file. If we think of a file that can hold 100 records, the first record has a relative key of 1, while the last one has a relative key of 100. Access to records in a file organized as relative is by reference to the relative key of each record. For instance, we may use the following two types of commands:

1. Write this record as the 20th record in the file.
2. Read the 68th record in the file.

As these examples show, reference is made to the relative location of a record. We say "relative" as distinguished from the *absolute* location of a given record. An absolute location would be specified in terms of the address of the record within a specific disk volume, within a specific cylinder, within a specific track, and the record number in that track.

Relative file organization is ideal for a case where records are identified by consecutive numbers. For instance, suppose that invoice records are numbered 0001, 0002, 0003, ... We can use relative organization and store the records in the order of the invoice number. If we want to access invoice number 0050, we can do so simply by accessing the record whose relative key is 50. It is rare, however, that records can be numbered exactly consecutively as in this example, and relative file organization requires some specific techniques to allow us to utilize this method of file organization.

Several *key-to-address transformation methods* can be used to transform record keys (identifiers) to relative location addresses. All such methods have one common property: they enable us to transform record identifiers, such as customer numbers and product numbers, to relative key values. Thus, if we want the record of product number 1234, we would apply a key-to-address transformation procedure that would transform product number 1234 into a relative key value, say, 371. Then we would retrieve the 371st record in the relative file, with the expectation that it would be the record of product number 1234.

As the preceding example illustrates, a relative file can be a high-performance file. We can compute the address of a record without having to use index structures, as is required with indexed files. It generally is true that relative files can provide fast, direct access to records, but it should be added that the level of performance depends on the specific file and the specific method chosen. Good performance in a relative file often requires some analysis and experimentation. The main reason for variability in performance is that all known key-to-address methods produce *synonyms,* which are said to occur when the key-to-address method generates the same relative key for two or more data records. For instance, it may be that product numbers 1234 and 4965 both generate the same relative key; therefore we need additional processing beyond the key-to-address methods.

There are many ways to handle the occurrence of synonyms, but we illustrate here one procedure that is often successful. At file creation time, go through the file and mark each record as a vacant record, using a special field in the record for this purpose. Then, as each data record is being stored in the file, we apply the chosen key-to-address method and compute a *home-address* relative key value. We now read that record space, and, if it is marked as vacant, we record the data in that space and then mark it as occupied. If we previously had stored a data record in that home-address space, we look at the next record space to see if it is vacant and, if it is, we write the data record there. If it is occupied, we continue looking for a vacancy in consecutive record spaces, and either we find a vacancy, or we come full circle in the case of a file that is completely filled. For example, suppose that V = vacant, and O = occupied. Let us assume that we want to store a product record for product number 2645 in the file. Further, let us assume that the chosen key-to-address method computes a relative key of 132. As can be observed in the following, the product record will be stored in relative record location 134, which is the first available vacancy.

RECORD RELATIVE KEY	130		131		132		133		134		135	
Content	V		O	7391	O	0935	O	5383	V		V	

If we wanted to retrieve the record of product number 2645 after it had been loaded into the file, we would compute its home address as 132 as before. We would attempt to retrieve the record at location 132 by comparing the record key of 2645 to the record key at location 132, which happens to be 0935. This comparison indicates that record 2645 is a synonym, and we would continue searching sequentially until the record was found at location 134. Notice that if we were trying to retrieve a record that, in fact, did not exist in the file, we would know that the record did not exist as soon as we came upon the first vacancy. We could conclude that the record did not exist, because if a record is a synonym, it is stored in the first available vacancy past the home address.

This procedure needs to be expanded to take account of deletion of records from the file. If we desire to free up the record space when a record is deleted, we recommend that the space be marked as deleted. If we want to add a new record, a deleted record then constitutes a vacancy. If we are retrieving a record and it is not at its home address, however, we should continue looking for it until we encounter the first vacancy, *not* counting deleted records as vacancies. In the preceding example of record 2645, whose home address was 132 but which was written at 134 due to synonyms, suppose that the record at location 133 was later deleted. To retrieve record 2645 from location 134, we would have to continue looking past the deleted record at location 133. Of course, if the record at location 133 were deleted *before* record 2645 was added to the file, then record 2645 would have been written at location 133.

When adding a new record to the file, we must check for the possibility of duplicate records, as illustrated by the following. Suppose the home address of the new record is 131, but that location is occupied. Record location 132 has been marked as deleted, location 133 is occupied, and location 134 is vacant. When we encounter a deleted record at location 132, we want to save that address; if the new record is not a duplicate, it should go to location 132. However, we must continue looking in the file until we find a vacant record to ascertain that there is not already a record in the file with the same key as the one to be added. Therefore we would proceed reading records until finding the first vacant location at 134, checking each occupied record to see if it is a duplicate. At that point, we want to return to location 132 and write the new record there.

We conclude this section by pointing out that the subject of creating efficient relative files is very broad. Many additional methods have been developed, and research on "efficient hashing functions" is active. As a brief illustration of an alternative method, consider now the practice of using a two-pass file creation process. In the first pass only those records that are not synonyms are loaded into the file. The remaining records then are loaded in the second pass. Such an approach to file creation often leads to a higher percentage of records being located in their home addresses.

R E V I E W . . . .

1. In a relative file the location of a record is described relative to the other _____ in the file.

records

2. Key-to-address transformation methods are concerned with converting a record key (identifier) into a relative _____.

location address

3. When two different record keys result in the same relative location address, it is said that a _____ has been produced.

synonym

4. When a synonym has occurred, a common solution is to store the synonym in the first vacant record space [preceding / following] the home-address space.

following

5. When records are deleted from a relative file and are marked as deleted, such record spaces then [are / are not] available for the storage of new records.

are

6. If a record is neither at its home address nor at the first vacancy after that address (not counting deleted records), then we can conclude that

_____.

the record does not exist

. . . .

THE DIVISION REMAINDER METHOD

In the preceding section we saw that use of relative file organization is predicated on a key-to-address transformation capability. There are several key-to-address methods available. One that is in wide use is the division remainder method.

To apply the division remainder method, we first must choose the file size. A rule of thumb to determine the file size is to divide the number of records in the file by 0.80, so that 80 percent of the file will be filled and 20 percent of the file will be unused.* This unused space serves two purposes: it cuts down the incidence of synonyms, and it also allows for file expansion. The term *packing factor* or *file density* is used to denote the percent of filled space in a relative file. If we divide the number of data records by 0.80, the result is an 80 percent packing factor, or density. In general, the lower the packing factor, the fewer the synonyms but the greater the unused file space. We can see now why relative files require analysis and experimentation. For instance, record size and frequency of access are factors that would be considered in the analysis for choosing a suitable packing factor.

Once the file size has been chosen, we select the prime number closest to the file size. A *prime number* is divisible only by itself and the number 1. For instance, the numbers 3 and 7 are prime numbers. Tables of prime numbers are available in mathematical handbooks. Use of a prime number is not critical, however. We also can use the file size instead of the prime number closest to it, and in most cases there is little difference in the number of synonyms generated. In general, however, the use of a prime number is likely to result in fewer synonyms.

---

* Where X = file size

If No. Records = .80X

Then $X = \dfrac{\text{No. Records}}{.80}$

Suppose a customer file contains 9,600 records. We decide on a packing factor of 80 percent; therefore the allocated file size is 9,600 / 0.80 = 12,000 record spaces. The prime number closest to 12,000 is 11,987. The customers are identified by a 6-digit customer number. The first step in the division remainder method is to divide the record identifier by the prime number (or the file size itself). Thus, if we want to compute the location address of customer 123456, we divide this record identifier by the prime number 11987, obtaining a whole-number quotient of 10 and a remainder of 3586. By the division remainder method, the remainder plus 1 is the computed home address. For our example, the address is thus 3586 + 1 = 3587. If we had used the file size instead of the prime number as the divisor, we would have divided 123456 by 12000, giving a whole-number quotient of 10 and a remainder of 3456. The home address in this case would have been 3456 + 1 = 3457.

Note that when we divide a number by any divisor, the remainder from the division can range from 0 to the value of the divisor minus 1. Thus, if we are dividing by 12000, the smallest possible remainder is 0 and the largest possible remainder is 11999. Since we add 1 to the remainder in the division remainder method, we can see that division by the file size results in the smallest computed value being 1 and the largest value being the file size itself. Thus, by taking the remainder plus 1, we generate addresses that correspond to the relative addresses in the file. In the case where a prime number is used that is smaller than the file size itself, a few addresses would be impossible to generate. For example, with a prime number of 11987 as a divisor and a file size of 12000, we would never generate addresses 11989, 11990, 11991, ... , 12000. Still, those addresses could be occupied by records if we happened to have enough synonyms in the addresses 11988 and before.

As indicated by this example, the division remainder method is rather easy to apply. In the sample program, given later in the chapter (Figure 21-7), the procedure is implemented as follows:

```
MOVE ITEM-NUMBER OF SOURCE-RECORD TO WORKFIELD
DIVIDE PRIME-NUMBER INTO WORKFIELD GIVING QUOTIENT
COMPUTE LOCATION-ADDRESS =
       WORKFIELD - (PRIME-NUMBER * QUOTIENT) + 1.
```

The QUOTIENT field must be defined as an integer field, of course. Then the remainder is computed by multiplying the divisor by the integer quotient and then subtracting the result from the dividend. The address is stored in LOCATION-ADDRESS as the remainder plus 1.

The division remainder method, as well as other methods for transforming record identifiers into file addresses, has the property of giving about an equal chance to every possible file address. The general relationship between the record identifier and the address computed is random, and this is the reason that key-to-address methods are referred to as randomizing methods. The term *hashing* also is used very widely to describe such randomizing key-to-address methods.

R E V I E W . . . .

1. A key-to-address transformation is required for relative files in order to convert a record key (identifier) into a relative file address. The widely used method described in this section is the _____ method.

division remainder

2. The percentage of filled space in a relative file is identified by the term
_____.

packing factor (or file density)

3. Suppose an accounts payable file includes 2,100 records. If a 70 percent packing factor is to be used, the allocated field size would be _____ (number) record spaces.

2,100 / 0.70 = 3,000

4. Given a file size of 3,000, transform Account No. 4211 into a file address by using the file size as the divisor.

Integer quotient: 1
Remainder: 1211
File Address: 1211 + 1 = 1212

5. Given a file size of 3,000, transform Account No. 911 into a file address by using the file size as the divisor.

Integer quotient: 0
Remainder: 911
File Address: 911 + 1 = 912

6. Key-to-address methods are called randomizing methods because the possible [record identifiers / file addresses] have about an equal chance of occurring.

file addresses

• •

OTHER KEY-TO-ADDRESS TRANSFORMATION METHODS

Digit Analysis Method

By this method a frequency count is performed in regard to the number of times each of the 10 digits occurs in each of the positions included in the record key. For example, Table 21-1 presents a frequency count for the number of times each digit occurred in a five-position numeric key for 2,800 records. In this tabulation we can observe that digits 0–9 occur with approximately uniform distribution in key positions 2, 3, and 5; therefore, if a 3-digit address were required, the digits in these three positions in the record keys could be used. Given that there are 2,800 records, however, a 4-digit address would be required. Suppose we desire the first digit to be a 0,1,2, or 3 only. Such assignment can be made with about equal frequency for each digit by using a rule such as the following: assign a "0" when digits in positions 2 and 3 both contain odd numbers, a "1" if position 2 is odd and position 3 is even, a "2" if position 2 is even and position 3 is odd, or a "3" if positions 2 and 3 both contain even numbers. Thus, the address for key 16258 would be 3628: the "3" from the fact that positions 2 and 3 both contain even numbers and the "628" from key positions 2, 3, and 5. Other rules for prefixing additional digits can be formulated for different circumstances. In any event the digit analysis method relies on the digits in some of the key positions being approximately equally distributed. If such is not the case, the method cannot be used with good results.

Mid-Square Method

The record key is multiplied by itself, and the product is truncated from both left and right so as to form a number equal to the desired address length. Thus key 36258 would be squared to give 1314642564. To form a 4-digit address,

TABLE 21-1

Frequency of Occurrence of the Digits 169 for 2,800 Five-Position Keys

DIGIT	KEY POSITION				
	1	2	3	4	5
0	2026				
1	618	250	218	1012	260
2	128	395	391	185	382
3	23	263	389	299	271
4	5	298	330	52	302
5		335	299	101	387
6		303	339	18	299
7		289	308	134	301
8		267	267	999	245
9		400	259		353

this number would be truncated from both the left and right, resulting in the address 4642.

Folding

The key is separated into two parts that then are added together to form the address. For example, suppose key 1234567 is to be transformed into a 4-digit address. We can add the first four positions to the last three positions to form the address; in this case: 1234 + 567 = 1801. As another possibility, we can begin with the middle 4 digits and add the other digits as follows:

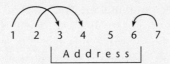

In general, the concept of folding does not refer to one standard method but to a general class of possibilities.

Alphabetic Keys

It is possible and sometimes common that the key is alphabetic, as in the case of a student file that utilizes an alphabetic key. To determine a numeric address, a procedure is defined by which letters are transformed into numbers. These numbers then might be used as addresses or, more likely, might be used in conjunction with one of the randomizing techniques discussed previously. Thus, if the transformation rule is that A = 00, B = 01, ... , Z = 25, then ADAM would become 00030012.

The key-to-address transformation methods that have been discussed are not the only ones that can be used, but they do represent the principal techniques. As indicated previously, the division remainder technique is used most frequently and generally works at least as well as other methods, but special circumstances may make some other method desirable for a given file.

R E V I E W . . . .

1. The transformation method for which the digits in at least some of the key positions must be dispersed about equally in terms of value is the _____ method.

   digit analysis

2. The transformation method in which the key is multiplied by itself as part of the procedure for determining the address for the record is the _____ method.

   mid-square

3. The transformation method in which one part of a key number is added to another part of the number to form the address is the _____ method.

   folding

4. Alphabetic keys generally are transformed [directly into a numeric address / into a numeric code for subsequent determination of an address].

   into a numeric code for subsequent
   determination of an address

5. The transformation technique most frequently used in conjunction with relative file organization is the _____ method.

   division remainder

. . . .

COBOL STATEMENTS FOR RELATIVE FILES

The SELECT Statement

Matters such as key-to-address transformations and handling of synonyms are not acknowledged by the language. COBOL assumes that the programmer handles these. The language provides only the basic mechanism by which relative files can be created and processed.

The general format for the SELECT statement in the ENVIRONMENT DIVISION is presented in Figure 21-1. ORGANIZATION IS RELATIVE has the obvious meaning. The ACCESS MODE clause has the same meaning as discussed for indexed files. Notice, however, RELATIVE KEY as contrasted to RECORD KEY. The data-name specified as RELATIVE KEY must be a WORKING-STORAGE unsigned integer item. Its function is to contain the location address for the record about to be accessed, or the location of the record that was just accessed.

FIGURE 21-1
General Format for the SELECT Statement

```
SELECT  file-name

                ⎧ implementor-name ⎫
ASSIGN TO       ⎨                  ⎬
                ⎩ literal          ⎭

[ORGANIZATION IS] RELATIVE

  ⎡                    ⎧ SEQUENTIAL ⎫  [RELATIVE KEY IS data-name-1] ⎤
  ⎢ ACCESS MODE IS     ⎨ RANDOM     ⎬                               ⎥
  ⎢                    ⎩ DYNAMIC    ⎭  RELATIVE KEY IS data-name-1   ⎥
  ⎣                                                                 ⎦

[FILE STATUS IS  data-name-2]
```

The reader should understand clearly the role of RELATIVE KEY, which is different from the RECORD KEY of indexed files. RECORD KEY is part of the file record. RELATIVE KEY is an item apart from the record. When we want to access the 3rd record, we move the value 3 to the RELATIVE KEY field and then we issue an I/O verb such as READ, WRITE, REWRITE, or DELETE. The system then uses the RELATIVE KEY value to determine where the I/O verb applies in the file.

Typically, rather than wanting the 3rd or some other record referenced by its location, a record whose key field has some particular value is desired. Given a record, the value of its identifier field is taken by the programmer and transformed through a key-to-address routine to a location address. Figure 21-2 illustrates the process.

The FILE STATUS clause in Figure 21-1 is identical to its counterpart in sequential and indexed files. Figure 21-3 is a list of selected status codes. For a complete list you should consult the appropriate manual for the computer system used.

FIGURE 21-2

Illustration of the Role of Relative Key

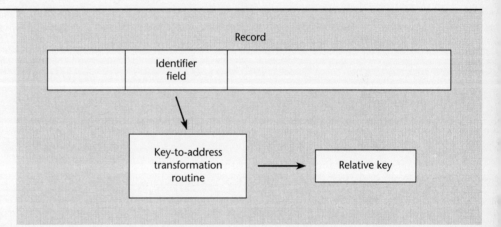

FIGURE 21-3

Selected File Status Codes and Their Meaning

STATUS CODE	DESCRIPTION
00	Successful execution.
04	Record length does not conform to file description.
10	End of file while attempting a sequential read.
22	Attempt to write a record where a record is already written (perhaps, a REWRITE should have been used).
23	Attempt to read a record that does not exist.
24	Attempt to write beyond the boundaries of the file.
41	Attempt to OPEN a file that is already opened.
42	Attempt to CLOSE a file that is not open.
43	Attempt to DELETE or REWRITE while in the sequential access mode, yet no preceding successful READ has been executed.
47	Attempt to READ or START a file not in the I-O mode.
48	Attempt to WRITE in a file not open in the OUTPUT, I-O, or EXTEND mode.
49	Attempt to DELETE or REWRITE in a file not in the I-O mode.

Creating a Relative File

A relative file may be created either sequentially or randomly. If it is to be created sequentially, we may omit the RELATIVE KEY clause, an option for the SELECT statement in Figure 21-1. In the format observe that the RELATIVE KEY clause is required if the access mode is RANDOM or DYNAMIC. To create the file sequentially, we can write

```
SELECT file-name ASSIGN TO ...
    ORGANIZATION IS RELATIVE
    ACCESS MODE IS SEQUENTIAL.
```

In the PROCEDURE DIVISION we then open the file as OUTPUT and we WRITE record-name. The first execution of WRITE results in writing in the first record location, the second execution results in writing in the second location, and so on.

The above procedure is used to create the file in the sequential mode. It is also possible to declare the file as ACCESS MODE IS RANDOM, in which case each WRITE execution results in writing a record in the location specified by the relative key. To illustrate the concept, consider this example:

```
SELECT CUSTOMER-FILE ASSIGN TO ...
        ORGANIZATION IS RELATIVE
        ACCESS MODE IS RANDOM
        RELATIVE KEY IS CUST-KEY.
    .
    .
    .
OPEN OUTPUT CUSTOMER-FILE
PERFORM WRITE-SAMPLE VARYING CUST-KEY FROM 1 BY 2
                    UNTIL CUST-KEY > 9.
    .
    .
    .
WRITE-SAMPLE.
    MOVE SPACES TO CUSTOMER-RECORD
    WRITE CUSTOMER-RECORD.
```

The above example writes (blank) records in record-locations 1, 3, 5, 7, and 9; all other record-locations do not contain data records at this point. If we attempted to read the 6th record, we would be attempting to read a nonexistent record. Also, if subsequent to the above example we accessed all the records sequentially, there would be five records accessed. In other words, the system keeps track of used and vacant record-locations. Still, we recommend that the programmer initialize all the records in the file with a distinguishing code in a special field. This method allows a more direct control method for sensing vacant and used record-locations. The following example illustrates the procedure:

```
SELECT DISK-FILE ASSIGN TO ...
        ORGANIZATION IS RELATIVE
        ACCESS MODE IS RANDOM
        RELATIVE KEY IS LOCATION-ADDRESS.
        .
        .
        .
```

```
01  DISK-RECORD.
    02  REC-STATUS-CODE        PIC 9.
        88  VACANT-RECORD       VALUE ZERO.
        88  USED-RECORD         VALUE 1.
        .
        .
        .

    OPEN OUTPUT DISK-FILE
    PERFORM ZERO-DISK
            VARYING I FROM 1 BY 1
                UNTIL I > MAX-NO-OF-LOCATIONS.
        .
        .
        .

ZERO-DISK.
    MOVE I TO LOCATION-ADDRESS
    MOVE SPACES TO DISK-RECORD
    MOVE ZERO TO REC-STATUS-CODE
    WRITE DISK-RECORD
        INVALID KEY PERFORM ...
```

Notice that the first field in the disk record is used to identify whether the record is vacant or occupied, as explained in the first section of this chapter. MAX-NO-Of-LOCATIONS is assumed to contain the number of record-locations in the file. The PERFORM ZERO-DISK loop writes a zero in the REC-STATUS-CODE of all the records, as a means of initializing the file.

In the above example the file was declared to be in RANDOM access mode. However, since the VARYING clause varies I through all the values from 1 on up, we could just as well have used sequential access.

I/O Verbs Used with Relative Files

Input/output verbs used with relative files are similar to the ones discussed in the preceding chapter on indexed files. Figure 21-4 presents the two general formats for the READ statement.

FIGURE 21-4
General Formats for the READ Statement

FORMAT 1 (for Sequential Access)

READ file-name-1 [NEXT] RECORD [INTO identifier-1]

    AT END imperative-statement-1]

    [NOT AT END imperative-statement-2]

[END-READ]

FORMAT 2 (for Random Access)

READ file-name-1 RECORD [INTO identifier-1]

    [INVALID KEY imperative-statement-1]

    [NOT INVALID KEY imperative-statement-2]

[END-READ]

Format 1 must be used if records are retrieved in sequential mode. NEXT must be used if DYNAMIC access mode is specified and records are retrieved sequentially.

Format 2 is used when the access mode is RANDOM, or when the access mode is DYNAMIC and records are retrieved in random order. The INVALID KEY condition occurs when RELATIVE KEY contains an address pointing to a record that was deleted previously (see DELETE verb, following) or to an address beyond the boundaries of the file.

The WRITE, REWRITE, DELETE, and START statements parallel the ones discussed in Chapter 20 with respect to indexed files. Figures 21-5 and 21-6 present the general format for these statements. In all cases, if the effective access mode is random, the RELATIVE KEY field must contain the record number of the record involved in the I/O operation. For instance, to DELETE a record, we must

FIGURE 21-5

General Format for the WRITE, REWRITE, and DELETE Statements

```
WRITE   record-name-1   [FROM identifier-1]
      [INVALID KEY imperative-statement-1]
      [NOT INVALID KEY imperative-statement-2]
[END-WRITE]


REWRITE   record-name-1   [FROM identifier-1]
      [INVALID KEY imperative-statement-1]
      [NOT INVALID KEY imperative-statement-2]
[END-REWRITE]


DELETE   file-name-1   RECORD
      [INVALID KEY imperative-statement-1]
      [NOT INVALID KEY imperative-statement-2]
[END-DELETE]
```

FIGURE 21-6

General Format for the START Verb

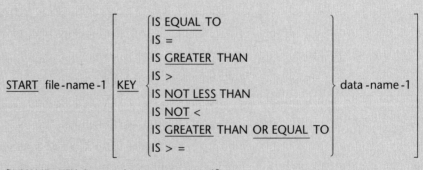

```
            ⎡    ⎧ IS EQUAL TO                         ⎫    ⎤
            ⎢    ⎪ IS =                                ⎪    ⎥
            ⎢    ⎪ IS GREATER THAN                     ⎪    ⎥
START file-name-1 KEY ⎨ IS >                           ⎬ data-name-1
            ⎢    ⎪ IS NOT LESS THAN                    ⎪    ⎥
            ⎢    ⎪ IS NOT <                            ⎪    ⎥
            ⎢    ⎪ IS GREATER THAN OR EQUAL TO         ⎪    ⎥
            ⎣    ⎩ IS > =                              ⎭    ⎦

[INVALID KEY imperative-statement-1]
[NOT INVALID KEY imperative-statement-2]
[END-START]
```

first determine its location address, put that address value in the RELATIVE KEY field, and then issue a DELETE command.

Sequential retrieval of records may be accomplished using the SEQUENTIAL or DYNAMIC access mode, the issuance of an OPEN INPUT instruction, and repetitive execution of READ or READ NEXT, respectively. Whenever sequential retrieval is desired from a point other than the beginning of a file, then the START command can be used. The same format applies as for indexed files, except that the starting record location is placed in the RELATIVE KEY field.

As was explained in Chapter 20 in connection with indexed files, the INVALID KEY and AT END options in the respective verb formats in Figures 21-4, 21-5, and 21-6 are optional. However, if these options are omitted, then the program must contain a DECLARATIVES portion with an appropriate USE AFTER STANDARD EXCEPTION PROCEDURE specification.

R E V I E W . . . .

1. The location address determined by a key-to-address routine is stored in the _____ field.

   RELATIVE KEY

2. For an indexed file the RECORD KEY [is / is not] part of the original file record. For a relative file, the RELATIVE KEY [is / is not] part of the original file record.

   is; is not

3. In the SELECT statement of the ENVIRONMENT DIVISION the RELATIVE KEY clause is not needed and may be omitted if the file is to be created [sequentially / randomly].

   sequentially

4. Records stored sequentially in a relative file [can / cannot] be accessed randomly.

   can

5. Records stored randomly in a relative file [can / cannot] be accessed sequentially.

   can

. . . .

AN EXAMPLE OF CREATING A RELATIVE FILE

A source file is to be transferred to disk, organized as a relative file. For simplicity, we assume that there will be no more than 50 records. Each record contains an ITEM-NUMBER in columns 1–5 and an ITEM-NAME in columns 6–25. We shall use ITEM-NUMBER as the identifier for each record and we shall compute disk addresses using this identifier and the prime number 47. By using the division remainder technique, we convert each ITEM-NUMBER value to a (relative) disk address in the range 1–50.

Figure 21-7 presents a program written to create such a relative file. In the 010-MAIN ROUTINE we perform 020-ZERO-DISK as many times as the value of MAX-NO-OF-LOCATIONS, which was set to 50 in the DATA DIVISION. The function of 020-ZERO-DISK is to initialize to zero the REC-STATUS-CODE of each record space, thereby indicating a vacant record space.

The second main task in 010-MAIN-ROUTINE is the repetitive reading of a record from SOURCE-FILE and execution of 030-LOAD-RECORD to "load" the record into the file. Loading involves execution of 040-RANDOMIZE-READ, which computes LOCATION-ADDRESS and executes 060-READ-DISK-REC to read the record at that LOCATION-ADDRESS.

FIGURE 21-7

*Sample Program for Creating a
Relative File*

```
IDENTIFICATION DIVISION
PROGRAM-I.D. RELATIVE-CREATE
*
ENVIRONMENT DIVISION.
CONFIGURATION SECTION.
SOURCE-COMPUTER. ABC-480.
OBJECT-COMPUTER. ABC-480.
INPUT-OUTPUT SECTION.
FILE-CONTROL.
    SELECT DISK FILE    ASSIGN TO DISK
                        ORGANIZATION IS RELATIVE
                        ACCESS MODE IS RANDOM
                        RELATIVE KEY IS LOCATION-ADDRESS.
*
    SELECT SOURCE-FILE  ASSIGN TO READER.
    SELECT PRINT-FILE   ASSIGN TO PRINTER.
*
DATA DIVISION.
FILE SECTION.
*

FD  DISK-FILE       LABEL RECORDS STANDARD
                    DATA RECORD IS DISK-RECORD
                    RECORD CONTAINS 26 CHARACTERS.
01  DISK-RECORD.
    02  REC-STATUS-CODE     PIC 9.
        88 VACANT-RECORD    VALUE ZERO.
        88 USED-RECORD      VALUE 1.
    02  ITEM-NUMBER         PIC 9(5).
    02  ITEM-NAME           PIC X(20).
*
FD  SOURCE-FILE     LABEL RECORDS OMITTED
                    DATA RECORD IS SOURCE-RECORD.
01  SOURCE-RECORD.
    02 ITEM-NUMBER          PIC 9(5).
    02 ITEM-NAME            PIC X(20).
    02 FILLER               PIC X(55).
*
FD  PRINT-FILE      LABEL RECORDS OMITTED
                    DATA RECORD IS PRINT-RECORD.
*
01  PRINT-RECORD            PIC X(132).
*
WORKING-STORAGE SECTION.
*
01  END-OF-DATA-FLAG        PIC XXX.
    88 END-OF-SOURCE        VALUE 'YES'.
    88 NOT-END-OF-SOURCE    VALUE 'NO '.
*
01  READ-VALIDITY-FLAG      PIC XXX.
    88 VALID-READ           VALUE 'YES'.
    88 INVALID-READ         VALUE 'NO '.
```

FIGURE 21-7
Sample Program for Creating a
Relative File (continued)

```
*
 01  WRITE-VALIDITY-FLAG    PIC XXX.
     88 VALID-WRITE         VALUE 'YES'.
     88 INVALID-WRITE       VALUE 'NO '.
*
 01  LOOP-FLAG              PIC XXX.
     88 FILE-IS-FULL        VALUE 'YES'.
     88 FILE-IS-NOT-FULL    VALUE 'NO '.
*
 01  LOCATION-ADDRESS       PIC 999.
 01  STARTING-ADDRESS       PIC 999.
 01  PRIME-NUMBER           PIC 99  VALUE 47.
 01  WORKFIELD              PIC S99999.
 01  QUOTIENT               PIC S999.
 01  MAX-NO-OF-LOCATIONS    PIC 999 VALUE 50.
 01  I                      PIC 999.
 01  ERROR-RECORD.
     02 FILLER              PIC X    VALUE SPACE.
     02 ERROR-LOCATION      PIC ZZ999.
     02 FILLER              PIC XX   VALUE SPACE.
     02 ERR-MESSAGE         PIC X(50).
*
 PROCEDURE DIVISION.
*
 010-MAIN-ROUTINE.
     OPEN INPUT  SOURCE-FILE
     OPEN OUTPUT DISK-FILE
                 PRINT-FILE.
     PERFORM 020-ZERO-DISK
        VARYING I FROM 1 BY 1
           UNTIL I > MAX-NO-OF-LOCATIONS
              OR INVALID-WRITE
*
     CLOSE DISK-FILE.
     OPEN I-O DISK-FILE
     SET NOT-END-OF-SOURCE TO TRUE
     SET FILE-IS-NOT-FULL  TO TRUE
     SET VALID-READ        TO TRUE
     PERFORM  UNTIL END-OF-SOURCE
                 OR INVALID-READ
                 OR FILE-IS-FULL
                 OR INVALID-WRITE
        READ SOURCE-FILE RECORD
           AT END
               SET END-OF-SOURCE TO TRUE
           NOT AT END
               PERFORM 030-LOAD-RECORD
        END-READ
     END-PERFORM
*
     CLOSE SOURCE-FILE
           PRINT-FILE
           DISK-FILE
     STOP RUN.
```

FIGURE 21-7
Sample Program for Creating a
Relative File (continued)

```
*
  020-ZERO-DISK.
     MOVE I TO LOCATION-ADDRESS
     MOVE SPACES TO DISK-RECORD
     MOVE ZERO TO REC-STATUS-CODE
*
     WRITE DISK-RECORD
        INVALID KEY
           MOVE 'INVALID KEY DURING ZERO-DISK'
                TO ERR-MESSAGE
           PERFORM 070-CANT-ACCESS
           SET INVALID-WRITE TO TRUE
        NOT INVALID KEY
           SET VALID-WRITE TO TRUE
     END-WRITE.
*
  030-LOAD-RECORD.
*
     PERFORM 040-RANDOMIZE-READ
*
     IF VALID-READ AND USED-RECORD
        MOVE LOCATION-ADDRESS TO STARTING-ADDRESS
        SET FILE-IS-NOT-FULL TO TRUE
        PERFORM 050-HANDLE-SYNONYMS
           UNTIL VALID-READ AND VACANT-RECORD
              OR INVALID-READ
              OR FILE-IS-FULL
     END-IF
     IF VALID-READ AND VACANT-RECORD
        MOVE 1 TO REC-STATUS-CODE
        MOVE ITEM-NUMBER OF SOURCE-RECORD
             TO ITEM-NUMBER OF DISK-RECORD
        MOVE ITEM-NAME OF SOURCE-RECORD
             TO ITEM-NAME OF DISK-RECORD
*
        REWRITE DISK-RECORD
           INVALID KEY
              MOVE 'ERROR DURING REWRITE' TO ERR-MESSAGE
              PERFORM 070-CANT-ACCESS
              STRING 'SOURCE RECORD INVOLVED = '
                     SOURCE-RECORD DELIMITED BY SIZE
                 INTO PRINT-RECORD
              WRITE PRINT-RECORD AFTER 2
              SET INVALID-WRITE TO TRUE
        END-REWRITE
*
     END-IF.
*
```

FIGURE 21-7

Sample Program for Creating a Relative File (continued)

```
040-RANDOMIZE-READ.
*
    MOVE ITEM-NUMBER OF SOURCE-RECORD TO WORKFIELD
    DIVIDE PRIME-NUMBER INTO WORKFIELD GIVING QUOTIENT
    COMPUTE LOCATION-ADDRESS =
        WORKFIELD - (PRIME-NUMBER * QUOTIENT) + 1
*
    PERFORM 060-READ-DISK-REC.
*
050-HANDLE-SYNONYMS.
*
    ADD 1 TO LOCATION-ADDRESS
    IF LOCATION-ADDRESS > MAX-NO-OF-LOCATIONS
       MOVE 1 TO LOCATION-ADDRESS
    END-IF
    IF LOCATION-ADDRESS = STARTING-ADDRESS
       MOVE SPACES TO PRINT-RECORD
       STRING 'FILE IS FULL; NEW RECORD IS = '
               SOURCE-RECORD DELIMITED BY SIZE
            INTO PRINT-RECORD
       WRITE PRINT-RECORD AFTER 2
       SET FILE-IS-FULL TO TRUE
    ELSE
       SET FILE-IS-NOT-FULL TO TRUE
       PERFORM 060-READ-DISK-REC
    END-IF.
*
060-READ-DISK-REC.
    READ DISK-FILE RECORD
       INVALID KEY
          MOVE 'ERROR WHILE READING ' TO ERR-MESSAGE
          PERFORM 070-CANT-ACCESS
          SET INVALID-READ TO TRUE
       NOT INVALID KEY
          SET VALID-READ TO TRUE
    END-READ.
*
070-CANT-ACCESS.
    MOVE LOCATION-ADDRESS TO ERROR-LOCATION
    WRITE PRINT-RECORD FROM ERROR-RECORD AFTER 2.
```

Continuing with the 030-LOAD-RECORD paragraph, following execution of 040-RANDOMIZE-READ we check to determine if the record read is already occupied (USED-RECORD), in which case the 050-HANDLE-SYNONYMS paragraph is executed. In either case, if a space is found (VALID-READ AND VACANT-RECORD), we proceed to write the data into the disk. Notice that we use the REWRITE rather than the WRITE verb. This is because the 020-ZERO-DISK procedure did WRITE all 50 records. From the standpoint of the language, records are being updated (REWRITE) in the 030-LOAD-RECORD paragraph.

As a final point, notice the two special cases handled in the 050-HANDLE-SYNONYMS paragraph. By the IF LOCATION-ADDRESS > MAX-NO-OF-LOCATIONS we MOVE 1 to LOCATION-ADDRESS to "wrap around" the file. Also, by the IF LOCATION-ADDRESS = STARTING-ADDRESS we recognize the FILE-IS-FULL condition, and the program then terminates execution because of the PERFORM UNTIL ... OR FILE-IS-FULL in 010-MAIN-ROUTINE.

AN EXAMPLE OF UPDATING A RELATIVE FILE

We illustrate the use of relative file organization by a sample program that updates the file created by the program in Figure 21-7. Figures 21-8 and 21-9 present the structure chart and the corresponding program for the update task.

Transaction records are submitted through a TRANS-FILE. Each transaction record has a code indicating the type of transaction:

```
01  TRANS-REC.
    02  TRANS-CODE            PIC 9.
        88  ADD-TRANS         VALUE ZERO.
        88  DELETE-TRANS      VALUE 1.
        88  MODIFY-TRANS      VALUE 2.
        88  ERROR-TRANS       VALUES 3 THRU 9.
    02  ITEM-NUMBER           PIC 9(5).
    02  ITEM-NAME             PIC X(20).
    02  FILLER                PIC X(54).
```

An ADD-TRANS indicates the addition of a new record to the disk file, a DELETE-TRANS indicates the deletion of a record existing in the file, while a MODIFY-TRANS represents a change in the ITEM-NAME of the disk record.

It should be noted that disk records are specified by the following description:

```
01  DISK-RECORD.
    02  REC-STATUS-CODE       PIC 9.
        88  VACANT-RECORD     VALUE ZERO.
        88  USED-RECORD       VALUE 1.
        88  DELETED-RECORD    VALUE 2.
    02  ITEM-NUMBER           PIC 9(5).
    02  ITEM-NAME             PIC X(20).
```

When a record is deleted, the REC-STATUS-CODE for that record space is set equal to 2. On any subsequent occasion we can identify the fact that the record space is available for a new record, and we ignore it when looking for synonyms, as explained in the first section of this chapter. For instance, suppose that a transaction record specifies deletion of an item number. In the 600-DELETE-RECORD paragraph of Figure 21-9 we see that we PERFORM 300-RANDOMIZE-READ to compute the home address of the item record and then read the record at the home address. Then we say

```
PERFORM 650-FIND-RECORD
    UNTIL RECORD-FOUND OR RECORD-NOT-FOUND
        OR INVALID-READ.
```

In the 650-FIND-RECORD paragraph we first check to determine if the record space at the home address is occupied (IF USED-RECORD). If it is occupied, we

FIGURE 21-8

Structure Chart for the Relative Update Program

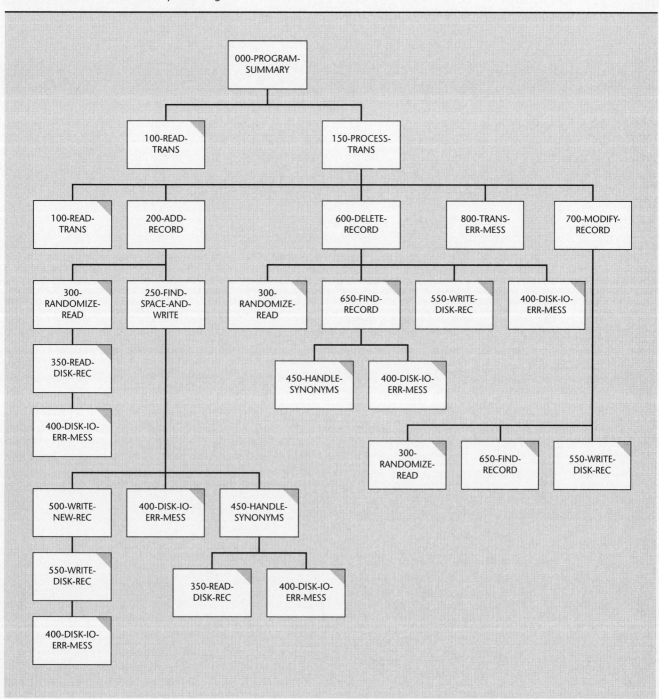

check to determine if the ITEM-NUMBER in the transaction record matches the one in the disk record, in which case that is the record to be deleted. If the record space is occupied but does not contain the record that we want, then the 650-FIND-RECORD paragraph PERFORMs 450-HANDLE-SYNONYMS. As a result the next disk record is read, and we repeat the process under control of the PERFORM 650-FIND-RECORD UNTIL ... loop in the 600-DELETE-RECORD paragraph.

FIGURE 21-9

Sample Program for Updating a Relative File

```
IDENTIFICATION DIVISION.
PROGRAM-ID. REL-UPDATE.
*
ENVIRONMENT DIVISION.
CONFIGURATION SECTION.
SOURCE-COMPUTER. ABC-480.
OBJECT-COMPUTER. ABC-480.
*
INPUT-OUTPUT SECTION.
FILE-CONTROL.
*
    SELECT DISK-FILE  ASSIGN TO DISK
                          ORGANIZATION IS RELATIVE
                          ACCESS MODE IS RANDOM
                          RELATIVE KEY IS LOCATION-ADDRESS.
*
    SELECT TRANS-FILE ASSIGN TO READER.
*
    SELECT PRINT-FILE ASSIGN TO PRINTER.
*
DATA DIVISION.
*
FILE SECTION.
*
FD  DISK-FILE    LABEL RECORDS OMITTED
                     DATA RECORD IS DISK-RECORD
                     RECORD CONTAINS 26 CHARACTERS.
01  DISK-RECORD.
    02 REC-STATUS-CODE    PIC 9.
        88 VACANT-RECORD   VALUE ZERO.
        88 USED-RECORD     VALUE 1.
        88 DELETED-RECORD  VALUE 2.
    02 ITEM-NUMBER        PIC 9(5).
    02 ITEM-NAME          PIC X(20).
*
FD  TRANS-FILE   LABEL RECORDS OMITTED
                     DATA RECORD IS TRANS-REC.
*
01  TRANS-REC.
    02 TRANS-CODE         PIC 9.
        88 ADD-TRANS       VALUE ZERO.
        88 DELETE-TRANS    VALUE 1.
        88 MODIFY-TRANS    VALUE 2.
        88 ERROR-TRANS     VALUES 3 THRU 9.
    02 ITEM-NUMBER        PIC 9(5).
    02 ITEM-NAME          PIC X(20).
    02 FILLER             PIC X(54).
*
FD  PRINT-FILE   LABEL RECORDS OMITTED
                     DATA RECORD IS PRINT-REC.
01  PRINT-REC            PIC X(132).
*
```

FIGURE 21-9

Sample Program for Updating a
Relative File (continued)

```
WORKING-STORAGE SECTION.
*
01  FLAGS.
    02 END-OF-TRANS-FLAG       PIC XXX VALUE 'NO'.
       88 END-OF-TRANS         VALUE 'YES'.
    02 SYNONYM-LOOP-FLAG       PIC XXX VALUE 'NO'.
       88 FILE-IS-FULL         VALUE 'YES'.
       88 FILE-IS-NOT-FULL     VALUE 'NO '.
*
    02 READ-VALIDITY-FLAG      PIC 9.
       88 VALID-READ           VALUE 0.
       88 INVALID-READ         VALUE 1.
*
    02 WRITE-VALIDITY-FLAG     PIC 9.
       88 VALID-WRITE          VALUE ZERO.
       88 INVALID-WRITE        VALUE 1.
*
    02 RECORD-FOUND-FLAG       PIC 9.
       88 RECORD-FOUND         VALUE ZERO.
       88 RECORD-NOT-FOUND     VALUE 1.
       88 STILL-LOOKING        VALUE 2.
*
    02 ADD-REC-FLAG           PIC 9.
       88 RECORD-ADDED         VALUE ZERO.
       88 RECORD-NOT-ADDED     VALUE 1.
       88 RECORD-TO-BE-ADDED   VALUE 2.
*
01  LOCATION-ADDRESS           PIC 9(3).
01  MAX-NO-OF-LOCATIONS        PIC 9(3) VALUE 50.
01  STARTING-ADDRESS           PIC 9(3).
01  PRIME-NUMBER               PIC 99   VALUE 47.
01  WORKFIELD                  PIC S9(5).
01  QUOTIENT                   PIC S9(3).
*
01  ERROR-RECORD.
    02 FILLER                  PIC X VALUE SPACE.
    02 ERROR-LOCATION          PIC ZZ999.
    02 FILLER                  PIC XX VALUE SPACES.
    02 ERR-MESSAGE             PIC X(50).
/
PROCEDURE DIVISION.
*
000-PROGRAM-SUMMARY.
*
    OPEN INPUT    TRANS-FILE
    OPEN OUTPUT   PRINT-FILE
    OPEN I-O      DISK-FILE
*
    PERFORM 100-READ-TRANS
    PERFORM 150-PROCESS-TRANS
            UNTIL END-OF-TRANS
                OR FILE-IS-FULL
                OR INVALID-READ
                OR INVALID-WRITE
```

FIGURE 21-9
Sample Program for Updating a Relative File (continued)

```
*
        CLOSE DISK-FILE
              PRINT-FILE
              TRANS-FILE
*
     STOP RUN.
*
 100-READ-TRANS.
     READ TRANS-FILE RECORD
          AT END SET END-OF-TRANS TO TRUE.
*
 150-PROCESS-TRANS.
     EVALUATE TRUE
        WHEN ADD-TRANS
             PERFORM 200-ADD-RECORD
        WHEN DELETE-TRANS
             PERFORM 600-DELETE-RECORD
        WHEN MODIFY-TRANS
             PERFORM 700-MODIFY-RECORD
        WHEN OTHER
             PERFORM 800-TRANS-ERR-MESS
     END-EVALUATE
      PERFORM 100-READ-TRANS.
*
 200-ADD-RECORD.
     PERFORM 300-RANDOMIZE-READ
     SET RECORD-TO-BE-ADDED TO TRUE
*
     PERFORM 250-FIND-SPACE-AND-WRITE
             UNTIL RECORD-ADDED
                OR RECORD-NOT-ADDED
                OR INVALID-READ
                OR FILE-IS-FULL.
*
 250-FIND-SPACE-AND-WRITE.
     IF VACANT-RECORD OR DELETED-RECORD
        PERFORM 500-WRITE-NEW-REC
        SET RECORD-ADDED TO TRUE
     ELSE
        IF ITEM-NUMBER OF TRANS-REC
             = ITEM-NUMBER OF DISK-RECORD
           MOVE 'ATTEMPT TO ADD DUPLICATE RECORD'
                TO ERR-MESSAGE
           PERFORM 400-DISK-IO-ERR-MESS
           SET RECORD-NOT-ADDED TO TRUE
        ELSE
           PERFORM 450-HANDLE-SYNONYMS.
*
```

FIGURE 21-9

*Sample Program for Updating a
Relative File (continued)*

```
300-RANDOMIZE-READ.
    MOVE ITEM-NUMBER OF TRANS-REC TO WORKFIELD
    DIVIDE PRIME-NUMBER INTO WORKFIELD GIVING QUOTIENT
    COMPUTE LOCATION-ADDRESS =
            WORKFIELD - (QUOTIENT * PRIME-NUMBER) + 1
    SET FILE-IS-NOT-FULL TO TRUE
*
    MOVE LOCATION-ADDRESS TO STARTING-ADDRESS
*
    PERFORM 350-READ-DISK-REC.
*
350-READ-DISK-REC.
    READ DISK-FILE RECORD
        INVALID KEY
            SET INVALID-READ TO TRUE
            MOVE 'THIS RECORD LOCATION CANNOT BE READ'
                TO ERR-MESSAGE
            PERFORM 400-DISK-IO-ERR-MESS
        NOT INVALID KEY
            SET VALID-READ TO TRUE
    END-READ.
*
400-DISK-IO-ERR-MESS.
*
    MOVE LOCATION-ADDRESS TO ERROR-LOCATION
    WRITE PRINT-REC FROM ERROR-RECORD AFTER 2 LINES
    MOVE SPACES TO ERROR-RECORD
    MOVE 'TRANSACTION RECORD IS' TO ERR-MESSAGE
    WRITE PRINT-REC FROM ERROR-RECORD AFTER 2 LINES
    MOVE TRANS-REC TO ERR-MESSAGE
    WRITE PRINT-REC FROM ERROR-RECORD AFTER 2 LINES.
*
450-HANDLE-SYNONYMS.
    SET FILE-IS-NOT-FULL TO TRUE
    ADD 1 TO LOCATION-ADDRESS
    IF LOCATION-ADDRESS > MAX-NO-OF-LOCATIONS
        MOVE 1 TO LOCATION-ADDRESS
    END-IF
*
    IF LOCATION-ADDRESS = STARTING-ADDRESS
        MOVE 'CAME FULL CIRCLE' TO ERR-MESSAGE
        PERFORM 400-DISK-IO-ERR-MESS
    ELSE
        PERFORM 350-READ-DISK-REC.
*
500-WRITE-NEW-REC.
    MOVE 1 TO REC-STATUS-CODE
    MOVE ITEM-NUMBER OF TRANS-REC
        TO ITEM-NUMBER OF DISK-RECORD
    MOVE ITEM-NAME OF TRANS-REC
        TO ITEM-NAME OF DISK-RECORD
    PERFORM 550-WRITE-DISK-REC.
```

FIGURE 21-9
Sample Program for Updating a
Relative File (continued)

```
*
  550-WRITE-DISK-REC.
      REWRITE DISK-RECORD
         INVALID KEY
           SET INVALID-WRITE TO TRUE
           MOVE 'THIS RECORD LOCATION CANNOT BE WRITTEN'
               TO ERR-MESSAGE
           PERFORM 400-DISK-IO-ERR-MESS
         NOT INVALID KEY
           SET VALID-WRITE TO TRUE
      END-REWRITE.
*
 600-DELETE-RECORD.
*
     PERFORM 300-RANDOMIZE-READ
*
     SET STILL-LOOKING TO TRUE
     PERFORM 650-FIND-RECORD
             UNTIL RECORD-FOUND
                OR RECORD-NOT-FOUND
                OR INVALID-READ
*
     IF RECORD-FOUND
        MOVE 2 TO REC-STATUS-CODE
        PERFORM 550-WRITE-DISK-REC
     ELSE
        IF RECORD-NOT-FOUND
           MOVE 'ATTEMPT TO DELETE NONEXISTENT RECORD'
               TO ERR-MESSAGE
           PERFORM 400-DISK-IO-ERR-MESS.
*
 650-FIND-RECORD.
     IF  VALID-READ AND USED-RECORD
          AND ITEM-NUMBER OF TRANS-REC
             = ITEM-NUMBER OF DISK-RECORD
        SET RECORD-FOUND TO TRUE
     ELSE
        IF (VALID-READ AND USED-RECORD
            AND ITEM-NUMBER OF TRANS-REC
            NOT = ITEM-NUMBER OF DISK-RECORD)
           OR
           (VALID-READ AND DELETED-RECORD)
*
           PERFORM 450-HANDLE-SYNONYMS
           IF FILE-IS-FULL OR INVALID-READ
              SET RECORD-NOT-FOUND TO TRUE
           END-IF
        ELSE
           IF VALID-READ AND VACANT-RECORD
              SET RECORD-NOT-FOUND TO TRUE
           ELSE
              SET RECORD-NOT-FOUND TO TRUE
           END-IF
        END-IF
     END-IF.
```

FIGURE 21-9
Sample Program for Updating a
Relative File (continued)

```
*
  700-MODIFY-RECORD.
*
      SET STILL-LOOKING TO TRUE
      PERFORM 300-RANDOMIZE-READ
*
      PERFORM 650-FIND-RECORD
              UNTIL RECORD-FOUND
                  OR RECORD-NOT-FOUND
                  OR INVALID-READ
      IF RECORD-FOUND
         MOVE ITEM-NAME OF TRANS-REC
              TO ITEM-NAME OF DISK-RECORD
         PERFORM 550-WRITE-DISK-REC
      ELSE
         IF RECORD-NOT-FOUND
            MOVE 'ATTEMPT TO MODIFY NONEXISTENT RECORD'
                 TO ERR-MESSAGE
            PERFORM 400-DISK-IO-ERR-MESS
         END-IF
      END-IF.
*
  800-TRANS-ERR-MESS.
      MOVE SPACES TO ERROR-RECORD
      MOVE 'THIS TRANSACTION HAS INVALID-CODE'
          TO ERR-MESSAGE
      WRITE PRINT-REC FROM ERROR-RECORD AFTER 2 LINES
      MOVE TRANS-REC TO ERR-MESSAGE
      WRITE PRINT-REC FROM ERROR-RECORD AFTER 2 LINES.
```

Continuing our analysis of the 650-FIND-RECORD paragraph,
note that we say:

```
IF... OR... (VALID-READ AND DELETED RECORD)
    PERFORM 450-HANDLE-SYNONYMS
```

If there is a deleted record, we simply PERFORM 450-HANDLE-SYNONYMS to
move to the next disk record space on the relative file. The FILE-IS-FULL check
included in this paragraph prevents us from searching the entire file repeatedly for
a nonexisting record, in the case where all the records are occupied or vacant
from deletions only. Notice that the 650-FIND-RECORD terminates (SET
RECORD-NOT-FOUND TO TRUE) when a vacant record is encountered (IF VALID-
READ AND VACANT-RECORD), since such an occurrence indicates that the record
does not exist.

The program is substantially self-documenting, and you should be able to
review it and follow the details. The overall task is typical of most such
update programs, and the sample program can be used as the basic structure for
most of them.

USING BUCKETS WITH RELATIVE FILES

Relative files can be very efficient for the purpose of achieving direct access to records. However, such files can be associated with serious inefficiencies if synonym chains are very long, thereby causing multiple disk access for each logical I/O operation. As we have discussed, choice of an appropriate hashing procedure is one critical factor that affects synonyms. A second factor under our control is the file density; by decreasing the packing factor and allowing more unused space, the probability of generating synonyms is decreased.

A third tool for controlling synonyms is the use of the concept of a *bucket*. A bucket is really a block of records. From the standpoint of this approach, a file is considered to consist of a number of buckets, with each bucket capable of holding a certain number of records. The hashing procedure is based on buckets rather than on individual records. As a result the incidence of effective synonyms is reduced. For example, if a bucket size of five records is defined, a synonym would be generated only when six or more records hashed to the same bucket.

The concept of using buckets works (1) because of the difference in speed between accessing a record on disk versus processing records in central storage, and (2) because once an I/O operation begins, data transfer rates are high compared to the time that it takes to get ready to carry out an I/O operation.

Let us consider an example to help explain how these concepts work. Suppose that a bucket size of five records is defined for a file that has already been created. We are about to read a record. The home address of the record is computed as a bucket number, and the entire bucket of five records is read from the disk in one READ operation. The bucket is a table in central storage, and it is searched to determine if it contains the desired record. Searching a table in central storage is very fast compared with reading multiple times from a disk. For example, if the given record and three other records happen to be synonyms, all four records would be in the same bucket and be accessed by one disk operation. On the other hand, in the absence of a bucket, as many as four disk reads could be required to access one particular record when there are four synonyms. It is true that with a bucket size of five, every disk read (or write) requires five times the number of bytes as accessing an individual record does. However, data transfer rates are very high. What is relatively slow is the time needed for initiating a read operation, due to the rotational delay of the disk and the time required to move from one cylinder or track to the next cylinder or track.

If the use of buckets is a good thing, the question then is how large a bucket should be in terms of number of records. Conceptually, we might try to balance the opposing factors of data transfer rates as contrasted to access times to disk. However, a practical approach is to consider the track size of the disks being used and aim for a bucket size that approaches the track size. Remember, though, that file I/O areas are double-buffered in most operating systems, so that for each relative file in use, the total I/O buffer size will be double the bucket size. This consideration may lead to the conclusion that the bucket size should be smaller than the track size. Finally, it is a general rule that a bucket size divided into a track size should yield an integer, to avoid unused track portions or spanned records across tracks.

To illustrate use of the bucket concept, Figure 21-10 is a modification of the program presented in Figure 21-7 to create a relative file. For ease of reference, repeated below is the file description that is concerned with the bucket:

```
FD  DISK-FILE LABEL RECORDS STANDARD
    DATA RECORD IS DISK-RECORD
    RECORD CONTAINS 127 CHARACTERS.
01  DISK-RECORD.
    02  BUCKET-STATUS-CODE      PIC 9.
        88 VACANT-BUCKET        VALUE ZERO.
        88 USED-BUCKET          VALUE 1.
```

```
02  NO-OF-RECS-IN-BUCKET   PIC 9.
    88 FULL-BUCKET            VALUE 5.
02  DISK-RECORD-BUCKET OCCURS 5 TIMES.
    03 ITEM-NUMBER            PIC 9(5).
    03 ITEM-NAME             PIC X(20).
```

The BUCKET-STATUS-CODE refers to the entire bucket. A bucket has a vacancy if there are four or fewer records stored in it, and it is full if it contains five records. The field NO-OF-RECS-IN-BUCKET is used to keep track of how many records are in the bucket. The FULL-BUCKET and USED-BUCKET condition-names are apparently redundant, leading to the thought that NO-OF-RECS-IN-BUCKET with suitable condition-names could serve the role of BUCKET-STATUS-CODE as well. While such is the case for this program, it would not be true for an updating program. Because of the need to know "delete" status codes for a bucket when files are being updated, it makes sense to use two "marker" fields in each bucket.

FIGURE 21-10

Sample Program to Create a Relative File with the Use of the Bucket Concept

```
IDENTIFICATION DIVISION.
PROGRAM-ID. REL-CREATE-BUCKETS.
*
ENVIRONMENT DIVISION.
CONFIGURATION SECTION.
SOURCE-COMPUTER. ABC-480.
OBJECT-COMPUTER. ABC-480.
INPUT-OUTPUT SECTION.
FILE-CONTROL.
    SELECT DISK-FILE    ASSIGN TO NEWMASTER
                        ORGANIZATION IS RELATIVE
                        ACCESS MODE IS RANDOM
                        RELATIVE KEY IS LOCATION-ADDRESS.
*
    SELECT SOURCE-FILE  ASSIGN TO SOURCEFL.
    SELECT PRINT-FILE   ASSIGN TO PRINTER.
*
DATA DIVISION.
FILE SECTION.
*
FD  DISK-FILE    LABEL RECORDS STANDARD
                 DATA RECORD IS DISK-RECORD
                 RECORD CONTAINS 127 CHARACTERS.
01  DISK-RECORD.
    02  BUCKET-STATUS-CODE   PIC 9.
        88 VACANT-BUCKET       VALUE ZERO.
        88 USED-BUCKET         VALUE 1.
    02  NO-OF-RECS-IN-BUCKET PIC 9.
        88 FULL-BUCKET         VALUE 5.
*
    02  DISK-RECORD-BUCKET   OCCURS 5 TIMES.
        03 ITEM-NUMBER         PIC 9(5).
        03 ITEM-NAME           PIC X(20).
```

FIGURE 21-10
Sample Program to Create a
Relative File with the Use of the
Bucket Concept (continued)

```
*
 FD  SOURCE-FILE   LABEL RECORDS OMITTED
                   DATA RECORD IS SOURCE-RECORD.
 01  SOURCE-RECORD.
     02  SOURCE-ITEM-NUMBER   PIC 9(5).
     02  SOURCE-ITEM-NAME     PIC X(20).
     02  FILLER               PIC X(55).
*
 FD  PRINT-FILE    LABEL RECORDS OMITTED
                   DATA RECORD IS PRINT-RECORD.
 01  PRINT-RECORD             PIC X(132).
*
 WORKING-STORAGE SECTION.
*
 01  END-OF-DATA-FLAG         PIC XXX.
     88  END-OF-SOURCE        VALUE 'YES'.
     88  NOT-END-OF-SOURCE    VALUE 'NO '.
 01  READ-VALIDITY-FLAG       PIC XXX.
     88  VALID-READ           VALUE 'YES'.
     88  INVALID-READ         VALUE 'NO '.
*
 01  LOOP-FLAG                PIC XXX.
     88  FILE-IS-FULL         VALUE 'YES'.
     88  FILE-IS-NOT-FULL     VALUE 'NO '.
*
 01  LOCATION-ADDRESS         PIC 999.
 01  STARTING-ADDRESS         PIC 999.
 01  PRIME-NUMBER             PIC 9       VALUE 7.
 01  WORKFIELD                PIC S99999 USAGE COMP.
 01  QUOTIENT                 PIC S999   USAGE COMP.
 01  MAX-NO-OF-LOCATIONS      PIC 999     VALUE 10.
 01  I                        PIC 999.
*
 01  ERROR-RECORD.
     02  FILLER               PIC X VALUE SPACE.
     02  ERROR-LOCATION       PIC ZZ999.
     02  FILLER               PIC XX VALUE SPACE.
     02  ERR-MESSAGE          PIC X(50).
/
 PROCEDURE DIVISION.
*
 010-MAIN-ROUTINE.
     OPEN INPUT  SOURCE-FILE
     OPEN OUTPUT DISK-FILE
                 PRINT-FILE.
*
```

FIGURE 21-10
*Sample Program to Create a
Relative File with the Use of the
Bucket Concept (continued)*

```
              PERFORM 020-ZERO-DISK
                 VARYING I FROM 1 BY 1 UNTIL I > MAX-NO-OF-LOCATIONS.
        *
              CLOSE DISK-FILE.
        *
              OPEN I-O DISK-FILE
              SET NOT-END-OF-SOURCE TO TRUE
              SET FILE-IS-NOT-FULL  TO TRUE
              SET VALID-READ        TO TRUE
              PERFORM  UNTIL END-OF-SOURCE
                          OR INVALID-READ
                          OR FILE-IS-FULL
                READ SOURCE-FILE RECORD
                  AT END
                        SET END-OF-SOURCE TO TRUE
                  NOT AT END
                        PERFORM 030-LOAD-RECORD
                END-READ
              END-PERFORM.
        *
              CLOSE SOURCE-FILE
                    PRINT-FILE
                    DISK-FILE.
              STOP RUN.
        *
         020-ZERO-DISK.
                MOVE I TO LOCATION-ADDRESS
                MOVE SPACES TO DISK-RECORD
                MOVE ZERO TO BUCKET-STATUS-CODE
                MOVE ZERO TO NO-OF-RECS-IN-BUCKET
        *
              WRITE DISK-RECORD
                 INVALID KEY
                    MOVE 'INVALID KEY DURING ZERO-DISK' TO ERR-MESSAGE
                    PERFORM 070-CANT-ACCESS
              END-WRITE.
        *
         030-LOAD-RECORD.
              PERFORM 040-RANDOMIZE-READ
        *
              IF VALID-READ AND USED-BUCKET
                 MOVE LOCATION-ADDRESS TO STARTING-ADDRESS
                 SET FILE-IS-NOT-FULL TO TRUE
                 PERFORM 050-HANDLE-SYNONYMS
                    UNTIL INVALID-READ
                          OR VACANT-BUCKET
                          OR FILE-IS-FULL.
        *
```

FIGURE 21-10

Sample Program to Create a
Relative File with the Use of the
Bucket Concept (continued)

```
            IF VALID-READ AND VACANT-BUCKET
               ADD 1 TO NO-OF-RECS-IN-BUCKET
               IF FULL-BUCKET
                  MOVE 1 TO BUCKET-STATUS-CODE
               END-IF
               MOVE SOURCE-ITEM-NUMBER
                     TO ITEM-NUMBER (NO-OF-RECS-IN-BUCKET)
               MOVE SOURCE-ITEM-NAME
                     TO ITEM-NAME (NO-OF-RECS-IN-BUCKET)
               REWRITE DISK-RECORD
                  INVALID KEY
                     MOVE 'ERROR DURING REWRITE' TO ERR-MESSAGE
                     PERFORM 070-CANT-ACCESS
                     STRING 'SOURCE RECORD INVOLVED = '
                           SOURCE-RECORD DELIMITED BY SIZE
                        INTO PRINT-RECORD
                     WRITE PRINT-RECORD AFTER 2
               END-REWRITE
            ELSE
               NEXT SENTENCE.
*
      040-RANDOMIZE-READ.
         MOVE SOURCE-ITEM-NUMBER TO WORKFIELD
         DIVIDE PRIME-NUMBER INTO WORKFIELD GIVING QUOTIENT
         COMPUTE LOCATION-ADDRESS =
             WORKFIELD - (PRIME-NUMBER * QUOTIENT) + 1
*
      PERFORM 060-READ-DISK-REC.
*
      050-HANDLE-SYNONYMS.
         ADD 1 TO LOCATION-ADDRESS
         IF LOCATION-ADDRESS > MAX-NO-OF-LOCATIONS
            MOVE 1 TO LOCATION-ADDRESS
         END-IF
         IF LOCATION-ADDRESS = STARTING-ADDRESS
            THEN
                MOVE SPACES TO PRINT-RECORD
                STRING 'FILE IS FULL; NEW RECORD IS = '
                      SOURCE-RECORD DELIMITED BY SIZE
                   INTO PRINT-RECORD
                WRITE PRINT-RECORD AFTER 2
                SET FILE-IS-FULL TO TRUE
             ELSE
                SET FILE-IS-NOT-FULL TO TRUE
                PERFORM 060-READ-DISK-REC
         END-IF.
*
      060-READ-DISK-REC.
         READ DISK-FILE RECORD
            INVALID KEY
               MOVE 'ERROR WHILE READING ' TO ERR-MESSAGE
               PERFORM 070-CANT-ACCESS
               SET INVALID-READ TO TRUE
            NOT INVALID KEY
               SET VALID-READ TO TRUE
         END-READ.
*
      070-CANT-ACCESS.
         MOVE LOCATION-ADDRESS TO ERROR-LOCATION
         WRITE PRINT-RECORD FROM ERROR-RECORD AFTER 2.
```

Again, keep in mind that the bucket *is* the record from the standpoint of the COBOL language and the operating system. It is up to the programming logic to "split" the bucket into five records during processing. Accordingly, in the DATA DIVISION included in Figure 21-10 notice that PRIME-NUMBER is initialized to 7 and MAX-NO-OF-LOCATIONS is initialized to 10. This corresponds to the total of 50 records in Figure 21-7 (10 buckets x 5 records = 50).

To initialize each bucket to an empty state, the 020-ZERO-DISK paragraph in Figure 21-10 moves a zero value to both the BUCKET-STATUS-CODE and the NO-OF-RECS-IN-BUCKET fields.

Finally, in the 030-LOAD-RECORD paragraph, notice that we ADD 1 TO NO-OF-RECS-IN-BUCKET as we are about to add a new record, and then that incremented value is used as a subscript. Also, if the bucket is full, we set BUCKET-STATUS-CODE to the appropriate value so that the bucket will be sensed as being full on any subsequent occasion. Again, a bucket is not full until all five record locations are filled.

Exercise 21.6 incorporates the bucket concept in an update procedure.

R E V I E W . . . .

1. A "bucket" essentially is a block, or group, of _____.

    records

2. When a bucket of, say, five records is read, it is entered into central
   _____ , where a search is then made for the particular _____
   that is desired.

    storage; record

3. The size of the bucket that is used should generally be [smaller / larger] than the track size.

    smaller

4. In program processing, a bucket with a record size of five records is full only when there are _____ (number) records stored in it.

    five

. . . .

SUMMARY

The three methods of file organization are the *sequential, indexed,* and *relative.* This chapter covered the creation and processing of relative files. Techniques for sequential files were described in Chapters 10 and 17, while indexed file processing was covered in Chapter 20.

A *relative file* is one in which the records are accessed by reference to their position *relative* to other records in the file. *Key-to-address transformation methods* are used to transform record keys (identifiers) to relative location addresses. When two different record keys result in the same relative location address, a *synonym* is said to have occurred. A common storage solution for a synonym is to store it in the first available space following the home-address space. The term *packing factor,* or *file density,* is used to denote the percent of filled space in a relative file.

The key-to-address transformation method most frequently used is the *division remainder method.* As the name indicates, the relative address is based on the remainder associated with a process of division that is explained and illustrated in the respective section of this chapter. Other, less frequently used, transformation methods are the *digit analysis method,* the *mid-square method,* and *folding.* The technique of transforming *alphabetic record keys* to relative addresses also was described.

COBOL language instructions for relative files then were considered. In the ENVIRONMENT DIVISION the ORGANIZATION IS RELATIVE clause of the SELECT statement specifies that the file is a relative file. The ACCESS MODE has the same meaning as for indexed files, as explained in the preceding chapter. The RELATIVE KEY is required as a WORKING-STORAGE unsigned integer item. This contrasts with the respective situation for indexed files, for which the RECORD KEY is part of the file record.

In the PROCEDURE DIVISION, use of the input/output verbs WRITE, REWRITE, DELETE, and START was briefly described. Use of these verbs parallels their use for indexed files, as covered in the preceding chapter.

Two example programs were then discussed. The first one (in Figure 21-7) was written to create a relative file, while the second one (in Figure 21-9) updates the file that was created.

The final section of this chapter described the use of the concept of a *bucket,* or block of records, for reducing access time in the processing of relative files. Overall access time is reduced because the incidence of synonyms is reduced when records are accessed as blocks of records, rather than individually. A sample program (in Figure 21-10) illustrates creation of relative files that incorporate the bucket concept.

EXERCISES

21.1　Do a digit analysis of the following set of customer account numbers: 8023, 9178, 9034, 8187, 8056, 9162, 9019.

21.2　Based on the digit analysis in Exercise 21.1, describe a key-to-address transformation method for a file that consists of 100 customer accounts. Demonstrate the procedure by computing the address for account numbers 8023 and 3456.

21.3　Outline what changes would be needed in the sample program for creating a relative file in Figure 21-7 to guarantee that there will be no duplicate records in the file. A duplicate record is one that has the same key as another record in the file.

21.4　Refer to Exercise 10.3 for the program description.

　　a.　Create the master file as a relative file, using the part number as the RELATIVE KEY.

　　b.　Update the master file on a random basis, using the part number as the RELATIVE KEY.

21.5　A manufacturer of three product classes has a sales force consisting of 100 salespeople, each person assigned a unique salesperson number of 5 digits. Salespeople are paid on commission, receiving monthly commission benefits as well as an annual bonus based on monthly performance. We want to maintain commission data for each salesperson, by product class and by month, on a disk file.

　　a.　Create a relative file that will contain a record of the commission data for each salesperson in the following form. Salesperson number will serve for the RELATIVE KEY.

FIELD	FIELD SIZE
Salesperson number	5 digits
Salesperson name	
Last name	15 characters
First name	10 characters
Middle initial	1 character
Commission totals by product class (3 classes) and by month (12 months).	Each total can be as large as 999,999.99.
	Note: There will be 36 totals.

The file is created by reading one record per salesperson, containing the salesperson-number and salesperson-name fields. After the randomizing technique has been employed to determine the disk location, all commission totals (36 fields) are set to zero. Then the record is written on the disk.

b. Update this file, using sales transaction data. Use the salesperson number as the RELATIVE KEY.

The transaction records have the following layout:

COLUMNS	FIELD
1–5	Salesperson number
6	Commission code (based on product class) 1 = 0.02 of sales 2 = 0.03 of sales 3 = 0.05 of sales
7–8	Month code (from 01 to 12)
9–14	Sales values in dollars and cents

Assume that the transaction records are sorted by salesperson number; therefore we need to access the relevant master record only once for each set of records corresponding to one salesperson. Of course, we may have transactions for only some of the salespeople. As each salesperson is processed, we want to print a report, as follows:

```
                    CURRENT COMMISSION DATA

                                            TOTALS
                                    --------------------------
    SALESPERSON    SALESPERSON-
    NUMBER         NAME             THIS MONTH    YEAR-TO-DATE
    12345          LAST, FIRST, M.    $870.35       $18,562.40
    24966          LAST, FIRST, M.    1020.20        12,112.96
      .               .                 .              .
      .               .                 .              .
      .               .                 .              .
```

In other words, we want to accumulate the commissions, regardless of product class, for the current month; as well as the year-to-date totals for all months through the present one.

21.6   Modify the sample program for updating a relative file in Figure 21-9 to incorporate the concept of a bucket. Use a bucket size of five records.

When a record is deleted from a bucket and it is not the last record in the table, shift the remaining records so that the "top" of the table is packed. In other words, do not leave any gaps in the table of records that constitutes a bucket.

Interactive Processing

IN THIS CHAPTER *you will learn the general principles and specific techniques for writing programs that display output and accept input from a terminal with a video monitor.*

The concepts apply only to some input and output processing. Reading from and writing to files is unaffected, and neither is the other logic of programming. However, since the programming features of standard COBOL for such use are not well developed, you will need some additional information about features and instructions that apply specifically to your own compiler.

The chapter begins with a brief overview of the ACCEPT and DISPLAY verbs that can be used to read from the keyboard and write onto the monitor screen. Then you will learn the basic concepts of interactive programming: defining and processing the desired contents and attributes of the screen and the inputting of data from the keyboard.

You will see the application of the general principles in two sample programs. The first program utilizes standard COBOL capabilities, but it requires that the programmer have available certain "escape code" definitions for the type of terminal that is used. Such escape codes tell the terminal to display a field in bold, to position the cursor to a desired location on the screen, to erase all or part of the screen, etc. Once such codes are available, you will be able to use the exact techniques that we illustrate and discuss in the sample program.

The second sample program demonstrates a nonstandard but widely used compiler sold by the Microsoft Corporation. The specific features are not standard, but most compilers have similar ones. These features simplify the programming code, and it is likely that many of them will be standardized in a future version of COBOL.

INTRODUCTION

Interactive programs are designed to carry on some kind of "dialogue" between the program and an individual utilizing a computer terminal or personal computer. Although such programs are widely used, the standard COBOL language lacks the types of specific features that several compilers provide to facilitate interactive processing. Consequently, individual vendors have written extensions to their COBOL compilers that can be used to write interactive programs. Because each vendor has a different product, it is difficult to present one unified set of concepts and techniques in this chapter. Still, the differences between vendors' compilers are not always dramatic, and it is easy to transfer the concepts and methods from one compiler to another.

ACCEPT AND DISPLAY

COBOL provides for interactive processing capability through the use of the ACCEPT and DISPLAY verbs, as represented in the following formats:

ACCEPT identifier [FROM mnemonic-name]

$$\text{DISPLAY} \begin{Bmatrix} \text{identifier -1} \\ \text{literal -1} \end{Bmatrix} \begin{Bmatrix} \text{identifier -2} \\ \text{literal -2} \end{Bmatrix} \dots [\text{UPON} \ \text{mnemonic-name}]$$

[WITH NO ADVANCING]

With respect to the above format specifications, when mnemonic names are used, they are defined in the SPECIAL-NAMES paragraph of the ENVIRONMENT DIVISION. A chosen mnemonic name can be an interactive terminal, and thus we can ACCEPT data from such a terminal and DISPLAY data upon the screen of such a terminal. In fact, the WITH NO ADVANCING clause in the DISPLAY format was added in the 1985 standard specifically to provide control over cursor positioning at a video terminal. Thus, if we DISPLAY ... WITH NO ADVANCING, we can present a message to the user and then ACCEPT input on the same line, as in the following:

```
DISPLAY 'ENTER YOUR NAME: ' WITH NO ADVANCING
ACCEPT NAME
```

When the user responds by entering data on the keyboard, the response will be on the same line as the above message. In the *absence* of the NO ADVANCING clause, a DISPLAY results in an automatic line-feed, thus making it impossible to arrange a simple dialogue.

The example above notwithstanding, the ACCEPT and DISPLAY verbs have inadequate features to support interactive programming. As a comparison of what is needed versus what is available, Figures 22-1 and 22-2 present the extensions of ACCEPT and DISPLAY verbs, respectively, in one of the compilers of the Digital Equipment Corporation. Unfortunately, the variability in terminals and their use has led the language designers away from adopting any standard set of specifications for interactive processing.

R E V I E W . . . .

1. The COBOL verb that provides capability to input data from a computer terminal is the _____ verb.

ACCEPT

FIGURE 22-1
*Digital Equipment Corporation
Implementation of the ACCEPT
Verb*

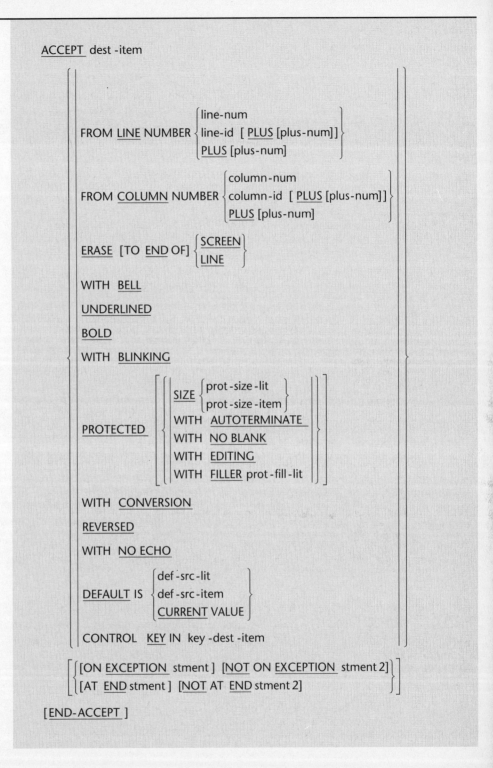

ACCEPT dest -item

$$
\begin{aligned}
&\text{FROM } \underline{\text{LINE}} \text{ NUMBER} \begin{cases} \text{line-num} \\ \text{line-id} \ [\ \underline{\text{PLUS}}\ [\text{plus-num}]\ ] \\ \underline{\text{PLUS}}\ [\text{plus-num}] \end{cases}
\end{aligned}
$$

$$
\text{FROM } \underline{\text{COLUMN}} \text{ NUMBER} \begin{cases} \text{column-num} \\ \text{column-id} \ [\ \underline{\text{PLUS}}\ [\text{plus-num}]\ ] \\ \underline{\text{PLUS}}\ [\text{plus-num}] \end{cases}
$$

$$
\underline{\text{ERASE}} \ [\text{TO } \underline{\text{END}} \text{ OF}] \begin{cases} \underline{\text{SCREEN}} \\ \underline{\text{LINE}} \end{cases}
$$

WITH BELL

UNDERLINED

BOLD

WITH BLINKING

$$
\underline{\text{PROTECTED}} \quad \left[\left[\begin{cases} \underline{\text{SIZE}} \begin{cases} \text{prot -size -lit} \\ \text{prot -size -item} \end{cases} \\ \text{WITH } \underline{\text{AUTOTERMINATE}} \\ \text{WITH } \underline{\text{NO BLANK}} \\ \text{WITH } \underline{\text{EDITING}} \\ \text{WITH } \underline{\text{FILLER}} \text{ prot -fill -lit} \end{cases}\right]\right]
$$

WITH CONVERSION

REVERSED

WITH NO ECHO

$$
\underline{\text{DEFAULT}} \text{ IS} \begin{cases} \text{def -src -lit} \\ \text{def -src -item} \\ \underline{\text{CURRENT}} \text{ VALUE} \end{cases}
$$

CONTROL KEY IN key -dest -item

$$
\begin{bmatrix} [\text{ON } \underline{\text{EXCEPTION}} \text{ stment}] \ [\underline{\text{NOT}} \text{ ON } \underline{\text{EXCEPTION}} \text{ stment 2}] \\ [\text{AT } \underline{\text{END}} \text{ stment}] \ [\underline{\text{NOT}} \text{ AT } \underline{\text{END}} \text{ stment 2}] \end{bmatrix}
$$

[END-ACCEPT]

2. The COBOL verb that provides the capability to present data at a terminal screen
   is the _____ verb.

   DISPLAY

3. When mnemonic names are used in an ACCEPT or DISPLAY statement, they are
   defined in the _____ paragraph of the ENVIRONMENT
   DIVISION.

   SPECIAL-NAMES

FIGURE 22-2
*Digital Equipment Corporation
Implementation of the DISPLAY
Verb*

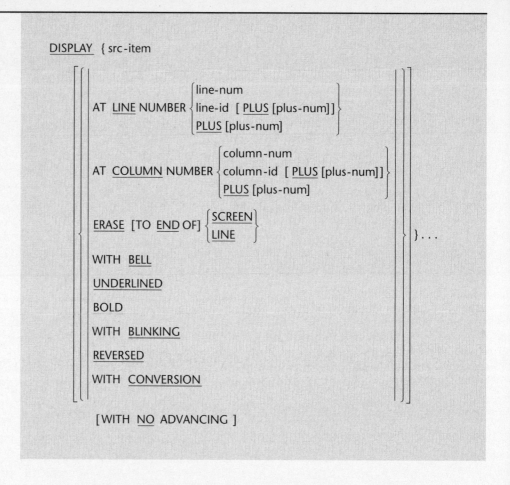

4. The COBOL language [does / does not] include the features that facilitate the development of programs for interactive processing.

                                                                        does not

• • • • • • • • • • • • • • • • • • • •

PROGRAMMING CONCEPTS FOR INTERACTIVE PROCESSING

Two main characteristic operations concern the programmer when writing interactive programs.

1. The need for control over the screen display, so that appropriate data and messages can be presented to the user.

2. The need for control over the sequence of the data entered by the user on the keyboard.

A typical interactive program involves presentation of a "menu" screen to the user, with instructions to enter one or more keystrokes in reply. When the user keys-in a chosen reply, the program analyzes the reply; and depending on its content, the program may do one of several things. For example, it can display a corrective message telling the user to give a different reply, or it can take some other action (including that of terminating the program).

All interactive programs are of the "question-answer" type. The program issues a "question," the user provides a reply and, based upon the reply, the program proceeds to the next question. Such questions may be direct, such as, "Do you want to make a deposit or a withdrawal?"; or they may be indirect, such as, "What do you want me to do next?" Programs that ask explicit questions of the user are called *menu driven,* while programs that ask implicit questions of the "What next?" type are called *command driven.* In either case the critical programming feature is the ability to examine keyboard input and, based on the input, to take the next step in the program logic. Once a data item has been made available to the program, its further processing is independent of its origin (the keyboard, magnetic disk, or magnetic tape, etc.). For example, given a product number, a routine to validate such a number would be the same whether the program is interactive or batch; thus the difference lies only in the method by which the data item is entered into the program and not on how it is processed.

As we stated at the beginning of this section, there are two main operations involved in interactive programs: controlling display output on the screen and controlling keyboard input. We now proceed to describe these two operations in turn.

Writing on the Screen

The screen display typically consists of 24 lines of 80 columns each, for a total of 1,920 characters (24 x 80). There are larger and smaller screens as well (for example, some portable machines often include displays of a few lines and fewer than 80 columns). For a given screen size, the programmer must specify the characters to be displayed in each of the available positions on the screen. However, there are typically a number of shortcuts available. For example, in most cases it is possible to issue one command to clear the screen instead of defining a field for the whole screen, such as

```
01   ENTIRE-SCREEN.
     03   FILLER  PIC X(1920) VALUE SPACES.
```

ENTIRE-SCREEN could be written (by use of the DISPLAY verb) to clear the screen. As we will explain in greater detail later, there are simpler alternatives for clearing the screen. Still, it is important to understand the relationship between the screen and data definitions that can refer to portions of the screen. For example, we can fill the first line with spaces and the second line with 26 spaces followed by the literal "AMERICAN SALES COMPANY", followed by 30 spaces, by the following:

```
01   SCREEN-TITLE.
     02   FILLER      PIC X(106) VALUE SPACES.
     02   FILLER      PIC X(24)  VALUE
          'AMERICAN SALES CORPORATION'.
     02   FILLER      PIC X(30) VALUE SPACES.
     .
     .
     .
```

Writing DISPLAY SCREEN-TITLE then will do the task.

In addition to determining what to write on the screen and where it is to be written, the programmer must control the special display *attributes* of the screen. For instance, we can show characters in a particular position on the screen as boldfaced, reversed foreground-background, underscored, or blinking. If color is available, we can display characters in blue, red, and so forth. Information about desired screen display attributes is usually provided by specialized commands as we will explain below. In some cases, however, to store such display-attribute information, we may need an additional "attribute" byte for each of the character bytes on the screen. Thus, if we have a 24 x 80 screen, we would define two fields to fully describe and control the screen display: one field of 1,920 (24 x 80) bytes to store the displayed data and another field of 1,920 bytes to describe the display attributes of the character bytes. Again, in most cases, there are simpler ways to define screen attributes, and we will discuss them below.

There is often a need to display a message or a field of data in a specific place on the screen, without displaying the entire screen. For instance, we may want to display the message "INVALID CHOICE. TRY AGAIN" on line 20, starting with column 30. One approach would be to define a specific field within the screen-defining field. For example:

```
01  INVALID-MESSAGE.
    02  FILLER                PIC X(1529).
    02  MESSAGE-FIELD         PIC X(26).
```

If we write MOVE "INVALID CHOICE. TRY AGAIN" to MESSAGE-FIELD and subsequently we DISPLAY INVALID-MESSAGE, we have a way of displaying that message in row 20, column 30 [(19 x 80) + 29 = 1,529]. However, this approach requires transmission of a lot of undesired data (1529 bytes).

A more common and simpler approach that we will describe below is to use the ability to specify a location on the screen by means of row-column coordinates. Thus we could position the cursor at line 20, column 30, for example, and write the desired message at that point. Positioning the cursor is specific to each device type. In general terms, we need to define a field containing special codes that mean "move the cursor," followed by the row-column values for the desired location.

A common method of handling writing on the screen, particularly when remote terminals are involved, is to send special codes to the receiving terminal that specify the desired action. The terminal then sorts out the special codes, does what these codes specify, and then displays the (remaining) data.

We will illustrate the process by means of examples based on the DEC VAX computer and the VT-series of terminals. Actually, terminals such as the VT-100 and VT-240, are somewhat industry standards in the sense that there are many terminals manufactured from companies other than DEC whose terminals operate in the VT-xxx mode. Following are a few selected codes:

CODE	MEANING
\<ESC\>[	The "escape" character sequence. The \<ESC\> stands for one character that is unprintable and has the ASCII value of 27. We will show these five characters with the understanding that they stand for just one character. Thus the escape sequence consists of two characters.
\<ESC\>[7m	Turn on the reverse-video attribute
\<ESC\>[m	Turn on the normal attribute (thus turning off any other attribute)
\<ESC\>[1m	Turn on the bold attribute
\<ESC\>[2;40H	Position the cursor to row 2 column 40. (We show a specific example to make clear the distinction between the variable parameters 2 and 40 and the constant symbols of the escape sequence \<ESC\>, [, ;, and H)
\<ESC\>[H\<ESC\>[J	Clear the entire screen
\<ESC\>[J	Clear from the cursor to the end of the screen

These are a few of the escape codes available. A variety of other codes can also be defined.

To illustrate the process of writing on the screen, we define the following fields:

```
01  REVERSE-ON.
    03 FILLER              PIC XXXX VALUE '<ESC>[7m'.
01  NORMAL-ON.
    03 FILLER              PIC XXX  VALUE '<ESC>[m'.
01  CURSOR-POSITION.
    03  ESCAPE-CODE        PIC X    VALUE '<ESC>['.
    03  ROW-POSITION       PIC 99.
    03  FILLER             PIC X    VALUE ';'
    03  COLUMN-POSITION    PIC 99.
    03  FILLER             PIC X    VALUE 'H'.
01  MESSAGE-FIELD          PIC X(15).
01  DISPLAY-LINE           PIC X(80).
```

To write the words "Type your NAME:" in reverse-video in row 10, column 20, and leave the cursor at the end of the message, we would write

```
MOVE 10 TO ROW-POSITION
MOVE 20 TO COLUMN-POSITION
DISPLAY CURSOR-POSITION WITH NO ADVANCING
DISPLAY REVERSE-ON       WITH NO ADVANCING
MOVE 'Type your NAME:' TO MESSAGE-FIELD
DISPLAY MESSAGE-FIELD    WITH NO ADVANCING
DISPLAY NORMAL-ON        WITH NO ADVANCING
```

Or, using the STRING verb:

```
MOVE SPACES TO DISPLAY-LINE
MOVE 10 TO ROW-POSITION
MOVE 20 TO COLUMN-POSITION
STRING   CURSOR-POSITION
         REVERSE-ON
         'Type your NAME:'
         NORMAL-ON
     DELIMITED BY SIZE
     INTO DISPLAY-LINE
DISPLAY DISPLAY-LINE WITH NO ADVANCING
```

In either version the above example illustrates that we incorporate the escape codes into the data to be displayed. However, when the terminal receives them, it "sorts through" them and knows which characters are commands to the terminal and which are characters to be displayed on the screen.

With respect to the version using the STRING statement, it should be noted that DISPLAY-LINE was defined by PIC X(80). However, since we are stringing escape characters into it as well as data, its effective capacity is less than 80. This could be a concern if the data to be displayed were near 80 characters, and/or there were a lot of escape codes involved in the STRING operation.

The above approach to writing on the screen is a general one. If we have a different terminal, what we need to do is find out its escape codes and replace the ones above with the new ones. The PROCEDURE DIVISION logic and statements would not be affected by the specific escape codes defined in the DATA DIVISION.

Handling Keyboard Input

Interactive COBOL programs handle keyboard input in one of two ways: Either the program contains logic to "look at" each incoming keystroke value and process it individually, or we can define a whole field and issue a command to receive from the keyboard a value for the entire field. In the latter case, while the user is keying in the data, our program cannot "see" what is being keyed-in until the entire field value is available. When data for the field are available, then the contents of the field can be examined, just as in batch processing. When a record is read from a disk, for example, the contents of a given field in the record are made available as a unit, *not* character by character.

If we are able to get character-by-character input, we can provide the user with an opportunity for exception input. For instance, in the middle of entering a customer's name, the user may want to issue a "cancel," or "redo from start," or "exit" command by pressing a special key. The program that senses each character senses such an exception key and takes immediate action. In contrast, a program that receives field-at-a-time input from the keyboard cannot sense the user's signal immediately. The user must wait until the right occasion comes along before the special command is given. The programmer chooses one method over the other depending on the specific applications and programming ease.

To receive data from the keyboard, we use the ACCEPT verb, as in the following example:

```
ACCEPT SALES-AMOUNT
IF SALES-AMOUNT NOT NUMERIC ...
```

Typically, if we are going to input a number of fields, we precede each ACCEPT by a suitable DISPLAY to position the cursor at the desired screen location, as explained in the preceding section. We may have program logic to examine each field immediately after it is entered, or we may wait till all the fields on the screen have been entered and then evaluate the input. The latter approach is just like reading data from a file. We receive all the fields of a given record before we evaluate some or all of them for further processing.

Business applications are mainly field-oriented rather than character-oriented. Still, most compilers provide for ways for the program to "sense" that a *function key* or other special key has been pressed and to allow the program to take appropriate action. However, there is wide variation among compilers for handling such processing, so we do not pursue the subject further.

R E V I E W . . . .

1. In interactive programs one area of required attention is control over display [input / output] on the screen.

   output

2. Another area of concern is control over keyboard _____.

   input

3. All interactive programs are "question-_____" types of programs.

   answer

4. Interactive programs that ask *explicit* questions of the user, in which the possible responses are identified, are called _____ driven.

   menu

5. Interactive programs that ask *implicit* questions of the "What next?" type are called _____ driven.

command

6. The screen display typically consists of _____ lines of_____ columns each.

24; 80

7. If particular positions on the screen are to be boldface, underscored, or in color, such required information is called display _____ information.

attribute

8. Data can also be displayed selectively on a screen by moving the _____ to a specified position and then displaying the desired data.

cursor

9. Such special effects as boldface can be obtained on a screen by sending special _____ to the terminal.

escape codes

10. Each code to be used to achieve a special effect on a screen can be defined in the DATA DIVISION, in the _____ clause for the data-item designating that effect.

VALUE

11. Keyboard entries can be handled character-by-_____ or as an entire _____.

character; field

• •

SAMPLE INTERACTIVE PROGRAM FOR STANDARD COBOL

In this section we present a sample interactive program to help illustrate in a specific context the general concepts already discussed.

The overall function of the program is indicated by Figures 22-3(a) and 22-3(b). Initially, the program shows the menu in Figure 22-3(a). The ENTER SELECTION > prompt asks the user to enter one of the four designated choices. If the user enters anything other than 1, 2, 3, or 4, the message *** INVALID CHARACTER-TRY AGAIN *** appears at the bottom of the screen, as shown in Figure 22-3(b). Otherwise, the program does one of the four specified choices.

If the user enters choice 1 in the main menu, the program displays the screen shown in Figure 22-4(a). At that point the user will enter the name (last, first, and middle) and a telephone number. When the user has finished entering the phone number, which is the last field to be input, then the three-choice menu appears at the bottom of the screen, as shown in Figure 22-4(b). The user responds with a choice to indicate the desired action.

To describe the sample program in greater detail, a full program listing is presented in Figure 22-5. The file CUST-FILE is defined so that we can write the data entered in the screen, as shown in Figures 22-4(a) and 22-4(b). When the user presses the C choice in Figure 22-4(b), the program will save the data displayed on the screen onto the name and telephone-number fields in CUST-FILE.

In the 000-MAIN-PARA there is an in-line PERFORM WITH TEST AFTER, so that we can keep iterating to and from the main menu until the PROGRAM-END condition is true. First, within this main outer loop, we PERFORM 100-DISPLAY-MENU to display the initial menu shown in Figure 22-3(a).

In the program listing in Figure 22-5, the first instruction in 100-DISPLAY-MENU is DISPLAY CLEAR-FULL-SCREEN, which is a field in WORKING-STORAGE whose content is the escape codes for clearing the entire screen. Next, we set the

FIGURE 22-3(a)
Sample Menu Screen

```
CUSTOMER FILE MENU


1   ADD A NEW CUSTOMER

2   CHANGE CUSTOMER DATA

3   DELETE CUSTOMER

4   EXIT PROGRAM


ENTER SELECTION >
```

FIGURE 22-3(b)
Sample Menu Screen After
Incorrect Selection Is Made

```
CUSTOMER FILE MENU


1   ADD A NEW CUSTOMER

2   CHANGE CUSTOMER DATA

3   DELETE CUSTOMER

4   EXIT PROGRAM


ENTER SELECTION > A



*** INVALID CHARACTER - TRY AGAIN ***
```

cursor position to row 2, column 26, and after moving the desired heading we DISPLAY EACH-LINE-DISPLAY. Observe in the DATA DIVISION definition of EACH-LINE-DISPLAY that it is a group item that incorporates the escape codes for positioning the cursor, followed by the 37-byte MENU-DISPLAY-LINE field.

After displaying the heading and increasing the row value by 2, we execute a PERFORM VARYING to display the four lines that constitute the four main menu choices. Notice the use of the STRING to put together the escape codes for bold display of the menu choice number and for resetting to normal display attribute, as well as the MENU-DETAIL-LINE (I), which was based on a REDEFINES of the CHOICE-LINES table of constants in the 01 MAIN-MENU-LINES paragraph of the WORKING-STORAGE SECTION. Finally, when all four lines have been displayed in 100-DISPLAY-MENU, we MOVE FOOTING-LN prior to displaying it to get the "ENTER SELECTION >" prompt.

Returning to the 000-MAIN-PARA, following execution of the 100-DISPLAY-MENU we keep PERFORMing 200-GET-MENU-CHOICE to enable us to receive the user's menu choice.

In 200-GET-MENU-CHOICE in Figure 22-5 we DISPLAY CURSOR-SPOT, which has been defined in the DATA DIVISION to contain the cursor position for

FIGURE 22-4(a)
Sample Input Screen

```
                    AMERICAN SALES COMPANY

                        CUSTOMER DATA


NAME (Last): [                ]   (First): [            ]   (Middle): [            ]


PHONE: [              ]
```

FIGURE 22-4(b)
Sample Input Screen After Input Has Been Entered

```
                    AMERICAN SALES COMPANY

                        CUSTOMER DATA


NAME (Last): [ ANDERSON       ]   (First): [ HELEN      ]   (Middle): [ KAY        ]


PHONE: [ (602)123-4567 ]




        R = RE-ENTER    C = INPUT COMPLETE    X = ESCAPE TO MENU
```

FIGURE 22-5

Sample Interactive Program Using Standard COBOL

```
        IDENTIFICATION DIVISION.
        PROGRAM-ID.  INTERACTIVE.
        *
        ENVIRONMENT DIVISION.
        CONFIGURATION SECTION.
        SOURCE-COMPUTER. ABC-480.
        OBJECT-COMPUTER. ABC-480.
        INPUT-OUTPUT SECTION.
        FILE-CONTROL.
            SELECT CUST-FILE ASSIGN TO CUSTRPT.
        *
        DATA DIVISION.
        FILE SECTION.
        *
        FD  CUST-FILE LABEL RECORD OMITTED
                        DATA RECORD CUST-RECORD.
        01  CUST-RECORD.
            05  CUST-NAME-OUT.
                10  L-NAME-OUT          PIC X(15).
                10  F-NAME-OUT          PIC X(12).
                10  M-NAME-OUT          PIC X(12).
            05  PHONE-CODE-OUT.
                10  AREA-CODE-OUT       PIC 9(3).
                10  PHONE-1-OUT         PIC 9(3).
                10  PHONE-2-OUT         PIC 9(4).
        *
        WORKING-STORAGE SECTION.
        *
        01  CLEAR-SCREEN.
            02  CLEAR-FULL-SCREEN       PIC X(6) VALUE "<ESC>[H<ESC>[J".
            02  CLEAR-ERR-MESSAGE.
                03  GO-TO-ROW-COL       PIC X(8) VALUE "<ESC>[16;44H".
                03  CLEAR-TILL-END      PIC X(3) VALUE "<ESC>[J".
        *
        01  ERROR-MES                   PIC X(37) VALUE
            "*** INVALID CHARACTER - TRY AGAIN ***".
        *
        01  MAIN-MENU-LINES.
            02  HEADER-1                PIC X(21) VALUE
                " CUSTOMER FILE MENU ".
            02  CHOICE-LINES.
                04  ADD-LINE            PIC X(22) VALUE
                    " ADD A NEW CUSTOMER".
                04  CHANGE-LINE         PIC X(22) VALUE
                    " CHANGE CUSTOMER DATA".
                04  DELETE-LINE         PIC X(22) VALUE
                    " DELETE CUSTOMER".
                04  EXIT-LINE           PIC X(22) VALUE
                    " EXIT PROGRAM".
            02  CHOICE-LN-TABLE REDEFINES CHOICE-LINES.
                04  MENU-DETAIL-LINE OCCURS 4 TIMES PIC X(22).
            02  FOOTING-LN              PIC X(18) VALUE
                "ENTER SELECTION > ".
```

FIGURE 22-5

Sample Interactive Program Using Standard COBOL (continued)

```
       *
        01  MAIN-MENU-DISPLAY.
            02  EACH-LINE DISPLAY.
                03  ESCAPE            PIC X(2) VALUE "<ESC>[".
                03  ROW-NO            PIC 99.
                03  FILLER            PIC X VALUE ";".
                03  COL-NO            PIC 99.
                03  FILLER            PIC X VALUE "H".
                03  MENU-DISPLAY-LINE PIC X(37).
            02  MENU-CHOICE-DISPLAY.
                03  BOLD-ON           PIC X(4) VALUE "<ESC>[1m".
                03  CHOICE-NO         PIC 9.
                03  BOLD-OFF          PIC X(3) VALUE "<ESC>[m".
       *
        01  CURSOR-SPOT               PIC X(8) VALUE "<ESC>[16;45H".
       *
        01  PROGRAM-END-FLAG          PIC X VALUE "0".
            88  PROGRAM-END           VALUE "1".
       *
        01  ADD-CUST-END-FLAG         PIC X.
            88 KEEP-ADDING            VALUE "0".
            88 BACK-TO-MENU           VALUE "1".
       *
        01  MENU-CHOICE               PIC X.
            88  VALID-CHOICE          VALUES ARE "1", "2", "3", "4".
            88  ADD-CUST              VALUE "1".
            88  CHANGE-CUST           VALUE "2".
            88  DELETE-CUST           VALUE "3".
            88  EXIT-PROGRAM          VALUE "4".
       *
        01  INPUT-SCREEN-DISPLAY.
            02  FILLER                PIC X(7) VALUE "<ESC>[4;26H".
            02  FILLER                PIC X(22) VALUE
                " AMERICAN SALES COMPANY " .
            02  FILLER                PIC X(7) VALUE "<ESC> [5;31H".
            02  FILLER                PIC X(13) VALUE "CUSTOMER DATA".
            02  FILLER                PIC X(7) VALUE "<ESC> [9;2H".
            02  FILLER                PIC X(12) VALUE "NAME(Last): ".
            02  FILLER                PIC X(4) VALUE "<ESC>[7m".
            02  FILLER                PIC X(15) VALUE SPACES.
            02  FILLER                PIC X(3) VALUE "<ESC>[m".
            02  FILLER                PIC X(11) VALUE " (First): ".
            02  FILLER                PIC X(4) VALUE "<ESC>[7m".
            02  FILLER                PIC X(12) VALUE SPACES.
            02  FILLER                PIC X(3) VALUE "<ESC>[m".
            02  FILLER                PIC X(11) VALUE " (Middle): ".
            02  FILLER                PIC X(4) VALUE "<ESC>[7m".
            02  FILLER                PIC X(12) VALUE SPACES.
            02  FILLER                PIC X(3) VALUE "<ESC>[m".
            02  FILLER                PIC X(7) VALUE "<ESC>[12;2H".
            02  FILLER                PIC X(9) VALUE " PHONE:  ".
            02  FILLER                PIC X(4) VALUE "<ESC>[7m".
            02  FILLER                PIC X(13) VALUE "(   )  -    ".
            02  FILLER                PIC X(3) VALUE "<ESC>[m".
       *
```

FIGURE 22-5
Sample Interactive Program Using
Standard COBOL (continued)

```
 01  BOX-TOP.
     02  TURN-ON               PIC XXX VALUE "<ESC>(0".
     02  GOTO-START            PIC X(6) VALUE "<ESC>[2;0H".
     02  DRAW-1-ROW.
         03  DRAW-LEFT-TOP     PIC X VALUE "l".
         03  DRAW-TOP-LINE     PIC X(76) VALUE ALL "q".
         03  DRAW-RIGHT-TOP    PIC X VALUE "k".
 *
 01  VERTICAL-LINES.
         03  FILLER            PIC X(11) VALUE "<ESC>["
         03  VERTICAL-ROW-1    PIC 99.
         03  FILLER            PIC X(6) VALUE ";0Hx<ESC>[".
         03  VERTICAL-ROW-2    PIC 99.
         03  FILLER            PIC X(5) VALUE ";77Hx".
 *
 01  HORIZONTAL-LINE.
         03  FILLER            PIC X(7) VALUE "<ESC>[21;0H".
         03  DRAW-LEFT-BOT     PIC X VALUE "m".
         03  DRAW-TOP-LINE     PIC X(76) VALUE ALL "q".
         03  DRAW-RIGHT-BOT    PIC X VALUE "j".
 *
 01  PLACE-CURSOR.
     02  FILLER               PIC XX VALUE "<ESC>[".
     02  CURSOR-ROW           PIC 99.
     02  FILLER               PIC X VALUE ";".
     02  CURSOR-COL           PIC 99.
     02  FILLER               PIC X VALUE "H".
 *
 01  I                        PIC 9(6).
 01  DUMMY                    PIC 9(6).
 *
 01  ROW-COUNT                PIC 99.
 01  SCREEN-LENGTH            PIC 99 VALUE 21.
 *
 01  ADD-SCREEN-OPTION        PIC X.
     88  GOOD-CHOICE          VALUES ARE "R", "C", "X".
     88  REDO                 VALUE "R".
     88  COMPLETED            VALUE "C".
     88  ESCAPE-EXIT          VALUE "X".
 *
 PROCEDURE DIVISION.
 *
 000-MAIN-PARA.
 *
     OPEN OUTPUT CUST-FILE.
 *
     PERFORM WITH TEST AFTER UNTIL PROGRAM-END
         PERFORM 100-DISPLAY-MENU
 *
         PERFORM 200-GET-MENU-CHOICE WITH TEST AFTER
             UNTIL VALID-CHOICE
 *
```

FIGURE 22-5
*Sample Interactive Program Using
Standard COBOL (continued)*

```
                                EVALUATE TRUE
                                    WHEN ADD-CUST
                                        SET KEEP-ADDING TO TRUE
                                        PERFORM 300-ADD-NEW-CUSTOMER
                                            UNTIL BACK-TO-MENU
                                    WHEN CHANGE-CUST
                                        PERFORM 500-CHANGE-CUSTOMER
                                    WHEN DELETE-CUST
                                        PERFORM 600-DELETE-CUSTOMER
                                    WHEN OTHER
                                        SET PROGRAM-END TO TRUE
                                END-EVALUATE
                    END-PERFORM
                    CLOSE CUST-FILE
                    STOP RUN.
        *
         100-DISPLAY-MENU.
                    DISPLAY CLEAR-FULL-SCREEN.
        *
                    MOVE 2 TO ROW-NO
                    MOVE 26 TO COL-NO
                    MOVE HEADER-1 TO MENU-DISPLAY-LINE
                    DISPLAY EACH-LINE-DISPLAY WITH NO ADVANCING
        *
                    ADD 2 TO ROW-NO
        *
                    PERFORM VARYING I FROM 1 BY 1 UNTIL I > 4
                        MOVE I TO CHOICE-NO
                        STRING MENU-CHOICE-DISPLAY DELIMITED BY SIZE
                                MENU-DETAIL-LINE (I) DELIMITED BY SIZE
                            INTO MENU-DISPLAY-LINE
                        ADD 2 TO ROW-NO
                        DISPLAY EACH-LINE-DISPLAY WITH NO ADVANCING
                    END-PERFORM
        *
                    ADD 4 TO ROW-NO
                    MOVE FOOTING-LN TO MENU-DISPLAY-LINE
                    DISPLAY EACH-LINE-DISPLAY WITH NO ADVANCING.
        *
         200-GET-MENU-CHOICE.
                    DISPLAY CURSOR-SPOT WITH NO ADVANCING
                    ACCEPT MENU-CHOICE
        *
                    IF NOT VALID-CHOICE
                        ADD 4 TO ROW-NO
                        MOVE ERROR-MES TO MENU-DISPLAY-LINE
                        DISPLAY EACH-LINE-DISPLAY WITH NO ADVANCING
        *
                        PERFORM VARYING I FROM I BY 1
                                    UNTIL I > 10000
                            MOVE I TO DUMMY
                        END-PERFORM
```

FIGURE 22-5

Sample Interactive Program Using
Standard COBOL (continued)

```
*
                    DISPLAY CLEAR-ERR-MESSAGE
                    DISPLAY CURSOR-SPOT WITH NO ADVANCING
          END-IF.
*
 300-ADD-NEW-CUSTOMER.
     DISPLAY CLEAR-FULL-SCREEN.
     PERFORM 310-BOX-DISPLAY.
     DISPLAY INPUT-SCREEN-DISPLAY.
*
     PERFORM 400-GET-INPUT
*
     PERFORM WITH TEST AFTER
         UNTIL GOOD-CHOICE
       MOVE 19 TO CURSOR-ROW
       MOVE 10 TO CURSOR-COL
       DISPLAY PLACE-CURSOR WITH NO ADVANCING
       DISPLAY "R = RE-ENTER    C = INPUT COMPLETE
           "X = ESCAPE TO MENU  " WITH NO ADVANCING
       ACCEPT ADD-SCREEN-OPTION
     END-PERFORM
*
     EVALUATE TRUE
         WHEN REDO
             CONTINUE
         WHEN COMPLETED
             WRITE CUST-RECORD
         WHEN ESCAPE-EXIT
             SET BACK-TO-MENU TO TRUE
     END-EVALUATE.
*
 310-BOX-DISPLAY.
     DISPLAY BOX-TOP WITH NO ADVANCING
     PERFORM VARYING ROW-COUNT FROM 3 BY 1
             UNTIL ROW-COUNT > SCREEN-LENGTH
         MOVE ROW-COUNT TO VERTICAL-ROW-1, VERTICAL-ROW-2
         DISPLAY VERTICAL-LINES WITH NO ADVANCING
     END-PERFORM
     DISPLAY HORIZONTAL-LINE WITH NO ADVANCING.
*
 400-GET-INPUT.
     MOVE 9 TO CURSOR-ROW
     MOVE 15 TO CURSOR-COL
*
     DISPLAY "<ESC>[7m" WITH NO ADVANCING
*
     DISPLAY PLACE-CURSOR WITH NO ADVANCING
     ACCEPT L-NAME-OUT
*
     MOVE 41 TO CURSOR-COL
     DISPLAY PLACE-CURSOR WITH NO ADVANCING
     ACCEPT F-NAME-OUT
```

FIGURE 22-5
Sample Interactive Program Using Standard COBOL (continued)

```
*
            MOVE 64 TO CURSOR-COL
            DISPLAY PLACE-CURSOR WITH NO ADVANCING
            ACCEPT M-NAME-OUT
*
            MOVE 12 TO CURSOR-ROW
            MOVE 12 TO CURSOR-COL
            DISPLAY PLACE-CURSOR WITH NO ADVANCING
            ACCEPT AREA-CODE-OUT
*
            MOVE 16 TO CURSOR-COL
            DISPLAY PLACE-CURSOR WITH NO ADVANCING
            ACCEPT PHONE-1-OUT
*
            MOVE 20 TO CURSOR-COL
            DISPLAY PLACE-CURSOR WITH NO ADVANCING
            ACCEPT PHONE-2-OUT
*
            DISPLAY "<ESC>[m".
*
    500-CHANGE-CUSTOMER.
*
*       This procedure not implemented.
*
    600-DELETE-CUSTOMER.
*
*       This procedure not implemented.
*
```

row 16, column 45. This illustrates an alternative to using MOVE to define the row and column parameters. After positioning the cursor, we ACCEPT MENU-CHOICE, which is a 1-byte field for which we defined five condition-names: VALID-CHOICE, ADD-CUST, CHANGE-CUST, DELETE-CUST, and EXIT-PROGRAM. If the user does not enter one of the four valid choices, we display the ERROR-MES, we execute a do-nothing delay loop (UNTIL I > 10000) to give the user enough time to see the error message, and then we clear the error message (DISPLAY CLEAR-ERR-MESSAGE) and reposition the cursor at CURSOR-SPOT.

If the user chooses the first menu item, the first WHEN in the 000-MAIN-PARA will be true and we will PERFORM 300-ADD-NEW-CUSTOMER. This 300-paragraph clears the screen, and then we PERFORM 310-BOX-DISPLAY. This latter is a routine to paint a box outline around the screen, as shown in Figure 22-4. If you are now studying this program for the first time, you may want to bypass the following explanation. Drawing the box outline involves several details that are not essential to the logic of the program, but that do demonstrate the kind of programming involved in achieving special effects on the screen.

In 310-BOX-DISPLAY in Figure 22-5 the first thing is to DISPLAY BOX-TOP. Studying the definition of BOX-TOP in WORKING-STORAGE, we see that it contains escape codes to begin the definition of special characters (in the TURN-ON field), to position the cursor to row 2 column zero, to define the special character for the upper left corner of the box, to define the 76-byte horizontal line, and to define the upper right corner of the box. We must keep in mind that the escape code in TURN-ON allows us to define special characters by means of ordinary characters. We referred to the manual of the terminal that we were using and read that "1", "q", and "k" define the top left, the horizontal line, and the top right, respectively, of a box outline. Of course, a different terminal might have different ways of specifying characters not on the keyboard.

Continuing with 310-BOX-DISPLAY, we wrote a PERFORM VARYING to print the vertical lines of the box for 21 lines (SCREEN-LENGTH was set to 21 in its VALUE clause). Finally, we DISPLAY HORIZONTAL-LINE, whose VALUE clauses define the bottom left and right corners as well as the horizontal bottom line of the box.

Returning to the 300-ADD-NEW-CUSTOMER paragraph in Figure 22-5, after drawing the line box we DISPLAY INPUT-SCREEN-DISPLAY, which produces the screen output illustrated in Figure 22-4(a). Notice in the DATA DIVISION definition of the INPUT-SCREEN-DISPLAY that, after the FILLER whose VALUE is "NAME(Last): ", the next FILLER defines the escape sequence "<ESC>[7m", which turns the reverse-video attribute on so that the next 15 blank bytes displayed by the following FILLER will be in reverse-video, as illustrated in Figure 22-4(a). Thus, defining a screen with multiple fields and a variety of attributes requires considerable detail.

After displaying the appropriate screen, we PERFORM 400-GET-INPUT in Figure 22-5. For each of the fields we position the cursor at the appropriate row and column coordinates, and ACCEPT the data for the field. Execution of an ACCEPT means that the program waits until the return key has been pressed to signify that the user has finished inputting to that field. When 400-GET-INPUT has been completed, we return to 300-ADD-NEW-CUSTOMER, where we execute a PERFORM ... UNTIL GOOD-CHOICE to elicit from the user one of the three options displayed at the bottom of Figure 22-4(b): R, C, or X. Upon ACCEPTing the ADD-SCREEN-CHOICE option, we EVALUATE to determine which of the three choices was selected. The RE-ENTER choice takes us back to the WHEN ADD-CUST loop in the 000-MAIN-PARA so that we execute the 300- paragraph again. If the INPUT COMPLETE choice is taken, then the record whose contents were ACCEPTed is written onto CUST-FILE. Finally, if the user chooses the ESCAPE TO MENU choice, then we return to the main PERFORM loop in the 000-MAIN-PARA to display the main menu and to continue until choice 4 is selected in the main menu in Figures 22-3(a) and 22-3(b), at which point we CLOSE CUST-FILE and STOP RUN.

The main menu provides for selections relating to changing customer data and deleting customers. Those options are left as stub paragraphs in Figure 22-5, since the objective of the sample program is limited to demonstrating the techniques of interactive processing. Implementation of those additions would add length to the program, but would not illustrate any new concepts about interactive processing.

The sample program contains the majority of interactive features and operations that any interactive program would contain. Thus you can use it as a basic framework for developing similar programs.

SAMPLE INTERACTIVE PROGRAM FOR NONSTANDARD COBOL

We will now illustrate the implementation of some extensions to COBOL that improve the ability of the language to handle interactive processing. These features apply to the Microsoft compiler and are not standard, but they are common in microcomputer compilers. We will use the same task as in the previous section, but we will incorporate two new features: use of the SCREEN section, and enhancements to the ACCEPT and DISPLAY VERBS.

FIGURE 22-6

Sample Interactive Program Using
Nonstandard COBOL (continued)

```
01  ADD-CUSTOMER-SCREEN  FOREGROUND-COLOR IS 7
                              BACKGROUND-COLOR IS 1.
    02  BLANK SCREEN.
    02  LINE 4      COLUMN 26 VALUE 'AMERICAN SALES COMPANY'.
    02  LINE + 1    COLUMN 31 VALUE 'CUSTOMER DATA'.
    02  LINE 9      COLUMN 2  VALUE 'NAME(Last): '.
    02              COLUMN 14 REVERSE-VIDEO
                              PIC X(15) FROM L-NAME-OUT.
    02              COLUMN 30 VALUE '(First): '.
    02              COLUMN 39 REVERSE-VIDEO
                              PIC X(12) FROM F-NAME-OUT.
    02              COLUMN 52 VALUE '(Middle): '.
    02              COLUMN 62 REVERSE-VIDEO
                              PIC X(12) FROM M-NAME-OUT.
    02  LINE 12     COLUMN 2  VALUE 'PHONE: '.
    02  LINE 12             REVERSE-VIDEO.
        04          COLUMN 9     VALUE '('.
        04          COLUMN + 1   PIC 9(3) FROM AREA-CODE-OUT.
        04          COLUMN + 1   VALUE ')'.
        04          COLUMN + 1   PIC 9(3) FROM PHONE-1-OUT.
        04          COLUMN + 1   VALUE '-'.
        04          COLUMN + 1   PIC 9(4) FROM PHONE-2-OUT.
*
 01 CONFIRM-ADD-MENU.
    02  LINE 19     COLUMN 10 VALUE
        "R = RE-ENTER   C = INPUT COMPLETE   X = ESCAPE TO MENU".
*
 PROCEDURE DIVISION.
*
 000-MAIN-PARA.
*
     OPEN OUTPUT CUST-FILE.
     PERFORM WITH TEST AFTER UNTIL PROGRAM-END
         PERFORM 100-DISPLAY-GET-MENU-CHOICE
*
                 EVALUATE TRUE
                     WHEN ADD-CUST
                         MOVE SPACES TO CUST-RECORD
                         SET KEEP-ADDING TO TRUE
                         PERFORM 200-ADD-NEW-CUSTOMER
                             UNTIL BACK-TO-MENU
                     WHEN CHANGE-CUST
                         PERFORM 300-CHANGE-CUSTOMER
                     WHEN DELETE-CUST
                         PERFORM 400-DELETE-CUSTOMER
                     WHEN OTHER
                         SET PROGRAM-END TO TRUE
                 END-EVALUATE
     END-PERFORM
     CLOSE CUST-FILE
     STOP RUN.
*
```

FIGURE 22-6
Sample Interactive Program Using Nonstandard COBOL (continued)

```
  100-DISPLAY-GET-MENU-CHOICE.
      DISPLAY MAIN-MENU-SCREEN
      MOVE SPACES TO MENU-CHOICE
      DISPLAY MENU-CHOICE AT LINE 14 COLUMN 44
      ACCEPT MENU-CHOICE AT LINE 14 COLUMN 44 WITH AUTO
      IF NOT VALID-CHOICE
          PERFORM UNTIL VALID-CHOICE
              DISPLAY INVALID-MAIN-MENU-CHOICE
              ACCEPT MENU-CHOICE AT LINE 14 COLUMN 44 WITH AUTO
          END-PERFORM
      END-IF.
*
  200-ADD-NEW-CUSTOMER.
      DISPLAY ADD-CUSTOMER-SCREEN
      ACCEPT L-NAME-OUT AT LINE 9 COLUMN 14 WITH REVERSE-VIDEO
                                               AUTO
      ACCEPT F-NAME-OUT AT LINE 9 COLUMN 39 WITH REVERSE-VIDEO
                                               AUTO
      ACCEPT M-NAME-OUT AT LINE 9 COLUMN 62 WITH REVERSE-VIDEO
                                               AUTO
      ACCEPT AREA-CODE-OUT AT LINE 12 COLUMN 10 WITH REVERSE-VIDEO
                                                  AUTO
      ACCEPT PHONE-1-OUT AT LINE l2 COLUMN 14 WITH REVERSE-VIDEO
                                               AUTO
      ACCEPT PHONE-2-OUT AT LINE 12 COLUMN 18 WITH REVERSE-VIDEO
                                               AUTO
      DISPLAY CONFIRM-ADD-MENU
      PERFORM WITH TEST AFTER
          UNTIL GOOD-CHOICE
            MOVE SPACES TO ADD-SCREEN-OPTION
            DISPLAY ADD-SCREEN-OPTION AT LINE 19 COLUMN 65
            ACCEPT ADD-SCREEN-OPTION AT LINE 19 COLUMN 65 WITH AUTO
      END-PERFORM
*
      EVALUATE TRUE
          WHEN REDO
              CONTINUE
          WHEN COMPLETED
              WRITE CUST-RECORD
              MOVE SPACES TO CUST-RECORD
          WHEN ESCAPE-EXIT
              SET BACK-TO-MENU TO TRUE
      END-EVALUATE.
*
  300-CHANGE-CUSTOMER.
*
*   This procedure not implemented.
*
  400-DELETE-CUSTOMER.
*
*   This procedure not implemented.
*
```

The PROCEDURE DIVISION is also simpler. 000-MAIN-PARA includes a main loop to present the main menu, process the resulting selection, and repeat until the user selects the exit-program type of option in the main menu. First, we PERFORM 100-DISPLAY-GET-MENU-CHOICE, which combines the two functions of displaying the menu and getting a choice.

In the 100- paragraph we DISPLAY MAIN-MENU-SCREEN, which includes within it all the necessary fields. Writing an iterative procedure to display the four individual menu items as we did in the program in Figure 22-5 is not necessary since the entire screen was defined in the SCREEN SECTION. Next, studying the 100-DISPLAY-GET-MENU-CHOICE paragraph, we see

```
ACCEPT MENU-CHOICE AT LINE 14 COLUMN 44 WITH AUTO
```

This illustrates use of the enhanced ACCEPT, which allows us to specify the cursor positioning, and the special AUTO feature, which specifies that if the user fills the field with data, there is no need for the user to press the return key. The last character typed serves as if the return key was pressed.

If the user does not supply a valid choice, then we stay in a loop that DISPLAYs INVALID-MAIN-MENU-CHOICE until a valid choice is made. Note that in the definition of INVALID-MAIN-MENU-CHOICE in the SCREEN SECTION, we used the BLINK attribute and we changed the background color to black (0) and the foreground color to red (4).

Once a main menu choice has been selected, program control returns to the EVALUATE statement of the 000-MAIN-PARA. If WHEN ADD-CUST is the choice, we keep PERFORMing 200-ADD-NEW-CUSTOMER. First, we DISPLAY ADD-CUSTOMER-SCREEN. Observing the SCREEN SECTION we see that it defines the screen illustrated in Figure 22-4(a), with the exception that we did not choose to implement a box outline. The features illustrated in this sample program do not make a significant change in the way of drawing a box, so there would not be a reason to illustrate the procedure for a second time. Notice that several 02 items under the 01 ADD-CUSTOMER-SCREEN do not have a LINE specification, since the line is the same as before. Also, notice the mnemonic REVERSE-VIDEO option.

After DISPLAYing the ADD-CUSTOMER-SCREEN, there is a series of ACCEPT statements in 200-ADD-NEW-CUSTOMER. They illustrate cursor positioning, display attribute specification, and AUTO features. The AUTO, again, does not require using the enter key if the field is completely filled with data.

The sample program and the nature of the features are largely self-documenting. If you have access to the Microsoft compiler or another compiler with similar features, you should be able to use the sample program as a basis for including additional features not illustrated here.

Overall, these nonstandard features simplify and expedite interactive programming. Still, until they are incorporated into the standard, their use binds the program to a particular compiler.

SUMMARY

This chapter has provided a comprehensive introduction to interactive programming, including standard and nonstandard, but common, features. An *interactive program* is one that carries on a dialogue with the user. Menus are presented, the user makes choices, and the program executes procedures depending on the selected choices and the data input by the user.

The ACCEPT and DISPLAY verbs constitute the cornerstone of COBOL interactive programming. The DISPLAY is used to write onto a screen. Positioning the cursor on desired locations on the screen and controlling special *attributes,* such as blinking and bold, are implemented in one of two ways. To use the standard COBOL, the programmer has to have available certain *escape codes* that control the behavior of the terminal in use. Once those codes are available, they are encoded into data fields and incorporated along with the data to be displayed. For instance, to display a given field in reverse-video, the code that sets the reverse-video attribute on is sent to the terminal preceding the content of the field, as if to say "display the following field in reverse-video."

Nonstandard COBOL features, such as those in the Microsoft compiler, employ a specialized SCREEN SECTION that uses mnemonic codes and other easy-to-use features for defining the contents and attributes of a screen. Another feature involves enhancements to the ACCEPT and DISPLAY verbs so that they contain clauses for cursor positioning and attribute control. Use of the nonstandard features simplifies both the DATA DIVISION and PROCEDURE DIVISION code.

EXERCISES

22.1 Adapt the sample program in Figure 22-5 to your computer system and execute it.

22.2 Take any previously written program that involved batch file input and change it so that input is entered via a keyboard.

23

Subprograms and Nested Programs

THROUGHOUT THIS BOOK *you have used the PERFORM verb to execute modular program structure. In this chapter you will learn how to implement a modular design by using subprograms and nested programs.*

*Subprograms are programs that can be written and compiled independently of other programs, but can be executed only under the control of a **main program**.*

*In COBOL '85 programs can also be **contained**, or **nested**, within a **containing** program. In addition to the modularity benefits associated with subprograms, nested programs facilitate data sharing among programs.*

In addition to the concepts and techniques, you will also study a sample program that has an associated subprogram, and a sample program with a nested program.

INTRODUCTION

The PERFORM verb is one basic control mechanism for implementing modular program structure. Still, it is often desirable to program a task in terms of one main program and one or more subprograms. In such a structure the main program is the executable program. *Subprograms* can be written and compiled independently, but they can be executed only in conjunction with a *main program*. There are three basic reasons why subprograms are desirable:

1. Whenever a task either is too large for one person or the time available requires the formation of a project team, subprograms are a natural way of partitioning one task among several persons. Because subprograms can be compiled independently, each team member can work individually to develop and test a portion of the total task. Communication among the team members is limited to brief coordinative activities assigned to a chief programmer, who is responsible for the overall project design and for effective and efficient interfacing between subtasks partitioned out as subprograms.

2. There is a frequent need to incorporate the same task into more than one program. In such a case a subprogram that is written and tested once can be recorded in a program library and can be used by several programs, thus avoiding the "reinvention-of-the-wheel" syndrome.

3. When using subprograms we can identify the data items specifically involved with the functions performed by each individual subprogram. In contrast, there is only one DATA DIVISION in a program, and it contains a description of the data for all modules in the program, as a group.

When using subprograms, there is one main program and one or more subprograms. The main program initiates and controls execution of the entire job, including the execution of subprograms, and eventually terminates the job. A given subprogram may be called into execution by the main program, or it may be called by another subprogram; however, in a given program there must be at least one call issued by the main program, and that must be the first call. After that point, subprograms may call each other—although they cannot call themselves (recursion is not allowed). You may have noticed the use of the word "call." It is standard terminology in reference to subprogram execution, and it is implemented in COBOL through the verb CALL.

R E V I E W . . . .

1. In lieu of using the PERFORM verb, modular program structure can be implemented by writing separate _____.

   subprograms

2. The use of subprograms makes the partitioning of a programming task among several individuals [easier / more difficult].

   easier

3. A subprogram [can / cannot] be used easily in conjunction with different programs.

   can

4. When a subprogram is written, the data involved in that subprogram are described specifically in the DATA DIVISION of the [main program / subprogram].

   subprogram

. . . .

CALLING AND CALLED PROGRAMS

Whenever subprograms are in use, we have one so-called *main* program and one or more subprograms. The main program is the executable program; execution of all subprograms is under the explicit or implicit control of the main program. Figure 23-1 illustrates the program execution process. Execution begins with the first executable statement in the main program and continues in that program until a CALL statement is encountered. The CALL statement transfers control to the subprogram referenced in the CALL statement, such as CALL A in Figure 23-1.

After the CALL is encountered, program execution continues within the called subprogram until an EXIT PROGRAM command is encountered, which then returns program execution and control to the statement immediately following the original CALL. EXIT PROGRAM is a COBOL statement that has the meaning "return to the calling program." A CALL is, in essence, a "Go to and Return" command.

As shown in Figure 23-1, a subprogram such as A may contain CALL statements to other subprograms, such as P in the example. In such a case A is the *calling* program and P is the *called* program. These two terms are more appropriate general terminology than the terms *main* and *subprogram,* since often a subprogram may serve as the controlling program for another subprogram. Of course, in any executable run unit (or job) there must be one main (calling) program, which must not be called. It initiates and terminates the run unit, and all subprograms are controlled by it, either directly or indirectly. In Figure 23-1 notice that after every CALL in the main program there is a return arrow to that program, and the main program is the only one that contains a STOP RUN statement.

In Figure 23-1 the combination of the CALL M statement in subprogram P and the CALL A statement in subprogram M illustrates an improper calling structure, as designated by the broken line. A subprogram may not be called by its dependents even indirectly, as in the case in the example. Subprograms are *link-edited* with the main program to form a run unit, or job. A COBOL subprogram is compiled and translated into object program form, and can be used immediately after compilation or can be saved in a *load library* for future use. In either case the link-edit processor will combine object-form subprograms together with the main program to form an executable job. The process is specified via Job Control Language statements.

FIGURE 23-1

Correct and Incorrect Subprogram Calls

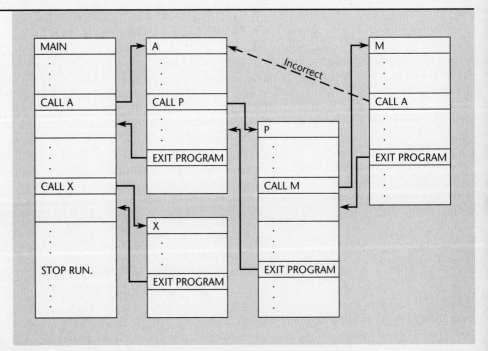

One type of job control setup is to submit the main program and the subprograms in source language form, compile each one into object form, use the link-edit processor to build an executable module (sometimes called *load module*), and then execute the job. This approach is not common, and it is not recommended because it involves recompilation of every program (calling and called) every time.

Another, more common, job stream setup is to compile subprograms and save them in a library in object form. Then job control statements include reference to this library so that the link-editor can access the modules needed. Most systems have facilities to create a load module library that contains the result of the link-edit process, which is, in turn, an executable job stream. Modules (subprograms) then may be added or deleted in such a load library without the need to recompile and link-edit the whole job.

The procedures for handling subprograms are specific to each system and each computer site, and the reader will need to obtain specific instructions with respect to any given computer system.

Considering the job execution phase, the main program and the subprograms are loaded into storage, as illustrated conceptually in Figure 23-2. The link-editor builds a storage layout where the main and the subprograms then are located relative to one another. (The actual physical storage layout is dependent on the operating system and will be dynamically varied during program execution due to swapping and/or virtual storage paging operations.)

As Figure 23-2 also illustrates, a subprogram may not be physically loaded into main storage until it is needed. The subprogram is held in secondary storage and is brought into and out of main storage dynamically, to save central storage space. This is accomplished by writing the CALL statements so that they have the format "CALL identifier." The identifier will have a value during execution that refers to a specific subprogram. By this procedure, at link-edit time the processor does not know which subprogram to actually link into the run unit. Linkage is instead performed dynamically during execution. To illustrate this concept, suppose that there are two subprograms for payroll processing: HOURLY and SALARIED. In a calling program we may have this:

```
IF condition
    MOVE 'HOURLY' TO SUB-NAME
ELSE
    MOVE 'SALARIED' TO SUB-NAME.
CALL SUB-NAME ...
```

FIGURE 23-2
Storage Layout of Subprograms

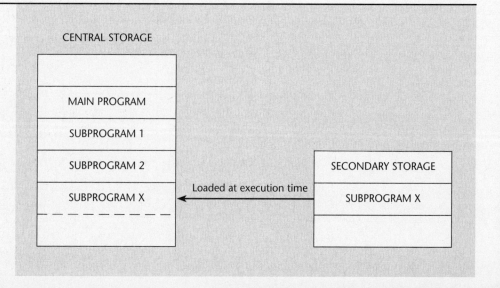

The CALL statement does not specify explicitly the subprogram to be called. The value in SUB-NAME is dependent on specific conditions during program execution.

We conclude this section by providing an outline of COBOL statements and program layouts used in subprograms. Figure 23-3 provides such an overview. In the calling program (which may or may not be a main program) there is a CALL statement that references a subprogram and the data names used to pass data to and from the subprogram. In the called program the PROGRAM-ID contains the name by which the calling program calls the called program ('SUBPR' in this example). In the DATA DIVISION of a subprogram, there is a LINKAGE SECTION that contains data descriptions for the data-names that are used to pass data to

FIGURE 23-3
Calling-Called Program Outline

CALLING PROGRAM	CALLED PROGRAM
| ```
IDENTIFICATION DIVISION.
PROGRAM-ID. MAINPROG.
ENVIRONMENT DIVISION.
    .
    .
    .
DATA DIVISION.
FILE SECTION.
    .
    .
    .
FD FILE-1 . . .
01 F-REC . . .
    .
    .
    .
WORKING-STORAGE SECTION.
    .
    .
    .
77 ABC . . .
01 XYZ . . .
LINKAGE SECTION.
[only if a subprogram]
    .
    .
    .
PROCEDURE DIVISION.
    .
    .
    .
    CALL 'SUBPR' USING F-REC
                    ABC
                    XYZ.
    .
    .
    .
``` | ```
IDENTIFICATION DIVISION.
PROGRAM-ID SUBPR.
ENVIRONMENT DIVISION.
    .
    .
    .
DATA DIVISION.
FILE SECTION.
    .
    .
    .
FD FILE-M . . .
    .
    .
    .
WORKING-STORAGE SECTION.
    .
    .
    .
77 FIELD-A . . .
    .
    .
01 FIELD-B . . .
LINKAGE SECTION.
77 PART-NO . . .
01 V-CODE . . . .
01 DATA-REC . . .

PROCEDURE DIVISION USING DATA-REC
                          PART-NO
                          V-CODE.
    .
    .
    .
RETURN-P.
    EXIT PROGRAM.
``` |

and from the subprogram. The PROCEDURE DIVISION header involves the USING clause, followed by a list of data-names that correspond to the ones in the CALL statement of the calling program (possibly using different names, as in the example). Finally, there is an EXIT PROGRAM statement that serves to return control to the calling program.

R E V I E W . . . .

1. When subprograms are used, there are always only one _____ program and one or more _____.

                                                                                        main; subprograms

2. The command that transfers program control from the main program to the subprogram is the _____ statement.

                                                                                                          CALL

3. The command that returns program execution and control from the subprogram back to the main program is the _____ statement.

                                                                                                  EXIT PROGRAM

4. A subprogram that has been called by a main program [may / may not] contain CALL statements to other subprograms.

                                                                                                           may

5. When subprogram B includes a CALL to subprogram C, B is referred to as the _____ program, and C is referred to as the _____ program.

                                                                                                calling; called

6. With respect to the relationships among the main program and several subprograms, the main program itself can [sometimes / never] be the object of a CALL statement.

                                                                                                          never

7. With respect to the relationships between a subprogram that is a calling program and the other called programs, the calling program can [sometimes / never] be called by its dependents.

                                                                                                          never

8. Object-form subprograms are combined with the main program to form an executable job by the _____ processor.

                                                                                                      link-edit

9. Linkage of a subprogram with a main program is said to be performed dynamically during program execution when the CALL statement [does / does not] specify explicitly the name of the subprogram to be called.

                                                                                                       does not

. . . .

SUBPROGRAM DATA LINKAGE

A subprogram may contain a FILE and a WORKING-STORAGE SECTION in its DATA DIVISION. Additionally, there may be a LINKAGE SECTION that contains data descriptions for items that serve as *arguments* in a subprogram call. In the typical case, arguments are data items that send data to a subprogram or receive data from a subprogram. For example, assume that we have a simplified subprogram whose function is to receive two numbers and return their sum to the calling program. The CALL will need as arguments the two fields containing the numbers and a third field to return the sum. Further, there could be a fourth argument, which is used to indicate whether some wrong condition exists, such as nonnumeric data in the incoming values or an arithmetic overflow condition.

The list of arguments appear both in the CALL statement and in the PROCEDURE DIVISION header of the subprogram. For example, we could have

```
Calling program:   CALL 'SUM-SUB' USING AMT-1, AMT-2, TOTAL, OK-FLAG

Called program:    PROCEDURE DIVISION USING A, B, TOT, FLAG.
```

The connecting lines inserted above serve to clarify the correspondence between arguments. For example, a reference to AMT-1 in the calling program and a reference to A in the called program are references to the same storage area. If either the calling program specifies MOVE ZERO TO AMT-1 or the called program specifies MOVE ZERO TO A, the field represented will be set to zero. It is important to write the arguments in the CALL and in the PROCEDURE DIVISION header of the subprogram in the right order, so that correct references are made.

When a subprogram is compiled, statements that involve items in the LINKAGE SECTION are not translated to addresses in the usual way. For instance, for the example we have been discussing, MOVE ZERO TO TOT in the subprogram would, in concept, be translated to "Move zero to the field whose beginning address will be identified by the third argument in the CALL statement and whose data description is provided in the LINKAGE SECTION under the name TOT."

One of the functions of the link-editor is to specify the address of linkage items. For example, if the CALL was written as CALL 'SUM-SUB' USING AMT-1, AMT-2, TOTAL, OK-FLAG, and if TOTAL was stored beginning with location 1,000, the MOVE ZERO TO TOT statement in the subprogram would be modified to "Move zero to the field beginning at address 1,000, whose data description is under TOT in the LINKAGE SECTION."

It is important to keep in mind that the (beginning) address of the arguments is passed by the calling program, but it is the LINKAGE SECTION that describes the assumed size and the data characteristics of the fields. Consider the illustration in Figure 23-4 as to why it is important to have consistent data definitions.

FIGURE 23-4
Illustration of Argument Definitions

```
CALLING PROGRAM                CALLED PROGRAM

01  A  PIC  X(4) VALUE 'MARY'.  LINKAGE SECTION.
01  B  PIC  9(3) VALUE 321      01  X  PIC  X(5).
        .                       01  Y  PIC  9(3).
        .                               .
        .                               .
CALL 'SUB' USING A, B.                  .
                                PROCEDURE DIVISION USING X, Y.
                                        .
                                        .
                                        .
                                    MOVE X TO . . .
                                        .
                                        .
                                    MOVE Y TO . . .
```

In Figure 23-4 notice that A has PIC X(4) but X has PIC X(5). If we assume that A and B were stored by the compiler next to each other, the MOVE X TO ... in the subprogram would move 'MARY3', since it refers to a move of 5 characters. However, the second move, MOVE Y TO ... , would correctly move '321', since the data descriptions in the calling and the called programs are consistent. The important point to observe is that it is the size of the data involved that is crucial to maintain consistency between the calling and the called program. The specific descriptions can vary according to the needs in each case. Figure 23-5 illustrates the point. Notice that X has PIC X(20) in the calling program, but A is broken down into several subfields whose PIC sizes add up to 20. Also, notice that table data may be specified in either program with or without OCCURS descriptors. As a general rule, however, it is a good idea to use identical data descriptions in both calling and called programs to avoid errors.

COBOL offers two options for associating argument fields in the calling and called programs. As explained in the next section of this chapter, the CALL statement provides a choice between BY REFERENCE and BY CONTENT. An argument field BY REFERENCE is treated as described in the discussion above. After its address is passed to the called program, that program can refer to the field by its corresponding name, with such use including the possibility of changing the content of the field. In the 1985 standard, however, it is possible to use an argument BY CONTENT, in which case the calling program cannot alter the content of the field in the called program. An argument declared BY CONTENT is used by the called program in a routine fashion during execution of the called program, including changing the original value. But when control returns to the calling program, the content of the BY CONTENT argument is unaltered. This option allows the programmer to provide certain immunity from contamination of data included in arguments because of errors in the subprogram.

In the 1974 standard you need to use two fields to achieve the BY CONTENT effect. The original data is moved to a field that is then used as an

---

FIGURE 23-5
Illustration of LINKAGE SECTION Data Descriptions

CALLING PROGRAM	CALLED PROGRAM
.	.
.	.
.	.
01 X PIC X(20).	PROGRAM-ID. SAMPLE.
01 Y PIC X(100).	.
01 W.	.
02 Z PIC X(6)	.
OCCURS 100 TIMES.	LINKAGE SECTION.
.	01 A.
.	02 B PIC X(4).
.	02 C.
	03 D PIC 9(8)V99.
	03 E PIC X(6).
CALL 'SAMPLE' USING X, Y, W.	01 L.
	02 N OCCURS 25 TIMES
	PIC 9(4).
	01 M PIC X(600).
	.
	.
	.
	.
	PROCEDURE DIVISION USING A, L, M.

argument in the CALL, thus preserving the original data by saving it as a separate field.

Another point to observe is that, in the 1974 standard, arguments must refer to fields described at the 01- or 77-level. In the 1985 standard, on the other hand, arguments can also be subordinate elementary items.

The LINKAGE SECTION may not contain a VALUE clause except one associated with a condition-name (level 88). Since arguments in the subprogram represent fields that are identified only by the CALL, it would make no sense to specify contents via a VALUE clause. This point is further reinforced when we consider that there may be several calls to the same subprogram with different sets of arguments. For instance, we could have the following in the same calling program:

```
CALL 'SUM-SUB' USING AMT-1, AMT-2, TOTAL, OK-FLAG
  .
  .
  .
CALL 'SUM-SUB' USING M, N, P, OK-FLAG.
```

The link-editor would associate each of these two different sets of arguments with the corresponding set in the PROCEDURE DIVISION header of SUM-SUB.

A special note should be added regarding INDEX items. Index items cannot be shared between calling and called programs. Rather, they are treated separately. Thus an index item defined in the subprogram is different from one in the main program, even if both items are associated with the same table. This makes sense, since index items do not represent defined storage locations, being registers used during processing of a table.

Arguments may be literals instead of data-names. Let us consider an example. Suppose that there is a subprogram designed to perform any of three functions on a 60-character field. These functions are identified by the following names: CENTER TITLE, CHECK, FORMAT. These names are included in Figure 23-6 as arguments in the sample CALL statements of the calling program.

In the LINKAGE SECTION of the subprogram, RENAMES is used to subdivide the first argument into 5-, 6-, and 12-character fields, which correspond to the lengths of the names of the three functions. It is important to recognize that if we issued a CALL 'CHR-PROC' USING 'FORMAT' DATA-FIELD and we wrote IF FUNCTION-CODE = 'FORMAT' in the subprogram, the condition would be false! Since FUNCTION-CODE is a 12-character field, we check the 12 characters that start with the 'F' of the literal 'FORMAT' to determine if they equal 'FORMAT'. The equality condition would be true only if, by coincidence, the 6 characters following FORMAT in storage happened to be spaces. Recall that unless we use the COBOL '85 BY CONTENT option, the arguments are passed to a subprogram as storage addresses, not as content. Thus it is necessary to check the first 6 characters of the 12-character FUNCTION-CODE to determine if they are equal to 'FORMAT', and the RENAMES provides a convenient mechanism for handling the task.

Generally, it is preferable not to pass literals as arguments. However, it is sometimes appropriate to use literals to make the CALL statement more understandable, as in the above example. As an alternative to the use of RENAMES, we could use the approach illustrated in Figure 23-7. In this figure three 12-character fields are defined, which contain the desired literals. Then each CALL specifies the data-name that contains the appropriate literal in each case. In the calling program we use 88-level condition-names to designate the five possibilities, and then the IF statement is used to identify the value in FUNCTION-CODE.

FIGURE 23-6

Illustration of Literals as Arguments

```
CALLING PROGRAM                        CALLED PROGRAM

                                       PROGRAM-ID. CHR-PROC.
    .
    .                                  LINKAGE SECTION.
    .                                  01  FUNCTION-CODE.
01  DATA-FIELD    PIC X(60).               02  A1      PIC  X(5).
    .                                      02  A2      PIC  X.
    .                                      02  A3      PIC  X(6).
    .                                  66  CHAR-5 RENAMES A1.
    CALL 'CHR-PROC' USING 'CHECK'      66  CHAR-6 RENAMES A1 THRU A2.
                       DATA-FIELD...
                                       66  CHAR-12 RENAMES A1 THRU A3.
      .                                01  DATA-FIELD  PIC X(60).
      .                                PROCEDURE DIVISION USING
      .                                    FUNCTION-CODE, DATA-FIELD.
    CALL 'CHR-PROC' USING 'CENTER TITLE'  A.  IF  CHAR-5 = 'CHECK'
                       DATA-FIELD                 PERFORM CHECK-ROUTINE
      .                                         ELSE
      .                                            IF  CHAR-6 = 'FORMAT'
      .                                                PERFORM FORMAT-ROUTINE
                                              ELSE...
```

FIGURE 23-7

Alternate Method of Handling Literals as Arguments

```
CALLING PROGRAM                        CALLED PROGRAM

01  CHECK        PIC X(12) VALUE 'CHECK'.   PROGRAM-ID. CHR-PROC.
01  FORMAT       PIC X(12) VALUE 'FORMAT'.      .
01  CENTER-TITLE PIC X(12) VALUE 'CENTER-TITLE'.  .
                                                .
    CALL 'CHR-PROC' USING CHECK, DATA-FIELD  LINKAGE SECTION.
      .                                      01  FUNCTION-CODE PIC X(12).
      .                                          88  CHECK VALUE 'CHECK'.
      .                                          88  FORMAT VALUE 'FORMAT'.
    CALL 'CHR-PROC' USING FORMAT, DATA-FIELD     .
      .                                          .
      .                                      01  DATA-FIELD   PIC X(12).
      .                                          .
    CALL 'CHR-PROC' USING CENTER-TITLE, DATA-FIELD  .
                                                .
                                           PROCEDURE DIVISION USING
                                               FUNCTION-CODE, DATA-FIELD.
                                           A.
                                               IF CHECK PERFORM CHECK-ROUTINE
                                               ELSE
                                                   IF FORMAT PERFORM . . .
                                                     .
                                                     .
                                                     .
```

As another approach we could define one field in the calling program, such as 01 FUNCTION-CODE-PIC X(12), and then precede each call by a MOVE-literal statement:

```
MOVE 'FORMAT' TO FUNCTION-CODE
CALL 'CHR-PROC' USING FUNCTION-CODE, DATA-FIELD
   .
   .
   .

MOVE 'CENTER TITLE' TO FUNCTION-CODE
CALL 'CHR-PROC' USING FUNCTION-CODE, DATA-FIELD
   .
   .
   .
```

In conclusion, it can be stated that improper argument definition is often a source of errors in conjunction with the use of subprograms. As a general rule, document clearly the meaning and description of each argument and avoid "tricks." For instance, never use the same argument for different purposes. If a subprogram is designed to take the square root of a number, provide a separate argument for the original number and for its square root. If the square root is stored in the same location as the original number, then by such an approach we destroy the original number. Further, always provide for some way of communicating error conditions back from a subprogram. What if there is an error in the input data? What should the subprogram do in such a case?

Another form of a confusing argument specification is the use of group items when elementary items would be more meaningful. If we write one item at the 01-level that includes all the arguments involved in the CALL, the item is not very meaningful in itself because we have to refer to the DATA DIVISION to determine what arguments are actually involved. Writing 5 to 10 argument names with each CALL is not really as time-consuming as the confusion that might result from using 1 or 2 group items that "hide" the specific arguments. On the other hand, if we have 30 arguments, it does make good sense to treat them as a group. It would be confusing to write them all every time a CALL is needed.

Sometimes arguments may not be used at all. For instance, a program may create a file that is to be processed further by a subprogram. The file is CLOSEd by the calling program and then it is OPENed as input by the called program. In such a case the file, in essence, serves as the means of data linkage, but in a totally different form from the use of arguments. We should add that files cannot be shared by calling and called programs. If the same file is to be used by both types of programs, it must be closed by the calling program before it can be opened by the called program, and vice-versa.

R E V I E W . . . .

1. The data items that send data to a subprogram or receive data from a subprogram are called _____.

   arguments

2. The list of arguments appears in the _____ statement of the main program and in the _____ header of the subprogram.

   CALL; PROCEDURE DIVISION

3. The data-name for an argument [need not be / must be] the same in both the main program and the subprogram.

   need not be

4. The overall PICTURE description associated with an argument [need not be / should be] the same in both the main program and the subprogram.

should be

5. In the 1974 standard, arguments are passed from a main program to a subprogram as [content / storage addresses].

storage addresses

6. In the 1985 standard the calling program cannot alter the content of the field in the called program when the _____ option is used.

BY CONTENT

7. In the 1974 standard the data items to be used as an argument should be described at the _____ or _____-level in the DATA DIVISION of the calling program.

01; 77

8. Although data-names generally serve as arguments, _____ can be used as arguments to make the CALL statement more understandable.

literals

9. To avoid argument specifications that are confusing, it is generally advisable that [elementary items / group items] serve as arguments.

elementary items

10. If a file, rather than a set of arguments, serves as the means of data linkage, it is CLOSEd by the [calling / called] program and OPENed as input by the [calling / called] program.

calling; called

. . . .

TRANSFER OF CONTROL

As explained previously in this chapter, a run unit or job that includes subprograms consists of one main program and one or more subprograms. Program execution is initiated by the main program and should also be terminated via a STOP RUN command in the main program. This main program transfers control to a subprogram via a CALL statement, while the subprogram transfers control back to the calling program via an EXIT PROGRAM command.

The main program may contain more than one CALL statement to one or several subprograms. The subprograms may, in turn, contain CALL statements to other subprograms. Transfer of control from the calling to the called programs and back is very much like a procedure in a program that invokes execution of another procedure via the PERFORM verb. The PERFORMed procedure may in turn PERFORM one or more other procedures, and so on, but no procedure may PERFORM the one that PERFORMed it, either directly or indirectly. Of course, the EXIT PROGRAM command has no explicit counterpart in PERFORM structures, but it is understood that this return function is implied by the end of the procedure being PERFORMed. Figure 23-1 illustrated correct and incorrect calling sequences.

Figure 23-8 presents the two formats of the CALL statement. Identifier-1 must be an alphanumeric field capable of storing a valid program-name. The identifier-1 option often is not available in some compilers. The option is designed to provide for dynamic specification of the subprogram name during execution. When the identifier-1 option is used, it is not known which subprogram is being called until the CALL statement is actually executed. At the time of CALL execution the content of identifier-1 is used to determine the subprogram name. For example, if we have CALL SUBNAME USING ARG-1, ARG-2, the calling program will need

FIGURE 23-8

General Formats for the CALL Statement

FORMAT 1

$$\underline{\text{CALL}} \quad \left\{ \begin{array}{l} \text{identifier -1} \\ \text{literal -1} \end{array} \right\}$$

$$\left[\underline{\text{USING}} \quad \left\{ \begin{array}{l} [\text{BY } \underline{\text{REFERENCE}}\text{] identifier -2 . . .} \\ \text{BY } \underline{\text{CONTENT}}\text{ identifier -2} \end{array} \right\} \cdot \cdot \cdot \right]$$

$$[\text{ON } \underline{\text{OVERFLOW}} \text{ imperative -statement -1] } [\underline{\text{END-CALL}}]$$

FORMAT 2

$$\underline{\text{CALL}} \quad \left\{ \begin{array}{l} \text{identifier -1} \\ \text{literal -1} \end{array} \right\}$$

$$\left[\underline{\text{USING}} \quad \left\{ \begin{array}{l} [\text{BY } \underline{\text{REFERENCE}}\text{] identifier -2 . . .} \\ \text{BY } \underline{\text{CONTENT}}\text{ identifier -2 . . .} \end{array} \right\} \cdot \cdot \cdot \right]$$

$$[\text{ON } \underline{\text{EXCEPTION}} \text{ imperative -statement -1]}$$

$$[\underline{\text{NOT}}\text{ ON } \underline{\text{EXCEPTION}} \text{ imperative -statement -2]}$$

$$[\underline{\text{END-CALL}}]$$

to first move a subprogram name into SUBNAME. The move may be explicit, such as MOVE 'CHECK-NAME' TO SUBNAME, or it may be indirect, as in the following example:

```
DISPLAY 'Do you want Names or Addresses?'
DISPLAY 'Type in either  N  or  A'
ACCEPT PROC-TYPE
IF PROC-TYPE NOT = 'N' OR PROC-TYPE NOT = 'A'
   PERFORM ERROR-CASE
ELSE
   IF PROC-TYPE = 'N'
      MOVE 'NAME' TO SUBNAME
   ELSE
      MOVE 'ADDR' TO SUBNAME
   END-IF
CALL SUBNAME USING ARG-1 ...
```

In this example we assume that 'NAME' and 'ADDR' are the names of two subprograms, and that the terminal user specifies the code for the appropriate subprogram.

When identifier-1 is used, the link-edit process cannot resolve the program being called, but it provides code to do that at execution time. When such a CALL is executed, the system looks for the subprogram in the object program library and loads the subprogram into main storage. Subsequently that subprogram is available in central storage. Therefore the subprogram is not copied every time that it is CALLed, but only once, when the first CALL for that subprogram is executed.

Literal-1 in Figure 23-8 must be an alphanumeric literal corresponding to a program-name; that is, it specifies the name of a subprogram as given in the PROGRAM-ID paragraph of the subprogram being called.

The BY REFERENCE clause may be omitted, in which case it is specified by default. BY REFERENCE means to associate subprogram data-names in the LINKAGE and PROCEDURE DIVISION USING ... specifications with the address of the corresponding data-names in the calling program.

When the BY CONTENT clause is used, the CALL statement makes available the content of the data-names listed in the CALL statement to the subprogram. The subprogram then does not make reference to the actual data-name storage locations in the calling program. In essence, the calling program passes data, not references, to the called program. As an example, we could write

```
CALL 'STATS' USING
          BY CONTENT NO-OF-RECS, SALES-DATA
          BY REFERENCE SALES-STAT, COMPLETION-CODE.
```

The ON OVERFLOW in Format 1 in Figure 23-8 and the [NOT] ON EXCEPTION clauses in Format 2 are designed for exception processing when it is determined, at the time of the CALL, that the program specified by the CALL statement cannot be made available for execution. The OVERFLOW in Format 1 and the ON EXCEPTION in Format 2 perform the same function. The difference in the two formats is the NOT ON EXCEPTION option in Format 2. The latter COBOL '85 option allows for more flexible structures, as in the following example, which also includes use of the END-CALL:

```
IF N > ZERO
   CALL 'STATS' USING ...
        ON EXCEPTION PERFORM CANT-CALL-STATS
        NOT ON EXCEPTION PERFORM AFTER-STATS
   END-CALL
ELSE ...
```

Referring to the example above, if the CALL is successful, we PERFORM AFTER-STATS; if it is not successful, then we PERFORM CANT-CALL-STATS. If Format 1 is used, we have to establish a flag type of field, set it to a specific value with the ON OVERFLOW condition, and then test whether an "overflow" condition occurs after the CALL.

A subprogram that is declared with the INITIAL option, which is described in a later section titled The COMMON and INITIAL Options, is initialized every time it is CALLed. Therefore each CALL to such a subprogram is like the first CALL, and the INITIAL option enables the CALL to act as if a CANCEL verb, described below, preceded each CALL.

It is apparent that identifier-1 can be a useful tool in saving storage by loading subprograms only when needed. This capability is further enhanced by the CANCEL verb:

$$\underline{\text{CANCEL}} \quad \left\{ \begin{array}{l} \text{identifier -1} \\ \text{literal -1} \end{array} \right\} \dots$$

Use of this verb in a calling program releases the memory areas occupied by the subprogram(s) referenced in the CANCEL statement. Thus a subprogram can be brought into storage by the use of CALL and can be removed by use of CANCEL. A subsequent CALL after a CANCEL will initiate the subprogram in its original state. Thus we must be careful not to assume resumption of the subprogram in its previous state. If the subprogram contained WORKING-STORAGE fields that had accumulated data as a result of previous CALLs, we should recognize that a CANCEL "erases" such accumulations, and a subsequent CALL will restore the subprogram as if it were the first CALL issued for that subprogram.

Care must be taken in using CANCEL whenever several subprograms in a job call a given subprogram that is CANCELed by one of them. Regardless of which subprogram cancels the subprogram, the action takes effect for that subprogram in general and affects all its calling programs.

The identifiers and literals in the above general format for the CANCEL statement refer to subprogram names in the same way as they are used in the CALL statement.

The CANCEL also provides an explicit mechanism for setting a subprogram to its initial state if it precedes a subsequent CALL to it. A CALL that follows a CANCEL for a given subprogram causes that subprogram to be executed as if it were the first execution during the job. Thus a CALL ... CANCEL ... CALL sequence has the same effect as achieved by each CALL for a subprogram that is declared with the INITIAL option.

The EXIT PROGRAM is a specialized verb for subprograms, and transfers control to the calling program. It must be written as the last executable statement in a paragraph. Although a subprogram may contain several EXIT PROGRAM paragraphs, it is recommended that only one such command be used in order to preserve the one-entry, one-exit principle of good program structures.

If an EXIT PROGRAM is executed for a subprogram that possesses the INITIAL attribute, the EXIT PROGRAM serves as an equivalent of a CANCEL statement. In other words, when a subsequent CALL is executed for that subprogram, the subprogram will be the same as it was at the first execution of the CALL verb.

R E V I E W . . . .

1. Transfer of control to a subprogram by use of the CALL command is very similar to transfer of control to another procedure *within* a program by use of the _____ verb.

    PERFORM

2. When the object of the CALL command is a literal, what is specified is an alphanumeric name of a subprogram, as given in the PROGRAM-ID paragraph of the [calling / called] program.

    called

3. Dynamic specification of the subprogram name is accomplished by use of the [identifier-1 / literal-1] option associated with the CALL verb.

    identifier-1

4. The option associated with the CALL verb that allows the calling program to specify the procedure to be executed for the specific case in which insufficient central storage space is encountered for a called program is the _____ option.

    ON OVERFLOW

5. The option associated with the CALL verb that is similar to the ON OVERFLOW option but is concerned with any situation in which the called program cannot be made available for execution and also allows for a more flexible programming structure is the [NOT] _____ option.

    ON EXCEPTION

6. A subprogram declared with the INITIAL option is initialized [only the first time / each time] that it is CALLed.

each time

7. Whereas a subprogram is brought into central storage by use of the CALL command, it can be removed from central storage by use of the _____ command in the calling program.

CANCEL

8. If a subprogram contains WORKING-STORAGE fields with accumulated data, use of the CANCEL command [does not affect the WORKING-STORAGE fields / deletes all accumulated values in the WORKING-STORAGE fields].

deletes all accumulated values in the WORKING-STORAGE fields

9. If a CALL is executed after an EXIT PROGRAM for a subprogram with the INITIAL attribute, the content of the CALLed program will be as it was [before / after] a previous call execution.

before

.   .   .   .

SAMPLE PROGRAM WITH A SUBPROGRAM

Figures 23-9 and 23-10 illustrate a main program and a subprogram. These sample programs were written as follows:

- MAIN PROGRAM. The main program reads source records containing sales data and stores them in a table. In the process the program counts the number of data items, up to a maximum of 100 items. When all the data are input, the main program calls a subprogram and provides the subprogram with the table of sales data and the number of items in the table. If the indication from the subprogram is that there were no errors, the main program prints the data processed by the subprogram; otherwise, the main program sets the results data to zero to indicate the presence of errors.

- SUBPROGRAM. This program finds the minimum and maximum values in the table of sales data and computes the average. If a SIZE ERROR condition occurs during accumulation of the total sales values, then the subprogram indicates the occurrence of such an error by putting spaces in a status field and then returns to the calling (main) program. If no error occurs, then the subprogram places the literal value 'O.K.' in the status field and returns to the main program.

Notice in Figures 23-9 and 23-10 that the list of arguments includes a table and that different names have been used for some of the arguments in the main program and subprogram. The corresponding arguments are illustrated in the following:

```
CALL 'STATS'                    PROCEDURE DIVISION
    USING NO-OF-RECS                USING NO-OF-VALUES
          SALES-TABLE                     INPUT-TABLE
          SALES-STATS                     OUTPUT-STATS
          COMPLETION-CODE                 STATUS-CODE.
```

The sample subprogram in Figure 23-10 could be thought of as having the following function: Receive a table of data and a value indicating the number of data items in the table, and compute the minimum, maximum, and average values in the table; if no error occurs in the process, indicate so by placing 'O.K.' in

FIGURE 23-9

Sample Main Program

```
        IDENTIFICATION DIVISION.
        PROGRAM-ID.  SALESTATS.
        *
        ENVIRONMENT DIVISION.
        *
        CONFIGURATION SECTION.
        SOURCE-COMPUTER. ABC-480.
        OBJECT-COMPUTER. ABC-480.
        *
        INPUT-OUTPUT SECTION.
        FILE-CONTROL.
            SELECT SOURCE-FILE   ASSIGN TO SOURCEFL.
            SELECT OUTPUT-FILE   ASSIGN TO PRINTER.
        *
        DATA DIVISION.
        *
        FILE SECTION.
        *
        FD   SOURCE-FILE            LABEL RECORDS STANDARD
                                    DATA RECORD IS SOURCE-REC.
        01   SOURCE-REC.
             02  SALES-AMOUNT       PIC 9(4)V99.
             02  FILLER             PIC X(74).
        *
        FD   OUTPUT-FILE            LABEL RECORDS OMITTED
                                    DATA RECORD IS OUTPUT-REC.
        01   OUTPUT-REC             PIC X(132).
        *
        WORKING-STORAGE SECTION.
        *
        01   END-OF-FILE-TEST       PIC XXX VALUE 'NO '.
             88  END-OF-FILE        VALUE 'YES'.
        *
        01   COMPLETION-CODE        PIC X(4).
        *
        01   NO-OF-RECS             PIC 9(3) VALUE ZERO.
        01   RECORD-COUNTERS.
             02  N-GOOD             PIC 9(3) VALUE ZERO.
             02  N-TOTAL            PIC 9(3) VALUE ZERO.
        *
        01   SALES-TABLE.
             02   SALES   OCCURS 100 TIMES PIC 9(4)V99.
        *
        01   SALES-STATS.
             02  MIN                PIC 9(4)V99.
             02  MAX                PIC 9(4)V99.
             02  AVG                PIC 9(4)V99.
        *
        01   WS-OUTPUT-REC.
             02  FILLER             PIC X(6) VALUE 'MIN = '.
             02  MIN-OUT            PIC Z(4)9.99.
             02  FILLER             PIC X(8) VALUE '  MAX = '.
             02  MAX-OUT            PIC Z(4)9.99.
             02  FILLER             PIC X(8) VALUE '  AVG = '.
             02  AVG-OUT            PIC Z(4)9.99.
             02  FILLER             PIC X(6) VALUE '  N = '.
             02  N-OUT              PIC ZZ9.
```

FIGURE 23-9

Sample Main Program (continued)

```
*
  PROCEDURE DIVISION.
*
  000-PROGRAM-SUMMARY.
      OPEN INPUT SOURCE-FILE
           OUTPUT OUTPUT-FILE
      PERFORM 100-READ-SOURCE-RECORDS
*
      IF N-GOOD > ZERO
         MOVE N-GOOD TO NO-OF-RECS
         CALL 'STATS' USING NO-OF-RECS,
                            SALES-TABLE,
                            SALES-STATS,
                            COMPLETION-CODE
         IF COMPLETION-CODE = 'O.K.'
            NEXT SENTENCE
         ELSE
            MOVE ZEROS TO SALES-STATS
      ELSE
         MOVE ZEROS TO SALES-STATS.
*
      PERFORM 400-PRINT-STATS
*
      CLOSE SOURCE-FILE
            OUTPUT-FILE
      STOP RUN.
*
  100-READ-SOURCE-RECORDS.
      PERFORM 200-READ-SOURCE
      PERFORM 300-STORE-SALES
          UNTIL  END-OF-FILE  OR N-GOOD = 100.
*
  200-READ-SOURCE.
      READ SOURCE-FILE
         AT END MOVE 'YES' TO END-OF-FILE-TEST.
*
  300-STORE-SALES.
      ADD 1 TO N-TOTAL
      IF SALES-AMOUNT IS NUMERIC
         ADD 1 TO N-GOOD
         MOVE SALES-AMOUNT TO SALES (N-GOOD)
      ELSE
         STRING 'RECORD ' N-TOTAL ' CONTAINS NON-NUMERIC DATA:
             SALES-AMOUNT
             DELIMITED BY SIZE
             INTO OUTPUT-REC
      WRITE OUTPUT-REC.
*
      PERFORM 200-READ-SOURCE.
*
  400-PRINT-STATS.
      MOVE MIN TO MIN-OUT
      MOVE MAX TO MAX-OUT
      MOVE AVG TO AVG-OUT
      MOVE NO-OF-RECS TO N-OUT
      WRITE OUTPUT-REC FROM WS-OUTPUT-REC.
```

FIGURE 23-10

Sample Subprogram

```
*
*   The following is the called program
*
    IDENTIFICATION DIVISION.
    PROGRAM-ID.  STATS.
*
    ENVIRONMENT DIVISION.
*
    CONFIGURATION SECTION.
    SOURCE-COMPUTER. ABC-480.
    OBJECT-COMPUTER. ABC-480.
*
    DATA DIVISION.
    WORKING-STORAGE SECTION.
    01  SALES-TOTAL              PIC 9(5)V99 VALUE ZERO.
    01  I                        PIC 999.
*
    LINKAGE SECTION.
*
    01  NO-OF-VALUES             PIC 9(3).
    01  INPUT-TABLE.
        02  DATA-VALUE   OCCURS 100 TIMES PIC 9(4)V99.
*
    01  OUTPUT-STATS.
        02  MIN                  PIC 9(4)V99.
        02  MAX                  PIC 9(4)V99.
        02  AVG                  PIC 9(4)V99.
*
    01  STATUS-CODE              PIC X(4).
*
    PROCEDURE DIVISION USING NO-OF-VALUES, INPUT-TABLE
                             OUTPUT-STATS, STATUS-CODE.
*
    000-PROGRAM-SUMMARY.
        MOVE 'O.K.' TO STATUS-CODE
        MOVE DATA-VALUE (1) TO MIN, MAX, SALES-TOTAL.
        PERFORM 100-STATISTICS VARYING I FROM 2 BY 1
                        UNTIL I > NO-OF-VALUES
                        OR STATUS-CODE = SPACES.
        DIVIDE SALES-TOTAL BY NO-OF-VALUES GIVING AVG
                ON SIZE ERROR MOVE SPACES TO STATUS-CODE.
*
    200-RETURN-TO-CALL.
        EXIT PROGRAM.
*
    100-STATISTICS.
        IF  MIN > DATA-VALUE (I)
            MOVE DATA-VALUE (I) TO MIN.
        IF  MAX < DATA-VALUE (I)
            MOVE DATA-VALUE (I) TO MAX.
        ADD DATA-VALUE (I) TO SALES-TOTAL
            ON SIZE ERROR MOVE SPACES TO STATUS-CODE.
```

a status field; otherwise, put spaces in that field. This description makes no reference to sales data or any other particular type of data. Thus generic data-names such as INPUT-TABLE and OUTPUT-STATS are reasonable choices and serve to emphasize the point that a subprogram may be designed to perform a general-purpose function and could therefore be used (CALLed) by *many* programs needing execution of the same function.

Incidentally, the OCCURS ... DEPENDING ON could have been used in the table description of the main program or the subprogram, but there was no particular reason, since we did not need to use the SEARCH verb, which takes direct advantage of that feature.

THE CONCEPT OF NESTED COBOL PROGRAMS

In the 1985 version of COBOL it is possible to write programs that contain other programs. Of course, a subprogram logically is a program contained within its calling program. However, COBOL '85 makes available an additional technique by which programs can be *contained,* or *nested,* within another program. One advantage of nested programs is that they not only allow the modularity benefits of subprograms but also further facilitate data sharing among programs.

Figure 23-11 illustrates a sample outline of nested programs. Each program begins with the keywords IDENTIFICATION DIVISION and ends with the keywords END PROGRAM ... . The outer *containing* program in Figure 23-11 is named MAS-TER-PROGRAM. It is shown as having all four divisions of a COBOL program. The MASTER-PROGRAM contains PROGRAM-A, which in turn contains PROGRAM-B. The latter two programs contain IDENTIFICATION and PROCEDURE divisions, and they could include ENVIRONMENT and/or DATA DIVISIONs as well, depending on the specific circumstances. Also, it could be the case that a contained program consisted of only its IDENTIFICATION DIVISION, as mentioned in Chapter 15 in the discussion about "stub" programs. The fact that a nested program need not include any or all of the ENVIRONMENT, DATA, and PROCEDURE DIVISIONs allows for greater flexibility in constructing modular, interrelated programs.

Each program terminates with the special END PROGRAM terminator, followed by the program-name that was given in the respective PROGRAM-ID. The large vertical brackets in Figure 23-11 identify the scope of each program.

Figure 23-12 further illustrates the concept of nested programs by showing a more extensive example of nesting. The name of the containing program in Figure 23-12 is MASTER-PROGRAM. This program directly contains two other programs: PROGRAM-A and PROGRAM-X. In turn, PROGRAM-A is the containing program for PROGRAM-B, which is the containing program for PROGRAM-C.

A program such as PROGRAM-C in Figure 23-12 is directly contained by PROGRAM-B and indirectly contained by MASTER-PROGRAM. On the other hand, PROGRAM-Y is directly contained by PROGRAM-X and indirectly contained by MASTER-PROGRAM. It is important to have a clear understanding of the direct and indirect containment of specific programs in a given nested structure, because several rules of the language apply according to whether a program is or is not contained by another program in the structure. For example, the GLOBAL clause (discussed in a subsequent section) can be used to declare data-names, which then become available to all programs contained directly or indirectly within the declaring program. In Figure 23-12 if PROGRAM-A declared item XYZ as GLOBAL, it would be GLOBAL for PROGRAM-B and PROGRAM-C, but it would not be GLOBAL for MASTER-PROGRAM, PROGRAM-X, or PROGRAM-Y.

A set of nested programs that includes the containing program and all contained programs constitutes a *run unit*. Thus the run unit in Figure 23-12

FIGURE 23-11
Sample Outline of Nested Programs

FIGURE 23-12
Sample Outline of Multiple-Nested Programs

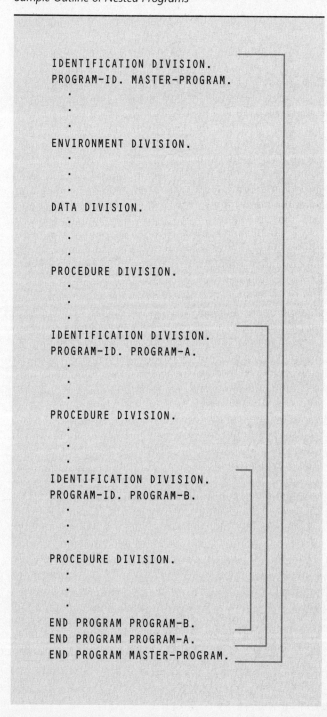

```
IDENTIFICATION DIVISION.
PROGRAM-ID. MASTER-PROGRAM.
        .
        .
        .

ENVIRONMENT DIVISION.
        .
        .
        .

DATA DIVISION.
        .
        .
        .

PROCEDURE DIVISION.
        .
        .
        .

IDENTIFICATION DIVISION.
PROGRAM-ID. PROGRAM-A.
        .
        .
        .

PROCEDURE DIVISION.
        .
        .
        .

IDENTIFICATION DIVISION.
PROGRAM-ID. PROGRAM-B.
        .
        .
        .

PROCEDURE DIVISION.
        .
        .
        .

END PROGRAM PROGRAM-B.
END PROGRAM PROGRAM-A.
END PROGRAM MASTER-PROGRAM.
```

```
IDENTIFICATION DIVISION.
PROGRAM-ID. MASTER-PROGRAM.
        .
        .
        .

IDENTIFICATION DIVISION.
PROGRAM-ID. PROGRAM-A.
        .
        .
        .

IDENTIFICATION DIVISION.
PROGRAM-ID. PROGRAM-B.
        .
        .
        .

IDENTIFICATION DIVISION.
PROGRAM-ID. PROGRAM-C.
        .
        .
        .

PROCEDURE DIVISION.
        .
        .
        .

END PROGRAM PROGRAM-C.
END PROGRAM PROGRAM-B.
END PROGRAM PROGRAM-A.

IDENTIFICATION DIVISION.
PROGRAM-ID. PROGRAM-X.
        .
        .
        .

IDENTIFICATION DIVISION.
PROGRAM-ID. PROGRAM-Y.
        .
        .
        .

PROCEDURE DIVISION.
        .
        .
        .

END PROGRAM PROGRAM-Y.
END PROGRAM PROGRAM-X.
END PROGRAM MASTER-PROGRAM.
```

consists of six programs. The concept of the run unit is used in the next two sections of this chapter in connection with the COMMON, INITIAL, and GLOBAL options. A sample complete nested program illustration is presented in the last section of this chapter.

R E V I E W . . . .

1. In addition to the use of subprograms, the 1985 version of COBOL makes it possible to have programs that are contained within another program through the process of _____.

    nesting

2. In the context of nesting, the main program is called the containing program while the nested programs are called _____ programs.

    contained

3. When nesting is used, the divisions of the COBOL program that are optional for all but the outer, containing (main) program are the _____, _____, and _____.

    ENVIRONMENT, DATA, PROCEDURE

4. A set of nested source programs is said to constitute a _____ unit.

    run

. . . .

THE COMMON AND INITIAL OPTIONS

As explained in the preceding section, a set of nested programs constitutes a run unit. In such a run unit, programs may be declared as being COMMON and/or INITIAL by the following format:

$$\text{PROGRAM-ID.} \quad \text{program-name} \quad \left[\text{IS} \left\{ \left| \begin{matrix} \underline{\text{COMMON}} \\ \underline{\text{INITIAL}} \end{matrix} \right| \right\} \text{PROGRAM} \right]$$

The straight vertical lines in the above format specify "choice indicators" that require that one or more of the unique options contained within the choice indicators must be specified, but any one option may be specified only once. Thus either COMMON or INITIAL, or both, may be written for the same program. (This is an infrequent COBOL format rule introduced in the 1985 version.)

A COMMON program may be called by any program contained directly or indirectly by the program that contains the COMMON program. For example, if PROGRAM-X has been declared COMMON in Figure 23-12, then PROGRAM-A, PROGRAM-B, and PROGRAM-C could call PROGRAM-X because the COMMON PROGRAM-X is contained by MASTER-PROGRAM and can be called from any program directly or indirectly contained by MASTER-PROGRAM. For instance, PROGRAM-B is indirectly contained by MASTER-PROGRAM.

An INITIAL program is initialized to its original state each time that such a program is called. Thus the state of an INITIAL program is the same on the tenth time that it is called, for example, as it was on the first call. The INITIAL option can be thought of as a shorthand way of initializing the data fields that are "local" to a given program. As explained in the next section of this chapter, the INITIAL option may be combined with the EXTERNAL option to effect selective initialization.

R E V I E W . . . .

1. A program that can be called by any program contained within a nested
    program structure is declared as being _____ in the PROGRAM-ID
    paragraph.

    COMMON

2. The option use in the PROGRAM-ID paragraph for a nested program that is to be
    initialized to its original state each time it is called is the _____ option.

    INITIAL

. . . .

EXTERNAL AND GLOBAL ITEMS

In a nested program structure it is possible to define a file or a record as being
EXTERNAL, GLOBAL, or both. The general format for such file description is
presented in Figure 23-13.

The EXTERNAL Option

The storage associated with an EXTERNAL object is not part of any particular
program in the run unit. Rather, EXTERNAL item storage is associated with the
run unit itself. Figure 23-14 illustrates the point. The run unit consists of three
programs, each of which occupies a certain storage area. For instance, data items
declared in PROGRAM-A that are *not* EXTERNAL are contained in the storage area
for PROGRAM-A. However, any items declared to be EXTERNAL are not in that
area. Rather, they are stored separately and may be referenced by any program
that belongs to the run unit and includes the same description of the item. Thus
several programs can make reference to the same storage area without that area
being exclusively associated with any one program. As a result a program whose
PROGRAM-ID is declared as INITIAL will not have its EXTERNAL items (if any)
affected by the INITIAL attribute upon a CALL to that program.

As a specific example, consider Figure 23-15. In this illustration the run
unit consists of two separately compiled nested structures. Notice that only the
MAIN-PROGRAM contains the STOP RUN statement. All other programs are
contained programs, including the separately compiled ones. Evidence that these
are contained programs (and are therefore CALLed) is provided in Figure 23-15 by
the EXIT PROGRAM statements. The WORKING-STORAGE item CUST-REC is
declared EXTERNAL in PROGRAM-A. Then the same declaration is made in
PROGRAM-X. Therefore CUST-REC is in reference to the same storage area, an

---

FIGURE 23-13

General Formats for EXTERNAL and GLOBAL Clauses

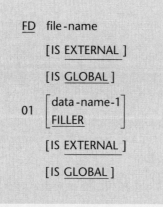

FIGURE 23-14
Illustration of External Storage

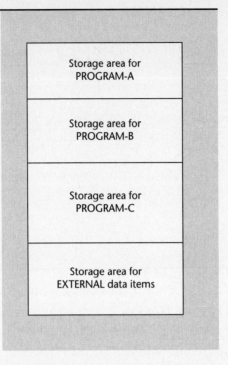

Storage area for
PROGRAM-A

Storage area for
PROGRAM-B

Storage area for
PROGRAM-C

Storage area for
EXTERNAL data items

area that applies to the run unit as a whole, not to any individual program in the run unit. As required, the 01 CUST-REC IS EXTERNAL statements are identical in both declarations. Further, the data descriptions (PIC clauses) are identical in both places, but the subordinate names may be different, as for instance, CUST-NO vs. ACCOUNT-ID.

The EXTERNAL option requires that each program describe the EXTERNAL item by the same data-name and general data description. However, any program so describing an EXTERNAL item may also use the REDEFINES clause to alter the description of that item to fit the needs of that program. For instance, we may have

```
01  CUST-REC IS EXTERNAL.
    02 ACCOUNT-NO        PIC X(5).
    02 ACCOUNT-NAME      PIC X(20).
01  ACCOUNT-REC REDEFINES CUST-REC.
    02 ACCOUNT-TYPE      PIC X.
    02 ACCOUNT-NUM       PIC X(4).
    02 LAST-NAME         PIC X(15).
    02 FILLER            PIC X(5).
```

As a final point about the EXTERNAL option, we mention that it may be attached to either a file name or a record. When a file name is declared as EXTERNAL, we understand that this is in reference to the "file connector" that associates the COBOL program file-name with the physical device on which the file is stored. As an example, we may have

```
FD  CUST-FILE IS EXTERNAL ...
```

The GLOBAL Option

The GLOBAL option allows us to describe items in one program and have them referenced either in that program or in any program contained in the program

FIGURE 23-15

Illustration of External Items

```
IDENTIFICATION DIVISION.
PROGRAM-ID.  MAIN-PROGRAM.
  .
  .
  .
PROCEDURE DIVISION.
  .
  .
  .
   STOP RUN.
IDENTIFICATION DIVISION.
PROGRAM-ID. PROGRAM-A.
  .
  .
  .
DATA DIVISION.
  .
  .
  .
WORKING-STORAGE SECTION.
  .
  .
  .
01  CUST-REC IS EXTERNAL.
    02  CUST-NO    PIC X(5).
    02  CUST-NAME  PIC X(20).
  .
  .
  .
PROCEDURE DIVISION
  .
  .
  .
   EXIT PROGRAM.
END PROGRAM PROGRAM-A
END PROGRAM MAIN-PROGRAM
```

The following is a separately compiled program.

```
IDENTIFICATION DIVISION
PROGRAM-ID. PROGRAM-X.
  .
  .
  .
DATA DIVISION.
  .
  .
  .
WORKING-STORAGE SECTION
  .
  .
  .
01  CUST-REC IS EXTERNAL.
    02  ACCOUNT-ID    PIC X(5).
    02  ACCOUNT-NAME PIC X(20).
  .
  .
  .
IDENTIFICATION DIVISION.
PROGRAM-ID. PROGRAM-Y.
  .
  .
  .
END PROGRAM PROGRAM-X
END PROGRAM PROGRAM-Y.
```

that declares the GLOBAL item. GLOBAL names provide a means of avoiding duplicate definitions for data items that need to be used by more than one program. When a name is declared as GLOBAL in a program, that item need not be described again in any of the contained programs.

Items that are not declared GLOBAL are *local* by default. A local item is defined and can be referenced only within the program that defines it. If another program defines an item by the same name, there is no relationship between the two identically named items. Thus, when working within a nested program, we need only keep in mind the names of GLOBAL items; otherwise, any name can be used without regard to its possible use in any other program. Further, if an item has been declared as GLOBAL and another, contained program, defines an item by the same name and with or without the GLOBAL declaration, that second item is totally separate from the original one. Consider this example:

```
PROGRAM-ID.  A.
   .
   .
   .
01  ITEM-A IS GLOBAL.
   .
   .
   .
01  ITEM-B IS GLOBAL.
       02 XYZ  PIC ...
   .
   .
   .
PROGRAM-ID.  B.
   .
   .
   .
01  ITEM-A.
   .
   .
   .
PROGRAM-ID.  C.
   .
   .
   .
01  ITEM-B IS GLOBAL.
       02 PDQ PIC ...
   .
   .
   .
PROGRAM-ID.  D.
   .
   .
   .
END PROGRAM D
END PROGRAM C
END PROGRAM B
END PROGRAM A.
```

In the above nested structure ITEM-A is GLOBAL for programs A, C, and D. In program B there is an ITEM-A defined, but it bears no relationship to the global one with the same name. Also, ITEM-B is declared as a GLOBAL item in both programs A and C. For programs A and B the first definition applies. For program C and its contained program D, the second definition applies. Thus the scope of a GLOBAL item may be overtaken by any identically named item in a contained program and the directly contained programs within that contained program. It is obvious that the practical solution to these semantic traps is to avoid using the same names as items that have been declared GLOBAL. Thus it is a good idea to pay attention to the global names when defining new names in a nested program structure.

An item may be declared as being both GLOBAL and EXTERNAL. In such a case the *name* is GLOBAL and the *storage* is EXTERNAL. As a GLOBAL item it is available to every program contained within the program that describes the item. As an EXTERNAL item it is available only to separately compiled programs in the run unit that include the same description for that item.

R E V I E W . . . .

1. When a data item is to be stored separately from any particular program in the run unit, it is declared as being _____ in its description.

    EXTERNAL

2. When the EXTERNAL option is used, each program that is to make reference to the item [must / need not] describe the item by the same data-name or file-name, and description.

    must

3. To fit the needs of a particular nested program, the description of an EXTERNAL item can be altered by use of the _____ clause in that nested program.

    REDEFINES

4. The declaration in the DATA DIVISION of the containing program that makes it possible to reference a data-name in all of its contained programs without definition of that data-name is the _____ declaration.

    GLOBAL

5. The DATA DIVISION of a contained program can include data-names that are not defined in the containing program. As opposed to GLOBAL data-names, such data-names are called _____.

    local

SAMPLE NESTED PROGRAMS

Figure 23-16 includes a sample nested program structure consisting of two programs. The outer, or containing, program is called SALESTATS and contains the STATS program nested within it. Essentially, the sample nested structure is for the same programming task as illustrated in Figures 23-9 and 23-10, which involved a main program and a subprogram. The programs perform the following tasks:

- Sales data are read from SOURCE-FILE and stored in SALES-TABLE, a table within the SALES-DATA record in working storage. The latter is declared as GLOBAL in the outer program. The 100-READ-SOURCE-RECORDS in the outer program reads and stores data until the END-OF-FILE OR N-GOOD = 100. N-GOOD is a counter for the number of valid ("good") data items stored in SALES-TABLE.

- If one or more (N-GOOD > ZERO) valid data items have been stored, then the outer program CALLs the contained STATS program. The STATS program determines the minimum, maximum, and average values for the

FIGURE 23-16

Sample Nested Programs

```
         IDENTIFICATION DIVISION.
         PROGRAM-ID.  SALESTATS.
         *
         ENVIRONMENT DIVISION.
         *
         CONFIGURATION SECTION.
         SOURCE-COMPUTER. ABC-480.
         OBJECT-COMPUTER. ABC-480.
         *
         INPUT-OUTPUT SECTION.
         FILE-CONTROL.
             SELECT SOURCE-FILE   ASSIGN TO SLSINP.
             SELECT OUTPUT-FILE   ASSIGN TO SLSOUT.
         *
         DATA DIVISION.
         *
         FILE SECTION.
         *
         FD   SOURCE-FILE            LABEL RECORDS STANDARD
                                     DATA RECORD IS SOURCE-REC.
         01   SOURCE-REC.
              02  SALES-AMOUNT       PIC 9(4)V99.
              02  FILLER             PIC X(74).
         *
         FD   OUTPUT-FILE            LABEL RECORDS OMITTED
                                     DATA RECORD IS OUTPUT-REC.
         01   OUTPUT-REC             PIC X(132).
         *
         WORKING-STORAGE SECTION.
         *
         01   END-OF-FILE-TEST       PIC XXX VALUE 'NO '.
              88 END-OF-FILE         VALUE 'YES'.
         *
         01   COMPLETION-CODE   IS GLOBAL.
              02 FILLER             PIC X(4).
         *
         01   SALES-DATA IS GLOBAL.
              02  N-GOOD            PIC 9(3).
              02  N-TOTAL           PIC 9(3).
              02  SALES-TABLE.
                  03  SALES         OCCURS 100 TIMES
                                    PIC 9(4)V99.
         *
         01   SALES-STATS IS EXTERNAL GLOBAL.
              02  MIN               PIC 9(4)V99.
              02  MAX               PIC 9(4)V99.
              02  AVG               PIC 9(4)V99.
         *
```

FIGURE 23-16

Sample Nested Programs (continued)

```
01  WS-OUTPUT-REC.
    02  FILLER              PIC X(6) VALUE 'MIN = '.
    02  MIN-OUT             PIC Z(4)9.99.
    02  FILLER              PIC X(8) VALUE '  MAX = '.
    02  MAX-OUT             PIC Z(4)9.99.
    02  FILLER              PIC X(8) VALUE '  AVG = '.
    02  AVG-OUT             PIC Z(4)9.99.
    02  FILLER              PIC X(6) VALUE ' N = '.
    02  N-OUT               PIC ZZ9.
*
 PROCEDURE DIVISION.
*
 000-PROGRAM-SUMMARY.
     OPEN INPUT SOURCE-FILE  OUTPUT OUTPUT-FILE
     INITIALIZE SALES-DATA
     PERFORM 100-READ-SOURCE-RECORDS
*
     IF N-GOOD > ZERO
        CALL 'STATS'
        IF  COMPLETION-CODE = 'O.K.'
            CONTINUE
        ELSE
            MOVE ZEROS TO SALES-STATS
        END-IF
     ELSE
         MOVE ZEROS TO SALES-STATS
     END-IF
     PERFORM 200-PRINT-STATS
*
     CLOSE SOURCE-FILE OUTPUT-FILE
     STOP RUN.
*
 100-READ-SOURCE-RECORDS.
     PERFORM WITH TEST AFTER
             UNTIL END-OF-FILE OR N-GOOD = 100
         READ SOURCE-FILE
           AT END SET END-OF-FILE TO TRUE
           NOT AT END
               ADD 1 TO N-TOTAL
               IF  SALES-AMOUNT IS NUMERIC
               ADD 1 TO N-GOOD
               MOVE SALES-AMOUNT TO SALES (N-GOOD)
             ELSE
               STRING 'RECORD ' N-TOTAL
                      ' CONTAINS NON-NUMERIC DATA:'
                      SOURCE-REC(1:6)
                    DELIMITED BY SIZE
                    INTO OUTPUT-REC
                 WRITE OUTPUT-REC
             END-IF
         END-READ
     END-PERFORM.
```

FIGURE 23-16

Sample Nested Programs
(continued)

```
*
 200-PRINT-STATS.
     MOVE MIN TO MIN-OUT
     MOVE MAX TO MAX-OUT
     MOVE AVG TO AVG-OUT
     MOVE N-GOOD TO N-OUT
     WRITE OUTPUT-REC FROM WS-OUTPUT-REC.
```

```
 IDENTIFICATION DIVISION.
 PROGRAM-ID.  STATS.
*
 DATA DIVISION.
 WORKING-STORAGE SECTION.
 01  SALES-TOTAL            PIC 9(5)V99 VALUE ZERO.
 01  I                      PIC 999.
*
 PROCEDURE DIVISION.
*
 000-PROGRAM-SUMMARY.
     MOVE 'O.K.' TO COMPLETION-CODE
     MOVE SALES (1) TO MIN, MAX, SALES-TOTAL.
     PERFORM VARYING I FROM 2 BY 1
             UNTIL I > N-GOOD
             OR COMPLETION-CODE = SPACES
         IF  MIN > SALES (I)
             MOVE SALES (I) TO MIN
         ELSE
             IF  MAX < SALES (I)
                 MOVE SALES (I) TO MAX
             ELSE
                 CONTINUE
             END-IF
         END-IF
         ADD SALES (I) TO SALES-TOTAL
             ON SIZE ERROR MOVE SPACES TO COMPLETION-CODE
         END-ADD
     END-PERFORM
*
     DIVIDE SALES-TOTAL BY N-GOOD GIVING AVG
         ON SIZE ERROR MOVE SPACES TO COMPLETION-CODE.
*
 100-RETURN-TO-CALL.
     EXIT PROGRAM.
*
 END PROGRAM STATS.
*
 END PROGRAM SALESTATS.
```

data in SALES-TABLE. If no SIZE ERROR occurs during execution of the contained STATS program, then COMPLETION-CODE is set to 'O.K.' Otherwise, COMPLETION-CODE is set to SPACES.

- The outer program continues by executing 200-PRINT-STATS, closing the files and terminating execution of the run unit.

In the outer program, SALESTATS, notice use of GLOBAL in the definition of SALES-DATA. Because of that, N-GOOD, N-TOTAL, and SALES-TABLE are not defined in the DATA DIVISION of the contained program STATS. Also, SALES-STATS has been declared GLOBAL, as well as EXTERNAL. In this example the EXTERNAL option is not needed, but it is included as an illustration.

In the contained program, notice that there are only two data items defined, SALES-TOTAL and I. These are both local items. For example, if the outer program had defined an item by the data-name I, then the two I's would refer to two totally different fields.

SUMMARY

This chapter covered the concepts and COBOL features associated with the use of *subprograms* and *nested programs*. These are alternatives to using the PERFORM verb to implement modular program structure.

When subprograms are used, there is one *main program* and one or more *subprograms*. Only the main program is directly executable, with execution of subprograms being under the control of the main program through the use of the CALL verb. The data items that send data to a subprogram or receive data from a subprogram are called *arguments*. These arguments appear in the CALL statement of the main program and in the PROCEDURE DIVISION header of the subprogram.

Whereas the main program transfers control to a subprogram via the CALL command, the subprogram transfers control back to the main program via the EXIT PROGRAM command. Overall program execution is terminated by the STOP RUN command in the main program. The various options associated with the CALL verb were explained in the section, "Transfer of Control," followed by a sample program with a subprogram in the following section of the chapter.

The use of *nested programs* is possible only in COBOL '85. Such programs not only provide the modularity benefits of subprograms, but also further facilitate data sharing among programs. As indicated by the name, a nested program is one that is contained within another program. The main program is called the *containing program,* while nested programs are called *contained programs*. A set of programs that includes the containing program and all associated contained programs is called a *run unit*. In such a unit, a COMMON program (as identified in the PROGRAM-ID paragraph) may be called by *any* program contained by that containing program. An INITIAL program is initialized to its original state each time that such a program is called.

In nested program structures, files or records can be EXTERNAL, GLOBAL, or both. The storage associated with an EXTERNAL object is not part of any particular program in the run unit. The GLOBAL option allows you to describe items in one program and have them referenced in that program *or* in any program contained by that program. A sample run unit consisting of a containing program and one contained (nested) program was presented and discussed for the same programming task for which the sample main program and subprogram were presented earlier in the chapter.

EXERCISES

23.1   Discuss three main reasons for using externally compiled subprograms rather than using PERFORM structures within a large program.

23.2   Consider the following:

```
MAIN PROGRAM

CALL 'CHR-PROC' USING X, 'SAMPLE'.
   .
   .
   .


SUBPROGRAM

LINKAGE SECTION.
01  A  PIC X(5).
01  B  PIC X(3).
   .
   .
   .
PROCEDURE DIVISION USING B, A.
   .
   .
   .
MOVE SPACES TO A.
```

What will happen as a result of the MOVE statement in the subprogram?

23.3   Employees pay FICA-RATE percent of their first FICA-LIMIT annual earnings as F.I.C.A. tax. We wish to write a subprogram that will compute the F.I.C.A. tax for each employee.

Outline a skeleton program structure for a main program and the subprogram. The main program CALLs the subprogram to compute the F.I.C.A. tax. Be sure to include argument definition and PROCEDURE DIVISION statements for both the main program and the subprogram.

23.4   A subprogram is to be written that can perform the following functions: (1) Open the printer file; (2) close the printer file; and (3) write a record, leaving a specified number of blank lines before printing.

Design such a subprogram by responding to the following requirements:

a.   Write the LINKAGE SECTION of the subprogram (named PRINTER).

b.   Write the entire PROCEDURE DIVISION of the subprogram.

c.   Write sample CALL statements for the main program.

23.5   Your task is to prepare a program to check for errors in transaction data pertaining to inventory. The source data items have the following format:

COLUMN	FIELD-NAME
1–5	ITEM-NUMBER
6–20	ITEM-NAME
21	ITEM-CODE
22–26	QUANTITY

The basic checking procedure is concerned with the value of ITEM-CODE, because this signifies the type of record. The value 1 means that the QUANTITY field contains the previous balance for the item specified by ITEM-NUMBER; the value 2 indicates the receipt of goods; and 3 indicates the issue of goods from inventory. Any other code is an error.

We assume that the records are sorted so that all records of the same item number are grouped together and the record with a 1 in column 21 leads the group.

We recognize four types of error conditions:

- *Duplicate balance record:* This condition arises whenever more than one record in a group of the same item number has a code of 1.

- *Misplaced balance record:* A record with a code of 1 exists, but it is not the first in the group.

- *Balance record missing:* The first record in a group is not a code 1 record.

- *Incorrect code:* A code other than 1, 2, or 3 exists.

On detection of a record meeting one of these conditions, the record is printed with the corresponding explanatory error message so that it can be corrected.

In addition to the error messages, we also desire a summary of totals. Figure 23-17 illustrates a set of sample input records and the resulting sample output.

We proceed to define the function of the main program and the subprogram as follows:

- *Main program:* This reads each transaction and gives each record to the subprogram to check for data validity. If execution of the subprogram indicates that the data are not valid, the record is printed by the calling program along with an error message. If execution of the subprogram indicates that the data are valid, then we accumulate the proper totals. We then proceed to read another record. When all the records have been read, we print a summary of the accumulated totals and terminate the program.

- *Subprogram:* The subprogram receives a transaction record from the main program. It checks for errors. If an error is found, an appropriate error message is supplied to the main program. If no error is found, a blank error message is supplied to the main program. Then the subprogram terminates.

The four error messages are

```
DUPLICATE BALANCE RECORD
MISPLACED BALANCE RECORD
BALANCE RECORD MISSING
INCORRECT CODE
```

Figure 23-18 is a decision table that facilitates complete enumeration of the possibilities.

FIGURE 23-17

Sample Input and Output for
Exercise 23.5

INPUT FILE

```
12345TEST-ITEM-1    100100
12345TEST-ITEM-1    200100
12345TEST-ITEM-1    300200
23456TEST-ITEM-2    300010
34567TEST-ITEM-3    100020
34567TEST-ITEM-3    200100
34567TEST-ITEM-3    300050
45678TEST-ITEM-4    200100
45678TEST-ITEM-4    100100
45678TEST-ITEM-4    300100
45678TEST-ITEM-4    100200
56789TEST-ITEM-5    100100
56789TEST-ITEM-5    40050
56789TEST-ITEM-5    300020
67890TEST-ITEM-6    100300
67890TEST-ITEM-6    300100
78901TEST-ITEM-7    100400
78901TEST-ITEM-7    100300
89012TEST-ITEM-8    100200
```

PROGRAM OUTPUT

```
23456TEST-ITEM-2    300010    BALANCE RECORD MISSING

45678TEST-ITEM-4    200100    BALANCE RECORD MISSING

45678TEST-ITEM-4    100100    MISPLACED BALANCE RECORD

45678TEST-ITEM-4    300100    BALANCE RECORD MISSING

45678TEST-ITEM-4    100200    MISPLACED BALANCE RECORD

56789TEST-ITEM-5    40050     INCORRECT CODE

78901TEST-ITEM-7    100300    DUPLICATE BALANCE RECORD


VALID-RECORDS =                         012

INVALID-RECORDS =                       007

BALANCE-TOTAL =                         1120

RECEIPTS TOTAL =                        200

ISSUES TOTAL =                          370
```

FIGURE 23-18

Decision Table for Exercise 23.5

CONDITION	POSSIBILITY							
	1	2	3	4	5	6	7	8
PREVIOUS-ITEM = CURRENT-ITEM	X	X	X					
PREVIOUS-ITEM NOT = CURRENT-ITEM				X	X	X	X	X
KODE = 1	X			X	X			
KODE = 2 OR 3		X				X		X
KODE NOT = 1 OR 2 OR 3			X				X	
BALANCE-CODE = 1				X		X		
BALANCE-CODE = 2					X			X
ACTION	1	2	3	4	5	6	7	8
BLANK ERROR MESSAGE	X					X		
DUPLICATE BALANCE CARD				X				
MISPLACED BALANCE CARD					X			
BALANCE CARD MISSING		X	X					X
INCORRECT CODE							X	

23.6 Modify Exercise 23.5 so that you use a two-program nested structure rather than a main program and a subprogram. The nested (inner) program should correspond in function to the subprogram description in Exercise 23.5.

24 The Report Writer Feature

YOU STUDIED THE PROCESS *of producing reports using COBOL in Chapter 9, which was concerned with control break processing. In this chapter you will extend your knowledge of producing reports by studying the COBOL* **report writer feature.** *In essence, the report writer feature is a specialized language embedded in COBOL for use in report-generating programs. Its use facilitates and simplifies the programming for such output.*

You will become familiar with the report writer feature through the discussion of three examples of its use in this chapter. The first example is relatively basic, followed by an example with control breaks, and culminating with an example that illustrates how a programmer can specify special types of output procedures that are not associated with the standard report groups.

After learning the basic features of the report writer by studying the three examples, you will then study the language specifications for the report writer from a more generalized point of view.

INTRODUCTION

As we discussed in Chapter 9, report generation constitutes a common and extensive activity in organizations. A report is a formatted collection of data recorded on paper, or a display screen, or microfilm, or some other medium, which is intended for managerial use. In the context of COBOL programming, many report-generating programs are coded in the usual fashion, as we did in Chapter 9. However, a special *report writer feature* that facilitates report programming and has the property of being standardized also is available. The report writer is a *language* type of feature; that is, it is essentially a specialized language for writing programs to produce reports.

The report writer module provides the facility for producing reports by specifying the physical appearance of a report through the use of special data definitions, rather than by requiring specification of detailed COBOL procedures necessary to produce the report. For most reports the report writer feature will prove an advantage by reducing program logic requirements and by reducing errors. The report writer is part of the COBOL language, and it can be incorporated into any program except in cases of compilers that do not include this feature.

THE REPORT WRITER FEATURE — A BASIC EXAMPLE

Our description of the report writer begins with a basic example, in an attempt to impart an overall view of the use of this language feature. Then additional capabilities are discussed in the context of more advanced examples.

Figure 24-1 presents the desired report format for the basic example on a printer spacing chart. In this case there are five parts to the report. The first one is a report heading, a title for the report. Such a heading will appear only once in a report, and, in this example, we desire it to be on a separate page. Then there is the page heading. This is a heading that we want to have printed at the beginning of each page of the report. The report detail consists of the actual data of the report. In this case we require four fields for each line of report detail. The first field includes 18 alphanumerics in columns 4–21, the second field includes 2 numerics in columns 27–28, the third field includes 4 alphanumerics in columns 39–42, and the fourth field is a numeric edited field in columns 52–61. A page footing is desired that consists of the literal PAGE and a Z9 field to print the page number. Finally, corresponding to the report heading, we desire a report footing, which will be printed at the very end of the report. In the report writer terminology, the report heading, the page heading, the detail, the page footing, and the report footing are called *report groups*. Additional report groups will be described later.

FIGURE 24-1
Desired Report Format

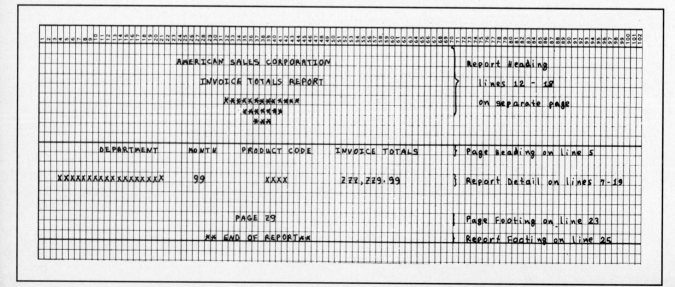

Now that we have described the horizontal format for each report group, we turn our attention to the vertical format of the report. Most reports consist of pages. For this example we assume that a page consists of 25 lines. Within the per-page limit of 25 lines, we define the desired vertical layout, as shown in the explanatory comments on the right side of Figure 24-1. Notice that the report heading will start on line 12 of the first page and will end on line 18. No other data will be presented on that page. The page heading will appear on line 5, and, since in this case it consists of only 1 line, it will also end on line 5. The first detail line will start on line 7 (we double-space between it and the page heading), while the last detail line will be printed on line 19. Then the page footing will appear on line 23, while the report footing will appear on line 25 of the last page only.

Figure 24-2 presents the header page, the second page, and the last page of the report. The design of the report format constitutes the major conceptual effort in report writing. The next step consists of translating the two-dimensional layout to COBOL instructions.

FIGURE 24-2

*Header Page, Page 2, and Last
Page of the Required Report*

```
                        AMERICAN SALES CORPORATION
                          INVOICE TOTALS REPORT
                          *************
                             *******
                               ***

            ---------- (page break here) -----------

            DEPARTMENT      MONTH     PRODUCT CODE    INVOICE-TOTALS

         APPLIANCES           01          A-10            100.25
         APPLIANCES           01          A-11             25.25
         APPLIANCES           01          A-15            250.00
         APPLIANCES           01          B-13             83.00
         APPLIANCES           01          B-20          9,008.30
         APPLIANCES           01          B-21            150.50
         APPLIANCES           01          B-22            326.60
         APPLIANCES           01          C-10              8.90
         APPLIANCES           02          A-10             90.20
         APPLIANCES           02          A-15             85.37
         APPLIANCES           02          A-25            654.92
         APPLIANCES           02          B-18            870.00
         APPLIANCES           02          B-20             50.00

                               PAGE 2

            ---------- (page break here) -----------

            DEPARTMENT      MONTH     PRODUCT CODE    INVOICE-TOTALS

      CHILDRENS CLOTHING      03          1-16            118.42
      CHILDRENS CLOTHING      03          1-17            100.00
      CHILDRENS CLOTHING      03          1-18             20.00
      CHILDRENS CLOTHING      03          1-19             70.00
      CHILDRENS CLOTHING      03          1-20             79.85
      CHILDRENS CLOTHING      03          1-21             85.42
      CHILDRENS CLOTHING      03          1-22            160.66
      CHILDRENS CLOTHING      03          1-23            158.18
      CHILDRENS CLOTHING      03          1-24            750.00

                               PAGE 6

                         **END OF REPORT**
```

Let us assume that our task is defined as follows. We desire to read data from a file and to produce a report with the format presented in Figure 24-1. The input file records have the following record description:

COLUMN	DATA-NAME	PICTURE
1–18	DEPARTMENT-N	X(18)
19–20	MONTH-IN	99
21–24	PRODUCT-CODE-IN	X(4)
25–32	INVOICE-TOTALS-IN	9(6)V99
33–80	FILLER	X(48)

Our task will involve printing a report with appropriate page headings, specified horizontal and vertical spacing, and page and report footings. The data for the report will be provided from a file. For each record read in, a report line will be printed. Figure 24-3 presents the first part of a program written to accomplish this task. It will be noted that it is just like any other COBOL program so far. The FD entry and the record description for SOURCE-REC are typical of COBOL programs in general.

We want to produce the report on the file called REPORTFILE, as indicated by the SELECT statement in the ENVIRONMENT DIVISION. Since this will be a report produced by the report writer, the FD for REPORTFILE in the complete program will be:

```
FD  REPORTFILE
        LABEL RECORDS ARE OMITTED
        REPORT IS INVOICE-REPORT.
```

FIGURE 24-3

First Part of the COBOL Program
for the Basic Example

```
IDENTIFICATION DIVISION.
PROGRAM-ID. REPGEN1.
*
ENVIRONMENT DIVISION.
CONFIGURATION SECTION.
SOURCE-COMPUTER. ABC-480.
OBJECT-COMPUTER. ABC-480.
INPUT-OUTPUT SECTION.
FILE-CONTROL.
    SELECT SOURCE-FILE  ASSIGN TO SOURCE-READER.
    SELECT REPORTFILE   ASSIGN TO PRINTER.
*
DATA DIVISION.
FILE SECTION.
FD  SOURCE-FILE
        LABEL RECORDS ARE OMITTED
        DATA RECORD IS SOURCE-REC.
01  SOURCE-REC.
    02 DEPARTMENT-IN       PIC X(18).
    02 MONTH-IN            PIC 99.
    02 PRODUCT-CODE-IN     PIC X(4).
    02 INVOICE-TOTALS-IN   PIC 9(6)V99.
    02 FILLER              PIC X(48).
```

The terms REPORTFILE and INVOICE-REPORT are arbitrary choices of the program author. That the LABEL RECORDS ARE OMITTED is no surprise, since this is a printer file, but they could have been STANDARD if, for example, the report were to be produced on disk or tape (for eventual transmission to printer or display terminal). What is new is the REPORT IS clause. Instead of saying DATA RECORD IS, as is the case for other files, we now use the reserved word REPORT IS.

Figure 24-4 presents the complete COBOL program. Notice that, following the FILE SECTION of the DATA DIVISION and the WORKING-STORAGE SECTION, we write the REPORT SECTION.

In the REPORT SECTION the report description RD level entry parallels the file description FD entry of an ordinary file. The report-name in RD INVOICE-REPORT must be the same name as specified in the FD entry of the report file, where the REPORT IS clause gives the report-name. The PAGE clause is optional, but it is commonly used unless we simply desire a report that is continuous and not broken into pages (in other words, a report consisting of one long page). In the example we have

```
RD  INVOICE-REPORT
        PAGE LIMIT IS 25 LINES
        HEADING 5
        FIRST DETAIL 7
        LAST DETAIL 19.
```

The indentations and the separate lines are used here for visual clarity. The RD must appear on columns 8–9, and the other clauses must be in column 12 or to the right of 12. PAGE LIMIT IS 25 LINES defines the vertical page size. This page

FIGURE 24-4

The Complete Program for the Basic Example

```
IDENTIFICATION DIVISION.
PROGRAM-ID. REPGEN1.
*
ENVIRONMENT DIVISION.
CONFIGURATION SECTION.
SOURCE-COMPUTER. ABC-480.
OBJECT-COMPUTER. ABC-480.
INPUT-OUTPUT SECTION.
FILE-CONTROL.
    SELECT SOURCE-FILE  ASSIGN TO SOURCEFILE.
    SELECT REPORTFILE   ASSIGN TO RPTFILE.
*
DATA DIVISION.
FILE SECTION.
FD  SOURCE-FILE
        LABEL RECORDS ARE OMITTED
        DATA RECORD IS SOURCE-REC.
01  SOURCE-REC.
        02 DEPARTMENT-IN        PIC X(18).
        02 MONTH-IN             PIC 99.
        02 PRODUCT-CODE-IN       PIC X(4).
        02 INVOICE-TOTALS-IN     PIC 9(6)V99.
        02 FILLER               PIC X(48).
```

```
*
FD   REPORTFILE
         LABEL RECORDS ARE OMITTED
         REPORT IS INVOICE-REPORT.
*
WORKING-STORAGE SECTION.
01   END-OF-DATA              PIC XXX.
*
REPORT SECTION.
RD   INVOICE-REPORT
         PAGE LIMIT IS 25 LINES
             HEADING 5
             FIRST DETAIL 7
             LAST DETAIL 19.
*
01   TYPE IS REPORT HEADING
        NEXT GROUP NEXT PAGE.
     02 LINE NUMBER IS 12
        COLUMN NUMBER IS 24
        PICTURE IS A(26)
        VALUE IS 'AMERICAN SALES CORPORATION'.
     02 LINE NUMBER IS PLUS 2
        COLUMN NUMBER IS 28
        PICTURE IS X(21)
        VALUE IS 'INVOICE TOTALS REPORT'.
     02 LINE NUMBER IS PLUS 2
        COLUMN NUMBER IS 32
        PICTURE IS X(13)
        VALUE IS ALL '*'.
     02 LINE NUMBER IS PLUS 1
        COLUMN NUMBER IS 35
        PICTURE IS X(7)
        VALUE ALL '*'.
     02 LINE NUMBER IS PLUS 1
        COLUMN NUMBER IS 37
        PICTURE IS XXX
        VALUE '***'.
*
01   TYPE PAGE HEADING
         LINE NUMBER IS 5.
     02 COLUMN NUMBER IS 11
        PICTURE IS X(20)
        VALUE IS 'DEPARTMENT    MONTH'.
     02 COLUMN NUMBER IS 35
        PICTURE IS X(30)
        VALUE IS 'PRODUCT CODE   INVOICE-TOTALS'.
*
```

FIGURE 24-4

The Complete Program for the
Basic Example (continued)

```
01   INVOICE-DATA
        TYPE IS DETAIL
        LINE NUMBER IS PLUS 1.
     02 COLUMN NUMBER IS 4
        PICTURE IS X(18)
        SOURCE IS DEPARTMENT-IN.
     02 COLUMN NUMBER IS 27
        PICTURE IS 99
        SOURCE IS MONTH-IN.
     02 COLUMN NUMBER IS 39
        SOURCE IS PRODUCT-CODE-IN
        PICTURE IS X(4).
     02 COLUMN NUMBER IS 52
        PICTURE IS ZZZ,ZZ9.99
        SOURCE IS INVOICE-TOTALS-IN.
*
 01   TYPE PAGE FOOTING.
      02 LINE 23.
         03 COLUMN 34
            PIC AAAA
            VALUE 'PAGE'.
         03 COLUMN 40
            PIC Z9
            SOURCE IS PAGE-COUNTER.
*
 01   TYPE REPORT FOOTING
      LINE 25.
      02 COLUMN 30
      PIC X(17).
      VALUE '**END OF REPORT**'
*
 PROCEDURE DIVISION.
 SET-UP.
     OPEN INPUT SOURCE-FILE
         OUTPUT REPORTFILE.
     MOVE 'NO' TO END-OF-DATA
     READ SOURCE-FILE RECORD
         AT END MOVE 'YES' TO END-OF-DATA.
     INITIATE INVOICE-REPORT.
     PERFORM READ-PRINT
         UNTIL END-OF-DATA = 'YES'.
     TERMINATE INVOICE-REPORT
     CLOSE SOURCE-FILE REPORTFILE
     STOP RUN.
 READ-PRINT.
     GENERATE INVOICE-DATA.
     READ SOURCE-FILE RECORD
         AT END MOVE 'YES' TO END-OF-DATA.
```

size is not required to be the same as the physical size of the paper, but typically the two sizes are identical.

The HEADING 5 entry means that page or report headings will start on line 5. The entries for FIRST DETAIL and LAST DETAIL define the inclusive range of lines on which detail report lines can be written.

It will be noted that in this example no mention is made in the PAGE entry about the page and report footing. The omission is intentional, so that the example can provide an illustration of defining vertical positioning apart from the PAGE option. A later example will include another option (FOOTING) in the PAGE description.

After the RD entry in Figure 24-4, it will be noted that there are five report groups described, each at the 01 level:

```
01   TYPE IS REPORT HEADING
.
.
.
01   TYPE PAGE HEADING ...
.
.
.
01   INVOICE-DATA TYPE IS DETAIL ...
.
.
.
01   TYPE PAGE FOOTING ...
.
.
.
01   TYPE REPORT FOOTING ...
```

Each 01-level in Figure 24-4 introduces a report group in a fashion analogous to the record descriptions in an ordinary file. A report group may consist of one or several lines of output, and within each line there may be one or several fields. Following is a description of each report group and an explanation of the options used.

The first report group is

```
01   TYPE IS REPORT HEADING
     NEXT GROUP NEXT PAGE.
     02 LINE NUMBER IS 12
        COLUMN NUMBER IS 24
        PICTURE IS A(26)
        VALUE IS 'AMERICAN SALES CORPORATION'.
     02 LINE NUMBER IS PLUS 2
        COLUMN NUMBER IS 28
        PICTURE IS X(21)
        VALUE IS 'INVOICE TOTALS REPORT'.
     02 LINE NUMBER IS PLUS 2
        COLUMN NUMBER IS 32
        PICTURE IS X(13)
        VALUE ALL '*'.
     02 LINE NUMBER IS PLUS 1
        COLUMN NUMBER IS 35
        PICTURE IS X(7)
        VALUE ALL '*'.
```

```
02 LINE NUMBER IS PLUS 1
   COLUMN NUMBER IS 37
   PICTURE IS XXX
   VALUE '***'.
```

The 01-level number introduces a new report group. The reserved words TYPE IS REPORT HEADING declare the type of report group about to be described. The NEXT GROUP specifies the positioning of the next group, and NEXT PAGE specifies that it should be on the next page. It will be recalled that the report heading was to be on a page by itself.

At the 02-level there are five entries. In this case each represents 1 line. The level numbers used are in the range 01–49, as usual. The first level 02 entry reads

```
02  LINE NUMBER IS 12
    COLUMN NUMBER IS 24
    PICTURE IS A(26)
    VALUE IS 'AMERICAN SALES CORPORATION'.
```

The LINE NUMBER IS 12 specifies that we want this item to be printed on line 12. Then, in column 24 (COLUMN NUMBER IS 24), we want to print a field whose PICTURE IS A(26) and whose content is supplied by the VALUE clause.

The second level 02 entry illustrates what is called *relative line spacing* with the option LINE NUMBER IS PLUS 2, meaning to double-space from the previous line. In our example the previous line was number 12, which was specified by *absolute line spacing;* therefore the PLUS 2 in this case has the same effect as having said LINE NUMBER IS 14.

The remaining three level 02 entries of this report group are similar to the first two and have the purpose of printing three lines of asterisks for visual effect.

The second report group in Figure 24-4—remember, a report group is introduced by a 01-level—is TYPE PAGE HEADING, which implies that this information will be printed once for each page as a heading on the page. The LINE NUMBER IS 5 specifies that the page heading will be printed on line 5. Notice that, for this report group, the LINE clause is not given at the 02-level, unlike the previous report group (the REPORT HEADING). The reason for the difference is that the PAGE HEADING will consist of one line only, so the LINE clause can be included in the 01-level.

Two level 02 entries now introduce two fields, one starting in column 11, the other starting in column 35. They both contain literals specified by VALUE clauses. The presence of two fields is simply for illustration. One longer field would have the same effect as two shorter ones, since the intent is simply to print a heading.

The third report group described is given a data-name (INVOICE-DATA) and is TYPE DETAIL. The data-name is optional for the other report groups but is required for this one because later on, in the PROCEDURE DIVISION, we will want to make direct reference to this report group. The first field of this group is

```
02  COLUMN NUMBER IS 4
    PICTURE IS X(18)
    SOURCE IS DEPARTMENT-IN.
```

The SOURCE clause specifies the source of the contents of this field. It is analogous in effect to a MOVE DEPARTMENT-IN TO the X(18) field starting in column 4. Whenever this report group is to be printed, the data contained in the field

DEPARTMENT-IN will be moved to the current field. (It will be recalled that DEPARTMENT-IN was a field in the input file in this example.) The remaining three fields of the INVOICE-DATA report group specify the location and source for the remainder of the line.

The next level 01 entry in Figure 24-4 introduces a TYPE PAGE FOOTING, which will be printed once for each page. The page footing will consist of one line of output as specified by 02 LINE 23. Notice that, for illustration of the available options, the LINE clause has been given its own 02-level and that the IS has been omitted, being optional in all cases. There are two fields in that line, each introduced at the 03-level (it could have been 04 or higher just as well). The first field starts at column 34 and has the VALUE clause, the second field is in columns 40–41 and has the SOURCE IS PAGE-COUNTER clause. The PAGE-COUNTER is a COBOL reserved word. It is a counter that contains an integer value indicating the page number of the current page. The counter is updated automatically each time a new page is to be printed, so no special instructions along this line are required. However, the programmer may access (but not alter) the content of PAGE-COUNTER both in the REPORT SECTION and in the PROCEDURE DIVISION. The effect of this page footing report group will be to print the page number at the bottom of each page, as can be observed in Figure 24-2.

The final report group described in Figure 24-4 is TYPE REPORT FOOTING, which indicates that the report footing will be printed on line 25. The effect of this report group will be to print **END OF REPORT** below the page number of the last page of the report, as can be observed in Figure 24-2.

Completion of the REPORT SECTION constitutes the end of the major task in the use of the report writer. The PROCEDURE DIVISION for this example is rather simple:

```
PROCEDURE DIVISION.
SET-UP.
    OPEN INPUT SOURCE-FILE
        OUTPUT REPORTFILE.
    MOVE 'NO' TO END-OF-DATA
    READ SOURCE-FILE RECORD
        AT END MOVE 'YES' TO END-OF-DATA.
    INITIATE INVOICE-REPORT
    PERFORM READ-PRINT
        UNTIL END-OF-DATA = 'YES'.
    TERMINATE INVOICE-REPORT
    CLOSE SOURCE-FILE REPORTFILE
    STOP RUN.
READ-PRINT.
    GENERATE INVOICE-DATA.
    READ SOURCE-FILE RECORD
        AT END MOVE 'YES' TO END-OF-DATA.
```

First, the files are opened and the first input record is read. Then comes the INITIATE INVOICE-REPORT, which is an instruction that is analogous to OPEN for files. For instance, the INITIATE will cause the PACE-COUNTER to be set to zero. Other actions resulting from the INITIATE will be described later. For now, it will suffice to say that before a report can be written, the INITIATE command must be issued once—and only once.

In the READ-PRINT paragraph the procedure consists of reading a record from the SOURCE-FILE and then generating INVOICE-DATA. It will be recalled that INVOICE-DATA was the data-name that we gave to the TYPE IS DETAIL report group. As a result of executing the GENERATE instruction, the report writer will control the printing of all other report groups (REPORT HEADING, PAGE HEADING, PAGE FOOTING) used in this example. Thus the report writer is concerned mainly with report format specifications, not with procedure specifications.

When all the records from SOURCE-FILE have been processed, we TERMINATE INVOICE-REPORT. As a result of the TERMINATE, the report footing will be printed. The TERMINATE is similar to CLOSE. To complete the program, we CLOSE the two files and STOP RUN.

R E V I E W . . . .

1. The report writer module of COBOL makes it possible for the programmer to arrange production of a report by specifying the [detailed programming procedures / format] for the report.

    format

2. In the terminology of the report writer such parts of the report as the report heading, page heading, and page footing are called report _____ .

    groups

3. Typically, the first step associated with using the report writer is to lay out the desired format of the report on a _____ chart.

    printer spacing

4. When the report writer module is used, the format of the report is described in the _____ DIVISION of the COBOL program.

    DATA

5. In the DATA DIVISION of the COBOL program the section in which the report format is described, and which typically follows the FILE SECTION and the WORKING-STORAGE SECTION, is the _____ .

    REPORT SECTION

6. In the REPORT SECTION of the DATA DIVISION each of the report groups associated with the report is assigned the level number _____ .

    01

7. Within each report group in the REPORT SECTION each item of output typically is described at the level-number _____ when several items (lines or fields) are included.

    02 (or higher)

8. If the report writer module is used, then in the PROCEDURE DIVISION the _____ command must be executed, both after the OPEN command for the files and before the report can be printed.

    INITIATE

9. In the PROCEDURE DIVISION the printed output for all of the report groups is achieved by execution of the _____ command.

    GENERATE

10. When the report writer module is used, the PROCEDURE DIVISION command that is analogous to the CLOSE and also results in the report footing being printed is the _____ command.

    TERMINATE

. . . .

REPORT WRITER WITH CONTROL BREAKS

The basic purpose of the example that follows is to illustrate the use of control breaks. Additionally, other features of the report writer will be illustrated. We begin with a description of the desired report, in terms of the format of the layout and in terms of the content. In discussing the basic example earlier, we illustrated the process of developing the report specifications. At this point we assume that the task specification stage has been completed, and we proceed to illustrate the desired report by presenting three sample pages in Figure 24-5. Notice that this report essentially is a revised version of the previous example in this chapter.

Figure 24-5(a) presents the first page of the report. The report header is now on the same page as the first page header and the first page detail. The page header has been modified by dropping the column DEPARTMENT and adding two new columns, MONTH TOTAL and DEPT. TOTAL.

A new report group appears that consists of the fixed header, DEPART-MENT:, and the department name (in the case of the first page it is APPLIANCES). This type of header is absent from the second page, in Figure 24-5(b), because we want department name to be printed only at the start of a new department listing.

The page footing remains the same as in the previous example. Figure 24-5(b) presents the second page of the report and serves to illustrate the accumulation of month and department totals. The page is short because the end of the first department (APPLIANCES) occurs on this page and we want to start each department at the top of a new page. The line of asterisks is used for visual effect.

Figure 24-5(c) presents the last page of the report. One item deserves special attention: the line GRAND TOTAL FOR INVOICE REPORT. The purpose is to show the grand total of all invoice totals processed in this report. It is, therefore, produced as a final control footing.

Now that we have a clear visualization of the desired report, let us consider the programming aspects. Figure 24-6 presents the entire program from which the sample report pages were produced. Up to the REPORT SECTION the program is identical to the one used in the basic example. The Report Description (RD) entry specifies the fields that will be used for control break purposes:

```
RD  INVOICE-REPORT
    CONTROLS ARE FINAL
    DEPARTMENT-IN
    MONTH-IN
```

Three control breaks are specified. One is declared with the reserved word FINAL. This is always the most inclusive control in the hierarchy. The next control field is DEPARTMENT-IN, which is a field in the input record. The minor control is MONTH-IN, which is also a field in the input record. The order of writing establishes the hierarchy. The FINAL must be the first control (if used); then the remaining order is established. Thus, if instead of having written MONTH-IN as the last item, we had written it as the second, we would have established DEPARTMENT-IN as the minor control.

In the present example we want control footings for month and department. Referring to the sample output in Figure 24-5, it should be noted that the data presented to the report writer were sorted by month within department. If the data were sorted by department within month and given the hierarchy of FINAL, DEPARTMENT-IN, MONTH-IN, then the report would be different. The difference would be that department totals would be produced for all departments for each month. Thus it is important to relate the input file sort order with the control breaks desired and, when required, to sort the input file in a different order or to change the format of the report.

The PAGE clause in the RD entry in Figure 24-6 is similar in form to the basic example. The FOOTING 20 clause specifies that line 20 will be the last line

FIGURE 24-5

(a) First Page of the Report (b) Second Page of the Report (c) Last Page of the Report

```
                        AMERICAN SALES CORPORATION
                          INVOICE TOTALS REPORT
             MONTH    PRODUCT CODE    INVOICE-TOTALS    MONTH TOTAL   DEPT. TOTAL
DEPARTMENT: APPLIANCES

              01         A-10            100.25
                         A-11             25.25
                         A-15            250.00
                         B-13             83.00
                         B-20          9,008.30
                         B-21            150.50
                         B-22            326.60
                         C-10              8.90
                                                          9,952.80


                              PAGE 1
(a)
```

```
             MONTH    PRODUCT CODE    INVOICE-TOTALS    MONTH TOTAL   DEPT. TOTAL

              02         A-10             90.20
                         A-15             85.37
                         A-25            654.92
                         B-18            870.00
                         B-20             50.00
                                                          1,750.49
              03         A-15             15.00
                         B-20            182.18
                                                            197.18
                                                                        11,900.47
**************************************************************************************

                              PAGE 2
(b)
```

```
             MONTH    PRODUCT CODE    INVOICE-TOTALS    MONTH TOTAL   DEPT. TOTAL
              03         1-19             70.00
                         1-20             79.85
                         1-21             85.42
                         1-22            160.66
                         1-23            158.18
                         1-24            750.00
                                                          2,041.16
                                                                         5,157.10
**************************************************************************************
**************************************************************************************
      GRAND TOTAL FOR INVOICE REPORT                     19,289.69

                              PAGE 7
                         **END OF REPORT**
(c)
```

FIGURE 24-6
*COBOL Program for the Example
with Control Breaks*

```
*
 IDENTIFICATION DIVISION.
 PROGRAM-ID. REPGEN2.
*
 ENVIRONMENT DIVISION.
 CONFIGURATION SECTION.
 SOURCE-COMPUTER. ABC-480.
 OBJECT-COMPUTER. ABC-480.
 INPUT-OUTPUT SECTION.
 FILE-CONTROL.
     SELECT SOURCE-FILE ASSIGN TO SOURCEFILE.
     SELECT REPORTFILE ASSIGN TO RPTFILE.
*
 DATA DIVISION.
 FILE SECTION.
 FD  SOURCE-FILE
         LABEL RECORDS ARE OMITTED
         DATA RECORD IS SOURCE-REC.
 01  SOURCE-REC.
         02 DEPARTMENT-IN        PIC X(18).
         02 MONTH-IN             PIC 99.
         02 PRODUCT-CODE-IN       PIC X(4).
         02 INVOICE-TOTALS-IN     PIC 9(6)V99.
         02 FILLER               PIC X(48).
*
 FD  REPORTFILE
         LABEL RECORDS ARE OMITTED
         REPORT IS INVOICE-REPORT.
 WORKING-STORAGE SECTION.
 01  END-OF-DATA            PIC XXX.
*
 REPORT SECTION.
 RD  INVOICE-REPORT
         CONTROLS ARE FINAL
                       DEPARTMENT-IN
                       MONTH-IN
         PAGE LIMIT IS 25 LINES
               HEADING 2
               FIRST DETAIL 8
               LAST DETAIL 18
               FOOTING 20.
*
 01  TYPE IS REPORT HEADING.
     02 LINE IS 2
         COLUMN NUMBER IS 35
         PICTURE IS A(26)
         VALUE IS 'AMERICAN SALES CORPORATION'.
     02 LINE NUMBER IS PLUS 2
         COLUMN NUMBER IS 38
         PICTURE IS X(21)
         VALUE IS 'INVOICE TOTALS REPORT'.
*
```

FIGURE 24-6
COBOL Program for the Example
with Control Breaks (continued)

```
01    PAGE-TOP TYPE IS PAGE HEADING
           LINE NUMBER IS PLUS 2.
      02 COLUMN NUMBER IS 25
         PICTURE IS XXXXX
         VALUE IS 'MONTH'.
      02 COLUMN NUMBER IS 35
         PICTURE IS X(30)
         VALUE IS 'PRODUCT CODE    INVOICE-TOTALS'.
      02 COLUMN NUMBER IS 72
          VALUE IS 'MONTH TOTAL    DEPT. TOTAL'
          PICTURE IS X(25).
*
01    TYPE IS CONTROL HEADING DEPARTMENT-IN
           LINE NUMBER IS PLUS 2
           NEXT GROUP IS PLUS 2.
      02 COLUMN 6
         PICTURE X(11)
         VALUE 'DEPARTMENT:'.
      02 COLUMN 18
         PICTURE X(18)
         SOURCE DEPARTMENT-IN.
*
01    INVOICE-DATA
           TYPE IS DETAIL
           LINE NUMBER IS PLUS 1.
      02 COLUMN NUMBER IS 4
         PIC IS X(18)
         SOURCE IS DEPARTMENT-IN
         GROUP INDICATE.
      02 COLUMN NUMBER IS 27
         PICTURE IS 99
         SOURCE IS MONTH-IN
         GROUP INDICATE.
      02 COLUMN NUMBER IS 39
         SOURCE IS PRODUCT-CODE-IN
         PIC X(4).
      02 COLUMN NUMBER IS 52
         PIC IS ZZZ,ZZ9.99
         SOURCE IS INVOICE-TOTALS-IN.
*
01    TYPE IS CONTROL FOOTING MONTH-IN
           LINE NUMBER IS PLUS 1.
      02 MONTH-TOTAL
         COLUMN NUMBER IS 69
         PICTURE IS Z,ZZZ,ZZ9.99
         SUM INVOICE-TOTALS-IN.
*
01    DEPT-TOTAL TYPE IS CONTROL FOOTING DEPARTMENT-IN
           NEXT GROUP NEXT PAGE.
      02 LINE NUMBER PLUS 1
         COLUMN NUMBER IS 82
         PICTURE IS ZZ,ZZZZ,ZZ9.99
         SUM MONTH-TOTAL.
```

FIGURE 24-6
*COBOL Program for the Example
with Control Breaks (continued)*

```
*
        02 LINE NUMBER IS PLUS 2
           PICTURE IS X(95)
           VALUE ALL '*'
           COLUMN NUMBER IS 2.
*
   01   TYPE IS CONTROL FOOTING FINAL.
        02 LINE NUMBER IS PLUS 2
           COLUMN NUMBER 2
           PICTURE X(95)
           VALUE ALL '*'.
        02 LINE NUMBER PLUS 2.
           03 COLUMN NUMBER 36
              PIC X(30)
              VALUE 'GRAND TOTAL FOR INVOICE REPORT'.
           03 COLUMN NUMBER 66
              PIC ZZZ,ZZZ,ZZ9.99
           SUM INVOICE-TOTALS-IN.
*
   01   TYPE PAGE FOOTING.
        02 LINE 23.
           03 COLUMN 46
              PIC AAAA
              VALUE 'PAGE'.
           03 COLUMN 54
              PIC Z9
              SOURCE IS PAGE-COUNTER.
   01   TYPE REPORT FOOTING
           LINE NUMBER IS PLUS 2.
        02 COLUMN NUMBER IS 41
           PICTURE X(17)
           VALUE '**END OF REPORT**'.
*
   PROCEDURE DIVISION.
   SET-UP.
        OPEN INPUT  SOURCE-FILE
             OUTPUT REPORTFILE.
        MOVE 'NO' TO END-OF-DATA
        INITIATE INVOICE-REPORT
        READ SOURCE-FILE RECORD
             AT END MOVE 'YES' TO END-OF-DATA.
        PERFORM READ-PRINT
           UNTIL END-OF-DATA = 'YES'.
        TERMINATE INVOICE-REPORT
        CLOSE SOURCE-FILE REPORTFILE
        STOP RUN.
*
   READ-PRINT.
        GENERATE INVOICE-DATA.
        READ SOURCE-FILE RECORD
             AT END MOVE 'YES' TO END-OF-DATA.
```

number on which a CONTROL FOOTING report group may be presented. PAGE FOOTING and REPORT FOOTING report groups must follow line 20.

The REPORT HEADING group is specified to begin on LINE 2. The absence of NEXT GROUP NEXT PAGE (as contrasted to Figure 24-4) implies that this heading will be on the first page of the report, along with the page heading.

The next report group is

```
01   PAGE-TOP TYPE IS PAGE HEADING
     LINE NUMBER IS PLUS 2.
```

For illustration, a data-name (PAGE-TOP) has been assigned to this TYPE PAGE HEADING report group, and this heading begins two lines below the previous line printed. Referring back to the REPORT HEADING description, it will be observed that the report heading begins on line 2 and consists of 2 lines with double spacing (PLUS 2). Thus the report heading will be printed on lines 2–4, and the page heading will begin on line 6 of the first page. On subsequent pages, however, the report heading will not be printed. Then the page heading will start on line 4, which is determined as follows: the PAGE clause established line 2 as the first line on which a heading (HEADING 2) can be printed. Since the PAGE HEADING has relative spacing (LINE NUMBER IS PLUS 2), it follows that the page heading will start on line 4 of the second and subsequent pages.

The next report group in Figure 24-6 is

```
01   TYPE IS CONTROL HEADING DEPARTMENT-IN
     LINE NUMBER IS PLUS 2
     NEXT GROUP IS PLUS 2.
     02   COLUMN 6     PICTURE X(11)
          VALUE 'DEPARTMENT:'.
     02   COLUMN 18    PICTURE X(18)
          SOURCE DEPARTMENT-IN.
```

This is a CONTROL HEADING group, and it will be printed every time the DEPARTMENT-IN field changes value. Referring to Figure 24-5, the header DEPARTMENT: XXXXXXXXXXXXXXXXXX (where the X's stand for the department name) is printed only when a new department is introduced in the input stream. (The fact that the DEPARTMENT-IN field is used both as a control heading break and as a source field is just a coincidence in this example.)

The clauses LINE NUMBER IS PLUS 2 and NEXT GROUP IS PLUS 2 specify that this report group will be printed 2 lines after the previous report group (the page header) and that the next group (which is a detail report group in this example) will be presented 2 lines below, thus double spacing before and after. The two 02 fields are similar to the type we have discussed already in the basic example.

The next report group specified in Figure 24-6 is 01 INVOICE-DATA TYPE IS DETAIL LINE NUMBER IS PLUS 1. As in the previous sample, this will be the report group referenced in the GENERATE statement in the PROCEDURE DIVISION. The only difference between this and the corresponding group in the basic example is the use of the GROUP INDICATE clause. Specifically, we have

```
02   COLUMN NUMBER IS 27
     PICTURE IS 99
     SOURCE IS MONTH-IN
     GROUP INDICATE.
```

The effect of the GROUP INDICATE is to print the data only at the beginning of a report, at the beginning of each page, and after each control break. A glance at the sample report output in Figure 24-5 will show the effect of the GROUP INDICATE. A good contrast is provided by the absence of this clause in the description of the detail group of the basic (first) example.

The next report group in Figure 24-6 is

```
01   TYPE IS CONTROL FOOTING MONTH-IN
          LINE NUMBER IS PLUS 1.
     02   MONTH-TOTAL
          COLUMN NUMBER IS 69
          PICTURE IS Z,ZZZ,ZZ9.99
          SUM INVOICE-TOTALS-IN.
```

The TYPE clause specifies this to be a CONTROL FOOTING associated with the data-name MONTH-IN, which is a data-name in the input file record. The meaning of this control footing is that whenever the value of the data-name MONTH-IN changes, a control break will occur that will, in turn, result in printing the edited sum of the values of the data-name INVOICE-TOTALS-IN, starting in column 69 of the next line. As each detail group is presented, the sum of the INVOICE-TOTALS-IN fields is formed in the MONTH-TOTAL field.

The ability to specify summation fields whose data are printed as a result of control breaks is a fundamental capability of the report writer. A SUM counter is set initially to zero by the report writer. Then, as each detail line is presented, the specified data are added to this sum counter. When a control break occurs, the value of the sum counter is printed and then it is reset to zero. In the present example, a name has been given to the accumulator: MONTH-TOTAL. As each input record is read and a detail report line is printed, MONTH-TOTAL is incremented by the value of INVOICE-TOTALS-IN. Then, when MONTH-IN changes value, the edited value of MONTH-TOTAL will be printed, starting in column 69. Referring to Figure 24-5(a), it will be observed that when the month changed from 01 to 02, a month total of 9,952.80 was printed.

The next report group introduced in Figure 24-6 is

```
01   DEPT-TOTAL TYPE IS CONTROL FOOTING DEPARTMENT-IN
          NEXT GROUP NEXT PAGE.
```

The effect of this control footing is to sum the values of the MONTH-TOTAL sum counter (SUM MONTH-TOTAL) and to print the edited sum, starting in column 82 of the next line. Reference to Figure 24-5 reveals that this sum counter is printed only when the department changes; thus, all the month totals for a given department are printed before the department total. Referring back to CONTROLS ARE FINAL DEPARTMENT-IN MONTH-IN serves to remind us that in this hierarchy of control breaks the MONTH-IN is subordinate to DEPARTMENT-IN. Thus, the expected order of control footings is that several MONTH-TOTALS will be printed for each DEPT-TOTAL. Incidentally, the order in which the control footing report groups are written is immaterial. The logic of report presentation is not related to the physical order in which the report groups are specified in the program.

Two additional features of the DEPT-TOTAL report group deserve attention. The NEXT GROUP NEXT PAGE clause specifies that, after this group, we want to start a new page. The second feature is that this group consists of two lines. The first one prints the value of the sum counter while the second line consists of asterisks.

The next group is

```
01   TYPE IS CONTROL FOOTING FINAL.
```

No name is given to this report group (names are optional). This kind of control footing will be printed after all control breaks have occurred, since it is the highest in the control hierarchy. Thus, after the last detail group has been presented and after all the control footings have been presented, the final control footing is presented in the report. In a sense it resembles a report footing, except that SUM clauses can appear only in control footing groups; therefore a CONTROL FOOTING FINAL is necessary.

The SUM INVOICE-TOTALS-IN specifies that this sum counter (and we have given it no name) will accumulate the sums of the INVOICE-TOTALS-IN values. Actually, it would be advisable to have said SUM DEPT-TOTAL to reduce the required number of additions, in a fashion similar to the SUM MONTH-TOTAL specified for the DEPT-TOTAL group. This inadvisable variation is shown here to illustrate the options available. If the report consisted of thousands of lines, the extra additions might be considered somewhat inefficient.

One point needs clarification. Referring to Figure 24-5(c), the question may be raised: Why is the final control footing not printed on a new page, since the previous control footing (DEPT-TOTAL) contained the NEXT GROUP NEXT PAGE clause? The reason is that the NEXT GROUP clause is ignored when it is specified on a control footing report group that is at a level other than the highest level at which a control break is detected. In this case a final control footing is at a higher level; therefore the NEXT GROUP clause associated with the DEPT-TOTAL control footing group is ignored.

The PAGE FOOTING and REPORT FOOTING groups in Figure 24-6 are similar to the ones in the basic example in Figure 24-4. The PROCEDURE DIVISION is identical to the one in the basic example, illustrating that the differences in the resulting report are attributable to the differences in the report description, rather than in the procedures specified.

R E V I E W . . . .

1. In the RD entry in the REPORT SECTION of the DATA DIVISION, if the FINAL control break is used, then it must be the [first one / last one] listed.

first one

2. When the major report groups are described at the 01-level in the DATA DIVISION, then the CONTROL HEADING and CONTROL FOOTING groups are described at the [01 / 02]-level.

01

3. The effect of the GROUP INDICATE clause in the description of a report group is to print the associated information only at the beginning of the report, at the beginning of each _____ , and after each _____ .

page; control break

4. A CONTROL HEADING report group typically involves the specification of descriptive _____ headings.

column (or report)

5. A CONTROL FOOTING report group typically involves the specification of various _____ which are to be reported.

sums (or totals)

6. Even though a report footing has been specified, it also is necessary to specify a FINAL control footing if the output of a(n) _____ clause is desired at the end of the report.

SUM

.   .   .   .

REPORT WRITER USING DECLARATIVES

Figure 24-7 illustrates the output of what appears similar to the report discussed in the preceding example, with one main exception: The line PAGE TOTAL = 10,128.37 is new. Suppose that we are interested in showing a PAGE TOTAL for the INVOICE-TOTALS printed on that page. This example will serve as a vehicle to illustrate how the programmer can specify procedures other than those made possible by the standard report groups.

What we desire is to have the INVOICE-TOTALS summarized and printed at the bottom of the page above the page footing. In a sense, we desire a control break associated with the end of a page, but the rules of the CONTROLS clause specify that we must not use control breaks associated with data-names defined in the REPORT SECTION. Further, a SUM counter cannot be used except with CONTROL FOOTING report groups.

To proceed directly to the illustration, consider the modification to the preceding program in Figure 24-8. A WORKING-STORAGE field has been added, called PAGE-ACCUMULATOR. Then, in the PROCEDURE DIVISION, the reserved word DECLARATIVES introduces a special-purpose section; in this example it is the PAGE-END SECTION. The USE verb specifies the condition under which the procedures in the DECLARATIVES portion will be executed; in this case it is

FIGURE 24-7
Output Resulting from the Modified Program Using DECLARATIVES

```
                          AMERICAN SALES CORPORATION

                           INVOICE TOTALS REPORT

   DEPARTMENT        MONTH     PRODUCT CODE    INVOICE-TOTALS    MONTH TOTAL   DEPT. TOTAL

   APPLIANCES         01          A-10             100.25
                                  A-11              25.25
                                  A-15             250.00
                                  B-13              83.00
                                  B-20           9,008.30
                                  B-21             150.50
                                  B-22             326.60
                                  C-10               8.90
                                                                  9,952.80
   APPLIANCES         02          A-10              90.20
                                  A-15              85.37


                      PAGE TOTAL =            10,128.37

                               PAGE    1
```

BEFORE REPORTING PAGE-TOP. It will be recalled that PAGE-TOP was the name given to the page heading report group. Thus the procedures specified in this section will be executed before printing the page header. Now, looking at PAR-A, the simple task of MOVE ZEROS TO PAGE-ACCUMULATOR is the only procedure specified in this section (PAR-B simply contains an EXIT command). In essence, then, we have said: before printing the heading on each page, zero out the WORKING-STORAGE field called PAGE-ACCUMULATOR. The END DECLARATIVES marks the end of the declarative part of the PROCEDURE DIVISION. (The DECLARATIVES feature was also discussed in Chapter 17, in connection with exception processing for sequential and other files.)

In the READ-PRINT paragraph observe the two statements:

```
GENERATE INVOICE-DATA.
ADD INVOICE-TOTALS-IN TO PAGE-ACCUMULATOR.
```

After each report detail group is generated, the value of PAGE-ACCUMULATOR is incremented by the amount of INVOICE-TOTALS-IN. When a page footing is printed, the value of PAGE-ACCUMULATOR serves as the SOURCE. Then the declarative portion takes effect, before the next page heading is printed, and the PAGE-ACCUMULATOR is set to zero to begin again the new page accumulation.

FIGURE 24-8
Modified Program for the Example Using DECLARATIVES

```
*
 IDENTIFICATION DIVISION.
 PROGRAM-ID. REPGEN3.
*
 ENVIRONMENT DIVISION.
 CONFIGURATION SECTION.
 SOURCE-COMPUTER. ABC-480.
 OBJECT-COMPUTER. ABC-480.
 INPUT-OUTPUT SECTION.
 FILE-CONTROL.
     SELECT SOURCE-FILE ASSIGN TO SOURCEFILE.
     SELECT REPORTFILE ASSIGN TO RPTFILE.
*
 DATA DIVISION.
 FILE SECTION.
 FD  SOURCE-FILE
         LABEL RECORDS ARE OMITTED
         DATA RECORD IS SOURCE-REC.
 01  SOURCE-REC.
     02 DEPARTMENT-IN        PIC X(18).
     02 MONTH-IN             PIC 99.
     02 PRODUCT-CODE-IN       PIC X(4).
     02 INVOICE-TOTALS-IN     PIC 9(6)V99.
     02 FILLER               PIC X(48).
 *
 FD  REPORTFILE
         LABEL RECORDS ARE OMITTED
         REPORT IS INVOICE-REPORT.
 *
 WORKING-STORAGE SECTION.
 01  END-OF-DATA            PIC XXX.
 01  PAGE-ACCUMULATOR       PIC 9(7)V99.
 *
```

```
REPORT SECTION.
RD   INVOICE-REPORT
          CONTROLS ARE FINAL
                          DEPARTMENT-IN
                          MONTH-IN
          PAGE LIMIT IS 25 LINES
               HEADING 2
               FIRST DETAIL 8
               LAST DETAIL 18
               FOOTING 20.
*
  01   TYPE IS REPORT HEADING.
       02 LINE IS 2
          COLUMN NUMBER IS 35
          PICTURE IS A(26)
          VALUE IS 'AMERICAN SALES CORPORATION'.
       02 LINE NUMBER IS PLUS 2
          COLUMN NUMBER IS 38
          PICTURE IS X(21)
          VALUE IS 'INVOICE TOTALS REPORT'.
*
  01   PAGE-TOP TYPE IS PAGE HEADING
          LINE NUMBER IS PLUS 2.
       02 COLUMN NUMBER IS 6
          PICTURE IS X(24)
          VALUE IS 'DEPARTMENT          MONTH'.
       02 COLUMN NUMBER IS 35
          PICTURE IS X(30)
          VALUE IS 'PRODUCT CODE    INVOICE-TOTALS'.
       02 COLUMN NUMBER IS 72
          VALUE IS 'MONTH TOTAL    DEPT. TOTAL'
          PICTURE IS X(25).
*
  01   INVOICE-DATA
          TYPE IS DETAIL
          LINE NUMBER IS PLUS 1.
       02 COLUMN NUMBER IS 4
          PIC IS X(18)
          SOURCE IS DEPARTMENT-IN
          GROUP INDICATE.
       02 COLUMN NUMBER IS 27
          PICTURE IS 99
          SOURCE IS MONTH-IN
          GROUP INDICATE.
       02 COLUMN NUMBER IS 39
          SOURCE IS PRODUCT-CODE-IN
          PIC X(4).
       02 COLUMN NUMBER IS 52
          PIC IS ZZZ,ZZ9.99
          SOURCE IS INVOICE-TOTALS-IN.
  01   TYPE IS CONTROL FOOTING MONTH-IN
          LINE NUMBER IS PLUS 1.
       02 MONTH-TOTAL
          COLUMN NUMBER IS 69
          PICTURE IS Z,ZZZ,ZZ9.99
          SUM INVOICE-TOTALS-IN.
```

FIGURE 24-8

*Modified Program for the Example
Using DECLARATIVES (continued)*

```
*
 01   DEPT-TOTAL TYPE IS CONTROL FOOTING DEPARTMENT-IN
           NEXT GROUP NEXT PAGE.
      02 LINE NUMBER IS PLUS 1
         COLUMN NUMBER IS 82
         PICTURE IS ZZ,ZZZZ,ZZ9.99
         SUM MONTH-TOTAL.
      02 LINE NUMBER IS PLUS 2
            PICTURE IS X(95)
         VALUE ALL '*'
         COLUMN NUMBER IS 2.
*
 01   TYPE IS CONTROL FOOTING FINAL.
      02 LINE NUMBER IS PLUS 2
         COLUMN NUMBER 2
         PICTURE X(95)
         VALUE ALL '*'.
      02 LINE NUMBER PLUS 2.
         03 COLUMN NUMBER 32
            PIC X(30)
            VALUE 'GRAND TOTAL FOR INVOICE REPORT'.
         03 COLUMN NUMBER 66
            PIC ZZZ,ZZZ,ZZ9.99
         SUM INVOICE-TOTALS-IN.
*
 01   TYPE PAGE FOOTING.
      02 LINE 21.
         03 COLUMN 34
            PIC A(12)
            VALUE 'PAGE TOTAL ='.
         03 COLUMN 49
            PIC ZZ,ZZZ,ZZ9.99
            SOURCE PAGE-ACCUMULATOR.
      02 LINE 23.
         03 COLUMN 46
            PIC AAAA
            VALUE 'PAGE'.
         03 COLUMN 52
            PIC Z9
            SOURCE IS PAGE-COUNTER.
*
 01   TYPE REPORT FOOTING
      LINE NUMBER IS PLUS 2.
      02 COLUMN NUMBER IS 41
         PICTURE X(17)
         VALUE '**END OF REPORT**'.
*
 PROCEDURE DIVISION.
*
 DECLARATIVES.
 PAGE-END SECTION.
      USE BEFORE REPORTING PAGE-TOP.
*
```

FIGURE 24-8
Modified Program for the Example
Using DECLARATIVES (continued)

```
    PAR-A.
        MOVE ZEROS TO PAGE-ACCUMULATOR.
    PAR-B.
        EXIT.
    END DECLARATIVES.
*
    PROCEDURAL SECTION.
    SET-UP.
        OPEN INPUT SOURCE-FILE
             OUTPUT REPORTFILE.
        MOVE 'NO' TO END-OF-DATA
        INITIATE INVOICE-REPORT
        READ SOURCE-FILE RECORD
             AT END MOVE 'YES' TO END-OF-DATA.
        PERFORM READ-PRINT
           UNTIL END-OF-DATA = 'YES'.
        TERMINATE INVOICE-REPORT
        CLOSE SOURCE-FILE REPORTFILE
        STOP RUN.
*
    READ-PRINT.
        GENERATE INVOICE-DATA.
        ADD INVOICE-TOTALS-IN TO PAGE-ACCUMULATOR
        READ SOURCE-FILE RECORD
             AT END MOVE 'YES' TO END-OF-DATA.
```

R E V I E W . . . .

1. The reserved word DECLARATIVES is used to introduce special-purpose sections in the _____ DIVISION of a COBOL program.

    PROCEDURE

2. The verb that specifies the condition under which the procedures under DECLARATIVES are to be executed is the _____ verb.

    USE

3. When presentation of the DECLARATIVES in the PROCEDURE DIVISION has been completed, this is indicated by the command _____ .

    END DECLARATIVES

. . . .

LANGUAGE SPECIFICATIONS FOR THE REPORT WRITER

A complete language specification description is beyond the scope of the present discussion; however, a full list of the language options is included in Appendix B. In the following description only the main options are highlighted.

One option is

$$
\left\{ \begin{matrix} \underline{CONTROL} \text{ IS} \\ \underline{CONTROLS} \text{ ARE} \end{matrix} \right\}
\left\{ \begin{matrix} \text{data-name-1 [data-name-2]} \\ \underline{FINAL} \text{ [data-name-1 [data-name-2] . . .]} \end{matrix} \right\}
$$

Data-name-1 and data-name-2 must not be defined in the report section. FINAL, if specified, is the highest control; data-name-1 is the major control; data-name-2 is an intermediate control, and so forth. The last data-name specified is the minor control.

A second option is

GROUP INDICATE

The GROUP INDICATE clause specifies that the associated printable item is presented only on the first occurrence of the associated report group, after a control break or page advance.

A third optional clause is

$$\text{LINE NUMBER IS} \begin{Bmatrix} \text{integer-1 [ON \underline{NEXT PAGE}]} \\ \underline{\text{PLUS}} \text{ integer-2} \end{Bmatrix}$$

This clause specifies vertical positioning information for the associated report group. The following rules apply:

1. Integer-1 and integer-2 must not be specified in such a way as to cause any line of a report group to be presented outside the vertical subdivisions of the page designated for the report group type, as defined by the PAGE clause (see discussion of the PAGE clause).

2. Within a given report group, an entry that contains a LINE NUMBER clause must not contain a subordinate entry that also contains a LINE NUMBER clause.

3. Within a given report description entry, a NEXT PAGE phrase can appear only once and, if present, must be in the first LINE NUMBER clause in that report group.

4. A LINE NUMBER clause with the NEXT PAGE phrase can appear only in the description of the CONTROL HEADING, DETAIL, CONTROL FOOTING, and REPORT FOOTING groups.

5. The first LINE NUMBER clause specified within a PAGE FOOTING report group must be an absolute LINE NUMBER clause.

A fourth optional clause is

$$\text{NEXT GROUP IS} \begin{Bmatrix} \text{integer-1} \\ \underline{\text{PLUS}} \text{ integer-2} \\ \underline{\text{NEXT PAGE}} \end{Bmatrix}$$

The NEXT GROUP clause specifies information for vertical positioning following presentation of the last line of a report group. However, it is ignored when it is specified on a CONTROL FOOTING report group that is at a level other than the highest level at which a control break is detected. These two rules apply:

1. The NEXT PAGE phrase of the NEXT GROUP clause must not be specified in a PAGE FOOTING report group.

2. The NEXT GROUP clause must not be specified in a REPORT FOOTING or PAGE HEADING report group.

A fifth option is

$$\underline{PAGE} \begin{bmatrix} \text{LIMIT IS} \\ \text{LIMITS ARE} \end{bmatrix} \text{integer -1} \begin{bmatrix} \text{LINE} \\ \text{LINES} \end{bmatrix}$$

[HEADING integer -2] [FIRST DETAIL integer -3]

[LAST DETAIL integer -4] [FOOTING integer -5]

The PAGE clause defines the length of a page and the vertical subdivisions within which report groups are presented. Use of the PAGE clause defines certain page regions that are described in this format. The integer-1, integer-2, and so on refer to the operands of the PAGE clause. As an illustration of using the format, notice that the CONTROL FOOTING report groups are allocated the region between integer-3 and integer-5. Thus, if the PAGE clause had contained FIRST DETAIL 6, FOOTING 20, the CONTROL FOOTING report group description should not contain, for example, an absolute LINE NUMBER clause referring to line 22.

Figure 24-9 clarifies the meaning of the PAGE clause with an example that illustrates the different regions defined by integer-1 through integer-5 in the general format.

A sixth option is

SOURCE IS identifier-1

The SOURCE clause identifies the sending data item that is moved to an associated printable item defined within a report group description entry. Identifier-1 may be defined in any section of the DATA DIVISION. If identifier-1 is a REPORT SECTION item, it can only be PAGE-COUNTER, LINE-COUNTER, or a sum counter.

A seventh optional clause is

[SUM identifier -1 [identifier -2] . . .

    [UPON data -name-1 [data -name-2] . . .] . . .

$$\begin{bmatrix} \underline{RESET} \text{ ON} \begin{Bmatrix} \text{data -name-3} \\ \text{FINAL} \end{Bmatrix} \end{bmatrix}$$

The SUM clause establishes a sum counter and names the data items to be summed. When more than one identifier is used, the sum counter is incremented by the sum of the identifiers. Thus

```
03 EX-TOTAL PIC Z(6).99 SUM DAT1, DAT2
```

indicates that EX-TOTAL will be incremented by both the value of DAT1 and DAT2 each time a summation is indicated. If DAT1 and DAT2 are items described in the same report group and on the same line, we refer to this sum as a *crossfooting*, as in this example:

```
DAT1    DAT2    EX-TOTAL
20       30       50
```

In contrast to crossfooting, we refer to *rolling forward* as the summation of sum counters at a lower hierarchical level. Thus

FIGURE 24-9

Sample Application of the PAGE Clause

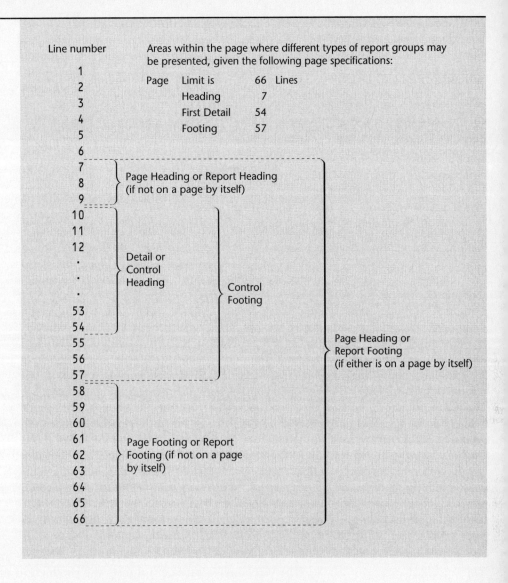

Line number

Areas within the page where different types of report groups may be presented, given the following page specifications:

Page	Limit is	66	Lines
	Heading	7	
	First Detail	54	
	Footing	57	

```
02  DEPT-TOTAL PIC ZZ,ZZZ,ZZ9.99 COLUMN 69
    SUM MONTH-TOTAL.
```

where MONTH-TOTAL was a sum counter specified earlier, is an example of a rolling forward total.

The following rules apply:

1. A SUM clause may appear only in the description of a CONTROL FOOTING report group.

2. The UPON phrase provides the capability to accomplish selective subtotaling for the detail report groups named in the phrase.

3. The RESET option inhibits automatic resetting to zero upon the occurrence of a control break. Thus the sum counter can be zeroed only when a control break occurs for data-name-3, or on the occurrence of FINAL. The latter case represents an accumulation for the entire report.

An eighth optional clause is

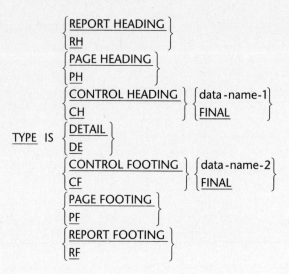

The TYPE clause specifies the particular type of report group that is described by this entry. Each option can be abbreviated in a two-letter reserved COBOL word, as shown.

A ninth option is

INITIATE report-name

The INITIATE statement causes the system to begin processing a report. As part of the initialization procedure, all sum counters are set to zero, and PAGE-COUNTER and LINE-COUNTER are initialized.

A tenth optional clause is

$$\underline{\text{GENERATE}} \quad \begin{Bmatrix} \text{data-name} \\ \text{report-name} \end{Bmatrix}$$

The GENERATE statement directs the production of a report in accordance with the report description in the REPORT SECTION of the DATA DIVISION. Data-name is a TYPE DETAIL report group. If report-name is used, no detail report groups are printed; instead, we produce what is called a summary report. The GENERATE statement causes report generation, including handling of control breaks, the start of page procedures, and so forth. A report may contain more than one type of detail report group. In such a case there will be more than one GENERATE statement in the PROCEDURE DIVISION, each referencing the proper detail group.

An eleventh option is

TERMINATE report-name

The TERMINATE statement causes the completion of the report processing. All CONTROL FOOTING and REPORT FOOTING groups are produced.

Finally, a twelfth optional clause is

USE BEFORE REPORTING identifier

The USE statement specifies PROCEDURE DIVISION statements that are executed just before a report group named in the REPORT SECTION of the DATA DIVISION is produced. The USE statement, when present, must follow immediately a section header in the DECLARATIVES section, and must be followed by a period and a space. The identifier is a report group.

SUMMARY

This chapter covered the *report writer* feature. As such, it is an extension of the coverage of control break processing for reports in Chapter 9.

The report writer feature is essentially a specialized report-generating language embedded in the framework of COBOL, and is an alternative to the use of the usual types of COBOL statements that can be used to produce reports. Instead of requiring the detailed program procedures, the format of the desired report is specified.

Three program examples were used to introduce you to the features of the report writer. The first example illustrated use of report headings, page headings, report footings, and page numbering. The associated specialized statements in the DATA DIVISION and PROCEDURE DIVISION also were discussed, and are included in the *Review* following the first example.

The second example program illustrates application of control headings and control footings. Again, some of the detailed programming considerations are included in the *Review* that follows the second example.

The third example demonstrates exception processing, that is, the ability to specify some special-purpose procedures when a defined condition exists. The reserved word DECLARATIVES is used to introduce such special-purpose sections in the PROCEDURE DIVISION, while the USE verb specifies the conditions under which those procedures are to be executed.

The last part of the chapter considered some of the most important and frequently used options associated with the report writer from a general point of view.

EXERCISES

24.1 A file contains data pertaining to student grades. Each record consists of the following:

COLUMN	CONTENT
1–15	Student name
16–27	Course name
28	Credits
29	Grade (A, B, C, D, or F)

Create a program whereby we can print a report as outlined on the print chart shown in Figure 24-10.

The report heading SEMESTER GRADE REPORT will be printed on the first page only.

Each student is enrolled in five courses.

A report footing is printed at the end of the report, as shown.

The grade point average (GPA) is computed by considering A = 4, B = 3, C = 2, D = 1, F = 0 points.

Hint: You may find it useful to use two DECLARATIVES procedures; one to compute the GPA before printing the line containing the GPA, and one to clear the total credits accumulator, which you will need to sum up the credits for each student.

FIGURE 24-10

*Print Chart Showing Desired
Report Format for Exercise 24.1*

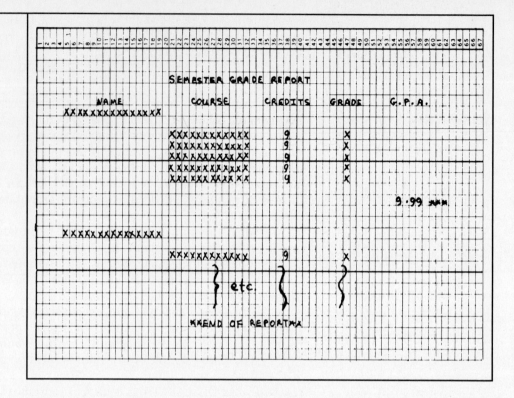

24.2   Incorporate the report writer feature into a program that you have already
       written.

25 Data Structures

IN THIS CHAPTER *you will cover some concepts and techniques by which the **structuring** and **referencing** of data can be extended beyond those provided directly by COBOL.*

*Logical data structure is concerned with defined data relationships apart from their physical storage representation. The file structures that you have considered in this book are **flat files.** Other types of logical data structures that you will study in this chapter are **tree hierarchies, networks,** and the **relational model.***

*Physical data structure is concerned with the actual storage representation of data and their relationships. A **pointer** is a data item whose value is the storage address of some other data item. The types of pointer structures that you will study are **stacks, queues, simple list chains,** and **rings.** A sample program will illustrate the application of pointer concepts.*

*Next, you will learn how to use **file inversion,** which, through **indexing,** can be used as a data structure that facilitates efficient database interrogation. Finally, you will study some overview concepts in **database management systems,** since the various types of data structures covered in this chapter are used mainly in such systems.*

INTRODUCTION

COBOL provides convenient ways for structuring data to meet the needs for certain applications. In particular, the language provides convenient ways by which data can be grouped and referenced within a record, including reference to level-numbers and associated elementary and group-item formations and the use of reference modification, the REDEFINES clause, and the RENAMES clause. Additionally, data can be structured in the form of tables; and files can be organized in sequential, indexed, or relative form.

Even though COBOL provides considerable flexibility in structuring and referencing data, there are some occasions in which the data need to be structured differently from the ways provided for by the language. This chapter presents an overview of data structures that extends beyond the capability included in the COBOL language.

LOGICAL DATA STRUCTURES

An important characteristic of data structures is the ability to represent inter-relationships among data items. Two levels of data structure can be considered: logical structure and physical structure. The *logical data structure* is concerned with the defined data relationships apart from their physical recording. *Physical data structure* is concerned with the actual storage representation of data and their relationships. In this section we consider four basic types of logical data structure: flat files, tree hierarchies, networks, and the relational model.

Flat Files

The sequential, indexed, and relative file structures that we have considered in this book are called *flat files*. We have viewed files as collections of records, each record consisting of a number of fields, such as shown in Figure 25-1. Each row in Figure 25-1 constitutes a record. Each record is identified by a unique key, called the *entity identifier* or the *primary key*. In Figure 25-1 the EMPLOYEE-NUMBER is an example of an entity identifier. The term *attribute* is often used in lieu of the term field. Thus a column in Figure 25-1, such as WAGE-RATE, constitutes an entity attribute. Flat files are often ordered on the basis of the entity identifier values, thereby establishing a logical relationship between records. However, no relationships are implied between the other attributes in the record.

Tree Hierarchies

A *hierarchical data structure* represents a relationship between a *parent* and a *child* data item. The relationship can be depicted in graphic form as a tree, as illustrated in Figure 25-2. At the head of the tree is an element called the *root;* all other elements are hierarchically lower and are referred to as *nodes* in the tree. A node that

---

FIGURE 25-1

An Example of a Flat File

EMPLOYEE-NUMBER	DEPARTMENT	SKILL CODE	WAGE RATE	YEAR-TO-DATE GROSS
1234	10	A	3	10000
5678	20	B	1	7500
9101	10	L	2	8425

has other dependent nodes is a parent element, while the dependent nodes are called the children. Children of the same parent are called (logical) *twins*. A node with no children is called a *leaf*.

Record descriptions in COBOL constitute hierarchies. The root element is the 01-level item, while subordinate group-items constitute nodes, and elementary items constitute leaves. Figure 25-3 illustrates the concept. The specific characteristic of a hierarchical structure is that each child has only one parent. (We will contrast this characteristic to network structures in the next section.)

Trees may be *balanced* (each parent has an equal number of children) or *unbalanced*. Balanced trees may be *binary* (each parent has two children). An

FIGURE 25-2

A Tree Structure

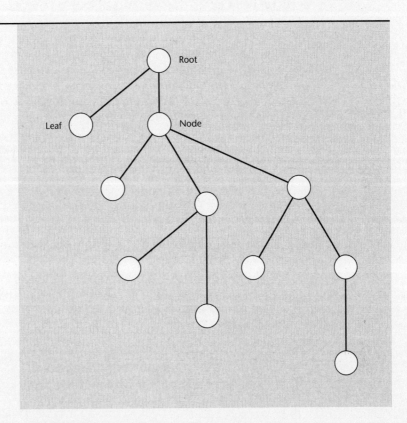

FIGURE 25-3

Hierarchical Representation of COBOL Record Description

```
01 A
    02 B
        03 C
        03 D
    02 E
    02 F
        03 G
            04 H
            04 I
        03 J
```

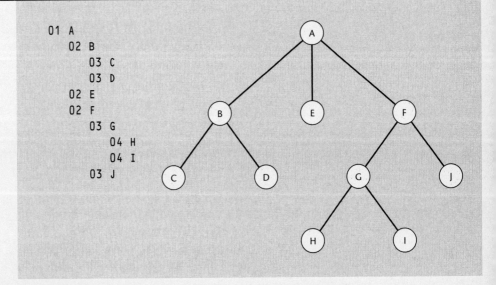

alternative to the parent-child terminology is *owner-member*. A hierarchy can be represented by a so-called CODASYL set, as illustrated in Figure 25-4. The set terminology comes from the database specifications of CODASYL.

Consider Figure 25-5, illustrating the hierarchical structure for a personnel file. The DEPT RECORD serves as the root of the tree hierarchy. EMPLOYEE RECORD and DEPT JOB RECORD are children of the root. Finally, EMPLOYEE RECORD is the parent to three logical children records: MAILING ADDRESS, JOB HISTORY, and DEPENDENTS.

Networks

A *network* is a data structure such that a child in a hierarchy may have more than one parent. Consider a case where a company operates on the basis of projects. Employees are assigned to projects, and machines are used by projects. The logical relationships are represented in Figure 25-6. A specific illustration is given in Figure 25-7, which is based on three employees, two projects, and three machines. The connecting lines indicate the relationships. For instance, Employee 1 has

FIGURE 25-4
A Codasyl Set

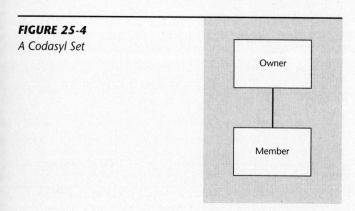

FIGURE 25-5
A Hierarchical File Structure

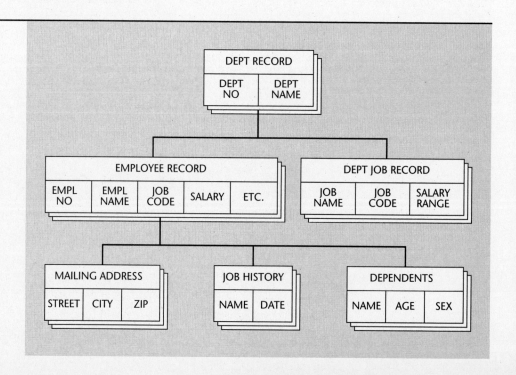

three parents, Project 1 and Machines 1 and 2. Similarly, Project 1 can be viewed to have as parents Machines 1 and 3 and Employees 1, 2, and 3. Actually, the term "child" may be substituted for "parent" in each of the two references in the preceding sentence. In a network the notions of child and parent are blurred.

Figure 25-8 illustrates the decomposition of the example network into six *set* hierarchies, while Figure 25-9 illustrates that the network could also be represented by six flat files (at the cost of great redundancy).

FIGURE 25-6
A Network Relationship

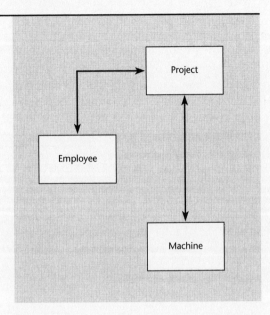

FIGURE 25-7

An Example of a Network Structure with Three Record Types

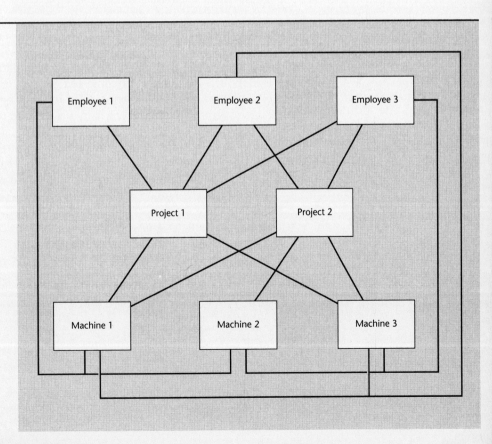

FIGURE 25-8

Substitution of Six Set Hierarchies for a Network

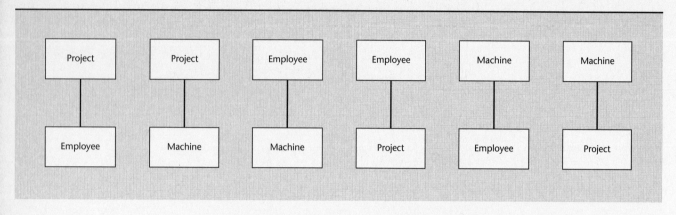

FIGURE 25-9

Representation of the Network as Six Flat Files

P1 E1	P1 M1	E1 M1	E1 P1	M1 E1	M1 P1
P1 E2	P1 M3	E1 M2	E2 P1	M1 E2	M1 P2
P1 E3	P2 M1	E2 M1	E2 P2	M2 E1	M2 P2
P2 E2	P2 M2	E2 M3	E3 P1	M2 E3	M3 P1
P2 E3	P2 M3	E3 M2	E3 P2	M3 E2	M3 P2
		E3 M3		M3 E3	

The Relational Model

The *relational model* is based on the fact that any data structure can be reduced to a set of flat files, provided that some redundancy is allowed. A *relation* is a two-dimensional table. The table consists of rows called *tuples* and a fixed number of *attributes* (columns) such that the data in a column represent a homogeneous set—the data represent values for the same attribute. The database user is equipped with language operators (relational algebra and/or relational calculus) that enable the formation of new tables (relations) by means of extracting a subset of columns or a subset of rows, or by combining columns and rows from two or more tables.

Consider Figure 25-10, which represents two relations, Project and Employee. The Project Table (relation) consists of two rows and two columns, while the Employee Table consists of five rows and two columns. Relationships can be formed by reference to these tables. Suppose that we present the request: Identify the employees who worked on Project 2. This request could be satisfied by forming a new table that would consist of the second and fifth rows of the Employee Table, as follows:

E3	P1
E3	P2

As another example, consider this request: Find the customer names for the projects on which Employee 3 (E3) worked. This request would be satisfied by

FIGURE 25-10

An Example of a Relational Model Data Representation

PROJECT TABLE

PROJECT NO	CUSTOMER NAME
P1	Jones
P2	Smith

EMPLOYEE TABLE

EMPLOYEE NO	PROJECT NO
E1	P1
E1	P2
E2	P1
E3	P1
E3	P2

joining the fourth and fifth rows of the Employee Table and the two rows of the Project Table in Figure 25-10 to form a new table:

EMPLOYEE NO	PROJECT NO
E3	P1
E3	P2

+

PROJECT NO	CUSTOMER NAME
P1	Jones
P2	Smith

=

CUSTOMER NAME
Jones
Smith

The appeal of the relational model is based on two factors. First, the concept of tabular structure seems easy to understand by users in general. In contrast, hierarchies and networks can become quite complex and difficult to comprehend. The second advantage of the relational model is that it is based on a formal, rational model whose logical manipulation can be described by means of the mathematical systems of relational algebra and relational calculus.

R E V I E W . . . .

1. The data structure concepts that are concerned with defined data relationships, but not the physical recording of the data, are associated with _____ data structure.

    logical

2. In the flat file structure, if each column represents a data field, or attribute, then each row represents a _____ .

    record

3. In the flat file structure each record is uniquely identified by one of the attributes, which is used as the _____ .

    entity identifier (or primary key)

4. In hierarchical tree structures the element at the head of the tree is called the _____ . All other elements, which are hierarchically lower, are called _____ .

    root; nodes

5. In hierarchical tree structures a node that has other dependent nodes is called a _____ element, while the dependent nodes are called _____ .

parent; children

6. In hierarchical tree structures a parent [can / cannot] have more than one child, and a child [can / cannot] have more than one parent.

can; cannot

7. In the network structure a parent [can / cannot] have more than one child, and a child [can / cannot] have more than one parent.

can; can

8. If a file that has a network structure is represented by several flat files instead, the result is that there will be considerable _____ in the data.

redundancy

9. When the relational model is used as the basis for logical data structure, the relation of interest can always be graphically portrayed as a two-dimensional _____ .

table

10. In comparison with hierarchical tree structures and network structures, logical data structures that follow the relational model are generally [easier / more difficult] to understand.

easier

·   ·   ·   ·   ·   ·   ·   ·   ·   ·   ·   ·   ·   ·   ·   ·   ·   ·

POINTER STRUCTURES

The preceding section presented the basic concepts associated with *logical data structures.* Our ability to understand and communicate logical structure concepts is dependent on our use of graphic representations. But computers can store and access characters of data, not graphic figures, and thus we must use some other method of representation when it comes to considerations of *physical data structures. Pointers* provide us with an effective physical means of implementing logical data relationships in computer storage. A pointer is a data item whose value is the storage address of some other data item. Commonly, a pointer is a record field that contains the storage address of some other record. The address may be *logical,* such as a name, or *physical,* such as a specific memory or disk address.

In this section we present some of the common pointer structures. It should be recognized, however, that many other pointer structures are also used.

Stacks

A *stack* is a one-dimensional table structure, also called a *linear list,* for which all additions and deletions take place at one end of the table. A simple example of a physical stack is the stack of trays in a cafeteria, given that new trays are added to the top of the stack and removals also are made from the top of the stack. In the terminology of the field of accounting, the term Last-In, First-Out (LIFO) describes the basic properties of a stack. In a data processing context a stack can be used to represent the inventory of available rooms in a hotel, given that the rooms are assigned according to which one was most recently cleaned. In a computer science context, a compiler can use a stack structure to store the return addresses of a series of nested PERFORM, or CALL, statements.

To implement a stack in COBOL, a table structure that includes a field to keep track of the head (or tail) of the stack can be used. Consider the following example:

```
01  STACK-STRUCTURE.
    02  STACK-HEAD      PIC 99.
    02  STACK-CAPACITY PIC 99 VALUE 50.
    02  STACK-DATA.
        03 STACK-TABLE OCCURS 50 TIMES.
            04  HOTEL-ROOM   PIC X(4).
            04  ROOM-RATE    PIC 9(3)V99.
```

Initially, we could store a zero value in STACK-HEAD for the above example. When a new item is to be added to the stack, say, the room number in the field CLEAN-ROOM, we would execute the following procedure:

```
ADD-TO-STACK.
    IF  STACK-HEAD = STACK-CAPACITY
        PERFORM STACK-IS-FULL
    ELSE
        ADD 1 TO STACK-HEAD
        MOVE CLEAN-ROOM-NO TO HOTEL-ROOM (STACK-HEAD)
        MOVE CLEAN-ROOM-RATE TO ROOM-RATE (STACK-HEAD)
    END-IF.
```

To assign (remove) the room that is at the head of the stack, the following procedure would be executed:

```
DELETE-FROM-STACK.
    IF  STACK-HEAD < 1
        PERFORM STACK-IS-EMPTY
    ELSE
        MOVE HOTEL-ROOM (STACK-HEAD) TO ROOM-ASSIGNMENT
        MOVE ROOM-RATE (STACK-HEAD) TO ASSIGNED-RATE
        SUBTRACT 1 FROM STACK-HEAD
    END-IF.
```

By the above examples we can observe that a stack can be maintained with relatively simple coding procedures. If a stack is stored in a relative file, common approach is to store the stack head information on the first record of the file and to use the remainder of the file for stack storage. Assuming that REL-KEY was declared as the RELATIVE KEY, we would write

```
MOVE 1 TO REL-KEY
READ STACK-FILE
    INVALID KEY ...
    .
    .
    .
MOVE STACK-FILE-REC TO STACK-HEAD.
```

Before terminating the program, the stack head would be saved by the following instructions:

```
MOVE STACK-HEAD TO STACK-FILE-REC
MOVE 1 TO REL-KEY
REWRITE STACK-FILE-REC
    INVALID KEY ...
```

In parallel with the table structure defined at the beginning of this subsection, the procedure to add a record to the stack might be written as follows:

```
ADD-TO-STACK.
    IF STACK-HEAD = MAX-RECS-ALLOWED-IN-FILE
        PERFORM STACK-IS-FULL
    ELSE
        ADD 1 TO STACK-HEAD
        MOVE STACK-HEAD TO REL-KEY
        MOVE appropriate data TO STACK-FILE-REC
        WRITE STACK-FILE-REC  (or use REWRITE if appropriate)
            INVALID KEY ...
```

Again, we conclude that a stack is fairly easy to implement, either as a table structure or as a relative file.

Queues

A *queue* is a one-dimensional table representation with defined beginning and end locations that is operated on a First-In, First-Out (FIFO) basis. Records are added to the end of the list and are removed from the beginning of the list. An everyday example of a queue is a waiting line of customers at a post-office service counter. New customers are added to the end of the line (list) while servicing (removal) takes place at the beginning of the line (list). In a data processing context a list of outstanding invoices (accounts payable) can be treated as a queue. A new invoice goes to the bottom of the list. When a payment is received, it is applied against the oldest invoice first. If the payment is larger than that particular amount due, the remainder of the payment is applied to succeeding invoices. In computer science a common use of a queue structure is in the scheduling algorithm for a multiprogramming operating system. Incoming jobs are stored as a queue, with the oldest job submitted being served first.

Referring to the hotel-room example in the previous subsection on stacks, a queue can be implemented with the following type of table structure, resulting in a FIFO basis for assigning rooms:

```
01  QUE-STRUCTURE.
    02  QUE-START    PIC 99    VALUE 1.
    02  QUE-END      PIC 99    VALUE 0.
    02  QUE-SIZE     PIC 99    VALUE 0.
    02  QUE-CAPACITY PIC 99    VALUE 50.
    02  QUE-DATA.
        03 QUE-TABLE OCCURS 50 TIMES.
            04 HOTEL-ROOM    PIC X(4).
            04 ROOM-RATE     PIC 9(3)V99.
```

Initially, we set the values for QUE-START, QUE-END, and QUE-SIZE as shown in the above specifications. When an item is to be added to the queue, we write

```
ADD-TO-QUE.
    IF  QUE-SIZE = QUE-CAPACITY
        PERFORM QUE-IS-FULL
    ELSE
        ADD 1 TO QUE-END
        IF QUE-END > QUE-CAPACITY
           MOVE 1 TO QUE-END
        END-IF
        ADD 1 TO QUE-SIZE
        MOVE CLEAN-ROOM-NO TO HOTEL-ROOM (QUE-END)
        MOVE CLEAN-ROOM-RATE TO ROOM-RATE (QUE-END)
    END-IF.
```

In the above program segment, notice that QUE-START is not involved and therefore not affected by an ADD-TO-QUE operation. As items are added to the queue, it may become full, hence the statement IF QUE-SIZE = QUE-CAPACITY PERFORM QUE-IS-FULL. Another special case is that in which the QUE-START value is greater than 1 because of previous deletions. In such a case we wrap around the queue by the statement IF QUE-END > QUE-CAPACITY THEN MOVE 1 TO QUE-END. Figure 25-11 presents some example possibilities for queue contents to illustrate the circular implementation used. An alternative approach is to keep the queue contents "packed" at the top of the queue. By the latter approach, when an item is removed, then every item in the queue is moved up one place. The result is that the value of QUE-END would always be equal to QUE-SIZE, thereby making QUE-START and QUE-END unnecessary. However, this mode of operation is not the preferred one, because physically moving the contents of the queue is time-consuming, especially for large queues.

Deletions from the queue can be handled by the following procedure:

```
DELETE-FROM-QUE.
    IF  QUE-SIZE > 0
        MOVE HOTEL-ROOM (QUE-START) TO ROOM-ASSIGNMENT
```

FIGURE 25-11

Sample Queue Contents and Structure Descriptors

A	Empty	K	Empty
B	Empty	L	L
C	Empty	Empty	M
Empty	G	G	Empty
Empty	Empty	H	Empty

QUE-START = 1	QUE-START = 4	QUE-START = 4	QUE-START = 2
QUE-END = 3	QUE-END = 4	QUE-END = 2	QUE-END = 3
QUE-SIZE = 3	QUE-SIZE = 1	QUE-SIZE = 4	QUE-SIZE = 2

```
            MOVE ROOM-RATE (QUE-START) TO ASSIGNED-RATE
            ADD 1 TO QUE-START
            IF QUE-START > QUE-CAPACITY
                MOVE 1 TO QUE-START
            END-IF
            SUBTRACT 1 FROM QUE-SIZE
            IF QUE-SIZE = 0
                MOVE 1 TO QUE-START
                MOVE 0 TO QUE-END
            END-IF
        ELSE
            PERFORM QUE-IS-EMPTY
        END-IF.
```

If the queue is not empty when the program segment above is executed (QUE-SIZE > 0), we advance the QUE-START by one position, wrapping around the queue if necessary. Notice that we do not bother to "erase" the deleted record in the sample procedure above. Deletion consists simply of advancing the value of QUE-START; thus the "empty" cells in Figure 25-11 need not be empty. They may contain previously deleted but not yet overwritten items. Of course, an item being deleted can be erased by executing MOVE SPACES TO QUE-TABLE (QUE-START) before executing ADD 1 TO QUE-START.

Implementing a queue structure in a relative file can be done in a manner paralleling the method discussed in the previous subsection on implementing stack structures.

List Chains

A *list* is a data structure such that there is one starting (head) record, and each record (including the head) contains a pointer to the next record in sequence. The last record in the sequence has a special pointer value to indicate the end of the list chain. Figure 25-12 represents a simple list structure for five "Project Records." The spatial separation of the records is intended to represent the possible physical separations that may exist between records. The arrows in Figure 25-12 provide a pictorial view of the pointer structure. In computer storage the value stored in the pointer field gives the storage address of the record to which the arrow points in the figure.

The basic advantage of a simple list chain is that we may preserve logical order even though we may have "random" physical order. One disadvantage is that it is a forward-only system. If we have accessed a particular record through a chain of pointers and we wish to access its logical predecessor, there is no way to go backward. Figure 25-13 shows how we can have both forward and backward access capability by utilizing two pointers in each record. One pointer gives the storage address of the succeeding record, while the other pointer gives the storage address of the preceding record.

Figure 25-14 illustrates the applications of two-way pointers in the case of hierarchical structure involving two projects and the relationships of employees and machines assigned to projects. We form two list chains, one for each project. The project records serve as heads of their respective chains. Each employee record contains two pointers. One pointer points to the next employee record for Project 1, while the other pointer points to the next employee record for Project 2. The employee pointer (EP) in the Project 1 record points to Employee 1. The Project 1 Pointer (P1P) in the Employee 1 record points to the Employee 2 record, which is the end of the chain. With respect to the Project 2 chain it should be noted that

FIGURE 25-12
A Simple List Structure

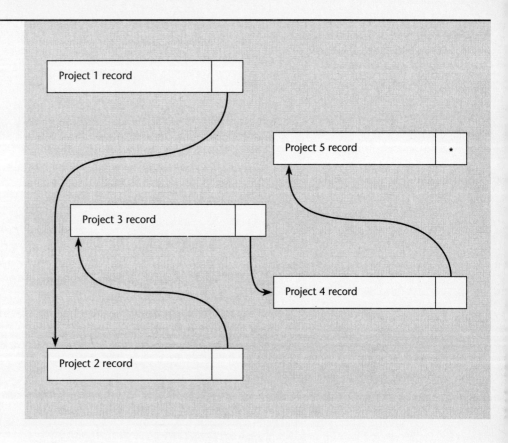

FIGURE 25-13
A List Chain with Forward and
Backward Pointers

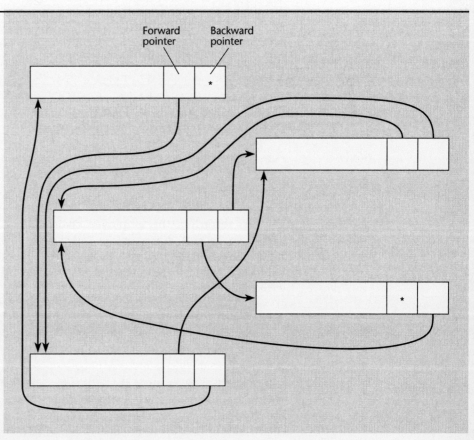

FIGURE 25-14

*An Illustration of a List Chain with
Two-Way Pointers*

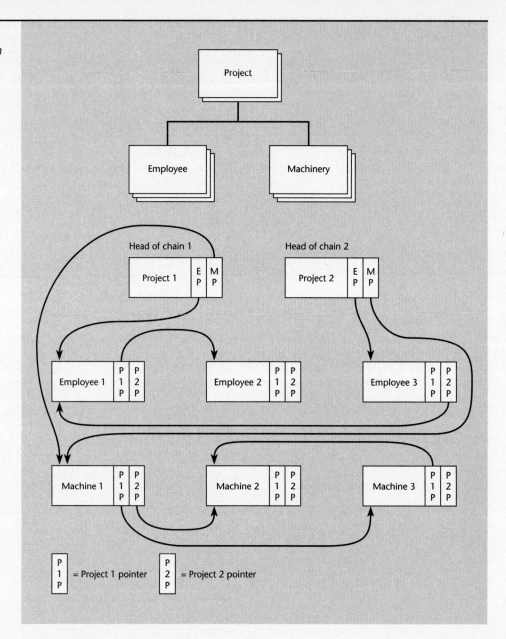

FIGURE 25-14

*An Illustration of a List Chain with
Two-Way Pointers*

the first record in the employee chain is Employee 3, which is followed by Employee 1. This last example illustrates the ability of pointer structures to represent logical orders that are impossible to represent as physical orders without redundancy. Specifically, the Employee 1 record is first in the Project 1 chain, while it is last in the Project 2 chain.

The machine records also contain two pointers to indicate which machines are utilized in which projects.

Rings

A *ring* is a list chain such that the last record in the chain points to the head record. Figure 25-15 shows a simple ring structure. A ring provides an access path that is circular, and care must be taken to distinguish the head record. Suppose that in a ring of 500 records we are looking for a record that does not exist. We could have an infinite loop if we did not mark the header record as such.

FIGURE 25-15
A Simple Ring Structure

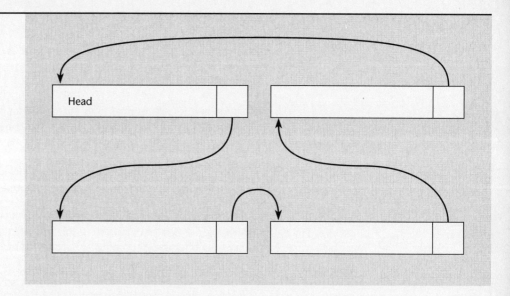

FIGURE 25-16
A Two-Pointer Ring Structure

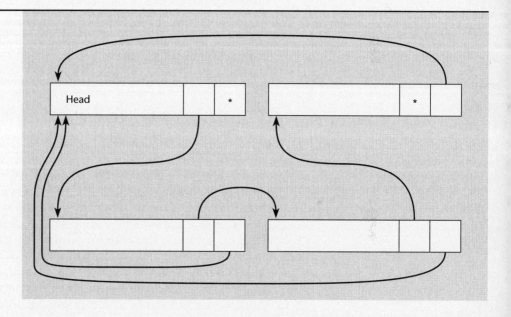

Sometimes it is desirable to be able to return to the head of a chain from the record that we have just accessed without completing the entire path of the ring. Figure 25-16 illustrates the use of two pointers for quick return to the head record. One pointer points to the next record, while the other points to the head record.

Reviewing Figure 25-16, it can be seen that the pointer structure allows return to the head of the chain, but is inefficient for returning to the predecessor record. Thus, in such a ring of 500 records, if we had accessed the 300th logical record and we wanted to access the 299th logical record, we would have to access all records from the first record (head) to the 299th record. We could consider the use of a third pointer to identify the predecessor record if we anticipate frequent need to backtrack. Obviously, pointer systems can proliferate as we strive for flexibility and efficiency. For instance, it is possible to have pointers that allow for "big jumps" instead of one record at a time. In general, as the number of pointers increases, file updating becomes more complex, since additions or deletions to the file require changes in many pointers.

R E V I E W . . . .

1. In terms of physical data structure a data item whose value indicates the storage location of some other record is called a _____ .

                                                                                    pointer

2. The type of one-dimensional table structure that can be described as a Last-In, First-Out (LIFO) system is the _____ structure.

                                                                                    stack

3. The type of one-dimensional table structure that can be described as a First-In, First-Out (FIFO) system is the _____ structure.

                                                                                    queue

4. In a simple list structure, if there is only one pointer per record, that pointer usually identifies the [preceding / succeeding] record.

                                                                                    succeeding

5. When a simple list structure is used, it [is / is not] necessary that the records in the file physically be in a logical order.

                                                                                    is not

6. The type of list chain structure in which one or more records in the chain point to the head record is called a _____ .

                                                                                    ring

. . . .

SAMPLE COBOL PROGRAM

In this section the application of the pointer concepts discussed in the preceding section is illustrated by means of a complete COBOL program.

Pointer structures will be used to sort the data in a table in both ascending and descending order. We refer to this as the *chained records sort algorithm*. By the use of this method two additional fields are defined for each record of a given table of records. The first field, call it the *predecessor field*, contains a value that defines the location of the record that logically precedes the record in question. The other field, call it the *successor field*, contains a value that defines the location of the record that logically follows the given record. If such predecessor and successor fields are defined for each record, we say that we have a *fully chained* set of records. Such a set has both a forward and a backward chain since, given any particular record, we can determine all the records that precede it and all the records that follow it. To designate the first and last records of the table, the first can be assigned a predecessor value of zero, while the last record can be assigned a successor value of zero.

To illustrate the procedure associated with the chained records sort algorithm, let us consider the table defined by the following DATA DIVISION statements:

```
01  DATA-TABLE.
    02 TABLE-ENTRIES OCCURS 50 TIMES.
        03  KEY-FIELD           PICTURE 9(4).
        03  DATA-FIELD          PICTURE X(76).
        03  PREDECESSOR         PICTURE 9(2).
        03  SUCCESSOR           PICTURE 9(2).
```

Conceptually, the table defined by the above statements has the following structure:

KEY-FIELD	DATA-FIELD	PREDECESSOR	SUCCESSOR

PREDECESSOR (1) and SUCCESSOR (1) refer to the predecessor and successor values of the first record in the table. Assume that the data to be stored consist of five records whose KEY-FIELDs are 3200, 3900, 2000, 4000, and 3500. For simplicity we ignore the DATA-FIELD values. Additionally, it is useful to define the following data-names, whose values will be stored outside of the table as such:

NEW:	new entry in the table
FIRST-PLACE:	physical position of the record that is logically the first entry in the table
LAST-PLACE:	physical position of the record that is logically the last entry in the table

For the five records whose keys are 3200, 3900, 2000, 4000, and 3500, we now consider the effects of entering each of these records into the table described above in a sequential fashion.

FIRST RECORD ENTERED

KEY-FIELD	DATA-FIELD	PREDECESSOR	SUCCESSOR
3200		00	00

NEW = 1, FIRST-PLACE = 1, LAST-PLACE = 1

Since there is only one record in the table at this point, the PREDECESSOR and SUCCESSOR fields are both set equal to zero. Similarly, this one record is both the FIRST-PLACE and LAST-PLACE entry in the table. The value of NEW indicates the location of the new record.

SECOND RECORD ENTERED

KEY-FIELD	DATA-FIELD	PREDECESSOR	SUCCESSOR
3200		00	02
3900		01	00

NEW = 2, FIRST-PLACE = 1, LAST-PLACE = 2

The KEY-FIELD of the second record is higher than the KEY-FIELD of the first record; therefore the second record logically succeeds the first, and SUCCESSOR (1) = 02. However, the first record is not logically preceded by any other record, and hence PREDECESSOR (1) = 00. Similarly, PREDECESSOR (2) = 01 and SUCCESSOR (2) = 00. The FIRST-PLACE in the table is at record 1, while the LAST-PLACE is at record 2.

THIRD RECORD ENTERED

KEY-FIELD	DATA-FIELD	PREDECESSOR	SUCCESSOR
3200		03	02
3900		01	00
2000		00	01

NEW = 3, FIRST-PLACE = 3, LAST-PLACE = 2

The KEY-FIELD of the third record (2000) is compared with the KEY-FIELD of FIRST-PLACE (3900), and it is found to be smaller. Thus the search is completed, and the predecessor and successor values are changed as indicated above.

The effects of processing the fourth and fifth records are illustrated in the following two tables. Note the logic of the changes in the predecessor and successor values in each table.

FOURTH RECORD ENTERED

KEY-FIELD	DATA-FIELD	PREDECESSOR	SUCCESSOR
3200		03	02
3900		01	04
2000		00	01
4000		02	00

NEW = 4, FIRST-PLACE = 3, LAST-PLACE = 4

FIFTH RECORD ENTERED

KEY-FIELD	DATA-FIELD	PREDECESSOR	SUCCESSOR
3200		03	05
3900		05	04
2000		00	01
4000		02	00
3500		01	02

NEW = 5, FIRST-PLACE = 3, LAST-PLACE = 4

Given the completed table above, suppose we wish to output the records in this table in ascending sequence. FIRST-PLACE indicates the location of the first record, that is, the record with the smallest key value. In the above example it is the third record, with the associated KEY-FIELD value of 2000. If the location of this record had not been stored in FIRST-PLACE, it could have been determined by checking the value of each PREDECESSOR field until the one with a value of zero was found. Of course, once the first record is identified, the location of each record that follows is determined by reference to the SUCCESSOR field.

Figure 25-17 presents a structure chart, while Figure 25-18 presents a complete COBOL program that implements the general procedure in a specific context. The DATA-TABLE definition includes a REC-NO field designed to store the record-number of each record for ease of reference. The program is designed to output three tables. The first table is a listing of the original input data in the order presented in the INPUT-FILE. The second table is a listing of the DATA-TABLE records in physical order. The third table is a listing of the records in ascending order, along with the respective PREDECESSOR and SUCCESSOR values.

In the PROCEDURE DIVISION, PERFORM 200-STORE-FIRST-RECORD is executed as a separate procedure to handle the very first record. One can reason that the same logic that adds any record to the table can be applied to the first such record as well. However, such an approach complicates the processing logic by requiring the program to differentiate first and nonfirst records. Reviewing the 200-STORE-FIRST-RECORD paragraph, we observe that it consists of setting the appropriate values to define the one-record condition.

FIGURE 25-17
Structure Chart for Sample
Program

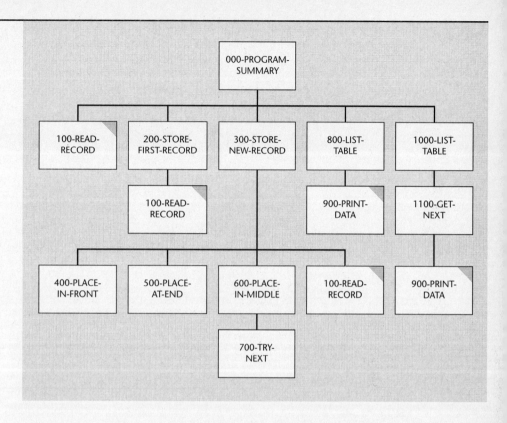

FIGURE 25-18
Sample COBOL Program

```
*
      IDENTIFICATION DIVISION.
      PROGRAM-ID.  CHAINPR.
*
      ENVIRONMENT DIVISION.
      CONFIGURATION SECTION.
      SOURCE-COMPUTER. ABC-380.
      OBJECT-COMPUTER. ABC-380.
      INPUT-OUTPUT SECTION.
      FILE-CONTROL.
          SELECT INPUT-FILE ASSIGN TO CARDS.
          SELECT OUTPUT-FILE ASSIGN TO PRINTER.
*
      DATA DIVISION.
      FILE SECTION.
      FD  INPUT-FILE LABEL RECORD OMITTED
                      DATA RECORD IN-RECORD.
      01  IN-RECORD.
          02 REC-ID-IN        PIC 9(4).
          02 REC-DATA-IN       PIC X(76).
      FD  OUTPUT-FILE LABEL RECORD OMITTED
                      DATA RECORD OUT-RECORD.
      01  OUT-RECORD          PIC X(132).
*
      WORKING-STORAGE SECTION.
*
```

FIGURE 25-18

Sample COBOL Program
(continued)

```
     01   DATA-END            PIC XXX VALUE 'NO'.
     *
        POINTERS
     *
     01   NEW                 PIC 99.
     01   FIRST-PLACE         PIC 99.
     01   LAST-PLACE          PIC 99.
     01   XTH                 PIC 99.
     01   I                   PIC 99.
     01   NO-OF-RECS          PIC 99 VALUE ZERO.
     *
     01   HEADER-1.
          02 FILLER           PIC X(13) VALUE 'ORIGINAL DATA'.
     01   HEADER-2.
          02 FILLER           PIC X(4)  VALUE SPACES.
          02 FILLER           PIC X(6)  VALUE 'REC-NO'.
          02 FILLER           PIC X(2)  VALUE SPACES.
          02 FILLER           PIC X(10) VALUE 'IDENTIFIER'.
          02 FILLER           PIC X(38) VALUE SPACES.
          02 FILLER           PIC X(4)  VALUE 'DATA'.
          02 FILLER           PIC X(38) VALUE SPACES.
          02 FILLER           PIC X(11) VALUE 'PREDECESSOR'.
          02 FILLER           PIC X(2)  VALUE SPACES.
          02 FILLER           PIC X(9)  VALUE 'SUCCESSOR'.
     *
     01   REC-OUT.
          02 FILLER           PIC X(6)  VALUE SPACES.
          02 REC-NO-OUT       PIC Z9.
          02 FILLER           PIC X(5)  VALUE SPACES.
          02 REC-ID-OUT       PIC 9(4).
          02 FILLER           PIC X(5)  VALUE SPACES.
          02 REC-DAT-OUT      PIC X(76).
          02 FILLER           PIC X(5)  VALUE SPACES.
          02 PREDEC-OUT       PIC 9(2).
          02 FILLER           PIC X(11) VALUE SPACES.
          02 SUCCES-OUT       PIC 9(2).
     *
     01   DATA-TABLE.
          02 TABLE-ENTRIES    OCCURS 50 TIMES.
             03 REC-NO        PIC 99.
             03 REC-ID        PIC 9(4).
             03 REC-DATA      PIC X(76).
             03 PREDECESSOR   PIC 9(2).
             03 SUCCESSOR     PIC 9(2).
     *
        PROCEDURE DIVISION.
        000-PROGRAM-SUMMARY.
           OPEN INPUT INPUT-FILE
           OPEN OUTPUT OUTPUT-FILE
           WRITE OUT-RECORD FROM HEADER-1 AFTER PAGE.
           PERFORM 100-READ-RECORD
```

FIGURE 25-18
Sample COBOL Program
(continued)

```
*
            PERFORM 200-STORE-FIRST-RECORD
*
       PERFORM 300-STORE-NEW-RECORD
               UNTIL DATA-END = 'YES' OR NEW = 50.
*
       PERFORM 800-LIST-TABLE.
*
       PERFORM 1000-LIST-SORTED-TABLE.
       CLOSE INPUT-FILE OUTPUT-FILE
       STOP RUN.
*
   100-READ-RECORD.
       READ INPUT-FILE
           AT END MOVE 'YES' TO DATA-END.
       IF DATA-END NOT = 'YES'
       MOVE SPACES TO REC-OUT
       MOVE REC-ID-IN TO REC-ID-OUT
       MOVE REC-DATA-IN TO REC-DAT-OUT
       WRITE OUT-RECORD FROM REC-OUT AFTER 2.
*
   200-STORE-FIRST-RECORD.
       MOVE 1 TO REC-NO (1)
       MOVE 1 TO NO-OF-RECS
       MOVE 1 TO NEW
       MOVE 1 TO FIRST-PLACE
       MOVE 1 TO LAST-PLACE
       MOVE ZEROS TO PREDECESSOR (1)
       MOVE ZEROS TO SUCCESSOR (1)
       MOVE REC-ID-IN TO REC-ID (1)
       MOVE REC-DATA-IN TO REC-DATA (1).
       PERFORM 100-READ-RECORD.
*
   300-STORE-NEW-RECORD.
       ADD 1 TO NO-OF-RECS
       ADD 1 TO NEW
       MOVE NEW TO REC-NO (NEW)
       MOVE REC-ID-IN TO REC-ID (NEW)
       MOVE REC-DATA-IN TO REC-DATA (NEW)
*
       IF REC-ID (NEW)  NOT > REC-ID (FIRST-PLACE)
          PERFORM 400-PLACE-IN-FRONT
       ELSE
          IF REC-ID (NEW)  NOT < REC-ID (LAST-PLACE)
              PERFORM 500-PLACE-AT-END
          ELSE
              PERFORM 600-PLACE-IN-MIDDLE.
*
       PERFORM 100-READ-RECORD.
*
```

FIGURE 25-18
Sample COBOL Program
(continued)

```
400-PLACE-IN-FRONT.
    MOVE FIRST-PLACE TO SUCCESSOR (NEW)
    MOVE NEW TO PREDECESSOR (FIRST-PLACE)
    MOVE ZERO TO PREDECESSOR (NEW)
    MOVE NEW TO FIRST-PLACE.
*
500-PLACE-AT-END.
    MOVE LAST-PLACE TO PREDECESSOR (NEW)
    MOVE NEW TO SUCCESSOR (LAST-PLACE)
    MOVE ZERO TO SUCCESSOR (NEW)
    MOVE NEW TO LAST-PLACE.
*
600-PLACE-IN-MIDDLE.
    MOVE FIRST-PLACE TO XTH
*
    PERFORM 700-TRY-NEXT UNTIL REC-ID (NEW) NOT > REC-ID (XTH)
*
    MOVE PREDECESSOR (XTH) TO I
    MOVE NEW TO SUCCESSOR (I)
                PREDECESSOR (XTH)
    MOVE I TO PREDECESSOR (NEW)
    MOVE XTH TO SUCCESSOR (NEW).
*
700-TRY-NEXT.
    MOVE SUCCESSOR (XTH) TO XTH.
*
800-LIST-TABLE.
    WRITE OUT-RECORD FROM HEADER-2 AFTER PAGE
    PERFORM 900-PRINT-DATA VARYING I FROM 1 BY 1
            UNTIL I > NO-OF-RECS.
*
1000-LIST-SORTED-TABLE.
    WRITE OUT-RECORD FROM HEADER-2 AFTER PAGE
    MOVE FIRST-PLACE TO I
    PERFORM 1100-GET-NEXT UNTIL I = ZERO.
*
900-PRINT-DATA.
    MOVE REC-NO (I) TO REC-NO-OUT
    MOVE REC-ID (I) TO REC-ID-OUT
    MOVE REC-DATA (I) TO REC-DAT-OUT
    MOVE PREDECESSOR (I) TO PREDEC-OUT
    MOVE SUCCESSOR (I) TO SUCCES-OUT
    WRITE OUT-RECORD FROM REC-OUT.
*
1100-GET-NEXT.
    PERFORM 900-PRINT-DATA
    MOVE SUCCESSOR (I) TO I.
```

FIGURE 25-19

Illustration of Adding a Record to the Chain

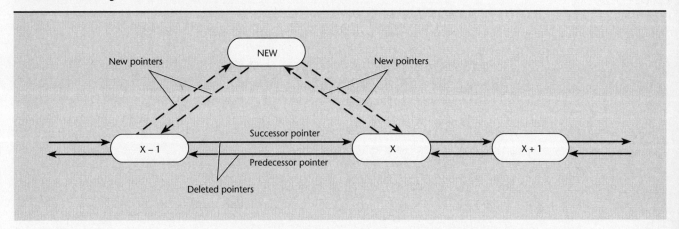

The 300-STORE-NEW-RECORD procedure controls the logic of adding a new record. Three possibilities are represented by the three distinct procedures: 400-PLACE-IN-FRONT, 500-PLACE-AT-END, and 600-PLACE-IN-MIDDLE. The last possibility represents the most complex case, since we need to travel through the chain until we find the position at which the new record "fits," as follows:

```
PERFORM 700-TRY-NEXT
        UNTIL REC-ID (NEW) NOT > REC-ID (XTH).
```

It is interesting to note the content of the 700-TRY-NEXT paragraph: MOVE SUCCESSOR (XTH) to XTH. That MOVE instruction provides the mechanism for accessing the next (XTH) record.

Figure 25-19 helps to illustrate the process of entering a new record "in the middle" of a file. NEW represents the new record, X represents the current record with which NEW is being compared, and X – 1 and X + 1 represent the records preceding and following X, respectively. The dashed lines represent new pointer values that need to be set, while the remark "deleted pointers" identifies the pointers that need to be changed. The program is substantially self-documenting, so the reader can follow the logic of the program by reading through it. However, the logic involving the pointers is rather difficult and terse; therefore the best approach to understanding such logic is to use some sample data and to desk-check the program step by step.

INDEXING AND FILE INVERSION

It is often desirable to query a file or data base in the following fashion: retrieve all the employees who have a particular characteristic. If the file is ordered by that particular characteristic, then the access to those records is easy. If, however, the file is ordered on some other basis, then the entire file has to be read to retrieve all of the appropriate records. *File inversion* through appropriate *indexing* is a data structure that facilitates efficient database interrogation. Let us consider an example, as presented in the following paragraphs.

Figure 25-20 presents an ordinary flat file. Records are identified by EMPLOYEE-NO, the primary key. The file is (partially) inverted in Figure 25-21, where we have created two indexes. The first index is ordered by the DEPT-NO values, and for each department it contains a pointer to the storage address of the EMPLOYEE-NO indicated. The second index is ordered according to JOB, and also contains a pointer to the storage address of the employee. The little arrow is

FIGURE 25-20

A Flat Employee File

EMPLOYEE- NO	DEPARTMENT	NAME	JOB	SALARY
100	30	Doe	Plumber	27,600
102	10	Johnson	Carpenter	24,400
105	30	Taylor	Welder	23,000
112	20	Prentice	Carpenter	25,000
113	10	Brown	Plumber	24,800
122	20	Smith	Carpenter	21,900
125	30	Burger	Carpenter	22,000

FIGURE 25-21

An Illustration of a Partially Inverted File

EMPLOYEE FILE

EMPLOYEE-NO	NAME	SALARY
100	Doe	27,600
102	Johnson	24,400
105	Taylor	23,000
112	Prentice	25,000
113	Brown	24,800
122	Smith	21,900
125	Burger	22,000

DEPARTMENT INDEX

DEPT-NO	POINTER TO EMPLOYEE FILE		
10	102 ↑	113 ↑	
20	100 ↑	112 ↑	122 ↑
30	105 ↑	125 ↑	

JOB INDEX

JOB	POINTER TO EMPLOYEE FILE			
Carpenter	102	112	122 ↑	125 ↑
Plumber	100	113		
Welder	105			

included to show that the value stored there would be the storage address for the record of the employee number shown, and not the employee number as such. The department index indicates, for instance, that the records of Employees 102 and 113 contain the department-number value of 10. Now look back at the Employee file. It consists of only three data items per record. The DEPARTMENT and JOB attributes have been eliminated on the assumption that the indexes suffice to provide this information. (We will return to this point shortly.)

Figure 25-21 is an example of partial inversion. A fully inverted file is one with an index for each attribute. In our example full inversion would also include an index for NAME and an index for SALARY. Indexes created for inversion are called *secondary indexes*. The *primary index* is, of course, based on the record identifier (primary key).

In general, only partial inversion is necessary. In our example in Figure 25-21 the file is not inverted on NAME or SALARY. On close observation it will be seen that an index for either of these two attributes would be as long as the original file, since the values of SALARY and NAME are unique. For that reason we might pause before deciding to invert fully, and consider whether queries about salary or name are going to be frequent. If it is expected that queries about names or salaries are going to be frequent, then it would be preferable to invert the file on those two fields, as well. In the absence of inversion, if we were looking for a name in the file, there would be no knowledge available as to where in the file that name is located. With inversion, however, the name index would be sorted and quick reference to a particular name would be possible.

One more observation is in order. In Figure 25-21 the Employee file does not contain data for DEPT-NO and JOB, which are the bases for the two secondary indexes. Suppose we ask the question: In what department is Employee 112 located? The required access path would be to search the Department Index in a serial fashion until we have satisfied the question. If we did want to have the ability to retrieve efficiently all the attributes of a given employee's record, then we could retain all the data in the Employee file. But redundancy would thereby be introduced, since now the values for DEPARTMENT-NO and JOB would be stored both in the respective indexes and in the Employee file.

R E V I E W . . . .

1. When a file is inverted, this means that one or more _____ are created to facilitate efficient database interrogation.

    indexes

2. When indexes are created for some but not all of the attributes in the records, the file is said to be _____ . When indexes are available for all attributes, the file is said to be _____ .

    partially inverted; fully inverted

3. An objective underlying file inversion is to facilitate database interrogation by [including / not including] redundancy in the file system.

    not including

4. Consider a file that is ordered on the basis of PART-NO and has an index for CUSTOMER-NO. If a report is prepared according to CUSTOMER-NO, then the efficiency of processing for this report is [greater than / equal to / less than] it would be if the file were ordered according to CUSTOMER-NO.

    less than

DATABASE MANAGEMENT SYSTEMS

We conclude this chapter by presenting some overview concepts with respect to *database management systems,* since the various types of data structures discussed in this chapter find their most common use in such systems. Database systems need to implement relationships among data without requiring that the data be physically moved or reorganized. Because of this requirement, pointers and other structures are the usual means of implementing database constructs.

The conceptual design of a database has to take into account the unique characteristics of each organization. However, the programming implementation need not be unique in the sense that file data definition and file processing as applied in different organizations are bound to include a great deal of common logic. Recognition of this fact has led to the development of a number of so-called database management systems. These are software packages designed to minimize individual programming efforts in both the creation and use of databases. Presently, they are mainly available from software firms for a rental or purchase fee. Based on their degree of sophistication, the purchase price for such systems varies from about a few hundred dollars for personal computers to over $100,000 for mainframes. These generalized software packages represent extensive programming efforts.

Basically, two types of database management systems have been developed: the *host-language systems* and the *self-contained systems.* The host-language systems are enhancements of procedure-oriented languages such as COBOL. Options within the language allow file management programming to be accomplished with a limited number of commands. The self-contained systems utilize their own language rules, and in this sense such a system can be thought of as a unique procedure-oriented language directed toward file management in database systems. The Data Base Task Group (DBTG), appointed by the CODASYL Committee that oversees the development of COBOL, has developed a set of specifications for incorporating database management capabilities within the COBOL language. However, the CODASYL recommendations have not been widely adopted. Instead, there are many database management systems, each with its own specific conceptual foundation and design.

As indicated above, from the user's standpoint the advantage of using a database management system is that it minimizes the amount of individual program development on the part of the user. In more specific terms the following advantages can be cited for using such a software package:

1. Allow the firm's programmer(s) to work on complex tasks rather than on routine file maintenance and report generation.

2. Since the program statements in such systems are shorter than those in standard programming languages, reduce the amount of effort to create programs.

3. Eliminate duplicate file design efforts through the availability of easily restructured file definitions.

4. Allow the execution of multiple tasks concurrently and the production of reports in many different sequences, given one set of specifications.

5. Give the user the advantage of a debugged common program logic, thereby making the user's own debugging task less complex and less time-consuming.

The term *schema* denotes the logical description of the database. Typically, there is a *Data Base Administrator* (DBA) in an organization, whose main responsibility is to define and maintain the database schema. Applications programmers need not be bound by the schema. Each applications program defines a *subschema,* which is a description of data from the viewpoint of this particular program. One of the main reasons for a database is to have the capability to look at data from different perspectives for individual uses (subschema), while at the same time the overall relationships of data are maintained in the background (schema).

Figure 25-22 presents the main elements in the operation of a database system. The *Data Base Management System* (DBMS) is the central element. The DBMS interacts with the operating system in controlling all aspects of database operations. The schema describes the overall logical blueprint of the database. The actual physical database resides in direct access storage devices, and it is stored and maintained there by the DBMS. Each subschema is used by the DBMS to access the physical database and make it available through some buffer storage, which serves as the staging point for data access and manipulation.

To implement the functions required of a DBMS, three types of languages are needed. One is a *Data Description Language* (DDL) to enable the DBA to construct and maintain the schema. A second language needed is a *Data Manipulation Language* (DML) that can provide the interface between the applications programmer and the DBMS. In many cases the DML can be used by the COBOL programmer as part of the application program. For instance, the DML may include commands such as CLOSE, DELETE, FIND, GET, INSERT, MODIFY, OPEN, ORDER, REMOVE, and STORE.

The third type of language needed is one to describe data storage and retrieval at the physical level—a *Device/Media Control Language* (DMCL). This third type of language has to be oriented toward specific hardware, and therefore there is less of an agreement as to what such a language should be for general use.

Many database software products are available. These products vary in the conceptual basis for the database and the features that are available, as well as the hardware for which they are programmed. Choosing among these many and varied software offerings is not an easy task. Lack of accepted standardization makes the choice rather critical, since portability from one system to another is nonexistent. CODASYL has proposed a standard, but there exists wide controversy

FIGURE 25-22

Basic Elements of a Data Management System in Operation

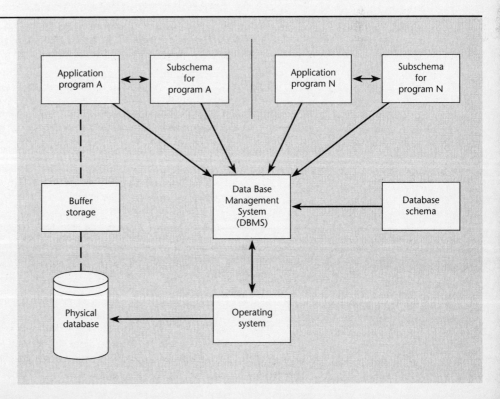

about this standard. In fact, there is an emerging de facto standard, and it is the relational database model.

R E V I E W . . . .

1. A database management system is essentially a specialized type of _____ package.

   software

2. Of the two types of database management systems, the type for which the program statements used are similar to a procedure-oriented language such as COBOL is the [self-contained / host-language] system.

   host-language

3. The main advantage associated with using a database management system is that

   _____ .

   it minimizes the amount of programming and
debugging that has to be done for a particular system (etc.)

4. The overall logical description of the database is included in the _____ for the database, while each applications program defines a _____ for specific uses of the data.

   schema; subschema

5. In the context of database management systems, DBA stands for _____ and DBMS stands for

   _____ .

   Data Base Administrator;
Data Base Management System

6. A language that enables the DBA to construct and maintain a schema is the DDL, or _____ .

   Data Description Language

7. A language that provides an interface between the applications programmer and the DBMS is the DML, or

   _____ .

   Data Manipulation Language

8. At the current stage of development, it can be said that the software to be used to implement the database approach [has / has not] been standardized.

   has not

. . . .

SUMMARY

This chapter covered concepts and techniques by which the *structuring* and *referencing* of data can be extended beyond the capabilities provided directly by COBOL.

Logical data structure is concerned with the defined data relationships apart from their physical storage representation. The sequential, indexed, and relative file structures that we have considered in this book are called *flat files*. In flat file structure, if each column represents a data field, then each row represents a record. Other types of logical data structures described in this chapter are tree hierarchies, networks, and the relational model.

In *hierarchical tree structures* the element at the head of the tree is called the *root,* while all other elements, which are hierarchically lower, are called *nodes.* In such a structure a *parent* can have more than one *child,* but a child cannot have more than one parent. In the *network structure* a parent can have more than one child, and a child *can* have more than one parent. For *relational models* the relation of interest can always be represented as a two-dimensional table.

Physical data structure is concerned with the actual storage representation of data, and data relationships. A *pointer* is a data item whose value indicates the storage location of some other record. The type of one-dimensional table structure that can be described as a Last-In, First-Out (LIFO) system is the *stack structure.* The type of one-dimensional table structure that can be described as a First-In, First-Out (FIFO) system is the *queue structure.* In the *simple list structure,* or *chain,* if there is only one pointer per record, that pointer usually identifies the immediately succeeding record. Finally, the type of list chain structure in which one or more records in the chain point to the head record is called a *ring.* The example COBOL program in the chapter illustrates the application of pointer concepts to form a forward and backward chain, in order to sort the records in a table in both ascending and descending order.

File inversion through appropriate *indexing* is a data structure that facilitates efficient database interrogation. When indexes are created for some but not all of the attributes in the records, the file is said to be *partially inverted.* When indexes are available for all attributes, the file is said to be *fully inverted.* The objective underlying file inversion is to facilitate database interrogation *without* including redundancy in the file system.

The final section of this chapter was devoted to concepts concerned with *database management systems* because the various types of data structures described in this chapter find their most common use in such systems. The systems essentially are specialized types of software packages. *Host-language systems* are enhancements of procedure-oriented languages such as COBOL. On the other hand, the *self-contained systems* use their own language rules and are unique procedure-oriented languages directed toward file management. The general advantage of using a self-contained commercial database management system is that it minimizes the amount of individual program development in the organization.

EXERCISES

25.1   Differentiate the concepts of logical data structure and physical data structure in the design of a database information system.

25.2   Give some examples of different logical data structures, and describe some of the differences among these structures.

25.3   Various types of pointer structures provide the physical basis for implementing logical data relationships in computer storage. Describe some of the common pointer structures that are available.

25.4   What is the main objective associated with file inversion? Describe how this objective is achieved.

25.5   What are "database management systems"? Describe the nature and availability of such systems at the present time, and the likely direction of future developments in this area.

25.6 Revise the sample program in Figure 25-18 to incorporate deletions as well as additions. Assume the source file records have the following format:

```
01  IN-RECORD.
       02 TRANS-CODE         PIC X.
          88 ADD-REC         VALUE 'A'.
          88 DELETE-REC      VALUE 'D'.
       02 KEY-FIELD-IN       PIC 9(4).
       02 REC-DATA-IN        PIC X(75).
```

To implement deletions, create a new chain whose head is in NEXT-PLACE. Initialize the table so that the SUCCESSOR values are 2, 3, 4, ... , 50, 0, while NEXT-PLACE is equal to 1. Thus, starting with the value in NEXT-PLACE (which initially has a value of 1), the chain of empty records is at locations 1, 2, 3, ... , 50. The successor of the 50th record is set to zero, indicating that there is no other empty record.

When you delete a record, place that record location as the head of the empty-record chain. Suppose that we have the following records:

RECORD LOCATION	KEY-FIELD	PREDECESSOR	SUCCESSOR
.	.	.	.
.	.	.	.
10	MARY	13	08
.	.	.	.
13	JOHN	33	10
.	.	.	.
.	.	.	.
33	ANN	40	13

We are about to delete the record at 13. Assume NEXT-PLACE = 17. We would MOVE NEXT-PLACE TO SUCCESSOR (13) and we would MOVE 13 TO NEXT-PLACE. Of course, the PREDECESSOR and SUCCESSOR values of the records at 10 and 33 also need to be adjusted to effect the deletion.

26

A Comprehensive File Processing Example

IN THIS CHAPTER *you will study a programming task that involves all three file organization methods:* **sequential,** **indexed,** *and* **relative.** *The main purpose of this "capstone" example is to demonstrate a simplified information system that includes more than one program and more than one type of file.*

OVERVIEW OF THE TASK

The basic task involves maintenance of a student master file and the processing of the enrollment of students in classes.

There are two master files: A *student master file* organized as a relative file based on a unique student-ID field, and a *class master file* that contains information about classes being offered during the semester of enrollment. The class master is an *indexed file,* whose primary key is the class "line number" that identifies each class uniquely.

There are two basic processing tasks. First, there is a transaction file containing updates to the student master file. When these transactions are processed, the student master is updated and an exception report is produced to identify any errors that are detected. Then, after the student master is updated, there is another transaction file that contains data about registration requests submitted by students. These requests contain information regarding the classes that have been requested by the students through their registration forms. Classes have a fixed capacity, so not all enrollment requests can be processed. Finally, each student is billed for his/her enrollment.

Figure 26-1 outlines the relationships between each task and the respective files.

STUDENT MASTER UPDATE

The student master file consists of the following records:

FIELD	COLUMNS	
Student ID Number	01–09	
Name	10–24	
Address	25–57	
Street	25–40	
City	41–50	
State	51–52	
Zip	53–57	
Telephone	58–64	
Class	65–66	(Fr,So,Jr,Sr)
Major	67–69	
GPA (Grade Point Average)	70–72	(PIC 9V99)
Balance	73–78	(PIC S9(4)V99) (+ = owe school) (– = refund)
Credit Hours	79–80	
Record Status	81	(0 = Vacant) (1 = Occupied) (2 = Deleted)

This student master file is a relative file consisting of a maximum of 20 record spaces. (Allocating 20 record spaces to a file is unrealistically small; however, in a learning environment, it allows us to visually inspect the file to review processing, etc.) The *relative key* is obtained by hashing the student ID number—we divide it by the prime number 19, then add 1 to the remainder.

Before class registration for a new semester begins, student records are updated. As a result of the registration process, new students will be added to the file, while the records of former students will be removed. Names, phone numbers,

FIGURE 26-1
Overview of the File Processing
Tasks

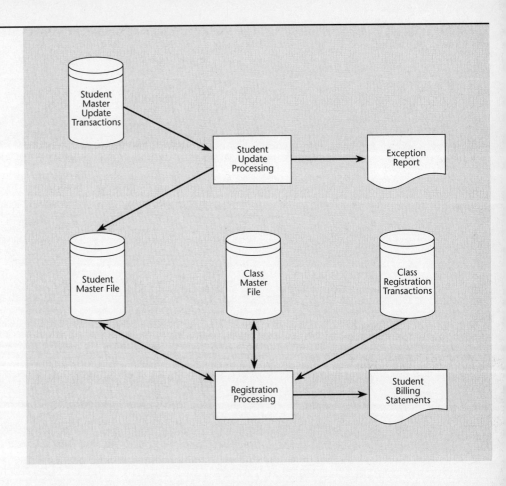

addresses, classes, majors, and GPAs (Grade Point Averages) will be updated, and the amount of money that a student owes to the school will be added (loan) or subtracted (payment of loan and/or scholarship).

Even the student identification number may be changed in the update process. (In some cases, such as with a foreign student, a temporary student ID is first assigned, and later a permanent ID is issued.) We handle such cases by first performing a "delete" and then an "add" transaction, making sure, of course, to save the original student information somewhere before deleting the record.

Transactions to update the student master file are of *four main types: Add* a new student; *Change* the record of an existing student; *Adjust* the balance amount; and *Delete* the record of a student. Actually, Change transactions may involve changes to any one of a number of fields, as indicated below. Notice that transaction codes are designated by a *two-digit code* such as 10 for an ADD type.

Student Master Update Transactions:

	FIXED PORTION	COLUMNS
	Trans. Code	01–02
	Student ID	03–11

TRANS CODE	VARIABLE PORTION	
10: ADD	Name	12–26
	Address	27–59
	Phone	60–66

TRANS CODE	VARIABLE PORTION	COLUMNS
	Class	67–68
	Major	69–71
	GPA	72–74
	Balance	75–80

(When adding a new student, Credit Hours is set to a 0 value and the Record Status is set to 1)

CHANGE

21: ID	New ID	12–20
22: Name	New Name	12–26
23: Addrs	New Address	12–44
24: Phone	New Phone	12–18
25: Class	New Class	12–13
26: Major	New Major	12–14
27: GPA	New GPA	12–14

ADJUST BALANCE (amount owed to school)

31: Increase   Amount added to balance

                    12–17 (PIC 9(4)V99)

32: Decrease   Amount subtracted from balance

                    12–17 (PIC 9(4)V99)

DELETE

40: Delete the student record

As the student records are updated, we generate a report that contains all the transactions that cannot be processed because of the following conditions.

1. Adding an existing student

2. Changing a nonexisting student

3. Deleting a nonexisting student

When one of these conditions is true, then the transaction is not processed, and a message that explains the problem along with the transaction record is printed in the exception summary report.

Figure 26-2 presents a listing of the initial contents of the student master file. Again, we have purposely limited the file size to 20 record positions so you can engage in visual review of individual records in the file.

Figure 26-3 presents a listing of the student transaction records involved in the sample student master update processing.

Figure 26-4 presents a program that updates the student master file. A *case structure* is used in 200-PROCESS-TRANS to EVALUATE the type of transaction. When there is a new student record to be added, we execute 300-ADD-RECORD, which reads the home address (310-RANDOMIZE-READ) and then iterates 320-FIND-SPACE-AND-WRITE until either we add the new record or we encounter an exception. In 320-FIND-SPACE-AND-WRITE, the condition-names NEVER-MET-

FIGURE 26-2

Initial Contents of the Student Master File

```
STUDENT MASTER FILE

922203456DAVID CHEUNG     324 N EMERSON    MESA      AZ852018342171SRACC400000000001
123065433SYLVESTER LEE  1123 APACHE BLVDTEMPE       AZ852879351023SRMKT310000000001
230886121MALISSA S BROWN4056 ELLIOT ROADCHANDLER    AZ853028683821FRECN350036030001
337820421JOHN BIGGS     1524 W CAMELBACKPHOENIX     AZ852348162438SRCIS333000000001
000000000                                                                          0
000000000                                                                          0
523098278EVONNE MECHUM  8284 CENTRAL AVEGLENDALE     AZ853139224321JRACC248002000001
000000000                                                                          0
000000000                                                                          0
000000000                                                                          0
000000000                                                                          0
472215903MIKE HOSSACK    323 W 1ST ST     THATCHER   AZ855237042826FRCIS299000000001
502447621ANNDEE SELKIRK 1024 E EXTENSIONMESA        AZ852038282716JRCIS389000000001
621023487KATHLEEN MCKAY 290 W 8TH AVE    MESA       AZ852088350982SOMGT399000000001
445320418CHUCK K GOODMAN3042 RURAL ROAD SCOTTSDALEAZ852549474502SOMGT234010200001
000000000                                                                          0
000000000                                                                          0
920346527MOHAMMAD AFAR   1028 E LEMON #4 TEMPE       AZ852849355336FRMKT102000000001
992043712CHIN CHON CHUNG628 MILL AVE #22TEMPE       AZ852899523412JRCIS289000000001
000000000                                                                          0
```

DELETE and MET-DELETE are used to keep track of whether we have or have not encountered a location whose status is "deleted." Recall, from Chapter 21, that in adding a record to a relative file we employ a procedure for checking for the possibility that the record about to be added already exists in the file by virtue of an existing record having the same student ID number. Thus we must search the file until we find a "vacant" record location. If we encounter such a vacancy before we encounter any "deleted" location, then we add the record at that vacancy. If, however, we encounter a deleted location, we save that LOCATION-ADDRESS in STARTING-ADDRESS, we SET MET-DELETE TO TRUE, and we continue looking for the first vacancy to guarantee that there is no duplicate record in the file. The record is added either in the first encountered "deleted" location, or the first vacancy if it occurs before any "deleted" location.

A fairly large number of "flag" fields are used in this program, as can be seen by reviewing the beginning of the WORKING-STORAGE SECTION. There are a number of possible conditions requiring conditional logic in this task and, as usual, flag fields provide a way of "remembering" or recognizing the set of conditions that prevail at a point in time. To follow the logic of this and similar programs, you need to spend some time becoming familiar with the definition and purpose of these flags. We hope that we have used names that are mnemonic enough to be recognized as to their purpose.

Because there is a large number of "change" type of transactions, we have set up a separate procedure, 420-MOVE-CHANGE-FIELDS, to handle the appropriate case logic. A special case (transaction code = 21) involves a change in the student

FIGURE 26-3
Listing of the Student Transaction Records

```
STUDENT TRANSACTION FILE

10326894037CAROL JOHNSON  949 W MAIN    MESA      AZ852078462033FRMKT000000000
22502447621ANNDEE BUYKIRK
31523098278200000
10472540205LONEY RANGER   1024 SILVER RD TOMBSTONE AZ892315522300FRCIS000000000
40123065432
40123065433
40230886121
31472540205125000
26326894037PED
25558645810FR
10472540205LONEY RANGER   1024 SILVER RD TOMBSTONE AZ892315522300FRCIS000000000
10558645810TONTO REDMAN   2861 SCOUT RD  APACHE JCTAZ850289863347JRACC228000000
21920346572
21920346527621508745
10228659871CONNIE CHUNG   3459 CAMELBACK  SCOTTSDALEAZ852659233485SRCIS395000000
242286598618203452
40621023487
10600619097ROB DOLE       4577 S 315T    PHOENIX   AZ852778839924SOACC103000000
21992043712468724313
22992043712CHIN CHON CHUNG
22468724313CHIN CHON CHUNG
25123065433JR
25230886121SO
25337820421JR
25472215903SO
25502447621SR
25445320418JR
25621508745SO
27502447621377
27445320418300
27337820421344
27468724313224
234687243132332 BASELINE RDTEMPE      AZ85383
32922203456065000
31337820421050000
32502447621030000
32445320418020000
32621508745100000
32230886121035000
```

identifier number. We PERFORM 421-SAVE-RECORD to save the original record in storage temporarily, we mark the original record as deleted, and then we PERFORM 300-ADD-RECORD as if the old saved record is a new record (having already, of course, changed the STUD-ID to its new value).

When a record is to be deleted, we process it in 500-DELETE-RECORD. We PERFORM 410-FIND-RECORD and, if the record is found, we change its STUD-REC-STATUS to a value of 2, signifying that it is a deleted record. Then we

FIGURE 26-4
The Progam to Update the
Student Master File

```
             IDENTIFICATION DIVISION.
             PROGRAM-ID. STUD-MAST-UPDATE.
      *
             ENVIRONMENT DIVISION.
             CONFIGURATION SECTION.
             SOURCE-COMPUTER. IBM-3090.
             OBJECT-COMPUTER. IBM-3090.
      *
             INPUT-OUTPUT SECTION.
      *
             FILE-CONTROL.
      *
                 SELECT STUDENT-MAS-FILE ASSIGN TO RELFILE
                     ORGANIZATION IS RELATIVE
                     ACCESS IS DYNAMIC
                     RELATIVE KEY IS LOCATION-ADDRESS.
                 SELECT STUDENT-TRANS-FILE ASSIGN TO TCARDS.
                 SELECT EXCEPTION-SUMMARY-REPORT ASSIGN TO ERROR1.
      *
             DATA DIVISION.
      *
             FILE SECTION.
      *
             FD  STUDENT-MAS-FILE
                     DATA RECORD IS STUD-REC.
      *
             01  STUD-REC.
                 02  STUD-ID                      PIC 9(09).
                 02  STUD-NAME                    PIC X(15).
                 02  STUD-ADDRESS.
                     03  STUD-STREET              PIC X(16).
                     03  STUD-CITY                PIC X(10).
                     03  STUD-STATE               PIC X(02).
                     03  STUD-ZIP                 PIC X(05).
                 02  STUD-PHONE                   PIC X(07).
                 02  STUD-CLASS                   PIC X(02).
                 02  STUD-MAJOR                   PIC X(03).
                 02  STUD-GPA                     PIC 9V99.
                 02  STUD-BALANCE                 PIC S9(4)V99.
                 02  STUD-CR-HRS                  PIC 9(02).
                 02  STUD-REC-STATUS              PIC 9.
                     88  VACANT-REC               VALUE 0.
                     88  OCCUPIED-REC             VALUE 1.
                     88  DELETED-REC              VALUE 2.
      *
             FD  STUDENT-TRANS-FILE
                     LABEL RECORDS ARE STANDARD
                     DATA RECORDS ARE   TRANS-REC, TRANS-REC10, TRANS-REC21,
                                        TRANS-REC22, TRANS-REC23, TRANS-REC24,
                                        TRANS-REC25, TRANS-REC26, TRANS-REC27,
                                        TRANS-REC30.
```

FIGURE 26-4

The Progam to Update the
Student Master File (continued)

```
      *
       01  TRANS-REC.
           02  TRANS-CODE.
               03  TRANS-CODE1              PIC 9(01).
                   88  ADD-REC              VALUE 1.
                   88  CHG-REC              VALUE 2.
                   88  CHG-BAL              VALUE 3.
                   88  DEL-REC              VALUE 4.
               03  TRANS-CODE2              PIC 9(01).
           02  T-STUD-ID                    PIC 9(09).
           02  FILLER                       PIC X(69).
      *
       01  TRANS-REC10.
           02  FILLER                       PIC X(11).
           02  T-STUD-NAME                  PIC X(15).
           02  T-STUD-ADDRESS               PIC X(33).
           02  T-STUD-PHONE                 PIC X(07).
           02  T-STUD-CLASS                 PIC X(02).
           02  T-STUD-MAJOR                 PIC X(03).
           02  T-STUD-GPA                   PIC 9V99.
           02  T-STUD-BALANCE               PIC S9(4)V99.
      *
       01  TRANS-REC21.
           02  FILLER                       PIC X(11).
           02  T-STUD-NEW-ID                PIC 9(09).
           02  FILLER                       PIC X(60).
      *
       01  TRANS-REC22.
           02  FILLER                       PIC X(11).
           02  T-STUD-NEW-NAME              PIC X(15).
           02  FILLER                       PIC X(54).
      *
       01  TRANS-REC23.
           02  FILLER                       PIC X(11).
           02  T-STUD-NEW-ADDRESS           PIC X(33).
           02  FILLER                       PIC X(36).
      *
       01  TRANS-REC24.
           02  FILLER                       PIC X(11).
           02  T-STUD-NEW-PHONE             PIC X(07).
           02  FILLER                       PIC X(62).
      *
       01  TRANS-REC25.
           02  FILLER                       PIC X(11).
           02  T-STUD-NEW-CLASS             PIC X(02).
           02  FILLER                       PIC X(67).
      *
       01  TRANS-REC26.
           02  FILLER                       PIC X(11).
           02  T-STUD-NEW-MAJOR             PIC X(03).
           02  FILLER                       PIC X(66).
```

FIGURE 26-4

*The Progam to Update the
Student Master File (continued)*

```
*
 01  TRANS-REC27.
     02  FILLER                      PIC X(11).
     02  T-STUD-NEW-GPA              PIC 9V99.
     02  FILLER                      PIC X(66).
*
 01  TRANS-REC30.
     02  FILLER                      PIC X(11).
     02  T-STUD-ADJ-AMT              PIC 9(4)V99.
     02  FILLER                      PIC X(63).
*
 FD  EXCEPTION-SUMMARY-REPORT
         LABEL RECORDS ARE STANDARD
         DATA RECORD IS ERROR-REC.
*
 01  ERROR-REC                       PIC X(132).
*
 WORKING-STORAGE SECTION.
*
 01  FLAGS.
     02  END-OF-TRANS-FLAG           PIC X(03)  VALUE 'NO '.
         88  END-OF-TRANS            VALUE 'YES'.
         88  NOT-END-OF-TRANS        VALUE 'NO '.
*
     02  LOOP-FLAG                   PIC X(03)  VALUE 'NO '.
         88  FILE-IS-FULL            VALUE 'YES'.
         88  FILE-IS-NOT-FULL        VALUE 'NO '.
         88  FILE-IS-DONE            VALUE 'XXX'.
*
     02  READ-VALIDITY-FLAG          PIC 9.
         88  VALID-READ              VALUE ZERO.
         88  INVALID-READ            VALUE 1.
*
     02  WRITE-VALIDITY-FLAG         PIC 9.
         88  VALID-WRITE             VALUE ZERO.
         88  INVALID-WRITE           VALUE 1.
*
     02  RECORD-FOUND-FLAG           PIC 9.
         88  RECORD-FOUND            VALUE ZERO.
         88  RECORD-NOT-FOUND        VALUE 1.
         88  STILL-LOOKING           VALUE 2.
*
     02  ADD-REC-FLAG                PIC 9.
         88  RECORD-ADDED            VALUE ZERO.
         88  RECORD-NOT-ADDED        VALUE 1.
*
     02  CHANGE-FLAG                 PIC 9.
         88  VALID-CHANGE            VALUE ZERO.
         88  INVALID-CHANGE          VALUE 1.
         88  VALID-CHANGE-DONE       VALUE 2.
```

FIGURE 26-4

The Progam to Update the
Student Master File (continued)

```
*
          02  DELETE-ENCOUNTER-FLAG          PIC 9 VALUE 1.
              88  NEVER-MET-DELETE           VALUE 0.
              88  MET-DELETE                 VALUE 1.
*
  01  LOCATION-ADDRESS                       PIC 99.
  01  STARTING-ADDRESS                       PIC 99.
  01  PRIME-NUMBER                           PIC 99  VALUE 19.
  01  WORKFIELD                              PIC S9(09).
  01  QUOTIENT                               PIC S9(07).
  01  MAX-NO-OF-LOCATIONS                    PIC 99  VALUE 20.
*
  01  HOLD-CHANGE-REC.
      02  HOLD-STUD-ID                       PIC 9(09).
      02  HOLD-REST                          PIC X(72).
*
* EXCEPTION REPORT FORMATS
*
  01  EXCEPTION-SUMMARY-FORMAT.
      02  E-HEAD1.
          03  FILLER                         PIC X(54)  VALUE SPACES.
          03  FILLER                         PIC X(24)  VALUE
              'EXCEPTION SUMMARY REPORT'.
          03  E-HEAD2.
          03  FILLER                         PIC X(10)  VALUE SPACES.
          03  FILLER                         PIC X(13)  VALUE
              'ERROR MESSAGE'.
          03  FILLER                         PIC X(27)  VALUE SPACES.
          03  FILLER                         PIC X(18)  VALUE
              'TRANSACTION RECORD'.
      02  E-HEAD3.
          03  FILLER                         PIC X(132) VALUE ALL '-'.
      02  E-BLANK.
          03  FILLER                         PIC X(132) VALUE SPACES.
      02  E-DETAIL.
          03  FILLER                         PIC X(10)  VALUE SPACES.
          03  ERROR-MESSAGE                  PIC X(40).
          03  ERROR-TRANS                    PIC X(82).
*
  PROCEDURE DIVISION.
*
  000-MAIN-ROUTINE.
      OPEN INPUT  STUDENT-TRANS-FILE
           OUTPUT EXCEPTION-SUMMARY-REPORT
           I-O    STUDENT-MAS-FILE.
*
      PERFORM 100-READ-TRANS.
      PERFORM 150-PRINT-HEADINGS.
      PERFORM 200-PROCESS-TRANS
          UNTIL END-OF-TRANS OR FILE-IS-FULL.
*
```

FIGURE 26-4

The Progam to Update the
Student Master File (continued)

```
            CLOSE STUDENT-TRANS-FILE
                  EXCEPTION-SUMMARY-REPORT
                  STUDENT-MAS-FILE.
    *
            STOP RUN.
    *
      100-READ-TRANS.
            READ STUDENT-TRANS-FILE RECORD
                AT END SET END-OF-TRANS TO TRUE.
    *
      150-PRINT-HEADINGS.
            WRITE ERROR-REC FROM E-HEAD1 AFTER PAGE
            WRITE ERROR-REC FROM E-HEAD2 AFTER 2 LINES
            WRITE ERROR-REC FROM E-HEAD3 AFTER 1 LINE
            WRITE ERROR-REC FROM E-BLANK AFTER 1 LINE.
    *
      200-PROCESS-TRANS.
            EVALUATE TRUE
                WHEN ADD-REC
                    PERFORM 300-ADD-RECORD
                WHEN CHG-REC
                    PERFORM 400-CHANGE-RECORD
                WHEN CHG-BAL
                    PERFORM 400-CHANGE-RECORD
                WHEN DEL-REC
                    PERFORM 500-DELETE-RECORD
                WHEN OTHER
                    MOVE 'INVALID TRANS CODE' TO ERROR-MESSAGE
                    PERFORM 322-PRINT-EXCEPTION-RECORD
            END-EVALUATE.
    *
            PERFORM 100-READ-TRANS.
    *
      300-ADD-RECORD.
            PERFORM 310-RANDOMIZE-READ.
            MOVE 1 TO ADD-REC-FLAG.
            MOVE ZERO TO READ-VALIDITY-FLAG.
    *
            SET NEVER-MET-DELETE TO TRUE.
            PERFORM 320-FIND-SPACE-AND-WRITE
                UNTIL RECORD-ADDED
                OR INVALID-READ
                OR FILE-IS-FULL
                OR FILE-IS-DONE.
            IF  MET-DELETE AND VALID-READ
                PERFORM 321-WRITE-NEW-REC.
    *
      310-RANDOMIZE-READ.
            MOVE T-STUD-ID TO WORKFIELD
            DIVIDE PRIME-NUMBER INTO WORKFIELD
                GIVING QUOTIENT
            COMPUTE LOCATION-ADDRESS = WORKFIELD -
                        (QUOTIENT * PRIME-NUMBER) + 1
            SET FILE-IS-NOT-FULL TO TRUE
            MOVE LOCATION-ADDRESS TO STARTING-ADDRESS
```

FIGURE 26-4

The Progam to Update the
Student Master File (continued)

```
*
        PERFORM 311-READ-MAS-REC.
*
 311-READ-MAS-REC.
    SET VALID-READ TO TRUE
    READ STUDENT-MAS-FILE RECORD
        INVALID KEY
           SET INVALID-READ TO TRUE
           MOVE 'THIS RECORD LOCATION CANNOT BE READ'
                  TO ERROR-MESSAGE
           PERFORM 322-PRINT-EXCEPTION-RECORD.
*
 320-FIND-SPACE-AND-WRITE.
    IF  VACANT-REC AND NEVER-MET-DELETE
        PERFORM 321-WRITE-NEW-REC
        MOVE ZERO TO ADD-REC-FLAG
    ELSE IF DELETED-REC AND NEVER-MET-DELETE
            SET MET-DELETE TO TRUE
            MOVE LOCATION-ADDRESS TO STARTING-ADDRESS
         ELSE IF (T-STUD-ID = STUD-ID) AND OCCUPIED-REC
                MOVE 'ADDING AN EXISTING STUDENT' TO
                      ERROR-MESSAGE
                PERFORM 322-PRINT-EXCEPTION-RECORD
                SET INVALID-READ TO TRUE
             ELSE
                PERFORM 323-HANDLE-SYNONYMS
             END-IF
        END-IF
    END-IF.
*
 321-WRITE-NEW-REC.
    MOVE 1 TO STUD-REC-STATUS
    MOVE 0 TO STUD-CR-HRS
    MOVE T-STUD-ID TO STUD-ID
    MOVE T-STUD-NAME TO STUD-NAME
    MOVE T-STUD-ADDRESS TO STUD-ADDRESS
    MOVE T-STUD-PHONE TO STUD-PHONE
    MOVE T-STUD-CLASS TO STUD-CLASS
    MOVE T-STUD-MAJOR TO STUD-MAJOR
    MOVE T-STUD-GPA TO STUD-GPA
    MOVE T-STUD-BALANCE TO STUD-BALANCE
    PERFORM 321A-WRITE-MAS-REC.
*
 321A-WRITE-MAS-REC.
    SET VALID-WRITE TO TRUE
    REWRITE STUD-REC
        INVALID KEY
           SET INVALID-WRITE TO TRUE
           MOVE 'THIS LOCATION CANNOT BE WRITTEN TO'
                  TO ERROR-MESSAGE
           PERFORM 322-PRINT-EXCEPTION-RECORD
    END-REWRITE.
```

FIGURE 26-4

*The Progam to Update the
Student Master File (continued)*

```
*
  322-PRINT-EXCEPTION-RECORD.
      MOVE TRANS-REC TO ERROR-TRANS
      WRITE ERROR-REC FROM E-DETAIL AFTER 2 LINES
      MOVE SPACES TO E-DETAIL.
*
  323-HANDLE-SYNONYMS.
      SET FILE-IS-NOT-FULL TO TRUE
      ADD 1 TO LOCATION-ADDRESS
      IF  LOCATION-ADDRESS > MAX-NO-OF-LOCATIONS
          MOVE 1 TO LOCATION-ADDRESS
      END-IF
*
      IF  LOCATION-ADDRESS = STARTING-ADDRESS
          IF  NEVER-MET-DELETE
              MOVE 'ENTIRE FILE READ FULL CIRCLE' TO
                    ERROR-MESSAGE
              PERFORM 322-PRINT-EXCEPTION-RECORD
              SET FILE-IS-FULL TO TRUE
          ELSE
              SET FILE-IS-DONE TO TRUE
          END-IF
      ELSE
          PERFORM 311-READ-MAS-REC
      END-IF.
*
  400-CHANGE-RECORD.
      SET STILL-LOOKING TO TRUE
      SET VALID-READ TO TRUE
      PERFORM 310-RANDOMIZE-READ.
      PERFORM 410-FIND-RECORD
            UNTIL RECORD-FOUND
            OR RECORD-NOT-FOUND
            OR INVALID-READ.
      IF RECORD-FOUND
          PERFORM 420-MOVE-CHANGE-FIELDS
          IF  VALID-CHANGE
              PERFORM 321A-WRITE-MAS-REC
          END-IF
      ELSE  IF RECORD-NOT-FOUND
              MOVE 'CHANGING NONEXISTING STUDENT'
                  TO ERROR-MESSAGE
              PERFORM 322-PRINT-EXCEPTION-RECORD
          END-IF
      END-IF.
*
```

FIGURE 26-4

*The Progam to Update the
Student Master File (continued)*

```
410-FIND-RECORD.
    IF  VALID-READ AND OCCUPIED-REC
        IF   T-STUD-ID = STUD-ID
            SET RECORD-FOUND TO TRUE
        ELSE
            PERFORM 323-HANDLE-SYNONYMS
            PERFORM 411-CHECK-FULL-CIRCLE
        END-IF
    ELSE
        IF  VALID-READ AND DELETED-REC
            PERFORM 323-HANDLE-SYNONYMS
            PERFORM 411-CHECK-FULL-CIRCLE
        ELSE
            IF  VALID-READ AND VACANT-REC
                SET RECORD-NOT-FOUND TO TRUE
            ELSE
                SET RECORD-NOT-FOUND TO TRUE
                MOVE 'STATUS CODE OF MASTER REC IS INVALID'
                    TO ERROR-MESSAGE
                PERFORM 322-PRINT-EXCEPTION-RECORD
            END-IF
        END-IF
    END-IF.
*
411-CHECK-FULL-CIRCLE.
    IF  FILE-IS-FULL
        SET RECORD-NOT-FOUND TO TRUE.
*
420-MOVE-CHANGE-FIELDS.
    SET VALID-CHANGE TO TRUE
*
    EVALUATE TRANS-CODE
        WHEN 21
                PERFORM 421-SAVE-RECORD
                PERFORM 300-ADD-RECORD
                SET VALID-CHANGE-DONE TO TRUE
        WHEN 22
            MOVE T-STUD-NEW-NAME TO STUD-NAME
        WHEN 23
            MOVE T-STUD-NEW-ADDRESS TO STUD-ADDRESS
        WHEN 24
            MOVE T-STUD-NEW-PHONE TO STUD-PHONE
        WHEN 25
            MOVE T-STUD-NEW-CLASS TO STUD-CLASS
        WHEN 26
            MOVE T-STUD-NEW-MAJOR TO STUD-MAJOR
        WHEN 27
            MOVE T-STUD-NEW-GPA TO STUD-GPA
        WHEN 31
            ADD T-STUD-ADJ-AMT TO STUD-BALANCE
        WHEN 32
            SUBTRACT T-STUD-ADJ-AMT FROM STUD-BALANCE
        WHEN OTHER
            SET INVALID-CHANGE TO TRUE
            MOVE 'INVALID CHANGE TRANS CODE' TO
                ERROR-MESSAGE
            PERFORM 322-PRINT-EXCEPTION-RECORD
    END-EVALUATE.
```

FIGURE 26-4

*The Progam to Update the
Student Master File (continued)*

```
*
    421-SAVE-RECORD.
        MOVE T-STUD-NEW-ID TO T-STUD-ID
        MOVE STUD-NAME TO T-STUD-NAME
        MOVE STUD-ADDRESS TO T-STUD-ADDRESS
        MOVE STUD-PHONE TO T-STUD-PHONE
        MOVE STUD-CLASS TO T-STUD-CLASS
        MOVE STUD-MAJOR TO T-STUD-MAJOR
        MOVE STUD-GPA TO T-STUD-GPA
        MOVE STUD-BALANCE TO T-STUD-BALANCE
        MOVE 2 TO STUD-REC-STATUS
        PERFORM 321A-WRITE-MAS-REC.
*
    500-DELETE-RECORD.
        SET STILL-LOOKING TO TRUE
        SET VALID-READ TO TRUE
*
        PERFORM 310-RANDOMIZE-READ
*
        PERFORM 410-FIND-RECORD
            UNTIL RECORD-FOUND
            OR RECORD-NOT-FOUND
            OR INVALID-READ.
*
        IF  RECORD-FOUND
            MOVE 2 TO STUD-REC-STATUS
            PERFORM 321A-WRITE-MAS-REC
        ELSE
            IF RECORD-NOT-FOUND
                MOVE 'DELETING NONEXISTING STUDENT' TO
                    ERROR-MESSAGE
                PERFORM 322-PRINT-EXCEPTION-RECORD
            END-IF
        END-IF.
```

PERFORM 321A-WRITE-MAS-REC to REWRITE the record so marked. As a further refinement, we could add logic to check if the immediately following record location was marked as vacant. If so, we could mark as vacant the location of the record to be deleted instead of marking it as deleted. The reasoning is that if the immediately following record is vacant, then marking as vacant the newly deleted location would be consistent with the reasons for which the distinction between "vacant" and "deleted" was made in the first place. You may want to so modify the program to incorporate this enhancement.

Figure 26-5 presents a listing of the updated master so that you can trace any or all of the transactions in Figure 26-3 against the original master file in Figure 26-2.

Finally, Figure 26-6 presents a copy of the EXCEPTION SUMMARY REPORT generated as a result of processing the transactions in Figure 26-3.

FIGURE 26-5

Contents of the Updated Student Master File Before Registration Processing

```
UPDATED STUDENT MASTER

922203456DAVID CHEUNG    324 N EMERSON    MESA      AZ852018342171SRACC40006500.001
558645810TONTO REDMAN    2861 SCOUT RD    APACHE JCTAZ850289863347JRACC228000000001
228659871CONNIE CHUNG    3459 CAMELBACK   SCOTTSDALEAZ852659233485SRCIS395000000001
337820421JOHN BIGGS      1524 W CAMELBACKPHOENIX    AZ852348162438JRCIS34405000.001
472540205LONEY RANGER    1024 SILVER RD   TOMBSTONE AZ892315522300FRCIS00012500.001
000000000                                                                         0
523098278EVONNE MECHUM   8284 CENTRAL AVEGLENDALE   AZ853139224321JRACC24820200.001
326894037CAROL JOHNSON   949 W MAIN       MESA      AZ852078462033FRPED000000000001
600619097ROB DOLE        4577 S 31ST      PHOENIX   AZ852778839924SOACC103000000001
000000000                                                                         0
000000000                                                                         0
472215903MIKE HOSSACK    323 W 1ST ST     THATCHER  AZ855237042826SOCIS299000000001
502447621ANNDEE BUYKIRK  1024 E EXTENSIONMESA       AZ852038282716SRCIS37703000.001
468724313CHIN CHON CHUN  2332 BASELINE RDTEMPE      AZ853839523412JRCIS224000000001
445320418CHUCK K GOODMAN3042 RURAL ROAD SCOTTSDALEAZ852549474502JRMGT30000980.001
621508745MOHAMMAD AFAR   1028 E LEMON #4 TEMPE      AZ852849355336SOMKT10210000.001
000000000                                                                         0
920346527MOHAMMAD AFAR   1028 E LEMON #4 TEMPE      AZ852849355336FRMKT102000000002
992043712CHIN CHON CHUNG628 MILL AVE #22TEMPE       AZ852899523412JRCIS289000000002
000000000                                                                         0
```

FIGURE 26-6

The Exception Summary Report

```
                                    EXCEPTION SUMMARY REPORT

    ERROR MESSAGE                    TRANSACTION RECORD
------------------------------------------------------------------------------------------

    DELETING NONEXISTING STUDENT     40123065432

    CHANGING NONEXISTING STUDENT     25558645810FR

    ADDING AN EXISTING STUDENT       10472540205LONEY RANGER    1024 SILVER RD   TOMBSTONE AZ892315

    CHANGING NONEXISTING STUDENT     21920346572

    CHANGING NONEXISTING STUDENT     242286598618203452

    CHANGING NONEXISTING STUDENT     22992043712CHIN CHON CHUN

    CHANGING NONEXISTING STUDENT     25123065433JR

    CHANGING NONEXISTING STUDENT     25230886121SO

    CHANGING NONEXISTING STUDENT     32230886121035000
```

REGISTRATION PROCESSING

After the student-record update, we are then ready for class registration. Information about classes is maintained in a *class master file,* which is an *indexed file,* and contains the following fields:

FIELD	COLUMNS
Class Line Number	01–05
Class Title	06–11
Credit Hours	12–13
Instructor	14–28
Time	29–37
Room	38–43
Seats Assigned	44–46
Seats Remaining	47–49

Registration is done on class request forms. Each request form can include a maximum of five requests, as follows:

FIELD	COLUMNS
Student ID	01–09
Number of Requests	10 (0–5)
Line Number	PIC X(05) Occurs 5 times (fixed)

The requests are processed in the same sequence as they are listed in each transaction record. (A class request form is considered a transaction, but each transaction can have up to five requests.) If the line number is not valid, or if the class is full, an appropriate message will be printed, along with the line number, on the billing statement.

When a course is requested, we update the seats-remaining field in the class file. If there are no seats remaining, the request for that class is not granted, and a message is printed along with the line number in the billing statement.

A billing statement is printed for each student, and as each class request (line number) is processed, the line number and class information for that class are printed on the billing statement. Each credit hour costs $65 up to 9 credit hours. Over 9 credit hours, a flat rate of $650.00 is applied. A student may have a beginning balance, so we make sure to include it when computing the new balance.

Figure 26-7 shows three sample billing statements that illustrate three different cases with respect to the balance field.

The Credit Hours field and the Balance field in the student master file also need to be updated when a transaction is processed. Thus, as can be seen in Figure 26-1, registration processing involves updating *both* the class and the student master file.

Figure 26-8 consists of a program listing that does the registration processing. Notice the RELATIVE and INDEXED organization of the STUDENT-MAS-FILE and the CLASS-MAS-FILE, respectively. Additionally, we have the sequential files for the transactions (REQUEST-FILE) and the bills (BILLING-FILE).

The 300-UPDATE-CLASS-RECORDS procedure is executed until all the registration request records have been input. First, we PERFORM 310-BILLING-REPORT-HEADINGS to obtain the name, address, and so forth, of the corresponding student record from the student master file. From 310-BILLING-REPORT-

FIGURE 26-7
Three Sample Billing Statements

```
DATE: 08/05/91          USA STATE UNIVERSITY SCHEDULE/BILLING STATEMENT

MIKE HOSSACK
323 W 1ST ST
THATCHER  , AZ 85523


========================================================================

              SCHEDULE/BILLING STATEMENT

    ACC222   23259   3       1140  MWF   BAC116      C. WHITE
    CIS200   13445   3       0940  MWF   BAC216      G. SMITH
    CIS420   14701   3       0840  MW    BA439       L. THOMPSON
    MGT301   43254   3       0740  TTH   BAC216      M. MAN
             58323   INVALID LINE NUMBER, CANNOT ADD

             TOTAL  12                    TUITION:     $650.00
                                      NEW BALANCE:     $650.00



_____


DATE: 08/05/91          USA STATE UNIVERSITY SCHEDULE/BILLING STATEMENT

DAVID CHEUNG
324 N EMERSON
MESA      , AZ 85201


========================================================================

              SCHEDULE/BILLING STATEMENT

    ACC351   24835   3       1040  TTH   BA258       W. TAX
             32250   INVALID LINE NUMBER, CANNOT ADD
    ECN102   32330   3       0940  MWF   BA212       P. PINK
    CIS420   14701   3       0840  MW    BA439       L. THOMPSON
    ECN101   31011   3       0840  MWF   BAC343      B. BROWN

             TOTAL  12                    TUITION:     $650.00
                                      NEW BALANCE:       $0.00



_____


DATE: 08/05/91          USA STATE UNIVERSITY SCHEDULE/BILLING STATEMENT

MOHAMMAD AFAR
1028 E LEMON #4
TEMPE     , AZ 85284


========================================================================

              SCHEDULE/BILLING STATEMENT

    ACC331   23737   3       1240  MWF   BA332       E. BLUE
    ACC501   29073   3       1215  TTH   BA218       H. ORANGE

             TOTAL   6                    TUITION:     $390.00
                                      NEW BALANCE:     $610.00CR
```

FIGURE 26-8

The Program to Do the
Registration Processing

```
            IDENTIFICATION DIVISION.
            PROGRAM-ID. CLASS-REG.
        *
            ENVIRONMENT DIVISION.
            CONFIGURATION SECTION.
            SOURCE-COMPUTER. IBM-3090.
            OBJECT-COMPUTER. IBM-3090.
        *
            INPUT-OUTPUT SECTION.
        *
            FILE-CONTROL.
        *
                SELECT STUDENT-MAS-FILE ASSIGN TO RELFILE
                    ORGANIZATION IS RELATIVE
                    ACCESS IS RANDOM
                    RELATIVE KEY IS LOCATION-ADDRESS.
                SELECT CLASS-MAS-FILE ASSIGN TO CLASMAS
                    ORGANIZATION IS INDEXED
                    ACCESS IS RANDOM
                    RECORD KEY IS LINE-NUMBER
                    FILE STATUS IS MASTER-FILE-STATUS.
                SELECT REQUEST-FILE ASSIGN TO RCARDS.
                SELECT BILLING-FILE ASSIGN TO BILLING.
        *
            DATA DIVISION.
        *
            FILE SECTION.
        *
            FD  STUDENT-MAS-FILE
                    DATA RECORD IS STUD-REC.
        *
            01  STUD-REC.
                02  STUD-ID            PIC 9(09).
                02  STUD-NAME          PIC X(15).
                02  STUD-ADDRESS.
                    03  STUD-STREET    PIC X(16).
                    03  STUD-CITY      PIC X(10).
                    03  STUD-STATE     PIC X(02).
                    03  STUD-ZIP       PIC X(05).
                02  STUD-PHONE         PIC X(07).
                02  STUD-CLASS         PIC X(02).
                02  STUD-MAJOR         PIC X(03).
                02  STUD-GPA           PIC 9V99.
                02  STUD-BALANCE       PIC S9(4)V99
                02  STUD-CR-HRS        PIC 9(02).
                02  STUD-REC-STATUS    PIC 9(01).
                    88  VACANT-REC     VALUE 0.
                    88  OCCUPIED-REC   VALUE 1.
                    88  DELETED-REC    VALUE 2.
```

FIGURE 26-8

*The Program to Do the
Registration Processing
(continued)*

```
*
   FD  CLASS-MAS-FILE
           DATA RECORD IS CLASS-REC.
*
   01  CLASS-REC.
       02  LINE-NUMBER              PIC X(05).
       02  CLASS-TITLE              PIC X(06).
       02  CR-HR                    PIC 9(02).
       02  INSTRUCTOR               PIC X(15).
       02  CLASS-DAYS               PIC X(04).
       02  CLASS-TIME               PIC X(04).
       02  FILLER                   PIC X(01).
       02  CLASS-ROOM               PIC X(06).
       02  SEATS-ASSIGNED           PIC 9(03).
       02  SEATS-REMAINING          PIC 9(03).
*
   FD  REQUEST-FILE
           LABEL RECORDS ARE STANDARD
           DATA RECORD IS REQUEST-REC.
*
   01  REQUEST-REC.
       02  R-STUD-ID                PIC 9(09).
       02  R-NUM-OF-REQUESTS        PIC 9(01).
       02  R-REQUESTS               OCCURS 5 TIMES.
           03  R-LINE-NUMBER        PIC X(05).
       02  FILLER                   PIC X(45).
*
   FD  BILLING-FILE
       LABEL RECORDS ARE STANDARD
       DATA RECORD IS BILLING-REC.
*
   01  BILLING-REC                  PIC X(132).
*
*
   WORKING-STORAGE SECTION.
*
   01  FLAGS.
       02  END-OF-REQUEST-FLAG      PIC X(03) VALUE 'NO '.
           88  END-OF-REQUEST           VALUE 'YES'.
           88  NOT-END-OF-REQUEST       VALUE 'NO '.
*
       02  LOOP-FLAG                PIC X(03) VALUE 'NO '.
           88  FILE-IS-FULL             VALUE 'YES'.
           88  FILE-IS-NOT-FULL         VALUE 'NO '.
*
       02  READ-VALIDITY-FLAG       PIC 9.
           88  VALID-READ               VALUE ZERO.
           88  INVALID-READ             VALUE 1.
*
       02  WRITE-VALIDITY-FLAG      PIC 9.
           88  VALID-WRITE              VALUE ZERO.
           88  INVALID-WRITE            VALUE 1.
```

```
*
            02  RECORD-FOUND-FLAG               PIC 9.
                88  RECORD-FOUND               VALUE ZERO.
                88  RECORD-NOT-FOUND           VALUE 1.
                88  STILL-LOOKING              VALUE 2.
*
            02  ADD-REC-FLAG                   PIC 9.
                88  RECORD-ADDED               VALUE ZERO.
                88  RECORD-NOT-ADDED           VALUE 1.
*
            02  CHANGE-FLAG                    PIC 9.
                88  VALID-CHANGE               VALUE ZERO.
                88  INVALID-CHANGE             VALUE 1.
*
            02  MASTER-FILE-STATUS             PIC X(02) VALUE ZERO.
                88  READ-FINE                  VALUE '00'.
                88  NO-RECORD                  VALUE '23'.
                88  EOF-MASTER                 VALUE '10'.
*
        01  TUITION                            PIC 9(3).
            88  PART-TIME                      VALUE 65.
            88  FULL-TIME                      VALUE 650.
*
        01  LOCATION-ADDRESS                   PIC 99.
        01  STARTING-ADDRESS                   PIC 99.
        01  PRIME-NUMBER                       PIC 99   VALUE 19.
        01  WORKFIELD                          PIC S9(09).
        01  QUOTIENT                           PIC S9(07).
        01  MAX-NO-OF-LOCATIONS                PIC 99   VALUE 20.
        01  SUBSCRIPT                          PIC 9.
        01  TOTAL-CR-HRS                       PIC 99   VALUE ZERO.
        01  TOTAL-BALANCE                      PIC S9(4)V99.
        01  PART-TIME-FEE                      PIC 9(03).
*
        01  WS-DATE.
            02  WS-YR                          PIC 9(02).
            02  WS-MO                          PIC 9(02).
            02  WS-DAY                         PIC 9(02).
*
* OUTPUT RECORD DESCRIPTIONS:
*
        01  BILLING-DETAIL-FORMAT.
            02  B-BLANK-LINE.
                03  FILLER                     PIC X(132) VALUE SPACES.
            02  B-DOUBLE-LINE.
                03  FILLER                     PIC X(10)  VALUE SPACES.
                03  FILLER                     PIC X(70)  VALUE ALL '='.
*
```

FIGURE 26-8

The Program to Do the Registration Processing (continued)

```
02  B-HEAD1.
    03  FILLER                  PIC X(10)  VALUE SPACES.
    03  FILLER                  PIC X(06)  VALUE 'DATE:'.
    03  B-MONTH                 PIC 9(02).
    03  FILLER                  PIC X(01)  VALUE '/'.
    03  B-DAY                   PIC 9(02).
    03  FILLER                  PIC X(01)  VALUE '/'.
    03  B-YEAR                  PIC 9(02).
    03  FILLER                  PIC X(09)  VALUE SPACES.
    03  FILLER                  PIC X(21)  VALUE
        'USA STATE UNIVERSITY'.
    03  FILLER                  PIC X(26)  VALUE
        'SCHEDULE/BILLING STATEMENT'.
02  B-HEAD2.
    03  FILLER                  PIC X(33)  VALUE SPACES.
    03  FILLER                  PIC X(26)  VALUE
        'SCHEDULE/BILLING STATEMENT'.
02  B-HEAD3.
    03  FILLER                  PIC X(19) VALUE SPACES.
    03  FILLER                  PIC X(09) VALUE 'COURSE'.
    03  FILLER                  PIC X(06) VALUE 'LINE'.
    03  FILLER                  PIC X(07) VALUE 'HRS'.
    03  FILLER                  PIC X(10) VALUE 'OPT TIME'.
    03  FILLER                  PIC X(06) VALUE 'DAYS'.
    03  FILLER                  PIC X(13) VALUE
        'BLDG/ROOM'.
    03  FILLER                  PIC X(10) VALUE
        'INSTRUCTOR'.
02  B-ADDRESS1.
    03  FILLER                  PIC X(10) VALUE SPACES.
    03  B-STUD-NAME             PIC X(15).
02  B-ADDRESS2.
    03  FILLER                  PIC X(10) VALUE SPACES.
    03  B-STUD-STREET           PIC X(16).
02  B-ADDRESS3.
    03  FILLER                  PIC X(10) VALUE SPACES.
    03  B-STUD-CITY             PIC X(10).
    03  FILLER                  PIC X(02) VALUE ', '.
    03  B-STUD-STATE            PIC X(02).
    03  FILLER                  PIC X(01) VALUE SPACES.
    03  B-STUD-ZIP              PIC X(05)
02  B-DETAIL1.
    03  FILLER                  PIC X(19) VALUE SPACES.
    03  B-CLASS-TITLE           PIC X(06).
    03  FILLER                  PIC X(03) VALUE SPACES.
    03  B-LINE-NUMBER1          PIC X(05).
    03  FILLER                  PIC X(02) VALUE SPACES.
    03  B-CR-HR                 PIC Z9.
    03  FILLER                  PIC X(08) VALUE SPACES.
    03  B-CLASS-TIME            PIC X(04).
    03  FILLER                  PIC X(02) VALUE SPACES.
    03  B-CLASS-DAYS            PIC X(05).
    03  FILLER                  PIC X(01) VALUE SPACES.
    03  B-CLASS-ROOM            PIC X(06).
    03  FILLER                  PIC X(07) VALUE SPACES.
    03  B-INSTRUCTOR            PIC X(15).
```

FIGURE 26-8
The Program to Do the
Registration Processing
(continued)

```
        02  B-DETAIL2.
            03  FILLER                PIC X(28) VALUE SPACES.
            03  B-LINE-NUMBER2        PIC X(05).
            03  FILLER                PIC X(03) VALUE SPACES.
            03  B-ERROR-MESSAGE       PIC X(35).
        02  B-TOTAL-LN1.
            03  FILLER                PIC X(28) VALUE SPACES.
            03  FILLER                PIC X(07) VALUE 'TOTAL'.
            03  B-TOTAL-HOURS         PIC Z9.
            03  FILLER                PIC X(24) VALUE SPACES.
            03  FILLER                PIC X(10) VALUE
                'TUITION:'.
            03  B-STUD-TUITION        PIC $$,$$9.99.
        02  B-TOTAL-LN2.
            03  FILLER                PIC X(57) VALUE SPACES.
            03  FILLER                PIC X(14) VALUE
                'NEW BALANCE:'.
            03  B-STUD-BALANCE        PIC $$,$$9.99CR.
*
    PROCEDURE DIVISION.
*
    000-MAIN-ROUTINE.
        PERFORM 100-INITIALIZATION.
        PERFORM 200-READ-REQUEST-REC.
        PERFORM 300-UPDATE-CLASS-RECORDS
            UNTIL END-OF-REQUEST.
        CLOSE STUDENT-MAS-FILE
              CLASS-MAS-FILE
              REQUEST-FILE
              BILLING-FILE.
        STOP RUN.
*
    100-INITIALIZATION.
        OPEN I-O  STUDENT-MAS-FILE
             I-O  CLASS-MAS-FILE
             INPUT REQUEST-FILE
             OUTPUT BILLING-FILE.
        ACCEPT WS-DATE FROM DATE.
        MOVE WS-YR TO B-YEAR.
        MOVE WS-MO TO B-MONTH.
        MOVE WS-DAY TO B-DAY.
*
    200-READ-REQUEST-REC.
        READ REQUEST-FILE AT END
             SET END-OF-REQUEST TO TRUE.
*
```

FIGURE 26-8

*The Program to Do the
Registration Processing
(continued)*

```
300-UPDATE-CLASS-RECORDS.
    PERFORM 310-BILLING-REPORT-HEADINGS
    MOVE ZERO TO TOTAL-CR-HRS
    PERFORM 320-UPDATE-CLASSES
        VARYING SUBSCRIPT FROM 1 BY 1
        UNTIL SUBSCRIPT > R-NUM-OF-REQUESTS.
    IF  TOTAL-CR-HRS > 9
        ADD 650 TO TOTAL-BALANCE
        MOVE 650 TO B-STUD-TUITION
    ELSE
        COMPUTE PART-TIME-FEE = 65 * TOTAL-CR-HRS
        MOVE PART-TIME-FEE TO B-STUD-TUITION
        ADD PART-TIME-FEE TO TOTAL-BALANCE
    END-IF
    MOVE TOTAL-CR-HRS TO B-TOTAL-HOURS
    WRITE BILLING-REC FROM B-TOTAL-LN1 AFTER 2
    MOVE TOTAL-BALANCE TO B-STUD-BALANCE
    WRITE BILLING-REC FROM B-TOTAL-LN2
    PERFORM 330-UPDATE-STUD-REC
    PERFORM 200-READ-REQUEST-REC.
*
310-BILLING-REPORT-HEADINGS.
    WRITE BILLING-REC FROM B-HEAD1 AFTER PAGE
    SET STILL-LOOKING TO TRUE
    SET VALID-READ TO TRUE
    PERFORM 311-RANDOMIZE-READ
    PERFORM 313-FIND-MATCH
        UNTIL RECORD-FOUND
        OR RECORD-NOT-FOUND
        OR INVALID-READ.
    IF  RECORD-FOUND
        MOVE STUD-NAME TO B-STUD-NAME
        MOVE STUD-STREET TO B-STUD-STREET
        MOVE STUD-CITY TO B-STUD-CITY
        MOVE STUD-STATE TO B-STUD-STATE
        MOVE STUD-ZIP TO B-STUD-ZIP
        MOVE STUD-BALANCE TO TOTAL-BALANCE
        WRITE BILLING-REC FROM B-ADDRESS1 AFTER 2
        WRITE BILLING-REC FROM B-ADDRESS2 AFTER 1
        WRITE BILLING-REC FROM B-ADDRESS3 AFTER 1
        WRITE BILLING-REC FROM B-DOUBLE-LINE AFTER 2
        WRITE BILLING-REC FROM B-HEAD2 AFTER 2
        WRITE BILLING-REC FROM B-BLANK-LINE
        SET VALID-WRITE TO TRUE
    ELSE
        SET INVALID-WRITE TO TRUE
    END-IF.
*
```

FIGURE 26-8

The Program to Do the Registration Processing (continued)

```
311-RANDOMIZE-READ.
    MOVE R-STUD-ID TO WORKFIELD
    DIVIDE PRIME-NUMBER INTO WORKFIELD
        GIVING QUOTIENT
    COMPUTE LOCATION-ADDRESS = WORKFIELD -
            (QUOTIENT * PRIME-NUMBER) + 1
    SET FILE-IS-NOT-FULL TO TRUE
    MOVE LOCATION-ADDRESS TO STARTING-ADDRESS
    PERFORM 312-READ-MAS-REC.
*
312-READ-MAS-REC.
    SET VALID-READ TO TRUE
    READ STUDENT-MAS-FILE RECORD
       INVALID KEY
          SET INVALID-READ TO TRUE
          DISPLAY 'THIS RECORD LOCATION CANNOT BE READ'.
*
313-FIND-MATCH.
    IF  VALID-READ AND OCCUPIED-REC
        IF   R-STUD-ID = STUD-ID
             SET RECORD-FOUND TO TRUE
        ELSE
             PERFORM 313A-HANDLE-SYNONYMS
             PERFORM 313B-CHECK-FULL-CIRCLE
        END-IF
    ELSE
        IF  VALID-READ AND DELETED-REC
            PERFORM 313A-HANDLE-SYNONYMS
            PERFORM 313B-CHECK-FULL-CIRCLE
        ELSE
            IF  VALID-READ AND VACANT-REC
                SET RECORD-NOT-FOUND TO TRUE
            ELSE
                SET RECORD-NOT-FOUND TO TRUE
                DISPLAY 'STATUS CODE OF MASTER REC IS INVALID'
            END-IF
        END-IF
    END-IF.
*
313A-HANDLE-SYNONYMS.
    SET FILE-IS-NOT-FULL TO TRUE
    ADD 1 TO LOCATION-ADDRESS
    IF  LOCATION-ADDRESS > MAX-NO-OF-LOCATIONS
        MOVE 1 TO LOCATION-ADDRESS
    END-IF
*
    IF  LOCATION-ADDRESS = STARTING-ADDRESS
        DISPLAY 'ENTIRE FILE READ FULL CIRCLE'
        SET FILE-IS-FULL TO TRUE
    ELSE
        PERFORM 312-READ-MAS-REC
    END-IF.
```

```
*
 313B-CHECK-FULL-CIRCLE.
     IF  FILE-IS-FULL
         SET RECORD-NOT-FOUND TO TRUE.
*
 320-UPDATE-CLASSES.
     MOVE R-LINE-NUMBER(SUBSCRIPT) TO LINE-NUMBER
     READ CLASS-MAS-FILE RECORD
     IF  NO-RECORD
         MOVE R-LINE-NUMBER(SUBSCRIPT) TO B-LINE-NUMBER2
         MOVE 'INVALID LINE NUMBER, CANNOT ADD' TO
                 B-ERROR-MESSAGE
         WRITE BILLING-REC FROM B-DETAIL2
     ELSE IF SEATS-REMAINING = 0
         MOVE R-LINE-NUMBER(SUBSCRIPT) TO B-LINE-NUMBER2
         MOVE 'NO SEATS AVAILABLE, CANNOT ADD' TO
                 B-ERROR-MESSAGE
         WRITE BILLING-REC FROM B-DETAIL2
     ELSE IF READ-FINE
         SUBTRACT 1 FROM SEATS-REMAINING
         REWRITE CLASS-REC
            INVALID KEY
                MOVE 'ERROR REWRITING RECORD' TO
                    B-ERROR-MESSAGE
                WRITE BILLING-REC FROM B-DETAIL2
         END-REWRITE
         PERFORM 321-MOVE-BILLING-INFO.
*
 321-MOVE-BILLING-INFO.
     MOVE LINE-NUMBER TO B-LINE-NUMBER1
     MOVE CLASS-TITLE TO B-CLASS-TITLE
     MOVE CR-HR TO B-CR-HR
     MOVE INSTRUCTOR TO B-INSTRUCTOR
     MOVE CLASS-DAYS TO B-CLASS-DAYS
     MOVE CLASS-TIME TO B-CLASS-TIME
     MOVE CLASS-ROOM TO B-CLASS-ROOM
     WRITE BILLING-REC FROM B-DETAIL1
*
     ADD CR-HR TO TOTAL-CR-HRS.
*
 330-UPDATE-STUD-REC.
     MOVE TOTAL-CR-HRS TO STUD-CR-HRS
     MOVE TOTAL-BALANCE TO STUD-BALANCE
     REWRITE STUD-REC
         INVALID KEY
             DISPLAY 'ERROR WRITING STUDENT MASTER REC'.
*
```

HEADINGS, we initiate execution of procedures such as 311-RANDOMIZE-READ and 313A-HANDLE-SYNONYMS via 313-FIND-MATCH, which access the relative file containing student records. Thus the program demonstrates the integration of several file access methods within the same program.

There may be, and generally are, multiple class requests for a given request transaction. Therefore in 300-UPDATE-CLASS-RECORDS we PERFORM 320-UP-DATE-CLASSES VARYING SUBSCRIPT FROM 1 BY 1 UNTIL SUBSCRIPT > R-NUM-OF-REQUESTS. In 320-UPDATE-CLASSES if the READ-FINE condition is true, we SUBTRACT 1 FROM SEATS-REMAINING, REWRITE the updated CLASS-REC, and WRITE a BILLING-REC for that student's bill.

When all the requests for a given student transaction record have been processed, we then compute the appropriate fees in 300-UPDATE-CLASS-RECORDS and proceed with the completion of the billing report. Finally, back at the end of 300-UPDATE-CLASS-RECORDS we PERFORM 330-UPDATE-STUD-REC to revise the total credits and the balance field in the student master file, and we PERFORM 200-READ-REQUEST-REC to read the next record from the transaction file.

Figures 26-9 and 26-10 show the contents of data files so you can trace any desired processing steps and their effects. Figure 26-9 presents the initial contents of the class master file, the registration transaction file, and the resulting updated class master file. The updated student master file is presented in Figure 26-10.

FIGURE 26-9

Initial Contents of the Class Master File, the Registration Transaction File, and the Updated Class Master File

```
CLASS MASTER FILE

13445CIS20003G. SMITH      MWF 0940 BAC216020020
14470CIS33003M. GOUL       TTH 0740 BAC357005005
14520CIS33503R. KEIM       TTH 0915 BAC351005005
14701CIS42003L. THOMPSON   MW  0840 BA439 007007
23221ACC22103M. GREEN      MWF 1040 BAC216010010
23259ACC22203C. WHITE      MWF 1140 BAC116010010
23737ACC33103E. BLUE       MWF 1240 BA332 005005
24835ACC35103W. TAX        TTH 1040 BA258 008008
28840ACC44703E. BORING     TTH 0915 BA358 008008
29073ACC50103H. ORANGE     TTH 1215 BA218 003003
31011ECN10103B. BROWN      MWF 0840 BAC343007007
32330ECN10203P. PINK       MWF 0940 BA212 006006
33344ECN20103K. KING       MWF 1040 BAC243005005
35242ECN20203L. LONG       MWF 1140 BA112 005005
43254MGT30103M. MAN        TTH 0740 BAC216008008
44523MGT46303J. BOND       TTH 0140 BA111 003003
57382ENG10103S. SMART      TTH 0315 LLA213005005
58232ENG10203M. J. FOX     TTH 0915 LLA313005005
67184PED10501F. FISH       MWF 0140 PEW101006006
68292PED10501S. SHOOT      MWF 0240 PEW102005005
68320PED10501B. BALL       MWF 0340 PEW103005005
73234MAT24202T. TOUGH      MW  0315 PSA205005005
```

FIGURE 26-9

Initial Contents of the Class Master File, the Registration Transaction File, and the Updated Class Master File (continued)

```
REGISTRATION TRANSACTION FILE

47221590352325913445147014325458323
32689403752322114470288406718473234
92220345652483532250323301470131011
46872431351447014702237373334473234
62150874522373729073
60061909731447031011135242
22865987126829229073
47254020541470122737310113524 2
33782042132483514701445 23
44532041841470133344732346829 2
50244762141470131011732334452 3
52309827831470173234290 73
55864581051470131011573826832032250


UPDATED CLASS MASTER FILE

13445CIS20003G. SMITH        MWF 0940 BAC216020019
14470CIS33003M. GOUL         TTH 0740 BAC357005002
14520CIS33503R. KEIM         TTH 0915 BAC351005005
14701CIS42003L. THOMPSON     MW  0840 BA439 007000
23221ACC22103M. GREEN        MWF 1040 BAC216010009
23259ACC22203C. WHITE        MWF 1140 BAC116010009
23737ACC33103E. BLUE         MWF 1240 BA332 005003
24835ACC35103W. TAX          TTH 1040 BA258 008006
28840ACC44703E. BORING       TTH 0915 BA358 008007
29073ACC50103H. ORANGE       TTH 1215 BA218 003000
31011ECN10103B. BROWN        MWF 0840 BAC343007002
32330ECN10203P. PINK         MWF 0940 BA212 006005
33344ECN20103K. KING         MWF 1040 BAC243005003
35242ECN20203L. LONG         MWF 1140 BA112 005003
43254MGT30103M. MAN          TTH 0740 BAC216008007
44523MGT46303J. BOND         TTH 0140 BA111 003001
57382ENG10103S. SMART        TTH 0315 LLA213005004
58232ENG10203M. J. FOX       TTH 0915 LLA313005005
67184PED10501F. FISH         MWF 0140 PEW101006005
68292PED10501S. SHOOT        MWF 0240 PEW102005003
68320PED10501B. BALL         MWF 0340 PEW103005004
73234MAT24202T. TOUGH        MW  0315 PSA205005001
```

A COBOL Reserved Words

ACCEPT
ACCESS
ADD
ADVANCING
AFTER
ALL
ALPHABET
ALPHABETIC
ALPHABETIC-LOWER
ALPHABETIC-UPPER
ALPHANUMERIC
ALPHANUMERIC-EDITED
ALSO
ALTER
ALTERNATE
AND
ANY
ARE
AREA
AREAS
ASCENDING
ASSIGN
AT
AUTHOR

BEFORE
BINARY
BLANK
BLOCK
BOTTOM
BY

CALL
CANCEL
CD
CF
CH
CHARACTER
CHARACTERS
CLASS
CLOSE
CODE
CODE-SET

COLLATING
COLUMN
COMMA
COMMON
COMMUNICATION
COMP
COMPUTATIONAL
COMPUTE
CONFIGURATION
CONTAINS
CONTENT
CONTINUE
CONTROL
CONTROLS
CONVERTING
COPY
CORR
CORRESPONDING
COUNT
CURRENCY

DATA
DATE
DATE-COMPILED
DATE-WRITTEN
DAY
DAY-OF-WEEK
DE
DEBUG-CONTENTS
DEBUG-ITEM
DEBUG-LINE
DEBUG-NAME
DEBUG-SUB-I
DEBUG-SUB-2
DEBUG-SUB-3
DEBUGGING
DECIMAL-POINT
DECLARATIVES
DELETE
DELIMITED
DELIMITER
DEPENDING
DESCENDING

DESTINATION
DETAIL
DISABLE
DISPLAY
DIVIDE
DIVISION
DOWN
DUPLICATES
DYNAMIC

EGI
ELSE
EMI
ENABLE
END
END-ADD
END-CALL
END-COMPUTE
END-DELETE
END-DIVIDE
END-EVALUATE
END-IF
END-MULTIPLY
END-OF-PAGE
END-PERFORM
END-READ
END-RECEIVE
END-RETURN
END-REWRITE
END-SEARCH
END-START
END-STRING
END-SUBTRACT
END-UNSTRING
END-WRITE
ENVIRONMENT
EOP
EQUAL
ERROR
ESI
EVALUATE
EXCEPTION
EXIT

EXTEND	LINE-COUNTER	QUOTES	STATUS
EXTERNAL	LINES		STOP
	LINKAGE	RANDOM	STRING
FALSE	LOCK	RD	SUB-QUEUE- I
FD	LOW-VALUE	READ	SUB-QUEUE-2
FILE	LOW-VALUES	RECEIVE	SUB-QUEUE-3
FILE-CONTROL		RECORD	SUBTRACT
FILLER	MERGE	RECORDS	SUM
FINAL	MESSAGE	REDEFINES	SUPPRESS
FIRST	MODE	REEL	SYMBOLIC
FOOTING	MOVE	REFERENCE	SYNC
FOR	MULTIPLE	REFERENCES	SYNCHRONIZED
FROM	MULTIPLY	RELATIVE	
		RELEASE	TABLE
GENERATE	NATIVE	REMAINDER	TALLYING
GIVING	NEGATIVE	REMOVAL	TAPE
GLOBAL	NEXT	RENAMES	TERMINAL
GO	NO	REPLACE	TERMINATE
GREATER	NOT	REPLACING	TEST
GROUP	NUMBER	REPORT	TEXT
	NUMERIC	REPORTING	THAN
HEADING	NUMERIC-EDITED	REPORTS	THEN
HIGH-VALUE		RESERVE	THROUGH
HIGH-VALUES	OBJECT-COMPUTER	RESET	THRU
	OCCURS	RETURN	TIME
I-O	OFF	REWIND	TIMES
I-O-CONTROL	OMITTED	REWRITE	TO
IDENTIFICATION	ON	RF	TOP
IF	OPEN	RH	TRAILING
IN	OPTIONAL	RIGHT	TRUE
INDEX	OR	ROUNDED	TYPE
INDEXED	ORDER	RUN	
INDICATE	ORGANIZATION		UNIT
INITIAL	OTHER	SAME	UNSTRING
INITIALIZE	OUTPUT	SD	UNTIL
INITIATE	OVERFLOW	SEARCH	UP
INPUT		SECTION	UPON
INPUT-OUTPUT	PACKED-DECIMAL	SECURITY	USAGE
INSPECT	PADDING	SEGMENT	USE
INSTALLATION	PAGE	SEGMENT-LIMIT	USING
INTO	PAGE-COUNTER	SELECT	
INVALID	PERFORM	SEND	VALUE
IS	PF	SENTENCE	VALUES
	PH	SEPARATE	VARYING
JUST	PIC	SEQUENCE	
JUSTIFIED	PICTURE	SEQUENTIAL	WHEN
	PLUS	SET	WITH
KEY	POINTER	SIGN	WORKING-STORAGE
	POSITION	SIZE	
LABEL	POSITIVE	SORT	ZERO
LAST	PRINTING	SORT-MERGE	ZEROES
LEADING	PROCEDURE	SOURCE	ZEROS
LEFT	PROCEDURES	SOURCE-COMPUTER	
LENGTH	PROCEED	SPACE	+ >
LESS	PROGRAM	SPACES	– <
LIMIT	PROGRAM-ID	SPECIAL-NAMES	=
LIMITS	PURGE	STANDARD	*
LINAGE		STANDARD- I	/ >=
LINAGE-COUNTER	QUEUE	STANDARD-2	<=
LINE	QUOTE	START	**

B

Complete COBOL Language Formats

THIS **APPENDIX CONTAINS** *the composite language skeleton of the revised version of the American National Standard COBOL. It is intended to display complete and syntactically correct formats.*

The leftmost margin on pages 834 through 844 is equivalent to margin A in a COBOL source program. The first indentation after the leftmost margin is equivalent to margin B in a COBOL source program.

On pages 845 through 857 the leftmost margin indicates the beginning of the format for a new COBOL verb. The first indentation after the leftmost margin indicates continuation of the format of the COBOL verb. The appearance of the italic letter **S**, **R**, **I**, *or* **W** *to the left of the format for the verbs CLOSE, OPEN, READ, and WRITE indicates the* **Sequential** *I-O module,* **Relative** *I-O module,* **Indexed** *I-O module, or Report* **Writer** *module in which that general format is used.*

The following formats are presented:

Identification Division

IDENTIFICATION DIVISION .

PROGRAM-ID. program-name $\left[\text{IS} \left\{ \begin{array}{l} \underline{\text{COMMON}} \\ \underline{\text{INITIAL}} \end{array} \right\} \text{PROGRAM} \right]$

[AUTHOR. [comment-entry]...]

[INSTALLATION . [comment-entry]...]

[DATE-WRITTEN . [comment-entry]...]

[DATE-COMPILED. [comment-entry]...]

[SECURITY. [comment-entry]...]

Environment Division

[ENVIRONMENT DIVISION .

[CONFIGURATION SECTION .

[SOURCE-COMPUTER. [computer-name [WITH DEBUGGING MODE].]]

[OBJECT- COMPUTER. [computer-name

    [PROGRAM COLLATING SEQUENCE IS alphabet-name-1]

    [SEGMENT-LIMIT IS segment-number].]]

[SPECIAL-NAMES. [[implementor-name-1

$$\left\{ \begin{array}{l} \text{IS mnemonic-name-1 } [\underline{\text{ON}} \text{ STATUS IS condition-name-1 } [\underline{\text{OFF}} \text{ STATUS IS condition-name-2}]] \\ \text{IS mnemonic-name-2 } [\underline{\text{OFF}} \text{ STATUS IS condition-name-2 } [\underline{\text{ON}} \text{ STATUS IS condition-name-1}]] \\ [\underline{\text{ON}} \text{ STATUS IS condition-name-1 } [\underline{\text{OFF}} \text{ STATUS IS condition-name-2}]] \\ [\underline{\text{OFF}} \text{ STATUS IS condition-name-2 } [\underline{\text{ON}} \text{ STATUS IS condition-name-1}]] \end{array} \right\}]...$$

    [ALPHABET alphabet-name-1 IS

$$\left\{ \begin{array}{l} \underline{\text{STANDARD}}\text{-1} \\ \underline{\text{STANDARD}}\text{-2} \\ \underline{\text{NATIVE}} \\ \text{implementor-name-2} \\ \left\{ \text{literal-1} \left[\left\{ \begin{array}{l} \underline{\text{THROUGH}} \\ \underline{\text{THRU}} \end{array} \right\} \text{literal-2} \\ \{\underline{\text{ALSO}} \text{ literal-3}\}... \right] \right\}... \end{array} \right\}]...$$

$$\left[\underline{\text{SYMBOLIC}} \text{ CHARACTERS} \left\{ \left\{ \{\text{symbolic-character-1}\}... \left\{ \begin{array}{l} \text{IS} \\ \text{ARE} \end{array} \right\} \{\text{integer-1}\}... \right\}... [\underline{\text{IN}} \text{ alphabet-name-2}] \right\} \right]...$$

$$\left[\underline{\text{CLASS}} \text{ class-name IS} \left\{ \text{literal-4} \left[\left\{ \begin{array}{l} \underline{\text{THROUGH}} \\ \underline{\text{THRU}} \end{array} \right\} \text{literal-5} \right] \right\}... \right]...$$

Environment Division *(continued)*

[<u>CURRENCY</u> SIGN IS literal -6]

[<u>DECIMAL -POINT</u> IS <u>COMMA</u>] .]]]

[<u>INPUT- OUTPUT SECTION</u> .

<u>FILE -CONTROL</u>.

　　{file -control -entry } . . .

[<u>I-O-CONTROL</u>.

$$
\left[\left[\underline{\text{SAME}}\begin{bmatrix}\underline{\text{RECORD}}\\\underline{\text{SORT}}\\\underline{\text{SORT-MERGE}}\end{bmatrix}\text{AREA FOR file -name-1 \{file -name-2\}} \dots\right] \dots\right]
$$

$$
\left[\underline{\text{MULTIPLE FILE}}\ \text{TAPE CONTAINS}\atop \text{\{file -name-3 [\underline{POSITION} IS integer -1]\} \dots}\right] \dots \quad .
$$

]]

File Control Entry

SEQUENTIAL FILE

<u>SELECT</u> [<u>OPTIONAL</u>] file -name-1

　　<u>ASSIGN</u> TO $\begin{Bmatrix}\text{implementor -name-1}\\\text{literal -1}\end{Bmatrix}$ . . .

　　$\left[\underline{\text{RESERVE}}\text{ integer -1}\begin{bmatrix}\text{AREA}\\\text{AREAS}\end{bmatrix}\right]$

　　[[<u>ORGANIZATION</u> IS] <u>SEQUENTIAL</u>]

　　$\left[\underline{\text{PADDING}}\text{ CHARACTER IS }\begin{Bmatrix}\text{data -name-1}\\\text{literal -2}\end{Bmatrix}\right]$

　　$\left[\underline{\text{RECORD DELIMITER}}\text{ IS }\begin{Bmatrix}\underline{\text{STANDARD -1}}\\\text{implementor -name-2}\end{Bmatrix}\right]$

　　[<u>ACCESS</u> MODE IS <u>SEQUENTIAL</u>]

　　[FILE <u>STATUS</u> IS data -name-2] .

RELATIVE FILE

<u>SELECT</u> [<u>OPTIONAL</u>] file -name-1

　　<u>ASSIGN</u> TO $\begin{Bmatrix}\text{implementor -name-1}\\\text{literal -1}\end{Bmatrix}$ . . .

　　$\left[\underline{\text{RESERVE}}\text{ integer -1}\begin{bmatrix}\text{AREA}\\\text{AREAS}\end{bmatrix}\right]$

　　[<u>ORGANIZATION</u> IS] <u>RELATIVE</u>

File Control Entry (continued)

$$\left[\text{\underline{ACCESS} MODE IS} \left\{\begin{array}{l}\text{\underline{SEQUENTIAL}} \quad [\underline{\text{RELATIVE}} \ \text{KEY IS data-name-1}] \\ \text{\underline{RANDOM}} \\ \text{\underline{DYNAMIC}}\end{array}\right\} \underline{\text{RELATIVE}} \ \text{KEY IS data-name-1}\right]$$

[FILE <u>STATUS</u> IS data-name-2].

INDEXED FILE

<u>SELECT</u> [<u>OPTIONAL</u>] file-name-1

    <u>ASSIGN</u> TO $\left\{\begin{array}{l}\text{implementor-name-1} \\ \text{literal-1}\end{array}\right\}$ ...

    $\left[\underline{\text{RESERVE}} \ \text{integer-1} \left[\begin{array}{l}\text{AREA} \\ \text{AREAS}\end{array}\right]\right]$

    [<u>ORGANIZATION</u> IS] <u>INDEXED</u>

    $\left[\underline{\text{ACCESS}} \ \text{MODE IS} \left\{\begin{array}{l}\text{\underline{SEQUENTIAL}} \\ \text{\underline{RANDOM}} \\ \text{\underline{DYNAMIC}}\end{array}\right\}\right]$

    <u>RECORD</u> KEY IS data-name-1

    [<u>ALTERNATE RECORD</u> KEY IS data-name-2 [WITH <u>DUPLICATES</u>]] ...

    [FILE <u>STATUS</u> IS data-name-3].

SORT OR MERGE FILE

<u>SELECT</u> file-name-1 <u>ASSIGN</u> TO $\left\{\begin{array}{l}\text{implementor-name-1} \\ \text{literal-1}\end{array}\right\}$ ...

REPORT FILE

<u>SELECT</u> [<u>OPTIONAL</u>] file-name-1

    <u>ASSIGN</u> TO $\left\{\begin{array}{l}\text{implementor-name-1} \\ \text{literal-1}\end{array}\right\}$ ...

    $\left[\underline{\text{RESERVE}} \ \text{integer-1} \left[\begin{array}{l}\text{AREA} \\ \text{AREAS}\end{array}\right]\right]$

    [[<u>ORGANIZATION</u> IS] <u>SEQUENTIAL</u>]

    $\left[\underline{\text{PADDING}} \ \text{CHARACTER IS} \left\{\begin{array}{l}\text{data-name-1} \\ \text{literal-2}\end{array}\right\}\right]$

    $\left[\underline{\text{RECORD DELIMITER}} \ \text{IS} \left\{\begin{array}{l}\text{\underline{STANDARD}-1} \\ \text{implementor-name-2}\end{array}\right\}\right]$

    [<u>ACCESS</u> MODE IS <u>SEQUENTIAL</u>]

    [FILE <u>STATUS</u> IS data-name-2].

Data Division

[DATA DIVISION .

[FILE SECTION .

[file-description-entry

{record-description-entry} . . .] . . .

[sort-merge-file-description-entry

{record-description-entry} . . .] . . .

[report-file-description-entry] . . .]

[WORKING-STORAGE SECTION .

$$\begin{bmatrix} \text{77-level-description-entry} \\ \text{record-description-entry} \end{bmatrix} . . .]$$

[LINKAGE SECTION .

$$\begin{bmatrix} \text{77-level-description-entry} \\ \text{record-description-entry} \end{bmatrix} . . .]$$

[COMMUNICATION SECTION .

[communication-description-entry

[record-description-entry] . . .] . . .]

[REPORT SECTION .

[report-description-entry

{record-group-description-entry} . . .] . . .]]

File Description Entry

SEQUENTIAL FILE

FD file-name-1

   [IS EXTERNAL]

   [IS GLOBAL]

$$\left[\underline{\text{BLOCK}} \text{ CONTAINS } [\text{integer-1 } \underline{\text{TO}}] \text{ integer-2} \begin{Bmatrix} \underline{\text{RECORDS}} \\ \text{CHARACTERS} \end{Bmatrix} \right]$$

$$\left[\underline{\text{RECORD}} \begin{Bmatrix} \text{CONTAINS integer-3 CHARACTERS} \\ \text{IS } \underline{\text{VARYING}} \text{ IN SIZE } [[\text{FROM integer-4}] [\underline{\text{TO}} \text{ integer-5}] \text{ CHARACTERS }] \\ \qquad [\underline{\text{DEPENDING}} \text{ ON data-name-1}] \\ \text{CONTAINS integer-6 } \underline{\text{TO}} \text{ integer-7 CHARACTERS} \end{Bmatrix} \right]$$

$$\left[\underline{\text{LABEL}} \begin{Bmatrix} \underline{\text{RECORD}} \text{ IS} \\ \underline{\text{RECORDS}} \text{ ARE} \end{Bmatrix} \begin{Bmatrix} \underline{\text{STANDARD}} \\ \underline{\text{OMITTED}} \end{Bmatrix} \right]$$

File Description Entry (continued)

$$\left[\underline{\text{VALUE OF}} \quad \left\{ \text{implementor -name-1 IS} \quad \left\{ \begin{array}{l} \text{data -name-2} \\ \text{literal -1} \end{array} \right\} \right\} \dots \right]$$

$$\left[\underline{\text{DATA}} \quad \left\{ \begin{array}{l} \underline{\text{RECORD}} \text{ IS} \\ \underline{\text{RECORDS}} \text{ ARE} \end{array} \right\} \{\text{data -name-3}\} \dots \right]$$

$$\left[\underline{\text{LINAGE}} \text{ IS} \left\{ \begin{array}{l} \text{data -name-4} \\ \text{integer -8} \end{array} \right\} \text{ LINES} \left[\text{WITH} \quad \underline{\text{FOOTING}} \text{ AT} \left\{ \begin{array}{l} \text{data -name-5} \\ \text{integer -9} \end{array} \right\} \right] \right.$$

$$\left. \left[\text{LINES AT } \underline{\text{TOP}} \left\{ \begin{array}{l} \text{data -name-6} \\ \text{integer -10} \end{array} \right\} \right] \left[\text{LINES AT } \underline{\text{BOTTOM}} \left\{ \begin{array}{l} \text{data -name-7} \\ \text{integer -11} \end{array} \right\} \right] \right]$$

[<u>CODE-SET</u> IS alphabet -name-1] .

RELATIVE FILE

<u>FD</u>   file -name-1

   [IS <u>EXTERNAL</u>]

   [IS <u>GLOBAL</u>]

$$\left[\underline{\text{BLOCK}} \text{ CONTAINS } [\text{ integer -1 } \underline{\text{TO}}] \text{ integer -2} \left\{ \begin{array}{l} \underline{\text{RECORDS}} \\ \text{CHARACTERS} \end{array} \right\} \right]$$

$$\left[\underline{\text{RECORD}} \left\{ \begin{array}{l} \text{CONTAINS integer -3 CHARACTERS} \\ \text{IS } \underline{\text{VARYING}} \text{ IN SIZE } [\, [\text{FROM integer -4}] \, [\underline{\text{TO}} \text{ integer -5}] \text{ CHARACTERS }] \\ \quad [\underline{\text{DEPENDING}} \text{ ON data -name-1}] \\ \text{CONTAINS integer -6 } \underline{\text{TO}} \text{ integer -7 CHARACTERS} \end{array} \right\} \right]$$

$$\left[\underline{\text{LABEL}} \left\{ \begin{array}{l} \underline{\text{RECORD}} \text{ IS} \\ \underline{\text{RECORDS}} \text{ ARE} \end{array} \right\} \left\{ \begin{array}{l} \underline{\text{STANDARD}} \\ \underline{\text{OMITTED}} \end{array} \right\} \right]$$

$$\left[\underline{\text{VALUE OF}} \left\{ \text{implementor -name-1 IS} \left\{ \begin{array}{l} \text{data -name-2} \\ \text{literal -1} \end{array} \right\} \right\} \dots \right]$$

$$\left[\underline{\text{DATA}} \left\{ \begin{array}{l} \underline{\text{RECORD}} \text{ IS} \\ \underline{\text{RECORDS}} \text{ ARE} \end{array} \right\} \{\text{data -name-3}\} \dots \right] .$$

SORT -MERGE FILE

<u>SD</u>   file -name-1

$$\left[\underline{\text{RECORD}} \left\{ \begin{array}{l} \text{CONTAINS integer -1 CHARACTERS} \\ \text{IS } \underline{\text{VARYING}} \text{ IN SIZE } [\, [\text{FROM integer -2}] \, [\underline{\text{TO}} \text{ integer -3}] \text{ CHARACTERS }] \\ \quad [\underline{\text{DEPENDING}} \text{ ON data -name-1}] \\ \text{CONTAINS integer -4 } \underline{\text{TO}} \text{ integer -5 CHARACTERS} \end{array} \right\} \right]$$

$$\left[\underline{\text{DATA}} \left\{ \begin{array}{l} \underline{\text{RECORD}} \text{ IS} \\ \underline{\text{RECORDS}} \text{ ARE} \end{array} \right\} \{\text{data -name-2}\} \dots \right]$$

File Description Entry *(continued)*

INDEXED FILE

<u>FD</u> file-name-1

 [IS <u>EXTERNAL</u>]

 [IS <u>GLOBAL</u>]

 $\left[\underline{\text{BLOCK}} \text{ CONTAINS [integer-1 } \underline{\text{TO}}] \text{ integer-2 } \begin{Bmatrix} \underline{\text{RECORDS}} \\ \text{CHARACTERS} \end{Bmatrix} \right]$

 $\left[\underline{\text{RECORD}} \begin{Bmatrix} \text{CONTAINS integer-3 CHARACTERS} \\ \text{IS } \underline{\text{VARYING}} \text{ IN SIZE [[FROM integer-4] [}\underline{\text{TO}} \text{ integer-5] CHARACTERS]} \\ \quad\quad \text{[}\underline{\text{DEPENDING}} \text{ ON data-name-1]} \\ \text{CONTAINS integer-6 } \underline{\text{TO}} \text{ integer-7 CHARACTERS} \end{Bmatrix} \right]$

 $\left[\underline{\text{LABEL}} \begin{Bmatrix} \underline{\text{RECORD}} \text{ IS} \\ \underline{\text{RECORDS}} \text{ ARE} \end{Bmatrix} \begin{Bmatrix} \underline{\text{STANDARD}} \\ \underline{\text{OMITTED}} \end{Bmatrix} \right]$

 $\left[\underline{\text{VALUE OF}} \begin{Bmatrix} \text{implementor-name-1 IS } \begin{Bmatrix} \text{data-name-2} \\ \text{literal-1} \end{Bmatrix} \end{Bmatrix} \ldots \right]$

 $\left[\underline{\text{DATA}} \begin{Bmatrix} \underline{\text{RECORD}} \text{ IS} \\ \underline{\text{RECORDS}} \text{ ARE} \end{Bmatrix} \text{\{data-name-3\} } \ldots \right]$.

REPORT FILE

<u>FD</u> file-name-1

 [IS <u>EXTERNAL</u>]

 [IS <u>GLOBAL</u>]

 $\left[\underline{\text{BLOCK}} \text{ CONTAINS [integer-1 } \underline{\text{TO}}] \text{ integer-2 } \begin{Bmatrix} \underline{\text{RECORDS}} \\ \text{CHARACTERS} \end{Bmatrix} \right]$

 $\left[\underline{\text{RECORD}} \begin{Bmatrix} \text{CONTAINS integer-3 CHARACTERS} \\ \text{IS } \underline{\text{VARYING}} \text{ IN SIZE [[FROM integer-4] [}\underline{\text{TO}} \text{ integer-5] CHARACTERS]} \\ \quad\quad \text{[}\underline{\text{DEPENDING}} \text{ ON data-name-1]} \\ \text{CONTAINS integer-6 } \underline{\text{TO}} \text{ integer-7 CHARACTERS} \end{Bmatrix} \right]$

 $\left[\underline{\text{LABEL}} \begin{Bmatrix} \underline{\text{RECORD}} \text{ IS} \\ \underline{\text{RECORDS}} \text{ ARE} \end{Bmatrix} \begin{Bmatrix} \underline{\text{STANDARD}} \\ \underline{\text{OMITTED}} \end{Bmatrix} \right]$

 $\left[\underline{\text{VALUE OF}} \begin{Bmatrix} \text{implementor-name-1 IS } \begin{Bmatrix} \text{data-name-2} \\ \text{literal-1} \end{Bmatrix} \end{Bmatrix} \ldots \right]$

 [<u>CODE-SET</u> IS alphabet-name-1]

 $\begin{Bmatrix} \underline{\text{REPORT}} \text{ IS} \\ \underline{\text{REPORTS}} \text{ ARE} \end{Bmatrix} \text{\{report-name-1\} } \ldots$

Data Description Entry

FORMAT 1

level -number $\begin{bmatrix} \text{data-name-1} \\ \underline{\text{FILLER}} \end{bmatrix}$

[REDEFINES data-name-2]

[IS EXTERNAL]

[IS GLOBAL]

$\left[\begin{Bmatrix} \underline{\text{PICTURE}} \\ \underline{\text{PIC}} \end{Bmatrix} \text{IS character -string} \right]$

$\left[\text{[USAGE IS]} \begin{Bmatrix} \underline{\text{BINARY}} \\ \underline{\text{COMPUTATIONAL}} \\ \underline{\text{COMP}} \\ \underline{\text{DISPLAY}} \\ \underline{\text{INDEX}} \\ \underline{\text{PACKED -DECIMAL}} \end{Bmatrix} \right]$

$\left[\text{[SIGN IS]} \begin{Bmatrix} \underline{\text{LEADING}} \\ \underline{\text{TRAILING}} \end{Bmatrix} \text{[SEPARATE CHARACTER]} \right]$

$\left[\begin{array}{l} \underline{\text{OCCURS}} \text{ integer -2 TIMES} \\ \quad \left[\begin{Bmatrix} \underline{\text{ASCENDING}} \\ \underline{\text{DESCENDING}} \end{Bmatrix} \text{KEY IS \{data-name-3\}} \ldots \right] \ldots \\ \quad \text{[\underline{INDEXED} BY \{index-name-1\} \ldots]} \\ \underline{\text{OCCURS}} \text{ integer -1 } \underline{\text{TO}} \text{ integer -2 TIMES } \underline{\text{DEPENDING}} \text{ ON data-name-4} \\ \quad \left[\begin{Bmatrix} \underline{\text{ASCENDING}} \\ \underline{\text{DESCENDING}} \end{Bmatrix} \text{KEY IS \{data-name-3\}} \ldots \right] \ldots \\ \quad \text{[\underline{INDEXED} BY \{index-name-1\} \ldots]} \end{array} \right]$

$\left[\begin{Bmatrix} \underline{\text{SYNCHRONIZED}} \\ \underline{\text{SYNC}} \end{Bmatrix} \begin{bmatrix} \underline{\text{LEFT}} \\ \underline{\text{RIGHT}} \end{bmatrix} \right]$

$\left[\begin{Bmatrix} \underline{\text{JUSTIFIED}} \\ \underline{\text{JUST}} \end{Bmatrix} \text{RIGHT} \right]$

[BLANK WHEN ZERO]

[VALUE IS literal -1] .

FORMAT 2

66 data -name-1 RENAMES data -name-2 $\left[\begin{Bmatrix} \underline{\text{THROUGH}} \\ \underline{\text{THRU}} \end{Bmatrix} \text{data -name-3} \right]$.

FORMAT 3

88 condition -name-1 $\begin{Bmatrix} \underline{\text{VALUE}} \text{ IS} \\ \underline{\text{VALUES}} \text{ ARE} \end{Bmatrix} \begin{Bmatrix} \text{literal -1} \left[\begin{Bmatrix} \underline{\text{THROUGH}} \\ \underline{\text{THRU}} \end{Bmatrix} \text{literal -2} \right] \end{Bmatrix} \ldots$.

Communication Description Entry

FORMAT 1

CD cd-name-1

FOR [INITIAL] INPUT

```
[ [SYMBOLIC  QUEUE IS data-name-1]
  [SYMBOLIC  SUB-QUEUE-1 IS data-name-2]
  [SYMBOLIC  SUB-QUEUE-2 IS data-name-3]
  [SYMBOLIC  SUB-QUEUE-3 IS data-name-4]
  [MESSAGE DATE  IS data-name-5]
  [MESSAGE TIME  IS data-name-6]
  [SYMBOLIC  SOURCE IS data-name-7]
  [TEXT LENGTH  IS data-name-8]
  [END KEY IS data-name-9]
  [STATUS KEY  IS data-name-10]
  [MESSAGE COUNT IS data-name-11] ]
[data-name-1, data-name-2, data-name-3,
  data-name-4, data-name-5, data-name-6,
  data-name-7, data-name-8, data-name-9,
  data-name-10, data-name-11]
```

FORMAT 2

CD cd-name-1 FOR OUTPUT

[DESTINATION COUNT IS data-name-1]

[TEXT LENGTH IS data-name-2]

[STATUS KEY IS data-name-3]

[DESTINATION TABLE OCCURS integer-1 TIMES

　　[INDEXED BY {index-name-1} ...]]

[ERROR KEY IS data-name-4]

[SYMBOLIC DESTINATION IS data-name-5] .

Communication Description Entry (continued)

FORMAT 3

CD cd-name-1

FOR [INITIAL] I-O
```
[ [MESSAGE DATE   IS  data-name-1]

    [MESSAGE TIME  IS  data-name-2]

    [SYMBOLIC  TERMINAL  IS  data-name-3]

    [TEXT LENGTH  IS  data-name-4]

    [END KEY  IS  data-name-5]

    [STATUS KEY  IS  data-name-6] ]

[data-name-1, data-name-2, data-name-3,

    data-name-4, data-name-5, data-name-6]
```

Report Description Entry

RD report-name-1

[IS GLOBAL]

[CODE literal-1]

$$\left[\left\{ \begin{matrix} \text{CONTROL IS} \\ \text{CONTROLS ARE} \end{matrix} \right\} \left\{ \begin{matrix} \{\text{data-name-1}\} \dots \\ \text{FINAL } [\text{data-name-1}] \dots \end{matrix} \right\} \right]$$

$$\left[\text{PAGE} \left[\begin{matrix} \text{LIMIT IS} \\ \text{LIMITS ARE} \end{matrix} \right] \text{integer-1} \left[\begin{matrix} \text{LINE} \\ \text{LINES} \end{matrix} \right] [\text{HEADING integer-2}] \right.$$

[FIRST DETAIL integer-3] [LAST DETAIL integer-4]

[FOOTING integer-5]] .

Report Group Description Entry

FORMAT 1

01   [data-name-1]

$$\left[\underline{\text{LINE}} \text{ NUMBER IS } \begin{Bmatrix} \text{integer-1 [ON } \underline{\text{NEXT PAGE}} \text{]} \\ \underline{\text{PLUS}} \text{ integer-2} \end{Bmatrix} \right]$$

$$\left[\underline{\text{NEXT GROUP}} \text{ IS } \begin{Bmatrix} \text{integer-3} \\ \underline{\text{PLUS}} \text{ integer-4} \\ \underline{\text{NEXT PAGE}} \end{Bmatrix} \right]$$

$$\underline{\text{TYPE}} \text{ IS } \begin{Bmatrix} \begin{Bmatrix} \underline{\text{REPORT HEADING}} \\ \underline{\text{RH}} \end{Bmatrix} \\ \begin{Bmatrix} \underline{\text{PAGE HEADING}} \\ \underline{\text{PH}} \end{Bmatrix} \\ \begin{Bmatrix} \underline{\text{CONTROL HEADING}} \\ \underline{\text{CH}} \end{Bmatrix} \begin{Bmatrix} \text{data-name-2} \\ \underline{\text{FINAL}} \end{Bmatrix} \\ \begin{Bmatrix} \underline{\text{DETAIL}} \\ \underline{\text{DE}} \end{Bmatrix} \\ \begin{Bmatrix} \underline{\text{CONTROL FOOTING}} \\ \underline{\text{CF}} \end{Bmatrix} \begin{Bmatrix} \text{data-name-3} \\ \underline{\text{FINAL}} \end{Bmatrix} \\ \begin{Bmatrix} \underline{\text{PAGE FOOTING}} \\ \underline{\text{PF}} \end{Bmatrix} \\ \begin{Bmatrix} \underline{\text{REPORT FOOTING}} \\ \underline{\text{RF}} \end{Bmatrix} \end{Bmatrix}$$

[[<u>USAGE</u> IS] <u>DISPLAY</u>] .

FORMAT 2

level-number [data-name-1]

$$\left[\underline{\text{LINE}} \text{ NUMBER IS } \begin{Bmatrix} \text{integer-1 [ON } \underline{\text{NEXT PAGE}} \text{]} \\ \underline{\text{PLUS}} \text{ integer-2} \end{Bmatrix} \right]$$

[[<u>USAGE</u> IS] <u>DISPLAY</u>] .

Report Group Description Entry (continued)

FORMAT 3

level -number [data -name-1]

$$\left\{ \begin{array}{l} \underline{PICTURE} \\ \underline{PIC} \end{array} \right\} \text{ IS character -string}$$

[[USAGE IS] DISPLAY]

$$\left[[SIGN \text{ IS}] \left\{ \begin{array}{l} \underline{LEADING} \\ \underline{TRAILING} \end{array} \right\} \underline{SEPARATE} \text{ CHARACTER} \right]$$

$$\left[\left\{ \begin{array}{l} \underline{JUSTIFIED} \\ \underline{JUST} \end{array} \right\} \text{ RIGHT} \right]$$

[BLANK WHEN ZERO]

$$\left[\underline{LINE} \text{ NUMBER IS } \left\{ \begin{array}{l} \text{integer -1 [ON } \underline{NEXT\ PAGE}] \\ \underline{PLUS} \text{ integer -2} \end{array} \right\} \right]$$

[COLUMN NUMBER IS integer -3]

$$\left\{ \begin{array}{l} \underline{SOURCE} \text{ IS identifier -1} \\ \underline{VALUE} \text{ IS literal -1} \\ \{ \underline{SUM} \text{ \{identifier -2\} . . . [\underline{UPON} \{data -name-2\} . . .]\} . . .} \\ \quad \left[\underline{RESET} \text{ ON } \left\{ \begin{array}{l} \text{data -name-3} \\ \underline{FINAL} \end{array} \right\} \right] \end{array} \right\}$$

[GROUP INDICATE] .

Procedure Division

FORMAT 1

[PROCEDURE DIVISION   [USING {data -name-1} . . .] .

[DECLARATIVES .

{section -name SECTION [segment -number] .

   USE statement .

[paragraph -name.

   [sentence] . . .] . . . } . . .

END DECLARATIVES .]

{section -name SECTION [segment -number] .

[paragraph -name.

   [sentence] . . .] . . . } . . .]

FORMAT 2

[PROCEDURE DIVISION   [USING {data -name-1} . . .] .

[paragraph -name.

   [sentence] . . . } . . .]

Cobol Verbs

ACCEPT identifier -1 [FROM mnemonic -name-1]

ACCEPT identifier -2 FROM $\begin{Bmatrix} \text{DATE} \\ \text{DAY} \\ \text{DAY-OF-WEEK} \\ \text{TIME} \end{Bmatrix}$

ACCEPT cd-name-1 MESSAGE COUNT

ADD $\begin{Bmatrix} \text{identifier -1} \\ \text{literal -1} \end{Bmatrix}$ . . . TO {identifier -2 [ROUNDED] } . . .

   [ON SIZE ERROR imperative -statement -1]

   [NOT ON SIZE ERROR imperative -statement -2]

   [END-ADD]

ADD $\begin{Bmatrix} \text{identifier -1} \\ \text{literal -1} \end{Bmatrix}$ . . . TO $\begin{Bmatrix} \text{identifier -2} \\ \text{literal -2} \end{Bmatrix}$

   GIVING {identifier -3} [ROUNDED] } . . .

   [ON SIZE ERROR imperative -statement -1]

   [NOT ON SIZE ERROR imperative -statement -2]

   [END-ADD]

ADD $\begin{Bmatrix} \text{CORRESPONDING} \\ \text{CORR} \end{Bmatrix}$ identifier -1 TO identifier -2 [ROUNDED]

   [ON SIZE ERROR imperative -statement -1]

   [NOT ON SIZE ERROR imperative -statement -2]

   [END-ADD]

ALTER {procedure -name-1 TO [PROCEED TO] procedure -name-2} . . .

CALL $\begin{Bmatrix} \text{identifier -1} \\ \text{literal -1} \end{Bmatrix}$ $\left[\text{USING} \begin{Bmatrix} \text{[BY REFERENCE] \{identifier -2\} . . .} \\ \text{BY CONTENT \{identifier -2\} . . .} \end{Bmatrix} \right]$ . . .

   [ON OVERFLOW imperative -statement -1] [END-CALL]

Cobol Verbs *(continued)*

CALL $\left\{ \begin{array}{l} \text{identifier -1} \\ \text{literal -1} \end{array} \right\}$ $\left[\underline{\text{USING}} \left\{ \begin{array}{l} [\text{BY } \underline{\text{REFERENCE}}] \ \{\text{identifier -2}\} \ldots \\ \text{BY } \underline{\text{CONTENT}} \ \{\text{identifier -2}\} \ldots \end{array} \right\} \ldots \right]$

    [ON $\underline{\text{EXCEPTION}}$ imperative -statement -1]

    [$\underline{\text{NOT}}$ ON $\underline{\text{EXCEPTION}}$ imperative -statement -2]

    [$\underline{\text{END-CALL}}$]

$\underline{\text{CANCEL}}$ $\left\{ \begin{array}{l} \text{identifier -1} \\ \text{literal -1} \end{array} \right\} \ldots$

S W $\underline{\text{CLOSE}}$ $\left\{ \text{file -name-1} \left[\begin{array}{l} \left\{ \begin{array}{l} \underline{\text{REEL}} \\ \underline{\text{UNIT}} \end{array} \right\} [\text{FOR } \underline{\text{REMOVAL}}] \\ \text{WITH } \left\{ \begin{array}{l} \underline{\text{NO REWIND}} \\ \underline{\text{LOCK}} \end{array} \right\} \end{array} \right] \right\} \ldots$

R I $\underline{\text{CLOSE}}$ {file -name-1} [WITH $\underline{\text{LOCK}}$] } . . .

$\underline{\text{COMPUTE}}$ {identifier -1 [$\underline{\text{ROUNDED}}$] } . . . = arithmetic -expression -1

    [ON $\underline{\text{SIZE ERROR}}$ imperative -statement -1]

    [$\underline{\text{NOT}}$ ON $\underline{\text{SIZE ERROR}}$ imperative -statement -2]

    [$\underline{\text{END-COMPUTE}}$]

$\underline{\text{CONTINUE}}$

$\underline{\text{DELETE}}$ file -name-1 RECORD

    [$\underline{\text{INVALID}}$ KEY imperative -statement -1]

    [$\underline{\text{NOT INVALID}}$ KEY imperative -statement -2]

    [$\underline{\text{END-DELETE}}$]

$\underline{\text{DISABLE}}$ $\left\{ \begin{array}{l} \text{INPUT [TERMINAL]} \\ \text{I-O TERMINAL} \\ \underline{\text{OUTPUT}} \end{array} \right\}$ cd -name-1

$\underline{\text{DISPLAY}}$ $\left\{ \begin{array}{l} \text{identifier -1} \\ \text{literal -1} \end{array} \right\} \ldots$ [$\underline{\text{UPON}}$ mnemonic -name-1] [WITH $\underline{\text{NO ADVANCING}}$]

Cobol Verbs *(continued)*

DIVIDE $\begin{Bmatrix} \text{identifier -1} \\ \text{literal -1} \end{Bmatrix}$ <u>INTO</u> {identifier -2 [<u>ROUNDED</u>]} . . .

    [ON <u>SIZE ERROR</u> imperative -statement -1]

    [<u>NOT</u> ON <u>SIZE ERROR</u> imperative -statement -2]

    [<u>END-DIVIDE</u>]

DIVIDE $\begin{Bmatrix} \text{identifier -1} \\ \text{literal -1} \end{Bmatrix}$ <u>INTO</u> $\begin{Bmatrix} \text{identifier -2} \\ \text{literal -2} \end{Bmatrix}$

    <u>GIVING</u> {identifier -3 [<u>ROUNDED</u>]} . . .

    [ON <u>SIZE ERROR</u> imperative -statement -1]

    [<u>NOT</u> ON <u>SIZE ERROR</u> imperative -statement -2]

    [<u>END-DIVIDE</u>]

DIVIDE $\begin{Bmatrix} \text{identifier -1} \\ \text{literal -1} \end{Bmatrix}$ <u>BY</u> $\begin{Bmatrix} \text{identifier -2} \\ \text{literal -2} \end{Bmatrix}$

    <u>GIVING</u> {identifier -3 [<u>ROUNDED</u>]} . . .

    [ON <u>SIZE ERROR</u> imperative -statement -1]

    [<u>NOT</u> ON <u>SIZE ERROR</u> imperative -statement -2]

    [<u>END-DIVIDE</u>]

DIVIDE $\begin{Bmatrix} \text{identifier -1} \\ \text{literal -1} \end{Bmatrix}$ <u>INTO</u> $\begin{Bmatrix} \text{identifier -2} \\ \text{literal -2} \end{Bmatrix}$ <u>GIVING</u> identifier -3 [<u>ROUNDED</u>]

    <u>REMAINDER</u> identifier -4

    [ON <u>SIZE ERROR</u> imperative -statement -1]

    [<u>NOT</u> ON <u>SIZE ERROR</u> imperative -statement -2]

    [<u>END-DIVIDE</u>]

DIVIDE $\begin{Bmatrix} \text{identifier -1} \\ \text{literal -1} \end{Bmatrix}$ <u>BY</u> $\begin{Bmatrix} \text{identifier -2} \\ \text{literal -2} \end{Bmatrix}$ <u>GIVING</u> identifier -3 [<u>ROUNDED</u>]

    <u>REMAINDER</u> identifier -4

    [ON <u>SIZE ERROR</u> imperative -statement -1]

    [<u>NOT</u> ON <u>SIZE ERROR</u> imperative -statement -2]

    [<u>END-DIVIDE</u>]

<u>ENABLE</u> $\begin{Bmatrix} \underline{\text{INPUT}} \text{ [}\underline{\text{TERMINAL}}\text{]} \\ \underline{\text{I-O TERMINAL}} \\ \underline{\text{OUTPUT}} \end{Bmatrix}$ cd -name-1

Cobol Verbs (continued)

$$\text{EVALUATE} \begin{Bmatrix} \begin{bmatrix} \text{identifier -1} \\ \text{literal -1} \\ \text{expression -1} \\ \underline{\text{TRUE}} \\ \underline{\text{FALSE}} \end{bmatrix} \end{Bmatrix} \begin{bmatrix} \underline{\text{ALSO}} \begin{Bmatrix} \text{identifier -2} \\ \text{literal -2} \\ \text{expression -2} \\ \underline{\text{TRUE}} \\ \underline{\text{FALSE}} \end{Bmatrix} \end{bmatrix} \dots$$

{ {WHEN

$$\begin{Bmatrix} \begin{bmatrix} \underline{\text{ANY}} \\ \text{condition -1} \\ \underline{\text{TRUE}} \\ \underline{\text{FALSE}} \\ [\underline{\text{NOT}}] \begin{Bmatrix} \text{identifier -3} \\ \text{literal -3} \\ \text{arithmetic -expression -1} \end{Bmatrix} \begin{bmatrix} \begin{Bmatrix} \underline{\text{THROUGH}} \\ \underline{\text{THRU}} \end{Bmatrix} \begin{Bmatrix} \text{identifier -4} \\ \text{literal -4} \\ \text{arithmetic -expression -2} \end{Bmatrix} \end{bmatrix} \end{bmatrix} \end{Bmatrix}$$

$$\begin{bmatrix} \underline{\text{ALSO}} \\ \begin{Bmatrix} \underline{\text{ANY}} \\ \text{condition -2} \\ \underline{\text{TRUE}} \\ \underline{\text{FALSE}} \\ [\underline{\text{NOT}}] \begin{Bmatrix} \text{identifier -5} \\ \text{literal -5} \\ \text{arithmetic -expression -3} \end{Bmatrix} \begin{bmatrix} \begin{Bmatrix} \underline{\text{THROUGH}} \\ \underline{\text{THRU}} \end{Bmatrix} \begin{Bmatrix} \text{identifier -6} \\ \text{literal -6} \\ \text{arithmetic -expression -4} \end{Bmatrix} \end{bmatrix} \end{Bmatrix} \end{bmatrix} \dots \} \dots$$

imperative -statement -1} . . .

[WHEN OTHER   imperative -statement -2]

[END-EVALUATE]

EXIT

EXIT PROGRAM

$$\underline{\text{GENERATE}} \begin{Bmatrix} \text{data -name-1} \\ \text{report -name-1} \end{Bmatrix}$$

GO TO [procedure -name-1]

GO TO { procedure -name-1} . . . DEPENDING ON identifier -1

$$\underline{\text{IF}} \text{ condition -1 THEN} \begin{Bmatrix} \{\text{statement -1}\} \dots \\ \underline{\text{NEXT SENTENCE}} \end{Bmatrix} \begin{Bmatrix} \underline{\text{ELSE}} \{\text{statement -2}\} \dots [\underline{\text{END-IF}}] \\ \underline{\text{ELSE NEXT SENTENCE}} \\ \underline{\text{END-IF}} \end{Bmatrix}$$

Cobol Verbs *(continued)*

INITIALIZE   {identifier -1} . . .

$$\left[\text{REPLACING} \left\{ \left\{ \begin{array}{l} \underline{\text{ALPHABETIC}} \\ \underline{\text{ALPHANUMERIC}} \\ \underline{\text{NUMERIC}} \\ \underline{\text{ALPHANUMERIC}} \text{-EDITED} \\ \underline{\text{NUMERIC}}\text{-EDITED} \end{array} \right\} \text{DATA} \ \underline{\text{BY}} \left\{ \begin{array}{l} \text{identifier -2} \\ \text{literal -1} \end{array} \right\} \right\} \dots \right]$$

INITIATE   {report -name-1} . . .

INSPECT identifier -1 <u>TALLYING</u>

$$\left\{ \text{identifier -2} \ \underline{\text{FOR}} \left\{ \begin{array}{l} \underline{\text{CHARACTERS}} \left[\left\{ \begin{array}{l} \underline{\text{BEFORE}} \\ \underline{\text{AFTER}} \end{array} \right\} \text{INITIAL} \left\{ \begin{array}{l} \text{identifier -4} \\ \text{literal -2} \end{array} \right\} \right] \dots \\ \left\{ \begin{array}{l} \underline{\text{ALL}} \\ \underline{\text{LEADING}} \end{array} \right\} \left\{ \begin{array}{l} \text{identifier -3} \\ \text{literal -1} \end{array} \right\} \left[\left\{ \begin{array}{l} \underline{\text{BEFORE}} \\ \underline{\text{AFTER}} \end{array} \right\} \text{INITIAL} \left\{ \begin{array}{l} \text{identifier -4} \\ \text{literal -2} \end{array} \right\} \right] \dots \right\} \dots \right\} \dots$$

INSPECT identifier -1 <u>REPLACING</u>

$$\left\{ \begin{array}{l} \underline{\text{CHARACTERS BY}} \left\{ \begin{array}{l} \text{identifier -5} \\ \text{literal -3} \end{array} \right\} \left[\left\{ \begin{array}{l} \underline{\text{BEFORE}} \\ \underline{\text{AFTER}} \end{array} \right\} \text{INITIAL} \left\{ \begin{array}{l} \text{identifier -4} \\ \text{literal -2} \end{array} \right\} \right] \dots \\ \left\{ \begin{array}{l} \underline{\text{ALL}} \\ \underline{\text{LEADING}} \\ \underline{\text{FIRST}} \end{array} \right\} \left\{ \begin{array}{l} \text{identifier -3} \\ \text{literal -1} \end{array} \right\} \underline{\text{BY}} \left\{ \begin{array}{l} \text{identifier -5} \\ \text{literal -3} \end{array} \right\} \left[\left\{ \begin{array}{l} \underline{\text{BEFORE}} \\ \underline{\text{AFTER}} \end{array} \right\} \text{INITIAL} \left\{ \begin{array}{l} \text{identifier -4} \\ \text{literal -2} \end{array} \right\} \right] \dots \right\} \dots$$

INSPECT identifier -1 <u>TALLYING</u>

$$\left\{ \text{identifier -2} \ \underline{\text{FOR}} \left\{ \begin{array}{l} \underline{\text{CHARACTERS}} \left[\left\{ \begin{array}{l} \underline{\text{BEFORE}} \\ \underline{\text{AFTER}} \end{array} \right\} \text{INITIAL} \left\{ \begin{array}{l} \text{identifier -4} \\ \text{literal -2} \end{array} \right\} \right] \dots \\ \left\{ \begin{array}{l} \underline{\text{ALL}} \\ \underline{\text{LEADING}} \end{array} \right\} \left\{ \begin{array}{l} \text{identifier -3} \\ \text{literal -1} \end{array} \right\} \left[\left\{ \begin{array}{l} \underline{\text{BEFORE}} \\ \underline{\text{AFTER}} \end{array} \right\} \text{INITIAL} \left\{ \begin{array}{l} \text{identifier -4} \\ \text{literal -2} \end{array} \right\} \right] \dots \right\} \dots \right\} \dots$$

<u>REPLACING</u>

$$\left\{ \begin{array}{l} \underline{\text{CHARACTERS BY}} \left\{ \begin{array}{l} \text{identifier -5} \\ \text{literal -3} \end{array} \right\} \left[\left\{ \begin{array}{l} \underline{\text{BEFORE}} \\ \underline{\text{AFTER}} \end{array} \right\} \text{INITIAL} \left\{ \begin{array}{l} \text{identifier -4} \\ \text{literal -2} \end{array} \right\} \right] \dots \\ \left\{ \begin{array}{l} \underline{\text{ALL}} \\ \underline{\text{LEADING}} \\ \underline{\text{FIRST}} \end{array} \right\} \left\{ \begin{array}{l} \text{identifier -3} \\ \text{literal -1} \end{array} \right\} \underline{\text{BY}} \left\{ \begin{array}{l} \text{identifier -5} \\ \text{literal -3} \end{array} \right\} \left[\left\{ \begin{array}{l} \underline{\text{BEFORE}} \\ \underline{\text{AFTER}} \end{array} \right\} \text{INITIAL} \left\{ \begin{array}{l} \text{identifier -4} \\ \text{literal -2} \end{array} \right\} \right] \dots \right\} \dots$$

Cobol Verbs *(continued)*

INSPECT identifier -1 <u>CONVERTING</u> $\left\{\begin{array}{l}\text{identifier -6}\\\text{literal -4}\end{array}\right\}$ <u>TO</u> $\left\{\begin{array}{l}\text{identifier -7}\\\text{literal -5}\end{array}\right\}$

$\left[\left\{\begin{array}{l}\underline{\text{BEFORE}}\\\underline{\text{AFTER}}\end{array}\right\}\text{ INITIAL }\left\{\begin{array}{l}\text{identifier -4}\\\text{literal -2}\end{array}\right\}\right]\ldots$

<u>MERGE</u> file-name-1 $\left\{\text{ON }\left\{\begin{array}{l}\underline{\text{ASCENDING}}\\\underline{\text{DESCENDING}}\end{array}\right\}\text{ KEY \{data-name-1\}}\ldots\right\}\ldots$

    [COLLATING <u>SEQUENCE</u> IS alphabet-name-1]

    <u>USING</u> file-name-2 {file-name-3}...

    $\left\{\begin{array}{l}\underline{\text{OUTPUT PROCEDURE}}\text{ IS procedure-name-1}\left[\left\{\begin{array}{l}\underline{\text{THROUGH}}\\\underline{\text{THRU}}\end{array}\right\}\text{procedure-name-2}\right]\\\underline{\text{GIVING}}\text{ \{file-name-4\}}\ldots\end{array}\right\}$

<u>MOVE</u> $\left\{\begin{array}{l}\text{identifier -1}\\\text{literal -1}\end{array}\right\}$ <u>TO</u> {identifier -2}...

<u>MOVE</u> $\left\{\begin{array}{l}\underline{\text{CORRESPONDING}}\\\underline{\text{CORR}}\end{array}\right\}$ identifier -1 <u>TO</u> identifier -2

<u>MULTIPLY</u> $\left\{\begin{array}{l}\text{identifier -1}\\\text{literal -1}\end{array}\right\}$ <u>BY</u> {identifier -2 [<u>ROUNDED</u>] }...

    [ON <u>SIZE ERROR</u> imperative-statement -1]

    [<u>NOT</u> ON <u>SIZE ERROR</u> imperative-statement -2]

    [<u>END-MULTIPLY</u>]

<u>MULTIPLY</u> $\left\{\begin{array}{l}\text{identifier -1}\\\text{literal -1}\end{array}\right\}$ <u>BY</u> $\left\{\begin{array}{l}\text{identifier -2}\\\text{literal -2}\end{array}\right\}$

    <u>GIVING</u> {identifier -3 [<u>ROUNDED</u>] }...

    [ON <u>SIZE ERROR</u> imperative-statement -1]

    [<u>NOT</u> ON <u>SIZE ERROR</u> imperative-statement -2]

    [<u>END-MULTIPLY</u>]

S   <u>OPEN</u> $\left\{\begin{array}{l}\underline{\text{INPUT}}\text{ \{file-name-1 [WITH }\underline{\text{NO REWIND}}\text{] \}}\ldots\\\underline{\text{OUTPUT}}\text{ \{file-name-2 [WITH }\underline{\text{NO REWIND}}\text{] \}}\ldots\\\underline{\text{I-O}}\text{ \{file-name-3\}}\ldots\\\underline{\text{EXTEND}}\text{ \{file-name-4\}}\ldots\end{array}\right\}\ldots$

Cobol Verbs (continued)

R I   OPEN $\left\{\begin{array}{l}\underline{\text{INPUT}}\ \{\text{file-name-1}\}\dots \\ \underline{\text{OUTPUT}}\ \{\text{file-name-2}\}\dots \\ \underline{\text{I-O}}\ \ \{\text{file-name-3}\}\dots \\ \underline{\text{EXTEND}}\ \ \{\text{file-name-4}\}\dots\end{array}\right\}\dots$

W   OPEN $\left\{\begin{array}{l}\underline{\text{OUTPUT}}\ \{\text{file-name-1}\ [\text{WITH}\ \underline{\text{NO REWIND}}\ ]\}\dots \\ \underline{\text{EXTEND}}\ \ \{\text{file-name-2}\}\dots\end{array}\right\}\dots$

$\underline{\text{PERFORM}}\ \left[\text{procedure-name-1}\ \left[\left\{\begin{array}{l}\underline{\text{THROUGH}}\\ \underline{\text{THRU}}\end{array}\right\}\text{procedure-name-2}\right]\right]$

[imperative-statement-1 $\underline{\text{END-PERFORM}}$]

$\underline{\text{PERFORM}}\ \left[\text{procedure-name-1}\ \left[\left\{\begin{array}{l}\underline{\text{THROUGH}}\\ \underline{\text{THRU}}\end{array}\right\}\text{procedure-name-2}\right]\right]$

$\left\{\begin{array}{l}\text{identifier-1}\\ \text{integer-1}\end{array}\right\}\ \underline{\text{TIMES}}\ $ [imperative-statement-1 $\underline{\text{END-PERFORM}}$]

$\underline{\text{PERFORM}}\ \left[\text{procedure-name-1}\ \left[\left\{\begin{array}{l}\underline{\text{THROUGH}}\\ \underline{\text{THRU}}\end{array}\right\}\text{procedure-name-2}\right]\right]$

$\left[\text{WITH}\ \underline{\text{TEST}}\ \left\{\begin{array}{l}\underline{\text{BEFORE}}\\ \underline{\text{AFTER}}\end{array}\right\}\right]\underline{\text{UNTIL}}\ \text{condition-1}$

[imperative-statement-1 $\underline{\text{END-PERFORM}}$]

$\underline{\text{PERFORM}}\ \left[\text{procedure-name-1}\ \left[\left\{\begin{array}{l}\underline{\text{THROUGH}}\\ \underline{\text{THRU}}\end{array}\right\}\text{procedure-name-2}\right]\right]$

$\left[\text{WITH}\ \underline{\text{TEST}}\ \left\{\begin{array}{l}\underline{\text{BEFORE}}\\ \underline{\text{AFTER}}\end{array}\right\}\right]$

$\underline{\text{VARYING}}\ \left\{\begin{array}{l}\text{identifier-2}\\ \text{index-name-1}\end{array}\right\}\ \underline{\text{FROM}}\ \left\{\begin{array}{l}\text{identifier-3}\\ \text{index-name-2}\\ \text{literal-1}\end{array}\right\}$

$\underline{\text{BY}}\ \left\{\begin{array}{l}\text{identifier-4}\\ \text{literal-2}\end{array}\right\}\ \underline{\text{UNTIL}}\ \text{condition-1}$

$\left[\underline{\text{AFTER}}\ \left\{\begin{array}{l}\text{identifier-5}\\ \text{literal-3}\end{array}\right\}\ \underline{\text{FROM}}\ \left\{\begin{array}{l}\text{identifier-6}\\ \text{index-name-4}\\ \text{literal-3}\end{array}\right\}\right.$

$\left.\underline{\text{BY}}\ \left\{\begin{array}{l}\text{identifier-7}\\ \text{literal-4}\end{array}\right\}\ \underline{\text{UNTIL}}\ \text{condition-2}\right]\dots$

[imperative-statement-1 $\underline{\text{END-PERFORM}}$]

Cobol Verbs *(continued)*

PURGE cd-name-1

S R I   READ file-name-1 [NEXT] RECORD [INTO identifier -1]

        [AT END imperative -statement -1]

        [NOT AT END imperative -statement -2]

        [END-READ]

R   READ file-name-1 RECORD [INTO identifier -1]

        [INVALID KEY imperative -statement -3]

        [NOT INVALID KEY imperative -statement -4]

        [END-READ]

I   READ file-name-1 RECORD [INTO identifier -1]

        [KEY IS data-name-1]

        [INVALID KEY imperative -statement -3]

        [NOT INVALID KEY imperative -statement -4]

        [END-READ]

RECEIVE cd-name-1 $\begin{Bmatrix} \text{MESSAGE} \\ \text{SEGMENT} \end{Bmatrix}$ INTO identifier -1

        [NO DATA imperative -statement -1]

        [WITH DATA imperative -statement -2]

        [END-RECEIVE]

RELEASE record -name-1 [FROM identifier -1]

RETURN file-name-1 RECORD [INTO identifier -1]

        AT END imperative -statement -1

        [NOT AT END imperative -statement -2]

        [END-RETURN]

S   REWRITE record -name-1 [FROM identifier -1]

Cobol Verbs *(continued)*

R I   REWRITE record -name-1 [FROM identifier -1]

      [INVALID KEY imperative -statement -1]

      [NOT INVALID KEY imperative -statement -2]

      [END-REWRITE]

SEARCH identifier -1 $\left[\text{VARYING} \begin{Bmatrix} \text{identifier -2} \\ \text{index -name-2} \end{Bmatrix} \right]$

  [AT END imperative -statement -1]

$\begin{Bmatrix} \underline{\text{WHEN}} \text{ condition -1} \begin{Bmatrix} \text{imperative -statement -2} \\ \text{NEXT- SENTENCE} \end{Bmatrix} \end{Bmatrix} \ldots$

  [END-SEARCH]

SEARCH ALL identifier -1 [AT END imperative -statement -1]

$\underline{\text{WHEN}} \begin{Bmatrix} \text{data -name-1} \begin{Bmatrix} \text{IS EQUAL TO} \\ \text{IS =} \end{Bmatrix} \begin{Bmatrix} \text{identifier -3} \\ \text{literal -1} \\ \text{arithmetic -expression -1} \end{Bmatrix} \\ \text{condition-name-2} \end{Bmatrix}$

$\left[\underline{\text{AND}} \begin{Bmatrix} \text{data -name-2} \begin{Bmatrix} \text{IS EQUAL TO} \\ \text{IS =} \end{Bmatrix} \begin{Bmatrix} \text{identifier -4} \\ \text{literal -2} \\ \text{arithmetic -expression -2} \end{Bmatrix} \\ \text{condition-name-2} \end{Bmatrix} \right] \ldots$

$\begin{Bmatrix} \text{imperative -statement -2} \\ \text{NEXT SENTENCE} \end{Bmatrix}$

  [END-SEARCH]

SEND cd -name-1 FROM identifier -1

SEND cd -name-1 [FROM identifier -1] $\begin{Bmatrix} \text{WITH identifier -2} \\ \text{WITH ESI} \\ \text{WITH EMI} \\ \text{WITH EGI} \end{Bmatrix}$

$\left[\begin{Bmatrix} \underline{\text{BEFORE}} \\ \underline{\text{AFTER}} \end{Bmatrix} \text{ADVANCING} \begin{Bmatrix} \begin{Bmatrix} \text{identifier -3} \\ \text{integer -1} \end{Bmatrix} \begin{Bmatrix} \text{LINE} \\ \text{LINES} \end{Bmatrix} \\ \begin{Bmatrix} \text{mnemonic-name-1} \\ \text{PAGE} \end{Bmatrix} \end{Bmatrix} \right]$

  [REPLACING LINE]

Cobol Verbs *(continued)*

$$\underline{SET} \begin{Bmatrix} \text{index-name-1} \\ \text{identifier-1} \end{Bmatrix} \dots \underline{TO} \begin{Bmatrix} \text{index-name-2} \\ \text{identifier-2} \\ \text{integer-1} \end{Bmatrix}$$

$$\underline{SET} \{\text{index-name-3}\} \dots \begin{Bmatrix} \underline{UP\ BY} \\ \underline{DOWN\ BY} \end{Bmatrix} \begin{Bmatrix} \text{identifier-3} \\ \text{integer-2} \end{Bmatrix}$$

$$\underline{SET} \begin{Bmatrix} \{\text{mnemonic-name-1}\} \dots \underline{TO} \begin{Bmatrix} \underline{ON} \\ \underline{OFF} \end{Bmatrix} \end{Bmatrix} \dots$$

$$\underline{SET} \{\text{condition-name-1}\} \dots \underline{TO\ TRUE}$$

$$\underline{SORT} \text{ file-name-1} \begin{Bmatrix} ON \begin{Bmatrix} \underline{ASCENDING} \\ \underline{DESCENDING} \end{Bmatrix} KEY \{\text{data-name-1}\} \dots \end{Bmatrix} \dots$$

  [WITH <u>DUPLICATES</u> IN ORDER]

  [COLLATING <u>SEQUENCE</u> IS alphabet-name-1]

$$\begin{Bmatrix} \underline{INPUT\ PROCEDURE} \text{ IS procedure-name-1} \left[\begin{Bmatrix} \underline{THROUGH} \\ \underline{THRU} \end{Bmatrix} \text{procedure-name-2} \right] \\ \underline{USING} \text{ [file-name-2]} \dots \end{Bmatrix}$$

$$\begin{Bmatrix} \underline{OUTPUT\ PROCEDURE} \text{ IS procedure-name-3} \left[\begin{Bmatrix} \underline{THROUGH} \\ \underline{THRU} \end{Bmatrix} \text{procedure-name-4} \right] \\ \underline{GIVING} \text{ [file-name-3]} \dots \end{Bmatrix}$$

$$\underline{START} \text{ file-name-1} \left[\underline{KEY} \begin{Bmatrix} \text{IS } \underline{EQUAL}\text{ TO} \\ \text{IS} = \\ \text{IS } \underline{GREATER}\text{ THAN} \\ \text{IS} > \\ \text{IS } \underline{NOT\ LESS}\text{ THAN} \\ \text{IS } \underline{NOT} < \\ \text{IS } \underline{GREATER}\text{ THAN OR } \underline{EQUAL}\text{ TO} \\ \text{IS} >= \end{Bmatrix} \text{data-name-1} \right]$$

  [<u>INVALID</u> KEY imperative-statement-1]

  [<u>NOT INVALID</u> KEY imperative-statement-2]

  [<u>END-START</u>]

$$\underline{STOP} \begin{Bmatrix} \underline{RUN} \\ \text{literal-1} \end{Bmatrix}$$

Cobol Verbs (continued)

STRING $\left\{\begin{array}{l}\text{identifier -1}\\\text{literal -1}\end{array}\right\}$ ... DELIMITED BY $\left\{\begin{array}{l}\text{identifier -2}\\\text{literal -2}\\\text{SIZE}\end{array}\right\}$ ...

    INTO identifier -3

    [WITH POINTER identifier -4]

    [ON OVERFLOW imperative -statement -1]

    [NOT ON OVERFLOW imperative -statement -2]

    [END-STRING]

SUBTRACT $\left\{\begin{array}{l}\text{identifier -1}\\\text{literal -1}\end{array}\right\}$ ... FROM {identifier -3 [ROUNDED] } ...

    [ON SIZE ERROR imperative -statement -1]

    [NOT ON SIZE ERROR imperative -statement -2]

    [END-SUBTRACT]

SUBTRACT $\left\{\begin{array}{l}\text{identifier -1}\\\text{literal -1}\end{array}\right\}$ ... FROM $\left\{\begin{array}{l}\text{identifier -2}\\\text{literal -2}\end{array}\right\}$

    GIVING {identifier -3} [ROUNDED] } ...

    [ON SIZE ERROR imperative -statement -1]

    [NOT ON SIZE ERROR imperative -statement -2]

    [END-SUBTRACT]

SUBTRACT $\left\{\begin{array}{l}\text{CORRESPONDING}\\\text{CORR}\end{array}\right\}$ identifier -1 FROM identifier -2 [ROUNDED]

    [ON SIZE ERROR imperative -statement -1]

    [NOT ON SIZE ERROR imperative -statement -2]

    [END-SUBTRACT]

SUPPRESS PRINTING

TERMINATE {report -name-1} ...

Cobol Verbs (continued)

UNSTRING identifier -1

$$\left[\text{\underline{DELIMITED}} \text{ BY } [\underline{ALL}] \begin{Bmatrix} \text{identifier -2} \\ \text{literal -1} \end{Bmatrix} \left[\underline{OR} \text{ } [\underline{ALL}] \begin{Bmatrix} \text{identifier -3} \\ \text{literal -2} \end{Bmatrix}\right] \dots \right]$$

INTO {identifier -4 [DELIMITER IN identifier -5] [COUNT IN identifier -6] } . . .

[WITH POINTER identifier -7]

[TALLYING IN identifier -8]

[ON OVERFLOW imperative -statement -1]

[NOT ON OVERFLOW imperative -statement -2]

[END-UNSTRING]

$$\text{\underline{USE}} \text{ } [\underline{GLOBAL}] \text{ } \underline{AFTER} \text{ STANDARD } \begin{Bmatrix} \text{EXCEPTION} \\ \text{ERROR} \end{Bmatrix} \text{\underline{PROCEDURE}} \text{ ON } \begin{Bmatrix} \{\text{file -name-1}\} \dots \\ \text{INPUT} \\ \text{OUTPUT} \\ \text{I-O} \\ \text{EXTEND} \end{Bmatrix}$$

USE [GLOBAL] BEFORE REPORTING identifier -1

$$\text{\underline{USE}} \text{ FOR } \underline{DEBUGGING} \text{ ON } \begin{Bmatrix} \text{cd -name-1} \\ [\underline{ALL} \text{ REFERENCES OF}] \text{ identifier -1} \\ \text{file -name-1} \\ \text{procedure -name-1} \\ \underline{ALL PROCEDURES} \end{Bmatrix} \dots$$

S   WRITE record -name-1 [FROM identifier -1]

$$\left[\begin{Bmatrix} \underline{BEFORE} \\ \underline{AFTER} \end{Bmatrix} \text{ADVANCING} \begin{Bmatrix} \begin{Bmatrix} \text{identifier -2} \\ \text{integer -1} \end{Bmatrix} \begin{bmatrix} \text{LINE} \\ \text{LINES} \end{bmatrix} \\ \text{mnemonic -name-1} \\ \underline{PAGE} \end{Bmatrix}\right]$$

$$\left[\underline{AT} \begin{Bmatrix} \text{END-OF-PAGE} \\ \underline{EOP} \end{Bmatrix} \text{imperative -statement -1}\right]$$

$$\left[\underline{NOT} \text{ AT } \begin{Bmatrix} \text{END-OF-PAGE} \\ \underline{EOP} \end{Bmatrix} \text{imperative -statement -2}\right]$$

[END-WRITE]

Cobol Verbs *(continued)*

R I   <u>WRITE</u> record -name-1 [<u>FROM</u> identifier -1]

      [<u>INVALID</u> KEY imperative -statement -1]

      [<u>NOT INVALID</u> KEY imperative -statement -2]

      [<u>END-WRITE</u>]

COPY and REPLACE Statements

<u>COPY</u> text -name-1 $\left[\begin{Bmatrix} \underline{OF} \\ \underline{IN} \end{Bmatrix} \text{library -name-1} \right]$

$\left[\underline{REPLACING} \begin{Bmatrix} \begin{Bmatrix} == \text{pseudo -text -1} == \\ \text{identifier -1} \\ \text{literal -1} \\ \text{word -1} \end{Bmatrix} \underline{BY} \begin{Bmatrix} == \text{pseudo -text -2} == \\ \text{identifier -2} \\ \text{literal -2} \\ \text{word -2} \end{Bmatrix} \end{Bmatrix} \dots \right]$

<u>REPLACE</u> {== pseudo -text -1 == BY == pseudo -text -2 ==} . . .

<u>REPLACE OFF</u>

Conditions

RELATION CONDITION

$\begin{Bmatrix} \text{identifier -1} \\ \text{literal -1} \\ \text{arithmetic -expression -1} \\ \text{index -name-1} \end{Bmatrix}$ $\begin{Bmatrix} \text{IS [\underline{NOT}] } \underline{\text{GREATER}} \text{ THAN} \\ \text{IS [\underline{NOT}] } > \\ \text{IS [\underline{NOT}] } \underline{\text{LESS}} \text{ THAN} \\ \text{IS [\underline{NOT}] } < \\ \text{IS [\underline{NOT}] } \underline{\text{EQUAL}} \text{ TO} \\ \text{IS [\underline{NOT}] } = \\ \text{IS } \underline{\text{GREATER}} \text{ THAN } \underline{\text{OR EQUAL}} \text{ TO} \\ \text{IS } > = \\ \text{IS } \underline{\text{LESS}} \text{ THAN } \underline{\text{OR EQUAL}} \text{ TO} \\ \text{IS } < = \end{Bmatrix}$ $\begin{Bmatrix} \text{identifier -2} \\ \text{literal -2} \\ \text{arithmetic -expression -2} \\ \text{index -name-2} \end{Bmatrix}$

Conditions (continued)

CLASS CONDITION

identifier -1 IS [NOT] { NUMERIC
ALPHABETIC
ALPHABETIC -LOWER
ALPHABETIC -UPPER
class -name }

CONDITION-NAME CONDITION

condition -name-1

SWITCH-STATUS CONDITION

condition -name-1

SIGN CONDITION

arithmetic -expression -1 IS [NOT] { POSITIVE
NEGATIVE
ZERO }

NEGATED CONDITION

NOT condition -1

COMBINED CONDITION

condition -1 { { AND
OR } condition -2 } . . .

ABBREVIATED COMBINED RELATION CONDITION

relation -condition { { AND
OR } [NOT] [relational -operator] object } . . .

Qualification

FORMAT 1

$$
\begin{Bmatrix} \text{data-name-1} \\ \text{condition-name} \end{Bmatrix}
\begin{Bmatrix}
\begin{Bmatrix} \begin{Bmatrix} \underline{\text{IN}} \\ \underline{\text{OF}} \end{Bmatrix} \text{data-name-2} \end{Bmatrix} \dots \left[\begin{Bmatrix} \underline{\text{IN}} \\ \underline{\text{OF}} \end{Bmatrix} \begin{Bmatrix} \text{file-name} \\ \text{cd-name} \end{Bmatrix} \right] \\
\begin{Bmatrix} \underline{\text{IN}} \\ \underline{\text{OF}} \end{Bmatrix} \begin{Bmatrix} \text{file-name} \\ \text{cd-name} \end{Bmatrix}
\end{Bmatrix}
$$

FORMAT 2

$$
\text{paragraph-name} \begin{Bmatrix} \underline{\text{IN}} \\ \underline{\text{OF}} \end{Bmatrix} \text{section-name}
$$

FORMAT 3

$$
\text{text-name} \begin{Bmatrix} \underline{\text{IN}} \\ \underline{\text{OF}} \end{Bmatrix} \text{library-name}
$$

FORMAT 4

$$
\underline{\text{LINAGE-COUNTER}} \begin{Bmatrix} \underline{\text{IN}} \\ \underline{\text{OF}} \end{Bmatrix} \text{report-name}
$$

FORMAT 5

$$
\begin{Bmatrix} \underline{\text{PAGE-COUNTER}} \\ \underline{\text{LINE-COUNTER}} \end{Bmatrix} \begin{Bmatrix} \underline{\text{IN}} \\ \underline{\text{OF}} \end{Bmatrix} \text{report-name}
$$

FORMAT 6

$$
\text{data-name-3} \begin{Bmatrix}
\begin{Bmatrix} \underline{\text{IN}} \\ \underline{\text{OF}} \end{Bmatrix} \text{data-name-4} \left[\begin{Bmatrix} \underline{\text{IN}} \\ \underline{\text{OF}} \end{Bmatrix} \text{report-name} \right] \\
\begin{Bmatrix} \underline{\text{IN}} \\ \underline{\text{OF}} \end{Bmatrix} \text{report-name}
\end{Bmatrix}
$$

Miscellaneous Formats

SUBSCRIPTING

$$\left\{ \begin{array}{l} \text{condition -name-1} \\ \text{data -name-1} \end{array} \right\} \left(\left\{ \begin{array}{l} \text{integer -1} \\ \text{data -name-2 } [\{\pm\} \text{ integer -2}] \\ \text{index -name-1 } [\{\pm\} \text{ integer -3}] \end{array} \right\} \dots \right)$$

REFERENCE MODIFICATION

data -name-1 (leftmost -character -position: [length])

IDENTIFIER

$$\text{data -name-1} \left[\left\{ \begin{array}{l} \text{IN} \\ \text{OF} \end{array} \right\} \text{data -name-2} \right] \dots \left[\left\{ \begin{array}{l} \text{IN} \\ \text{OF} \end{array} \right\} \left\{ \begin{array}{l} \text{cd -name} \\ \text{file -name} \\ \text{report -name} \end{array} \right\} \right]$$

[({subscript } . . .)] [(leftmost -character -position : [length])]

Nested Source Programs

IDENTIFICATION DIVISION.

PROGRAM -ID. program -name-1 [IS INITIAL PROGRAM] .

[ENVIRONMENT DIVISION . environment -division -content]

[DATA DIVISION . data -division -content]

[PROCEDURE DIVISION. procedure -division -content]

[[nested -source-program] . . .

END PROGRAM program -name-1.]

NESTED-SOURCE-PROGRAM

IDENTIFICATION DIVISION.

$$\text{PROGRAM -ID. program -name-2} \left[\text{IS} \left\{ \left| \begin{array}{l} \underline{\text{COMMON}} \\ \underline{\text{INITIAL}} \end{array} \right| \right\} \text{PROGRAM} \right].$$

[ENVIRONMENT DIVISION . environment -division -content]

[DATA DIVISION . data -division -content]

[PROCEDURE DIVISION. procedure -division -content]

[nested -source-program] . . .

END PROGRAM program -name-2.

A Sequence of Source Programs

{IDENTIFICATION DIVISION.

PROGRAM-ID. program-name-3 [IS INITIAL PROGRAM].

[ENVIRONMENT DIVISION . environment -division -content]

[DATA DIVISION . data -division -content]

[PROCEDURE DIVISION . procedure -division -content]

[nested -source-program] . . .

END PROGRAM program-name-3.} . . .

IDENTIFICATION DIVISION.

PROGRAM-ID. program-name-4 [IS INITIAL PROGRAM].

[ENVIRONMENT DIVISION . environment -division -content]

[DATA DIVISION . data -division -content]

[PROCEDURE DIVISION . procedure -division -content]

[[nested -source-program] . . .

END PROGRAM program-name-4.]

Index

COBOL Coding Form

System				Punching Instructions								Sheet		of	
Program				Graphic							Card #		Identification		
Programmer		Date		Punch							Form		73		80

Sequence		Cont.	A	B	COBOL Statement
(Page)	(Serial)				

COBOL Coding Form

System					Punching Instructions									Sheet		of		
Program					Graphic							Card #			Identification			
Programmer				Date	Punch							Form			73]			[80

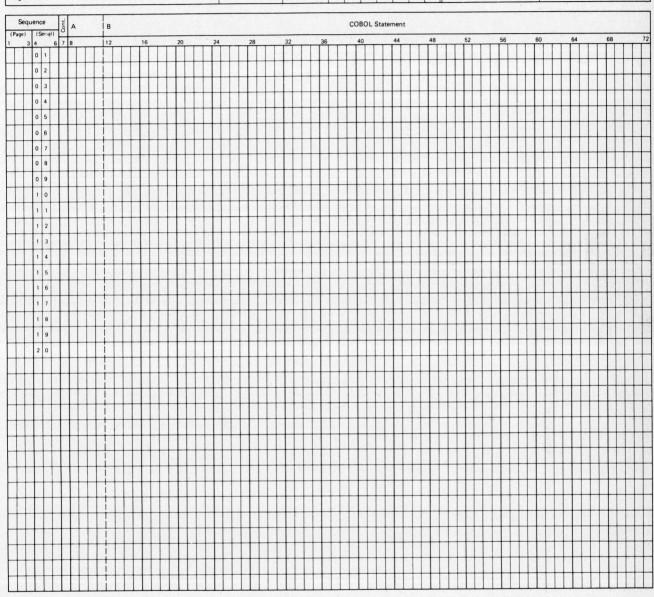

Sequence		Cont.	A	B	COBOL Statement
(Page)	(Serial)				
1 3	4 6	7	8	12 16 20 24 28 32 36 40 44 48 52 56 60 64 68 72	
	0 1				
	0 2				
	0 3				
	0 4				
	0 5				
	0 6				
	0 7				
	0 8				
	0 9				
	1 0				
	1 1				
	1 2				
	1 3				
	1 4				
	1 5				
	1 6				
	1 7				
	1 8				
	1 9				
	2 0				

COBOL Coding Form

System				Punching Instructions									Sheet	of	
Program				Graphic						Card #			Identification		
Programmer		Date		Punch						Form			73		80

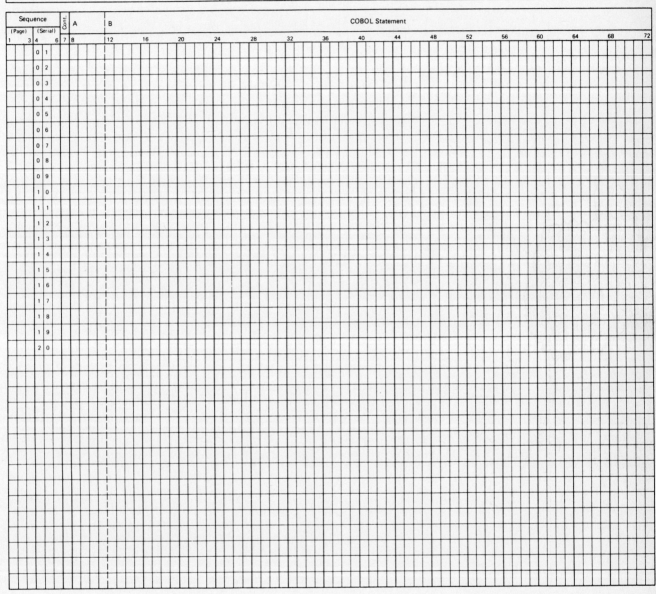

COBOL Coding Form

System				Punching Instructions											Sheet	of
Program				Graphic							Card #				Identification	
Programmer			Date	Punch							Form				73] [80	

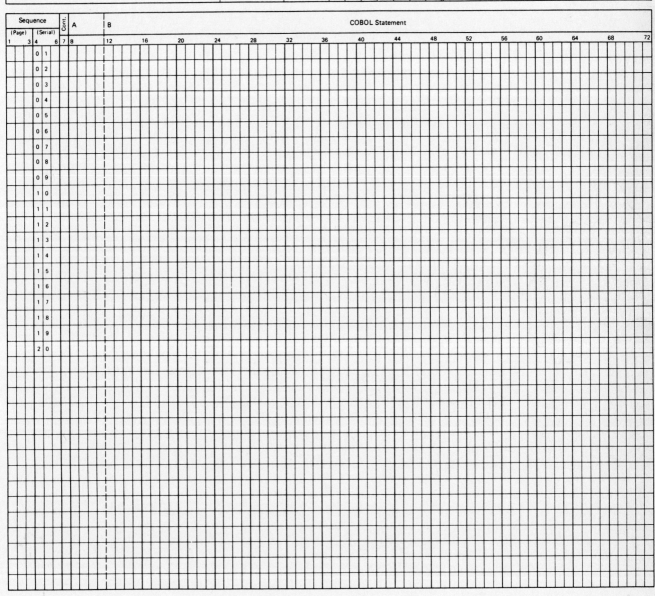

COBOL Coding Form

System						Punching Instructions								Sheet	of	

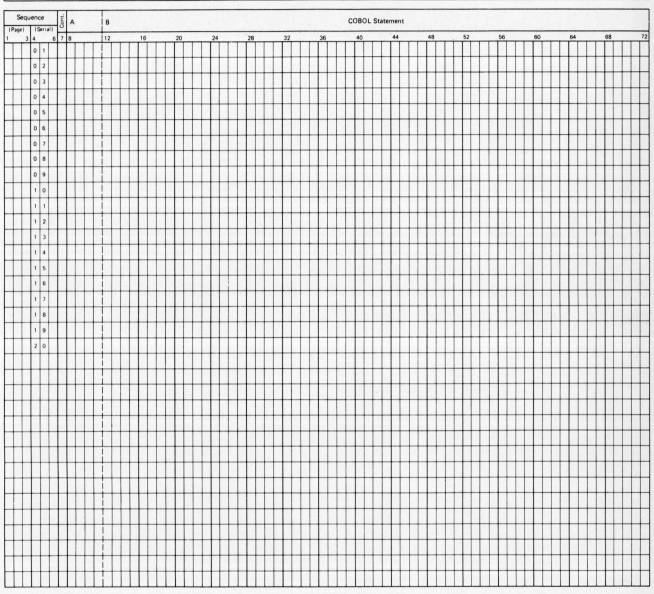

Printer Spacing Chart

Printer Spacing Chart

Printer Spacing Chart

Printer Spacing Chart

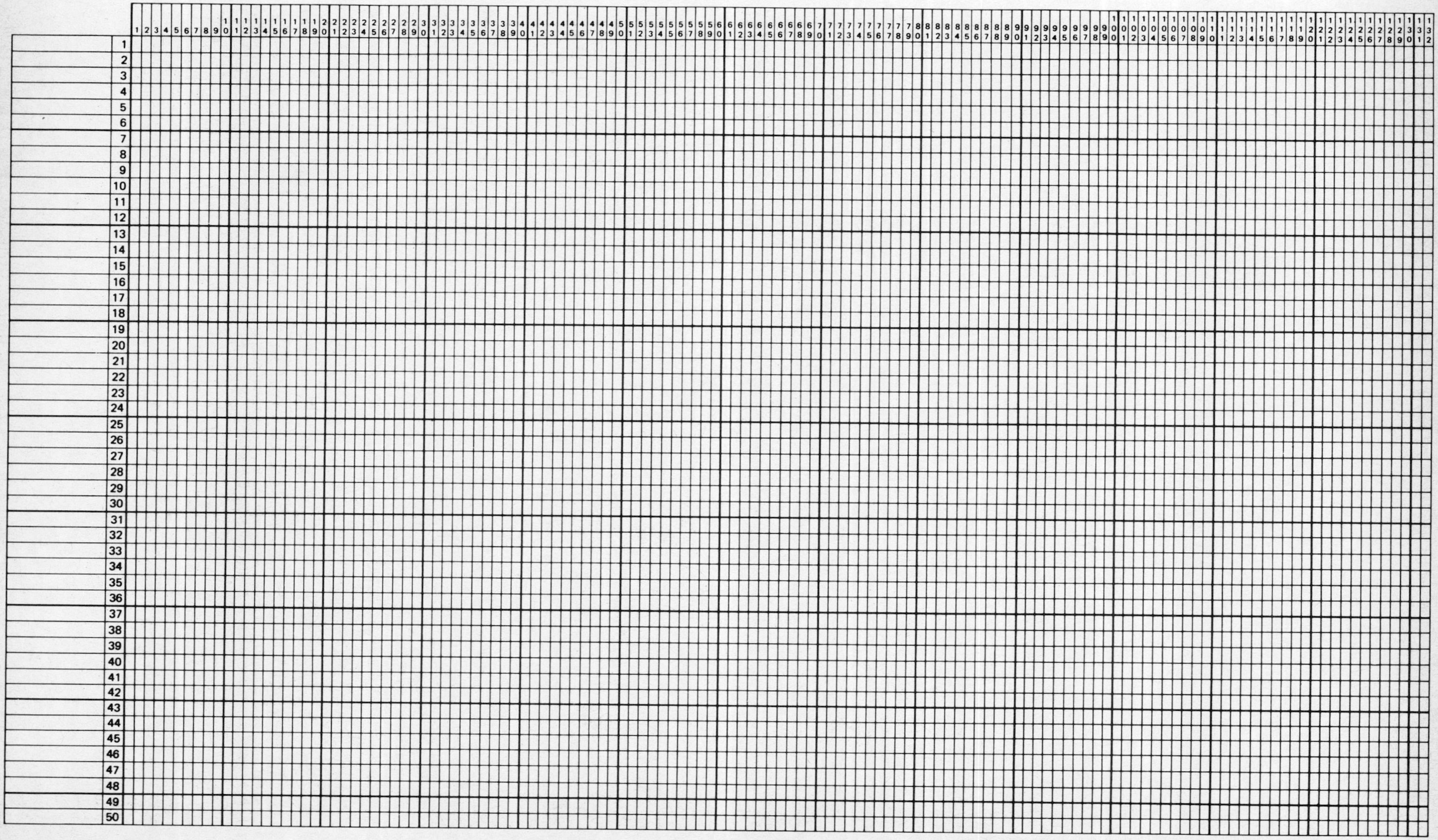